RIGHTS OF PRISONERS

Third Edition

**Volume 1
Chapters 1-7**

Michael B. Mushlin
Professor of Law
Pace University School of Law

For Customer Assistance Call 1-800-328-4880

Mat #17837605

SOUTH UNIVERSITY
709 MALL BLVD.
SAVANNAH, GA 31406

© 2002 West Group
All Rights Reserved.

West Group has created this publication to provide you with accurate and authoritative information concerning the subject matter covered. However, this publication was not necessarily prepared by persons licensed to practice law in a particular jurisdiction. West Group is not engaged in rendering legal or other professional advice, and this publication is not a substitute for the advice of an attorney. If you require legal or other expert advice, you should seek the services of a competent attorney or other professional.

ISBN # 0-07-172514-8

TO THEA

Preface

In the decade since the last edition of this work the United States prison population has grown, doubling to a level that is an historic high surpassing that of any industrialized nation in the world. Two million American adults on any given day are now behind bars. As the prison population swells, so, too, has the law defining prisoners' rights grown more complex. Since the Second Edition the United States Supreme Court has decided a number of key cases, several by five to four votes. These decisions for the most part do not overrule prior cases. Instead, in more instances than not, the decisions generate a new set of requirements that must be met before inmates can prevail in their claims. Thus, rather than remodel the house, the Supreme Court has added new rooms to the structure. Hundreds of decisions from the lower courts each year supply further structural refinement. And Congress joined the fray when in 1996 it passed the Prison Litigation Reform Act. That Act makes as major an impact on prison litigation as the Supreme Court decisions. The PLRA has been described as a charter of restrictions unprecedented in American law that have the effect of limiting access to the courts for inmates in ways that are more restrictive that those imposed on any other set of litigants.

In this, the Third Edition, the numerous developments occurring over the past decade are thoroughly digested and described. I hope that the reader will find that this has been done in a straightforward, clear manner, without sacrificing detail or nuance. To do this, and to make the transition to this Edition easier for the reader familiar with that text, the basic structure of the Second Edition is preserved. The chapters are organized basically in the same manner and remain in the same order. Each chapter has been comprehensively revised and rewritten to incorporate all changes since the last Edition. In addition, two new chapters have been added, Chapter Sixteen, describing the Prison Litigation

Reform Act, and Chapter Seventeen, discussing the unique issues presented by the use of private prisons. To stay abreast of changes in this rapidly changing field, these volumes, as was the case with prior editions, will be kept current through annual supplements. The goal of the Third Edition remains identical to that of the Second Edition, "to set out in one place a comprehensive description of the complex body of law that has developed governing the law of prisoners' rights."

In the final analysis, the message of this book is that despite the new barriers and difficulties, the "hands off" doctrine -- under which courts refused for decades to even consider prisoner pleas regarding conditions of confinement -- has not returned. Courts continue to have a role to play in ensuring that the constitutional rights of inmates are not left purely to the discretion of prison administrators. This book aims to describe that role, which is an essential one if all the citizens of this country are to be governed by the rule of law. My sincere hope is that these volumes will contribute to the understanding of this body of law and that the work will help shape its appropriate development.

I could not have completed this project by myself. I am indebted to my student research assistants, Sarah Courtman, Victoria Handy, Adam Tracy and Kevin Wilson, all law students at Pace University School of Law, all of whom were of enormous help to me in the preparation of this Edition. Bill Chabb, my research assistant for several years prior to the publication of this work and now a practicing attorney, also made contributions to this work for which I express my appreciation. I am grateful to my assistant Elizabeth Fraser who did important and tedious technical work on this project. The Pace Law Library staff is exceptional. Under the leadership of Professor Marie Newman the staff provided superb assistance and were always available to help whenever I asked. John Boston, Project Director of the Prisoners' Rights Project of the Legal Aid Society of New York, who is one of the great minds in this field, was of incalculable help to me in a host of ways including answering a constant barrage of questions and providing access to his summaries of decided prison cases. I am indebted to him for his assistance. I am also grateful to Russ Davis of West Group for his helpful editorial suggestions. My friend Dan Wise was a constant source of encouragement. My wife Thea and my two sons,

PREFACE

Rory and Ben are the center of my life. I am especially grateful to my wife for her support and encouragement at every step of the way. Finally, I thank Pace University School of Law for the institutional support provided, and for an environment in which a professor is free to create a work such as this.

>Michael B. Mushlin
>White Plains, New York
>November 2002

SUMMARY OF CONTENTS

Volume 1

Chapter 1 Prisoners' Rights-Historical Background and General Overview

Chapter 2 The Eighth Amendment—Solitary Confinement, Prevention of Violence, Protection Against Overcrowding, and Provision of the Necessities of Life

Chapter 3 The Eighth Amendment: Medical Care

Chapter 4 Equal Protection Clause-Discrimination Issues

Chapter 5 Communication and Expression: Speech in Prison

Chapter 6 First Amendment Rights: Religion

Chapter 7 Prison Labor

Volume 2

Chapter 8 Fourth Amendment Rights: Privacy and Related Issues

Chapter 9 Disciplinary Proceedings

Chapter 10 Classifications, Transfers, and Detainers

Chapter 11 Access to Courts

Chapter 12 Visiting

Chapter 13 Personal Correspondence: Mail, Telephone, Email

Chapter 14 Access to the Media

Volume 3

Chapter 15 Civil Disabilities

TABLE OF CONTENTS

Chapter 16　The Prison Litigation Reform Act and In Forma Pauperis Proceedings

Chapter 17　Private Prisons

Appendices

Table of Cases

Index

Detailed Volume Table of Contents

Chapter 1
Prisoners' Rights-Historical Background and General Overview

§ 1:1 Introduction
§ 1:2 A Brief History of Prisons in the United States
§ 1:3 The Hands-Off Doctrine
§ 1:4 The Demise of the Hands-Off Doctrine and the Beginning of Prisoners' Rights Law
§ 1:5 A Brief Overview of the Law of Prisoners' Rights
§ 1:6 —Rights Retained by Prisoners
§ 1:7 —Standards for Determining whether Prisoners' Rights Have Been Violated
§ 1:8 —Prison Litigation Reform Act
§ 1:9 An Introduction to the Four-Factor *Turner v. Safley* Analysis
§ 1:10 —The First *Turner* Factor: The Valid, Rational Connection Test
§ 1:11 —The Second *Turner* Factor: The Search for Alternative Means
§ 1:12 —The Third *Turner* Factor: The Cost of Accommodation
§ 1:13 —The Fourth *Turner* Factor: The Presence of a *De Minimis* Alternative
§ 1:14 —The Weight to Be Assigned to the Four *Turner* Factors
§ 1:15 Development of Private Prisons
§ 1:16 The Scope and Organization of This Book

xi

Chapter 2

The Eighth Amendment—Solitary Confinement, Prevention of Violence, Protection Against Overcrowding, and Provision of the Necessities of Life

§ 2:1   Introduction
§ 2:2   The Supreme Court's Definition of Cruel and Unusual Punishment
§ 2:3   Restrictive Confinement: Punitive Segregation, Solitary Confinement and "Supermax" Units
§ 2:4   Corporal Punishment and Physical and Mechanical Restraints
§ 2:5   Use of Force by Guards
§ 2:6   —Riots
§ 2:7   Assaults by Other Inmates
§ 2:8   Escape from Prison to Avoid Assaults
§ 2:9   Conditions of Confinement-Basic Human Needs and the Prisoner's Physical Well-Being
§ 2:10 —Diet
§ 2:11 —Exercise and Outside Recreation
§ 2:12 —Shelter, Clothing, Personal Hygiene, Sanitation, Ventilation, Fire Safety, and Hazardous Substances
§ 2:13 —Overcrowding
§ 2:14 —Idleness, Programs, and Rehabilitation
§ 2:15 —Large Scale Litigations: Totality of the Conditions, Inadequate Finances, and Remedies

Chapter 3

The Eighth Amendment: Medical Care

§ 3:1   • Introduction

TABLE OF CONTENTS

§ 3:2 *Estelle v Gamble*
§ 3:3 Rights of Pretrial Detainees to Medical Care
§ 3:4 What is a "Serious Medical Need"?
§ 3:5 Initial Screening When Entering Facility
§ 3:6 Emergency Care and Sick Call Procedures
§ 3:7 Periodic Examinations and Necessary Treatment
§ 3:8 Facilities and Equipment
§ 3:9 Staff
§ 3:10 Records
§ 3:11 Dental Care
§ 3:12 Eye Care
§ 3:13 Diet
§ 3:14 Health Needs of Women
§ 3:15 Mental Health
§ 3:16 Suicide
§ 3:17 Drug and Alcohol Treatment and Treatment for Tobacco Addiction
§ 3:18 Disabled Prisoners
§ 3:19 Prisoners and the Americans With Disabilities Act
§ 3:20 AIDS
§ 3:21 Transsexuals
§ 3:22 Experimentation and Research
§ 3:23 Right to Refuse Treatment
§ 3:24 Prison Co-Payment Plans For Medical Care

Chapter 4
Equal Protection Clause-Discrimination Issues

§ 4:1 Introduction
§ 4:2 The Theory of Equal Protection and Equal Protection standards
§ 4:3 Equal Protection Applied
§ 4:4 —Racial Discrimination
§ 4:5 —Sexual Discrimination

Chapter 5

Communication and Expression: Speech in Prison

- § 5:1 Introduction
- § 5:2 The Supreme Court's Approach to Speech in Prison
- § 5:3 Censorship and Limitations on Receipt of Publications
- § 5:4 Publisher-Only Rules
- § 5:5 Access to Literature in Punitive Segregation
- § 5:6 Prisoner Writings
- § 5:7 The Right to Political Activity: The Right to Associate, to Communicate, and to Present Grievances in Prison

Chapter 6

First Amendment Rights: Religion

- § 6:1 Introduction
- § 6:2 The Search for a Governing Standard
- § 6:3 *O'Lone v Estate of Shabazz*
- § 6:4 Congress and the Supreme Court Battle Over a Governing Standard
- § 6:5 Equal Protection
- § 6:6 Establishment of Religion
- § 6:7 Defining Religion
- § 6:8 Religious Practices
- § 6:9 —Personal Appearance and Clothing
- § 6:10 —Meals
- § 6:11 —Religious Services
- § 6:12 —Name Changes
- § 6:13 —Access to Clergy
- § 6:14 —Access to Religious Mail and Publications
- § 6:15 —Access to Religious Accouterments
- § 6:16 —Work-Religion Conflicts
- § 6:17 —Medical Treatment-Religion Conflicts

TABLE OF CONTENTS

Chapter 7
Prison Labor

§ 7:1 Introduction
§ 7:2 Historical Background
§ 7:3 Prison-Made Goods
§ 7:4 Thirteenth Amendment—Involuntary Servitude Exception: Can Inmates Be Forced to Work?
§ 7:5 The Right to Work or Be Employed
§ 7:6 Job Seniority and Security; The Right to a Particular Job
§ 7:7 The Right to a Particular Job as Affected by Civil Rights Laws
§ 7:8 The Right to a Particular Job as Affected by AIDS and Other Conditions
§ 7:9 Wages—The Right to Be Paid in General
§ 7:10 —The Right to Be Paid Minimum Wages
§ 7:11 Withholding Wages and Payment of Interest on Inmate Accounts
§ 7:12 The Right to Be Compensated for Work-Related Injuries
§ 7:13 The Right to Unemployment Compensation
§ 7:14 The Right to Form Prisoners' Unions
§ 7:15 The Right to Engage in Work Stoppages and Strikes
§ 7:16 The Right to Participate in Work Release Programs Generally
§ 7:17 Work Release Participation and Due Process Requirement
§ 7:18 Conclusion—The Legislative Challenge

Chapter 1

Prisoners' Rights-Historical Background and General Overview

Research References

Nahmod, Civil Rights and Civil Liberties Litigation: The Law of Section 1983 § 3:35
Prisoners and the Law, Ch 1, 22
Am. Jur. 2d, Penal and Correctional Institutions §§ 27, 120 to 146
Constitutional Law ⚖82(13)
A.L.R. Index: Constitutional Law; Prisons and Prisoners

> **KeyCite®:** Cases and other legal materials listed in KeyCite Scope can be researched through West Group's KeyCite service on Westlaw®. Use KeyCite to check citations for form, parallel references, prior and later history, and comprehensive citator information, including citations to other decisions and secondary materials.

§ 1:1   Introduction
§ 1:2   A Brief History of Prisons in the United States
§ 1:3   The Hands-Off Doctrine
§ 1:4   The Demise of the Hands-Off Doctrine and the Beginning of Prisoners' Rights Law
§ 1:5   A Brief Overview of the Law of Prisoners' Rights
§ 1:6   —Rights Retained by Prisoners
§ 1:7   —Standards for Determining whether Prisoners' Rights Have Been Violated
§ 1:8   —Prison Litigation Reform Act
§ 1:9   An Introduction to the Four-Factor *Turner v. Safley* Analysis
§ 1:10 —The First *Turner* Factor: The Valid, Rational Connection Test
§ 1:11 —The Second *Turner* Factor: The Search for Alternative Means
§ 1:12 —The Third *Turner* Factor: The Cost of Accommodation

§ 1:13 —The Fourth *Turner* Factor: The Presence of a *De Minimis* Alternative
§ 1:14 —The Weight to Be Assigned to the Four *Turner* Factors
§ 1:15 Development of Private Prisons
§ 1:16 The Scope and Organization of This Book

§ 1:1 Introduction

This is a book about prison law in the United States. It synthesizes and describes a large body of primarily constitutional law that has developed in the past four decades defining the rights of prisoners who are held in America's prisons. The law described here is applicable to the enormous and historically high population of American prisons and jails. The numbers by any past measure are staggering. On any given day there are currently over two million inmates in the United States jails and prisons.[1] The number of adults held in prisons and jails in the United States has increased by more

---

[Section 1:1]

[1]Overall, the United States incarcerated 2,100,146 persons at yearend 2001 in federal and state prisons, local jails, territorial prisons, Immigration and Naturalization Service Facilities, military facilities, Indian country jails and juvenile facilities. At yearend of 2001, 1,406,031 prisoners were incarcerated in federal or state adult correctional facilities. For the first time in two decades in 2001, there was a slight reduction in the total prison population, which is now at historic highs. Between July 1, 2001, and December 31, 2001, the number of inmates under state jurisdiction declined by 3,705 inmates (down 0.3%), repeating the same pattern of decline first observed in the last 6 months of 2000. In fact, during 2001, 10 States experienced prison population decreases, led by New Jersey (down 5.5%), followed by Utah (-5.2%), New York (-3.8%), and Texas (-2.8%). However, the Federal Bureau of Prisons population continued to grow rapidly, up 4,205 inmates since midyear 2001. At yearend 2001, the federal system was the third largest prison system, behind Texas (162,070) and California (159,444). If growth rates remain unchanged, the federal system will be the largest by yearend 2002. United States Department of Justice, Office of Justice Programs, Bureau of Justice Statistics Bulletin, Prisoners in 2001 (July 2002).

BACKGROUND AND OVERVIEW   § 1:1

than five fold in less than thirty years.[2] In the past decade alone the prison population has doubled.[3]

Because of the huge numbers involved, the law described in this book governs almost every aspect of

---

[2]Michael B. Mushlin, Legal Rights of Prisoners, 1161 Encyclopedia of Crime and Justice (2d Ed 2001) ("Americans live in a time of the greatest prison expansion in . . . modern history"). Minorities are represented in the prison population in numbers that far exceed the percentage of their representation in the general population. African-Americans comprise less than thirteen percent of the population of the country, yet forty eight percent of the prison population is African-American. Michael B. Mushlin, Legal Rights of Prisoners, 1161 Encyclopedia of Crime and Justice (2d Ed 2001), citing U.S. Census Bureau, Statistical Abstract of the United States: 1999 (119th Edition) Washington, DC, 1999, and United States Department of Justice, Bureau of Justice Statistics at www.USDOJ.gov (2000). If the country continues to incarcerate at the same rate as it does now, it means that a black male child born in the year 2000 will have a twenty nine percent chance of serving time in prison at some point in his life. A Hispanic male baby will have a sixteen percent chance. By contrast, the odds of a white male going to prison at sometime in his life are only four percent. The Sentencing Project, Facts about Prisons and Prisoners (April 2000). While the numbers of people in prison have increased dramatically, people who are imprisoned are no longer predominantly violent felons. In 1996, for example, seventy one percent of those sent to prison were there because they were convicted of non-violent crimes. Thirty percent of all prisoners were in prison because of drug offenses; twenty nine percent because of property crimes. An indication in the growth of imprisonment for non-violent offenses is that in 1983 one out of every ten inmates were drug offenders; seventeen years later that number had risen to one in four. The Sentencing Project, Facts about Prisons and Prisoners (April 2000).

[3]See Bureau of the Census, US Dept. of Commerce, Statistical Abstract of the United States (112th ed 1992) (reporting the prison population of the United States in 1990 as 774,375) and United States Department of Justice, Office of Justice Programs, Bureau of Justice Statistics Bulletin, Prisoners in 2001 (July 2002) (reporting the prison population of the United States at the end of 2001 was 1,406,031).

the lives of one out of every 142 Americans.[4] Understanding prisoners' rights law is important to lawyers and judges who will confront the many prisoners' rights cases filed every year.[5] This law also affects the interests of the hundreds of thousands of people who work in prisons, since their lives are directly affected by it. In addition, this law is of more than passing interest to the legal profession generally. In it, our constitutional principles are implemented in the day-to-day operation of some of our most important public institutions. Finally, the public at large should be vitally interested in this subject. Aside from concern about the treatment of fellow citizens who will almost all one day return to free society,[6] the operation of prisons commands public attention because imprisonment on the present scale imposes a sizeable drain on the pubic treasury.[7]

It was not always the case that a work such as this would have been needed. Indeed, had this work been written as late as the 1960s, it would have been a slender volume. The list of prisoners' rights recognized by the judiciary could have been comprehensively discussed in a few pages. By the time the last edition of

---

[4]United States Department of Justice, Bureau of Justice Statistics 2000 available at www.ojp.usdoj.gov/bjs.

[5]During 2000, 58,257 prisoner petitions were filed in U.S. District Courts-80% by state prison inmates and 20% by federal inmates. United States Department of Justice, Bureau of Justice, Prisoner Petitions Filed in U.S. District Courts 2000, with Trend 1980-2000, available at www.ojp.usdoj.gov/bjs/abstract/ppfusd00.htm.

[6]Approximately half a million men and women are released every year from American prisons. Michael B. Mushlin, Legal Rights of Prisoners, 1161 Encyclopedia of Crime and Justice (2d Ed 2001).

[7]To build new prisons costs an average of $36,000 to $42,000 per maximum-security bed. In 1995, state and federal governments allocated over five billion dollars for new prison construction. The operational cost of running the prisons is now over thirty eight billion dollars per year. In some states, more tax money goes to the operation of prisons and jails than is spent on educating a comparable age group. Marc Mauer, Race to Incarcerate (1999).

this book was written in 1993, a body of law concerning prisoners' rights had developed.[8] The size of the present work is proof that, in almost a decade since the last edition, prisoners' rights law has grown considerably—with no sign that it will diminish.

In this chapter, the stage is set for the description of prison law that follows. This chapter begins with a brief history of prisons in the United States. Next, it describes the hands-off doctrine, which reigned supreme until the 1960s and which, as much as anything, was responsible for the lack of development of almost any prisoners' rights law before that time. The chapter then describes the developments which lead to the increasing willingness of the judiciary to explore the rights of inmates, after which it sets out in broad strokes the Supreme Court's evolving treatment of prisoners' rights, including a more extensive discussion of the *Turner v. Safley* test for deciding whether prison rules are valid. The chapter discusses the appearance of private prisons and discusses briefly their significance. Finally, the chapter concludes with a roadmap of the topics covered by this work.

§ 1:2 A Brief History of Prisons in the United States

The development of prisons in this country began in

---

[8]For surveys of prison law, see Lynn S. Branham, The Law of Sentencing, Corrections and Prisoners' Rights (6th ed. 2002); Columbia Human Rights Law Review, A Jailhouse Lawyer's Manual 622 (5th ed. 2000); John Boston & Daniel E. Manville, Prisoners' Self-help Litigation Manual (3d ed. 1995). See also Stephen S. Sypherd and Gary M. Ronan, Thirtieth Annual Review of Criminal Procedure: Introduction and Guide for Users VI. Prisoners' Rights: Substantive Rights Retained by Prisoners, 89 Geo. L.J. 1897 (2001); Rahul Patel and Ann N. Sagerson, Thirtieth Annual Review of Criminal Procedure: Introduction and Guide for Users VI. Prisoners' Rights: Procedural Means of Enforcement Under 42 U.S.C.A. § 1983, 89 Geo. L.J. 1938 (2001).

the early nineteenth century.[1] In colonial times, jails were used primarily to hold defendants awaiting trial. Persons who had been convicted of crimes rarely were imprisoned; instead they were fined, whipped, placed in the stockade, banished, or hanged, depending on the seriousness of their offense. These sentences reflected the then-prevalent Calvinist philosophy that, because people were inherently evil, attempts at reformation were destined to fail. All that could be done when a crime occurred was to punish the wrongdoer.[2]

By the early nineteenth century, the social order was changing; cities were becoming crowded, industry was growing rapidly, and the Calvinist influence was on the decline. The harsh punishments of the colonists were looked on with increasing disfavor. More moderate sanctions were thought to be in order, and imprisonment replaced death as the penalty for the most serious offenses.[3]

It was not until the Jacksonian period, the 1820s, that the modern penitentiary came into wide-scale use.[4] In part this occurred because the more moderate punishments employed in the early part of the century failed to stem criminal activity, but it also represented a new ideology fashioned by criminal justice reformers.

[Section 1:2]

[1] See, generally, David J. Rothman, The Discovery of the Asylum: Social Order and Disorder in the New Republic (1971). See also George Fisher, The Birth of the Prison Retold, 104 Yale L.J. 1235 (1995) (discussing the modern British prison system by tracing its roots back to the eighteenth century, and concluding that the motivating concern for the effort was the problem of juvenile crime).

[2] David J. Rothman, The Discovery of the Asylum: Social Order and Disorder in the New Republic at chapters 1 & 2 (1971).

[3] *Id.* at chapter 3 (1971). The Pennsylvania Quakers began to utilize prison as a penal sanction in the latter part of the seventeenth century. Donald R. Cressey, Adult Felons in Prison, Prisoners in America 120 (Lloyd E. Ohlin ed. 1973).

[4] See, generally, David J. Rothman, The Discovery of the Asylum: Social Order and Disorder in the New Republic at chapter 4 (1971).

After having assiduously studied criminal biographies, the reformers had reached the conclusion, contrary to the colonists' belief that crime was inherent in human nature, that the roots of crime were traceable to the family and community.[5]

The Jacksonian penitentiary, therefore, was designed for the purpose of rehabilitating offenders. The prototypical institutions were the Auburn prison in New York and the prisons in Pennsylvania.[6] Although at the time widespread debate raged over whether the New York or Pennsylvania model was superior, the prisons were more notable for their similarities than for their differences. In each, inmates worked during the day and slept alone at night,[7] prisoners were not allowed to talk,[8] rigid discipline prevailed,[9] and the only reading material allowed was the Bible.[10] The major difference between the two models was that at Auburn prisoners worked together (although they were not permitted to speak to each other), while in Pennsylvania prisoners were isolated even during work periods.[11]

The theoretical foundation of the prison regimen was the belief that criminal activity was the product of an inappropriate upbringing and/or improper community influences. By physically isolating offenders, prisons effectively removed them from the corruption of the community. In turn, the prison routine provided the

---

[5]David J. Rothman, The Discovery of the Asylum: Social Order and Disorder in the New Republic at 65-66 (1971).

[6]These are described in detail in David J. Rothman, The Discovery of the Asylum: Social Order and Disorder in the New Republic at chapter 4 (1971).

[7]David J. Rothman, The Discovery of the Asylum: Social Order and Disorder in the New Republic at 82 (1971).

[8]*Id.*

[9]*Id.*

[10]*Id.* The Bible was provided because early prison reformers believed that religion had an important role to play in rehabilitating inmates. See Ch 6 for a more complete discussion of that topic.

[11]David J. Rothman, The Discovery of the Asylum: Social Order and Disorder in the New Republic at 82 (1971).

discipline, order, and values that the inmate's family had failed to inculcate. The emphasis on labor reflected the perceived relationship between idleness and crime. The ban on interprisoner communication prevented prisoners from corrupting each other. To cut the prisoner's links with the outside world, visitors were carefully screened, correspondence was strictly curtailed, and newspapers were disallowed. As one historian observed, the walls of the penitentiary "were not only to keep the inmates in, but the rest of the world out."[12] Thus, the Jacksonian prison was marked by isolation, silence, religiosity, constant labor, and harsh discipline. Regimentation prevailed, and prisoners, when moving from place to place, marched in lockstep, single file, with heads pointed to the right.[13]

The Jacksonian approach to prisons and prisoner reform came under attack at the beginning of the twentieth century. Reformers argued that the Auburn and Pennsylvania prisons did not, in fact, reduce crime. Moreover, the reformers claimed that the harshness of prison life established by that system had a debilitating effect on inmates that, if anything, hardened them further to a criminal way of life that they were likely to resume after they were released from prison.[14] The reformers pointed out that the promise of the founders of American prisons rang hollow in practice. Prisons were "overcrowded and in sad disrepair, without

---

[12]David J. Rothman, The Discovery of the Asylum: Social Order and Disorder in the New Republic at 96 (1971). This assertion is subject to some dispute. Recent scholarship suggests that, contrary to accepted notions, early American prisons were subject to oversight by outside groups interested in prison reform. Leonard G. Leverson, Constitutional Limits on the Power to Restrict Access to Prisons: A Historical Re-Examination, 18 Harv. CR-CL L Rev 409 (1983).

[13]David J. Rothman, The Discovery of the Asylum: Social Order and Disorder in the New Republic at 105 (1971).

[14]For a fascinating description of the harsh prison conditions at Auburn prison at the beginning of the twentieth century, see Thomas M. Osborne, Within Prison Walls (D. Appelton 1991) (1915).

BACKGROUND AND OVERVIEW § 1:2

internal discipline, disorderly, enervating, monotonous and cruel."[15] Under the reformers' prodding, eventually the rigidity of the routine and the requirement of silence were relaxed. Moreover, alternatives to endless periods of incarceration were put into place, including use of probation for first offenders and parole for the earlier release of inmates.

Although the Progressive period reformers had high hopes that their efforts would lead to vast improvements in prisons, these desires were not fully realized. Confinement of dangerous individuals within a penitentiary's walls neutralized their threat to free society, at least for the duration of the incarceration, and served society's appetite to punish people who had transgressed the criminal law, but there was a general acknowledgement by mid-century that prisons did not serve the rehabilitative role intended for them. The conditions of confinement, while eased somewhat from the harsh deprivations of the early nineteenth century penitentiaries, continued to be overly restrictive and, in many instances, inhumane.[16]

While the goal of a humane and rehabilitative penal system remained on the books in some states,[17] in truth, it was more rhetoric than reality. The modern prison was primarily a place of confinement for society's criminals with little regard to how they were kept. The judiciary did little to alter that reality until the beginning of the prisoners' rights movement in the 1960s. The reason was the so-called hands-off doctrine.

---

[15]David J. Rothman, History of Prisons, Asylums, and Other Decaying Institutions 9, in Prisoners' Rights Sourcebook (1973).

[16]See, e.g., National Advisory Commn. on Criminal Justice Standards & Goals, Corrections 1 (1973) (reporting the view that mid-twentieth century prisons were characterized by "crippling idleness, anonymous brutality and destructive impact").

[17]See, e.g., RI Gen Laws § 42-56-1. See also Pell v. Procunier, 417 U.S. 817, 822-23, 94 S. Ct. 2800, 41 L. Ed. 2d 495 (1974) (rehabilitation cited as one of three primary functions of a penal system).

§ 1:3 The Hands-Off Doctrine

The Constitution did not breach prison walls for over 170 years. Indeed, during most of the history of this country, there was some question as to whether prisoners had any constitutional rights at all. An often-quoted early decision characterized convicts as slaves of the states.[1] This view, both among judges and penologists, had probably lost substantial support by the mid-twentieth century. Yet it was difficult to be sure. The so-called hands-off doctrine[2] precluded judges from ever reaching the question of what rights survived incarceration. Under this doctrine, federal courts refused to intervene on the ground that "it is not the function of the courts to superintend the treatment and discipline of prisoners in penitentiaries, but only to deliver from imprisonment those who are illegally confined."[3]

The doctrine was invoked even when inmates' safety was at stake. In one illustrative case, a federal court refused to adjudicate a claim that lives were endangered when inmates were held in an area containing a coal stove presenting a grave risk of fire to the inmates who were in locked, overcrowded cells without any means of retreat.[4] Even though the court recognized that these conditions were a "fabulous obscenity," the judge felt

---

[Section 1:3]

[1] Ruffin v. Commonwealth, 62 Va. 790, 21 Gratt. 790, 1871 WL 4928 (1871).

[2] The origin of the term has been attributed to Fritch, Civil Rights of Federal Prison Inmates 31 (1961) (document prepared for the Federal Bureau of Prisons), cited in Note, Beyond the Ken of the Courts: A Critique of Judicial Refusal to Hear the Complaints of Convicts, 72 Yale L.J. 506, n.4 (1963).

[3] Stroud v. Swope, 187 F.2d 850, 851-52 (9th Cir. 1951). See also Bethea v. Crouse, 417 F.2d 504, 505 (10th Cir. 1969) ("We have consistently adhered to the so-called 'hands off' policy in matters of prison administration . . .").

[4] Ex parte Pickens, 13 Alaska 477, 101 F. Supp. 285, 287, 290 (Terr. Alaska 1951).

§ 1:3 BACKGROUND AND OVERVIEW

powerless to act because of the hands-off doctrine.[5] Indeed, the pull of the doctrine was so strong that even claims of racial discrimination were not cognizable.[6]

Lurking behind the hands-off doctrine were concerns regarding the appropriate reach of judicial power.[7] One concern had to do with separation of powers. The management and control of prisons are generally viewed as executive and legislative functions. That courts should tell these co-equal branches of government how to run penal institutions was troublesome. Courts also doubted their power to fashion meaningful relief when improvement in prison conditions required the appropriation of funds. Another consideration involved principles of federalism. State inmates brought many prisoner suits in federal court. Federal courts expressed concern that, by adjudicating these claims in a way that was favorable to the inmates, they would be using federal power to dictate to the states how to run their own institutions.[8]

Another factor counseling hesitation was the belief that courts lacked the expertise to become involved. Courts proceeded from the assumption that the management of prisons requires considerable skill, training, and experience. Corrections officials perceived judicial review as threatening to internal prison discipline and

---

[5]*Id.*

[6]U.S. ex rel. Morris v. Radio Station WENR, 209 F.2d 105 (7th Cir. 1953) (overruled by, Wartman v. Branch 7, Civil Division, County Court, Milwaukee County, State of Wis., 510 F.2d 130 (7th Cir. 1975)). See also Note, Constitutional Rights of Prisoners: The Developing Law, 110 U. Pa. L. Rev. 985 (1962).

[7]See, generally, Kenneth C. Haas, Judicial Politics and Correctional Reform: An Analysis of the Decline of the "Hands-Off Doctrine," 1977 Det. L. Rev. 795; Note, Beyond the Ken of the Courts: A Critique of Judicial Refusal to Hear the Complaints of Convicts, 72 Yale L.J. 506 (1963).

[8]Note, Beyond the Ken of the Courts: A Critique of Judicial Refusal to Hear the Complaints of Convicts, 72 Yale L.J. 506, 515 (1963).

authority.⁹ Finally, although not expressly stated, questions of judicial workload also may have influenced judges. With large numbers of inmates potentially willing to present their complaints, and with a large variety of claims that might be pressed, judges who invoked the hands-off doctrine may have done so to protect themselves from becoming inundated with prisoner petitions, many of which may have been baseless. Even if the petitions proved meritorious, a judge would have to spend a great deal of time processing the case and monitoring the remedy. The hands-off doctrine made the court's work easier. All a court had to determine was the nature of the claim; once that fact was established, the suit was automatically dismissed.

Nevertheless, the doctrine imposed serious costs. The most serious loss was that the merits of potentially worthy complaints were never reached. Moreover, there was little judicial pressure to improve institutional conditions, resulting in bitter inmates whose prospects of rehabilitation were less than when they entered the system.

These costs could not be justified on any principled basis. The hands-off doctrine was based on erroneous quasi-constitutional and policy objections. Separation of powers does not foreclose judicial scrutiny when the legislature or executive acts unconstitutionally. Courts regularly invalidate laws that violate citizens' constitutional rights. In fact, a major function of courts in our constitutional system is to ensure that constitutional rights are preserved and protected.¹⁰

The argument that federal judges lack the expertise to run prisons rests on a misconception of the judiciary's

---

⁹Note, Beyond the Ken of the Courts: A Critique of Judicial Refusal to Hear the Complaints of Convicts, 72 Yale L.J. 506, 516 (1963).

¹⁰Pennsylvania v. Union Gas Co., 491 U.S. 1, 27-28, 109 S. Ct. 2273, 105 L. Ed. 2d 1 (1989) (overruled on other grounds by, Seminole Tribe of Florida v. Florida, 517 U.S. 44, 116 S. Ct. 1114, 134 L. Ed. 2d 252 (1996)); Harris v. Reed, 489 U.S. 255, 267, 109 S. Ct. 1038, 103 L. Ed. 2d 308 (1989).

role in prison cases. The invalidation of a particular prison practice on constitutional grounds rarely, if ever, requires a court to assume management of the penal institution. Courts are the experts in constitutional law, and that is the basic issue in most prison suits. To the extent that other expertise is needed for accurate decision-making, courts have been willing to be informed by the arguments of counsel and the taking of testimony, including the testimony of expert witnesses.[11] In addition, courts have the capacity to use appointed masters to assist in carrying out their orders. Finally, the possibility of being swamped with frivolous petitions always has been one of the costs of operating a judicial system, yet it never has been deemed a valid excuse for denial of constitutional rights. Justice Harlan addressed this point when he wrote that fear of burgeoning caseloads cannot "be permitted to stand in the way of the recognition of otherwise sound constitutional principles."[12] In addition, problems of frivolous suits can be handled in other ways that do not involve shutting the courthouse door to meritorious claims out of fear that too many non-meritorious lawsuits will be brought.[13]

---

[11]For examples of decisions in which an extensive record of testimony of expert witnesses has been made, see, e.g., Rhem v. Malcolm, 371 F. Supp. 594, 627 (S.D. N.Y. 1974), opinion supplemented, 377 F. Supp. 995 (S.D. N.Y. 1974), aff'd and remanded, 507 F.2d 333 (2d Cir. 1974); Fisher v. Koehler, 692 F. Supp. 1519 (S.D. N.Y. 1988).

[12]Bivens v. Six Unknown Named Agents of Federal Bureau of Narcotics, 403 U.S. 388, 411, 91 S. Ct. 1999, 29 L. Ed. 2d 619 (1971) (Harlan, J, concurring).

[13]For a discussion of that topic, see Ch 16. Moreover, the available evidence suggests that prisoners' rights lawsuits have not overloaded the courts. See, e.g., Theodore Eisenberg & Stewart Schwab, The Reality of Constitutional Tort Litigation, 72 Cornell L. Rev. 641 (1987).

§ 1:4 The Demise of the Hands-Off Doctrine and the Beginning of Prisoners' Rights Law

On balance, the costs of the hands-off doctrine were ultimately recognized to be too high a price to pay. This conclusion was implicit in the numerous lower court cases in the 1960s in which judges, for the first time, began to address prisoner petitions on their merits. It was made explicit by two decisions of the United States Supreme Court in the early 1970s. In the first, Justice White sounded the death knell to the hands-off doctrine in a single line: "[T]here is no iron curtain drawn between the Constitution and the prisons of this country."[1] In the second, a year later, Justice Powell, writing for the court, proclaimed:

> [A] policy of judicial restraint cannot encompass any failure to take cognizance of valid constitutional claims whether arising in a federal or state institution. When a prison regulation or practice offends a fundamental constitutional guarantee, federal courts will discharge their duty to protect constitutional rights.[2]

With these statements, the hands-off doctrine formally ended. Since then, the Court has continually asserted that the doctrine has no place in its constitutional jurisprudence.[3] It is now settled law that the hands-off doctrine ends where the abridgement of constitutional rights begins. With the decline of the doctrine, the law

---

[Section 1:4]

[1] Wolff v. McDonnell, 418 U.S. 539, 555-56, 94 S. Ct. 2963, 41 L. Ed. 2d 935 (1974).

[2] Procunier v. Martinez, 416 U.S. 396, 405-06, 94 S. Ct. 1800, 40 L. Ed. 2d 224 (1974) (overruled by, Thornburgh v. Abbott, 490 U.S. 401, 109 S. Ct. 1874, 104 L. Ed. 2d 459 (1989)).

[3] See, e.g., Thornburgh v. Abbott, 490 U.S. 401, 407, 109 S. Ct. 1874, 104 L. Ed. 2d 459 (1989) ("[p]rison walls do not form a barrier separating prison inmates from the protections of the Constitution"); Turner v. Safley, 482 U.S. 78, 84, 107 S. Ct. 2254, 96 L. Ed. 2d 64 (1987) (same); Rhodes v. Chapman, 452 U.S. 337, 352, 101 S. Ct. 2392, 69 L. Ed. 2d 59 (1981) ("Courts certainly have a responsibility to scrutinize [prisoners'] claims . . ."); Bell v. Wolfish, 441 U.S. 520, 562, 99 S. Ct. 1861, 60 L. Ed. 2d 447 (1979).

§ 1:4

of prisoners' rights began to take shape.

Several forces combined in the 1960s to increase the number of prison cases reaching the judiciary and to shake the foundations of the doctrine.[4] First, prisoners were becoming increasingly militant and assertive. This was particularly true of the Black Muslims, whose efforts to practice their religion were sometimes ignored or punished by corrections officials.[5] The Black Muslim First Amendment challenges represented some of the initial judicial victories for prisoners[6] and opened the door to a flood of litigation on a variety of prison-related issues.

Second, a civil rights-civil liberties bar was gradually emerging in the legal profession. Government and private foundation funding made possible litigation that otherwise would have been economically infeasible.[7] The importance of lawyer involvement should not be underestimated. Pro se prisoner complaints, too frequently authored by inmates with limited education and little or no legal training, were often confused and

---

[4]See, generally, David J. Rothman, Decarcerating Prisoners and Patients, 1 Civ. Lib. Rev. 8 (1973).

[5]See, e.g., Pierce v. La Vallee, 293 F.2d 233 (2d Cir. 1961); Sewell v. Pegelow, 291 F.2d 196 (4th Cir. 1961) (disapproved of by, District of Columbia v. Carter, 409 U.S. 418, 93 S. Ct. 602, 34 L. Ed. 2d 613 (1973)); Fulwood v. Clemmer, 206 F. Supp. 370 (D. D.C. 1962); Brown v. McGinnis, 10 N.Y.2d 531, 225 N.Y.S.2d 497, 180 N.E.2d 791 (1962). See also Ch 6.

[6]See Pierce v. La Vallee, 293 F.2d 233 (2d Cir. 1961); Sewell v. Pegelow, 291 F.2d 196 (4th Cir. 1961) (disapproved of by, District of Columbia v. Carter, 409 U.S. 418, 93 S. Ct. 602, 34 L. Ed. 2d 613 (1973)); Fulwood v. Clemmer, 206 F. Supp. 370 (D. D.C. 1962); Brown v. McGinnis, 10 N.Y.2d 531, 225 N.Y.S.2d 497, 180 N.E.2d 791 (1962).

[7]For examples of federal statutes authorizing government payment of attorneys, see 18 U.S.C. § 3006A(d); 42 U.S.C. § 1988. For a description of the growing use of legal services programs devoted to the needs of prisoners, see, e.g., Robert C. Hauhart, The First Year of Operating a Prisoners' Legal Services Program: Part I, 24 Clearinghouse Rev 106 (June 1990) (describing the legal services program established for inmates of the District of Columbia).

were easily dismissed by overburdened courts. Those same complaints, cast by attorneys into proper forms and buttressed by legal precedent, could not be ignored as readily.

Third, the judiciary was becoming more responsive to the plight of society's underprivileged. On the national level, the United States Supreme Court greatly expanded the rights of individuals vis-à-vis the state.[8] These opinions began to establish the principle that federal courts have a special role to play in protecting the rights of "discrete and insular minorities" who lack access to the political process necessary to effectively protect their own interests.[9] As one commentator put it: "The judicial obligation to enforce the rights of the politically powerless is at the heart of the American political system."[10] Prisoners, who are by and large poor, minority persons, generally feared and even despised by members of the public, are quintessential members of "discrete and insular" minorities whose needs command little respect in state legislatures.

---

[8]See, e.g., Brown v. Board of Educ. of Topeka, Kan., 349 U.S. 294, 75 S. Ct. 753, 99 L. Ed. 1083, 71 Ohio L. Abs. 584 (1955) (discrimination); Street v. New York, 394 U.S. 576, 89 S. Ct. 1354, 22 L. Ed. 2d 572 (1969) (free speech); Sherbert v. Verner, 374 U.S. 398, 83 S. Ct. 1790, 10 L. Ed. 2d 965 (1963) (free exercise). See also Katz v. U.S., 389 U.S. 347, 88 S. Ct. 507, 19 L. Ed. 2d 576 (1967) (Fourth Amendment protects privacy interests); U.S. v. Wade, 388 U.S. 218, 87 S. Ct. 1926, 18 L. Ed. 2d 1149 (1967) (right to an attorney at lineup); Miranda v. Arizona, 384 U.S. 436, 86 S. Ct. 1602, 16 L. Ed. 2d 694, 10 A.L.R.3d 974 (1966) (right to warnings before interrogations); Mapp v. Ohio, 367 U.S. 643, 81 S. Ct. 1684, 6 L. Ed. 2d 1081, 86 Ohio L. Abs. 513, 84 A.L.R.2d 933 (1961) (exclusionary rule applies to state prosecutions and bars illegally seized evidence).

[9]The term "discrete and insular minority" was first used by Chief Justice Harlan F. Stone in his now famous footnote in U.S. v. Carolene Products Co., 304 U.S. 144, 152 n4, 58 S. Ct. 778, 82 L. Ed. 1234 (1938) to describe those groups that most require judicial protection in order to enjoy their constitutional rights.

[10]John H. Ely, Democracy and Distrust 135 (1980). See also Robert M. Cover, The Origins of Judicial Activism in the Protection of Minorities, 91 Yale L.J. 1287 (1982).

BACKGROUND AND OVERVIEW § 1:4

Supreme Court decisions were also instrumental in two other respects. During this period, the Court extended most of the provisions of the Bill of Rights to the states through incorporation into the Due Process Clause.[11] This development allowed prisoners in state institutions to sue for violations of federal constitutional rights. In addition, the Supreme Court, by resurrecting the functional utility of the Civil Rights Statute (42 U.S.C.A. § 1983)[12] provided prisoners with an attractive procedural vehicle for challenging prison conditions and practices.

Finally, the public, including judges, was becoming increasingly aware of the sordid conditions that often characterized prison life. Penitentiaries traditionally have been built in remote locations, and this practice,

---

[11] By the 1960s, virtually all of the provisions of the Bill of Rights relating to prisoner rights were selectively incorporated into the Due Process Clause and thereby became binding on the states. See, e.g., John E. Nowak & Ronald D. Rotunda, Constitutional Law, Chapter 10 (6th ed 2000). Specifically, the Court incorporated the right to be free from unreasonable searches and seizures, Mapp v. Ohio, 367 U.S. 643, 81 S. Ct. 1684, 6 L. Ed. 2d 1081, 86 Ohio L. Abs. 513, 84 A.L.R.2d 933 (1961); the privilege against self-incrimination, Malloy v. Hogan, 378 U.S. 1, 84 S. Ct. 1489, 12 L. Ed. 2d 653 (1964); the right to counsel, Gideon v. Wainwright, 372 U.S. 335, 83 S. Ct. 792, 9 L. Ed. 2d 799, 93 A.L.R.2d 733 (1963); the right to confrontation, Pointer v. Texas, 380 U.S. 400, 85 S. Ct. 1065, 13 L. Ed. 2d 923 (1965), Washington v. Texas, 388 U.S. 14, 87 S. Ct. 1920, 18 L. Ed. 2d 1019 (1967), and the prohibition against cruel and unusual punishment, Robinson v. California, 370 U.S. 660, 82 S. Ct. 1417, 8 L. Ed. 2d 758 (1962). First Amendment rights, including freedom of speech, religion, and assembly, had previously been incorporated. See, e.g., Gitlow v. People of State of New York, 268 U.S. 652, 45 S. Ct. 625, 69 L. Ed. 1138 (1925); Whitney v. California, 274 U.S. 357, 47 S. Ct. 641, 71 L. Ed. 1095 (1927)(overruled in part by, Brandenburg v. Ohio, 395 U.S. 444, 89 S. Ct. 1827, 23 L. Ed. 2d 430 (1969)); De Jonge v. State of Oregon, 299 U.S. 353, 57 S. Ct. 255, 81 L. Ed. 278 (1937).

[12] See Monroe v. Pape, 365 U.S. 167, 81 S. Ct. 473, 5 L. Ed. 2d 492 (1961) (overruled by, Monell v. Department of Social Services of City of New York, 436 U.S. 658, 98 S. Ct. 2018, 56 L. Ed. 2d 611 (1978)).

coupled with highly restrictive institutional visitation and mail policies, complicated discovery of activities behind prison walls. This changed dramatically when prisoner strikes and riots, most notably the uprising at Attica, New York, dramatically brought the reality of prisons to public attention.[13] Widely read books written by convicts such as Caryl Chessman and Eldridge Cleaver also contributed to this consciousness-raising process.[14] These independent sources of knowledge regarding prison conditions may have made prisoner complaints more credible to judges. With these ingredients, the stage was set for the courts to begin the development of the prisoners' rights law.

§ 1:5 A Brief Overview of the Law of Prisoners' Rights

With the decline of the hands-off doctrine and the incorporation of most provisions of the Bill of Rights into the Fourteenth Amendment, courts increasingly faced the task of determining the scope of prisoners' constitutional rights. Building from the early cases dealing with the rights of Black Muslims to practice religion in prisons, lower courts in the 1970s came face-to-face with the grimmest conditions of confinement through litigation about the horrendous prison systems

---

[13]See Justin Brooks, Essay, How Can We Sleep While the Beds Are Burning? The Tumultuous Prison Culture of Attica Flourishes in American Prisons Twenty-Five Years Later, 45 Syracuse L. Rev. 159 (1996) (drawing comparisons between the prison culture in Attica and contemporary prisons; predicting that without prison reform, the prison culture of "Attica" will return).

[14]See, e.g., Eldridge Cleaver, Soul on Ice (1968); Caryl Chessman, Cell 2455 Death Row (1954); Caryl Chessman, The Face of Justice (1957); Caryl Chessman, Trial by Ordeal (1955). Popular writings on the problems in American prisons continue. See, e.g., Jennifer Wynn, Inside Rikers (2001); Joseph T. Hallinan, Going Up the River (2001); Ted Conover, Newjack: Guarding Sing Sing (2000).

BACKGROUND AND OVERVIEW § 1:5

in Arkansas, Alabama, and Mississippi.[1] The litigation quickly moved to more urban settings addressing equally detrimental conditions of confinement at such places as the infamous "Tombs" jail in lower Manhattan.[2] These cases collectively stood for the proposition that judicial review of the complaints of prisoners for more humane treatment was the new reality.

The United States Supreme Court began to be involved in this litigation shortly after the initial period of exploration of the rights of prisoners by the lower courts. Starting in 1964 with *Cooper v Pate*[3] and continuing to the present, the Court has regularly addressed the question of the rights of prisoners in a variety of contexts. In the chapters that follow, the many decisions of the Supreme Court that bear on the rights of prisoners will be discussed in some detail.[4] It might be useful here, however, to draw out of the Court's decisions some of the commonalties that govern the law of prisoners' rights, since the Court obviously plays "a critical role" in this effort.[5]

[Section 1:5]

[1] Pugh v. Locke, 406 F. Supp. 318 (M.D. Ala. 1976), judgment aff'd and remanded, 559 F.2d 283 (5th Cir. 1977), cert. granted in part, judgment rev'd in part, 438 U.S. 781, 98 S. Ct. 3057, 57 L. Ed. 2d 1114 (1978); Gates v. Collier, 501 F2d 129 (5th Cir 1974), amended, 390 F. Supp. 482 (ND Miss 1975), aff'd, 525 F.2d 965 (5th Cir 1976); Holt v. Sarver, 309 F. Supp. 362 (E.D. Ark. 1970), aff'd and remanded, 442 F.2d 304 (8th Cir. 1971).

[2] Rhem v. Malcolm, 371 F. Supp. 594, 627 (S.D. N.Y. 1974), opinion supplemented, 377 F. Supp. 995 (S.D. N.Y. 1974), aff'd and remanded, 507 F.2d 333 (2d Cir. 1974).

[3] Cooper v. Pate, 378 U.S. 546, 84 S. Ct. 1733, 12 L. Ed. 2d 1030 (1964) (per curiam).

[4] For a brief summary of the Supreme Court's prison opinions to 1995, see Jack E. Call, The Supreme Court and Prisoners' Rights, 59 Fed. Prob. 36 (1995).

[5] Barry R. Bell, Note, Prisoners' Rights, Institutional Needs and the Burger Court, 72 Va. L. Rev. 161, 162 (1986).

§ 1:6 —Rights Retained by Prisoners

Some general principles are now established. First, the Court has made clear that prisoners do not forfeit all constitutional rights.[1] Although this statement may not appear startling, it has real significance. For one thing, it stands in marked contrast to the earlier view that a prisoner was the slave of the state.[2] For another, by definition, it means that there are some limits to the deference that is owed to the views of prison administrators. The statement that prisoners do not forfeit all constitutional rights carries with it the promise of some level of judicial review of the actions of prison administrators to ensure that the rights that prisoners do enjoy are not taken from them.

But to say that inmates have rights is not to list what constitutional rights they retain. One way in which courts have addressed that question is to make the general observation that a prisoner "[r]etains all the rights of an ordinary citizen except those expressly, or by necessary implication, taken from him by law.[3] This superficial formula fails to identify which constitutional rights are taken by law, but it does make the point that

---

[Section 1:6]

[1]See, e.g., Jones v. North Carolina Prisoners' Labor Union, Inc., 433 U.S. 119, 129, 97 S. Ct. 2532, 53 L. Ed. 2d 629 (1977); Meachum v. Fano, 427 U.S. 215, 225, 96 S. Ct. 2532, 49 L. Ed. 2d 451 (1976); Wolff v. McDonnell, 418 U.S. 539, 555-56, 94 S. Ct. 2963, 41 L. Ed. 2d 935 (1974); Pell v. Procunier, 417 U.S. 817, 94 S. Ct. 2800, 41 L. Ed. 2d 495 (1974). See also Bell v. Wolfish, 441 U.S. 520, 545, 99 S. Ct. 1861, 60 L. Ed. 2d 447 (1979) (pretrial detainees also do not forfeit all constitutional rights).

[2]Ruffin v. Commonwealth, 62 Va. 790, 21 Gratt. 790, 1871 WL 4928 (1871).

[3]Procunier v. Martinez, 416 U.S. 396, 422-23, 94 S. Ct. 1800, 40 L. Ed. 2d 224 (1974) (overruled on other grounds by, Thornburgh v. Abbott, 490 U.S. 401, 109 S. Ct. 1874, 104 L. Ed. 2d 459 (1989)) (Marshall, J, concurring) (quoting Coffin v. Reichard, 143 F.2d 443, 445, 155 A.L.R. 143 (C.C.A. 6th Cir. 1944)).

BACKGROUND AND OVERVIEW § 1:6

important rights survive incarceration.[4]

While many rights survive, it is not difficult to discern that some rights retained by free citizens are lost or necessarily diminished by imprisonment. To take an obvious example, the right to travel, which has been deemed fundamental by the Court,[5] cannot be enjoyed by prisoners because of their forced confinement. Other rights are necessarily restricted by confinement. Housed in a congregate setting under the supervision of agents of the state, prisoners inevitably do not benefit from the same expectations of privacy available to persons living in private quarters.[6]

Nevertheless, the Court has determined that most of the constitutional rights contained in the Bill of Rights survive incarceration, albeit in a diminished state. First Amendment rights to free speech and the free exercise of religion, the Eighth Amendment right to be free of cruel and inhumane punishment, the right not to be deprived of a liberty interest without due process, the right to petition courts for relief, and the right to be protected from discrimination are all examples of constitutional rights that the Court has held are available to prisoners.[7]

---

[4]See Turner v. Safley, 482 U.S. 78, 84, 107 S. Ct. 2254, 96 L. Ed. 2d 64 (1987) (freedom of expression and right to marry); O'Lone v. Estate of Shabazz, 482 U.S. 342, 348, 107 S. Ct. 2400, 96 L. Ed. 2d 282 (1987) (freedom of religion); Wolff v. McDonnell, 418 U.S. 539, 555, 94 S. Ct. 2963, 41 L. Ed. 2d 935 (1974) (liberty interests survive); Pell v. Procunier, 417 U.S. 817, 94 S. Ct. 2800, 41 L. Ed. 2d 495 (1974).

[5]Shapiro v. Thompson, 394 U.S. 618, 89 S. Ct. 1322, 22 L. Ed. 2d 600 (1969) (overruled in part on other grounds by, Edelman v. Jordan, 415 U.S. 651, 94 S. Ct. 1347, 39 L. Ed. 2d 662 (1974)).

[6]Hudson v. Palmer, 468 U.S. 517, 526, 104 S. Ct. 3194, 82 L. Ed. 2d 393 (1984).

[7]Wilson v. Seiter, 501 U.S. 294, 111 S. Ct. 2321, 115 L. Ed. 2d 271 (1991) (cruel and unusual punishment); Rhodes v. Chapman, 452 U.S. 337, 101 S. Ct. 2392, 69 L. Ed. 2d 59 (1981) (same); Turner v. Safley, 482 U.S. 78, 84, 107 S. Ct. 2254, 96 L. Ed. 2d 64 (1987) (freedom of expression and right to marry); O'Lone v. Estate

§ 1:7 —Standards for Determining whether Prisoners' Rights Have Been Violated

A separate question from a determination of what rights inmates retain is the issue of the standard that is utilized to determine whether those rights have been violated. In many ways, this is a key question around which much of the current debate rages. If the standard for violation of prisoners' rights is high, then more rights will be recognized in practice. If, on the other hand, the standard is lax and the burden placed on prisoners difficult to meet, prisoners' rights might remain more theoretical than real.

Currently, at this stage in its development, no unified theory of prisoners' rights law setting a single standard has emerged from the Supreme Court. Rather, the Court has marked out at least four distinct approaches depending on the nature of the right at stake. These approaches, which are discussed at length in the chapters of the book to which they apply, include:

(1) the rational relationship test of *Turner v Safley* for the determination of most substantive constitutional rights;[1]

(2) the objective and subjective tests for determination of Eighth Amendment violations;[2]

(3) the procedural due process model for determination of issues relating to individual disciplinary decisions to which an inmate is subjected;[3] and

(4) the analysis reserved for specially protected

---

of Shabazz, 482 U.S. 342, 348, 107 S. Ct. 2400, 96 L. Ed. 2d 282 (1987) (freedom of religion); Bounds v. Smith, 430 U.S. 817, 97 S. Ct. 1491, 52 L. Ed. 2d 72 (1977) (right of access to courts); Lee v. Washington, 390 U.S. 333, 88 S. Ct. 994, 19 L. Ed. 2d 1212 (1968) (racial discrimination).

[Section 1:7]

[1]Discussed in Chs 5, 6. The rational relationship test is discussed at some length in §§ 1:9 et seq.

[2]Discussed in Ch 2.

[3]Discussed in Chs 9, 10.

rights in prison, including the right of access to the courts and the right to be free from discrimination.[4]

The first three of these approaches share the common notion that caution and considerable deference is in order when adjudicating the claims of inmates. In the leading case on this subject, *Turner v Safley*,[5] for example, a closely divided (5-4) Court held that a variant of the reasonable relationship test was the appropriate test for cases dealing even with preferred First Amendment rights in a prison setting. While the Court recognized that "prison walls do not form a barrier separating inmates from the protections of the Constitution,"[6] it expressed serious reservations about an overly aggressive role for the federal courts in prison cases. Prisons, the Court said, are difficult to operate, and courts lack the "expertise, planning and the commitment of resources" powers that the legislative and executive branches of government have to run them.[7] Moreover, prison administration is a function that has been committed to the legislatures and the executive. Therefore, "separation of powers concerns counsel a policy of judicial restraint."[8] The Court further noted that federalism problems are raised when federal courts are involved in determining the rights of inmates in state prison systems.[9]

Because of these concerns, the Court held that strict scrutiny analysis, which is normally called for when the state impinges on the First Amendment interests of citizens, was not appropriate in prisoners' rights cases. To apply the normal constitutional standard, the Court

---

[4]Discussed in Ch 11.
[5]Turner v. Safley, 482 U.S. 78, 107 S. Ct. 2254, 96 L. Ed. 2d 64 (1987).
[6]*Id.*
[7]*Id.*
[8]*Id.*
[9]*Id.*

held, "would seriously hamper [prison officials'] ability to anticipate security problems and to adopt innovative solutions to the intractable problems of prison administration."[10] In addition, applying a strict scrutiny analysis would mean that "[c]ourts inevitably would become the primary arbiters of what constitutes the best solution to every administrative problem" in the prisons.[11] Instead, the Court chose a variation of a reasonable relationship test. Under that standard, a prison rule that restricts prisoners' rights "is valid if it is reasonably related to legitimate penological interests."[12]

Echoing this passion for deference, the Supreme Court also held that there can be no violation of the Eighth Amendment without a finding that the prison officials' subjective intent was to subject an inmate to cruel and unusual punishment[13] and that, when dealing with prison disturbances, a greater level of culpability is required in order to accommodate the need of prison officials to deal aggressively with explosive situations.[14] Moreover, in the procedural due process arena, the Court has stressed the need for "mutual accommodation" to the "needs and exigencies of the institutional environment."[15]

The Court's deferential standards can be criticized on a number of grounds. In the words of one commentator, the Court's approach "places prisoners' constitutional rights in a very precarious situation . . . [it] provides [prison] officials with great discretion to curtail and

---

[10]*Id.*

[11]*Id.*

[12]*Id.* The four-part test devised by the *Turner* Court is described in Chs 5, 6.

[13]Wilson v. Seiter, 501 U.S. 294, 111 S. Ct. 2321, 115 L. Ed. 2d 271 (1991).

[14]Whitley v. Albers, 475 U.S. 312, 106 S. Ct. 1078, 89 L. Ed. 2d 251 (1986).

[15]Wolff v. McDonnell, 418 U.S. 539, 555, 94 S. Ct. 2963, 41 L. Ed. 2d 935 (1974).

§ 1:7 BACKGROUND AND OVERVIEW

abolish many basic . . . rights of the incarcerated."[16] "[W]ith only minimal justification" prison officials can extinguish these rights.[17] In addition, with the tendency of the Court to subject infringements of fundamental constitutional rights of prisoners to a low-level reasonable relationship test, the Court has refused to recognize any hierarchy of values among important constitutionally protected interests. This trivializes important constitutional rights by treating the First Amendment rights to go to church or to read a book in the same manner as the right of an inmate to possess small items of personal property in his or her cell. Moreover, there is-as the discussions in the relevant chapters reveal-a substantial amount of ambiguity in the nature of judicial scrutiny called for by the Court's deferential tests. Perhaps most telling is the complaint that the Court has been inching the law back to the now thoroughly discredited hands-off doctrine.[18]

Given these criticisms, it is possible that the standards will evolve, in the coming years, toward a posture more protective of prisoners' constitutional rights. Indeed, the best testimony of the unstable nature of much of the current Supreme Court doctrine in the field of prisoners' rights is that many of the major recent decisions in this field are very closely divided.[19] An example of the opposing approach on the Court to the

---

[16]Matthew P. Blischak, Note, O'Lone v Shabazz: The State of Prisoners' Religious Free Exercise Rights, 37 Am. U. L. Rev. 453, 483 (1988).

[17]*Id.* at 478. See also Hedieh Nasheri, A Spirit of Meanness: Courts, Prisons and Prisoners, 27 Cumb. L. Rev. 1173 (1997).

[18]See, e.g., Susan Herman, Slashing and Burning Prisoners' Rights: Congress and the Supreme Court in Dialogue, 77 Or. L. Rev. 1229, 1258 (1998); Cheryl Dunn Giles, Turner v Safley and Its Progeny: A Gradual Retreat to the "Hands-Off" Doctrine?, 35 Ariz. L. Rev. 219 (1993).

[19]Several important prisoners' rights cases were 5-4 decisions. See, e.g., Sandin v. Conner, 515 U.S. 472, 115 S. Ct. 2293, 132 L. Ed. 2d 418 (1995); Wilson v. Seiter, 501 U.S. 294, 111 S. Ct. 2321, 115 L. Ed. 2d 271 (1991); O'Lone v. Estate of Shabazz, 482 U.S. 342, 107 S. Ct. 2400, 96 L. Ed. 2d 282 (1987); Turner v. Safley, 482

§ 1:7

current doctrine was well expressed in a dissenting opinion by Justice Brennan, who wrote that a high level of deference to prison officials was not justified. He explained:

> The Constitution was not adopted as a means of enhancing the efficiency with which government officials conduct their affairs, nor as a blueprint for ensuring sufficient reliance on administrative expertise. Rather it was meant to provide a bulwark against infringements that might otherwise be justified as necessary expedients of governing.[20]

At this stage in the development of prison law, with the ultimate pattern of that law still unsettled, it is possible that the current standards will change over time.[21]

In any event, as the ensuing chapters and the length of this book reveal, it is an overreaction to maintain that the Supreme Court's current jurisprudence has eliminated prisoners' rights. To the contrary, while in some areas of the law the hurdles to judicial relief are not insubstantial, there can be little doubt that the courts remain open and available to enforce constitutional rights of inmates. Indeed, in these pages, one can discern a conscientious struggle by many members of the judiciary to ensure respect for constitutional rights while, at the same time, not unduly interfering with the prerogatives of prison officials. In the process, many entitlements that ordinary citizens take for granted, but were only prisoners' dreams a few short years ago, are now realistic guarantees for prisoners, at least in a

---

U.S. 78, 107 S. Ct. 2254, 96 L. Ed. 2d 64 (1987); Whitley v. Albers, 475 U.S. 312, 106 S. Ct. 1078, 89 L. Ed. 2d 251 (1986).

[20]O'Lone v. Estate of Shabazz, 482 U.S. 342, 356, 107 S. Ct. 2400, 96 L. Ed. 2d 282 (1987) (Brennan, J, dissenting).

[21]As Justice White stated, "Our conclusion . . . is not graven in stone. As the nature of the prison disciplinary process changes in future years, circumstances may then exist which will require further consideration and reflection of this Court." Wolff v. McDonnell, 418 U.S. 539, 571-72, 94 S. Ct. 2963, 41 L. Ed. 2d 935 (1974).

modified form. The real story of this book is the story of how courts and litigators struggle to resolve the inherent tension between the need to safeguard prisoners' rights and preserving the legitimate institutional requirements of prison officials.

§ 1:8 —Prison Litigation Reform Act

A major development in this field occurred in 1996 with the passage of the Prison Litigation Reform Act (PLRA).[1] The PLRA contains a host of barriers enacted by Congress that restrict inmates seeking to litigate claims regarding the condition of confinement in prison. This Act, which has had a profound impact on prison litigation, is discussed in detail in this book.[2]

§ 1:9 An Introduction to the Four-Factor *Turner v. Safley* Analysis

As mentioned earlier, in *Turner v. Safley*[1] the United States Supreme Court set out a four-factor test for determining the reasonableness of the many kinds of prison regulations. The four-part analysis enunciated in *Turner v. Safley*[2] is the standard that is used most often by courts to determine the constitutionality of prison practices. It is now the governing standard for First Amendment claims, including speech and religion claims and normally is used in determining the constitutionality of any prison rule which is not governed by the Eighth Amendment or some other specific constitutional provision. Because of its importance to so many areas covered by this book, and because it is so indicative of the Supreme Court's approach to prison cases, it

---

[Section 1:8]
  [1]Pub L No 104-134, 110 Stat 1321, (1996).
  [2]See Ch 16.

[Section 1:9]
  [1]Turner v. Safley, 482 U.S. 78, 107 S. Ct. 2254, 96 L. Ed. 2d 64 (1987).
  [2]*Id.*

is worth taking the time to examine the *Turner* test in this first chapter of the book.

In *Turner*, the Court held that four factors determine whether a prison rule is reasonable. The first factor requires a determination that there is "a valid, rational connection" between the regulation and legitimate governmental objectives. The second factor asks whether there are "alternative means of exercising the right at issue." The third factor is a consideration of the effect that the claimed right of the prisoner would have on the institution including other inmates and corrections officers and government resources. The fourth and final factor examines whether there are obvious, easy alternatives available to prison officials to meet their legitimate interests without impinging on prisoner rights.

Turner is less precise in its discussion of how to apply this four-part test. The opinion is ambiguous about how each of the four branches of the test are to be applied and provides no guidance about the relative weight of each of these factors. Each of these ambiguities has caused problems for lower courts that have struggled to apply the *Turner* test. The discussion that follows addresses these issues.

§ 1:10 —The First *Turner* Factor: The Valid, Rational Connection Test

The first-and seemingly the most clear-cut-branch of the inquiry asks whether there is a "valid, rational connection" between the restriction and the governmental interests invoked to justify the restriction. To satisfy this requirement, the interests invoked need to be "legitimate."[1] Given the breadth of the government's interest in maintaining security, providing for rehabili-

---

[Section 1:10]
[1]Turner v. Safley, 482 U.S. 78, 89, 107 S. Ct. 2254, 96 L. Ed. 2d 64 (1987).

tation of inmates, and conserving resources,[2] it is not terribly difficult for prison officials to tie a restriction to one of these sweeping, and valid, interests.[3] Nevertheless, courts will require prison officials to provide an articulable reason linking the restriction to some valid interest of the prison.[4] Manufactured reasons are not permitted.[5] Moreover, the reason must relate to valid penological interests of the state.[6] Without a valid articulable reason for the restriction, summary judgment will not be granted in favor of the prison.[7]

---

[2] All of these have been identified by the Court as legitimate governmental interests in the operation of prisons. Procunier v. Martinez, 416 U.S. 396, 412, 94 S. Ct. 1800, 40 L. Ed. 2d 224 (1974).

[3] See Powell v. Estelle, 959 F.2d 22, 22 Fed. R. Serv. 3d 904 (5th Cir. 1992) (prohibition of facial hair and long hair upheld based on the rationally related test); see also Brown v. Wallace, 957 F.2d 564, 22 Fed. R. Serv. 3d 285 (8th Cir. 1992) (court upheld prohibition on long hair, finding equal protection claim of plaintiff no bar even though female inmates and male inmates at halfway houses were allowed to wear long hair).

[4] See, e.g., L'Heureux v. Ashton, 181 F.3d 79 (1st Cir. 1998) (finding that prison officials presented sufficient justification for the restricting the inmates' associational rights); Allen v. Cuomo, 100 F.3d 253 (2d Cir. 1996) (agreeing with district court that the interests enhanced by a five dollar surcharge for violating prison rules-deterring inmate misbehavior and raising revenues-were legitimate interests that passed constitutional muster); Young v. Coughlin, 866 F.2d 567 (2d Cir. 1989).

[5] Turner v. Safley, 482 U.S. 78, 79, 107 S. Ct. 2254, 96 L. Ed. 2d 64 (1987).

[6] See, e.g., O'Lone v. Estate of Shabazz, 482 U.S. 342, 349, 107 S. Ct. 2400, 96 L. Ed. 2d 282 (1987); Duamutef v. Hollins, 297 F.3d 108 (2d Cir. 2002); Mauro v. Arpaio, 188 F.3d 1054 (9th Cir. 1999), cert. denied, 529 U.S. 1018, 120 S. Ct. 1419, 146 L. Ed. 2d 311 (2000) (finding the relationship between the jail's policy of prohibiting the possession of sexually explicit materials and the goals of preventing sexual harassment of female officers, inmate rehabilitation, and maintenance of jail security rationally related).

[7] See, e.g., Gill v. Defrank, 2000 WL 897152 (S.D. N.Y. 2000), judgment aff'd, 8 Fed. Appx. 35 (2d Cir. 2001); Street v. Maloney, 991 F.2d 786 (1st Cir. 1993).

§ 1:10

The more formidable task is determining whether the link between the restriction and the governmental interest, when one is offered, is a logical one. The problem most frequently arises in two situations in which prison officials attempt to show that restrictions are reasonably related to the officials' important interests. The first situation occurs when defendants claim that the restriction is reasonably related to a valid interest, but fail to offer evidence demonstrating that there were any problems before the restriction was imposed. The second situation arises when the record shows that the prison, without any apparent difficulty, allows other practices that are similar in nature to the barred practice. In these two situations, the question will be: have the prison officials done enough to forge the bond between their interests and the restriction to satisfy the *Turner* reasonable relationship test?

Some courts have ruled that, in these situations, the prison officials have satisfied the reasonable relationship test. They justify this conclusion by pointing to language in *Turner* that corrections officials may "anticipate security problems and adopt innovative solutions."[8] These courts will uphold restrictions as rationally related to prison security even if there is no concrete evidence that the restriction will prevent a collapse of security or other problems for the facility.[9] For similar reasons, even though evidence demonstrates

---

[8] O'Lone v. Estate of Shabazz, 482 U.S. 342, 349, 107 S. Ct. 2400, 96 L. Ed. 2d 282 (1987) (quoting Turner v. Safley, 482 U.S. 78, 89, 107 S. Ct. 2254, 96 L. Ed. 2d 64 (1987)).

[9] See, e.g., Amatel v. Reno, 156 F.3d 192 (D.C. Cir. 1998) (holding that there was a rational connection between the interest of rehabilitation and regulations on pornography in the prison even though there was no concrete evidence that pornography had a negative effect on rehabilitation); Giano v. Senkowski, 54 F.3d 1050 (2d Cir. 1995) (holding the mere threat of violence established a rational connection between the regulation banning nude pictures of prisoners' significant others and the penological interest of preventing violence); Standing Deer v Carlson, 831 F.2d 1525 (9th Cir. 1987) (holding that native American inmates could be prevented from wearing headbands in the dining halls even

Background and Overview § 1:10

that the prison officials were inconsistent in practices that they restricted and those that they did not, some courts have held, nevertheless, that the reasonable relationship test is satisfied.[10]

However, other courts are more wary. In *Aiello v. Litscher*,[11] for example defendant prison officials enacted a state regulation prohibiting access to allegedly sexually explicit materials.[12] The defendants claimed that the regulation was related to legitimate correctional goals of maintaining security, promoting rehabilitation, and preventing sexual harassment of female guards. The court disagreed, concluding that that "in the absence of both scientific or expert credible evidence and common sense, a trier of fact could conclude reasonably that there is no rational connection between the asserted objectives and the ban."[13] The challenged rule was so broad that it encompassed banning such items as Michelangelo's Sistine Chapel, artwork by Herrera, a Sports Illustrated swimsuit issue and issues of Vanity Fair, Rolling Stone, Maxim and various fitness and motorcycle magazines.[14]

A similar willingness to carefully analyze the justifications that prison officials offer for restrictions on

---

though prison officials did not offer evidence to show that the headbands caused any sanitation problem); Muhammad v Lynaugh, 966 F.2d 901 (5th Cir. 1992) (restricted wearing of "Kufis" except in cell and chapel in order to control possible spread of contraband).

[10]Higgins v Burroughs, 834 F.2d 76 (3d Cir. 1987).

[11]Aiello v. Litscher, 104 F. Supp. 2d 1068 (W.D. Wis. 2000).

[12]These materials included any "written, visual, video, or audio representation or reproduction that depicts any of the following: (a) human sexual behavior, (b) sadomasochistic abuse, (c) unnatural preoccupation with human excretion, (d) nudity which appeals to the prurient interest in sex, and (e) nudity which is not part of any published or printed material, such as a personal nude photograph." Aiello v. Litscher, 104 F. Supp. 2d 1068, 1072 (W.D. Wis. 2000).

[13]Aiello v. Litscher, 104 F. Supp. 2d 1068, 1072 (W.D. Wis. 2000).
[14]*Id.*

religious practices is found in the Sixth Circuit's decision in *Whitney v Brown*.[15]

The plaintiffs, Jewish inmates of different security classifications at a Michigan prison, challenged a prison rule that prevented them from gathering together for religious services and for a Passover observance. The defendants argued that the rule was necessary because of concerns for the safety of the minimum and medium security Jewish inmates who would have to travel into the maximum-security area to attend the services. The Sixth Circuit held that this justification was not rational, given the prison's inconsistent practice of permitting an outside rabbi and his volunteers into the maximum-security wing on a regular basis.[16]

Thus, the better reasoned decisions indicate that, while prison officials are entitled, under the *Turner* standard, to deference if they can show a valid, rational connection between a rule that restricts certain practices and a legitimate governmental interest, prison officials do not have carte blanche to tender reasons which are "arbitrary, exaggerated and pretextual."[17]

Whether a challenged regulation is reasonably related to a valid governmental interest, therefore, should properly be considered a question of fact, not supposition.[18]

To do this, courts must closely examine the factual premises on which the defendants rely and must independently assess their connection to the challenged practices.

§ 1:11 —The Second *Turner* Factor: The Search for Alternative Means

The second of the four *Turner* factors asks whether

---

[15]Whitney v. Brown, 882 F.2d 1068 (6th Cir. 1989).

[16]Whitney v. Brown, 882 F.2d 1068, 1076 (6th Cir. 1989).

[17]Williams v. Lane, 851 F.2d 867, 875, 11 Fed. R. Serv. 3d 753 (7th Cir. 1988).

[18]Hunafa v. Murphy, 907 F.2d 46, 48 (7th Cir. 1990) (Posner, J).

there are "alternative means of exercising the right at issue."¹ If there are alternative means of exercising a certain right, the courts will be more willing to uphold the restriction or regulation. In *Turner*, the Court dealt with a challenge to a rule that restricted mail correspondence with inmates at other institutions. Although the Court upheld the rule, it found that the practice had only a limited effect on prisoners' rights to correspond with others. The Court stated that the "regulation does not deprive prisoners of all means of expression. Rather, it bars communication only with a limited class of other people with whom prison officials have particular cause to be concerned-inmates at other institutions. . . ."²

The Court did not deal with other, more generic alternatives to free expression in the prison, thus lending support to the idea that what the Court had in mind in this branch of the test is alternatives to the particular, not the general, right invoked.³

However, in *O'Lone v. Estate of Shabazz*,⁴ the Court appeared to embrace the more generic approach when it found that, although Friday services for Muslims were an important part of their faith, alternative means of generally practicing their faith, such as observances of other Muslim holidays and services, were sufficient substitutes. This leaves uncertainty in the lower courts; should they look for particular alternatives means or generic alternatives means of exercising the right at issue?⁵

[Section 1:11]

¹Turner v. Safley, 482 U.S. 78, 86, 107 S. Ct. 2254, 96 L. Ed. 2d 64 (1987).

²*Id.* at 92.

³See Turner v. Safley, 482 U.S. 78, 86, 107 S. Ct. 2254, 96 L. Ed. 2d 64 (1987).

⁴O'Lone v. Estate of Shabazz, 482 U.S. 342, 107 S. Ct. 2400, 96 L. Ed. 2d 282 (1987).

⁵An illustrative recent case is Mauro v. Arpaio, 188 F.3d 1054 (9th Cir. 1999), cert. denied, 529 U.S. 1018, 120 S. Ct. 1419, 146 L.

§ 1:11

The difference between these competing alternatives can also determine the outcome of a case. Two cases, both dealing with the rights of Jewish inmates to practice their faiths, illustrate the difference. In the first, *Whitney v Brown*,[6] the plaintiffs complained that they were not able to attend a congregate Passover service. The court, applying the "particular alternative interpretation" of this branch of the *Turner* test, held that there were no alternative means available to prisoners to observe the Passover holiday.[7] Even though there were other ways that the prison allowed the inmate to practice his faith, this was enough for the court to find that the prisoner had met his burden of showing that there were no alternatives. In the second case, *Fromer v Scully*,[8] however, the court adhered to the generic approach with dramatically different results. Fromer dealt with a challenge by Jewish inmates to a rule that prevented them from growing beards. Even though this was an important religious practice of Orthodox Jews, and the rule, if enforced, precluded any alternative method of practicing that tenet of the faith, the court held that alternative means of exercising the right to practice religion were available to the plaintiff. who was "freely [able to] observe a

---

Ed. 2d 311 (2000). There, an inmate challenged a jail policy that denied access to sexually explicit materials. The court held that there were alternative means of obtaining explicit material other than the prohibited sexually explicit materials that showed frontal nudity, for example, sexually explicit letters between inmates and others or sexually explicit articles, or photographs of clothed females. In its analysis, the *Mauro* case seems to adopt the more generic approach of *O'Lone*.

[6]Whitney v Brown, 882 F.2d 1068 (6th Cir. 1989).

[7]The court held that the only alternative available, celebrating Passover alone, while permissible as a matter of religious law, was not an acceptable alternative since it would be a "miserable" experience. Whitney v. Brown, 882 F.2d 1068, 1070 (6th Cir. 1989).

[8]Fromer v Scully, 874 F.2d 69 (2d Cir. 1989).

34

number of [his] religious obligations."[9]

Given the vagueness of the Court's articulation of this branch of its test, it not surprising that lower courts have reached different results and are presently in a "state of confusion" over how to handle this part of the Turner test.

§ 1:12 —The Third *Turner* Factor: The Cost of Accommodation

The third *Turner* factor is designed to take into account the impact that the accommodation of the asserted constitutional right would have on prison personnel, other inmates, and the allocation of prison resources. To undertake this analysis, the courts should consider whether there are practical options available to defendants that, if implemented, would allow the plaintiff the practice that he or she requests without causing unreasonable difficulties for the prison.

Several aspects of this branch of the test are worth noting. One is that the burden is on the plaintiff to propose the alternatives that the court must evaluate. As Chief Justice Rehnquist stated in *Turner*, "we have rejected the notion that 'prison officials. . . have to set up and then shoot down every conceivable alternative method of accommodating the claimant's constitutional rights.'"[1] Another is that, in evaluating the alternatives suggested by the plaintiff, a court must examine all of the costs of implementation, including not only the direct financial costs, but also other related costs, including costs of prison security and management of the facility.[2]

In making this determination, the Supreme Court forewarned lower courts to be aware of the "ripple ef-

---

[9]*Id.*

[Section 1:12]
[1]Turner v. Safley, 482 U.S. 78, 90-91, 107 S. Ct. 2254, 96 L. Ed. 2d 64 (1987).
[2]*Id.* at 90.

fect" that a proposed accommodation might have on prison life.[3] The allusion to the ripple effect phenomenon is intended to sensitize the reviewing courts to the fact that changes to one area of prison administration can often cause problems in other areas. If the court finds that the ripple effect in a particular case will be significant-and undesirable-it must reject the alternate methods proposed by the plaintiffs.[4]

The analysis called for by this branch of the *Turner* test is similar in nature to the analysis required under the valid, rational connection test discussed earlier.[5] However, while the two tests are similar in that they both trigger a reasonableness analysis, they are not the same. It is important, therefore, not to confuse them. The first *Turner* factor is intended to determine the rational connection between the prison rule and the governmental interest that is allegedly furthered by the rule. To do this, one considers the reasonableness of the rule in the context of the prison as it currently is operated. The third *Turner* factor, by contrast, considers a more hypothetical state of affairs in which the court considers the reasonableness of the prohibition in light of alternative ways of operating the prison proposed by the plaintiff. Evaluating this factor, the court must necessarily envision what prison life would probably be like if the prohibition did not exist.

In the aftermath of *Turner*, a common argument made under the third branch of the test by defendants deserves consideration here. The argument asserts that, if plaintiffs prevail and are permitted to exercise a particular right, other inmates will become jealous on ac-

---

[3]*Id.*

[4]*Id.* at 92.

[5]In evaluating both the first and third factors of the test, the court is likely to hear security, administrative convenience, and fiscal concerns voiced by prison officials, and these arguments must be considered seriously by courts. The arguments are subject to a reasonableness standard, that is to say, if the arguments of the defendants in support of either of these factors do not stand up to logical reflection, they should not be credited.

§ 1:12

count of the special favors granted the plaintiffs. This, the argument runs, will create an improper ripple effect that should not be permitted.[6]

There are two difficulties with this line of thought. Using the right to exercise one's religion as an example, the first difficulty is that it can only be true if the practice that the plaintiff desires to participate in is one that would appeal to nonreligious inmates as well as religious ones. This is not invariably the case. Not everyone, for example, would accept a vegetarian[7] or a pork-free[8] diet, nor is it fair to say that a non-Muslim prisoner would covet a Muslim prisoner's status when he or she is given special dispensation to observe the month-long holiday of Ramadan. (To observe this holiday, a Muslim is enjoined from eating any food from sunup to sundown.)[9] One, therefore, needs to use care to distinguish between those practices that might engender intra-inmate jealousies and those that will not.

The second difficulty is even more fundamental, at least in the context of religion, where this issue often arises: the argument fails to recognize that, in an important sense, all free exercise claims are, by definition, appeals for special treatment when there are sincere and important reasons for such treatment. If favoritism could be used routinely in every free exercise case to provide a rationale for refusing to grant exemptions from state-imposed regulations, this important constitutional right would be rendered a nullity.

This is not to say that jealousy should not be a factor to consider. When envy realistically threatens to rise to the level of violence, as might occur on occasion in a

---

[6]See Turner v. Safley, 482 U.S. 78, 107 S. Ct. 2254, 96 L. Ed. 2d 64 (1987); Dawson v. Scurr, 986 F.2d 257 (8th Cir. 1993); Koenig v Vannelli, 971 F.2d 422 (9th Cir. 1992); Goodwin v. Turner, 908 F.2d 1395 (8th Cir. 1990).

[7]Johnson v. Moore, 948 F.2d 517 (9th Cir. 1991).

[8]Kahey v. Jones, 836 F.2d 948 (5th Cir. 1988).

[9]Al-Alamin v. Gramley, 926 F.2d 680 (7th Cir. 1991).

§ 1:12   Rights of Prisoners, Third Edition

penal setting, a court can, consistent with the teachings of *Turner*, conclude that accommodation of plaintiff's rights is not worth the price. However, before reaching this conclusion, a court ought to have been shown proof that jealousy is extremely likely and will incite undesired conduct.

§ 1:13   —The Fourth *Turner* Factor: The Presence of a *De Minimis* Alternative

The fourth *Turner* factor considers whether the policy is an exaggerated response to the jail's concerns. The *Turner* Court stated that "the existence of obvious, easy alternatives may be evidence that the regulation is not reasonable, but is an exaggerated response to prison concerns."[1] The burden is on the prisoner challenging the regulation, not on the prison officials, to show that there are obvious, easy alternatives to the regulation. The prisoner must show an alternative that accommodates their rights at *de minimis* cost to security interests. However, it is difficult to understand what this factor adds to the analysis that is not already encompassed within the contemplation of the third factor.

Thus, if the defendants prevail under the third factor, it follows a fortiori that there are no *de minimis* alternatives helpful to prisoners.[2] By parity of reasoning, if the plaintiffs prevail under the third test, the fourth is, almost by definition, met. The only plausible value of the fourth factor is that it can serve as a means of informing the analysis under the third factor by assisting the court in weighing the costs of alternatives suggested by the plaintiff. As an independent mode of review, it is possible, but not very likely, that the *de minimis* factor might be useful if the deliberation under the third factor is inconclusive. If that is the case, a

---

[Section 1:13]
   [1]Turner v. Safley, 482 U.S. 78, 90-91, 107 S. Ct. 2254, 96 L. Ed. 2d 64 (1987).
   [2]U.S. v. Stotts, 925 F.2d 83 (4th Cir. 1991).

court might reasonably decide that the fourth factor ought to play a determinative role in resolving the case.

§ 1:14 —The Weight to Be Assigned to the Four *Turner* Factors

How should a court rule if the *Turner* factors do not all point in the same direction? This question can easily arise. To take one straightforward example: a court determines that a prison rule bears a rational relationship to a legitimate state interest, thereby satisfying the first *Turner* test, but also holds that the plaintiff's constitutional rights are so completely abridged by the prohibition that he or she is left without realistic alternative methods of exercising those rights, so that the rule running afoul of the second test. Or to take another plain illustration: a court decides that there are alternative methods of exercising a certain right available to the plaintiff, thereby satisfying the second test, but also determines that there are obvious, easy means available to the defendants to achieve their interests without enforcing the rule, thereby leading to the result that the fourth *Turner* factor is not satisfied.

Unfortunately, *Turner* itself does not tell us what a court should do in either of these situations. In fact, the question these hypotheticals raise was not addressed in *Turner*, perhaps because the Court determined that the facts of that case favored the defendants on each of the four factors. *Turner*, therefore, does not indicate the relative weight assigned to each of the four factors, or the interrelationships among them.

Without guidance from the Supreme Court, lower courts have not reached a consensus about how to deal with this question, nor have they contributed any meaningful discussion as to how the problem might be resolved. In fact, no clear method of approaching the four *Turner* factors has emerged. Until the Supreme Court provides guidance on this question, courts and attorneys will have to struggle to find a way to apply the four factors in a manner that is sensitive to the purposes of the test. What follows are several suggestions about how this evaluation should be conducted.

The primary recommendation is that the first factor ought to be determinative if it favors the prisoner's claim. The reason is that the first test itself deals with the rational connection between the rule and valid institutional goals. This is a qualitative question: does the restriction make sense? If that threshold determination results in a finding that the rule is not logically connected, then the other factors add little to the analysis that is not already present, since the overriding purpose of *Turner* is to determine the reasonableness of restrictions on prisoners' rights. Given that purpose, logic compels the conclusion that, if the first test is not satisfied, there is no reason for a court to resolve the remaining three.

However, if the first factor leads to a finding in favor of the defendants, then the other factors need to be considered. The reason for this is that the remaining factors aid the court in determining the quantitative question: is the restriction excessive? These questions include asking: are there legitimate alternatives to the exercising the right at issue that might easily accommodate the plaintiff at small cost, and what is the impact of the prohibition on the plaintiff's exercise of his or her rights? These are important considerations that, depending on the facts in a particular case, might lead a court to decide that a prohibition is unconstitutional even though at first blush it appeared to be reasonable.

If the remaining factors need to be examined, the question remains: what weight ought to be given to them? Inevitably, the answer to this question will vary depending on the facts of individual cases. Nevertheless, two preliminary observations are in order. The first is the importance of the fourth factor dealing with the presence or absence of *de minimis* alternatives. If a court determines that there are such alternatives, that finding is powerful evidence of the unconstitutionality of the prison policy.[1] A contrary finding would lead to the absurd result that deprivations of important constitutional rights are permissible even if there are easy alternative means of avoiding them.

A final observation concerns the second factor under the *Turner* test, dealing with alternative methods of exercising a particular right, and its relationship with the third branch of the test, which deals with examination of the effect that the claimed right of the prisoner would have on the institution, including other inmates and corrections officers and government resources. If, using the particular approach under the second factor, a court determines that the deprivation of the right is complete, not merely a regulation of, for example, the time, place, or manner of its exercise, then the third factor becomes more important than it would otherwise be. In such a case, a more searching examination ought to be called for under the third *Turner* factor than would be true if the plaintiff is not being completely deprived of the right. By similar reasoning, if the rule does not work a total deprivation of plaintiff's rights, then the inquiry under the third factor need not be as intense.

By recognizing the relationships between the *Turner* factors, courts should be better able to weigh the competing interests between plaintiffs' rights and defendants' valid administrative concerns, which the *Turner* rule, after all, is designed to accomplish.

§ 1:15 Development of Private Prisons

A new phenomenon in modern corrections is the increasing "privatization" of imprisonment. Although in the eighteenth and nineteenth centuries it was not uncommon for prisons and jails to be operated privately, in the twentieth century imprisonment has almost

---

[Section 1:14]

[1]Turner v. Safley, 482 U.S. 78, 90, 107 S. Ct. 2254, 96 L. Ed. 2d 64 (1987).

always been the exclusive province of the government.[1] However, in the last decade or so there has been an increasing tendency for state and local governments to contract with for profit entities to operate their prisons.[2] As of November 1999, one report revealed that that there were 162 private prisons or jails in thirty-one states, with a capacity of 125,000.[3] At the end of 2000 87,369 state and federal prisoners were housed in private penal facilities in the United States.[4] Private correctional facilities still make up less then seven percent of the entire United States correction facilities market and house less than five percent of the total U.S. prison population.[5]

§ 1:16 The Scope and Organization of This Book

The book is divided into seventeen chapters. Chapters 2-7 concern the basic entitlements that make up normal prison life. Included here is a discussion of the Eighth Amendment's protection against cruel and unusual punishment, the right to medical care, discrimination issues, particularly with regard to racial and sexual

---

[Section 1:15]

[1]See David Yarden, Book Note, 21 Am J Crim L 325 (1994) (reviewing Gary W. Bowman et al., Privatizing Correctional Institutions (1993)); Martin E. Gold, The Privatization of Prisons, 28 Urb. Law. 359 (1996).

[2]Martin Gold, The Privatization of Prisons, 28 Urb Law 359, 369-70 (1996). See also U.S. Department of Justice, Bureau of Justice Assistance, Emerging Issues on Privatized Prisons, ix (February 2001). Texas has the most facilities (43), followed by California (24), Florida (10) and Colorado (9). Most of the private facilities tend to be in the Southern and Western United States. *Id.*

[3]See University of Florida Center for Studies in Criminology and Law, at web.crim.ufl.edu/pcp.

[4]Developments in the Law, The Law of Prisons A Tale of Two Systems:Cost, Quality and Accountability in Private Prisons, 115 Harv. L. Rev. 1868, n.6 (2002) (citing Bureau of Justice Statistics, U.S. Dep't of Justice, Bulletin: Prisoners in 1999, at 7 Tbl.10 (2000)).

[5]U.S. Department of Justice, Bureau of Justice Assistance, Emerging Issues on Privatized Prisons, X (February 2001).

BACKGROUND AND OVERVIEW § 1:16

discrimination, and First Amendment rights, including the right to communication and expression and the right to free exercise of religion. Chapter 7 comprises a discussion of prison labor.

Chapters 8-10 deal with issues revolving around practices specifically designed by prison officials to maintain security in the institutions. This part of the book covers searches of prisoners and their property, disciplinary proceedings and the due process rights available to inmates at those proceedings, and finally, legal issues that arise when inmates are classified or transferred transferred, or when detainers are placed on them by officials from other jurisdictions.

Chapters 10-15 are concerned with the law surrounding prisoners' relationships with the outside world. Topics include access to the courts, visiting, personal correspondence, and access to the media. The section concludes with a discussion of the civil disabilities which prisoners may experience.

The book concludes with chapters new to this edition: Chapter 16 is a discussion of the Prison Litigation Reform Act. The Act is a major development in the field and deserves separate treatment because of the barriers it creates to the assertion of rights described in this book. Chapter 17 discusses the increasingly important role of private persons in American corrections.

While the book attempts to discuss comprehensively the topics it addresses, it is important to note that the book does not address issues that arise relating to criminal convictions or charges that led to the confinement of inmates in prisons or jails. A final word about the style of this book is in order. Because the structure of prison law is incomplete in many areas, in some cases decisions are in conflict and it is unclear which approaches will ultimately prevail. In other areas, an emerging pattern can be identified. In still others, the law is now relatively settled. An attempt has been made to indicate which of these possibilities characterize the precise area of the law that is being addressed. When the law is unsettled, in many instances the book sets

§ 1:16

forth the author's notion of the correct way to properly complete the embryonic or partially completed picture.

As the following discussion demonstrates, the analysis of traditional legal doctrines, even relatively straightforward ones, becomes complex when the petitioner is a prisoner. If there is one underlying issue in every area addressed, it is how much of their "humanity" individuals convicted of crime retain. This question permeates, sometimes on a visible and sometimes on a sub silentio level, litigation involving prisoners' rights, which almost by definition involves people who are confined in places that traditionally have not been subject to scrutiny. Justice Brennan perhaps captured this thought best when he wrote:

> Prisoners are persons whom most of us would rather not think about. Banished from everyday sight, they exist in a shadow world that only dimly enters our awareness. . . . When prisoners emerge from the shadows to press a constitutional claim, they invoke no alien set of principles drawn from a distant culture. Rather they speak the language of the charter upon which all of us rely to hold official power accountable. They ask us to acknowledge that power exercised in the shadows must be restrained at least as diligently as power that acts in the sunlight.[1]

It remains the challenge, and the responsibility, of the judiciary and the bar to continue to address the issue of the meaning of our fundamental charter to persons behind the prison walls.

[Section 1:16]

[1]O'Lone v. Estate of Shabazz, 482 U.S. 342, 354-55, 107 S. Ct. 2400, 96 L. Ed. 2d 282 (1987) (Brennan, J, dissenting).

Chapter 2

The Eighth Amendment—Solitary Confinement, Prevention of Violence, Protection Against Overcrowding, and Provision of the Necessities of Life

Research References

Prisoners and the Law, Ch 1B, 6, 7
Am. Jur. 2d, Penal and Correctional Institutions §§ 87 to 90, 110
Prisons ⚖13(5), 17
A.L.R. Index: Cruel and Unusual Punishment; Prisons and Prisoners

> **KeyCite®:** Cases and other legal materials listed in KeyCite Scope can be researched through West Group's KeyCite service on Westlaw®. Use KeyCite to check citations for form, parallel references, prior and later history, and comprehensive citator information, including citations to other decisions and secondary materials.

§ 2:1 Introduction
§ 2:2 The Supreme Court's Definition of Cruel and Unusual Punishment
§ 2:3 Restrictive Confinement: Punitive Segregation, Solitary Confinement and "Supermax" Units
§ 2:4 Corporal Punishment and Physical and Mechanical Restraints
§ 2:5 Use of Force by Guards
§ 2:6 —Riots
§ 2:7 Assaults by Other Inmates
§ 2:8 Escape from Prison to Avoid Assaults
§ 2:9 Conditions of Confinement-Basic Human Needs and the Prisoner's Physical Well-Being
§ 2:10 —Diet

§ 2:11 —Exercise and Outside Recreation
§ 2:12 —Shelter, Clothing, Personal Hygiene, Sanitation, Ventilation, Fire Safety, and Hazardous Substances
§ 2:13 —Overcrowding
§ 2:14 —Idleness, Programs, and Rehabilitation
§ 2:15 —Large Scale Litigations: Totality of the Conditions, Inadequate Finances, and Remedies

§ 2:1 Introduction

The Eighth Amendment bars cruel and unusual punishment.[1] As such, it is the only provision of the Bill of Rights that is applicable by its own terms to prisoners.[2] The Eighth Amendment potentially sweeps within its ambit virtually all aspects of prison life that might be claimed to be unconstitutionally punitive. Because of its broad thrust, the Eighth Amendment is a central source of the rights of prisoners, particularly in regard to the physical conditions and restrictions of their confinement. Indeed, the Eighth Amendment defines the floor below which the treatment of prisoners cannot fall.

In this and the next chapter, the operation of the Eighth Amendment in prison will be examined in some detail, but before we do so there are two important preliminary observations. First, there are aspects of the Eighth Amendment that touch on subjects beyond the scope of this work. For example, the Eighth Amendment bans excessive criminal sanctions. Under this branch of the Eighth Amendment, a violation may occur when the state formally imposes prison sentences

---

[Section 2:1]

[1] US Const Amend VIII: "Excessive bail shall not be required, nor excessive fines imposed, nor cruel and unusual punishment inflicted."

[2] See, e.g., Whitley v. Albers, 475 U.S. 312, 327, 106 S. Ct. 1078, 89 L. Ed. 2d 251 (1986) ("the Eighth Amendment . . . is specifically concerned with the unnecessary and wanton infliction of pain in penal institutions").

CRUEL & UNUSUAL PUNISHMENT § 2:1

that are wantonly cruel.³ The Eighth Amendment is also called into play when defendants challenge the imposition of the death penalty.⁴ An Eighth Amendment violation can also occur when the state undertakes to criminalize conduct which is not culpable, such as when penal sanctions are imposed for the mere status of drug addiction.⁵ These uses of the Eighth Amendment are not discussed in this text because they all raise issues concerning the penalty that may be

---

³Gregg v. Georgia, 428 U.S. 153, 173, 96 S. Ct. 2909, 49 L. Ed. 2d 859 (1976); McGruder v. Puckett, 954 F.2d 313 (5th Cir. 1992); U.S. v. Buckner, 894 F.2d 975 (8th Cir. 1990); U.S. v. Elkins, 885 F.2d 775, 28 Fed. R. Evid. Serv. 1469 (11th Cir. 1989); U.S. v. Cook, 859 F.2d 777 (9th Cir. 1988); U.S. v. Persico, 853 F.2d 134 (2d Cir. 1988). But see Harmelin v. Michigan, 501 U.S. 957, 111 S. Ct. 2680, 115 L. Ed. 2d 836 (1991) (holding that Eighth Amendment contains no guarantee of proportionality).

⁴See, e.g., Coker v. Georgia, 433 U.S. 584, 97 S. Ct. 2861, 53 L. Ed. 2d 982 (1977) (death penalty for rape unconstitutional); Gregg v. Georgia, 428 U.S. 153, 96 S. Ct. 2909, 49 L. Ed. 2d 859 (1976) (death penalty is not unconstitutional per se); Woodson v. North Carolina, 428 U.S. 280, 96 S. Ct. 2978, 49 L. Ed. 2d 944 (1976) (mandatory death penalty for first degree murder unconstitutional); Furman v. Georgia, 408 U.S. 238, 92 S. Ct. 2726, 33 L. Ed. 2d 346 (1972) (death penalty is unconstitutional). For decisions dealing with death by electrocution see, e.g., Dawson v. State, 274 Ga. 327, 554 S.E.2d 137 (2001) (carrying out the death penalty by electrocution violates the Eight Amendment); but see Provenzano v. Moore, 744 So. 2d 413 (Fla. 1999), cert. denied, 528 U.S. 1182, 120 S. Ct. 1222, 145 L. Ed. 2d 1122 (2000) (electrocution does not cause the lingering death or the infliction of unnecessary or wanton pain necessary for an Eighth Amendment violation); see also, State v. Shuttles, 30 S.W.3d 352 (Tenn. Sup. Ct. East. Sec. 2000); Bryant v. State, 1999 WL 1046430 (Ala. Crim. App. 1999); Poyner v. Murray, 1993 U.S. App. LEXIS 38227 (4th Cir. January 19, 1993) (citing numerous federal court decisions in rejecting inmate's Eighth Amendment objection to electrocution).

⁵See, e.g., Robinson v. California, 370 U.S. 660, 82 S. Ct. 1417, 8 L. Ed. 2d 758 (1962) (striking California law which made it a crime to be a drug addict).

formally imposed for the commission of a crime.[6] The focus of this book is not on that subject, but rather on the applicability of the Eighth Amendment to prison practices and procedures generally, without regard to whether they are imposed as a formal part of the criminal conviction.

A second preliminary point is that even when the Eighth Amendment is raised, it is not always the dispositive or central issue in a prison case. The amendment is sometimes invoked by prisoners when they challenge violations of other constitutional provisions. A Jewish or Muslim inmate, for example, might allege that the prison's failure to serve religiously prepared food contravenes First Amendment free exercise rights as well as the Eighth Amendment right to be free of cruel and unusual punishment.[7] Other examples include challenges to prison visitation rules, hair length restrictions, and inter-institutional transfers.[8] Courts normally, but not always, decide these claims by reference to the more specific of the constitutional provisions invoked. Thus, the Eighth Amendment argument normally does little to add to the determination of the case. This is because, if the challenged practice does not violate the more specific provision, such as the First Amendment's guarantee of free exercise of religion, it

---

[6]Justices Scalia and Thomas apparently believe that the Eighth Amendment is confined to this topic and has no bearing on conditions of confinement. See, e.g., Hudson v. McMillian, 503 U.S. 1, 112 S. Ct. 995, 1005, 117 L. Ed. 2d 156 (1992) (Thomas, J, dissenting); Helling v. McKinney, 509 U.S. 25, 113 S. Ct. 2475, 2482, 125 L. Ed. 2d 22 (1993) (Thomas, J, dissenting). However, this viewpoint has been rejected by a majority of the Court. See Landry, Article: "Punishment" and the Eighth Amendment, 57 Ohio St. L.J. 1607 (1996).

[7]U.S. v. Kahane, 396 F. Supp. 687 (E.D. N.Y. 1975).

[8]See, e.g., Laaman v. Helgemoe, 437 F. Supp. 269, 322 (D.N.H. 1977) (visitation); Rinehart v. Brewer, 360 F. Supp. 105 (S.D. Iowa 1973), judgment aff'd, 491 F.2d 705 (8th Cir. 1974) (hair regulations); Blake v. Pryse, 315 F. Supp. 625 (D. Minn. 1970), judgment aff'd, 444 F.2d 218 (8th Cir. 1971) (hair regulations); Lindsay v. Mitchell, 455 F.2d 917 (5th Cir. 1972) (transfers).

will rarely be an Eighth Amendment infraction. Conversely, if it does transgress the First Amendment, as might be the case in the kosher food example,[9] then the Eighth Amendment adds little to the disposition of the case.[10] Decisions involving other, more specific constitutional guarantees are discussed in chapters dealing with those subjects and will not be considered in this chapter.

The focus of this chapter, instead, will be on the standards that govern Eighth Amendment jurisprudence and on the most common topics to which the amendment applies, including conditions in special housing units, prevention of violence, protection from overcrowding, and conditions of confinement.

§ 2:2 The Supreme Court's Definition of Cruel and Unusual Punishment

In the past two decades the Supreme Court has decided no fewer than six cases directly addressing this topic. Before that time the Court had not discussed the scope of the Eighth Amendment's protections within prison walls.[1] This section will review that body of law by discussing each relevant Supreme Court case and then by summarizing the approach developed by the Court for analyzing an Eighth Amendment prison

---

[9]See Ch 6.

[10]There are, to be sure, rare exceptions to this. For example, the Ninth Circuit held that a search procedure violated the Eighth Amendment, although a Fourth Amendment issue was presented by the case as well. Jordan v. Gardner, 986 F.2d 1521 (9th Cir. 1993) (en banc). See also Hudson v. Palmer, 468 U.S. 517, 104 S. Ct. 3194, 82 L. Ed. 2d 393 (1984) (holding that a search which does not violate the Fourth Amendment might violate the Eighth Amendment).

[Section 2:2]

[1]Twenty years ago when the first edition of this book appeared, the Court had barely touched the topic. James J. Gobert & Neil P. Cohen, Rights of Prisoners 308 (Shepard's/McGraw-Hill 1981) (stating that the Supreme Court has "decided relatively few Eighth Amendment cases involving prisoners or prison conditions").

conditions case.

Before the Supreme Court considered prison conditions cases, the Eighth Amendment was invoked, if at all, in cases dealing with the appropriateness of a particular formally imposed sanction. Thus, in 1910, the Supreme Court struck down a minimum imprisonment of 12 years and a day, in chains, at hard and painful labor, accompanied by the loss of many basic civil rights and lifetime surveillance, for the relatively minor crime of falsifying an official document.[2] Similarly, in 1958, the Court found unconstitutional under the Eighth Amendment the denationalization of an American soldier who had deserted in wartime for one day.[3] In these cases, the Court made clear that the Eighth Amendment is not a static provision, but it takes its meaning from "the evolving standards of decency that mark the progress of a maturing society."[4]

It was not until 1976, in *Estelle v. Gamble*,[5] that the Supreme Court first squarely considered the applicability of the Eighth Amendment to a prison conditions case.

Estelle v. Gamble

Estelle dealt with a claim that the failure to provide medical attention to a prisoner was an Eighth Amendment violation. The Court noted that the government has an "obligation to provide medical care for those whom it is punishing by incarceration" and held that "deliberate indifference to a prisoner's serious illness or injury" would violate the Eighth Amendment.[6] *Estelle* is an important case for its role in breaking the barrier

---

[2]Weems v. U.S., 217 U.S. 349, 30 S. Ct. 544, 54 L. Ed. 793 (1910).

[3]Trop v. Dulles, 356 U.S. 86, 78 S. Ct. 590, 2 L. Ed. 2d 630 (1958).

[4]*Id.* at 101.

[5]Estelle v. Gamble, 429 U.S. 97, 97 S. Ct. 285, 50 L. Ed. 2d 251 (1976).

[6]*Id.* at 103, 105.

between the Eighth Amendment and prison conditions. However, it was a case involving the relatively discrete question of medical care in the context of a single denial of care to a particular prisoner and did not address the wider issue of the role of the Eighth Amendment in examining general prison conditions.[7] Moreover, the Court used the term "deliberate indifference" for the first time as the governing standard for determining violations of the right to medical care, but it made no affirmative effort to define this important term.[8]

Rhodes v. Chapman

Five years later in *Rhodes v. Chapman,* the Court for the first time reached the issue of the role of the Eighth Amendment in examining general prison conditions.[9] *Rhodes* involved a challenge to double celling at the Lucasville State Prison in Ohio. In that case, the Court

---

[7]*Estelle* is discussed in depth in Ch 3.

[8]The term evidently had not been used by the Supreme Court prior to *Estelle*. John Boston, Wilson v. Seiter: A Preliminary Analysis, in 8 Civil Rights Litigation and Attorney Fees Annual Handbook 43 (1992) (reporting the results of computer search of all Supreme Court cases back to 1790 revealing that the term had not been used previously).

[9]Rhodes v. Chapman, 452 U.S. 337, 344, 101 S. Ct. 2392, 69 L. Ed. 2d 59 (1981) ("We consider here for the first time the limitation that the Eighth Amendment . . . imposes upon the conditions in which a State may confine those convicted of crimes"). Previously, in Hutto v. Finney, 437 U.S. 678, 98 S. Ct. 2565, 57 L. Ed. 2d 522 (1978), and Bell v. Wolfish, 441 U.S. 520, 99 S. Ct. 1861, 60 L. Ed. 2d 447 (1979), the Court touched on general prison conditions but not in a definitive manner. *Hutto* was primarily an attorney's fees case that arose in the context of a prison conditions case, but the case also involved an appeal from the lower court's decision that inmates could not be held in punitive isolation beyond a set period of time. The district court had ruled that conditions of confinement in the prison violated the Eighth Amendment, but on appeal to the Supreme Court the defendants did not challenge that finding. See Hutto v. Finney, 437 U.S. 678, 684, 98 S. Ct. 2565, 57 L. Ed. 2d 522 (1978). The Court upheld both the attorney's fee award and the limitation on the amount of time that could be spent in isolation. However, the discussion was not

§ 2:2

held that the conditions of confinement, either alone or in combination, can violate the Constitution when they deprive inmates of "the minimal civilized measure of life's necessities."[10] This is so, the Court held, because "[c]onditions [of confinement] must not involve the wanton and unnecessary infliction of pain, nor may they be grossly disproportionate to the severity of the crime warranting imprisonment."[11]

At the same time, the Court made clear that not all prison conditions violate the Eighth Amendment; most prison conditions —even those that are harsh — are simply "part of the penalty that criminal offenders pay for their offenses against society."[12] As Justice Powell, writing for the Court, put it, "the Constitution does not mandate comfortable prisons."[13] While *Rhodes* establishes that the Eighth Amendment provides protection against prison conditions that fall below the level of human decency, the Court provided little guidance about how to determine when a prison condition crosses the line between the merely harsh and the impermissibly unconstitutional.[14]

The Court, however, implied that the issue did not depend on the state of mind of prison officials. Support for this point of view is that the Court "conducted an objective analysis of the prison conditions" to determine

---

extended, since the prison officials conceded that the conditions in isolation violated the Constitution.

Bell was a conditions case, but it involved a pretrial detention facility. The Court held that, since the rights of nonconvicted persons were at stake, the Eighth Amendment did not apply to the case at all but, instead, was resolved under the due process clause. Bell v. Wolfish, 441 U.S. 520, 535 n16, 99 S. Ct. 1861, 60 L. Ed. 2d 447 (1979).

[10]Rhodes v. Chapman, 452 U.S. 337, 347, 101 S. Ct. 2392, 69 L. Ed. 2d 59 (1981).

[11]*Id.*

[12]*Id.*

[13]*Id.*

[14]For a discussion of *Rhodes* as it bears on prison overcrowding, see § 2:13.

whether they violated the Constitution.[15] Moreover, the Court's discussion did not mention that an Eighth Amendment violation depended in any way upon the state of mind of prison officials. Instead, the Court's analysis insinuated that the Constitution is violated whenever the condition falls below constitutional minimums regardless of the motivation for the imposition of the conditions on inmates.[16] This approach to the determination of the Eighth Amendment question was unlike the approach used by the Court in *Estelle v. Gamble*. In that case, the Court used a "deliberate indifference" standard, which requires some inquiry into the defendant's state of mind. Thus, *Estelle* and *Rhodes* present divergent approaches. In its next case, the Court returned to a subjective analysis.

Whitley v. Albers

In *Whitley v. Albers*,[17] several prisoners rioted and took a prison guard hostage. During the effort to restore control over the prison and free the hostage, a guard shot Albers, an inmate who was not involved in the disturbance and who had attempted to assist officials in their efforts to quell it.[18] Albers brought suit contending that the shooting violated the Eighth Amendment.

The Court rejected his claim. The Court focused on the emergency facing the prison. The Court held that the Eighth Amendment must be applied "with due regard for differences in the kind of conduct against which an Eighth Amendment objection is lodged."[19] Decisions made in the context of a prison riot are "neces-

---

[15]Arthur B. Berger, Note, Wilson v. Seiter, An Unsatisfying Attempt at Resolving the Imbroglio of Eighth Amendment Prisoners' Rights Standards, 1992 Utah L. Rev. 565, 584.

[16]See, e.g., Rhodes v. Chapman, 452 U.S. 337, 347-50, 101 S. Ct. 2392, 69 L. Ed. 2d 59 (1981) (majority opinion by Justice Powell).

[17]Whitley v. Albers, 475 U.S. 312, 106 S. Ct. 1078, 89 L. Ed. 2d 251 (1986).

[18]*Id.* at 315-16.

[19]*Id.* at 320.

sarily made in haste, under pressure, and frequently without the luxury of a second chance."[20] Because in this case the shooting took place during an emergency situation, the Court held that the deliberate indifference standard of *Estelle* did not appropriately take into account the circumstances of the case. Rather, when prison officials were responding to an explosive emergency situation, an Eighth Amendment violation could only be made out if the inmate could prove that the shooting was done "maliciously and sadistically for the very purpose of causing harm."[21] If this showing could not be made, the Court held, an Eighth Amendment violation did not occur because the force was applied in a "good faith effort to maintain or restore discipline."[22]

Thus, *Whitley,* by focusing on the maliciousness of the conduct of the defendants, restored a subjective element to the determination of when an Eighth Amendment violation occurs within the prison walls. However, the opinion was vague in describing when a court should use the subjective test and when the objective test would suffice. *Whitley* also addressed a discrete incident and not an ongoing condition of confinement, as was the case in *Rhodes.*

Harmonizing *Estelle, Rhodes,* and *Whitley* is anything but simple. Indeed, the trilogy suggested three distinct tests for determining whether the Eighth Amendment was violated in a prison setting, depending on the circumstances in which the case arose. If the plaintiff's complaint challenged specific isolated actions of defendants, as was the case in *Estelle,* deliberate indifference appeared to be the standard. If, instead, inmates challenged overall prison conditions, as was the case in *Rhodes,* then the dissimilar, objective, decency test was applicable. Finally, if the challenge was to actions of prison officials during a riot situation, then the heightened, subjective, maliciousness standard of *Whitley*

---

[20]*Id.*
[21]*Id.*
[22]*Id.* at 320-21.

applied. This was the state of the law in 1991 when the Court decided *Wilson v. Seiter*.[23]

Wilson v. Seiter

In *Wilson*, the Court attempted "to rationalize and harmonize its decisions regarding the applicability of the Eighth Amendment to prison conditions and practices."[24] *Wilson*, like *Rhodes*, was a challenge to prison conditions. The case began when Pearly Wilson, an inmate at the Hicking Correctional Facility in Ohio, brought a pro se lawsuit alleging that various conditions in the prison, including overcrowding, excessive noise, inadequate heating and ventilation, and unsanitary dining facilities violated the Eighth Amendment.[25] The Sixth Circuit upheld the district court's grant of summary judgment to the defendants, holding that some of the conditions were not serious enough to be considered Eighth Amendment violations[26] and others did not violate the Eighth Amendment absent proof that the defendants had acted with "persistent mali-

---

[23]Wilson v. Seiter, 501 U.S. 294, 111 S. Ct. 2321, 115 L. Ed. 2d 271 (1991).

[24]Elizabeth Alexander, The Overall Context of Prison Litigation, in Section 1983 Civil Rights Litigation and Attorney's Fees 1992: Current Developments 401, (PLI Litig. & Admin. Practice Course Handbook Series No. 449, 1992).

[25]Wilson v. Seiter, 501 U.S. 294, 111 S. Ct. 2321, 2323, 115 L. Ed. 2d 271 (1991). *Wilson* also challenged unclean and unsanitary restrooms, insufficient locker space, and the housing of mentally and physically ill inmates with the general population. He sought declaratory and injunctive relief as well as damages. Wilson v. Seiter, 501 U.S. 294, 111 S. Ct. 2321, 2323, 115 L. Ed. 2d 271 (1991).

[26]These included the claim of inadequate cooling, housing with mentally ill inmates, and overcrowding. Wilson v. Seiter, 893 F.2d 861, 865 (6th Cir. 1990), cert. granted, 498 U.S. 808, 111 S. Ct. 41, 112 L. Ed. 2d 17 (1990) and judgment vacated, 501 U.S. 294, 111 S. Ct. 2321, 115 L. Ed. 2d 271 (1991).

§ 2:2   Rights of Prisoners, Third Edition

cious cruelty."[27]

Writing for a five-member majority, Justice Scalia held that all Eighth Amendment prison claims have to be supported by proof of an objective and a subjective component. Justice Scalia rejected the argument that *Rhodes* had endorsed using only an objective standard when the case involved a challenge to prison conditions. It was true, he noted, that *Rhodes* "turned on the objective component of an Eighth Amendment prison claim (was the deprivation sufficiently serious?), and . . . did not consider the subjective component (did the officials act with a sufficiently culpable state of mind?),"[28] but that was because there was no need to consider the subjective component, since the conditions themselves were not sufficiently serious to trigger Eighth Amendment concerns.[29]

In so ruling, Justice Scalia rejected as "neither . . . logical nor practical" the distinction offered by inmate's attorneys between "one time" conditions, such as were involved in *Estelle* and *Whitley,* where state of mind is relevant, and "systemic" conditions, such as those involved in *Rhodes,* where state of mind should not be an issue. It was not logical because the ordinary meaning of the term "punishment" requires "some form of intent."[30] It was not practical because there is no principled basis on which a court can distinguish between short-term and long-term conditions.[31]

The plaintiffs argued that if the Eighth Amendment

---

[27]Wilson v. Seiter, 893 F.2d 861, 867 (6th Cir. 1990), cert. granted, 498 U.S. 808, 111 S. Ct. 41, 112 L. Ed. 2d 17 (1990) and judgment vacated, 501 U.S. 294, 111 S. Ct. 2321, 115 L. Ed. 2d 271 (1991).

[28]Wilson v. Seiter, 501 U.S. 294, 111 S. Ct. 2321, 2324, 115 L. Ed. 2d 271 (1991).

[29]Wilson v. Seiter, 501 U.S. 294, 111 S. Ct. 2321, 2324, 115 L. Ed. 2d 271 (1991). *Id.*

[30]Wilson v. Seiter, 501 U.S. 294, 111 S. Ct. 2321, 2325-26, 115 L. Ed. 2d 271 (1991).

[31]Wilson v. Seiter, 501 U.S. 294, 111 S. Ct. 2321, 2325, 115 L. Ed. 2d 271 (1991). Although the *Wilson* Court was troubled by the

had a subjective component, many prison conditions cases would be doomed, because prison officials would evade responsibility by pleading poverty. In other words, prison officials would be able to argue that when they were prevented from alleviating the conditions by the lack of adequate funds, they lack the subjective intent to deprive inmates of constitutional rights. The majority refused to address this contention, since the defendants had not made it a defense.[32] In any event, Justice Scalia stated that this contention was a policy argument that had no bearing on the meaning of the Eighth Amendment. "An intent requirement is either implicit in the word 'punishment' or is not; it cannot be

---

practical problems of drawing time lines, in fact the Court in other instances has made exactly these kinds of decisions. See, e.g., County of Riverside v. McLaughlin, 500 U.S. 44, 111 S. Ct. 1661, 114 L. Ed. 2d 49 (1991) (holding that arrestees must be arraigned within 48 hours).

[32]Justice Scalia also opined that the issue was unlikely to come up since, as a practical matter, prison officials do not routinely raise this defense. Wilson v. Seiter, 501 U.S. 294, 111 S. Ct. 2321, 2326, 115 L. Ed. 2d 271 (1991). However, this is not entirely accurate. An examination of the case law reveals that the defense has been raised in other prison reform cases. See, e.g., Ramos v. Lamm, 639 F.2d 559, 578 (10th Cir. 1980) (disallowing funding problems as excuse for unconstitutional confinement conditions caused by overcrowding); Todaro v. Ward, 565 F.2d 48, 54 n8 (2d Cir. 1977). It also has been raised on occasion in cases after *Wilson*. See, e.g., Alberti v. Sheriff of Harris County, Tex., 978 F.2d 893 (5th Cir. 1992) (defense raised lack of funding as a defense in an overcrowding case; the court never reached the question of validity of the defense, but noted that *Seiter* left the question open); Carty v. Schneider, 986 F. Supp. 933 (D.V.I. 1997) (noting that a defense of lack of funding does not apply where efforts to provide free exercise of religion, and access to the outdoors and to the library, would involve no cost, and remedying physical plant deficiencies could be accomplished with little cost); Flournoy v. Sheahan, 1994 WL 605584 (N.D. Ill. 1994) (noting that lack of funding is to be considered when analyzing the circumstances surrounding a deliberate indifference inquiry); Pugh v. Rockwall County, TX, 2000 WL 730426 (N.D. Tex. 2000) (that a sheriff has made repeated attempts to secure funding to fix problems at a jail does not allow the sheriff to "sit on his hands" until funding arrives).

§ 2:2   Rights of Prisoners, Third Edition

alternately required and ignored as policy considerations might dictate."[33]

Thus, *Wilson* held that in an Eighth Amendment prison case, the plaintiffs must not only show that the conditions are objectively cruel and unusual, but also that the conditions are the result of culpable acts by agents of the state. While the *Wilson* Court held that the Eighth Amendment had a subjective component, it disagreed with the Sixth Circuit's adaptation of the *Whitley* maliciousness standard. The Court held that the deliberate indifference standard of *Estelle* was more appropriate to a prison conditions case. The Court held that the "very high state of mind prescribed in *Whitley*" does not apply to prison conditions cases because the maliciousness standard is reserved for cases in which prison officials have to act "in haste, under pressure."[34] Prison conditions cases, like prison medical care cases, do not arise from situations that pose those dangers.[35]

Finally, Justice Scalia dealt with the the plaintiff's argument that courts should consider all of the prison conditions challenged as a "totality" in order to determine whether the Eighth Amendment is violated. This argument was drawn from the Court's observation in *Rhodes* that prison conditions "alone or in combination" can violate the Eighth Amendment.[36] Justice Scalia agreed that "some conditions of confinement may establish an Eighth Amendment violation 'in combination'

---

[33]Wilson v. Seiter, 501 U.S. 294, 111 S. Ct. 2321, 2326, 115 L. Ed. 2d 271 (1991). For a discussion of the viability of the inadequate resources argument, see § 2:15.

[34]*Id.*

[35]For this reason, the Court remanded the case to the Sixth Circuit for a determination of whether the plaintiff had made the required showing of deliberate indifference to make out an Eighth Amendment violation. Wilson v. Seiter, 501 U.S. 294, 111 S. Ct. 2321, 2328, 115 L. Ed. 2d 271 (1991).

[36]Rhodes v. Chapman, 452 U.S. 337, 347, 101 S. Ct. 2392, 69 L. Ed. 2d 59 (1981).

when each would not do so alone."[37] However, this is only the case when the conditions "have a mutually enforcing effect that produces the deprivation of a single, identifiable human need such as food, warmth, or exercise."[38] Justice Scalia stated that an example of prison conditions that were mutually reinforcing is the combination of a low temperature cell with a failure to issue blankets. But in acknowledging this, he was quick to caution that this did not mean that prison conditions are a "seamless web" that must invariably be viewed in combination before a determination can be made whether the Eighth Amendment is violated.[39]

Justice Scalia's opinion for a bare five-member majority sparked a spirited dissent from Justice White on behalf of the four-member minority.[40] Justice White rejected the majority's holding that the Eighth Amendment contained a subjective component applicable to prison conditions cases. Justice White wrote that the subjective intent of prison officials should not be relevant to an Eighth Amendment determination when prison conditions fall below "broad and idealistic concepts of dignity, civilized standards, humanity, and decency."[41] He distinguished *Estelle* and *Whitley* on the grounds that those cases "involved challenges to specific acts or omissions directed at individual prisoners," not

---

[37]Wilson v. Seiter, 501 U.S. 294, 111 S. Ct. 2321, 2327, 115 L. Ed. 2d 271 (1991).

[38]*Id.*

[39]*Id.* For a discussion of the impact of this holding on the "totality of conditions" approach to prison Eighth Amendment litigation, see § 2:15.

[40]Since the majority agreed to remand the case to the lower courts, Justice White technically concurred in the judgment. However, in his reasoning he took a position that was in disagreement with almost all aspects of Justice Scalia's opinion. Therefore, it is appropriate to label his opinion a dissent.

[41]Wilson v. Seiter, 501 U.S. 294, 111 S. Ct. 2321, 2328, 115 L. Ed. 2d 271 (1991) (White, J, concurring in the judgment) (quoting Jackson v. Bishop, 404 F.2d 571, 579 (8th Cir. 1968)).

general conditions of confinement.[42]

Most troubling to Justice White was the concern that under the majority's reasoning, serious deprivations of basic human needs would go unredressed. He gave two reasons for this conclusion. First, the search for intent is difficult and often impossible because "inhumane prison conditions often are the result of cumulative actions and inactions by numerous officials inside and outside a prison, sometimes over a long period of time."[43] Second, and even more disturbing, the subjective test "leaves open the possibility . . . that prison officials will be able to defeat . . . [a prison conditions case] by showing that the conditions are caused by insufficient funding from the state legislature rather than by any deliberate indifference on the part of prison officials."[44]

Hudson v. McMillian

The next Supreme Court opinion interpreting the Eighth Amendment in the prison context was *Hudson v. McMillian*.[45] In that case the Court addressed the standard for determining when the use of force by prison guards in a non-riot situation violates the Eighth Amendment.

Hudson, an inmate, was beaten by two corrections officers after an argument between Hudson and one of the guards. The supervisor on duty simply watched the beating and intervened only to admonish the guards "not to have too much fun."[46] Hudson was left with facial swelling, loosened teeth, a cracked dental plate, and

---

[42]Wilson v. Seiter, 501 U.S. 294, 111 S. Ct. 2321, 2330, 115 L. Ed. 2d 271 (1991) (White, J, concurring in the judgment).

[43]Wilson v. Seiter, 501 U.S. 294, 111 S. Ct. 2321, 2330, 115 L. Ed. 2d 271 (1991) (White, J, concurring in the judgment).

[44]Wilson v. Seiter, 501 U.S. 294, 111 S. Ct. 2321, 2330-31, 115 L. Ed. 2d 271 (1991) (White, J, concurring in the judgment).

[45]Hudson v. McMillian, 503 U.S. 1, 112 S. Ct. 995, 117 L. Ed. 2d 156 (1992).

[46]Hudson v. McMillian, 503 U.S. 1, 112 S. Ct. 995, 997, 117 L. Ed. 2d 156 (1992).

CRUEL & UNUSUAL PUNISHMENT § 2:2

minor bruises but no lasting injury.[47] His suit for damages based on the Eighth Amendment was dismissed by the Fifth Circuit on the ground that an inmate must suffer a "serious injury" for the objective component of the Eighth Amendment to be violated.[48]

In a 7-2 opinion, the Supreme Court reversed. Justice O'Connor, writing for the Court, held that serious injury is not required to make out an Eighth Amendment claim of excessive force. She rejected the notion that significant injury is always a requirement for an Eighth Amendment claim, and wrote that the injury needed to violate "'contemporary standards of decency'"[49] will vary from situation to situation. In some contexts, more injury is required than in others.

Prison conditions cases illustrate a context in which more injury is needed. There, since routine discomfort is "part of the penalty that inmates pay for their offenses against society,"[50] the Eighth Amendment objective test is not satisfied unless the inmate is able to establish that the conditions cause "extreme deprivations."[51] However, "[i]n the excessive force context, society's expectations are different."[52] When prison officials inflict physical force on an inmate in a malicious or sadistic manner, "contemporary standards of decency always are violated."[53]

Regarding the subjective branch of the test, the Court

---

[47]*Id.*

[48]Hudson v. McMillian, 929 F.2d 1014, 1015 (5th Cir. 1990), judgment rev'd, 503 U.S. 1, 112 S. Ct. 995, 117 L. Ed. 2d 156 (1992).

[49]Hudson v. McMillian, 503 U.S. 1, 112 S. Ct. 995, 1000, 117 L. Ed. 2d 156 (1992).

[50]Hudson v. McMillian, 503 U.S. 1, 112 S. Ct. 995, 1000, 117 L. Ed. 2d 156 (1992) (quoting Rhodes v. Chapman, 452 U.S. 337, 347, 101 S. Ct. 2392, 69 L. Ed. 2d 59 (1981)).

[51]Hudson v. McMillian, 503 U.S. 1, 112 S. Ct. 995, 1000, 117 L. Ed. 2d 156 (1992).

[52]*Id.*

[53]*Id.* The Court, nevertheless, cautioned that "not every malevolent touch by a prison guard gives rise" to an Eighth Amendment violation; there is a "de minimis" level of harm which is not action-

held that it too is contextual and the standard used depends on the kind of Eighth Amendment claim that is being asserted. Choosing between the *Estelle* "deliberate indifference" standard, used by the Court for prison conditions and prison medical care cases, and the *Whitley* "malicious and sadistic" test, used by the Court for prison riot situations, the Court selected the *Whitley* standard as appropriate for all excessive force cases, regardless of whether the force was used in an emergency riot situation or otherwise.

Justice O'Connor explained that even with minor prison disturbances, guards must balance the need to restore discipline with the risk of harm resulting from the use of force.[54] The *Whitley* standard is the best one to accommodate that balance, Justice O'Connor held. Thus, in a prison excessive force case, "the core judicial inquiry is that set out in *Whitley:* whether force was applied in a good-faith effort to maintain or restore discipline, or maliciously and sadistically to cause harm."[55]

---

able even though the subjective component of the Eighth Amendment is transgressed. Hudson v. McMillian, 503 U.S. 1, 112 S. Ct. 995, 1000, 117 L. Ed. 2d 156 (1992). The Court did not further define this term. See § 2:5.

[54]Hudson v. McMillian, 503 U.S. 1, 112 S. Ct. 995, 998-99, 117 L. Ed. 2d 156 (1992).

[55]Hudson v. McMillian, 503 U.S. 1, 112 S. Ct. 995, 999, 117 L. Ed. 2d 156 (1992). Justice O'Connor also observed that the extent of the injury suffered by the inmate-plaintiff might be relevant in determining whether the use of force violated the Eighth Amendment, but it is not necessarily dispositive. Other factors need to be considered as well, including "the need for application of force, the relationship between that need and the amount of force used, the threat 'reasonably perceived by the responsible officials' and 'any efforts made to temper the severity of a forceful response.'" Hudson v. McMillian, 503 U.S. 1, 112 S. Ct. 995, 999, 117 L. Ed. 2d 156 (1992) (quoting Whitley v. Albers, 475 U.S. 312, 321, 106 S. Ct. 1078, 89 L. Ed. 2d 251 (1986)). This aspect of the Court's holding has been the subject of some litigation which is discussed in § 2:5.

Helling v. McKinney

Helling v. McKinney,[56] decided in June 1993, dealt with the issue of whether an inmate who was involuntarily subjected to exposure to tobacco smoke stated an Eighth Amendment claim even if at the time of the suit he had not suffered physical injury.[57] Justice White, writing for the Court, ruled that the plaintiff stated a valid claim for relief under the Eighth Amendment. Exposure to conditions that are "demonstrably unsafe" can violate the Eighth Amendment if the inmate can prove that the risk is "so grave that it violates contemporary standards of decency to expose anyone unwilling to such a risk."[58] However, the Court did not determine whether tobacco smoke fits within this category; it remanded to the lower courts for a determination of that issue. The Court explicitly ruled that the plaintiff did not have to show actual present injury. The Eighth Amendment protects against "imminent dangers" as well as against present harms. The Court offered the example of a prison inmate who complained about unsafe drinking water. Such an inmate could bring this claim for relief "without waiting for an attack of dysentery."[59]

Farmer v. Brennan

In *Farmer v. Brennan*,[60] the latest case decided by the Supreme Court that deals with prison conditions, the

---

[56]Helling v. McKinney, 509 U.S. 25, 113 S. Ct. 2475, 125 L. Ed. 2d 22 (1993).

[57]In *Helling,* plaintiff complained that he had been subjected involuntarily to being housed with another inmate who smoked five packs of cigarettes per day. Helling v. McKinney, 509 U.S. 25, 113 S. Ct. 2475, 2478, 125 L. Ed. 2d 22 (1993).

[58]Helling v. McKinney, 509 U.S. 25, 113 S. Ct. 2475, 2482, 125 L. Ed. 2d 22 (1993).

[59]Helling v. McKinney, 509 U.S. 25, 113 S. Ct. 2475, 2480, 125 L. Ed. 2d 22 (1993).

[60]Farmer v. Brennan, 511 U.S. 825, 114 S. Ct. 1970, 128 L. Ed. 2d 811 (1994).

Supreme Court directly addressed the appropriate standard for determining whether the Eighth Amendment is violated by inmate-on-inmate violence. The plaintiff in *Farmer* was a transsexual serving a twenty-year sentence in a federal prison. Although a biological male, *Farmer* had undergone treatment to bring about a sex change, including silicone breast implants and unsuccessful surgery to have his testicles removed. While in prison, plaintiff apparently continued to receive hormonal treatment and wore his clothing in a "feminine manner."[61] Although having a feminine appearance and manner, plaintiff was incarcerated in male federal prisons.

The case arose when the plaintiff was transferred to a high security prison in Terre Haute, Indiana, and placed in the general population. Within two weeks of arrival, the plaintiff was beaten and raped by another inmate. The plaintiff brought suit seeking damages and an injunction alleging that the transfer of a transsexual with feminine characteristics to a high security prison with a history of inmate assaults amounted to deliberate indifference in violation of the Eighth Amendment.

The district court granted summary judgment to the defendants, holding that in the absence of actual knowledge of a potential danger there was no constitutional violation. Since the plaintiff did not protest the transfer, or alert prison officials to any danger, the defendants lacked the requisite knowledge to impose liability. Following affirmance by the Seventh Circuit Court of Appeals, the Supreme Court granted certiorari and unanimously reversed.

The majority opinion, written by Justice Souter and joined by all of the Justices except Justices Stevens and Thomas, noted that while the Constitution does not mandate comfortable prisons, "neither does it permit

---

[61]*Id.* at 1975.

inhumane ones."[62] Justice Souter quickly disposed of the argument that the Constitution offers no protection from inmate assaults. Prisons hold dangerous persons. Since inmates are forced to be there, and are stripped "of virtually every means of self-protection and foreclosed their access to outside aid," prison officials "are not free to let the state of nature take its course."[63]

The Court also had little difficulty in determining that liability is predicated upon a showing of deliberate indifference.[64] The key issue for the Court was determining the proper test for deliberate indifference. Justice Souter began that analysis by locating the boundaries of the dispute. Deliberate indifference requires something more than mere negligence and something less than maliciousness. Within these poles lies the recklessness standard widely adopted by the Courts of Appeals. However, recklessness, the Court noted, is not self-defining.

The plaintiff advanced an objective test of recklessness, while the defendants offered a subjective test. Under the subjective test, liability could be found only if prison officials had actual knowledge of the danger to the plaintiff and then failed to act. Under the objective test, liability could be found even if there was no actual knowledge that the prison officials failed to react to an obviously unjustifiably high risk of harm. Rejecting the objective standard, the Court held that "a prison official cannot be found liable under the Eighth Amendment . . . unless the official knows of and disregards an excessive risk to inmate health or safety."[65]

While the Court rejected the objective standard, its description of the manner in which the subjective test is applied suggests that the defendants may have won only a Pyrrhic victory. First, the Court stated that de-

---

[62]Farmer v. Brennan, 511 U.S. 825, 114 S. Ct. 1970, 1976, 128 L. Ed. 2d 811 (1994).

[63]*Id.*

[64]*Id.*

[65]*Id.*

liberate indifference could properly be found even if the prison officials had no direct knowledge that harm would befall a particular inmate; it is enough that the prison officials be aware of a risk sufficiently broad to encompass inmates in the plaintiff's category. If the risk is present and is known "it would obviously be irrelevant to liability that the officials could not guess beforehand precisely who would attack whom."[66]

Second, the Court made clear that the subjective standard is not intended as a refuge for an ignorant prison official to escape liability by simply claiming that he was unaware of obvious dangers in the facility, and therefore lacked knowledge of the danger. In that connection, the Court carefully distinguished between the standard of proof that requires subjective knowledge and the evidence necessary to establish that standard, which does require direct evidence that the defendant knew of the risk to the plaintiff. Actual knowledge of a serious risk of danger, the Court held, can be satisfied by circumstantial evidence of an objective nature.

Using circumstantial evidence, liability can be premised upon objective proof, showing that the substantial risk of inmate attacks was "longstanding, pervasive, well documented, or expressly noted by prison officials in the past and the circumstances suggest that the defendant-official being sued had been exposed to information concerning the risk and thus 'must have known' about it. . . ."[67] In these circumstances, a prison official cannot escape liability by arguing that "he merely refused to verify underlying facts that he strongly suspected to be true, or declined to confirm inferences of risk that he strongly suspected to exist . . ."[68]

Prison officials can escape liability only if they can affirmatively show in the face of this evidence that they did not know of the underlying facts indicating a suf-

---

[66] Id.
[67] Id. at 1981.
[68] Id. at 1982 n8.

ficiently substantial danger and that they were therefore unaware of a danger, or that they knew the underlying facts, but believed (albeit unsoundly) that the risk to which the facts gave rise was insubstantial or nonexistent.[69] Of course, the Court noted, if prison officials respond reasonably to a known danger, they are not liable if harm ultimately occurs.[70] Finally, the Court held that under its standard an inmate does not have to wait to be assaulted in order to bring suit. The requisite showing of deliberate indifference can be made in absence of actual injury.[71]

Applying this test to the facts of Farmer's case, the Court reversed the grant of summary judgment. Justice Souter explained that the lower courts may have placed undue weight on the fact that the plaintiff had not complained about the transfer to the general population at the Terre Haute prison. "[T]he failure to give advance notice is not dispositive" if it can be shown that plaintiff's condition and appearance, coupled with the knowledge of violent assaults in the prison, make it reasonable to believe that the defendants were aware of a serious risk to the plaintiff and took no protective action.[72] The case, therefore, was remanded to the lower courts for reconsideration.

Justices Blackmun and Stevens concurred. Both Justices took the occasion to express their dissatisfaction with the use of the deliberate indifference standard to judge the constitutionality of prison conditions. In Justice Blackmun's view, the Eighth Amendment is violated whenever an inmate is unreasonably subjected to danger, regardless of whether prison officials intend that to occur or not.[73] He concurred in the opinion, however, because it "sends a clear message to prison officials that their affirmative duty under the Constitu-

---

[69] *Id.* at 1982.
[70] *Id.* at 1982-83, 128 L. Ed. 2d 811 (1994).
[71] *Id.*
[72] *Id.* at 1984-85.
[73] *Id.* at 1985-89.

tion to provide for the safety of inmates is not to be taken lightly."[74]

Justice Thomas concurred to register his continuing view that the Eighth Amendment does not cover treatment an inmate receives in prison unless that treatment is formally imposed by a sentencing court.[75]

Summary of the Standards for Determining Whether the Eighth Amendment is Violated

The decisions just reviewed cover many aspects of the Eighth Amendment, some of them quite discrete, but three general principles of Eighth Amendment law governing prison life emerge from the decisions.

The first, established by *Estelle, Rhodes* and *Farmer,* is that the Eighth Amendment applies to cases involving prison conditions and practices. The second principle, established by *Wilson,* is that the Eighth Amendment has both a subjective and an objective component. For an inmate to be successful in a challenge to prison policies or practices based on the Eighth Amendment, both components must be satisfied. The final general principle is that the test for the subjective component will depend on the particular Eighth Amendment claim that is being raised. If the claim is one involving prison conditions (*Wilson*), protection from inmate violence (*Farmer*) or medical care (*Estelle*), for example, deliberate indifference is the standard. If, however, the case deals with guard brutality (*Whitley; Hudson*), the maliciousness standard will be invoked. Beyond these three general principles, a number of observations about both the objective and the subjective branches of Eighth Amendment analysis merit further discussion.

---

[74]*Id.* at 1986, 128 L. Ed. 2d 811 (1994).
[75]Farmer v. Brennan, *Id.* at 1990.

The Objective Component: What is Cruel and Unusual Punishment?[76]

As the Supreme Court has repeatedly stressed, the Eighth Amendment takes its meaning from "the evolving standards of decency that mark the progress of a maturing society."[77] To fulfill the objective component of the Eighth Amendment, therefore, the inmate must prove that the conduct of the defendants violates "contemporary standards of decency."[78] What violates "contemporary standards of decency" defies precise definition. Notwithstanding the lack of specificity in the language of the Amendment, certain rough standards and guidelines have been developed.

First, at its most basic level, the Eighth Amendment forbids practices that were contrary to Eighteenth Century notions of civilized behavior. The primary concern of the drafters of the Eighth Amendment appears to have been with torture and other barbarous modes of physical punishment.[79] Because of the similarity of this form of treatment to physical brutality of inmates by prison guards, the Supreme Court in *Hudson* was quite willing to declare that any but the most

---

[76]Cruel and unusual punishment is generally treated as a phrase, a three-word term of art; there appears to be little attempt to examine separately the meaning of either of the two principal words. This is just as well, for major conceptual difficulties might arise if the term "unusual" were interpreted to have independent definitional significance. For example, if all prison guards routinely beat inmates for the sheer sadistic pleasure of the experience, it could hardly be said that such beatings were unusual. Yet, surely courts would agree that the practice violates the Eighth Amendment.

[77]Trop v. Dulles, 356 U.S. 86, 101, 78 S. Ct. 590, 2 L. Ed. 2d 630 (1958).

[78]Hudson v. McMillian, 503 U.S. 1, 112 S. Ct. 995, 1000, 117 L. Ed. 2d 156 (1992).

[79]See Gregg v. Georgia, 428 U.S. 153, 170, 96 S. Ct. 2909, 49 L. Ed. 2d 859 (1976); Wilkerson v. State of Utah, 99 U.S. 130, 136, 25 L. Ed. 345 (1878). For the early history and roots of the Amendment, see Anthony F. Granucci, Nor Cruel and Unusual Punishment Inflicted: The Original Meaning, 57 Cal L. Rev. 839 (1969).

de minimus physical beating of an inmate by a prison guard would contravene the objective branch of the Eighth Amendment, even if there was no serious or lasting physical injury as a result.[80]

But the Eighth Amendment is not limited to Eighteenth Century norms of civilized conduct. It also covers practices deemed cruel by contemporary society.[81] As Judge Posner wrote, "[l]ike much of the rest of the Bill of Rights, the Eighth Amendment would be obsolete if its meaning were thought bounded by the mental horizons of its eighteenth-century framers, broad as those horizons were."[82] Given evolving standards of decency, it is now established that the reach of the Amendment goes beyond physical brutality by prison guards. The Supreme Court has held that it is no longer tolerable for prison conditions and practices to deprive inmates of the "minimal civilized measure of life's necessities."[83] Justice Souter made much the same point when in the *Farmer v. Brennan* case he wrote

---

[80]Hudson v. McMillian, 503 U.S. 1, 112 S. Ct. 995, 117 L. Ed. 2d 156 (1992). However, the Fourth Circuit appears to have challenged this notion. The case law on that topic is discussed in Section 2:5.

[81]Helling v. McKinney, 509 U.S. 25, 113 S. Ct. 2475, 2482, 125 L. Ed. 2d 22 (1993). Thus, despite the views of Justices Thomas and Scalia to the contrary, see, e.g., Hudson v. McMillian, 503 U.S. 1, 112 S. Ct. 995, 1004, 117 L. Ed. 2d 156 (1992) (Thomas, J, dissenting for himself and Scalia, J,), the Supreme Court has clearly ruled that the Eighth Amendment is not frozen so as to forbid only punishments seen as barbaric in 1789.

[82]Davenport v. DeRobertis, 844 F.2d 1310, 1315 (7th Cir. 1988). Judge Posner also wrote in that case that the evolving nature of the Eighth Amendment means that "[t]he conditions in which prisoners are housed, like the poverty line, is a function of a society's standard of living. As that standard rises, the standard of minimum decency of prison conditions, like the poverty line, rises too." Davenport v. DeRobertis, 844 F.2d 1310, 1315 (7th Cir. 1988). See also Delaney v. DeTella, 256 F.3d 679 (7th Cir. 2001).

[83]Hudson v. McMillian, 503 U.S. 1, 112 S. Ct. 995, 1000, 117 L. Ed. 2d 156 (1992) (citing Rhodes v. Chapman, 452 U.S. 337, 347, 101 S. Ct. 2392, 69 L. Ed. 2d 59 (1981)).

that the Constitution does not allow "inhumane" prisons.[84] This raises the question of what are the "minimal civilized measure(s) of life's necessities" and what constitutes an "inhumane" prison?

In *Wilson v. Seiter,* the Court suggested that this term refers to the state's responsibility to meet the "identifiable human need[s]" of inmates.[85] The *Wilson* Court described food, warmth, exercise, and safety as falling into this category of essentials.[86] *Estelle* also identified "adequate medical care" as fitting into this grouping.[87] *Farmer* added to the list protection from physical abuse by other inmates.[88] Perhaps the clearest definition of what courts consider the human needs encompassed by the Eighth Amendment comes from a non-prison Supreme Court opinion written by Chief Justice Rhenquist. In that case, Chief Justice Rhenquist wrote a fuller explanation of the essentials that a civilized society must provide to persons who are in state custody:

> W]hen the State by the affirmative exercise of its power so restrains an individual's liberty that it renders him unable to care for himself, and at the same time fails to provide for his basic human needs-e.g., food clothing, shelter, medical care and reasonable safety-it transgresses the substantive limits on state action set by the Eighth Amendment.[89]

This concept of civilized decency is broad enough to encompass many, but by no means all, aspects of prison

---

[84]Farmer v. Brennan, 511 U.S. 825, 114 S. Ct. 1970, 1976, 128 L. Ed. 2d 811 (1994).

[85]Wilson v. Seiter, 501 U.S. 294, 111 S. Ct. 2321, 2327, 115 L. Ed. 2d 271 (1991).

[86]*Id.*

[87]Whitley v. Albers, 475 U.S. 312, 319, 106 S. Ct. 1078, 89 L. Ed. 2d 251 (1986).

[88]Farmer v. Brennan, 511 U.S. 825, 114 S. Ct. 1970, 1976-77, 128 L. Ed. 2d 811 (1994).

[89]DeShaney v. Winnebago County Dept. of Social Services, 489 U.S. 189, 109 S. Ct. 998, 1005, 103 L. Ed. 2d 249 (1989).

§ 2:2

life.[90] The role of model standards proposed by such diverse organizations as the National Advisory Commission on Criminal Justice Standards and Goals,[91] the American Law Institute,[92] the United Nations,[93] the American Correctional Association,[94] and the American Bar Association[95] in making the determination of what violates standards of decency has been controversial. While lower courts have often placed great reliance on these standards in making their determinations,[96] the Supreme Court has taken a different position, holding that the standards, which collectively constitute the considered judgment of professionals about what prison practices are and are not acceptable,[97] are relevant but

---

[90]See, e.g., §§ 2:9, 2:10, and 2:11, but it is not without its limits. See, e.g., § 2:14 for discussion of prison programs.

[91]See National Advisory Commission on Criminal Justice Standards and Goals, Corrections (1973).

[92]See Model Penal Code art 6 (1985).

[93]See United Nations, Standard Minimum Rules for the Treatment of Prisoners (1955); see also International Covenant on Civil and Political Rights, G.A. res. 2200A (XXI), 21 U.N. GAOR Supp. (No. 16) at 52, U.N. Doc. A/6316 (1966), 999 U.N.T.S. 171, entered into force Mar. 23, 1976; Body of Principles for the Protection of All Persons under Any Form of Detention or Imprisonment, G.A. res. 43/173, annex, 43 U.N. GAOR Supp. (No. 49) at 298, U.N. Doc. A/43/49 (1988); Basic Principles for the Treatment of Prisoners, G.A. res. 45/111, annex, 45 U.N. GAOR Supp. (No. 49A) at 200, U.N. Doc. A/45/49 (1990).

[94]The American Correctional Association sponsored the Commission on Accreditation for Corrections, which has published the Manual of Standards for Adult Correctional Institutions (2002) and the Manual of Standards for Adult Local Detention Facilities (2002).

[95]See ABA, Standards for Criminal Justice (1986).

[96]See, e.g., Rhem v. Malcolm, 371 F. Supp. 594, 627 (S.D. N.Y. 1974), aff'd and remanded, 507 F.2d 333 (2d Cir. 1974).

[97]The West Virginia Supreme Court of Appeals felt that these standards were the result of such a deliberate and thoughtful process and were so well thought out that it adopted them as law. Cooper v. Gwinn, 171 W. Va. 245, 298 S.E.2d 781, 794-95 (1981) (noting that the standards are the "product of a long and thought-

§ 2:2

not controlling.[98] The Court has taken a similar position on the opinions of experts.[99]

Does the nature of the injury play a role in determining whether "contemporary standards of decency" have been violated? The answer is yes, but there is no uniform requirement about the type of injury required, which is true for all Eighth Amendment cases. The nature of the injury required will depend on the particular claim. In *Hudson v. McMillian*, for example, a serious physical injury was not required to make out an Eighth Amendment case when the injury was the result of an unjustified beating by a prison guard.[100] Likewise, in *Helling v. McKinney*, the Court held that an Eighth Amendment violation can occur in the absence of any present injury if the threat of actual injury is imminent and is posed by some environmental hazard that prison officials ought to have prevented. *Farmer v. Brennan* stands for the same proposition. Any inmate need not be actually attacked before a court will act in the face of a pervasive threat of violence that if left uncorrected will surely cause injury. For traditional conditions of confinement cases, however, the Court has suggested that more may be necessary than was required in *Hudson*, *Helling*, or *Farmer*. Prisoner discomfort, for example, may not be enough to establish an Eighth Amendment violation.

In this connection, an open question not yet answered by the Supreme Court is whether the Eighth Amendment can be violated when the only injury suffered is

---

ful process of debate and deliberation and represent the best consensus of professionals in the corrections field.").

[98]See Bell v. Wolfish, 441 U.S. 520, 543-44 n.27, 99 S. Ct. 1861, 60 L. Ed. 2d 447 (1979) (standards of organizations express only the goals of the group in question, not constitutional minima). See also Rhodes v. Chapman, 452 U.S. 337, 348-40 n13, 101 S. Ct. 2392, 69 L. Ed. 2d 59 (1981).

[99]See, e.g., Rhodes v. Chapman, 452 U.S. 337, 348-40 n.13, 101 S. Ct. 2392, 69 L. Ed. 2d 59 (1981).

[100]Hudson v. McMillian, 503 U.S. 1, 112 S. Ct. 995, 997-98, 117 L. Ed. 2d 156 (1992).

§ 2:2   Rights of Prisoners, Third Edition

psychological. In *Hudson,* Justice Blackmun suggested in a concurring opinion[101] that the unnecessary pain prohibited by the Eighth Amendment could include psychological as well as physical pain. This point of view makes a great deal of sense, particularly after the Court's decision in *Helling,* which did not require any present injury to state a claim. Psychological pain can be every bit as debilitating as physical pain. What is more, in a prison setting, where prison officials have such total control over inmates, the potential for the infliction of severe psychological harm is quite real. To fence out psychological pain from Eighth Amendment protection would be to open up opportunities to maltreat inmates without constitutional review.[102] Thus, most lower courts have interpreted the Supreme Court's holdings in *Hudson* and *Helling* to stand for the proposition that physical injury is not required to make an Eighth Amendment violation.[103] While there is general agreement among the lower courts on this general

---

[101]Hudson v. McMillian, 503 U.S. 1, 112 S. Ct. 995, 1004, 117 L. Ed. 2d 156 (1992). (Blackmun, J, concurring).

[102]Solitary confinement, for example, is a device that is fraught with dangers of psychological injury. In this regard Eighth Amendment litigation has had a great deal of impact in setting limits on how solitary confinement can operate. See § 2:3.

[103]See, e.g., Jordan v. Gardner, 986 F.2d 1521 (9th Cir. 1993) (en banc) (holding that severe psychological pain can violate the Eighth Amendment); Northington v. Jackson, 973 F.2d 1518, 23 Fed. R. Serv. 3d 934 (10th Cir. 1992) (holding that placing a revolver to a prisoner's head without justification is actionable infliction of "psychological injury"); Chandler v. Baird, 926 F.2d 1057 (11th Cir. 1991) (holding that statement of inmate that "I'm sure I was depressed from it" was sufficient to state a claim for violation of the Eighth Amendment standards for prison conditions); Babcock v. White, 102 F.3d 267, 273 (7th Cir. 1996) (observing that "the Constitution does not countenance psychological torture merely because it fails to inflict physical injury"); Shakka v. Smith, 71 F.3d 162, 166 (4th Cir. 1995) (holding that a "significant . . . emotional injury" can constitute Eighth Amendment pain; citation and internal quotation marks omitted); Hobbs v. Lockhart, 46 F.3d 864, 869, 31 Fed. R. Serv. 3d 380 (8th Cir. 1995) (ruling that allegations of severe emotional distress, nightmares and constant

principal, there is a split in authority on the question of whether a damage award can be imposed when the only injury suffered is psychological.[104] These issues are discussed in greater detail in the sections that follow.[105]

In the final analysis, it is extremely difficult to discuss in the abstract the meaning and parameters of the cruel and unusual punishment clause. Concrete factual situations must be examined, and many of the more common of these will be explored in the subsequent sections. But first the subjective component of the Eighth Amendment must be explored.

---

fears stated a constitutionally cognizable claim); Thomas v. Farley, 31 F.3d 557, 559 (7th Cir. 1994) ("Mental torture is not an oxymoron, and has been held or assumed in a number of prisoner cases . . . to be actionable as cruel and unusual punishment."); Strickler v. Waters, 989 F.2d 1375 (4th Cir. 1993) (observing that in unusual instances an emotional injury "would be cognizable" under the Eighth Amendment); Scher v. Engelke, 943 F.2d 921, 924 (8th Cir. 1991) (ruling that "fear, mental anguish, and misery" can cause sufficient pain to violate the Eighth Amendment); White v. Napoleon, 897 F.2d 103, 111 (3d Cir. 1990) (finding that "allegations [of mental anxiety] are sufficient to state a claim under the Eighth Amendment"); Delaney v. DeTella, 256 F.3d 679 (7th Cir. 2001) (claim can be based on the presence of a "strong likelihood" of psychological damage due to the denial of exercise privileges for 90 days); Benefield v. McDowall, 241 F.3d 1267 (10th Cir. 2001) (the pervasiveness of psychological injury is taken into account in proving substantial risk of serious harm); Chandler v. District of Columbia Dept. of Corrections, 145 F.3d 1355 (D.C. Cir. 1998) (a claim of psychological injury due to a verbal threat may be sufficient to implicate the Eighth Amendment); Wilson v. Silcox, 151 F. Supp. 2d 1345 (N.D. Fla. 2001) (verbal threats can lead to an Eighth Amendment claim for psychological injury).

[104]Contrast e.g., Doe v. Welborn, 110 F.3d 520, 523-24 (7th Cir. 1997) and Babcock v. White, 102 F.3d 267, 272-273 (7th Cir. 1996), holding that damages can not be awarded for psychological fear caused by living in fear of other inmates, with Benefield v. McDowall, 241 F.3d 1267, 1272 (10th Cir. 2001), holding that damages could be awarded for this injury.

[105]See §§ 2:5, 2:7. The impact of the Prison Reform Litigation Act's prohibition on suits not based on physical injury on this branch of the law is discussed in that section.

The Subjective Component: What Is Punishment?

The Supreme Court has engrafted a subjective element into all Eighth Amendment analysis.[106] The reason given by the Supreme Court for this controversial requirement is that the Eighth Amendment bars cruel and unusual "punishment." If a practice cannot be characterized as punishment, the Eighth Amendment does not prohibit it, no matter how cruel and unusual it may be. Accordingly, the Court has held that in a case involving pain that is not "formally meted out as punishment by the statute or the sentencing judge," there must be an inquiry into the state of mind of the person or persons responsible for the conduct that is at issue in the case.[107] Furthermore, the Court has held that the requisite state of mind depends on the type of Eighth Amendment claim being asserted. If the claim concerns brutality by prison guards, in a riot situation or not, then, in order to recover, the inmate must prove that the defendants acted with malice.[108] If, however, the claim concerns a prison condition, the right to safety and protection from inmate assaults, or prison medical care, then the lesser standard of "deliberate indiffer-

---

[106]Wilson v. Seiter, 501 U.S. 294, 111 S. Ct. 2321, 115 L. Ed. 2d 271 (1991).

[107]Wilson v. Seiter, 501 U.S. 294, 111 S. Ct. 2321, 2325, 115 L. Ed. 2d 271 (1991). It is, of course, possible to argue that because individuals convicted of crime are sent to prison for punishment, whatever happens to them in prison should be deemed punishment. See Wilson v. Seiter, 501 U.S. 294, 111 S. Ct. 2321, 115 L. Ed. 2d 271 (1991) (White, J, concurring in the judgment). Cf. Landman v. Royster, 333 F. Supp. 621, 645 (E.D. Va. 1971) (any treatment to which a prisoner is exposed is a form of punishment and subject to Eighth Amendment standards). This broad, but logical, approach to punishment, however, was rejected by the majority in *Wilson*. Wilson v. Seiter, 501 U.S. 294, 111 S. Ct. 2321, 2325, 115 L. Ed. 2d 271 (1991).

[108]Hudson v. McMillian, 503 U.S. 1, 112 S. Ct. 995, 998, 117 L. Ed. 2d 156 (1992); Whitley v. Albers, 475 U.S. 312, 320, 106 S. Ct. 1078, 89 L. Ed. 2d 251 (1986). The prerequisites for a finding of malice are found in the section of this chapter discussing violence in prison. See § 2:6.

ence" applies.[109] Thus, a prison condition, no matter how objectively deplorable, conceivably can be found constitutional because it was not imposed with the requisite scienter by prison officials.

The holding that prison conditions are not violative of the Eighth Amendment unless deliberate indifference is proven has been criticized.[110] The primary objection to the requirement is that it opens up the possibility that courts will refuse to remedy prison conditions that objectively fall below civilized standards on the ground that the defendants did not act with deliberate indifference in causing them. According to the critics, shocking prison conditions are unconstitutional regardless of their cause. As Justice Stevens trenchantly

---

[109]Wilson v. Seiter, 501 U.S. 294, 111 S. Ct. 2321, 2323, 115 L. Ed. 2d 271 (1991); Estelle v. Gamble, 429 U.S. 97, 104-05, 97 S. Ct. 285, 50 L. Ed. 2d 251 (1976). But see LeMaire v. Maass, 12 F.3d 1444 (9th Cir. 1993) (holding that, even in a conditions case, the maliciousness standard can apply if the conditions are imposed on an incorrigible inmate for the purpose of preventing him from engaging in violence).

[110]For scholarly criticism of this branch of *Wilson v. Seiter,* see Elizabeth Alexander, The Overall Context of Prison Litigation, in Section 1983 Civil Rights Litigation and Attorney's Fees 1992: Current Developments 401 (PLI Litig. & Admin. Practice Course Handbook Series No 449, 1992); Arthur B. Berger, Note, Wilson v. Sieter, An Unsatisfying Attempt at Resolving the Imbroglio of Eighth Amendment Prisoners' Rights Standards, 1992 Utah L Rev 565; Russell W. Gray, Wilson v. Seiter, Defining the Components of and Proposing A Direction for Eighth Amendment Prison Condition Law, 41 Am U L Rev 1339 (1992); Note, Cruel and Unusual Punishments Clause-Prison Conditions: Wilson v. Seiter, 105 Harv L Rev 235 (1991); Siegal, Note: Rape in Prison and AIDS: A Challenge for the Eighth Amendment Framework of Wilson v.Seiter, 44 Stan. L. Rev. 1541 (1992); Note & Comment: The "Deliberate Indifference" Test Defined: Mere Lip Service to the Protection of Prisoners' Civil Rights, 5 Temple Pol & Civ. Rts. L.R. 121. But see Richard H. Kuhlman, Comment, Prison Conditions and the Deliberate Indifference Standard Under the Eighth Amendment: Wilson v. Seiter 111 S Ct 2321, 42 Wash UJ Urb & Contemp L 369 (1992).

§ 2:2   Rights of Prisoners, Third Edition

observed: "[w]hether the conditions in Andersonville[111] were the product of design, negligence, or mere poverty, they were cruel and inhuman."[112]

A related objection to the deliberate indifference standard is that it is unworkable when applied to prison conditions litigation. Justice White made this point when he commented that intent is difficult to determine in the diffused, bureaucratic setting of a prison, where many persons-some known, some unknowable-over an extended period of time can contribute to making, or failing to correct, a particular prison condition.[113] Further complicating the search for intent is the reality that grievous prison conditions often result, not from the actions of prison officials, but rather from the unwillingness of state legislatures to fund prison operations adequately.[114]

A subjective, in addition to an objective, approach to punishment complicates a prisoner's assertion of an Eighth Amendment claim. It remains to be seen, however, how the Court will ultimately answer these questions. To date, the Court has said little affirmatively about what the test means. For the most part, it has defined deliberate indifference more by saying what it is not. In *Estelle,* for example, the Court gave little definition of deliberate indifference other than to distin-

---

[111]Andersonville was the infamous prison camp run by the Confederacy during the Civil War for captured Union solders. Thirteen thousand prisoners died there. James M. McPherson, Battle Cry of Freedom 796 (1988).

[112]Estelle v. Gamble, 429 U.S. 97, 116-17, 97 S. Ct. 285, 50 L. Ed. 2d 251 (1976) (Stevens, J, dissenting). See also Bell v. Wolfish, 441 U.S. 520, 585, 99 S. Ct. 1861, 60 L. Ed. 2d 447 (1979) (Stevens, J, dissenting) (quoting from H. Packer, The Limits of the Criminal Sanction 33 (1968), and noting that the emphasis on subjective intent "can only 'encourage hypocrisy and unconscious self-deception'").

[113]Wilson v. Seiter, 501 U.S. 294, 111 S. Ct. 2321, 2331, 115 L. Ed. 2d 271 (1991) (White, J, concurring in the judgment).

[114]For a discussion of whether the defense of inadequate resources can counter an argument of deliberate indifference, see § 2:15.

guish it from medical malpractice or negligence. At the other end of the spectrum, in *Whitley,* the Court held that a finding of deliberate indifference involved less culpability than a finding that the defendant's actions were taken "maliciously and sadistically for the very purpose of causing harm."[115] Thus, "deliberate indifference occupies a middle ground between negligence and malice or intentional misconduct."[116]

The most extensive discussion of the subject is the *Farmer* case, which dealt with a claim that a vulnerable inmate was not adequately protected from assault. In that case, the Court made clear that while the term required a subjective knowledge on the part of the defendant of the conditions to which the plaintiffs were exposed, that knowledge can be inferred from objective circumstances.[117] In other words, if a condition is obviously harmful to the mental well being of an inmate, and if it serves no valid penological purpose to impose the condition, then it is permissible to infer that the defendant must have known of the risk, and the failure to correct it can be evidence of the subjective state of mind of the defendant to be deliberately indifferent.[118]

This approach conforms to the constitutional stan-

---

[115]Whitley v. Albers, 475 U.S. 312, 320, 106 S. Ct. 1078, 89 L. Ed. 2d 251 (1986).

[116]John Boston, Wilson v. Seiter: A Preliminary Analysis, in 8 Civil Rights Litigation and Attorney Fees Annual Handbook 42 (1992).

[117]Farmer v. Brennan, 511 U.S. 825, 114 S. Ct. 1970, 1983, 128 L. Ed. 2d 811 (1994).

[118]This approach is mirrored in another Supreme Court case, City of Canton, Ohio v. Harris, 489 U.S. 378, 109 S. Ct. 1197, 103 L. Ed. 2d 412 (1989). That case involved a failure to provide psychiatric assistance to a person arrested by the police. Justice O'Connor indicated that a municipal defendant could be liable under the civil rights law for failure to train its police officers in how to handle persons who are arrested and suffer from psychiatric conditions. The Court held that deliberate indifference can be inferred from the failure of defendants to take affirmative actions to cure a problem where it can be shown that the conditions or practices objectively violate the Eighth Amendment. Justice

§ 2:2   Rights of Prisoners, Third Edition

dard of established tort principles. In tort law, the middle ground between negligence and maliciousness is "wanton" or "reckless" conduct. According to Professors Prosser and Keeton, wanton or reckless conduct is described as meaning:

> . . . that the actor has intentionally done an act of an unreasonable character in disregard of a known or obvious risk that was so great as to make it highly probable that harm would follow, and which thus is usually accompanied by conscious indifference to the consequences.[119]

The key to this definition of the deliberate indifference standard is that it does not literally compel an inquiry into a person's actual state of mind. As Prosser and Keeton point out:

> Since [conscious indifference] is almost never admitted, and can be proved only by the conduct and the circumstances, an objective standard must of necessity in practice be applied. The "willful" requirement, therefore, breaks down and receives at best lip service, where it is clear from the facts that the defendant, *whatever his state of*

O'Connor cited with approval four lower court cases to support this proposition. Fiacco v. City of Rensselaer, N.Y., 783 F.2d 319, 20 Fed. R. Evid. Serv. 49 (2d Cir. 1986) (holding that knowledge of unconstitutional police brutality, combined with a failure to act, is sufficient to establish that police supervisors were guilty of deliberate indifference); Patzner v. Burkett, 779 F.2d 1363, 1367 (8th Cir. 1985) (failure to take remedial steps after receiving notice constitutes deliberate indifference); Languirand v. Hayden, 717 F.2d 220, 226-27 n.7, 70 A.L.R. Fed. 1 (5th Cir. 1983) (same); Wellington v. Daniels, 717 F.2d 932, 936 (4th Cir. 1983) (history of widespread abuse gives rise to an inference of knowledge sufficient to trigger a finding of deliberate indifference when no remedial action is taken).

[119]W.P. Keeton et al, Prosser and Keeton on Torts § 34, at 212-13 (5th ed 1984); Saccenti, Comment: Preventing Summary Judgment Against Inmates Who Have Been Sexually Assaulted by Showing That the Risk Was Obvious, 59 Md. L. Rev. 642 (2000); Byrd, Comment: Reflections on Willful, Wanton, Reckless, and Gross Negligence, 48 La. L. Rev. 1383 (1988); Monte, Casenote: "Gross Negligence" and "Wilful and Wanton Misconduct"-Thanks to Jennings v. Southwood, Michigan Now Knows What They Mean, 1995 Det. C.L. Rev. 1379 (1995).

mind, has proceeded in disregard of a high and excessive degree of danger, either known to him or apparent to a reasonable person in his position.[120]

Thus, "plaintiffs need not psychoanalyze prison officials to prove their Eighth Amendment claims. If prison officials know, or *should* know, of deprivations of basic human needs in their institutions, and have not remedied them, deliberate indifference" is established.[121] This point addresses the concern that the deliberate indifference standard is unworkable because "intent simply is not very meaningful when considering a challenge to an institution."[122] If the crux of the issue is that the defendant knowingly acts with disregard of what, to a reasonable person, is objectively a prison condition that is a violation of the Eighth Amendment, or if the official proceeds in obvious disregard of risks that ought to be obvious objective violations of the Eighth Amendment, then accountability can be laid at the door of prison officials with responsibility for the institution.[123]

Under this theory, the showing of deliberate indiffer-

---

[120]W.P. Keeton et al, Prosser and Keeton on Torts § 34, at 212-13 (5th ed 1984) (emphasis supplied).

[121]John Boston, Wilson v. Seiter: A Preliminary Analysis, in 8 Civil Rights Litigation and Attorney Fees Annual Handbook 45 (1992) (emphasis in original). See also; Hope v. Pelzer, 240 F.3d 975 (11th Cir. 2001), rev'd on other grounds, 122 S. Ct. 2508, 153 L. Ed. 2d 666 (U.S. 2002); Oxendine v. Kaplan, 241 F.3d 1272 (10th Cir. 2001); Johnson v. Herman, 132 F. Supp. 2d 1130 (N.D. Ind. 2001).

[122]Wilson v. Seiter, 501 U.S. 294, 111 S. Ct. 2321, 2330, 115 L. Ed. 2d 271 (1991) (White, J, concurring in the judgment).

[123]A number of lower courts take this position. See, e.g., LaMarca v. Turner, 995 F.2d 1526, 1535 (11th Cir. 1993) ("To be deliberately indifferent, a prison official must knowingly or recklessly disregard an inmate's basic needs so that knowledge can be inferred"); Hendricks v. Coughlin, 942 F.2d 109, 113 (2d Cir. 1991); Redman v. County of San Diego, 942 F.2d 1435, 1443 (9th Cir. 1991); Berry v. City of Muskogee, Okl., 900 F.2d 1489, 1499 (10th Cir. 1990). However, some circuits have taken a contrary position. In McGill v. Duckworth, 944 F.2d 344, 348-49, 20 Fed. R. Serv. 3d 1247 (7th Cir. 1991), for example, the Seventh Circuit ruled that a

§ 2:2   RIGHTS OF PRISONERS, THIRD EDITION

ence might vary depending on whether the case is a damages action or an injunction action. Since damages actions involve findings of individual responsibility, courts are wary of finding liability for actions beyond a defendant's control.[124] This could occur if, for example, the condition was caused by the absence of adequate funding and the defendant prison official had attempted to secure adequate funds from the state to address the problem but was unsuccessful.[125]

Where an injunction is sought, however, the plaintiffs

---

prison official could not be held liable for failing to address risks that they were unaware of even if they "should have known of them." See also, Curry v. Scott, 249 F.3d 493 (6th Cir. 2001) (the court held that the district court erred in finding that prison officials should have been aware of the danger a prison guard posed to African American prisoners, as it was a question that was to be left to the jury whether the officials had actual knowledge of the danger based on obvious facts). This holding is inconsistent with the Supreme Court's statement in *Canton* that deliberate indifference can be shown by a failure to respond to "obvious risks." City of Canton, Ohio v. Harris, 489 U.S. 378, 389-90, 109 S. Ct. 1197, 103 L. Ed. 2d 412 (1989); Jensen v. Clarke, 73 F.3d 808 (8th Cir. 1996). For a further discussion of *McGill*, see § 2:6.

[124]See, e.g., Cortes-Quinones v. Jimenez-Nettleship, 842 F.2d 556, 559-60 (1st Cir. 1988) (defendants are not responsible for conditions they cannot control, but each defendant can be found liable for deliberate indifference based on his own actions or omissions that contribute to the unconstitutional condition), cited in Wilson v. Seiter, 501 U.S. 294, 111 S. Ct. 2321, 2327, 115 L. Ed. 2d 271 (1991).

[125]See, e.g., Birrell v. Brown, 867 F.2d 956, 959-60 (6th Cir. 1989) (where unconstitutional conditions resulted from budgetary constraints, prison officials were entitled to qualified immunity); Williams v. Bennett, 689 F.2d 1370, 1387-88 (11th Cir. 1982); Hale v. Tallapoosa County, 50 F.3d 1579 (11th Cir. 1995). This defense, however, is not valid if the official does have the power to allocate the funds to correct the problem but does not do so. See, e.g., Boswell v. Sherburne County, 849 F.2d 1117, 1123 (8th Cir. 1988) (refusing to allocate funds in order to save money does not excuse unconstitutional condition); Jones v. Johnson, 781 F.2d 769, 771-72 (9th Cir. 1986). Cf LaMarca v. Turner, 995 F.2d 1526, 1533 (11th Cir. 1993) (holding that, even in a damage action, the lack of funding defense is not sufficient if plaintiffs can show that the de-

do not seek to impose individual liability on the defendants; rather, they seek only a court order remedying the problem. Therefore, with injunctive cases, the focus on deliberate indifference is "broader and more generalized" than in damage cases, with the emphasis on the "combined acts or omissions" of the prison officials.[126] In such cases, courts have held that liability can be premised on a showing of "'repeated examples of negligent acts which disclose a pattern of conduct . . .' or by showing 'systemic or gross deficiencies in staffing, facilities, equipment or procedures.'"[127] This is in keeping with the notion that, with injunctive actions, the defendant is being sued in his or her "official capacity," and, thus, in reality, the case is a suit against the governmental entity charged with operating the facility.[128] The Eleventh Circuit relied on this theory when it held that injunctive relief could appropriately be granted based on a finding of institutional deliberate indifference even though the prison warden who was the named defendant was a "dedicated public servant who is trying very hard. . . to make [the prison] an efficient and effective correctional institution."[129]

If this theory of deliberate indifference is generally adopted by courts following *Wilson*,[130] then the decision to impose a subjective element on prison conditions

---

fendant, nevertheless, had the capability to ameliorate the conditions).

[126]Leer v. Murphy, 844 F.2d 628, 633 (9th Cir. 1988).

[127]French v. Owens, 777 F.2d 1250 (7th Cir. 1985) (quoting Ramos v. Lamm, 639 F.2d 559, 575 (10th Cir. 1980)). See also Fisher v. Koehler, 692 F. Supp. 1519, 1561-62 (S.D. N.Y. 1988).

[128]Kentucky v. Graham, 473 U.S. 159, 166-67, 105 S. Ct. 3099, 87 L. Ed. 2d 114 (1985) (suit against an individual in his official capacity is the same as a suit against the state).

[129]LaMarca v. Turner, 995 F.2d 1526, 1542 (11th Cir. 1993).

[130]There is further support for this theory in the Supreme Court's opinion in Bell v. Wolfish, 441 U.S. 520, 99 S. Ct. 1861, 60 L. Ed. 2d 447 (1979). In that case, the Court held that the due process clause of the Fourteenth Amendment was not violated unless harsh jail conditions were imposed on pretrial detainees with intent to

§ 2:2

Eighth Amendment cases will result in no major break from preexisting law.[131] Indeed, for the reasons sketched above, one commentator noted "[i]n case[s] involving . . . conditions of confinement, something like the deliberate indifference standard has been routinely applied [by the lower courts], though often without using the term."[132]

With this summary of the objective and subjective components of the Eighth Amendment, an analysis of the types of claims that are raised under an Eighth Amendment rubric will be meaningful.

---

punish. However, the majority in *Wolfish* indicated at least one tactical method by which inmate petitioners can ease their burden. In a footnote they hypothesized:

> [L]oading a detainee with chains and shackles and throwing him in a dungeon may ensure his presence at trial and preserve the security of the institution. But it would be difficult to conceive of a situation where conditions so harsh, employed to achieve objectives that could be accomplished in so many alternative and less harsh methods, would not support a conclusion that the purpose for which they were imposed was to punish.

Bell v. Wolfish, 441 U.S. 520, 539 n.20, 99 S. Ct. 1861, 60 L. Ed. 2d 447 (1979). This language strongly suggests that intent to punish can be inferred from an examination of objective facts by, for instance, showing that other, less drastic means for accomplishing a concededly legitimate governmental purpose are available. See also Hutto v. Finney, 437 U.S. 678, 699, 98 S. Ct. 2565, 57 L. Ed. 2d 522 (1978) (holding that an injunctive suit is, for practical purposes, a suit against the state).

[131]See, e.g., Young v. Ballis, 762 F. Supp. 823 (S.D. Ind. 1990); Warren v. State of Mo., 754 F. Supp. 150 (W.D. Mo. 1990), judgment aff'd, 995 F.2d 130 (8th Cir. 1993).

[132]John Boston, Wilson v. Seiter: A Preliminary Analysis in 8 Civil Rights Litigation and Attorney Fees Annual Handbook 42 (1992).

§ 2:3 Restrictive Confinement: Punitive Segregation, Solitary Confinement and "Supermax" Units

Research References
West's Key Number Digest, Prisons ⌐13(5)

Punitive segregation has a long pedigree in this country.[1] Historically, ever since prisons were established in the early nineteenth century[2] officials have used this type of confinement for various reasons, including using it as a sanction for the serious violation of institutional rules.[3] In more recent times, the units have continued to be used as punishment for rules infractions, but increasingly they have also been designated as a place to isolate inmates whom prison officials consider unduly violent or disruptive regardless of whether specific rules were violated. While there is wide variation on the conditions of confinement in the units, they are all characterized by more severe restrictions than imposed on inmates in general population.[4] Typically, an inmate in this status is locked into his cell for 23 or more hours per day with limited

---

[Section 2:3]

[1] Model Sentencing and Corrections Act § 4-502, cmt. at 173 (2001) (noting that solitary confinement "has been the most persistently inflicted punishment in the past").

[2] See, e.g., Sally Mann Romano, If the Shu Fits: Cruel and Unusual Punishment at California's Pelican Bay State Prison, 45 Emory L. J. 1089, 1093 (1996) (citing Blake McKelvey, American Prisons: A History of Good Intentions 3 (1977); Thomas O. Murton, Prison Management: The Past, The Present, and The Possible Future, in Prisons: Present and Possible 5, 9 (Marvin E. Wolfgang ed. 1979).

[3] See, e.g., Sostre v. McGinnis, 442 F.2d 178, 192 (2d Cir. 1971) (describing solitary confinement as one of "the main traditional disciplinary tools of our prison system").

[4] See, e.g., Craig Haney and Monia Lynch, Regulating Prisons of the Future: A Psychological Analysis of Supermax and Solitary Confinement, 23 NYU Rev. L. & Soc. Change 477 (1997) (describing the wide variety in the conditions in these units varying from units in which inmates are totally isolated from one another and

opportunities for exercise or programming. As a result, the conditions impose "at least partial social isolation and partial reduction of certain forms of stimulations as compared to general population prisoners."[5]

While this type of confinement has a long history, in the past relatively few inmates were subjected to it. However, that has changed. The use of restrictive housing has increased to the point that now tens of thousands of inmates are confined in these units. According to some estimates as many as 7 to 10% of all inmates are currently confined in some form of punitive segregation or solitary confinement.[6] Most of the increase in the use of this kind of confinement is caused by the development of what have come to be known as "supermax" units or "supermax" prisons.[7] These are special housing units (SHU) or prisons that are designed to

---

subjected to severe sensory deprivation to units in which the opposite is true; that is that the units have multiple cell occupancy).

[5]Craig Haney and Monia Lynch, Regulating Prisons of the Future: A Psychological Analysis of Supermax and Solitary Confinement, 23 NYU Rev. L. & Soc. Change 497 (1997).

[6]See, e.g., Craig Haney and Monia Lynch, Regulating Prisons of the Future: A Psychological Analysis of Supermax and Solitary Confinement, 23 NYU Rev. L. & Soc. Change 477, 497 (1997) (indicating that the precentages of inmates in restrictive housing ranges from 2.3% to 27.2% with an average nationally of 7.7%). In New York 8% of the prison population is housed in supermax facilities. Correctional Association of New York, State of the Prison: Conditions of Confinement in 25 Correctional Facilities, 12 (2002).

[7]Jerry R. DeMaio, If You Build It, They Will Come: The Threat of Overclassification in Wisconsin's Supermax Prison, 2001 Wisc. L. Rev. 207 (2001). Although "supermax" is the most common term for this type of prison, some agencies also use "maximum control facility," "control unit," "maxi-maxi," "special (or secured) housing unit (SHU)," "administrative maximum (ad- max or ADX)" or "intensive housing unit." Nat'l Inst. of Corrections, Supermax Prisons: Overview and General Considerations 5 (1999). See also, Cassandra Shaylor, "It's Like Living In A Black Hole": Women Of Color And Solitary Confinement In The Prison Industrial Complex, 24 New Eng. J. On Crim. & Civil Confinement 385 (1998), where the author examines the emerging use of the control unit, a "prison within a prison," for women prisoners.

house inmates who are considered the most incorrigible or difficult. The Department of Justice has describes as supermax unit as:

> a highly restrictive, high-custody housing unit within a secure facility, or an entire secure facility, that isolates inmates from the general prison population and from each other.[8]

Supermax units are often entire prisons.[9] In them, inmates are held under conditions that are similar to punitive segregation. Prisoners are locked in their cells for virtually the entire day and night with very limited opportunities for programs or recreation and with minimal visiting and other activities.

The movement to build such units has grown significantly in recent years.[10] According to one report, as of March 1997, thirty-four agencies in the United States,

---

[8]U.S. Dep't of Justice, National Institute of Corrections, Supermax Prisons: Overview and General Considerations (1999).

[9]Madrid v. Gomez, 889 F. Supp. 1146 (N.D. Cal. 1995), mandamus denied, 103 F.3d 828 (9th Cir. 1996). The case dealt with conditions at the Pelican Bay State Prison, a correctional facility located in northwest California. The facility is a "state-of-the-art prison" housing between 3,500 and 3,900 inmates at a time, a maximum security facility of 2,000 "general population" inmates, and a Security Housing Unit (SHU) reserved for 1,000 to 1,500 inmates who allegedly posed serious disciplinary problems such as gang activity.

[10]Tachiki, Comment: Indeterminate Sentences in Supermax Prisons Based Upon Alleged Gang Affiliations: A Reexamination of Procedural Protection and a Proposal for Greater Procedural Requirements, 83 Calif. L. Rev. 1115 (1995). A description of the Wisconsin Supermax facility is typical in that prison. In that facility:

> Prisoners . . . are subjected to the most intense and restrictive confinement available in the Wisconsin corrections system. Inmates spend over twenty-three hours every day in a twelve-foot by six-foot cell, only leaving for recreation time approximately four hours each week. Nearly all of an inmate's contact with the outside world—visitors, education, and even religious services—comes through a video teleconferencing system; even an inmate's direct contact with prison staff members is minimal. While in their cells, inmates receive no direct sunlight—only what comes in indirectly through a thin window at the top of the cell. They can be monitored at all times through

including the federal government, were either operating or had plans to open a supermax facility.[11] Indeed, the growth is so dramatic that two authors of a recent study of the use of supermax facilities concluded, "at no point in the modern history of imprisonment have so many prisoners been so completely isolated for so long a period of time in facilities designed so completely for the purpose of near isolation."[12]

There are several rationales offered for the creation of "Supermax" facilities. First, they are part of an overall "get tough" policy, which has characterized criminal justice matters in the last two decades. With the decline in the rehabilitation model, this type of confinement has grown more attractive. Second, by concentrating disruptive inmates to one place in prison, officials argue that they are able to be less restrictive with general population inmates. Finally, staff at these facilities can be trained in how to handle inmates who present behavior problems.[13]

The "severe deprivation of liberty" involved in the operation of these prisons has engendered much recent litigation.[14] Since punitive segregation and solitary confinement are normally intended at least to some

---

cameras and audio hookups in their cells, and a high technology security system can control and track inmate movement throughout the facility. In short, when inmates are identified for transfer and moved to [the supermax facility] they give up significantly more freedom than in a normal prison setting.

Jerry R. DeMaio, If You Build It, They Will Come: The Threat of Overclassification in Wisconsin's Supermax Prison, 2001 Wisc. L. Rev. 207, 207-208 (2001).

[11]*Id.* at 215.

[12]Craig Haney and Monia Lynch, Regulating Prisons of the Future: A Psychological Analysis of Supermax and Solitary Confinement, 23 NYU Rev. L. & Soc. Change 477, 480 (1997).

[13]*Id.* at 481.

[14]Jerry R. DeMaio, If You Build It, They Will Come: The Threat of Overclassification in Wisconsin's Supermax Prison, 2001 Wisc. L. Rev. 216 (2001).

extent as punishment,[15] one might first suppose that a challenge to conditions in a solitary confinement unit automatically satisfies the subjective component of the Eighth Amendment.[16] This is a bit too glib, however. While assignment to such a unit may be generally intended as punishment, the particular practice of the unit that is being challenged may not be one that prison officials consciously sought to impose.[17] In addition, sometimes the claim might involve an alleged deviation by individual staff members, in which case there is a further question of whose intent is at issue. Finally, there may be correctional justifications other than intent to punish for particular practices. Thus, in litigation about conditions in these units both the objective and the subjective branches of the Eight Amendment test must be considered.[18]

Nevertheless, the crucial question in most of the

---

[15]Segregation may also be used to protect inmates, to observe them, or prior to classification. See, e.g., 28 C.F.R. § 541.23 (calling for the establishment of administrative detention for inmates who need protection).

[16]The Supreme Court, in addition, has recognized that prisoner liberty interests might be implicated by punitive confinement to solitary, and has prescribed the minimum due process safeguards that must be complied with prior to its imposition in prison disciplinary proceedings. See, e.g., Wolff v. McDonnell, 418 U.S. 539, 571 n19, 94 S. Ct. 2963, 41 L. Ed. 2d 935 (1974); Sandin v. Conner, 515 U.S. 472, 115 S. Ct. 2293, 132 L. Ed. 2d 418 (1995). For a discussion of this point, see Ch 9.

[17]See, e.g., Bracewell v. Lobmiller, 938 F. Supp. 1571 (M.D. Ala. 1996), aff'd, 116 F.3d 1493 (11th Cir. 1997) (inmate confined to disciplinary segregation claimed prison officials were deliberately indifferent to her health and safety; the plaintiff was subjected to the presence of a mentally disturbed inmate who threw feces and urine, and constantly made noise; while the court held that the objective component of the Eighth Amendment was satisfied, the plaintiff failed to satisfy the subjective component; the court found prison officials did not have actual knowledge that conditions in the segregation unit were so serious that they were injuring the plaintiff).

[18]For pretrial detainees, challenging restrictive housing practices in a jail setting is governed by the Fourteenth Amendment;

§ 2:3

many cases that have touched on this subject focuses on the objective side of the equation. The issue in most cases is whether the conditions in the punitive segregation unit, or the way in which a particular punitive segregation unit operates, falls below "contemporary standards of decency"[19] through "the unnecessary and wanton infliction of pain."[20]

There is a strong case to be made for the proposition that this kind of restrictive confinement, with the severe sensory deprivation that it entails, at least when used for extended periods of time, violates the Eighth Amendment.[21] The potential for serious harm to inmates confined in isolation has long been realized. Over a century ago, the Supreme Court recounted this country's initial experiences with penitentiaries where convicts were kept in complete isolation.[22] The effects of this regimen were described by the Court:

> A considerable number of prisoners fell, after even a short confinement, into a semi-fatuous condition, from which it was next to impossible to arouse them, and others became violently insane; others still, committed suicide; while those who stood the ordeal better were not generally reformed, and in most cases did not recover sufficient

---

however, the standard to be applied is the Eighth Amendment test. See, e.g., Landfair v. Sheahan, 878 F. Supp. 1106 (N.D. Ill. 1995); Bowman v. Campbell, 850 F. Supp. 144 (N.D. N.Y. 1994).

[19]Hudson v. McMillian, 503 U.S. 1, 112 S. Ct. 995, 1000, 117 L. Ed. 2d 156 (1992).

[20]Rhodes v. Chapman, 452 U.S. 337, 347, 101 S. Ct. 2392, 69 L. Ed. 2d 59 (1981).

[21]For a discussion of the international standards regarding solitary confinement see Nan D. Miller, International Protection of the Rights of Prisoners: Is Solitary Confinement In The United States A Violation of International Standards?, 26 Cal. W. Int'l. L.J. 138 (1995).

[22]In re Medley, 134 U.S. 160, 10 S. Ct. 384, 33 L. Ed. 835 (1890). (the issue in *Medley* was whether a sentence to solitary confinement was so drastically different from a sentence to the general population of a prison that it could not be imposed on an inmate who had been sentenced originally to a term that did not include solitary confinement; the Court held that it was).

mental activity to be of any subsequent service to the community.[23]

Research validates these observations.[24] Studies confirm that "serious emotional consequences" result when isolation is utilized as a form of imprisonment.[25] The studies reveal that, even in the absence of physical brutality or unhygienic conditions, inmates who are exposed to solitary confinement suffer "declines in mental functioning" and, in a number of cases, extreme reactions, such as hallucinations and delusions.[26] An exhaustive review of the extensive psychological and psychiatric research that has been done on the effects of this type of confinement concluded that almost all studies show that this type of confinement produces

---

[23]In re Medley, 134 U.S. 160, 168, 10 S. Ct. 384, 33 L. Ed. 835 (1890). In 1922, Justice Brandeis echoed this sentiment when he noted in dissent that "the most severe punishment inflicted" in American prisons "was solitary confinement without labor." U.S. v. Moreland, 258 U.S. 433, 449, 42 S. Ct. 368, 66 L. Ed. 700, 24 A.L.R. 992 (1922) (Brandeis, J., dissenting). For another graphic account of the way in which solitary confinement units operated at the turn of the century, see Thomas M. Osborne, Within Prison Walls (D. Appelton ed. 1915 & 1991).

[24]For a comprehensive discussion of that literature, see Craig Haney and Monia Lynch, Regulating Prisons of the Future: A Psychological Analysis of Supermax and Solitary Confinement, 23 N.Y.U. Rev. L. & Soc. Change 477 (1997). See also Maria A. Luise, Note, Solitary Confinement: Legal and Psychological Considerations, 15 N.E. J. on Crim. & Civ. Conf. 310 (1989). Courts, too, have come to similar conclusions. See, e.g., Davenport v. DeRobertis, 844 F.2d 1310, 1313 (7th Cir. 1988) ("the record shows, what anyway seems pretty obvious, that isolating a human being from other human beings year after year or even month after month can cause substantial psychological damage, even if the isolation is not total").

[25]Maria A. Luise, Note, Solitary Confinement: Legal and Psychological Considerations, 15 New Eng. J. on Crim. & Civ. Confinement 310, 317 (1989).

[26]*Id.* at 319 (citing Thomas B. Benjamin & Kenneth Lux, Solitary Confinement as Psychological Punishment, 13 Cal. W.L. Rev. 265, 268 (1977)).

"strikingly similar negative psychological effects."[27] These included anxiety, panic, rage, loss of control, appetite and sleep disturbances, self-mutilations, paranoia, and suicidal impulses.[28] The evidence is so strong that some authorities have concluded that "[t]he empirical record compels an unmistakable conclusion: this experience is psychologically painful, can be traumatic and harmful and puts many of those who have been subjected to it at risk of long term emotional and even physical damage."[29]

Because of concerns about the human consequences, some respected groups have called for the drastic curtailment of the use of this kind of confinement.[30] The views of these groups, and some reputable penologists notwithstanding, virtually every court which has considered the issue has held that the imposition of

---

[27] Craig Haney and Monia Lynch, Regulating Prisons of the Future: A Psychological Analysis of Supermax and Solitary Confinement, 23 N.Y.U. Rev. L. & Soc. Change 477, 530 (1997).

[28] *Id.* at 500.

[29] Craig Haney and Monia Lynch, Regulating Prisons of the Future: A Psychological Analysis of Supermax and Solitary Confinement, 23 N.Y.U. Rev. L. & Soc. Change 477, 500 (1997).

[30] See National Sheriffs' Assn, Inmates' Legal Rights 47 (1987) (noting that "the practice [of solitary confinement] is condemned by many groups with correctional interests"). See also National Advisory Comm'n on Criminal Justice Standards & Goals, Corrections Standard 2.4 (1973) (isolation should be punishment of last resort and then should not extend beyond 10 days); American Correctional Assn, Standards for Adult Correctional Institutions Standard 3-4243 (1990) (outside limit should be set on duration of disciplinary detention; 30 days sufficient for most cases; all cases in which sanction is extended over 60 days requires the provision of the same services and privileges as are available to persons in protective custody and administrative segregation); Model Sentencing and Corrections Act § 4-502 (1983) (limited confinement to solitary confinement to no more than 90 days). But see ABA, Standards for Criminal Justice Standard 23-6.13(d) (1986) (refusing to adopt the recommendation of the drafting committee that solitary confinement be abolished but decreeing that the conditions must not deprive the inmates of "items necessary for the maintenance of psychological and physical well-being").

solitary confinement, without more, does not violate the Eighth Amendment.[31] Arguments that isolation offends evolving standards of decency, that it constitutes psychological torture,[32] and that it is excessive because less severe sanctions would be equally efficacious, have routinely failed.[33]

However, courts have by no means been insensitive to the potential for serious harm posed by its use. Indeed, the courts have been actively involved in policing the use of solitary confinement.[34] Even though inmates with serious disciplinary problems may be housed in these units, one court aptly observed, "even

---

[31]See, e.g., Young v. Quinlan, 960 F.2d 351, 364, 22 Fed. R. Serv. 3d 530 (3d Cir. 1992) (holding that solitary confinement "is not cruel and unusual punishment per se"); Smith v. Coughlin, 748 F.2d 783, 787 (2d Cir. 1984); Gregory v. Wyse, 512 F.2d 378 (10th Cir. 1975); Gates v. Collier, 501 F.2d 1291 (5th Cir. 1974); Novak v. Beto, 453 F.2d 661 (5th Cir. 1971); Adams v. Pate, 445 F.2d 105 (7th Cir. 1971); Sostre v. McGinnis, 442 F.2d 178 (2d Cir. 1971); Ford v. Board of Managers of New Jersey State Prison, 407 F.2d 937, 18 A.L.R. Fed. 1 (3d Cir. 1969).

[32]But see Falkenstein v. City of Bismarck, 268 N.W.2d 787 (N.D. 1978) (city held liable where conditions in isolation induced suicide).

[33]See, generally, Maria A. Luise, Note, Solitary Confinement: Legal and Psychological Considerations, 15 New Eng. J. on Crim. & Civ. Confinement 310 (1989); Thomas B. Benjamin & Kenneth Lux, Solitary Confinement as Psychological Punishment, 13 Cal. W.L. Rev. 265 (1977); Richard G. Singer, Confining Solitary Confinement, Constitutional Arguments for a "New Penology, " 56 Iowa L. Rev. 1251; Raymond H. Thoenig, Punishment Within the Letter of the Law, or Psychological Torture?, 1972 Wis. L. 971; Raymond H. Thoenig, Comment, Solitary Confinement- Rev. 223.

[34]The National Sheriff's Association was not exaggerating when it reported that "no single correctional practice has caused as much controversy and as many lawsuits as the use of solitary confinement." National Sheriffs' Assn., Inmates' Legal Rights 47 (1987). See also David Rudovsky, Alvin J. Bronstein, Edward I. Koren, & Julia Cade, The Rights of Prisoners 4 (4th ed. 1988) ("It should surprise no one that most cases raising the issue of cruel and unusual punishment concern confinement in segregation, stripcells, or solitary").

§ 2:3

nasty prisoners cannot be knowingly housed in ghastly conditions reminiscent of the Black Hole of Calcutta."[35]

The United States Supreme Court set an example when, over a two decades ago in *Hutto v. Finney*,[36] the Court upheld a lower court's order limiting the length of stay in the punitive segregation unit of the Arkansas prison system to 30 days. The *Hutto* Court held that in light of the inadequate diet, overcrowding,[37] rampant violence, vandalism, and lack of professionalism and good judgment on the part of maximum security personnel, the prohibition against cruel and unusual punishment had been violated by stays in the prison solitary confinement unit that exceeded that length of time.[38] Thus, the Court established a mutual dependence between "duration" of confinement in solitary confinement and the conditions in the unit. In other words, conditions that might be endurable for short periods become insufferable if inflicted for longer periods. As the Court put it, confinement in a "filthy, overcrowded cell and a

---

[35] Isby v. Clark, 100 F.3d 502, 503 (7th Cir. 1996).

[36] Hutto v. Finney, 437 U.S. 678, 98 S. Ct. 2565, 57 L. Ed. 2d 522 (1978).

[37] While the terms punitive segregation and solitary confinement used in this section imply that prisoners are separated from all other inmates, often in punitive segregation units several convicts are confined in relatively small isolation cells designed for fewer persons than are held in them, thereby creating a serious overcrowding problem. This was certainly the case in *Hutto*. There, it was common for an average of four and sometimes as many as ten or eleven inmates to be confined in a punitive segregation cell that measured 8 feet by 10 feet. Hutto v. Finney, 437 U.S. 678, 682, 98 S. Ct. 2565, 57 L. Ed. 2d 522 (1978). See also Chavis v. Rowe, 643 F.2d 1281 (7th Cir. 1981) (confinement of five prisoners in a 5 foot by 7 foot cell for six months would violate the Eighth Amendment); Landman v. Royster, 333 F. Supp. 621 (E.D. Va. 1971). The common characteristic of either pure solitary confinement or restrictive housing is that both rely on a regime of severe deprivation of activity and stimulation.

[38] Hutto v. Finney, 437 U.S. 678, 686, 98 S. Ct. 2565, 57 L. Ed. 2d 522 (1978).

diet of 'grue'[39] might be tolerable for a few days and intolerably cruel after weeks and months."[40] Following the example of *Hutto,* "courts have drawn limits as to what kinds of physical conditions and treatment may be tolerated" in punitive segregation units.[41] Courts have not hesitated to find Eighth Amendment violations when the conditions in solitary confinement "are unsanitary, degrading or unhealthful."[42]

Specially singled out for careful consideration are the so-called "strip cells." These are isolation cells to which inmates are confined without normal clothing (usually nude or clad only in underwear) or bedding as punishment for rules infractions. Sometimes these cells lack such essentials as toilet facilities.[43] Courts have taken special care to examine the conditions in these units and have held that they are unconstitutional unless there are special circumstances.[44] These circumstances

---

[39]A concoction resulting from the mixing and baking of mashed meat, potatoes, oleo, syrup, vegetables, eggs, and seasoning.

[40]Hutto v. Finney, 437 U.S. 678, 686-87, 98 S. Ct. 2565, 57 L. Ed. 2d 522 (1978). See also O'Brien v. Moriarty, 489 F.2d 941, 944 (1st Cir. 1974). But compare Griffin v. DeRobertis, 557 F. Supp. 302 (N.D. Ill. 1983) (brevity of period during which prisoner is exposed to excessively harsh punishments cannot in itself defeat an Eighth Amendment claim). See also Ind. Code Ann. § 11-11-5-4(6) (Supp. 1992); Vt. Stat. Ann. Tit. 28, § 853(a)(2) (1986).

[41]David Rudovsky, Alvin J. Bronstein, Edward I. Koren, & Julia Cade, The Rights of Prisoners 4 (4th ed. 1988). Sometimes legislatures themselves have taken the initiative to set standards for the operation of solitary confinement units in their states. See, e.g., N.Y. Correct. Law § 137(6) (McKinney 1987 & Supp. 1993); Vt. Stat. Ann. Tit. 28, § 853(a) (1986).

[42]Daniel E. Manville & John Boston, Prisoners' Self-Help Litigation Manual 141 (3d ed 1995).

[43]Young v. Quinlan, 960 F.2d 351, 22 Fed. R. Serv. 3d 530 (3d Cir. 1992) (disclosing the use by the Federal Bureau of Prisons of a "dry cell" that did not contain a toilet and was used for segregated confinement). Cf. Anderson v. County of Kern, 45 F.3d 1310 (9th Cir. 1995) (cell with only a "pit toilet").

[44]See, e.g. DeSpain v. Uphoff, 229 F.3d 1162 (10th Cir. 2000) (prisoner's claims that he was held in a "strip cell" for 72 hours

§ 2:3

include extremely aggressive conduct of the inmate that make use of a strip cell the only alternative available,[45] or the limited duration of the confinement.[46]

without a mattress, bedding, or hygiene items, and that he was left in his boxer shorts in an unheated cell in cold weather, stated a claim for relief); Blissett v. Coughlin, 66 F.3d 531 (2d Cir. 1995) (holding that jury could find that incarceration of a naked prisoner for several days in a a dark, stuffy, feces-smeared mental observations unit was an Eighth Amendment violation); Porth v. Farrier, 934 F.2d 154 (8th Cir. 1991) (upholding jury verdict against inmate who was held in strip cell without clothes for twelve hours); Maxwell v. Mason, 668 F.2d 361 (8th Cir. 1981) (14 days in solitary cell with no clothing except undershorts and no bedding except mattress in cold temperatures was cruel and unusual punishment); McCray v. Burrell, 516 F.2d 357 (4th Cir. 1975), cert. granted, 423 U.S. 923, 96 S. Ct. 264, 46 L. Ed. 2d 249 (1975) and cert. dismissed, 426 U.S. 471, 96 S. Ct. 2640, 48 L. Ed. 2d 788 (1976) (two-day confinement in a cell without clothing, blanket, or mattress was unconstitutional); Wright v. McMann, 387 F.2d 519 (2d Cir. 1967) (holding that 11 days of confinement in a "strip cell," naked, without soap, towels or toilet paper and without bedding of any kind, with inmate sleeping on the floor, being exposed to cold temperatures was cruel and unusual punishment). It is worth noting that the American Correctional Association is on record in opposition to the use of strip cells. American Correctional Assn, Standards for Adult Correctional Institutions Standards 3-4249 & 3-4250 (1990) (requiring clothing for all inmates in solitary). See also U.S. Dept. of Justice, Federal Standards for Prisons and Jails § 11.14 (1980) (inmates in disciplinary detention must be fully clothed).

[45]See, e.g., Anderson v. County of Kern, 45 F.3d 1310 (9th Cir. 1995) (holding that some inmates become so violent and such a danger that placement in a "safety cell" is necessary to protect them from harming themselves); LeMaire v. Maass, 12 F.3d 1444 (9th Cir. 1993) (upholding severe restrictions when inmate refuses to conform his behavior to prison rules); McMahon v. Beard, 583 F.2d 172 (5th Cir. 1978) (upholding use of strip cell when it was necessary in order to protect an inmate who had suicidal tendencies, and when medical personnel visited regularly).

[46]See, e.g., O'Leary v. Iowa State Men's Reformatory, 79 F.3d 82 (8th Cir. 1996) (conditions in progressive four-day behavior management program did not violate Eighth Amendment, court noting that on the first day of the program, inmates were denied visitation, mattress, blankets, underwear, and exercise, and that

It is not strip cells alone that transgress the limits imposed by the Eighth Amendment. Rather, conditions have been found unconstitutional, either alone or in combination, when they lead to: (1) a deprivation of the basic elements of hygiene (soap, showers, etc.);[47] or (2)

---

on the second day of the program, inmates regained these privileges so long as they demonstrated satisfactory behavior; court noted that inmates were never denied food, water, or the opportunity to read their mail); Seltzer-Bey v. Delo, 66 F.3d 961 (8th Cir. 1995) (two days without clothing, bedding or concrete floor, a concrete slab for a bed, and cold air blowing on inmate); Johnson v. Boreani, 946 F.2d 67 (8th Cir. 1991) (use of "quiet" room for short periods of less than 24 hours after a disturbance by the inmate did not violate the Constitution); Benford v. Wright, 782 F. Supp. 1263 (N.D. Ill. 1991) (placement in a strip cell for a few hours not unconstitutional); Fillmore v. Eichkorn, 891 F. Supp. 1482 (D. Kan. 1995), judgment aff'd, 77 F.3d 492 (10th Cir. 1996) (prison officials did not violate Eighth Amendment where inmate alleged that over 48 hours, officials placed him in a padded cell with a drain for a toilet and then moved him to a standard cell, where he was given only a pen, paper, and a telephone call; court noted that the treatment was constitutional given its limited duration).

[47]See, e.g., Keenan v. Hall, 83 F.3d 1083 (9th Cir. 1996) (allegation that inmate in disciplinary unit had to choose between legal supplies and hygiene products stated an Eighth Amendment claim); Young v. Quinlan, 960 F.2d 351, 22 Fed. R. Serv. 3d 530 (3d Cir. 1992) (deprivation of basic hygiene items is even more "revolting" when inmate is HIV positive); Toussaint v. McCarthy, 597 F. Supp. 1388 (N.D. Cal. 1984), judgment aff'd in part, rev'd in part on other grounds, 801 F.2d 1080 (9th Cir. 1986); Walker v. Mintzes, 771 F.2d 920 (6th Cir. 1985) (right to at least a weekly shower); Gates v. Collier, 501 F.2d 1291 (5th Cir. 1974); Wright v. McMann, 387 F.2d 519 (2d Cir. 1967); Hancock v. Avery, 301 F. Supp. 786 (M.D. Tenn. 1969); Jordan v. Fitzharris, 257 F. Supp. 674 (N.D. Cal. 1966); Trammel v. Coombe, 170 Misc. 2d 471, 649 N.Y.S.2d 964 (Sup 1996) (prison officials may not deprive an inmate of basic hygienic requirements for the purpose of imposing disciplinary sanctions; thus, plaintiff who was deprived of hot water, showers, soap, toothbrush and toilet paper while in prison Special Housing Unit (SHU) properly raised an Eighth Amendment violation). But see May v. Baldwin, 895 F. Supp. 1398 (D. Or. 1995), judgment aff'd, 109 F.3d 557 (9th Cir. 1997) (prison officials did not violate Eighth Amendment where prison refused to

§ 2:3 RIGHTS OF PRISONERS, THIRD EDITION

exposure to the cold;[48] or (3) inadequate toilet[49] or (4)

provide inmate in disciplinary segregation with shampoo, conditioner, and body lotion, despite inmate's dry skin; prison officials provided inmate with towel, soap. toothbrush, and baking soda); Ramirez v. Holmes, 921 F. Supp. 204, 208 (S.D. N.Y. 1996) (prison officials did not violate Eighth Amendment where inmate alleged that officials denied inmate the opportunity to shower three times; court found that prison officials did not act with a culpable state of mind); see also 28 C.F.R. § 541.21(5) (segregated inmates must have the opportunity to maintain an acceptable level of personal hygiene); Ind. Code Ann. § 11-11-5-4(4) (1992). See also American Correctional Assn, Standards for Adult Correctional Institutions Standards 3-4249 & 3-4250 (1990) (requiring "basic items needed for personal hygiene" and opportunity to shave and shower at least three times a week); National Sheriffs' Assn, Inmates' Legal Rights 46 (1987) ("segregated inmates should be able to maintain the same level of personal hygiene as other inmates"; should be provided with the same toilet articles and have the same bathing and shaving schedule as other inmates); Model Sentencing and Corrections Act § 4-502(b)(4) (1985) (deprivation of cosmetic or hygienic implements is not authorized); US Dept of Justice, Federal Standards for Prisons and Jails § 11.15 (1980) ("inmates in disciplinary detention . . . should be provided basic items needed for personal hygiene"). But compare Thomas v. Smith, 559 F. Supp. 223 (W.D. N.Y. 1983) (mere failure to supply deodorants, soap, and shampoo does not create a constitutional violation).

[48]See, e.g., Antonelli v. Sheahan, 81 F.3d 1422 (7th Cir. 1996) (inmate stated a claim where he alleged that prison officials violated Eighth Amendment, where officials failed to adequately regulate the cold temperature of his cell and refused to provide him with blankets); Isby v. Clark, 100 F.3d 502, 505 (7th Cir. 1996); Gerakaris v. Champagne, 913 F. Supp. 646, 649 (D. Mass. 1996) (claim stated where pre-trial detainee alleged that he was required to wear jail issued pants, a short sleeve shirt, and sandals, while other prisoners were allowed to wear warm clothes; was placed in a small, cold solitary confinement cell that lacked mattress, pillow, or blanket; and his requests for additional blankets or clothing were denied); Jones v. Bishop, 981 F. Supp. 290 (S.D. N.Y. 1997) (inmate at Sing Sing Correctional facility brought this action alleging, inter alia, that he had to endure two weeks in the Special Housing Unit with no underwear or insulated clothing, only possessing the clothes on his back and a very thin blanket in a cell with open windows in February; the court granted defendant's' motion for summary judgment, holding that there was no

§ 2:3

evidence that plaintiff ever informed officials that he was cold or that officials possessed a wanton state of mind when leaving the windows open); Henderson v. DeRobertis, 940 F.2d 1055 (7th Cir. 1991) (exposing inmates to temperatures below freezing for four days without any protection violated the Eighth Amendment); Chandler v. Baird, 926 F.2d 1057 (11th Cir. 1991) (claim of exposure to cold temperatures in solitary confinement stated a claim for relief); Wright v. McMann, 387 F.2d 519 (2d Cir. 1967); Robinson v. Illinois State Correctional Center (Stateville) Warden, 890 F. Supp. 715 (N.D. Ill. 1995) (inmate stated a claim under the Eighth Amendment where he alleged that inadequate heating and cooling in prison caused serious health risk to inmates); Thomas v. Jabe, 760 F. Supp. 120 (E.D. Mich. 1991) (placement of inmate naked in cell flooded with sewage stated a claim under the Eighth Amendment); Landman v. Royster, 333 F. Supp. 621 (E.D. Va. 1971); Hancock v. Avery, 301 F. Supp. 786 (M.D. Tenn. 1969); Jordan v. Fitzharris, 257 F. Supp. 674 (N.D. Cal. 1966). See also 28 C.F.R. § 541.19(3) (normal institutional clothing must be provided); Ind. Code Ann. § 11-11-5-4(4) (1992) (clothing may not be restricted); American Correctional Assn, Standards for Adult Correctional Institutions Standards 3-4249 & 3-4250 (1990) (requiring clothing for all inmates in solitary); National Sheriffs' Assn, Inmates' Legal Rights 46 (1987) (requiring "adequate heat and ventilation in all segregation cells" and the provision of normal clothing to inmates); US Dept of Justice, Federal Standards for Prisons and Jails § 11.14 (1980) (inmates in disciplinary detention must be fully clothed).

[49]See, e.g., Young v. Quinlan, 960 F.2d 351, 22 Fed. R. Serv. 3d 530 (3d Cir. 1992) (holding unconstitutional confinement of an inmate in a "dry cell" that did not contain a toilet and that forced him to beg permission, which was often denied, to be let out to urinate or defecate); Williams v. Adams, 935 F.2d 960 (8th Cir. 1991) (allegation that the plaintiff was placed for thirteen days in "the hole," a cell with a broken toilet that leaked filth onto the floor of the cell, stated a constitutional claim); Toussaint v. McCarthy, 597 F. Supp. 1388 (N.D. Cal. 1984), judgment aff'd in part, rev'd in part on other grounds, 801 F.2d 1080 (9th Cir. 1986); Flakes v. Percy, 511 F. Supp. 1325, 1329 (W.D. Wis. 1981) ("However primitive and ordinary the right to defecate and to urinate without awaiting the permission of government, and while eating or at rest, the right to avoid the odor of one's earlier emitted feces and urine, are rights close to the core of the liberty guaranteed by the due process clause of the Fourteenth Amendment"); Kirby v. Blackledge, 530 F.2d 583 (4th Cir. 1976); LaReau

§ 2:3   Rights of Prisoners, Third Edition

lack of, or limited, opportunities for exercise;[50] or (5) the

---

v. MacDougall, 473 F.2d 974 (2d Cir. 1972); Masonoff v. DuBois, 899 F. Supp. 782 (D. Mass. 1995) (material issue of fact precluded summary judgment where inmate alleged that use and maintenance of chemical toilets caused chemical burns, stench, nausea, and rashes and that infestation of vermin created inadequate sanitation and health risk); Jordan v. Fitzharris, 257 F. Supp. 674 (N.D. Cal. 1966). See also National Sheriffs' Assn, Inmates' Legal Rights 46 (1987) (segregated inmates should have toilets in their cells). But see Neal v. Clark, 938 F. Supp. 484 (N.D. Ill. 1996) (conditions in a segregation unit did not violate the Eighth Amendment where an inmate for 20 days had a broken toilet in which the water did not flush adequately; court justified conditions on the ground that prison officials allowed the inmate to keep a plunger for the toilet in his cell at all times); Douglas v. DeBruyn, 936 F. Supp. 572 (S.D. Ind. 1996) (prisoner confined in double-occupancy cell for sixteen hours without a toilet failed to state an Eighth Amendment violation; court justified conditions on the ground that prison officers did not deny inmate access to a restroom upon request).

[50]See, e.g., Antonelli v. Sheahan, 81 F.3d 1422, 1432 (7th Cir. 1996) (inmate stated a claim where he alleged that prison officials violated Eighth Amendment where they prohibited inmate from "recreat[ing] for periods up to seven weeks in succession, and at most, was called once every two weeks for sessions of no longer than one hour at a time"); Keenan v. Hall, 83 F.3d 1083 (9th Cir. 1996) (denial of outdoor exercise for six months while in disciplinary segregation violated the Eighth Amendment); Divers v. Department of Corrections, 921 F.2d 191 (8th Cir. 1990) (45 minutes per week exercise in segregation violated the Eighth Amendment); Toussaint v. McCarthy, 597 F. Supp. 1388 (N.D. Cal. 1984), judgment aff'd in part, rev'd in part on other grounds, 801 F.2d 1080 (9th Cir. 1986); Kirby v. Blackledge, 530 F.2d 583 (4th Cir. 1976); Hardwick v. Ault, 447 F. Supp. 116 (M.D. Ga. 1978) (two hours per week); Sinclair v. Henderson, 331 F. Supp. 1123 (E.D. La. 1971). See also Roby v. Department of Corrections, 427 F. Supp. 251 (D. Neb. 1977). See § 2:11. See also 28 C.F.R. § 541.21 (6) (five hours of exercise per week must be permitted); Ind Code Ann § 11-11-5-4(2) (one and a half hours daily exercise required). See also American Correctional Assn, Standards for Adult Correctional Institutions Standard 3-4258 (1990) (requiring minimum of one hour per day five days a week of exercise outside of the cell for solitary confinement inmates); National Sheriffs' Assn, Inmates' Legal Rights 46 (1987) (segregated inmates should be given the

§ 2:3

absence of mattresses (necessitating sleeping on a cold, often concrete floor);[51] or (6) excessive noise[52] or (7) the

---

same opportunities for physical exercise as general population inmates); Model Sentencing and Corrections Act § 4-502(b)(2) (1985) (solitary confinement must be permitted seven hours per week of physical exercise); U.S. Dept of Justice, Federal Standards for Prisons and Jails § 11.19 (1980) (requiring that inmates in disciplinary detention be provided with a minimum of one hour a day of outside exercise at least five days per week). But see Kropp v. McCaughtry, 915 F. Supp. 85 (E.D. Wis. 1996) (prison officials did not violate Eighth Amendment where inmate was denied outdoor exercise while confined to administrative segregation for one month; court noted that inmate could exercise in his cell and was allowed to exercise outdoors twice a week once he was transferred back to general population); May v. Baldwin, 895 F. Supp. 1398 (D. Or. 1995), judgment aff'd, 109 F.3d 557 (9th Cir. 1997) (denial of inmate's requests for outdoor exercise while in disciplinary segregation for four weeks was not a violation of Eighth Amendment; court noted that inmate was never denied the opportunity to exercise in his cell and that inmate had the opportunity to walk for ten minutes three times per week); Stone-Bey v. Barnes, 913 F. Supp. 1226, 1234 (N.D. Ind. 1996), opinion vacated on other grounds, 120 F.3d 718 (7th Cir. 1997) (overruled on other grounds by, DeWalt v. Carter, 224 F.3d 607 (7th Cir. 2000) (prison officials did not violate Eighth Amendment where inmate alleged that officials denied him access to recreation); Brewton v. Hollister, 948 F. Supp. 244 (W.D. N.Y. 1996) (where inmate was confined in prison's special housing unit (SHU) for 74 days and was allowed only one hour of exercise daily, the court held such allotment of time for exercise did not violate the Eighth Amendment).

[51]See, e.g., Mitchell v. Maynard, 80 F.3d 1433, 34 Fed. R. Serv. 3d 1018 (10th Cir. 1996) (bedding is required); Toussaint v. McCarthy, 597 F. Supp. 1388 (N.D. Cal. 1984), judgment aff'd in part, rev'd in part on other grounds, 801 F.2d 1080 (9th Cir. 1986); Gates v. Collier, 501 F.2d 1291 (5th Cir. 1974); Maguire v. Coughlin, 901 F. Supp. 101 (N.D. N.Y. 1995) (denial of bed linen stated a claim); Kelly v. Brewer, 378 F. Supp. 447 (S.D. Iowa 1974); Hancock v. Avery, 301 F. Supp. 786 (M.D. Tenn. 1969); Jordan v. Fitzharris, 257 F. Supp. 674 (N.D. Cal. 1966). See also 28 C.F.R. § 541.21(c)(3) (mattress and bedding required); American Correctional Assn, Standards for Adult Correctional Institutions Standard 3-4251 (1990) (requiring that all inmates in solitary receive bedding); National Sheriffs' Assn, Inmates' Legal Rights 46 (1987) (same); US Dept of Justice, Federal Standards for Prisons and

§ 2:3 RIGHTS OF PRISONERS, THIRD EDITION

presence of rats, mice, roaches and vermin;[53] or (8) lack of adequate lighting or ventilation;[54] or (9) intrusive

---

Jails § 11.17 (1980) (same). See also Blissett v. Coughlin, 66 F.3d 531 (2d Cir. 1995) (prison officials violated Eighth Amendment where they beat inmate, smeared feces on him, and placed him in mental observation cell without furnishings for eight days; court affirmed jury award of $75,000 in compensatory damages and $15,000 in punitive damages). But compare Mann v. Smith, 796 F.2d 79 (5th Cir. 1986) (prisoners have no right to elevated beds). But see Anderson v. County of Kern, 45 F.3d 1310 (9th Cir. 1995) (holding that lack of bedding in a padded cell that was used to temporarily confine violent or suicidal or mentally ill prisoners who might injure themselves, known as a safety cell, was not a violation of Eighth Amendment, where convicted prisoner had a violent episode and there had been a psychological evaluation as well as regular monitoring of the inmate's activity).

[52]Keenan v. Hall, 83 F.3d 1083, 1089 (9th Cir. 1996).

[53]Cf, e.g., Antonelli v. Sheahan, 81 F.3d 1422 (7th Cir. 1996) (inmate stated an Eighth Amendment claim where he alleged that there was a pest control problem in prison regarding mice and cockroaches and correctional officials only fumigated twice in a sixteen month period); Toussaint v. McCarthy, 597 F. Supp. 1388 (N.D. Cal. 1984), judgment aff'd in part, rev'd in part on other grounds, 801 F.2d 1080 (9th Cir. 1986); Berryman v. Johnson, 940 F.2d 658 (6th Cir. 1991) (allegation of birds, mice, and cockroaches infesting cells and running through the food and serving trays stated an Eighth Amendment claim); Hamilton v. Schiro, 338 F. Supp. 1016 (E.D. La. 1970) (such conditions in prison contributed to a finding of an Eighth Amendment violation). But see Harris v. Ostrout, 65 F.3d 912 (11th Cir. 1995) (prison officials did not violate First Amendment and Eighth Amendment where inmate alleged that he was incarcerated in an insect-infected cell in retaliation for his prior litigation; court found that cell conditions were not hazardous to human life); Robinson v. Illinois State Correctional Center (Stateville) Warden, 890 F. Supp. 715 (N.D. Ill. 1995) (prison officials did not violate Eighth Amendment where inmate alleged that vermin infested prison; court noted that the allegations were not that severe, since inmate was unable to demonstrate that he had any medical problems as a result of the conditions).

[54]See, e.g., Keenan v. Hall, 83 F.3d 1083, 1090 (9th Cir. 1996) (cell "permeated with stale air that was saturated with the fumes of feces [thrown by inmates], the smell of urine and vomit, as well as other odors" was an Eight Amendment violation); Antonelli v. Sheahan, 81 F.3d 1422 (7th Cir. 1996) (inmate stated a claim

§ 2:3

and unnecessary surveillance[55] or the use of closed front

---

where he alleged that prison officials violated Eight Amendment where the lighting in his cell was insufficient to read by; court noted that inmate alleged that the poor light made it difficult for him to read and hurt his eyes); Toussaint v. McCarthy, 597 F. Supp. 1388 (N.D. Cal. 1984), judgment aff'd in part, rev'd in part on other grounds, 801 F.2d 1080 (9th Cir. 1986); Hoptowit v. Ray, 682 F.2d 1237, 1257, 9 Fed. R. Evid. Serv. 1511 (9th Cir. 1982); Kirby v. Blackledge, 530 F.2d 583 (4th Cir. 1976); Hancock v. Avery, 301 F. Supp. 786 (M.D. Tenn. 1969); Jordan v. Fitzharris, 257 F. Supp. 674 (N.D. Cal. 1966). See also 28 C.F.R. § 541.21(c)(l) (segregation facilities must be adequately lighted, well ventilated, appropriately heated, and maintained in a sanitary condition); Ind. Code Ann. § 11-11-5-4(3) (1992); National Sheriffs' Assn, Inmates' Legal Rights 46 (1987) (requiring "well lighted" and adequately ventilated cells in segregation); US Dept of Justice, Federal Standards for Prisons and Jails § 11.10 (1980) (requiring "healthful" conditions in cells). In an interesting case, a federal District Court found that the use of continual lighting of cells 24 hours per day can cause psychological harm and thus was unconstitutional. LeMaire v. Maass, 745 F. Supp. 623 (D. Or. 1990), vacated, 12 F.3d 1444 (9th Cir. 1993) (on appeal, the state agreed to modify the lighting in the cell). See also, Keenan v. Hall, 83 F.3d 1083, 1090 (9th Cir. 1996) (disputed issue of material fact as to whether prison lighting constantly illuminated inmate's cell precluded summary judgment on inmate's claim alleging cruel and unusual punishment).

The Seventh Circuit remanded a case for a determination of the adequacy of the lighting in a segregation unit. The court implied that confinement in a cell without sufficient reading light constitutes cruel and unusual punishment. Bono v. Saxbe, 620 F.2d 609, 617 (7th Cir. 1980). On remand, the District Court ordered that each inmate be provided with a 40-, 60-, or 100-watt bulb. Bono v. Saxbe, 527 F. Supp. 1182 (S.D. Ill. 1980).

[55]See, e.g., Keenan v. Hall, 83 F.3d 1083, 1090 (9th Cir. 1996) (constant illumination may violate Eighth Amendment if it causes sleeping problems; not a sufficient answer to say that inmate can sleep with his head toward the back of the cell); Lewis v. Lane, 816 F.2d 1165 (7th Cir. 1987) (holding that practice of "bar-banging" on the cells of death row inmates violates the Eighth Amendment if it can be shown that it is done by guards merely to harass); Hardwick v. Ault, 447 F. Supp. 116 (M.D. Ga. 1978).

cells that cut off all contact with the outside world.[56]

"The touchstone [of these cases] is the health of the inmate."[57] Where the conditions jeopardize the physical or mental health of the inmate, they have been "universally condemned."[58] However, while the Eighth Amendment guards against the most disastrous conditions of confinement in punitive segregation, it by no means decrees that punitive segregation be a pleasant, or even a comfortable, place.[59] Therefore, conditions in punitive segregation that are merely restrictive or boring are

---

[56]See, e.g., Bono v. Saxbe, 450 F. Supp. 934 (E.D. Ill. 1978), aff'd in part, 620 F.2d 609 (7th Cir. 1980); LeMaire v. Maass, 745 F. Supp. 623 (D. Or. 1990), vacated on other grounds, 12 F.3d 1444 (9th Cir. 1993) (use of solid steel doors is unlawful when inmates with serious medical needs are placed in them; Court of Appeals remanded for determination whether certain conditions imposed on inmates in control unit were reasonably related to need for institutional security); Kelly v. Brewer, 378 F. Supp. 447 (S.D. Iowa 1974) aff'd, 525 F.2d 394 (8th Cir. 1975). See also U.S. Dept. of Justice, Federal Standards for Prisons and Jails § 11.13 (1980) (segregation cells must be situated so that "the inmates assigned to them can converse with others and be observed by staff members"). But see Libby v. Commissioner of Correction, 385 Mass. 421, 432 N.E.2d 486 (1982) (closed solid doors on isolation cells were not cruel and unusual punishment absent other significant deprivations).

Conversely, inmates should not be exposed to excessive noise in the unit. See, e.g., Toussaint v. McCarthy, 597 F. Supp. 1388 (N.D. Cal. 1984), judgment aff'd in part, rev'd in part on other grounds, 801 F.2d 1080 (9th Cir. 1986).

[57]Young v. Quinlan, 960 F.2d 351, 364, 22 Fed. R. Serv. 3d 530 (3d Cir. 1992).

[58]*Id.*

[59]Some courts have gone beyond this point to reach the questionable result that shackling, handcuffing, and in extreme instances "spread-eagled" handcuffing of segregated prisoners is permissible treatment of segregated inmates. Bruscino v. Carlson, 854 F.2d 162, 164 (7th Cir. 1988); LeMaire v. Maass, 12 F.3d 1444 (9th Cir. 1993) (placing inmate in restraints, including handcuffs and shackles, while inmate showered was not "cruel and unusual punishment" in violation of Eighth Amendment, despite inmate's concern that he might fall down and hurt himself while showering; purpose of restraints was to protect staff, which was security im-

not forbidden. As one court put it: "[i]nactivity, lack of companionship, and a low level of intellectual stimulation do not constitute cruel and unusual punishment. . .."[60] Furthermore, while courts have required that nutritious food be served, some courts have permitted a monotonous diet for inmates in solitary confinement.[61]

The determination of the constitutionality of the conditions of solitary confinement is an intensely fact-specific inquiry.[62] To resolve these cases, it is often important for prisoners to sensitize judges to their plight by persuading them to visit and examine the facilities in question.[63] In the absence of personal judicial inspection, documentation of the existence of the challenged conditions, either through photographs, depositions, or live testimony, is essential.

---

perative, particularly in view of damage inmate had inflicted on staff and inmates). But see Roy v. Jenkins, No. 86 C 5738, 1991 W.L. 202587 (N.D. Ill. Oct 3, 1991) (indicating that it may be impermissible to handcuff an inmate's arms and legs to a bed without providing due process protections).

[60]Bono v. Saxbe, 620 F.2d 609, 614 (7th Cir. 1980). See also Toussaint v. McCarthy, 597 F. Supp. 1388 (N.D. Cal. 1984), judgment aff'd in part, rev'd in part on other grounds, 801 F.2d 1080 (9th Cir. 1986) (no constitutional right for inmates in segregation to be free of enforced idleness); Smith v. Coughlin, 748 F.2d 783 (2d Cir. 1984) (restrictions on plaintiff's activities while in segregation do not render the confinement unconstitutional); Gibson v. Lynch, 652 F.2d 348 (3d Cir. 1981) (no constitutional violation as long as basic needs are met).

[61]See, e.g., LeMaire v. Maass, 12 F.3d 1444 (9th Cir. 1993) (where the court upheld a diet of Nutraloaf for a limited time because it provided an adequate balanced diet); Bono v. Saxbe, 620 F.2d 609, 613 (7th Cir. 1980); Dorrough v. Hogan, 563 F.2d 1259 (5th Cir. 1977). See also Miles v. Konvalenka, 791 F. Supp. 212 (N.D. Ill. 1992) (upholding the denial of coffee to inmates in punitive segregation).

[62]Chandler v. Baird, 926 F.2d 1057, 1063 (11th Cir. 1991) (noting the importance of a "fact-intensive inquiry" in these cases).

[63]See, e.g., Tillery v. Owens, 907 F.2d 418 (3d Cir. 1990) (reporting that the district judge conducted a trial and made an "unannounced tour" of the facility).

§ 2:3

There is a clear relationship between the conditions of solitary confinement and the amount of time to which an inmate can be exposed to those conditions.[64] Thus, in an Eighth Amendment challenge to conditions of confinement, a court should also consider the length of time that the inmate has been exposed to the conditions. This is aptly illustrated by a North Carolina case in which the court found Eighth Amendment violations in the punitive confinement of a prisoner in a metal "box" for more than 24 hours, in a solid-door solitary cell for more than 15 days, and in a barred-door solitary cell for more than 30 days.[65] In *Hutto v. Finney*, the Supreme Court approved a 30-day limit under the circumstances disclosed by the evidence.[66]

However, there does not appear to be an agreed-upon time limit beyond which confinement in isolation can be said to be per se cruel and unusual. Both 400 days[67] and two years[68] in segregation have been upheld. More

---

[64] Gibson v. Lynch, 652 F.2d 348 (3d Cir. 1981) (balancing length and conditions of confinement); Friends v. Moore, 776 F. Supp. 1382 (E.D. Mo. 1991) (confinement of inmate in enclosed recreation area for two hours in mild weather without clothing did not violate Constitution even though inmate was wet); Benford v. Wright, 782 F. Supp. 1263, 1266 (N.D. Ill. 1991) ("duration of the conditions under which the inmate suffers is a legitimate concern and may enhance or minimize the actual severity of the condition"). But compare Isaac v. Jones, 529 F. Supp. 175, 181 (N.D. Ill. 1981) (brevity of confinement does not necessarily defeat the claim).

[65] Berch v. Stahl, 373 F. Supp. 412 (W.D. N.C. 1974).

[66] Hutto v. Finney, 437 U.S. 678, 98 S. Ct. 2565, 57 L. Ed. 2d 522 (1978).

[67] Knuckles v. Prasse, 302 F. Supp. 1036 (E.D. Pa. 1969), judgment aff'd, 435 F.2d 1255 (3d Cir. 1970).

[68] Davidson v. Coughlin, 219 A.D.2d 843, 631 N.Y.S.2d 949 (4th Dep't 1995) (placement of inmate in SHU for two years with loss of telephone privileges was not so disproportionate as to be shocking where officials found that inmate had ordered magazines in prison officials' names and caused officials to be billed personally). Graham v. Willingham, 384 F.2d 367 (10th Cir. 1967). See also Williams v. Ramos, 71 F.3d 1246 (7th Cir. 1995) (where inmate was placed in twenty-four hour per day administrative segregation

significantly, confinement to solitary for an indefinite term has been sustained.[69] Nevertheless, at the outer extremes, when confinement in a disciplinary segregation unit stretches into years, courts have held that "excessive confinement" may well violate the Constitution.[70] In addition, there is some case law that limits solitary to very short periods of time. An example is a New Hampshire federal case imposing a maximum 14-day limit on the number of consecutive days that could be spent in isolation.[71] In addition, various states have set similar limits by statute.[72] For inmates who are confined in isolation while awaiting the death sentence, there may be special considerations. Often, but not always, these inmates are held in severely restricted housing conditions.[73] There is an unresolved issue of whether prolonged confinement in these conditions while under a sentence of death violates the

---

for 19 days, prison officials did not violate Eighth Amendment, since inmate was not denied life's basic necessities);

[69]Adams v. Carlson, 352 F. Supp. 882 (E.D. Ill. 1973); Sostre v. McGinnis, 442 F.2d 178 (2d Cir. 1971).

[70]See, e.g., Jackson v. Meachum, 699 F.2d 578, 584-85 (1st Cir. 1983); Morris v. Travisono, 549 F. Supp. 291 (D.R.I. 1982), judgment aff'd, 707 F.2d 28 (1st Cir. 1983) (Eighth Amendment violated by eight and a half year confinement in solitary). See also Sheley v. Dugger, 833 F.2d 1420, 1429 (11th Cir. 1987) (12-year confinement in solitary confinement unit "raises serious constitutional questions"); Sealey v. Giltner, 116 F.3d 47 (2d Cir. 1997) (inmate placed in administrative segregation based on confidential information claimed his civil rights were violated; court held that since plaintiff actually served 152 days in confinement, which deprived him of "all programming opportunities and privileges that prisoners in general population enjoyed," summary judgment for defendants was inappropriate).

[71]Laaman v. Helgemoe, 437 F. Supp. 269, 326 (D.N.H. 1977).

[72]See, e.g., Mass. Gen. Laws Ann. Ch. 127, § 41 (West 1993) (10 days); Tenn. Code Ann. § 41-21-402 (1990) (30 days); Vt. Stat. Ann. Tit. 28, § 853(a)(1) (1986) (30 days).

[73]Dying Twice: Conditions On New York's Death Row, Report of Joint Subcommittee of Committee on Corrections and Committee on Capital Punishment, Association of the Bar of the City of New York.

Eighth Amendment.[74]

Another potentially significant fact in cases challenging the conditions or duration of solitary is the extent to which prisoners retain control over their stay. When inmates hold the keys to release in their pocket, so to speak, courts are less receptive to their Eighth Amendment claims.[75] Thus, where a prisoner could have

---

[74]See, e.g., Lackey v. State, 819 S.W.2d 111 (Tex. Crim. App. 1989), reh'g granted, (Sept. 13, 1989) and on reh'g, (May 29, 1991) and reh'g dismissed, (Sept. 25, 1991) (although the court denied certiorari in a case rejecting an Eighth Amendment claim of death row inmate who spent 17 years waiting for sentence to be carried out, Justice Stevens filed a special statement indicating the importance of this issue and urging lower courts to seriously consider it; Justice Stevens indicated that the Court might decide to give the matter full consideration after the issue had percolated in the lower courts); see also In re Soering, 28 I.L.M. 1063 (1989) (the European Court of Human Rights ruled that a German national who confessed to murdering two people in the United States could not be extradited to the United States because he would face the death penalty; Court held that the jurisdiction's death penalty policy violated Article 3 of the European Convention for the Protection of Human Rights and Fundamental Freedoms because of the protracted delays associated with administering the death penalty in the United States and the long stays on death row prior to execution).

For a discussion of whether extended stays in solitary confinement pending execution violate the Eighth Amendment, see Richard E. Shugrue, "A Fate Worse Than Death," An Essay On Whether Long Times On Death Row Are Cruel Times, 29 Creighton L. Rev. 1 (1995). For a discussion of the psychological effects of protracted death row confinement and its potential Eighth Amendment implications, see Kathleen M. Flynn, Note, The Agony of Suspense: How Protracted Death Row Confinement Gives Rise to an Eighth Amendment Claim of Cruel and Unusual Punishment, 54 Wash & Lee L. Rev. 291 (1997).

[75]See, e.g., Isby v. Clark, 100 F.3d 502 (7th Cir. 1996) (if an inmate through his own conduct causes foul conditions to exist in solitary confinement, he may not maintain an Eighth Amendment claim of cruel and unusual punishment, although normally such repugnant conditions would lead to such a violation); Anderson v. County of Kern, 45 F.3d 1310 (9th Cir. 1995) (holding that lack of sinks or toilets in a safety cell did not violate the Eighth Amend-

obtained release by agreeing to comply with reasonable grooming regulations, the court found that his 10-month confinement in isolation was not cruel and unusual.[76] Similarly, the Second Circuit Court of Appeals appears to have been influenced by the fact that a petitioner could have returned to the general prison population by either participating in group therapy or by agreeing to obey institutional rules.[77] Conversely, in

---

ment provided that the confinement was temporary and inmate's prior violent episode evidenced that he could potentially be harmful to himself); Shakka v. Smith, 71 F.3d 162 (4th Cir. 1995) (prison officials did not violate Eighth Amendment where they denied disabled inmate's request to take a shower for three days after inmates in tier threw feces at disabled inmate; court noted that disabled inmate had intentionally broken his toilet with a pipe, flooding the tier with sewage; court found that inmate was given materials to clean himself within his cell); Hameed v. Coughlin, 37 F. Supp. 2d 133 (N.D. N.Y. 1999) (inmate brought a § 1983 action against prison officials for alleged constitutional violations arising out of his administrative segregation; inmate was confined after he was found to have played a leadership role in the disobedience of several other inmates; after the confinement term relating to the violation was over the inmate was kept in administrative confinement because prison officials believed that his presence in the general population would pose a threat to the safety and security of the facility; in granting summary judgment for the defendants, the district court held that it was the inmate's own affirmative conduct which necessitated that others be protected from him and therefore the defendants had a rational basis for placing greater restrictions on inmates in administrative segregation than inmates confined for nonpunitive reasons).

[76]Winsby v. Walsh, 321 F. Supp. 523 (C.D. Cal. 1971).

[77]Sostre v. McGinnis, 442 F.2d 178 (2d Cir. 1971). See also LeMaire v. Maass, 12 F.3d 1444 (9th Cir. 1993) (use of both full mechanical restraints and full in-cell restraints, when imposed in strict compliance with existing prison regulations, did not violate Eighth Amendment, and injunction should therefore not have required more than adherence to established regulations; regulations provided that full restraints could be used only upon demonstration that inmate was out of control and engaged in behavior which could result in major destruction of property, constitute serious health or injury hazard to inmate or others, or escalate into serious disturbance, and that inmate was to be released as

Bono v. Saxbe,[78] the failure of institutional authorities to provide inmates with clear criteria for working their way out of punitive confinement was a major contributing factor to the court's finding of an Eighth Amendment violation.[79] To guard against arbitrary stays in solitary and to ensure that persons do not remain in limbo in that status, courts stress the necessity to have periodic reviews of the need for continued segregated confinement in each case.[80]

Challenges to conditions of confinement by inmates on death row, which in many but not all states resemble conditions in punitive segregation, have been treated similarly to challenges of conditions by inmates who have been placed in segregation or solitary confinement.[81] Even where inmates have alleged deprivations unique to death row procedures, courts will

---

soon as it was reasonable to believe that behavior leading to use of restraints would not immediately resume).

[78]Bono v. Saxbe, 450 F. Supp. 934 (E.D. Ill. 1978), aff'd in part, 620 F.2d 609 (7th Cir. 1980).

[79]*Id.* at 945. But compare McGruder v. Phelps, 608 F.2d 1023, 1026 (5th Cir. 1979) (no right to have criteria made known as to how to be classified out of a unit).

[80]See, e.g., Toussaint v. McCarthy, 597 F. Supp. 1388 (N.D. Cal. 1984), judgment aff'd in part, rev'd in part on other grounds, 801 F.2d 1080, 1101 (9th Cir. 1986) (yearly reviews are insufficient to satisfy the Constitution); Sourbeer v. Robinson, 791 F.2d 1094 (3d Cir. 1986) (monthly reviews are adequate as long as they are not performed in a perfunctory manner); Clark v. Brewer, 776 F.2d 226 (8th Cir. 1985) (holding that periodic reviews are constitutionally required, but not mandating specific time periods for reviews); Mims v. Shapp, 744 F.2d 946 (3d Cir. 1984) (periodic reviews of every 30 days are constitutional); Jackson v. Meachum, 699 F.2d 578 (1st Cir. 1983). See also US Dept of Justice, Federal Standards for Prisons and Jails § 11.06 (1980) requiring review every 30 days when inmate is held for more than two months in segregation). But compare Smith v. Coughlin, 748 F.2d 783 (2d Cir. 1984) (no requirement for periodic review when length of stay is 13 months).

[81]See e.g., Peterkin v. Jeffes, 855 F.2d 1021 (3d Cir. 1988) (fact that inmates confined to cells for 22 hours a day did not violate Eighth Amendment; two hours a day of exercise was adequate; court also found that the size of the cells were adequate, dirty

analyze the claims under the same standard as claims brought by inmates placed in solitary or punitive segregation.[82]

One Eighth Amendment challenge that may be available to death row inmates in certain circumstances in the future concerns whether the amount of time they have spent on death row amounts to cruel and unusual punishment. In a 1995 decision, Justice Stevens opened the door to this possibility when he wrote separately where the full court refused to hear a case making just such a claim.[83] The case concerned an inmate's claim that to execute him after he had spent 17 years on death row would amount to cruel and unusual

---

toilets did not violate the Eighth Amendment, lack of stimulating activity was not cruel and unusual punishment); Simon v. Norris, 57 F.3d 1070 (6th Cir. 1995) (treating conditions of confinement claims by death row inmates the same as claims by prisoners throughout the Tennessee prison system); Smith v. Coughlin, 748 F.2d 783 (2d Cir. 1984) (fact that death row prisoner faced numerous restrictions due to security concerns did not violate Eighth Amendment, where prisoner was provided more than adequate facilities, visitation, and exercise); but see, Lewis v. Lane, 816 F.2d 1165 (7th Cir. 1987) (trial court's grant of summary judgment was vacated and remanded where the court held that death row inmate could have proved an Eighth Amendment claim of lack of heat, and that guards tapped on bars to harass inmates, but that prisoner had no chance to prove claim as appointed counsel failed to put any effort into the case).

[82]See e.g., Nicks v. Bullard, 1997 U.S. Dist. LEXIS 21184 (S.D. Ala. January 24, 1997) (inmate was placed on single walk status, which meant that inmate was restricted from walking with other inmates; inmate claimed Eighth Amendment violation due to restrictions placed on him as result of the status, and alleged, inter alia that he was denied access to an education program, television, and exercise with other inmates; court held that none of these deprivations implicated Eighth Amendment).

[83]Lackey v. Texas, 514 U.S. 1045, 115 S. Ct. 1421, 131 L. Ed. 2d 304 (1995), leave to file for reh'g denied, 520 U.S. 1183, 117 S. Ct. 1465, 137 L. Ed. 2d 568 (1997) (statement of Stevens, J.).

punishment.[84] Justice Stevens stated that the goal of the death penalty is deterrence and retribution, and that the "state interest in retribution has arguably been satisfied by the severe punishment already inflicted."[85] The Court recognized that a delay of years could have significant psychological effects on the inmate, as it produces uncertainty, which is "one of the most horrible feelings to which he can be subjected."[86] The Court pointed out that deterrence due to actual execution at this point "as compared to 17 years on death row" followed by life imprisonment "seems minimal."[87]

However, Justice Stevens noted that the claim was novel, and that it warranted "postponing consideration of the issue until after it has been addressed by other courts."[88]

In 1999, the Supreme Court again denied certiorari to the claim of two inmates, who had spent nearly 20 years on death row, that the length of their confinement on death row violated the Eighth Amendment.[89] Justice Thomas wrote a concurring opinion in the denial, recalling Justice Stevens' opinion in *Lackey* suggesting that lower state and federal courts be used as "laboratories" on the question.[90] Thomas cited several lower court decisions rejecting inmate claims that lengthy stays on death row violate the Eighth Amendment,[91] and opined, "I submit that the Court should

---

[84]Lackey v. Texas, 514 U.S. 1045, 115 S. Ct. 1421, 131 L. Ed. 2d 304 (1995), leave to file for reh'g denied, 520 U.S. 1183, 117 S. Ct. 1465, 137 L. Ed. 2d 568 (1997).

[85]*Id.*

[86]*Id.*

[87]*Id.*

[88]*Id.*

[89]Knight v. Florida, 528 U.S. 990, 120 S. Ct. 459, 145 L. Ed. 2d 370 (1999).

[90]Knight v. Florida, 528 U.S. 990, 992, 120 S. Ct. 459, 145 L. Ed. 2d 370 (1999).

[91]*Id.* at 992-93, 120 S. Ct. 459, 145 L. Ed. 2d 370 (1999) (in reaching his conclusion, Justice Thomas cited People v. Frye, 18

CRUEL & UNUSUAL PUNISHMENT § 2:3

consider the experiment concluded."[92] Justice Breyer, however, had the opposite view of Thomas.[93] Since *Knight,* lower courts have rejected Eighth Amendment challenges based on length of confinement.[94]

In addition to length of confinement, another aspect of solitary confinement that determines its legality is the offense that lead to the confinement. Conditions and duration of solitary confinement, even when not considered cruel and unusual in the abstract, may become so if the punishment is disproportionate to the inmate's offense.[95] In one case, the incarceration of

---

Cal. 4th 894, 19 Cal. 4th 253d, 77 Cal. Rptr. 2d 25, 959 P.2d 183 (1998)); People v. Massie, 19 Cal. 4th 550, 79 Cal. Rptr. 2d 816, 967 P.2d 29 (1998); Ex parte Bush, 695 So. 2d 138 (Ala. 1997); State v. Schackart, 190 Ariz. 238, 947 P.2d 315 (1997); Bell v. State, 938 S.W.2d 35 (Tex. Crim. App. 1996); State v. Smith, 280 Mont. 158, 931 P.2d 1272 (1996); White v. Johnson, 79 F.3d 432 (5th Cir. 1996); Stafford v. Ward, 59 F.3d 1025 (10th Cir. 1995).

[92]Knight v. Florida, 528 U.S. 990, 993, 120 S. Ct. 459, 145 L. Ed. 2d 370 (1999).

[93]*Id.* at 994.

[94]Jones v. Gibson, 206 F.3d 946 (10th Cir. 2000), cert. denied, 531 U.S. 998, 121 S. Ct. 496, 148 L. Ed. 2d 467 (2000); People v. Ochoa, 26 Cal. 4th 398, 110 Cal. Rptr. 2d 324, 28 P.3d 78 (2001), cert. denied, 122 S. Ct. 1803, 152 L. Ed. 2d 660 (U.S. 2002) (rejecting the claim that length of confinement nullified the deterrence or retribution goals of the death penalty); Booker v. State, 773 So. 2d 1079 (Fla. 2000), cert. denied, 532 U.S. 1033, 121 S. Ct. 1989, 149 L. Ed. 2d 779 (2001) (court quoted its opinion in the precursor decision to *Knight* in rejecting the notion that the claim may succeed where the state is responsible for part of the delay); McKinney v. State, 133 Idaho 695, 992 P.2d 144 (1999), cert. denied, 530 U.S. 1208, 120 S. Ct. 2207, 147 L. Ed. 2d 240 (2000); Jordan v. State, 786 So. 2d 987 (Miss. 2001), cert. denied, 122 S. Ct. 823, 151 L. Ed. 2d 705 (U.S. 2002); State v. Lafferty, 2001 UT 19, 20 P.3d 342 (Utah 2001), cert. denied, 122 S. Ct. 542, 151 L. Ed. 2d 420 (U.S. 2001).

[95]Rodriguez v. Coughlin, 216 A.D.2d 617, 627 N.Y.S.2d 470, 471 (3d Dep't 1995) (where prison officials found drug paraphernalia, marijuana, heroin, and $550 in inmate's cell and inmate was found to have violated prison regulation regarding possession of contraband, sentence of 48 months confinement and loss of privi-

prisoners in administrative segregation for 16 months for inciting a work stoppage was deemed disproportionate punishment under the Eighth Amendment.[96] A like result was reached where a prisoner was confined in solitary for two years for participating in an illegal religious service.[97] Punishment in solitary for no offense or for exercise of protected constitutional rights would be, a fortiori, disproportionate and cruel and unusual.[98]

---

leges was not "so disproportionate as to be shocking"); Jones v. State, 545 N.W.2d 313 (Iowa 1996) (inmate was afforded due process where he was sentenced to 365 days of disciplinary segregation, loss of 365 days of good time, and restitution of $16,000 for violating a prison regulation; court noted that while hearing officer gave inmate a stiffer sentence than administrative law judge had in the past, sentence comported with due process since it was in accordance with the maximum sentence allowable); Hoyer v. Coombe, 224 A.D.2d 879, 638 N.Y.S.2d 514 (3d Dep't 1996) (sentence of one year in Special Housing Unit and loss of certain privileges was not excessive where "correctional officials confiscated a life sized, wooden monkey head and other unfinished imitation wooden body parts from inmate's cell"). See Black v. Brown, 524 F. Supp. 856 (N.D. Ill. 1981), aff'd in part, rev'd in part, 688 F.2d 841 (7th Cir. 1982) (18-month punishment for running in prison yard held disproportionate to the offense); Hutto v. Finney, 437 U.S. 678, 98 S. Ct. 2565, 57 L. Ed. 2d 522 (1978); Johnson v. Anderson, 370 F. Supp. 1373 (D. Del. 1974). Prison accreditation standards provide that the duration of disciplinary detention should be proportionate to the offense committed, but other relevant factors, such as the prisoner's record, can also be considered. American Correctional Assn, Standards for Adult Correctional Institutions Standard 3-4243, commentary (1990); Model Sentencing and Corrections Act § 4-501(b)(2) (1985); U.S. Dept. of Justice, Federal Standards for Prisons and Jails § 10.01 (1980).

[96]Adams v. Carlson, 368 F. Supp. 1050 (E.D. Ill. 1973).

[97]Fulwood v. Clemmer, 206 F. Supp. 370 (D. D.C. 1962). But compare Knuckles v. Prasse, 302 F. Supp. 1036 (E.D. Pa. 1969), judgment aff'd, 435 F.2d 1255 (3d Cir. 1970).

[98]See, e.g., Morgan v. LaVallee, 526 F.2d 221 (2d Cir. 1975); Bono v. Saxbe, 450 F. Supp. 934, 944 (E.D. Ill. 1978), aff'd in part, 620 F.2d 609 (7th Cir. 1980) (no offense); Johnson v. Anderson, 370 F. Supp. 1373, 1388 n31 (D. Del. 1974). Cf., Davidson v. Chestnut, 1998 WL 436527 (S.D. N.Y. 1998), vacated on other grounds, 193 F.3d 144 (2d Cir. 1999) (rejecting allegation that inmate was placed

Thus, for example, where an inmate was placed in disciplinary segregation for seven months for refusing, on religious grounds, to handle pork, the Sixth Circuit Court of Appeals found an Eighth Amendment violation.[99] Arbitrary or discriminatory imposition of solitary would also come within the Amendment's prohibition.[100]

Of course, as stated at the beginning of this section, not every confinement to isolation is for punitive purposes. Sometimes persons are placed in isolation for administrative reasons having nothing to do with misconduct. They may be isolated, for example, because they are unable to protect themselves in the general population or because they have not yet been classified.[101] Often the confinement for such purposes is

---

in solitary confinement in retaliation for filing his lawsuit, holding by implication that placement in isolation in retaliation for filing a lawsuit would state a claim).

[99]Chapman v. Pickett, 586 F.2d 22 (7th Cir. 1978).

[100]See, e.g., Johnson v. Anderson, 370 F. Supp. 1373, 1388 n.31 (D. Del. 1974; Breece v. Swenson, 332 F. Supp. 837 (W.D. Mo. 1971). See Ch 10.

[101]Griffin v. Vaughn, 112 F.3d 703 (3d Cir. 1997) (confinement of inmate for 15 months in administrative custody, pending charge of raping female prison guard, did not violate the Eighth Amendment; plaintiff failed to present evidence that he was deprived of food, clothing, shelter, sanitation, medical and personal safety); Giano v. Selsky, 37 F. Supp. 2d 162 (N.D. N.Y. 1999), vacated and remanded, 238 F.3d 223 (2d Cir. 2001) (district court held that prisoner's 92-day confinement in administrative segregation following two prior escape attempts and a stab wound received from another prisoner did not rise to the level of atypical, significant hardship and granted defendant summary judgment on prisoner's due process claim); Zimmerman v. Tippecanoe Sheriff's Dept., 25 F. Supp. 2d 915 (N.D. Ind. 1998) (where pre-trial detainee attempted to escape and handcuff key used in the attempt was never located, district court held that sheriff's order that inmate be held in disciplinary segregation unit without hearing did not violate prisoner's due process rights, as sheriff was advancing "jail security" and was not attempting to punish inmate). See, e.g., 28 C.F.R.

§ 2:3　　　　　Rights of Prisoners, Third Edition

for indefinite periods that can stretch out for years.[102] The constitutionality of conditions in these units is often subjected to a different analysis.[103] The reason for this is that the conditions are not inflicted for the express purpose of punishment.[104] Thus, under the Supreme Court's analysis in *Wilson v. Seiter*,[105] no Eighth Amendment violation arises unless the court can determine that the subjective branch of the Eighth Amendment has been satisfied.[106]

However, this is more an academic problem than a real one. Since the threat to health is so readily apparent in segregation and since conditions that fall below the levels of human decency are likely to be well known to prison officials, such conditions constitute deliberate

---

§ 541.23 (calling for the establishment of administrative detention for inmates who need protection)

[102]Hershberger v. Scaletta, 33 F.3d 955 (8th Cir. 1994) (holding that confinement to administrative segregation for nine years does not constitute cruel and unusual punishment);

[103]Griffin v. Vaughn, 112 F.3d 703 (3d Cir. 1997) (confinement of inmate for 15 months in administrative custody, pending charge of raping female prison guard, did not violate Eighth Amendment; plaintiff failed to present evidence that he was deprived of food, clothing, shelter, sanitation, medical and personal safety); Giano v. Selsky, 37 F. Supp. 2d 162 (N.D. N.Y. 1999), vacated and remanded, 238 F.3d 223 (2d Cir. 2001) (district court held that prisoner's 92-day confinement in administrative segregation following two prior escape attempts and stab wound received from another prisoner did not rise to level of atypical, significant hardship and granted defendant summary judgment on prisoner's due process claim).

[104]See, e.g., Zimmerman v. Tippecanoe Sheriff's Dept., 25 F. Supp. 2d 915 (N.D. Ind. 1998) (where pre-trial detainee attempted to escape, and handcuff key used in the attempt was never located, district court held that sheriff's order that inmate be held in disciplinary segregation unit without a hearing did not violate prisoner's due process rights, as sheriff was advancing "jail security" and was not attempting to punish inmate).

[105]Wilson v. Seiter, 501 U.S. 294, 111 S. Ct. 2321, 115 L. Ed. 2d 271 (1991), discussed in § 2:2.

[106]See § 2:2.

indifference and, thereby, are "punishment."[107] It would be ironic if the law were otherwise. If it were, prisoners convicted of serious violations of institutional rules could challenge harsh conditions in a segregation unit on cruel and unusual punishment grounds, but inmates confined for classification, observation, or self-protection could not, despite the fact (actually, because of the fact) that they have committed no rule infraction.[108]

The deprivation of some entitlements for inmates in segregation may raise distinct constitutional issues other than those under the Eighth Amendment. For example, deprivation of visiting or mail privileges to inmates in solitary confinement raises First Amendment issues, and denial of access to the law library raises questions dealing with the right of access to the courts. Those important issues are discussed separately in the chapters of this text dealing with those topics.[109]

Increasingly, courts have been called upon to adjudicate conditions in the new "supermax" facilities that have been established with increasing regularity. Two district judges have issued sweeping opinions regarding this topic.[110] In the first case, the district court held that while "conditions of extreme social isolation and

---

[107]See, e.g., Young v. Quinlan, 960 F.2d 351, 22 Fed. R. Serv. 3d 530 (3d Cir. 1992); Henderson v. DeRobertis, 940 F.2d 1055 (7th Cir. 1991). But see Lavine v. Wright, 423 F. Supp. 357 (D. Utah 1976) (holding that conditions in isolation unit for observation, classification, or protection of an inmate from harm were not punishment, because they were not intended as punishment).

[108]Another way to avoid this questionable result would be to allow the challenge to conditions in administrative segregation units to proceed on an equal protection basis. For a discussion of equal protection in prison, see Ch 4. See also Madden v. Kemna, 739 F. Supp. 1358 (W.D. Mo. 1990).

[109]See §§ 11:8, 12:9, 13:8.

[110]Madrid v. Gomez, 889 F. Supp. 1146 (N.D. Cal. 1995), mandamus denied, 103 F.3d 828 (9th Cir. 1996). The case dealt with conditions at the Pelican Bay State Prison, a correctional facility located in northwest California. The facility was a "state-of-the-art prison" housing between 3,500 and 3,900 inmates at a time, a maximum security facility of 2,000 "general population"

reduced environmental stimulation" are likely to cause "some degree of psychological trauma upon most inmates confined there for more than brief periods,"[111] this kind of "generalized psychological pain" is not suf-

---

inmates, and a Security Housing Unit (SHU) reserved for 1,000 to 1,500 inmates who allegedly posed serious disciplinary problems such as gang activity. Inmates in this last category were restricted to windowless cells with no exercise, recreational, or work opportunities. The court found that the conditions were especially severe in the SHU. Inmates were incarcerated in windowless drab rooms, ate their meals by themselves in their cells, and were not exposed to any form of human contact. Indeed, the SHU was constructed with the idea of providing as little human contact as possible. Though the court did not find the living conditions in the SHU to be unconstitutional as far as mentally stable inmates were concerned, for mentally ill prisoners or those inmates who were prone to mental illness, the court found that the conditions were unconstitutional. The severity of the living conditions in the SHU caused many mentally ill prisoners to deteriorate. However, prison officials provided few mental health services for these inmates. Moreover, the court found that, as operated, the unit precluded any form of social activity and caused a psychological condition known as Reduced Environmental Stimulation (RES). RES results in semi-fatuous behavior, violent insanity, and, in yet more extreme cases, suicide. In a study conducted in the SHU, prisoners were found to be suffering from "confused thought process, hallucinations, irrational anger, emotional flatness, and violent depression." Furthermore, the risk of psychosis increased where inmates were housed in double-cell units. Cellmates were exposed to potential paranoia, hostility and violent tendencies. *Id.* at 1230. Due to these extreme pressures put on mentally ill prisoners and prisoners with a propensity towards mental illness, the court held that the SHU in operation deprived inmates of the basic human needs protected by the Eighth Amendment. The court held that if segregation conditions "inflict a serious mental illness, greatly exacerbate mental illness, or deprive inmates of sanity, then defendants have deprived inmates of a basic necessity of human existence. Indeed, they have crossed into the realm of psychological torture." *Id.* at 1264. See also Jones "El v. Berge, 164 F. Supp. 2d 1096 (W.D. Wis. 2001).

[111]Madrid v. Gomez, 889 F. Supp. 1146, 1265 (N.D. Cal. 1995), mandamus denied, 103 F.3d 828 (9th Cir. 1996).

ficient to show an Eighth Amendment violation.[112] Thus, even when conditions "press the outer boundaries of what humans can psychologically tolerate," restrictive confinement is not unconstitutional unless it can be demonstrated that there is a high risk that inmates exposed to these conditions will develop serious mental illness.[113]

In the second case, the district court dealt with conditions in a supermax facility in Wisconsin and reached a similar decision on a motion for a preliminary injunction.[114] In some units of that facility, inmates were held in

> almost total sensory deprivation . . .kept confined alone in their cells for all but four hours a week. The exercise cell is devoid of equipment. The constant illumination is

---

[112]Madrid v. Gomez, 889 F. Supp. 1146, 1265 (N.D. Cal. 1995), mandamus denied, 103 F.3d 828 (9th Cir. 1996). (holding that the conditions did not violate constitutional rights of inmates who did not suffer mental illness but that they did for inmates who were confined in the unit with preexisting mental problems).

[113]Madrid v. Gomez, 889 F. Supp. 1146, 1267 (N.D. Cal. 1995), mandamus denied, 103 F.3d 828 (9th Cir. 1996). Thus, one commentator noted that "the emotional consequences of isolation play a minor role in determining whether a constitutional violation exists." Maria A. Luise, Solitary Confinement: Legal and Psychological Considerations, 15 New Eng. J. Crim. & Civ. Confinement 301, 317 (1989). See also Jason Sanabria, Farmer v. Brennan: Do Prisoners Have Any Rights Left Under the Eighth Amendment, 16 Whittier L. Rev. 1113, 1145 (1995) (suggesting that courts are hesitant to consider psychological implications of solitary confinement). But see Ruiz v. Johnson, 37 F. Supp. 2d 855, 914 (S.D. Tex. 1999), rev'd on other grounds and remanded, 243 F.3d 941 (5th Cir. 2001) (holding that conditions in the administrative segregation units of the Texas prison system caused such extreme levels of psychological harm as to violate the Eighth Amendment; the court held that "[a]s the pain and suffering caused by a cat-o'-nine-tails lashing an inmate's back are cruel and unusual punishment by today's standards of humanity and decency, the pain and suffering caused by extreme levels of psychological deprivation are equally, if not more, cruel and unusual. The wounds and resulting scars, while less tangible, are no less painful and permanent when they are inflicted on the human psyche.").

[114]Jones "El v. Berge, 164 F. Supp. 2d 1096 (W.D. Wis. 2001).

disorienting, as is the difficulty in knowing the time of day. The vestibule architecture and solid boxcar doors prevent any incidental interaction between inmates and guards . . .[115]

The court held that these conditions "pose a grave risk of harm to seriously mentally ill inmates. These risks include the development of serious mental illness, such as the extreme and bizarre behavior of feces smearing and refusing to eat. . .and the exacerbation of existing symptoms such as increased depression, hallucination, derealization and acute suicidality."[116]

If these decisions evidence a hesitancy to hold that supermax confinement is unconstitutional per se, they certainly reflect a judicial appreciation of the severe impact of sensory deprivation conditions and an unwillingness to tolerate subjecting the most vulnerable inmates to them.

§ 2:4 Corporal Punishment and Physical and Mechanical Restraints

The history of corporal punishment (i.e. the physical beating of inmates) may reflect "the evolving standards of decency that mark the progress of a maturing society."[1] Once fairly commonplace, its employment today as punishment for crime or violations of prison rules is rare. Several states specifically outlaw it by statute.[2] The American Correctional Association has

---

[115]*Id.*

[116]*Id.*

[Section 2:4]

[1]Trop v. Dulles, 356 U.S. 86, 101, 78 S. Ct. 590, 2 L. Ed. 2d 630 (1958). See § 2:1.

[2]E.g., Cal. Penal Code § 2652; NC Gen Stat § 148-20 (1992); ND Cent Code § 12-47-26; Del. Code Ann. Tit. 11, § 6517(4). A comprehensive, although somewhat dated, statutory compilation appears in Robert Platkin, Surviving Justice: Prisoners' Rights to be Free From Physical Assault, 23 Clev. St. L. Rev. 387, app. at 411-21 (1974).

declared its opposition to corporal punishment,[3] and many corrections officials have quietly abandoned its use.

These legislative and administrative actions have rendered litigation largely unnecessary. While there are some early cases that uphold the use of corporal punishment,[4] the law is now well established that corporal punishment is banned. The leading case is *Jackson v. Bishop*,[5] an opinion written by then Circuit Judge Blackmun. At issue in *Jackson* was the Arkansas practice of whipping inmates for disciplinary violations. In an earlier decision, procedural safeguards governing use of the strap had been ordered.[6] In *Jackson,* however, the Eighth Circuit Court of Appeals concluded that, irrespective of safeguards, whipping was cruel and unusual.[7] Justice (then Judge) Blackmun, provided nine distinct reasons for this conclusion, in many instances broadening his attack to encompass all forms of corporal punishment. Over half of his points had to do with the difficulty of controlling and regulating whipping, were it to be judicially sanctioned. Rules, he stated, often go unobserved, are easily circumvented, and do not

---

[3] American Correctional Assn., Standards for Adult Correctional Institutions Standard 3-4268 (2002); National Sheriffs' Assn, Inmates' Legal Rights Right 17 (1987) (banning the use of physical punishment). See also National Advisory Comm. on Criminal Justice Standards & Goals, Corrections, Standard 2.4 (1973).

[4] See, e.g., Bryant v. Harrelson, 187 F. Supp. 738 (S.D. Tex. 1960). Even these cases, however, established no trend since there were a number of cases to the contrary. See, e.g., U.S. v. Jones, 108 F. Supp. 266 (S.D. Fla. 1952), judgment rev'd, 207 F.2d 785 (5th Cir. 1953) (Court of Appeals, reversing, held that allegations of beating of prisoner for purpose of imposing illegal summary punishment upon prisoner and to extort information form him sufficiently charged violation of Civil Rights Act); State v. Nipper, 166 N.C. 272, 81 S.E. 164 (1914).

[5] Jackson v. Bishop, 404 F.2d 571 (8th Cir. 1968) (Blackmun, J).

[6] Talley v. Stephens, 247 F. Supp. 683 (E.D. Ark. 1965).

[7] Jackson v. Bishop, 404 F.2d 571, 579 (8th Cir. 1968).

prevent abuse.[8] Furthermore, drawing and enforcing a line between permissible and impermissible use of the strap would be extremely difficult.[9] His remaining points were more general in nature. Corporal punishment, he maintained, was subject to abuse in the hands of the sadistic or unscrupulous person; it generated hatred toward the punisher and the system which allowed it; it was degrading to both the person inflicting the punishment and the person being punished; it frustrated rehabilitative goals; and it rendered more difficult ultimate readjustment to society.[10] Finally, he noted that public opinion was opposed to whipping.[11] Other courts have since adopted the *Jackson* reasoning.[12]

Physical and Mechanical Restraints

The employment of some forms of mechanical restraints has been condemned on a similar rationale: that these passive devices bear the markings of the infliction of punishment in the same way that, in the eighteenth century, the use of the stocks and pillory did. One case involved the excessive use of neck chains;[13] another, four-way restraints, with which prisoners were chained on their backs to a metal bed frame by means of handcuffs and leg irons.[14]

---

[8]*Id.* at 579.

[9]*Id.* at 579-80.

[10]*Id.* at 580.

[11]*Id.*

[12]See, e.g., Gates v. Collier, 501 F.2d 1291, 1306 (5th Cir. 1974). See also Landman v. Royster, 333 F. Supp. 621 (E.D. Va. 1971).

[13]Spain v. Procunier, 600 F.2d 189 (9th Cir. 1979). See also Cal Penal Code § 2652.5 (unlawful to place a chain around the neck of any prisoner).

[14]Stewart v. Rhodes, 473 F. Supp. 1185 (S.D. Ohio 1979), judgment aff'd, 785 F.2d 310 (6th Cir. 1986). While there are occasions where the use of physical restraints might be permissible to prevent an inmate from injuring himself or herself, the use must be carefully monitored and cannot be excessive. See, e.g., Ferola v.

§ 2:4

The Supreme Court in *Hope v. Pelzer*[15] recently dealt with a case involving the use of restraints. In that case an inmate in Alabama was handcuffed to a "hitching post." A "hitching post" is a "horizontal bar placed between 45 to 57 inches from the ground. Inmates are handcuffed to it in a standing position and remain standing during the entire time they are placed on the hitching post."[16] The plaintiff alleged that he was attached to the post for approximately seven hours in the hot June Alabama sun and that during that time he was given water only once or twice and was given no bathroom breaks. The Supreme Court held that these allegations, if proven, violated clearly established constitutional law. The Court noted that the practice smacked of "obvious cruelty" and that its use was "antithetical to human dignity." The Court held that it was obvious from its past precedents that it was unconstitutional to be "hitched to a post for an extended period of time in a position that was painful and under circumstances that were both degrading and dangerous."[17]

This does not mean that restraints can never be employed. In *Hope,* the hitching post was not imposed

---

Moran, 622 F. Supp. 814 (D.R.I. 1985) (holding that it was unconstitutional to use restraints for medical reasons without careful medical monitoring; chaining an inmate spread-eagled to a bed for a total of 20 hours is excessive). But see LeMaire v. Maass, 12 F.3d 1444 (9th Cir. 1993) (chaining on incorrigible inmate who had a long history of violence and showed no inclination to change was proper); Bruscino v. Carlson, 854 F.2d 162, 164 (7th Cir. 1988) (upholding chaining of inmates to a bed in prison dealing with "the nation's least corrigible inmates"); Laws v. Cleaver, 140 F. Supp. 2d 145, 56 Fed. R. Evid. Serv. 941 (D. Conn. 2001) (holding prisoner in four-point restraints for four hours following an altercation not a violation of the Eighth Amendment).

[15]Hope v. Pelzer, 122 S. Ct. 2508, 153 L. Ed. 2d 666 (U.S. 2002).

[16]Hope v. Pelzer, 122 S. Ct. 2508 n1, 153 L. Ed. 2d 666 (U.S. 2002) (citing Austin v. Hopper, 15 F. Supp. 2d 1210 (M.D. Ala. 1998).

[17]Hope v. Pelzer, 122 S. Ct. 2508, 2518, 153 L. Ed. 2d 666 (U.S. 2002).

§ 2:4 RIGHTS OF PRISONERS, THIRD EDITION

in an emergency situation to maintain control.[18] Courts generally have upheld the use of restraints when their use poses no danger to the inmate, where their use is required to control behavior, and when appropriate safeguards are in place, including medical supervision and monitoring.[19] However, where the restraints have been imposed on "gratuitously" or barbarically,[20] without necessity, as was the case in *Hope,* or upon

---

[18]*Id.*

[19]See, e.g., Baumer v. Hampton, 238 F.3d 427 (9th Cir. 2000) (holding that "cross chaining" inmate to a bench for an hour was not a constitutional violation); Thielman v. Leean, 140 F. Supp. 2d 982 (W.D. Wis. 2001), judgment aff'd, 282 F.3d 478 (7th Cir. 2002) (supporting the notion that transportation of sexually violent persons in full restraints is not unconstitutional); Price v. Dixon, 961 F. Supp. 894 (E.D. N.C. 1997) (confinement of prisoner in four-point metal restraints by prison officials for a time period of twenty-eight hours did not violate the Eighth Amendment, where inmate had a history of disobedience and had continuously been disruptive towards prison personnel, and where prison officials checked his condition every fifteen minutes and allowed him regular bathroom and meal breaks; defendant's motion for summary judgment was granted). See Keenan v. Hall, 83 F.3d 1083 (9th Cir. 1996) (prison officials did not violate Eighth Amendment where inmate alleged that officials used chains and shackles when transferring inmate; court noted that the objects caused inmates cuts and pain, but the court held that these precautions may be exercised to maintain safety of prison guards); Fitts v. Witkowski, 920 F. Supp. 679, 687 (D.S.C. 1996) (prison officials were entitled to qualified immunity where inmate alleged that prison officials violated Eighth Amendment where they stripped inmate naked and placed him spread-eagle, face down on a bunk with four point restraints for four hours after he assaulted a corrections officer; court acknowledged that after settlement of a prior suit, department of corrections officials implemented a policy stating that four point restraints would not be used unless they were the method of last resort and there was prior medical approval; however, court found that "simply because a settlement agreement set forth clear guidelines on the use of four point restraints does not mean that the Decree automatically created a liberty interest protectable by the due process clause").

[20]For another hitching post case see Fountain v. Talley, 104 F. Supp. 2d 1345 (M.D. Ala. 2000), aff'd, 275 F.3d 57 (11th Cir. 2001).

vulnerable subjects, such as pregnant inmates, they have been judicially banned.[21]

§ 2:5 Use of Force by Guards

Although formal corporal punishment has virtually disappeared from the correctional scene, the use of force by guards against prisoners has not. The law books abound with cases of inmates who claim that they have been the victims of excessive force by prison guards.[1] After a period of uncertainty,[2] the basic parameters for resolving these cases have now emerged.

---

[21]Women Prisoners of District of Columbia Dept. of Corrections v. District of Columbia, 877 F. Supp. 634, 98 Ed. Law Rep. 681 (D. D.C. 1994), vacated in part on other grounds, modified in part on other grounds, 899 F. Supp. 659, 104 Ed. Law Rep. 213 (D.D.C. 1995). (shackling of women prisoners in third trimester of pregnancy and immediately after giving birth posed serious risk to female inmates' well-being as to be violative of Eighth Amendment).

[Section 2:5]

[1]See, e.g., Miller v. Leathers, 885 F.2d 151, 153 (4th Cir. 1989), reh'g granted, 893 F.2d 57 (4th Cir. 1989) and on reh'g, 913 F.2d 1085 (4th Cir. 1990) ("confrontations between guards and inmates in the prison setting are legion").

[2]Before Hudson v. McMillian, 503 U.S. 1, 112 S. Ct. 995, 1000, 117 L. Ed. 2d 156 (1992), there was a great deal of uncertainty about the appropriate standard to use in a prison excessive force case. Compare, e.g., Meriwether v. Coughlin, 879 F.2d 1037, 14 Fed. R. Serv. 3d 1251 (2d Cir. 1989) (holding that deliberate indifference standard applies) with Huguet v. Barnett, 900 F.2d 838, 841 (5th Cir. 1990) (applying the "maliciousness standard"). It was also unclear whether serious injury was a prerequisite for bringing such a case. See, e.g., Johnson v. Morel, 876 F.2d 477, 480 (5th Cir. 1989) (en banc). *Hudson* settled both questions. Hudson v. McMillian, 503 U.S. 1, 112 S. Ct. 995, 998-1001, 117 L. Ed. 2d 156 (1992) (holding that the *Whitley* maliciousness standard applies and that serious injury is not required). Some earlier cases relied on the due process clause rather than the Eighth Amendment. With *Hudson* it is now clear that, at least for prisoners, the Eighth Amendment is the relevant provision for analyzing an excessive force case.

§ 2:5   RIGHTS OF PRISONERS, THIRD EDITION

Hudson v. McMillian,³ is the most important case. In *Hudson,* the Court held that the use of force by prison guards violates the Eighth Amendment when it is not applied "in a good-faith effort to maintain or restore discipline" but, rather, is administered "maliciously and sadistically to cause harm."⁴ To determine whether the use of force is unconstitutional, a court must consider such factors as "the need for application of force, the relationship between that need and the amount of force used, the threat 'reasonably perceived by the responsible officials,' and 'any efforts made to temper the severity of a forceful response.'"⁵ In addition, factored into this equation is the extent of the injury to the inmate from the use of force by the prison guards.⁶ This standard is decidedly different from the negligence standard that governs the common law tort of assault and battery. Under the constitutional standard, "[n]ot every push or shove, even if it may later seem unnecessary in the peace of a judge's chambers, violates a prisoner's constitutional rights."⁷

While *Hudson* deals directly with convicted prison-

---

³Hudson v. McMillian, 503 U.S. 1, 112 S. Ct. 995, 117 L. Ed. 2d 156 (1992). See § 2:1.

⁴Hudson v. McMillian, 503 U.S. 1, 112 S. Ct. 995, 999, 117 L. Ed. 2d 156 (1992).

⁵Hudson v. McMillian, 503 U.S. 1, 112 S. Ct. 995, 999, 117 L. Ed. 2d 156 (1992) (quoting Whitley v. Albers, 475 U.S. 312, 321, 106 S. Ct. 1078, 89 L. Ed. 2d 251 (1986)).

⁶Hudson v. McMillian, 503 U.S. 1, 112 S. Ct. 995, 999, 117 L. Ed. 2d 156 (1992).

⁷Johnson v. Glick, 481 F.2d 1028, 1033 (2d Cir. 1973), quoted in Hudson v. McMillian, 503 U.S. 1, 112 S. Ct. 995, 1000, 117 L. Ed. 2d 156 (1992). One of the reasons for this conclusion is that "[t]he management by a few guards of large numbers of prisoners, not usually the most gentle or tractable of men and women, may require and justify the occasional use of a degree of intentional force." Johnson v. Glick, 481 F.2d 1028, 1033 (2d Cir. 1973). See also Miller v. Glanz, 948 F.2d 1562 (10th Cir. 1991) (causing inmate to be stretched out in an awkward position for two hours is not unconstitutional); Ricketts v. Derello, 574 F. Supp. 645 (E.D. Pa. 1983) (mere unwelcome shove of prisoner is not actionable);

CRUEL & UNUSUAL PUNISHMENT § 2:5

ers, it is relevant to cases involving pretrial detainees and arrestees as well. However, there are some legal distinctions between these two groups and convicted inmates that need to be made. For pretrial detainees, the Eighth Amendment does not formally apply, since they have not been convicted. Pretrial detainees draw their protection from the due process clause of the Fourteenth Amendment and not the Eighth Amendment. In *Bell v. Wolfish*[8] the Supreme Court held that pretrial detainees who have not been convicted of a crime could not be punished at all. While the Supreme Court has not specifically addressed what standard to apply to determine an excessive force case when a pretrial detainee is involved, lower courts have almost universally held that the maliciousness standard of *Hudson* applies to a jail setting via the due process clause.[9] As one court observed, since it is "impracticable to draw a line between convicted prisoners and pretrial detainees for the purpose of maintaining jail security," the proper framework for analyzing an excessive force case for pretrial detainees is the *Hudson* standard.[10] Thus, for pre trial detainees, *Hudson* is fully applicable in an excessive force case but it is applicable by dint of the Fourteenth, not the Eighth, Amendment.

Black Spotted Horse v. Else, 767 F.2d 516 (8th Cir. 1985) (pokes in the back or use of belligerent tone by guard does not violate the Eighth Amendment). But see H.C. by Hewett v. Jarrard, 786 F.2d 1080, 1085-86 (11th Cir. 1986); Winder v. Leak, 790 F. Supp. 1403, 1407 (N.D. Ill. 1992) (pushes did, under the circumstances, violate the Eighth Amendment).

[8]Bell v. Wolfish, 441 U.S. 520, 99 S. Ct. 1861, 60 L. Ed. 2d 447 (1979).

[9]See, e.g., Taylor v. McDuffie, 155 F.3d 479 (4th Cir. 1998); Valencia v. Wiggins, 981 F.2d 1440, 1446 (5th Cir. 1993). See also Daniel E. Manville & John Boston, Prisoners' Self-Help Litigation Manual 105 (3rd ed 1995) (noting that the due process clause and the Eighth Amendment the standards "are generally similar"). For a discussion of the development of the modern standard for resolving excessive force cases, see § 2:2.

[10]Rankin v. Klevenhagen, 5 F.3d 103, 105 (5th Cir. 1993) citing Valencia v. Wiggins, 981 F.2d 1440, 1446 (5th Cir. 1993),

Arrestees invoke different constitutional protections from those invoked by either pretrial detainees or convicts. In *Grahman v. Connor*,[11] the Supreme Court held that the Fourth Amendment, which regulates and prohibits "unreasonable seizures." governs an excessive force claim by a person who has been arrested and who has not yet become a pretrial detainee. The question in such a case is "whether the officers' actions are 'objectively reasonable' in light of the facts and circumstances confronting them, without regard to their underlying intent or motivation."[12] In making this determination it is not necessary to know whether the defendant was acting maliciously as is the case for convicts. There is a controversy over who is an arrestee. Some courts hold that one remains in this status until the initial arraignment before a judge.[13] Others hold that the period is much shorter, ending after the initial arrest itself takes place.[14]

Thus, the three groups of potential plaintiffs (convicts, pretrial detainees and arrestees) invoke three different provisions of the Constitution when they allege an excessive use of force. Nevertheless, in practice the

---

[11]Graham v. Connor, 490 U.S. 386, 109 S. Ct. 1865, 104 L. Ed. 2d 443 (1989).

[12]*Id.* at 397. See also Kostrzewa v. City of Troy, 247 F.3d 633 (6th Cir. 2001) (holding that the plaintiff was handcuffed too tightly and complained repeatedly about it to the arresting officers; that the officers amused themselves by speeding unnecessarily, braking abruptly so the plaintiff was thrown around in the police car; that when he was taken to the hospital he was cuffed again despite the fact that his wrists were swollen; and that the officers would only remove one cuff for examination and replaced it after the examination all amounted to a Fourth Amendment claim).

[13]See, e.g., Powell v. Gardner, 891 F.2d 1039, 1044 (2d Cir. 1989); McDowell v. Rogers, 863 F.2d 1302, 1306 (6th Cir. 1988); Robins v. Harum, 773 F.2d 1004, 1010 (9th Cir. 1985).

[14]See.e.g., Taylor v. McDuffie, 155 F.3d 479, 482-83 (4th Cir. 1998) (citing cases); Wilkins v. May, 872 F.2d 190, 192 (7th Cir. 1989) (overruled on other grounds as stated in, Muhammad v. Chicago Bd. of Educ., 1995 WL 89013 (N.D. Ill. 1995)); Riley v. Dorton, 115 F.3d 1159, 1164-65 (4th Cir. 1997) (en banc).

CRUEL & UNUSUAL PUNISHMENT § 2:5

outcomes are largely the same regardless of the category of plaintiff bringing the case. Indeed, one court remarked that the similarities between the standards for the three groups "far outweigh any differences."[15]

For in any excessive force case regardless of the status of the plaintiff (prisoner, pretrial detainee or arrestee) two hurdles must be cleared. First, is the threshold requirement that the plaintiff demonstrate that he or she was harmed by the use of force. Second, the plaintiff must show that the use of force was not justified at all or, if it was, that its use in the context of the case was excessive.[16]

What Kind of Harm is Required?

In *Hudson*, the Supreme Court held that the Eighth Amendment "excludes from constitutional recognition de minimis uses of physical force. . .."[17] Does this mean that a plaintiff must show a serious injury to prove that force that was used was excessive and not de mimimis? The Court said that serious injury is not required. Writing for the Court, Justice O'Connor observed that "when prison officials maliciously and sadistically use force to cause harm, contemporary standards of decency always are violated. This is true whether or not significant injury is evident. Otherwise the Eighth Amendment would permit any physical punishment, no matter how diabolical or inhumane, inflicting less than some

---

[15]Davis v. Little, 851 F.2d 605, 610 (2d Cir. 1988) (citing Martin v. Malhoyt, 830 F.2d 237, 261 n.76 (D.C. Cir. 1987)); Titran v. Ackman, 893 F.2d 145, 147 (7th Cir. 1990). See also Daniel E. Manville & John Boston, Prisoners' Self-Help Litigation Manual 105 (3rd ed 1995).

[16]For a discussion of the degree of force that prison officials may use, see Jeffery T. Walker, Police and Correctional Use of Force: Legal and Policy Standards and Implications, 42 Crime & Delinquency 144 (1996).

[17]Hudson v. McMillian, 503 U.S. 1, 112 S. Ct. 995, 1000, 117 L. Ed. 2d 156 (1992) (quoting Whitley v. Albers, 475 U.S. 312, 327, 106 S. Ct. 1078, 89 L. Ed. 2d 251 (1986)).

§ 2:5   Rights of Prisoners, Third Edition

arbitrary quantity of injury."[18]

The Court made clear that the extent of the injury is but one of several important factors that must be considered in resolving an excessive force case. The Court stated that:

> the extent of injury suffered by an inmate is one factor that may suggest "whether the use of force could plausibly have been thought necessary" in a particular situation, "or instead evidenced such wantonness with respect to the unjustified infliction of harm as is tantamount to knowing willingness that it occur." In determining whether the use of force was wanton and unnecessary it may also be relevant to evaluate the need for application of force, the relationship between that need and the amount of force used, the threat "reasonably perceived by the responsible officials" and "any efforts made to temper the severity of a forceful response." *The absence of serious injury is therefore relevant to the Eighth Amendment injury but does not end it.* (emphasis supplied)[19]

Accordingly, most lower court decisions following *Hudson* have held that while an inmate must demonstrate some "actual" injury,[20] the injury need not be significant.[21] In most cases, this requirement is satisfied

---

[18]Hudson v. McMillian, 503 U.S. 1, 112 S. Ct. 995, 1000, 117 L. Ed. 2d 156 (1992).

[19]Hudson v. McMillian, 503 U.S. 1, 112 S. Ct. 995, 117 L. Ed. 2d 156 (1992).

[20]Cummings v. Malone, 995 F.2d 817, 37 Fed. R. Evid. Serv. 177 (8th Cir. 1993). See also Risdal v. Martin, 810 F. Supp. 1049 (S.D. Iowa 1993) (taunting and jostling of inmate on the way back from a forced shower is not an injury); Brown v. Croce, 967 F. Supp. 101 (S.D. N.Y. 1997) (inmate claimed that a corrections officer violated the Eighth Amendment when he slapped him twice and used a racial epithet; court held that since plaintiff suffered no injury the two slaps only amounted to de minimis use of force that could not support an Eighth Amendment claim); Glenn v. City of Tyler, 242 F.3d 307 (5th Cir. 2001) (finding that handcuffing too tightly, with nothing more, does not amount to excessive force).

[21]See, e.g., Sims v. Artuz, 230 F.3d 14 (2d Cir. 2000) (significant harm is not required): Davidson v. Flynn, 32 F.3d 27, 29, n.1 (2d Cir. 1994); Ikerd v. Blair, 101 F.3d 430, 434 (5th Cir. 1996);

CRUEL & UNUSUAL PUNISHMENT § 2:5

by showing some physical injury.[22] While this is the view of almost all the circuits,[23] there is a line of cases in the Fourth Circuit that take a contrary view.[24] Those cases hold that "absent the most extraordinary circumstances, a plaintiff cannot prevail on an Eight Amendment excessive force claim if his injury is *de minimis*."[25] The reason given for this conclusion is that if there is "de minimis" injury, the force must have been de

---

Lunsford v. Bennett, 17 F.3d 1574, 1582 (7th Cir. 1994); White v. Holmes, 21 F.3d 277, 281 (8th Cir. 1994); Harris v. Chapman, 97 F.3d 499, 505, 45 Fed. R. Evid. Serv. 1063 (11th Cir. 1996) (where prison official snapped an inmate's head back with a towel and slapped him twice in the face, causing back injuries, such injuries were more than "de minimis"). However, if the injury is so slight as to be de mimimis then recovery cannot occur. Siglar v. Hightower, 112 F.3d 191 (5th Cir. 1997).

[22]See, e.g., Rankin v. Klevenhagen, 5 F.3d 103, 107 (5th Cir. 1993) (*Hudson* removed the "serious" or "significant" injury requirement); Bender v. Brumley, 1 F.3d 271, 277 (5th Cir. 1993) (holding that "signficant injury is not required to establish liability in an excessive force case involving an arrestee).

[23]Taylor v. McDuffie, 155 F.3d 479, 485-86 (4th Cir. 1998) (dissenting opinion) (citing cases). See also Sims v. Artuz, 230 F.3d 14 (2d Cir. 2000) (significant harm is not required): Davidson v. Flynn, 32 F.3d 27, 29, n.1 (2d Cir. 1994); Ikerd v. Blair, 101 F.3d 430, 434 (5th Cir. 1996); Lunsford v. Bennett, 17 F.3d 1574, 1582 (7th Cir. 1994); White v. Holmes, 21 F.3d 277, 281 (8th Cir. 1994); Harris v. Chapman, 97 F.3d 499, 505, 45 Fed. R. Evid. Serv. 1063 (11th Cir. 1996) (where prison official snapped an inmate's head back with a towel and slapped him twice in the face, causing back injuries, such injuries were more than "de minimis"); Siglar v. Hightower, 112 F.3d 191 (5th Cir. 1997).

[24]See e.g., Riley v. Dorton, 115 F.3d 1159 (4th Cir. 1997) (en banc); Taylor v. McDuffie, 155 F.3d 479, 482-83 (4th Cir. 1998); Norman v. Taylor, 25 F.3d 1259 (4th Cir. 1994).

[25]Norman v. Taylor, 25 F.3d 1259, 1263 (4th Cir. 1994) (en banc). The court indicated that the extraordinary circumstances that it was referring to include situations in which the force uses is of a "sort repugnant to the conscience of mankind." Norman v. Taylor, 25 F.3d 1259, 1263 (4th Cir. 1994).

§ 2:5   Rights of Prisoners, Third Edition

minimis.[26] Applying this approach in one of the cases, the Fourth Circuit held that there was no viable excessive force claim even if the plaintiff could prove that he was maliciously attacked by government officials who grabbed him by the collar, pointed his gun at him, threatened to "blow his brains out," placed his knee in the lower part of his back, grabbed his head and pulled it backwards, and stuck a small wooden baton inside his nose and mouth with sufficient force to cause his nose to bleed and to crack a tooth.[27]

The reason the court assigned for this conclusion is that the injuries that the plaintiff suffered were not serious. The court relied upon medical records[28] that, if believed, indicated that while there was "slight swelling in the jaw" and some irritation of the mucous membranes of the mouth," the plaintiff's tooth was not cracked and his nose was not injured in the encounter.[29] Thus, the injuries in the court's opinion were de mimimis and for that reason there was no excessive use of force.

This line of decisions, the rule of which is decidedly the minority rule,[30] is difficult, if not impossible, to reconcile with *Hudson*. As the dissenting judge in the case

---

[26]See, Germain v. Ruzicka, 205 F.3d 1333 (4th Cir. 2000); Taylor v. McDuffie, 155 F.3d 479 (4th Cir. 1998); Jackson v. Morgan, 19 Fed. Appx. 97 (4th Cir. 2001), cert. denied, 122 S. Ct. 1437, 152 L. Ed. 2d 381 (U.S. 2002); Williams v. Dehay, 81 F.3d 153 (4th Cir. 1996).

[27]Taylor v. McDuffie, 155 F.3d 479 (4th Cir. 1998).

[28]It is questionable whether medical records should be accepted as incontrovertible on a motion for summary judgment. See Taylor v. McDuffie, 155 F.3d 479, 487 (4th Cir. 1998) (dissenting opinion).

[29]Taylor v. McDuffie, 155 F.3d 479, 487 (4th Cir. 1998).

[30]Germain v. Ruzicka, 205 F.3d 1333 (4th Cir. 2000); Taylor v. McDuffie, 155 F.3d 479 (4th Cir. 1998); Jackson v. Morgan, 19 Fed. Appx. 97 (4th Cir. 2001), cert. denied, 122 S. Ct. 1437, 152 L. Ed. 2d 381 (U.S. 2002); Williams v. Dehay, 81 F.3d 153 (4th Cir. 1996). For a discussion and critique of these cases, see Troy J. Aramburu, The Role of "De Minimis" Injury in the Excessive Force Determination: Taylor v. McDuffie and the Fourth Circuit Stand Alone, 14 BYU J. Pub. L. 313 (2000). See also Ostrander v. Horn, 145 F.

CRUEL & UNUSUAL PUNISHMENT § 2:5

just discussed noted, it is entirely possible that excessive force may be used without causing serious physical injury. The judge gave two examples of situations in which this could occur:

> [I]magine an inmate who, although thrown from a prison balcony, is fortunate to incur only minor scrapes and bruises. Or imagine an inmate who although beaten intensely in the stomach, back, chest or groin, displays no greater outward signs of physical injury than that which the majority terms "temporary swelling.[31]

Supp. 2d 614 (M.D. Pa. 2001) (where inmate was forcefully extracted from his cell during a training drill, was handcuffed, and had his face pushed into a corner, injuries were de minimus); Outlaw v. Newkirk, 259 F.3d 833 (7th Cir. 2001) (where correction officer accidentally slammed a food service slot on inmate's hand, causing minor injury, use of force was de minimus and officer had legitimate reason because evidence proved that inmate said "take this garbage, you bitch," and other inmates often used food service slots to throw garbage at guards); Collins v. Bopson, 816 F. Supp. 335 (E.D. Pa. 1993) (holding physical injuries were so minimal that use of force must have been de minimis); Barber v. Grow, 929 F. Supp. 820 (E.D. Pa. 1996) (where inmate sustained cuts and bruises to his arm and knee as a result of a prison guard intentionally pulling a chair out from under him, injuries were "de minimis" and failed to rise to a constitutionally impermissible level of "unnecessary and wanton" infliction of pain); Acosta v. McGrady, 1999 WL 158471 (E.D. Pa. 1999) (inmate claimed that, as he was being led to a misconduct hearing, his handcuffed arms were pulled sharply and he was slammed into the wall by corrections officer resulting in swollen hands and headaches for a few days thereafter; even assuming the inmate's disputed account was true, court granted summary judgment for the corrections officer because the physical contact was de minimis and thus not rising to the level of an Eighth Amendment violation). But see, Romaine v. Rawson, 140 F. Supp. 2d 204 (N.D. N.Y. 2001), where an inmate was slapped three times by a guard, and the court found an Eighth Amendment violation though the use of force was de minimis, since force was clearly not necessary and therefore was "repugnant to the conscience of mankind." Romaine v. Rawson, 140 F. Supp. 2d 204, 212 (N.D. N.Y. 2001) (quoting Romano v. Howarth, 998 F.2d 101, 105, 39 Fed. R. Evid. Serv. 196 (2d Cir. 1993)).

[31]Taylor v. McDuffie, 155 F.3d 479, 486 (4th Cir. 1998) (dissenting opinion).

§ 2:5   RIGHTS OF PRISONERS, THIRD EDITION

For these reasons and because of the strong language in *Hudson* on this point, almost all courts take the position that there is no *per se* requirement that an inmate plead and prove a serious physical injury in order to prevail in an excessive force claim.[32]

If, therefore, it is true that slight physical injury can be sufficient to establish an excessive force claim, what of a situation where no physical injury results? Can a plaintiff prevail in a situation where there is no physical injury, but there is psychological trauma? The Supreme Court has not definitely answered that question. There is, however, a significant body of precedent for the proposition that unconstitutional use of force can be found even in the absence of physical injury if the force causes intense psychological suffering.

An opinion from the Tenth Circuit Court of Appeals chillingly illustrates this point.[33] In that case, the plaintiff, a prisoner, alleged that a prison official put a revolver to his head and threatened to kill him unless he took steps to help apprehend another inmate who was engaged in illegal activities.[34] In reinstating the dismissed complaint, the court held that when an inmate is exposed to the "terror of instant and unexpected death at the hands of [his] keepers" a constitutional violation occurs even if there is no physical

---

[32]Because the language of *Hudson* is so clear, a district court in the Fourth Circuit declined to follow *Taylor v. McDuffie* and held that a claim of bruising, scarring and swelling as a result of an assault, without more, did not disqualify the plaintiff from recovery for an alleged unlawful beating by prison officials. Watford v. Bruce, 126 F. Supp. 2d 425 (E.D. Va. 2001). See B.L. Taylor, Use of Excessive Physical Force Against a Prisoner May Constitute Cruel and Unusual Punishment Under the Eighth Amendment Even Though the Prisoner Does Not Suffer Significant Injury,43 Drake L Rev 765 (1995).

[33]Northington v. Jackson, 973 F.2d 1518, 23 Fed. R. Serv. 3d 934 (10th Cir. 1992). See also, e.g., Smith v. Aldingers, 999 F.2d 109 (5th Cir. 1993) (inmate forced to watch a beating of another inmate and threatened with possibly receiving similar treatment).

[34]Northington v. Jackson, 973 F.2d 1518, 1522, 23 Fed. R. Serv. 3d 934 (10th Cir. 1992).

injury.[35] The court distinguished this kind of psychological terror from "an idle and laughing threat" from prison guards, which, while unpleasant, is not enough to trigger the protection of the Eighth Amendment.[36] By the same token, verbal abuse by guards, without more, does not fall within the ambit of this branch of the Eighth Amendment.[37] However, verbal abuse and

---

[35]*Id.* at 1524. See also Wisniewski v. Kennard, 901 F.2d 1276, 1277 (5th Cir. 1990) (guard placing a revolver in an inmate's mouth and threatening to blow the inmate's head off); Oses v. Fair, 739 F. Supp. 707 (D. Mass. 1990) (guard stuck .38 caliber revolver into plaintiff's mouth and forced the inmate to play Russian Roulette); Burton v. Livingston, 791 F.2d 97, 100 (8th Cir. 1986) (guard drew weapon and threatened to shoot); Douglas v. Marino, 684 F. Supp. 395 (D.N.J. 1988) (prison employee wielded knife and threatened to stab inmate).

[36]See, e.g., Hopson v. Fredericksen, 961 F.2d 1374 (8th Cir. 1992) (mere threat to inflict injury, without brandishing weapon or taking any further steps, does not violate the Eighth Amendment); Martin v. Sargent, 780 F.2d 1334, 1338 (8th Cir. 1985) (mere threatening language and gestures do not violate the Constitution); Collins v. Cundy, 603 F.2d 825, 827 (10th Cir. 1979) (idle threat of sheriff that he would hang a prisoner is not enough to invoke the Eighth Amendment). See also James W. Marquart, Prison Guards and the Use of Physical Coercion as a Mechanism of Prisoner Control, 24 Criminology 347 (1986).

[37]See, e.g., Siglar v. Hightower, 112 F.3d 191 (5th Cir. 1997); Keenan v. Hall, 83 F.3d 1083, 1091 (9th Cir. 1996) (prison guards did not violate Eighth Amendment where inmate alleged that guards verbally harassed inmates; court noted that "disrespectful and assaultive comments" which denied inmate "peace of mind" were insufficient to state a claim where the comments were not "unusually gross even for a prison setting"); Tatro v. Kervin, 41 F.3d 9 (1st Cir. 1994); Oltarzewski v. Ruggiero, 830 F.2d 136 (9th Cir. 1987) (verbal harassment or abuse is not sufficient to state a constitutional claim); Ramirez v. Holmes, 921 F. Supp. 204 (S.D. N.Y. 1996) ("mere verbal abuse, slander, threats, and harassment are not judicially cognizable injuries"); Partee v. Cook County Sheriff's Office, 863 F. Supp. 778 (N.D. Ill. 1994) (no violation of Eighth Amendment where prisoner was subjected to prison officer's verbal threats, racial slurs, and other harassment); Davis v. Sancegraw, 850 F. Supp. 809 (E.D. Mo. 1993); but see Burton v. Livingston, 791 F.2d 97 (8th Cir. 1986) (death threat by guard was

§ 2:5   Rights of Prisoners, Third Edition

taunts, when accompanied by a beating, can be legitimately considered part of the injury inflicted on the inmate.[38]

The recognition that physical injury is not an indispensable requirement is in keeping with the reality-all too apparent in recent times of terrorist attacks and threats-that mental pain can be intentionally inflicted without necessarily leaving physical scars.[39] To hold otherwise would be to "place various kinds of state-sponsored torture and abuse-of the kind ingeniously designed to cause pain but without a tell-tale 'significant injury'-entirely beyond the pale of the Constitution."[40] For this reason, as the Sixth Circuit Court of Appeals held, "claims of excessive force do not

---

actionable where evidence showed that the threat was made in response to the prisoner's exercise of constitutional rights). There is one notable exception to this: where guards state to other inmates that a particular prisoner is a "snitch." Watson v. McGinnis, 981 F. Supp. 815 (S.D. N.Y. 1997) (inmate claimed that the guard used excessive force when he called him a snitch; court recognized that the guard calling an inmate a snitch in order to cause him harm is an Eighth Amendment excessive force violation); Benefield v. McDowall, 241 F.3d 1267 (10th Cir. 2001) (labeling an inmate a "snitch" to other inmates meets deliberate indifference standard).

[38]Harris v. Chapman, 97 F.3d 499, 45 Fed. R. Evid. Serv. 1063 (11th Cir. 1996) (prison official snapped an inmate's head back with a towel and slapped him twice in the face causing back injuries; court noted that the defendant's use of racial epithets and taunts during the beating supported the award of punitive damages).

[39]See also Hudson v. McMillian, 503 U.S. 1, 112 S. Ct. 995, 1004, 117 L. Ed. 2d 156 (1992) (observing that pain "in its ordinary meaning surely includes a notion of psychological harm") (Blackmun, J, concurring). See also Jordan v. Gardner, 986 F.2d 1521 (9th Cir. 1993) (psychological harm from cross-gender body searches of women prisoners presents an Eighth Amendment claim).

[40]Hudson v. McMillian, 503 U.S. 1, 112 S. Ct. 995, 1003, 117 L. Ed. 2d 156 (1992) (Blackmun, J, concurring) (citing the examples of such infamous torture devices as the "Tucker Telephone" a device that generated electric shocks to sensitive body parts).

necessarily require allegations of assault."[41] Psychological injury, therefore, fits within the zone protected by the Eighth Amendment. Of course, as mentioned earlier,[42] this does not mean the type or severity of the injury is irrelevant. It can play an important rule in answering the next series of questions.

The second hurdle to clear in order to successfully establish an excessive force claim is to show that the force was applied maliciously and sadistically.[43] This is the "core inquiry."[44] The malicious and sadistic use of force can occur in two situations. The first is when prison officials in the particular case are not justified in using force, in other words, that the use of force in the first instance in whatever degree was not justified by the situation. The second is when, even though the decision to use force was justifiable, force used, in the circumstances, is badly out of proportion to the need.

When Is the Use of Force Justified?

The first question raised by these requirements is: when can prison officials use force? As an initial matter, prison guards occupy the role of police in prison and, therefore, have the same general authority to use force that is granted to law enforcement personnel

---

[41]Cornwell v. Dahlberg, 963 F.2d 912, 915 (6th Cir. 1992) (holding that forcing an inmate to lie on the cold ground constituted excessive use of force).

[42]See Hudson v. McMillian, 503 U.S. 1, 112 S. Ct. 995, 117 L. Ed. 2d 156 (1992), discussed earlier in this section.

[43]It is not enough that force was "excessive," it must have been used maliciously and sadistically. Romano v. Howarth, 998 F.2d 101, 105, 39 Fed. R. Evid. Serv. 196 (2d Cir. 1993). Both words are important. One court held that it was reversible error to instruct the jury in an excessive force case using one word but not the other. Howard v. Barnett, 21 F.3d 868 (8th Cir. 1994).

[44]Cummings v. Malone, 995 F.2d 817, 822, 37 Fed. R. Evid. Serv. 177 (8th Cir. 1993).

outside of prison.[45] This authority includes the right to use reasonable force to effectuate a lawful arrest, to prevent the commission of a crime, and to prevent the escape of one who has committed a crime. However, this does not mean that prison officials, any more than police officers, are justified in using force simply to gain information that can be used in a criminal investigation.[46] In the prison context, of course, the reference is to a crime other than the one that is the basis for the prisoner's incarceration. In addition, as is the case with civilians, prison guards are authorized to use reasonable force in self-defense, in defense of others, and in defense of property.

None of the above justifications for the use of force in a prison setting are controversial. But there is an additional justification for the use of force by prison guards that has stirred controversy. That is whether guards may use force to compel prisoners to obey prison rules. The argument has been made that the orderly internal operation of a prison requires the authorization to use reasonable force on the spot to compel immediate compliance.

There is little doubt that prisons may establish rules of conduct for inmates.[47] Sanctions for infractions of these rules are usually imposed by a disciplinary committee pursuant to a hearing.[48] This much is clear. But does it follow that guards can use force to compel compliance with their orders? In an interesting Seventh Circuit Court of Appeals case, inmates argued that they could not.[49] In that case, the inmates asserted that when an inmate refuses to obey an order, the institution's

---

[45]See, e.g., Ala Code § 14-3-14 (1982); State v. Rhea, 94 N.M. 168, 608 P.2d 144 (1980) (jailer held to be a peace officer); Kennibrew v. Russell, 578 F. Supp. 164 (E.D. Tenn. 1983) (as peace officers, guards are entitled to carry, firearms).

[46]See, e.g., Gray v. Spillman, 925 F.2d 90, 93 (4th Cir. 1991).

[47]See Ch 9.

[48]See Ch 9.

[49]Soto v. Dickey, 744 F.2d 1260 (7th Cir. 1984).

§ 2:5

exclusive remedy lies with the formal disciplinary procedures and not with the use of force.[50] However, the Seventh Circuit rejected this contention. The court reasoned that "[w]hen an inmate refuse(s) to obey a proper order, he is attempting to assert his authority over a portion of the institution and its officials. Such refusal and denial of authority places the staff and other inmates in danger."[51] This opinion echoes the institution's strong interest in compliance with its rules and regulations. Achieving prompt compliance with institutional norms can be more important for the maintenance of institutional security than the imposition of punishment for violations. Therefore, the weight of authority establishes that, in prison, obedience to rules may be secured through the employment of "forceful" persuasion.[52] For these reasons, it has been held that a convict has no right to physically resist an arguably in-

---

[50]An ABA Committee also expressed its opposition to the use of any physical force for this purpose. ABA, Joint Committee on the Legal Status of Prisoners Proposed Standard 6.11(b)(iii). The Committee did, however, allow the use of force to isolate or confine an inmate. In its final draft of its standards for prisons, the ABA rejected this position. ABA, Standards for Criminal Justice Standard 23-6.12(a)(ii)(B) (1986) authorizes the use of force to maintain control of the institution; this section applies when property is being destroyed or the prisoner constitutes a threat to himself or herself or another, disrupts the order of a living area, or threatens the security of an institution.

[51]Soto v. Dickey, 744 F.2d 1260, 1267 (7th Cir. 1984). The court continued by saying "[w]hen an order is given to an inmate there are only so many choices available to the correctional officer. If it is an order that requires action by the institution, and the inmate cannot be persuaded to obey the order, some means must be used to compel compliance, such as a chemical agent or physical force." Soto v. Dickey, 744 F.2d 1260, 1267 (7th Cir. 1984).

[52]See also Caldwell v. Moore, 968 F.2d 595, 601 (6th Cir. 1992) (holding that an institution "has a legitimate interest in having inmates obey orders"); Johnson v. Glick, 481 F.2d 1028, 1033 (2d Cir. 1973); Giroux v. Sherman, 807 F. Supp. 1182 (E.D. Pa. 1992) (blows to inmate were justified by the difficulties prison authorities faced in maintaining discipline); Theus v. Angelone, 895 F. Supp. 265 (D. Nev. 1995) (where ten high-security Muslim inmates

§ 2:5   Rights of Prisoners, Third Edition

valid order but must, instead, submit and subsequently pursue legal redress.[53]

Nevertheless, some have raised serious questions about whether force should be used to compel compliance with an order where the failure to do so would not

---

protested prison regulation regarding chapel restroom by throwing a chair through chapel window, guards used a constitutional degree of force when they placed the individuals in hand cuffs and leg restraints after they surrendered; court noted that none of the inmates were injured and that no chemical agents were used); Dennis v. Thurman, 959 F. Supp. 1253 (C.D. Cal. 1997) (inmate suffered injuries after being hit by a ricocheting bullet fired from a prison official's 37 mm gas gun after the inmate refused to voluntarily leave his cell; court held prison officials had a legitimate penological need to perform cell extractions; further, the prison official did not shoot directly at the plaintiff; thus, the use of such a dangerous weapon was not employed in a "sadistic and malicious" manner so as to constitute an Eighth Amendment violation); Jackson v. Allen, 376 F. Supp. 1393 (E.D. Ark. 1974); In re Riddle, 57 Cal. 2d 848, 22 Cal. Rptr. 472, 372 P.2d 304 (1962); Colo Rev Stat § 17-20-122 (1986) (force, including deadly force, may be used to require obedience to lawful commands); Minn Stat Ann § 243.52 (West 1992). See also National Sheriffs' Assn, Inmates' Legal Rights 21 (1987) (force should be used only when necessary for self-defense, to protect other inmates, to maintain order, or to prevent escape or a riot); Model Sentencing and Corrections Act § 4-102, cmt. at 173 (2001) (physical force is limited to situations where necessary to protect the safety of the public or security or safety within the institution). But see U.S. Dept. of Justice, Federal Standards for Prisons and Jails § 6.15 (1980) (force may only be used in "instances of justifiable self-protection, protection of others, protection of property and prevention of escapes"); American Correctional Assn., Standards for Adult Correctional Institutions Standard 3-4198 (2002) (same).

[53]Hasenmeier-McCarthy v. Rose, 986 F. Supp. 464 (S.D. Ohio 1998) (force may be used to administer a tuberculosis test); Jackson v. Allen, 376 F. Supp. 1393, 1395 (E.D. Ark. 1974) (ad hoc personal decisions by prisoners regarding the propriety of the use of force by guards would inevitably lead to undesirable confrontation and would undermine prison discipline; an exception, however, exists where submission would result in death or serious, irreparable, and potentially permanent mental or physical injury).

§ 2:5

jeopardize the security of the institution.[54] They argue that in some situations there is nothing to be gained by asserting force to compel an inmate to do an act that is not essential such as leaving his cell. It may be better in such situations to allow the inmate to remain in his cell if he is secure in that place than to force a confrontation in which the inmate is injured and in which guards are exposed to the potential for harm to themselves.[55]

That there are reasons that justify the use of force implies that there are situations in which force is not proper. Using force on an inmate in retaliation for using an approved grievance procedure is a prime example of a situation in which force is not appropriate.[56] The same is true when force is applied "gratuitously to degrade" an inmate."[57] In addition, the use of force to interrogate inmates to uncover information about contraband or about an attempted prison escape is not lawful.[58] In sum, the Eighth Amendment does not sanction the use of force in "unprovoked and unjustified at-

---

[54]Committee on Corrections, The Use of Stun Shields on Rikers Island, The Record (2001).

[55]*Id.*

[56]See, e.g., Flowers v. Phelps, 956 F.2d 488, 22 Fed. R. Serv. 3d 328 (5th Cir. 1992), vacated and superseded in part on other grounds on denial of reh'g, 964 F.2d 400 (5th Cir. 1992); Tijerina v. Plentl, 958 F.2d 133, 23 Fed. R. Serv. 3d 187 (5th Cir. 1992), opinion withdrawn and superseded on other grounds on denial of reh'g, 984 F.2d 148, 24 Fed. R. Serv. 3d 1289 (5th Cir. 1993).

[57]See, e.g., Felix v. McCarthy, 939 F.2d 699, 701 (9th Cir. 1991) (guard deliberately spat on the floor and ordered inmate to clean it up; when inmate refused, guard pushed inmate to the wall and handcuffed him).

[58]Cohen v. Coahoma County, Miss., 805 F. Supp. 398, 403-04 (N.D. Miss. 1992) ("the Constitution does not accept the whipping of inmates in order to extract information concerning the location of contraband"); Cohen v. Coahoma County, Miss., 805 F. Supp. 398 (N.D. Miss. 1992) (force may not be used to coerce an inmate to give information about an escape plan).

tack(s) by prison guards."[59]

If Force Is Justified, Under What Circumstances Is Its Application Excessive?

Even if the circumstances indicate that force may be legitimately employed, the next question that arises is whether the force applied under the circumstances is excessive. The general rule under *Hudson* is that even if the use of force is justified, it cannot be applied maliciously and sadistically.[60] In making this determination, it is useful to distinguish between deadly and nondeadly force.

In the civilian world, deadly force may only be used by civilians in self-defense against a life-threatening attack or one that threatens serious bodily injury,[61] although state law may require one to retreat before resorting to deadly force.[62] While state law may vary, deadly force is also often permitted in defense of another who reasonably appears threatened by a life-endangering attack.[63] Some states limit this use of deadly force to instances in which the attacked person

---

[59]Felix v. McCarthy, 939 F.2d 699, 702 (9th Cir. 1991).

[60]Hudson v. McMillian, 503 U.S. 1, 112 S. Ct. 995, 998, 117 L. Ed. 2d 156 (1992). See also Johnson v. Glick, 481 F.2d 1028 (2d Cir. 1973); Jackson v. Allen, 376 F. Supp. 1393 (E.D. Ark. 1974). See also Colo Rev Stat § 27-20-122 (1986); Minn Stat Ann § 243.52 (West 1992). See, generally, Andre Sansoucy, Note, Applying the Eighth Amendment to the Use of Force against Prison Inmates, 60 BU L Rev 332 (1980).

[61]W.P. Keeton, Prosser & Keeton on Torts § 19, at 126-27 (5th ed 1984).

[62]W.P. Keeton, Prosser & Keeton on Torts § 19, at 127-28 (5th ed 1984). See also Spain v. Procunier, 600 F.2d 189, 195 (9th Cir. 1979).

[63]See, generally, Wayne R. LaFave & Austin W. Scott, Criminal Law § 5.7(b), at 456 (2d ed 1986). Unlike in civilian society where citizens usually are not legally obliged to come to the aid of another in distress, prison guards may be under a legal duty to protect visitors and other inmates from harm. See, e.g., 18 U.S.C. § 4042; Mich Comp Laws Ann § 800.41 (West 1982 & Supp 1993). See § 2:7.

would have been privileged to use such force.[64] Deadly force is not permitted in defense of property.[65]

Deadly force also may be employed by law enforcement personnel in two additional defined situations. One deals with escape. In some circumstances, deadly force may be justified to prevent the escape of an inmate.[66] However, the answer to the question of exactly when deadly force may be used for this purpose is muddled.[67] Several distinct approaches have been identified.[68] Of the competing approaches, the one taken by the American Bar Association is perhaps the most persuasive. It states that deadly force is not justified to prevent the escape of a person from an institution used principally to hold misdemeanants or persons awaiting trial, when the officer has reason to know that the escapee has not committed earlier felonies or that the

---

[64]Wayne R. LaFave & Austin W. Scott, Criminal Law § 5.7(b), at 456 (2d ed 1986).

[65]See, generally, Wayne R. LaFave & Austin W. Scott, Criminal Law § 5.9 at 465.

[66]Cf. Kinney v. Indiana Youth Center, 950 F.2d 462 (7th Cir. 1991) (holding that it was proper to shoot an inmate who was escaping as long as a warning was issued before firing shots); Newby v. Serviss, 590 F. Supp. 591 (W.D. Mich. 1984) (holding that the use of deadly force to prevent an escape is justifiable when warning shots were fired and failed to end the attempt).

[67]Many state statutes are not helpful, speaking only in terms of using that amount of force required under the circumstances. See, e.g., Ala Code § 14-3-15; Mich Comp Laws Ann § 800.41 (West 1982 & Supp 1993); Tenn Code Ann § 41-21-401.

[68]Compare, e.g., Holloway v. Moser, 136 SE 375 (NC 1927) (deadly force may be used if the crime for which the person is committed is one for which deadly force could be used to prevent escape from arrest) with National Commn. on Reform of the Federal Criminal Law, Study Draft § 607 (1970) (deadly force may only be used to prevent escape by dangerous convicts or those posing a substantial risk to the public) and State v. Turlington, 102 Mo. 642, 15 S.W. 141 (1891) (deadly force may only be used if the crime of escape is a felony) and Model Penal Code § 3.07(3) (1985) (deadly force may be used to prevent the escape of anyone from a penal institution).

§ 2:5

escapee is unlikely to endanger human life.[69] This approach would base the permissible amount of force on the nature of the institutions-deadly force could be used only in preventing escapes from institutions housing felons; it could not be used even then against an escapee known not to be dangerous.[70] The merit in this approach is that it attempts to narrow the circumstances in which deadly force is permissible to only those cases in which public safety demands it. In any event, the single unifying theme in all of these approaches is that deadly force is not permissible when lesser force would effectively frustrate the escape attempt.[71]

The second rationale for law enforcement personnel using deadly force is to arrest someone who is in the process of committing a felony.[72] However, deadly force is not permitted when the crime involved is a misdemeanor,[73] and state laws differ as to what felonies may be prevented or terminated by the use of deadly force.[74]

Reasonable nondeadly force may be used in a civilian society in self-defense, in defense of others, and in

---

[69]ABA, Standards for Criminal Justice Standard 6.12(a)(A) (1986).

[70]ABA, Standards for Criminal Justice Standard 6.12(a)(A) (1986).

[71]See, e.g., Andry v. Parish of Orleans, 309 So. 2d 814 (La. Ct. App. 4th Cir. 1975); Lamma v. State, 46 Neb. 236, 64 N.W. 956 (1895). See also Handley v. State, 96 Ala. 48, 11 So. 322 (1892); Ark Code Ann § 5-2-613 (1987).

[72]Wayne R. LaFave & Austin W. Scott, Criminal Law § 5.10.

[73]See, generally, Wayne R. LaFave & Austin W. Scott Criminal Law § 5.10, at 472. Even where deadly force would not be initially appropriate (for example, in the arrest of a misdemeanant), if life threatening resistance is offered, deadly force may become justified on a self-defense basis. Wayne R. LaFave & Austin W. Scott, Criminal Law § 5.10(a), at 471; Arnold H. Loewy, Criminal Law in a Nutshell § 5.07, at 77-8 (2d ed 1987).

[74]Wayne R. LaFave & Austin W. Scott, Criminal Law § 5.10(a), at 472.

§ 2:5

defense of property.[75] It may also be used by law enforcement personnel to effectuate a lawful arrest, to prevent an escape from custody, or to maintain civil order.[76]

These standards for the use of force have applicability to a prison context. Thus, deadly force is unwarranted, except where essential to protect life,[77] and also, possibly, when necessary to prevent the escape of a dangerous felon from prison. Therefore, in the overwhelming majority of cases in which force is permissible, the force employed must not be lethal. Furthermore, prison officials are not justified in using far greater force than necessary to accomplish a lawful purpose.[78] The words of the Ninth Circuit Court of Appeals that "guards may use force only in proportion to the need in each situation"[79] capture one of the factors that courts must examine in determining whether force

---

[75]W. P. Keeton, Prosser & Keeton on Torts §§ 19, 20, 21 (5th ed 1984).

[76]Wayne R. LaFave & Austin W. Scott, Criminal Law § 5.10(a), (b), (c).

[77]See, e.g., Jeffers v. Gomez, 267 F.3d 895 (9th Cir. 2001) (holding that shooting inmate in the neck was justifiable when shots were fired to prevent inmates from stabbing other inmates).

[78]National Sheriffs' Assn, Inmates' Legal Rights 21 (1987) ("the force used must be only the smallest degree or amount required to accomplish [legitimate] ends under the circumstances"). See also American Correctional Assn., Standards for Adult Correctional Institutions Standard 3-4198 (2002) (force should only be used as a last resort).

[79]Hoptowit v. Ray, 682 F.2d 1237, 1251, 9 Fed. R. Evid. Serv. 1511 (9th Cir. 1982). See also Johnston v. Lucas, 786 F.2d 1254 (5th Cir. 1986) (amount of force used should be proportionate to the need); Norris v. District of Columbia, 737 F.2d 1148 (D.C. Cir. 1984) (amount of force that may be used varies with the necessities of the situation); Williams v. Henry, 596 F. Supp. 925 (N.D. Ill. 1984) (unlawful for guard to use greater force than necessary to accomplish a lawful purpose). But see Hines v. Boothe, 841 F.2d 623 (5th Cir. 1988) (holding that guard is not liable even if he was the instigator; it does not matter "who started it" because the Eighth Amendment does not protect against "rough and unfair treatment"); Zimmerman v. Tippecanoe Sheriff's Dept., 25 F. Supp.

§ 2:5

is excessive.

Force may be excessive and, therefore, unreasonable even if the prisoner was the original aggressor.[80] This can occur when the situation provoked by the inmate is under control, but the guard in the fury of the moment fails to exercise professional restraint and continues to inflict blows on the inmate.[81] Even when force is used to compel compliance with a lawful order, for example, the force employed must not be excessive.[82] Thus, it may be permissible to use coercive force to grab the inmate or

---

2d 915 (N.D. Ind. 1998) (after an unsuccessful escape attempt, pretrial detainee asserted that defendant prison guard violated his Eighth Amendment rights when he was handcuffed so tightly that he suffered permanent radial nerve damage to his wrist; court denied summary judgment for the defendant, saying that a finder of fact could conclude that placing handcuffs on an inmate, if done with sufficient force, could cause permanent nerve injury).

[80]See, e.g., Ridley v. Leavitt, 631 F.2d 358, 360 (4th Cir. 1980) ("While prison officials should be afforded broad discretion in maintaining order and discipline . . . we do not think that any amount of force is justified, especially if the threat of disorder has subsided."); Jones v. Huff, 789 F. Supp. 526 (N.D. N.Y. 1992) (continued beating and stripping of an inmate after he is handcuffed is unlawful); King v. Meekins, 593 F. Supp. 59 (D.D.C. 1984).

[81]For this reason, a prisoner's complaint regarding excessive force cannot be dismissed because the inmate is convicted for assault during the incident. In such a case, the inmate's claim that the guard continued to beat him after the need to do so no longer existed is not adjudicated in the inmate's criminal trial, since the use of unlawful force to subdue the inmate would not have been a defense to the assault charge. Ridley v. Leavitt, 631 F.2d 358 (4th Cir. 1980). See also Bogan v. Stroud, 958 F.2d 180 (7th Cir. 1992) (plea of guilty to attempted murder charge did not establish that prisoner was not unjustifiably beaten during the incident).

[82]See, e.g., Triplett v. District of Columbia, 108 F.3d 1450 (D.C. Cir. 1997) (prison official used "excessive force" when inmate disobeyed prison rules; use of force resulted in a broken neck and permanent loss of feeling in inmate's left arm; court affirmed the lower court's determination that the plaintiff was entitled to $135,000 in damages); Hill v. Shelander, 992 F.2d 714 (7th Cir. 1993) (when inmate refuses to leave his cell it is not permissible to pull the inmate from the cell by the shoulder and hair, slam the inmate's head against the bars of an adjacent cell and strike him

to immobilize him,[83] but it would be impermissible to use injurious force, for example, by inflicting pain or injury until he follows orders.[84] Nevertheless, in these

---

twice in the face and knee him in the groin); Mitchell v. Maynard, 80 F.3d 1433, 34 Fed. R. Serv. 3d 1018 (10th Cir. 1996) (material issue of fact precluded summary judgment regarding Eighth Amendment violation where inmate alleged that officials beat him as they transported him across the yard, naked, and shackled; court noted that at that point inmate posed no threat to prison guards); see, e.g., Madrid v. Gomez, 889 F. Supp. 1146 (N.D. Cal. 1995), mandamus denied, 103 F.3d 828 (9th Cir. 1996) (beating unarmed prisoners after disciplinary incidents were over, a bath of scalding water administered to a mentally ill prisoner, and the use of a taser gun to extract a prisoner from a cell after he did not return his meal tray were examples of excessive force); Holmes v. Dailey, 1998 WL 709621 (D. Kan. 1998) (where, after plaintiff, using improperly acquired handcuff key to free his arms and legs, bolted from transport van, defendant deputy fired three shots, striking plaintiff in the leg with the third shot, and as plaintiff stumbled and slowed, defendant fired a fourth shot paralyzing plaintiff from the chest down, summary judgment denied defendant because plaintiff met his burden to demonstrate that defendant shot plaintiff "maliciously and sadistically for the very purpose of causing harm," thus violating plaintiff's Eighth Amendment right against infliction of cruel and unusual punishment); Evans v. Hennessy, 934 F. Supp. 127 (D. Del. 1996) (prison official "maliciously and sadistically" sought to cause harm when he hit an inmate twice in the face with a clenched fist; prison official claimed he sought to maintain order and control of the inmate who was verbally abusing prison officials and attempting to incite other inmates; but court held that under the circumstances the force was not applied in a "good faith effort to maintain or restore discipline" because the prison official was surrounded by at least three other prison guards and the inmate made no attempt to physically assault a prison official; court awarded plaintiff $7,500 in damages).

[83]See, e.g., Carson v. Harrington, 12 Fed. Appx. 299 (6th Cir. 2001) (force used was warranted and reasonable where the defendant grabbed the prisoner, threw him to the ground, and sat on him until help arrived, and where the prisoner started the altercation by kicking the guard in the groin).

[84]For example, the district court for the Northern District of New York held that that it is impermissible to use excessive force to compel compliance with an order. The case involved a juvenile who when he disobeyed an order, was put in a physical restraint

§ 2:5   RIGHTS OF PRISONERS, THIRD EDITION

circumstances some of the cases appear to give defendants a wide berth in assessing the moment when a legitimate response to inmate provocation crosses the line into revenge.[85]

Another unresolved question is whether the Eighth

---

hold a half an hour, rendering the boy unconscious. When the boy was revived, he remained sluggish, and couldn't answer simple questions correctly. An hour later, while in the cafeteria, the boy again disobeyed an order and was once again put in a restraining hold. He was once again rendered unconscious, but this time, he could not be revived. He was in a coma for two months, and suffers from permanent physical and brain injuries. Employee claims of threatening behavior by the boy were not sufficient to show that they used only the force necessary to restore discipline, as the employees were much larger than the boy, and they kept the boy in the hold long after he had gone limp and had become unresponsive. Jackson v. Johnson, 118 F. Supp. 2d 278 (N.D. N.Y. 2000), aff'd in part, appeal dismissed in part, 13 Fed. Appx. 51 (2d Cir. 2001). See also Fisher v. Koehler, 692 F. Supp. 1519 (S.D. N.Y. 1988).

[85]See, e.g., Lunsford v. Bennett, 17 F.3d 1574 (7th Cir. 1994) (where prisoner flooded cell, being shackled to bars of cell and subsequently doused with water while a cleanup was underway did not violate the Eighth Amendment even though alternatives in retrospect were available); Scarbough v. Halliburton, 2001 WL 283105 (N.D. Tex. 2001)(consistent and escalating refusal to cooperate, that is, refusal to comply with lawful orders, especially in the face of repeated warnings, may justify some use of force); Miller v. Leathers, 885 F.2d 151 (4th Cir. 1989), reh'g granted, 893 F.2d 57 (4th Cir. 1989) and on reh'g, 913 F.2d 1085 (4th Cir. 1990) (holding that deference should be accorded prison guards in making the determination as to whether the inmate's provocation and threats of violence are ended); Williams v. Kelley, 624 F.2d 695 (5th Cir. 1980) (guards not liable where they accidentally strangled a prisoner while trying to subdue him); Shearin v. Pennington, 867 F. Supp. 1250 (E.D. Va. 1994) (prison officer's actions of thrusting metal window rod into inmate's cell and subsequently lunging at inmate after inmate had thrown dissolved human waste at the officer was not cruel and unusual punishment). Conversely, the use of force to retaliate is forbidden. Mitchell v. Keane, 974 F. Supp. 332 (S.D. N.Y. 1997), aff'd, 175 F.3d 1008 (2d Cir. 1999) (before use-of-force incident, plaintiff was involved in altercation with another guard; court held that Eighth Amendment does not allow guards to use force as retaliation, therefore, plaintiff's claim not dismissed).

Amendment is violated by the isolated and unauthorized beating of an inmate by a rogue prison guard. There is some old authority for the proposition that this does not violate the Eighth Amendment.[86] The issue was raised in *Hudson,* but the Supreme Court found it unnecessary to reach it.[87] On analysis, however, the argument has little to recommend it. Judge Posner, writing for the Seventh Circuit, observed that there is no common sense reason for such a position. As he wrote: "[i]f a guard decided to supplement a prisoner's official punishment by beating him, this would be punishment . . ." whether it was authorized by higher officials or not.[88] The same undoubtedly can be said for an isolated case of brutality by a prison guard; even though it is isolated, it is difficult to understand why it is not infliction of punishment by a state actor. The questions of authorization and of the prevalence of misuse of force are surely germane to the liability of supervisors or the governmental entity, but not the question of whether the Constitution has been violated.[89]

---

[86]George v. Evans, 633 F.2d 413, 416 (5th Cir. 1980) ("[A] single unauthorized assault by a guard does not constitute cruel and unusual punishment . . ."); Johnson v. Glick, 481 F.2d 1028, 1032 (2d Cir. 1973); Townsend v. Frame, 587 F. Supp. 369, 371 (E.D. Pa. 1984).

[87]Hudson v. McMillian, 503 U.S. 1, 112 S. Ct. 995, 1001-02, 117 L. Ed. 2d 156 (1992).

[88]Duckworth v. Franzen, 780 F.2d 645, 652 (7th Cir. 1985). The Tenth Circuit gave another reason for rejecting the argument. In Estelle v. Gamble, 429 U.S. 97, 97 S. Ct. 285, 50 L. Ed. 2d 251 (1976), the Supreme Court held that a prison guard's deliberate indifference to a known serious medical need violates the Eighth Amendment. If an individual's unauthorized denial of medical care can violate the Constitution, it is difficult to understand why an unauthorized beating should be immune. Sampley v. Ruettgers, 704 F.2d 491, 495 (10th Cir. 1983).

[89]When guard brutality occurs, other prison officials who are aware of it have the responsibility to intervene. If they do not, they may be held responsible for the ensuing injury. See, e.g., Webb v. Hiykel, 713 F.2d 405 (8th Cir. 1983) (holding that guard had a responsibility to protect an inmate subject to his charge

§ 2:5   RIGHTS OF PRISONERS, THIRD EDITION

On the other end of the scale from isolated acts of brutality of prison guards is the situation that arises when physical brutality by guards becomes "part of the daily routine" of prison life.[90] When the state allows the operation of its prisons to deteriorate to that point, there is no doubt that the courts have authority to act vigorously to remedy the problem.[91] Remedies in such

---

from physical assault by other officers, despite the fact that the officers were his superiors); Murray v. Koehler, 734 F. Supp. 605 (S.D. N.Y. 1990) (holding that supervising official is liable for the brutality of his subordinate if the supervising official has knowledge of the propensity of the guard to employ excessive force); Korin v. Department of Corrections, State Correctional Inst. at Graterford, 137 Pa. Commw. 94, 585 A.2d 559 (1991) (guard who observed, but failed to report, excessive use of force by other guards was properly suspended from his position).

[90]Hoptowit v. Ray, 682 F.2d 1237, 1251, 9 Fed. R. Evid. Serv. 1511 (9th Cir. 1982). See also Carty v. Farrelly, 957 F. Supp. 727, 22 A.D.D. 333 (D.V.I. 1997) (prison officials at the Criminal Justice Complex (CJC) regularly beat inmates with batons; court held that the CJC prison officials "maliciously and sadistically" sought to cause harm, thus violating the Eighth Amendment, and held the defendants in civil contempt for their failure to comply with a previous court order to remedy such continuing abuses); Ruiz v. Johnson, 37 F. Supp. 2d 855 (S.D. Tex. 1999), rev'd on other grounds and remanded, 243 F.3d 941 (5th Cir. 2001) (holding in a class action context that prisoners in the Texas prison system were subjected to excessive force in violation of their Eighth Amendment rights, where inmates presented evidence of broken jaws, bruised faces, broken bones and other injuries shown to be the result of wholly unnecessary physical aggression by prison employees; pattern of uncalled for "slamming, hitting and kicking" by corrections officers was found to be so prevalent as to implicate the Constitution; such a culture of sadistic and malicious violence, pervading the Texas prison system, violated contemporary standards of decency).

[91]See, e.g., Hoptowit v. Ray, 682 F.2d 1237, 1251, 9 Fed. R. Evid. Serv. 1511 (9th Cir. 1982); Spain v. Procunier, 600 F.2d 189 (9th Cir. 1979); Inmates of Attica Correctional Facility v. Rockefeller, 453 F.2d 12 (2d Cir. 1971); Ruiz v. Johnson, 37 F. Supp. 2d 855 (S.D. Tex. 1999), rev'd on other grounds and remanded, 243 F.3d 941 (5th Cir. 2001) (holding in a class action context that prisoners in the Texas prison system were subjected

CRUEL & UNUSUAL PUNISHMENT § 2:5

cases may include damages, injunctive relief, or both. In one significant case, the West Virginia Supreme Court issued an innovative order requiring psychological testing of all correctional employee applicants as well as at least annual reexamination during their employment.[92] Those found psychologically unsuitable, or those whose brutality was established in proceedings consistent with civil service regulations, were to be discharged.[93] The court also warned that it would consider releasing prisoners if constitutional violations continued.[94] In another case involving allegations of systemic violence against inmates by prison guards, a

---

to excessive force in violation of their Eighth Amendment rights, where inmates presented evidence of broken jaws, bruised faces, broken bones and other injuries shown to be the result of wholly unnecessary physical aggression by prison employees; pattern of uncalled for "slamming, hitting and kicking" by corrections officers was found to be so prevalent as to implicate the Constitution; such a culture of sadistic and malicious violence, pervading the Texas prison system, violated contemporary standards of decency); Harrah v. Leverette, 165 W. Va. 665, 271 S.E.2d 322 (1980).

[92]Harrah v. Leverette, 165 W. Va. 665, 271 S.E.2d 322, 332 (1980). See also ABA, Standards for Criminal Justice Standard 6.12(c) (1986) (requiring physical, mental and temperamental evaluation of guards to determine their fitness to use force); Natl. Advisory Commn. on Criminal Justice Standards and Goals, Corrections Standard 2.4(1973) (recommending periodic evaluation of staff and reassignment or discharge of those who pose a threat to inmates).

[93]Harrah v. Leverette, 165 W. Va. 665, 271 S.E.2d 322 (1980). But compare Hoptowit v. Ray, 682 F.2d 1237, 1251, 9 Fed. R. Evid. Serv. 1511 (9th Cir. 1982) (screening, testing, and training of guards is not constitutionally required).

[94]Harrah v. Leverette, 165 W. Va. 665, 271 S.E.2d 322, 332 (1980). It is also within the state's authority to criminally prosecute guards who employ excessive force. Even if not convicted, the guard may still be discharged for the transgression. See Smith v. Roosevelt County, 242 Mont. 27, 788 P.2d 895 (1990) (holding that guard may be dismissed for "gross inefficiency in the performance" of his duties even though he was acquitted in criminal trial). But see New Mexico, ex rel. Ortiz v. Reed, 524 U.S. 151, 118 S. Ct. 1860, 141 L. Ed. 2d 131 (1998), where the Supreme Court held that state courts have no power to prevent extradition of an inmate

§ 2:5 Rights of Prisoners, Third Edition

district court approved a comprehensive consent decree that contained numerous provisions designed to address the problem.[95] In cases such as these, where it

---

to another state even if the inmate claims that he will be subject to prison violence if he is returned. In *Reed,* the plaintiff was sentenced to twenty-five years in the Ohio correctional system for armed robbery and theft of drugs. In 1992 he was paroled. The following year, Ohio prison authorities informed him that his parole status was to be revoked. Consequently, the plaintiff fled from Ohio to New Mexico. Ohio sought extradition and the Governor of New Mexico issued a warrant directing the plaintiff's return to Ohio. In October 1994 he was arrested. He sought a writ of habeas corpus from the New Mexico state district court. The plaintiff alleged that he was not a fugitive for purposes of extradition because he fled under duress, believing that he would sustain physical harm if returned to Ohio prison, and that Ohio authorities intended to revoke his parole without due process of law. The New Mexico state district court granted the plaintiff's request for a writ of habeas corpus and ordered his release from custody. The Supreme Court of New Mexico affirmed the lower court and declared that the plaintiff was a "refugee from injustice." The Supreme Court of the United States granted certiorari and unanimously reversed. In a per curium opinion, the Court held that the determination of whether the plaintiff was in danger of prison harm could not be considered by the New Mexico courts. The Court noted that in "case after case we have held that claims relating to what actually happened in the demanding State, the law of the demanding State, and what may be expected to happen in the demanding State when the fugitive returns, are issues that must be tried in the courts of that State and not in those of the asylum State." New Mexico, ex rel. Ortiz v. Reed, 524 U.S. 151, 118 S. Ct. 1860, 141 L. Ed. 2d 131 (1998).

[95]Sheppard v. Phoenix, 1998 WL 397846 (S.D. N.Y. 1998) (order approving stipulation of settlement of class action law suit alleging a pattern of brutality in the New York City Department of Correction's Central Punitive Segregation Unit ("CPSU"); the settlement (1) required the department to direct and train staff to respond to inmate misconduct without force, and if force was necessary, to utilize control techniques that minimized injuries; (2) required the development of an operating manual; (3) required a written plan for provision of mental health services; (4) prohibited withholding access to services in retaliation for misconduct; (5) required a system of video monitoring of staff interactions with inmates; (6) imposed requirements to ensure that experienced staff

can be established that systemic breakdowns in training or supervision led to the use of excessive force, liability can be imposed on supervisory personnel even if they did not themselves inflict the violence.[96] Since these systemic failures are "conditions of confinement," the proper standard to be applied is the deliberate indifference standard, not the malicious and sadistic standard.[97]

---

were assigned to the unit; (7) mandated transfer of staff with poor records; (8) required review and evaluation of staff on a regular basis to weed out incompetents; (9) required detailed reports of use of force; (10) required collection of physical evidence of use of force; (11) required detailed investigations of use of force; (12) established an "integrity control officer" for the unit to act as the "eyes and ears" of the Investigation Division; (13) established a computerized record keeping system; (14) imposed time frames for resolution of disciplinary charges against staff; and (15) required that outside experts be employed to assist the department in complying with the settlement). See also Fisher v. Koehler, 692 F. Supp. 1519 (S.D. N.Y. 1988) (Correctional Institution for Men); Jackson v. Montemagno, CV 85-2384 (Order Approving Stipulation for Entry of Judgment, November 26, 1991) (Brooklyn House of Detention); Reynolds v. Ward, 81 Civ. 101 (Order and Consent Judgment, October 1, 1990) (Bellevue Prison Psychiatric Ward).

[96]See, e.g,, Madrid v. Gomez, 889 F. Supp. 1146 (N.D. Cal. 1995), mandamus denied, 103 F.3d 828 (9th Cir. 1996) (where prison officials lacked written policies on proper staff training and staff evaluation standards, there could not be adequate supervision and safeguards to control the use of force within the prison).

[97]Estate of Davis by Ostenfeld v. Delo, 115 F.3d 1388 (8th Cir. 1997) (finding liability based on a deliberate indifference theory when a "movement team" repeatedly struck Davis as he was lying motionless on the floor; the other officers failed to stop the assault, and did not report it to supervisors); Vineyard v. County of Murray, Ga., 990 F.2d 1207, 1212 (11th Cir. 1993) (police department had no policy for logging complaints against officers so that problems could be corrected; this was held to be deliberate indifference); Noguera v. Hasty, 2001 WL 243535 (S.D. N.Y. 2001) (inmate claimed a guard raped and sexually abused her, then retaliated against her when she reported it to prison officials, and that two supervisory officials were deliberately indifferent to serious risks of allowing guard to remain on duty; supervisory officials claimed they were not personally involved, as the last attack occurred before their tenure at facility began; court disagreed, holding that

§ 2:5   Rights of Prisoners, Third Edition

Finally, if a claim is made out, it is appropriate to award compensatory damages and in proper cases punitive damages for violation of the right to be free from excessive force.[98]

Tear Gas, Mace, Stun Guns

A question that has arisen with some frequency concerns whether prison officials are ever justified in using tear gas, mace, and stun guns to subdue prisoners. While the unnecessary use of tear gas and other chemical agents has been held unlawful,[99] courts have rejected the view that these agents should not be allowed in a prison arsenal.[100] Chemical agents have been permitted "in non-dangerous quantities" to

---

inmate sufficiently alleged that possibility for harm still existed at time the two officials arrived at facility, and that they had been informed of the danger; officials can be held liable for deliberate indifference that creates a serious risk of substantial harm, even where no actual harm occurs).

[98]See e.g., Cooper v. Casey, 97 F.3d 914 (7th Cir. 1996) (upholding an award of compensatory and punitive damages in the total sum of $130,000); Johnson v. Howard, 24 Fed. Appx. 480 (6th Cir. 2001) (upholding an award of $15,000 in compensatory damages and $300,000 in punitive damages). But see, Johnson v. Breeden, 280 F.3d 1308 (11th Cir. 2002) (upholding an award of $25,000 in compensatory damages but overturning award of $35,000 in punitive damages. The court found that punitive damages were prospective relief, and must be no larger than necessary to deter the kind of violations of the federal right that occurred in the case).

[99]See, e.g., Ruiz v. Estelle, 503 F. Supp. 1265, 1305 (S.D. Tex. 1980), aff'd in part, rev'd in part on other grounds, 679 F.2d 1115, 10 Fed. R. Evid. Serv. 1483 (5th Cir. 1982), amended in part, vacated in part on other grounds, 688 F.2d 266 (5th Cir. 1982) (citing cases); Spain v. Procunier, 600 F.2d 189, 195-96 (9th Cir. 1979).

[100]See, e.g., Soto v. Dickey, 744 F.2d 1260, 1270 (7th Cir. 1984) (refusing to ban the use of mace and holding that "the appropriateness of the use must be determined by the facts and circumstances of the case"); Lock v. Jenkins, 641 F.2d 488 (7th Cir. 1981) (upholding the use of tear gas to restrain inmates who were inciting a riot but not for minor offenses such as stopping an inmate from shouting); Spain v. Procunier, 600 F.2d 189 (9th Cir. 1979); Blair-El v. Tinsman, 666 F. Supp. 1218 (S.D. Ill. 1987).

CRUEL & UNUSUAL PUNISHMENT § 2:5

prevent future danger to security and even in "dangerous quantities" where the use of deadly force might be resorted to instead.[101] Nevertheless, because of the potential for wide dispersal of these gases, care must be taken to ensure that innocent inmates are not made victims of their use.[102] Prison officials also must take steps to ensure that treatment is promptly given to

---

[101]See, e.g., Collins v. Kahelski, 828 F. Supp. 614 (E.D. Wis. 1993), (holding that the use of tear gas is a reasonable means of quelling a prison disturbance); Cummings v. Caspari, 821 F. Supp. 1291, 1293 (E.D. Mo. 1993) (summary judgment was granted in a case where force was used to restrain a prisoner, including spraying mace, because the force was used in good faith in an effort to restore discipline and not maliciously or sadistically to cause harm); Price v. Dixon, 961 F. Supp. 894 (E.D. N.C. 1997) (where inmate was disorderly and threw urine on prison officials, use of mace to restrain inmate was appropriate under the circumstances; further, denying the inmate the ability to wash after being sprayed with mace did not violate the Eighth Amendment; accordingly, the defendant's motion for summary judgment was granted); Norris v. Detrick, 918 F. Supp. 977 (N.D. W. Va. 1996), aff'd, 108 F.3d 1373 (4th Cir. 1997) (prison guards did not violate Eighth Amendment where inmate alleged that guards fired two doses of CN gas at inmates; court noted that an inmate, who was proficient in martial arts, had refused to return to his cell for lock down and instead charged an officer); Soto v. Dickey, 744 F.2d 1260, 1270 (7th Cir. 1984); Norris v. District of Columbia, 737 F.2d 1148 (D.C. Cir. 1984) (use of mace under restricted conditions is not unconstitutional); Peterson v. Davis, 551 F. Supp. 137, 12 Fed. R. Evid. Serv. 112 (D. Md. 1982), judgment aff'd, 729 F.2d 1453 (4th Cir. 1984) (upholding use of tear gas to remove recalcitrant inmates from dormitory). Courts have refused to draw the line against the use of tear gas in a closed cell area, although this use of tear gas is obviously more dangerous than using it in a more open area. Lock v. Jenkins, 641 F.2d 488 (7th Cir. 1981). But see McCargo v. Mister, 462 F. Supp. 813 (D. Md. 1978) (use of crop dusting gas against inmates without justification violates prisoners' rights).

[102]See, e.g., Holloway v. Lockhart, 813 F.2d 874, 22 Fed. R. Evid. Serv. 959, 7 Fed. R. Serv. 3d 453 (8th Cir. 1987) (innocent inmates who were exposed to tear gas that was used to quell a disturbance by three other inmates stated a claim under the Eighth Amendment).

§ 2:5 RIGHTS OF PRISONERS, THIRD EDITION

people who have been gassed and need help.[103]

Stun or Taser guns, which administer an electrical shock, are another means of subduing inmates. These are relatively new devises whose long-term effects are unknown. Indeed, there is some evidence that they may not be as safe as has been generally assumed.[104] Courts have recognized that the "long-term effects [of Tasers] are unknown" and that research may "uncover . . . evidence of an adverse long-term effect that would call into question the use of Tasers."[105] In the absence of such proof, however, two circuit courts of appeals, in questionable opinions, approved the use of Tasers by prison officials in subduing inmates, at least in situations where "resort to even greater force may be necessary."[106] A study conducted by the Association of the Bar of The City of New York concluded that without

---

[103]Cooper v. Casey, 97 F.3d 914 (7th Cir. 1996) (where cellmates sustained cuts, muscular pain and burning sensation in eyes and skin as a result of being sprayed by mace and assaulted by prison guards such conduct constituted excessive force; further, court held that two-day delay in providing plaintiffs medical assistance after beating violated Eighth Amendment; court awarded each plaintiff $5,000 in compensatory damages and $60,000 in punitive damages).

[104]See, e.g., Jesus Amena, "L.A. Man Dies after Jolts from Police Taser Gun," Los Angeles Herald Examiner, Aug 29, 1986, at A1; Steve Eddy, "Taser Guns No Panacea for Police," Orange County Register, June 15, 1986, at A1 (reporting that five persons in Los Angeles had died after having been shot with Taser darts).

[105]Michenfelder v. Sumner, 860 F.2d 328, 336 (9th Cir. 1988) (disapproved of by, Duamutef v. Leonardo, 1993 WL 428509 (N.D. N.Y. 1993)); accord McKenzie v. City of Milpitas, 738 F. Supp. 1293, 1298-99 (N.D. Cal. 1990), aff'd, 953 F.2d 1387 (9th Cir. 1992). Tasers have been outlawed in New York because of concern about the effect of their use on persons with heart problems. People v. Sullivan, 116 A.D.2d 101, 500 N.Y.S.2d 644, 647 (1st Dep't 1986), order rev'd on other grounds, 68 N.Y.2d 495, 510 N.Y.S.2d 518, 503 N.E.2d 74 (1986). Because of similar concerns, they are classified by the Georgia state prison system as deadly weapons. McCranie v. State, 172 Ga. App. 188, 322 S.E.2d 360, 361 n1 (1984).

[106]See, e.g., Caldwell v. Moore, 968 F.2d 595, 600 (6th Cir. 1992); Michenfelder v. Sumner, 860 F.2d 328, 336 (9th Cir. 1988)

serious medical safeguards the use of stun shields posed an unacceptable risk of harm.[107]

Without proof that stun guns can be safely employed when used as they are intended, the use of these devices by prison officials expose inmates to the possible needless infliction of injury and even death. There are, for these reasons, cases holding that the use of these weapons can violate the Eighth Amendment.[108] These courts have noted that weaponry such as stun guns, Tasers, high-pressure hoses, gas, and batons, "though legitimate forms of control in certain circumstances, become instruments of brutality when used indiscriminately against a defenseless prisoner. . . .[A prisoner's abusive language] assuredly did not justify subjecting him to steady blasts of water from two high-pressure hoses or beating him savagely around the head and body with billy clubs."[109]

(disapproved of by, Duamutef v. Leonardo, 1993 WL 428509 (N.D. N.Y. 1993)). See also Rubins v. Roetker, 737 F. Supp. 1140 (D. Colo. 1990), aff'd, 936 F.2d 583 (10th Cir. 1991). See also Jasper v. Thalacker, 999 F.2d 353 (8th Cir. 1993) (holding use of stun gun not unconstitutional because it was not used maliciously or sadistically); Collins v. Scott, 961 F. Supp. 1009 (E.D. Tex. 1997) (no constitutional violation when officers used stun shield when plaintiff refused to submit to strip search, since the shield was the least restrictive means of maintaining control of the prisoner);

[107]Committee on Corrections, The Use of Stun Shields on Rikers Island, The Record (2001).

[108]Skrtich v. Thornton, 280 F.3d 1295 (11th Cir. 2002) (absent any evidence that force was necessary, Eighth Amendment violated when prisoner was shocked by electric shield and subsequently beaten, sustaining serious injury); Hickey v. Reeder, 12 F.3d 754, 758-59 (8th Cir. 1993) (shooting prisoner with stun gun because he refused to clean cell violated Eighth Amendment).

[109]Slakan v. Porter, 737 F.2d 368, 372, 16 Fed. R. Evid. Serv. 59 (4th Cir. 1984); see also Hickey v. Reeder, 12 F.3d 754, 757 (8th Cir. 1993) (use of force on inmate who refused to sweep his cell unconstitutional: "This is exactly the sort of torment without marks with which the Supreme Court was concerned in [Hudson] and which, if inflicted without legitimate reason, supports the Eighth Amendment's objective component."); U.S. v. Tines, 70 F.3d 891,

Sexual Assault

Forced sexual contact is certainly an assault[110] that can cause severe physical and psychological harm.[111] "[S]exual abuse of a prisoner by a corrections officer has no legitimate penological purpose and is 'simply not part of the penalty that criminal offenders pay for their offenses against society.'"[112] . For this reason, courts are clear that "severe or repetitive sexual abuse of an inmate by a prison official" is an Eighth Amendment violation.[113] Sexual assault, of course, includes rape.

---

43 Fed. R. Evid. Serv. 478, 1995 FED App. 339P (6th Cir. 1995) (affirming criminal convictions of jail guards for beating and stunning prisoners as punishment for stealing another prisoner's shoes); Madrid v. Gomez, 889 F. Supp. 1146 (N.D. Cal. 1995), mandamus denied, 103 F.3d 828 (9th Cir. 1996) (Eighth Amendment violation found in staff's use of force at Pelican Bay Security Housing Unit based on record of staff beatings, use of "fetal restraints," use of firearms, and use of batons, gas and Taser guns unnecessarily and sometimes recklessly in cell extractions where there was no imminent security risk).

[110]An "assault" is a "violent physical . . . attack." Webster's Ninth New Collegiate Dictionary 108 (1986).

[111]Boddie v. Schnieder, 105 F.3d 857, 860-61 (2d Cir. 1997).

[112]Boddie v. Schnieder, 105 F.3d 857, 861 (2d Cir. 1997) (quoting Farmer v. Brennan, 511 U.S. 825, 114 S. Ct. 1970, 128 L. Ed. 2d 811 (1994)).

[113]Boddie v. Schnieder, 105 F.3d 857, 861 (2d Cir. 1997). See also Mathie v. Fries, 935 F. Supp. 1284 (E.D. N.Y. 1996), aff'd, 121 F.3d 808 (2d Cir. 1997), where a former inmate brought suit claiming that the prison director sexually abused him, causing him emotional distress. The plaintiff met with the director 25 to 30 times. During the first few meetings, the director would hold the plaintiff's hand and rub his thighs. Subsequently, the defendant rubbed the plaintiff's genitals and tried to perform oral sex on him. The final episode that led to the suit happened in mid-March almost two months later. At this encounter the defendant locked the door after the plaintiff entered. He then "grabbed him from behind in a bear hug, handcuffed him to two vertical pipes in a corner of the room, pulled down his own and plaintiff's pants, rubbed lotion on their bodies, and anally penetrated plaintiff." From this the plaintiff suffered physical pain and bleeding in the anal area for the following week. The plaintiff informed other

CRUEL & UNUSUAL PUNISHMENT § 2:5

But it also includes "unwanted physical contact of a sexual nature such as fondling of the breasts and/or

---

prison officials about the assault but no action was ever taken. The district court awarded the plaintiff $250,000 in compensatory damages and $500,000 in punitive damages, and the Second Circuit affirmed the judgment but reduced the amount of punitive damages to $200,000.

In Walker v. Taylorville Correctional Center, 129 F.3d 410 (7th Cir. 1997), an inmate brought an action for sexual assault, retaliation and unfair discipline. The plaintiff claimed that a prison counselor sexually assaulted him when he went to her for help concerning threats from other inmates. He claimed that she rubbed his arm and called him "honey." He further alleged that on another occasion she came into his cell while he was sleeping, grabbed his genitals, and stated "you know you like it " Finally, he stated that she saw him in the shower and said, "I've seen bigger, but you have enough for me." The Court of Appeals affirmed the dismissal of retaliation and unfair discipline claims, holding that the plaintiff produced no evidence to support his claim;, however, the court reinstated his sexual assault claim, holding that his allegations "satisfy the threshold standard for sexual harassment claims in section 1983" actions.

In Collins v. Union County Jail, 150 N.J. 407, 696 A.2d 625 (1997), an inmate brought an action against a county jail after allegedly being raped by a corrections officer. The incident occurred when the plaintiff was escorted from his living area to a consultation area. Once there, the guard began to fondle and kiss the plaintiff. Next the guard pulled down the plaintiff's pants and sodomized him. The plaintiff suffered no physical injury but did suffer psychological problems. The plaintiff was awarded $100,000 in compensatory damages, $150,000 in punitive damages, and $3,220 for medical expenses. The New Jersey Supreme Court reinstated the jury verdict.

See also English v. Colorado Dept. of Corrections, 248 F.3d 1002 (10th Cir. 2001), where the plaintiff, an African-American correction officer who was fired for having sex with a prisoner produced enough evidence to make out a prima facie case of racial discrimination, but did not show that the proffered legitimate nondiscriminatory reason for termination was pretextual. The fact that one white female officer was not fired after kissing an inmate did not suffice, since that conduct was not of comparable seriousness to multiple acts of sexual intercourse.

§ 2:5

genital areas."[114] The proscription against sexual assault protects inmates from homosexual as well as heterosexual assault;[115] and protects male as well as female inmates. Although the protection from sexual assault is well established, in questionable rulings courts have been unwilling to hold that consensual sexual relations between prison guards and inmates as an Eighth Amendment violation.[116] The rulings are questionable because it is doubtful that in a prison setting where guards and prison officials have such unbridled control over inmates that an inmate who has been propositioned by a prison official is in a position to freely "consent" to sexual contact.[117] Recognizing this in a number of jurisdictions, the legislature has decreed that it is a criminal offense for corrections officials to

---

[114]Moore-Bey v. Washington, No. 99-2962 2000 U.S. Dist. LEXIS 13875 (D.D.C. September 19, 2000) (Eighth Amendment claim stated that prison guard squeezed plaintiff's penis and testicles); see also Women Prisoners of District of Columbia Dept. of Corrections v. District of Columbia, 877 F. Supp. 634, 98 Ed. Law Rep. 681 (D.D.C. 1994), vacated in part on other grounds, modified in part on other grounds, 899 F. Supp. 659, 104 Ed. Law Rep. 213 (D. D.C. 1995); Columbia Human Rights Law Review, A Jailhouse Lawyer's Manual, 603 (2000).

[115]Schwenk v. Hartford, 204 F.3d 1187 (9th Cir. 2000) (preoperative male-to-female transsexual sued a state prison guard and other prison authorities under 42 U.S.C. § 1983 and the Gender Motivated Violence Act (GMVA), alleging attempted rape by the male guard; guard's contention that it was not clearly established at the time of the assault that same-sex harassment of prisoners was unconstitutional did not qualify the guard for immunity).

[116]See, e.g., Fisher v. Goord, 981 F. Supp. 140 (W.D. N.Y. 1997) (inmate claimed her civil rights were violated when correction and state prison officials allegedly raped and sexually abused her; plaintiff's claim failed because the sexual relations with prison staff were consensual; the one instance which was not consensual was a kiss).

[117]See e.g., Paz v. Weir, 137 F. Supp. 2d 782 (S.D. Tex. 2001) (summary judgment for defendant prison clergy member denied on issue of whether a sexual relationship with a female inmate was consensual; court recognized that clergy in a prison setting have tremendous power of coercion).

CRUEL & UNUSUAL PUNISHMENT § 2:5

have sexual contact with inmates without regard to whether or not the inmate "consents" to the conduct.[118]

Claims regarding verbal sexual harassment are more difficult to maintain. There is no firm rule that has yet emerged as to whether sexual harassment without physical contact can give rise to an Eighth Amendment claim, however, some commentators have argued that it should give rise to such a claim.[119] There is also some well-reasoned case law that supports this theory,[120] but the law is not yet settled. There are numerically more

---

[118]18 U.S.C. § 2241 (1999) (criminalizing sexual intercourse or any type of sexual physical contact between prisoners and any persons with "custodial supervisory or disciplinary" authority over prisoners in federal prisons); see also NY Penal Law § 130.05(3)(e)-(f) (McKinney 1997) (stating that inmates are incapable of consenting to sexual relations with prison employees). According to one survey, 27 states have similar laws. Columbia Human Rights Law Review, A Jailhouse Lawyer's Manual, 607-08 (2000).

[119]See, e.g., Amy Laderberg, The Dirty Little Secret": Why Class Actions Have Emerged as the only Viable Option for Women Inmates Attempting to Satisfy the Subjective Prong of the Eighth Amendment in Suits for Custodial Sexual Abuse, 40 Wm & Mary L Rev 323 (1998): Delisa Springfield, Sisters in Misery: Utilizing International Law to Protect United States Female Prisoners from Sexual Abuse, 10 Ind. Int'l Comp. L. Rev. 457 (2000); Iman R. Soliman, Male Officers in Women's Prisons: The Need for Segregation of Officers in Certain Positions, 10 Tex. J. Women & L. 45 (2000).

[120]See, e.g., Women Prisoners of District of Columbia Dept. of Corrections v. District of Columbia, 877 F. Supp. 634, 98 Ed. Law Rep. 681 (D.D.C. 1994), vacated in part on other grounds, modified in part on other grounds, 899 F. Supp. 659, 104 Ed. Law Rep. 213 (D.D.C. 1995) (sexual harassment in the form of sexual assaults, vulgar sexual profanities directed at female inmates by prison officials, lack of privacy within cells, and a refusal of male guards to announce themselves upon entering living areas resulting in psychological trauma to women prisoners constituted a violation of the Eighth Amendment); Galvan v. Carothers, 855 F. Supp. 285 (D. Alaska 1994), aff'd, 122 F.3d 1071 (9th Cir. 1997) (holding that sexual harassment of women held in a prison with men can violate the Eighth Amendment); Jordan v. Gardner, 986 F.2d 1521 (9th Cir. 1993) (injunction against non emergency random clothed searches of female inmates by male guards upheld as searches served no valid penological purpose, caused severe emotional

§ 2:5

cases that take the position that verbal sexual harassment is not a violation of the Eighth Amendment. *Somers v. Thurman*[121] is an example. In that case female prison guards gawked, pointed, and joked at a male inmate while performing a body cavity search. Even though this conduct was harmful, the court held that since the plaintiff did not allege that any of the officials intended to humiliate him, the conduct did not violate the Eighth Amendment.[122] This does not mean that verbal harassment is irrelevant. If an inmate is a victim of both a physical and verbal sexual advance, then the harassment is considered part and parcel of a sexual assault and is actionable.[123]

§ 2:6 —Riots

The potential for "violent confrontation and conflagra-

---

distress in some of the prisoners, and therefore violated the Eighth Amendment).

[121]Somers v. Thurman, 109 F.3d 614 (9th Cir. 1997).

[122]*Id.* A similar case is Kent v. Johnson, 821 F.2d 1220 (6th Cir. 1987) (holding that lack of privacy in showers and harassing conduct by guards did not violate the Eighth Amendment). See also Boddie v. Schnieder, 105 F.3d 857 (2d Cir. 1997) (small number of incidents where inmate was verbally harassed, touched and pressed against by a prison official without his consent was insufficient to state an Eighth Amendment violation; however, the court held such offensive conduct may be the basis for a state tort action); Jones v. Bishop, 981 F. Supp. 290 (S.D. N.Y. 1997) (inmate claimed inter alia that guards called him derogatory names such as "Super-rape-po" and "tree jumper" and they "toyed" with his recreation privileges; court held that the name calling and taunting was insufficient to support a claim).

[123]See, e.g. Daskalea v. District of Columbia, 227 F.3d 433 (D.C. Cir. 2000) (plaintiff was forced by guards to dance naked on a table in front of other inmates and guards in addition to being sexually assaulted); Galvan v. Carothers, 855 F. Supp. 285 (D. Alaska 1994), aff'd, 122 F.3d 1071 (9th Cir. 1997).

tion" is an unfortunate aspect of prison life.[1] According to one commentator, riots will continue to occur "as long as the dominant function of prisons is the custodial confinement of inmates."[2] Obviously, riots and widespread disorders are serious matters. When they come to pass, force may be necessary to regain control of the institution from rebellious inmates. There are limits, however, to the amount of force that may constitutionally be employed even in a riotous situation.

The law gives prison officials latitude in determining how best to respond to these emergencies, but they are not insulated from accountability for actions "taken in bad faith and for no legitimate purpose."[3] The leading case on this topic is *Whitley v. Albers.*[4] *Whitley,* as we

---

[Section 2:6]

[1]Jones v. North Carolina Prisoners' Labor Union, Inc., 433 U.S. 119, 132, 97 S. Ct. 2532, 53 L. Ed. 2d 629 (1977).

[2]Ira P. Robbins, Legal Aspects of Prison Riots, 16 Harv CR-CL L Rev 735 (1982). See also Vernon Fox, Why Prisoners Riot, 35 Fed Prob 1, 9-10 (Mar 1971) ("The way to make a strong bomb is to build a strong perimeter and generate pressure inside. Similarly, riots occur where . . . pressures and demands are generated in the presence of strong custodial confinement."). These predictions have unhappily proven accurate. Major riots have been, and continue to be, all too commonplace events. In February 1980, for example, a riot at the New Mexico Penitentiary in Sante Fe left 36 inmates dead and 90 inmates seriously injured. See Reid H. Montgomery, Gordon A. Crews, A History of Correctional Violence : An Examination of Reported Causes of Riots and Disturbances (American Correctional Associates 1998); Office of the Attorney General, Report of the Attorney General on February 2 and 3, 1980, Riot at the Penitentiary of New Mexico (1980); Ronald Smothers, "Talks Over Hostages Go on at Ohio Prison," Houston Chronicle, Apr 13, 1993, at A2; "Seventh Ohio Prison Riot Victim Found," Chicago Tribune, Apr 13, 1993, at 1; Sharon LaFraniere, "In Wake of Deadly Riot in Montana, Prisons Are on Edge," Washington Post, Sept 26, 1991, at A3. See also American Correctional Assn, Riots and Disturbances in Correctional Institutions (1981).

[3]Whitley v. Albers, 475 U.S. 312, 322, 106 S. Ct. 1078, 89 L. Ed. 2d 251 (1986).

[4]Whitley v. Albers, 475 U.S. 312, 106 S. Ct. 1078, 89 L. Ed. 2d 251 (1986).

§ 2:6

have seen, dealt with a prison disturbance involving the taking of a prison guard as a hostage.

In an attempt to regain control of the facility and to free the hostage, Albers, an inmate who was not a participant in the disturbance and, in fact, was attempting to assist officials, was shot in the leg and seriously injured. At trial, Albers contended that the force used was excessive. He presented evidence that there were alternative means of quelling the disturbance that should have been employed. Specifically, Albers challenged the failure of prison officials to pursue nonviolent means of calming the situation, their failure to provide a verbal warning to the inmates before firing shotgun blasts at them, and their failure to direct the officers not to shoot at him, since he had already disclosed his noninvolvement in the disturbance.

The Supreme Court by a 5-4 vote held for the prison officials. The Court placed great weight on the need for deference to prison security measures "taken in response to an actual confrontation with riotous inmates.[5] The Eighth Amendment is not violated even if there is a dispute about the "reasonableness of a particular use of force or the existence of arguably superior alternatives."[6] The Court cautioned that "[o]fficials cannot be expected to consider every contingency or minimize every risk. . .."[7] Thus, the availability of alternative approaches that might have prevented the shooting were not relevant as long as the choices that were made were not the product of an act done "maliciously and sadistically for the very purpose of causing harm."[8]

Whitley establishes that prison officials will not be held liable under the Constitution for actions taken to restore order in the face of a riot or disturbance even if

---

[5] Whitley v. Albers, 475 U.S. 312, 322, 106 S. Ct. 1078, 89 L. Ed. 2d 251 (1986).

[6] *Id.*

[7] *Id.* at 325.

[8] *Id.* at 322-21, (quoting Johnson v. Glick, 481 F.2d 1028, 1033 (2d Cir. 1973)).

CRUEL & UNUSUAL PUNISHMENT § 2:6

their behavior, in hindsight, was unreasonable, unless they deliberately set out to cause harm or acted with such disregard to the safety of inmates that maliciousness can be inferred.[9] When such a showing can be made, however, courts have found prison officials culpable.[10] This required showing was made in *Campbell v. Grammer*.[11] In that case, the Eighth Circuit Court of Appeals upheld a verdict finding the defendants liable for intentionally spraying inmates with a high-powered fire hose "with absolutely no justification for this application of force."[12] *Albers*, therefore, "does not mean that a prison riot affords prison administrators limitless authority to employ any means, no matter how brutal, to restore order."[13]

While prison officials are given a wide scope of discretion in deciding how best to quell a disturbance, courts have shown more willingness to review the circumstances that frequently arise in the aftermath of riots. Not infrequently, violence against inmates has continued to be inflicted even after the riot is repressed. A notorious example of this is found in the case of *Inmates*

---

[9]See, e.g., Al-Jundi v. Mancusi, 926 F.2d 235 (2d Cir. 1991) (the retaking of Attica and the decisions not to issue an ultimatum and to use prison guards who had a motive to be brutal was not a deliberate attempt to inflict harm and, while possibly unreasonable, was not a violation of *Albers*); Cunningham v. List, 543 F. Supp. 102 (D. Nev. 1982) (unintentional injuries to innocent inmates caused by use of tear gas to quell disturbance not actionable); Poindexter v. Woodson, 510 F.2d 464 (10th Cir. 1975); Clemmons v. Greggs, 509 F.2d 1338 (5th Cir. 1975).

[10]White v. McEwing, 1991 WL 127579 (N.D. Ill. 1991) (firing gun into crowd of fighting inmates immediately after warning shot and without waiting to determine whether order could be restored would violate the Eighth Amendment); Spain v. Procunier, 600 F.2d 189, 195 (9th Cir. 1979); Battle v. Anderson, 376 F. Supp. 402, 423 (E.D. Okla. 1974), judgment aff'd in part, rev'd in part on other grounds, 993 F.2d 1551 (10th Cir. 1993).

[11]Campbell v. Grammer, 889 F.2d 797 (8th Cir. 1989).

[12]Campbell v. Grammer, 889 F.2d 797, 802 (8th Cir. 1989).

[13]Al-Jundi v. Mancusi, 926 F.2d 235, 238 (2d Cir. 1991).

of the Attica Correctional Facility v. Rockefeller.[14] In September 1971, an insurrection occurred at New York's Attica prison with inmates capturing part of the facility and seizing numerous hostages. Efforts at negotiations failed, and corrections officials subsequently resorted to force in order to recover control of the institution, at the cost of 43 lives. The prisoners alleged that state troopers and correctional personnel had engaged in cruel and inhuman conduct in the aftermath of the riot. The actions taken by prison guards after the episode were described by the court in these words:

> Injured prisoners, some on stretchers, were struck, prodded or beaten with sticks, belts, bats, or other weapons. Others were forced to strip and run naked through gauntlets of guards armed with clubs, which they used to strike the bodies of the inmates as they passed. Some were dragged on the ground, some marked with an "X" on their backs, some spat upon or burned with matches, and others poked in the genitals or anus with sticks.[15]

Given these events, the Second Circuit Court of Appeals held that the force used went beyond that necessary to maintain order, and constituted cruel and unusual punishment.[16] The court granted injunctive relief against further physical abuse, tortures, beatings, or similar conduct.[17] In a more recent opinion, the Second Circuit held that prison officials should stand trial for damages for these events. The court held that the law is now clearly established that prison administrators have no authority for "summary infliction of

---

[14]Inmates of Attica Correctional Facility v. Rockefeller, 453 F.2d 12 (2d Cir. 1971).

[15]Inmates of Attica Correctional Facility v. Rockefeller, 453 F.2d 12, 18-19 (2d Cir. 1971).

[16]*Id.* at 23.

[17]*Id.* at 24-25. For a similar case, see Harrah v. Leverette, 165 W. Va. 665, 271 S.E.2d 322 (1980).

§ 2:6

brutal punishment once the riot is quelled."[18] For similar reasons, the failure to plan for medical care of inmates who might be injured in the effort to end the riot, if proven, would violate the Eighth Amendment rights of inmates.[19] Liability is a two way street, according to one state court opinion, which held that a damage award against inmates who instigate riots was proper.[20]

In a recent case, the Ninth Circuit pointed out cor-

---

[18]Al-Jundi v. Mancusi, 926 F.2d 235, 240 (2d Cir. 1991). A jury's finding that prison officials were liable for violent reprisals against inmates was upheld by a district judge. A separate trial will be held to determine damages. "Attica Riot Verdict Upheld by Judge," Wash Times, Jan 21, 1993, at B10. Inmates have already won $1.325 million in a state court action. Gary Spencer, "Attica Inmates Win $1.3 Million from State," NYLJ, Oct 26, 1989, at 1. For an additional case holding prison officials liable for the unjustified use of force against groups of inmates after a riot, see Bolin v. Black, 875 F.2d 1343 (8th Cir. 1989). Cf Meriwether v. Coughlin, 879 F.2d 1037, 14 Fed. R. Serv. 3d 1251 (2d Cir. 1989) (use of force against a group of inmates who were being transferred from the prison unconstitutional).

[19]Al-Jundi v. Mancusi, 926 F.2d 235, 239 (2d Cir. 1991) ("Once it was decided to retake the prison by force, the duty to make adequate provision for medical needs arose to at least the same extent as it does with respect to the normal operation of a prison").

In Blyden v. Mancusi, 186 F.3d 252 (2d Cir. 1999), the Second Circuit reversed a four million dollar jury award for brutality toward an inmate by guards during the retaking of Attica. The judgment was in favor of one of the plaintiffs in a class action suit by inmates who were present at the prison when it was retaken. The judgment was reversed because of faulty jury instructions which did not clearly specify what issues the jury was to decide in assessing damages in the case of the particular inmate whose claim was tried. In reversing the decision and remanding for a new trial the court stated that "given the long history of this case we direct the district court to give it expedited treatment." The case was finally settled for $8,000,000. See Associated Press, $8 Million Attica Settlement Approved, NYLJ, Feb. 16, 2000, at 8.

[20]See Shroyer v. Pennsylvania Dept. of Corrections, 743 A.2d 534 (Pa. Commw. Ct. 1999) (indicating that an administrative order requiring the an inmate to pay $99,014.00 as his fair share of damages arising out of a fire he and other inmates started during

§ 2:6   RIGHTS OF PRISONERS, THIRD EDITION

rectly that in such situations after order has been restored, the correct standard to apply in determining whether prison officials actions violated the Constitution is the deliberate indifference standard, not the *Whitley* malicious and sadistic standard.[21]

The case involved inmates who had been kept out of doors while prison officials searched prison buildings after quelling disturbances. The inmates were kept outside for four days and did not receive protection from the elements sufficient to ward off heat-related illnesses. They received inedible food, little water, and inadequate access to toilets to avoid soiling themselves, and were not allowed to clean themselves afterwards.

The court held that the inmates' evidence if believed, would establish deprivations serious enough to satisfy the objective component of a § 1983 claim.[22] The court went on to hold that until the officials were able to successfully remove the inmates from the buildings and secure them in the prison yard, the officials' state of mind should be measured against the *Whitley* good faith standard, and, that their actions did not violate that standard.[23] However, after the inmates were removed to the yard and were handcuffed, prone, and under armed guard, the state-of-mind requirement was deliberate indifference. The court found that the evidence was sufficient, if believed, to justify a finding that the defendants were deliberately indifferent, in that they had actual knowledge of the inmates' exposure to the elements and of their need for sanitation, edible food, and adequate drinking water, and that they intentionally

---

a prison riot could be proper, but remanding the matter for a new hearing on due process grounds).

[21]Johnson v. Lewis, 217 F.3d 726 (9th Cir. 2000), cert. denied, 532 U.S. 1065, 121 S. Ct. 2215, 150 L. Ed. 2d 209 (2001).

[22]Johnson v. Lewis, 217 F.3d 726, 732 (9th Cir. 2000), cert. denied, 532 U.S. 1065, 121 S. Ct. 2215, 150 L. Ed. 2d 209 (2001).

[23]*Id.*

disregarded these conditions.[24]

§ 2:7 Assaults by Other Inmates

"Prisons are dangerous places."[1] It is undeniable that there are violent persons housed in our nation's prisons. These persons, left unchecked, can make prey of weaker inmates.[2] The explosive mixture of personalities inherent in any prison setting is made even more incendiary by the overcrowding prevalent in numerous prisons, the lack of supervision and control in others, and the presence of acquired immune deficiency syndrome (AIDS) and other sexually transmitted diseases, which makes the prospect of sexual assault even more frightening than it already is. The result is that, in all too many prisons, the risk of serious violence is pervasive.[3]

No one knows for certain how much violence takes place in American prisons since so much of it is not reported.[4] However, what is known is alarming. One commentator reported, "incarceration subjects convicts

---

[24]*Id.* See also DeSpain v. Uphoff, 264 F.3d 965, 975 (10th Cir. 2001) (holding that the failure to clean up a flooded area after a disturbance is actionable and that the *Whitley* standard should not apply if there was no longer "an ongoing threat to safety . . .").

[Section 2:7]

[1]McGill v. Duckworth, 944 F.2d 344, 345, 20 Fed. R. Serv. 3d 1247 (7th Cir. 1991).

[2]Not all prisoners are so inclined. For example, in 1999 over 70% of commitments in New York were for nonviolent offenses, see www.Correctionalassociation.org./fact.html (July 22, 2002), and many others have no appetite for violence.

[3]On the general subject of violence in prison, see David M. Siegal, Rape in Prison and AIDS: A Challenge for the Eighth Amendment Framework of Wilson v. Seiter, 44 Stan L Rev 1541 (1992); James E. Robertson, The Constitution in Protective Custody: An Analysis of the Rights of Protective Custody Inmates, 56 Cin L Rev 91 (1987); James E. Robertson, Surviving Incarceration: Constitutional Protection from Inmate Violence, 35 Drake L Rev 101 (1985-86); Barbara H. Hendrie, Note, Physical Security in Prison: Rights Without Remedies?, 12 New Eng L Rev 269 (1976).

[4]The actual incidence of inmate assaults is often difficult to gauge. Fear of retaliation may prevent reporting. Also, an informal

§ 2:7   Rights of Prisoners, Third Edition

to a murder rate eight times greater than that found outside prison and an assault rate exceeding the prison murder rate by twenty-fold."[5] In 1998, seventy nine inmates were killed in prison by other prisoners and many thousands more injured.[6] In 1997, 10% of state inmates and 3% of federal inmates reported being injured in a fight since entering prisons.[7]

The incidence of homosexual rape and sexual assault, at least among male prisoners, may be even greater.[8] Recently a five-year study of male rape in United States prisons was published.[9] This comprehensive and sober-

---

code among prisoners strongly discourages "snitching" on fellow prisoners. In addition, prison officials have themselves displayed an unwillingness to accurately report the violence occurring within their domain; courts have frequently commented on the fear of reporting crimes committed by other inmates, and on the not uncommon discouragement and inaccurate reporting by prison officials. See, e.g., Vosburg v. Solem, 845 F.2d 763, 766 (8th Cir. 1988); Roland v. Johnson, 856 F.2d 764, 770 (6th Cir. 1988); Fisher v. Koehler, 692 F. Supp. 1519, 1529-30 (S.D. N.Y. 1988).

[5]James E. Robertson, The Constitution in Protective Custody: An Analysis of the Rights of Protective Custody Inmates, 56 U Cin L Rev 91, 94 (1987).

[6]The Corrections Yearbook 1998 pp. 30, 40.

[7]Laura M. Maruschak and Allen J. Beck, Medical Problems of Inmates, 1997, 1, 4 (Bureau of Justice Statistics Special Report, January 2001).

[8]David M. Siegal, Rape in Prison and AIDS: A Challenge for the Eight Amendment Framework of Wilson v. Seiter, 44 Stan L Rev 1541, 1544-47 (1992). See also Carl Weiss & David James Friar, Terror in the Prisons (1974); Davis, Sexual Assault in the Philadelphia Prison and Sheriff's Vans, 6 Transaction 8 (1968). But see David Lockwood, Issues in Prison Sexual Violence, in Prison Violence in America 89, 90 (Michael Braswell, Steven Dillingham & Reid Montgomery eds 1985) (noting that prison conditions vary and some prisons are much safer than others) and Richard G. Singer, Prisoners' Rights Litigation: A Look at the Past Decade and a Look at the Coming Decade, 44 Fed Prob 3, 7 (Dec 1980) (rejecting the claim that prison violence is continuing and arguing that the evidence is inconclusive).

[9]See Joanne Mariner, No Escape: Male Rape in the U.S. Prisons (Human Rights Watch 2001).

ing report demonstrates that the rape and sexual abuse of male prisoners by fellow prisoners is a systemic problem in United States prisons. In addition to graphic and disturbing stories by rape victims describing their horrible experiences, the report surveys the empirical research on the topic. The studies reach various conclusions about the level of sexual abuse and rape in male prisons. But they uniformly find that the rate of sexual abuse is far more than is reported by prison officials. Some of the recent studies find alarmingly high rates of sexual assault. One such study in 1996 in one state found that that 22 percent of male inmates had been "sexually pressured or abused since being incarcerated."[10] A confidential internal survey of guards in a southern state by the author of the report found that those prison guards who directly supervise inmates estimated that approximately one-fifth of all prisoners were victims of coerced sexual abuse."[11] Surveying the data, the report concludes that "even taking only the lowest of the . . . estimates of coerced sexual activity - and even framing that one conservatively — more than one in ten inmates in prisons surveyed was subject to sexual abuse."[12]

In many jurisdictions, there is a duty imposed by statute to protect inmates from violence from other inmates.[13] In addition, there is little doubt that inmates may be criminally prosecuted for assaulting other

---

[10]*Id.* at 137.

[11]*Id.* at 135.

[12]Richard G. Singer, Prisoners' Rights Litigation: A Look at the Past Decade and a Look at the Coming Decade, 44 Fed Prob 3, 5 (Dec 1980).

[13]See, e.g., 18 U.S.C. § 4042(a); Cal Penal Code § 2650 (West 2002); NY Correct Law § 137(2) (West 2002); Ariz Rev Stat Ann § 31-122(B) (West 2002). A comprehensive, but somewhat dated, statutory compilation appears in Robert Plotkin, Surviving Justice: Prisoners' Rights to be Free From Physical Assault, 23 Clev State L Rev 387, app at 411-21 (1974). See also Model Sentencing and Corrections Act § 4-104 (2001) (director shall take appropriate action to protect the inmates' physical security); Natl Sheriffs' Assn,

§ 2:7   Rights of Prisoners, Third Edition

inmates.[14] But independent of the vagaries of a particu-

Inmates' Legal Rights, Right 2 (1987); American Correctional Assn., Standards for Adult Correctional Institutions Standard 3-4268, commentary (2002) (protect inmate from self and others); ABA, Standards for Criminal Justice Standard 23-6.9 (1986) (prisoners are entitled to protection from injury and abuse). See also Caruso v. County of Suffolk, 234 A.D.2d 495, 652 N.Y.S.2d 58 (2d Dep't 1996) (pursuant to New York law, prison officials "have a duty to use reasonable care to protect inmates from the foreseeable risks of harm, including risks of attack by other prisoners); 9 NYCRR 7003.3(a) (active supervision shall be maintained in all facility housing areas, including multiple occupancy housing units, when any prisoners are confined in such areas but not secured in their individual housing units); 9 NYCRR 7003.2(c)(4) (active supervision is "the continuous occupation of a security post within any facility housing area in which more than twenty inmates are housed"); Millette v. Ohio Dept. of Rehab. & Corr., 83 Ohio Misc. 2d 44, 677 N.E.2d 1293 (Ct. Cl. 1996), aff'd, 1997 WL 606873 (Ohio Ct. App. 10th Dist. Franklin County 1997) (pursuant to Ohio law, state prison officials are not "liable for the intentional attack on an inmate by another inmate unless there is adequate notice of an impending assault."); Sherrod v. State Dept. of Correctional Services, 251 Neb. 355, 557 N.W.2d 634 (1997) (pursuant to Nebraska law a "jailer is bound to exercise, in the control and management of the jail, the degree of care required to provide reasonably adequate protection for his inmates.").

See also Arnold v. County of Nassau, 89 F. Supp. 2d 285 (E.D. N.Y. 2000), judgment vacated on other grounds, 252 F.3d 599 (2d Cir. 2001) (county inmate beaten by fellow inmates because he was arrested for sexual assault was awarded $475,000.00 for past injury and $425,000.00 for future injury; court held that the violation of the state statute requiring the providing of the safety for inmates was negligence per se and that the jury could find that the county displayed deliberate indifference to the inmate by adopting the policy of housing accused sex offenders, considered in danger from the general population, in a special section reserved for mentally-ill inmates, who might be more prone to harm inmate than would general population; Court of Appeals vacated and ordered new trial because district court failed to define for the jury crucial term "housing area"); Kemp v. Waldron, 115 A.D.2d 869, 497 N.Y.S.2d 158 (3d Dep't 1985) (under state law sheriff has a nondelegable duty to keep prisoners in county jail safe).

[14]See, e.g., Com. v. DeMarco, 281 Pa. Super. 62, 421 A.2d 1147 (1980); State v. Barnes, 122 R.I. 451, 409 A.2d 988 (1979); Birch v.

lar state's statutory scheme and the limitations inherent in criminal prosecution, is there a constitutional right to protection from inmate violence? The first response one might have in answering this question is to wonder why the government should be held responsible when a convict attacks a fellow prisoner? Inmate-on-inmate violence, after all, differs from violence perpetuated by prison guards. Guards are the agents of the state and there is liability for unjustifiable uses of force by them.[15] But a violent inmate generally is a private actor not associated with the government.[16] Given this difference, is there a constitutional right to protection

---

State, 401 N.E.2d 750 (Ind. Ct. App. 3d Dist. 1980). While there is no impediment to criminal prosecutions, this remedy has its limitations. For one thing, it provides no direct compensation to the victim. For another, there is limited deterrent effect when the prosecution is brought against an inmate already serving a lengthy sentence. An additional reason for doubting the efficacy of this remedy is that prison officials often are disinclined to report assaults to the local prosecutors. See, e.g., Martin v. White, 742 F.2d 469 (8th Cir. 1984) (critizing this failure to report assaults).

In addition to criminal penalties against prisoners who assault other inmates, civil remedies may be available under state tort law. In Ruley v. Nevada Bd. of Prison Com'rs, 628 F. Supp. 108 (D. Nev. 1986), for example, the court upheld a state scheme which allowed a prison disciplinary committee to order a restitutionary award against a prisoner found guilty of assault, the money to be paid from the inmates' trust fund.

[15]See § 2:5.

[16]There are some exceptions to this that have all but vanished from the modern correctional scene. In the past, some prison systems, especially in the South, gave some inmates custodial duties. The most egregious examples of this involved the institutional use of armed inmate trustees. In some instances incompetent, unscreened, and untrained prisoners were assigned custodial responsibility over other inmates. See, e.g., Gates v. Collier, 501 F.2d 1291 (5th Cir. 1974); Holt v. Sarver, 309 F. Supp. 362 (E.D. Ark. 1970), aff'd and remanded, 442 F.2d 304 (8th Cir. 1971); Roberts v. Williams, 302 F. Supp. 972 (N.D. Miss. 1969), decision rescinded, 456 F.2d 819 (5th Cir. 1971). The potential dangers were compounded when, as sometimes occurred, the inmate trustees were armed and given virtually unchecked authority. The result in one case, for instance, was the unprovoked, grossly

from violence by inmates against fellow inmates? The Supreme Court in *Farmer v. Brennan*[17] definitely answered this question by holding that prison officials commit an Eighth Amendment violation if they are deliberately indifferent to the risk that inmate might be attacked.

Even before *Farmer,* the Court signaled its understanding that there must be such a right in *Estelle v. Gamble*[18] when it held that the state has responsibility to provide inmates with medical care[19] and in *Rhodes v. Chapman*[20] when it held that there was an obligation to provide other "minimal civilized measure(s) of life's

---

negligent shooting of a prisoner. Holt v. Sarver, 309 F. Supp. 362 (E.D. Ark. 1970), aff'd and remanded, 442 F.2d 304 (8th Cir. 1971). See also Alberti v. Sheriff of Harris County, Texas, 406 F. Supp. 649 (S.D. Tex. 1975).

While these practices have largely disappeared, there continue to be reported instances of violence by inmates that are inspired by prison officials. See, e.g., Mayoral v. Sheahan, 245 F.3d 934 (7th Cir. 2001) (describing an instance where prison officials "put the fate of the inmates in the hands of another inmate"); Northington v. Jackson, 973 F.2d 1518, 1525, 23 Fed. R. Serv. 3d 934 (10th Cir. 1992); Vaughn v. Willis, 853 F.2d 1372, 1377, 26 Fed. R. Evid. Serv. 423 (7th Cir. 1988); Glover v. Alabama Dept. of Corrections, 734 F.2d 691, 15 Fed. R. Evid. Serv. 1844 (11th Cir. 1984), cert. granted, judgment vacated, 474 U.S. 806, 106 S. Ct. 40, 88 L. Ed. 2d 33 (1985) (prison official offered cigarettes for killing of subsequently assaulted prisoner). In this and similar situations, the courts have had little difficulty finding an Eighth Amendment violation. *Id.* See also Gates v. Collier, 501 F.2d 1291 (5th Cir. 1974).

[17]Farmer v. Brennan, 511 U.S. 825, 114 S. Ct. 1970, 128 L. Ed. 2d 811 (1994). This case is discussed extensively in § 2:2.

[18]Estelle v. Gamble, 429 U.S. 97, 97 S. Ct. 285, 50 L. Ed. 2d 251 (1976).

[19]*Id.*

[20]Rhodes v. Chapman, 452 U.S. 337, 347, 101 S. Ct. 2392, 69 L. Ed. 2d 59 (1981) (holding that under certain conditions double celling is unconstitutional).

necessities" to prisoners.[21] These opinions did not in so many terms identify a right to safety in prison. But the logic of the holdings compels the conclusion that there is.

If there is a right to medical care to prevent the unnecessary infliction of pain and injury, how could there not be a similar right to be free of preventable injury inflicted by inmates? Just as a prisoner is not able to receive medical care if it is not given by the state so, too, an inmate who is housed with dangerous people involuntarily must necessarily depend upon the state for protection. There is little difference between an untreated disease and an unprevented attack. In both situations, the harm comes because the state fails to take affirmative steps to prevent imminent harm. In both situations the inmate-victim is posing no potential danger to institutional authority and only seeks services that the institution has an interest in providing.[22] Thus, if medical care is a "life's necessity" so, too, is safety from assault and rape.

In other decisions before *Farmer,* the Supreme Court continued to lay the groundwork for the *Farmer* holding. In *Wilson v. Seiter,*[23] the Court in dicta included protection from violence as one of the "necessities of life" that prisons were obligated by the Eighth Amend-

---

[21]Rhodes v. Chapman, 452 U.S. 337, 101 S. Ct. 2392, 69 L. Ed. 2d 59 (1981).

[22]But see Dudley v. Stubbs, 489 U.S. 1034, 109 S. Ct. 1095, 103 L. Ed. 2d 230 (1989) (O'Connor, J, dissenting from denial of certiorari) (observing that on occasion a guard may fail to stop an attack in order to protect himself or herself).

[23]Wilson v. Seiter, 501 U.S. 294, 111 S. Ct. 2321, 115 L. Ed. 2d 271 (1991). See also Rhodes v. Chapman, 452 U.S. 337, 348, 101 S. Ct. 2392, 69 L. Ed. 2d 59 (1981) (holding that "violence among inmates" is one of several deprivations of essential human needs constituting intolerable prison conditions prohibited by the Eighth Amendment).

§ 2:7   Rights of Prisoners, Third Edition

ment to provide.[24] In *Helling v. McKinney,* decided a year before *Farmer,* the Supreme Court all but settled this point when it wrote:

> When the State takes a person into its custody and holds him there against his will, the Constitution imposed upon it a corresponding duty to assume some responsibility for his safety and well-being. . . . The rationale for this principle is simple enough: when the state by the affirmative exercise of its power so restrains an individual's liberty that it renders him unable to care for himself, and at the same time fails to provide for his basic human needs-e.g., food, clothing, shelter, medical care, and reasonable safety-it transgresses . . . the Eighth Amendment.[25]

With such clear signals it is not surprising that lower courts anticipated the direction that the Court would take in *Farmer.*[26] In a statement that captured an essential understanding of the underpinnings of the right-

---

[24] Wilson v. Seiter, 501 U.S. 294, 111 S. Ct. 2321, 2323-24, 115 L. Ed. 2d 271 (1991). See also Davidson v. Cannon, 474 U.S. 344, 106 S. Ct. 668, 88 L. Ed. 2d 677 (1986). In *Davidson,* the Supreme Court held that the negligent failure to protect was not actionable. It assumed that if a sufficient showing of culpability was made then there would be liability. Davidson v. Cannon, 474 U.S. 344, 106 S. Ct. 668, 88 L. Ed. 2d 677 (1986).

[25] Helling v. McKinney, 509 U.S. 25, 113 S. Ct. 2475, 2480, 125 L. Ed. 2d 22 (1993) (emphasis supplied) (quoting DeShaney v. Winnebago County Dept. of Social Services, 489 U.S. 189, 199-200, 109 S. Ct. 998, 103 L. Ed. 2d 249 (1989)). See also Hewitt v. Helms, 459 U.S. 460, 473, 103 S. Ct. 864, 74 L. Ed. 2d 675 (1983), history on other grounds (Chief Justice (then Justice) Rehnquist remarked: "[t]he safety of the institution's guards and inmates is perhaps the most fundamental responsibility of the prison administration.").

[26] McGill v. Duckworth, 944 F.2d 344, 347, 20 Fed. R. Serv. 3d 1247 (7th Cir. 1991). See also Butler v. Dowd, 979 F.2d 661, 675 (8th Cir. 1992) ("This Court has clearly held that prisoners have a constitutional right to be free of sexual attacks by other inmates"); Young v. Quinlan, 960 F.2d 351, 361, 22 Fed. R. Serv. 3d 530 (3d Cir. 1992) ("It is well established that the Eighth Amendment affords an inmate a right to be protected from violence inflicted by other inmates"); Hendricks v. Coughlin, 942 F.2d 109 (2d Cir. 1991) (holding that there is a constitutional right to be protected from violence by other inmates); Vosburg v. Solem, 845 F.2d 763

to-protection doctrine, Judge Posner observed in a case decided prior to *Farmer:* "If the state puts a man in a position of danger from private persons and then fails to protect him, it will not be heard to say that its role was merely passive; it is as much an active [role] as if it had thrown him into a snake pit."[27]

In *Farmer,* the Supreme Court made clear and held explicitly what was apparent from these precedents: that there is a right to be protected from harm.[28] In an opinion by Justice Souter, the Court began with the proposition that the Eighth Amendment imposes a duty on prison officials to provide humane conditions of confinement.[29] The Court observed that the beating and rape of one prisoner by another serves no "legitimate penologocial objective."[30] Having stripped inmates of the means of self-protection and having confined them with dangerous people and having foreclosed their ability to enlist outside support, the state may not stand idly by and "let the state of nature take its course." Thus, there is a governmental obligation to "protect prisoners from violence at the hands of other prisoners,"[31] and the assault of one inmate by another can violate the Constitution even though the inmate inflicting the injury is not an agent of the state.

Justice Souter went on to explain that an inmate invoking this right must meet two conditions. First he musts show that he is "incarcerated under conditions

---

(8th Cir. 1988) (holding that inmates have the constitutional right to be free from sexual attacks by other inmates); Leonardo v. Moran, 611 F.2d 397, 398-99 (1st Cir. 1979) ("prison officials have a duty to protect prisoners from violence at the hands of other prisoners").

[27]Bowers v. DeVito, 686 F.2d 616, 618 (7th Cir. 1982).

[28]Farmer v. Brennan, 511 U.S. 825, 114 S. Ct. 1970, 128 L. Ed. 2d 811 (1994). *Farmer* is discussed in detail in § 2:2.

[29]*Id.* at 1976.

[30]*Id.*

[31]*Id.*, quoting Cortes-Quinones v. Jimenez-Nettleship, 842 F.2d 556, 558 (1st Cir. 1988).

§ 2:7   Rights of Prisoners, Third Edition

posing a substantial risk of serious harm."[32] Second, he must prove that the defendants were "deliberately indifferent" to the plaintiff's plight.[33]

The first requirement is not difficult to meet. A beating, an assault, or a rape is not part of the sentence that a prisoner has received. It is an infliction of punishment that offends contemporary standards of decency and is thus a violation of the objective component of the Eighth Amendment.[34] Because of the importance of protecting inmates from this kind of conduct, the Supreme Court made clear that actual injury need not take place to satisfy this requirement. It is enough if plaintiff can show there is "substantial risk of serious harm."

The more difficult component is the second one: showing that the prison officials' conduct constituted "deliberate indifference" to the risk facing the inmate. The Supreme Court had not previously defined the meaning of the term "deliberate indifference." Before *Farmer*, Judge Easterbrook of the Seventh Circuit expressed the frustration felt by many judges when he remarked, "this seeming oxymoron has given us, in company with other courts of appeals, fits."[35] The difficulty comes from trying to "simultaneously honor both the 'deliberate' and the 'indifference' aspects" of the standard.[36] Before *Farmer*, courts had somewhat divergent views on what constituted deliberate indifference.[37] All courts agreed that deliberate indifference requires something more than mere negligence and something less than

---

[32]*Id.*

[33]*Id.* at 1977.

[34]See § 2:4.

[35]McGill v. Duckworth, 944 F.2d 344, 351, 20 Fed. R. Serv. 3d 1247 (7th Cir. 1991).

[36]*Id.*

[37]See, e.g., Young v. Quinlan, 960 F.2d 351, 360, 22 Fed. R. Serv. 3d 530 (3d Cir. 1992) (noting the split "among the circuit courts regarding the quantum of knowledge possessed by a prison officials, necessary to satisfy the deliberate indifference requirement").

maliciousness. Thus, the failure to exercise reasonable care is not deliberate indifference.

The disagreement came from a dispute about what needed to be shown beyond negligence to establish liability under the deliberate indifference standard. Some courts held that the standard was not satisfied unless it was established that the prison officials knew of danger to the inmate but failed to take steps to avoid it.[38] This view presupposed that there was no liability unless the defendant was "reckless" in the criminal law sense of actually knowing about a danger but not responding to it. Other courts, however, held that deliberate indifference could be established in the absence of knowledge of a threat if the plaintiffs could prove that the defendant should have known of the threat.[39] Under this view, the defendant was "reckless" in the civil law context if the defendant failed to act in the face of a risk that a reasonable person in that circumstance could not fail to notice. This issue is discussed at some length earlier in this chapter.[40]

The Supreme Court in *Farmer* resolved this debate by holding that actual knowledge must be proven. To be deliberately indifferent, the Court held, the defendants must "know" of the risk to the plaintiff, but be indifferent and unresponsive to it. This is a subjective test, which is surely met if the defendant is shown to be aware of the risk to the inmate and then fails to re-

---

[38] See, e.g. McGill v. Duckworth, 944 F.2d 344, 349, 20 Fed. R. Serv. 3d 1247 (7th Cir. 1991) (to recover, plaintiff "had to show that the defendants had actual knowledge of the threat"); Rodriguez v. Connecticut, 169 F. Supp. 2d 39 (D. Conn. 2001) (in a close custody unit designed to manage gang members, plaintiff's murder by rival inmate when they were housed together supported Eighth Amendment claim; however, commissioner and warden were not shown to have any knowledge of the informal practice and could not be held liable for the resulting Eighth Amendment violation).

[39] See, e.g., Young v. Quinlan, 960 F.2d 351, 361, 22 Fed. R. Serv. 3d 530 (3d Cir. 1992); Redman v. County of San Diego, 942 F.2d 1435, 1442 (9th Cir. 1991).

[40] § 2:2.

spond to it. But the *Farmer* Court also held that the standard is met even without such direct evidence. Knowledge, the Court held, may be proved by circumstantial evidence.[41] For example, even if the prison officials had no direct knowledge that harm would befall a particular inmate, deliberate indifference to that risk can be found through proof that prison officials were aware of a risk to inmates in the same general category as the plaintiff.[42] Put another way, actual knowledge of a serious risk of danger can be premised upon objective proof, showing that the substantial risk of inmate attacks was "longstanding, pervasive, well documented, or expressly noted by prison officials in the past and the circumstances suggest that the defendant-official being sued had been exposed to information concerning the risk and thus 'must have known' about it."[43] In these circumstances, a prison official cannot escape liability by arguing that "he merely refused to verify underlying facts that he strongly suspected to be true, or declined to confirm inferences of risk that he strongly suspected to exist."[44]

Therefore, under the holding in *Farmer,* if there is evidence that there was a serious risk of danger that an inmate would be attacked or assaulted by another inmate, prison officials prison officials cannot escape accountability unless there is evidence from which the trier of fact can find that the defendants did not know of the underlying facts indicating a sufficiently substantial danger and that they were therefore unaware of the danger, or that they knew the underlying facts, but believed (albeit unsoundly) that the risk to which the

---

[41]Farmer v. Brennan, 511 U.S. 825, 842, 114 S. Ct. 1970, 1981, 128 L. Ed. 2d 811 (1994).

[42]*Id.* at 1982 ("it does not matter whether the risk comes from a single source or multiple sources any more than it matters whether a prisoner faces an excessive risk of attack for reasons personal to him or because all prisoners in his situation face such a risk").

[43]*Id.* at 1981.

[44]*Id.* at 1982 n 8.

facts gave rise was insubstantial or nonexistent.[45]

By the same token, the Court noted if prison officials respond reasonably to a known danger, they are not liable even if they are unsuccessful and harm ultimately occurs.[46] Finally, the Court held that under its standard an inmate does not have to wait to be assaulted in order to bring suit. The requisite showing of deliberate indifference can be made in the absence of actual injury.[47] The Court also said if the other conditions are met, the failure to give notice of the specific threat facing the inmate is not "dispositive."[48] Thus, *Farmer* establishes that inmates enjoy a right, secured by the Eighth Amendment, to be protected from violence committed by other inmates.[49]

Farmer is an important case that has attracted a great deal of scholarly attention.[50] Because violence is

---

[45]*Id.* at 1982.

[46]*Id.* at 1982-83.

[47]*Id.* at 1982-83.

[48]*Id.* at 1984-85.

[49]Whether the right imposes a duty on persons who are not in a custodial relationship with the defendant is an open question. See e.g, Latimore v. Widseth, 7 F.3d 709, 713 (8th Cir. 1993).(holding that a prosecutor was not liable for disclosing information about the defendant that caused the defendant to be subjected to an assault by gang members who were inmates).

[50]For a sampling of the rich literature discussing *Farmer* see Marjorie Rifkin, Farmer v. Brennan [114 S.Ct 1970 (1994)]: Spotlight on an Obvious Risk of Rape in a Hidden World, 26 Colum Hum Rts L Rev 203 (1995); James J. Park, Redefining the Liability of Prison Officials For Failing to Protect Inmates From Serious Harm, 20 Quinnipiac L.Rev. 407 (2001); Cheryl Bell, Martha Coven, John P. Cronan, Christian A. Garza, Janet Gugemos and Laura Storto, Rape and Sexual Misconduct in the Prison System: Analyzing America's "Open" Secret, 18 Yale L & Pol'y Rev 195 (1999); Stacy Lancaster Cozad, Cruel But Not So Unusual: Farmer v. Brennan and the Devolving Standards of Decency, 23 Pepperdine L Rev 175 (1995); Jason D Sanabria, Do Prisoners Have Any Rights Left Under the Eighth Amendment?, 16 Whittier L Rev 1113 (1995); Richard D. Vetstein, Rape and AIDS in Prison: a Collision Course to a New Death Penalty, 30

such a major problem in prisons, it is not surprising that over the years there has been a great deal of litigation on this topic in the lower courts. In the years following *Farmer*, how have the lower courts interpreted that seminal decision?

Because of *Farmer* some things are now clear.[51] There are a number of benchmarks for when the right to safety has not been violated. The clearest is that regardless of the nature of the risk, mere negligence on the part of prison officials is insufficient to establish Eighth Amendment culpability.[52] More is required. For this reason, courts have not found deliberate indifference

---

Suffolk UL Rev 863 (1997). See also James E. Robertson, Cruel And Unusual Punishment in United States Prisons: Sexual Harassment Among Male Inmates, 36 Am Crim L Rev 1 (1999) (Eighth Amendment imposes upon prison staff constitutional duty not to be deliberately indifferent to sexual harassment among male inmates and such duty is frequently ignored; sexual harassment among male inmates can inflict the type and degree of injury prohibited by the Eighth Amendment and yet prison officials know of and tolerate pervasive sexual harassment). See also Joanne Mariner, No Escape: Male Rape In The U.S. Prisons, 11 (Human Rights Watch 2001) (maintaining that the deliberate indifference standard provides "perverse incentives" for prison officials to want to be unaware of risks to inmates).

[51]The deliberate indifference standard applies to cases involving pretrial detainees. See, e.g., Pugh v. Rockwall County, TX, 2000 WL 730426 (N.D. Tex. 2000).

[52]Davidson v. Cannon, 474 U.S. 344, 106 S. Ct. 668, 88 L. Ed. 2d 677 (1986) (holding that mere negligence is insufficient to establish a claim under the Fourteenth Amendment for failure to protect an inmate from harm); Wilson v. Seiter, 501 U.S. 294, 111 S. Ct. 2321, 115 L. Ed. 2d 271 (1991) (holding that more than negligence is required to prove a violation of the Eighth Amendment in a prison conditions case). See also U.S. ex rel. Miller v. Twomey, 479 F.2d 701, 721 (7th Cir. 1973); Penn v. Oliver, 351 F. Supp. 1292 (E.D. Va. 1972).

While negligence is insufficient for liability under the Eighth Amendment, it might very well suffice under a common law tort theory under state or local law. See, e.g., Finkelstein v. District of Columbia, 593 A.2d 591 (D.C. 1991) (en banc) (upholding verdict based on a negligence theory); White v. State, 167 A.D.2d 646, 563

CRUEL & UNUSUAL PUNISHMENT § 2:7

when the attack by another inmate was unanticipated.[53] This can occur when the plaintiff fails to inform correctional officials of any potential danger[54] or when the

N.Y.S.2d 239 (3d Dep't 1990) (using negligence theory but also applying comparative negligence standards).

[53]See, e.g., Doe v. Bowles, 254 F.3d 617 (6th Cir. 2001) (plaintiff assaulted by fellow inmate in protective custody unit could not prove that captain was deliberately indifferent to attack, because captain took steps to address the danger by asking reporting officer if the prisoners should be formally segregated and the officer said that wasn't necessary); Grimsley v. MacKay, 93 F.3d 676 (10th Cir. 1996) (inmate who lost an eye during an altercation with a fellow inmate failed to show that there was an basis for believing that the perpetrator of the assault posed a threat to the plaintiff); Farmer v. Brennan, 81 F.3d 1444, 35 Fed. R. Serv. 3d 71 (7th Cir. 1996) (Director of Federal Bureau of Prisons did not violate Eighth Amendment where local prison officials placed a male transsexual in general population and inmate was subject to assaults by other inmates; court noted that the Director had no knowledge of the conduct of local officials); Walden v. State, 430 So. 2d 1224 (La. Ct. App. 1st Cir. 1983), writ denied, 435 So. 2d 430 (La. 1983) (no liability when there was reason to anticipate attack)

[54]See, e.g., Soto v. Johansen, 137 F.3d 980 (7th Cir. 1998) (inmate was attacked by other inmates for not paying "cell rent"; plaintiff told a prison counselor about his fear that he would be attacked and he requested protective custody; the counselor could not remember whom he told but thought it could have been the defendant; court found in favor of the defendant because the plaintiff's testimony did not prove that defendant was aware of the situation and acted with deliberate indifference); Davis v. Scott, 94 F.3d 444 (8th Cir. 1996) (court held that inmate failed to state an Eighth Amendment violation because he could not provide prison officials with specific list of potential attackers prior to the transfer; thus, prison officials could not identify a serious risk to the inmate's safety); Delgado-Brunet v. Clark, 93 F.3d 339, 35 Fed. R. Serv. 3d 885 (7th Cir. 1996) (inmate did not satisfy the subjective component of Farmer when he failed to convey his fear of inmate violence); Robinson v. Cavanaugh, 20 F.3d 892 (8th Cir. 1994) (failure to identify inmate's potential attackers); Smith v. Ullman, 874 F. Supp. 979 (D. Neb. 1994), on reconsideration, (July 22, 1994) (in order to maintain a claim, inmate must communicate to prison officials a specific identifiable harm from other inmate(s), and prison officials must ignore the threat); Luong v. Hatt, 979 F. Supp. 481

§ 2:7   RIGHTS OF PRISONERS, THIRD EDITION

attack is an isolated episode.[55] When this happens,

(N.D. Tex. 1997) (plaintiff's attackers were friends of two prisoners he informed on in another prison; court held that the defendants' did not violate their duty to protect him since they were not aware of the threat and his injuries, such as cuts, bruises and abrasions, were de minimis); Agosto v. Gilless, 229 F.3d 1150 (6th Cir. 2000) (inmate told guards that another inmate had a pocket knife, but the court held summary judgment was properly granted for the defendants where the inmate's statement was not made in a way that would have alarmed the guards to a possible attack); Busch v. Gammon, 2000 WL 1514753 (E.D. Mo. 2000) (guards had no warning of an impending attack, and there was no history of attacks in the receiving and orientation unit of the prison; court held that plaintiff failed to show guards were deliberately indifferent to a possible attack by failing to patrol the housing unit at the instant the attack occurred); Falls v. Nesbitt, 966 F.2d 375 (8th Cir. 1992) (no liability if inmate states that he had no reason to believe that he would be attacked and failed to inform prison officials of any danger before he was attacked); Duane v. Lane, 959 F.2d 673, 677 (7th Cir. 1992) (noting that plaintiff "does not allege that any defendant had antecedent knowledge" of an attack); McGill v. Duckworth, 944 F.2d 344, 348, 20 Fed. R. Serv. 3d 1247 (7th Cir. 1991) (holding that "failure to tell prison officials about threats is fatal" to the action); Ruefly v. Landon, 825 F.2d 792 (4th Cir. 1987); Saunders v. State of R.I., 731 F.2d 81 (1st Cir. 1984) (no liability where no notice of danger to plaintiff); Hopkins v. Britton, 742 F.2d 1308, 16 Fed. R. Evid. Serv. 651 (11th Cir. 1984) (no liability where prisoner admitted that he was totally surprised by the attack); Sinnett v. Simmons, 45 F. Supp. 2d 1210 (D. Kan. 1999) (plaintiff never reported any concerns to prison officials about the attacker, even though he was in the best position to assess the threats to his safety).

[55]See, e.g., Stanley v. State, 239 A.D.2d 700, 657 N.Y.S.2d 481 (3d Dep't 1997) (no liability where the attack was sudden and committed by an unknown assailant; plaintiff failed to present any evidence that the state failed to take reasonable measures to protect him from a foreseeable risk of attack); Inmates, Washington County Jail v. England, 516 F. Supp. 132 (E.D. Tenn. 1980), aff'd, 659 F.2d 1081 (6th Cir. 1981); Woodhous v. Com. of Va., 487 F.2d 889 (4th Cir. 1973); Williams v. Field, 416 F.2d 483 (9th Cir. 1969); Swarts v. Johnson, 628 F. Supp. 549 (W.D. Mich. 1986), judgment aff'd, 826 F.2d 1065 (6th Cir. 1987); Lovell v. Brennan, 566 F. Supp. 672 (D. Me. 1983), judgment aff'd, 728 F.2d 560 (1st Cir. 1984); Van Horn v. Lukhard, 392 F. Supp. 384 (E.D. Va. 1975).

courts are prone to label the attack an "unfortunate by-product" of the penal system.[56] In addition, courts will not second guess officials by imposing liability when an anticipated attack occurs if officials have taken reasonable steps to prevent it, even if those measures failed.[57] If the defendants did respond to the risk prior to the attack, the only way that liability would be imposed is if there is other evidence which proves that the defendants intended to harm the plaintiff, or that they were indifferent to a known risk.[58] While prison officials must re-

---

[56]See, e.g., Falls v. Nesbitt, 966 F.2d 375, 380 (8th Cir. 1992). See also McGill v. Duckworth, 944 F.2d 344, 348, 20 Fed. R. Serv. 3d 1247 (7th Cir. 1991) (observing that "[s]ome level of brutality and sexual aggression among [inmates] is inevitable no matter what the guards do"). See also Golden v. Waters, 211 F.3d 1278 (10th Cir. 2000) (inmate plaintiff sustained injuries from being stabbed with a pencil by another inmate during a prison fight; prior to the fight, the attacker had not threatened or assaulted any other prisoner; therefore, defendant prison authority, who was not present at the time of the fight, did not consider the attacker a threat to other prisoners and there was no Eighth Amendment violation); Cupples v. State, 18 Kan. App. 2d 864, 861 P.2d 1360 (1993) (holding that although the state has a duty to protect inmates from foreseeable harm, there is no liability when the prison officials had no reason to anticipate the attack).

[57]See, e.g., Bagola v. Kindt, 131 F.3d 632, 646 (7th Cir. 1997) ("reasonable measures taken to avert known risks will insulate a prison official from Eighth Amendment liability, even if those measures prove unsuccessful"); Woods v. Lecureux, 110 F.3d 1215, 46 Fed. R. Evid. Serv. 1111, 1997 FED App. 116P (6th Cir. 1997) (warden took steps to reduce violence in a cell block housing violent prisoners); Duane v. Lane, 959 F.2d 673, 677 (7th Cir. 1992) (defendants did use measures, although unsuccessful, to thwart threat to plaintiff); Berg v. Kincheloe, 794 F.2d 457 (9th Cir. 1986) (indicating that liability might not attach if officials took "prophylactic or preventative" measures to protect the prisoner).

[58]See, e.g., Curry v. Crist, 226 F.3d 974 (8th Cir. 2000) (summary judgment for defendants was proper where inmate threatened he would commit mass murder 16 months before murder by inmate of plaintiff's relative; court found defendants were not deliberately indifferent where they reacted to the threat, and determined that it was only a cry for help by the inmate before returning him to the general prison population; attacker had not been disciplined

§ 2:7   Rights of Prisoners, Third Edition

spond to threats of harm to inmates, there is some authority that they do not have a constitutional duty to prosecute inmates who attack fellow inmates.[59] In addition, to prove an Eighth Amendment violation, the plaintiff must be able to identify the prison officials who

---

and there was no warning of an impending attack in the months following the threat); Thomas v. Keane, 2001 WL 410095 (S.D. N.Y. 2001) (where guards interviewed prisoners regarding a rumor of a planned retaliation attack and found no information, they were not deliberately indifferent to a likely attack); Langston v. Peters, 100 F.3d 1235 (7th Cir. 1996) (court held that prison officials were not deliberately indifferent to risk of inmate retaliation after inmate was transferred from administrative segregation to punitive segregation and was raped by his cellmate; court found that prison officials were not sufficiently aware that plaintiff would be subject to assault in retaliation for his cooperation with prosecutors in a case); Jelinek v. Greer, 90 F.3d 242 (7th Cir. 1996) (inmate was brutally beaten by a fellow inmate after transfer from protective custody; court held that inmate failed to state an Eighth Amendment violation; court reasoned that while he was removed from protective custody, he was not transferred to the general prison population but only to a less protective area than protective custody); Mooreman v. Sargent, 991 F.2d 472 (8th Cir. 1993) (no Eighth Amendment violation found when prison officials responded immediately to a report that an inmate had been raped and had no prior knowledge that such an event was likely to occur); Prater v. Dahm, 89 F.3d 538 (8th Cir. 1996) (inmate who was beaten by fellow inmate failed to state an Eighth Amendment claim despite prison officials' knowledge of a substantial risk of harm to inmate; court held prison officials acted reasonably in response to the risk; court noted that prison officials consulted with plaintiff prior to attacker's transfer and received assurances from both inmates that there would be no problems).

However, a belated response after the violence has actually occurred is not sufficient. See, e.g., Bradley v. Puckett, 157 F.3d 1022, 1026 (5th Cir. 1998).

[59]See Gangloff v. Poccia, 888 F. Supp. 1549 (M.D. Fla. 1995) (prison officials did not violate Constitution when they failed to prosecute inmate who attacked plaintiff). See also Joanne Mariner, No Escape: Male Rape in the U.S. Prisons 154-156 (Human Rights Watch 2001) (reporting on the failure of corrections officials to initiate prosecutions for rape in prison; of the over 100 prison rapes reported to Human Rights Watch "not a single one led to a criminal prosecution").

knew of the risk yet failed to act.[60] However, leave to amend should be granted to allow the plaintiff to supply the names if it appears at all possible that the plaintiff can correct the defect.[61] [62]

There are also established benchmarks for when the right to safety has been violated. The clearest examples are unfortunate instances in which prison officials encourage inmates to attack other inmates either

---

[60]Lopez v. Smith, 203 F.3d 1122, 46 Fed. R. Serv. 3d 494 (9th Cir. 2000) (district court abused its discretion in dismissing claims, without leave to amend, based on prisoner's failure to name correct defendants); K.F.P. v. Dane County, 110 F.3d 516 (7th Cir. 1997) (in order to satisfy the subjective component under a theory of "deliberate indifference" a showing of scienter is necessary; thus, when an inmate fails to specifically identify prison officials allegedly responsible for disregarding a substantial risk of harm, individualized inquiries into the prison official's state of mind are legally impossible and an Eighth Amendment claim cannot prevail).

[61]Lopez v. Smith, 203 F.3d 1122, 46 Fed. R. Serv. 3d 494 (9th Cir. 2000)

It can be dangerous to intervene when an attack is underway. For this reason lower courts have not required that defendants make "superhuman" efforts to stem prison violence, particularly where doing so will subject guards to risk to their own personal safety. If intervention by the guards would pose a serious risk of harm to the guards, it is not deliberate indifference for the guards to delay until it is safe for them to act to stem the violence.

[62]Prosser v. Ross, 70 F.3d 1005 (8th Cir. 1995) (prison guards not constitutionally required to intervene in violent fight between inmates when inmates outnumber guards); Arnold v. Jones, 891 F.2d 1370, 1373 (8th Cir. 1989) (holding that prison guards have no constitutional duty to intervene in the armed assault of one inmate upon another when intervention would place the guards in danger of physical harm); Lacy v. Berge, 921 F. Supp. 600, 609 (E.D. Wis. 1996), decision aff'd, 132 F.3d 36 (7th Cir. 1997) (prison officials did not violate Eighth Amendment where inmate alleged that guard failed to break up fight between inmates; court noted that intervention by prison guard without reinforcements would have been unsafe to the officer and that even if guard did intervene the fight would not have ended sooner than it in fact did).

through direct incitement or through name-calling.[63] When this occurs, of course, prison officials are as liable as they would be were they the ones that actually inflicted the injury.[64] Even if they are not instigators of

---

[63]See, e.g., Benefield v. McDowall, 241 F.3d 1267 (10th Cir. 2001) (inmate claimed defendant guard labeled him a "snitch" and fabricated letters he allegedly wrote providing investigators with information; court affirmed district court's denial of dismissal of the complaint, finding that the guard was not entitled to qualified immunity, as the inmate's constitutional rights were obviously violated if the allegations were true; court also found that claim could go forward even though inmate had not actually been assaulted; pursuant to Farmer, court held that the inmate sufficiently alleged facts that, if proved, would satisfy the subject element needed for finding of deliberate indifference subjecting inmate to threat of serious harm, and that no actual assault was needed to find an Eighth Amendment violation); Montero v. Crusie, 153 F. Supp. 2d 368 (S.D. N.Y. 2001) (no summary judgment where plaintiff alleged that guards incited a fight between inmates, and spread rumors that plaintiff inmate was gay, a child molester, and a rapist). But see Law v. Tillman, 2001 WL 103304 (S.D. Ala. 2001) (summary judgment granted for defendant, even though guard stated over intercom that the plaintiff is a snitch and encouraged other inmates to beat the plaintiff; court held the inmate did not show that the statement caused the alleged attack).

[64]See, e.g., Fischl v. Armitage, 128 F.3d 50, 48 Fed. R. Evid. Serv. 211 (2d Cir. 1997), where an inmate brought suit against correctional officers after he was assaulted by other inmates in his cell, allegedly with the consent of the guards. The plaintiff was placed in protective custody, where the doors on the cells could only be opened by means of a control panel in the officer's cage. The plaintiff flooded his cell after a dispute with another inmate. The water caused damage to nearby cells. The next morning the officer on duty was informed about the incident and resulting property damage. Sometime between 9:00 and 9:30 that morning the plaintiff was assaulted. He claimed that he heard other inmates say, "Sergeant says no steel. No steel. As far as a weapon, no steel. He said we got ten minutes. The sergeant said we got ten minutes. No steel." The inmates then entered through the plaintiff's unlocked cell door and punched, kicked, and beat him with a broom for approximately ten minutes. During this time the plaintiff screamed but no guards appeared to stop the assault. Almost two hours later, the plaintiff was taken to the hospital. The plaintiff suffered injuries. The plaintiff claimed that while he was in the

violence, guards may not stand by in the face of an attack and refuse to intervene if they can safely do so and can end the assault. Where it can be demonstrated that prison officials who know about impending violence stood by when violence was about to occur and did nothing to prevent it, there is a violation of the right to safety.[65]

It is also clear that there is no need for explicit advance notice of an attack if the circumstances made

---

hospital one of the guards brought two of the attackers to his room and threatened him. The court reversed the finding of summary judgment in favor of defendants. A hospital doctor testified that the plaintiff's injuries could not have been self-inflicted due to their severity. Further, the allegation that the officer arrived with two of the assailants could lead a jury to believe that there was a conspiracy between the officer and these inmates; the court found that this evidence was sufficient if believed by a jury to warrant recovery.

See Stubbs v. Dudley, 849 F.2d 83, 86 (2d Cir. 1988); Curtis v. Everette, 489 F.2d 516 (3d Cir. 1973); Vance v. Bordenkircher, 533 F. Supp. 429 (N.D. W. Va. 1982) (corrections officer stood by and watched inmate stab plaintiff). However, it is not deliberate indifference for guards to fail to break up a fight when they reasonably believe that their intervention would threaten their own safety. Williams v. Willits, 853 F.2d 586 (8th Cir. 1988).

[65]Payne v. Collins, 986 F. Supp. 1036 (E.D. Tex. 1997) (Plaintiffs brought action against officials of the Texas Department of Criminal Justice for failing to protect their son. Their son suffered injuries from assaults by other inmates that led to his death. He was killed after he refused to pay "protection money." The Court denied defendant's motion for summary judgment holding that since there was some evidence that a prison guard witnessed the violence but failed to stop it, there were triable issues on the question of government liability). Earrey v. Chickasaw County, Miss., 965 F. Supp. 870 (N.D. Miss. 1997) (Plaintiff brought an action against the county after being beaten for fifteen minutes by other inmates while detained in the county jail. The jail plaintiff was held in consisted of six cells, of which most had broken locks. As a result, the prisoners were allowed to move about freely. Defendants' motion for summary judgment was denied; court stated that the defendant might have heard the assault over the intercom that left a question of fact as to the existence of subjective knowledge on the part of the defendant).

§ 2:7 Rights of Prisoners, Third Edition

clear that an assault was imminent.[66] Indeed, prison officials cannot go "out of . . . the way to avoid acquiring unwelcome knowledge."[67] In such a case, knowledge of the danger to the inmate is imputed to the prison officials.[68] This point is perhaps best summarized with the observation that prison officials cannot constitutionally act like ostriches with their heads in the sand, pretending that an easily determinable risk to an inmate's safety does not exist.[69] Thus, the law is fairly clear that prison officials can be held liable for injuries caused by other inmates if the danger of an attack was known or readily apparent, but the defendants failed to take steps to prevent it.[70] This is true even if the plaintiff did not disclose information to defendants in

---

[66]Woods v. Lecureux, 110 F.3d 1215, 46 Fed. R. Evid. Serv. 1111, 1997 FED App. 116P (6th Cir. 1997) (". . . warnings from the prisoner himself are not required when other evidence discloses a substantial risk of serious harm.").

[67]McGill v. Duckworth, 944 F.2d 344, 351, 20 Fed. R. Serv. 3d 1247 (7th Cir. 1991).

[68]See, e.g., Marsh v. Butler County, Ala., 268 F.3d 1014 (11th Cir. 2001) (en banc) (holding that a "jail facility that allows prisoners ready access to weapons, fails to provide an ability to lock down inmates, and fails to allow for surveillance of inmates poses a substantial risk of serious harm to inmates" and plaintiff's allegations that the county had received reports of the conditions, but took no remedial measures states a claim for deliberate indifference against it); James v. Milwaukee County, 956 F.2d 696, 700 (7th Cir. 1992); McGill v. Duckworth, 944 F.2d 344, 348, 20 Fed. R. Serv. 3d 1247 (7th Cir. 1991); Elliott v. Cheshire County, N.H., 940 F.2d 7, 10 (1st Cir. 1991).

[69]McGill v. Duckworth, 944 F.2d 344, 351, 20 Fed. R. Serv. 3d 1247 (7th Cir. 1991).

[70]See, e.g., Pope v. Shafer, 86 F.3d 90 (7th Cir. 1996) (where prison officials were aware of threats made to inmate's safety and disregarded those threats by failing to immediately transfer inmate, evidence was sufficient to support a finding that prison officials were deliberately indifferent to inmate's safety; court affirmed the lower court's award of $75,000 in compensatory damages).

§ 2:7

advance.[71]

Another prominent benchmark of deliberate indifference is the failure of prison officials to respond to information about a danger to a specific inmate.[72] A failure to investigate instances of abuse of inmates by other inmates can give rise to liability under this standard,[73] as can a failure to adequately supervise.[74] In all of these situations, a prisoner need not wait until actually

---

[71]Hayes v. New York City Dept. of Corrections, 84 F.3d 614 (2d Cir. 1996) (plaintiff's refusal to identify his attackers is not dispositive when there is other evidence that defendants knew of the risk).

[72]See, e.g., Young v. Quinlan, 960 F.2d 351, 22 Fed. R. Serv. 3d 530 (3d Cir. 1992) (failure to respond to repeated appeals by inmate to prison guards that another inmate was threatening to rape him is actionable); Anderson v. Gutschenritter, 836 F.2d 346, 349 (7th Cir. 1988); Frett v. Government of Virgin Islands, 839 F.2d 968, 978 (3d Cir. 1988).

The fact that the assaulted inmate may have knowledge that an assault against him is imminent does not exonerate prison officials. They still have the obligation to protect the inmate from harm. Bell v. State, 143 Ariz. 305, 693 P.2d 960 (Ct. App. Div. 1 1984) (holding that the inmate's knowledge of the possibility of an assault is not relevant to defendant's liability). But see Doe v. Bowles, 254 F.3d 617 (6th Cir. 2001) (plaintiff assaulted by fellow inmate in protective custody unit could not prove that captain was deliberately indifferent to attack, because captain took steps to address the danger by asking reporting officer if the prisoners should be formally segregated and the officer said that was not necessary).

[73]See, e.g., Butler v. Dowd, 979 F.2d 661 (8th Cir. 1992); Vosburg v. Solem, 845 F.2d 763 (8th Cir. 1988).

[74]See, e.g., Vosburg v. Solem, 845 F.2d 763 (8th Cir. 1988) (only one guard at night stationed in area holding 175 cells in four tiers, many of them double celled); Bass v. Jackson, 790 F.2d 260, 263 (2d Cir. 1986); Martin v. White, 742 F.2d 469 (8th Cir. 1984) (inadequate surveillance, failure to detect defective cell locks, and failure to report assaults to prosecutor constitutes deliberate indifference); Fisher v. Koehler, 692 F. Supp. 1519, 1549 (S.D. N.Y. 1988); McMurry v. Phelps, 533 F. Supp. 742 (W.D. La. 1982) overruled on other grounds by, Thorne v. Jones, 765 F.2d 1270 (5th Cir. 1985).

assaulted.[75]

There is no requirement that the plaintiffs provide direct proof that the defendant actually knew of the specific risk to the plaintiff.[76] The risk of harm can be proved by circumstantial evidence.[77] Moreover, the risk need not be unique to a particular inmate but rather can be to a particularly vulnerable group of inmates to which he belongs.[78]

---

[75]Helling v. McKinney, 509 U.S. 25, 113 S. Ct. 2475, 2480, 125 L. Ed. 2d 22 (1993) (holding that Eighth Amendment protects against conduct that poses a serious risk of future harm to inmates); Woodhous v. Com. of Va., 487 F.2d 889, 890 (4th Cir. 1973).

[76]See Newman v. Holmes, 122 F.3d 650 (8th Cir. 1997) (upholding liability on circumstantial evidence that the defendants were aware of the risk to plaintiff).

[77]Horton v. Cockrell, 70 F.3d 397, 410 (5th Cir. 1995) (during two-week period inmate filed three grievances and made one oral complaint regarding fears of possible attack; the inmate who he feared had a history of assault; this circumstantial evidence was sufficient to prove knowledge). See also Knowles v. New York City Dept. of Corrections, 904 F. Supp. 217 (S.D. N.Y. 1995) (circumstantial evidence sufficient to show knowledge).

[78]See Clark v. State, 1996 WL 628221 (N.D. Cal. 1996), aff'd, 123 F.3d 1267, 25 A.D.D. 146 (9th Cir. 1997) (court denied defendant's motion for summary judgment where a class of developmentally disabled prisoners claimed that prison officials were deliberately indifferent to their safety and welfare; court held that a genuine issue of material fact existed as to whether defendants knew plaintiff's were vulnerable to physical and mental abuse and failed to take reasonable efforts to protect them); Pugh v. Rockwall County, TX, 2000 WL 730426 (N.D. Tex. 2000) (plaintiff, incarcerated on a charge of injury to a child, was assaulted over a substantial period of time by other inmates, and alleged that defendants unconstitutionally failed to protect him; court held that the defendant administrator's failure to take any action after being advised of the assaults, his failure to correct jail conditions, and improper practices by the guards demonstrated deliberate indifference to the risk to the plaintiff; such indifference was also shown on the part of defendant sheriff, who failed to supervise jail operations and personnel, and whose sole response to overcrowding, understaffing, disrepair, and inmate violence at the jail was to seek budgetary relief).

In one instructive case that illustrates this point, a 78-pound mildly retarded inmate was sexually assaulted after he transferred to a facility that housed prisoners in a dormitory style barracks. The defendant argued that there was no evidence that he was personally aware of any specific risk that the plaintiff would be attacked at the new facility. The Sixth Circuit held that this was not enough to avoid liability, since there was evidence that the warden failed to implement any procedures to "protect vulnerable inmates from dangerous transfers."[79] The court held that the "correct inquiry" is not whether the defendant had personal knowledge of the plaintiff's "particular vulnerabilities." Rather, the "correct inquiry is whether he had knowledge about the substantial risk to a particular class of persons, not whether he knew who the particular victim turned out to be."[80] The evidence that showed that the warden had responsibility for approving all transfers to the facility.

In the same vein, there can be liability for conditions that pose a risk of harm to all prisoners. This can be shown by a "series of incidents closely related in time" or by systematic deficiencies in staffing, facilities or procedures [that] make suffering inevitable."[81] Thus, there is a constitutional violation when plaintiffs demonstrate that there was a "constant threat of violence" in the institution or a "pervasive risk of harm," either to all the inmates in the facility or to an identifiable group, and that the authorities took no action to address the problem.[82] When this occurs, courts have found liability, even in the absence of specific knowl-

---

[79]Taylor v. Michigan Department of Corrections, Taylor v. Michigan Dept. of Corrections, 69 F.3d 76, 1995 FED App. 318P (6th Cir. 1995).

[80]*Id.* at 81.

[81]Fisher v. Koehler, 692 F. Supp. 1519, 1561 (S.D. N.Y. 1988).

[82]See, e.g., LaMarca v. Turner, 995 F.2d 1526 (11th Cir. 1993) (finding pervasive risk of harm where prisoners were exposed to constant violence in dark, overcrowded cells); Butler v. Dowd, 979 F.2d 661 (8th Cir. 1992) (100 assaults in three-year period created

§ 2:7   Rights of Prisoners, Third Edition

edge of the situation, on the theory that the failure to act is the equivalent of "[s]uspecting that something is true but shutting your eyes for fear of what you will learn."[83] A common example of this phenomenon is when correctional officials transfer a known informer to the general population without taking steps to protect him or her in that exposed position[84] Other examples include placing a general population inmate with violent propensities in a work detail in protective custody where the inmate can have access to inmates who are considered "snitches,"[85] allowing conditions of violence so pandemic that prison officials should have been

---

a pervasive risk of harm); Doe v. Sullivan County, Tenn., 956 F.2d 545, 35 Fed. R. Evid. Serv. 117 (6th Cir. 1992) (four incidents per month per 100 inmates created a pervasive risk of harm that was actionable); Withers v. Levine, 615 F.2d 158 (4th Cir. 1980) (finding a pervasive risk of harm); Ruiz v. Estelle, 679 F.2d 1115, 1140-42, 10 Fed. R. Evid. Serv. 1483 (5th Cir. 1982), amended in part, vacated in part on other grounds, 688 F.2d 266 (5th Cir. 1982); Ramos v. Lamm, 639 F.2d 559, 572 (10th Cir. 1980). See also Robinson v. Prunty, 249 F.3d 862 (9th Cir. 2001) (prisoner in administrative segregation alleged that he was attacked by other prisoners as a result of a policy of racial integration in prison yards, in the context of intense race-based gang rivalries). According to commentary, a pervasive risk of harm can be shown by the number or incidents recorded in prison records or by testimony or other evidence showing that serious violence is endemic to the institution. The authors point out that prison records may actually underreport the level of violence, since prisoners are afraid to "snitch" or because prison officials discount their reports or fail to observe them or to report them accurately." John Bost, Daniel E. Manville, Prisoners' Self Help Litigation Manual, 93, N.480 (1995).

[83]McGill v. Duckworth, 944 F.2d 344, 351, 20 Fed. R. Serv. 3d 1247 (7th Cir. 1991).

[84]See, e.g., Gullatte v. Potts, 654 F.2d 1007 (5th Cir. 1981) (transfer of known "snitch" to the general population of maximum security prison where he was murdered); Blizzard v. Quillen, 579 F. Supp. 1446 (D. Del. 1984) (holding prison officials liable for failing to realize that an inmate who had cooperated with a state investigation of prison corruption was in danger when transferred to the general population).

[85]Reece v. Groose, 60 F.3d 487 (8th Cir. 1995) (plaintiff, a known informer, was injured by a general population inmate on janitorial

aware of the need for protective measures without proof of knowledge of a specific risk to the plaintiff,[86] and failing to implement security measures controlling tools or other implements that can be used as weapons.[87] It is not enough simply to allege that such dangerous conditions exist; solid proof must be offered establishing that this is the case.[88]

In some disturbing cases courts have found entire prison systems to be rife with the potential for unnecessary violence and therefore unconstitutional. A prime, but by no means the only, example is *Ruiz v. Johnson,*

---

duty in the protective custody unit when the inmate threw hot water on the plaintiff; the court held that a fact finder could conclude that the risk posed by allowing the attacker into the protective custody unit was so obvious that liability should be imposed).

[86]Gibson v. Babcox, 601 F. Supp. 1156 (N.D. Ill. 1984). See also Shrader v. White, 761 F.2d 975 (4th Cir. 1985).

[87]See, e.g., Smith v. Norris, 877 F. Supp. 1296 (E.D. Ark. 1995), aff'd in part, rev'd in part on other grounds, 103 F.3d 637 (8th Cir. 1996) (inmates' possession of sharp hobby craft tools in an open barracks unit created an obvious risk of harm and demonstrated officials' deliberate indifference); Berry v. City of Muskogee, Okl., 900 F.2d 1489 (10th Cir. 1990) (wire brooms).

[88]See, e.g., Davis v. Scott, 94 F.3d 444, 446-47 (8th Cir. 1996) (claim dismissed because of lack of "solid evidence"); Lewis v. Richards, 107 F.3d 549, 553-54 (7th Cir. 1997) (prisoner must present evidence that official knew of the risk and disregarded it); Franklin v. District of Columbia, 960 F. Supp. 394 (D.D.C. 1997), supplemented, 1997 WL 403418 (D.D.C. 1997), vacated in part, 163 F.3d 625 (D.C. Cir. 1998), reh'g and reh'g en banc denied, 168 F.3d 1360 (D.C. Cir. 1999) and rev'd in part, vacated in part on other grounds, 163 F.3d 625 (D.C. Cir. 1998) supra (class of Hispanic inmates failed to demonstrate prison officials were deliberately indifferent to racially motivated attacks against Hispanic prisoners; rather, evidence showed prison officials "acted promptly to investigate incidents involving Hispanic prisoners and took appropriate action); Cooney v. Hooks, 535 N.W.2d 609 (Minn. 1995) (prison officials did not violate Eighth Amendment regarding failure to protect inmate from other inmates where they placed individual arrested for DWI in cell with two other inmates, one of whom sexually assaulted plaintiff; court noted that there was no evidence that inmate was so intoxicated that he would be easy prey for violent attacks).

§ 2:7   RIGHTS OF PRISONERS, THIRD EDITION

involving the Texas prison system.[89] In that 1999 case, the district court held that institutional resistance to resolving serious safety problems pervaded the system. The lack of protection for the inmates evidenced a lack of control by the prison officials. The evidence revealed a prison underworld in which rapes, beatings, and servitude were the "currency of power." To preserve their physical safety, some vulnerable inmates allowed themselves to be bought and sold among prison predator groups, providing their oppressors with goods, domestic services or sexual favors. The lucky were allowed to pay money for their protection. Others found violating prison rules in order to get locked away in administrative segregation a rational means of self-protection, despite the loss of good-time credits. Accordingly, the court noted that "to expect such a world to rehabilitate wrong-doers is absurd, to allow such a world to exist is unconstitutional."[90]

To say that there is general agreement these matters does not mean that there are no differences about the results that courts reach in these cases. While there are clear aspects of the *Farmer* decision, not all questions have been answered by the opinion. In fact, courts do differ in their judgments about a number of common situations where plaintiffs claim that the risk of harm to an inmate was so serious that the failure to act constituted an Eighth Amendment violation. In these situ-

---

[89]Ruiz v. Johnson, 37 F. Supp. 2d 855 (S.D. Tex. 1999), rev'd on other grounds and remanded, 243 F.3d 941 (5th Cir. 2001). See also Carty v. Farrelly, 957 F. Supp. 727, 22 A.D.D. 333 (D.V.I. 1997) (prison officials at the Criminal Justice Complex (CJC) were held in violation of the Eighth Amendment for their failure to maintain and operate a viable prison classification and security system; prison officials knew of, and failed to adequately respond to, rampant inmate-on-inmate violence; thus, plaintiffs demonstrated that prison officials knowingly disregarded a serious threat of risk to "inmate health and safety"; court held the defendants in civil contempt for their failure to comply with a previous court order to remedy such conditions).

[90]Ruiz v. Johnson, 37 F. Supp. 2d 855 (S.D. Tex. 1999), rev'd on other grounds and remanded, 243 F.3d 941 (5th Cir. 2001).

ations, while courts agree basically on the formulation of the standard, they part company on its application in particular fact patterns. In part, this divergence is caused by the fact that the line between deliberate indifference and negligence is not always easy to draw.[91]

One example of this disagreement arises in cases where the plaintiff claims that the failure of the prison system to adequately separate potential victim-prisoners from inmates who would prey on them violated the Eighth Amendment where the alleged failure led to an assault on a weaker inmate. Some courts have held that the failure to classify, at least into separate categories of persons who pose grave risks to particular groups of inmates, is deliberate indifference;[92] others have not found an Eighth Amendment violation in this kind of case.[93]

An additional illustration is overcrowding. Some

---

[91]Newman v. Holmes, 122 F.3d 650 (8th Cir. 1997) (in a case in which liability was premised on the violation of prison regulations by a guard who wrongfully opened a cell door, allowing an inmate in isolation to escape and attack the plaintiff, the court noted that liability was a "very close" question, since more than mere negligence is required)

[92]See, e.g., Redman v. County of San Diego, 942 F.2d 1435, 1442 (9th Cir. 1991); Vosburg v. Solem, 845 F.2d 763 (8th Cir. 1988); Cortes-Quinones v. Jimenez-Nettleship, 842 F.2d 556, 559-61 (1st Cir. 1988) (placement of mentally disturbed inmate in general population of prison with no psychiatric facilities); Withers v. Levine, 615 F.2d 158 (4th Cir. 1980) (finding a pervasive risk of harm); Jones v. Sheahan, 2000 WL 1377114 (N.D. Ill. 2000) (inmate claimed jail officials were deliberately indifferent to likely harm when it housed gang members and non-gang members together; court held the inmate stated a valid claim of failure to protect); Pagan v. County of Orange, New York, 2001 WL 32785 (S.D. N.Y. 2001) (defendant's motion for summary judgment denied where the incident occurred in a mental health dorm, and officials could have foreseen a substantial risk of harm should the inmates with mental problems be left unsupervised); Fisher v. Koehler, 692 F. Supp. 1519, 1560 (S.D. N.Y. 1988).

[93]See, e.g., James v. Milwaukee County, 956 F.2d 696 (7th Cir. 1992) (failure to separate parole violators from probation violators did not violate the Eighth Amendment); McGill v. Duckworth, 944

§ 2:7

courts have held that the placement of inmates in a severely overcrowded facility, particularly one that makes use of open dormitories[94] or that uses double cells,[95] invites assault, especially where there is no attempt made to classify those inmates who are security risks. Other courts have held that these circumstances alone do not give rise to responsibility for resulting assaults.[96] Some courts interpret indications of pending violence as not serious enough to warrant a finding of deliberate indifference even though the signs, had they been heeded, would have prevented violence.[97] Other

---

F.2d 344, 20 Fed. R. Serv. 3d 1247 (7th Cir. 1991) (holding that placing a small young protective custody inmate in a segregation unit with inmates on disciplinary status did not violate the Eighth Amendment).

[94]See, e.g., Ruiz v. Estelle, 679 F.2d 1115, 10 Fed. R. Evid. Serv. 1483 (5th Cir. 1982), amended in part, vacated in part on other grounds, 688 F.2d 266 (5th Cir. 1982); Fisher v. Koehler, 692 F. Supp. 1519, 1546-47, (S.D. N.Y. 1988); Grubbs v. Bradley, 552 F. Supp. 1052, 1128 (M.D. Tenn. 1982) (holding that overcrowding can contribute to high levels of violence).

[95]See, e.g., Jensen v. Clarke, 94 F.3d 1191 (8th Cir. 1996) (inmates at Nebraska State Penitentiary brought a class action claiming prison procedures regarding double-cell assignments created "pervasive risk of harm"; court held that the double-celling of inmates did not violate the Eighth Amendment per se but the "manner in which the defendants were conducting the practice did"; in particular, prison authorities failed to determine if cellmates were compatible; as evidence, plaintiffs submitted statistics demonstrating the increase in violent incidents since double-celling was increased; court affirmed lower court's requirement of injunctive relief, consisting of the employment of prison classification procedures to determine inmate compatibility).

[96]See, e.g., James v. Milwaukee County, 956 F.2d 696 (7th Cir. 1992) (housing an inmate in an open dormitory does not create liability for inmate assaults); Marsh v. Arn, 937 F.2d 1056, 1062 (6th Cir. 1991) (same).

[97]See, e.g., Torrence v. Musilek, 899 F. Supp. 380 (N.D. Ill. 1995) (where prison officials received a letter from two inmates, which stated that they were going "to kick someone's ass" if they weren't transferred, prison officials were not deliberately indifferent, in violation of Eighth Amendment, to well-being of a third

§ 2:7

courts take a contrary view.[98]

It is difficult to reconcile all the cases. The divergence may result from the inherently subjective approach of the deliberate indifference standard that requires courts and factfinders to make delicate judgments about the state of mind of prison officials. In part, it may reflect the factual differences in the cases. In part, it may reflect the records that were made in the particular cases.[99] A final explanation may lie in the fact that the courts that are unwilling to find a violation when the assault can be attributed to a failure to classify or to overcrowding tend to overlook the systemic failures in

---

inmate whom they assaulted; court found that the letter did not threaten any inmate specifically); Gangloff v. Poccia, 888 F. Supp. 1549 (M.D. Fla. 1995) (prison officials did not violate Eighth Amendment where inmate alleged that officials failed to adequately protect inmate from another inmate; court found that inmate's statement to prison officials that he believed he might be in danger because he informed prison officials that other inmates had failed to lock their cells that evening, and prison official's failure to act, were insufficient to establish that prison officials acted with deliberate indifference to inmate's warnings).

[98]See, e.g., Evans v. Federal Bureau of Prisons, 28 F.3d 105 (9th Cir. 1994), as amended, (Oct. 6, 1994)(Eighth Amendment requires prison officials to protect prisoners from the threat of violence; to establish an Eighth Amendment violation, a prisoner must show that prison personnel acted with "deliberate indifference" to the inmate's need for a safe environment; deliberate indifference requires that a prison official "knows of and disregards an excessive risk" to the inmate's safety; prison official may be found to have known of a substantial risk if that risk was obvious); Riddle v. Mondragon, 83 F.3d 1197 (10th Cir. 1996)(inmate's Eighth Amendment claim for failure to protect is comprised of two elements: first, inmate must show that he is incarcerated under conditions posing substantial risk of serious harm, then must establish that prison official has sufficiently culpable state of mind, in that he or she is deliberately indifferent to inmate's health or safety).

[99]See, e.g., Fisher v. Koehler, 692 F. Supp. 1519, 1546-47, (S.D. N.Y. 1988) (commending plaintiffs' counsel for marshalling a mass of facts necessary to deal with a violence case and for presenting testimony that enabled court to make connections between the levels of violence and its causes).

management of the prison that contribute to a climate of violence and focus more on the individual actions of guards working in that environment.[100]

Remedies for Assaults by Inmates

If an inmate is a victim of an assault and proves that the defendants violated his right to safety, he is entitled to recover damages compensating him for his injuries.[101] Damages are not available unless the defendant is actually physically injured.[102] Of course, prison officials are not responsible for injuries that occur to an inmate as a result of an altercation that the inmate initiates.[103] There is no recovery in damages for living in fear of assault unless it can be proven that the prison officials

---

[100]See, e.g., McGill v. Duckworth, 944 F.2d 344, 348, 20 Fed. R. Serv. 3d 1247 (7th Cir. 1991) (holding that "the size of prisons, the number of separate areas, and so on, are in the hands of the state," not in the hands of the defendants); Walsh v. Brewer, 733 F.2d 473 (7th Cir. 1984) (finding no liability for assault by cellmate despite warnings to officials when defendant had no control over cell assignments); Wheeler v. Sullivan, 599 F. Supp. 630 (D. Del. 1984) (overcrowded conditions must be taken into account where they led to an assault against a young inmate, but responsibility for overcrowding that caused the assault could not be attributed to the defendants).

[101]Pope v. Shafer, 86 F.3d 90 (7th Cir. 1996) (affirming award of $75,000).

[102]See, e.g., Bracewell v. Lobmiller, 938 F. Supp. 1571 (M.D. Ala. 1996), aff'd, 116 F.3d 1493 (11th Cir. 1997) (inmate confined to a segregated housing unit failed to satisfy the subjective component of *Farmer*; plaintiff was subjected to presence of a mentally disturbed inmate who threw feces, urine, and constantly made noise; such conditions caused the plaintiff severe emotional and psychological harm, but no physical harm); Hopkins v. Campbell, 870 F. Supp. 316 (D. Kan. 1994) (no cause of action can be maintained unless the prisoner was subjected to some form of physical violence).

[103]Hailey v. Kaiser, 201 F.3d 447 (10th Cir. 1999) (plaintiff inmate sued prison authorities, claiming they were deliberately indifferent to his safety and security but the claim failed because the district court found that plaintiff was the aggressor in the altercation and admitted that he could have avoided it).

were not merely deliberately indifferent to the risk of harm but instead acted maliciously and sadistically.[104] However, the Supreme Court has established that an inmate need not wait to be injured before bringing suit.[105] Therefore, there are remedies additional to damage awards that may be granted. One remedy involves isolating the potential perpetrator and potential victim of assault. Another involves ordering injunctive relief to alleviate the conditions that give rise to an unacceptable level of violence.

Court-Ordered Remedies for Inmate Assaults

When plaintiffs seeking injunctive relief have successfully established that there is a constant threat of violence or a pervasive risk of harm in the institution, courts have ordered changes in the administration of the prison to address the problem.[106] One court, after concluding that conditions at a state penitentiary violated the Eighth Amendment, ordered the presence of two guards in open dormitories at all times as a means of increasing control of homosexual activity.[107] In the same vein, the Fifth Circuit Court of Appeals up-

---

[104]See e.g., Doe v. Welborn, 110 F.3d 520 (7th Cir. 1997); Babcock v. White, 102 F.3d 267 (7th Cir. 1996).

[105]See Farmer v. Brennan, 511 U.S. 825, 114 S. Ct. 1970, 128 L. Ed. 2d 811 (1994). See also Benefield v. McDowall, 241 F.3d 1267 (10th Cir. 2001) (inmate claimed defendant guard labeled him a "snitch" and fabricated letters he allegedly wrote to provide investigators with information; court found that the claim could go forward even though the inmate had not actually been assaulted; pursuant to Farmer, the court held that the inmate sufficiently alleged facts that, if proved, would satisfy the subjective element needed for a finding of deliberate indifference subjecting the inmate to the threat of serious harm: no actual assault was needed to find an Eighth Amendment violation).

[106]See, e.g., Fisher v. Koehler, 692 F. Supp. 1519, 1565-66 (S.D. N.Y. 1988).

[107]Williams v. Edwards, 547 F.2d 1206, 1213-14 (5th Cir. 1977). See also Balla v. Idaho State Bd. of Corrections, 595 F. Supp. 1558 (D. Idaho 1984) (ordering a doubling of security in units which were double-celled).

held a directive that a guard visit each occupied area once an hour.[108] To accomplish the goal of ensuring adequate supervision of inmates, courts have ordered the hiring of additional staff.[109] In addition, other changes designed to ameliorate the causes of violence[110] have been required in such areas as classification, overcrowding, and lack of sufficient cell housing.[111]

Isolating the Attacker or Victim

Another more limited approach to the problem of prison violence is for prison officials to create separate administrative segregation areas for inmates who might be assaultive and for inmates who might be victims of assault. Prison accreditation standards specifically ap-

---

[108]Smith v. Sullivan, 553 F.2d 373 (5th Cir. 1977). See also Smith v. Norris, 877 F. Supp. 1296 (E.D. Ark. 1995), aff'd in part, rev'd in part on other grounds, 103 F.3d 637 (8th Cir. 1996) (prison must take reasonable measures to protect inmates, including regular spot checks of open barracks).

[109]See, e.g., Smith v. Norris, 877 F. Supp. 1296 (E.D. Ark. 1995), aff'd in part, rev'd in part on other grounds, 103 F.3d 637 (8th Cir. 1996) (holding that where 92 prison guard positions were needed for adequate supervision of open barracks, an Eighth Amendment violation existed); Alberti v. Heard, 600 F. Supp. 443 (S.D. Tex. 1984), order aff'd, 790 F.2d 1220 (5th Cir. 1986); Alberti v. Klevenhagen, 606 F. Supp. 478 (S.D. Tex. 1985).

[110]Courts have found the use of expert witnesses helpful in determining what the causes are of excessive violence in a particular prison. See, e.g., Fisher v. Koehler, 692 F. Supp. 1519, 1541-51 (S.D. N.Y. 1988) (making extensive use of expert testimony to determine causes of violence); Hughes v. District of Columbia, 425 A.2d 1299 (D.C. 1981).

[111]See, e.g., Fisher v. Koehler, 692 F. Supp. 1519, 1567-69 (S.D. N.Y. 1988). One court has also suggested, but not mandated, the use of surveillance cameras as a means of increasing surveillance and reducing violence. Lovell v. Brennan, 566 F. Supp. 672 (D. Me. 1983), judgment aff'd, 728 F.2d 560 (1st Cir. 1984). See also Villante v. Department of Corrections of City of New York, 786 F.2d 516, 5 Fed. R. Serv. 3d 141 (2d Cir. 1986). But see National Advisory Commn on Criminal Justice Standards and Goals, Corrections Standard 2.4 (1973) (recommending against excessive reliance on such devices).

§ 2:7

prove of administrative segregation to protect the inmate who is segregated, other inmates, staff, or prison security.[112] The administrative segregation unit can hold either the potential assailant or the intended victim. The decision on which to isolate generally turns on administrative feasibility. When one or a handful of inmates, because of their violent propensities, threaten a large number of prisoners, the response is to isolate the violent minority from the majority. Conversely, when there is an identifiable victim, but a large unidentifiable group of potential assailants, such as when a young male prisoner is likely to be the target of a homosexual attack by other convicts, the victim is generally segregated to prevent the assault.[113] Prison officials have been given wide discretion by the courts in setting up these units.[114]

In *Hewitt v. Helms*,[115] the Supreme Court held that confining (to an administrative segregation unit) an inmate who might pose a threat to the safety of other inmates and staff did not by itself implicate a constitutional liberty interest entitling the inmate to due process protections against transfer.[116] The Court distinguished administrative segregation from punitive segregation, where due process protections are

---

[112]See e.g., US Dept of Justice, Federal Standards for Prisons and Jails § 11.05 (1980); Natl Sheriffs' Assn, Inmates' Legal Rights Right 12 (1987); Model Corrections and Sentencing Act § 4-411 (2001); American Correctional Assn., Standards for Adult Correctional Institutions Standard 3-4268 (2002).

[113]See, e.g., 28 CFR § 541.23.

[114]See, e.g., Hewitt v. Helms, 459 U.S. 460, 103 S. Ct. 864, 74 L. Ed. 2d 675 (1983); U.S. v. Smith, 464 F.2d 194 (10th Cir. 1972); Faison v. Riddle, 425 F. Supp. 648 (E.D. Va. 1977); Hancock v. Avery, 301 F. Supp. 786 (M.D. Tenn. 1969); State v. Brown, 643 S.W.2d 68 (Mo. Ct. App. W.D. 1982).

[115]Hewitt v. Helms, 459 U.S. 460, 103 S. Ct. 864, 74 L. Ed. 2d 675 (1983).

[116]*Id.* at 468.

§ 2:7   Rights of Prisoners, Third Edition

required.[117] Punitive segregation is intended as punishment for acts in violation of prison rules. Administrative segregation, by contrast, is not meant to be punitive. Since there is no intent to punish, and since confinement in administrative segregation does not entail loss of other benefits such as good-time credits-as is often the case with punitive segregation-confinement to these "less amenable and more restrictive quarters for nonpunitive reasons is well within the terms of confinement ordinarily contemplated by a prison sentence."[118]

Therefore, confinement in administrative segregation can be accomplished without the full panoply of due process protections. All that the inmate normally is entitled to is an informal, nonadversary review of the information supporting the inmate's transfer to administrative segregation and some opportunity to refute the claims.[119] In addition to this review, due process may require some method of periodic review of the necessity for continued confinement in administrative segregation.[120]

Semantics, however, should not cloud the reality of

---

[117]*Id.* at 468-78. In Wolff v. McDonnell, 418 U.S. 539, 94 S. Ct. 2963, 41 L. Ed. 2d 935 (1974), the Court held that inmates may not be confined in punitive segregation without procedural safeguards. See also U.S. ex rel. Hoss v. Cuyler, 452 F. Supp. 256, 286 (E.D. Pa. 1978) (greater deference should be given to administrative judgment when purpose is to prevent violence rather than to punish the confined prisoner). *Wolff* is discussed at length in Ch 9.

[118]Hewitt v. Helms, 459 U.S. 460, 468, 103 S. Ct. 864, 74 L. Ed. 2d 675 (1983).

[119]*Id.* at 472. *Hewitt* is discussed in full in Ch 10.

[120]Hewitt v. Helms, 459 U.S. 460, 479 n. 8, 103 S. Ct. 864, 74 L. Ed. 2d 675 (1983). This review must occur at regular intervals at least once every several months. See, e.g., McQueen v. Tabah, 839 F.2d 1525 (11th Cir. 1988); Toussaint v. McCarthy, 801 F.2d 1080 (9th Cir. 1986) (12 months without review violates due process). See, e.g., US Dept of Justice, Federal Standards for Prisons and Jails § 11.06 (1980) (review every seven days for the first two months, then every 30 days); Natl Sheriffs' Assn, Inmates' Legal

what is happening. If the prisoner's confinement to administrative segregation is, in fact, a punishment for past conduct, then disciplinary proceedings for that conduct should be brought. The significant due process requirements established by the Supreme Court in *Wolff v. McDonnell*,[121] which govern disciplinary proceedings, should not be circumvented by the expedient of labeling a prisoner's isolation as administrative rather than punitive.[122]

The isolation of potential victims poses other problems. Surely, society's collective conscience would be shocked if a woman were confined in jail to protect her from being raped. Yet, is it not the same reasoning that allows a male prisoner to be administratively segregated in protective custody to protect him from homosexual rape? The issue is rarely litigated, because, in most instances, the administrative segregation is at the request of the potential victim, who has presumably waived all objections to such confinement.[123] This argument is not persuasive, however, because a valid waiver must be voluntary, which it arguably is not when

---

Rights, Right 12 (1987) (every two weeks); Model Corrections and Sentencing Act § 4-411(c) (2001) (every 30 days); American Correctional Assn., Standards for Adult Correctional Institutions Standard 3-4241 (2001) (every seven days for first two weeks, then every 30 days). For a fuller discussion of the due process rights involved in administrative segregation see Ch 8.

[121]Wolff v. McDonnell, 418 U.S. 539, 94 S. Ct. 2963, 41 L. Ed. 2d 935 (1974). See Ch 8.

[122]See, e.g., Peranzo v. Coughlin, 850 F.2d 125 (2d Cir. 1988); Woodson v. Lack, 865 F.2d 107 (6th Cir. 1989) (administrative segregation for rules violations requires *Wolff* protections); Bishop v. McCoy, 174 W. Va. 99, 323 S.E.2d 140 (1984) (transfer of prisoner purportedly for protective custody purposes was in fact punitive and violated the Eighth Amendment). For a full discussion of this point, see Ch 10.

[123]James E. Robertson, The Constitution in Protective Custody: An Analysis of the Rights of Protective Custody Inmates, 56 Cin L Rev 91 (1987) (noting that 6.5% of all inmates are held in protective custody and that approximately 80% have voluntarily requested placement in that status).

§ 2:7   Rights of Prisoners, Third Edition

prompted by prison conditions highly conducive to physical assault. Despite this, courts have ruled that there is no interest inherent in the Constitution that would prevent prison officials from involuntarily transferring an inmate to protective custody for his or her protection.[124] Similarly, there is no right to be confined in such units if prison officials do not deem it necessary.[125] However, there may be liability if prison officials fail to classify inmates and as a result violent inmates are placed in close confinement with vulnerable ones.[126]

When challenges to protective custody do occur, it is usually because the conditions in protective segregation are as bad as those in solitary confinement.[127] Where

---

[124]See, e.g., Hewitt v. Helms, 459 U.S. 460, 103 S. Ct. 864, 74 L. Ed. 2d 675 (1983); Deane v. Dunbar, 777 F.2d 871 (2d Cir. 1985) (holding that there is no due process right to be free of confinement in protective custody). But see 28 CFR § 541.23(b) (inmates placed in administrative segregation for protection but not at their request are entitled to a hearing with due process safeguards).

[125]See, e.g., Adams v. Rice, 40 F.3d 72 (4th Cir. 1994) (prisoner had no constitutional right to protective or minimum custody nor to parole or its attendant administrative procedures where prisoner was housed in single-cell unit and other inmates posed no threat); Roudette v. State, 224 A.D.2d 808, 638 N.Y.S.2d 185 (3d Dep't 1996) (prison officials were not negligent where they failed to place inmate in protective custody after he requested it and inmate was later attacked by another inmate; court noted that inmate failed to alert interviewing officer of the reason for his request or the degree of urgency); Jones v. Russell, 950 F. Supp. 855 (N.D. Ill. 1996) (court held inmate had no constitutional right to be housed in protective custody on demand; thus, the placement of the plaintiff in disciplinary segregation for his refusal to re-enter the general prison population did not violate the Eighth Amendment); Lovell v. Brennan, 566 F. Supp. 672 (D. Me. 1983), judgment aff'd, 728 F.2d 560 (1st Cir. 1984); Young v. Scully, 515 F. Supp. 8 (S.D. N.Y. 1981).

[126]Trout v. Buie, 653 N.E.2d 1002 (Ind. Ct. App. 1995) (placing plaintiff, charged with DWI, in cell with inmate charged with murder and arson may violate right to be protected from harm).

[127]See, e.g., Young v. Quinlan, 960 F.2d 351, 22 Fed. R. Serv. 3d 530 (3d Cir. 1992); Henderson v. DeRobertis, 940 F.2d 1055 (7th

§ 2:7

they are not, the fact that inmates segregated at their own request suffer deprivations, such as limited recreational opportunities, an inferior prison menu, and restricted shaving and bathing privileges, has been held not to give rise to an Eighth Amendment claim.[128] Conversely, prisoners in protective custody may not be denied fundamental rights, such as access to courts or the free exercise of religion, absent a compelling state interest.[129] It is worth noting that the willingness of courts to uphold restrictions in protective custody that are not shared by inmates in the general population runs counter to correctional standards which call for protective custody inmates to be given treatment similar to that of other inmates.[130]

Cir. 1991); Hancock v. Avery, 301 F. Supp. 786 (M.D. Tenn. 1969). Cf. People ex rel. Schipski v. Flood, 88 A.D.2d 197, 452 N.Y.S.2d 652 (2d Dep't 1982) (holding that 22-hour per day lock-in procedure violated rights under state constitution). See § 2:3.

[128]French v. Owens, 777 F.2d 1250 (7th Cir. 1985); Taylor v. Rogers, 781 F.2d 1047 (4th Cir. 1986); Breeden v. Jackson, 457 F.2d 578 (4th Cir. 1972). But see Wojtczak v. Cuyler, 480 F. Supp. 1288 (E.D. Pa. 1979) (holding that denial of privileges available to general population inmates violates the Eighth Amendment); Nadeau v. Helgemoe, 423 F. Supp. 1250 (D.N.H. 1976), aff'd in part, vacated in part on other grounds, remanded, 561 F.2d 411 (1st Cir. 1977) (equal protection claim upheld where protective custody inmates were denied privileges available to the general population).

[129]The issue of the rights of persons in protective custody to these specific entitlements are discussed in the chapters devoted to these topics. See Chs 6 and 11.

[130]See, e.g., US Dept of Justice, Federal Standards for Prisons and Jails § 11.07 (1980) (inmates in administrative segregation to be accorded same general privileges as inmates in general population); Model Sentencing and Corrections Act § 4-411(a) (2001) (a person in protective custody may not be denied privileges available in general population unless essential to ensure his or her protection); Natl. Sheriffs' Assn., Inmates' Legal Rights, Right 12 (1987) (inmates in segregation have same rights as general population); American Correctional Assn., Standards for Adult Correctional Institutions Standards 3-4251, 3-4254 (2002) (inmates in segregation have same rights to laundry, barber, and mail as others).

Given the rationale of protecting inmates from violence through segregation, prison officials may not create rules that have the opposite effect. Thus, the court in *Nadeau v. Helgemoe*[131] invalidated a prison policy requiring administratively segregated inmates to receive visitors in the same room as members of the general prison population, where the inmates were exposed to verbal abuse and the threat of physical assault.[132]

§ 2:8 Escape from Prison to Avoid Assaults

The question of whether there is a right to be free from homosexual or physical assault can arise in an oblique manner. An inmate in fear of such an assault may escape. Recaptured and tried for escape, the defendant may raise the defense of necessity or duress, citing the threat of the homosexual attack. Earlier decisions tended to reject this defense.[1] Some courts invoked the requirement that the threat had to be imminent,[2] even though this would likely nullify all possibility of

---

[131]Nadeau v. Helgemoe, 423 F. Supp. 1250 (D.N.H. 1976), aff'd in part, vacated in part, remanded, 561 F.2d 411 (1st Cir. 1977).

[132]*Id.* at 1274. See also Balla v. Idaho State Bd. of Corrections, 595 F. Supp. 1558 (D. Idaho 1984) (prison officials should be sensitive to predatory attacks on prisoners placed in protective custody). But see McGill v. Duckworth, 944 F.2d 344, 20 Fed. R. Serv. 3d 1247 (7th Cir. 1991) (no liability even when protective custody inmate was assaulted by general population inmates); Godinez v. Lane, 733 F.2d 1250 (7th Cir. 1984) (holding that it did not violate the Eighth Amendment to permit general population inmates access to protective custody unit where no particular instance of serious harm had occurred).

[Section 2:8]

[1]See, e.g., State v. Green, 470 S.W.2d 565 (Mo. 1971); People v. Richards, 269 Cal. App. 2d 768, 75 Cal. Rptr. 597 (1st Dist. 1969); People v. Whipple, 100 Cal. App. 261, 279 P. 1008 (2d Dist. 1929). For an example of a more recent case rejecting the defense, see People v. Waters, 163 Cal. App. 3d 935, 209 Cal. Rptr. 661 (6th Dist. 1985).

[2]See, e.g., People v. Richards, 269 Cal. App. 2d 768, 75 Cal. Rptr. 597, 604 (1st Dist. 1969).

avoiding the attack. Others reasoned that for a duress defense to succeed, the escaping inmate must have been compelled to escape by other inmates.[3]

There is now a growing trend to accept a limited justification defense.[4] The leading case is *People v. Lovercamp*,[5] where the court accepted the defense, but only under the following carefully circumscribed conditions. There had to be: (1) a specific threat of death, forcible sexual attack, or substantial bodily injury in the immediate future;[6] (2) no time for complaint to the appropriate officials, or a history indicating that a complaint would prove futile;[7] (3) no time or opportunity to resort to the judiciary;[8] (4) no use of force or violence against

---

[3] See, e.g., People v. Richards, 269 Cal. App. 2d 768, 75 Cal. Rptr. 597, 601 (1st Dist. 1969).

[4] For scholarly commentary on this defense, see, e.g., Michael G. Levin, Flight, Flee, Submit, Sue: Alternatives for Sexually Assaulted Prisoners, 18 Colum JL & Soc Probs 505 (1985); Herbert Fingarette, Victimization: A Legalist Analysis of Coercion, Deception, Undue Influence and Excusable Prison Escape, 42 Wash & Lee 65 (1985); Philip D. Webb, Necessity as a Defense to Prison Escape in Texas, 21 S Tex LJ 211 (1981).

[5] People v. Lovercamp, 43 Cal. App. 3d 823, 118 Cal. Rptr. 110, 69 A.L.R.3d 668 (4th Dist. 1974).

[6] A single threat from an unknown source occurring two to four weeks before the escape was held insufficient to justify an instruction on duress. State v. Watkins, 316 N.W.2d 627 (S.D. 1982). See also Com. v. Brown, 314 Pa. Super. 311, 460 A.2d 1155 (1983) (most recent threat coming one week before escape); State v. Kirkland, 684 S.W.2d 402 (Mo. Ct. App. W.D. 1984) (subjective fear of harm or injury, standing alone, is not sufficient to establish the defense).

[7] See People v. McKnight, 626 P.2d 678 (Colo. 1981). See also Joanne Mariner No Escape: Male Rape in the U.S. Prisons, 154-156 (Human Rights Watch 2001) (indicating that prison officials tend to downplay claims of sexual abuse and rarely prosecute offenders).

[8] See State v. Heald, 443 A.2d 954 (Me. 1982).

§ 2:8   Rights of Prisoners, Third Edition

prison personnel or other "innocent" persons;[9] and (5) the prisoner had to turn himself or herself in to the proper authorities after attaining a position of safety in regard to the threatened harm.[10]

The modern trend, therefore, is to accept this defense if the rigid *Lovercamp* guidelines are met. Thus, in one case, the court permitted the defense to be raised when the defendant escaped after he was faced with an imminent transfer to another prison holding gang members against whom he had testified and who had threatened to kill him.[11] The United States Supreme Court in *United States v. Bailey*,[12] also has indicated that it would accept this defense in construing a comparable defense to a federal escape charge, as long as the defendant could show that the fifth criterion was satisfied; that is, that there was a bona fide effort to surrender after the claimed duress had lost its coercive force.[13] Whenever the defense is used, the burden is on the defendant to establish that the criteria have been met.[14]

If this defense is permitted for an escape charge, it

---

[9] Cf U.S. v. Mauchlin, 670 F.2d 746, 10 Fed. R. Evid. Serv. 256 (7th Cir. 1982) (firing of weapon undercut necessity defense to charge of illegal conveyance of weapons in prison).

[10] People v. Lovercamp, 43 Cal. App. 3d 823, 118 Cal. Rptr. 110, 115, 69 A.L.R.3d 668 (4th Dist. 1974). See also State v. Little, 67 N.C. App. 128, 312 S.E.2d 695 (1984); Com. v. Brown, 314 Pa. Super. 311, 460 A.2d 1155 (1983); People v. Pelate, 49 Ill. App. 3d 11, 6 Ill. Dec. 913, 363 N.E.2d 860 (5th Dist. 1977); State v. Horn, 58 Haw. 252, 566 P.2d 1378 (1977). But compare People v. Unger, 66 Ill. 2d 333, 5 Ill. Dec. 848, 362 N.E.2d 319 (1977) (*Lovercamp* criteria are relevant but all do not necessarily have to be present).

[11] Com. v. O'Malley, 14 Mass. App. Ct. 314, 439 N.E.2d 832 (1982).

[12] U.S. v. Bailey, 444 U.S. 394, 100 S. Ct. 624, 62 L. Ed. 2d 575 (1980).

[13] *Id.* Accord Holdren v. State, 415 So. 2d 39 (Fla. Dist. Ct. App. 2d Dist. 1982); Com. v. Slavik, 297 Pa. Super. 135, 443 A.2d 336 (1982).

[14] See, e.g., People v. Waters, 163 Cal. App. 3d 935, 209 Cal. Rptr. 661 (6th Dist. 1985).

would follow, a fortiori, that it would be permitted as a defense to a lesser crime, such as possession of contraband where the contraband is a weapon obtained for self-defense.[15]

While there is support for a justification defense to a criminal charge where the offense was motivated by the desire to forestall an assault, there does not appear to be a comparable judicial movement toward accepting this defense in situations where the escape was motivated by a desire to avoid the imposition of unconstitutional conditions of confinement.[16]

§ 2:9 Conditions of Confinement-Basic Human Needs and the Prisoner's Physical Well-Being

Research References

West's Key Number Digest, Prisons ⚿17

---

[15]See, e.g., People v. Green, 98 A.D.2d 908, 471 N.Y.S.2d 371 (3d Dep't 1983). See also People v. Perry, 145 Mich. App. 778, 377 N.W.2d 911 (1985) (prisoner charged with possession of weapon could be acquitted if jury found that the weapon was obtained for self-defense and that the inmate intended to surrender it at first opportunity); Cook v. Coughlin, 97 A.D.2d 663, 469 N.Y.S.2d 204 (3d Dep't 1983) (justification was a valid defense to charge of assault and possession of a dangerous weapon). But compare People v. Velasquez, 158 Cal. App. 3d 418, 204 Cal. Rptr. 640 (2d Dist. 1984) (necessity does not justify arming oneself against future unanticipated attack by fellow prisoners); People v. Crooks, 151 Mich. App. 389, 390 N.W.2d 250 (1986) (duress not available where inmate had been offered, but declined, protective custody).

[16]See, e.g., People v. McKnight, 626 P.2d 678 (Colo. 1981); People v. Mendoza, 108 Mich. App. 733, 310 N.W.2d 860 (1981); State v. Green, 470 S.W.2d 565 (Mo. 1971); State v. Palmer, 45 Del. 308, 72 A.2d 442 (Gen. Sess. 1950). But see People v. Martin, 100 Mich. App. 447, 298 N.W.2d 900 (1980) (disapproved of by, People v. Ruff, 108 Mich. App. 716, 310 N.W.2d 852 (1981)) (noting that medical necessity might justify escape). See, generally, George P. Fletcher, Should Intolerable Prison Conditions Generate a Justification or an Excuse for Escape, 26 UCLA L Rev 1355 (1979); Cynthia R. Farina, Note, Escape from Cruel and Unusual Punishment: A Theory of Constitutional Necessity, 59 BU L Rev 334 (1979).

§ 2:9   RIGHTS OF PRISONERS, THIRD EDITION

When a government imprisons individuals, it must assume responsibility for their well-being, as incarceration in many respects prevents inmates from caring for themselves. For example, a state, having foreclosed access to private physicians, cannot then deliberately ignore a convict's medical complaints. Similarly, the state must provide prisoners with the minimal necessities of life, including adequate food, clothing, and shelter, since prisoners are not free to provide these essentials themselves. As the Supreme Court noted:

> [W]hen the state by the affirmative exercise of its power so restrains an individual's liberty that it renders him unable to care for himself, and at the same time fails to provide for his basic human needs—e.g., food, clothing, shelter, medical care, and reasonable safety-it transgresses . . . the Eighth Amendment.[1]

Thus, with imprisonment, the state assumes the obligation of caring for inmates and providing them with the essentials of life. The Eighth Amendment stands as a barrier against prison "subhuman" conditions that, if left unchecked, could make those conditions "reminis-

---

[Section 2:9]

[1]Helling v. McKinney, 509 U.S. 25, 113 S. Ct. 2475, 2480, 125 L. Ed. 2d 22 (1993) (emphasis supplied) (quoting DeShaney v. Winnebago County Dept. of Social Services, 489 U.S. 189, 199-200, 109 S. Ct. 998, 103 L. Ed. 2d 249 (1989)). See also Rhodes v. Chapman, 452 U.S. 337, 347, 101 S. Ct. 2392, 69 L. Ed. 2d 59 (1981) (holding that the state is obligated under the Eighth Amendment to provide "the minimal civilized measure of life's necessities"). Not every inmate desire is included within the ambit of life's necessities covered by the Eighth Amendment. See, e.g., Austin v. Lehman, 893 F. Supp. 448 (E.D. Pa. 1995) (prison officials did not violate Eighth Amendment where they denied inmate his biweekly allotment of cigarettes while he was in disciplinary segregation; court noted that inmate was not denied life's basics necessities); May v. Baldwin, 895 F. Supp. 1398, 1408 (D. Or. 1995), judgment aff'd, 109 F.3d 557 (9th Cir. 1997) (prison officials did not violate Eighth Amendment regarding cruel and unusual punishment where inmate was given 24 hours to unbraid his dreadlocks).

cent of the Black Hole of Calcutta."[2] Courts, utilizing the Eighth Amendment, have played an important role in policing the conditions of confinement to ensure that "the numerous aspects of prison confinement that have the potential for causing deleterious effects on the physical and mental well-being of prisoners" are remedied.[3] The sections that follow will survey the conditions that, alone or in combination, may fall so far below the "contemporary standards of decency" as to call for judicial scrutiny.[4]

§ 2:10 —Diet

It has long been held that the failure to properly prepare and serve nutritionally adequate meals consti-

---

[2]Jackson v. Duckworth, 955 F.2d 21 (7th Cir. 1992) (so labeled a complaint that conditions of confinement included forcing an inmate to live with "filth, leaking and inadequate plumbing, roaches, rodents, the constant smell of human waste, poor lighting, dirty and unclean bedding, without toilet paper, rusted out toilets, broken windows, [and] drinking water contain[ing] small black worms which would eventually turn into small black flies").

[3]Anderson v. Coughlin, 757 F.2d 33, 35 (2d Cir. 1985). See also Jordan v. Gardner, 986 F.2d 1521 (9th Cir. 1993) (holding cross gender clothed body searches violative of the Eighth Amendment because of its psychological effect on inmates). While work assignments are considered conditions of confinement subject to scrutiny under the Eighth Amendment, Choate v. Lockhart, 7 F.3d 1370, 1373 (8th Cir. 1993), not every violation of safety rules violates the Eighth Amendment. See, e.g., Bagola v. Kindt, 131 F.3d 632 (7th Cir. 1997) (inmate claimed that prison officials failed to protect him, which resulted in the loss of his hand by a textile machine; earlier the prison was cited for safety violations pertaining to these machines; court held that the incident did not rise to the level of an Eighth Amendment violation simply because the accident occurred within prison walls). For a discussion of minimum conditions of confinement which prison officials must provide inmates see Jay P. Kesan & Stephan L. Teischer, Prisoner's Substantive Rights, 83 Georgetown L Rev 1462 (1995).

[4]Helling v. McKinney, 509 U.S. 25, 113 S. Ct. 2475, 125 L. Ed. 2d 22 (1993).

§ 2:10 RIGHTS OF PRISONERS, THIRD EDITION

tutes an Eighth Amendment violation.[1] Since prisoners depend on the state to feed them, they are entitled to "nutritionally adequate food that is prepared and served . . . under conditions which do not present an immediate danger to the health and well being of the inmates who consume it."[2] Not surprisingly, then, the refusal to provide food for 50 ½ hours was held to be a violation of the Eighth Amendment,[3] as was a diet that caused

[Section 2:10]

[1] See, e.g., Adams v. Mathis, 458 F. Supp. 302 (M.D. Ala. 1978), judgment aff'd, 614 F.2d 42 (5th Cir. 1980).

[2] Ramos v. Lamm, 639 F.2d 559, 570-71 (10th Cir. 1980). Accord, Antonelli v. Sheahan, 81 F.3d 1422 (7th Cir. 1996) (inmate stated a claim where he alleged that prison officials violated Eighth Amendment where prison food was rancid and nutritionally deficient; court noted that inmate alleged that these conditions caused a health risk to inmates); Keenan v. Hall, 83 F.3d 1083, 1090 (9th Cir. 1996) (prison officials violated Eighth Amendment if it could be proved that they failed to provide inmates with adequate food and water; inmate stated that the food was "spoiled, tampered with, cold, raw, and failed to meet a balanced nutritional level," and that the water was "blue green in color and foul tasting"); Leach v. Dufrain, 103 F. Supp. 2d 542 (N.D. N.Y. 2000) (to prevail, plaintiff must show that "the food served to inmates is nutritionally inadequate, and that it is served under conditions that present an immediate danger to the health and well-being of those inmates"); Masonoff v. DuBois, 899 F. Supp. 782, 799 (D. Mass. 1995) (material issue of fact precluded summary judgment where inmate alleged that water in prison is "rusty and has a disagreeable taste and smell"). See also Hazen v. Pasley, 768 F.2d 226, 228 n. 2 (8th Cir. 1985); Dawson v. Kendrick, 527 F. Supp. 1252, 1297-98 (S.D. W. Va. 1981); Palmigiano v. Garrahy, 443 F. Supp. 956, 981 (D.R.I. 1977); Anderson v. Redman, 429 F. Supp. 1105, 1120-23 (D. Del. 1977).

[3] Dearman v. Woodson, 429 F.2d 1288 (10th Cir. 1970). See also Williams v. Coughlin, 875 F. Supp. 1004 (W.D. N.Y. 1995) (where prisoner alleged that he was denied food for two consecutive days, an Eighth Amendment challenge could be mounted); DeMaio v. Mann, 877 F. Supp. 89 (N.D. N.Y. 1995), judgment aff'd, 122 F.3d 1055 (2d Cir. 1995) (where inmate was allegedly deprived of food and clothing for 12 consecutive days, an Eighth Amendment challenge was maintained). But see Williams v. Coughlin, 875 F. Supp. 1004 (W.D. N.Y. 1995) (where prisoner informed prison counselor

"notable weight loss and mildly diminished health."[4] Some state statutes impose similar requirements.[5] In addition, correctional standards are unequivocal in declaring that prisons must serve inmates three nutritionally adequate meals per day.[6] In addition to

---

that he had been deprived of five consecutive meals over two days and the counselor promised to discuss the matter with prison officials, no evidence of deliberate indifference was established).

[4]Hazen v. Pasley, 768 F.2d 226, 228 n2 (8th Cir. 1985); Campbell v. Cauthron, 623 F.2d 503 (8th Cir. 1980). See also Barnes v. Government of Virgin Islands, 415 F. Supp. 1218, 1234 (D.V.I. 1976) (holding that the prison must provide "three wholesome and nutritious meals" per day for every inmate).

[5]See, e.g., Ala Code § 14-3-45 (sound and wholesome diet); Tex Govt Code Ann § 501.003 (department of corrections hall ensure that inmates housed in facilities operated by the department are fed good and wholesome food, prepared under sanitary conditions, and provided in sufficient quantity and reasonable variety). See also Hickson v. Kellison, 170 W. Va. 732, 296 S.E.2d 855 (1982). But see Gardner v. Beale, 780 F. Supp. 1073 (E.D. Va. 1991), judgment aff'd, 998 F.2d 1008 (4th Cir. 1993) (providing inmates with two meals per day three times per week for sixteen weeks with 18.5 hours between the evening meal and brunch the following day did not violate the Eighth Amendment).

[6]ABA, Standards for Criminal Justice, Standard 23-6.13(c)(iv) (1986) (balanced diet); American Correctional Assn., Standards for Adult Correctional Institutions, Standards 3-4297, 3-4298, 3-4309 (2002) (three meals per day including two hot meals; food should be nutritionally adequate, palatable, and attractive, and produced under sanitary conditions); U.S. Dept of Justice, Federal Standards for Prisons and Jails §§ 4.02, 4.08 (1980) (all meals must meet or exceed dietary allowances recommended by National Academy of Sciences; at least three meals a day, two of which must be hot, must be served every day); United Nations, Standard Minimum Rules for the Treatment of Prisoners, Rule 20 (1955) ("at the usual hours food of nutritional value adequate for health and strength, of wholesome quality and well prepared and served"). But see White v. Gregory, 1 F.3d 267, 269 (4th Cir. 1993) (holding two meals on weekends and holidays did not state a constitutional claim because there was no serious or significant physical or mental injury, particularly when at other times the plaintiff had unlimited access to a refrigerator that was filled with food); Gardner v. Beale, 780 F. Supp. 1073 (E.D. Va. 1991), judgment aff'd,

§ 2:10 RIGHTS OF PRISONERS, THIRD EDITION

food, inmates are also entitled to be given water fit for drinking.[7]

On the other hand, to comply with constitutional minimums, corrections officials need not duplicate the offerings and service of a fine restaurant.[8] In this connection, there is no right to order from a menu.[9] Courts have held that there is no constitutional right to coffee.[10] In addition, there is some authority for the proposition that prisons need not supply hot meals as long as prisoners are adequately fed.[11] This, however, runs

---

998 F.2d 1008 (4th Cir. 1993) (two meals a day, for 48 days, with 18 hours between dinner and brunch did not violate the Eighth Amendment).

[7]Jackson v. Duckworth, 955 F.2d 21, 22 (7th Cir. 1992).

[8]Although nutritional standards are imposed by the Eighth Amendment, unless a deprivation of the "minimal civilized measure of life's necessities" is alleged, a small dining room is not unconstitutional. Chandler v. Moore, 2 F.3d 847, 848 (8th Cir. 1993); see also Hopkins v. Campbell, 870 F. Supp. 316 (D. Kan. 1994) (where dietitian prepares balanced and varied diet plan, there is no violation of Eighth Amendment); Zingmond v. Harger, 602 F. Supp. 256 (N.D. Ind. 1985) (nutritious albeit "plain" food did not violate the Constitution); Featherman v. DiGiacinto, 617 F. Supp. 431 (E.D. Pa. 1985) (no right to have covered food brought to cell); Chase v. Quick, 596 F. Supp. 33 (D.R.I. 1984); Loren v. Jackson, 57 N.C. App. 216, 291 S.E.2d 310 (1982) (no right to home-cooked food).

[9]See Bijeol v. Nelson, 579 F.2d 423 (7th Cir. 1978). See also Miles v. Konvalenka, 791 F. Supp. 212 (N.D. Ill. 1992) (no constitutional right for inmate in punitive segregation to be served hot coffee).

[10]Lane v. Hutcheson, 794 F. Supp. 877, 882-82 (E.D. Mo. 1992).

[11]See, e.g., Leach v. Dufrain, 103 F. Supp. 2d 542 (N.D. N.Y. 2000) (corrections officers denial of hot food for a two month period as discipline for defendant prisoner's misconduct was not cruel and unusual punishment, absent a showing of nutritional inadequacy or immediate danger to prisoner's health and well-being). See also Hoitt v. Vitek, 495 F.2d 219 (1st Cir. 1974); Johnson v. Williams, 768 F. Supp. 1161 (E.D. Va. 1991) (upholding service of cold sack lunches during prison lockdown); Boston v. Stanton, 450 F. Supp. 1049, 1055 (W.D. Mo. 1978). Of course, it depends on why the food is cold. These cases provide no license to serve food that is intended

counter to correctional standards, and it is doubtful that such a practice would be upheld if it were imposed for an extended period of time.[12]

It also has been held that inmates may be restricted in their ability to linger over their meals, as long as they are allowed not less than 15 minutes at the meal table.[13] Correctional standards require that food be served in congregate settings and advises against serving meals in cells except where necessary for security.[14] To accomplish this, correctional officials have the right to impose security measures to ensure that congregate

---

to be hot cold; nor is it proper to serve cold foods warm. See, e.g., Ramos v. Lamm, 639 F.2d 559, 571 (10th Cir. 1980); Toussaint v. McCarthy, 597 F. Supp. 1388, 1401 (N.D. Cal. 1984), judgment aff'd in part, rev'd in part on other grounds, 801 F.2d 1080 (9th Cir. 1986); Palmigiano v. Garrahy, 443 F. Supp. 956, 963 (D.R.I. 1977). But see Abdul-Akbar v. Department of Corrections, 910 F. Supp. 986, 1006 (D. Del. 1995), judgment aff'd, 111 F.3d 125 (3d Cir. 1997) (prison officials did not violate Eighth Amendment where inmate alleged that officials served cold meals on unsanitary carts. Court denied inmate relief because inmate was unable to demonstrate that he was denied an "identifiable human need").

[12]See, e.g., American Correctional Assn., Standards for Adult Correctional Institutions, Standard 3-4309 (2002) (requiring three meals per day, including two hot meals); U.S. Dept of Justice, Federal Standards for Prisons and Jails § 4.08 (1980) (same).

[13]See, e.g., Robbins v. South, 595 F. Supp. 785 (D. Mont. 1984) (allocation of 12 to 15 minutes for eating meals is not unconstitutional): Rutherford v. Pitchess, 457 F. Supp. 104, 116 (C.D. Cal. 1978) (quoting Stewart v. Gates, 450 F. Supp. 583, 588 (C.D. Cal. 1978)).

[14]See, e.g., U.S. Dept of Justice, Federal Standards for Prisons and Jails § 4.10 (1980) (meals should be served under conditions minimizing regimentation); American Pub. Health Assn., Standards for Health Services in Correctional Institutions § VIIE3 (1976); American Correctional Assn., Standards for Adult Correctional Institutions, Standard 3-4308 (2002) (meals should be served under conditions minimizing regimentation). Courts have upheld the service of food in cells when there was a legitimate security reason for doing so. See. e.g., Johnson v. Williams, 768 F. Supp. 1161 (E.D. Va. 1991) (upholding service of food in cell during an emergency prison lockdown).

§ 2:10   Rights of Prisoners, Third Edition

dining is conducted in safety.[15]

The deprivation of food as a punishment has a long history in this country.[16] The refrain that the inmate be sent to solitary confinement on a diet of bread and water is distressingly familiar, but there is reason to think that society has now evolved to the point that such a regime would run afoul of the Eighth Amendment.[17] Support for this proposition is found at the Supreme Court level. The Justices in *Hutto v. Finney*[18] spoke disapprovingly of the prison staple of grue, a substance created by mashing and mixing meat, potatoes, oleo, syrup, vegetables, eggs and seasoning, imposed as punishment on inmates sent to disciplinary segregation.[19] The Justices noted that the prison's meals provided less than 1,000 calories per day, compared to a recommended average of 2,700. The Court implied that such a diet could be intolerably cruel, at least if maintained for a substantial time period.[20] Following this lead, lower courts have condemned diets of bread and water.[21] Many states by "statute or regulation forbid the use of food as punishment or require that

---

[15]See, e.g., Walker v. Johnson, 544 F. Supp. 345 (E.D. Mich. 1982), aff'd in part, rev'd in part on other grounds, 771 F.2d 920 (6th Cir. 1985).

[16]See, e.g., Tenn Code Ann § 41-21-402(b) (prisoners in solitary to be fed bread and water only, unless the physician certifies to the warden that the health of the convict requires other diet).

[17]Modern correctional standards uniformly provide that an inmate may not be deprived of three nutritious meals a day as punishment. U.S. Dept of Justice, Federal Standards for Prisons and Jails § 4.09 (1980); National Sheriffs' Assn., Inmates Legal Rights 20-21 (1987); Model Sentencing and Corrections Act § 4-502(b)(4) (1985); American Correctional Assn., Standards for Adult Correctional Institutions, Standard 3-4301 (2002); ABA, Standards for Criminal Justice, Standard 23-6.13(a) (1986).

[18]Hutto v. Finney, 437 U.S. 678, 98 S. Ct. 2565, 57 L. Ed. 2d 522 (1978).

[19]*Id.* at 686-87.

[20]*Id.*

[21]Jenkins v. Werger, 564 F. Supp. 806 (D. Wyo. 1983) (diet of bread and water for up to five days is cruel and unusual); People v.

segregated inmates receive the same meals as other prisoners."[22] In a recent case, the Ninth Circuit held that an Eighth Amendment violation was made out when inmates alleged that they were held for four days in handcuffs in an outside yard while prison officials investigated the cause of a disturbance. During this time food was left in the sun and spoiled before it was served and there was no drinking water until well into the second day.[23]

Two cases from the Fifth Circuit Court of Appeals address the topic of using deprivation of food as a punishment.[24] In the first, the prison had a rule requiring inmates to be "fully dressed" to receive a meal. Prison officials enforced the rule by depriving any inmate who violated the rule of food for that meal. The plaintiff alleged that the defendant had enforced this rule against him in a manner that deprived him of food for 13 days, 12 of which were consecutive. The Fifth Circuit reversed the district court's dismissal of the

---

Joseph, 105 Ill. App. 3d 568, 61 Ill. Dec. 300, 434 N.E.2d 453 (1st Dist. 1982) (impermissible for trial court to order a defendant placed in solitary confinement and fed bread and water on the anniversary of his offense); Landman v. Royster, 333 F. Supp. 621, 647 (E.D. Va. 1971), opinion supplemented, 354 F. Supp. 1302 (E.D. Va. 1973) (condemning diet of bread and water as a staple, but noting it might be upheld if periodically supplemented by full meals). See also Ford v. Board of Managers of New Jersey State Prison, 407 F.2d 937, 18 A.L.R. Fed. 1 (3d Cir. 1969); Novak v. Beto, 320 F. Supp. 1206 (S.D. Tex. 1970), judgment aff'd in part, rev'd in part on other grounds, 453 F.2d 661 (5th Cir. 1971).

[22]John Boston, Daniel E. Manville, Prisoners' Self Help Litigation Manual 34 (Oceana 1995). See, e.g., Rust v. Grammer, 858 F.2d 411 (8th Cir. 1988) (citing Neb. Rev. Stat. 33-4,114); Domegan v. Fair, 859 F.2d 1059, 1064, 105 A.L.R. Fed. 741 (1st Cir. 1988) (citing Mass.Gen.Laws. Ch 127 §§ 39-40); Thomas v. Jabe, 760 F. Supp. 120, 123 (E.D. Mich. 1991) (citing Mich. Admin. Code r. 791.5510 (2)(f)).

[23]Johnson v. Lewis, 217 F.3d 726 (9th Cir. 2000), cert. denied, 532 U.S. 1065, 121 S. Ct. 2215, 150 L. Ed. 2d 209 (2001).

[24]Cooper v. Sheriff, Lubbock County, Tex., 929 F.2d 1078, 19 Fed. R. Serv. 3d 1270 (5th Cir. 1991); Talib v. Gilley, 138 F.3d 211 (5th Cir. 1998).

§ 2:10   Rights of Prisoners, Third Edition

claim. In doing so, the court disapproved of the practice, holding that the forfeiture of adequate food for significant periods of time is a "form of corporal punishment" forbidden by the Eighth Amendment.[25]

However, in the second case, the court upheld the deprivation of food. In that case, the plaintiff, who was confined to his cell for disciplinary reasons, refused to comply with a policy which required an inmate to face the wall of his cell kneeling with his hands behind his back in order to be served a meal. The plaintiff alleged that, because of his non-compliance with this policy, he missed almost fifty meals over a five-month period. The court did not believe this deprivation was particularly severe. It observed that "[m]issing a mere one out of every nine meals is hardly more than that missed by many working citizens over the same time period."[26] The court also held that the policy requiring inmates to kneel was a legitimate safety precaution to avoid assaults of guards by inmates. Since to the court the deprivation was not great, and since the security need was rational, the court held that the policy was not unconstitutional. Moreover, the court noted, the inmate need not have missed any meals. Had he complied with what the court considered a reasonable prison rule, he would have been fed. Thus, the plaintiff "in a very real sense 'carried the keys' to the kitchen cupboard."[27]

In addition to this case, which permits the depriva-

---

[25]Cooper v. Sheriff, Lubbock County, Tex., 929 F.2d 1078, 1084, 19 Fed. R. Serv. 3d 1270 (5th Cir. 1991); see also Gates v. Collier, 501 F.2d 1291, 1301-03, 1306 (5th Cir. 1974); Cunningham v. Jones, 567 F.2d 653, 656-57 (6th Cir. 1977). But see Cunningham v. Jones, 667 F.2d 565 (6th Cir. 1982) (holding that one meal a day of sufficient caloric content does not violate the Eighth Amendment). For this reason, inmates in administrative segregation are entitled to the same quality of food as inmates in general population. Divers v. Department of Corrections, 921 F.2d 191 (8th Cir. 1990) (holding that claim of inadequate food in administrative segregation is actionable).

[26]Talib v. Gilley, 138 F.3d 211, 213 n3 (5th Cir. 1998).

[27]*Id.* at 217.

tion of food to further an administrative rule, courts have held that as a punishment prison officials can deprive inmates for limited periods of the food normally served to the general population.[28] To impose this penalty, prison officials must make sure that the food that it is given (in most cases it is a "food loaf," a substance made by mixing foods together into one unappetizing product) is nutritionally adequate.[29] They also must only impose this deprivation for behavior related to the service of food. Thus, courts have upheld the use of food loafs when the food loaf was served because the inmate involved had earlier been involved in throwing food or misusing food utensils.[30]

Other food-related issues concern kitchen conditions. "Food served to inmates is deficient . . . even when nutritionally complete if it is prepared under conditions so unsanitary as to make it unwholesome and a threat to the health of those inmates who consume it."[31] Kitchens must be kept sanitary. Courts have held that the failure to ensure sanitary conditions, including the health and cleanliness of kitchen personnel, violates prisoners' rights to live in conditions which do not threaten their physical safety.[32]

While there is an obligation to maintain acceptable

---

[28]Johnson v. Gummerson, 198 F.3d 233 (2d Cir. 1999) (restricted diet, consisting of a "food loaf" for seven days, was not an Eighth Amendment violation without an allegation that the restricted diet was nutritionally inadequate or otherwise posed a threat to plaintiff-appellant's physical well-being).

[29]Cunningham v. Jones, 567 F.2d 653, 657-60 (6th Cir. 1977).

[30]See e.g., LeMaire v. Maass, 745 F. Supp. 623, 633 (D. Or. 1990), vacated on other grounds, 12 F.3d 1444 (9th Cir. 1993); Adams v. Kincheloe, 743 F. Supp. 1393 (E.D. Wash. 1990) (upholding a policy of feeding an inmate in solitary confinement a "nutra-loaf" diet when inmate had a habit of throwing food at guards).

[31]Adams v. Kincheloe, 743 F. Supp. 1393, 1397 (E.D. Wash. 1990); Toussaint v. McCarthy, 597 F. Supp. 1388 (N.D. Cal. 1984), judgment aff'd in part, rev'd in part on other grounds, 801 F.2d 1080 (9th Cir. 1986).

[32]See, e.g., French v. Owens, 777 F.2d 1250, 1255 (7th Cir. 1985) (finding kitchen and food storage areas unsanitary and un-

§ 2:10 RIGHTS OF PRISONERS, THIRD EDITION

sanitary conditions, occasional lapses do not constitute cruel and unusual punishment. Thus, the sporadic discovery of a "foreign object" in food does not establish a constitutional violation.[33] Some courts have gone a step further and, in questionable decisions, have held that the inmate must allege that he or she was actually harmed by the conditions in order to establish a claim of unsanitary food services.[34] These decisions are not in

---

constitutional); Ramos v. Lamm, 639 F.2d 559, 570 (10th Cir. 1980); Carty v. Farrelly, 957 F. Supp. 727, 22 A.D.D. 333 (D.V.I. 1997) (kitchen infested with vermin and roaches at the Criminal Justice Complex (CJC) violated the Eighth Amendment; court held such problems presented "an immediate threat to the health and safety of inmates," and held the defendants in civil contempt for their failure to comply with a previous court order to remedy such conditions); Lightfoot v. Walker, 486 F. Supp. 504, 524 (S.D. Ill. 1980) ("improper food storage, inadequate dishwashers, untrained personnel, . . . open garbage tins and leaking water lines lead to the inevitable conclusion that lack of sanitation in food services presents an imminent danger to the health of each and every inmate"); Capps v. Atiyeh, 559 F. Supp. 894 (D. Or. 1982) (constitutional deficiency in process of milk pasteurization); Laaman v. Helgemoe, 437 F. Supp. 269, 323 (D.N.H. 1977). See also Hamilton v. Schiro, 338 F. Supp. 1016 (E.D. La. 1970).

[33]LeMaire v. Maass, 12 F.3d 1444 (9th Cir. 1993); Tucker v. Rose, 955 F. Supp. 810 (N.D. Ohio 1997) (inmates who were served contaminated cornstarch failed to establish that prison officials violated the Eighth Amendment; court held that prison officials were not sufficiently aware that the cornstarch was tainted and it was an isolated incident; further, prison officials implemented pest control measures to maintain a healthy food supply). See also Hamm v. DeKalb County, 774 F.2d 1567 (11th Cir. 1985); Miles v. Konvalenka, 791 F. Supp. 212 (N.D. Ill. 1992) (single instance of finding mouse in food not actionable); Islam v. Jackson, 782 F. Supp. 1111 (E.D. Va. 1992) (single instance of serving food contaminated with maggots was not a violation of Eighth Amendment); Johnson v. Bruce, 771 F. Supp. 327 (D. Kan. 1991), aff'd, 961 F.2d 220 (10th Cir. 1992) (isolated instance of serving undercooked chicken not actionable); Lunsford v. Reynolds, 376 F. Supp. 526 (W.D. Va. 1974); Sinclair v. Henderson, 331 F. Supp. 1123 (E.D. La. 1971).

[34]See, e.g., Landfair v. Sheahan, 878 F. Supp. 1106 (N.D. Ill. 1995) (where foreign objects surfaced in food, absent a showing of

accord with the pronouncements of the United States Supreme Court that "the Eighth Amendment protects against sufficiently imminent dangers" without the necessity of showing present injury.[35] However, it is proper for a court to require proof that the conditions under which food is prepared are in fact unsanitary. Thus, simply pleading that the food is "lethal to those who ate it" without presenting any evidentiary allegations in support of this claim was not sufficient.[36] In addition, if prison officials are genuinely responsive to the identifiable problems, courts have deferred even if there is a suggestion that the problem should be handled

---

actual harm no Eighth Amendment claim could be maintained); Antonelli v. Sheahan, 863 F Supp 756 (ND Ill 1994) (where spoiled food did not pose an immediate danger of harm to inmates, there was no constitutional violation); Kennibrew v. Russell, 578 F Supp 164 (ED Tenn 1983) (absent allegation of inadequate diet or illness resulting from food preparation, unsanitary conditions did not amount to constitutional violation, at least where good faith efforts were made to maintain sanitary conditions); Loern v. Jackson, 291 SE2d 310 (NC Ct App 1982).

[35]Helling v. McKinney, 113 S Ct 2475, 2480 (1993) ("We would think that a prison inmate also could successfully complain about demonstrably unsafe drinking water without waiting for an attack of dysentery."). See also Knop v. Johnson, 667 F Supp 512, 525 (WD Mich 1987) (serious illness or death need not be proved to establish a claim for unsanitary kitchen facilities). Of course, evidence of injury is not irrelevant to the determination of whether a constitutional violation has occurred. See, e.g., Shrader v. White, 761 F2d 975 (4th Cir 1985) (holding that a pattern of food-related injuries was revealing).

[36]May v. Baldwin, 895 F Supp 1398, 1408 (D Or 1995) (prison officials did not violate Eighth Amendment where inmate alleged that food in prison was inedible; court noted that no evidence was presented that the food was "inadequate to maintain inmates' health"; prison officials did not violate Eighth Amendment where inmate alleged that water in prison was unsafe and caused kidney stones, arteriosclerosis, emphysema, constipation, and inflamed gastro-intestinal tracts; court noted that inmate presented no evidence other than conclusory allegations).

§ 2:10

differently.[37]

Beyond those obligations owed to the general prison population, in two instances corrections officials have to provide individual inmates with specialized meals. First, the state has an obligation to provide a special diet to a person whose physical condition requires it.[38] Likewise, diet restrictions imposed by an inmate's religion may have to be honored because of the prisoner's First Amendment free exercise rights.[39]

A final topic regarding food-or, more accurately, the absence of food-is hunger strikes. Sometimes inmates go on hunger strikes to dramatize some aspect of their

---

[37] See, e.g, Gholson v. Murry, 953 F. Supp. 709 (E.D. Va. 1997) (inmates who were exposed to lead-polluted water claimed such conditions violated the Eighth Amendment; court held that the defendants were not deliberately indifferent to the risks of inmate health and welfare; evidence demonstrated that prison officials reacted reasonably in response to the problem where they informed inmates of the contaminated water and suggested they let the water run for fifteen to thirty seconds before drinking it; court granted the defendant's motion for summary judgment).

[38] See, e.g., Massey v. Hutto, 545 F.2d 45 (8th Cir. 1976) (holding that a state breaches its medical duty to prisoners with stomach ulcers if it fails to provide them a prescribed bland diet). See also Balla v. Idaho State Bd. of Corrections, 595 F. Supp. 1558 (D. Idaho 1984); Ronson v. Commissioner of Correction, 112 A.D.2d 488, 491 N.Y.S.2d 209 (3d Dep't 1985) (diet for diabetic prisoner); Brown v. State, Through Dept. of Correction, 354 So. 2d 633 (La. Ct. App. 1st Cir. 1977). Prison accreditation standards require provision of medically necessary diets. See, e.g, American Correctional Assn., Standards for Adult Correctional Institutions, Standard 4229 (2002) (requiring special diets as prescribed by medical or dental personnel). But see Ayers v. Uphoff, 1 Fed. Appx. 851 (10th Cir. 2001) (summary judgment affirmed where inmate claimed that prison failed to provide him with the precise special diet recommended by a physician; court held that an inmate is not entitled to choose which foods the prison will prepare for him; no constitutional violation where the inmate simply did not like the substitute diet prepared by the prison kitchen). For a full discussion of this topic, see Ch 3.

[39] See, e.g., Kahane v. Carlson, 527 F.2d 492 (2d Cir. 1975) (Orthodox Jewish prisoner entitled to kosher meals). See Ch 6 for a full discussion of this point.

treatment[40] or simply to die.[41] The question that arises in these cases is whether the state has the right, indeed the obligation, to force feed hunger-striking inmates? The cases are split. Some cases hold that an inmate has a privacy right in refusing force-feeding.[42] The majority have held that the state has the right to intervene to prevent death.[43]

---

[40]See, e.g., Zant v. Prevatte, 248 Ga. 832, 286 S.E.2d 715 (1982) (hunger strike to protest failure to transfer inmate for his protection).

[41]See, e.g., In re Caulk, 125 N.H. 226, 480 A.2d 93 (1984) (hunger strike by inmate sentenced to long prison term who sought to die).

[42]Singletary v. Costello, 665 So. 2d 1099, 1104 (Fla. Dist. Ct. App. 4th Dist. 1996) (court denied department of corrections petition for a court order to allow prison doctor to force feed inmate on a hunger strike if his life became threatened; court found that inmate as a "competent person has a right to choose or refuse medical treatment and that right extends to all relevant decisions concerning one's health"; however, court noted that there are state interests which must be addressed as well, including "the preservation of life, protection of innocent third parties, prevention of suicide, and maintenance of the ethical integrity of the medical profession"; court found that these factors weighed in favor of the inmate's right to choose); Zant v. Prevatte, 248 Ga. 832, 286 S.E.2d 715 (1982).

[43]See, e.g., Martinez v. Turner, 977 F.2d 421, 423 (8th Cir. 1992); Com., Dept. of Public Welfare, Farview State Hosp. v. Kallinger, 134 Pa. Commw. 415, 580 A.2d 887 (1990) (inmate of hunger strike may be force fed); In re Caulk, 125 N.H. 226, 480 A.2d 93 (1984); In re Sanchez, 577 F. Supp. 7 (S.D. N.Y. 1983); State ex rel. White v. Narick, 170 W. Va. 195, 292 S.E.2d 54 (1982); Von Holden v. Chapman, 87 A.D.2d 66, 450 N.Y.S.2d 623 (4th Dep't 1982). See, generally, D. Snead, Harry W. Stonecipher, Prisoner Fasting as Symbolic Speech: The Ultimate Speech-Action Test, 32 Howard L. J. 549 (1989); Steven C. Bennett, Note, The Privacy and Procedural Due Process Rights of Hunger Striking Prisoners, 58 NYU L Rev 1157 (1983); Joel K. Greenberg, Note, Hunger Striking Prisoners: The Constitutionality of Force, Civ Confinement 169 (1984); Stephanie C. Powell, Comment, Constitutional Law-Forced Feeding of a Prisoner on a Hunger Strike: A Violation of an Inmate's Right to Privacy, 61 NC L Rev 714 (1983); Steven C. Sunshine,

§ 2:11 —Exercise and Outside Recreation

Another critical aspect of a prisoner's physical well-being involves exercise and outside recreation. As the Seventh Circuit Court of Appeals observed, "[w]here movement is denied and muscles are allowed to atrophy, the health of the individual is threatened."[1] Recently, the Seventh Circuit made the point again when it recognized that "exercise is now regarded in many quarters as an indispensable component of preventive medicine."[2] The court continued, "exercise is no longer considered an optional form of recreation, but is instead a necessary requirement for physical and mental well-being."[3] Courts also have noted that the failure to provide opportunities for outdoor exercise can be psychologically stultifying.[4] Since deprivations of exercise and outside recreation can lead to the serious impairment of health,[5] deliberate indifference to these needs has long been considered a matter that raises

---

Note, Should a Hunger Striking Prisoner be Allowed to Die?, 25 BC L Rev 423 (1984).

[Section 2:11]

[1]French v. Owens, 777 F.2d 1250, 1255 (7th Cir. 1985). See also Pressley v. Brown, 754 F. Supp. 112 (W.D. Mich. 1990) (noting that it was uncontested that lack of recreation had caused inmate to suffer stomach and bowel problems).

[2]Delaney v. DeTella, 256 F.3d 679, 681-82 (7th Cir. 2001), (citing Anderson v. Romero, 72 F.3d 518 (7th Cir. 1995)).

[3]Delaney v. DeTella, 256 F.3d 679, 682 (7th Cir. 2001). See also Perkins v. Kansas Dept. of Corrections, 165 F.3d 803, 809 (10th Cir. 1999) (Exercise "is extremely important to the psychological and physical well being of inmates").

[4]Housley v. Dodson, 41 F.3d 597 (10th Cir. 1994) (pointing out the "denial of fresh air" can jeopardize the psychological and physical well being of inmates); LeMaire v. Maass, 745 F. Supp. 623 (D. Or. 1990), vacated on other grounds, 12 F.3d 1444 (9th Cir. 1993) (outdoor exercise is needed to "prevent physical and mental deterioration"). See also Davenport v. DeRobertis, 844 F.2d 1310 (7th Cir. 1988).

[5]In regard to exercise, see Delaney v. DeTella, 256 F.3d 679, 681-82 (7th Cir. 2001). See also National Advisory Commission on

serious Eighth Amendment issues.[6]

While the cases speak of the right to exercise, the fundamental question that is not always answered (or even asked) explicitly in the cases is what is exercise for? Is it to prevent physical deterioration? Or is it to meet a broader and more humanistic and psychological need for exposure to the elements and to be relieved of constant confinement in a small space? If the former, recreation does not become an issue unless people are deprived of the ability to move their extremities and lack the space to engage in physical activities such as running in place, push ups and sit ups. If it is the latter, then exercise is a more comprehensive entitlement and one that permits inmates some respite out of the cell, and perhaps out of doors, to break up unrelieved cell confinement.

The Supreme Court has not addressed this issue directly. In the absence of direction from the Court, the majority of the federal Court of Appeals opinions to one degree or another seem to utilize the broader of the two theories.[7] As Judge Posner cogently observed in rejecting the first theory, "an inmate can preserve his cardiovascular fitness and overall muscle tone by running in place or by engaging in other forms of exercise that are feasible; *but this misses the point.*"[8] In the taut closed environment of a prison the right to "exercise"

Criminal Justice Standards and Goals, Corrections Standard 2.5 (1973).

[6]See Allen v. Sakai, 48 F.3d 1082 (9th Cir. 1994) ("defendants cannot legitimately claim that their duty to provide regular outdoor exercise . . . was not clearly established"); Williams v. Goord, 142 F. Supp. 2d 416 (S.D. N.Y. 2001) ("exercise is one of the basic human needs protected by the Eighth Amendment").

[7]See, e.g., Lopez v. Smith, 203 F.3d 1122, 46 Fed. R. Serv. 3d 494 (9th Cir. 2000) (en banc); Housley v. Dodson, 41 F.3d 597, 599 (10th Cir. 1994); Davenport v. DeRobertis, 844 F.2d 1310, 1313 (7th Cir. 1988).

[8]Davenport v. DeRobertis, 844 F.2d 1310, 1313 (7th Cir. 1988) (emphasis supplied). Unfortunately some courts have apparently missed this point. Roop v. Squadrito, 70 F. Supp. 2d 868 (N.D. Ind.

§ 2:11 Rights of Prisoners, Third Edition

ought also embrace the need to be out of doors and away from unyielding confinement in a cell. If the Eighth Amendment is to truly protect against psychological debilitation and to be a barrier to the operation of inhumane prisons, the right should mean more than merely the ability to move muscles.

Nevertheless, courts have made many pronouncements about the constitutional right to exercise.[9] One reason why it is difficult to draw a controlling theory from the cases is in part because the issue arises in a wide variety of factual situations. The issue may be posed in a case in which the policy challenged governs the entire facility,[10] or it may arise in a case in which the restriction is placed upon inmates in special housing units,[11] or it may involve a suspension of recreation for an institution that has been locked down,[12] or it may

---

1999) (lack of exercise not unconstitutional if inmate could do push-ups and sit-ups in his cell); Leslie v. Doyle, 868 F. Supp. 1039 (N.D. Ill. 1994), aff'd, 125 F.3d 1132 (7th Cir. 1997) (temporary restrictions on sports activities did not constitute cruel and unusual punishment where inmate could exercise in cell and maintained duties as a porter which could reasonably lead to rehabilitation of leg).

[9]See, e.g., Delaney v. DeTella, 256 F.3d 679 (7th Cir. 2001); Lopez v. Smith, 203 F.3d 1122, 46 Fed. R. Serv. 3d 494 (9th Cir. 2000) (en banc); Perkins v. Kansas Dept. of Corrections, 165 F.3d 803 (10th Cir. 1999); Williams v. Greifinger, 97 F.3d 699 (2d Cir. 1996); Sweet v. South Carolina Dept. of Corrections, 529 F.2d 854 (4th Cir. 1975). An occasional statute provides inmates with the right to exercise. See, e.g, Pa Stat Ann tit 61, § 101 (at least two hours daily exercise); Inmates of B-Block v. Marks, 61 Pa. Commw. 421, 434 A.2d 211 (1981) (compelling compliance with statute requiring two hours a day of exercise). But see Brooks v. Kleiman, 743 F. Supp. 350 (E.D. Pa. 1989) (state law may be relaxed for "proper purposes").

[10]See, e.g., Shelby County Jail Inmates v. Westlake, 798 F.2d 1085 (7th Cir. 1986).

[11]Leonard v. Norris, 797 F.2d 683 (8th Cir. 1986); Williams v. Goord, 142 F. Supp. 2d 416 (S.D. N.Y. 2001).

[12]Delaney v. DeTella, 256 F.3d 679 (7th Cir. 2001).

CRUEL & UNUSUAL PUNISHMENT § 2:11

involve a loss of recreation by just one person.[13] Moreover, the case may involve a deprivation that is just days long or one that stretches for months or even years.[14] Finally, the case may involve an absolute deprivation of exercise opportunities,[15] or restrictions on the conditions under which exercise is permitted, including whether outdoor exercise is permitted.[16] Thus, an examination of the case law indicates, "what constitutes adequate exercise will depend upon the circumstances of each case."[17]

While each case must be examined on its own facts, it is now well-established law that there is a right to exercise protected by the Eighth Amendment.[18] This does not mean that exercise cannot be restricted. It can. The critical question is by how much. To sketch the parameters of the right requires a look at a number of critical issues.

At What Point Does the Right to Exercise Arise?

The first is when does the right accrue? Or, to put it another way, are short-term deprivations of recreation permissible? The answer is that courts are willing to tolerate a "short term" denial of the right on the appar-

---

[13]Perkins v. Kansas Dept. of Corrections, 165 F.3d 803 (10th Cir. 1999) (inmate with AIDS subjected to a limitation on recreation); Williams v. Greifinger, 97 F.3d 699 (2d Cir. 1996) (inmate who refused TB test denied recreation).

[14]Compare Delaney v. DeTella, 256 F.3d 679 (7th Cir. 2001) (six months); Sostre v. McGinnis, 442 F.2d 178 (2d Cir. 1971) (en banc) (several years) with Harris v. Fleming, 839 F.2d 1232, 1236 (7th Cir. 1988) (28 days).

[15]Williams v. Goord, 111 F. Supp. 2d 280 (S.D. N.Y. 2000).

[16]Toussaint v. Yockey, 722 F.2d 1490 (9th Cir. 1984).

[17]Housley v. Dodson, 41 F.3d 597, 599 (10th Cir. 1994).

[18]See, e.g., Williams v. Greifinger, 97 F.3d 699 (2d Cir. 1996). ("The availability of exercise is a key ingredient of a court's analysis whether an inmate's conditions of confinement pass muster under the Eight Amendment.").

§ 2:11   Rights of Prisoners, Third Edition

ent ground that such a deprivation is de minimis.[19] What constitutes more than a short term denial of the right? There is no single answer to this question, although the cases seem to draw the line somewhere between one to three months.[20] Beyond that point, because of their concern that a deprivation that is long term will carry with it serious consequences for the health and well-being of prisoners, courts no longer tolerate

---

[19]See, e.g., Lopez v. Smith, 203 F.3d 1122, 1133, 46 Fed. R. Serv. 3d 494 (9th Cir. 2000) (temporary denial of outdoor recreation with no medical effects not a substantial deprivation); May v. Baldwin, 109 F.3d 557, 565 (9th Cir. 1997); Delaney v. DeTella, 256 F.3d 679 (7th Cir. 2001) ("we have consistently held that short-term denials of exercise may be inevitable in the prison context and are not so detrimental as to constitute a constitutional deprivation") (citing cases); Davidson v. Chestnut, 1998 WL 463527 (SDNY 1998), vacated in part on other grounds, remanded by, 193 F.3d 144 (2nd Cir. 1999) (denial of exercise claim dismissed because a short deprivation of exercise, here at most two days out of a five day stay, does not rise to the level of a constitutional violation); Davidson v. Coughlin, 968 F. Supp. 121 (S.D. N.Y. 1997) (less than an hour of exercise per day for almost four and a half months while plaintiff was in keeplock did not violate the Constitution; deprivation was for a short period and plaintiff was allowed to participate in other out-of-cell exercise activities); Kropp v. McCaughtry, 915 F. Supp. 85 (E.D. Wis. 1996) (prison officials did not violate Eighth Amendment where inmate was denied outdoor exercise while confined to administrative segregation for one month; inmate could exercise in his cell and was allowed to exercise outdoors twice a week once he was transferred back to general population).

[20]Pearson v. Ramos, 237 F.3d 881, 885 (7th Cir. 2001) (holding that after 90 days the right to exercise accrues); Delaney v. DeTella, 256 F.3d 679 (7th Cir. 2001) (citing cases approving short term denials of 70 days, 28 days, 10 days, and 30 days and holding that a denial for six months is unconstitutional); Thomas v. Ramos, 918 F. Supp. 228 (N.D. Ill. 1996), judgment aff'd, 130 F.3d 754 (7th Cir. 1997) (prison officials did not violate Eighth Amendment where inmate was placed in disciplinary segregation for 70 days pending the completion of investigation; deprivation of access to outdoor exercise, law library, day room, telephones, and gym was not a significant hardship).

CRUEL & UNUSUAL PUNISHMENT   § 2:11

deprivation of the right to exercise.[21]

How Much Recreation Time is Required?

Another question about the right to exercise is what is the minimum amount of out-of-cell recreation time that is constitutionally necessary?[22] One court held that seven hours per week was required.[23] Conversely, an-

---

[21]Lopez v. Smith, 203 F.3d 1122, 46 Fed. R. Serv. 3d 494 (9th Cir. 2000) (en banc) (when deprivation is long term, six weeks, the plaintiff was "not required to show adverse medical effects"; 45 minutes of outdoor exercise per week over a six week period was objectively unconstitutional); Perkins v. Kansas Dept. of Corrections, 165 F.3d 803 (10th Cir. 1999) (holding that a denial of outdoor recreation for a period of nine months is unconstitutional); Antonelli v. Sheahan, 81 F.3d 1422, 1432 (7th Cir. 1996) (inmate stated a claim where he alleged that prison officials violated Eighth Amendment where they prohibited inmate from "recreat[ing] for periods up to seven weeks in succession, and at most, was called once every two weeks for sessions of no longer than one hour at a time"); Allen v. Sakai, 48 F.3d 1082 (9th Cir. 1994) (a six-week period in which inmate was provided only 45 minutes per week of outdoor recreation was unconstitutional); Housley v. Dodson, 41 F.3d 597 (10th Cir. 1994) (holding that providing only 30 minutes of recreation over three months is unconstitutional); Watts v. Ramos, 948 F. Supp. 739 (N.D. Ill. 1996) (inmate was fully deprived of recreation time for one year while in prison segregation unit; court held that such an absolute restriction on recreation time constituted "cruel and unusual punishment," noting the absence of a compelling penological reason to deny the inmate recreation time, and denied the defendant's motion for summary judgment).

[22]See, e.g., Gawloski v. Dallman, 803 F. Supp. 103 (S.D. Ohio 1992) (noting that the law on the amount of exercise that is required was not yet clearly established).

[23]Bono v. Saxbe, 462 F. Supp. 146 (E.D. Ill. 1978), aff'd in part, 620 F.2d 609 (7th Cir. 1980). See American Correctional Assn., Standards for Adult Correctional Institutions, Standard 3-4147 (1990) (requiring one hour of outside exercise per day); U.S. Dept of Justice, Federal Standards for Prisons and Jails § 16.02 (1980) (requiring one hour of physical exercise per day with "frequent opportunities" for outdoor exercise). A United Nations standard calls for one hour per day of exercise in the open air. United Nations, Standard Minimum Rules for the Treatment of Prisoners, Rule 21 (1955).

§ 2:11 RIGHTS OF PRISONERS, THIRD EDITION

other stated that the two hours and twenty minutes outdoor recreation time allotted weekly by the institution was sufficient.[24] Taking a more individualistic approach, the Fourth Circuit reasoned that, while only two weekly one-hour exercise periods might not be cruel and unusual, an indefinite limitation on exercise might be harmful to a prisoner's health and, if so, would violate the Eighth Amendment.[25] After canvassing the opinions in this area, the Seventh Circuit Court of Appeals came to the conclusion that inmates must be provided with at least five hours of exercise time per week in order to comply with the Eighth Amendment.[26] While there is by no means unanimity of view, that position does seem to have attracted the most support.[27] Correctional experts, on the other hand, advise that a prison provide opportunities for at least one hour per day of physical activity.[28]

Further complicating any inquiry is the view expressed by one court that the amount of exercise required depends on individual factors, and that each

---

[24] Stewart v. Gates, 450 F. Supp. 583 (C.D. Cal. 1978).

[25] Sweet v. South Carolina Dept. of Corrections, 529 F.2d 854 (4th Cir. 1975).

[26] Davenport v. DeRobertis, 844 F.2d 1310, 1315 (7th Cir. 1988).

[27] See, e.g., John Boston, Daniel E. Manville, Prisoners' Self Help Litigation Manual 136 (Oceana 1995) ("many courts have held that prison officials must permit at least five hours a week of out-of- cell exercise"). But see Thomas v. Leslie, 176 F.3d 489 (10th Cir. 1999) ("We have declined to adopt a set weekly total for regular or daily exercise").

[28] See, e.g., American Correctional Assn., Standards for Adult Correctional Institutions, Standard 3-4147 (2002). See also Walker v. Mintzes, 771 F.2d 920 (6th Cir. 1985) (same); Anderson v. Coughlin, 757 F.2d 33 (2d Cir. 1985) (same); Campbell v. Cauthron, 623 F.2d 503, 507 (8th Cir. 1980) (same); Albro v. Onondaga County, N.Y., 681 F. Supp. 991 (N.D. N.Y. 1988) (one hour of recreation per day is required); Parnell v. Waldrep, 511 F. Supp. 764 (W.D. N.C. 1981) (one hour of recreation per day, five days per week); Hutchings v. Corum, 501 F. Supp. 1276 (W.D. Mo. 1980) (one hour per day of exercise); Frazier v. Ward, 426 F. Supp. 1354 (N.D. N.Y. 1977).

convict is entitled to the exercise necessary to satisfy that person's health needs.[29] A corollary notion is that unless an inmate can show specific and identifiable physical injury resulting from restrictions on exercise, there has been no deprivation of a constitutional right.[30] The administrative feasibility of an individualistic approach, however, is highly questionable. Moreover, in tying the amount of exercise required to a determination of whether a particular inmate has been damaged by the failure to provide it,[31] courts may fall into the trap of ignoring conditions that pose a threat to health by forcing the inmate to wait until he or she is actually injured before allowing suit.[32] The better approach was taken recently in *Delaney v. DeTella*.[33] In that case the plaintiff challenged the complete denial of recreation for a period of six months due to a prison wide lockdown. The defendants acknowledged the deprivation, but argued that there was no proof that the plaintiff had suffered any physical injury as a result. They claimed that without such proof there was no constitutional violation. The court rejected this argument, holding that when a person has been denied recreation for a period that exceeds 90 days there is a "strong likelihood

---

[29]Laaman v. Helgemoe, 437 F. Supp. 269, 309 (D.N.H. 1977).

[30]See, e.g., Wishon v. Gammon, 978 F.2d 446 (8th Cir. 1992) (Eighth Circuit held that forty-five minutes of out-of-cell exercise per week was sufficient because the inmate did not suffer any injury).

[31]See, e.g., Arey v. Warden, Connecticut Correctional Inst., 187 Conn. 324, 445 A.2d 916 (1982) (no Eighth Amendment violation when no evidence is provided that the plaintiff's health has been injured). See also Dominguez v. Figel, 626 F. Supp. 368 (N.D. Ind. 1986).

[32]The Supreme Court has rejected this approach. Helling v. McKinney, 509 U.S. 25, 113 S. Ct. 2475, 2480, 125 L. Ed. 2d 22 (1993) (Eighth Amendment protects against conduct that poses a serious risk of future harm to inmates, without requiring proof of injury).

[33]Delaney v. DeTella, 256 F.3d 679 (7th Cir. 2001).

§ 2:11   Rights of Prisoners, Third Edition

of psychological injury."[34] The court also rejected the notion that only physical injury can satisfy an Eighth Amendment claim.[35] The Ninth Circuit, sitting en banc, also adopted this view when it held that there was no need to prove specific injury if the deprivation is long term.[36]

Is Outdoor Exercise Required?

There is also disagreement about whether exercise time should be out of cell and out of doors. A strong majority that has dealt with this issue has held that exercise should be out of the cell in some location.[37] Whether the location should be out of doors is not always litigated or firmly decided. A majority of the courts, particularly in recent opinions that have specifically addressed the issue, hold that there is a right to outdoor exercise.[38] But there are cases to the contrary,[39] and in still others the issue is not clearly addressed.

---

[34]Delaney v. DeTella, 256 F.3d 679, 685 (7th Cir. 2001).

[35]*Id.* at 685. See also § 2:4.

[36]Lopez v. Smith, 203 F.3d 1122, 46 Fed. R. Serv. 3d 494 (9th Cir. 2000) (en banc) (when deprivation was long term—six weeks—the plaintiff was "not required to show adverse medical effects").

[37]See, e.g., Davenport v. DeRobertis, 844 F.2d 1310 (7th Cir. 1988) (holding that there is a right to out-of-cell time but not specifying that it be outdoors and not addressing the issue); Williams v. Greifinger, 97 F.3d 699 (2d Cir. 1996) (not addressing the issue but holding that exercise is required); Williams v. Goord, 142 F. Supp. 2d 416 (S.D. N.Y. 2001) (same). Hopkins v. Campbell, 870 F. Supp. 316 (D. Kan. 1994) (holding that inmates were provided adequate recreational facilities even if prison did not have formal exercise area if jail had a day room for inmates to watch television, listen to the radio, and conduct limited exercises).

[38]See, e.g., Lopez v. Smith, 203 F.3d 1122, 46 Fed. R. Serv. 3d 494 (9th Cir. 2000) (en banc) (holding that outdoor exercise is required); Perkins v. Kansas Dept. of Corrections, 165 F.3d 803 (10th Cir. 1999) ("Some form of regular outdoor exercise is extremely important to the psychological and physical well being of inmates"); Allen v. Sakai, 48 F.3d 1082 (9th Cir. 1994) (holding that the deprivation of outdoor exercise can violate the Eighth Amendment); Bailey v. Shillinger, 828 F.2d 651, 653 (10th Cir.

1987); Housley v. Dodson, 41 F.3d 597 (10th Cir. 1994) (holding that the denial of fresh air can be cruel and unusual punishment); Carver v. Knox County, Tenn., 753 F. Supp. 1370 (E.D. Tenn. 1989), aff'd in part, rev'd in part on other grounds, 887 F.2d 1287 (6th Cir. 1989) (implying that denial of outdoor recreation for persons serving sentences of longer than one year is unconstitutional); Preston v. Thompson, 589 F.2d 300 (7th Cir. 1978) (one hour a day in outside yard is required); LeMaire v. Maass, 745 F. Supp. 623 (D. Or. 1990), vacated on other grounds, 12 F.3d 1444 (9th Cir. 1993) (outdoor exercise is needed to "prevent physical and mental deterioration"); Adams v. Wolff, 624 F. Supp. 1036 (D. Nev. 1985) (denial of outdoor recreation to protective custody inmate violates the Eighth Amendment); New York State Com'n of Correction v. Ruffo, 139 Misc. 2d 1087, 530 N.Y.S.2d 469 (Sup 1988), judgment aff'd as modified, 157 A.D.2d 987, 550 N.Y.S.2d 746 (3d Dep't 1990) (ordering one hour a day of outdoor exercise); Sinclair v. Henderson, 331 F. Supp. 1123 (E.D. La. 1971) (confinement for long periods without the opportunity for regular outdoor exercise violated the Eighth Amendment). Cf. Keenan v. Hall, 83 F.3d 1083 (9th Cir. 1996) (denying summary judgment to defendant, where inmate alleged that prison officials violated Eighth Amendment in that inmate was denied outdoor exercise for six months while in disciplinary segregation).

If outdoor exercise is permitted, courts have insisted that it be meaningful. Thus, one court held that exercise in special well-lighted rooms with fresh air was not outdoor exercise. Mathis v. Henderson, 108 Misc. 2d 63, 437 N.Y.S.2d 34 (Sup 1980).

[39]Bailey v. Shillinger, 828 F.2d 651 (10th Cir. 1987) (lack of exercise in the fresh air is "restrictive," but not unconstitutional); Shelby County Jail Inmates v. Westlake, 798 F.2d 1085 (7th Cir. 1986) (no right to outdoor exercise if opportunities for indoor exercise are provided); Wilkerson v. Maggio, 703 F.2d 909 (5th Cir. 1983) (constitutional to deny inmate outdoor exercise for five years when one hour a day of indoor exercise was provided); Antonelli v. Sheahan, 863 F. Supp. 756 (N.D. Ill. 1994), judgment aff'd in part, rev'd in part on other grounds, 81 F.3d 1422 (7th Cir. 1996). (if the prison offers indoor forms of recreation, severe restrictions on outdoor exercise may be placed on prisoners without offending any constitutional rights); Leslie v. Doyle, 868 F. Supp. 1039 (N.D. Ill. 1994), aff'd, 125 F.3d 1132 (7th Cir. 1997) (inmate does not have Eighth Amendment right to yard recreation time); Brewton v. Hollister, 948 F. Supp. 244 (W.D. N.Y. 1996) (confinement in prison's special housing unit (SHU) for 74 days with one hour of exercise per day did not violate the Eighth Amendment); Grace v.

§ 2:11   Rights of Prisoners, Third Edition

For an activity period to be meaningful, there must be not only space, but also equipment and facilities. While few courts have addressed this issue directly, a North Carolina court did. It held that the recreation area must be arranged with equipment sufficient for "full-fledged physical exercise, for example, weightlifting, basketball, volleyball or running."[40] On the other hand, another court held that as long as there is opportunity for some form of vigorous exercise, there is no constitutional requirement that the exercise area be equipped for a variety of activities.[41]

What are the Exercise Rights of Inmates in Segregation?

The question of the amount and type of recreation that inmates in administrative or punitive detention are to be permitted has been much litigated.[42] Since the opportunity to exercise is essential to maintenance of

---

Wainwright, 761 F. Supp. 1520, 1525 (M.D. Fla. 1991) ("The fact that plaintiff has been denied *outside* exercise, sunlight, and fresh outdoor air does not present a condition which is so foul, so inhuman, and so violative of the basic concepts of decency that it falls within the proscriptions of the Eighth Amendment.") (emphasis in original). Cf. Estep v. Dent, 914 F. Supp. 1462 (W.D. Ky. 1996) (prison officials did not violate Eighth Amendment where inmate alleged that prison officials failed to provide inmate access to outdoor exercise; court noted that inmate failed to establish that prison officials were acting with deliberate indifference, since officials were in the process of constructing a yard in accordance with inmates' security level).

[40]Parnell v. Waldrep, 511 F. Supp. 764 (W.D. N.C. 1981).

[41]Anderson v. Coughlin, 757 F.2d 33 (2d Cir. 1985). It is worth noting that *Anderson* arose after many recreation issue had been settled and the recreation program considerably enhanced. See also Gholson v. Murry, 953 F. Supp. 709 (E.D. Va. 1997) (inmates confined to a segregated housing unit claimed prison officials provided inadequate recreational facilities, specifically, that recreation facilities were too small and did not provide access to water and restrooms; court held that there is no constitutional right to adequate exercise facilities, only an adequate opportunity to exercise). Sellers v. Roper, 554 F. Supp. 202 (E.D. Va. 1982).

[42]In fact, most of the cases cited above involve segregation.

physical and mental health, courts have held that it is unconstitutional to confine a person in segregation for lengthy periods of time without making provisions for exercise out of their cells.[43] However, as long as the bare minimum is provided,[44] it is permissible for prison officials to provide less opportunities for recreation to inmates in segregation than is provided to their counterparts in the general population.[45] Likewise, prison officials have been allowed to curtail exercise periods during institutional emergency or "lock down" situations as long as the suspension is short lived.[46]

---

[43]Toussaint v. Rushen, 553 F. Supp. 1365 (N.D. Cal. 1983), aff'd in part, 722 F.2d 1490 (9th Cir. 1984) (opportunity for exercise must be extended to inmates in segregation); Grubbs v. Bradley, 552 F. Supp. 1052 (M.D. Tenn. 1982). Courts, however, have upheld the denial of recreation for short periods for persons in punitive segregation, in part, on the ground that it serves the legitimate purpose of making punitive segregation unpleasant. Leonard v. Norris, 797 F.2d 683 (8th Cir. 1986). See also Knight v. Armontrout, 878 F.2d 1093 (8th Cir. 1989) (short-term deprivation of recreation is constitutional); Brightwell v. Smarkola, 1988 WL 124913 (E.D. Pa. 1988).

[44]Davenport v. DeRobertis, 844 F.2d 1310 (7th Cir. 1988) (noting that less than five hours a week out-of-cell exercise time for inmates in segregation would violate the Constitution). See also Divers v. Department of Corrections, 921 F.2d 191 (8th Cir. 1990) (a claim that inmates in protective custody only received one 45-minute exercise period a week stated a claim that the Eighth Amendment had been violated).

[45]See, e.g., Wishon v. Gammon, 978 F.2d 446 (8th Cir. 1992) (restriction to one 45-minute period a week of outdoor recreation for protective custody inmate upheld); Peterkin v. Jeffes, 855 F.2d 1021 (3d Cir. 1988) (inmates in death row can be provided less recreation time then general population); Harris v. Fleming, 839 F.2d 1232 (7th Cir. 1988) (failure to provide exercise for protective custody inmate for 28 days did not violate Constitution); Bailey v. Shillinger, 828 F.2d 651 (10th Cir. 1987) (restriction of segregated inmate to one hour a week of outdoor exercise upheld); Pendleton v. Housewright, 651 F. Supp. 631 (D. Nev. 1986) (upholding brief denials of yard access for administrative segregation unit inmates).

[46]Knight v. Armontrout, 878 F.2d 1093, 1096 (8th Cir. 1989) ("Denial of recreation for a short period, per se, is not a constitu-

§ 2:11　　　　　　Rights of Prisoners, Third Edition

Thus, it is clearly established law[47] that some program of regular physical activity is now constitutionally required.[48] Only the most compelling reasons, such as assaultive behavior, can justify the total denial of out-of-cell time for recreation, and then only after all alternatives to the denial are shown to be unworkable.[49]

---

tional violation."); Harris v. Fleming, 839 F.2d 1232, 1236 (7th Cir. 1988); Miller v. Campbell, 804 F. Supp. 159, 162-63 (D. Kan. 1992); Stewart v. McGinnis, 800 F. Supp. 604 (N.D. Ill. 1992), judgment aff'd, 5 F.3d 1031, 26 Fed. R. Serv. 3d 1299 (7th Cir. 1993) (three-month lockdown with denial of outdoor recreation did not violate the Eighth Amendment where inmates were permitted out of their cells regularly); Johnson v. Williams, 768 F. Supp. 1161 (E.D. Va. 1991) (limited recreation during 10-week lockdown period did not violate Constitution); Martin v. Lane, 766 F. Supp. 641, 647 (N.D. Ill. 1991); Dominguez v. Figel, 626 F. Supp. 368 (N.D. Ind. 1986) (upholding failure to let inmate out of his cell for exercise during prison lockdown); Frazier v. Ward, 426 F. Supp. 1354 (N.D. N.Y. 1977).

[47]Housley v. Dodson, 41 F.3d 597, 599 (10th Cir. 1994) ("Although we have never expressly held that prisoners have a constitutional right to exercise, there can be no doubt that total denial of exercise for an extended period of time would constitute cruel and unusual punishment prohibited by the Eighth Amendment."). See also Williams v. Greifinger, 97 F.3d 699, 703-705 (2d Cir. 1996); Mitchell v. Rice, 954 F.2d 187, 191 (4th Cir. 1992); Bailey v. Shillinger, 828 F.2d 651, 653 (10th Cir. 1987).

[48]Williams v. Greifinger, 97 F.3d 699, 704 n.5 (2d Cir. 1996) (Circuit cases are uniform in concluding that the Eighth Amendment requires that prison inmates be allowed some out-of-cell exercise); Mitchell v. Rice, 954 F.2d 187, 192 (4th Cir. 1992); Davenport v. DeRobertis, 844 F.2d 1310, 1315 (7th Cir. 1988); Toussaint v. Yockey, 722 F.2d 1490, 1492-93 (9th Cir. 1984); French v. Owens, 777 F.2d 1250, 1255 (7th Cir. 1985); Preston v. Thompson, 589 F.2d 300 (7th Cir. 1978); Spain v. Procunier, 600 F.2d 189, 199 (9th Cir. 1979); Reece v. Gragg, 650 F. Supp. 1297 (D. Kan. 1986) (total absence of recreation area contributed to a finding of unconstitutionality). Merely allowing inmates to walk in a narrow corridor between cells does not provide adequate exercise. See, e.g., Campbell v. Cauthron, 623 F.2d 503 (8th Cir. 1980); Hickson v. Kellison, 170 W. Va. 732, 296 S.E.2d 855 (1982).

[49]See, e.g., Delaney v. DeTella, 256 F.3d 679 (7th Cir. 2001); Williams v. Greifinger, 97 F.3d 699 (2d Cir. 1996). A few courts

There has been a great deal of case law defining the "compelling" circumstances that would justify suspension of the right to exercise. These cases establish the proposition that the right can be suspended for inmates who are so violent and disruptive in prison that it is not safe to allow them out of their cells for exercise.[50] This is the so called "safety exception."[51] The safety exception is consistent with other areas of Eighth Amendment jurisprudence that permit prison officials to deny aspects of basic rights to prisoners who, through their behavior, make it impossible for prison officials to operate safe facilities if they are granted the full right.[52]

The "Safety Exception"

The safety exception permits a direct infringement on a constitutional right. The infringement is one that can cause a threat to the mental and physical health of inmates. For these reasons, courts have been especially careful to ensure that the safety exception is only invoked where the inmate is exhibiting demonstratively

---

have taken the view that there is no right to out-of-cell recreation, since inmates can always "jog in place, perform aerobics and do pushups" in their cells. Grace v. Wainwright, 761 F. Supp. 1520, 1525 (M.D. Fla. 1991). However, this view is not in accord with the majority viewpoint on this subject and fails to recognize the severe limitations on physical movement imposed when one is limited to a small cell for moving large muscle groups. As noted in the beginning of this section, this view also "misses the point" that the right to exercise includes the psychological benefit of allowing inmates to be in each other's presence. Davenport v. DeRobertis, 844 F.2d 1310, 1314 (7th Cir. 1988).

[50]See e.g., Pearson v. Ramos, 237 F.3d 881, 885 (7th Cir. 2001) (4 consecutive 90-day denials of out-of-cell exercise privileges for serious violations upheld): LeMaire v. Maass, 12 F.3d 1444, 1457-58 (9th Cir. 1993) (5-year denial of out-of-cell exercise justified because inmate posed constant threat of attack).

[51]The term "safety exception" was first coined by Judge Pollack speaking for the Second Circuit in Williams v. Greifinger, 97 F.3d 699 (2d Cir. 1996).

[52]§ 2:10, discussing situations in which inmates can be deprived of food.

§ 2:11　　　　　　　　　Rights of Prisoners, Third Edition

harmful conduct that cannot be controlled in any way than other through depriving the inmate of recreation and exercise. The exception must be limited to "unusual circumstances" or circumstances in which exercise is "impossible" because of disciplinary needs.[53] Courts will not accept an "unsupported statement" of reasons for depriving an inmate of this important right.[54]

One such "unsupported" reason for the denial of recreation is the crime that led to the inmate's imprisonment. The Tenth Circuit Court of Appeals expressed this idea when it said, "even a convicted murdered who had murdered another inmate and represented a major security risk was entitled to outdoor recreation."[55] The fact that an inmate is violent may "justify segregating him or her from the general population but does not necessarily justify a prison's failure to make 'other exercise arrangements.'"[56] On similar reasoning, exercise cannot be denied on the ground that the inmate "holds the keys to his cell." In other words, conditioning the right to recreation on a modification of behavior is not a justification for failing to provide this basic human need.[57] Finally, courts have held that administrative obstacles are not an excuse for

---

[53]Williams v. Greifinger, 97 F.3d 699 (2d Cir. 1996); Mitchell v. Rice, 954 F.2d 187, 192 (4th Cir. 1992); Spain v. Procunier, 600 F.2d 189, 199 (9th Cir. 1979).

[54]See, e.g., Delaney v. DeTella, 256 F.3d 679 (7th Cir. 2001). See also Davenport v. DeRobertis, 844 F.2d 1310, 1312 (7th Cir. 1988) (upholding injunction which permits the denial "for a reasonable time" of recreation if an inmate violates prison rules during that time).

[55]Housley v. Dodson, 41 F.3d 597, 599 (10th Cir. 1994) (citing Bailey v. Shillinger, 828 F.2d 651, 653 (10th Cir. 1987)).

[56]Williams v. Greifinger, 97 F.3d 699 (2d Cir. 1996).

[57]Williams v. Greifinger, 97 F.3d 699 (2d Cir. 1996) (the fact that the inmate could resume normal activities if he modified his behavior "in no way relax(es) the court's inquiry into the adequacy of the conditions to which (the prisoner) was subjected").

totally depriving an inmate of the right to recreation.[58]

Pearson v. Ramos[59] is an illustration of a case in which the safety exception was invoked. It demonstrates that the only permissible reason to deny recreation is conduct of the inmate that clearly establishes the danger to other inmates or staff that would result if the inmate were granted the right. In *Pearson,* the conduct that led to the suspension of recreation was "not trivial."[60] The inmate had attacked and beaten a guard seriously enough to require his hospitalization, set fire to blankets, coats, and cardboard boxes, requiring the evacuation of inmates with respiratory problems, spit in the face of a guard, and thrown "bodily fluids" at a medical technician.[61] The court found that since these infractions all occurred while the inmate was out of his cell and since they marked the plaintiff as "violent and incorrigible," it was not a violation of the Eighth Amendment to deprive him of out-of-cell exercise for a period of a year.

The court gave two reasons for this conclusion. First, "[p]reventing access to the yard was a reasonable method of protecting the staff and the other prisoners from his violent propensities."[62] Second, there was no evidence that the plaintiff suffered any psychological or physical injury as a result of the loss of recreation.[63]

§ 2:12 —Shelter, Clothing, Personal Hygiene, Sanitation, Ventilation, Fire Safety, and Hazardous Substances

While government officials have a great deal of discre-

---

[58]Allen v. Sakai, 48 F.3d 1082 (9th Cir. 1994) (administrative problems involved in providing recreation do not excuse the denial of recreation even if to do so would be "difficult" for defendants).

[59]Pearson v. Ramos, 237 F.3d 881 (7th Cir. 2001).

[60]*Id.* at 885.

[61]*Id.*

[62]Pearson v. Ramos, 237 F.3d 881, 885 (7th Cir. 2001).

[63]*Id.* at 886.

tion in deciding how to maintain and furnish prisons,[1] in doing so they must comply with the requirements of the Eighth Amendment. The Supreme Court has made clear that prison conditions may be "restrictive and even harsh," but they may not deprive inmates of "the minimal civilized measure of life's necessities."[2] Thus, under the Eighth Amendment, prisons must provide adequate shelter, ventilation, clothing, sanitation, and protection from hazards such as fire and dangerous substances. These are essential if the Eighth Amendment goal of a "healthy habilitative environment" is to be met.[3] These essentials are also needed to ensure that inmates do not live in conditions which cause "degeneration or threaten . . . mental and physical well being."[4]

Applying these principles, lower courts have determined in a great many cases that the conditions in many American prisons fall distressingly below civilized standards of decency. The best way to approach the catalog of items that fit within the rubric of general prison conditions is to discuss them individually.

Shelter

While many consider shelter a basic human need,[5] the Supreme Court has not established an entitlement

[Section 2:12]

[1] See, e.g., Martin v. Tyson, 845 F.2d 1451 (7th Cir. 1988) (holding that there is no obligation to design prisons to "duplicate the amenities of . . . hotels."); Isby v. Clark, 100 F.3d 502, 505 (7th Cir. 1996) ("Prisons, of course, are not Hilton hotels").

[2] Rhodes v. Chapman, 452 U.S. 337, 347, 101 S. Ct. 2392, 69 L. Ed. 2d 59 (1981). See also Helling v. McKinney, 509 U.S. 25, 113 S. Ct. 2475, 125 L. Ed. 2d 22 (1993); Wilson v. Seiter, 501 U.S. 294, 111 S. Ct. 2321, 115 L. Ed. 2d 271 (1991); Farmer v. Brennan, 511 U.S. 825, 114 S. Ct. 1970, 128 L. Ed. 2d 811 (1994).

[3] Ramos v. Lamm, 639 F.2d 559, 568 (10th Cir. 1980).

[4] Id. at 568.

[5] See, e.g., DeShaney v. Winnebago County Dept. of Social Services, 489 U.S. 189, 109 S. Ct. 998, 1005-06, 103 L. Ed. 2d 249 (1989).

in the free world to shelter.⁶ However, for prisoners who have no choice where they will live, adequate shelter is clearly a necessity of life.⁷ If it is not provided for them they will not be able to procure it for themselves. The Supreme Court has identified shelter⁸ and warmth⁹ as Eighth Amendment entitlements. Adequate shelter includes such basics as sufficient temperature control, ventilation, lighting, and bedding. The failure to provide any of these rudiments of decent living can give rise to liability under the Eighth Amendment.

Temperature and Ventilation

Courts have condemned prison conditions that fail to supply inmates with sufficient heat[10] and ventilation.[11] The reason for this is that extreme temperatures or

---

[6]Lindsey v. Normet, 405 U.S. 56, 92 S. Ct. 862, 31 L. Ed. 2d 36 (1972) ("We are unable to perceive in that document any constitutional guarantee of access to dwellings of a particular quality, or any recognition of the right of a tenant to occupy the real property of his landlord beyond the term of his lease without the payment of rent").

[7]Farmer v. Brennan, 511 U.S. 825, 832, 114 S. Ct. 1970, 128 L. Ed. 2d 811 (1994) ("prison officials must ensure that inmates receive adequate food, clothing, shelter, and medical care, and must 'take reasonable measures to guarantee the safety of the inmates'") (quoting Hudson v. Palmer, 468 U.S. 517, 526-527, 104 S. Ct. 3194, 82 L. Ed. 2d 393 (1984)).

[8]Helling v. McKinney, 509 U.S. 25, 32, 113 S. Ct. 2475, 125 L. Ed. 2d 22 (1993) (citing DeShaney v. Winnebago County Dept. of Social Services, 489 U.S. 189, 199-2000, 109 S. Ct. 998, 103 L. Ed. 2d 249 (1989)).

[9]Wilson v. Seiter, 501 U.S. 294, 304, 111 S. Ct. 2321, 115 L. Ed. 2d 271 (1991).

[10]See, e.g., Mitchell v. Maynard, 80 F.3d 1433, 34 Fed. R. Serv. 3d 1018 (10th Cir. 1996); Del Raine v. Williford, 32 F.3d 1024, 29 Fed. R. Serv. 3d 1370 (7th Cir. 1994) (collecting cases); Henderson v. DeRobertis, 940 F.2d 1055 (7th Cir. 1991) (holding that the right to adequate heat is premised on the notion that "constitutional rights don't come and go with the weather"); Ramos v. Lamm, 639 F.2d 559, 572 (10th Cir. 1980) (holding lack of heating to be constitutional violation); Inmates of the Allegheny County

§ 2:12　　　　　　　　Rights of Prisoners, Third Edition

insufficient ventilation "undermines the health of the inmates" and "increases the likelihood of disease as well as frustration brought on by uncomfortable temperatures and odors."[12]

An example of the harm that can befall inmates who are confined in facilities without adequate ventilation is *Brock v. Warren County*.[13] In that case, an inmate was placed in a cell with no ventilation except for a pan hole for food dishes. The cell had a window, but a steel plate was placed over it. Temperatures in the cell reached 110 degrees during the day.[14] These conditions were known by the defendants but were not corrected, in part because the government refused to allocate funds to correct the problem. As a result of these conditions, the inmate died of heat prostration.[15] The court found that the defendants' conduct in housing the inmate in these deplorable conditions was a shocking

---

Jail v. Wecht, 699 F. Supp. 1137 (W.D. Pa. 1988), aff'd in part, appeal dismissed in part, 874 F.2d 147 (3d Cir. 1989), cert. granted, judgment vacated on other grounds, 493 U.S. 948, 110 S. Ct. 355, 107 L. Ed. 2d 343 (1989) (holding inadequate a heating plant that broke down every winter); Lewis v. Lane, 816 F.2d 1165 (7th Cir. 1987) (allegation of inadequate heating raises a claim under the Eighth Amendment).

[11]See, e.g., Blake v. Hall, 668 F.2d 52 (1st Cir. 1981); Brock v. Warren County, Tenn., 713 F. Supp. 238 (E.D. Tenn. 1989) (holding lack of adequate ventilation caused plaintiff's death); Inmates of Occoquan v. Barry, 717 F. Supp. 854 (D.D.C. 1989) (holding that defendants must submit a plan to remedy the "nonexistent ventilation system"). Although adequate ventilation is essential, air conditioning is not. See, e.g., Lane v. Hutcheson, 794 F. Supp. 877 (E.D. Mo. 1992).

[12]Tillery v. Owens, 719 F. Supp. 1256 (W.D. Pa. 1989), order aff'd, 907 F.2d 418 (3d Cir. 1990).

[13]Brock v. Warren County, Tenn., 713 F. Supp. 238 (E.D. Tenn. 1989).

[14]The cell was so stifling that one of the guards testified that "he would only put his pet cat in Cell 1505 if the 'cat had rabies.'" Brock v. Warren County, Tenn., 713 F. Supp. 238, 241 (E.D. Tenn. 1989).

[15]See also Mays v. Rhodes, 255 F.3d 644 (8th Cir. 2001) (defendant died of heat exhaustion during work detail).

violation of the Eighth Amendment.[16] The cases abound with allegations of exposure to the cold.[17] Typical is a complaint that the plaintiff was forced to stand in the rain and cold without adequate protective clothing.[18] Another is one in which the plaintiff "was stripped of his clothing, placed in a concrete cell, with no heat."[19]

Even if the temperatures are not excessive, a poor ventilation system can cause severe problems. For example, in *Keenan v. Hall*,[20] an inmate stated that his cell was "permeated with stale air that was saturated with the fumes of feces (thrown by inmates), the smell of urine and vomit, as well as other odors."[21] In yet another case, the court found that the air in the prison cells was "fetid and odorous, smelling of sweat and unwashed human bodies."[22] The court found that this contributed to the spread of disease.[23] Because these failures jeopardize the health of prisoners, courts have found that the failure to properly maintain a prison

---

[16]Mays v. Rhodes, 255 F.3d 644 (8th Cir. 2001).

[17]Allegations of excessive cold are not unusual. See, e.g., Wright v. McMann, 460 F.2d 126, 129 (2d Cir. 1972) (finding an inmate was placed in a cell naked without bedding in temperatures that were "sufficiently cold to cause extreme discomfort."); McCray v. Burrell, 516 F.2d 357 (4th Cir. 1975), cert. granted, 423 U.S. 923, 96 S. Ct. 264, 46 L. Ed. 2d 249 (1975) and cert. dismissed, 426 U.S. 471, 96 S. Ct. 2640, 48 L. Ed. 2d 788 (1976) (temperature so cold that inmate tore open the mattress and nestled inside); Maxwell v. Mason, 668 F.2d 361 (8th Cir. 1981); Lewis v. Lane, 816 F.2d 1165 (7th Cir. 1987).

[18]Chandler v. Moore, 2 F.3d 847 (8th Cir. 1993).

[19]Mitchell v. Maynard, 80 F.3d 1433, 1442, 34 Fed. R. Serv. 3d 1018 (10th Cir. 1996). See also Oladipupo v. Austin, 104 F. Supp. 2d 654 (W.D. La. 2000) (allegation that officer took away mattress that plantiff had been using as a makeshift device to keep out cold and left him to sleep on a cold wet floor for seven hours).

[20]Keenan v. Hall, 83 F.3d 1083 (9th Cir. 1996).

[21]*Id.* at 1090.

[22]Carty v. Farrelly, 957 F. Supp. 727, 22 A.D.D. 333 (D.V.I. 1997) (Criminal Justice Complex in Puerto Rico).

[23]Carty v. Farrelly, 957 F. Supp. 727, 22 A.D.D. 333 (D.V.I. 1997).

§ 2:12   Rights of Prisoners, Third Edition

ventilation system is a constitutional violation.[24]

To make out a constitutional violation, the inmate must offer proof that the conditions are not just uncomfortable, but that they are seriously deficient and have caused severe discomfort. If there is no such showing, there is no liability. Thus, for example, an inmate's claim of inadequate heat failed where the evidence showed that the temperature of cellblocks was monitored and records indicated that the temperature was suitable.[25] However, if the conditions are deficient, the plaintiff need not prove that the conditions are fatal or

---

[24]See, e.g., Mitchell v. Maynard, 80 F.3d 1433, 34 Fed. R. Serv. 3d 1018 (10th Cir. 1996) (material issue of fact precluded summary judgment regarding Eighth Amendment violation where inmate alleged that officials failed to maintain adequate ventilation and hot water); Robinson v. Illinois State Correctional Center (Stateville) Warden, 890 F. Supp. 715 (N.D. Ill. 1995) (inmate stated a claim under the Eighth Amendment where he alleged that inadequate heating and cooling in prison caused serious health risk to inmates); Women Prisoners of District of Columbia Dept. of Corrections v. District of Columbia, 877 F. Supp. 634, 98 Ed. Law Rep. 681 (D.D.C. 1994), vacated in part on other grounds, modified in part on other grounds, 899 F. Supp. 659, 104 Ed. Law Rep. 213 (D.D.C. 1995) (objective violation of Eighth Amendment established where a combination of heating unit problems resulted in freezing temperatures in cells and not all prisoners were given a sufficient amount of blankets; where prison officials knew of the situation and did not act, deliberate indifference was exhibited); see also Gordon v. Faber, 800 F. Supp. 797 (N.D. Iowa 1992), aff'd, 973 F.2d 686 (8th Cir. 1992) (hats and gloves in subfreezing temperatures are necessities).

[25]Hopkins v. Campbell, 870 F. Supp. 316 (D. Kan. 1994). See also Leach v. Dufrain, 103 F. Supp. 2d 542 (N.D. N.Y. 2000) (without proof of inadequate ventilation, claim was dismissed); Benson v. Godinez, 919 F. Supp. 285 (N.D. Ill. 1996) (prison officials did not violate Eighth Amendment where inmate alleged that officials placed him in a cell with inadequate heating and ventilation; inmate was provided with warm clothes and there was a "chuckhole" in cell door for ventilation; in addition, inmate only suffered from colds and a sore throat); DeMaio v. Mann, 877 F. Supp. 89 (N.D. N.Y. 1995), judgment aff'd, 122 F.3d 1055 (2d Cir. 1995) (plexiglass-shielded cell was not a violation of Eighth Amendment because the shield did not prevent air circulation and there

that they have already caused serious harm. It is enough to show that the conditions cause serious discomfort and/or that they pose a serious threat to the health and safety of the inmate.[26] Plaintiffs can meet this standard, one court stressed, without having to show that conditions are so bad that "frostbite, hypothermia or a similar affliction" is certain to occur.[27] In addition, the obligation to provide "this basic need" is not relieved by an emergency once the most exigent circumstances are past.[28]

Bedding

The Eighth Amendment is violated by the failure to supply adequate bedding.[29] While at least a mattress,[30] sheets, and a blanket in appropriate weather is re-

---

was a legitimate interest in protecting prison officials who had been previously pelted with human waste).

[26]Del Raine v. Williford, 32 F.3d 1024, 29 Fed. R. Serv. 3d 1370 (7th Cir. 1994).

[27]Del Raine v. Williford, 32 F.3d 1024, 1033, 29 Fed. R. Serv. 3d 1370 (7th Cir. 1994). (emphasis supplied). This does not mean that there is no need for some injury. Sarro v. Essex County Correctional Facility, 84 F. Supp. 2d 175 (D. Mass. 2000) (allegation that plaintiff was ordered to keep his cell shut for three days and nights was not sufficient when the plaintiff failed to prove how he was injured by this order).

[28]Johnson v. Lewis, 217 F.3d 726, 731-32 (9th Cir. 2000), cert. denied, 532 U.S. 1065, 121 S. Ct. 2215, 150 L. Ed. 2d 209 (2001) (allegation that inmates were made to lie down in prison yard outside for four days after a riot and not given shelter when temperatures were hot stated a "harm of sufficient magnitude to satisfy the objective prong of an Eighth Amendment violation").

[29]Landfair v. Sheahan, 878 F. Supp. 1106 (N.D. Ill. 1995); Maguire v. Coughlin, 901 F. Supp. 101 (N.D. N.Y. 1995) (material issue of fact precluded summary judgment where inmate alleged that prison officials denied him bed linen while he was incarcerated in SHU). Beyond bedding, courts have had little to say about cell furnishings. Correctional standards, however, require more than simply bedding: at least a writing surface, place to sit, storage spaces for personal items, a place to hang clothes. American Correctional Assn., Standards for Adult Correctional Institutions, Standard 3-4128-1(2002).

§ 2:12   Rights of Prisoners, Third Edition

quired, courts have split on whether more is necessary. Some courts have deplored the practice of providing a mattress without a bed.[31] Others have not been troubled by the lack of a bed if a mattress on the floor is available.[32] Moreover, the deprivation of a pillow may not be unconstitutional as long as a bed and mattress are provided.[33] Temporary denials for good reason have been held to be *de minimis* violations.[34] Some courts have insisted that inmates must present detailed proof of the absence of these essentials before liability will be

---

[30]See, e.g., Oladipupo v. Austin, 104 F. Supp. 2d 654 (W.D. La. 2000) ("A mattress is a basic human need").

[31]See, e.g., Lyons v. Powell, 838 F.2d 28 (1st Cir. 1988) (subjecting inmates to use of a floor mattress without a bed, except for brief emergencies, is unlawful); Lareau v. Manson, 651 F.2d 96 (2d Cir. 1981) (failure to supply bed violates the Eighth Amendment).

[32]See, e.g., Brown v. Crawford, 906 F.2d 667 (11th Cir. 1990) (sleeping on a mattress on the floor is not unconstitutional unless this is imposed arbitrarily). See also Roop v. Squadrito, 70 F. Supp. 2d 868 (N.D. Ind. 1999) (sleeping on a mattress on a concrete floor is not unconstitutional); Castillo v. Bowles, 687 F. Supp. 277 (N.D. Tex. 1988) (being forced to sleep on the floor without an elevated bed for a few days does not violate the Constitution). Hopkins v. Campbell, 870 F. Supp. 316 (D. Kan. 1994) (holding that combination of pillow, sheets, mattresses, and two wool blankets provided adequate bedding).

[33]Martin v. Tyson, 845 F.2d 1451 (7th Cir. 1988).

[34]Antonelli v. Sheahan, 81 F.3d 1422 (7th Cir. 1996) (prison officials did not violate Eighth Amendment where inmate alleged that he was forced to sleep on the floor for one night due to overcrowding and situation was unintended and temporary); Jordan v. Doe, 38 F.3d 1559 (11th Cir. 1994) (temporary use of a mattress on the floor or on a table is not unconstitutional); Pierce v. King, 918 F. Supp. 932, 15 A.D.D. 246 (E.D. N.C. 1996), aff'd, 131 F.3d 136 (4th Cir. 1997), cert. granted, judgment vacated on other grounds, 525 U.S. 802, 119 S. Ct. 33, 142 L. Ed. 2d 25 (1998) (deprivation of disabled inmate's double mattresses, prescribed by prison physician, for ten minutes did not violate Eighth Amendment where the second mattress was confiscated due to a shortage of mattresses in the institution and was returned once the officers learned of the inmate's prescription).

imposed.[35] Where serious deprivations are proved, courts will act.[36]

Furnishings

Courts have not found a right in the Eighth Amendment to a particular interior design or particular furnishings, except that some courts have indicated that there should be some space to store some personal effects, and that if an inmate is locked into a cell for extended periods of time, a chair should be provided.[37] Another important aspect of shelter is clothing. There

---

[35]See, e.g., Lopez v. Smith, 160 F.3d 567 (9th Cir. 1998),reh'g granted, opinion withdrawn, 173 F.3d 749 (9th Cir. 1999) and on reh'g en banc, 203 F.3d 1122, 46 Fed. R. Serv. 3d 494 (9th Cir. 2000) (defendant granted summary judgment because inmate failed to produce any evidence that he was denied adequate warmth or heating or that he suffered from a cold, even though prison officials failed to provide a blanket and pillow in his cell); Robinson v. Illinois State Correctional Center (Stateville) Warden, 890 F. Supp. 715 (N.D. Ill. 1995) (prison officials did not violate Eighth Amendment where inmate alleged that there was a lack of weekly fresh bedding but inmate was unable to demonstrate that he had any medical problems as a result of the conditions); Antonelli v. Sheahan, 863 F. Supp. 756 (N.D. Ill. 1994), judgment aff'd in part, rev'd in part on other grounds, 81 F.3d 1422 (7th Cir. 1996) (holding no violation of due process where pretrial detainee sustained no injury as a result of sleeping on the floor);Gawloski v. Dallman, 803 F. Supp. 103 (S.D. Ohio 1992).

[36]Carty v. Farrelly, 957 F. Supp. 727, 22 A.D.D. 333 (D.V.I. 1997) (ripped and soiled mattresses which inmates were forced to sleep on violated the Eighth Amendment at the Criminal Justice Complex (CJC; the CJC regularly failed to sanitize and replace the mattresses; court held the defendants in civil contempt for failure to comply with a prior court order to remedy such conditions); Landfair v. Sheahan, 878 F. Supp. 1106 (N.D. Ill. 1995) (where pretrial detainee caught meningitis as a result of sleeping on floor of unsanitary cell, conditions held violative of Eighth Amendment).

[37]Lightfoot v. Walker, 486 F. Supp. 504, 528 (S.D. Ill. 1980) (lockers); Wojtczak v. Cuyler, 480 F. Supp. 1288, 1307 (E.D. Pa. 1979) (chair in protective custody). Other courts disagree. Luedtke v. Gudmanson, 971 F. Supp. 1263 (E.D. Wis. 1997) (inmate claimed, inter alia, that the conditions of his confinement violated the Eighth Amendment; court held that prison officials' failure

§ 2:12   Rights of Prisoners, Third Edition

is no right to a particular kind of clothing amenable to a person's individual tastes[38] but there is a right to suitable clothing to protect from the elements.[39] The cloth-

---

provide a desk and chair in plaintiff's segregation cell did not rise to the level of cruel and unusual punishment); Peterkin v. Jeffes, 661 F. Supp. 895, 917 (E.D. Pa. 1987), decision aff'd in part and vacated in part on other grounds, 855 F.2d 1021 (3d Cir. 1988) (no right to lockers).

[38]Even pretrial detainees may be required to wear uniforms. Wolfish v. Levi, 573 F.2d 118, 132-33 (2d Cir. 1978), cert. granted, 439 U.S. 816, 99 S. Ct. 76, 58 L. Ed. 2d 107 (1978) and judgment rev'd on other grounds, 441 U.S. 520, 99 S. Ct. 1861, 60 L. Ed. 2d 447 (1979); see also Bullock v. Horn, 720 A2d 1079 (Commw Ct Pa 1998) (petition for review of prison policy and practice allegedly denying inmate adequate clothing in which to exercise in winter; Eighth Amendment does not entitle a prisoner to clothing of his choice, unless the clothing provided is insufficient to protect him from the elements; where petitioner did not dispute that he received a coat, hat, footwear and gloves when he went outside during the winter months, the court would not issue a declaration requiring respondents to supply him with additional winter clothing).

[39]See, e.g., Palmer v. Johnson, 193 F.3d 346 (5th Cir. 1999) (inmate was forced to withstand strong winds and cold without the protection of jackets or blankets, and claimed that he and others were reduced to digging in the dirt to construct earthen walls as feeble wind barriers; court found that, although the degree to which the temperature actually fell was relevant to a conclusive determination, the inmate's exposure to the elements arising out of this incident could have risen to the level of a constitutional deprivation; accordingly, the court denied the defendants' motion for summary judgment on the basis of qualified immunity and remanded the cause for further proceedings); Mitchell v. Maynard, 80 F.3d 1433, 34 Fed. R. Serv. 3d 1018 (10th Cir. 1996) (material issue of fact precluded summary judgment regarding Eighth Amendment violation where inmate alleged that officials failed to provide him with adequate clothing); Gordon v. Faber, 973 F.2d 686 (8th Cir. 1992) (unconstitutional to send inmates into freezing weather without hats and gloves); Davidson v. Coughlin, 920 F. Supp. 305 (N.D. N.Y. 1996) (material issue of fact precluded summary judgment where inmate alleged that prison officials denied inmate winter underwear, socks, sweater, boots, and gloves during harsh winter season); Davidson v. Scully, 914 F. Supp. 1011 (S.D. N.Y. 1996) (material issue of fact precluded summary judgment

ing must also be clean.[40]

Lighting

"Adequate lighting is one of the fundamental attributes of adequate shelter."[41] Courts have been concerned with lighting that is too dim for an inmate to read by.[42] They also have expressed concern with a growing practice of keeping inmate living quarters constantly illuminated, making sleep difficult for inmates.[43] However, here, as in other areas, the Constitution does not

where inmate alleged that prison officials failed to provide warm outdoor clothing in violation of Eighth Amendment); Balla v. Idaho State Bd. of Corrections, 595 F. Supp. 1558, 1575 (D. Idaho 1984) (prison officials violated the Constitution when they provided inmates with clothing that was "patently insufficient to protect [them] from the cold in the winter months").

[40]See, e.g., Divers v. Department of Corrections, 921 F.2d 191, 194 (8th Cir. 1990).

[41]Tillery v. Owens, 719 F. Supp. 1256 (W.D. Pa. 1989), order aff'd, 907 F.2d 418 (3d Cir. 1990). See also Antonelli v. Sheahan, 81 F.3d 1422 (7th Cir. 1996); Jackson v. Duckworth, 955 F.2d 21 (7th Cir. 1992) (inadequate lighting can violate the Eighth Amendment); Gillespie v. Crawford, 833 F.2d 47 (5th Cir. 1987), on reh'g, 858 F.2d 1101 (5th Cir. 1988) (allegation of inadequate lighting stated an Eighth Amendment violation); French v. Owens, 777 F.2d 1250 (7th Cir. 1985) (inadequate lighting contributed to a finding of unconstitutional prison conditions); Ramos v. Lamm, 639 F.2d 559, 572 (10th Cir. 1980); Rhem v. Malcolm, 371 F. Supp. 594, 627 (S.D. N.Y. 1974), opinion supplemented, 377 F. Supp. 995 (S.D. N.Y. 1974), aff'd and remanded, 507 F.2d 333 (2d Cir. 1974); Carty v. Farrelly, 957 F. Supp. 727, 22 A.D.D. 333 (D.V.I. 1997) (where inmates lived in dark cells with no light at the Criminal Justice Complex (CJC), such conditions violated the Eighth Amendment; court held the CJC in civil contempt for failure to comply with a previous court order to remedy such conditions).

[42]Antonelli v. Sheahan, 81 F.3d 1422 (7th Cir. 1996) (inmate stated a claim where he alleged that prison officials violated First Amendment where the lighting in his cell was insufficient to read by; inmate alleged that the poor light made it difficult for him to read and hurt his eyes).

[43]Keenan v. Hall, 83 F.3d 1083 (9th Cir. 1996) (material issue of fact precluded summary judgment where inmate alleged that prison officials violated Eighth Amendment where his cell was il-

§ 2:12   Rights of Prisoners, Third Edition

guarantee perfection. Thus, the failure to replace a burned out light bulb will not support an Eighth Amendment claim.[44]

Whether natural light and sunlight is a necessary attribute of adequate lighting is an issue that has received scant attention. The best treatment of the topic is *Richard v. Reed*.[45] In that case, the plaintiff was confined in a unit that consisted of ten cells and a dayroom containing no windows. There was a window in his cell but he was not allowed access to the cell from 8 a.m. until 5:30 p.m. The plaintiff complained that he had not had exposure to direct sunlight for a period of over 100 days and that this placed his health in danger. The district court dismissed the complaint, holding that the plaintiff had not alleged a severe enough deprivation to make out an Eighth Amendment violation, but in dicta stated that "there may be extreme circumstances where deprivation of sunlight or light for an extended period of time might amount to a sufficiently serious deprivation."[46]

In sketching scenarios in which a serious deprivation might occur, the court gave as an example the description that Charles Dickens offered in *A Tale of Two Cities* of the punishment inflicted on Dr. Alexandre Manette, who was imprisoned in darkened cell in the Bastille in a place where "the light of day has never

---

luminated on a constant basis, making it difficult for him to rest); LeMaire v. Maass, 745 F. Supp. 623 (D. Or. 1990), vacated on other grounds, 12 F.3d 1444 (9th Cir. 1993) (conditions in a solitary confinement unit were unconstitutional because in each cell lights were left burning 24 hours a day).

[44]Young v. Ballis, 762 F. Supp. 823 (S.D. Ind. 1990). See also Vega v. Parsley, 700 F. Supp. 879 (W.D. Tex. 1988) (a burned-out light bulb, promptly replaced, does not violate the Eighth Amendment).

[45]Richard v. Reed, 49 F. Supp. 2d 485 (E.D. Va. 1999), aff'd, 188 F.3d 503 (4th Cir. 1999) (table).

[46]Richard v. Reed, 49 F. Supp. 2d 485, 487 (E.D. Va. 1999), aff'd, 188 F.3d 503 (4th Cir. 1999) (table).

shone."[47] The court made clear that the threshold of a constitutional deprivation "occurs well short of the Dickens example," but that in the case before it that threshold had not been met.[48] The court thus recognized that a severe deprivation of sunlight and natural light could be sufficiently threatening to violate the Eighth Amendment.[49]

Sanitation

Inadequate sanitation violates the Eighth Amendment.[50] The reason is self-evident. As one court in an extreme case recognized:

> No human being should be required to frequent bathrooms with slime oozing down the walls, stalactites hanging from

---

[47]*Id.* at 488, citing Charles Dickens, A Tale of Two Cities, Chapter XXI, "Echoing Footsteps."

[48]*Id.* at fn. 6. In *Richard,* the plaintiff's cell had a window. In the summer when he returned to his cell at 5:30 p.m. he would be exposed to sunlight, *Id.* at 487, therefore, this was not a case of year-round deprivation of exposure to the outside world.

[49]See in this connection the discussion about access to outdoor recreation, in § 2:11.

[50]See, e.g., Young v. Quinlan, 960 F.2d 351, 22 Fed. R. Serv. 3d 530 (3d Cir. 1992); Jackson v. Duckworth, 955 F.2d 21 (7th Cir. 1992); .Curry v. Kerik, 163 F. Supp. 2d 232 (S.D. N.Y. 2001) (plaintiff's allegation that he was exposed to an unsanitary and hazardous showering area for over nine months was sufficiently serious to state a constitutional claim); Benjamin v. Fraser, 161 F. Supp. 2d 151 (S.D. N.Y. 2001), on reconsideration in part on other grounds, 2001 WL 282705 (S.D. N.Y. 2001); Gilland v. Owens, 718 F. Supp. 665, 684 (W.D. Tenn. 1989) ("Sanitary living conditions and personal hygiene are among the necessities of life protected by the Eighth Amendment."); Fambro v. Fulton County, Ga., 713 F. Supp. 1426, 1431 (N.D. Ga. 1989) (correctional facilities "are constitutionally obligated to provide reasonably adequate sanitation for their inmates."). An extreme example of subjecting an inmate to unsanitary practices occurred in Blissett v. Coughlin, 66 F.3d 531 (2d Cir. 1995), where a jury found that prison officials violated Eighth Amendment where they beat inmate, smeared feces on him, and placed him in mental observation cell without furnishings for eight days; court affirmed a jury award of $75,000 in compensatory damages and 15,000 in punitive damages.

§ 2:12 Rights of Prisoners, Third Edition

the ceiling, thick soap scum on the walls and floors, and sewer water dripping into the toilet.[51]

A prison can be found wanting in its sanitation practices when it has defective plumbing[52] and the presence of sewage,[53] lack of cleaning and garbage disposal,[54] or

---

[51]Inmates of Occoquan v. Barry, 717 F. Supp. 854, 866-67 (D. D.C. 1989).

[52]Palmer v. Johnson, 193 F.3d 346 (5th Cir. 1999) (plaintiff claimed that he was not allowed to use a bathroom during a seventeen hour outdoor confinement and was told that his only option was to urinate and defecate in the confined area he shared with 48 other inmates; court found that this complete deprivation of toilets for scores of inmates confined in the same small area constituted "deprivation of basic elements of hygiene"). But see Anderson v. County of Kern, 45 F.3d 1310, 1315 (9th Cir. 1995) (explaining that providing pit toilet in safety cell as only means of sanitation was not violative of the Eighth Amendment where the prisoner was considered suicidal or mentally disturbed and could potentially harm himself); Robinson v. Illinois State Correctional Center (Stateville) Warden, 890 F. Supp. 715 (N.D. Ill. 1995) (prison officials did not violate Eighth Amendment where inmate alleged that toilets were unsanitary; court noted that allegations were not that severe, since inmate was unable to demonstrate that he had any medical problems as a result of the conditions); Neal v. Clark, 938 F. Supp. 484 (N.D. Ill. 1996) (conditions in a segregation unit did not violate the Eighth Amendment where for 20 days an inmate had a broken toilet in which the water did not flush adequately; court justified conditions on ground that prison officials allowed inmate to keep plunger for the toilet in his cell at all times).

[53]DeSpain v. Uphoff, 264 F.3d 965 (10th Cir. 2001) (finding that the lack of access to working toilets led to exposure to other inmate's urine and feces and was unconstitutional); Williams v. Griffin, 952 F.2d 820 (4th Cir. 1991) (insufficient showers, flooding with sewage from leaking toilets); Young v. Quinlan, 960 F.2d 351, 22 Fed. R. Serv. 3d 530 (3d Cir. 1992) (lack of toilet in cell in which inmate was locked); McCord v. Maggio, 927 F.2d 844 (5th Cir. 1991) (living in cell flooded with sewage and foul water violates the Eighth Amendment); Morales Feliciano v. Hernandez Colon, 754 F. Supp. 942 (D.P.R. 1991) (absence of running water in some sections of prison); Tillery v. Owens, 719 F. Supp. 1256, 1271 (W.D. Pa. 1989), order aff'd, 907 F.2d 418 (3d Cir. 1990) (inadequate plumbing violates the Constitution); Inmates of Occoquan v.

CRUEL & UNUSUAL PUNISHMENT   § 2:12

pest infestation.[55] Running water is also important.[56]

Barry, 717 F. Supp. 854, 866-67 (D.D.C. 1989) (leaking pipes and defective plumbing); Carver v. Knox County, Tenn., 753 F. Supp. 1370, 1389 (E.D. Tenn. 1989), aff'd in part, rev'd in part on other grounds, 887 F.2d 1287 (6th Cir. 1989) ("functioning sinks, toilets, and showers are basic necessities of modern life, particularly within the confines of a wholly self-contained environment such as a jail"). Some courts have gone even further and ordered refinements to the plumbing. See, e.g., Toussaint v. McCarthy, 801 F.2d 1080 (9th Cir. 1986) (upholding order requiring that showers have adjustable valves).

[54]Ramos v. Lamm, 639 F.2d 559, 569 (10th Cir. 1980); Johnson v. Pelker, 891 F.2d 136 (7th Cir. 1989) (allegation that inmate was placed in cell with feces smeared on the wall and that no cleaning supplies were provided stated an Eighth Amendment claim); Kyle v. Allen, 732 F. Supp. 1157 (S.D. Fla. 1990) (denial of means to clean cell).

[55]Gaston v. Coughlin, 249 F.3d 156 (2d Cir. 2001) (Eighth Amendment claim supported by plaintiff's claim that mice were constantly entering his cell, and that for several days the area in front of his cell was filled with urine, feces, and sewage water); Antonelli v. Sheahan, 81 F.3d 1422 (7th Cir. 1996) (inmate stated a claim where he alleged that prison officials violated Eighth Amendment where there was a pest control problem regarding mice and cockroaches and correctional officials only fumigated twice in a sixteen month period); Gillespie v. Crawford, 833 F.2d 47 (5th Cir. 1987), on reh'g, 858 F.2d 1101 (5th Cir. 1988) (allegation of insect infestation stated an Eighth Amendment violation); Ramos v. Lamm, 639 F.2d 559, 569 (10th Cir. 1980). Carty v. Farrelly, 957 F. Supp. 727, 22 A.D.D. 333 (D.V.I. 1997) (rampant presence of vermin and roaches throughout the entire Criminal Justice Complex (CJC), including housing, kitchen and medical areas, violated the Eighth Amendment; court held such problems presented "an immediate threat to the health and safety of inmates," and held the CJC in civil contempt for failure to comply with a previous court order to remedy such problems); Masonoff v. DuBois, 899 F. Supp. 782 (D. Mass. 1995) (material issue of fact precluded summary judgment where inmate alleged that infestation of vermin created a inadequate sanitation and health risk); Walton v. Fairman, 836 F. Supp. 511 (N.D. Ill. 1993) (holding objective prong of *Wilson* test satisfied by allegations of inmates being bitten and attacked by mice and rats). But see Warren v. Stempson, 800 F. Supp. 991 (D.D.C. 1992), aff'd, 995 F.2d 306 (D.C. Cir. 1993) (allegation that unit is "plagued with rats, mice,

§ 2:12   RIGHTS OF PRISONERS, THIRD EDITION

Access to toilets is required[57] and a toilet in a cell is required if an inmate is locked into his cell for an extended period of time.[58] Moreover, courts have condemned the use of so called "Chinese toilets," which are pits in the floor of a cell for segregated prisoners.[59] Unfortunately, these concerns continue to be important. Recent cases suggest that some prisons and jails continued to be plagued with serious sanitation problems.[60] Sometimes the problems are not simply because of poor facilities. For example in one recent

---

roaches, spiders, flying bugs, and insects, birds, lice . . ." did not state a claim). As long as the problem of infestation is addressed, courts will not intervene even if some rodents or insects remain. See, e.g., Wishon v. Gammon, 978 F.2d 446 (8th Cir. 1992); Dailey v. Byrnes, 605 F.2d 858 (5th Cir. 1979), opinion withdrawn on reh'g, (Jan. 7, 1980).

[56]An allegation that there was no running water in the cell for thirty-three days stated a claim of an Eighth Amendment violation. Thomas v. Brown, 824 F. Supp. 160 (N.D. Ind. 1993). Denying hot water for bathing for a period of months stated a claim for constitutional violation. Matthews v. Peters, 818 F. Supp. 224 (N.D. Ill. 1993). However, depriving inmates of a sink with running water for a period of five to six consecutive days was held insufficient to state an Eighth Amendment claim without any other deprivations enhancing the punishment. McNeal v. Ellerd, 823 F. Supp. 627 (E.D. Wis. 1993).

[57]Palmer v. Johnson, 193 F.3d 346, 352 (5th Cir. 1999) (lack of toilet facilities violates the Eighth Amendment).

[58]U.S. ex rel. Wolfish v. Levi, 439 F. Supp. 114 (S.D. N.Y. 1977), order aff'd, 573 F.2d 118 (2d Cir. 1978), cert. granted, 439 U.S. 816, 99 S. Ct. 76, 58 L. Ed. 2d 107 (1978) and judgment rev'd, 441 U.S. 520, 99 S. Ct. 1861, 60 L. Ed. 2d 447 (1979).

[59]See LaReau v. MacDougall, 473 F.2d 974 (2d Cir. 1972) ("What is most offensive to this Court was the use of the 'Chinese toilet." Causing a man to live, eat and perhaps sleep in close confines with his own human waste is too debasing and degrading to be permitted."). But see Anderson v. County of Kern, 45 F.3d 1310, 1315 (9th Cir. 1995) (upholding the temporary use of pit toilets)

[60]See, e.g., Benjamin v. Fraser, 161 F. Supp. 2d 151 (S.D. N.Y. 2001), on reconsideration in part on other grounds, 2001 WL 282705 (S.D. N.Y. 2001) (finding serious sanitation violations at numerous New York City Jails); Maynor v. Morgan County, Alabama, 147 F. Supp. 2d 1185 (N.D. Ala. 2001) (finding serious

case an inmate brought suit after a prison disturbance in which some inmates deliberately clogged their toilets and flooded the area with rancid water. Prison officials turned off the water to the system, but left the entire cellblock locked in their cells with no toilet facilities to use and with exposure to other inmates' "urine and feces via standing water"[61] These conditions allegedly continued well after any emergency had ended. The Tenth Circuit held that these conditions, if proven, ran afoul of the Eighth Amendment.[62]

Hygienic Supplies and Showers

Another attribute of sanitation is the provision of basic hygienic supplies to inmates, including toothbrushes, toothpaste, toilet paper, soap, and cleaning supplies.[63] In that regard, the Seventh Circuit in *Davenport v.*

---

sanitation problems at a county jail, including dirty cells, poor ventilation, lack of personal hygiene supplies, and poor heating and cooling).

[61]DeSpain v. Uphoff, 264 F.3d 965, 974 (10th Cir. 2001).

[62]*Id.*

[63]See, e.g., Keenan v. Hall, 83 F.3d 1083 (9th Cir. 1996) (material issue of fact precluded summary judgment where inmate alleged that prison officials violated Eighth Amendment by failing to provide inmate with basic hygiene products, forcing inmate to choose between legal supplies and hygiene products); Penrod v. Zavaras, 94 F.3d 1399 (10th Cir. 1996) (inmate who was deprived by prison officials of toothpaste and razors for approximately two months brought an Eighth Amendment action, claiming that the denial of dental products caused gum problems and tooth decay, which had to be treated by a dentist; court reversed the lower court and remanded to determine whether prison officials caused serious harm by failing to provide basic hygienic supplies). Divers v. Department of Corrections, 921 F.2d 191, 194 (8th Cir. 1990) ("Inmates are also entitled to adequate laundry facilities. . .as well as sufficient cleaning supplies."); Landfair v. Sheahan, 878 F. Supp. 1106 (N.D. Ill. 1995) (where pretrial detainee did not receive cleaning supplies, such as toothbrush, toothpaste, towels, toilet paper or any detergent to clean the soiled clothing that was provided for him, prisoner must prove that a substantial period of time elapsed for an Eighth Amendment challenge to be maintained); Carver v. Knox County, Tenn., 753 F. Supp. 1370, 1389

§ 2:12   Rights of Prisoners, Third Edition

DeRobertis[64] engaged in a fascinating discussion about whether the Constitution specifies a minimum number of showers that an inmate should be permitted to take to maintain good hygiene. In that case, the district court held that inmates in segregation were entitled to three showers per week.[65] The Seventh Circuit reversed. Writing for the majority, Judge Posner held that the Eighth Amendment protects against physical deterioration, but it does not protect cultural American norms about how often a person should shower. On that issue Judge Posner wrote:

> No doubt Americans take the most showers per capita of any people in the history of the world, but many millions of Americans take fewer than three showers (or baths) a week without endangering their physical or mental health, and abroad people as civilized and healthy as Americans take many fewer showers on average, as every tourist knows. . ...The importance of the daily shower to the average American is cultural rather than hygienic.[66]

Judge Cudahy in dissent observed that:

> A one shower a week regimen takes us back in memory to

(E.D. Tenn. 1989), aff'd in part, rev'd in part on other grounds, 887 F.2d 1287 (6th Cir. 1989) ("The failure to regularly provide prisoners with clean bedding, towels, clothing, and sanitary mattresses, as well as toilet articles including soap, razors, combs, toothpaste, toilet paper, access to a mirror, and sanitary napkins for female prisoners constitutes a denial of personal hygiene and sanitary living conditions"; Sixth Circuit reversed because district court applied "totality of the circumstances" standard in finding Eighth Amendment violation). However, if there are valid reasons, courts will permit limitations on the provision of these supplies. Rivera v. Leaming, 2000 WL 382035 (D. Kan. 2000) (holding that it is proper to provide only three squares of toilet paper at a time when there was evidence that toilet paper was used to cover the security cameras so that jailors could no longer observe plaintiff).

[64]Davenport v. DeRobertis, 844 F.2d 1310 (7th Cir. 1988).

[65]The court relied on a prior district court opinion, which held that only one shower per week "promotes deterioration of inmates physically." Lightfoot v. Walker, 486 F. Supp. 504, 511 (S.D. Ill. 1980).

[66]Davenport v. DeRobertis, 844 F.2d 1310, 1316 (7th Cir. 1988). Accord Henderson v. Lane, 979 F.2d 466 (7th Cir. 1992).

§ 2:12

the days of the Saturday night bath in a washtub with water heated on a wood stove. But that is history. Indoor plumbing has now been with us for some years — even in prisons. . ..The medical director of the [department of corrections] testified that three showers are the weekly minimum necessary to prevent serious adverse effects on the physical and mental health of inmates. . ."[67]

Sanitation is such an elementary requirement that responsibility for unsanitary conditions cannot be evaded by pointing a finger at the sloppiness of inmates. The government has the ultimate responsibility to ensure that the conditions are sanitary for everyone, notwithstanding the actions of some prisoners.[68] Again, perfection is not required. Courts will excuse violations if they do not pose serious risks to an inmate's health[69]

---

[67]Davenport v. DeRobertis, 844 F.2d 1310, 1317 (7th Cir. 1988) (Cudahy, C.J., dissenting). There is support for the dissent's position that more than one shower per week is constitutionally required. See, e.g., Walker v. Mintzes, 771 F.2d 920, 928-29 (6th Cir. 1985); Preston v. Thompson, 589 F.2d 300, 308 (7th Cir. 1978). See also Peterkin v. Jeffes, 661 F. Supp. 895, 914-15 (E.D. Pa. 1987), decision aff'd in part and vacated in part on other grounds, 855 F.2d 1021 (3d Cir. 1988) (three showers per week at a death row unit is constitutional). Certainly when an inmate contracts an illness or develops a medical condition as a result of a failure to shower or bath there is a constitutional violation. See Bradley v. Puckett, 157 F.3d 1022, 1025 (5th Cir. 1998) (inability to bath for two months resulting in fungal infection).

[68]See, e.g., McCord v. Maggio, 927 F.2d 844, 847 (5th Cir. 1991) (constitutional violation can occur even if sewage backup is caused by inmate vandalism); Blake v. Hall, 668 F.2d 52 (1st Cir. 1981); Women Prisoners of the District of Columbia Dept. of Corrections v. District of Columbia, 968 F. Supp. 744 (D.D.C. 1997); Inmates of Occoquan v. Barry, 717 F. Supp. 854, 866-67 (D.D.C. 1989).(argument that conditions were caused by failure of inmates to apply "elbow grease" rejected).

[69]Landfair v. Sheahan, 878 F. Supp. 1106 (N.D. Ill. 1995) (where pretrial detainee did not receive supplies such as toothbrush, toothpaste, towels, toilet paper or any detergent to clean the soiled clothing that was provided for him, prisoner must prove a substantial period of time elapsed for an Eighth Amendment challenge to be maintained); Lunsford v. Bennett, 17 F.3d 1574 (7th

§ 2:12   RIGHTS OF PRISONERS, THIRD EDITION

and if the prison officials are responsive to the problem.[70]

Cir. 1994) (deprivation of hygiene supplies for 24 hour period did not constitute an Eighth Amendment violation). Ishaaq v. Compton, 900 F. Supp. 935 (W.D. Tenn. 1995) (prison officials did not violate Eighth Amendment where inmate alleged that the walls of the prison shower were dirty; court found no serious threat to inmate's health); Landfair v. Sheahan, 878 F. Supp. 1106 (N.D. Ill. 1995) (athlete's foot contracted in clogged shower stall not a sufficiently serious injury to warrant Fourteenth Amendment claim); Gaston v. Coughlin, 861 F. Supp. 199 (W.D. N.Y. 1994), judgment aff'd in part, vacated in part, 249 F.3d 156 (2d Cir. 2001) (holding that inmate's confinement in unsanitary special housing unit for three days before cleaning was not cruel and unusual punishment); Harris v. Ostrout, 65 F.3d 912 (11th Cir. 1995) (prison officials did not violate First Amendment and Eighth Amendment where inmate alleged that he was incarcerated in an insect infected cell in retaliation for his prior litigation; court found that cell conditions were not hazardous to human life); Robinson v. Illinois State Correctional Center (Stateville) Warden, 890 F. Supp. 715 (N.D. Ill. 1995) (prison officials did not violate Eighth Amendment where inmate alleged that vermin infested prison; court noted that the allegations were not that severe since inmate was unable to demonstrate that he had any medical problems as a result of the conditions); Buckley v. Barlow, 997 F.2d 494 (8th Cir. 1993) (holding denial of personal hygiene items such as body lotions and hair grease insufficient to state an Eighth Amendment claim).

[70]Wilson v. Horn, 971 F. Supp. 943 (E.D. Pa. 1997), judgment aff'd, 142 F.3d 430 (3d Cir. 1998) (inmate claimed the Eighth Amendment was violated when the area he was housed in a cell was vermin-infested; court held that since defendants sprayed for mice and provided plaintiff with a blanket the conditions complained of did not violate the Eighth Amendment); May v. Baldwin, 895 F. Supp. 1398 (D. Or. 1995), judgment aff'd, 109 F.3d 557 (9th Cir. 1997) (prison officials did not violate Eighth Amendment where prison refused to provide inmate in disciplinary segregation with shampoo, conditioner, and body lotion, despite inmate's dry skin; court noted that prison officials provided inmate with towel, soap, toothbrush, and baking soda); Smith v. Copeland, 87 F.3d 265 (8th Cir. 1996) (conditions were "de minimis" where pretrial detainee was exposed to "raw sewage" for a period of four days and "made to endure the stench of his own feces and urine; court reasoned that the inmate was afforded a sufficient opportunity to remove the sewage and flush the toilet); Antonelli v. Sheahan, 863 F. Supp. 756 (N.D. Ill. 1994), judgment aff'd in part,

Environmental Hazards

The Supreme Court, in *Helling v. McKinney*,[71] established that the Eighth Amendment protects inmates from involuntary exposure to environmental hazards. In *Helling*, the plaintiff complained that he had been subjected involuntarily to being housed with another inmate who smoked five packs of cigarettes per day. Justice White, writing for the Court, ruled that exposure to conditions that are "demonstrably unsafe" can violate the Eighth Amendment if the inmate can prove that the risk is "so grave that it violates contemporary standards of decency to expose anyone unwillingly to such a risk."[72] Although the Court did not determine whether tobacco smoke fit within this category, it remanded the case for a determination of that issue, thereby rejecting the defendants' argument that the Eighth Amendment is not violated unless the prisoner is actually injured.[73]

---

rev'd in part, 81 F.3d 1422 (7th Cir. 1996) (where prison was sprayed twice during pretrial detainee's stay and rodent and roach problem persisted, there was no due process violation); Eason v. Thaler, 73 F.3d 1322 (5th Cir. 1996) (prison officials did not violate Eighth Amendment where inmate alleged that officials failed to remove inmates from their cells during a gas leak; court found that when a "gas leak occurred in the building while repairs were being made to the central heating system, officials responded quickly to the outcry by the inmates, releasing the inmates in A-Wing . . . within a matter of minutes and using exhaust fans in B-Wing"; court noted that plaintiff failed to establish deliberate indifference);

[71]Helling v. McKinney, 509 U.S. 25, 113 S. Ct. 2475, 125 L. Ed. 2d 22 (1993).

[72]Helling v. McKinney, 509 U.S. 25, 113 S. Ct. 2475, 2482, 125 L. Ed. 2d 22 (1993).

[73]Helling v. McKinney, 509 U.S. 25, 113 S. Ct. 2475, 2482, 125 L. Ed. 2d 22 (1993). There was a great deal of litigation on this topic in the lower courts prior to the Supreme Court's decision in *Helling*. See, e.g., Clemmons v. Bohannon, 956 F.2d 1523 (10th Cir. 1992),opinion corrected, (Feb. 14, 1992) (en banc); Hunt v. Reynolds, 974 F.2d 734 (6th Cir. 1992); Steading v. Thompson, 941 F.2d 498 (7th Cir. 1991). On the other side of the coin, inmates have challenged prison rules that ban smoking. To date, these

§ 2:12   RIGHTS OF PRISONERS, THIRD EDITION

Helling has engendered a great deal of scholarly interest and debate.[74] Many issues are left in its wake.

---

challenges have not met with success. See, e.g., Murphy v. Dowd, 975 F.2d 435 (8th Cir. 1992); Addison v. Pash, 961 F.2d 731 (8th Cir. 1992); Washington v. Tinsley, 809 F. Supp. 504 (S.D. Tex. 1992); Doughty v. Board of County Com'rs for County of Weld, State of Colo., 731 F. Supp. 423 (D. Colo. 1989).

[74]See, C.M. Kiggen, Note, Helling v. McKinney: Warning. . .Second-Hand Smoke May be Cruel and Unusual Punishment, 20 New Eng. J. Crim. & Civ. Confinement 453 (1994) (discussing legal history leading to decision in the case); J.S. Kinsler, Note, Sensible Application of Stare Decisis or a Rewriting of the Constitution: An Examination of Helling v. McKinney, 13 St. Louis U. Pub. L Rev. 705 (1994) (arguing that *Helling* is consistent with prior case law); Gizzi, Note: Helling v. McKinney and Smoking in the Cell Block: Cruel and Unusual Punishment? 43 Am. U. L. Rev. 1091 (1994) (calling for a lowering of the standard to satisfy an Eighth Amendment claim for future harm involving ETS, claiming the contemporary standards requirement to hard to prove); Vold, Note: The Eighth Amendment "Punishment" Clause After Helling v. McKinney: Four Terms, Two Standards, and a Search For Definition, 44 Depaul L. Rev. 215 (1994) (using *Helling* to analyze the "punishment" component of the Eighth Amendment); Kraft, Casenote: Second-Hand Smoke as Cruel and Unusual Punishment: Helling v. McKinney: The Insurmountable Burden of Proof and the Role of the Court, 3 Geo. Mason Ind. L. Rev. 257 (1994) (*Helling* decision requires proof access to which an inmate is not likely to have, to be victorious on an ETS claim); Ginestra, Comments: Environmental Tobacco Smoke: Cruel and Unusual Punishment? 42 Kan. L. Rev. 169 (1993) (prisoners will have hard time proving future harm from long term ETS exposure); Frazier, Case Comment: Constitutional Law-Helling v. McKinney: Future Risks of Harm Actionable Under the Eighth Amendment, 25 U.Mem.L.Rev. 1479 (1995) (*Helling* leaves many unanswered questions); Kane, Note: You've Come a Long Way, Felon: Helling v. McKinney Extends the Eighth Amendment to Grant Prisoners the Exclusive Constitutional Right to a Smoke-Free Environment, 72 N.C.L. Rev. 1399 (1994) (Eighth Amendment should be reserved for actual cases of punishment, legislatures should decide smoking policy); Schwartman, Note: Constitutional Law—Eighth Amendment - Involuntary Exposure to Second-Hand Smoke in Prison Supports a Valid Cruel and Unusual Punishment Claim if the Risk to One's Health is Unreasonable and Prison Officials Are Indifferent to that Risk-Helling v. McKinney, 113 S. Ct. 2475

What kind of showing does a plaintiff who alleges future harm have to make in order to prove that he has been exposed to "unreasonably high levels" of a toxicant? Does this require scientific and expert testimony? How does one prove that the risk, if it does exist, is "so grave that it violates contemporary standards of decency to expose anyone unwillingly to such a risk?" Does the term "contemporary standards" refer to what society is unwilling to tolerate for members of the general public? Or, instead, does it require an inquiry as to the risks that society is willing to tolerate for prisoners specifically? Can a plaintiff recover damages for future injuries that have not yet occurred? Does *Helling* mandate smoke free prisons? Does the *Helling* decision apply to other toxic substances in addition to tobacco smoke? The Supreme Court has not revisited the issue. However, there has been a great deal of litigation in the lower courts addressing many of these issues. As result of the litigation, there are answers to a few of these questions but for most of them the answers are still developing.

Tobacco Smoke

Since the Supreme Court's decision in *Helling,* most, but by no means all, of the litigation has centered on Environmental Tobacco Smoke (ETS). Some of these cases have involved inmates who claimed that they had been physically injured by involuntary exposure to tobacco smoke in prison. A number have presented

---

(1993), 25 Seton Hall L. Rev. 314 (1994); Mopett, Case Comments: Constitutional Law—Extending Eighth Amendment Protections to Prisoners Involuntarily Exposed to Unreasonable Levels of Environmental Tobacco Smoke—Helling v. McKinney, 113 S. Ct. 2475 (1993), 28 Suffolk U. L. Rev. 200 (1993); Weiss, Note: Helling v. McKinney: Creating a Constitutional Right to be Free From Environmental Tobacco Smoke, 7 Tul. Envtl. L.J. 249 (the ETS in prisons issue will remain a matter for judicial interpretation, and the Supreme Court will eventually have to either extend *Helling* to provide more protection for non-smokers, or make it a right to privacy issue).

what appear to be strong cases. For example, there are cases in which the plaintiffs suffered from asthma, an affliction that would make a person sensitive to tobacco smoke.[75] Another case involved an inmate who had just recovered from lung cancer. He sued claiming that the ETS exposure could cause a reemergence of the illness.[76] In yet another case, the plaintiff alleged that as a result of second hand tobacco smoke he had experienced difficulty in breathing, chest pains, dizziness, sinus problems, burning sensations in his throat and headaches.[77] Another case involved an inmate who suffered from angina and emphysema, but who had to share a housing area with smokers.[78]

What Proof of Injury Is Required?

Despite the natural appeal of these claims, damages have been denied in almost all of the cases, primarily on the ground that the plaintiff did not offer strong enough proof of a serious medical condition that was made demonstrably worse by tobacco smoke. In the case involving generalized complaints about difficulty in breathing and chest pains, the court held that that there was no proof from a physician that the plaintiff either had a medical condition which mandated a smoke

---

[75]Alvarado v. Litscher, 267 F.3d 648 (7th Cir. 2001) (plaintiff alleged constitutional violation where he suffered from severe chronic asthma and continued to be housed in units where no-smoking rules were not enforced); Oliver v. Deen, 77 F.3d 156 (7th Cir. 1996) (plaintiff who complained about ETS suffered from asthma); See also Scott v. District of Columbia, 139 F.3d 940 (D.C. Cir. 1998) (inmate suffered from asthma and had been treated for thyroid cancer); Reilly v. Grayson, 157 F. Supp. 2d 762 (E.D. Mich. 2001).

[76]Goffman v. Gross, 59 F.3d 668 (7th Cir. 1995).

[77]Henderson v. Sheahan, 196 F.3d 839 (7th Cir. 1999), cert. denied, 530 U.S. 1244, 120 S. Ct. 2691, 147 L. Ed. 2d 962 (2000).

[78]Jacobs v. Young, 134 F.3d 371 (6th Cir. 1997). See also McIntyre v. Robinson, 126 F. Supp. 2d 394 (D. Md. 2000) (describing a host of medical conditions which inmates suffered that were made worse by tobacco smoke).

free environment, or that he had been treated for a condition that was caused by second hand smoke.[79]

In the case where the inmate had suffered from lung cancer, the court found that there was no credible evidence that suggested that the ETS posed a serious risk of triggering a reoccurrence of the disease. The inmate submitted testimony from fellow prisoners that he had difficulty breathing when exposed to cigarette smoke, but the court rejected this testimony. The court ruled that "the medical effects of secondhand smoke are not within the ken of the ordinary person so these inmates' lay testimony by itself cannot establish the showing of medical causation necessary to sustain [the plaintiff's] claim."[80]

Thus, in order to recover damages for a present injury the plaintiff will need solid scientific proof that the affliction he complains of was actually either caused by ETS or materially exacerbated by smoke.[81] One court suggested that recovery might even require an additional showing that that a physician recommended that plaintiff be given a smoke free environment

---

[79]Henderson v. Sheahan, 196 F.3d 839, 846 (7th Cir. 1999), cert. denied, 530 U.S. 1244, 120 S. Ct. 2691, 147 L. Ed. 2d 962 (2000).

[80]Goffman v. Gross, 59 F.3d 668, 671 (7th Cir. 1995).

[81]See also Jackson v. Berge, 864 F. Supp. 873 (E.D. Wis. 1994) (where prison resorted to double-celling due to overcrowding, inmate did not present sufficient evidence that he had a serious medical condition or that cellmate's smoking aggravated his condition; therefore, he could not establish a constitutional violation under second-hand smoke theory); Davidson v. Coughlin, 920 F. Supp. 305 (N.D. N.Y. 1996) (prison officials did not violate Eighth Amendment where inmate alleged that officials exposed inmate to environmental tobacco smoke (ETS); court found that inmate failed to present an estimate of the amount of smoke which was in his cell or that the smoke in fact significantly affected his health); Pryor-El v. Kelly, 892 F. Supp. 261 (D.D.C. 1995) (prison officials did not violate Eighth Amendment where inmate alleged only that he was exposed to smoke while in the TV room, game room, and letter room; court noted that inmate failed to establish that there was a significant health risk or that officials acted with a culpable state of mind).

§ 2:12 RIGHTS OF PRISONERS, THIRD EDITION

because of his medical condition.[82] In addition to showing that the plaintiff's medical condition was made worse by tobacco smoke, to establish liability the plaintiff would need to prove that the level of ETS in the prison was unreasonably high, higher than society is willing to tolerate.[83] Finally, the plaintiff would need to prove that plaintiffs were aware of the problem but were deliberately indifferent to the consequences.[84]

---

[82]Henderson v. Sheahan, 196 F.3d 839, 846 (7th Cir. 1999), cert. denied, 530 U.S. 1244, 120 S. Ct. 2691, 147 L. Ed. 2d 962 (2000).

[83]*Id.* at 847. See also, Alamin v. Scully, 96 Civ. 1630 2000 U.S. Dist. LEXIS 13143 (S.D.N.Y. September 13, 2000) (plaintiff successfully stated a claim where he alleged he had serious medical needs that could be exacerbated by exposure to ETS from prison personnel smoking five packs of cigarettes a day; he stated a valid claim that the level of ETS was higher than society would tolerate by pointing to New York state's Clean Air Act); Simmons v. Sager, 964 F. Supp. 210 (W.D. Va. 1997) (inmate's ETS exposure claim failed because he did not show any current physical condition that was being or could be worsened by exposure to ETS); Davidson v. Coughlin, 920 F. Supp. 305 (N.D. N.Y. 1996) (prison officials did not violate Eighth Amendment where inmate alleged that officials exposed inmate to environmental tobacco smoke (ETS); court found that inmate failed to present an estimate of the amount of smoke which was in his cell or that the smoke in fact significantly affected his health); Pryor-El v. Kelly, 892 F. Supp. 261 (D.D.C. 1995) (prison officials did not violate Eighth Amendment where inmate alleged only that he was exposed to smoke while in the TV room, game room, and letter room; court noted that inmate failed to establish that there was a significant health risk or that officials acted with a culpable state of mind). Davidson v. Scully, 155 F. Supp. 2d 77 (S.D. N.Y. 2001) (plaintiff's claim of exposure to second-hand smoke was defeated by qualified immunity because in an earlier case the Second Circuit said that the law was not clearly established that single-celling in an environment where ambient tobacco smoke is present is unconstitutional).

[84]See, e.g., Little v. Lycoming County, 912 F. Supp. 809, 15 A.D.D. 561 (M.D. Pa. 1996), aff'd, 101 F.3d 691 (3d Cir. 1996) (where inmate was examined and treated by prison medical staff on twenty-one separate occasions during a 93 day period for congestion and persistent cough relating to environmental tobacco smoke (ETS), prison officials were not deliberately indifferent to inmate's health in violation of the Eighth Amendment; court noted

In one of the damage cases, *Reilly v. Grayson*,[85] these elements came together to justify recovery. There, plaintiff was an asthmatic. The prison had a system of noting recommendations for medical treatment of the prisoners that were called Individual Management Plans (IMP). In 1994, the plaintiff was given an IMP by prison officials that required that he be placed in a smoke-free environment. Nevertheless, he was placed in a unit in which the non-smoking policy was not enforced. In the face of this acknowledgement by prison officials of the plaintiff's serious medical need for a smoke free environment, and their further acknowledgement that it was not made available to the plaintiff for over five years, the court found liability and ordered the defendants to pay $54,750 to the plaintiff.[86]

Requirements for Relief from Future Injury

In addition to claims for damages for present injury caused by ETS, there is another set of claims in the tobacco cases: these are cases in which the plaintiff seeks relief not for present injury but for the future injury that will occur because of the exposure to tobacco. These kinds of cases are of two types. The first seeks damages for anticipated future medical problems causes by ETS. The second seeks injunctive relief eliminating the exposure to tobacco smoke.

Damage Claims for Future Injuries

In the first type of action, there is a question whether a prisoner who has not yet suffered physical injury can recover damages. The Supreme Court in *Helling* indicated that an Eighth Amendment violation from

---

that each time inmate visited the infirmary, she was given the appropriate level of care).

[85]Reilly v. Grayson, 157 F. Supp. 2d 762 (E.D. Mich. 2001).

[86]*Id.* at 774. (compensatory damages were set at $20 per day for 1,825 days confinement with smokers and punitive damages were assessed in the amount of $18,250).

§ 2:12

exposure to toxic substances could result even if the inmate "shows no serious current symptoms."[87] The Court, however, did not indicate that damages were the remedy for this exposure or how damages for such conjectural harm can be calculated. The opinion certainly concentrated on the action for an injunction and not the damages claim.[88] On the other hand, the Court did not hold that damages for future injury could not be recovered; indeed, the Court remanded the entire case including the damage claim.[89]

In the aftermath of *Helling,* there is authority that it is possible to recover damages in this situation. *Henderson v. Sheahan*[90] is the leading case. Henderson sued for damages for future injury that he said would occur as a result of his exposure to tobacco smoke in jail.[91] The court interpreted *Helling* as authorizing damage awards if liability is established.[92] Since *Helling* did not give any guidance on this question and since there was no statutory rule describing how to award future damages, the *Henderson* court held that it would apply state tort law on the subject.[93] Applying Illinois state law the court found that there could be no recovery for future

---

[87]Helling v. McKinney, 509 U.S. 25, 113 S. Ct. 2475, 2480, 125 L. Ed. 2d 22 (1993).

[88]In *Helling* itself, plaintiff made a claim for damages as well as injunction but the Court focused most of its discussion on injunctive relief. Scott v. District of Columbia, 139 F.3d 940, 942 (D.C. Cir. 1998) ("Most of the [*Helling*] opinion's legal analysis concerned injunctive relief.'). See also Fontroy v. Owens, 23 F.3d 63, 66 (3d Cir. 1994) ("Supreme Court [in *Helling*] did not have the occasion to comment on the request for damages by plaintiff who alleged only risk of future injury").

[89]Helling v. McKinney, 509 U.S. 25, 113 S. Ct. 2475, 2482, 125 L. Ed. 2d 22 (1993).

[90]Henderson v. Sheahan, 196 F.3d 839 (7th Cir. 1999), cert. denied, 530 U.S. 1244, 120 S. Ct. 2691, 147 L. Ed. 2d 962 (2000).

[91]He also sued for injunctive relief and for damages for a present injury. *Id.* at 843.

[92]*Id.* at 848-851.

[93]Henderson v. Sheahan, 196 F.3d 839, 849 n.3 (7th Cir. 1999), cert. denied, 530 U.S. 1244, 120 S. Ct. 2691, 147 L. Ed. 2d 962

injury unless it was "reasonably certain" to occur.[94] The court further held that that standard had not been satisfied in the case before it, and dismissed the action.[95]

Injunctive Relief to Prevent Future Injury

The second type of action seeks an injunction ending the exposure to ETS. This is the most common type of post *Helling* case.[96] It is hardly a great surprise that such claims are brought. Indeed, the discussion in *Helling* was devoted in large part on the assumption that this was the type of relief which federal courts were most likely to grant if a case were proven.

Since *Helling,* it has proven difficult for plaintiffs to prevail. Some courts have denied an injunction without reaching the merits. This has occurred in situations in which the plaintiff(s) were transferred to another prison while the motion was pending. This moots the action.[97] A claim for injunctive relief can also be mooted by a

---

(2000). See also Fontroy v. Owens, 150 F.3d 239, 242-44 (3d Cir. 1998) (applying Pennsylvania law on damages).

[94]*Id.*

[95]*Id.* at 852-53.

[96]See e.g., Scott v. District of Columbia, 139 F.3d 940 (D.C. Cir. 1998); Ahlers v. Goord, 2001 WL 477238 (E.D. N.Y. 2001); Mcintyre v. Robinson, 126 F2d 394 (D MD. 2000); Henderson v. Sheahan, 196 F.3d 839 (7th Cir. 1999), cert. denied, 530 U.S. 1244, 120 S. Ct. 2691, 147 L. Ed. 2d 962 (2000).

[97]See, e.g., Henderson v. Sheahan, 196 F.3d 839, 849 n.3 (7th Cir. 1999), cert. denied, 530 U.S. 1244, 120 S. Ct. 2691, 147 L. Ed. 2d 962 (2000); Scott v. District of Columbia, 139 F.3d 940 (D.C. Cir. 1998); Jacobs v. Young, 134 F.3d 371 (6th Cir. 1997) (unpublished opinion); Reilly v. Grayson, 157 F. Supp. 2d 762, 765 (E.D. Mich. 2001); Blackiston v. Vaughn, 1998 WL 665477 (E.D. Pa. 1998) (plaintiff no longer housed in smokers' cellblock). Curiously, the plaintiff in *Helling* was transferred, but the Supreme Court did not find the case moot. This could be either because the issue was not raised and the court did not see it in Helling, or because the case involved a claim for damages as well as an injunction. Transfer would not defeat a damages action. See Scott v. District of Columbia, 139 F.3d 940 (D.C. Cir. 1998) for a discussion of this issue.

§ 2:12   Rights of Prisoners, Third Edition

change in the prison smoking policy.[98]

When they do reach the merits, courts have indicated that they do not read *Helling* as mandating smoke-free prisons[99] or a risk-free environment.[100] Therefore, the District of Columbia Circuit Court of Appeals reversed a lower court injunction that prevented "any direct exposure to tobacco smoke whether from the same room or from an adjacent area."[101] The court held that "before an injunction may issue the inmate must prove that he currently *is being* exposed to unreasonably high levels of smoke." (emphasis in original).[102] Courts have granted summary judgment for defendants where the evidence

---

[98] See Helling v. McKinney, 509 U.S. 25, 36, 113 S. Ct. 2475, 125 L. Ed. 2d 22 (1993). See also Ahlers v. Goord, 2001 WL 477273 (E.D. N.Y. 2001) (implementation of a 100% smoke-free policy mooted the case).

[99] See Henderson v. Sheahan, 196 F.3d 839, 845 (7th Cir. 1999), cert. denied, 530 U.S. 1244, 120 S. Ct. 2691, 147 L. Ed. 2d 962 (2000) (exposure to ETS is not a per se constitutional violation; plaintiff has to prove that the level of ETS is unreasonably high); Henderson v. Fews, 2001 WL 873016 (N.D. Ill. 2001) ("Absent extreme individual sensitivity . . . . requiring a prisoner to breath smoke-polluted air occasionally does not rise to the level of cruel and unusual punishment."). See also State ex rel. Kincaid v. Parsons, 191 W. Va. 608, 447 S.E.2d 543 (1994) (prison officials may not institute a total ban on smoking in a prison facility without following state administrative procedures, which include public comment and legislative review); State ex rel. White v. Parsons, 199 W. Va. 1, 483 S.E.2d 1, 66 A.L.R.5th 737 (1996), reh'g refused, (Feb. 11, 1997) (pretrial detainee challenged a regulation banning smoking promulgated by the Jail and Correctional Facility Standards Commission; plaintiff did not allege that he had a constitutional right to smoke, rather, he claimed defects in the rulemaking process denied him of basic procedural due process rights; court held the Commission's rulemaking process was arbitrary and capricious). See also Nowaczyk v. Shaheen, 49 Fed. R. Serv. 3d 107, 2001 DNH 13 (D.N.H. 2001) (smoking ban not a denial of a basic need; no constitutional right to smoke).

[100] Henderson v. Fews, 2001 WL 873016 (N.D. Ill. 2001).

[101] Scott v. District of Columbia, 139 F.3d 940, 942 (D.C. Cir. 1998).

[102] *Id.* at 943.

suggests only low levels of ETS exposure, or exposure that is intermittent or occurs over a short period of time.[103] This body of case law indicates that courts will insist on clearly convincing evidence that the level of tobacco smoke is "unreasonably high." How is this done? Anecdotal evidence will not suffice.[104] Scientific evidence establishing the level of tobacco smoke to which the plaintiff is exposed will be required.[105] Courts have indicated that that evidence will be carefully

---

[103]Compare Boblett v. Angelone, 957 F. Supp. 808, 22 A.D.D. 373 (W.D. Va. 1997) (evidence that inmate was exposed to ETS over a four day period did not establish exposure to an unreasonably high risk); Pryor-El v. Kelly, 892 F. Supp. 261 (D.D.C. 1995) (exposure to ETS in TV room, not in cell, did not state a claim upon which relief could be granted); Richardson v. Spurlock, 260 F.3d 495 (5th Cir. 2001) (complaint dismissed where inmate alleged exposure only on intermittent bus rides); Blackiston v. Vaughn, 1998 WL 665477 (E.D. Pa. 1998) (complaint dismissed where alleged exposure came, not from plaintiff's own cell, but from neighboring cells, and exposure lasted only 20 days); Hamilton v. Peters, 919 F. Supp. 1168 (N.D. Ill. 1996) (court granted summary judgment for defendants where asthmatic prisoner's exposure to ETS was only for a brief time). But see Harris v. Ashby, F.Supp.2d 2001 U.S. Dist. LEXIS 12092 (May 31, 2001) (plaintiff's testimony that he was housed for six months with between 15 and 23 inmates who all smoked from early in the morning until late at night stated sufficient facts to survive summary judgment).

[104]Scott v. District of Columbia, 139 F.3d 940, 942 (D.C. Cir. 1998).

[105]See e.g., Scott v. District of Columbia, 139 F.3d 940 (D.C. Cir. 1998) (court reversed district court's grant of summary judgment for the plaintiffs, where there was no evidence presented as to level of exposure of ETS, and evidence actually pointed to a lack of exposure rising to the "unreasonably high" risk standard); Davidson v. Coughlin, 920 F. Supp. 305 (N.D. N.Y. 1996) (plaintiff presented no evidence of the level of ETS exposure, unlike plaintiff in *Helling* who alleged he was housed with an inmate who smoked five packs a day); but see Warren v. Keane, 196 F.3d 330 (2d Cir. 1999) (court rejected defendants' claims that plaintiff had to allege facts mirroring those in *Helling* in order to survive summary judgment).

scrutinized. For example, in *McIntyre v. Robinson*,[106] the court indicated that at trial it would look carefully at the scientific evidence of the level of tobacco smoke in the prison and would not accept the evidence unless the plaintiff could show that the experts used reliable methodology.[107]

Even if the plaintiff is successful in establishing that there is a high level of tobacco smoke in the prison, there is still no entitlement to relief unless the plaintiff can show that the levels violate contemporary standards of decency. Unlike the question of the effect of tobacco smoke, which is decidedly a medical and scientific question, this issue is one not of science but of judicial judgment. Here the courts are split. One view is that prisoners do not have any greater right to escape tobacco smoke than do citizens in the free world.[108] In the words of one judge:

> Many Americans spend eight hours or more every day in the company of smokers . . . True, non-smoking workers can choose a non-smoking workplace while [prisoners cannot]. . . To the extent [the plaintiff] is required to breathe the air in the dayroom from time to time, the court

---

[106] McIntyre v. Robinson, 126 F. Supp. 2d 394 (D. Md. 2000).

[107] McIntyre v. Robinson, 126 F. Supp. 2d 394 (D. Md. 2000) (plaintiffs introduced both the results of urinalysis tests of prisoners and measurements of ETS in the air from smoke monitors set out in the prison in order to prove future risk of harm; court rejected the magistrate judge's recommendation that summary judgment be granted for the plaintiffs, as defendants introduced the results of earlier urinalysis tests that put the facts alleged by the plaintiffs at issue, as well as expert's report challenging the methodology the plaintiff used in making the measurements).

[108] See, e.g., McIntyre v. Robinson, 126 F. Supp. 2d 394, 406 (D. Md. 2000) (test is not whether society will accept exposing prisoners to ETS, but whether society will accept anyone to be exposed to ETS; further, that "current standards of decency must be measured by evidence from the nation as a whole, not merely what the state legislatures have done").

is not prepared to view as cruel and unusual something many free world persons freely tolerate.[109]

The contrary view is that there are different considerations that come into play in prison cases raising the issue of exposure to tobacco smoke, because prisoners do not have a choice to avoid tobacco smoke.[110]

This view was well expressed by Judge Nickerson when he wrote that:

> [d]efendants appear to assume that if society is willing to tolerate a level of smoke for the general public, that level is tolerable for prisoners. That cannot be the criterion for the reality of a life in prison. Unlike the general public, prisoners are subjected to the conditions against their will, without freedom or power to avoid or change those conditions. Their only recourse is either escape or litigation. Would large numbers of the general public tolerate pumping of high levels of second hand smoke into their bedrooms against their will?[111]

At least one commentator has expressed concern that another view might win acceptance: that society would tolerate greater health risks in the form of high levels of ETS in prisons than it would in the free world. The basis for this view is that society devalues the lives of inmates and does not mind their languishing in toxic conditions.[112] To date, this view, which appears unwarranted, has not found expression in the cases.

---

[109]Henderson v. Fews, 2001 WL 873016 (N.D. Ill. 2001).

[110]Compare, with Ahlers v. Goord, 2001 WL 477238 (E.D. N.Y. 2001) (court rejects the notion that the level of ETS society will accept for the general public also stands for prisoners, noting that prisoners are held against their will and have no way to avoid certain conditions other than escape or litigation).

[111]Ahlers v. Goord, 2001 WL 477238 (E.D. N.Y. 2001).

[112]Lisa Grizzi, Helling v. McKinney and Smoking in the Cell Block: Cruel and Unusual Punishment? 43 Am. U. L. Rev. 1091, 1111 (1994) ("[Some] people. . .argue that criminals must bear harsh, unhealthy living conditions as a price to pay for violating the law.").

Other Environmental Hazards

While the risks associated with passive exposure to tobacco smoke may be in doubt,[113] there is little question that other environmental hazards are well-known. Thus, exposure to asbestos has been held to violate the Eighth Amendment,[114] as has exposure to pesticides in large quantities, such as when they are sprayed directly in an area occupied by an inmate.[115] Moreover, it is unconstitutional to house an inmate in an area where there is faulty or exposed electrical wiring.[116] By parity

---

[113]But see US Dept of Health & Human Serv., The Health Consequences of Involuntary Smoking: A Report of the Surgeon General (1986) (noting the health risks of passive smoke).

[114]LaBounty v. Coughlin, 137 F.3d 68 (2d Cir. 1998) (inmate stated a claim that survived summary judgment where he alleged he was exposed to friable asbestos, where defendants did not dispute that the pipes holding the asbestos were sometimes damaged, possibly releasing the carcinogen); Powell v. Lennon, 914 F.2d 1459 (11th Cir. 1990) (housing an inmate in an area with an asbestos hazard is unconstitutional); Masonoff v. DuBois, 899 F. Supp. 782 (D. Mass. 1995) (material issue of fact precluded summary judgment where inmate alleged that asbestos fell off old pipes and into inmates' water and clothing, causing a health risk); Diaz v. Edgar, 831 F. Supp. 621 (N.D. Ill. 1993) (intentionally exposing an inmate to a dangerous condition, such as asbestos, constitutes cruel and unusual punishment, provided prison officials acted maliciously or sadistically for the very purpose of causing harm); Inmates of Occoquan v. Barry, 717 F. Supp. 854, 866 (D. D.C. 1989) (holding that asbestos must be removed before renovations of certain housing areas may begin). The mere presence of asbestos which is not exposed and in the air and is not a health hazard is not an Eighth Amendment violation. McNeil v. Lane, 16 F.3d 123 (7th Cir. 1993).

[115]Johnson-El v. Schoemehl, 878 F.2d 1043 (8th Cir. 1989) (allegation of spraying pesticides so that prisoners had to breathe the fumes states a constitutional claim); but compare McBride v. Illinois Dept. of Corrections, 677 F. Supp. 537 (N.D. Ill. 1987) (merely being subjected to the odors of insect spray not unlawful).

[116]Inmates of Allegheny County Jail v. Wecht, 874 F.2d 147 (3d Cir. 1989), cert. granted, judgment vacated on other grounds, 493 U.S. 948, 110 S. Ct. 355, 107 L. Ed. 2d 343 (1989) (faulty wiring contributed to a finding that the facility was unconstitutional);

of reasoning, housing inmates in institutions that do not have adequate fire protection contravenes the Eighth Amendment.[117] The test for these cases is the same for the ETS cases, there must be proof that the inmate has been exposed to a level of asbestos that poses an unreasonable risk to future health, and of course there must be a standard finding of deliberate indifference on the part of the defendants.[118] Courts have also

---

Inmates of Occoquan v. Barry, 717 F. Supp. 854, 867 (D.D.C. 1989) (ordering that all exposed electrical wiring and fixtures be covered or safely secured).

[117]See, e.g., French v. Owens, 777 F.2d 1250, 1257 (7th Cir. 1985) (holding that "fire and occupational safety are legitimate concerns under the Eighth Amendment"); Palmigiano v. DiPrete, 737 F. Supp. 1257 (D.R.I. 1990) (defendants were required to assign staff to fire safety duties, maintain all fire prevention equipment and have equipment inspected by state fire marshal); Tillery v. Owens, 719 F. Supp. 1256 (W.D. Pa. 1989), order aff'd, 907 F.2d 418 (3d Cir. 1990) ("prisoners have a right to be free from an unreasonable risk of injury or death by fire"); Women Prisoners of the District of Columbia Dept. of Corrections v. District of Columbia, 968 F. Supp. 744 (D.D.C. 1997); Carty v. Farrelly, 957 F. Supp. 727, 22 A.D.D. 333 (D.V.I. 1997); Inmates of the Allegheny County Jail v. Wecht, 699 F. Supp. 1137 (W.D. Pa. 1988), aff'd in part, appeal dismissed in part, 874 F.2d 147 (3d Cir. 1989), cert. granted, judgment vacated, 493 U.S. 948, 110 S. Ct. 355, 107 L. Ed. 2d 343 (1989) (ordering correction of fire safety hazards). While courts will order improvements, there is some reluctance to require compliance with local fire codes. French v. Owens, 777 F.2d 1250 (7th Cir. 1985) ("the Eighth Amendment does not constitutionalize the Indiana Fire Code"); Miles v. Bell, 621 F. Supp. 51 (D. Conn. 1985) (one clear violation of Safety Code does not violate the Eighth Amendment).

[118]See Robinson v. Page, 170 F.3d 747 (7th Cir. 1999) (allegation of lead in drinking water could not be dismissed even though plaintiff was not yet ill); LaBounty v. Coughlin, 137 F.3d 68, 73 (2d Cir. 1998) (court remanded to the district court for further development of the facts to show the level of asbestos, if any, plaintiff was exposed to, and if it posed an unreasonable risk to his future health); Eason v. Thaler, 73 F.3d 1322 (5th Cir. 1996) (prison officials did not violate Eight Amendment where inmate alleged that officials failed to remove inmates from their cells during a gas leak; court found that when a "gas leak occurred in the building

§ 2:12　　　　　　　　Rights of Prisoners, Third Edition

applied *Helling* in a variety of other situations, including exposure to "chemical toilets,"[119] exposure to tuberculosis,[120] the risk resulting from improperly constructed

---

while repairs were being made to the central heating system, officials responded quickly to the outcry by the inmates, releasing the inmates in A-Wing . . . within a matter of minutes and using exhaust fans in B-Wing"; court noted that plaintiff failed to establish deliberate indifference); McNeil v. Lane, 16 F.3d 123 (7th Cir. 1993) (though inmate alleged pipes containing asbestos were located outside of his cell, and defendants refused to transfer him, summary judgment was granted for defendants as plaintiff never alleged any actual exposure to asbestos); Crawford v. Artuz, 143 F. Supp. 2d 249 (S.D. N.Y. 2001) (plaintiff alleged that there is no safe level of asbestos exposure, and cited a government report showing exposure for only a day could cause serious health problems; summary judgment was still granted for defendant on testimony of expert who classified plaintiff's exposure as "trivial" and testified that it was unlikely that the exposure would ever cause any health problem; court held the expert's testimony more reliable than the inmate's conclusory statement based on a 20-year-old government pamphlet); Napoleoni v. Scully, 932 F. Supp. 559 (S.D. N.Y. 1996) (inmate exposed to asbestos while working on the prison roof failed to state an Eighth Amendment violation; court found that prison officials were not aware that asbestos was in the work area, and that after the incident the plaintiff immediately ceased working in the area and was not exposed to asbestos again).

[119]Masonoff v. DuBois, 899 F. Supp. 782 (D. Mass. 1995) (plaintiffs were forced to use "chemical toilets," which used no running water and had to be emptied by the inmates into a sink daily; defendants never disputed the plaintiffs' claim that the toilets were unsanitary; in granting summary judgment on the objective component of the plaintiffs'claim, the court noted, "if the future harm resulting from exposure to second-hand smoke can give rise to an Eighth Amendment claim," than daily contact with the chemical toilets could, as the chemicals caused rashes, burning, teary eyes, and headaches); see also Crawford v. Myer, 1999 WL 1390245 (W.D. N.Y. 1999) (court refused to grant summary judgment where inmate claimed he was repeatedly forced to work near various toxic chemicals, had suffered some health effects and feared future harm, and had been provided no safety data on the chemicals).

[120]See Loftin v. Dalessandri, 3 Fed. Appx. 658 (10th Cir. 2001) (inmate claimed jail officials refused to move him to another cell

§ 2:12

bunks,[121] contaminated water,[122] and the risk of fire hazards.[123]

---

after two cellmates tested positive for TB; inmate later tested positive for exposure to TB; reversing summary judgment for defendants, court noted that the Helling opinion specifically stated that communicable diseases could satisfy the test for an Eighth Amendment violation based on future harm); but see, Wright v. Baker, 849 F. Supp. 569 (N.D. Ohio 1994) (court held that inmate's negative TB test was conclusive evidence that there was no exposure to the disease, and granted summary judgment for the defendants).

[121]See Brown v. Bargery, 207 F.3d 863, 2000 FED App. 109P (6th Cir. 2000) (court reversed trial court's dismissal of plaintiff's claim, where he alleged that improper installation of cell bunks caused inmates to slide off of the beds onto the concrete floor, creating an unreasonable risk of harm).

[122]See, e.g., Robinson v. Page, 170 F.3d 747 (7th Cir. 1999) (allegation of lead in drinking water stated a claim under the Eighth Amendment); Ford v. Page, 2000 WL 960732 (N.D. Ill. 2000) (court denied defendant's motion to dismiss for failure to state a claim, where inmate alleged the water at the facility was contaminated; court held that the Eighth Amendment protects against future health problems as well as current serious health problems, and that defendants could not claim qualified immunity if they had knowledge of the contamination, since violated clearly established law). But see Carroll v. DeTella, 255 F.3d 470 (7th Cir. 2001) (plaintiff sued prison officials, the state environmental protection agency, and two EPA employees alleging that the drinking water was contaminated by radium and lead; claim was dismissed and court noted that "if the prison authorities are violating federal antipollution laws, the plaintiff may have a remedy under those laws. . . ..His remedy is not under the Eighth Amendment.").

[123]See Benjamin v. Kerik, 1998 WL 799161 (S.D. N.Y. 1998) (plaintiff pretrial detainees alleged violation of due process, but court held their claims of risk of injury due to lack of working fire equipment should be analyzed under the *Helling* Eighth Amendment rule; court held the fire safety protections at defendant jail exposed inmates to an unreasonable risk of serious damage to their future health, and ordered defendants to improve fire safety at the jail). See also Carty v. Farrelly, 957 F. Supp. 727, 22 A.D.D. 333 (D.V.I. 1997) (inoperable manual alarm systems, smoke dampers and heat detectors at the Criminal Justice Complex (CJC) violated the Eighth Amendment; court declared the prison facility itself "cannot adequately protect the occupants during a fire," and

§ 2:12　　　　Rights of Prisoners, Third Edition

Somewhat more ambiguous is excessive noise. At first blush, it may seem that noise is a minor irritant and not constitutionally prohibited.[124] It is well recognized in scientific circles, however, that exposure to excessive

---

court held the CJC in civil contempt for failure to comply with a previous court order to remedy such problems); Masonoff v. DuBois, 899 F. Supp. 782 (D. Mass. 1995) (material issue of fact precluded summary judgment where inmate alleged that structural conditions within prison were not in accordance with building codes; inmates alleged that facility was a fire hazard since cells were not equipped with automatic locks and sprinklers); Women Prisoners of District of Columbia Dept. of Corrections v. District of Columbia, 877 F. Supp. 634, 98 Ed. Law Rep. 681 (D.D.C. 1994), vacated in part on other grounds, modified in part on other grounds, 899 F. Supp. 659, 104 Ed. Law Rep. 213 (D.D.C. 1995) (where the prison maintained one unlocked fire door, no fire alarm system, no sprinkler system, no regularly scheduled fire drills, combustible material in living areas, and overcrowded open dormitories, the conditions were violative of the Eighth Amendment). But see Standish v. Bommel, 82 F.3d 190 (8th Cir. 1996) (prison officials did not violate Eighth Amendment where inmate alleged there was an absence of smoke detectors and sprinklers, inadequate ventilation, and deficient emergency procedures; court noted that the only fires that had occurred were started by inmates themselves and that there had been no injuries; court found that inmates failed to establish deliberate indifference since after the fires, prison officials prohibited inmates from smoking in their cells); Morissette v. Peters, 45 F.3d 1119, 31 Fed. R. Serv. 3d 1466 (7th Cir. 1995) (holding no violation of the Eighth Amendment where prisoner was temporarily exposed to electrical wires in a controlled segregation cell even if the prison guards knew of hazard and failed to remedy it); Carlton v. Department of Corrections, 215 Mich. App. 490, 546 N.W.2d 671 (1996) (prison officials did not violate Eighth Amendment where they failed to immediately remove inmate from his cell during a fire; inmate had intentionally set fire to the cell and prison officials first extinguished the fire and then removed inmate once he was handcuffed in accordance with prison regulations).

[124]Several courts have so held. See, e.g., Givens v. Jones, 900 F.2d 1229 (8th Cir. 1990); Peterkin v. Jeffes, 855 F.2d 1021 (3d Cir. 1988) (noise, while "irritating," is not unconstitutional); Griffin v. Coughlin, 743 F. Supp. 1006 (N.D. N.Y. 1990).

noise can cause physical and mental problems.[125] Thus, the better reasoned cases hold that excessive noise in a penal facility can violate the Eighth Amendment.[126]

---

[125]Rhem v. Malcolm, 371 F. Supp. 594, 608, 628 (S.D. N.Y. 1974), opinion supplemented, 377 F. Supp. 995 (S.D. N.Y. 1974), aff'd and remanded, 507 F.2d 333 (2d Cir. 1974) (citing studies).

[126]Keenan v. Hall, 83 F.3d 1083, 1090 (9th Cir. 1996) (material issue of fact precluded summary judgment where inmate alleged that prison officials violated Eighth Amendment where there was constant noise in the prison; plaintiff stated that inmates screamed, wailed, cried, and sang in groups during the night and day and that there was a constant loud banging); Toussaint v. McCarthy, 801 F.2d 1080 (9th Cir. 1986) (ordering installation of sound-absorbing wall on the ground that excessive noise "inflicts pain without penological justification"); Williams v. Lehigh Dept. of Corrections, 79 F. Supp. 2d 514 (E.D. Pa. 1999) (excessive noise can violate the Constitution but there was no evidence that noise was excessive in this case); Langley v. Coughlin, 709 F. Supp. 482 (S.D. N.Y. 1989) (housing inmates amid "noise and squalor" violated the Eighth Amendment); Reece v. Gragg, 650 F. Supp. 1297 (D. Kan. 1986) (excessive noise contributed to finding of unconstitutionality); Palmigiano v. Garrahy, 443 F. Supp. 956, 979 (D.R.I. 1977); Anderson v. Redman, 429 F. Supp. 1105, 1112 (D. Del. 1977); Rhem v. Malcolm, 371 F. Supp. 594, 627 (S.D. N.Y. 1974), opinion supplemented, 377 F. Supp. 995 (S.D. N.Y. 1974), aff'd and remanded, 507 F.2d 333 (2d Cir. 1974). But see Lunsford v. Bennett, 17 F.3d 1574 (7th Cir. 1994) (loud noise emanating from intercom for a period of hours did not constitute cruel and unusual punishment); Women Prisoners of District of Columbia Dept. of Corrections v. District of Columbia, 877 F. Supp. 634, 98 Ed. Law Rep. 681 (D.D.C. 1994), vacated in part on other grounds, modified in part on other grounds, 899 F. Supp. 659, 104 Ed. Law Rep. 213 (D.D.C. 1995) (daytime noise which was stressful did not present a sufficient health threat to female inmates); Abdul-Akbar v. Department of Corrections, 910 F. Supp. 986, 1006 (D. Del. 1995), judgment aff'd, 111 F.3d 125 (3d Cir. 1997) (prison officials did not violate Eighth Amendment where inmate alleged that there was excessive noise in the prison; court denied inmate relief because inmate was unable to demonstrate that he was denied an "identifiable human need"); Hector v. Thaler, 927 S.W.2d 95 (Tex. App. Houston 1st Dist. 1996) (inmates contended exposure to excessive noise constituted a health threat; court noted that the noise plaintiffs complained of was not work related, but resulted from housing many inmates close together; under such circumstances,

§ 2:12   Rights of Prisoners, Third Edition

This list is merely illustrative. The world, unfortunately, is filled with environmental hazards. Whenever one is introduced into a prison, the cases strongly imply that inmates-who have no option to go elsewhere to avoid exposure-are protected from the risk if they can show that it would be unacceptable to expose free-world citizens to the hazardous substance.[127]

§ 2:13 —Overcrowding

Overcrowding is perhaps the most serious problem facing American prisons today. At the time of the first edition of this text, there were approximately 325,00 inmates in state and federal jails; by the time of the second edition the number had more than doubled, rising in 1991 to over 755,000.[1] Experts at that time projected that by the end of 1994, the state and federal prison population would continue to climb, going over the one million mark.[2] These experts proved to be correct in their forecast of a continued dramatic increase.

---

noise is not a judicially cognizable health threat, thus the court affirmed the lower court's grant of summary judgment).

[127]See, e.g., Jackson v. Duckworth, 955 F.2d 21 (7th Cir. 1992) (exposure to contaminated drinking water would violate the Eighth Amendment); Burton v. Armontrout, 975 F.2d 543 (8th Cir. 1992) (injunction granted against requiring inmates to be involved in large scale cleanup of sewage contaminated with the HIV virus without supplying protective clothing); Fruit v. Norris, 905 F.2d 1147, 17 Fed. R. Serv. 3d 300 (8th Cir. 1990) ("forcing inmates to work in a shower of human excrement without protective clothing and equipment would be 'inconsistent with a standard of decency'"); Clark v. Moran, 749 F. Supp. 1186 (D.R.I. 1990), aff'd, 942 F.2d 24 (1st Cir. 1991) (unconstitutional to subject a suspect in a prison murder to a chemical test on his skin using benzidine, a known carcinogen).

[Section 2:13]

[1]Edna M. Clark Foundation, Americans Behind Bars 3 (1992). See also US Dept of Justice, Prisoners in 1989, at 1 (1990) (reporting a prison population in 1989 of 710,054).

[2]Edna M. Clark Foundation, Americans Behind Bars 3 (1992) (reporting the forecast of the National Council on Crime and Delinquency). This figure does not include persons held in county

In fact, if anything, they underestimated. By midyear 2000 there were over 1.3 million people in federal and state prisons.[3] When the jail population is added to these figures the numbers are even more astounding: at the same time there were over 600,000 people in American jails, making the total adult population behind bars in the United States over 1.9 million people.[4] The explosion in incarceration is unprecedented in American history. The United States now has the "world's largest overall prison population."[5]

"The alarming growth in the prison population in the United States has reached a point of crisis . . ."[6] Much

---

and city jails. With those inmates included, the American penal population exceeded one million in 1990. *Id.* This chapter does not discuss the unique problems caused by jail overcrowding, or the unique solutions to those problems devised by courts and public officials.

[3]Bureau of Justice Statistics Bulletin: Prison and Jail Inmates at Midyear 2000 at www.ojp.usdoj.gov/bjs/pub/pdf/pjim00.pdf (2001); see also The Sentencing Project: New Prison Population Figures Show Slowing Growth But Uncertain Trends, at www.sentencingproject.org/brief/pub1044.pdf (2001).

[4]Bureau of Justice Statistics Bulletin: Prison and Jail inmates at Midyear 2001 at www.ojp.usdoj.gov/bjs/pub/pdf/pjim00.pdf (2001).

[5]Susanna Y. Chung, Prison Overcrowding: Standards in Determining Eighth Amendment Violations, 66 Fordh. L. Rev. 2351 (2000) (citing Human Rights Watch, Human Rights Watch World Report 2000 at 392 (1990)). The Justice Policy Institute estimated that the prison population would top 2 million in 2000. It noted that the U.S. has a quarter of the world's prison population, despite holding only 5% of the world's population. Justice Policy Institute: Two Million Americans Behind Bars, Press Release (December 1999) at www.cjcj.org/punishingdecade/punishingpr.html. Some have argued that prison overcrowding is the most significant cause of human rights abuses in the United States prison system. Human Rights Watch & American Civil Liberties Union, Human Rights Violations in the United States 101-03 (1993).

[6]Susanna Y. Chung, Prison Overcrowding: Standards in Determining Eighth Amendment Violations, 66 Fordh. L. Rev. 2351, 2400 (2000).

of the growth is not attributable to an increase in violent crime or an increase in the incarceration of violent criminals. Rather, the single greatest cause is the commitment of large numbers of non-violent, lower level drug offenders, longer sentences, and a decrease in the possibility of parole.[7] This dramatic growth has overwhelmed the criminal justice system. "More prisoners are taken into our prisons each week than existing cells can hold.[8] As a consequence, most prison systems operate substantially over capacity. In 1998, for example, the federal prison system operated at 27% over capacity and state prisons were on the average 13 to 22% overcapacity.[9] The repercussions of this overcrowding on prisoners have been described this way:

> In many prisons throughout the country, inmates are double-bunked in small cells designed for one or forced to sleep on mattresses in unheated prison gyms or on the floors of dayrooms, hallways, or basements. Others sleep in makeshift trailers or tents, or converted ferries. Space that had once been devoted to work, study, and recreational programs is now often occupied by dormitories. Violent, predatory inmates can no longer be reliably segregated from nonviolent offenders. . . . Overcrowding has

---

[7] See Marc Mauer, Race To Incarerate (The New Press 1999); Riveland, Article: Prison Management Trends, 1975-2025, 26 Crime & Just. 163 (1999) (harsh sentences for low-level drug offenders led to over- crowding in New York Prisons); Fried, Reflections on Crime and Punishment, 30 Suffolk U. L. Rev. 681 (1997) (low-level drug offenses account for about half of the increase in the prison population over the last two decades); Brown, Note: Drug Diversion Courts: Are They Needed and Will They Succeed in Breaking the Cycle of Drug-Related Crime?, 23 N.E. J. on Crim. & Civ. Con. 63 (1997) (drug convictions have led to prison overcrowding); Comment: Mandatory Minimum Sentences: Exemplifying the Law of Unintended Consequences, 28 Fla. St. U.L. Rev. 935 (2001) (mandatory minimum sentences lead to overcrowding and force the release of some prisoners who would not otherwise be eligible for parole).

[8] See Marc Mauer, Race to Incarerate (The New Press 1999).

[9] Susanna Y. Chung, Prison Overcrowding: Standards in Determining Eighth Amendment Violations, 66 Fordh. L. Rev. 2351 (2000) (citing Department of Justice statistics).

also contributed to the spread of tuberculosis, particularly in its more virulent form, among prisoners and corrections staff.[10]

Consider another description of the same phenomena:

> Prison overcrowding has . . . resulted in a lack of privacy, deleterious physical conditions, inadequate sanitation, and decreased availability of basic necessities such as staff supervision and medical services.[11]

Prison overcrowding has led to double-celling of inmates, and in some cases, random assignments of prisoners to the same cells without use of classification information and without assessing inmate compatibility. Moreover, over-

---

[10]*Id.* See also Robert B. McKay, Prison Overcrowding: The Threat of the 1980s, in Prisoners and the Law (Ira Robbins, editor) (noting that in an overcrowded prison there are increased assaults, suicides, mental disorders, fatal medical conditions, and idleness).

There is, in addition, a considerable body of scientific evidence that overcrowding exacts a high toll on inmates. See, e.g., Fisher v. Koehler, 692 F. Supp. 1519, 1542-46 (S.D. N.Y. 1988) (recounting the scientific evidence which demonstrates, among other things, that overcrowding causes stress and increased violence, and holding that recent scientific knowledge buttresses the conclusions reached by social scientists on this point in the 1970s); Terrence B. Thornberry & Jack E. Call, Constitutional Challenges to Prison Overcrowding: The Scientific Evidence of Harmful Effects, 35 Hast L Rev 313 (1983); C. McCain, V. Cox & P. Paulus, US Dept of Justice, The Effect of Prison Crowding on Inmate Behavior (1980); Bailus Walker, Jr & Theodore Gordon, Health and High Density Confinement in Jails and Prisons, 34 Fed Prob 53 (Mar 1980); see, generally, Peter L. Nacci, Hugh E. Teitelbaum, & Jerry Prather, Population Density and Inmate Misconduct Rates in the Federal Prison System, 41 Fed Prob 26 (June 1977); D'Atre & Ostfield, Crowding: Its Effects on the Elevation of Blood Pressure in a Prison Setting, 4 Preventive Medicine 550 (1975).

Prison conditions may also adversely affect a prisoner's mental health. See Ruthanne DeWolfe & Allen S. DeWolfe, Impact of Prison Conditions on the Mental Health of Inmates, 1979 S Ill U LJ 497 (1979).

[11]Susanna Y. Chung, Prison Overcrowding: Standards in Determining Eighth Amendment Violations, 66 Fordh. L. Rev. 2351, 2352 (2000).

§ 2:13

crowding has resulted in deteriorating physical plants, inadequate medical care, lack of staffing and unsanitary conditions. For example, prison overpopulation has forced inmates to sleep on the floor, has "increased stress, anxiety . . . and 'the opportunity for predatory activities and [has] facilitated the spread of disease, already extant due to the unsanitary conditions.'" It has also heightened the level of tension and violence among prisoners within correctional facilities as evidenced by increased accounts of sexual assaults. Furthermore as a result of overcrowding, inmates are often denied rehabilitation and recreational programs as some prisoners spend almost twenty-four hours each day in their cells.[12]

In addition to the human costs, the financial price exacted by the expanded prison population is staggering. In fiscal year 1999, the latest year for which figures are available, the United States spent over $49 billion on corrections, making corrections one of the fastest rising government expenses and draining many state treasuries.[13]

---

[12]Susanna Y. Chung, Prison Overcrowding: Standards in Determining Eighth Amendment Violations, 66 Fordh. L. Rev. 2351, 2355 (2000) (citing El Tabech v. Gunter, 922 F. Supp. 244 (D. Neb. 1996), order aff'd, 94 F.3d 1191 (8th Cir. 1996) and Tillery v. Owens, 907 F.2d 418 (3d Cir. 1990).

[13]Bureau of Justice Statistics Bulletin: Justice Expenditure and Employment in the United States, 1999, at www.ojp.usdoj.gov/bjs/pub/pdf/jeeus99.pdf (2002). See also Edna M. Clark, Foundation, Americans Behind Bars 5 (1992) (putting cost in 1990 at over $20 billion and noting that only the cost of Medicaid has grown at a higher rate). Experts estimate that in 1987 the cost of construction to add one bed to a prison system was at least $66,000. Prison Projections: Can the United States Keep Pace? Hearing before the Subcommittee on Federal Spending, Budget, and Accounting of the Sen Comm on Governmental Affairs, 100th Cong, 1st Sess 49 (1987) (statement of William J. Anderson). The cost of housing one prisoner in 1988, including the cost of food, staff, medical care and other operations costs, was estimated to be $16,315. George Camp, Criminal Justice Inst, The Corrections Yearbook 28 (1989). For further discussion of the prison overcrowding crisis, see Colloquium, The Prison Overcrowding Crisis, 12 NYU Rev L & Soc Change 1 (1983-84); Symposium, Prison Overcrowding, 1984 U Ill L Rev 203. Because of the severe overcrowding now plaguing Amer-

It is not surprising, therefore, that overcrowding has been a major topic for prison litigation. It is a problem that has also attracted some, but not enough, scholarly attention.[14]

---

ican prisons, there are signs that the country is beginning to respond. Some states, for example, have enacted laws that grant reductions in sentences whenever the prison population rises above a specified level. See, e.g., Fla Stat § 944.277 (Supp 1993) (authorizing up to 60 days reduction in sentence whenever the prison population reaches 97.5% of lawful capacity, unless the inmate was convicted of certain specified serious crimes). See also Skow v. Goodrich, 162 Wis. 2d 448, 469 N.W.2d 888 (Ct. App. 1991) (similar Wisconsin law); Muskegon County Bd. of Com'rs v. Muskegon Circuit Judge, 188 Mich. App. 270, 469 N.W.2d 441 (1991) (Michigan Law).

Another response to the crisis is found in sentencing decisions. Some courts have begun to explicitly consider prison overcrowding when fashioning a sentence. See, e.g., State v. Van Robinson, 248 Mont. 528, 813 P.2d 967 (1991) (upholding sentence which was reduced in part because the trial judge determined that overcrowding made it less likely that rehabilitative programs would be made available to the defendant).

For a thoughtful listing of programs and alternatives that can be adopted to ease the crisis, see Edna M. Clark, Foundation, Americans Behind Bars (1992); for a discussion of the causes and impact of the jail population explosion, see Tyler v. U.S., 737 F. Supp. 531 (E.D. Mo. 1990).

[14]See, e.g., Susanna Y. Chung, Prison Overcrowding: Standards in Determining Eighth Amendment Violations, 66 Fordh. L. Rev. 2351 (2000) (arguing that international standards on prison overcrowding be used domestically); Kerry L. Pyle, Note, Prison Employment: A Long-Term Solution To The Overcrowding Crisis, 77 BU L Rev 151 (1997) (arguing that prison employment is a solution to prison overcrowding; it provides job skills, is an effective tool of rehabilitation and reduces rates of recidivism); Jason Orndorff, Releasing the Elderly Inmate: A Solution to Prison Overcrowding, 4 Elder LJ 173 (1996) (arguing that because prisons have been transformed into veritable nursing homes, the release of the elderly prisoner provides a solution to the problems of prison overcrowding). See also Pamela M. Rosenblatt, Note, The Dilemma of Overcrowding in the Nations Prisons: What are Constitutional Conditions and What can Be Done?, 8 N.Y.L.S. J. Hum. Rts. 489 (1991).

Rhodes v. Chapman

Although overcrowing has been a major problem from the beginning of the prisoner's rights period,[15] it was not until 1981, in the case of *Rhodes v. Chapman*,[16] that the United States Supreme Court first squarely addressed the issue of whether and when the Eighth Amendment is transgressed by prison overcrowding.[17] *Rhodes* was a challenge to double-celling at a maximum-security state prison at Lucasville, Ohio. The Lucasville prison was a new facility. Unlike the bulk of American prisons, Lucasville was described by the district court as "unquestionably a top-flight, first class facility.[18]

Nevertheless, the prison was operating over capacity, with the result that many inmates were double-celled in 63 square-foot cells designed for only one person.[19] The plaintiffs claimed that the double-celling violated their Eighth Amendment rights. At trial, however, the plaintiffs were unable to prove that the crowding was the source of increased violence at the prison or that it caused any notable diminution of services to the

---

[15]See, e.g., Leeds v. Watson, 630 F.2d 674 (9th Cir. 1980); Battle v. Anderson, 564 F.2d 388 (10th Cir. 1977); Williams v. Edwards, 547 F.2d 1206 (5th Cir. 1977).

[16]Rhodes v. Chapman, 452 U.S. 337, 101 S. Ct. 2392, 69 L. Ed. 2d 59 (1981).

[17]The Court earlier had confronted the question of overcrowding in pretrial detention facilities, but that case was decided under a due process, not an Eighth Amendment, analysis. Bell v. Wolfish, 441 U.S. 520, 99 S. Ct. 1861, 60 L. Ed. 2d 447 (1979).

[18]Rhodes v. Chapman, 452 U.S. 337, 341, 101 S. Ct. 2392, 69 L. Ed. 2d 59 (1981).

[19]Approximately 1,400 of the 2,000 inmates at the prison were double-celled. Rhodes v. Chapman, 452 U.S. 337, 341, 101 S. Ct. 2392, 69 L. Ed. 2d 59 (1981). The cells, though small, were "exceptionally modern and functional." Each cell was heated and ventilated and had hot and cold running water and a sanitary toilet. In addition, each cell was equipped with a radio. *Id.* at 349 n 13.

§ 2:13

inmates.[20] Still, the district court entered judgment for the plaintiffs, finding that the double-celling was not temporary, that it was imposed on prisoners serving long sentences who were required to spend most of their time in cells with their cellmates,[21] and that it violated correctional standards.[22] In its decision, the district court also gave weight to views of correctional experts that double-celling was not an acceptable correctional practice.[23]

The Supreme Court reversed. Speaking for the Court, Justice Powell wrote that the Eighth Amendment is not violated by overcrowding unless the plaintiffs are able to demonstrate that the overcrowding has been the cause of serious hardships. Justice Powell held that such a showing had not been made. While the plaintiffs may have proved that the overcrowding was inherently

---

[20]The district court, for example, found that food service was adequate, the ventilation and heating systems were not overly taxed, and space for dayrooms, visiting, library, and school remained sufficient to accommodate the inmates. Although there were some "isolated instances of failure to provide medical and dental care," there was no major systemic breakdown in the delivery of health care. The increase in violence was not out of proportion to the increase in the prison population, and the ratio of guards to prisoners remained acceptable. Finally, the plaintiffs failed to show that double-celling caused an increase in violence beyond what could be attributed to the increased population. *Id.* at 342-43. The only demonstrable consequences of the double-celling was a loss of privacy, a watering down of the jobs and the number of hours worked per inmate, and a reduction in the availability of psychiatrists and social workers. *Id.* at 343. See also Chilcote v. Mitchell, 166 F. Supp. 2d 1313 (D. Or. 2001) (crowding did not violate the Eighth Amendment because the prisoners received their "basic needs" of shelter, food and water, clothes, and medical care).

[21]Justice Powell noted that this factual finding may have been erroneous, since the record showed that most inmates were only locked into their cells from 9:00 p.m. to 6:30 a.m., leaving them free to move about for approximately fourteen hours per day. *Id.* at 350 n. 15.

[22]*Id.* at 343-44.

[23]*Id.*

§ 2:13

unpleasant, and even painful,[24] Justice Powell wrote, the Eighth Amendment does not require that prisons be comfortable places. "[R]estrictive and even harsh" prison conditions are simply "part of the penalty that criminal offenders pay for their offenses against society."[25]

The Court held that the other factors cited by the district court for enjoining double-celling were not sufficient to support a finding that the practice "inflicts unnecessary or wanton pain. . . ."[26] Expert testimony and correctional standards, for example, while relevant and helpful, were not dispositive. The views of experts often express aspirations about how to best accomplish correctional goals rather than assessments about what the constitutional minima are.[27] The same was said about correctional standards. These, too, do not describe enforceable minimum standards.[28] Finally, Justice Powell saw no magic in the fact that the population violated the rated capacity of the institution. Since prison populations are driven upward by a variety of factors, prisons that house more people than they are designed to hold are simply, in Justice Powell's opinion, facilities that are designed by officials who "guessed incorrectly about the future prison population[s], and no more."[29] *Rhodes,* thus, rejects the argument that double-celling

---

[24]Rhodes v. Chapman, 452 U.S. 337, 349, 101 S. Ct. 2392, 69 L. Ed. 2d 59 (1981) (noting that the double-celling at Lucasville could inflict pain).

[25]*Id.* at 347.

[26]*Id.* at 348.

[27]*Id.* at 348 n 13. For a criticism of this branch of the decision see Elizabeth Alexander, Prisoners' Lawyers Face Critical Issues, 13 J Natl Prison Projects 23, 25 (1987) ("By limiting the use of expert witnesses, the Court was able to continue to articulate a concern for minimum constitutional standards while making it more difficult for plaintiffs to show that constitutional standards have been violated.").

[28]Rhodes v. Chapman, 452 U.S. 337, 348, 101 S. Ct. 2392, 69 L. Ed. 2d 59 (1981).

[29]*Id.* at 349 n15.

and overcrowding are *per se* unconstitutional.[30] Rather, the totality of conditions and the effects of overcrowding must be closely examined.[31]

Given the seriousness of the overcrowding crisis, there are troubling aspects of the *Rhodes* decision.[32] Most troubling is the holding of the Court raising the requirements of proof for a finding of unconstitutional overcrowding. Proving that many more prisoners are

---

[30]See also Akao v. Shimoda, 832 F.2d 119 (9th Cir. 1987).

[31]See, e.g., Palmigiano v. Garrahy, 639 F. Supp. 244 (D.R.I. 1986). *Rhodes,* as might be expected, has spawned a great deal of scholarly commentary. For a sampling, see, e.g., David J. Gottlieb, The Legacy of Wolfish and Chapman: Some Thoughts about "Big Prison Case" Litigation in the 1980s, in Prisoners and the Law (Ira Robbins editor); Susan N. Herman, Institutional Litigation in the Post-Chapman World, 12 NYU Rev L & Soc Change 299 (1983-84); James E. Robertson, When the Supreme Court Commands, Do the Lower Courts Obey? The Impact of *Rhodes v. Chapman* on Correctional Litigation, 7 Hamline L Rev 79 (1984); Randall B. Pooler, Prison Overcrowding and the Eighth Amendment: the Rhodes not Taken, 9 NE J Crim & Civ Confinement 1 (1983); Eric B. Woodbury, Note, Prison Overcrowding and Rhodes v. Chapman: Double-Celling by What Standard?, 23 BC L Rev 713 (1982); David R. Cianflone, Comment, Prisons: Confinement and the Eighth Amendment: Rhodes v. Chapman, 3 U Bridgeport L Rev 363 (1982).

[32]One problem with the *Rhodes* decision is the imprecision of the opinion. It tells us what is not unconstitutional and what benchmarks are not dispositive but it does not give us in their place a clear standard for determining when overcrowding is unconstitutional. Is it when the totality of conditions in the institution fall below accepted notions of decency? Is it when, because of overcrowding, the prison is unable to meet a basic human need? The Court failed to specify which of these approaches a court should take in resolving these claims. See Susanna Y. Chung, Prison Overcrowding: Standards in Determining Eighth Amendment Violations, 66 Fordh. L. Rev. 2351 (2000) (stating that *Rhodes* does not indicate whether a totality or a "core conditions" approach should be used in these cases). The lack of a clearly articulated and easy to apply rule of decision can lead lower courts to use conflicting standards, which results in "uncertainty for both prison officials and inmates" who bring law suits about overcrowding. *Id.* at 2370.

§ 2:13

housed in a prison than it was designed to hold will not mandate a finding of an Eighth Amendment violation; nor will proof that professionally recognized standards have been violated, or that the weight of expert testimony is against the overcrowding, compel court-ordered population reductions.

This does not mean that the views of experts, the positions of correctional standards, and rated capacities were rejected by the *Rhodes* Court. Under that ruling they continue to be relevant, although no longer dispositive.[33] However, to prevail after *Rhodes,* in addition, a plaintiff must prove in vivid detail the actual effect of prison overcrowding. To succeed, plaintiffs must show that the conditions caused by the overcrowding fall below the bottom line of human existence forbidden by the Eighth Amendment.

This can be done by showing "the effects of overcrowding on the way in which the facility meets basic human needs for food, clothing, shelter, sanitation, medical

---

[33]See, e.g., Tillery v. Owens, 907 F.2d 418 (3d Cir. 1990) (opinions of experts and positions of correctional standards are useful and serve to put conditions in "perspective"); Inmates of Occoquan v. Barry, 850 F.2d 796, 800 (D.C. Cir. 1988) (denying leave for en banc consideration, noting that there is no quarrel with the view that expert testimony can be pertinent in overcrowding cases) (Starr, J); Inmates of the Allegheny County Jail v. Wecht, 699 F. Supp. 1137 (W.D. Pa. 1988), aff'd in part, appeal dismissed in part, 874 F.2d 147 (3d Cir. 1989), cert. granted, judgment vacated, 493 U.S. 948, 110 S. Ct. 355, 107 L. Ed. 2d 343 (1989) (standards are relevant and "provide guidance" to the court).

Correctional standards provide for at least 35 square feet of cell space for prisoners who spend no more than 10 hours a day in their cells, and 80 square feet for inmates who spend longer than that in their cells. American Correctional Assn., Standards for Adult Correctional Institutions, Standard 3-4128 (2002); see also American Public Health Assn, Standards for Health Services in Correctional Institutions (1976) (requiring 60 square feet per inmate); US Dept of Justice Federal, Standards for Prisons and Jails §§ 2.04, 2.05 (1980) (requiring 80 square feet per inmate for long term institutions and 60 square feet otherwise); Model Corrections and Sentencing Act § 2-704(4) (2001) (requiring 70 square feet per person).

care, and personal safety."[34] What is important is a showing through "objective facts" that "essential human needs" are not being met.[35]

Lower Court Decisions Since *Rhodes*

Since *Rhodes,* federal courts have acted when faced with proven claims of inhumane conditions brought about by overcrowding. In those cases, lower courts have found overcrowding to be unconstitutional when it has been shown to cause deplorable prison conditions. These decisions focus sharply on the totality of conditions brought on, or associated with, overcrowding. The decisions assess the basic architecture and design of the facilities and calibrate the impact made by the increased numbers on such basic components of a living environment as heat, ventilation, lighting, sanitation, and food services. The decisions also evaluate the effect of overcrowding on the level of activities that can be provided, on the medical services that can be delivered, and on the impact of overcrowding on the ever-present danger of violence in the institution.

When, as frequently happens with overcrowding, conditions in the institution fall below the standards of elemental decency, overcrowding has been found by courts, even after *Rhodes,* to be unconstitutional.[36] Thus, in one recent case where crowding had caused es-

---

[34]Fischer v. Winter, 564 F. Supp. 281, 298-99 (N.D. Cal. 1983).

[35]Inmates of Occoquan v. Barry, 844 F.2d 828, 836 (D.C. Cir. 1988).

[36]See, e.g., Maynor v. Morgan County, Alabama, 147 F. Supp. 2d 1185 (N.D. Ala. 2001) (holding that overcrowding in which inmates were forced to sleep on concrete floor space under bunks was unconstitutional); Zolnowski v. County of Erie, 944 F. Supp. 1096 (W.D. N.Y. 1996); Moore v. Morgan, 922 F.2d 1553, 18 Fed. R. Serv. 3d 831 (11th Cir. 1991) (holding that there was an Eighth Amendment violation when inmates were routinely forced to sleep on the floor with only 15 square feet of space); Tillery v. Owens, 907 F.2d 418 (3d Cir. 1990) (finding overcrowding to be unconstitutional in a Pennsylvania prison and reporting that, as of 1990, 42 states were under some type of court order to reduce overcrowd-

§ 2:13   RIGHTS OF PRISONERS, THIRD EDITION

sential services in the facility to break down and "[t]he sardine-can appearance of its cell units more nearly resemble the holding units of slave ships during the Middle Passage of the eighteenth century," conditions were held to be unconstitutional.[37]

However, where the requisite showing has not been made, overcrowding has been tolerated even if it makes incarceration more unpleasant or uncomfortable. In one

---

ing); Balla v. Idaho State Bd. of Corrections, 869 F.2d 461, 13 Fed. R. Serv. 3d 646 (9th Cir. 1989) (population cap imposed to end double-celling); Ruiz v. Estelle, 679 F.2d 1115, 10 Fed. R. Evid. Serv. 1483 (5th Cir. 1982), amended in part, vacated in part on other grounds, 688 F.2d 266 (5th Cir. 1982) (overcrowding caused an increase in violence); Wellman v. Faulkner, 715 F.2d 269 (7th Cir. 1983) (affirming imposition of population cap); French v. Owens, 777 F.2d 1250 (7th Cir. 1985) (double-celling unconstitutional); Fisher v. Koehler, 692 F. Supp. 1519 (S.D. N.Y. 1988) (overcrowding explains vast increase in violence); Jackson v. Gardner, 639 F. Supp. 1005 (E.D. Tenn. 1986); Reece v. Gragg, 650 F. Supp. 1297 (D. Kan. 1986); Palmigiano v. Garrahy, 639 F. Supp. 244 (D. R.I. 1986). See also Williams v. Griffin, 952 F.2d 820 (4th Cir. 1991) (holding that allegations that crowding causes problems with sanitation and infestation states a claim under the Eighth Amendment). Cf. Bell v. Wolfish, 441 U.S. 520, 542, 99 S. Ct. 1861, 60 L. Ed. 2d 447 (1979) ("confining a given number of people in a given amount of space in such a manner as to cause genuine privations and hardship over an extended period of time might raise serious questions under the Due Process Clause as to whether those conditions amounted to punishment"). See also Carty v. Farrelly, 957 F. Supp. 727, 22 A.D.D. 333 (D.V.I. 1997) (court held defendants in civil contempt for their failure to comply with a prior court order to remedy overcrowded conditions at the Criminal Justice Complex (CJC); prison cells housed up to four times as many inmates as they were designed to accommodate, causing inmates to have to sleep on the floor with their heads against the toilets and to urinate on one another during the night; where overcrowding causes such "adverse effects, the overcrowding is unconstitutional"). Newkirk v. Sheers, 834 F. Supp. 772, 781-83 (E.D. Pa. 1993) (the district court found housing five inmates in a cell designed for a single person violated the pretrial detainees' rights).

[37]Maynor v. Morgan County, Alabama, 147 F. Supp. 2d 1185 (N.D. Ala. 2001).

case the court noted that the evidence of overcrowding painted "a picture of a prison overtaxed by the number of inmates it is housing with resulting breakdowns in the timely delivery of services and maintenance." However, since none of the evidence was sufficient to allow a trier of fact to conclude that the plaintiff was deprived of any basic human need such as food, clothing, shelter, sanitation, warmth, medical care or exercise, relief was denied.[38]

Double-Celling

Double-celling cases are a subset of the overcrowding cases. With the rapid rise of prison populations, prisons have resorted to housing two inmates in a cell designed for only one. Locking two people into a small cell for many hours each day entails a substantial loss of privacy and creates serious issues of prison violence. In addition, since the practice is normally just a consequence of overcrowding, all of the problems associated with overcrowding also come into play when double-celling is used. Double-celling has thus spawned a substantial number of cases. A close examination of a representative sampling of recent cases reveals that here, too, there is no *per se* rule, and that a dtermination of whether the practice is constitutional or not involves an intense fact-specific inquiry of the context in which the practice occurs. Two sets of cases illustrate this trend.

In the first set, courts have held that double-celling is not unconstitutional. In *Bolton v. Goord*,[39] inmates at Woodbourne, a medium security prison in New York, claimed that the practice of housing two prisoners in a

---

[38]Simpson v. Horn, 25 F. Supp. 2d 563, 571 (E.D. Pa. 1998). See also Taylor v. Freeman, 34 F.3d 266 (4th Cir. 1994) (holding that without firm proof that overcrowding has caused violence, it is inappropriate for a district judge to mandate a 30% reduction in the inmate population).

[39]Bolton v. Goord, 992 F. Supp. 604 (S.D. N.Y. 1998).

§ 2:13   Rights of Prisoners, Third Edition

small cell[40] designed for one constituted cruel and unusual punishment. The court held a three-week trial to examine the consequences of double-celling and overcrowding at the facility. At trial, the court heard from 39 witnesses and considered over 150 exhibits.[41]

The massive record showed that the inmates who were sent to the facility were older inmates who had amassed a good conduct record for at least two years at other prisons in the state before they were transferred. Once transferred, an inmate's record was carefully evaluated and a decision was made whether to place the inmate in a double cell. This depended upon personality and medical characteristics of the inmate.[42] Most inmates were only double-celled for a short period of time, usually no more than two to four months.[43] Inmates who were double-celled were locked into their cells for 10 to 12 hours per day and were allowed out of the cells for programs, meals, and recreation for the remainder of the time.[44]

The court also carefully examined the consequences of the increased population on the conditions of confinement in the institution, concluding that double-celling and the increased inmate population did not lead to breakdowns in food service, sanitation, medical care, or ventilation. Although there were only two reported incidents of cellmates fighting one another in their cells, there was an increase in violence at the institution. However, the court found that this was probably the result of other causes such as the increase in gang re-

---

[40]Bolton v. Goord, 992 F. Supp. 604, 609 (S.D. N.Y. 1998). (cells at the prison were between 53 and 58 square feet.).

[41]Bolton v. Goord, 992 F. Supp. 604, 607 (S.D. N.Y. 1998).

[42]For example, inmates who were mentally disturbed, physically disabled, or victim-prone, or who exhibited aggressive behavior or who had communicable diseases, were not double-celled. *Id.* at 608.

[43]*Id.* at 628.

[44]Bolton v. Goord, 992 F. Supp. 604, 610 (S.D. N.Y. 1998).

lated activity in the prison system.[45]

The court did find that double-celling led to a loss of privacy, particularly when inmates had to use the toilet in the presence of one another in the small cell. This was "undoubtedly embarrassing and uncomfortable," the court observed.[46] However, "[it] does not approach the standard of inhumane conditions that violate the Eighth Amendment."[47]

On these facts, the court found that double-celling, while difficult for inmates, was not unconstitutional because it did not lead to denials of essential services such as food, exercise, medical care, reasonable physical safety or protection from disease.[48] Other courts have reached similar conclusions.[49] In *Smith v. Fairman*,[50] for example, the Seventh Circuit reversed a district court judgment ordering an end to overcrowding in a

---

[45]*Id.* at 629.

[46]*Id.* at 627. See also Simpson v. Horn, 25 F. Supp. 2d 563, 571 (E.D. Pa. 1998) ("Privacy is an inevitable casualty of incarceration and is not recognized as a basic human in this context.").

[47]*Id.* at 627.

[48]*Id.* at 626-28.

[49]Simpson v. Horn, 25 F. Supp. 2d 563 (E.D. Pa. 1998) (plaintiff alleged that double-celling inmates caused overcrowding which contributed to a long list of deficiencies in the prison's ventilation, sanitation, plumbing, laundry, heating, bedding, clothing, seating, recreational equipment, telephones, medical, and food services, and that overcrowding was a threat to security of inmates and guards; defendants acknowledged that many of the conditions were the unavoidable and temporary result of the overcrowding; while overcrowding in prisons, specifically double-celling of inmates in cells designed to house one inmate, may be violative of the Eighth Amendment if it results in a deprivation of any basic human need, court granted summary judgment in favor of defendants because the evidence failed to show such a deprivation, and if there was a deprivation, that defendants acted with deliberate indifference); see also Jackson v. Pataki, 2001 WL 228136 (S.D. N.Y. 2001) (plaintiff could state a claim of an Eighth Amendment violation based on double-celling in conjunction with other conditions, but claim was dismissed as state officials acting in their official capacity enjoyed sovereign immunity); Walker v. Dept. of Corrections, 238 F.3d 426 (6th Cir. 2000) (officials were protected by sovereign

§ 2:13   Rights of Prisoners, Third Edition

100-year-old facility in which 56 per cent of the inmates were double-celled. In another case, the court recognized that double-celling is "among the most debasing and most dehumanizing aspects of present prison life. It rips away the sense of privacy-of dignity, which can make bearable many things which could not otherwise be endured."[51] Nevertheless, the court held that, absent proof that the double-celling caused the prison to fail to provide the minimal essentials, it was not unconstitutional.[52]

In a second set of cases, double-celling was held unconstitutional. *Jensen v. Clarke*[53] is one example. There, inmates at the Nebraska State Penitentiary brought a class action suit, claiming that prison procedures regarding double-cell assignments created a "pervasive risk of harm." Based on an extensive record developed by the trial court, the Eighth Circuit held

---

immunity, and double-celling in and of itself is not unconstitutional).

But see, Jones v. Goord, 190 F.R.D. 103 (S.D. N.Y. 1999) (court denied defendants' motion to dismiss as to double-celling claim, as plaintiff should get the chance to prove that the double-celling, in combination with other conditions, violated plaintiff's Eighth Amendment rights).

[50]Smith v. Fairman, 690 F.2d 122 (7th Cir. 1982).

[51]Delgado v. Cady, 576 F. Supp. 1446, 1448 (E.D. Wis. 1983).

[52]*Id.* For additional cases which deny relief even though the prison was overcrowded, see, e.g., C.H. v. Sullivan, 920 F.2d 483 (8th Cir. 1990) ("double-celling is not unconstitutional . . . absent deprivation of food, medical care, sanitation, increased violence or other conditions intolerable for incarceration"); Inmates of Occoquan v. Barry, 850 F.2d 796 (D.C. Cir. 1988); Cody v. Hillard, 830 F.2d 912 (8th Cir. 1987) (en banc); Nelson v. Collins, 659 F.2d 420 (4th Cir. 1981); Miles v. Bell, 621 F. Supp. 51, 62 (D. Conn. 1985) (although overcrowding made the prison uncomfortable and inconvenient, conditions were not unconstitutional); Lovell v. Brennan, 566 F. Supp. 672 (D. Me. 1983), judgment aff'd, 728 F.2d 560 (1st Cir. 1984); Alston v. Coughlin, 668 F. Supp. 822 (S.D. N.Y. 1987). See also Ruark v. Solano, 928 F.2d 947 (10th Cir. 1991) (double-celling which meant sharing a cell with a new cellmate every few days was not unconstitutional).

[53]Jensen v. Clarke, 94 F.3d 1191 (8th Cir. 1996).

unconstitutional the "manner in which the defendants were conducting the practice."[54] In particular, prison authorities failed to determine if cellmates were compatible with each other. The plaintiffs submitted statistics demonstrating a significant increase in violent incidents since double-celling was instituted because of overcrowding. Unlike the situation in *Bolton* where inmates were carefully screened before they were double-celled with a particular inmate, in *Jensen,* the inmates, who were maximum- security inmates, were placed with one another at random. As the district court recounted, the consequences of this practice could be horrific:

> Imagine you committed a crime and are entering the Nebraska State Penitentiary for the first time as a convicted felon. . ..
>
> In the cell you find a monster in the form of a man. . .. Imagine further that this creature has a well-documented history of taking his recreation by sodomizing any available prey. If the prey resists, the monster may use a razor to slice the victim. . ..
>
> Imagine also that your keepers . . . have consciously decided that efficiently packing the available cells is more important than . . . reasonably providing for your safety. Space is valuable, and you, as a prisoner, are not.[55]

To alleviate this unconstitutional condition, the court enjoined the use of double-cells unless it was done with prior screening of inmates.[56]

Another case is *Tillery v. Owens.*[57] There, following a six-week trial which included an unannounced visit of the prison by the court, double-celling was found unconstitutional. The district court made "detailed and

---

[54]Jensen v. Clarke, 94 F.3d 1191, 1194 (8th Cir. 1996).

[55]El Tabech v. Gunter, 922 F. Supp. 244, 245-46 (D. Neb. 1996), order aff'd, 94 F.3d 1191 (8th Cir. 1996).

[56]Jensen v. Clarke, 94 F.3d 1191 (8th Cir. 1996).

[57]Tillery v. Owens, 719 F. Supp. 1256 (W.D. Pa. 1989), order aff'd, 907 F.2d 418 (3d Cir. 1990).

§ 2:13   Rights of Prisoners, Third Edition

meticulous findings of fact"[58] about the effect of double-celling on staff shortages, heating, ventilation, exercise, plumbing, sanitation, and safety. The court found that inmates were forced by double-celling to live "elbow to elbow," causing "squalid, dangerous" conditions that were in violation of the Eighth Amendment.[59] The court found that there did not have to be an epidemic, "an outbreak of AIDS, a deadly fire, or a prison riot" before it acted to alleviate the unconstitutional conditions.[60]

What emerges from these seemingly disparate cases is that the determination of whether there are unconstitutional conditions caused by overcrowding and/or double-celling depends upon a close examination of the effect of the overcrowding or double-celling on the operation of the prison.[61] It is clear that overcrowding and double-celling are not per se unconstitutional.[62] It is equally true that they are not per se constitutional.

---

[58]Tillery v. Owens, 907 F.2d 418, 421 (3d Cir. 1990).

[59]*Id.* at 423-24.

[60]*Id.* at 428.

[61]It is possible to argue that the difference between several of these cases can only be explained by the greater allowance of some judges than others for harsh and even debilitating prison conditions. Compare, e.g., Inmates of Occoquan v. Barry, 844 F.2d 828 (D.C. Cir. 1988) (Starr, J.) (holding that overcrowded conditions are not unconstitutional in part because not similar to well known cases of squalid conditions) with Inmates of Inmates of Occoquan v. Barry, 850 F.2d 796, 797 (D.C. Cir. 1988) (Wald, C.J.) (arguing in dissent that the conditions fall below standards of human decency).

[62]Strickler v. Waters, 989 F.2d 1375, 1382 (4th Cir. 1993) (double bunking alone "does not constitute a cognizable Eighth Amendment deprivation"); Harris v. Maloughney, 827 F. Supp. 1488 (D. Mont. 1993) (overcrowding does not state a constitutional claim without a deprivation of a human necessity); Jensen v. County of Lake, 958 F. Supp. 397 (N.D. Ind. 1997) (overcrowding is not per se unconstitutional); Barajas v. Waters, 815 F. Supp. 222, 225 (E.D. Mich. 1993), aff'd, 21 F.3d 427 (6th Cir. 1994) (double-celling is not unconstitutional per se); Counts v. Newhart, 951 F. Supp. 579 (E.D. Va. 1996), aff'd, 116 F.3d 1473 (4th Cir. 1997) (plaintiff failed to present any evidence suggesting his physical and emotional injuries were "attributable to the deprivation of

One court described the law well when it observed that "*Rhodes* does not stand for the proposition that double-celling can never be an Eighth Amendment violation . . . implicit in *Rhodes* is that double-celling can amount to an Eighth Amendment violation if combined with other adverse conditions."[63]

Thus, courts must examine such factors as the length of confinement (if the lengths of stay are short, the conditions are more likely to be satisfactory than if the stays are lengthy),[64] amount of time in the cell, sanitation, lighting, ventilation, noise, programs, including educational and rehabilitative programs, activities out of the cell, state of repair of the facility, plumbing and showers, and levels of violence in the facility.[65] In addition, courts take into account the type of prison and who is being held in the conditions complained about.

---

a single human need," and therefore was unable to demonstrate that prison overcrowding caused his injuries); Abdul-Akbar v. Department of Corrections, 910 F. Supp. 986, 1006 (D. Del. 1995), judgment aff'd, 111 F.3d 125 (3d Cir. 1997) (overcrowding did not deprive inmates of an "identifiable human need."); Walker v. Dept. of Corrections, 238 F.3d 426 (6th Cir. 2000) (double-celling in and of itself is not unconstitutional); see also Jackson v. Pataki, 2001 WL 228136 (S.D. N.Y. 2001) (plaintiff could state a claim of an Eighth Amendment violation based on double-celling in conjunction with other conditions, but claim was dismissed as state officials acting in their official capacity enjoyed sovereign immunity).

But see, Jones v. Goord, 190 F.R.D. 103 (S.D. N.Y. 1999) (court denied defendants' motion to dismiss as to double-celling claim, as plaintiff should get the chance to prove that the double-celling, in combination with other conditions, violated plaintiff's Eighth Amendment rights).

[63]Nami v. Fauver, 82 F.3d 63, 67 (3d Cir. 1996).

[64]See, e.g., Hall v. Dalton, 34 F.3d 648 (8th Cir. 1994); Moore v. Morgan, 922 F.2d 1553, 18 Fed. R. Serv. 3d 831 (11th Cir. 1991).

[65]See, e.g., Maynor v. Morgan County, Alabama, 147 F. Supp. 2d 1185 (N.D. Ala. 2001) (citing breakdown in essential services); Carty v. Farrelly, 957 F. Supp. 727, 22 A.D.D. 333 (D.V.I. 1997) ("Overcrowding of inmates in correctional facilities can lead to violence among prisoners, breakdowns in classification systems, deterioration of physical conditions and other safety hazards. When overcrowding causes such adverse effects, the overcrowding is

§ 2:13   RIGHTS OF PRISONERS, THIRD EDITION

If, for example, the inmates have psychological problems or are suicidal, then conditions that might be acceptable for other inmates without those problems might be found unacceptable for them.[66] If the court's examination reveals that the conditions are below levels of decency and that the defendants were aware of these conditions, then an Eighth Amendment violation has been proven.[67] In cases denying relief, the conditions, by and large, were not as subhuman as conditions in those

---

unconstitutional."). See also John Boston & Daniel E. Manville, Prisoner Self-Help Litigation Manual, 22 (1995) (citing cases).

[66]See, e.g., Balla v. Board of Corrections, 656 F. Supp. 1108 (D. Idaho 1987) (psychiatric inmates); Delgado v. Cady, 576 F. Supp. 1446 (E.D. Wis. 1983) (double-celling of suicidal inmates prohibited).

[67]See, e.g., Nami v. Fauver, 82 F.3d 63, 66 (3d Cir. 1996), in which an inmate in a youth correctional institution stated a claim where he alleged that prison officials violated the Eighth Amendment when inmates were doubled-celled and housed two to a single room, 80 square foot cell with only one bed, so that one of them must sleep on the floor by the toilet. The inmate stated that the cells had solid doors with only a four-inch wide window for cell inspection, making it difficult to summon help, and furthermore, that inmates often shared cells with others who suffered from psychiatric problems and/or who were violent felons, and non-smokers must often share cells with smokers. Moreover, the inmate alleged, this double-celling had resulted in rapes, assaults, and psychological stress. If proven, the court held, these conditions were unconstitutional. See also Maynor v. Morgan County, Alabama, 147 F. Supp. 2d 1185 (N.D. Ala. 2001) (holding that overcrowding that forced inmates in a county jail to sleep on concrete floors and that taxed ventilation, sanitation, exercise, fire safety, and medical care violated the Eighth Amendment); Jones v. Goord, 190 F.R.D. 103 (S.D. N.Y. 1999) (holding that double-celling is unconstitutional if it causes "real hardship."). See also John Boston & Daniel E. Manville, Prisoner Self-Help Litigation Manual, 22 (1995) ("[C]ourts are more likely to find crowding unconstitutional if it is linked with violence and other safety hazards, breakdowns in classification, food services or medical care, or deteriorated physical conditions.").

cases in which courts did intervene.[68] Moreover, the good faith efforts of prison administrators to cope in a less chaotic way with the effects of the overcrowding is a factor that explains some of these cases.[69]

---

[68]See, e.g., Parton v. White, 203 F.3d 552 (8th Cir. 2000), cert. denied, 531 U.S. 963, 121 S. Ct. 392, 148 L. Ed. 2d 302 (2000) (finding despite overcrowding that medical services, food, and other services were maintained); Waldo v. Goord, 1998 WL 713809 (N.D. N.Y. 1998) (allegation that overcrowding causes fear is not enough to state a claim when there was no allegation that overcrowding caused the deprivation of basic needs).

Another factor that is relevant is the amount of time that inmates are locked into their cells. When it is for long periods of time, the effects of the overcrowding in doubled-up cells is obviously greater. See, e.g., Rhodes v. Chapman, 452 U.S. 337, 101 S. Ct. 2392, 69 L. Ed. 2d 59 (1981); Bell v. Wolfish, 441 U.S. 520, 543, 99 S. Ct. 1861, 60 L. Ed. 2d 447 (1979); Moore v. Morgan, 922 F.2d 1553, 18 Fed. R. Serv. 3d 831 (11th Cir. 1991) (overcrowding combined with lack of out-of-cell time violated the Constitution); Lyons v. Powell, 838 F.2d 28, 31 (1st Cir. 1988); Hoptowit v. Ray, 682 F.2d 1237, 1249, 9 Fed. R. Evid. Serv. 1511 (9th Cir. 1982).

[69]Compare, Inmates of Occoquan v. Barry, 844 F.2d 828, 840 n 17 (D.C. Cir. 1988) (citing "litany of improvements" made by defendants to cope with the overcrowding); Cody v. Hillard, 830 F.2d 912, 914 (8th Cir. 1987) (en banc) (citing the effort of prison administrators to reduce the negative impact of double-celling) with Maynor v. Morgan County, Alabama, 147 F. Supp. 2d 1185 (N.D. Ala. 2001) (finding that the failure of the state department of social services to remove "state ready" inmates from the county jail to the state prison contributed to the severe overcrowding in the county jail). See also Parton v. White, 203 F.3d 552 (8th Cir. 2000), cert. denied, 531 U.S. 963, 121 S. Ct. 392, 148 L. Ed. 2d 302 (2000) (finding that hiring of extra staff to cope with rising numbers of inmates militated against a finding of unconstitutionality); Pratt v. Rowland, 65 F.3d 802 (9th Cir. 1995) (inmate was not entitled to a preliminary injunction requiring inmate to be incarcerated in a single cell; court noted that where inmate, a former Black Panther, was transferred to a medium security prison to allow him to visit local psychiatric program and was double-celled, officials did not act with deliberate indifference to inmate's health; court found that while there were documented health reasons which required inmate to be single-celled, officials were unable to give inmate a single cell because institution was over capacity).

While conditions may not have been as horrendous in the cases denying relief as they were in the cases in which the courts have held overcrowding unconstitutional, the consequences of the overcrowding in many of the cases denying relief were, nonetheless, quite serious. Moreover, the good-faith attempts of administrators to cope with the problems created by overcrowding-seized on by many of the courts that denied relief-while admirable, cannot compensate for conditions that reduce life to a quest for survival.

Summary of Post—*Rhodes* Decisions

To the extent that *Rhodes* makes it more difficult for courts to enjoin serious overcrowding demonstrates that the decision has had a discouraging effect on the conduct of prison overcrowding litigation. It has persuaded some courts to tolerate debilitating levels of overcrowding, and it has limited others to acting only when the conditions caused by the overcrowding deteriorated to a point of near collapse. Nevertheless, activity of the lower courts after *Rhodes* illustrates that courts have an important role to play in ensuring that the prison overcrowding crisis does not produce prisons that fail to provide the essentials of human existence mandated by the Eighth Amendment.

Remedies for Overcrowding

The first priority, of course, is for the states themselves to deal with the problem.[70] For this reason,

---

[70]Maynor v. Morgan County, Alabama, 147 F. Supp. 2d 1185 (N.D. Ala. 2001) (requiring state to take "state ready" inmates to state prison and thereby reduce county jail crowding). See also Smith v. Cleary, 24 P.3d 1245 (Alaska 2001), where, in order to comply with a settlement requiring the state to relieve overcrowding in its prisons, the state asked the court's permission to transfer prisoners to a privately run facility in Arizona. The superior court granted the request on the condition that the Arizona facility complied with the settlement requirements. The state appealed, claiming that the settlement expressly stated that its require-

CRUEL & UNUSUAL PUNISHMENT § 2:13

federal courts have tended to defer to remedies that state prison officials have implemented to alleviate overcrowding.[71] In addition, because overcrowding is so problematic, whether or not it is unconstitutional, a number of states have enacted legislation to alleviate the conditions.[72] Overcrowding has also raised issues for state courts that have been confronted with ques-

---

ments applied only to facilities owned and operated by the state. The Supreme Court affirmed, however, holding that it was within the superior court's discretion to impose requirements based on its view of the intentions of the parties at the time the settlement was reached).

[71]See, e.g., Leslie v. Wisconsin Dept. of Corrections, 215 F.3d 1330 (7th Cir. 2000) (plaintiff inmates challenged Wisconsin transfer policy's purpose, the easing of overcrowding in the state's prisons, as a rational basis for transferring them; district court upheld the policy, finding that its goal of easing overcrowding in the state prisons was a sufficient rational basis for the transfer of prisoners); Austin v. Pennsylvania Dept. of Corrections, 876 F. Supp. 1437, 10 A.D.D. 1042 (E.D. Pa. 1995) (commending the state for addressing the overcrowding problem by building new prisons to accommodate the rising numbers of inmates).

[72]Code of Ala. § 12-25-2 (establishing sentencing commission, one goal of which was to ease prison overcrowding); Alaska Stat. § 33.30.031 (allows commissioner of corrections to contract with out of state prisons for the care of prisoners where there is no space in Alaska prisons); A.R.S. § 31-233 (Arizona statute aimed at reducing overcrowding by allowing early parole); A.C.A. § 12-28-601 (Arkansas statute authorizing a declaration of a prison overcrowding state of emergency, and authorizes the Director of the Department of Correction to move up prisoners' transfer, parole eligibility, or release dates if the prison population reaches 98 percent capacity for 30 consecutive days); Cal Pub Contract Code § 20134 (California statute allows a bypass of the normal process for constructing jails where it is shown that a county's jails are 20 percent above capacity); Conn. Gen. Stat. § 18-87k (provides for a commission to look at ways to reduce overcrowding); D.C. Code § 24-201.42 (allows the mayor to declare a prison overcrowding state of emergency if prisons exceed capacity for 30 consecutive days; during such emergency, the mayor can reduce the sentences of eligible prisoners by 90 days); O.C.G.A. § 42-2-14 (allows Georgia officials to seek out alternative temporary and permanent site at which to house inmates if an overcrowding emergency is declared).

§ 2:13   Rights of Prisoners, Third Edition

tions concerning how to calculate sentences that have been delayed or disturbed as a result of overcrowding.[73]

During the 1996-1997 term, the United States Supreme Court decided two cases related to statutes designed to alleviate prison overcrowding. In *Lynce v. Mathis*,[74] the Supreme Court considered whether a Florida statute that retroactively canceled early release credits awarded to alleviate prison overcrowding violated the Ex Post Facto Clause of the Constitution. The plaintiff, a Florida state prisoner who was convicted of attempted murder, was granted early release by the Florida Department of Corrections after earning a sufficient number of good time credits. The early release was granted under the Correctional Reform Act of 1983, which was enacted to alleviate prison overcrowding. Under provisions of Fla. Stat. § 944.275, prisoners could earn up to sixty days good-time when the prison population reached 97.5 percent. Shortly after the plaintiff's release, the Florida legislature passed a statute retroactively canceling the award of good time credits

---

[73]See, e.g., N. Canton v. Hutchinson, 75 Ohio St. 3d 112, 1996-Ohio-170, 661 N.E.2d 1000 (1996) (court refused to disturb decision of jail supervisor suspending commencement of criminal sentences for five years because prison system was overcrowded); State v. Walker, 905 S.W.2d 554 (Tenn. 1995) (court held that "where persons under a criminal sentence immediately present themselves to the appropriate authorities for incarceration and are turned away, the sentences . . . shall begin to run when the judgment of conviction becomes final or the prisoner is actually incarcerated, whichever is earlier"; in context, the court found that where two inmates were sentenced for DWI, presented themselves, and were turned away by prison officials due to overcrowding, their sentence began to run at that time; when prison officials called them over two years later and informed them that there was now room for them, their sentence had already expired). See also Shifrin v. Fields, 39 F.3d 1112 (10th Cir. 1994) (Eighth Amendment not violated where a repeat violent offender could not benefit from the Oklahoma Prison Overcrowding Emergency Powers Act, which provided extra time credits to allow inmates convicted of lesser offenses to be released sooner).

[74]Lynce v. Mathis, 519 U.S. 433, 117 S. Ct. 891, 137 L. Ed. 2d 63 (1997).

CRUEL & UNUSUAL PUNISHMENT § 2:13

to prisoners convicted of murder or attempted murder. Consequently, the plaintiff was rearrested and returned to prison. The plaintiff sought a writ of habeas corpus, claiming the statute violated the Ex Post Facto Clause of the Constitution.

The Court, in a majority opinion written by Justice Stevens, agreed with the plaintiff. Relying on the court's prior decision in *Weaver v. Graham*,[75] the Court held that "to fall within the ex post facto prohibition, a law must be retrospective and disadvantage the offender affected by it."[76]

The Court noted that the operation of the statute disadvantaged the plaintiff by increasing his sentence and therefore was unconstitutional. The court rejected the defendant's contention that *Weaver* was not "controlling because it was the overcrowded condition of the prison system, rather than the character of the prisoner's conduct, that gave rise to the award" of good time credits.[77]

In *Young v. Harper*,[78] the Supreme Court considered whether a pre-parole program entitled a prisoner to the same due process protections as parole. The plaintiff, an Oklahoma state prisoner, was conditionally released pursuant to Okla. Stat. Tit. 57, § 365(A), a statute designed to alleviate prison overcrowding when the prison population exceeded 95 percent of its capacity. After five months without incident, the Governor denied the plaintiff parole and ordered him back to prison. The plaintiff sought a writ of habeas corpus, claiming his arbitrary return to prison violated the Due Process Clause of the Fourteenth Amendment. The Court, in a unanimous opinion by Justice Thomas, held that pre-

---

[75] Weaver v. Graham, 450 U.S. 24, 101 S. Ct. 960, 67 L. Ed. 2d 17 (1981).

[76] Lynce v. Mathis, 519 U.S. 433, 117 S. Ct. 891, 896, 137 L. Ed. 2d 63 (1997).

[77] *Id.*

[78] Young v. Harper, 520 U.S. 143, 117 S. Ct. 1148, 137 L. Ed. 2d 270 (1997).

§ 2:13   Rights of Prisoners, Third Edition

parole "differed from parole in name alone" and that the plaintiff was entitled to the due process protections outlined in *Morrissey v. Brewer*.[79] The *Morrissey* Court held that because a parolee was released from prison, there was at least an "implicit promise that parole will be revoked only if he fails to live up to the parole conditions."[80] Consequently, summary revocation violated the Due Process Clause.

In extending the *Morrissey* protections to the instant case, Justice Thomas rejected the defendant's argument that pre-parole differed from parole. He described the defendant's proffered distinctions between pre-parole and parole as "phantom," "non-existent," and "illusory."[81]

When, despite efforts (or because of lack of them), prison overcrowding causes prison conditions to fall below the level of the Eighth Amendment, historically courts have had wide discretion in shaping the relief.[82] One common remedy that was used by many courts was to set a population cap on the facility.[83] Some courts went beyond merely setting population caps; for example, some courts ordered that overcrowding not be shifted to local jails where inmates ready for transfer to

---

[79]Morrissey v. Brewer, 408 U.S. 471, 92 S. Ct. 2593, 33 L. Ed. 2d 484 (1972).

[80]Young v. Harper, 520 U.S. 143, 117 S. Ct. 1148, 1152, 137 L. Ed. 2d 270 (1997).

[81]*Id.*

[82]See, e.g., Tillery v. Owens, 907 F.2d 418 (3d Cir. 1990) (citing cases and holding that courts have broad remedial powers to eliminate unconstitutional prison conditions).

[83]See, e.g., Tillery v. Owens, 907 F.2d 418 (3d Cir. 1990); French v. Owens, 777 F.2d 1250 (7th Cir. 1985); Wellman v. Faulkner, 715 F.2d 269 (7th Cir. 1983) (affirming imposition of population cap); Ruiz v. Estelle, 679 F.2d 1115, 10 Fed. R. Evid. Serv. 1483 (5th Cir. 1982), amended in part, vacated in part on other grounds, 688 F.2d 266 (5th Cir. 1982); Morales Feliciano v. Hernandez Colon, 754 F. Supp. 942 (D.P.R. 1991) (setting population cap); Fisher v. Koehler, 718 F. Supp. 1111 (S.D. N.Y. 1989), judgment aff'd, 902 F.2d 2 (2d Cir. 1990) (setting population cap to remedy violence).

§ 2:13

state prisons were backed up.[84] In addition, before the passage of the Prison Reform Litigation Act, courts indicated a willingness to consider release orders, particularly where the defendants fail to comply with other remedies designed to end the overpopulation.[85]

In a divided opinion from the District of Columbia Court of Appeals, however, Circuit Judge Starr questioned whether these population control remedies were the proper way to address the problem.[86] Judge Starr urged that, rather than make use of a "global remedy" for overcrowding such as a court order that double-celling be ended, or an order setting a population cap at the facility, a court should only impose a remedy limited to correction of the specific constitutionally deficient conditions that have been found to exist.[87] In other words, under this approach, if the prison was so overcrowded that the prison was unable to provide basic services such as sanitation, food, medical care, and the like, rather than entering an order reducing the

---

[84]See, e.g., Alberti v. Sheriff of Harris County, Tex., 978 F.2d 893 (5th Cir. 1992) (setting population cap at facility where inmates are backed up); Williams v. McKeithen, 963 F.2d 70 (5th Cir. 1992) (upholding order setting population limits at local jails where inmates are backed up); Roberts v. Tennessee Dept. of Correction, 887 F.2d 1281 (6th Cir. 1989) (approving settlement addressing this problem). See also Maynor v. Morgan County, Alabama, 147 F. Supp. 2d 1185 (N.D. Ala. 2001) (ordering state to take state-ready inmates).

[85]See, e.g., Plyler v. Evatt, 924 F.2d 1321, 1329 (4th Cir. 1991) (indicating that while release orders should be considered the accommodation of last resort, they may be used if no other remedy will work). Another option is civil contempt. See, e.g., Twelve John Does v. District of Columbia, 855 F.2d 874 (D.C. Cir. 1988) (holding officials in contempt for failure to abide by a population cap order); Badgley v. Santacroce, 800 F.2d 33 (2d Cir. 1986) (failure to implement population cap can, in an appropriate case, lead to a finding of civil contempt); Morales Feliciano v. Hernandez Colon, 754 F. Supp. 942 (D.P.R. 1991) (imposing fine of $10 per prisoner per day for violation of population cap).

[86]Inmates of Occoquan v. Barry, 850 F.2d 796 (D.C. Cir. 1988).

[87]Inmates of Occoquan v. Barry, 844 F.2d 828, 841 (D.C. Cir. 1988).

§ 2:13   Rights of Prisoners, Third Edition

prison population, a court would enter an order requiring improvements in the provision of services.

The benefit of this approach, according to Judge Starr, is that it is less intrusive. "[A]bsent a complete abdication of [government's] responsibility to remedy ongoing constitutional violations,"[88] Judge Starr wrote, "[s]uch fundamental decisions as how many prisons to build and how large to build them-basic political decisions regarding the allocation of public resources- are simply outside the domain of federal courts."[89]

This idea was assailed in a thoughtful opinion by Chief Judge Wald, who wrote that Judge Starr's theory "denies district courts the right to go to the heart of the problem."[90] Judge Wald also pointed out that Judge Starr's approach somewhat ironically poses a danger of being even more intrusive than a population cap. A population cap does not dictate how a prison must operate; it only sets a limit on the number of people the fa-

---

[88]*Id.* at 842 n 21.

[89]*Id.* at 842. See also Women Prisoners of District of Columbia Dept. of Corrections v. District of Columbia, 93 F.3d 910, 113 Ed. Law Rep. 30 (D.C. Cir. 1996), where the court held that the imposition of "population caps" to alleviate the effects of prison overcrowding are remedies of "last resort." In the instant case, the lower court prematurely imposed a population cap on the defendants. Prison overcrowding caused unsanitary conditions to exist in the prison facility, and the lower court properly determined such conditions violated the Eighth Amendment. However, the lower court should have ordered the defendants to remedy those conditions rather than imposing a population cap. Thus, the court vacated the lower court's order. See also Cody v. Hillard, 830 F.2d 912, 914 (8th Cir. 1987) (en banc).

[90]Inmates of Occoquan v. Barry, 850 F.2d 796, 799 (D.C. Cir. 1988) (Wald, C.J., dissenting from denial of petition for rehearing en banc). A subsequent opinion in the case demonstrates this point. Inmates of Occoquan v. Barry, 717 F. Supp. 854, 868-69 (D.D.C. 1989) ("as long as more inmates are placed in Occoquan, the bathroom facilities will be overburdened, the dorms will be filled beyond capacity, the food will become cold due to extended feedings, appointments for medical care will be postponed as more and more inmates seek help, and sanitation will remain a problem while far too many inmates scuffle to use limited facilities").

cility can hold while the defendants design their own solutions to problems of managing the institution. Moreover, a population cap is easily rescinded when constitutional conditions are restored to the institution and there is no longer a realistic threat of a return to unconstitutional conditions.[91] By contrast, under Judge Starr's approach, the district court would be required to decree, in some detail, how prison administrators manage their facilities.[92] The Fifth Circuit followed the approach outlined by Judge Wald when it observed, "[a] numerical cap on the number of prisoners is not an overly intrusive remedy. It gives [government] maximum flexibility in determining on its own how to meet [constitutional requirements]."[93]

---

[91]See, e.g., Diaz v. Romer, 801 F. Supp. 405 (D. Colo. 1992), aff'd, 9 F.3d 116 (10th Cir. 1993) (removing population cap after improvements to the facility were made); French v. Owens, 777 F.2d 1250 (7th Cir. 1985) (noting that order enjoining double-celling could be reconsidered when constitutional conditions are established at the prison).

[92]Inmates of Occoquan v. Barry, 850 F.2d 796, 800 (D.C. Cir. 1988) (Ruth Bader Ginsburg, J, dissenting from denial of rehearing en banc) (noting that a population cap is less intrusive than an injunction relating to specific conditions). Tillery v. Owens, 907 F.2d 418 (3d Cir. 1990) (rejecting the argument that district court should not be permitted to set a population cap after a finding of unconstitutional overcrowding; holding that courts have the "moral and legal obligation to relieve the inhumane and unconstitutional conditions" even if this means decreeing an end to double-celling); Inmates of Occoquan v. Barry, 717 F. Supp. 854, 869 (D. D.C. 1989) (inability to impose a population cap and instead order specific improvements "comes painfully close to treading in the area of prison administration").

[93]Alberti v. Sheriff of Harris County, Tex., 978 F.2d 893, 896 (5th Cir. 1992). But cf. McClendon v. City of Albuquerque, 79 F.3d 1014, 35 Fed. R. Serv. 3d 679 (10th Cir. 1996) (prison officials were entitled to emergency stay of district court's injunction which prohibited prison officials from admitting inmates in excess of the institutional capacity; court noted that stay of injunction was appropriate where prison officials demonstrated strong likelihood of success on appeal since district court did not hold that the overcrowding was at a level which violated the Eighth Amendment).

§ 2:13

Congress largely ended this debate when it passed the Prison Reform Litigation Act in 1996.

That Act, which is discussed in detail elsewhere in this book,[94] restricts the use of prison release orders. It provides that no release order can be entered unless the court has previously tried a less restrictive remedy that has failed, and unless the defendant is given a "reasonable period of time to comply with the previous court orders."[95] In addition, these orders can no longer be entered by a single district judge; only a specially empaneled three-judge court has the authority to issue a release order.[96] The court may not grant the relief unless it finds that overcrowding is the primary cause of the violation of a federal right and that no other relief will remedy the violation.[97] Moreover, the Act gives the right to intervene in the action to oppose a release order not only to the named defendants but also to other government officials whose jurisdiction "includes the appropriation of funds for construction, operation, or maintenance of program faculties or the prosecution or custody of persons who may be released from, or not admitted to, a prison as a result . . .[of the order].[98] This provision makes a broad variety of officials including district attorneys, local jail officials, and other state and local officials eligible to participate formally in these proceedings. To date, since the passage of the PLRA, research has not disclosed any prison release orders entered nor have any three-judge courts been convened.

This is not to say that courts are not uninvolved. For example, recently in *Maynor v. Morgan County*,[99] when faced with unconscionable overcrowding conditions in a

---

[94]See Ch 16.

[95]18 U.S.C. § 3626 (C)(3)(A)(i) and (ii).

[96]18 U.S.C. § 3626 (C)(3)(C).

[97]18 U.S.C. § 3626 (C)(3)(E).

[98]18 U.S.C. § 3626 (C)(3)(F).

[99]Maynor v. Morgan County, Alabama, 147 F. Supp. 2d 1185 (N.D. Ala. 2001).

county jail, the court acted. Conditions at the jail were so severe that inmates were forced to sleep on concrete floors, sometimes within two feet of commodes or showers. Inmates were sometimes not even provided with sleeping mats, blankets and sheets, and those that were provided were often unclean. Because of overcrowding, the cells were dirty and poorly ventilated, food was inadequate in amount and unsanitary in preparation, medical needs went unattended and the jail was a fire hazard. The court ordered changes in all these conditions and entered an order requiring the defendants to present a plan to eliminate overcrowding by removing from the jail sentenced inmates who had not been sent to state prison.[100] Since the court did not order the release of inmates from confinement, but instead the transfer of state ready inmates from jail to prison, the order did not run afoul of the PLRA.[101]

§ 2:14 —Idleness, Programs, and Rehabilitation

Many penologists and members of the public believe that it is a good idea to attempt to rehabilitate prisoners. Enlightened self-interest explains this view. If recidivism can be reduced, then society can breathe easier when, as is the normally the case, prisoners are released from incarceration. A number of states, by statute, have endorsed the goal of rehabilitation.[1] Correctional standards also uniformly call for the provision

---

[100]*Id.* at 1188-89.

[101]See also Morales Feliciano v. Rosello Gonzalez, 124 F. Supp. 2d 774 (D.P.R. 2000) (holding defendants in contempt of previous court order for continuing to allow overcrowded admissions cells, inmates sleeping on the floor with mattresses or bedding, inadequate toilet facilities, grossly unsanitary conditions, and a lack of adequate hygienic supplies).

[Section 2:14]

[1]See, e.g., Ark Code Ann §§ 12-29-306 to -310; Cal Penal Code §§ 2002, 2022, 2032; Ga Code Ann § 42-5-57; NY Correct Law § 136; RI Gen Laws § 42-56-1. See also 28 CFR §§ 544.20-.72. See, generally, National Advisory Commn on Criminal Justice Standards and Goals, Corrections Standard 2.9 (1973). But see Cal Penal

§ 2:14

of programs.[2] In *Pell v. Procunier*,[3] the Supreme Court cited rehabilitation as one of three primary functions of a penal system.[4]

Ironically, however, it has been argued that conditions in most prisons are, in fact, anti-rehabilitative.[5]

Code § 1170(a)(1) (the purpose of confinement in California is punishment, not rehabilitation).

[2]See, e.g., ABA Standards for Criminal Justice, Standard 4.3 (1986); American Correctional Assn., Standards for Adult Correctional Institutions, Standard 3-4294 (2002) (requiring full-time work and/or program assignments for all inmates in the general population); US Dept of Justice, Federal Standards for Prisons and Jails § 17.01 (1980).

[3]Pell v. Procunier, 417 U.S. 817, 94 S. Ct. 2800, 41 L. Ed. 2d 495 (1974).

[4]Pell v. Procunier, 417 U.S. 817, 822-23, 94 S. Ct. 2800, 41 L. Ed. 2d 495 (1974); The Court's acceptance of rehabilitation as a legitimate function of the penal system does not, of course, mean that everyone agrees that rehabilitation should be vigorously pursued. Some commentators have suggested that rehabilitation should be curtailed or eliminated as a goal of the penal system. See, generally, David Fogel, We Are the Living Proof (1975); James Q. Wilson, Thinking About Crime 181-203 (1975). Recently, the pendulum may be swinging back toward rehabilitation. See, e.g., Rotman, Article: Criminal Law: Do Criminal Offenders Have a Constitutional Right to Rehabilitation? 77 J. Crim. L. & Criminology 1023 (1986) (normal prison conditions have detrimental effects on the mental health of prisoners, and rehabilitation is essential to combat this); Sheffer, Note: Serious and Habitual Juvenile Offender Statutes: Reconciling Punishment and Rehabilitation Within the Juvenile Justice System, 48 Vand. L. Rev. 479 (1995) (goal of rehabilitation can be effectively achieved in tandem with effectuating the goal of punishment); Lamparello, Note & Comment: Reaching Across Legal Boundaries: How Mediation Can Help the Criminal Law in Adjudicating "Crimes of Addiction," 16 Ohio St. J. on Disp. Resol. 335 (2001) (rehabilitation is a better goal than punishment for "crimes of addiction").

[5]Ruthanne DeWolfe & Allan S. DeWolfe, Impact of Prison Conditions on the Mental Health of Inmates, 1979 So Ill LJ 497 (1979); Ogloff, Mental Health Services in Jails and Prisons: Legal, Clinical, and Policy Issues, 18 Law & Psychol. Rev. 109 (1994) (15% to 40% of inmates suffer from a "moderate" mental illness); Rotman, Article: Criminal Law: Do Criminal Offenders Have a

One of the primary reasons for this is the dearth of programs, or even activities, for prisoners. In fact, for far too many prisoners, idleness is the order of the day. Today, in part because of the overcrowding that is swelling the populations of prisons,[6] in part because of rising indifference to the plight of prisoners, and in part because of a sense of frustration that "nothing works,"[7]

Constitutional Right to Rehabilitation? 77 J. Crim. L. & Criminology 1023 (1986) (normal prison conditions have detrimental effects on the mental health of prisoners, and rehabilitation is essential to combat this); Sheffer, Note: Serious and Habitual Juvenile Offender Statutes: Reconciling Punishment and Rehabilitation Within the Juvenile Justice System, 48 Vand. L. Rev. 479 (1995) (goal of rehabilitation can be effectively achieved in tandem with effectuating the goal of punishment); Lamparello, Note & Comment: Reaching Across Legal Boundaries: How Mediation Can Help the Criminal Law in Adjudicating "Crimes of Addiction," 16 Ohio St. J. on Disp. Resol. 335 (2001) (rehabilitation is a better goal than punishment for "crimes of addiction").

[6]See § 2:13.

[7]Many types of programs ranging from vocational training to education to religious counseling have been attempted with mixed success. No doubt this is attributable in part to inadequate funding and the lack of skilled personnel, but the theoretical merits of many of the programs are also subject to dispute. See, generally, Daniel Glaser, The Effectiveness of a Prison and Parole System (1964). More importantly, "there has been a shift in the view that rehabilitation is the overriding goal of prisons." Sheldon Kranz, Corrections and Prisoners' Rights 207 (1989). See also Francis A. Allen, The Decline in the Rehabilitative Ideal in American Criminal Justice, 27 Clev St L Rev 147 (1978) (noting that prison programs have declined because of the views of many that they do not work and that their availability shows that the public is being too soft on offenders). As a result, some states have even changed their laws to indicate that the purpose of confinement is punishment, not rehabilitation. See Cal Penal Code § 1170(a)(1). But see, Rotman, Article: Criminal Law: Do Criminal Offenders Have a Constitutional Right to Rehabilitation? 77 J. Crim. L. & Criminology 1023 (1986) (normal prison conditions have detrimental effects on the mental health of prisoners, and rehabilitation is essential to combat this).

§ 2:14 RIGHTS OF PRISONERS, THIRD EDITION

idleness has become "a major feature of prison life.⁸

The question that arises from this set of facts is whether the absence of rehabilitation programs and activities violates the Eighth Amendment. Several courts have identified a right to treatment for involuntarily committed mental patients⁹ and juveniles.¹⁰ While some of these cases were decided on statutory grounds,¹¹ others were based on a constitutionally derived right to treatment.¹² The theory is that if states deprive individuals of their freedom because of mental illness or for the express purpose of "curing" juvenile delinquency,

---

⁸Barbara B. Knight & Stephen T. Early, Jr, Prisoners' Rights in America 160 (1986).

⁹E.g., Wyatt v. Aderholt, 503 F.2d 1305 (5th Cir. 1974)(civilly committed mental patients have constitutional rights to such individual treatment as will help each of them to be cured or to improve his or her mental condition); Welsch v. Likins, 373 F. Supp. 487 (D. Minn. 1974), judgment aff'd, 525 F.2d 987 (8th Cir. 1975).

¹⁰e.g., Nelson v. Heyne, 491 F.2d 352 (7th Cir. 1974); Martarella v. Kelley, 359 F. Supp. 478 (S.D. N.Y. 1973); Alexander S. By and Through Bowers v. Boyd, 876 F. Supp. 773, 8 A.D.D. 919, 98 Ed. Law Rep. 72 (D.S.C. 1995) (where the goal of a state's juvenile system is treatment and rehabilitation, the Due Process Clause requires the programs and services at a particular institution must be reasonably related for that purpose).

¹¹See, e.g., Rouse v. Cameron, 373 F.2d 451 (D.C. Cir. 1966). See also Handberry v. Thompson, 92 F. Supp. 2d 244, 143 Ed. Law Rep. 799 (S.D. N.Y. 2000) (state law requires that juveniles in confinement be given an education; requiring that the defendants devise a plan for providing "full and complete educational services to all eligible inmates on Rikers Island"). But see Tremblay v. Riley, 917 F. Supp. 195, 107 Ed. Law Rep. 817 (W.D. N.Y. 1996) (amendment to Violent Crimes Control Act (VCCA) that struck provision of Higher Education Act allowing inmates to receive Pell Grants was not a violation of Ex Post Facto Clause; court found that the denial of grants was not a punishment and was only temporary, since inmates would be eligible again upon release).

¹²See, e.g., Wyatt v. Aderholt, 503 F.2d 1305 (5th Cir. 1974) (civilly committed mental patients have constitutional rights to such individual treatment as will help each of them to be cured or to improve his or her mental condition). It might be noted that when provided the opportunity to affirm this constitutional right to

§ 2:14

the states are constitutionally obligated to provide treatment that has some possibility of addressing the problem. In other words, treatment is the quid pro quo for commitment.

These developments received some limited recognition by the United States Supreme Court in *O'Connor v. Donaldson*.[13] In that case, the Court held that it was unconstitutional to confine a nondangerous mentally ill person without providing treatment if the person was capable of living outside the institution either alone or with some limited help from others. However, the Court left open the possibility that confinement without treatment was permissible if the confinement was for the purpose of preventing harm from a dangerous person.[14] The Court, in addition, did not address whether mentally ill persons have the right to demand treatment if they are not confined.[15]

In *Kansas v. Hendricks*[16] the Supreme Court contributed to this trend when by a 5 to 4 vote it upheld a statute which authorized the confinement of sex offenders who had served their sentences but who were found to be still a danger to the community. The court held that the scheme provided for a civil commitment of

---

treatment, the Supreme Court chose to avoid the issue. O'Connor v. Donaldson, 422 U.S. 563, 95 S. Ct. 2486, 45 L. Ed. 2d 396 (1975).

[13]O'Connor v. Donaldson, 422 U.S. 563, 95 S. Ct. 2486, 45 L. Ed. 2d 396 (1975).

[14]*Id.* at 573-74.

[15]O'Connor v. Donaldson, 422 U.S. 563, 95 S. Ct. 2486, 45 L. Ed. 2d 396 (1975). See also Youngberg v. Romeo, 457 U.S. 307, 102 S. Ct. 2452, 73 L. Ed. 2d 28 (1982) (holding that mentally retarded persons have the right to minimally adequate training to effectuate their right to be free from bodily restraint and to have reasonably safe conditions of confinement).

[16]Kansas v. Hendricks, 521 U.S. 346, 117 S. Ct. 2072, 138 L. Ed. 2d 501 (1997). See alsoSeling v. Young, 531 U.S. 250, 121 S. Ct. 727, 148 L. Ed. 2d 734 (2001) (holding that such statutes do not violate Double Jeopardy or become Ex Post Facto provisions of the constitution on an "as applied" basis in an individual case, but noting that treatment for treatable conditions are constitutionally required in such cases so as not to violate the Due Process Clause).

315

§ 2:14   Rights of Prisoners, Third Edition

these persons and thus was "civil," not criminal. The place of confinement was not the prison itself and the *quid pro quo* for the commitment was treatment of those inmates whom had treatable conditions. In *Sharp v. Weston*,[17] the Ninth Circuit held that the constitution must give persons who are so committed "a realistic opportunity to be cured or to improve the mental condition for which they were confined."[18]

The question raised by these decisions is whether prison inmates can claim the limited right to treatment and rehabilitation that has been developed in these cases for civilly committed mental patients, for juveniles, and for sex offenders who are held after the expiration of their sentences. In the 1970's there were some holdings answering this question in the affirmative and establishing a semblance of a constitutional right of rehabilitation for prisoners. The opinions spoke in terms of preventing the "torpor induced by prolonged mental and physical inactivity."[19] To prevent this "dehabilitation," these opinions ordered corrections officials to institute or expand educational, vocational, and work study/work release programs.[20]

This trend did not develop into established law. The analogy of prisoners to the nondangerous mentally ill and to juveniles is difficult to maintain. For one thing, prisoners, unlike mental patients, have run afoul of the criminal law. The institutionalization of nondangerous mental patients and released sex offenders could not be

---

[17]Sharp v. Weston, 233 F.3d 1166 (9th Cir. 2000).

[18]*Id.* at 1172.

[19]Laaman v. Helgemoe, 437 F. Supp. 269, 318 (D.N.H. 1977).

[20]*Id.*; Hamilton v. Landrieu, 351 F. Supp. 549, 552 (E.D. La. 1972) (ordering that the prison maintain a rehabilitation and education program); Barnes v. Government of Virgin Islands, 415 F. Supp. 1218, 1234 (D.V.I. 1976) (each inmate is entitled to basic education, work release, college release, or vocational training programs); Pugh v. Locke, 406 F. Supp. 318 (M.D. Ala. 1976), judgment aff'd and remanded, 559 F.2d 283 (5th Cir. 1977), cert. granted in part, judgment rev'd in part on other grounds , 438 U.S. 781, 98 S. Ct. 3057, 57 L. Ed. 2d 1114 (1978).

§ 2:14

justified were it not for their illness; conviction in a criminal court affords an independent and self-sufficient basis for incarceration. Unlike the case of juveniles, where the sole rationale for confinement is said to be rehabilitation, there are other reasons than rehabilitation for imprisoning those convicted of crime. Retribution, general and special deterrence, and restraint, among others, are penologically accepted rationales for imprisonment.[21] These objectives can still be accomplished despite the absence of rehabilitation programs. Thus, the quid pro quo relied on in the cases of the nondangerous mentally ill and juvenile offenders is not present in the case of prisoners.[22]

Courts, therefore, have not validated a right to rehabilitative treatment for prisoners. The Fifth Circuit Court of Appeals, for example, starting with the dubious proposition that the mental, physical, and emotional status of all adults, whether in or out of custody, deteriorates over time, held that "[t]he Constitution does not require that prisoners as individuals or as a group, be provided with any and every amenity which some person may think is needed to avoid mental, physical, and emotional deterioration."[23] This line of thinking has now become an accepted mantra. The Ninth Circuit invoked it when it wrotethat, "[a]lthough methods of analysis differ, each circuit that has considered the issue has held that enforced idleness does not

---

[21]The United States Supreme Court has specifically upheld the death penalty as serving, in some cases, the goal of retribution. Gregg v. Georgia, 428 U.S. 153, 185-87, 96 S. Ct. 2909, 49 L. Ed. 2d 859 (1976) (plurality opinion). Obviously the death penalty does not serve any rehabilitative function for the defendant.

[22]One exception to this may be the case of a prisoner assigned to a mental institution. See, e.g., Cameron v. Tomes, 990 F.2d 14 (1st Cir. 1993); Flakes v. Percy, 511 F. Supp. 1325 (W.D. Wis. 1981).

[23]Newman v. State of Ala., 559 F.2d 283, 291 (5th Cir. 1977), cert. granted in part, judgment rev'd in part on other grounds, 438 U.S. 781, 98 S. Ct. 3057, 57 L. Ed. 2d 1114 (1978).

§ 2:14　　　　　　　Rights of Prisoners, Third Edition

constitute cruel and unusual punishment."[24]

While the courts have not recognized an unequivocal right to rehabilitation for prisoners, a closer examination of the cases indicated that there were two more limited circumstances in which a right to programs might arise for prisoners. The first occurs when the inmate's confinement is made expressly contingent on receiving some form of rehabilitation. *Ohlinger v. Watson*[25] provides one example of this. In *Ohlinger,* the inmate, a sex offender, was sentenced under an Oregon law that provided that child sex offenders would receive indeterminate life sentences rather than 15-year sentences, and would receive treatment. The court held that "[h]aving chosen to incarcerate [inmates] on the basis of their mental illness," the state was constitution-

---

[24]Toussaint v. McCarthy, 801 F.2d 1080, 1107 n28 (9th Cir. 1986). See also Peterkin v. Jeffes, 855 F.2d 1021, 1029-30 (3d Cir. 1988); Women Prisoners of District of Columbia Dept. of Corrections v. District of Columbia, 899 F. Supp. 659, 675, 104 Ed. Law Rep. 213 (D.D.C. 1995) (the lack of child placement counseling does not rise to the level of an Eighth Amendment violation"; court explained that "[t]hough the Court regards such matters as exceedingly important, it does not believe that the lack of child placement counseling is a deprivation which denies the minimal civilized measure of life's necessities"); Byrd v. Moseley, 942 F. Supp. 642 (D.D.C. 1996) ("well-established that an inmate has no constitutional right to participate in a particular educational or vocational program"); Gabel v. Estelle, 677 F. Supp. 514, 515 (S.D. Tex. 1987) (no right to creation of educational, vocational, or counseling programs). See also Gholson v. Murry, 953 F. Supp. 709 (E.D. Va. 1997) (denial of work opportunities and educational programs to inmates confined in segregated housing did not violate the Eighth Amendment); Hargett v. Logan, 688 So. 2d 217 (Miss. 1996) (no right to educational programs for inmates in protective custody; prison officials had a rational basis for restricting inmates in protective custody from such programs; further, inmates in protective custody could take correspondence courses to further their education); Vargas v. Pataki, 899 F. Supp. 96 (N.D. N.Y. 1995) (court held that prison regulation which prohibited inmates convicted of homicide from participating in work release did not violate Ex Post Facto Clause; court found that policy was rationally related to public safety and was not punitive).

[25]Ohlinger v. Watson, 652 F.2d 775 (9th Cir. 1980).

ally obligated to provide meaningful treatment.[26] Similarly, in *Cooper v. Gwinn*,[27] the West Virginia Supreme Court held that a state statute which provided that inmates "shall be afforded individual and group treatment to reestablish their ability to live peaceably and consistent with the protection of the community . . . ."[28] established that the state legislature "requires that rehabilitation be the primary goal of the West Virginia corrections system."[29] Therefore, inmates had a right to treatment.[30]

The other situation in which a right to programs might arise is when the absence of activity contributes to prison conditions falling below "the minimal civilized measure of life's necessities" prohibited by the Eighth Amendment.[31] This occurred in a case involving the Puerto Rico prison system. There, the court found that idleness was one of the causes of violence in the prison. Since the right to safety is a recognized entitlement under the Eighth Amendment,[32] the court determined that it could order the establishment of prison programs

---

[26]*Id.* at 777. See also Cameron v. Tomes, 990 F.2d 14 (1st Cir. 1993) (holding that the state has a due process obligation to provide treatment in order to limit the extent to which it worsens a prisoner's mental condition and therefore extends his detention indefinitely under a sex offender law).

[27]Cooper v. Gwinn, 171 W. Va. 245, 298 S.E.2d 781 (1981).

[28]*Id.* at 788 (citing W Va Code § 62-13-1).

[29]*Id.* at 778.

[30]*Id.* See also Ferguson v. State, Dept. of Corrections, 816 P.2d 134 (Alaska 1991) (holding that in Alaska there is a state constitutional right to rehabilitation); Williams v. Lane, 851 F.2d 867, 879-81, 11 Fed. R. Serv. 3d 753 (7th Cir. 1988); Palmigiano v. Garrahy, 443 F. Supp. 956 (D.R.I. 1977); Bishop v. McCoy, 174 W. Va. 99, 323 S.E.2d 140 (1984) (extending the right to programs to inmates in protective custody). But see Hoptowit v. Ray, 682 F.2d 1237, 1255, 9 Fed. R. Evid. Serv. 1511 (9th Cir. 1982) (state rehabilitation laws create no right to treatment under the Constitution).

[31]Rhodes v. Chapman, 452 U.S. 337, 347, 101 S. Ct. 2392, 69 L. Ed. 2d 59 (1981).

[32]§ 2:12.

as a way of ensuring that right.[33] Thus, there is a derivative right to programs where necessary to avoid a stultifying and degenerative environment that would otherwise violate the Eighth Amendment.[34]

Exclusion of Inmates from Established Programs

Although it may not be constitutionally required, most prisons have offered at least some rehabilitative programs because of the perceived beneficial effects. Whenever programs are in place, inmates want to get into them. If they are excluded, how, if at all, can they challenge their exclusion? Since, as demonstrated above, there is at best a limited Eighth Amendment right to programs and no right to a particular program unless one of the exceptions described above is met, most of the Eighth Amendment challenges are not successful.[35]

Without a reliable Eighth Amendment anchor, a va-

---

[33]Morales Feliciano v. Romero Barcelo, 672 F. Supp. 591, 619-20 (D.P.R. 1986). See also Capps v. Atiyeh, 559 F. Supp. 894, 909 (D. Or. 1982) (indicating that the power to order programs exists if programs would lessen the amount of prison violence); Palmigiano v. Garrahy, 443 F. Supp. 956 (D.R.I. 1977).

[34]See, e.g., Battle v. Anderson, 564 F.2d 388 (10th Cir. 1977); Lewis v. Washington, 197 F.R.D. 611 (N.D. Ill. 2000) (failure to provide vocational rehabilitative and educational programs may constitute an Eighth Amendment violation if it tied to the totality of conditions in the institution); Laaman v. Helgemoe, 437 F. Supp. 269 (D.N.H. 1977). See also Knop v. Johnson, 667 F. Supp. 512, 8 Fed. R. Serv. 3d 1109 (W.D. Mich. 1987) (although idleness does not violate the Eighth Amendment, a court may remedy it if it results in high levels of violence); Barnes v. Government of Virgin Islands, 415 F. Supp. 1218 (D.V.I. 1976); Alberti v. Sheriff of Harris County, Texas, 406 F. Supp. 649 (S.D. Tex. 1975). See also Davenport v. DeRobertis, 844 F.2d 1310 (7th Cir. 1988) (holding that the Eighth Amendment forbids enforced idleness in a severely confined situation when it causes severe psychological harm).

[35]When the challenges are on Eighth Amendment grounds they are unsuccessful, since there is no general right under the Eighth Amendment to participate in a particular program. Higgason v. Farley, 83 F.3d 807 (7th Cir. 1996). But when the challenge is on

riety of other theories to challenge exclusions from programs have been tried. If an inmate alleges that he is excluded from an existing program because the program maintains discriminatory admissions standards, the claim is analyzed under the Equal Protection Clause. Most, but not all of these cases, deal with claims of racial or religious discrimination. The case law on this topic is discussed in Chapter 4 of this book, dealing with discrimination issues.[36]

If the inmate claims that he has been barred from a program in retaliation for protected activity, the claim is brought under the First Amendment. Courts have held that this is a valid theory for recovery if the inmate can prove that the motivation for the denial of access to a program was retaliation against a prisoner for his exercise of a valid First Amendment right, such as fil-

---

Eighth Amendment grounds combined with a claim of discrimination, relief has been granted. See Women Prisoners of the District of Columbia Dept. of Corrections v. District of Columbia, 968 F. Supp. 744 (D.D.C. 1997).

[36]On these issues see, generally, Glover v. Johnson, 931 F. Supp. 1360 (E.D. Mich. 1996), aff'd in part, rev'd in part on other grounds and remanded, 138 F.3d 229, 1998 FED App. 72P (6th Cir. 1998) (sex discrimination case involving prison programs, court holding defendants in contempt for their failure to comply with prior court orders to remedy insufficient vocational, educational, and apprenticeship programs at women's correctional facilities); Franklin v. District of Columbia, 960 F. Supp. 394 (D.D.C. 1997), vacated in part, 163 F.3d 625 (D.C. Cir. 1998) (class of Hispanic inmates claimed the failure of defendants to provide vocational, rehabilitative and educational programs in the Spanish language violated their rights; in vacating in part, Court of Appeals noted that shortly before trial, the defendants compiled a list of all Hispanic inmates, revised its master roster of bilingual employees, trained bilingual coordinators, appointed health and mental health service coordinators, designed and administered the language assessment test, and color coded medical charts regarding Hispanic inmates' language proficiency; court concluded that such efforts—stretching over the course of years—did not resemble cruel and unusual punishment).

§ 2:14

ing a lawsuit[37]

Generalized due process claims not grounded on the Equal Protection Clause or the First Amendment normally do not fair well. Prison officials have wide discretion in the manner in which they administer programs and make eligibility decisions.[38] Inmates may be denied access to programs for disciplinary infractions.[39] Also, where limited spaces are available, authorities can select those most likely to profit from the program.[40]

At the time of the last edition of this book, there was some case law that supported a "liberty interest" theory for inmates who attacked denial of access to a particular program. The theory could be invoked if there was a state statutory or state constitutional right to a particular rehabilitative program. In such a case, the theory was that the state law created a liberty interest for people who met the criteria that could not be taken away without due process protections.[41] However, the Supreme Court's decision in *Sandin v. Conner*,[42] discussed in Chapter 9, has almost, but not entirely, eviscerated that line of authority. Under *Sandin* there

---

[37]See, e.g., Friedl v. City of New York, 210 F.3d 79, 46 Fed. R. Serv. 3d 146 (2d Cir. 2000); Harris v. Fleming, 839 F.2d 1232, 1236-38 (7th Cir. 1988); Higgason v. Farley, 83 F.3d 807 (7th Cir. 1996).

[38]See, e.g., Newman v. State of Ala., 559 F.2d 283, 292 (5th Cir. 1977), cert. granted in part, judgment rev'd in part on other grounds, 438 U.S. 781, 98 S. Ct. 3057, 57 L. Ed. 2d 1114 (1978).

[39]See, e.g., Russell v. Oliver, 392 F. Supp. 470 (W.D. Va. 1975), aff'd in part, vacated in part on other grounds, 552 F.2d 115 (4th Cir. 1977); Pinkston v. Bensinger, 359 F. Supp. 95 (N.D. Ill. 1973). See also Numer v. Miller, 165 F.2d 986 (C.C.A. 9th Cir. 1948).

[40]See, e.g., Sellers v. Ciccone, 530 F.2d 199 (8th Cir. 1976); Queen v. South Carolina Dept. of Corrections, 307 F. Supp. 841 (D. S.C. 1970).

[41]See, e.g., Williams v. Lane, 851 F.2d 867, 880, 11 Fed. R. Serv. 3d 753 (7th Cir. 1988); Perrote v. Percy, 444 F. Supp. 1288 (E.D. Wis. 1978). See Ch 8.

[42]Sandin v. Conner, 515 U.S. 472, 115 S. Ct. 2293, 132 L. Ed. 2d 418 (1995).

is no federal due process entitlement to participate in any prison activity unless the denial of the right works an "atypical and significant hardship" in relation to the "ordinary incidents of prison life."[43] This is so regardless of whether state law provides criteria for the program that the inmate meets.

Under *Sandin,* there is no longer a due process right to participate in prison programs, since courts have held that denial of participation in these programs is not an "atypical and significant hardship."[44] There are two possible exceptions to this. The first is where the inmate can show that the denial of the right to participate will "inevitably affect the duration of the inmate's sentence."[45] The second is where there is a termination of participation in work release programs. On the latter question there is a split in the Circuits. The Second Circuit held that there is a liberty interest in continuation in work release, since work release allows a person to leave prison walls and enter free society. Therefore, revocation of the status is an "atypical and significant" change in the conditions of confinement sufficient to

---

[43]*Id.* at 2300.

[44]Higgason v. Farley, 83 F.3d 807 (7th Cir. 1996). See also Nicholas v. Pataki, 233 A.D.2d 657, 650 N.Y.S.2d 317 (3d Dep't 1996) (inmate challenged the denial of his petition for educational leave; pursuant to 7 NYCRR § 1900.3(e) inmates were ineligible for educational release where their crimes were homicide-related; court held that such determinations are best relegated to the discretion of the Department of Correctional Services).

[45]Higgason v. Farley, 83 F.3d 807 (7th Cir. 1996). See also Chambers v. Colorado Dept. of Corrections, 205 F.3d 1237 (10th Cir. 2000), cert. denied, 531 U.S. 974, 121 S. Ct. 419, 148 L. Ed. 2d 323 (2000) and cert. denied, 531 U.S. 962, 121 S. Ct. 391, 148 L. Ed. 2d 301 (2000) (holding that labeling an inmate a sex offender implicates a liberty interest, since it will lead to less earned time credit, although there may be an alternative ground for decision in that the inmate was granted extra earned time and then it was taken away without a hearing).

§ 2:14   RIGHTS OF PRISONERS, THIRD EDITION

satisfy *Sandin*.[46] The First and Eighth Circuits do not agree.[47]

Conditions Attached to Participation in Programs

An increasing number of rehabilitation programs require the inmate to confess to his criminal act as a condition for entry. This arises most frequently in programs established to treat sex offenders. There has been a significant amount of litigation involving challenges to such provisions on the theory that they violate the Fifth Amendment. The issue attracted the attention of the United States Supreme Court. The case, *Lile v. McKune*,[48] arose when the Kansas Department of Corrections established the Sexual Abuse Treatment Program. The program required that the inmate describe the crime that he was convicted of, and any other uncharged crimes. The philosophy of the program was that the act of confession would increase the chances of successful treatment. The program carried important benefits for those who participated, including housing in a medium security prison, increased visitation rights, a greater chance of gaining parole eligibility, and other privileges. The plaintiff, who refused to confess to his crime, argued that the Fifth Amendment right against self-incrimination was violated by this provision.

The Tenth Circuit rejected the defendant's argument

---

[46] Kim v. Hurston, 182 F.3d 113 (2d Cir. 1999). Accord, Friedl v. City of New York, 210 F.3d 79, 46 Fed. R. Serv. 3d 146 (2d Cir. 2000). Admission to temporary release has been held not to create a liberty interest. Lee v. Governor of State of N.Y., 87 F.3d 55 (2d Cir. 1996).

[47] Dominique v. Weld, 73 F.3d 1156 (1st Cir. 1996) (no liberty interest in termination of work release status); Callender v. Sioux City Residential Treatment Facility, 88 F.3d 666 (8th Cir. 1996) (no liberty interest in remaining in a work release program). See also Bankes v. Simmons, 265 Kan. 341, 963 P.2d 412 (1998).

[48] Lile v. McKune, 224 F.3d 1175 (10th Cir. 2000), cert. granted, 532 U.S. 1018, 121 S. Ct. 1955, 149 L. Ed. 2d 752 (2001) and rev'd, 122 S. Ct. 2017, 153 L. Ed. 2d 47 (U.S. 2002).

the Fifth Amendment was not implicated because the program was voluntary.[49] The First Circuit, however, came to the opposite conclusion in deciding the same issue. The facts in *Ainsworth v. Risley*[50] were almost identical to the facts in *Lile*. The First Circuit held that since the lack of participation in the treatment program did not, in itself, lead to the loss of parole eligibility, or the loss of desired housing status, the program did not constitute a Fifth Amendment violation. The court applied the *Turner* test and found that the state had an interest in reducing recidivism, and considering the voluntary nature of the program, and the fact that parole was not lost inevitably by failing to participate, there was no violation of the Fifth Amendment.[51]

The Supreme Court resolved this issue in June 2002 by ruling 6 to 3 that requiring an inmate to confess to the crime as a condition for entering a treatment program for sex offenders did not transgress the Fifth Amendment.[52] The Court held that prison officials had a valid penological interest in imposing this requirement, and that the conditions for entry into the program did not work a "significant and atypical" hardship, since they did not extend the length of the prison sentence nor was the prisoner sent to punitive segregation for refusing to disclose past criminal acts. While the prisoner was put to a difficult choice, the court held

---

[49]*Id.*

[50]Ainsworth v. Risley, 244 F.3d 209 (1st Cir. 2001), cert. granted, judgment vacated, 122 S. Ct. 2652, 153 L. Ed. 2d 829 (U.S. 2002).

[51]Accord, Neal v. Shimoda, 905 F. Supp. 813 (D. Haw. 1995), aff'd in part, rev'd in part, 131 F.3d 818 (9th Cir. 1997); State v. Carter, 146 N.H. 359, 772 A.2d 326 (2001) (necessary compulsion absent where the inmate is not forced to participate in the program). For a discussion of whether requiring inmates to admit their guilt to gain access to sex offender treatment programs violates their constitutional right against self-incrimination, see, Stefan J. Padfield, Self-Incrimination and Acceptance of Responsibility in Prison Sex Offender Treatment Programs, 49 Kan. L. Rev. 487 (2001).

[52]McKune v. Lile, 122 S. Ct. 2017, 153 L. Ed. 2d 47 (U.S. 2002).

that it was not an unconstitutional one.[53]

Finally, prison officials may compel inmates to participate in rehabilitation programs by imposing punishment for their refusal,[54] unless the inmates' failure to participate is motivated by a valid constitutionally based objection.[55]

§ 2:15 —Large Scale Litigations: Totality of the Conditions, Inadequate Finances, and Remedies

Prison suits come in several distinct varieties. Sometimes, they are individual actions, often brought pro se, raising one or two discrete issues. These suits account for the bulk of the statistics on prisoners' rights litigation. However, there is another kind of prison suit that, while less frequent, has had a more profound effect on the operation of American prisons. It is an

---

[53]*Id.*

[54]See, e.g., Jackson v. McLemore, 523 F.2d 838 (8th Cir. 1975) (sustaining punishment imposed on inmate for failure to enroll in compulsory education class); Muhammad v. Moore, 760 F. Supp. 869 (D. Kan. 1991) (refusal to cooperate with inmate financial responsibility program justifies sanction).

[55]See, e.g., Williams v. Greifinger, 918 F. Supp. 91 (S.D. N.Y. 1996), order rev'd in part on other grounds, 97 F.3d 699 (2d Cir. 1996) (holding that New York Department of Corrections policy which required inmates to consent to TB testing or be "confined to their cell at all times except for one shower per week and legal visits, until such time as they agree to be tested" violates the Eighth Amendment); Mace v. Amestoy, 765 F. Supp. 847 (D. Vt. 1991) (state could not compel participation in treatment program that required inmate to take responsibility for his sex offenses unless it granted immunity from criminal prosecutions). But compare Stafford v. Harrison, 766 F. Supp. 1014 (D. Kan. 1991) (participation in Alcoholics Anonymous (AA) did not violate free exercise rights of prisoner since AA is not a religious program). See also Parton v. Armontrout, 895 F.2d 1214 (8th Cir. 1990) (cancellation of parole based on inmate's failure to complete state sexual offender program violates the Ex Post Facto Clause of the Constitution).

"institutional reform litigation"[1] class action brought on behalf of large numbers of inmates. These suits seek comprehensive injunctive relief to cure systemic problems in the operation of the prison or prison system or in some major aspect of its operation. The lawsuit might be addressed to the elimination of overcrowding,[2] or it might it might seek to reform some other aspect of the system such as inadequate medical care.[3] Unlike the normal prison case, which is filed without the assistance of counsel,[4] the large-scale prison case is normally handled by experienced civil rights lawyers who have the resources and know-how to conduct complex litigation.[5]

[Section 2:15]

[1]Institutional reform litigation or litigation seeking a "structural injunction" are terms used to define lawsuits that are aimed at remedying constitutional violations in operation of government-run services such as schools, prisons, and other public institutions. For a discussion of the utility of these lawsuits generally, see, e.g., David Rudenstine, Institutional Injunctions, 4 Cardoza L Rev 611 (1983); Orin Fiss, Foreword: The Forms of Justice, 93 Harv L Rev 1 (1979).

[2]See, e.g., David J. Gottlieb, The Legacy of Wolfish and Chapman: Some Thoughts about "Big Prison Case" Litigation in the 1980s, in Prisoners and the Law § 2, at 3 (Ira Robbins editor) (defining a large scale prison case as one in which inmates claim that the "basic ambient conditions of confinement-food, clothing, shelter, recreation, prison programs and personal safety-are so inadequate that exposure to them constitutes cruel and unusual punishment").

[3]See, e.g., Rouse v. Plantier, 182 F.3d 192 (3d Cir. 1999). Sometimes these suits challenge discrete aspects of the prison operation. See, e.g., Von Colln v. County of Ventura, 189 F.R.D. 583 (C.D. Cal. 1999) (certifying a class action by detainees at a county jail challenging the use of a Pro-straint chair, a devise with built-in restraints for the wrist and arms and shackles for the legs).

[4]See Ch 11.

[5]On rare occasion there may be some dispute about who is best able to represent the class. See e.g., Gates v. Cook, 234 F.3d 221, 48 Fed. R. Serv. 3d 147 (5th Cir. 2000), reh'g and reh'g en banc denied, 253 F.3d 707 (5th Cir. 2001).

§ 2:15

These lawsuits have altered the landscape of American corrections.[6] At the height of these actions in 1993, 40 states, plus the District of Columbia, Puerto Rico, and the Virgin Islands were under court order or consent decree as a result of suits covering some aspect of their operations.[7] Twelve jurisdictions were under court orders covering their entire systems.[8] By 1995, 33 states remained under court order to limit prison populations or to improve prison conditions either in the entire state system or in some of its major institu-

---

[6]Litigation has had a profound effect on the operation of the nation's prisons. Malcolm Feeley, Judicial Policy Making and the Modern State: How the Courts Reformed America's Prisons (1998); Wayne N. Welsh, Counties in Court : Jail Overcrowding and Court-Ordered Reform (1995); Susan L. Rhodes, Prison Reform and Prison Life: Four Books on the Process of Court-Ordered Change, 26 Law & Socy Rev 189 (1992). See also Ben M. Crouch & James W. Marquart, An Appeal to Justice: Litigated Reform in Texas Prisons (1989); Larry W. Yackle, Reform and Regret: The Story of Federal Judicial Involvement in the Alabama Prison System (1989); James E. Robertson, Surviving Incarceration: Constitutional Protection from Inmate Violence, 35 Drake L Rev 101 (1985-86) (surveying the results of four prison cases and concluding that the cases "result[ed] in a significant lessening of prison violence"); M.K. Harris & Dudley P. Spiller, Jr, US Dept of Justice, After Decision: Implementation of Judicial Decrees in Correctional Settings, Natl Inst L Enforcement & Crim Just L Enforcement Assistance Admin (1985). Courts have noted the many positive changes produced by this litigation as well. See Celestineo v. Singletary, 147 F.R.D. 258, 262 (M.D. Fla. 1993) ("many prison lawsuits have effected dramatic improvements in the correctional systems"); Grubbs v. Bradley, 821 F. Supp. 496 (M.D. Tenn. 1993) (noting dramatic improvements to the Tennessee prison system and terminating the decree after finding that the defendants had complied with constitutional standards).

[7]Edward I. Koren, Status Report: State Prisons and the Courts-January 1993, 8 J Natl Prison Project 3 (1993).

[8]*Id.* at 3-11. These jurisdictions are Alabama, Alaska, Arkansas, Delaware, Florida, Mississippi, New Mexico, Rhode Island, South Carolina, Tennessee, Texas, and the District of Columbia.

tions,[9] and nine states were under court order covering their entire prison system.[10]

There is currently no reliable data on the precise number of jurisdictions under court order. However, it is clear that in recent years the number of such cases has decreased. In part, the decrease was caused by compliance with the terms of the court orders and the subsequent lifting of the court order.[11] In part, the decrease is caused by the passage of the Prison Litigation Reform Act (PLRA), which imposes barriers to these cases that did not exist previously.[12] While the number of these cases has decreased, these lawsuits continue to play an important role.[13]

---

[9]American Civil Liberties Union Foundation, Status Report: State Prisons and the Courts January 1, 1995, National Prison Project J 5 (Winter 1994/95).

[10]*Id.*

[11]See, e.g., Grubbs v. Bradley, 821 F. Supp. 496 (M.D. Tenn. 1993) (noting dramatic improvements to the Tennessee prison system and terminating the decree after finding that the defendants had achieved compliance with constitutional standards); Glover v. Johnson, 198 F.3d 557, 1999 FED App. 415P (6th Cir. 1999) (court upheld termination of court oversight of prisons where it was found that the prison system had achieved parity between programs offered to male and female prisoners, satisfying a consent decree); see also Bobby M. v. Chiles, 907 F. Supp. 368 (N.D. Fla. 1995).

[12]For a discussion of the PLRA see Prison Litigation Reform Act of 1995, Pub. L. No. 104-134 (codified as amended in scattered titles and sections of the United States Code); see also H.R. 3019, 104th Cong. (1996). The Act is discussed in Chapter 16, *Infra*

[13]See, e.g., Carty v. Farrelly, 957 F. Supp. 727, 22 A.D.D. 333 (D.V.I. 1997) (citing cases). Most of the cases have been in federal court; however, state courts have by no means been uninvolved. See, e.g., State ex rel. Sams v. Kirby, 208 W. Va. 726, 542 S.E.2d 889 (2000) (holding that that housing state prisoners in county jails violated the right to rehabilitation created by West Virginia state law; regional and county jails did not offer the recreational and rehabilitative programs offered by DOC-operated facilities; court appointed a new special master to establish a long range plan to transfer the prisoners to DOC-operated facilities, and ordered the DOC to find a temporary solution to transfer the

§ 2:15

A complete canvas of the myriad legal issues that are presented by these lawsuits is beyond the present scope of this work. However, three aspects of these lawsuits raise significant Eighth Amendment issues that will be briefly discussed here. These are: (1) a theory of liability often employed in large-scale litigation, called the "totality of the conditions" theory; (2) the defense of inadequate resources to correct unconstitutional conditions; and (3) the remedies available to a court finding unconstitutional conditions.

The Totality of the Conditions Theory

The totality of the conditions theory asserts that conditions that, by themselves, may not be constitutionally offensive, may become so when occurring in combination. The constitutional totality, in effect, becomes greater than the sum of its parts. This theory has played an important role in several large-scale prison litigation cases.

The first of the totality of conditions cases was *Holt v. Sarver*.[14] The court reserved its harshest criticism for the open, overcrowded barracks, (which encouraged sexual attacks and violence) and for the use of armed inmates as guards. But the court also noted the inadequate medical and dental facilities, the unsanitary kitchen conditions, the inability to maintain personal hygiene, and the lack of rehabilitation programs as conditions which, while perhaps not rising in and of themselves to the level of a constitutional violation, "aggravate the more serious defects and deficiencies."[15] These conditions, taken as a whole, were held to be

---

inmates to DOC-operated facilities until a new prison was completed).

[14] Holt v. Sarver, 309 F. Supp. 362 (E.D. Ark. 1970), aff'd and remanded, 442 F.2d 304 (8th Cir. 1971).

[15] *Id.* at 380.

cruel and unusual.[16]

Other courts followed the lead of *Holt*. A famous example was in Alabama, where federal district Judge (later Circuit Judge) Frank Johnson examined conditions in the state prison system and found severe overcrowding, a nonfunctioning classification system, inadequate medical and mental health care, rampant violence, overwhelming idleness, barbaric segregation conditions, and so many public health violations that a public health officer testified that, in combination, these conditions rendered the four major penitentiaries "wholly unfit for human habitation."[17] Making use of the totality approach, Judge Johnson had little trouble concluding that the conditions violated "any current judicial definition of cruel and unusual punishment."[18]

Similarly, a Rhode Island district court, examining the Rhode Island Adult Correctional Institutions, found that the:

> lack of sanitation, lighting, heating, and ventilation, and the noise, idleness, fear and violence, and the absence or inadequacy of programs of classification, education, physical exercise, vocational training or other constructive activity create a total environment where debilitation is inevitable, and which is unfit for human habitation and shocking to the conscience of a reasonably civilized person.[19]

---

[16]*Id.* at 381. See, generally, Michael S. Feldberg, Confronting the Conditions of Confinement: An Expanded Role for Courts in Prison Reform, 12 Harv CR- CL L Rev 367 (1977).

[17]Pugh v. Locke, 406 F. Supp. 318 (M.D. Ala. 1976), judgment aff'd and remanded, 559 F.2d 283 (5th Cir. 1977), cert. granted in part, judgment rev'd in part on other grounds, 438 U.S. 781, 98 S. Ct. 3057, 57 L. Ed. 2d 1114 (1978).

[18]Pugh v. Locke, 406 F. Supp. 318, 329 (M.D. Ala. 1976), judgment aff'd and remanded, 559 F.2d 283 (5th Cir. 1977), cert. granted in part, judgment rev'd in part on other grounds, 438 U.S. 781, 98 S. Ct. 3057, 57 L. Ed. 2d 1114 (1978).

[19]Palmigiano v. Garrahy, 443 F. Supp. 956, 979 (D.R.I. 1977).

§ 2:15   Rights of Prisoners, Third Edition

Other courts have reached similar results.[20]

It has been suggested that the cases reveal eleven distinct factors on which the courts focus in "totality" suits:[21]

1. the health and safety hazards created by the physical facilities
2. overcrowding
3. absence of a classification system
4. conditions in isolation and segregation cells
5. medical facilities and treatment
6. food service
7. personal hygiene and sanitation
8. the incidence of violence and homosexual attacks
9. the quantity and training of prison personnel
10. lack of rehabilitation programs
11. the presence of other constitutional violations

No particular condition, however, is necessarily critical to a court's decision. For instance, while most of the cases have identified overcrowding as a key condition, a district court found the totality of conditions in the state's prisons to be cruel and unusual despite the fact that prisoners were housed either in single cells or uncrowded dormitories.[22] Because conditions that might not be found unconstitutional if attacked individually may be held unconstitutional in a totality suit, relief can encompass aspects of prison life that would not

---

[20]See, e.g., Tillery v. Owens, 907 F.2d 418 (3d Cir. 1990); Battle v. Anderson, 564 F.2d 388, 403 (10th Cir. 1977); Williams v. Edwards, 547 F.2d 1206 (5th Cir. 1977); Laaman v. Helgemoe, 437 F. Supp. 269 (D.N.H. 1977); Barnes v. Government of Virgin Islands, 415 F. Supp. 1218 (D.V.I. 1976).

[21]Ira P. Robbins & Michael B. Buser, Punitive Conditions of Prison Confinement: An Analysis of Pugh v. Locke and Federal Court Supervision of State Penal Administration Under the Eighth Amendment, 29 Stan L Rev 893, 909-14 (1977).

[22]Palmigiano v. Garrahy, 443 F. Supp. 956 (D.R.I. 1977).

otherwise be addressed. For example, the absence of rehabilitative programs is not generally actionable by itself.[23] Yet in totality suits, courts have prescribed the development of educational and vocational programs as part of an overall remedy, if necessary to ensure that basic human needs are being met by the institution.[24]

The Supreme Court appeared at first to espouse the totality approach. Thus, in *Hutto v. Finney*,[25] the Court, in affirming a lower court order setting a limit on the amount of time that inmates could be held in a notorious punitive segregation unit, held that the order was supported by the "the *interdependence* of the conditions causing the violation."[26] And, in *Rhodes v. Chapman*,[27] the Court again stressed that conditions "alone or *in combination*," may deprive inmates of Eighth Amendment rights.[28]

However, in *Wilson v. Seiter*,[29] the Court revisited the topic, and, in the process, appeared to limit the reach of the theory.[30] In *Wilson*, Justice Scalia, writing for the Court, agreed that "some conditions of confinement may establish an Eighth Amendment violation 'in combina-

---

[23]See § 2:14.

[24]See, e.g., Palmigiano v. Garrahy, 443 F. Supp. 956, 988 (D.R.I. 1977); Laaman v. Helgemoe, 437 F. Supp. 269, 330 (D.N.H. 1977).

[25]Hutto v. Finney, 437 U.S. 678, 98 S. Ct. 2565, 57 L. Ed. 2d 522 (1978).

[26]*Id.* at 688 (emphasis supplied).

[27]Rhodes v. Chapman, 452 U.S. 337, 101 S. Ct. 2392, 69 L. Ed. 2d 59 (1981).

[28]*Id.* at 347 (emphasis supplied).

[29]Wilson v. Seiter, 501 U.S. 294, 111 S. Ct. 2321, 115 L. Ed. 2d 271 (1991).

[30]Elizabeth Alexander, The Overall Context of Prison Litigation, in Section 1983 Civil Rights Litigation and Attorney's Fees 1992: Current Developments, at 401 (PLI Litig & Admin Practice Course Handbook Series No 449, 1992) (noting that in Wilson the court "attempted to explain the concept of interacting prison conditions with greater precision").

tion' when each would not do so alone."³¹ However, this is only true when the conditions "have a mutually enforcing effect that produces the deprivation of a single, identifiable human need such as food, warmth, or exercise. . . ."³² Justice Scalia stated that an example of prison conditions that were mutually reinforcing is the combination of a low temperature cell with a failure to issue blankets. But he added that this did not mean that prison conditions are a "seamless web" that must invariably be viewed in combination before a determination can be made whether the Eighth Amendment is violated.³³

This language, while it does not reject the totality approach, as had some lower court opinions prior to *Wilson*,³⁴ suggests that it might not be given the full sweep that some lower courts had used prior to *Wilson*. The phraseology certainly implies that courts may not simply add up conditions and throw them onto a scale to be weighed to determine whether the conditions of confinement violate the Eighth Amendment. After *Wilson*, only those prison conditions that correlate with one another to produce "a mutually enforcing effect" causing a deprivation of an identifiable human need can be cumulated together under the totality theory.

The *Wilson* Court, however, did not address in detail which conditions interact in the prescribed way and which do not. It remains for the lower courts, which to date have handled this question on a case-by-case, and not a systemic, basis, and perhaps a future decision from the Supreme Court, to flesh out in more detail how to make this determination. In the absence of

---

[31]Wilson v. Seiter, 501 U.S. 294, 111 S. Ct. 2321, 2327, 115 L. Ed. 2d 271 (1991).

[32]*Id.*

[33]*Id.*

[34]See, e.g., Hoptowit v. Ray, 682 F.2d 1237, 1247, 9 Fed. R. Evid. Serv. 1511 (9th Cir. 1982) ("A number of conditions, each of which satisf[ies] Eighth Amendment requirements, cannot in combination amount to an Eighth Amendment violation.").

settled precedent in this area,[35] one observation can be made: in the closed world of a prison environment, interrelationships between different types of conditions are not hard to find.[36]

Take a case of dormitory overcrowding, inadequate ventilation, and the mixing of physically ill prisoners into the general dormitory population.[37] These claims do interact in a way that makes the use of the totality approach pertinent. It is evident, for example, that the claim of inadequate ventilation cannot be evaluated without considering the numbers of people that the ventilation system will serve. The greater the number of people, the more demand on the existing system, so that a system that provides a sufficient quantity and

---

[35]Even prior to *Wilson,* lower courts were not altogether in unison about how to apply the totality approach. Compare, e.g., Tillery v. Owens, 907 F.2d 418 (3d Cir. 1990) (double-celling might be unbearable" in light of other conditions even if those conditions are not caused by the overcrowding) with Toussaint v. McCarthy, 801 F.2d 1080, 1106-07 (9th Cir. 1986) (only "related conditions" can be considered together). For an interesting counterspin on the totality approach, see Fisher v. Koehler, 692 F. Supp. 1519, 1564 (S.D. N.Y. 1988) (clean building in good condition could not compensate for unconstitutional levels of violence).

[36]Cf. John Boston, Wilson v. Seiter: A Preliminary Analysis, 8 Civil Rights Litigation and Attorney Fees Annual Handbook 49-50 (1992) (arguing that many seemingly unrelated conditions can combine to affect human beings, and that it is impossible to know how this process works without expert psychological testimony since the totality doctrine, properly understood, involves "nothing less than the way that the human consciousness processes and integrates experience"). See also Women Prisoners of District of Columbia Dept. of Corrections v. District of Columbia, 877 F. Supp. 634, 98 Ed. Law Rep. 681 (D.D.C. 1994), vacated in part on other grounds, modified in part on other grounds, 899 F. Supp. 659, 104 Ed. Law Rep. 213 (D.D.C. 1995) (a combination of conditions can be violative of the Eighth Amendment even if any one of the conditions, taken alone, would be insufficient to establish a violation).

[37]These are some of the allegations made in *Wilson.* See Wilson v. Seiter, 501 U.S. 294, 111 S. Ct. 2321, 2323, 115 L. Ed. 2d 271 (1991).

§ 2:15

quality of air for a given prison population might very well be insufficient for greater numbers in the same space. Thus, overcrowding would have a mutually enforcing effect on adequacy of ventilation.

Likewise, it makes sense to evaluate the claim that physically ill persons are placed in the dormitory in conjunction with the claims regarding ventilation and crowding. The greater the crowding, the more the pressure on the ventilation system, the more danger that is posed to inmates by the presence of physically ill inmates who may have contagious diseases that are spread more readily in congested, poorly ventilated quarters. Thus, here too, the conditions would have a mutually enforcing effect.[38] In any event, if conditions do "interact" to cause the deprivation of an identifiable need, then liability is established even if a particular condition may not by itself violate the Constitution. In *Benjamin v. Fraser,* a recent case dealing with New York City Jails, the district court applied this theory by holding that a variety of environmental and sanitary conditions, including some that in isolation are not unconstitutional, can be unconstitutional in combination.[39]

However, where the evidence establishes that there

---

[38]See, e.g., Tokar v. Armontrout, 97 F.3d 1078 (8th Cir. 1996) (giving examples of "mutually enforcing" including a broken windows and a leaky roof in one case and, in another, sealed windows, inadequate ventilation, and crowded cells); Moore v. Mabus, 976 F.2d 268, 271 (5th Cir. 1992); Young v. Quinlan, 960 F.2d 351, 22 Fed. R. Serv. 3d 530 (3d Cir. 1992) (protection from harm and sanitation are "mutually enforcing" conditions). Williams v. Griffin, 952 F.2d 820, 824 (4th Cir. 1991) (overcrowding and unsanitary and dangerous conditions are mutually reenforcing). But see Strickler v. Waters, 989 F.2d 1375 (4th Cir. 1993) (finding that overcrowding and temperatures are not mutually enforcing).

[39]Benjamin v. Fraser, 161 F. Supp. 2d 151 (S.D. N.Y. 2001), on reconsideration in part on other grounds, 2001 WL 282705 (S.D. N.Y. 2001). See also Carty v. Farrelly, 957 F. Supp. 727, 22 A.D.D. 333 (D.V.I. 1997) (court held defendants in civil contempt for failure to comply with a prior court order to remedy a myriad of problematic conditions at the Criminal Justice Complex (CJC); in

CRUEL & UNUSUAL PUNISHMENT § 2:15

is no mutually enforcing effect, courts will not apply the totality theory. A case which illustrates this is *Tokar v. Armontrout*.[40] In that case the plaintiff complained that there were a leaky roof and broken windows in the prison, but these conditions were not mutually enforcing because the plaintiff did not have a window in his cubicle, and in any event, he could use a blanket while waiting for the window to be repaired.[41] Other cases hold that the totality theory is not applicable when the plaintiff is unable to establish an interrelationship between the challenged conditions and the deprivation of a human need.[42]

The Defense of Inadequate Resources

A potential defense to a prison institutional reform case is that prison officials lack the resources to make the needed changes. In fact, often, the stumbling block to institutional prison reform that leads to litigation in the first place is the lack of funding. Prison officials, after all, have little desire to take charge of an overcrowded, poorly ventilated, infested, or decrepit institution. Usually, the reason that conditions get that

---

determining whether conditions at the CJC violated the Eighth Amendment, the court evaluated the totality of the prison circumstances, including: (1) prison overcrowding; (2) problems with regard to inmate shelter, the physical plant, and the overall effects of these on the environmental health of inmates; (3) non-functioning fire safety system; (4) inadequate medical care; (5) failure to properly segregate mentally ill inmates from the general prison population; (6) failure to implement an inmate classification system and an adequate security system; (7) non-compliance with the America with Disabilities Act; (8) failure to acknowledge the religious rights of pretrial detainees; and (9) insufficient law library and irregular and arbitrary access to the law library).

[40]Tokar v. Armontrout, 97 F.3d 1078 (8th Cir. 1996).

[41]*Id.* at 1082.

[42]See, e.g., Tran v. Roscizewski, 202 F.3d 275 (7th Cir. 1999), cert. denied, 530 U.S. 1207, 120 S. Ct. 2205, 147 L. Ed. 2d 238 (2000); Lunsford v. Bennett, 17 F.3d 1574 (7th Cir. 1994); Counts v. Newhart, 951 F. Supp. 579 (E.D. Va. 1996), aff'd, 116 F.3d 1473 (4th Cir. 1997).

§ 2:15   Rights of Prisoners, Third Edition

way is that legislatures, faced with competing demands, or unsympathetic to the needs of prisoners, view prison reform as a low priority budget item, particularly given the convicts' lack of political clout. If financial resources are needed to correct unconstitutional conditions, but legislatures are unwilling to allocate the necessary funds, should this fact be a defense to the action?

Historically, in cases seeking injunctive relief,[43] the answer was a resounding no. Courts have consistently held that inadequate funding is not a legitimate defense to constitutional violations.[44] However, the Supreme Court's decision in *Wilson v. Seiter*[45] casts doubt on that canon. In *Wilson,* as we have seen, the Court introduced a subjective component into Eighth Amendment analysis.[46] To satisfy this component, the plaintiff must show the defendant has been "deliberately indifferent"

---

[43]The answer for damages cases is more equivocal. In such cases, courts have held that personal liability "may not be imposed on a defendant for matters outside his or her control, and the unavailability of funding may fall into that category." John Boston, Wilson v. Seiter: A Preliminary Analysis, 8 Civil Rights Litigation and Attorney Fees Annual Handbook 48-49 (West 1992). See also Williams v. Bennett, 689 F.2d 1370, 1378-88 (11th Cir. 1982). If the official had no power over funding and if the lack of funding caused the constitutional violation, then the defense can defeat a claim for damages. See, e.g., Birrell v. Brown, 867 F.2d 956, 959-60 (6th Cir. 1989). See also LaMarca v. Turner, 995 F.2d 1526 (11th Cir. 1993).

[44]See, e.g., Monmouth County Correctional Institutional Inmates v. Lanzaro, 834 F.2d 326, 336-37, 90 A.L.R. Fed. 631 (3d Cir. 1987); Tyler v. Black, 811 F.2d 424, 435 (8th Cir. 1987), reh'g granted, 825 F.2d 1219 (8th Cir. 1987) and opinion withdrawn in part, vacated in part on other grounds, adopted in part on reh'g, 865 F.2d 181 (8th Cir. 1989) (en banc); Ramos v. Lamm, 639 F.2d 559, 573 n. 19 (10th Cir. 1980); Smith v. Sullivan, 611 F.2d 1039, 1043-44 (5th Cir. 1980); Duran v. Anaya, 642 F. Supp. 510, 525 (D. N.M. 1986). See also Toussaint v. McCarthy, 801 F.2d 1080, 1110 (9th Cir. 1986) ("fact that a remedy is costly does not preclude a court from ordering the remedy").

[45]Wilson v. Seiter, 501 U.S. 294, 111 S. Ct. 2321, 2326, 115 L. Ed. 2d 271 (1991).

[46]See § 2:2.

to his or her Eighth Amendment rights.[47] Can a prison warden be said to be deliberately indifferent if the cause of the problem is the failure of the state to appropriate sufficient funds to cure the constitutional violations?

The *Wilson* majority did not respond to this other than to say that the argument was not raised in the case before it,[48] and that, in any event, this was a policy argument that had no bearing on the meaning of the Eighth Amendment.[49] The four-member *Wilson* minority, however, met the argument head on and rejected it. They chided the majority for failing to acknowledge that "inhumane prison conditions often are the result of cumulative actions and inactions by numerous officials inside and outside a prison, sometimes over a long period of time."[50] The state, therefore, should not be permitted to escape responsibility for the consequences of its inactions. As Justice White wrote: "having chosen to use imprisonment as a form of punishment, a state must ensure that the conditions in its prisons comport with the 'contemporary standard of decency' required by the Eighth Amendment."[51]

The case law after *Wilson* provides no definitive answer to whether the inadequate resources argument, in fact, has been vitalized by the *Wilson* Court's failure to reject it. In the absence of a definitive statement from the Supreme Court, some lower courts have

---

[47]Wilson v. Seiter, 501 U.S. 294, 111 S. Ct. 2321, 2327, 115 L. Ed. 2d 271 (1991).

[48]The Court also said the issue had not been raised in other prison reform cases, Wilson v. Seiter, 501 U.S. 294, 111 S. Ct. 2321, 2326, 115 L. Ed. 2d 271 (1991), but this assertion is plainly wrong. See, e.g., Ramos v. Lamm, 639 F.2d 559, 578 (10th Cir. 1980) (disallowing funding problems as excuse for unconstitutional confinement conditions caused by overcrowding).

[49]Wilson v. Seiter, 501 U.S. 294, 111 S. Ct. 2321, 2326, 115 L. Ed. 2d 271 (1991).

[50]*Id.* at 2330 (White, J, concurring in the judgment).

[51]*Id.* 2331 (White, J, concurring in the judgment).

§ 2:15   RIGHTS OF PRISONERS, THIRD EDITION

indicated that the issue is now unsettled.[52] Nevertheless, there are at least two reasons for concluding that, even after *Wilson,* this defense will not defeat a claim for injunctive relief against unconstitutional conditions of confinement.

The primary reason for this conclusion is that a suit against an individual defendant in his or her official capacity is, in reality, a suit against the state. As the Supreme Court explained in *Kentucky v. Graham,*[53] suits against state officials in their official capacity generally represent only another way of pleading an action against an entity of which an officer is an agent. "As long as the government entity receives notice and an opportunity to respond, an official capacity suit is, *in all respects other than name, to be treated as a suit against the entity. It is not a suit against the official personally, for the real party in interest is the entity.*"[54]

Since an institutional prison reform case is a suit, not against the individual defendant, who may very well be powerless when it comes to obtaining funding to remedy the unconstitutional conditions, but is instead a suit against the state, which does have the authority to allocate the funds, the defense should not be available to excuse noncompliance with Eighth Amendment

---

[52]See, e.g., Alberti v. Sheriff of Harris County, Tex., 978 F.2d 893, 895 (5th Cir. 1992) ("How the Supreme Court will develop the funding defense to Eighth Amendment violations is not certain."). See also Russell W. Gray, Wilson v. Seiter, Defining the Components of and Proposing A Direction for Eighth Amendment Prison Condition Law, 41 Amer U L Rev 1339, 1382 (1992) (noting that the Supreme Court's flirting with this issue in Wilson, "is both surprising and troubling").

[53]Kentucky v. Graham, 473 U.S. 159, 105 S. Ct. 3099, 87 L. Ed. 2d 114 (1985).

[54]*Id.* at 165-66 (emphasis supplied). See also Will v. Michigan Dept. of State Police, 491 U.S. 58, 71, 109 S. Ct. 2304, 105 L. Ed. 2d 45 (1989) ("[A] suit against a state official in his or her official capacity is not a suit against the official but rather is a suit against the official's office"); LaMarca v. Turner, 995 F.2d 1526 (11th Cir. 1993) (holding that a suit for injunctive relief against a prison warden is, in reality, a suit against the state).

strictures.

A second reason for rejecting the defense is that it would balkanize the guarantees of the Eighth Amendment, making its meaning vary from state to state. If the Eighth Amendment is measured by each state's ability to pay, prisoners who are lucky enough to be confined in wealthy states would be entitled to greater Eighth Amendment protections than those inmates who have the misfortune of being imprisoned in states that are not as prosperous. The difficulty with this result is that the Eighth Amendment is intended to provide a constitutional minimum for all Americans, not simply those few who find themselves in circumstances where their needs are not as comparatively costly to the local government.

Thus, taken to its logical conclusion, the inadequate funding defense is reduced to a statement that Eighth Amendment rights are worth no more and no less than the state government is willing to pay for. This conclusion would drain the Eighth Amendment's important constitutional protections of much of their meaning.[55] It is hardly remarkable, therefore, that no court has yet been willing to endorse this theory, even after the subject was reopened in *Wilson*.[56] Indeed, in the years since *Wilson*, defendants who have been sued for injunc-

---

[55]See, e.g., Harris v. Thigpen, 941 F.2d 1495, 1509 (11th Cir. 1991) (rejecting an inadequate resources argument by a "poor state" because it could be used to deny inmates' basic rights).

[56]This is not to say that cost is not relevant in other situations. For example cost plays a role in determining the rights of disabled prisoners to reasonable accommodation under the ADA. See Onishea v. Hopper, 171 F.3d 1289, 162 A.L.R. Fed. 651 (11th Cir. 1999), cert. denied, 528 U.S. 1114, 120 S. Ct. 931, 145 L. Ed. 2d 811 (2000) (hiring of additional prison guards imposed undue burden on state's prison system, and thus was not reasonable accommodation for purposes of challenge to segregated prison programs asserted by inmates who tested positive for human immunodeficiency virus (HIV) under Rehabilitation Act, was not clearly erroneous, given estimated costs of approximately $1.7 million to hire guards needed to prevent high-risk behavior in integrated programs and prison system's financial condition). It

§ 2:15   Rights of Prisoners, Third Edition

tive relief apparently have only very rarely even raised the defense.

Alberti v. Sheriff of Harris County Texas[57] is a case where the defense was raised. There, state officials were sued for failure to accept felons from a county jail system for transfer to the state prison system, thus contributing to the unconstitutional overcrowding of the local jails. The district court directed the state officials to accept these "state ready" prisoners. On appeal, the state officials argued that because the state legislature had not appropriated more funds for prison expansion, it lacked the resources to comply with the constitutional directive. While recognizing that the Supreme Court's discussion of the defense leaves "open how difficulty in funding might negate the intent requirement [of the Eighth Amendment],"[58] the Court of Appeals did not credit the defense. It noted that the evidence of an absence of funding was equivocal, since the state at earlier times in the litigation had pointed to other issues as the cause for its unwillingness to accept "state ready" prisoners. Moreover, the court indicated that the decree could be complied with, if necessary, without expenditure of funds by releasing prisoners (as

---

also plays a role in damages cases where an individual defendant is sued. There is some authority that if the defendant can demonstrate that he has no power to remedy the problem complained of, this will constitute a good faith defense to the action. See, e.g., Wilson v. Blankenship, 163 F.3d 1284 (11th Cir. 1998) (wardens of city jail did not have authority or ability to provide jail with law library and exercise area, as required to support federal pretrial detainee's § 1983 claim that lack of law library and jail violated his constitutional rights of access to courts and due process, where federal pretrial detainees were housed at city jail pursuant to intergovernmental agreement between city and marshals service, wardens' duty with respect to pretrial detainee was to administer jail pursuant to agreement, marshals service was aware of lack of exercise space, and wardens had no ability to cause appropriation of funds to provide law library).

[57]Alberti v. Sheriff of Harris County, Tex., 978 F.2d 893 (5th Cir. 1992).

[58]*Id.* at 895.

unpalatable and as unnecessary as that might be).[59] If nothing else, *Alberti* demonstrates that courts are not eager to embrace the limited funds defense.[60] The Supreme Court itself has suggested that the *dicta* in *Wilson* may open a road that it does not wish to travel. In *Rufo v. Inmates of Suffolk County Jail*,[61] decided the term after *Wilson,* the Court observed that "[f]inancial constraints may not be used to justify the creation or perpetuation of constitutional violations. . . ."[62] If this is a signal, then it is one that the Court does not welcome this defense.

---

[59]*Id.* In a number of cases courts have fashioned remedies in a manner which may make the defense difficult to assert. Those cases have essentially said that the defendants are not being forced to expend funds to remedy conditions. They are merely being told that if they choose to have a prison system they must comply with the terms of the constitution. See, e.g., Rhem v. Malcolm, 507 F.2d 333 (2d Cir. 1974). Whether this approach runs afoul of the PLRA proscription against prison release orders has not been tested.

[60]See also LaMarca v. Turner, 995 F.2d 1526 (11th Cir. 1993) (holding that the defendant did have the means available to avoid constitutional injury and therefore the defense was not properly asserted); Carty v. Farrelly, 957 F. Supp. 727, 22 A.D.D. 333 (D. V.I. 1997) (rejecting a defense of inadequate resources on the grounds that insufficient resources cannot justify the perpetuation of constitutional violations and that defendants had significant sources of money under their control that they failed to use).

[61]Rufo v. Inmates of Suffolk County Jail, 502 U.S. 367, 112 S. Ct. 748, 116 L. Ed. 2d 867, 21 Fed. R. Serv. 3d 737 (1992).

[62]*Id.* at 764. Lower courts, as well, even after *Wilson,* are on record as rejecting the defense. See, e.g., Stone v. City and County of San Francisco, 968 F.2d 850, 24 Fed. R. Serv. 3d 98 (9th Cir. 1992) ("federal courts have repeatedly held that financial constraints do not allow states to deprive persons of their constitutional rights"); U.S. v. State of Ill., 803 F. Supp. 1338 (N.D. Ill. 1992) (rejecting the argument).

Remedies

Even if corrections officials are willing to cooperate with a court,[63] effectuating change may not prove easy. If institutional reform suits require a great amount of preparation on the part of litigants and judicial investment of considerable time at the liability stage, they also, when successful, tax the judicial ingenuity of the court that must fashion a remedy. The issue of remedies raises many thorny problems, both from legal and practical perspectives.[64] These are subjects that require extensive discussion that is beyond the scope of this text.[65] For the purposes of providing merely an overview of this important subject, however, it is worth discuss-

---

[63]Often a court order in these cases is issued as a consent decree without full formal litigation at the liability stage. The enforceability of these consent judgments and the new rules covering them are discussed in the chapter on the PLRA. See Ch 16.

[64]See, generally, Susan L. Rhodes, Prison Reform and Prison Life: Four Books on the Process of Court-Ordered Change, 26 Law & Socy Rev 189 (1992); Herbert A. Eastman, Triumph of the Prison: The True Limits of Prison Reform Litigation, 20 Toledo L Rev 69 (1989); Morris Lasker, Judicial Supervision of Institutional Reform, 5 Crim Just Ethics 2 (1986); David Rudenstine, Institutional Injunctions, 4 Cardoza L Rev 611 (1983); Gary R. Terrill & Terrill L. Unruh, Note, Eighth Amendment Challenges to Conditions of Confinement: State Prison Reform by Federal Judicial Decree, 18 Washburn LJ 288 (1979); H. Mary McKeown & William M. Midyette, III, Comment, Cruel But Not so Unusual Punishment: The Role of the Federal Judiciary in State Prison Reform, 7 Cumb L Rev 31 (1976).

[65]See, generally, Susan L. Rhodes, Prison Reform and Prison Life: Four Books on the Process of Court-Ordered Change, 26 Law & Socy Rev 189 (1992); Herbert A. Eastman, Triumph of the Prison: The True Limits of Prison Reform Litigation, 20 Toledo L Rev 69 (1989); Morris Lasker, Judicial Supervision of Institutional Reform, 5 Crim Just Ethics 2 (1986); David Rudenstine, Institutional Injunctions, 4 Cardoza L Rev 611 (1983); Gary R. Terrill & Terrill L. Unruh, Note, Eighth Amendment Challenges to Conditions of Confinement: State Prison Reform by Federal Judicial Decree, 18 Washburn LJ 288 (1979); H. Mary McKeown & William M. Midyette, III, Comment, Cruel But Not so Unusual Punishment: The Role of the Federal Judiciary in State Prison Reform, 7

ing two critical topics: (1) the standards for fashioning injunctive relief and (2) the remedies for violation of a court order.

Standards for Fashioning Injunctive Relief

Courts, having found a violation, historically have had broad powers to ensure that the unconstitutional condition is remedied. In the words of the Supreme Court, "[t]he controlling principle consistently expounded in our holdings is that the scope of the remedy is determined by the nature and extent of the constitutional violation."[66] To be sure, the remedy must be tailored to the constitutional violation. This concept is now embedded by Congress in the Prison Reform Litigation Act, which codified this basic constitutional law doctrine.[67]

The remedy stage, however, does not provide an excuse for a federal judge to undertake managing the day-to-day affairs of the prison.[68]

The United States Supreme Court has cautioned that "one of the most important considerations governing the exercise of equitable power is a proper respect for the integrity and function of local government

---

Cumb L Rev 31 (1976). Future additions to this text may address these issues.

[66]Milliken v. Bradley, 418 U.S. 717, 744, 94 S. Ct. 3112, 41 L. Ed. 2d 1069 (1974). See also Hutto v. Finney, 437 U.S. 678, 687 n9, 98 S. Ct. 2565, 57 L. Ed. 2d 522 (1978).

[67]The Prison Reform Litigation Act provides that judicial relief must "extend no further than necessary to correct the violation of the Federal right. . . .The court shall not grant or approve any prospective relief unless the court finds that such relief is narrowly tailored, extends no further than necessary to correct the violation of the federal right and is the least intrusive means necessary to correct the violation of the Federal right. . . ." 18 U.S.C. § 3626(a)(1). The PLRA is discussed in Ch 16.

[68]See, e.g., Inmates of Occoquan v. Barry, 844 F.2d 828, 841 (D.C. Cir. 1988).

institutions."[69] The concern is particularly acute in prison cases. The Supreme Court more than once has emphasized that prison administration is an important state and local concern and moreover, that "the problems of prisons in America are complex and intractable and . . . not readily susceptible of resolution by decree."[70]

Nevertheless, having found a constitutional violation, "the scope of [a court's] equitable powers to remedy past wrongs is broad, for breadth and flexibility are inherent in equitable powers."[71] The question is what technique works best to accomplish this result and to honor the principles of federalism and comity? The cases reveal three basic approaches.

In *Holt v. Sarver,* the first of the totality suits, the court simply instructed the defendants to begin improving conditions and to file periodic progress reports.[72]

The result was a series of hearings over the next several years, all of which resulted in findings of continued constitutional violations.[73] Seven years after the original decision, the district and appellate courts unhappily concluded that the unconstitutional conditions had not

---

[69]Missouri v. Jenkins, 495 U.S. 33, 110 S. Ct. 1651, 1663, 109 L. Ed. 2d 31, 59 Ed. Law Rep. 298 (1990).

[70]Rhodes v. Chapman, 452 U.S. 337, 101 S. Ct. 2392, 2401, 69 L. Ed. 2d 59 (1981), quoting Procunier v. Martinez, 416 U.S. 396, 94 S. Ct. 1800, 1807, 40 L. Ed. 2d 224 (1974).

[71]Swann v. Charlotte-Mecklenburg Bd. of Ed., 402 U.S. 1, 15, 91 S. Ct. 1267, 28 L. Ed. 2d 554 (1971).

[72]Holt v. Sarver, 300 F. Supp. 825 (E.D. Ark. 1969) (original holding of unconstitutionality in the litigation).

[73]Holt v. Sarver, 309 F. Supp. 362 (E.D. Ark. 1970), aff'd and remanded, 442 F.2d 304 (8th Cir. 1971); Holt v. Hutto, 363 F. Supp. 194 (E.D. Ark. 1973), judgment rev'd, 505 F.2d 194 (8th Cir. 1974); Finney v. Hutto, 410 F. Supp. 251 (E.D. Ark. 1976), judgment aff'd, 548 F.2d 740 (8th Cir. 1977), cert. granted, 434 U.S. 901, 98 S. Ct. 295, 54 L. Ed. 2d 187 (1977) and judgment aff'd, 437 U.S. 678, 98 S. Ct. 2565, 57 L. Ed. 2d 522 (1978) (implied overruling recognized by, Wolpoff v. Cuomo, 792 F. Supp. 964 (S.D. N.Y. 1992)).

yet been fully rectified.[74] It was not until 1982 that compliance with the decree was achieved.[75]

The second approach is at the other end of the spectrum. It is illustrated by *Pugh v. Locke*.[76] In that case, instead of allowing corrections officials a free hand to achieve constitutional standards, the court set forth detailed minimum standards to be met.[77]

The third approach, which has the endorsement of the Supreme Court, is described in the Court's opinion in *Lewis v. Casey*.[78] There, in the process of disapproving a court order that was overly intrusive, Justice Scalia, speaking for the Court, explained that district courts must exercise care in fashioning relief to avoid intruding on the need and responsibility for prison officials to manage their own affairs.[79] The way to accomplish this result, Justice Scalia stated, is to give the state "the first opportunity to correct the errors made

---

[74]Finney v. Hutto, 410 F. Supp. 251 (E.D. Ark. 1976), judgment aff'd, 548 F.2d 740 (8th Cir. 1977), cert. granted, 434 U.S. 901, 98 S. Ct. 295, 54 L. Ed. 2d 187 (1977) and judgment aff'd, 437 U.S. 678, 98 S. Ct. 2565, 57 L. Ed. 2d 522 (1978) (implied overruling recognized by, Wolpoff v. Cuomo, 792 F. Supp. 964 (S.D. N.Y. 1992)).

[75]Finney v. Mabry, 546 F. Supp. 628 (E.D. Ark. 1982) (finding compliance and relinquishing jurisdiction).

[76]Pugh v. Locke, 406 F. Supp. 318 (M.D. Ala. 1976), judgment aff'd and remanded, 559 F.2d 283 (5th Cir. 1977), cert. granted in part, judgment rev'd in part, 438 U.S. 781, 98 S. Ct. 3057, 57 L. Ed. 2d 1114 (1978).

[77]Pugh v. Locke, 406 F. Supp. 318, 332-37(M.D. Ala. 1976), judgment aff'd and remanded, 559 F.2d 283 (5th Cir. 1977), cert. granted in part, judgment rev'd in part, 438 U.S. 781, 98 S. Ct. 3057, 57 L. Ed. 2d 1114 (1978).

[78]Lewis v. Casey, 518 U.S. 343, 116 S. Ct. 2174, 135 L. Ed. 2d 606 (1996). The Lewis court also warned that courts must not "in the name of the Constitution, becom[e] . . . enmeshed in the minutiae of prison operations." *Id.* at 362 (quoting Bell v. Wolfish, 441 U.S. 520, 562, 99 S. Ct. 1861, 1886, 60 L. Ed. 2d 447 (1979)).

[79]*Id.* at 2185.

§ 2:15

in the internal administration of their prisons."[80] The court cited *Bounds v. Smith*[81] as an example of a case in which the district court followed this approach. In that case, rather than " 'dictat[ing] precisely what course the State should follow,' " the district court directed prison officials to devise and present to the court a plan for addressing the unconstitutional condition or conditions identified in the court's opinion.[82] Under this approach, the district court reviews the plan, obtains the reactions of the plaintiffs to it, and unless it is completely unresponsive approves it as is or with modifications. This approach, Justice Scalia added, "scrupulously respected the limits on [the judiciary's] role," by "not . . . thrust[ing] itself into prison administration" and instead permitting "[p]rison administrators [to] exercis[e] wide discretion within the bounds of constitutional requirements."[83]

In addition to entering a decree, courts have the authority to appoint persons to help monitor compli-

---

[80]*Id.*, quoting Preiser v. Rodriguez, 411 U.S. 475, 492, 93 S. Ct. 1827, 1837-1838, 36 L. Ed. 2d 439 (1973).

[81]Bounds v. Smith, 430 U.S. 817, 97 S. Ct. 1491, 52 L. Ed. 2d 72 (1977).

[82]*Id.* at 818.

[83]Lewis v. Casey, 518 U.S. 343, 116 S. Ct. 2174, 2185, 135 L. Ed. 2d 606 (1996). quoting Bounds v. Smith, 430 U.S. 817, 97 S. Ct. 1491, 1500, 52 L. Ed. 2d 72 (1977). Lower courts have followed this approach even before *Lewis*. Several circuit courts urged district courts to allow the defendants to propose their own detailed plan for obtaining compliance and to defer to it rather than fashioning their own, unless the defendants' plan is deficient. See, e.g., Dean v. Coughlin, 804 F.2d 207 (2d Cir. 1986); Toussaint v. McCarthy, 801 F.2d 1080 (9th Cir. 1986). For decisions since taking this tack, see, e.g., Johnson v. Levine, 588 F.2d 1378 (4th Cir. 1978); Newman v. State of Ala., 466 F. Supp. 628 (M.D. Ala. 1979) (court ordered Alabama to remedy Eighth Amendment violations, and only imposed its own specific remedy after the state had failed to implement its own plan after six years); Goff v. Nix, 113 F.3d 887 (8th Cir. 1997) (court reversed trial court's injunction ordering prison to allow sending of interprison legal mail between inmates, as the ban on such correspondence served a valid penological interest, but the court of appeals held that the prison must formulate a

ance with the decree and may also give them other specific enforcement powers.[84] Courts have also made use of remedial mechanisms, including reporting requirements.[85]

Remedies for violation of a court order

Securing a court order to change conditions found to be unconstitutional is no easy task. However, obtaining the order is often "just the beginning of the litigation battle."[86] What follows is the difficult period of obtaining compliance with a decree that may require extensive changes. There is no magic in how to best achieve this result. While achieving compliance with a court order is a complicated art, in this phase of the litigation courts are not powerless. They have a wide arsenal of enforcement tools to use to achieve the goal of compliance with

---

procedure by which inmates could return legal materials to their owners).

[84]See, e.g., Ruiz v. Estelle, 679 F.2d 1115, 10 Fed. R. Evid. Serv. 1483 (5th Cir. 1982), amended in part, vacated in part on other grounds, 688 F.2d 266 (5th Cir. 1982); Palmigiano v. Garrahy, 443 F. Supp. 956, 989 (D.R.I. 1977); Jones v. Wittenberg, 73 F.R.D. 82 (N.D. Ohio 1976), conformed to, 440 F. Supp. 60 (N.D. Ohio 1977). But see Tillery v. Owens, 719 F. Supp. 1256 (W.D. Pa. 1989), order aff'd, 907 F.2d 418 (3d Cir. 1990) (declining to appoint a monitor). See, generally, Samuel J. Brakel, "Mastering" the Legal Access Rights of Prison Inmates, 12 New Eng J on Crim & Civ Confinement 1 (1986); Vincent Nathan, The Use of Masters in Institutional Reform Litigation, 10 Toledo L Rev 419 (1979); Susan P. Sturm, Note, "Mastering" Intervention in Prisons, 88 Yale LJ 1062 (1979). The PLRA, however, has imposed some limitation on the way in which courts can use Special Masters. This topic is discussed in the chapter on the PLRA. See Ch 16.

[85]Note, Implementation Problems in Institutional Reform Litigation, 91 Harv L Rev 428, 441 (1979); Michael S. Lottman, Enforcement of Judicial Decrees: Now Comes the Hard Part, 1 Mental Disability L Rep 69, 70 (1976).

[86]Lynn S. Branham, The Law Of Sentencing Corrections and Prisoners' Rights 369 (1998).

§ 2:15　　　　　　　　Rights of Prisoners, Third Edition

their orders.[87] Among the remedies that courts have made use of in this connection in injunction cases is the civil contempt remedy.[88] In addition, in prison institutional reform litigation, courts have ordered, *inter alia,*

---

[87]To avoid federal court involvement in achieving compliance, some states have enacted legislation or agreed in consent decrees to establish independent oversight bodies to assist in achieving compliance with constitutional standards. For example, in Florida, to solve the problem of federal involvement in state prisons,the state legislature enacted Fla Stat Ann §§ 945.602-.6036. The statute provides for the creation of a Correctional Medical Authority to monitor prison compliance with constitutional standards. Celestineo v. Singletary, 147 F.R.D. 258 (M.D. Fla. 1993). See also Austin v. Pennsylvania Dept of Corrections, 876 F Supp 1437 (ED Pa 1995) (consent agreement which provided that prison was to establish a quality assurance program to monitor the prison's progress in implementing a medical delivery system including a peer review committee that would be comprised of physicians from outside the prison community).

[88]See, e.g., Glover v. Johnson, 199 F3d 301 (6th Cir. 1999) (upholding a contempt fine of $385,000 at a rate of $5,000 per day for failure to provide programming for women prisoners equivalent to that provided to male inmates); Turay v. Seling, 108 F. Supp. 2d 1148 (W.D. Wash. 2000), aff'd in part, rev'd in part on other grounds, 12 Fed. Appx. 618 (9th Cir. 2001) (holding defendants in contempt for failing to comply with terms of order for improving services to "sexually violent predators" and noting that the sanction has resulted in a "genuine and sustained effort to comply with the decree."); Carty v. Farrelly, 957 F. Supp. 727, 22 A.D.D. 333 (D.V.I. 1997) (holding defendants in contempt for not complying with a court order to improve conditions at a prison in the U.S. Virgin Islands); Mobile County Jail Inmates v. Purvis, 581 F. Supp. 222 (S.D. Ala. 1984) (finding defendants in contempt and imposing a $5,000 per day fine; subsequent opinion orders that $2 million in contempt fines be used to establish a bail fund); Benjamin v. Sielaff, 752 F. Supp. 140 (S.D. N.Y. 1990) (contempt order); Palmigiano v. DiPrete, 710 F Supp 875 (DRI 1989) (finding defendants in contempt and describing steps to be taken to purge the finding). See also Lynn S. Branham, The Law Of Sentencing Corrections and Prisoners' Rights 369 (1998) ("One of the ways in which the plaintiff may seek to secure the defendants' compliance is by asking the court to hold the defendants in contempt."). For a discussion of the law of civil contempt, see John Boston & Daniel E. Manville, Prisoner Self-Help Litigation Manual, 642-44 (1995).

§ 2:15

the construction of new facilities, provision of new programs, closing of facilities,[89] and even, in extreme cases, the release of prisoners.[90] The later remedy is now subject to special provisions of the PLRA.[91] Once compliance with the order is achieved then judicial supervision comes to an end.[92] The strategy of determining which of the available devises to use and when to

---

[89]For cases in which courts have ordered that portions of penal institutions be closed, see, e.g., Inmates of Suffolk County Jail v. Eisenstadt, 360 F. Supp. 676 (D. Mass. 1973), judgment aff'd, 494 F.2d 1196 (1st Cir. 1974); Williams v. Wainwright, 350 F. Supp. 33 (M.D. Fla. 1972).

[90]See, e.g., McMurry v. Phelps, 533 F. Supp. 742 (W.D. La. 1982) (overruled on other grounds by, Thorne v. Jones, 765 F.2d 1270 (5th Cir. 1985); Duran v. Elrod, 713 F.2d 292 (7th Cir. 1983) (upholding release of low-bail pretrial detainees to reach population cap); Jackson v. Gardner, 639 F. Supp. 1005 (E.D. Tenn. 1986). See, generally, Edward A. Hopson, Note, Courts, Corrections and the Eighth Amendment: Encouraging Prison Reform by Releasing Inmates, 44 S Cal L Rev 1060 (1971); Kim R. Tulsky, Comment, After the Stalemate: Releasing Prisoners to Compel State Prison Reform, 56 Temple LQ 95 (1983). See also Natl Advisory Commn on Criminal Justice Standards and Goals, Corrections Standard 2.5 (1973) (institution that does not meet state health and sanitation laws should be deemed a nuisance and abated). An alternative approach is to bar the prison from accepting any new inmates that would result in a population in excess of the maximum set by the court. See Ruiz v. Estelle, 679 F.2d 1115, 1148, 10 Fed. R. Evid. Serv. 1483 (5th Cir. 1982), amended in part, vacated in part on other grounds, 688 F.2d 266 (5th Cir. 1982); Badgley v. Varelas, 729 F.2d 894 (2d Cir. 1984).

[91]For a discussion of the PLRA provisions dealing with prisoner release orders see Ch 16.

[92]See, e.g., Collins v. Thompson, 8 F.3d 657 (9th Cir. 1993) (refusing to continue court monitoring after defendants had achieved compliance with the terms of the decree). See also Grubbs v. Bradley, 821 F. Supp. 496 (M.D. Tenn. 1993) (noting dramatic improvements to the Tennessee prison system and terminating the decree after finding that the defendants had achieved compliance with constitutional standards). Under the PLRA it is possible that judicial supervision might end even before that time. See Ch 16 for a discussion of the PLRA's provision on this subject.

§ 2:15   RIGHTS OF PRISONERS, THIRD EDITION

use it has engendered a great deal of discussion.[93] Suffice it to say here that judicial ingenuity as well as the creativity of counsel is called for in making these judgments. The effort is surely worthwhile. As one observer remarked:

> Even skeptical observers . . . have concluded that the quality of prisoners' lives has been improved by [this] remedial litigation. Inmates' housing, health care, nutrition and personal safety have gotten better as a result of judicial decisions, and in some states the changes have been dramatic.
>
> These benefits are important and have saved the lives and health of many prisoners, to the ultimate benefit of society generally.[94]

---

[93]See, e.g., Michael B. Mushlin, Unsafe Havens: the Case for Constitutional Protection of Foster Children from Abuse and Neglect, 23 Harv CR-CL L Rev 199, 271-80 (1988) (discussing strategies for implementing an institutional reform decree). See also Robert E. Buckholz, Jr et al, Special Project, The Remedial Process Institutional Reform Litigation, 78 Colum L Rev 784 (1978); Note, Implementation Problems in Institutional Reform Litigation, 91 Harv L Rev 428, 441 (1979).

[94]Susan L. Rhodes, Prison Reform and Prison Life: Four Books on the Process of Court-Ordered Change, 26 Law & Socy Rev 189, 211-12 (1992).

Chapter 3

The Eighth Amendment: Medical Care[1]

Research References

Prisoners and the Law, Ch 7, 14A, 14B, 17C, 17E

Am. Jur. 2d, Penal and Correctional Institutions §§ 91 to 97, 116

1 Americans with Disabilities: Practice and Compliance Manual, §§ 1:186 to 1:191

Prisons ⚖17(2); Sentencing and Punishment ⚖1546, 1547

A.L.R. Index: Cruel and Unusual Punishment; Prisons and Prisoners

Prisoner's right to die or refuse medical treatment, 66 A.L.R. 5th 111

Actions Brought Under Americans with Disabilities Act, 42 U.S.C.A. §§ 12101 et seq.—Supreme Court Cases, 173 A.L.R. Fed. 639

Rights of prisoners under Americans with Disabilities Act and Rehabilitation Act, 163 A.L.R. Fed. 285

Federal constitutional and statutory claims by HIV-positive inmates as to medical treatment or conditions of confinement, 162 A.L.R. Fed. 181

Propriety and construction of "totality of conditions" analysis in federal court's consideration of Eighth Amendment challenge to prison conditions, 85 A.L.R. Fed. 750

---

[1]This chapter was researched and written by Chris Hansen for the second edition. It has been revised for the third edition of this book by Michael B. Mushlin with assistance from Sara Courtman and Victoria Handy.

> **KeyCite®:** Cases and other legal materials listed in KeyCite Scope can be researched through West Group's KeyCite service on Westlaw®. Use KeyCite to check citations for form, parallel references, prior and later history, and comprehensive citator information, including citations to other decisions and secondary materials.

§ 3:1 Introduction
§ 3:2 *Estelle v Gamble*
§ 3:3 Rights of Pretrial Detainees to Medical Care
§ 3:4 What is a "Serious Medical Need"?
§ 3:5 Initial Screening When Entering Facility
§ 3:6 Emergency Care and Sick Call Procedures
§ 3:7 Periodic Examinations and Necessary Treatment
§ 3:8 Facilities and Equipment
§ 3:9 Staff
§ 3:10 Records
§ 3:11 Dental Care
§ 3:12 Eye Care
§ 3:13 Diet
§ 3:14 Health Needs of Women
§ 3:15 Mental Health
§ 3:16 Suicide
§ 3:17 Drug and Alcohol Treatment and Treatment for Tobacco Addiction
§ 3:18 Disabled Prisoners
§ 3:19 Prisoners and the Americans With Disabilities Act
§ 3:20 AIDS
§ 3:21 Transsexuals
§ 3:22 Experimentation and Research
§ 3:23 Right to Refuse Treatment
§ 3:24 Prison Co-Payment Plans For Medical Care

§ 3:1 Introduction

One of the most common complaints of inmates is that they are being provided with inadequate health care.¹ Inmates, like free individuals, have health needs; however, at least two features distinguish the provision of health care to inmates. First, inmates cannot provide for their own medical care.² They are wholly dependent on prison or jail officials for that care. "An individual incarcerated . . . becomes both vulnerable *and* dependent upon the state . . . denial of necessary medical attention may well result in disabilities beyond that contemplated by the incarceration itself . . . *restrained by the authority of the state,* the individual cannot himself seek medical aid."³ The Supreme Court has noted that "[a]n inmate must rely on prison authorities to treat his medical needs; if the authorities fail to do so, those needs will not be met."⁴ At the most simple level, an inmate cannot self-treat by calling in sick, changing a diet, or purchasing and using simple reme-

---

[Section 3:1]

[1]For this section, see, generally, Eric Neisser, Is There A Doctor In The Joint? The Search for Constitutional Standards for Prison Health Care, 63 Va L Rev 921 (1977); see also Ira P. Robbins, Managed Healthcare in Prisons as Cruel and Unusual Punishment, 90 J Crim L & Criminology 195 (Fall 1999) (regarding the use of managed care in prisons and arguing that the use of managed care in certain instances rises to the level of deliberate indifference, thereby violating the Eighth Amendment.); Michael C. Friedman, Comment, Cruel and Unusual Punishment in the Provision of Prison Medical Care: Challenging the Deliberate Indifference Standard, 45 Vand L Rev 921 (May 1992); Damon Martin, Comment, State Prisoner's Rights To Medical Treatment: Merely Elusive or Wholly Illusory, 8 Black LJ 427 (1983); Wendy L. Adams, Comment, Inadequate Medical Treatment of State Prisoners: Cruel and Unusual Punishment, 27 Am U L Rev 92 (1977).

[2]Eric Neisser, Is There A Doctor In The Joint? The Search for Constitutional Standards for Prison Health Care, 63 Va L Rev 921, 938-39 (1977).

[3]Fitzke v. Shappell, 468 F.2d 1072, 1076 (6th Cir. 1972) (emphasis in original).

[4]Estelle v. Gamble, 429 U.S. 97, 103, 97 S. Ct. 285, 50 L. Ed. 2d 251 (1976); West v. Atkins, 487 U.S. 42, 54-55, 108 S. Ct. 2250, 101 L. Ed. 2d 40 (1988).

§ 3:1 RIGHTS OF PRISONERS, THIRD EDITION

dies such as aspirin, cold pills, laxatives, or bandages.[5] More significantly, the inmate cannot choose a doctor or form of treatment. Because inmates cannot go to the emergency room of a local hospital, inmates will have medical needs that must be met on an emergency basis and around the clock. Prohibitions on the individual possession of drugs or medical devices, in addition to other security restrictions regulating medical care, result in the need for constant medical care.

Second, there is substantial evidence that inmates have a greater need for medical services than non-inmates.[6] One recent study reported that nearly a third of all inmates reported suffering from some physical or mental impairment. The percentage of inmates with mental health problems was estimated at 16.2% in 2000 by the Department of Justice prison census.[7] As many

---

[5]Todaro v. Ward, 431 F. Supp. 1129, 1133 (S.D. N.Y. 1977), judgment aff'd, 565 F.2d 48 (2d Cir. 1977) and aff'd, 652 F.2d 54 (2d Cir. 1981).

[6]Medical Problems of Inmates in 1997, www.ojp.usdoj.gov/bjs/pub/ascii/mpi97.txt (2002); See also Eric Neisser, Is There A Doctor In The Joint? The Search for Constitutional Standards for Prison Health Care, 63 Va L Rev 921, 942-46 (1977); Tillery v. Owens, 719 F. Supp. 1256, 1290 (W.D. Pa. 1989), order aff'd, 907 F.2d 418 (3d Cir. 1990) (greater incidence due to smoking, alcoholism, and drug addiction); Todaro v. Ward, 431 F. Supp. 1129, 1134-35 (S.D. N.Y. 1977), judgment aff'd, 565 F.2d 48 (2d Cir. 1977) and aff'd, 652 F.2d 54 (2d Cir. 1981).

[7]Mental Health Treatment in State Prisons in 2000, http://www.ojp.usdoj.gov/bjs/pub/pdf/mhtsp00.pdf (2002). See also Richard Freeman & Ronald Roesch, Mental Disorder and the Criminal Justice System: A Review, 12 Int J of L & Psych 105, 109 (1989) (10% have "major mental disorder" on arrival); Joel Droshin & Henry Steadman, Chronically Mentally Ill Inmates: The Wrong Concept for the Right Services, 12 Intl JL & Psych 203 (1989) (15% "severely" or " significantly" psychiatrically disabled and 25% need mental health services); Inmates of Allegheny County Jail v. Pierce, 612 F.2d 754 (3d Cir. 1979) (15-20% had psychiatric problems); Williams v. Edwards, 547 F.2d 1206 (5th Cir. 1977) (40% had psychiatric problems); Laaman v. Helgemoe, 437 F. Supp. 269 (D.N.H. 1977) (40% needed mental health services);

MEDICAL CARE § 3:1

as 70 percent have histories of drug or alcohol abuse.[8] Acquired Immune Deficiency Syndrome (AIDS) and tuberculosis (TB) are quite common in prisons and jails. The rate of HIV/AIDS infection in prison is between five and twelve times the rate of infection in the general population.[9] It was estimated in 1992 that approximately 23 percent of New York's prisoners "are infected with active or inactive TB."[10]

While prisoners enter prison with preexisting medical problems prison conditions, such as overcrowding, inadequate nutrition and exercise, and poor sanitation, will create or aggravate medical conditions.[11] A Department of Justice study in 1997 found that over 318,000 inmates reported suffering some form of injury since they were admitted to prison.[12] In addition, "incarceration appears to intensify normal concerns for bodily

---

Inmates of Allegheny County Jail v. Peirce, 487 F. Supp. 638 (W.D. Pa. 1980). For a critique of the health care services delivered to prisoners suffering from mental health disorders, see T. Howard Stone, Therapeutic Implications of Incarceration for Persons With Severe Mental Disorders: Searching for Rational Health Policy, 24 Am J Crim L 283 (1997).

[8]Palmigiano v. Garrahy, 443 F. Supp. 956 (D.R.I. 1977); Colburn v. Upper Darby Tp., 946 F.2d 1017, 1026 (3d Cir. 1991) ($\frac{2}{3}$ of all admitted to local jails were intoxicated).

[9]The Osborne Association: AIDS in Prison Project, www.osborneny.org/health_services.htm (2002); AIDS and HIV in Prisons and Jails, 1999, www.ojp.usdoj.gov/bjs/pub/pdf/hivpj99.pdf (2002).

[10]Correctional Assn of New York, Correctional Assn Reporter, Nov, 1992, at 4.

[11]Wendy L. Adams, Comment, Inadequate Medical Treatment of State Prisoners: Cruel and Unusual Punishment?, 27 Am U L Rev 92, n1 (1977); Lightfoot v. Walker, 486 F. Supp. 504, 511 (S.D. Ill. 1980).

[12]Medical Problems of Inmates in 1997, www.ojp.usdoj.gov/bjs/pub/ascii/mpi97.txt (2002); Eric Neisser, Is There A Doctor In The Joint? The Search for Constitutional Standards for Prison Health Care, 63 Va L Rev 921, 942 n48 (1977) (noting that 60% of inmates in New York City Jails were diagnosed on admission as having at least one medical problem; quoting Novick et al, Health Status of the New York City Prison Population, 15 Med Care 205 (1977)).

§ 3:1   Rights of Prisoners, Third Edition

well-being and integrity" due to its boredom and trauma.[13]

Historically, inmate medical care has been inadequate,[14] and thus case law is replete with examples of both individual stories[15] and prison medical care systems[16] that would shock even those most hostile to

---

[13] Eric Neisser, Is There A Doctor In The Joint? The Search for Constitutional Standards for Prison Health Care, 63 Va L Rev 921, 942-43 (1977).

[14] Wendy L. Adams, Comment, Inadequate Medical Treatment of State Prisoners: Cruel and Unusual Punishment?, 27 Am U L Rev 92, n.1 (1977). See also Jennifer Wynn, Health Care in New York State Prisons, A Report of Findings and Recommendations by the Prison Visiting Committee of the Correctional Association of New York (2000) (discussing such problems in New York as lack of oversight of medical care, lack of a uniform, statewide quality assurance program, non-competitive salaries, under-qualified doctors, unevenness in the care of HIV/AIDS infected inmates, inadequate services for Spanish-speaking inmates, and insufficient discharge planning).

[15] See, e.g., Ellen Barry, Recent Developments-Pregnant Prisoners, 12 Harv Women's LJ 189 (1980); Newman v. State of Ala., 349 F. Supp. 278, 284-85 (M.D. Ala. 1972), aff'd in part, 503 F.2d 1320 (5th Cir. 1974) and judgment vacated in part on other grounds, 522 F.2d 71 (5th Cir. 1975) (inmate who couldn't eat was given no intravenous food and died; quadriplegic inmate died of infections when dressings not changed); Lightfoot v. Walker, 486 F. Supp. 504, 518-21 (S.D. Ill. 1980) (inmates who died due to inadequate care); Ancata v. Prison Health Services, Inc., 769 F.2d 700, 704 (11th Cir. 1985) (inmate died because prison officials refused to provide access to specialists thought necessary until plaintiff agreed to pay for them).

[16] See, e.g., Ramos v. Lamm, 485 F. Supp. 122 (D. Colo. 1979), judgment aff'd in part, set aside in part on other grounds, 639 F.2d 559 (10th Cir. 1980); Todaro v Ward, 431 F Supp 1224 (SDNY), affd, 565 F2d 48 (2d Cir 1977); Battle v. Anderson, 376 F. Supp. 402 (E.D. Okla. 1974), judgment aff'd in part, rev'd in part on other grounds, 993 F.2d 1551 (10th Cir. 1993); Laaman v. Helgemoe, 437 F. Supp. 269 (D.N.H. 1977); Holt v. Sarver, 309 F. Supp. 362 (E.D. Ark. 1970), aff'd and remanded, 442 F.2d 304 (8th Cir. 1971).

MEDICAL CARE § 3:1

rights of prisoners.[17] Institutional concerns, including security and funding, often adversely affect the adequacy of medical care.[18]

There are many legal approaches to inadequate medical care in a prison setting. Medical malpractice remains a tort for which inmates may seek damages in state courts.[19] Many states have statutes, regulations, or policies requiring adequate medical care, which can

---

[17]Rhodes v. Chapman, 452 U.S. 337, 354, 101 S. Ct. 2392, 69 L. Ed. 2d 59 (1981) (Brennan, J, concurring) (judicial opinions in this area do not make pleasant reading). At the time of *Rhodes,* "individual prisons or entire prison systems in at least 24 States ha[d] been declared unconstitutional"), *Id.* at 353 n.1.

[18]West v. Atkins, 487 U.S. 42, 57 n15, 108 S. Ct. 2250, 101 L. Ed. 2d 40 (1988). In addition, class action cases finding prison medical systems inadequate are replete with observations that funding has been inadequate but that lack of funds is no defense to violation of constitutional rights. See, e.g., Gates v. Collier, 501 F.2d 1291, 1319-20 (5th Cir. 1974). See also Ancata v Prison Health Services, Inc., 769 F.2d 700 (11th Cir. 1985) (5%-40% estimates by experts); Newman v. State of Ala., 349 F. Supp. 278, 284 (M.D. Ala. 1972), aff'd in part, 503 F.2d 1320 (5th Cir. 1974) and judgment vacated in part on other grounds, 522 F.2d 71 (5th Cir. 1975). For a discussion on the constitutionality of denying funding for transplants and problems funding prisoner health care needs, see Jessica Wright, Medically Necessary Organ Transplants For Prisoners: Who Is Responsible For Payment? 39 BC L Rev 1175 (1998).

[19]See, e.g., ARA Health Services v. Stitt, 250 Ga. App. 420, 551 S.E.2d 793 (2001), cert. denied, (Nov. 30, 2001) (holding under state law that prison doctor caused inmate "egregious" and "permanent" injuries); Simmons v. City of Philadelphia, 947 F.2d 1042, 21 Fed. R. Serv. 3d 966 (3d Cir. 1991) (jail suicide case in which plaintiffs also prevail on state law claim); Roberts v. City of Troy, 773 F.2d 720 (6th Cir. 1985) (state negligence claims allowed to proceed in prison suicide case); Kanayurak v. North Slope Borough, 677 P.2d 893, 897 (Alaska 1984) ("a jailer owes a duty to the prisoner to exercise reasonable care for the protection of his life and health"); Roy v. Phelps, 488 So. 2d 468 (La. Ct. App. 3d Cir. 1986).

§ 3:1   Rights of Prisoners, Third Edition

form the basis for a state court action.[20] In addition, suits utilizing state constitutional protections, analogous to the federal Constitution, are available in state court.[21]

However, these approaches have not been used very often. There are several reasons for this. First, a number of defenses, including sovereign immunity, civil disability statutes, and budgetary limitations, may be available to defendants, consequently making such state law based cases difficult to win.[22] Even where the plaintiff is successful in persuading a court that a state

---

[20]State statutes are collected in Wendy L. Adams, Comment, Inadequate Medical Treatment of State Prisoners: Cruel and Unusual Punishment?, 27 Am U L Rev 92, 110 n87 (1977); Damon Martin, Comment, State Prisoner's Rights to Medical Treatment: Merely Elusive or Wholly Illusory?, 8 Black LJ 427, 435 n.52 (1983); Anthony L. Paccione, Note, The Federal Judiciary's Role in the Prevention of Communicable Diseases in State Prisons, 12 Ford Urb LJ 873, 889 nn.120-24 (1984); see also West v. Atkins, 487 U.S. 42, 55 n.12, 108 S. Ct. 2250, 101 L. Ed. 2d 40 (1988); Brown v. State, Through Dept. of Correction, 354 So. 2d 633 (La. Ct. App. 1st Cir. 1977). Molton v. City of Cleveland, 839 F.2d 240, 247 (6th Cir. 1988) (jail suicide case where the plaintiffs lost the constitutional claims, but succeeded on the basis of a state law duty "to exercise reasonable care"); U.S. ex rel. Walker v. Fayette County, Pa., 599 F.2d 573 (3d Cir. 1979) (plaintiff prevailed based on state statute); Model Sentencing and Corrections Act § 2-501 (July 2001); Kagan v. State, 221 A.D.2d 7, 646 N.Y.S.2d 336 (2nd Dept. 1996) (court held that the failure of prison medical personnel to properly follow its own protocols (non-discretionary medical standards governing the administration of medical care) were a direct cause of the plaintiff's loss of hearing; accordingly, the court affirmed the court of claims award of $304,000 in damages to the plaintiff); Ramsey v. Schauble, 141 F. Supp. 2d 584 (W.D. N.C. 2001) (federal court exercised supplemental jurisdiction over claim under state statute for treble damages against a jail keeper who intentionally caused plaintiff harm by shutting his finger in a cell window; burden of proof under this state statute was beyond a reasonable doubt, as a guilty finding included a misdemeanor charge).

[21]See, e.g., Smith v. Maloney, 2001 WL 755849 (Mass. Super. Ct. 2001).

[22]Wendy L. Adams, Comment, Inadequate Medical Treatment of State Prisoners: Cruel and Unusual Punishment?, 27 Am U L Rev

MEDICAL CARE § 3:1

statute has been violated, to avoid an injunction a state may simply change the law.[23] In addition, in a damage case under state law, it will ordinarily be difficult for an inmate to show damages caused by lack of employment since the inmate is not employed in free world anyway due to his imprisonment; therefore, only pain and suffering may justify damages.[24] The dearth of state court

---

92, 116-19 (1977); Comment, Prisoner Tort Recovery, 41 U Mo KC 308 (1972); Paxton R. Guymon, Utah Prison Physicians: Can They Commit Malpractice with Immunity or Does Their Official Immunity Violate the Open Courts Clause?, 1997 Utah L Rev 873 (1997). See, e.g., Buffington v. Baltimore County, Md., 913 F.2d 113, 123-26, 17 Fed. R. Serv. 3d 577 (4th Cir. 1990) (jail suicide case in which the court upheld immunity from state law claims).

In Herbert v. District of Columbia, 716 A.2d 196 (D.C. 1998), an inmate sued the District of Columbia, a corporate health care provider, and parties employed by the provider, claiming that she received improper medical treatment. The superior court's granting of a directed verdict for the defendants was reversed by the court of appeals holding that the District's limited obligation under the Eighth Amendment not to inflict cruel and unusual punishment could not be avoided by delegation to an independent contractor. On rehearing en banc, the court of appeals held that there was no evidence that the District failed to carry out its constitutional responsibilities. Further, the District had meaningful responsibilities pursuant to DC Code § 24-442, but it could satisfy these statutory responsibilities by exercising reasonable care in the supervision of its independent contractors, and the inmate did not demonstrate that the district failed to carry out its statutory duties. Accordingly, the District's obligation to exercise reasonable care in providing medical services could be delegated, and the District could not be held liable for medical malpractice committed on the inmate by employees of the independent contractor without proof of negligence on the part of District's officials or employees. The judgment of the trial court was affirmed.

[23]Lightfoot v. Walker, 486 F. Supp. 504, 508 (S.D. Ill. 1980) (court refused to rely solely on state law because "[a] decision predicated solely on state law may give the state the impetus to change that law and thereby perhaps, circumvent the relief, particularly where that relief is prospective and will be awarded to an unfavored, disenfranchised class of persons").

[24]Wendy L. Adams, Comment, Inadequate Medical Treatment of State Prisoners: Cruel and Unusual Punishment?, 27 Am U L Rev

litigation may also be a result of the usual justification given by civil rights lawyers for preferring federal court-that the judges are, on the whole, more competent, more receptive, and more independent. Given the enormous number of cases in this area that are brought by prisoners pro se, it may also simply be a matter of doing things the way they have always been done.

In some circumstances, there are federal statutory approaches available. The Federal Tort Claims Act[25] provides a cause of action against the United States for negligence, including medical negligence.[26] The Americans With Disabilities Act (ADA)[27] prohibits discrimination against handicapped people and applies, in appropriate cases, to inmates.[28] The Rehabilitation Act also prohibits discrimination against handicapped

---

92, 118-19 (1977); Comment, Prisoner Tort Recovery, 41 U Mo KC 308 (1972); Ancata v. Prison Health Services, Inc., 769 F.2d 700, 704 (11th Cir. 1985); Duran v. Anaya, 642 F. Supp. 510 (D.N.M. 1986) (enjoining staff reductions caused by budget cuts).

[25]42 U.S.C. § 2674 (1986).

[26]McNeil v. U.S., 508 U.S. 106, 113 S. Ct. 1980, 124 L. Ed. 2d 21 (1993); Castillo v. U.S., 44 Fed. Appx. 732 (7th Cir. 2002) (prisoner stated a claim for medical malpractice although not for deliberate indifference); U.S. v. Muniz, 374 U.S. 150, 83 S. Ct. 1850, 10 L. Ed. 2d 805 (1963); Henderson v. Harris, 672 F. Supp. 1054 (N.D. Ill. 1987) (Federal Tort Claims Act does not preempt a right to sue under the United States Constitution); Carlson v. Green, 446 U.S. 14, 100 S. Ct. 1468, 64 L. Ed. 2d 15 (1980) (Federal Tort Claims Act does contain a requirement that administrative remedies be exhausted); 28 U.S.C. § 2675(a); Deutsch v. Federal Bureau of Prisons, 737 F. Supp. 261 (S.D. N.Y. 1990), aff'd, 930 F.2d 909 (2d Cir. 1991). See also 18 U.S.C. § 4126 (exclusive remedy for prisoner injured at prison job).

[27]42 U.S.C. §§ 12101 et seq.

[28]Pennsylvania Dept. of Corrections v. Yeskey, 524 U.S. 206, 118 S. Ct. 1952, 141 L. Ed. 2d 215, 163 A.L.R. Fed. 671 (1998) (affirming the lower court's reversal of the trial court, because the Americans with Disabilities Act (ADA), 42 U.S.C.S. §§ 12131 et seq., clearly applied to boot camp programs administered by state prisons, and denial of the program to a prisoner with hypertension violated the ADA); the Act provided in 42 U.S.C. § 12312 that "[s]ubject to the provisions of this subchapter, no qualified individ-

MEDICAL CARE § 3:1

people in any federally funded "program or activity."[29]

Despite the availability of other approaches, virtually all of the litigation in this area is based on federal constitutional grounds, specifically the Eighth and Fourteenth Amendments.[30] Accordingly, the bulk of this chapter will concentrate on those rights.

There are literally hundreds of cases in which inmates have challenged the adequacy of their medical care, but the cases fall into two large categories. First, there are cases where inmates challenged the adequacy of the medical care system, either alone or in combination with other allegations of inadequacies in the general prison conditions. These cases are generally class actions. They concentrate on the inadequate procedures used to identify individual medical needs and deliver medical care to those who need that care and on the structural prerequisites to a medical care system, such as having a sufficient number of doctors available.[31] Perhaps the most commonly cited case challenging a

---

ual with a disability shall, by reason of such disability, be excluded from participation in or be denied the benefits of the services, programs, or activities of a public entity, or be subjected to discrimination by any such agency"). See Clarkson v. Coughlin, 145 F.R.D. 339, 348, 2 A.D.D. 639 (S.D. N.Y. 1993). See, generally, Steven J. Wright, Note, Bonner v. Lewis: Testing Society's Commitment to Aid Individuals With Handicaps, 1989 BYU L Rev 943.

[29]29 U.S.C. § 794.

[30]There may be relevant actions under other amendments. For example, a prosecutor's desire to force a prisoner to have surgery so that a bullet can be removed presents Fourth Amendment problems. See Winston v. Lee, 470 U.S. 753, 105 S. Ct. 1611, 84 L. Ed. 2d 662 (1985).

[31]The two general standards applied in class actions are quite clear and well-established. Ramos v Lamm, 639 F2d 559 (10th Cir 1980) ("In class actions challenging the entire system of health care, deliberate indifference to inmates' health needs may be shown by proving repeated examples of negligent acts which disclose a pattern of conduct by prison medical staff . . . or by proving there are such systemic and gross deficiencies in staffing, facilities, equipment, or procedures that the inmate population is effectively denied access to adequate medical care."); Todaro v. Ward, 431 F. Supp. 1129, 1133 (S.D. N.Y. 1977), judgment aff'd, 565 F.2d 48, 52

complete medical delivery system is *Newman v Alabama.*[32]

Typically, if the inmates are successful in an action claiming that the medical care system at the institution is inadequate, the relief granted is to require adequate procedures, such as a sick call system that ensures that those who need to see a doctor are able to do so with sufficient promptness. The relief often involves resolving the structural inadequacies by, for example, requiring the hiring of a sufficient number of doctors and ensuring that doctors and other medical personnel are sufficiently trained and equipped.

The other large category of cases comprises those in which individual inmates challenge the medical care given to them specifically. If there is one general rule that emerges from the individual cases, it is that inadequate medical care will be seen as a constitutional violation if the medical need was a serious one but was not attended to. This rule, while often unstated or couched in other language such as "deliberate indifference," explains most of the cases.

One general point should be made about the relationship between class actions and individual cases. Deficiencies that would justify class-wide relief may not justify relief in individual cases. Although this may ap-

---

(2d Cir. 1977) and aff'd, 652 F.2d 54 (2d Cir. 1981) ("When systemic deficiencies in staffing, facilities, or procedures make unnecessary suffering inevitable, a court will not hesitate to use its injunctive powers").

[32]Newman v. State of Ala., 349 F. Supp. 278 (M.D. Ala. 1972), aff'd in part, 503 F.2d 1320 (5th Cir. 1974) and judgment vacated in part on other grounds, 522 F.2d 71 (5th Cir. 1975). For other examples of thorough, though not always persuasive, discussions of medical care systems, see Todaro v. Ward, 431 F. Supp. 1129 (S.D. N.Y. 1977), judgment aff'd, 565 F.2d 48 (2d Cir. 1977) and aff'd, 652 F.2d 54 (2d Cir. 1981); Lightfoot v. Walker, 486 F. Supp. 504 (S.D. Ill. 1980); Burks v. Teasdale, 492 F. Supp. 650 (W.D. Mo. 1980) On extensive and detailed consent decree is Hines v. Anderson, 439 F. Supp. 12 (D. Minn. 1977). See also Goldsby v. Carnes, 365 F. Supp. 395, 406-07 (W.D. Mo. 1973), judgment amended on other grounds, 429 F. Supp. 370 (W.D. Mo. 1977).

MEDICAL CARE § 3:1

pear inconsistent on its face, it is logical. It can be fairly said that a prison is "deliberately indifferent" to the medical needs of all of the inmates if (1) it allows guards to prevent inmates from having access to doctors; (2) it allows untrained inmates to provide medical care, (3) it fails to follow through on ensuring that prescribed medicine is delivered to inmates, or (4) it has no doctors on staff. It can be said with certainty that these conditions will inevitably result in serious medical harm to inmates. These conditions, alone or in combination, however, do not guarantee that harm will come to a particular inmate. Thus, if there is no doctor on duty, but the inmate has no medical condition, the institution will not have been deliberately indifferent to his or her individual needs. The individual inmate will be unable to prevail in a suit for damages since he or she, individually, was not harmed by the institution's actions. If, however, the condition is chronic or even common, the inmate may still be able to seek injunctive relief on behalf of all of the inmates of the institution to ensure that when a need does arise, that need will be met.[33]

This chapter first discusses the leading Supreme Court case, *Estelle v Gamble*.[34] It then discusses the procedural issues involved in providing medical care to inmates, such as sick call, and addresses the structural issues, such as adequacy of staff. It also reviews specific types of treatment needs, such as mental health needs and the problems raised by particular inmates, such as women or transsexuals. Finally, the chapter will discuss the right of inmates to refuse treatment and the issue of human experimentation in prisons.

---

[33]Helling v. McKinney, 509 U.S. 25, 113 S. Ct. 2475, 125 L. Ed. 2d 22 (1993).

[34]Estelle v. Gamble, 429 U.S. 97, 97 S. Ct. 285, 50 L. Ed. 2d 251 (1976).

§ 3:2 *Estelle v Gamble*

Research References

West's Key Number Digest, Sentencing and Punishment ⚷1546

The leading case involving an allegation of inadequate medical care is *Estelle v Gamble*.[1] J.W. Gamble, an inmate in a Texas prison, alleged that he had hurt his back during a work assignment and that the medical care he had received for that injury was inadequate. He conceded that he had been given some treatment, having been seen by doctors eleven times, and by a medical assistant an additional six times, in the three months after the injury. He claimed, however, that "more should have been done by way of diagnosis and treatment and suggest[ed] a number of options that were not being pursued."[2]

The Supreme Court noted that the Eighth Amendment prohibits punishments that "involve the unnecessary and wanton infliction of pain."[3] This principle "establish[es] the government's obligation to provide medical care for those whom it is punishing by incarceration."[4] The Court concluded that "deliberate indifference to serious medical needs of prisoners constitutes the 'unnecessary and wanton infliction of pain' . . . proscribed by the Eighth Amendment."[5] It is this standard that has since governed all cases of prisoners seeking to challenge the adequacy of medical care given them.[6]

The Court gave little guidance concerning the mean-

[Section 3:2]

[1]*Id.*

[2]*Id.* at 107.

[3]*Id.* at 103 (quoting Gregg v. Georgia, 428 U.S. 153, 173, 96 S. Ct. 2909, 49 L. Ed. 2d 859 (1976)).

[4]*Id.* at 103.

[5]*Id.* at 104.

[6]The Court found that this standard was substantially identical to the standards that had been adopted by the circuit courts.

MEDICAL CARE § 3:2

ing of "deliberate indifference" or "serious medical needs." It did suggest three examples of behavior that would violate the standard. First, it said that a violation could be established when "indifference is manifested by prison doctors in their response to the prisoner's needs."[7] As examples of this type of violation, it cited cases in which prison doctors provided an "easier and less efficacious treatment" than was appropriate,[8] an inmate nurse gave the inmate an inappropriate treatment and then the doctor refused to treat the consequences,[9] and a prison doctor failed to follow the express post-operative directions of the surgeon who had operated on the prisoner.[10]

Id. at 104 n.14. The applicability of this standard to pretrial detainees is discussed later in this section.

[7]*Id.* at 104. This rule applies to prison doctors who are not state employees but are working on a contract basis. In West v. Atkins, 487 U.S. 42, 108 S. Ct. 2250, 101 L. Ed. 2d 40 (1988), the Supreme Court found that the actions of contract doctors were "state action" for purposes of the Eighth Amendment.

[8]*Id.* at 104 n.10, quoting Williams v Vincent, 508 F2d 541, 544 (2d Cir 1974) (inmate lost a "large portion of [his] right ear" in a fight; doctor told him "he did not need his ear" and refused to attempt to reattach the missing portion, an action the court found "one would expect a concerned doctor to have tried"). *Williams* is often cited as an example of "deliberate indifference." See, e.g., Tomarkin v. Ward, 534 F. Supp. 1224, 1230 (S.D. N.Y. 1982).

[9]*Id.* at 104 n.10, citing Thomas v. Pate, 493 F.2d 151, 158 (7th Cir. 1974), judgment vacated on other grounds, 419 U.S. 813, 95 S. Ct. 288, 42 L. Ed. 2d 39 (1974) (inmate nurse gave the inmate a shot of penicillin even though the inmate was allergic; doctor, "without examining him concluded that no further treatment was needed"). See also Carlson v. Green, 446 U.S. 14, 16 n.1, 100 S. Ct. 1468, 64 L. Ed. 2d 15 (1980) (treatment of asthmatic with "contraindicated drugs" and "inoperative" respirator).

[10]*Id.* at 104, citing Martinez v. Mancusi, 443 F.2d 921, 924 (2d Cir. 1970) (surgeons had recommended the inmate be kept prone and be given medication for pain; prison doctor said, "he did not know of those orders"); see also Holmes v. Dailey, 1998 WL 709621 (D. Kan. 1998) (plaintiff stated a claim for deliberate indifference sufficient to withstand motion for summary judgment where he alleged that he, attempting to escape, bolted from transport van and

§ 3:2

Second, the Court said that a violation would be established where "the indifference is manifested . . . by prison guards in intentionally denying or delaying access to medical care."[11] The Court cited eight cases that were examples of "denying" or "delaying" access.[12] Third, the Court said a violation would be established where guards "intentionally interfer[ed] with the treatment once prescribed."[13] Five case examples were cited.[14]

---

defendant deputy fired four shots, the fourth of which paralyzed the plaintiff from the chest down; defendant prison officials allegedly ignored paramedics' directions that handcuffs must be removed for proper spinal immobilization).

[11]Estelle v. Gamble, 429 U.S. 97, 104-5, 97 S. Ct. 285, 50 L. Ed. 2d 251 (1976). See also Carlson v. Green, 446 U.S. 14, 16 n1, 100 S. Ct. 1468, 64 L. Ed. 2d 15 (1980) (delay in treatment after asthma attack and delay in transfer to hospital); Shiflet v. Cornell, 933 F. Supp. 1549 (M.D. Fla. 1996) (inmate who suffered a stroke claimed prison officials acted with deliberate indifference when they failed to immediately bring him to a physician after he collapsed; since the plaintiff was immediately brought to an emergency room where he was treated by the prison nurse's office, the court held that at most the plaintiff stated a claim for medical negligence or malpractice).

[12]Westlake v. Lucas, 537 F.2d 857, 859 (6th Cir. 1976) (inmate denied access to doctor for bleeding ulcer for eight days, during which he "continued to suffer and his repeated requests for medical assistance went unanswered"); Thomas v. Pate, 493 F.2d 151, 158 (7th Cir. 1974), judgment vacated on other grounds, 419 U.S. 813, 95 S. Ct. 288, 42 L. Ed. 2d 39 (1974) (a delay of 15 days in removing some sutures while the inmate was in punitive confinement caused his ear to be infected); Fitzke v. Shappell, 468 F.2d 1072 (6th Cir. 1972) (allegation of a denial of medical attention for brain and leg injuries for 17 hours); Hutchens v. State of Ala., 466 F.2d 507, 508 (5th Cir. 1972) (denial of "medical attention and medication which both produces intolerable pain and further shortens life expectancy" for inmate with fatal cancer); Riley v. Rhay, 407 F.2d 496 (9th Cir. 1969) (alleged failure to treat tuberculosis); Edwards v. Duncan, 355 F.2d 993 (4th Cir. 1966) (alleged denial of medical care for heart condition recognized by doctor); Hughes v. Noble, 295 F.2d 495 (5th Cir. 1961) (denied medical attention for dislocated and fractured cervical vertebrae).

[13]Estelle v. Gamble, 429 U.S. 97, 105, 97 S. Ct. 285, 50 L. Ed. 2d 251 (1976).

§ 3:2

The Court also gave examples of conduct that would not establish a violation. First, an "accident, although it may produce added anguish, is not, on that basis alone, to be characterized as wanton infliction of unnecessary pain."[15] Thus, infliction of pain is not sufficient by itself to establish a violation.[16] Second, "an inadvertent failure to provide adequate medical care" or "a complaint that a physician has been negligent in diagnosing or treating a medical condition does not state a valid claim . . . medical malpractice does not become a constitutional violation merely because the victim is a prisoner."[17] The Court applied this last example in denying relief to Gamble, holding that the "question whether an X-ray-or additional diagnostic techniques or forms of treatment-is indicated is a clas-

---

[14]Wilbron v. Hutto, 509 F.2d 621 (8th Cir. 1975) (forced to work despite hand injury); Campbell v. Beto, 460 F.2d 765 (5th Cir. 1972) (made to work in fields and denied medication for heart problem, both in direct violation of doctor's orders, causing heart attack); Martinez v. Mancusi, 443 F.2d 921 (2d Cir. 1970) (prison doctor failed to follow the express post-operative directions of the surgeon who had operated on the prisoner); Tolbert v. Eyman, 434 F.2d 625 (9th Cir. 1970) (prison officials deny diabetic access to insulin); Edwards v. Duncan, 355 F.2d 993 (4th Cir. 1966) (alleged denial of medical care for heart condition recognized by doctor).

[15]Estelle v. Gamble, 429 U.S. 97, 105, 97 S. Ct. 285, 50 L. Ed. 2d 251 (1976).

[16]Wilson v. Seiter, 501 U.S. 294, 111 S. Ct. 2321, 115 L. Ed. 2d 271 (1991). See also Snipes v. DeTella, 95 F.3d 586 (7th Cir. 1996) (holding that a physician's failure to anesthetize an inmate's toe before removing a toenail did not constitute cruel and unusual punishment). Thus, pain itself is not enough to show a violation. It is equally true that, "an express intent to inflict unnecessary pain is not required." Whitley v. Albers, 475 U.S. 312, 319, 106 S. Ct. 1078, 89 L. Ed. 2d 251 (1986).

[17]Estelle v. Gamble, 429 U.S. 97, 105-6, 97 S. Ct. 285, 50 L. Ed. 2d 251 (1976); Jones v. Hannigan, 959 F. Supp. 1400 (D. Kan. 1997); Coppage v. Mann, 906 F. Supp. 1025 (E.D. Va. 1995) (holding that prison physician was not deliberately indifferent to inmate's medical condition where physician ordered tests which were less efficient in detecting spinal cancer than a MRI).

sic example of a matter for medical judgment."[18]

Since *Estelle,* the Supreme Court has provided some additional guidance concerning facts that would establish a violation. In *Carlson v Green,*[19] both parties agreed that a violation would be established if plaintiff could prove her allegations that the prison had inadequate facilities for treating her son's asthma, that he was kept in the facility despite the advice of doctors, that there was a delay of eight hours before treating him after he had an asthma attack, that "contraindicated drugs" were administered, that a respirator known to be inoperative was used, and that there was a delay in transferring him to an outside hospital, all of which caused his death.[20]

More recently, the Court has emphasized that the *Estelle* standard does include a subjective, state-of-mind requirement.[21] The requirement of " wantonness," the Court held, is an essential element of the Eighth Amendment, though in the context of the "state's

---

[18]*Id* at 107.

[19]Carlson v. Green, 446 U.S. 14, 100 S. Ct. 1468, 64 L. Ed. 2d 15 (1980).

[20]*Id* at 16 n.1, 17 n.3.

[21]Wilson v. Seiter, 501 U.S. 294, 111 S. Ct. 2321, 2331, 115 L. Ed. 2d 271 (1991); Helling v. McKinney, 509 U.S. 25, 113 S. Ct. 2475, 125 L. Ed. 2d 22 (1993); Vance v. Peters, 97 F.3d 987, 45 Fed. R. Evid. Serv. 1068 (7th Cir. 1996) (inmate who suffered a broken arm claimed prison officials acted with deliberate indifference when they denied her medical treatment for thirteen days; court held that to establish a constitutional violation under the Eighth Amendment, the denial or delay of medical care "requires evidence of a defendant's actual knowledge of, or reckless disregard for, a substantial risk of harm"; the plaintiff failed to meet this standard, thus, the court affirmed the lower court's grant of summary judgment for the defendants); Forbes v. Edgar, 112 F.3d 262 (7th Cir. 1997) (inmate who contracted tuberculosis claimed that prison officials were deliberately indifferent to her medical needs when they allowed tuberculosis to be spread in prison; court found that the defendants implemented tuberculosis control procedures recommended by the Center for Disease Control and the American Thoracic Society, and affirmed the lower court's grant of summary judgment for the defendants).

responsibility to attend to the medical needs of prisoners . . . 'deliberate indifference' would constitute wantonness."[22] The Court also rejected any notion that a different standard would apply when the violations were "continuing" or "systemic.[23] Thus, the same "deliberate indifference" standard must be met in class action challenges to medical care systems as in individual cases.

The "deliberate indifference" portion of the *Estelle* standard is similar to the "deliberate indifference" required for other Eighth Amendment violations, discussed in prior chapters.[24]

§ 3:3 Rights of Pretrial Detainees to Medical Care

The rights of pretrial detainees are analyzed under the Fourteenth Amendment, not the Eighth.[1] The Supreme Court has not yet decided whether the stan-

---

[22]Wilson v. Seiter, 501 U.S. 294, 111 S. Ct. 2321, 115 L. Ed. 2d 271 (1991) (quoting Whitley v. Albers, 475 U.S. 312, 320, 106 S. Ct. 1078, 89 L. Ed. 2d 251 (1986)).

[23]Wilson v. Seiter, 501 U.S. 294, 111 S. Ct. 2321, 2330, 115 L. Ed. 2d 271 (1991).

[24]See also Michael C. Friedman, Comment, Cruel and Unusual Punishment in the Provision of Prison Medical Care: Challenging the Deliberate Indifference Standard, 45 Vand L Rev 921 (May 1992). Compare Miller v. Glanz, 948 F.2d 1562, 1569 (10th Cir. 1991) (failure to allege "the state of mind required to meet the subjective or intent component of the standard" fatal to claim) with Weeks v. Chaboudy, 984 F.2d 185, 187 (6th Cir. 1993) (Constitution "does not require proof of intent to harm or a detailed inquiry into his state of mind").

Whether "deliberate indifference" will become a more important, independent factor, as *Miller* suggests, is still an open question, but there seems little reason for adopting the *Miller* notion that some type of evil intent is required. Weeks represents the better approach.

[Section 3:3]

[1]Bell v. Wolfish, 441 U.S. 520, 99 S. Ct. 1861, 60 L. Ed. 2d 447 (1979); Chicago Osteopathic Medical Centers v. City of Chicago, 271 Ill. App. 3d 165, 207 Ill. Dec. 837, 648 N.E.2d 293 (1st Dist.

§ 3:3   RIGHTS OF PRISONERS, THIRD EDITION

dard for the inadequate provision of medical care for pretrial detainees is the same as that for sentenced prisoners. In *City of Revere v Massachusetts General Hospital*,[2] the Supreme Court found that pretrial detainees are entitled to "rights . . . at least as great as the Eighth Amendment protections available to a convicted prisoner." Other courts have taken the similar approach of avoiding decision but analyzing the facts under Eighth Amendment standards.[3] Still others, recognizing the different status of pretrial prisoners and the different general standards set by the Supreme Court for them, have held that pretrial detainees have greater rights to medical care and that they cannot be deprived of medical care unless the deprivation is "rea-

---

1995) (holding that arresting authority was liable for medical expenses of arrestee until in custody of county sheriff but not if arrestee incurred injuries prior to being charged with a crime; county was liable for medical expenses of juvenile detainee whether injury was incurred before or after detainee was placed in juvenile detention center); Osteopathic Hosp. Founders Ass'n v. Oklahoma Dept. of Public Safety Through Oklahoma Highway Patrol Dept., 1995 OK CIV APP 34, 892 P.2d 671 (Okla. Ct. App. Div. 3 1995) (department of public safety was liable for hospital bills of arrested drunk driver despite county's statutory obligation that arrestee be in county custody); United Hosp. v. D'Annunzio, 514 N.W.2d 681 (N.D. 1994) (holding county as a governmental entity responsible for prisoner's medical bills, but county could seek reimbursement from prisoner).

[2]City of Revere v. Massachusetts General Hosp., 463 U.S. 239, 244, 103 S. Ct. 2979, 77 L. Ed. 2d 605 (1983).

[3]Some have held that the standards for analyzing the rights of pretrial detainees to adequate medical care are identical to those found in *Estelle,* which were applicable to sentenced prisoners. Estate of Cole by Pardue v. Fromm, 94 F.3d 254 (7th Cir. 1996); Brownell v. Figel, 950 F.2d 1285 (7th Cir. 1991); Shelby County Jail Inmates v. Westlake, 798 F.2d 1085 (7th Cir. 1986); Jones v. Johnson, 781 F.2d 769 (9th Cir. 1986); Hamm v. DeKalb County, 774 F.2d 1567, 1574 (11th Cir. 1985); Garcia v. Salt Lake County, 768 F.2d 303 (10th Cir. 1985).

MEDICAL CARE § 3:4

sonably related to a legitimate government objective."[4] It is doubtful that there is a practical difference in the application of these two standards. There is rarely, if ever, a genuine reason for denying an inmate or detainee adequate medical care for prison-related or punishment reasons. There seems no real reason to distinguish the medical needs of inmates from those of detainees.

§ 3:4 What is a "Serious Medical Need"?

Estelle makes clear that there is no constitutional violation unless the inmate can show that defendants were deliberately indifferent to a "serious medical need."[1] Thus, the determination of whether or not the plaintiff's medical condition is "serious" is a critical determination. Indeed, many if not most, of the medical care cases, whether challenging entire medical care

---

[4]Nerren v. Livingston Police Dept., 86 F.3d 469 (5th Cir. 1996) (court held that an arrestee's right to medical attention is equivalent to the rights of pretrial detainees, and are derived from the Fourteenth Amendment; pretrial detainees are entitled to medical care "unless the failure to supply that care is reasonably related to a legitimate governmental objective"); Alberti v. Klevenhagen, 790 F.2d 1220, 1224 (5th Cir. 1986) (citing Bell v. Wolfish, 441 U.S. 520, 539, 99 S. Ct. 1861, 60 L. Ed. 2d 447 (1979)); Partridge v. Two Unknown Police Officers of City of Houston, Tex., 791 F.2d 1182, 1186 (5th Cir. 1986); Rhyne v. Henderson County, 973 F.2d 386, 391 (5th Cir. 1992); Mayweather v. Foti, 958 F.2d 91 (5th Cir. 1992); Whisenant v. Yuam, 739 F.2d 160 (4th Cir. 1984); Norris v. Frame, 585 F.2d 1183 (3d Cir. 1978) (cited with approval by the Supreme Court in *Revere* and West v. Atkins, 487 U.S. 42, 108 S. Ct. 2250, 101 L. Ed. 2d 40 (1988)). The Third Circuit appears to be retreating from this view, holding in Boring v. Kozakiewicz, 833 F.2d 468 (3d Cir. 1987), that the Supreme Court's decision in *Bell* has undercut the doctrinal basis for *Norris* and that, at least in the context of an institution that houses both pretrial detainees and sentenced prisoners, the management problems of applying different standards to the two types of inmates justifies using the *Estelle* standard in both cases).

[Section 3:4]

[1]Estelle v. Gamble, 429 U.S. 97, 105, 97 S. Ct. 285, 50 L. Ed. 2d 251 (1976).

§ 3:4

systems or individual medical care, can be explained by application of the "serious medical need" standard.[2] If the court perceives the need as serious but unmet, the plaintiffs will win; otherwise, they will have little success.

Despite the importance of the concept, lower courts have sometimes been less than precise in defining serious medical need.[3] In these cases the analysis has

---

[2]McGuckin v. Smith, 974 F.2d 1050, 1061, 23 Fed. R. Serv. 3d 922 (9th Cir. 1992) (overruled on other grounds by, WMX Technologies, Inc. v. Miller, 104 F.3d 1133, 36 Fed. R. Serv. 3d 1042 (9th Cir. 1997)).

[3]Brown v. Hughes, 894 F.2d 1533, 1538 n4, 16 Fed. R. Serv. 3d 118 (11th Cir. 1990); Clemmons v. Bohannon, 956 F.2d 1523 (10th Cir. 1992), opinion corrected, (Feb. 14, 1992) (en banc). Sometimes, the cases are contradictory. Compare Hartbarger v. Blackford County Dept. of Public Welfare, 733 F. Supp. 300, 303 (N.D. Ind. 1990) (pregnancy not a serious medical condition without distress) with Monmouth County Correctional Institutional Inmates v. Lanzaro, 834 F.2d 326, 347, 90 A.L.R. Fed. 631 (3d Cir. 1987) (abortion is "serious medical need").

For a sampling of cases holding that particular conditions did not constitute a serious medical need, see, e.g., Brown v. Briscoe, 998 F.2d 201 (4th Cir. 1993) (second administration of tuberculosis vaccine was not a serious medical need); Doty v. County of Lassen, 37 F.3d 540 (9th Cir. 1994) (stress-related ailments, including nausea, headache, and depressed appetite arising from incarceration, did not constitute a "serious medical need"); Ashford v. Barry, 737 F. Supp. 1, 3 (D.D.C. 1990) (unspecified injury from being kicked in leg not serious); Wesson v. Oglesby, 910 F.2d 278, 284 (5th Cir. 1990) (swollen wrists "with some bleeding" not serious); Shabazz v. Barnauskas, 790 F.2d 1536, 1538 (11th Cir. 1986) (not serious when forced to shave despite doctor's orders and inmate developed "sensitive skin and other problems"); Borrelli v. Askey, 582 F. Supp. 512, 513 (E.D. Pa. 1984), judgment aff'd, 751 F.2d 375 (3d Cir. 1984) (inmate with "very slight visual impairment" was denied glasses and suffered at most "mild headaches and mild tension" and, thus, not serious); Pierce v. King, 918 F. Supp. 932, 15 A.D.D. 246 (E.D. N.C. 1996), aff'd, 131 F.3d 136 (4th Cir. 1997), cert. granted, judgment vacated on other grounds, 525 U.S. 802, 119 S. Ct. 33, 142 L. Ed. 2d 25 (1998) (holding that a swollen finger was not a serious medical need); Davidson v. Scully, 914 F. Supp. 1011 (S.D. N.Y. 1996) (holding that tinnitus, a ringing in the inner ear,

MEDICAL CARE § 3:4

consisted of little more than the assertion that "itching"[4] or a one-inch cut[5] are not serious medical needs, but broken bones are,[6] or that serious medical needs

___

was not serious enough to justify treatment and also holding that plaintiff's allergies, podiatric condition, hernia problem, knee condition, and cardiological problems were not severe or life threatening enough to constitute a serious medical need); Benson v. Godinez, 919 F. Supp. 285 (N.D. Ill. 1996) (holding colds and a sore throat are not serious medical needs); Vaughn v. Kerley, 897 F. Supp. 1413 (M.D. Fla. 1995) (holding that complaints of gastro-intestinal pain was not sufficiently serious); Abdul-Akbar v. Department of Corrections, 910 F. Supp. 986 (D. Del. 1995), judgment aff'd, 111 F.3d 125 (3d Cir. 1997) (holding that request for a hernia operation not serious); Flowers v. Dalsheim, 826 F. Supp. 772 (S.D. N.Y. 1993) (holding that if injury due to delay of medication is only "emotional" there is no serious medical need); Cummings v. Caspari, 821 F. Supp. 1291 (E.D. Mo. 1993) (injuries received from mace, including bruises, were not serious medical need); Tyler v. Rapone, 603 F. Supp. 268, 271-72 (E.D. Pa. 1985) (toothache and cut not serious); Griffin v. DeRobertis, 557 F. Supp. 302, 306 (N.D. Ill. 1983) ("aches and a sore throat" not serious, "spitting up blood" was); Lile v. Tippecanoe County Jail, 844 F. Supp. 1301 (N.D. Ind. 1992) (holding that prisoner's nose polyps were not a "serious medical need" so as to compel county sheriff's office to pay for their removal); Pace v. Fauver, 479 F. Supp. 456 (D.N.J. 1979), aff'd, 649 F.2d 860 (3d Cir. 1981) (alcoholism not serious); Shaw v. Jones, 81 N.C. App. 486, 344 S.E.2d 321 (1986) (overweight not serious).

For a sampling of cases holding conditions to be serious see, e.g., Oxendine v. Kaplan, 241 F.3d 1272 (10th Cir. 2001) (gangrene was serious medical need); Gutierrez v. Peters, 111 F.3d 1364 (7th Cir. 1997) (inmate's infected cyst constituted a "serious medical need."); Cameron v. Sarraf, 128 F. Supp. 2d 906 (E.D. Va. 2000), aff'd, 232 F.3d 886 (4th Cir. 2000) (degenerative disc condition was a serious medical need); De La Paz v. Peters, 959 F. Supp. 909 (N.D. Ill. 1997) (incontinence was a "serious medical need."); Arnold on Behalf of H.B. v. Lewis, 803 F. Supp. 246, 248 (D. Ariz. 1992) (schizophrenia).

[4]Wilson v. Franceschi, 735 F. Supp. 395 (M.D. Fla. 1990).

[5]Davis v. Jones, 936 F.2d 971 (7th Cir. 1991).

[6]Brown v. Hughes, 894 F.2d 1533, 16 Fed. R. Serv. 3d 118 (11th Cir. 1990).

§ 3:4

are different from "minor injuries."[7]

Other courts, however, have attempted to further define a "serious medical need," and their definitions do provide some additional and important guidance. For example, a condition need not be life threatening to be deemed serious.[8] Five factors have been held to be indicative of a "serious medical need."

- First, "a medical need is 'serious' if it is one that has been diagnosed by a physician as mandating treatment."[9]
- Second, a need is serious if it is "one that is so obvious that even a lay person would easily recognize the necessity for a doctor's attention."[10]

---

[7]Brownell v. Figel, 950 F.2d 1285, 1291 (7th Cir. 1991).

[8]Washington v. Dugger, 860 F.2d 1018 (11th Cir. 1988); Wright v. Baker, 849 F. Supp. 569 (N.D. Ohio 1994); Laaman v. Helgemoe, 437 F. Supp. 269, 311 (D.N.H. 1977) ("Even elective treatment recommended by a physician but not 'necessary' in life or health saving sense, may be constitutionally mandated upon a prisoner's election").

[9]Hill v. Dekalb Regional Youth Detention Center, 40 F.3d 1176, 1187 (11th Cir. 1994); Gaudreault v. Municipality of Salem, Mass., 923 F.2d 203, 208 (1st Cir. 1990); Laaman v. Helgemoe, 437 F. Supp. 269, 311 (D.N.H. 1977). But see Shabazz v. Barnauskas, 790 F.2d 1536, 1538 (11th Cir. 1986).

[10]Greeno v. Litscher, 13 Fed. Appx. 370 (7th Cir. 2001) (layperson should be able to ascertain that an inmate had a serious medical problem when he constantly complained of serious stomach pains and often vomited. Prison doctors, however, responded by telling him he would have to live with the condition, and gave him antacids. Eventually he was diagnosed with an ulcer); Sanderson v. Friedman, 2000 WL 1721052 (N.D. Cal. 2000) (any reasonable person should know that inmate who was suffering from numerous serious health conditions, including cancer, and end stage liver disease had serious medical needs); Hill v. Dekalb Regional Youth Detention Center, 40 F.3d 1176, 1187 (11th Cir. 1994); Gaudreault v. Municipality of Salem, Mass., 923 F.2d 203, 208 (1st Cir. 1990); Laaman v. Helgemoe, 437 F. Supp. 269, 311 (D.N.H. 1977).

MEDICAL CARE § 3:4

- Third, a need is serious if it causes pain.[11]
- Fourth, if the medical condition "significantly affects an individual's daily acts," it may be deemed serious.[12]
- Finally, if the condition offers the possibility of a life-long handicap or permanent loss, it may be considered serious.[13]

The seriousness of the medical need cannot be judged with the benefit of hindsight. Thus, the relevant facts

---

[11]Cooper v. Casey, 97 F.3d 914, 916-17 (7th Cir. 1996) (holding that pain from beating constituted serious medical need); McGuckin v. Smith, 974 F.2d 1050, 1059-60, 23 Fed. R. Serv. 3d 922 (9th Cir. 1992) (overruled on other grounds by, WMX Technologies, Inc. v. Miller, 104 F.3d 1133, 36 Fed. R. Serv. 3d 1042 (9th Cir. 1997)) ("chronic and substantial pain"); Monmouth County Correctional Institutional Inmates v. Lanzaro, 834 F.2d 326, 347, 90 A.L.R. Fed. 631 (3d Cir. 1987); White v. Napoleon, 897 F.2d 103, 109 (3d Cir. 1990) (intended to inflict pain without medical justification); Boretti v. Wiscomb, 930 F.2d 1150, 1155 (6th Cir. 1991) (pain inflicted "when relief is readily available" is actionable even if no lasting impact); East v. Lemons, 768 F.2d 1000 (8th Cir. 1985) (leg cramps); Hathaway v. Coughlin, 841 F.2d 48 (2d Cir. 1988); Billings v. Gates, 133 Or. App. 236, 890 P.2d 995 (1995), review allowed, 321 Or. 512, 900 P.2d 509 (1995) and decision aff'd and remanded, 323 Or. 167, 916 P.2d 291 (1996) (relief was appropriate where inmate was in great pain due to denial of arch supports); Wright v. Dee, 54 F. Supp. 2d 199 (S.D. N.Y. 1999) (pain from beating); Farinaro v. Coughlin, 642 F. Supp. 276, 279 (S.D. N.Y. 1986) ("pain, discomfort, or risk to health"); Young v. Harris, 509 F. Supp. 1111 (S.D. N.Y. 1981). But see Givens v. Jones, 900 F.2d 1229, 1233 (8th Cir. 1990) (one month of pain insufficient).

[12]Long v. Nix, 86 F.3d 761 (8th Cir. 1996) (inmate suffering for 20 years from dysphoria, a gender identity disorder); Koehl v. Dalsheim, 85 F.3d 86, 88 (2d Cir. 1996) (loss of vision); McGuckin v. Smith, 974 F.2d 1050, 1059-60, 23 Fed. R. Serv. 3d 922 (9th Cir. 1992) (overruled on other grounds by, WMX Technologies, Inc. v. Miller, 104 F.3d 1133, 36 Fed. R. Serv. 3d 1042 (9th Cir. 1997)).

[13]Johnson v. Bowers, 884 F.2d 1053, 1056 (8th Cir. 1989), and as modified on other grounds on reh'g, (Oct. 27, 1989); Monmouth County Correctional Institutional Inmates v. Lanzaro, 834 F.2d 326, 347, 90 A.L.R. Fed. 631 (3d Cir. 1987) (life-long handicap or permanent loss is "serious medical need").

are those known at the time of the incident. Officials will not be held liable for conditions that appeared nonserious but turned out to be serious. Likewise, prison officials will be held liable for conditions that appeared serious even if they did not ultimately turn out to be serious.[14] In addition, inmates need not wait until harm occurs for a court to find that serious needs are unmet.[15]

§ 3:5 Initial Screening When Entering Facility

A wide variety of cases have challenged the failure of an institution to engage in medical screening of inmates on their arrival at the institution.[1] Virtually all of those cases have held that an adequate medical system must

---

[14]Davis v. Jones, 936 F.2d 971 (7th Cir. 1991) (police must offer medical care to pretrial detainee whenever jail authorities have reason to suspect that injury is serious, whether or not problem turns out to be serious after further investigation; whether injury is actually serious is question best left to physician); Matzker v. Herr, 748 F.2d 1142, 1147 n3 (7th Cir. 1984); Boretti v. Wiscomb, 930 F.2d 1150 (6th Cir. 1991).

[15]Helling v. McKinney, 509 U.S. 25, 113 S. Ct. 2475, 125 L. Ed. 2d 22 (1993); Laaman v. Helgemoe, 437 F. Supp. 269, 312 (D.N.H. 1977). For a general discussion of the concept of "serious medical need," see Michael C. Friedman, Comment, Cruel and Unusual Punishment in the Provision of Prison Medical Care: Challenging the Deliberate Indifference Standard, 45 Vand L Rev 921 (1992).

[Section 3:5]

[1]Lareau v. Manson, 651 F.2d 96, 109 (2d Cir. 1981); Monmouth County Correctional Institution Inmates v. Lanzaro, 595 F. Supp. 1417, 1422 (D.N.J. 1984); Cody v. Hillard, 599 F. Supp. 1025 (D. S.D. 1984), decision aff'd, 799 F.2d 447 (8th Cir. 1986), reh'g granted, 804 F.2d 440 (8th Cir. 1986) and on reh'g, 830 F.2d 912 (8th Cir. 1987); Fambro v. Fulton County, Ga., 713 F. Supp. 1426 (N.D. Ga. 1989); Inmates of Occoquan v. Barry, 717 F. Supp. 854, 859-66, (D.D.C. 1989); Tillery v. Owens, 719 F. Supp. 1256, 1284-309 (W.D. Pa. 1989), order aff'd, 907 F.2d 418 (3d Cir. 1990); Barnes v. Government of Virgin Islands, 415 F. Supp. 1218 (D.V.I. 1976); Hines v. Anderson, 439 F. Supp. 12 (D. Minn. 1977); Inmates of Allegheny County Jail v. Peirce, 487 F. Supp. 638 (W.D. Pa. 1980); Todaro v. Ward, 431 F. Supp. 1129 (S.D. N.Y. 1977), judgment aff'd, 565 F.2d 48 (2d Cir. 1977) and aff'd, 652 F.2d 54 (2d Cir. 1981); Battle v. Anderson, 376 F. Supp. 402 (E.D.

MEDICAL CARE § 3:5

include a screening of all incoming inmates within a reasonable period in order to determine if the inmate has any condition that requires treatment and to check for the existence of any contagious disease.[2] The reason

---

Okla. 1974), judgment aff'd in part, rev'd in part, 993 F.2d 1551 (10th Cir. 1993); Palmigiano v. Garrahy, 443 F. Supp. 956 (D.R.I. 1977); Alberti v. Sheriff of Harris County, Texas, 406 F. Supp. 649 (S.D. Tex. 1975); O'Bryan v. Saginaw County, Mich., 437 F. Supp. 582 (E.D. Mich. 1977), judgment entered, 446 F. Supp. 436 (E.D. Mich. 1978); Miller v. Carson, 401 F. Supp. 835, 878 (M.D. Fla. 1975), aff'd in part, modified in part and remanded, 563 F.2d 741 (5th Cir. 1977); Hamilton v. Landrieu, 351 F. Supp. 549, 550 (E.D. La. 1972); Jones v. Wittenberg, 323 F. Supp. 93, 28 Ohio Misc. 81, 57 Ohio Op. 2d 109 (N.D. Ohio 1971), opinion supplemented, 330 F. Supp. 707, 29 Ohio Misc. 35, 58 Ohio Op. 2d 47 (N.D. Ohio 1971), aff'd, 456 F.2d 854, 62 Ohio Op. 2d 232 (6th Cir. 1972); Lightfoot v. Walker, 486 F. Supp. 504, 524 (S.D. Ill. 1980); Laaman v. Helgemoe, 437 F. Supp. 269, 327 (D.N.H. 1977); Dawson v. Kendrick, 527 F. Supp. 1252, 1307 (S.D. W. Va. 1981) ("It is generally recognized that prompt medical screening is a medical necessity in pretrial detention facilities"); Feliciano v. Barcelo, 497 F. Supp. 14, 37 (D.P.R. 1979) (requiring initial screening within one week of admission); Yarbaugh v. Roach, 736 F. Supp. 318, 320 (D. D.C. 1990) (failure to initially screen inmate with multiple sclerosis to determine treatment plan); see also Eric Neisser, Is There a Doctor in the Joint? The Search for Constitutional Standards for Prison Health Care, 63 Vand L Rev 921, 963 n168 (1977); C. Mayer, Survey of Case Law Establishing Constitutional Minima for the Provision of Mental Health Services to Psychiatrically Involved Inmates, 15 New Eng J on Crim & Civ Comm 243 (1989); Michael C. Friedman, Comment, Prison Medical Care, 45 Vand L Rev 921 (1992); Model Sentencing and Corrections Act § 4-105(b)(1)(2) (July 2001); U.S. Dept of Justice, Federal Standards for Prisons and Jails § 5.15-18 (Dec 16, 1980); ABA Standards for Criminal Justice § 23.5-3 (1986); American Correctional Assn, Standards for Adult Correctional Institutions, Standard 3-4343 (1990); National Commn on Correctional Health Care, Standards for Health Services in Jails, J-31 (Jan 1987); Commission on Accreditation for Corrections, Certification Standards for Health Care Programs, HC-058 (1989).

[2]This is generally true even if the inmate objects to the test on religious grounds. See, e.g., Karolis v. New Jersey Dept. of Corrections, 935 F. Supp. 523 (D.N.J. 1996) (holding that punishment of Christian Scientist inmate for refusal to submit to

§ 3:5 RIGHTS OF PRISONERS, THIRD EDITION

for this is that medically unskilled jail guards cannot be expected to recognize "hidden medical problems" that can be observed only by experts.[3]

For the most part, the parties to such cases have been able to reach easy agreement on the tests that need to be done at an initial screening.[4] However, where there has been a dispute, the courts have generally left it up to prison health officials to determine the specific tests required at an initial screening.[5] Seriously substandard

---

tuberculosis screening test did not violated his rights under the Religious Freedom Restoration Act (RFRA) or First Amendment); Jones-Bey v. Wright, 944 F. Supp. 723 (N.D. Ind. 1996) (court held that requiring Muslim inmate to either take a tuberculosis injection test or be placed in medical separation unit did not violate the Free Exercise Clause).

Todaro v. Ward, 431 F. Supp. 1129 (S.D. N.Y. 1977), judgment aff'd, 565 F.2d 48 (2d Cir. 1977) and aff'd, 652 F.2d 54 (2d Cir. 1981) is a notable exception to the requirement that screening take place when the inmate is admitted to the facility; court there found that even though initial screening took, on the average, 43 days and should only take one week, no violation existed without evidence of harm to inmates.

[3]Boston v. Lafayette County, Miss., 743 F. Supp. 462, 473 (N.D. Miss. 1990).

[4]Commission on Accreditation for Corrections, Certification Standards for Health Care Programs HC-058 (1989).

[5]Mills v. Rogers, 457 U.S. 291, 102 S. Ct. 2442, 73 L. Ed. 2d 16 (1982); Winters v. Miller, 446 F.2d 65 (2d Cir. 1971); Scott v. Plante, 532 F.2d 939 (3d Cir. 1976); Souder v. McGuire, 423 F. Supp. 830 (M.D. Pa. 1976); Rennie v. Klein, 653 F.2d 836 (3d Cir. 1981), cert. granted, judgment vacated on other grounds, 458 U.S. 1119, 102 S. Ct. 3506, 73 L. Ed. 2d 1381 (1982); Anderson v. Nosser, 438 F.2d 183 (5th Cir. 1971), decision modified on other grounds on denial of reargument, 456 F.2d 835 (5th Cir. 1972); Wyatt v. Stickney, 344 F. Supp. 387 (M.D. Ala. 1972), aff'd in part, rev'd in part on other grounds and remanded, 503 F.2d 1305 (5th Cir. 1974); U.S. v. Charters, 863 F.2d 302 (4th Cir. 1988) (person confined as incompetent to stand trial); Robert Plotkin, Limiting the Therapeutic Orgy: Mental Patients' Right to Refuse Treatment, 72 NW U L Rev 461 (1977).

Medical Care § 3:6

screening, however, will not be countenanced.[6]

The requirement that every prison medical system screen incoming inmates does not mean that any inmate who is not screened will be able to sue the prison officials. For example, an isolated failure to screen an inmate will ordinarily not result in liability.[7]

§ 3:6 Emergency Care and Sick Call Procedures

Inmates are entitled to medical attention to their problem. Aside from screening, inmates are entitled to emergency care and to some reasonable system of making their need for care known in non-emergency situations as well. This section discusses these access issues.

Access to Emergency Care

Virtually every case finds that the institution must

---

[6]Tillery v. Owens, 719 F. Supp. 1256, 1294, (W.D. Pa. 1989), order aff'd, 907 F.2d 418 (3d Cir. 1990) (doctor averaged 3 minutes per inmate and never touched inmate; must do X-rays "for new inmates with histories of heart or chest disease," test and monitor diabetics, do more to recognize AIDS); Barnes v. Government of Virgin Islands, 415 F. Supp. 1218, 1235 (D.V.I. 1976) (must include mental status examination); Inmates of Allegheny County Jail v. Peirce, 487 F. Supp. 638, 644 (W.D. Pa. 1980) (must be mental health screening); Lightfoot v. Walker, 486 F. Supp. 504, 526 (S.D. Ill. 1980) (delays of 13-162 days unacceptable and would require screening within seven days by physician).

[7]Boston v. Lafayette County, Miss., 743 F. Supp. 462 (N.D. Miss. 1990) (normal screening required would have detected heart problem and saved life of detainee). The same court later erroneously found that the requirement that incoming inmates be screened was not clearly established and retreated, inexplicably, from its previous finding that the screening would have identified the problem. Boston v. Lafayette County, Miss., 744 F. Supp. 746 (N.D. Miss. 1990), aff'd, 933 F.2d 1003 (5th Cir. 1991). See also Grim v. Moore, 745 F. Supp. 1280, 1284 (S.D. Ohio 1988), dismissed, 869 F.2d 1490 (6th Cir. 1989) (failure to screen person detained in jail for 13 hours for prescribed medication needs not a violation where no evidence of harm). But see U.S. ex rel. Walker v. Fayette County, Pa., 599 F.2d 573 (3d Cir. 1979) (failure to screen for drug addiction as required by state law stated cause of action).

§ 3:6   Rights of Prisoners, Third Edition

be properly organized to effectively respond to medical emergencies.[1] Failure to respond to a serious medical emergency will result in a finding of liability.[2]

[Section 3:6]

[1]Hoptowit v. Ray, 682 F.2d 1237, 1252-55, 9 Fed. R. Evid. Serv. 1511 (9th Cir. 1982); Nicholson v. Choctaw County, Ala., 498 F. Supp. 295, 308 (S.D. Ala. 1980); Cody v. Hillard, 599 F. Supp. 1025, 1056 (D.S.D. 1984), decision aff'd, 799 F.2d 447 (8th Cir. 1986), reh'g granted, 804 F.2d 440 (8th Cir. 1986) and on reh'g, 830 F.2d 912 (8th Cir. 1987); Tillery v. Owens, 719 F. Supp. 1256, 1307-08 (W.D. Pa. 1989), order aff'd, 907 F.2d 418 (3d Cir. 1990); Barnes v. Government of Virgin Islands, 415 F. Supp. 1218, 1235 (D.V.I. 1976); Newman v. State of Ala., 349 F. Supp. 278, 285, (M.D. Ala. 1972), aff'd in part, 503 F.2d 1320 (5th Cir. 1974) and judgment vacated in part on other grounds, 522 F.2d 71 (5th Cir. 1975); Lightfoot v. Walker, 486 F. Supp. 504, 527 (S.D. Ill. 1980) (must include adequate personnel, procedures, equipment); Laaman v. Helgemoe, 437 F. Supp. 269, 327 (D.N.H. 1977); Balla v. Idaho State Bd. of Corrections, 595 F. Supp. 1558 (D. Idaho 1984) (required 24 hours a day, quoting ACA mandatory standards that there be a four-minute response). See also Model Sentencing and Corrections Act § 2-503(2), 4-105(a), (b)(3)(ii), (4) (July 2001); U.S. Dept of Justice, Federal Standards for Prisons and Jails § 5.22-24 (1980); ABA Standards for Criminal Justice §§ 23.5-1, 5-2 (1986); Correctional Health Care, Standards for Health Services in Jails J-20-21 (1987); National Commission on Correctional Health Care, Standards for Health Services in Jails J-44 (May 1999); Commission on Accreditation for Corrections, Certification Standards for Health Care Programs HC-048, -053 (1989). But see Estate of Cartwright v. City of Concord, Cal., 618 F. Supp. 722 (N.D. Cal. 1985), judgment aff'd, 856 F.2d 1437 (9th Cir. 1988) (jailers need not be trained in CPR and use it).

    For a discussion of whether prison officials may charge inmates for health care, see Wesley P. Shields, Prison Health Care: Is It Proper to Charge Inmates For Health Services?, 32 Houston L Rev 271 (1995). For a discussion of the prison co-payment system, see § 3:24.

[2]Bass by Lewis v. Wallenstein, 769 F.2d 1173 (7th Cir. 1985) (upholding jury verdict for representative of inmate who died of cardiac failure based on 15-minute delay in response, unqualified medical technicians, inadequate equipment, and doctor who wrongly pronounced inmate dead). See also Colle v. Brazos County, Tex., 981 F.2d 237, 245, 24 Fed. R. Serv. 3d 655 (5th Cir. 1993) (may be municipal liability where there was policy of inade-

MEDICAL CARE § 3:6

Sick Call Procedures

The courts have also held that inmates must have access to doctors for non-emergency situations. The procedure by which such access is provided is often called sick call, and some form of a sick call procedure is constitutionally required.[3] There are several recurrent problems that arise in setting up an adequate sick call procedure:

---

quate staffing, monitoring and capability to respond appropriately by transferring to hospital); Flowers v. Bennett, 123 F. Supp. 2d 595 (N.D. Ala. 2000) (holding that a failure to give attend to give insulin to a diabetic prisoner who suffered a life threatening attack stated a valid constitutional deprivation claim, and denying summary judgment); Adams v. Franklin, 111 F. Supp. 2d 1255 (M.D. Ala. 2000) (holding that it was a constitutional violation not to provide prompt emergency care to a pretrial detainee who was experiencing shortness of breath and chest pains).

[3]Todaro v. Ward, 431 F. Supp. 1129, 1146 (S.D. N.Y. 1977), judgment aff'd, 565 F.2d 48 (2d Cir. 1977) and aff'd, 652 F.2d 54 (2d Cir. 1981) ("Courts have held that a sick call procedure for prompt referrals of those in need of a physician is constitutionally required."); Williams v. Edwards, 547 F.2d 1206, 1217 (5th Cir. 1977) (part of violation is that, in some cases, there was no sick call for three weeks); Casey v. Lewis, 834 F. Supp. 1477 (D. Ariz. 1993) (sick call system which discourages use because inmates must stand in line for long periods of time violates the Constitution); Lightfoot v. Walker, 486 F. Supp. 504, 526 (S.D. Ill. 1980) (procedure must exist); Laaman v. Helgemoe, 437 F. Supp. 269, 327 (D.N.H. 1977) (sick call procedure required); Dawson v. Kendrick, 527 F. Supp. 1252, 1273, (S.D. W. Va. 1981) (no regular sick call part of violations); Hoptowit v. Ray, 682 F.2d 1237, 1252-55, 9 Fed. R. Evid. Serv. 1511 (9th Cir. 1982) (must have "ready access to adequate medical care," lack of sick call every day part of inadequacy). See also Model Sentencing and Corrections Act § 4-105(b)(4) (July 2001); U.S. Dept of Justice, Federal Standards for Prisons and Jails §§ 5.19-20 (1980); ABA Standards for Criminal Justice §§ 23.5-1, 23.5-2; American Correctional Assn, Standards for Adult Correctional Institutions Standards 3-4331, 3-4353 (1990); National Commission on Correctional Health Care, Standards for Health Services in Jails J-32, J-35 through J-36 (May 1999); Commission on Accreditation for Corrections, Certification Standards for Health Care Programs HC-069 through HC-070 (1989).

§ 3:6   RIGHTS OF PRISONERS, THIRD EDITION

First, often the person doing the screening is untrained, and sometimes that person is another inmate. The case law is clear that if screening is to take place, the person doing the screening need not be a doctor but must be adequately trained to identify medical needs and determine the urgency with which the inmate must see the doctor.[4]

---

[4]Carty v. Farrelly, 957 F. Supp. 727, 22 A.D.D. 333 (D.V.I. 1997) (medical care screenings conducted by the prison security staff violated the Eighth Amendment); Todaro v. Ward, 431 F. Supp. 1129, 1143-46 (S.D. N.Y. 1977), judgment aff'd, 565 F.2d 48 (2d Cir. 1977) and aff'd, 652 F.2d 54 (2d Cir. 1981) (lobby clinic system prevented adequate examination and inadequately recorded need so that nurse could not determine who needed priority appointment with doctor); Battle v. Anderson, 376 F. Supp. 402, 434 (E.D. Okla. 1974), judgment aff'd in part, rev'd in part on other grounds, 993 F.2d 1551 (10th Cir. 1993) (must be seen by at least a "fully qualified health para-professional"); Miller v. Carson, 401 F. Supp. 835, 876 (M.D. Fla. 1975), aff'd in part, modified in part on other grounds and remanded, 563 F.2d 741 (5th Cir. 1977) (guards screened access to doctors and often inmate cannot obtain access; death had resulted); Newman v. State of Ala., 349 F. Supp. 278, 284 (M.D. Ala. 1972), aff'd in part, 503 F.2d 1320 (5th Cir. 1974) and judgment vacated in part on other grounds, 522 F.2d 71 (5th Cir. 1975) (untrained people screened and often denied access); Lightfoot v. Walker, 486 F. Supp. 504, 516, 526 (S.D. Ill. 1980) (system inadequate where no protocols and inadequately trained staff); Laaman v. Helgemoe, 437 F. Supp. 269, 313, 327 (D. N.H. 1977) (need trained personnel to screen access); Balla v. Idaho State Bd. of Corrections, 595 F. Supp. 1558, 1566-67, 1576 (D. Idaho 1984) (requests required guard's permission and often ignored); Gates v. Collier, 349 F. Supp. 881, 888, (N.D. Miss. 1972), judgment aff'd, 489 F.2d 298 (5th Cir. 1973), reh'g granted, 500 F.2d 1382 (5th Cir. 1974) and judgment aff'd, 501 F.2d 1291 (5th Cir. 1974) and order amended, 390 F. Supp. 482 (N.D. Miss. 1975), judgment aff'd, 525 F.2d 965 (5th Cir. 1976) and order supplemented, 423 F. Supp. 732 (N.D. Miss. 1976), judgment aff'd and remanded, 548 F.2d 1241 (5th Cir. 1977) (guards discouraged seeking medical attention and, upon express finding by superintendent, punished those who "unnecessarily request[ed] aid of a doctor"); see also U.S. Dept. of Justice, Federal Standards for Prisons and Jails § 5.37 (1980); American Correctional Assn, Standards for Adult Correctional Institutions, Standard § 3-4331 (1990); National Commission on Correctional Health Care, Stan-

MEDICAL CARE § 3:6

Second, if the screening process is not working properly, those doing the screening may improperly deny an inmate access to a doctor.[5] Denial of access to a doctor in cases where there is a clear need to see a physician is a violation of the Constitution.[6] It is not necessary, however, that access be completely denied

---

dards for Health Services in Jails J-17, J-19 (May 1999); Commission on Accreditation for Corrections, Certification Standards for Health Care Programs HC-049, H-057 (1989). All of the standards generally prohibit use of inmates to perform screening, no matter how well-trained.

[5]See, e.g., Rosen v. Chang, 811 F. Supp. 754, 760 (D.R.I. 1993) (nurse failed to make simple diagnosis of appendicitis and delayed access to doctor, and inmate died).

[6]Estelle v. Gamble, 429 U.S. 97, 104-05, 97 S. Ct. 285, 50 L. Ed. 2d 251 (1976); Watson v. Caton, 984 F.2d 537, 540 (1st Cir. 1993) (holding that allegation that inmate was denied medical treatment on the erroneous grounds that the institution was not liable for injuries that occurred prior to incarceration stated a claim); Hoptowit v. Ray, 682 F.2d 1237, 1252-55, 9 Fed. R. Evid. Serv. 1511 (9th Cir. 1982) (guards sometimes denied access to physicians, and this was part of inadequacy); Newman v. State of Ala., 349 F. Supp. 278, 284 (M.D. Ala. 1972), aff'd in part, 503 F.2d 1320 (5th Cir. 1974) and judgment vacated in part on other grounds, 522 F.2d 71 (5th Cir. 1975) (denied access to doctor and prescribed medication; denied needed surgery); Balla v. Idaho State Bd. of Corrections, 595 F. Supp. 1558, 1567, 1576 (D. Idaho 1984); Ancata v. Prison Health Services, Inc., 769 F.2d 700, 704 (11th Cir. 1985) (failure to meet known health needs is a violation and thus cause of action stated when alleged failure to provide access to specialists until inmate agreed to pay for them, resulting in death);Bass by Lewis v. Wallenstein, 769 F.2d 1173 (7th Cir. 1985) (upholding jury verdict for plaintiff who died of cardiac failure based on entire night when sick call procedure failed to bring attention, 15-minute delay in response, unqualified medical technicians, inadequate equipment, and doctor who wrongly pronounced inmate dead); French v. Owens, 777 F.2d 1250, 1254 (7th Cir. 1985) (inmates untreated for tuberculosis, broken back, abscessed rectum as a result of inadequate staff); Kaminsky v. Rosenblum, 929 F.2d 922 (2d Cir. 1991) (no treatment for critical three months); Kelsey v. Ewing, 652 F.2d 4 (8th Cir. 1981) (denied examination following surgery); Barksdale v. King, 699 F.2d 744 (5th Cir. 1983) (sickle cell anemia); Maclin v. Freake, 650 F.2d 885 (7th Cir. 1981) (paraplegic given no physical therapy); Aswegan v.

§ 3:6 RIGHTS OF PRISONERS, THIRD EDITION

for there to be a violation. If there is a delay in providing access to the doctor, a violation may exist.[7] The

---

Bruhl, 965 F.2d 676, 677-78 (8th Cir. 1992) (upholding jury verdict for plaintiffs against senior prison officials who denied access to medical personnel); Tucker v. Randall, 948 F.2d 388, 391 (7th Cir. 1991) (denial of treatment for nine and one half months for broken ribs and hand); Rubeck v. Sheriff of Wabash County, 824 F. Supp. 1291 (N.D. Ind. 1993) (failure to treat infected insect bites is actionable).

In Bailey v. Yu, 2000 WL 33127866 (N.D. Ill. 2000), the plaintiff injured his hand when it went through a window while he was working. Doctors stitched the wound, but scheduled him for further surgery. The surgery was repeatedly cancelled and postponed in favor of other inmates with more serious needs. The prison doctor regularly examined the plaintiff. The court held there was no showing that the defendants acted with deliberate indifference toward the inmate's serious medical needs. See also Tajeddini v. Gluch, 942 F. Supp. 772 (D. Conn. 1996) (holding that failure to treat dizziness, trembling and permanent pain was actionable); Model Sentencing and Corrections Act §§ 2-503(2), 4-105(a), (e) (July 2001).

[7]Estelle v. Gamble, 429 U.S. 97, 104-05, 97 S. Ct. 285, 50 L. Ed. 2d 251 (1976); Martin v. Tyson, 845 F.2d 1451 (7th Cir. 1988) (delay of one month in treating ear infection); Ramos v Lamm, 639 F2d 559, 577 (10th Cir 1980) (where officials rely on outside facilities, must have adequate transportation to prevent delay); Matzker v. Herr, 748 F.2d 1142 (7th Cir. 1984) (delay of three months in examining inmate with allegation of eye injury, though inmate seen for broken nose, causing pain and permanent injury stated cause of action); Toussaint v. Rushen, 553 F. Supp. 1365 (N.D. Cal. 1983), aff'd in part, 722 F.2d 1490 (9th Cir. 1984) (delay of weeks or months was part of violation); Nicholson v. Choctaw County, Ala., 498 F. Supp. 295, 308 (S.D. Ala. 1980) (delays part of violations); Fambro v. Fulton County, Ga., 713 F. Supp. 1426, 1429 (N.D. Ga. 1989) (delays of up to three days for medication, including critical medication, such as insulin or epileptic medication, and delay of up to a week for over-the-counter medication constituted part of findings of violation); Inmates of Occoquan v. Barry, 717 F. Supp. 854, 867 (D.D.C. 1989) (delay of months for appointments to specialty clinics); Todaro v. Ward, 431 F. Supp. 1129, 1133, (S.D. N.Y. 1977), judgment aff'd, 565 F.2d 48 (2d Cir. 1977) and aff'd, 652 F.2d 54 (2d Cir. 1981) (delays of two weeks to two months; however, delay in reporting venereal disease tests and pap tests, standing alone, did not rise to the level of constitutional violation

MEDICAL CARE § 3:6

amount of acceptable delay cannot be stated in terms of minutes or hours because it depends heavily on the seriousness of the need. Thus, a delay of 15 minutes in responding to a heart attack, a delay of 12-15 hours for an inmate with numbness in his leg, and a delay of 5 hours with the express purpose of making the inmate suffer have all been found to state a cause of action for damages.[8] On the other hand, a delay of a month for an

---

that would require judicial intervention); Newman v. State of Ala., 349 F. Supp. 278, 288 (M.D. Ala. 1972), aff'd in part, 503 F.2d 1320 (5th Cir. 1974) and judgment vacated in part on other grounds, 522 F.2d 71 (5th Cir. 1975) (delays of weeks or months unacceptable; if sent for medical care, must be seen within 12 hours); Archer v. Dutcher, 733 F.2d 14 (2d Cir. 1984) (delay of five hours "in order to make Archer suffer" stated cause of action); Bass by Lewis v. Wallenstein, 769 F.2d 1173 (7th Cir. 1985) (upholding jury verdict for representative of inmate who died of cardiac failure based on 15-minute delay in response, unqualified medical technicians, inadequate equipment, and doctor who wrongly pronounced inmate dead); Kaminsky v. Rosenblum, 929 F.2d 922 (2d Cir. 1991) (delay of five days in hospitalizing); McGuckin v. Smith, 974 F.2d 1050, 1062, 23 Fed. R. Serv. 3d 922 (9th Cir. 1992) (overruled on other grounds by, WMX Technologies, Inc. v. Miller, 104 F.3d 1133, 36 Fed. R. Serv. 3d 1042 (9th Cir. 1997)) (seven-month delay for surgery during which inmate was in pain); Johnson v. Bowers, 884 F.2d 1053 (8th Cir. 1989), reh'g en banc denied, (Oct. 27, 1989) and as modified on reh'g, (Oct. 27, 1989) (where nine-year delay for hand surgery, upheld jury verdict for defendants but ordered surgery take place); Women Prisoners of District of Columbia Dept. of Corrections v. District of Columbia, 877 F. Supp. 634, 98 Ed. Law Rep. 681 (D.D.C. 1994), vacated in part on other grounds, modified in part on other grounds, 899 F. Supp. 659, 104 Ed. Law Rep. 213 (D.D.C. 1995) (holding that delay of five months in granting a request for a mammogram and breast examination by a physician was a constitutional violation); See also Model Sentencing and Corrections Act § 4-105(e) (July 2001); ABA Standards for Criminal Justice § 23.5-2 (1986).

[8]Fitzke v. Shappell, 468 F.2d 1072 (6th Cir. 1972) (delay of 12-17 hours where inmate limping and complaining of numbness in leg stated cause of action); Archer v. Dutcher, 733 F.2d 14 (2d Cir. 1984) (delay of five hours "in order to make Archer suffer" stated cause of action); Bass by Lewis v. Wallenstein, 769 F.2d 1173 (7th Cir. 1985) (upholding jury verdict for representative of

§ 3:6   RIGHTS OF PRISONERS, THIRD EDITION

ear infection, where no permanent damage resulted, did not confer liability on the prison.[9] Systematic delays

---

inmate who died of cardiac failure based on 15-minute delay in response, unqualified medical technicians, inadequate equipment, and doctor who wrongly pronounced inmate dead); see also Cooper v. Casey, 97 F.3d 914 (7th Cir. 1996) (two-day delay in providing two inmates who shared a cell medical care for cuts, muscular pain and burning sensation in eyes and skin as a result of being sprayed by mace and assaulted by prison guards constituted deliberate indifference); Antonelli v. Sheahan, 81 F.3d 1422 (7th Cir. 1996) (holding that delay in providing psychological treatment and psychological medication stated a claim); Reece v. Groose, 60 F.3d 487 (8th Cir. 1995) (delay of two hours after another inmate threw hot water on plaintiff); Durmer v. O'Carroll, 991 F.2d 64 (3d Cir. 1993) (delayed physical therapy for stroke victim until it was too late to be effective was a constitutional violation); Pedraza v. Meyer, 919 F.2d 317 (5th Cir. 1990) (delay of several days in withdrawal); Duncan v. Duckworth, 644 F.2d 653, 654 (7th Cir. 1981) (delay of over a year of surgery for broken wrist when inmate in pain); Toombs v. Bell, 798 F.2d 297 (8th Cir. 1986) (not treated for three weeks and lost gall bladder as a result); Kelsey v. Ewing, 652 F.2d 4, 6 (8th Cir. 1981) (ten-year delay in hernia operation and six-year delay in operation on vein in right leg); Hathaway v. Coughlin, 841 F.2d 48 (2d Cir. 1988) (two years for hip surgery); Nelson v. Prison Health Services, Inc., 991 F. Supp. 1452 (M.D. Fla. 1997) (delay of seventeen hours of medication and treatment constituted deliberate indifference where inmate died of an acute heart attack); Mandala v. Coughlin, 920 F. Supp. 342 (E.D. N.Y. 1996) (holding that two-year delay in providing high fiber diet prescribed by physician and surgeon and physical therapy for two years stated a claim); Casey v. Lewis, 834 F. Supp. 1477 (D. Ariz. 1993) (one-month delay in treatment of serious gynecological problem was a constitutional violation); Senisais v. Fitzgerald, 940 F. Supp. 196 (N.D. Ill. 1996) (delay of nine days before inmate's broken hand was set in a cast was sufficient to state a cause of action for deliberate indifference);Abdush-Shahid v. Coughlin, 933 F. Supp. 168 (N.D. N.Y. 1996) (wait of almost three years to remove a salivary gallstone was a violation); Young v. Harris, 509 F. Supp. 1111 (S.D. N.Y. 1981) (one and one-half years for leg brace).

[9]Martin v. Tyson, 845 F.2d 1451 (7th Cir. 1988) (claim of delay of one month in treating ear infection insufficient when no permanent damage alleged). See also Vance v. Peters, 97 F.3d 987, 45 Fed. R. Evid. Serv. 1068 (7th Cir. 1996) (delay of 13 days after inmate suffered a broken arm was insufficient to state a cause of

MEDICAL CARE § 3:6

of weeks or months, regardless of the severity of the

action for deliberate indifference where prison officials were not "sufficiently informed of the situation to require their intervention."); Gutierrez v. Peters, 111 F.3d 1364 (7th Cir. 1997) (delay of six days where prison officials failed to attend to an inmate's infected cyst did not amount to deliberate indifference; given the benign nature of the plaintiff's condition); White v. State of Colo., 82 F.3d 364, 366, 15 A.D.D. 18 (10th Cir. 1996) ("one or two year delay in having the surgery until the plaintiff's release from prison, would not cause further damage to the plaintiff's leg"); Mahan v. Plymouth County House of Corrections, 64 F.3d 14 (1st Cir. 1995) (delay of one week in giving medication for depression and severe anxiety not actionable where prison officials were unaware of the severity of the condition); Olson v. Stotts, 9 F.3d 1475 (10th Cir. 1993) (11-day delay in heart surgery, termed elective, was acceptable, where evidence showed that inmate's recurrent chest pains were treated effectively with nitroglycerin); Ervin v. Busby, 992 F.2d 147 (8th Cir. 1993) (one-month delay in receiving Elavil after transfer to new facility was not a constitutional violation); Peterson v. Davis, 551 F. Supp. 137, 147, 12 Fed. R. Evid. Serv. 112 (D. Md. 1982), judgment aff'd, 729 F.2d 1453 (4th Cir. 1984) (excusing delays in treating minor injuries incurred by large number of inmates after prison disturbance); Gaudreault v. Municipality of Salem, Mass., 923 F.2d 203, 208 (1st Cir. 1990) (harmless delay of 10 hours in treating minor bruises and abrasions); Pierce v. King, 918 F. Supp. 932, 15 A.D.D. 246 (E.D. N.C. 1996), aff'd, 131 F.3d 136 (4th Cir. 1997), cert. granted, judgment vacated on other grounds, 525 U.S. 802, 119 S. Ct. 33, 142 L. Ed. 2d 25 (1998) (delay of one day in treatment of a swollen finger not a violation where injury appeared minor and the inmate was treated the next day by the prison doctor); Williams v. Keane, 940 F. Supp. 566 (S.D. N.Y. 1996) (delay of several months for a corrective shoe insert did not violate the Eighth Amendment); Jeffries v. Block, 940 F. Supp. 1509 (C.D. Cal. 1996) (delay in TB test not actionable where no injury occurred); Shiflet v. Cornell, 933 F. Supp. 1549 (M.D. Fla. 1996) (29-hour delay of access to a physician after inmate suffered a stroke was insufficient to state a cause of action for deliberate indifference where inmate was immediately brought to the emergency room, where he was treated by nurses); Coppage v. Mann, 906 F. Supp. 1025 (E.D. Va. 1995) (delay in removing inmate's waste during the evening hours was not actionable where inmate's spinal cancer caused incontinence and prison medical staff was understaffed at night); Caldwell v. District of Columbia, 901 F. Supp. 7 (D.D.C. 1995) (failure to provide medical treatment for 35 minutes after staff was informed that inmate was stabbed

§ 3:6 RIGHTS OF PRISONERS, THIRD EDITION

needs, are unacceptable.[10]

---

by three prisoners with ball point pens not a violation); Fillmore v. Eichkorn, 891 F. Supp. 1482 (D. Kan. 1995), judgment aff'd, 77 F.3d 492 (10th Cir. 1996) (prison officials did not violate Eighth Amendment where they failed to provide inmate with psychological counselor during the first 48 hours of incarceration); Cummings v. McCarter, 826 F. Supp. 299 (E.D. Mo. 1993) (two-day delay in treatment of headaches not a violation); Inmates, Washington County Jail v. England, 516 F. Supp. 132, 139 (E.D. Tenn. 1980), aff'd, 659 F.2d 1081 (6th Cir. 1981) (sufficient that "eventually" treated for 100% permanent disability and back and leg injury); Tyler v. Rapone, 603 F. Supp. 268, 271-72 (E.D. Pa. 1985) (delay of two weeks in treating toothache and cut not significant); McGuckin v. Smith, 974 F.2d 1050, 1060, 23 Fed. R. Serv. 3d 922 (9th Cir. 1992) (overruled on other grounds by, WMX Technologies, Inc. v. Miller, 104 F.3d 1133, 36 Fed. R. Serv. 3d 1042 (9th Cir. 1997)) ("mere delay" insufficient); Barnes v. Parker, 972 F.2d 978 (8th Cir. 1992) (upholding jury dismissal despite allegations of two and one half month delay in seeing specialist and over seven months in reading MRI); Taylor v. Bowers, 966 F.2d 417, 421 (8th Cir. 1992), opinion modified on other grounds on reh'g, (July 31, 1992) (delay alone not enough for liability); Aaron v. Finkbinder, 793 F. Supp. 734 (E.D. Mich. 1992), judgment aff'd, 4 F.3d 993 (6th Cir. 1993) (one day delay in insulin with no lasting effects); Sires v. Berman, 834 F.2d 9, 13 (1st Cir. 1987) (delay of several hours in applying nitropaste).

[10]Shannon v. White, 992 F.2d 791 (8th Cir. 1993) (noting with approval, the magistrate judge's observation that, "[w]hile it may be permissible to ignore a rash's origin for a short time, overlooking the origin of a rash for two or three years seems inappropriate"); Ramos v Lamm, 639 F2d 559, 577 (10th Cir 1980) (where prison relies on outside facilities, it must have adequate transportation to prevent delay); Toussaint v. Rushen, 553 F. Supp. 1365 (N.D. Cal. 1983), aff'd in part, 722 F.2d 1490 (9th Cir. 1984) (delay of weeks or months is part of violation); Nicholson v. Choctaw County, Ala., 498 F. Supp. 295, 308 (S.D. Ala. 1980) (delays part of violations); Fambro v. Fulton County, Ga., 713 F. Supp. 1426, 1429 (N.D. Ga. 1989) (delays of up to three days for medication, including critical medication such as insulin or epileptic medication, and delay of up to a week for over-the-counter medication, constituted part of findings of violation); Inmates of Occoquan v. Barry, 717 F. Supp. 854, 867 (D.D.C. 1989) (delay of months for appointments to specialty clinics); Todaro v. Ward, 431 F. Supp. 1129, 1133, (S.D. N.Y. 1977), judgment aff'd, 565 F.2d 48 (2d Cir. 1977) and aff'd,

MEDICAL CARE § 3:7

Where medical procedures do not work to ensure access to medical care, courts have looked to determine the reason, and where there have been no procedures or where the procedures have been inadequate, part of the remedy has been an injunction requiring that procedures be developed or changed. This includes development of medical protocols, emergency procedures, required staff meetings, supervisory rules, and quality assurance systems.[11]

§ 3:7 Periodic Examinations and Necessary Treatment

Periodic Examinations

In addition to reviewing the initial screening and

---

652 F.2d 54 (2d Cir. 1981) (delays of two weeks to two months; however, delay in reporting venereal disease tests and pap tests, standing alone, did not rise to the level of constitutional violation that would require judicial intervention); Newman v. State of Ala., 349 F. Supp. 278, 288 (M.D. Ala. 1972), aff'd in part, 503 F.2d 1320 (5th Cir. 1974) and judgment vacated in part on other grounds, 522 F.2d 71 (5th Cir. 1975) (delays of weeks or months unacceptable; if inmate sent for medical care, must be seen within 12 hours); Williams v. Edwards, 547 F.2d 1206, 1217 (5th Cir. 1977) (delays of up to six months for needed surgery).

[11]Grubbs v. Bradley, 821 F. Supp. 496 (M.D. Tenn. 1993) (injunction issued requiring institution to develop a quality assurance plan for medical services, with reports to plaintiffs' counsel for one year); Cody v. Hillard, 599 F. Supp. 1025, 1057-58 (D.S.D. 1984), decision aff'd, 799 F.2d 447 (8th Cir. 1986), reh'g granted, 804 F.2d 440 (8th Cir. 1986) and on reh'g, 830 F.2d 912 (8th Cir. 1987) (must be medical protocols and quality assurance system); Tillery v. Owens, 719 F. Supp. 1256, 1305-06, 1308 (W.D. Pa. 1989), order aff'd, 907 F.2d 418 (3d Cir. 1990) (need protocols, emergency plan); Todaro v. Ward, 431 F. Supp. 1129, 1147-49 (S.D. N.Y. 1977), judgment aff'd, 565 F.2d 48 (2d Cir. 1977) and aff'd, 652 F.2d 54 (2d Cir. 1981) (poor system for ensuring all labs tests done and positive results followed up, doctor follow up visits conducted); Palmigiano v. Garrahy, 443 F. Supp. 956, 975 (D.R.I. 1977) (inadequate system including evaluation, protocols, statistics); Newman v. State of Ala., 349 F. Supp. 278, 286-88 (M.D. Ala. 1972), aff'd in part, 503 F.2d 1320 (5th Cir. 1974) and judgment vacated in part on other grounds, 522 F.2d 71 (5th Cir. 1975).

§ 3:7 RIGHTS OF PRISONERS, THIRD EDITION

emergency and sick call procedures courts have reviewed both the frequency and the adequacy of routine examinations and, where they were deficient, ordered improvements.[1] One case required routine examinations at least every two years and another required them every year.[2] The content of the examinations is largely left to the discretion of prison officials. However,

---

[Section 3:7]
[1]Fambro v. Fulton County, Ga., 713 F. Supp. 1426, 1429 (N.D. Ga. 1989) (delays of up to 20 days for examinations part of violations); Tillery v. Owens, 719 F. Supp. 1256, 1295, 1306-07 (W.D. Pa. 1989), order aff'd, 907 F.2d 418 (3d Cir. 1990) (examinations at sick call too cursory, especially in restrictive unit where done "by looking at the inmate through the mesh window in the cell door;" when the noise level was too high, "the doctor leaves because he cannot hear the inmate's complaint"); Todaro v. Ward, 431 F. Supp. 1129 (S.D. N.Y. 1977), judgment aff'd, 565 F.2d 48 (2d Cir. 1977) and aff'd, 652 F.2d 54 (2d Cir. 1981) (screening system that prohibited examination impermissible); Newman v. State of Ala., 349 F. Supp. 278, 287 (M.D. Ala. 1972), aff'd in part, 503 F.2d 1320 (5th Cir. 1974) and judgment vacated in part on other grounds, 522 F.2d 71 (5th Cir. 1975) (must be regular examinations every two years); Lightfoot v. Walker, 486 F. Supp. 504, 518, 527 (S.D. Ill. 1980) (not enough doctors to assure examinations done "on a timely and regular basis" and of adequate quality); Laaman v. Helgemoe, 437 F. Supp. 269, 312, 327 (D.N.H. 1977) ("systemic absence of complete routine physical examinations, blood tests, syphilis tests, and other ordinary preventative measures can endanger the entire prison community"; these tests must be done annually).

[2]Newman v. State of Ala., 349 F. Supp. 278, 287 (M.D. Ala. 1972), aff'd in part, 503 F.2d 1320 (5th Cir. 1974) and judgment vacated in part on other grounds, 522 F.2d 71 (5th Cir. 1975) (must be regular examinations every two years); Laaman v. Helgemoe, 437 F. Supp. 269, 312, 327 (D.N.H. 1977) (annual). See also Model Sentencing and Corrections Act § 4-105(b)(2)(ii) (July 2001) (every two years); U.S. Dept of Justice Federal Standards for Prisons and Jails § 5.45 (1980); ABA Standards for Criminal Justice § 23.5-3 (1986) (generally every two years); American Correctional Assn, Standards for Adult Correctional Institutions, Standard 3-4348 (1990); National Commn on Correctional Health Care, Standards for Health Services in Jails J-33 (May 1999); Commission on Accreditation for Corrections, Certification Standards for Health Care Programs HC-059 through HC-061,HC-071 (1989). Most of

MEDICAL CARE § 3:7

clearly inadequate medical examinations are not countenanced. In one egregious case, "examinations" were done by trying to shout to the inmate through a mesh window in the cell door.[3]

Necessary Treatment

Four important principles relating to treatment have emerged from the prison medical care cases:

First, prison officials must ensure that officials follow through and that prescribed treatment is provided to inmates in a competent fashion.[4] One of the most commonly discussed deficiencies is the failure to ensure

---

the standard-setting organizations also require an examination shortly after arrival at the institution (in addition to the initial screening) and prior to release. *Id.*

[3]Tillery v. Owens, 719 F. Supp. 1256, 1295, 1306-07 (W.D. Pa. 1989), order aff'd, 907 F.2d 418 (3d Cir. 1990) (examinations at sick call too cursory, especially in restrictive unit where done "by looking at the inmate through the mesh window in the cell door. If the noise level . . . is too high, the doctor leaves because he cannot hear the inmate's complaint").

[4]Estelle v. Gamble, 429 U.S. 97, 104, 97 S. Ct. 285, 50 L. Ed. 2d 251 (1976); Todaro v. Ward, 431 F. Supp. 1129, 1133, 1151-54 (S.D. N.Y. 1977), judgment aff'd, 565 F.2d 48 (2d Cir. 1977) and aff'd, 652 F.2d 54 (2d Cir. 1981) ("The failure to carry out physician-ordered treatment is not constitutionally tolerable."); Battle v. Anderson, 457 F. Supp. 719, 730 (E.D. Okla. 1978) (lack of follow-up "contributed to death, pain, permanent injury and unnecessary suffering); Hoptowit v. Ray, 682 F.2d 1237, 1252, 9 Fed. R. Evid. Serv. 1511 (9th Cir. 1982); Nicholson v. Choctaw County, Ala., 498 F. Supp. 295, 308 (S.D. Ala. 1980) (inadequate system for ensuring inmates received medication); Cody v. Hillard, 599 F. Supp. 1025, 1056 (D.S.D. 1984), decision aff'd, 799 F.2d 447 (8th Cir. 1986), reh'g granted, 804 F.2d 440 (8th Cir. 1986) and on reh'g, 830 F.2d 912 (8th Cir. 1987) (acceptable to use guards to dispense medication if they are appropriately trained); Inmates of Occoquan v. Barry, 717 F. Supp. 854, 867 (D.D.C. 1989) (no system for follow-up of treatment of contagious diseases); Tillery v. Owens, 719 F. Supp. 1256, 1307 (W.D. Pa. 1989), order aff'd, 907 F.2d 418 (3d Cir. 1990) (inadequate monitoring of drug and inmate match); Newman v. State of Ala., 349 F. Supp. 278, 284 (M.D. Ala. 1972), aff'd in part, 503 F.2d 1320 (5th Cir. 1974) and judgment vacated in part on other grounds, 522 F.2d 71 (5th Cir. 1975) (no

§ 3:7 RIGHTS OF PRISONERS, THIRD EDITION

that inmates get prescribed medication; consequently, medication distribution systems are frequently found to be inadequate.[5] In addition to ensuring that inmates

---

follow-up on diet, medications, bandages and other doctor's orders); Lightfoot v. Walker, 486 F. Supp. 504, 517 (S.D. Ill. 1980) ("haphazard system of distribution" including guards must be cured so that only trained and supervised staff dispensed medication); Dawson v. Kendrick, 527 F. Supp. 1252, 1273, (S.D. W. Va. 1981) (jailers dispensed medication haphazardly); Eades v. Thompson, 823 F.2d 1055 (7th Cir. 1987) (failure to follow post-surgical orders); Johnson v. Hay, 931 F.2d 456 (8th Cir. 1991) (prison pharmacist refused to fill prescription for seizure medication); Boretti v. Wiscomb, 930 F.2d 1150 (6th Cir. 1991) (post-surgical care); Garcia v. Salt Lake County, 768 F.2d 303 (10th Cir. 1985) (upholding jury verdict where policy required frequent monitoring of unconscious inmate but not done); Aswegan v. Bruhl, 965 F.2d 676, 677-78 (8th Cir. 1992) (upholding jury verdict for plaintiffs against senior prison officials who failed to take steps to eliminate repeated violations of orders that inmate's medications be delivered in a timely manner); Hill v. Marshall, 962 F.2d 1209, 35 Fed. R. Evid. Serv. 602 (6th Cir. 1992) (upholding jury verdict and reinstating punitive damage award where medication not given to inmate to prevent tuberculosis); Colle v. Brazos County, Tex., 981 F.2d 237, 245, 24 Fed. R. Serv. 3d 655 (5th Cir. 1993)(may be municipal liability where policy of inadequate monitoring as required by doctor); Hamilton v. Endell, 981 F.2d 1062, 1066-67, 24 Fed. R. Serv. 3d 1392 (9th Cir. 1992) (may be liability where treating surgeon's orders ignored, based on opinion of another doctor and inmate recovering from ear surgery forced to fly); White v. Napoleon, 897 F.2d 103, 111 (3d Cir. 1990) (may be liability where prison doctor ignored a dose of medication).

[5]Jones v. U.S., 91 F.3d 623 (3d Cir. 1996) (prison officials owed duty of care to prisoner for purposes of prisoner's action alleging that prison officials' negligent failure to provide him with blood pressure medication caused cerebral hemorrhage; statute specifically required Bureau of Prisons to provide for safekeeping, care, subsistence and protection of all prisoners; material issue of fact as to whether prison officials negligently failed to provide prisoner with his blood pressure medication within 12 hours of its normal prescription time precluded summary judgment for United States); Wakefield v. Thompson, 177 F.3d 1160 (9th Cir. 1999) (holding that prison officials must be sure that inmates who were released had a sufficient supply of prescribed medication); Ralston v. McGovern, 167 F.3d 1160 (7th Cir. 1999) (holding that allegations

MEDICAL CARE § 3:7

receive and take the medication prescribed for them, an additional component of medication delivery systems is that trained personnel must administer the medication to ensure that the medication is in fact taken and that

---

of failure to give pain medication to inmate suffering from Hodgkin's disease who was being treated with radiation that caused painful blisters in his throat and pain in his mouth stated a claim); Antonelli v. Sheahan, 81 F.3d 1422 (7th Cir. 1996) (holding that inmate stated a claim where he alleged that prison officials violated Eighth Amendment when they ignored his repeated requests for psychological medication); Hoptowit v. Ray, 682 F.2d 1237, 1252, 9 Fed. R. Evid. Serv. 1511 (9th Cir. 1982) (part of inadequacy was that medication system resulted in "denial or delay of distribution of proper medicine"); Nicholson v. Choctaw County, Ala., 498 F. Supp. 295, 308 (S.D. Ala. 1980) (inadequate system for ensuring inmates got medication); Tillery v. Owens, 719 F. Supp. 1256, 1307 (W.D. Pa. 1989), order aff'd, 907 F.2d 418 (3d Cir. 1990) (inadequate monitoring of drug and inmate match); Newman v. State of Ala., 349 F. Supp. 278, 284 (M.D. Ala. 1972), aff'd in part, 503 F.2d 1320 (5th Cir. 1974) and judgment vacated in part on other grounds, 522 F.2d 71 (5th Cir. 1975) (no follow-up on diet, medications, bandages and other doctor's orders); Patrick v. Staples, 780 F. Supp. 1528, 1545 (N.D. Ind. 1991) (failure to supply prescribed medication, "for the purpose of causing him unnecessary pain," stated cause of action). For a discussion of cases involving the failure to provide inmates adequate medication, see Michael S. Vaughn, Section 1983 Civil Liability of Prison Officials For Denying and Delaying Medication and Drugs to Prison Inmates, 11 Issues in L & Medicine 47 (1995). See also U.S. Dept of Justice, Federal Standards for Prisons and Jails §§ 5.34, 5.46 (1980); American Correctional Assn, Standards for Adult Correctional Institutions Standard 3-4341 (1990); Commission on Accreditation for Corrections, Certification Standards for Health Care Programs HC-086 (1989). But see Williams v. Cearlock, 993 F. Supp. 1192 (C.D. Ill. 1998) (occasional delays in giving medication and denials of medication are not actionable if inmate had otherwise been receiving comprehensive on-going medical treatment); Bundrick v. Hammond, 817 F. Supp. 470 (D. Del. 1993) (holding that there was no violation where delay in medication resulted from inmate's failure to make timely request); Moyers v. Buescher, 806 F. Supp. 218 (E.D. Mo. 1992) (holding that there was no violation where medical unit was open four times daily to dispense prescriptions and inmate did not receive medication because he was late).

§ 3:7   Rights of Prisoners, Third Edition

the proper inmate takes it, and to observe any effects, especially adverse effects, of the medication.[6] These personnel can be guards if, but only if, they are adequately trained. Following through on doctor's orders may also include obeying any restrictions set by the doctor on work assignments.[7] Additionally, prison officials may not block access to treatment for reasons

---

[6] Miller v. Carson, 401 F. Supp. 835, 879 (M.D. Fla. 1975), aff'd in part, modified in part on other grounds and remanded, 563 F.2d 741 (5th Cir. 1977) (guards sometimes administered medications and did it inadequately, mixing up medications); Dawson v. Kendrick, 527 F. Supp. 1252, 1273, (S.D. W. Va. 1981) (jailers dispensed medication haphazardly); Cody v. Hillard, 599 F. Supp. 1025, 1056 (D.S.D. 1984), decision aff'd, 799 F.2d 447 (8th Cir. 1986), reh'g granted, 804 F.2d 440 (8th Cir. 1986) and on reh'g, 830 F.2d 912 (8th Cir. 1987) (acceptable to use guards to dispense medication if they are appropriately trained); Lightfoot v. Walker, 486 F. Supp. 504, 517 (S.D. Ill. 1980) ("haphazard system of distribution" including guards must be cured so that only trained and supervised staff dispensed medication); Laaman v. Helgemoe, 437 F. Supp. 269, 313, 327 (D.N.H. 1977) (unacceptable for untrained personnel to dispensed medication); Dawson v. Kendrick, 527 F. Supp. 1252, 1273, (S.D. W. Va. 1981) (jailers haphazardly give medication); Inmates of Allegheny County Jail v. Peirce, 487 F. Supp. 638 (W.D. Pa. 1980) (medication must be dispensed by nurses). See also U.S. Dept of Justice, Federal Standards for Prisons and Jails §§ 5.36-37 (1980); ABA Standards for Criminal Justice § 23.5-23.6 (1986); American Correctional Assn, Standards for Adult Correctional Institutions, Standard 3-4341 (1990); National Commn on Correctional Health Care, Standards for Health Services in Jails J-24, -30 (May 1999); Commission on Accreditation for Corrections, Certification Standards for Health Care Programs HC-057, H-086 (1989).

[7] See Johnson v. Clinton, 763 F.2d 326, 328 (8th Cir. 1985); Speed v. Adams, 502 F. Supp. 426 (E.D. Ark. 1980) (doctor refused to alter work assignment of obese inmate); Roy v. Phelps, 488 So. 2d 468 (La. Ct. App. 3d Cir. 1986) (state law violation for improper work assignment); Taylor v. Bowers, 966 F.2d 417, 421 (8th Cir. 1992), opinion modified on reh'g, (July 31, 1992); Patrick v. Staples, 780 F. Supp. 1528, 1543 (N.D. Ind. 1991); Madewell v. Roberts, 909 F.2d 1203 (8th Cir. 1990).

§ 3:7

of prison management.[8] If treatment is provided, even if it does not rectify the medical problem, an inmate cannot claim that his constitutional rights have been violated.[9] But if obvious problems are ignored and not

---

[8]Estelle v. Gamble, 429 U.S. 97, 105, 97 S. Ct. 285, 50 L. Ed. 2d 251 (1976); Johnson v. Meltzer, 134 F.3d 1393 (9th Cir. 1998) (holding that waking a prisoner from the medically induced coma he was in so he could be questioned was unconstitutional); Cody v. Hillard, 599 F. Supp. 1025, 1056 (D.S.D. 1984), decision aff'd, 799 F.2d 447 (8th Cir. 1986), reh'g granted, 804 F.2d 440 (8th Cir. 1986) and on reh'g, 830 F.2d 912 (8th Cir. 1987) (violation for prison to discourage certain prescription drugs); Williams v. Vincent, 508 F.2d 541, 544-45 (2d Cir. 1974) (denial of pain medication for 22 days while in solitary stated cause of action); Eades v. Thompson, 823 F.2d 1055 (7th Cir. 1987) (discouraged trip to infirmary); Ancata v. Prison Health Services, Inc., 769 F.2d 700, 704 (11th Cir. 1985) (no care unless prisoner paid); Taylor v. Bowers, 966 F.2d 417, 421 (8th Cir. 1992), opinion modified on reh'g, (July 31, 1992) (violation stated if treatment withheld to coerce confession); Arnold on Behalf of H.B. v. Lewis, 803 F. Supp. 246, 257 (D. Ariz. 1992) (security personnel overrode medical decisions); Gill v. Mooney, 824 F.2d 192, 196 (2d Cir. 1987). But see Lucien v. Godinez, 814 F. Supp. 754 (N.D. Ill. 1993) (denial of medical treatment for non-emergency ailment in knee during prison lockdown did not rise to the level of an Eighth Amendment violation); Oldham v. Chandler-Halford, 877 F. Supp. 1340 (N.D. Iowa 1995) (no constitutional violation where prison officials refused to let prisoner with a wrist injury sleep on bottom bunk bed because sleeping on the top bunk was not a restricted strenuous activity). See also U.S. Dept of Justice, Federal Standards for Prisons and Jails §§ 5.02, 5.19 (1980); ABA Standards for Criminal Justice § 23.5-2 (1986); American Correctional Assn, Standards for Adult Correctional Institutions, Standard 3-4327 (1990); National Commn on Correctional Health Care, Standards for Health Services in Jails J-02 (May 1999); Commission on Accreditation for Corrections, Certification Standards for Health Care Programs HC-041 (1989).

[9]See, e.g., Jolly v. Knudsen, 205 F.3d 1094 (8th Cir. 2000) (physician's treatment of prisoner's seizure disorder, including changes in prisoner's dosage levels and referral to a specialist, did not constitute deliberate indifference to the prisoner's serious medical needs; evidence showed that the physician's actions were aimed at correcting perceived difficulties in the prisoner's dosage levels, and even if the prisoner did not have seizure disorder, as he later claimed, the treatment of the nonexistent disorder did not consti-

§ 3:7

tute deliberate indifference); Sherrer v. Stephens, 50 F.3d 496 (8th Cir. 1994) (inmate received adequate medical care when painkillers were administered, X-rays were taken, several orthopedists examined his injured index finger, and application of ice and motion therapy were recommended); Douglas v. Stanwick, 93 F. Supp. 2d 320 (W.D. N.Y. 2000) (jail physician's actions in instructing the nursing staff to hold the plaintiff's narcotic prescription, written by an outside doctor, until the nurses could determine if a non-narcotic would control the pain did not show sufficient culpability); Goosman v. Foti, 2000 WL 423902 (E.D. La. 2000), appeal dismissed, 240 F.3d 1074 (5th Cir. 2000) (plaintiff had received "extensive treatment" for cancer as well as broken facial bones and back pain from an injury received prior to incarceration; treatment included repeated referrals to hospital clinics, numerous clinic visits, diagnostic testing, and provision of medicines such as Tylenol, Motrin, Naprozen, and a vitamin-enriched drink); Kenney v. Hawaii, 109 F. Supp. 2d 1271 (D. Haw. 2000) (inmate stated a valid deliberate indifference claim where officials denied him a controlled substance he said he was required to take in order to control a neurological disorder); White v. Mitchell, 2001 WL 64756 (E.D. N.Y. 2001) (holding that refusal to respond to inmate's complaints about serious hearing loss raised a violation of Eighth Amendment claim); Petrichko v. Kurtz, 117 F. Supp. 2d 467 (E.D. Pa. 2000) (holding that inmate's claims that prison officials denied him a visit to the hospital for two weeks after he separated his shoulder, leading to permanent disability, was sufficient to state a claim that officials were deliberately indifferent); Verser v. Elyea, 113 F. Supp. 2d 1211 (N.D. Ill. 2000) (holding that there was a violation when directions from a private orthopedic doctor that inmate receive physical therapy three times a week and a knee brace were not followed); Williams v. One Female Corrections Officer Sergeant Kolaczyk, 940 F. Supp. 31, 20 A.D.D. 1285 (D. Mass. 1996) (medical treatment on a daily basis and hospitalization on four separate occasions was not deliberate indifference); West v. McCaughtry, 971 F. Supp. 1272 (E.D. Wis. 1997) (defendants were not deliberately indifferent, because during the course of this action plaintiff was taken to a neurology clinic and given physical therapy); Trammel v. Coombe, 170 Misc. 2d 471, 649 N.Y.S.2d 964 (Sup 1996) (inmate confined to special housing unit failed to state a claim that prison officials were deliberately indifferent to his medical needs when he was seen daily by a nurse and weekly by a physician; court dismissed plaintiff's claim).

MEDICAL CARE § 3:7

diagnosed then liability will follow.[10] However, inmates have a responsibility to make their needs known. If they do not report problems, then obviously prison officials cannot be held liable for failure to treat them.[11] There is also no constitutional violation if the treatment failure is due to the defendants' failure to follow instructions,[12] or to accept treatment.[13]

---

[10]See, e.g., Bartley v. Artuz, 1999 WL 942425 (S.D. N.Y. 1999), where the court held that deliberate indifference was established by defendant doctor's failure to diagnose and treat the deceased prisoner for smoke inhalation, even though the prisoner medical records indicated that he had been "involved in a fire in blk [sic]," that his voice was "hoarse" and that his throat exhibited "slight redness." Two days later, the prisoner died as a result of the smoke inhalation. The Court held that given the timing of the events and the defendant doctor's history of licensing problems in two different states, failure to diagnose and treat the deceased prisoner could raise a colorable inference of culpability.

In Nieto v. State, 952 P.2d 834 (Colo. Ct. App. 1997), cert. granted, (Mar. 23, 1998) and aff'd in part, rev'd in part on other grounds, 993 P.2d 493 (Colo. 2000), the court found deliberate indifference where the plaintiff complained of pain and a swollen right eye, was given flu medication and sent away. When days later he complained that his condition was worsening, he was told to continue with his medication. After a third complaint, he was told that if he returned he would be disciplined. The plaintiff, however, did return and told the nurse he believed that he was having a stroke. He was only given an antibiotic and decongestant. Twice over the next three days, he tried to seek help. Shortly after that the plaintiff was "found in his cell, unconscious and incontinent, his right eye bulging from its socket." He was taken to the hospital, where it was discovered that he had a severe sinus infection that had spread to his brain. The plaintiff had to undergo five surgeries, three of which were to the brain. The Colorado Court of Appeals affirmed the judgment of $150,000 in favor of the plaintiff, also reversing the dismissal of the plaintiff's 1983 action.

[11]See, e.g., Mitchell v. Maynard, 80 F.3d 1433, 34 Fed. R. Serv. 3d 1018 (10th Cir. 1996) (no deliberate indifference where inmate never advised prison officials of injury sustained in a confrontation with guards).

[12]See, e.g., Webber v. Hammack, 973 F. Supp. 116 (N.D. N.Y. 1997) (holding that when inmate failed to follow doctor's instructions, prison officials could not be held liable); Garcia v.

§ 3:7 RIGHTS OF PRISONERS, THIRD EDITION

Second, negligent administration of medical care is not unconstitutional, and an inmate has no constitutional right to have the treatment he or she prefers.[14]

Senkowski, 919 F. Supp. 609 (N.D. N.Y. 1996) (where inmate failed to use pain medication, crutches, knee brace, and physical therapy that prison medical officials provided for him, inmate was unable to demonstrate that prison officials acted with deliberate indifference).

[13]See, e.g., Dorsey v. St. Joseph County Jail Officials, 910 F. Supp. 1343 (N.D. Ind. 1996), judgment rev'd on other grounds, 98 F.3d 1527 (7th Cir. 1996) and (overruling recognized by, Bowden ex rel. Bowden v. Wal-Mart Stores, Inc., 124 F. Supp. 2d 1228 (M.D. Ala. 2000)) (inmate was belligerent and actually refused treatment); Staples v. Virginia Dept. of Corrections, 904 F. Supp. 487, 16 A.D.D. 1258 (E.D. Va. 1995) (holding that inmate's complaint regarding assistance at night to move his bowels was caused by his own failure to comply with medical officials requests); Zatko v. Rowland, 835 F. Supp. 1174 (N.D. Cal. 1993) (inmate who refused treatment for broken jaw could not bring 42 U.S.C. § 1983 claim).

[14]Estelle v. Gamble, 429 U.S. 97, 105-06, 97 S. Ct. 285, 50 L. Ed. 2d 251 (1976); McGuckin v. Smith, 974 F.2d 1050, 1059, 23 Fed. R. Serv. 3d 922 (9th Cir. 1992) (overruled on other grounds by, WMX Technologies, Inc. v. Miller, 104 F.3d 1133, 36 Fed. R. Serv. 3d 1042 (9th Cir. 1997)) (negligence not sufficient); Mayweather v. Foti, 958 F.2d 91 (5th Cir. 1992) (no violation by reason of the fact that "[t]he treatment may not have been the best that money could buy . . ."); Ledoux v. Davies, 961 F.2d 1536, 1537 (10th Cir. 1992) (inmate's desire for additional medication just a disagreement with doctor and not basis for liability); Taylor v. Bowers, 966 F.2d 417, 421 (8th Cir. 1992), opinion modified on reh'g, (July 31, 1992); Watson v. Caton, 984 F.2d 537, 540 (1st Cir. 1993) (disagreement about treatment for back injury did not suffice for violation); Mason v. City of Denver, 221 F.3d 1352 (10th Cir. 2000) (negligence not enough); Freeman v. Strack, 2000 WL 1459782 (S.D. N.Y. 2000) (holding that prison nurse's misdiagnosis of inmate's appendicitis for indigestion was not sufficient); Evans v. Ayers, F.Supp.2d 2000 LEXIS 18481 (N.D.Cal. November 29, 2000) (holding that disagreement between physicians regarding the effectiveness of the treatment did not raise a constitutional claim); Tillery v. Owens, 719 F. Supp. 1256, 1305 (W.D. Pa. 1989), order aff'd, 907 F.2d 418 (3d Cir. 1990) ("Constitution does not guarantee a prisoner the treatment of his choice"); Patrick v. Staples, 780 F. Supp. 1528, 1543-44 (N.D. Ind. 1991) (negligent ex-

MEDICAL CARE § 3:7

For this reason, differences of opinion between a prisoner and physicians concerning the need for, or the adequacy of, the treatment do not constitute deliberate indifference to serious medical need.[15] By the same token, prison officials are not liable for following the directions of physicians even if those directions are erroneous.[16] Nor is there liability if staff are rude to inmates as they provide treatment.[17] Seriously substandard treatment, however, can evidence deliberate indifference to serious medical needs and justify relief.[18] Where the incidents are repeated, it is more likely that

---

amination and disagreement about treatment insufficient for constitutional violations); Tomarkin v. Ward, 534 F. Supp. 1224, 1228-29 (S.D. N.Y. 1982); Givens v. Jones, 900 F.2d 1229, 1232-33 (8th Cir. 1990) (no violation for giving inmate medication he said he was allergic to). But see Greeno v. Litscher, 13 Fed. Appx. 370 (7th Cir. 2001) (disagreement over treatment due to misdiagnosis may state a claim). Cf., Model Sentencing and Corrections Act § 4-105(c) (July 2001) (inmates should be permitted to use own resources to obtain outside medical help); ABA Standards for Criminal Justice § 23.5-1 (1986) (commentary).

[15]McGee v. Bloor, 216 F.3d 1087 (10th Cir. 2000); Lewis v Booker, 189 F.3d 478 (10th Cir 1999); Guy v Graham, 188 F3d 513 (9th Cir 1999); Callaway v. Smith County, 991 F. Supp. 801 (E.D. Tex. 1998) (holding that disagreement with medical treatment received "is insufficient to set forth a constitutional claim").

[16]See, e.g., Coppage v. Mann, 906 F. Supp. 1025 (E.D. Va. 1995) (superintendent of prison was not deliberately indifferent to inmate's medical condition where he failed to have inmate transferred to another institution for treatment of his bed sores, despite his advisement of inmate's condition by prison nurse; court noted that superintendent relied on prison physician's judgment in care of inmate).

[17]Arce v. Banks, 913 F. Supp. 307 (S.D. N.Y. 1996), as amended, (Apr. 8, 1996)(holding mere yelling by the nurse was insufficient to state a claim).

[18]Estelle v. Gamble, 429 U.S. 97, 104-05, 97 S. Ct. 285, 50 L. Ed. 2d 251 (1976); Hathaway v. Coughlin, 37 F.3d 63 (2d Cir. 1994) (holding that allegation that doctor failed to inform inmate that hip pins had deteriorated, ignored the inmate's repeated complaints of pain, and failed to refer prisoner to a specialist was actionable); Harris v. Coweta County, 21 F.3d 388 (11th Cir. 1994) (failure to treat hand injury caused by handcuffs during arrest);

§ 3:7

Lee v. Akture, 827 F. Supp. 556 (E.D. Wis. 1993) (allegation that doctor refused to treat ear infection in retaliation for grievance filed by plaintiff stated an Eighth Amendment claim); Wellman v. Faulkner, 715 F.2d 269, 273-74 (7th Cir. 1983) (where sufficiently bad, part of pattern justifying class-wide relief); Ancata v. Prison Health Services, Inc., 769 F.2d 700, 704 (11th Cir. 1985) (if treatment is "so cursory as to amount to no treatment at all . . . in the case of serious medical problems," cause of action stated); Bass by Lewis v. Wallenstein, 769 F.2d 1173 (7th Cir. 1985) (upholding jury verdict for representative of plaintiff who died of cardiac failure based on 15-minute delay in response, unqualified medical technicians, inadequate equipment, and doctor who wrongly pronounced plaintiff dead). See also Wellman v. Faulkner, 715 F.2d 269, 272 (7th Cir. 1983) ("the policy of deferring to the judgment of prison officials in matters of prison discipline and security does not usually apply in the context of medical care to the same degree as in other contexts"); Greason v. Kemp, 891 F.2d 829, 835 (11th Cir. 1990) (rejecting qualified immunity where doctor "provided [grossly incompetent] care and, moreover, . . . realized that he was doing so at the time" in ignoring clear threat of suicide); Eades v. Thompson, 823 F.2d 1055 (7th Cir. 1987) (inmate transferred with open wound and no medical records); Mullen v. Smith, 738 F.2d 317, 318 (8th Cir. 1984) ("complaints were answered with ridicule and derision"); Ingalls v. Florio, 968 F. Supp. 193 (D.N.J. 1997) (allegations of systemic breakdowns in care at Camden County Correctional Facility stated a claim);Nelson v. Prison Health Services, Inc., 991 F. Supp. 1452 (M.D. Fla. 1997) (holding that ignoring the pleas of a extremely sick inmate who was not given medication for heart condition and who died was a case of potentially gross negligence); Rosen v. Chang, 811 F. Supp. 754, 760 (D.R.I. 1993) ("Grossly incompetent and recklessly inadequate examinations by a licensed physician is a deliberately indifferent examination. This is ineluctably so when the manifested symptoms scream of a diagnosis that virtually lies within the knowledge of a lay person."); Arnold on Behalf of H.B. v. Lewis, 803 F. Supp. 246, 258 (D. Ariz. 1992) ("The defendants' treatment . . . has been worse than grossly inadequate or inhumane. It has been barbaric."); Waldrop v. Evans, 681 F. Supp. 840, 854 (M.D. Ga. 1988), judgment aff'd, 871 F.2d 1030 (11th Cir. 1989) (doctor removed inmate from medicine prescribed by outside doctor); Dace v. Solem, 858 F.2d 385, 388 (8th Cir. 1988) (improper administration of medication); Lair v. Oglesby, 859 F.2d 605 (8th Cir. 1988) (drug given to inmate who said he is allergic to it); Medcalf v. State of Kan., 626 F. Supp. 1179, 1183 (D. Kan. 1986) (finding no

MEDICAL CARE § 3:8

the court will find a violation.[19]

Third, at least some courts have held that a medical care system is deficient if it does not include preventative as well as curative treatment.[20]

Finally, prison officials may impose reasonable security restrictions on the receipt of medical care.[21]

§ 3:8 Facilities and Equipment

There is certain basic equipment that must be pres-

---

cause of action where there is "a mere difference of opinion between the inmate and the institution's medical staff" but determining that genuine issue of material fact existed as to allegations that gross failure to diagnose and treat inmate's brain tumor led to death). See also U.S. Dept of Justice, Federal Standards for Prisons and Jails § 5.51 (1980).

[19]Kost v. Kozakiewicz, 1 F.3d 176 (3d Cir. 1993) (eight untreated heat strokes were a serious medical need and sufficient to establish deliberate indifference); White v. Napoleon, 897 F.2d 103, 109 (3d Cir. 1990).

[20]Hoptowit v. Ray, 682 F.2d 1237, 1253, 9 Fed. R. Evid. Serv. 1511 (9th Cir. 1982) ("lacks preventive health care"); Miller v. Carson, 401 F. Supp. 835, 876 (M.D. Fla. 1975), aff'd in part, modified in part on other grounds and remanded, 563 F.2d 741 (5th Cir. 1977) (none provided). See also U.S. Dept of Justice, Federal Standards for Prisons and Jails § 5.26 (1980); American Correctional Assn, Standards for Adult Correctional Institutions, Standard 3-4363 (1990); Commission on Accreditation for Corrections, Certification Standards for Health Care Programs HC-072 (1989).

[21]See, e.g., Haslar v. Megerman, 104 F.3d 178 (8th Cir. 1997) (held not violation when prison officials refused to remove leg shackles while inmate received medical treatment); May v. Baldwin, 895 F. Supp. 1398 (D. Or. 1995), judgment aff'd, 109 F.3d 557 (9th Cir. 1997) (prison officials did not act with deliberate indifference to inmate's medical needs where they prohibited inmate from seeing prison doctor until he unbraided his dreadlocks; court noted that prison officials encouraged inmate to seek post operative treatment for vocal cord tumor, but inmate declined to unbraid his dreadlocks). See also Aswegan v. Henry, 49 F.3d 461 (8th Cir. 1995) (holding that plaintiff afflicted with asthma did not show that prison officials acted with deliberate indifference when he was subjected to a cell shakedown, where the shakedown was conducted in an open shower stall with no water running, and the incident lasted only 30 minutes).

§ 3:8   Rights of Prisoners, Third Edition

ent in any medical care facility in order to provide adequate medical care, and the failure to have that equipment violates minimal constitutional standards. The minimal equipment necessary ordinarily includes all equipment needed for response to emergencies, such as defibrillation and suctioning equipment, and all equipment needed for the routine care that provided in the prison, such as X-ray equipment and routine laboratory testing equipment.[1] Where, as in most prisons, medica-

---

[Section 3:8]
[1]Loftin v. Dalessandri, 3 Fed. Appx. 658 (10th Cir. 2001) (failure to have isolation room for inmates who tested positive for tuberculosis); Wellman v. Faulkner, 715 F.2d 269, 274 (7th Cir. 1983) (lack of equipment such as "waste-collection bags for those inmates who have had a colostomy"); Austin v. Pennsylvania Dept. of Corrections, 876 F. Supp. 1437, 10 A.D.D. 1042 (E.D. Pa. 1995) (consent agreement provided that Department of Corrections must request funding for "standard medical equipment" in each of its facilities, including "call bell systems, an oxygen concentrator, a peak flow meter, a word processor, a computer, a pulse oximeter, crash carts (without defibrillator), hospital beds, Hoyer lifts, two autoclaves (one for dental, one for medical), an addressograph and embossers, a locked medicine cabinet for drug delivery, geriatric chairs, shower chairs, an ultrasonic dental machine, gurneys, a paper shredder, two refrigerators, equipment for restricted housing unit examination rooms and examination room areas and a motorized vehicle (such as a golf cart) for emergency use"); Miller v. Carson, 401 F. Supp. 835, 876-78 (M.D. Fla. 1975), aff'd in part, modified in part on other grounds and remanded, 563 F.2d 741 (5th Cir. 1977) (no X-ray facilities, no lab, no convalescent beds, no medications or necessary "small equipment," existing equipment inadequate, transportation van had no medical equipment); Williams v. Edwards, 547 F.2d 1206, 1216-17 (5th Cir. 1977) (no adequate lab, lab records, or statistics; lab supervision and equipment poor; no pharmacy records or supervision; surgery unit so poor surgeon refused to use it; fish to be cooked kept in whirlpool); Payne v Lynaugh, 843 F2d 177 (5th Cir 1988) (lack of oxygen equipment for severe emphysema stated cause of action); Carty v. Farrelly, 957 F. Supp. 727, 22 A.D.D. 333 (D.V.I. 1997) (prison medical facility violated the Eighth Amendment by its failure to maintain adequate equipment for medical emergencies.); Sappington v. Ulrich, 868 F. Supp. 194 (E.D. Tex. 1994) (no facilities to treat ankle injury); Inmates of Occoquan v. Barry, 717 F. Supp.

MEDICAL CARE § 3:8

tion is dispensed, minimal facilities must also include an adequate pharmacy.[2] Other kinds of equipment are also required where essential to the proper care of an inmate.[3]

The facilities within which care is delivered must

854, 862 (D.D.C. 1989) (no X-ray equipment); Palmigiano v. Garrahy, 443 F. Supp. 956, 974 (D.R.I. 1977) (no routine equipment to do lab tests, for suctioning, or for defibrillation); Dawson v. Kendrick, 527 F. Supp. 1252, 1308 (S.D. W. Va. 1981) ("total absence of medical supplies or a medical room"); Gates v. Collier, 349 F. Supp. 881, 888, (N.D. Miss. 1972), judgment aff'd, 489 F.2d 298 (5th Cir. 1973), reh'g granted, 500 F.2d 1382 (5th Cir. 1974) and judgment aff'd, 501 F.2d 1291 (5th Cir. 1974) and order amended, 390 F. Supp. 482 (N.D. Miss. 1975), judgment aff'd, 525 F.2d 965 (5th Cir. 1976) and order supplemented, 423 F. Supp. 732 (N.D. Miss. 1976), judgment aff'd and remanded, 548 F.2d 1241 (5th Cir. 1977) (hospital without basic equipment); Newman v. State of Ala., 349 F. Supp. 278, 283, (M.D. Ala. 1972), aff'd in part, 503 F.2d 1320 (5th Cir. 1974) and judgment vacated in part on other grounds, 522 F.2d 71 (5th Cir. 1975) (material shortages, including of drugs and oxygen, must be eliminated), subsequent opinion, 466 F Supp 628 (MD Ala 1979) (still problems). See also U.S. Dept of Justice, Federal Standards for Prisons and Jails § 5.13 (1980); American Correctional Assn, Standards for Adult Correctional Institutions, Standards 3-4332 to 3-4333, 3-4352 (1990); National Commn on Correctional Health Care, Standards for Health Services in Jails J-26-28 (May 1999); Commission on Accreditation for Corrections, Certification Standards for Health Care Programs HC-046 through H-047 (1989).

[2]Palmigiano v. Garrahy, 443 F. Supp. 956 (D.R.I. 1977) (must set up pharmacy and hire pharmacist); Williams v. Edwards, 547 F.2d 1206, 1216-17 (5th Cir. 1977) (no pharmacy records or supervision). See also U.S. Dept of Justice, Federal Standards for Prisons and Jails § 5.34 (1980); American Correctional Assn, Standards for Adult Correctional Institutions, Standard § 3-4341 (1990); National Commn on Correctional Health Care, Standards for Health Services in Jails J-26 (May 1999); Commission on Accreditation for Corrections, Certification Standards for Health Care Programs HC-086 (1989).

[3]See, e.g., Berthelot v. Stadler, 2001 WL 69410 (E.D. La. 2001) (holding that there was evidence of deliberate indifference where, after inmate's leg was amputated after complications stemming from diabetes, the prison provided him with crutches, a wheelchair, and physical therapy, but failed to give him a knee immobilizer

§ 3:8   RIGHTS OF PRISONERS, THIRD EDITION

also be adequate. Thus, if separate facilities for examination and treatment do not exist, if they are unsanitary, or if they are isolated in such a way that they are not adequately supervised and inmates cannot easily and confidentially communicate their needs to medical personnel, they will be found unacceptable.[4]

---

until 7 months after the surgery, and refused to allow him to purchase a prescribed prosthetic leg).

[4]Miller v. Carson, 401 F. Supp. 835, 876-78 (M.D. Fla. 1975), aff'd in part, modified in part on other grounds and remanded, 563 F.2d 741 (5th Cir. 1977) (no convalescent beds); Hamilton v. Landrieu, 351 F. Supp. 549, 550 (E.D. La. 1972) (must build infirmary); Jones v. Wittenberg, 323 F. Supp. 93, 28 Ohio Misc. 81, 57 Ohio Op. 2d 109 (N.D. Ohio 1971), opinion supplemented, 330 F. Supp. 707, 29 Ohio Misc. 35, 58 Ohio Op. 2d 47 (N.D. Ohio 1971), aff'd, 456 F.2d 854, 62 Ohio Op. 2d 232 (6th Cir. 1972) (must be examination rooms, treatment rooms, place for inmates who are ill but do not need hospitalization); Todaro v. Ward, 431 F. Supp. 1129, 1140, 1144 (S.D. N.Y. 1977), judgment aff'd, 565 F.2d 48 (2d Cir. 1977) and aff'd, 652 F.2d 54 (2d Cir. 1981) ("sick wing" inadequate due to lack of observation and communication; clinic inadequate due to lack of ability to do examination); Battle v. Anderson, 376 F. Supp. 402, 434 (E.D. Okla. 1974), judgment aff'd in part, rev'd in part on other grounds, 993 F.2d 1551 (10th Cir. 1993) (must be hospital facility consistent with state standards); Newman v. State of Ala., 349 F. Supp. 278, 282 (M.D. Ala. 1972), aff'd in part, 503 F.2d 1320 (5th Cir. 1974) and judgment vacated in part on other grounds, 522 F.2d 71 (5th Cir. 1975) ("small, overcrowded infirmaries with only rudimentary laboratory facilities"); Williams v. Edwards, 547 F.2d 1206, 1216-17 (5th Cir. 1977) (no adequate lab, lab records, or statistics; lab supervision and equipment poor; no pharmacy records or supervision; surgery unit so poor surgeon refused to use it; fish to be cooked kept in whirlpool); Lightfoot v. Walker, 486 F. Supp. 504, 511, 525-27 (S.D. Ill. 1980) (unacceptable to put sick inmates in cells with no observation or communication; medical unit unsanitary and unsafe, labs inadequate, microbiology services inadequate, radiology services inadequate); Laaman v. Helgemoe, 437 F. Supp. 269, 313-14, 328 (D.N.H. 1977) (adequacy of facilities and equipment to be judged "in reference to the task to be accomplished" and specific facilities required that allowed monitoring and communication). See also U.S. Dept of Justice, Federal Standards for Prisons and Jails §§ 5.09-5.10 (1980); ABA Standards for Criminal Justice § 23.5-1 (1986); American Correctional Assn, Standards for Adult

MEDICAL CARE § 3:8

If the prison relies on outside medical facilities for some of the medical care it delivers (and it must do so unless facilities within the prison are adequate), there must be adequate transportation available to the outside facility and the transportation vehicles must have all equipment needed to ensure the safety of the person being transported.[5]

When there are inmates who have contagious diseases, adequate isolation facilities must be established and maintained to permit the treatment of those inmates and to protect other inmates from exposure to the disease.[6]

Correctional Institutions, Standards 3-4332 to 3-4333, 3-4354 (1990); National Commn. on Correctional Health Care, Standards for Health Services in Jails J-27 through J-29 (May 1999); Commission on Accreditation for Corrections, Certification Standards for Health Care Programs HC-020, H-044 through H-045 (1989).

[5]Ramos v Lamm, 639 F2d 559, 577 (10th Cir 1980) (where rely on outside facilities, must have adequate transportation to prevent delay); Miller v. Carson, 401 F. Supp. 835, 876-78 (M.D. Fla. 1975), aff'd in part, modified in part on other grounds and remanded, 563 F.2d 741 (5th Cir. 1977) (transportation van has no medical equipment); Hamilton v. Landrieu, 351 F. Supp. 549, 550 (E.D. La. 1972) (must provide transportation). See also Model Sentencing and Corrections Act § 4-105(b)(6) (July 2001); U.S. Dept of Justice, Federal Standards for Prisons and Jails §§ 5.12, 5.42-.43 (1980); ABA Standards for Criminal Justice § 23.5-1 (1986); American Correctional Assn, Standards for Adult Correctional Institutions Standards 3-4330, -4360 through -4361 (1990); National Commn on Correctional Health Care, Standards for Health Services in Jails J-29 (May 1999); Commission on Accreditation for Corrections, Certification Standards for Health Care Programs HC-048, -068, -079 through -080 (1989).

[6]Loftin v. Dalessandri, 3 Fed. Appx. 658 (10th Cir. 2001) (failure to have isolation room for inmates who tested positive for tuberculosis); Alberti v. Sheriff of Harris County, Texas, 406 F. Supp. 649, 677 (S.D. Tex. 1975) (must isolate those with contagious diseases); Miller v. Carson, 401 F. Supp. 835, 877-78 (M.D. Fla. 1975), aff'd in part, modified in part on other grounds and remanded, 563 F.2d 741 (5th Cir. 1977) (people with contagious diseases not always isolated and, thus, "epidemic possibilities"); Newman v. State of Ala., 349 F. Supp. 278, 282 (M.D. Ala. 1972),

§ 3:9 Staff

Each institution must employ or have available an adequate number of appropriately trained staff to provide needed treatment.[1] If there are inadequate

---

aff'd in part, 503 F.2d 1320 (5th Cir. 1974) and judgment vacated in part on other grounds, 522 F.2d 71 (5th Cir. 1975) (two prisons with no way to "isolate contagious diseases"); Laaman v. Helgemoe, 437 F. Supp. 269, 314 (D.N.H. 1977) (ward for inmates with contagious diseases required); Smith v. Sullivan, 553 F.2d 373, 380 (5th Cir. 1977) (failure to isolate those with contagious diseases a violation); Gates v. Collier, 349 F. Supp. 881, 888, (N.D. Miss. 1972), judgment aff'd, 489 F.2d 298 (5th Cir. 1973), reh'g granted, 500 F.2d 1382 (5th Cir. 1974) and judgment aff'd, 501 F.2d 1291 (5th Cir. 1974) and order amended, 390 F. Supp. 482 (N.D. Miss. 1975), judgment aff'd, 525 F.2d 965 (5th Cir. 1976) and order supplemented, 423 F. Supp. 732 (N.D. Miss. 1976), judgment aff'd and remanded, 548 F.2d 1241 (5th Cir. 1977) (part of violation); DeGidio v. Perpich, 612 F. Supp. 1383, 2 Fed. R. Serv. 3d 824 (D. Minn. 1985) (may seek class-wide damages for failure to take adequate steps to prevent tuberculosis outbreak). See also Anthony L. Paccione, Note, The Federal Judiciary's Role in the Prevention of Communicable Diseases in State Prisons, 12 Ford Urb LJ 873 (1984); Model Sentencing and Corrections Act § 4-105(b)(5) (July 2001); American Correctional Assn, Standards for Adult Correctional Institutions Standard 3-4365 (1990); National Commn on Correctional Health Care, Standards for Health Services in Jails J-41, J-54 (May 1999); But see Rish v. Johnson, 131 F.3d 1092 (4th Cir. 1997) (holding that there was no constitutional right that inmate orderlies be provided with proper protective clothing when they had to clean blood and other bodily fluids from surfaces); Jeffries v. Block, 940 F. Supp. 1509 (C.D. Cal. 1996) (where it was clear from the evidence that prison procedures adequately isolated inmates infected with tuberculosis, plaintiff failed to state a constitutional claim of deliberate indifference).

[Section 3:9]

[1]Battle v. Anderson, 457 F. Supp. 719 (E.D. Okla. 1978) (extensive list of needed staff; the most detailed ratios published); Ramos v Lamm, 639 F2d 559, 575-77 (10th Cir 1980) (for 1,400 inmates, need 40 hours per week of on-site primary physician coverage; need registered nurse on all three shifts and more than three physician assistants in 24-hour infirmary); Austin v. Pennsylvania Dept. of Corrections, 876 F. Supp. 1437, 10 A.D.D. 1042 (E.D. Pa. 1995) (consent agreement mandating a request of

MEDICAL CARE § 3:9

numbers of staff or if the staff is unqualified, there may

legislature funding for 40 hours of primary physician time, 150 registered nurses for every 1,000 inmates, and one nurse on-call 24 hours daily at each prison facility); Cody v. Hillard, 599 F. Supp. 1025, 1058 (D.S.D. 1984), decision aff'd, 799 F.2d 447 (8th Cir. 1986), reh'g granted, 804 F.2d 440 (8th Cir. 1986) and on reh'g, 830 F.2d 912 (8th Cir. 1987) (inadequate number of nurses); Miller v. Carson, 401 F. Supp. 835, 876 (M.D. Fla. 1975), aff'd in part, modified in part on other grounds and remanded, 563 F.2d 741 (5th Cir. 1977) (one doctor one-half day per week and four registered nurses insufficient for jail housing over 400 inmates); Hamilton v. Landrieu, 351 F. Supp. 549, 550 (E.D. La. 1972) (must have medical aid 24 hours a day); Inmates of Occoquan v. Barry, 717 F. Supp. 854 (D.D.C. 1989) (two doctors, four assistants, and three technical assistants insufficient in jail with 1,600-2,000 inmates); Tillery v. Owens, 719 F. Supp. 1256, 1291 (W.D. Pa. 1989), order aff'd, 907 F.2d 418 (3d Cir. 1990) (doctor present only three hours per weekday and 14 nurses were inadequate for 1,800 inmates; there must be at least one doctor present 24 hours, 7 days a week.); Barnes v. Government of Virgin Islands, 415 F. Supp. 1218, 1235 (D.V.I. 1976) (doctor must be on call at all times); Palmigiano v. Garrahy, 443 F. Supp. 956, 974 (D.R.I. 1977) (one full-time and two part-time doctors who work 24 hours per week would be acceptable for institution with 650 inmates if nurses were adequately trained and supervised); Battle v. Anderson, 376 F. Supp. 402, 434 (E.D. Okla. 1974), judgment aff'd in part, rev'd in part on other grounds, 993 F.2d 1551 (10th Cir. 1993) (must be one full-time doctor, "adequate" support staff, and 24-hour, 7-day-a-week nursing for over 3,000 inmates; must set up in-patient medical facility that complies with state standards); Newman v. State of Ala., 349 F. Supp. 278 (M.D. Ala. 1972), aff'd in part, 503 F.2d 1320 (5th Cir. 1974) and judgment vacated in part on other grounds, 522 F.2d 71 (5th Cir. 1975) (five prisons, none with full-time doctors, 800 prisoners at facilities with no medical personnel); Newman v. State of Ala., 466 F. Supp. 628 (M.D. Ala. 1979) (one licensed doctor for whole Alabama prison system); Lightfoot v. Walker, 486 F. Supp. 504, 514, 516, 527 (S.D. Ill. 1980) (need 100 hours of on-site physician per week with "sufficient number of physician extenders" for institution of 1,000; also need a medical technician for every 200 inmates); Laaman v. Helgemoe, 437 F. Supp. 269, 312-13 (D.N.H. 1977) (ratios are not relevant but "failure to staff a prison around the clock with qualified personnel trained to identify and cope with medical emergencies and reliance upon unqualified and untrained inmates, civilians, and employees of the prison to make medical decisions and to perform medical

§ 3:9   Rights of Prisoners, Third Edition

be grounds not only for an order for injunctive relief seeking additional staff or additional training, but also for damages if harm results.[2]

---

functions infringe on the constitutional rights of prisoners"; court later required one doctor and five registered nurses for restitution with 280 inmates); Balla v. Idaho State Bd. of Corrections, 595 F. Supp. 1558, 1575-76 (D. Idaho 1984) (eight hours of doctor visits per week for over 1,100 inmates insufficient and must hire one full-time doctor); Gates v. Collier, 349 F. Supp. 881, 888, (N.D. Miss. 1972), judgment aff'd, 489 F.2d 298 (5th Cir. 1973), reh'g granted, 500 F.2d 1382 (5th Cir. 1974) and judgment aff'd, 501 F.2d 1291 (5th Cir. 1974) and order amended, 390 F. Supp. 482 (N.D. Miss. 1975), judgment aff'd, 525 F.2d 965 (5th Cir. 1976) and order supplemented, 423 F. Supp. 732 (N.D. Miss. 1976), judgment aff'd and remanded, 548 F.2d 1241 (5th Cir. 1977) (one doctor for 1,900 inmates not enough, and must hire three plus two assistants, six nurses, one records librarian, and two clerical staff, none of whom may be inmates); French v. Owens, 777 F.2d 1250, 1254 (7th Cir. 1985) (inmates untreated for tuberculosis, broken back, abscessed rectum as a result of inadequate staff; for institution of 2,000 inmates, must have two full-time doctors, five physician assistants, hospital administrator, and full-time pharmacist); Duran v. Anaya, 642 F. Supp. 510 (D.N.M. 1986) (enjoining staff reductions caused by budget cuts). See also Model Sentencing and Corrections Act § 4-105(b)(3) (July 2001); U.S. Dept of Justice, Federal Standards for Prisons and Jails §§ 5.05-.07, 5.05-.21 (1980); ABA Standards for Criminal Justice §§ 23.5-1, 23.5-2 (1986); American Correctional Assn, Standards for Adult Correctional Institutions Standards 3-4334, 3-4338 to 3-4340 (1990); National Commn on Correctional Health Care, Standards for Health Services in Jails J-17 through J-24 (May 1999).

[2]Cabrales v. County of Los Angeles, 864 F.2d 1454, 1461 (9th Cir. 1988), cert. granted, judgment vacated on other grounds, 490 U.S. 1087, 109 S. Ct. 2425, 104 L. Ed. 2d 982 (1989) and opinion reinstated, 886 F.2d 235 (9th Cir. 1989) supra (upholding jury verdict in jail suicide case against county based on inadequate staffing that prevented adequate diagnosis and treatment; "access to the medical staff has no meaning if the medical staff is not competent to deal with the prisoners' problems"); Greason v. Kemp, 891 F.2d 829, 835 (11th Cir. 1990) (in prison suicide case, rejecting qualified immunity where supervisor ignored repeated information that staff and facilities were inadequate and incompetent); Garcia v. Salt Lake County, 768 F.2d 303 (10th Cir. 1985) (upholding jury verdict when unconscious prisoner not seen by

MEDICAL CARE § 3:9

It is not possible, of course, to identify a specific number of doctors or other types of medical care workers that must be present in each institution, because the number will depend, in part, on the size of the inmate population,[3] as well as on the mix of staff, such as the number of nurses, physician assistants, and other aides that can perform some of the tasks of a physician. Despite these problems, some courts have required ratios of various kinds of medical workers to inmates.[4] There are also state statutes or regulations that require specified numbers of physicians.[5]

No general rule governing ratios can be determined from cases that have specified a ratio or found that a particular number of staff was insufficient. To the extent that rules can be determined, the bulk of the cases hold that: there must be one doctor on call at all times for all but the smallest facilities; when the population gets above 500, the facility must hire more than one full-time doctor; and when the population gets

---

doctor due to lack of staff); Colle v. Brazos County, Tex., 981 F.2d 237, 245, 24 Fed. R. Serv. 3d 655 (5th Cir. 1993) (may be municipal liability where policy of inadequate staffing and monitoring, and inability to respond appropriately by transferring to hospital); Simpkins v. Bellevue Hosp., 832 F. Supp. 69 (S.D. N.Y. 1993) (municipality liable for hiring untrained doctor who caused severe sinus damage to inmate); Casey v. Lewis, 834 F. Supp. 1477 (D. Ariz. 1993) (where staff shortage through inadequate funding and inability to fill positions created delays, a constitutional violation existed). But see Rosen v. Chang, 811 F. Supp. 754, 761 (D.R.I. 1993) (no liability where doctors present only once a week).

[3]Laaman v. Helgemoe, 437 F. Supp. 269, 312-13 (D.N.H. 1977) (court says that ratios are not relevant but instead "failure to staff a prison around the clock with qualified personnel trained to identify and cope with medical emergencies and reliance upon unqualified and untrained inmates, civilians, and employees of the prison to make medical decisions and to perform medical functions infringe upon the constitutional rights of prisoners").

[4]Battle v. Anderson, 457 F. Supp. 719 (E.D. Okla. 1978) (extensive list of needed staff; the most detailed ratios published).

[5]See, e.g., Cal Penal Code § 4023, quoted in Dillard v. Pitchess, 399 F. Supp. 1225, 1239-40 (C.D. Cal. 1975) (one doctor "available at all times" if jail has more than 100 inmates).

§ 3:9   Rights of Prisoners, Third Edition

above 1,500, the facility must hire more than two fulltime doctors.[6]

---

[6]Laaman v. Helgemoe, 437 F. Supp. 269, 312-13 (D.N.H. 1977) (one doctor and five registered nurses for institution with 280 inmates); Miller v. Carson, 401 F. Supp. 835, 876 (M.D. Fla. 1975), aff'd in part, modified in part on other grounds and remanded, 563 F.2d 741 (5th Cir. 1977) (one doctor one-half day per week and four registered nurses insufficient for jail of over 400 inmates); Palmigiano v. Garrahy, 443 F. Supp. 956, 974 (D.R.I. 1977) (one full-time and two part-time doctors who work 24 hours per week would be acceptable for institution with 650 inmates if nurses were adequately trained and supervised); Lightfoot v. Walker, 486 F. Supp. 504, 514, 516, 527 (S.D. Ill. 1980) (institution of 1000 needed 100 hours of on-site physician per week with "sufficient number of physician extenders; also needed a medical technician for every 200 inmates); Balla v. Idaho State Bd. of Corrections, 595 F. Supp. 1558, 1575-76 (D. Idaho 1984) (eight hours of doctor visits per week for over 1,100 inmates insufficient and must hire one full-time doctor); Ramos v Lamm, 639 F2d 559, 575-77 (10th Cir 1980) (for 1,400 inmates, need 40 hours per week of on-site primary physician coverage; need registered nurse on all three shifts and more than three physician assistants in 24-hour infirmary); Inmates of Occoquan v. Barry, 717 F. Supp. 854 (D.D.C. 1989) (two doctors, four assistants, and three technical assistants insufficient in jail with 1,600-2,000 inmates); Tillery v. Owens, 719 F. Supp. 1256, 1291 (W.D. Pa. 1989), order aff'd, 907 F.2d 418 (3d Cir. 1990) (doctor present only three hours per weekday and 14 nurses inadequate for 1,800 inmates; must be at least one doctor present 24 hours a day, 7 days a week); Gates v. Collier, 349 F. Supp. 881, 888, (N.D. Miss. 1972), judgment aff'd, 489 F.2d 298 (5th Cir. 1973), reh'g granted, 500 F.2d 1382 (5th Cir. 1974) and judgment aff'd, 501 F.2d 1291 (5th Cir. 1974) and order amended, 390 F. Supp. 482 (N.D. Miss. 1975), judgment aff'd, 525 F.2d 965 (5th Cir. 1976) and order supplemented, 423 F. Supp. 732 (N.D. Miss. 1976), judgment aff'd and remanded, 548 F.2d 1241 (5th Cir. 1977) (one doctor for 1,900 inmates not enough and must hire three, plus two assistants, six nurses, one records librarian, and two clerical staff, none of whom may be inmates); French v. Owens, 777 F.2d 1250, 1254 (7th Cir. 1985) (inmates untreated for tuberculosis, broken back, abscessed rectum as a result of inadequate staff; for institution of 2,000 inmates, must have two full-time doctors, five physician assistants, a hospital administrator, and a full-time pharmacist); Battle v. Anderson, 376 F. Supp. 402, 434 (E.D. Okla. 1974), judgment aff'd in part, rev'd in part on other grounds, 993

MEDICAL CARE § 3:9

Where courts have found entire medical systems to be inadequate, part of the remedy has often been to require the hiring or appointment of a medical director who is then responsible for assuring that proper supervision occurs and that needed corrections are made.[7]

Staff must not only be sufficient in number, but also be sufficiently qualified. Guards, inmates, nurses, or other non-physicians cannot prescribe medication or perform surgery, and untrained staff cannot provide treatment to inmates.[8] Even physicians, nurses, and other health care professionals employed by the facility

---

F.2d 1551 (10th Cir. 1993) (must be one full-time doctor, "adequate" support staff, and 24 hour, 7-day a week nursing for over 3000 inmates). See also National Commn on Correctional Health Care, Standards for Health Services in Jails J-23 (May 1999).

[7]Tillery v. Owens, 719 F. Supp. 1256, 1305-06, 1308 (W.D. Pa. 1989), order aff'd, 907 F.2d 418 (3d Cir. 1990) (need administrator of medicine and of nursing, protocols, and emergency plan); Inmates of Allegheny County Jail v. Peirce, 487 F. Supp. 638 (W.D. Pa. 1980) (must hire psychiatric administrator); Lightfoot v. Walker, 486 F. Supp. 504, 515-29 (S.D. Ill. 1980) (problems due to inadequate administration, including lack of chief medical officer, no sick call protocols, no health screening of health personnel, no education, no peer review, heavy doctor turnover; budgeting and monitoring of quality of care and corrections required, including hiring chief medical officer); Feliciano v. Barcelo, 497 F. Supp. 14, 40 (D.P.R. 1979) (requiring hiring of medical director who must set up procedures and hire all staff "as they may be necessary to provide adequate medical care and attention"). See also American Correctional Assn, Standards for Adult Correctional Institutions, Standard 3-4334 (1990); ABA Standards for Criminal Justice § 23.5-1 (1986); U.S. Dept of Justice, Federal Standards for Prisons and Jails § 5.06 (1980); National Commn on Correctional Health Care, Standards for Health Services in Jails J-23 through J24 (May 1999); Commission on Accreditation for Corrections, Certification Standards for Health Care Programs HC-010 to HC-017 (pre-service and in-service training requirements), HC-052 (licensure) (1989).

[8]Ramos v Lamm, 639 F2d 559, 576, 577 (10th Cir 1980) (use of untrained "physician substitutes" and "standing orders" inadequate and caused "potentially life threatening situations along with needless pain and suffering"; use of inmates as technicians

§ 3:9   Rights of Prisoners, Third Edition

impermissible); Hoptowit v. Ray, 682 F.2d 1237, 1253, 9 Fed. R. Evid. Serv. 1511 (9th Cir. 1982) (staff must be "competent to examine prisoners and diagnose illnesses . . . to treat medical problems or to refer prisoners to others who can"); Madrid v. Gomez, 889 F. Supp. 1146 (N.D. Cal. 1995), mandamus denied, 103 F.3d 828 (9th Cir. 1996) (holding violation of Eighth Amendment where untrained staff performed emergency medical treatment); Casey v. Lewis, 834 F. Supp. 1477 (D. Ariz. 1993) (where security staff was used to provide medical treatment and could overrule medical orders, level of deliberate indifference was reached that was a constitutional violation); Nicholson v. Choctaw County, Ala., 498 F. Supp. 295, 309 (S.D. Ala. 1980) (staff must be properly trained); Cody v. Hillard, 599 F. Supp. 1025, 1056 (D.S.D. 1984), decision aff'd, 799 F.2d 447 (8th Cir. 1986), reh'g granted, 804 F.2d 440 (8th Cir. 1986) and on reh'g, 830 F.2d 912 (8th Cir. 1987)(use of untrained inmate workers for treatment was a violation); Inmates of Occoquan v. Barry, 717 F. Supp. 854 (D.D.C. 1989) (too much reliance on unsupervised assistants to prescribe and deliver medication); Newman v. State of Ala., 349 F. Supp. 278, 288 (M.D. Ala. 1972), aff'd in part, 503 F.2d 1320 (5th Cir. 1974) and judgment vacated in part on other grounds, 522 F.2d 71 (5th Cir. 1975) (still true); Williams v. Edwards, 547 F.2d 1206, 1216 (5th Cir. 1977) (untrained and unqualified inmates filled most medical positions; no pharmacist, no consulting pathologist); Lightfoot v. Walker, 486 F. Supp. 504, 515, 527 (S.D. Ill. 1980) ("extremely dangerous and questionable" to let untrained staff and inmates prescribe and administer controlled medication pursuant to standing orders and "appropriate and effective in-service training programs for all medical personnel" required); Laaman v. Helgemoe, 437 F. Supp. 269, 313 (D.N.H. 1977) (untrained personnel dispensed medication); Balla v. Idaho State Bd. of Corrections, 595 F. Supp. 1558, 1566-67, 1575 (D. Idaho 1984) (unqualified staff providing diagnosis and treatment); Gates v. Collier, 349 F. Supp. 881, 888 (N.D. Miss. 1972), judgment aff'd, 489 F.2d 298 (5th Cir. 1973), reh'g granted, 500 F.2d 1382 (5th Cir. 1974) and judgment aff'd, 501 F.2d 1291, 1303 (5th Cir. 1974) and order amended, 390 F. Supp. 482 (N.D. Miss. 1975), judgment aff'd, 525 F.2d 965 (5th Cir. 1976) and order supplemented, 423 F. Supp. 732 (N.D. Miss. 1976), judgment aff'd and remanded, 548 F.2d 1241 (5th Cir. 1977) (unqualified staff provided "medical functions"); Burks v. Teasdale, 492 F. Supp. 650, 676-78 (W.D. Mo. 1980) (use of nonphysicians for surgery "shocks the conscience" of the court but there need not be nurse or licensed physical therapist if staff is qualified). See also U.S. Dept of Justice, Federal Standards for Prisons and Jails

MEDICAL CARE § 3:9

must be qualified and adequately trained.[9] For all but the most minor injuries, courts have held that non-inmate translators must be provided to Spanish-speaking inmates to ensure that they can communicate their medical problems to the medical staff who do not speak the language.[10]

---

§§ 5.08, 5.37 (1980); American Correctional Assn, Standards for Adult Correctional Institutions Standard 3-4335 (1990); National Commn on Correctional Health Care, Standards for Health Services in Jails J-17, J-19 (May 1999); Commission on Accreditation for Corrections, Certification Standards for Health Care Programs HC-055 through HC-057 (1989). But see, Boston v. Lafayette County, Miss., 743 F. Supp. 462, 473 (N.D. Miss. 1990) (need not train jail guards to recognize "hidden medical problems" that can be observed only by experts).

[9]Wellman v. Faulkner, 715 F.2d 269, 272 (7th Cir. 1983) (violation where two of three doctors did not adequately speak English because this could lead to misdiagnosis and "unnecessary pain and suffering"); Andrews v. Camden County, 95 F. Supp. 2d 217 (D. N.J. 2000) (holding that jail must have a medical director on staff at the prison); Palmigiano v. Garrahy, 443 F. Supp. 956, 974 (D. R.I. 1977)(nurses insufficiently trained in a variety of conditions). See also Cabrales v. County of Los Angeles, 864 F.2d 1454, 1461 (9th Cir. 1988), cert. granted, judgment vacated, 490 U.S. 1087, 109 S. Ct. 2425, 104 L. Ed. 2d 982 (1989) and opinion reinstated, 886 F.2d 235 (9th Cir. 1989) supra (upholding jury verdict against county based on inadequate staffing that prevented adequate diagnosis and treatment; "access to the medical staff has no meaning if the medical staff is not competent to deal with the prisoners' problems"; on remand from Supreme Court, Court of Appeals held that disputed issues of fact existed about whether the county's policy of understaffing its jail with psychiatrists amounted to a policy of "deliberate indifference" to the medical needs of pretrial detainees).

[10]Anderson v. County of Kern, 45 F.3d 1310 (9th Cir. 1995) (holding that district court properly required that jail must provide a non-inmate translator for medical visits upon the inmate's request); Franklin v. District of Columbia, 960 F. Supp. 394 (D. D.C. 1997), supplemented, 1997 WL 403418 (D.D.C. 1997), vacated in part, 163 F.3d 625, 42 Fed. R. Serv. 3d 1013 (D.C. Cir. 1998), reh'g and reh'g en banc denied, 168 F.3d 1360 (D.C. Cir. 1999) and rev'd in part, vacated in part, 163 F.3d 625, 42 Fed. R. Serv. 3d 1013 (D.C. Cir. 1998) supra (where a class of Hispanic inmates

§ 3:9   RIGHTS OF PRISONERS, THIRD EDITION

Inmates may not choose their own doctor or opt to see doctors outside the institution instead of those provided by the facility.[11] Inmates must, however, have access to appropriate specialists.[12] Where a demonstrated need has existed, courts have required that those specialists be employed by the institution and have established ratios of specialists required.[13] In other

---

claimed the prison medical system failed to provide sufficient bilingual staff or qualified translators for medical care visits, the court held that such deficiencies violated the Eighth Amendment and ordered the defendants to submit a memorandum to the court detailing a plan to remedy the violation); Cortes v. Johnson, 114 F. Supp. 2d 182 (W.D. N.Y. 2000) (having other inmates translate for an inmate seeking medical care did not violate privacy rights, where the inmate suffered from an minor condition that would not adversely affect prison interests if disclosed to other prisoners). But see Camberos v. Branstad, 73 F.3d 174 (8th Cir. 1995) (holding that prison officials did not violate Eighth Amendment where inmate alleged that officials failed to provide him with an interpreter to facilitate communication between himself and health care worker).

[11]Berman v. Lamer, 874 F. Supp. 102 (E.D. Pa. 1995) (where prisoner received regular medical treatment and was examined by seven doctors for chronic gastrointestinal problem, inmate could not demand to be escorted to doctor of his choice, nor could he receive injunction enjoining prison from transferring him to another facility to rectify his condition by surgery); Trout v. Buie, 653 N.E.2d 1002 (Ind. Ct. App. 1995) (sheriff had no duty to reimburse plaintiff's surgeon for medical treatment which inmate obtained after he was released from incarceration). But see Harris v. Jacobs, 621 F.2d 341 (9th Cir. 1980) (due process right to see outside doctor may be created by state law); Model Sentencing and Corrections Act § 4-105(c) (July 2001) (inmates should be permitted to use own resources to obtain outside medical help).

[12]See, e.g., Williams v. Patel, 104 F. Supp. 2d 984 (C.D. Ill. 2000) (holding that where evidence showed that the prison doctor refused to treat the inmate's eye injury on several occasions, and it was nearly two months before the inmate was taken to an optometrist, and he later lost his eye, there was sufficient evidence to support a constitutional violation based on deliberate indifference).

[13]Ramos v Lamm, 639 F. 2d 559, 576 (10th Cir 1980) (for 1,400 inmates, need four hours per week on-site from internist and general surgeon and four hours every other week from ear, nose, and

MEDICAL CARE § 3:10

instances, courts have simply specified that access to specialists must be provided and left it up to the institution to determine the method of providing that access.[14]

§ 3:10 Records

There must be a medical records system that assures complete and accurate records of the medical needs and treatments for each inmate. The reason that this "paper work" requirement is of constitutional significance should be obvious: a doctor cannot adequately determine the medical needs of the inmate without a medical history. The doctor cannot treat the inmate without knowing such elementary facts as the inmate's allergies to certain medications or his history with certain treatments. It is impossible to determine the effectiveness of a treatment, and thus whether alternative treatments should be considered, without records verifying the effects of the treatment. Thus, one common finding

---

throat specialist and orthopedic surgeon); Miller v. Carson, 401 F. Supp. 835, 878 (M.D. Fla. 1975), aff'd in part, modified in part on other grounds and remanded, 563 F.2d 741 (5th Cir. 1977) (need part-time dermatologist and ophthalmologist); Tillery v. Owens, 719 F. Supp. 1256, 1307 (W.D. Pa. 1989), order aff'd, 907 F.2d 418 (3d Cir. 1990) (need on-site dermatologist and cardiologist); Gates v. Collier, 349 F. Supp. 881, 901 (N.D. Miss. 1972), judgment aff'd, 489 F.2d 298 (5th Cir. 1973), reh'g granted, 500 F.2d 1382 (5th Cir. 1974) and judgment aff'd, 501 F.2d 1291 (5th Cir. 1974) and order amended, 390 F. Supp. 482 (N.D. Miss. 1975), judgment aff'd, 525 F.2d 965 (5th Cir. 1976) and order supplemented, 423 F. Supp. 732 (N.D. Miss. 1976), judgment aff'd and remanded, 548 F.2d 1241 (5th Cir. 1977) (must have consultant radiologist and pharmacist).

[14]See, e.g, Oxendine v. Kaplan, 241 F.3d 1272 (10th Cir. 2001) (holding that failure to provide outside surgeons for surgery of inmate's severed finger would be a constitutional violation); Inmates of Inmates of Occoquan v. Barry, 717 F. Supp. 854 (D. D.C. 1989) (delays in neurology, urology); Burks v. Teasdale, 492 F. Supp. 650, 656 (W.D. Mo. 1980) (specialists available to institution). See also American Correctional Assn, Standards for Adult Correctional Institutions, Standard 3-4356 (1990); Commission on Accreditation for Corrections, Certification Standards for Health Care Programs HC-050 (1989).

§ 3:10

is that an institution's medical records system is inadequate and must be reformed.[1]

One special problem arises concerning inmates' medi-

[Section 3:10]

[1]Hoptowit v. Ray, 682 F.2d 1237, 1252-55, 9 Fed. R. Evid. Serv. 1511 (9th Cir. 1982) (record system inadequate because histories were not kept and not reviewed); Nicholson v. Choctaw County, Ala., 498 F. Supp. 295, 308 (S.D. Ala. 1980) (inadequate health records); Cody v. Hillard, 599 F. Supp. 1025, 1057-58 (D.S.D. 1984), decision aff'd, 799 F.2d 447 (8th Cir. 1986), reh'g granted, 804 F.2d 440 (8th Cir. 1986) and on reh'g, 830 F.2d 912 (8th Cir. 1987) (lack of adequate records constituted serious risk and a violation); Inmates of Occoquan v. Barry, 717 F. Supp. 854, 861, 867 (D.D.C. 1989) (records lost, not current, or not used at sick call); Newman v. State of Ala., 349 F. Supp. 278, 283, (M.D. Ala. 1972), aff'd in part, 503 F.2d 1320 (5th Cir. 1974) and judgment vacated in part on other grounds, 522 F.2d 71 (5th Cir. 1975) (records "not standardized, are inaccurate, and incomplete," did not reveal treatment given; records lost; deficiencies must be cured"); Lightfoot v. Walker, 486 F. Supp. 504, 517, 527 (S.D. Ill. 1980) (records "disorganized and failed to meet minimal standards"; delays in recording test results of up to a year; institution must set up adequate system); Laaman v. Helgemoe, 437 F. Supp. 269, 313, 327 (D.N.H. 1977) (with inadequate records, staff cannot know what treatment has been given or monitor it); Dawson v. Kendrick, 527 F. Supp. 1252, 1273, (S.D. W. Va. 1981) (records of drugs inadequate); Feliciano v. Barcelo, 497 F. Supp. 14, 37-38 (D.P.R. 1979) (must be adequate records); Burks v. Teasdale, 492 F. Supp. 650, 676 (W.D. Mo. 1980) (records "constitutionally infirm . . . inadequate, inaccurate, and unprofessionally maintained [and] results in a very grave risk of unnecessary pain and suffering"). See also Model Sentencing and Corrections Act § 4-105(b)(7) (July 2001); U.S. Dept of Justice, Federal Standards for Prisons and Jails § 5.38 (1980); ABA Standards for Criminal Justice §§ 23.5-.4 (1986); American Correctional Assn, Standards for Adult Correctional Institutions Standards 3-4346 through 3-4376 (3d ed. 1990); National Commn on Correctional Health Care, Standards for Health Services in Jails J-61-63 (May 1999); Commission on Accreditation for Corrections, Certification Standards for Health Care Programs HC-087 (1989). But see Abdush-Shahid v. Coughlin, 933 F. Supp. 168 (N.D. N.Y. 1996) (holding that failure of prison medical staff to maintain a record of all his visits did not cause the plaintiff any injuries or delay in treatment for a medical condition); Mitchell v. Keane, 974 F. Supp. 332 (S.D. N.Y. 1997),

MEDICAL CARE § 3:10

cal records. Obviously, medical records contain a great deal of information that most people would like to have kept confidential. Thus, all states provide for the confidentiality of the doctor-patient relationship. Many prisons or jails have used inmates in the medical records rooms and thus have given those inmates access to confidential medical information about other inmates. Although the cases are not unanimous, the majority, and better reasoned, find that practice unacceptable.[2]

---

aff'd, 175 F.3d 1008 (2d Cir. 1999) (holding that failure to file an injury report was not a constitutional violation).

[2]Tillery v. Owens, 719 F. Supp. 1256, 1305 (W.D. Pa. 1989), order aff'd, 907 F.2d 418 (3d Cir. 1990) (inmate cannot keep records); Williams v. Edwards, 547 F.2d 1206, 1207 (5th Cir. 1977) (confidentiality not maintained from other inmates or staff); Gates v. Collier, 349 F. Supp. 881, 901 (N.D. Miss. 1972), judgment aff'd, 489 F.2d 298 (5th Cir. 1973), reh'g granted, 500 F.2d 1382 (5th Cir. 1974) and judgment aff'd, 501 F.2d 1291 (5th Cir. 1974) and order amended, 390 F. Supp. 482 (N.D. Miss. 1975), judgment aff'd, 525 F.2d 965 (5th Cir. 1976) and order supplemented, 423 F. Supp. 732 (N.D. Miss. 1976), judgment aff'd and remanded, 548 F.2d 1241 (5th Cir. 1977) (inmates may not have access to records). See also Model Sentencing and Corrections Act § 4-105(b)(7) (July 2001); U.S. Dept of Justice, Federal Standards for Prisons and Jails §§ 5.39-.41 (1980); ABA Standards for Criminal Justice Standard 23.6.11 (1986); American Correctional Assn, Standards for Adult Correctional Institutions § 3-4377 (3d ed. 1990); National Commn on Correctional Health Care, Standards for Health Services in Jails J-61 (May 1999); Commission on Accreditation for Corrections, Certification Standards for Health Care Programs HC-088 (1989). But see Webb v. Goldstein, 117 F. Supp. 2d 289 (E.D. N.Y. 2000) (holding that there was no liability where inmate claimed that his medical records were disseminated to other prisoners. The court granted defendants qualified immunity, as there was no evidence that the officials would have known that the conditions in the records were sufficiently serious to implicate the inmate's privacy rights); Faison v. Parker, 823 F. Supp. 1198 (E.D. Pa. 1993) (medical and mental health information deserves a high degree of protection; disclosure of this information at sentencing, however, is in the interest of the inmate in order to send the inmate to the proper facility; disclosed information concerned cervical cancer, syphilis, HIV and severe character disorder); Burks v. Teasdale, 492 F. Supp. 650, 676 (W.D. Mo. 1980) (inmate workers

§ 3:11 Dental Care

"Prisoners generally have more extensive dental problems than the average citizen. Consequently dental care is one of the most important medical needs of inmates."[1] Those cases seeking to establish the necessary components of a minimally adequate medical care system invariably require that there be a dental care system.[2] The elements of a dental care system are similar to the elements of a medical care system and, for

---

could be used in the records department in the absence of evidence of problems that result).

[Section 3:11]

[1]Ramos v Lamm, 639 F2d 559, 576 (10th Cir 1980).

[2]Kinney v Kalfus, 25 F3d 633 (8th Cir 1994) (refusal of repeated requests for dental attention can rise to the level of an Eighth Amendment violation); Barnes v. Government of Virgin Islands, 415 F. Supp. 1218 (D.V.I. 1976); Cody v. Hillard, 599 F. Supp. 1025 (D.S.D. 1984), decision aff'd, 799 F.2d 447 (8th Cir. 1986), reh'g granted, 804 F.2d 440 (8th Cir. 1986) and on reh'g, 830 F.2d 912 (8th Cir. 1987); Ramos v. Lamm, 485 F. Supp. 122 (D. Colo. 1979), judgment aff'd in part, set aside in part on other grounds, 639 F.2d 559 (10th Cir. 1980); Williams v. Edwards, 547 F.2d 1206, 1217 (5th Cir. 1977); Hoptowit v Ray, 682 F2d 1237 (9th Cir 1982); Nicholson v. Choctaw County, Ala., 498 F. Supp. 295 (S.D. Ala. 1980); Toussaint v. Rushen, 553 F. Supp. 1365, 1381 (N.D. Cal. 1983), aff'd in part, 722 F.2d 1490 (9th Cir. 1984); Heitman v. Gabriel, 524 F. Supp. 622, 627 (W.D. Mo. 1981); Finney v. Arkansas Bd. of Correction, 505 F.2d 194, 204 (8th Cir. 1974); Fambro v. Fulton County, Ga., 713 F. Supp. 1426 (N.D. Ga. 1989); Miller v. Carson, 401 F. Supp. 835, 877 (M.D. Fla. 1975), aff'd in part, modified in part on other grounds and remanded, 563 F.2d 741 (5th Cir. 1977); Hamilton v. Landrieu, 351 F. Supp. 549, 550 (E.D. La. 1972); Jones v. Wittenberg, 323 F. Supp. 93, 28 Ohio Misc. 81, 57 Ohio Op. 2d 109 (N.D. Ohio 1971), opinion supplemented, 330 F. Supp. 707, 29 Ohio Misc. 35, 58 Ohio Op. 2d 47 (N.D. Ohio 1971), aff'd, 456 F.2d 854, 62 Ohio Op. 2d 232 (6th Cir. 1972); Inmates of Occoquan v. Barry, 717 F. Supp. 854 (D. D.C. 1989); Tillery v. Owens, 719 F. Supp. 1256, 1309 (W.D. Pa. 1989), order aff'd, 907 F.2d 418 (3d Cir. 1990); Battle v. Anderson, 376 F. Supp. 402, 434 (E.D. Okla. 1974), judgment aff'd in part, rev'd in part on other grounds, 993 F.2d 1551 (10th Cir. 1993); Newman v. State of Ala., 466 F. Supp. 628, 634 (M.D. Ala. 1979); Laaman v. Helgemoe, 437 F. Supp. 269, 313 (D.N.H. 1977); Gates

MEDICAL CARE § 3:11

example, involve ensuring that an adequate number of appropriately qualified staff be available.[3]

The most extensive discussion of the components of an adequate dental system is contained in a class action challenge to the adequacy of dental services at a New York prison for women, *Dean v Coughlin*.[4] After certifying the class,[5] the court made extensive findings concerning the inadequacies of the dental system at the prison. It found that there were delays of up to four or five months in initial screening of inmates to determine

---

v. Collier, 349 F. Supp. 881, 901 (N.D. Miss. 1972), judgment aff'd, 489 F.2d 298 (5th Cir. 1973), reh'g granted, 500 F.2d 1382 (5th Cir. 1974) and judgment aff'd, 501 F.2d 1291 (5th Cir. 1974) and order amended, 390 F. Supp. 482 (N.D. Miss. 1975), judgment aff'd, 525 F.2d 965 (5th Cir. 1976) and order supplemented, 423 F. Supp. 732 (N.D. Miss. 1976), judgment aff'd and remanded, 548 F.2d 1241 (5th Cir. 1977) (must hire two dentists for 1,900 inmates). See also Hunt v. Dental Dept., 865 F.2d 198 (9th Cir. 1989); Michael C. Friedman, Comment, Prison Medical Care, 45 Vand L Rev 921 (1992); U.S. Dept of Justice, Federal Standards for Prisons and Jails §§ 5.27-5.28 (1980); ABA Standards for Criminal Justice §§ 23.5-1 through 23.5-2 (1986); National Commn on Correctional Health Care, Standards for Health Services in Jails J-40 (May 1999).

[3]Cody v. Hillard, 599 F. Supp. 1025 (D.S.D. 1984), decision aff'd, 799 F.2d 447 (8th Cir. 1986), reh'g granted, 804 F.2d 440 (8th Cir. 1986) and on reh'g, 830 F.2d 912 (8th Cir. 1987) (improper for untrained inmates to take dental X-rays and, in some instances, to provide dental treatment); Ramos v Lamm, 639 F.2d 559 (10th Cir. 1980) (on site coverage of 40 hours a week sufficient for 800-1,000 inmates but not for 1,400); Jones v. Wittenberg, 323 F. Supp. 93, 28 Ohio Misc. 81, 57 Ohio Op. 2d 109 (N.D. Ohio 1971), opinion supplemented, 330 F. Supp. 707, 29 Ohio Misc. 35, 58 Ohio Op. 2d 47 (N.D. Ohio 1971), aff'd, 456 F.2d 854, 62 Ohio Op. 2d 232 (6th Cir. 1972) (part-time dentist must be on call; court also required adequate facilities for dentistry); Tillery v. Owens, 719 F. Supp. 1256, 1309 (W.D. Pa. 1989), order aff'd, 907 F.2d 418 (3d Cir. 1990) (adequate staff required); Inmates of Occoquan v. Barry, 717 F. Supp. 854 (D.D.C. 1989) (delays unacceptable).

[4]Dean v. Coughlin, 623 F. Supp. 392 (S.D. N.Y. 1985).

[5]Dean v. Coughlin, 107 F.R.D. 331 (S.D. N.Y. 1985).

§ 3:11

their dental needs,⁶ requests for routine care were largely ignored,⁷ requests for emergency care resulted in "long delays,"⁸ follow-up appointments did not occur as required or were seriously delayed,⁹ the institution rarely provided prophylactic care to inmates,¹⁰ and there were lengthy delays that, in many instances, caused serious pain and irreparable damage to "restorative care," such as "filling cavities, doing root canal work, and crowning broken teeth," "extractions," and " prosthetic services" including bridges and dentures.¹¹ The court concluded that most of these deficiencies violated the Eighth Amendment rights of the inmates based on a pattern of delay or denial of dental care that caused "pain, discomfort, or damage."¹² The sole exceptions were for prophylactic care and initial screening, both of which the court found were good ideas but were not necessary to respond "to inmates' pain and discomfort" as long as there was an adequate system for inmates to make their needs known.¹³

Dean is generally consistent with other cases discuss-

---

⁶Dean v. Coughlin, 623 F. Supp. 392, 394-95 (S.D. N.Y. 1985).

⁷*Id.* at 395.

⁸*Id.* at 395-96.

⁹*Id.* at 396.

¹⁰*Id.* at 397.

¹¹*Id.* at 397-99; Tillery v. Owens, 719 F. Supp. 1256, 1309 (W.D. Pa. 1989), order aff'd, 907 F.2d 418 (3d Cir. 1990) (delay of a year "regardless of the seriousness of the condition").

¹²Dean v. Coughlin, 623 F. Supp. 392, 400-05 (S.D. N.Y. 1985) ("denial of treatment regardless of mental state can also constitute deliberate indifference"); American Correctional Assn, Standards for Adult Correctional Institutions Standards 3-4350, 3-4358 (1990) (emergency care and prostheses, respectively); Commission on Accreditation for Corrections, Certification Standards for Health Care Programs HC-064, HC-077 (1989).

¹³Dean v. Coughlin, 623 F. Supp. 392, 404 (S.D. N.Y. 1985) ("burden is on the prisoner to make the needs known"). The district court later entered a detailed remedial order that was vacated because the district court failed to give sufficient deference to the institution's remedial plan. Dean v. Coughlin, 633 F. Supp. 308 (S.D. N.Y. 1986), vacated, 804 F.2d 207 (2d Cir. 1986). Despite

MEDICAL CARE   § 3:11

ing prison dental care. More specifically, denial of serious dental needs violates the Constitution.[14] Delay in providing dental care is not necessarily a violation of the Eighth Amendment, but a lengthy delay or one that results in serious pain or permanent damage does violate the Constitution.[15] The courts are split as to the holding in *Dean* that routine cleaning of teeth is not

---

this, the district court's remedial plan does provide excellent guidance on some of the aspects of a prison dental care system. But see American Correctional Assn, Standards for Adult Correctional Institutions Standard 3-4343 (1990) (initial screening should include dental care).

[14]Brownlee v. Conine, 957 F.2d 353, 355, 22 Fed. R. Serv. 3d 147 (7th Cir. 1992) (cause of action stated when it was alleged that guard refused to allow prisoner to see dentist "though he was in severe pain"); Heitman v. Gabriel, 524 F. Supp. 622, 627 (W.D. Mo. 1981) (limitation on dental care to just extraction impermissible); Jackson v. Whitman, 642 F. Supp. 816, 824-25 (W.D. La. 1986) (same).

[15]Moore v. Jackson, 123 F.3d 1082, 38 Fed. R. Serv. 3d 1450 (8th Cir. 1997) (holding that a delay of seven months to extract plaintiff's infected tooth provided evidence of deliberate indifference); Hunt v. Dental Dept., 865 F.2d 198, 200 (9th Cir. 1989) (delay of three months with "severe pain and resulting in permanent damage to his teeth . . . bleeding gums, breaking teeth and his inability to eat properly" stated cause of action for failure to give dentures); Martin v. Tyson, 845 F.2d 1451, 1457 (7th Cir. 1988); Fields v. Gander, 734 F.2d 1313 (8th Cir. 1984) (three-week delay accompanied by swelling and pain stated cause of action); Matzker v. Herr, 748 F.2d 1142 (7th Cir. 1984) (delay of three months in examining inmate with three broken teeth, causing pain and permanent injury stated cause of action); Ramos v Lamm, 639 F.2d 559, 576 (10th Cir. 1980) (inordinate delay causing "infections and abscesses leading to continued and unnecessary pain and loss of teeth"); Williams v. Scully, 552 F. Supp. 431 (S.D. N.Y. 1982) (five and one half month delay in filling caused by lack of staff, during which plaintiff "suffered considerable pain," stated cause of action); Fambro v. Fulton County, Ga., 713 F. Supp. 1426, 1429 (N.D. Ga. 1989) (delays of three weeks with acute problems and one month with less serious problems part of finding of violations); Robbins v. South, 595 F. Supp. 785 (D. Mont. 1984) (three-month delay in fixing gum infection and providing missing plate did not state cause of action); Jackson v. Wharton, 687 F. Supp. 595 (M.D. Ga. 1988) (dentures for cosmetic reasons not

§ 3:11

required, but, given the importance of routine care in preventing much more serious and perhaps permanent problems, the better reasoned cases find that prophylactic care, such as routine cleaning, must be provided to inmates.[16] Here, as is true with medical care, the standard is "deliberate indifference,"[17] not negligence, so inmates are not entitled to the best dental care and differences of opinion about the course of treatment, if at all legitimate, are resolved in favor of a finding of no

---

required); Vester v. Murray, 683 F. Supp. 140 (E.D. Va. 1988), judgment aff'd in part, vacated in part on other grounds, 878 F.2d 380 (4th Cir. 1989) (delay without harm was not a violation); Clifton v. Robinson, 500 F. Supp. 30, 35 (E.D. Pa. 1980) ("substantial harm" is the "sine qua non in denial of dental care cases"). For cases holding that the delays were not long enough in the particular case to constitute deliberate indifference, see, e.g., Reeves v. Caldwell, 1999 WL 375580 (D. Or. 1999) (delay of 21 days to treat tooth pain); Bout v. Bolden, 22 F. Supp. 2d 646, 42 Fed. R. Serv. 3d 562 (E.D. Mich. 1998), aff'd, 225 F.3d 658 (6th Cir. 2000) (three weeks for defendant dentist to treat and send inmate to an off-site hospital not actionable when prison officials offered to drill tooth without anesthesia).

[16]Compare Barnes v. Government of Virgin Islands, 415 F. Supp. 1218, 1235 (D.V.I. 1976); Jones v. Wittenberg, 323 F. Supp. 93, 28 Ohio Misc. 81, 57 Ohio Op. 2d 109 (N.D. Ohio 1971), opinion supplemented, 330 F. Supp. 707, 29 Ohio Misc. 35, 58 Ohio Op. 2d 47 (N.D. Ohio 1971), aff'd, 456 F.2d 854, 62 Ohio Op. 2d 232 (6th Cir. 1972) ("curative and preventive" dentistry required); Dawson v. Kendrick, 527 F. Supp. 1252, 1273 (S.D. W. Va. 1981) (court found that preventive dental care not provided but not clear if this is legal violation), with Jackson v. Lane, 688 F. Supp. 1291 (N.D. Ill. 1988) (claim frivolous); Rial v. McGinnis, 756 F. Supp. 1070 (N.D. Ill. 1991) (same). See also ABA Standards for Criminal Justice § 23.5-.2 (1986); American Correctional Assn, Standards for Adult Correctional Institutions Standard 3-4347 (1990); Commission on Accreditation for Corrections, Certification Standards for Health Care Programs HC-064 (1989).

[17]See, e.g., Harrison v. Barkley, 219 F.3d 132 (2d Cir. 2000) (holding that the correct standard is deliberate indifference and that if the dentists indeed refused to remove a diseased tooth only because inmate failed to consent to the removal of another tooth, there was deliberate indifference).

MEDICAL CARE § 3:12

liability.[18] If the state does not pay for preventative care there may be an entitlement to have it if the inmate is willing to pay.[19] However, if the dental need is significant and known, then it cannot be avoided or minimized. Moreover, the state may not opt for a substandard treatment of a serious problem by arguing that the required dental treatment is more expensive.[20]

§ 3:12 Eye Care

The same general principles apply to eye care that apply to any other form of medical care. Thus, delay or denial of care, if sufficiently serious, is a violation of the Constitution.[1] Inmates are entitled to corrective glasses and a failure to provide them, unless only for a short

---

[18]See, e.g., Hogan v. Russ, 890 F. Supp. 146 (N.D. N.Y. 1995) (holding that where prison officials offered to remove inmate's tooth or allow inmate to seek private dental treatment at his on expense there was no constitutional violation when prison officials refused to provide periodontal care); Malsh v. Austin, 901 F. Supp. 757 (S.D. N.Y. 1995) (holding that prison officials did not violate Eighth Amendment where inmate failed to attend the rescheduled dental appointment); Zimmerman v. Tippecanoe Sheriff's Dept., 25 F. Supp. 2d 915 (N.D. Ind. 1998).

[19]See, e.g., Hogan v. Russ, 890 F. Supp. 146, 149 (N.D. N.Y. 1995).

[20]Chance v. Armstrong, 143 F.3d 698, 703-04 (2d Cir. 1998) (holding that extracting teeth rather than filling cavities was deliberate indifference when the extraction caused pain and when it led to the loss of three other teeth).

[Section 3:12]

[1]Inmates of Occoquan v. Barry, 717 F. Supp. 854, 862, (D.D.C. 1989) (delay in eye clinic part of violations); Newman v. State of Ala., 349 F. Supp. 278, 287 (M.D. Ala. 1972), aff'd in part, 503 F.2d 1320 (5th Cir. 1974) and judgment vacated in part on other grounds, 522 F.2d 71 (5th Cir. 1975) (delay of a year for glasses must be cured and inmates must get them within "reasonable time"); Kersh v. Derozier, 851 F.2d 1509, 11 Fed. R. Serv. 3d 1505 (5th Cir. 1988) (upholding jury verdict against jailers who would not let detainee get piece of hay out of his eye even when it began to bleed and plaintiff ultimately lost eye as a result); Harris v. O'Grady, 803 F. Supp. 1361, 1366 (N.D. Ill. 1992) (cause of action stated when it was alleged that inmate was denied medical care

§ 3:12   Rights of Prisoners, Third Edition

time, will result in liability.[2]

§ 3:13   Diet

There are certain medical conditions that require special diets.[1] Failure to provide those diets can cause very serious consequences, including extended hospital-

---

for eye problem for eight months and denied glasses); Cox v. District of Columbia, 834 F. Supp. 439 (D.D.C. 1992) (consistent delays in timely refills of glaucoma medication stated a cause of action); Figueroa v. Vose, 874 F. Supp. 500, 503 (D.R.I. 1994), aff'd, 66 F.3d 306 (1st Cir. 1995) (finding no deliberate indifference; even though there were some delays there was no denial of care).

[2]Mitchell v. Maynard, 80 F.3d 1433, 34 Fed. R. Serv. 3d 1018 (10th Cir. 1996) (holding that failure to provide inmate with eyeglasses, if proved, violated the Constitution); Davidson v. Scully, 914 F. Supp. 1011 (S.D. N.Y. 1996) (holding that since prison officials did make attempts to provide inmate with eyeglasses, there was no constitutional violation); Williams v. ICC Committee, 812 F. Supp. 1029 (N.D. Cal. 1992) (depriving legally blind inmate of glasses stated a claim for deliberate indifference); Newman v. State of Ala., 349 F. Supp. 278, 287 (M.D. Ala. 1972), aff'd in part, 503 F.2d 1320 (5th Cir. 1974) and judgment vacated in part on other grounds, 522 F.2d 71 (5th Cir. 1975) (delay of a year for glasses must be cured and inmates get must them within "reasonable time"); Harris v. O'Grady, 803 F. Supp. 1361, 1366 (N.D. Ill. 1992) (cause of action stated when inmate alleged he was denied medical care for eye problem for eight months and was denied glasses); Harris v. O'Grady, 803 F. Supp. 1361, 1366 (N.D. Ill. 1992) (cause of action stated).

But see Nicholson v. Choctaw County, Ala., 498 F. Supp. 295, 308 (S.D. Ala. 1980) (pretrial detainees not entitled to glasses since services not provided to noninmates and in jail so short a time); Harris v. Murray, 758 F. Supp. 1114, 1118 (E.D. Va. 1991), published at 761 F.Supp. 409 (no violation when denied glasses for 10 days while in solitary). See also Borrelli v. Askey, 582 F. Supp. 512, 513 (E.D. Pa. 1984), judgment aff'd, 751 F.2d 375 (3d Cir. 1984) (inmate with "very slight visual impairment" was denied glasses and suffered at most "mild headaches and mild tension").

[Section 3:13]
  [1]This section only discusses medically required diets.

MEDICAL CARE § 3:13

ization and blindness.[2] As a result, many of the cases that set prerequisites for a minimally adequate medical care system require that medically necessary diets be provided.[3]

In individual cases, some courts order that medically necessary diets be provided,[4] and others deny such an order.[5] Small and non-serious delays in providing

---

[2]Balla v. Idaho State Bd. of Corrections, 595 F. Supp. 1558, 1574-75 (D. Idaho 1984).

[3]*Id*; Mandala v. Coughlin, 920 F. Supp. 342 (E.D. N.Y. 1996) (denial of high fiber diet prescribed by physician and surgeon, if proved, would be a constitutional violation); Barnes v. Government of Virgin Islands, 415 F. Supp. 1218, 1234 (D.V.I. 1976); Hines v. Anderson, 439 F. Supp. 12, 21-22 (D. Minn. 1977); Laaman v. Helgemoe, 437 F. Supp. 269 (D.N.H. 1977); Jackson v. Whitman, 642 F. Supp. 816, 822 (W.D. La. 1986); Miller v. Carson, 401 F. Supp. 835, 876 (M.D. Fla. 1975), aff'd in part, modified in part on other grounds and remanded, 563 F.2d 741 (5th Cir. 1977). See also U.S. v. State of Mich., 680 F. Supp. 270 (W.D. Mich. 1988) ("food loaf," which is mashed together food, could be impermissible in the case of inmates requiring special diets); Newman v. State of Ala., 349 F. Supp. 278 (M.D. Ala. 1972), aff'd in part, 503 F.2d 1320 (5th Cir. 1974) and judgment vacated in part, 522 F.2d 71 (5th Cir. 1975) (lack of diet system part of violation); Williams v. Edwards, 547 F.2d 1206 (5th Cir. 1977) (same); Laaman v. Helgemoe, 437 F. Supp. 269, 314 (D.N.H. 1977); Feliciano v. Barcelo, 497 F. Supp. 14, 38 (D.P.R. 1979). See also Brown v. State, Through Dept. of Correction, 354 So. 2d 633 (La. Ct. App. 1st Cir. 1977) (failure to give special diet was negligent violation of state statutory duty of care); National Commn on Correctional Health Care, Standards for Health Services in Jails J-45 (May 1999).

[4]Kyle v. Allen, 732 F. Supp. 1157 (S.D. Fla. 1990); Johnson v. Harris, 479 F. Supp. 333 (S.D. N.Y. 1979) (denied diet despite doctor's orders); Riddick v. Bass, 586 F. Supp. 881 (E.D. Va. 1984) (denied diet because of medical opinion, but court acknowledged that failure to provide medically indicated diet would be a violation); McCargo v. Vaughn, 778 F. Supp. 1341 (E.D. Pa. 1991); Massey v. Hutto, 545 F.2d 45, 46-47 (8th Cir. 1976).

[5]Stroud v. Roth, 741 F. Supp. 559 (E.D. Pa. 1990); Boring v. Kozakiewicz, 833 F.2d 468, 473 (3d Cir. 1987) (need for special diet for migraines not "serious medical need"); Cody v. Hillard, 599 F. Supp. 1025 (D.S.D. 1984), decision aff'd, 799 F.2d 447 (8th Cir.

§ 3:13   Rights of Prisoners, Third Edition

special diets have been found not to violate the Eighth Amendment.[6] Given the serious harm that can occur as a result of a failure to provide a medically indicated diet, it is apparent that a violation will be shown in cases where serious harm may occur, such as with diabetics, but will not be shown when the medical condition, or the consequences of not providing the diet, are less severe.[7]

§ 3:14   Health Needs of Women

There are surprisingly few cases specifically addressing the unique medical needs of women, including pregnancy and abortion.[1] Even *Todaro v. Ward*,[2] a case involving health care in a women's prison, had no

---

1986), reh'g granted, 804 F.2d 440 (8th Cir. 1986) and on reh'g, 830 F.2d 912 (8th Cir. 1987) (diabetics not entitled to special diet when getting dietary counseling sufficient to enable them to regulate their own diet); Startz v. Cullen, 468 F.2d 560 (2d Cir. 1972); Twyman v. Crisp, 584 F.2d 352, 354-55 (10th Cir. 1978) (allegations lack "gravity" where inmate got diet through connections with kitchen personnel).

[6]Toussaint v. McCarthy, 801 F.2d 1080, 1112 (9th Cir. 1986) ("Neither precedent nor common sense suggests that delay in providing a special diet rises to the level of deliberate indifference."); Hunt v. Dental Dept., 865 F.2d 198, 201 n2 (9th Cir. 1989).

[7]Compare Balla v. Idaho State Bd. of Corrections, 595 F. Supp. 1558 (D. Idaho 1984) (lack of diabetic diet caused inmate to become blind) with Boring v. Kozakiewicz, 833 F.2d 468 (3d Cir. 1987) (migraines) and Hunt v. Dental Dept., 865 F.2d 198 (9th Cir. 1989) (soft food for loss of dentures). See also Abdush-Shahid v. Coughlin, 933 F. Supp. 168 (N.D. N.Y. 1996) (holding that there is no violation where inmate is served special foods but refused to eat them).

[Section 3:14]

[1]Women Prisoners of District of Columbia Dept. of Corrections v. District of Columbia, 899 F. Supp. 659, 104 Ed. Law Rep. 213 (D.D.C. 1995) (injunctive relief was appropriate where female inmates alleged that prison officials failed to provide inmates with sufficient obstetrical and gynecological education; court noted that monetary relief was not suitable where the failure to provide health education caused a health risk to female inmates). For

§ 3:14

discussion of the particular needs of women. There have been studies indicating the extent of the need. One study indicates that as many as 10 percent of all women in prisons and jails are pregnant.[3] Some of the general class action cases discuss these needs incidental to other medical issues.[4] The few cases specific to the issues of pregnancy largely appear to have been settled

---

articles specific to the medical needs of women, see Mary Catherine McGurrin, Pregnant Inmates' Right to Heath Care, 20 New Eng. J. on Crim. & Civ. Confinement 163 (1992); Ellen Barry, Pregnant Prisoners, 12 Harv Women's LJ 189 (1989); Shelley Geballe & Martha Stone, The New Focus on Medical Care Issues in Women's Prison Cases, 15 J Natl Prison Project 1 (1988). These articles discuss pending cases more than reported cases and identify a number of horrible examples of inadequate care given to women. See also 28 CFR §§ 551.20 et seq. (federal regulations require medical care for pregnancy, birth control, and abortion); U.S. Dept of Justice, Federal Standards for Prisons and Jails § 5.49 (1980); ABA Standards for Criminal Justice § 23.5-23.7 (1986).

[2]Todaro v. Ward, 431 F.2d 1129 (S.D. N.Y.), aff'd, 565 F.2d 48 (2d Cir 1977).

[3]Ellen Barry, Pregnant Prisoners, 12 Harv Women's LJ 189 (1989) (quoting Stein & Mistiaen, Pregnant in Prison, The Progressive, Feb, 1988, at 18); Berrios-Berrios v. Thornburg, 716 F. Supp. 987, 990 (E.D. Ky. 1989) (at any time, 50 of 1,300 female inmates are pregnant); Columbia Human Rights Law Review, A Jailhouse Lawyer's Manual, 694 (5th ed. 2000) (reporting that as of 1991 about 6% of the women entering prison were pregnant and that in 1997 and 1998, 2,200 pregnant women were incarcerated in the United States).

[4]Newman v. State of Ala., 349 F. Supp. 278, 282-83 (M.D. Ala. 1972), aff'd in part, 503 F.2d 1320 (5th Cir. 1974) and judgment vacated in part on other grounds, 522 F.2d 71 (5th Cir. 1975) (inadequate facilities for delivery and no provisions for complicated delivery). See also Canterino v. Wilson, 546 F. Supp. 174 (W.D. Ky. 1982), judgment aff'd, 875 F.2d 862 (6th Cir. 1989) (women inmates seeking equal and adequate treatment); Women Prisoners of District of Columbia Dept. of Corrections v. District of Columbia, 877 F. Supp. 634, 98 Ed. Law Rep. 681 (D.D.C. 1994), vacated in part on other grounds, modified in part on other grounds, 899 F. Supp. 659, 104 Ed. Law Rep. 213 (D.D.C. 1995).

§ 3:14   Rights of Prisoners, Third Edition

with orders requiring comprehensive reform.[5] Failure to provide adequate services for delivery of a child, like other failures to provide medical care, can state violations of the Eighth Amendment.[6] In one shocking case, a court found that it was inhumane to shackle a pregnant prisoner to her bed during delivery and im-

---

[5]See, e.g., Archer v. Dutcher, 733 F.2d 14 (2d Cir. 1984) (holding that the state cannot punish a pregnant prisoner by denying her prenatal care); Calloway v. City of New Orleans, 524 So. 2d 182, 6 A.L.R.5th 1108 (La. Ct. App. 4th Cir. 1988), writ denied, 530 So. 2d 84 (La. 1988) (holding that a wrongful death action can be brought against prison officials who fail to provide adequate prenatal care to pregnant inmate). Cf. Daniels v. State of Delaware, 120 F.Supp. 2d 411 (D.Del. 2000) (woman's claim for wrongful life dismissed as state law did not recognize such a claim). For a discussion of the medical needs of pregnant prisoners see Columbia Human Rights Law Review, A Jailhouse Lawyer's Manual, 696-99 (5th ed. 2000); Ellen Barry, Pregnant Prisoners, 12 Harv Women's LJ 189, 194-201 (1989).

[6]Coleman v. Rahija, 114 F.3d 778 (8th Cir. 1997) (holding that ignoring fact that inmate was in labor for two hours when nurse was aware that plaintiff had a history of early labor, and the resulting unnecessary delay in transferring plaintiff to the hospital, constituted deliberate indifference); Boswell v. Sherburne County, 849 F.2d 1117 (8th Cir. 1988) (jailer knew of difficult pregnancy and severe cramping but did nothing); Archer v. Dutcher, 733 F.2d 14 (2d Cir. 1984); Women Prisoners of District of Columbia Dept. of Corrections v. District of Columbia, 877 F. Supp. 634, 98 Ed. Law Rep. 681 (D.D.C. 1994), vacated in part on other grounds , modified in part on other grounds, 899 F. Supp. 659, 104 Ed. Law Rep. 213 (D.D.C. 1995) (finding an Eighth Amendment violation where no prenatal care was provided, women were confined in lock-up while waiting to see doctor during pregnancy emergency, and woman with severe labor pains because her water had not broken was shackled and held); Williams v. Delcambre, 413 So. 2d 324, 326 (La. Ct. App. 3d Cir. 1982), writ denied, 416 So. 2d 115 (La. 1982) (failure to give treatment to pregnant woman stated claim). See also National Commn on Correctional Health Care, Standards for Health Services in Jails J-53, J-56 (May 1999). But see Pohlman v. Stokes, 687 F. Supp. 1179 (S.D. Ohio 1987) (at most, malpractice).

MEDICAL CARE § 3:14

mediately thereafter.[7]

At least one case has held that restrictions on abortion are impermissible.[8] Several other cases, however, have excused officials who delayed so long that abortion was no longer a viable option.[9]

Although women who are incarcerated are generally separated from their children shortly after birth, several women have sought to breast feed their infants either directly or by expressing the milk, with mixed

---

[7]Women Prisoners of District of Columbia Dept. of Corrections v. District of Columbia, 877 F. Supp. 634, 98 Ed. Law Rep. 681 (D. D.C. 1994), vacated in part on other grounds, modified in part on other grounds, 899 F. Supp. 659, 104 Ed. Law Rep. 213 (D.D.C. 1995).

[8]Monmouth County Correctional Institutional Inmates v. Lanzaro, 834 F.2d 326, 347, 90 A.L.R. Fed. 631 (3d Cir. 1987) (abortion is "serious medical need). But see Victoria W. v. Larpenter, 205 F. Supp. 2d 580 (E.D. La. 2002) (court order policy requiring prison inmate to hire an attorney, obtain a court order, and pay all attendant costs of non- therapeutic abortion did not deprive inmate of a right guaranteed by the Fourteenth Amendment, and a non-therapeutic abortion sought due to financial and emotional reasons was not a serious medical need for Eighth Amendment purposes); Gibson v. Matthews, 926 F.2d 532 (6th Cir. 1991) (no clearly established right to abortion, at least in third trimester); Bryant v. Maffucci, 923 F.2d 979 (2d Cir. 1991). Federal regulations permit abortions if paid for by the inmate. 28 CFR § 551.23. See also National Commn on Correctional Health Care, Standards for Health Services in Jails J-56 (May 1999). See also Columbia Human Rights Law Review, A Jailhouse Lawyer's Manual, 693 (5th ed. 2000) ("As a prisoner, you are supposed to have the right to an abortion.").

[9]Gibson v. Matthews, 926 F.2d 532 (6th Cir. 1991) (no clearly established right to abortion, at least in third trimester); Bryant v. Maffucci, 923 F.2d 979 (2d Cir. 1991) (mis-estimate of length of pregnancy only negligent). For a discussion of the abortion rights of female prisoners, see Sarah Tankersley, Note, Reproductive Freedom: Abortion Rights of Incarcerated and Non-Incarcerated Women, 85 Ky LJ 219 (1997) (arguing that incarcerated women have more reproductive freedom than nonincarcerated women).

§ 3:14   Rights of Prisoners, Third Edition

results.[10] In addition to Eighth Amendment concerns, the medical care available to female prisoners must comply with the Equal Protection Clause.[11]

§ 3:15 Mental Health

Research References

West's Key Number Digest, Prisons ⌾17(2); Sentencing and Punishment ⌾1547

Increasingly, mentally ill people are being sent to prison.[1] One recent comprehensive study reported that in western countries, including the United States, about

---

[10]Berrios-Berrios v. Thornburg, 716 F. Supp. 987, 990 (E.D. Ky. 1989) (no interest in denying breast feeding in person when will allow bottle feeding, but practicalities legitimately prevent storage of expressed milk given that at any time, 50 of 1,300 female inmates pregnant); Southerland v. Thigpen, 784 F.2d 713, 717 (5th Cir. 1986) (quoting Hudson v. Palmer, 468 U.S. 517, 104 S. Ct. 3194, 82 L. Ed. 2d 393 (1984)) (penological interests, including lack of facilities and the state's interest in deterrence and retribution, make breast feeding "fundamentally inconsistent with the objectives of incarceration" and justify denying "fundamental right" to breast feed; child's rights outweighed by state interests). See also Women Prisoners of District of Columbia Dept. of Corrections v. District of Columbia, 877 F. Supp. 634, 98 Ed. Law Rep. 681 (D. D.C. 1994), vacated in part on other grounds, modified in part on other grounds, 899 F. Supp. 659, 104 Ed. Law Rep. 213 (D.D.C. 1995) (holding Eighth Amendment violation where no child placement counseling was provided to pregnant women, inadequate staffing at the prison infirmary caused unusually high number of boarder babies to be housed in hospital, and there was a lack of adequate transportation for new mothers to see newborns in hospital).

[11]This applies to all health services, including medical, dental, and mental health. Further discussion of this issue may be found in § 3:2. For a discussion of the equal protection rights of inmates, see Ch 4.

[Section 3:15]

[1]Among inmates in state correctional facilities, a reported 17,354 (1.6%) are under 24-hour mental health care, 137,492 (12.9%) receive therapy or counseling, and 105,403 (9.7%) are prescribed psychotropic medications. According to the Bureau of Justice Statistics, more than 14 percent of inmates released on pa-

MEDICAL CARE § 3:15

one in seven prisoners have psychotic illnesses or major depression.[2] There can now be no doubt that the requirement that inmates receive needed medical care includes the requirement that they receive needed mental health care. Innumerable class actions have held that psychiatric care is as much an element of a minimally adequate medical care system as any other form of care.[3] Psychiatric care raises many of the same

---

role during 1999 had a mental illness. See American Corrections Association at www.aca.org/publications/questions.htm (visited September 17, 2002).

[2]Seena Fazel, John Banesh, Serious Mental Disorder in 23,000 Prisoners: A Systematic Review of 62 Surveys, 359 The Lancet 545 (2002).

[3]For a detailed discussion of the rights of prisoners to receive mental health care, see Fred Cohen, Captives' Legal Rights to Mental Health Care, 17 Law & Psychology Rev 1 (1993). See also Young v. City of Augusta, Ga. Through DeVaney, 59 F.3d 1160, 32 Fed. R. Serv. 3d 1438 (11th Cir. 1995) (holding that if city policy makers were aware of problems regarding mental illness in prison and failed to draft policy which addressed these concerns they would be liable); Doty v. County of Lassen, 37 F.3d 540 (9th Cir. 1994); Ramos v Lamm, 639 F2d 559, 574 (10th Cir 1980); Hoptowit v. Ray, 682 F.2d 1237, 1253, 9 Fed. R. Evid. Serv. 1511 (9th Cir. 1982); Wellman v. Faulkner, 715 F.2d 269, 272 (7th Cir. 1983); Finney v. Arkansas Bd. of Correction, 505 F.2d 194, 202-04 (8th Cir. 1974); Cody v. Hillard, 599 F. Supp. 1025, 1058-59 (D.S.D. 1984), decision aff'd, 799 F.2d 447 (8th Cir. 1986), reh'g granted, 804 F.2d 440 (8th Cir. 1986) and on reh'g, 830 F.2d 912 (8th Cir. 1987) (inadequate number of staff); Alberti v. Sheriff of Harris County, Texas, 406 F. Supp. 649, 677 (S.D. Tex. 1975) (must screen and treat and, where needed, transfer); Miller v. Carson, 401 F. Supp. 835, 876 (M.D. Fla. 1975), aff'd in part, modified in part and remanded, 563 F.2d 741 (5th Cir. 1977); Hamilton v. Landrieu, 351 F. Supp. 549, 550 (E.D. La. 1972) (must have psychiatric program); Inmates of Occoquan v. Barry, 717 F. Supp. 854 (D.D.C. 1989); Tillery v. Owens, 719 F. Supp. 1256, 1301 (W.D. Pa. 1989), order aff'd, 907 F.2d 418 (3d Cir. 1990); Palmigiano v. Garrahy, 443 F. Supp. 956 (D.R.I. 1977); Newman v. State of Ala., 349 F. Supp. 278 (M.D. Ala. 1972), aff'd in part, 503 F.2d 1320 (5th Cir. 1974) and judgment vacated in part on other grounds, 522 F.2d 71 (5th Cir. 1975); Williams v. Edwards, 547 F.2d 1206, 1217 (5th Cir. 1977) (no unit though 40% "would benefit"); Laaman v.

§ 3:15　　　　Rights of Prisoners, Third Edition

problems as general medical care. Screening of inmates for psychiatric problems is required.[4] A number of courts have reviewed the adequacy of the number of psychiatric staff at institutions and found it wanting.[5]

Helgemoe, 437 F. Supp. 269, 313, (D.N.H. 1977); Balla v. Idaho State Bd. of Corrections, 595 F. Supp. 1558, 1568-69, (D. Idaho 1984); See also Arnold on Behalf of H.B. v. Lewis, 803 F. Supp. 246, 248 (D. Ariz. 1992); U.S. Dept of Justice, Federal Standards for Prisons and Jails §§ 5.29-5.30 (1980); ABA Standards for Criminal Justice § 23.5-1 (1986) (commentary); American Correctional Assn, Standards for Adult Correctional Institutions, Standards 3-4336 through 3-4337 (3d ed. 1990); National Commn on Correctional Health Care, Standards for Health Services in Jails J-39 (May 1999); Commission on Accreditation for Corrections, Certification Standards for Health Care Programs HC-051, H-063, H-065 (1989). See also S. Hodgins, Assessing Mental Disorders in the Criminal Justice System: Feasibility versus Clinical Accuracy, 18 Int'l JL & Psychiatry 15 (1995). For a discussion of mental health care, see Richard C. McCorkle, Gender, Psychopathology, and Institutional Behavior: A Comparison of Male and Female Mentally Ill Prison Inmates, 23 J Crim Justice 53 (1995).

[4]Carty v. Farrelly, 957 F. Supp. 727, 22 A.D.D. 333 (D.V.I. 1997) (prison medical staff that was unqualified to properly identify mental illnesses violated the Eighth Amendment); Balla v. Idaho State Bd. of Corrections, 595 F. Supp. 1558, 1577 (D. Idaho 1984) (quoting Ruiz v. Estelle, 503 F. Supp. 1265 (S.D. Tex. 1980), aff'd in part, rev'd in part on other grounds, 679 F.2d 1115, 10 Fed. R. Evid. Serv. 1483 (5th Cir. 1982), amended in part on other grounds, vacated in part on other grounds, 688 F.2d 266 (5th Cir. 1982), and citing cases); Arnold on Behalf of H.B. v. Lewis, 803 F. Supp. 246, 253 (D. Ariz. 1992) (lack of screening part of liability). See also cases cited above in §§ 3:5, 3:16; U.S. Dept of Justice, Federal Standards for Prisons and Jails § 5.29 (1980); ABA Standards for Criminal Justice § 23.5-3 (1986); American Correctional Assn, Standards for Adult Correctional Institutions, Standards 3-4343 through 3-4345, 3-4349 (1990); National Commn on Correctional Health Care, Standards for Health Services in Jails J-39 (May 1999); Commission on Accreditation for Corrections, Certification Standards for Health Care Programs HC-062 (1989).

[5]Casey v. Lewis, 834 F. Supp. 1477 (D. Ariz. 1993) (where mentally ill inmates are put in lockdown because of lack of diagnosis due to lack of qualified staff, there is a violation); Madrid v. Gomez, 889 F. Supp. 1146 (N.D. Cal. 1995), mandamus denied, 103 F.3d 828 (9th Cir. 1996) (holding that that where prison of-

MEDICAL CARE § 3:15

Delays in providing needed psychiatric care violate the

ficials hired a visiting psychiatrist for periodic visits and then substituted a psychiatrist who resigned after one month, further substitution of nine on-call psychiatrists did not meet the mental health needs of prisoners in a population of 1,000 to 1,500 in the security housing unit alone). See also Ramos v Lamm, 639 F. 2d 559, 578 (10th Cir 1980) (need one full-time psychiatrist for 1,400 inmates, with estimate that 5-10% were "seriously mentally ill"); Wellman v. Faulkner, 715 F.2d 269, 272 (7th Cir. 1983) (need on-site psychiatrist); Cody v. Hillard, 599 F. Supp. 1025, 1058-59 (D. S.D. 1984), decision aff'd, 799 F.2d 447 (8th Cir. 1986), reh'g granted, 804 F.2d 440 (8th Cir. 1986) and on reh'g, 830 F.2d 912 (8th Cir. 1987) (inadequate number of staff); Alberti v. Sheriff of Harris County, Texas, 406 F. Supp. 649, 677 (S.D. Tex. 1975) (must obtain services of psychiatrist); Miller v. Carson, 401 F. Supp. 835, 879 (M.D. Fla. 1975), aff'd in part, modified in part on other grounds and remanded, 563 F.2d 741 (5th Cir. 1977) ("no trained personnel"); Jones v. Wittenberg, 323 F. Supp. 93, 28 Ohio Misc. 81, 57 Ohio Op. 2d 109 (N.D. Ohio 1971), opinion supplemented, 330 F. Supp. 707, 29 Ohio Misc. 35, 58 Ohio Op. 2d 47 (N.D. Ohio 1971), aff'd, 456 F.2d 854, 62 Ohio Op. 2d 232 (6th Cir. 1972) (must be doctor on call at all times); Inmates of Occoquan v. Barry, 717 F. Supp. 854, 868 (D.D.C. 1989) (need five psychologists and clerical staff for jail with 1,600-2,000 inmates); Tillery v. Owens, 719 F. Supp. 1256, 1284-86, (W.D. Pa. 1989), order aff'd, 907 F.2d 418 (3d Cir. 1990) (1,800 inmates had 33 hours of psychiatric care; one psychologist with three assistants, no psychiatric nurses or social workers); Barnes v. Government of Virgin Islands, 415 F. Supp. 1218, 1235 (D.V.I. 1976) (psychiatrist must be available one day per week); Inmates of Allegheny County Jail v. Pierce, 612 F.2d 754, 761-63 (3d Cir. 1979) (one nurse each shift for 450-500 inmates, two part-time psychiatrists with one always on call); Battle v. Anderson, 376 F. Supp. 402, 434 (E.D. Okla. 1974), judgment aff'd in part, rev'd in part on other grounds, 993 F.2d 1551 (10th Cir. 1993) (no psychiatrist for treatment); Newman v. State of Ala., 349 F. Supp. 278 (M.D. Ala. 1972), aff'd in part, 503 F.2d 1320 (5th Cir. 1974) and judgment vacated in part on other grounds, 522 F.2d 71 (5th Cir. 1975); Lightfoot v. Walker, 486 F. Supp. 504, 521-22, (S.D. Ill. 1980) (not enough counselors, clinical psychologists, and need two full-time psychiatrists for 2,650 inmate facility); Feliciano v. Barcelo, 497 F. Supp. 14, 38 (D.P.R. 1979) (court will not order specific number of staff but "it should be obvious" that institutions need "a full-time director of psychiatric services"); Ruiz v. Johnson, 37 F. Supp. 2d 855 (S.D. Tex. 1999), rev'd on other grounds and remanded, 243 F.3d 941 (5th Cir. 2001)

Constitution.[6] Failure to follow through on needed treatment ordered by a doctor violates the Eighth Amendment.[7] Courts have carefully examined the adequacy of mental health facilities and equipment, often requiring separate units, an adequate staff, sufficient equipment, and adequate sanitation for mentally ill inmates.[8] Records must also be adequate.[9] Here, as with

---

(consent decree providing for increased psychiatric care in Texas prisons); French v. Owens, 777 F.2d 1250, 1255 (7th Cir. 1985) (for institution of 2,000 inmates, must hire one psychiatrist, two psychiatric social workers, a clinical psychologist, and two behavioral clinicians); Duran v. Anaya, 642 F. Supp. 510 (D.N.M. 1986) (enjoining staff reductions caused by budget cuts); Burks v. Teasdale, 492 F. Supp. 650 (W.D. Mo. 1980) (psychologist and trained assistants can run ward when they work in close supervision with psychiatrist); Arnold on Behalf of H.B. v. Lewis, 803 F. Supp. 246, 253 (D. Ariz. 1992) (not enough staff to treat inmates). See also American Correctional Assn, Standards for Adult Correctional Institutions, Standard 3-4336 (1990); Commission on Accreditation for Corrections, Certification Standards for Health Care Programs HC-051.

[6]Ramos v Lamm, 639 F. 2d 559, 577 (10th Cir 1980) (lack of psychiatrist caused impermissible delay in mental health services); Lightfoot v. Walker, 486 F. Supp. 504, 521-22 (S.D. Ill. 1980) (delays in transferring to hospital and in referring to psychiatrists); Dawson v. Kendrick, 527 F. Supp. 1252, 1308 (S.D. W. Va. 1981) (failure to provide timely access); Arnold on Behalf of H.B. v. Lewis, 803 F. Supp. 246, 248 (D. Ariz. 1992) (lack of timely treatment).

[7]Steele v. Shah, 87 F.3d 1266, 45 Fed. R. Evid. Serv. 240 (11th Cir. 1996), as amended, (Sept. 6, 1996) (holding that if proved, discontinuing an inmate's prescribed psychotropic medication without examining prior medical records of the inmate would be unconstitutional); Arnold on Behalf of H.B. v. Lewis, 803 F. Supp. 246, 251 (D. Ariz. 1992) (medication); Waldrop v. Evans, 681 F. Supp. 840, 853-61 (M.D. Ga. 1988), judgment aff'd, 871 F.2d 1030 (11th Cir. 1989) (medication).

[8]Madrid v. Gomez, 889 F. Supp. 1146 (N.D. Cal. 1995), mandamus denied, 103 F.3d 828 (9th Cir. 1996) (holding that substandard conditions in security housing unit, which contained the most troubled and violent inmates, created a self-perpetuating situation in which inmates deteriorated further due to lack of proper mental health care and guidance); Casey v. Lewis, 834 F.

MEDICAL CARE § 3:15

medical care generally, while there is a right to treatment for serious mental conditions, the plaintiff must show that any failure was the result of deliberate indifference; otherwise, there is no liability.[10]

There are some issues that arise in the mental health context that are largely limited to that context.[11] For

---

Supp. 1477 (D. Ariz. 1993) (defendants ordered to develop plan for mental health housing); Inmates of Occoquan v. Barry, 717 F. Supp. 854, 863-64, (D.D.C. 1989) (must find alternative to unit where inmates kept in cell 23 hours a day and given no therapy); Tillery v. Owens, 719 F. Supp. 1256, 1303 (W.D. Pa. 1989), order aff'd, 907 F.2d 418 (3d Cir. 1990) (need adequate facilities including segregated unit); Inmates of Allegheny County Jail v. Peirce, 487 F. Supp. 638 (W.D. Pa. 1980) (must set up separate facility); Newman v. State of Ala., 466 F. Supp. 628, 631 (M.D. Ala. 1979) (segregation cells "unfit for the housing of persons with mental problems"); Lightfoot v. Walker, 486 F. Supp. 504, 521-24 (S.D. Ill. 1980) (placing inmates in unobserved cell without means of communication, inadequate in-patient facilities, both unacceptable). See also Balla v. Idaho State Bd. of Corrections, 595 F. Supp. 1558, 1577 (D. Idaho 1984) (segregation alone was insufficient); U.S. Dept of Justice, Federal Standards for Prisons and Jails § 5.31 (1980).

[9]Balla v. Idaho State Bd. of Corrections, 595 F. Supp. 1558, 1577 (D. Idaho 1984).

[10]For cases finding no violation, see Riddle v Mondragon, 83 F3d 1197 (10th Cir 1996) (failure to provide psychological treatment to inmate convicted of sex offenses for his compulsive sex drive and lack of self esteem was not deliberate indifference); Rodney v. Romano, 814 F. Supp. 311 (E.D. N.Y. 1993) (denial of access to psychologist trained in hypno-therapy was not a violation of the Eighth Amendment, particularly in light of the fact that evidence showed that hypno-therapy would not help, and might actually hurt).

For cases finding a deliberate indifference, see Perri v. Coughlin, 1999 WL 395374 (N.D. N.Y. 1999) (holding that mental health care constitutionally inadequate due to defendants' failure to carry out their statutory obligations to establish appropriate treatment programs for mentally ill inmates, and awarding damages of $50,000).

[11]Although it is beyond the scope of this chapter, when inmates are confined under "sexually dangerous persons" statutes or other statutes combining prison and mental health rationales, other

§ 3:15   Rights of Prisoners, Third Edition

example, a number of institutions have been found to have inadequate mental health systems when they have improperly or indiscriminately used physical restraints on mentally ill people.[12] Misuse of seclusion or observation is actionable.[13] In recent years more and more mentally ill inmates have been placed in so called

---

constitutional rights, such as the right to treatment, may apply. Balla v. Idaho State Bd. of Corrections, 595 F. Supp. 1558, 1577-78, (D. Idaho 1984).

[12]Jones v. Thompson, 818 F. Supp. 1263 (S.D. Ind. 1993) (holding that placing a pre-trial detainee in three-way restraints that prevented standing up and sitting down after suicide attempt violated the Fourteenth Amendment); Hamilton v. Landrieu, 351 F. Supp. 549, 552 (E.D. La. 1972) (prisons cannot chain "inmates manifesting symptoms of psychosis" and must use "humane means of restraint"); Inmates of Allegheny County Jail v. Pierce, 612 F.2d 754 (3d Cir. 1979) (cannot use restraints); Owens-El v. Robinson, 442 F. Supp. 1368, 1380 (W.D. Pa. 1978) (improper use of restraints for women); French v. Owens, 777 F.2d 1250, 1253-54 (7th Cir. 1985); Arnold on Behalf of H.B. v. Lewis, 803 F. Supp. 246, 256 (D. Ariz. 1992) (improper use of lockdown); Burks v. Teasdale, 492 F. Supp. 650, 679 (W.D. Mo. 1980) ("Insofar as the use of seclusion and/or restraints for mentally disturbed inmates can be used only for *medical* purposes without running afoul of due process, this Court holds that custody personnel are unqualified to make such determinations on a non-emergency basis"; in addition, there must be a "systemic policy for the use of seclusion and restraint" (emphasis in original)); Ferola v. Moran, 622 F. Supp. 814, 820-25 (D.R.I. 1985) (spreadeagle restraint without monitoring and without access to toilet); But see Rehbein v. Terry, 836 F. Supp. 677 (D. Neb. 1992), judgment aff'd, 7 F.3d 1042 (8th Cir. 1993) (psychiatrist not liable for keeping pre-trial detainee in restraints for 39 hours because professional judgment used); American Correctional Assn, Standards for Adult Correctional Institutions, Standard 3-4362 (1990); National Commn on Correctional Health Care, Standards for Health Services in Jails J-49 (May 1999); Commission on Accreditation for Corrections, Certification Standards for Health Care Programs HC-081.2 (1989).

[13]McCray v. Burrell, 516 F.2d 357 (4th Cir. 1975), cert. granted, 423 U.S. 923, 96 S. Ct. 264, 46 L. Ed. 2d 249 (1975) and cert. dismissed, 426 U.S. 471, 96 S. Ct. 2640, 48 L. Ed. 2d 788 (1976) (conditions of isolation cells); Negron v. Preiser, 382 F. Supp. 535 (S.D. N.Y. 1974); Johnson v. Levine, 588 F.2d 1378 (4th Cir. 1978); National Commn on Correctional Health Care, Standards for

MEDICAL CARE § 3:15

"Supermax" facilities in which conditions are especially harsh. As discussed in Chapter 2, there is a developing case law holding this practice, which exacerbates mental illness, unconstitutional.[14] Furthermore, misuse of powerful psychiatric drugs, either through their use for control purposes or through polypharmacy, is part of some courts' findings that the system is inadequate.[15] One court, after noting the huge increase in the use of psychiatric drugs, apparently for purposes of control and not treatment, held that "prescription and administration of behavior-altering medications in dangerous amounts by dangerous methods, or without appropriate supervision and periodic evaluation, is an unacceptable

---

Health Services in Jails J-26 (May 1999); Commission on Accreditation for Corrections, Certification Standards for Health Care Programs 1381; Wright v. McMann, 460 F.2d 126, 129 (2d Cir. 1972) (may not confine in psychiatric observation cells "for disciplinary purposes and without psychiatric justification"); Negron v. Ward, 458 F. Supp. 748 (S.D. N.Y. 1978) (upholding jury verdict for plaintiffs). But see Green v. Baron, 879 F.2d 305 (8th Cir. 1989) (committing pretrial detainee for behavior modification treatment so that he could personally participate in his criminal trial represented a legitimate government objective that would not violate rights of pretrial detainee). This issue is discussed in greater detail in § 2:3.

[14]§ 2:2.

[15]Lightfoot v. Walker, 486 F. Supp. 504, 522 (S.D. Ill. 1980). Woodland v. Angus, 820 F. Supp. 1497 (D. Utah 1993) (administration of psychotropic drugs to create competency for trial not justified; no reasonable medical certainty that plan would be successful). See also Knecht v. Gillman, 488 F.2d 1136, 71 Ohio Op. 2d 101 (8th Cir. 1973); Nelson v. Heyne, 491 F.2d 352 (7th Cir. 1974); but see Sullivan v. Flannigan, 8 F.3d 591 (7th Cir. 1993) (prisoner not allowed to refuse involuntary administration of medication in order to prove that it was no longer necessary); U.S. Dept of Justice, Federal Standards for Prisons and Jails § 5.35 (1980); American Correctional Assn, Standards for Adult Correctional Institutions, Standards 3-4341 through 3-4342 (1990); Commission on Accreditation for Corrections, Certification Standards for Health Care Programs HC-086, HC-091 (1989).

method of treatment."[16]

One recurrent issue is the transfer of mentally ill inmates to psychiatric institutions. A number of courts have held such transfers required in appropriate circumstances, because prisons are not set up to provide the intensive psychiatric care that should be provided in a mental health facility.[17] The Supreme Court has held that such transfers can be made only after proce-

---

[16]Balla v. Idaho State Bd. of Corrections, 595 F. Supp. 1558, 1568-69, (D. Idaho 1984) (increase "five and one half times in the course of three years"). See also Vaughan v. Lacey, 49 F.3d 1344 (8th Cir. 1995); Austin v. Pennsylvania Dept. of Corrections, 876 F. Supp. 1437, 10 A.D.D. 1042 (E.D. Pa. 1995) (consent agreement provided that inmates on psychotropic drugs must be re-evaluated every six months); Walker v. Shansky, 28 F.3d 666 (7th Cir. 1994); Franklin v. District of Columbia, 960 F. Supp. 394 (D.D.C. 1997), rev'd in part, vacated in part, 163 F.3d 625, 42 Fed. R. Serv. 3d 1013 (D.C. Cir. 1998) supra (prison medical system was deliberately indifferent to the mental health needs of a class of Hispanic inmates when it failed to make treatment available; such systemic deficiencies included a failure to properly administer mental health treatment in a consistent and continuous manner; court ordered the defendants to submit a memorandum to the court detailing a plan to redress the violations; on appeal, Court of Appeals held that District's failure to always provide interpreters for prisoners during medical consultations was not cruel and unusual punishment and that prisoners did not have constitutional privacy right in having medical personnel serve as interpreters).

[17]Cameron v. Tomes, 990 F.2d 14 (1st Cir. 1993) (holding that procedures such as 10-minute movement restriction, oral cavity searches, and armed guard and shackles during transport within a sexual offender treatment center could violate Eighth Amendment rights of an inmate if the procedures worsened the inmate's mental condition); Feliciano v. Barcelo, 497 F. Supp. 14, 38 (D.P.R. 1979); Inmates of Allegheny County Jail v. Wecht, 565 F. Supp. 1278, 1288 (W.D. Pa. 1983) (contempt for failure to institute commitment within 72 hours); Arnold on Behalf of H.B. v. Lewis, 803 F. Supp. 246, 251-53 (D. Ariz. 1992) (liability for failure to transfer); Campbell v. McGruder, 580 F.2d 521, 548-50 (D.C. Cir. 1978). See also American Correctional Assn, Standards for Adult Correctional Institutions, Standard 3-4367 (1990).

MEDICAL CARE § 3:15

dural due process protections are provided.[18]

Another issue that is beginning to receive attention is discharge planning. It makes little sense to stabilize a mentally ill inmate in prison and then release the inmate to the free world without making adequate provision for continued care. In one recent interesting case, a class of inmates who were mentally ill and were being released from New York City jails with no provision for continuation of medication or plans for housing filed suit in state court claiming that they were entitled under state law[19] to adequate discharge planning. The plaintiffs stated that approximately 25,000 pretrial detainees, sentenced individuals, and other inmates received mental health care while incarcerated in New York City jails. These services included the prescription of psychotropic medications as well as inpatient and outpatient individual and group therapy. Upon release from Rikers Island, however, inmates generally were not provided any mental health services, government benefits assistance, housing referrals, or other services or planning. Rather, all that was done for these inmates was that they are taken by bus to a subway station between 2:00 and 6:00 a.m. and given $1.50 plus two subway tokens or a two-fare transit card. The trial court issued a preliminary injunction, noting that there was no effective transition from inmate mental health services received while incarcerated to services in the

---

[18]Vitek v. Jones, 445 U.S. 480, 100 S. Ct. 1254, 63 L. Ed. 2d 552 (1980). See also American Correctional Assn, Standards for Adult Correctional Institutions § 3-4368 (3d ed. 1990); Commission on Accreditation for Corrections, Certification Standards for Health Care Programs HC-066 (1989). For a discussion of the transfer of mentally ill inmates from general population see B.D. Shannon, Diversion of Offenders With Mental Illness: Recent Legislative Reforms, 59 Tex B J 300 (1996).

[19]Mental Hygiene Law § 29.15, 14 NYCRR §§ 587.1 et seq.; N.Y. Const art. I, §§ 5, 6.

community.[20]

§ 3:16 Suicide

Prison suicide, and particularly jail suicide, is a serious problem, and there is now quite a bit known about the characteristics of those inmates who are at risk of suicide. People who are arrested are normally in high state of anxiety. These people may suffer from numerous medical problems, and they may be intoxicated when brought to the jail (indeed, the vast majority of jail suicides are committed by people who are intoxicated). All these factors make inmates as a group more prone to suicide than other populations.[1] A system that can identify, treat, and supervise inmates who are suicidal is often seen as part of an adequate mental health program.[2] The fact that suicide is an action taken by the inmate is irrelevant; there is a clear duty "to protect prisoners from self-destruction or self-injury."[3]

Most of the jail suicide cases are not class actions but

---

[20]Brad H. v. City of New York, 185 Misc. 2d 420, 712 N.Y.S.2d 336 (Sup 2000), order aff'd, 276 A.D.2d 440, 716 N.Y.S.2d 852 (1st Dep't 2000).

[Section 3:16]

[1]National Commn on Correctional Health Care, Standards for Health Services in Jails J-51 (May 1999) (identifying high risk periods). See also Simmons v. City of Philadelphia, 947 F.2d 1042, 1051, 21 Fed. R. Serv. 3d 966 (3d Cir. 1991) (plaintiff's expert testified that $\frac{2}{3}$ of jail suicides occur when the detainee is intoxicated, $\frac{3}{4}$ when detainee is isolated in cell, that most occur between midnight and 6:00 a.m., and that most who commit suicide are young).

[2]Balla v. Idaho State Bd. of Corrections, 595 F. Supp. 1558, 1577 (D. Idaho 1984); American Correctional Assn, Standards for Adult Correctional Institutions, Standards 3-4364 (1990); National Commn on Correctional Health Care, Standards for Health Services in Jails J-51 (May 1999); Commission on Accreditation for Corrections, Certification Standards for Health Care Programs HC-054 (1989).

[3]Lee v. Downs, 641 F.2d 1117, 1121 (4th Cir. 1981) (officials have a "duty to protect prisoners from self-destruction or self-injury"); Guglielmoni v. Alexander, 583 F. Supp. 821, 827 (D.

§ 3:16

individual suits for damages. In the earliest of those cases, there was a dispute about whether the proper mode of analysis was to treat these cases as analogous to the prisoner assault cases or as medical care cases.[4] Although this distinction appears to have little consequence,[5] the better reasoned cases treat the prevention of suicide as a medical care issue,[6] that is, inmates have a constitutional right to be protected from suicide and that prison officials will be held liable if it is determined that they are "deliberately indifferent" to an inmate's risk of suicide.[7]

The first critical question in any jail suicide case, as in any case, is the identity of the defendant, and more particularly, whether the governmental entity, city or county, is named as a defendant. Although it is beyond the scope of this book to discuss the elaborate doctrines that apply to suits against governmental entities, the jail suicide cases emphasize the two competing interests when those entities are named as defendants. First, the city or county is not entitled to the qualified immunity

---

Conn. 1984); Martin v. Harrison County Jail, 975 F.2d 192, 24 Fed. R. Serv. 3d 347 (5th Cir. 1992) (guards had duty to try to stop suicide and when they struck inmate while doing so, there was no liability). For an in-depth discussion of jail suicides, see George J. Franks, The Conundrum of Federal Jail Suicide Case Law Under Section 1983 and Its Double Bind for Jail Administrators, 17 Law & Psychology Rev 117 (1993).

[4]State Bank of St. Charles v. Camic, 712 F.2d 1140, 1145 n.3 (7th Cir. 1983) (using prisoner assault cases as analogous to *Estelle*); Roberts v. City of Troy, 773 F.2d 720 (6th Cir. 1985) (rejecting prison assault cases for medical cases); Partridge v. Two Unknown Police Officers of City of Houston, Tex., 791 F.2d 1182, 1191 (5th Cir. 1986) (dissent) (prisoner assault, not medical care cases).

[5]State Bank of St. Charles v. Camic, 712 F.2d 1140, 1145 n3 (7th Cir. 1983) (prisoner assault cases analogous to *Estelle*).

[6]Bell v. Stigers, 937 F.2d 1340, 1343 (8th Cir. 1991).

[7]See, e.g., Jacobs v. West Feliciana Sheriff's Dept., 228 F.3d 388 (5th Cir. 2000).

§ 3:16   RIGHTS OF PRISONERS, THIRD EDITION

defense available to individuals named as defendants.[8] On the other hand, cities and counties will not be held liable unless there is a causal link between the suicide and an official city or county policy.[9]

These factors can be critical and applied in wildly divergent ways. One critical feature of the inquiry into qualified immunity is the particularity of the right that was or was not clearly established. In the Sixth Circuit, in a case taking an extremely narrow view of the right that must be established, the plaintiffs lost because there was no clearly established right for an inmate who had hanged himself to be cut down immediately.[10] By contrast, the Seventh Circuit found in the same year

---

[8]County of Sacramento v. Lewis, 523 U.S. 833, 118 S. Ct. 1708, 140 L. Ed. 2d 1043 (1998); Monell v. Department of Social Services of City of New York, 436 U.S. 658, 98 S. Ct. 2018, 56 L. Ed. 2d 611 (1978).

[9]City of Canton, Ohio v. Harris, 489 U.S. 378, 109 S. Ct. 1197, 103 L. Ed. 2d 412 (1989); Molton v. City of Cleveland, 839 F.2d 240 (6th Cir. 1988) (city not liable where no custom or policy which "caused the officers to be deliberately indifferent to Molton's serious needs"); Buffington v. Baltimore County, Md., 913 F.2d 113, 17 Fed. R. Serv. 3d 577 (4th Cir. 1990) (upholding, in part, verdict against defendants where defendants knew inmate was suicidal and, in violation of policy, did not keep him under observation; but since policy would have prevented suicide, no municipal liability); Tittle v. Jefferson County Com'n, 10 F.3d 1535 (11th Cir. 1994) (county was not liable under respondeat superior theory for acts and omissions of jail personnel that were contrary to county policy of screening prisoners for suicidal tendencies, even if deputies were properly considered agents of the county); Gordon v. Kidd, 971 F.2d 1087 (4th Cir. 1992), as amended, (July 7, 1992) (city not liable because a failure of policy, not lack of one, citing Monell v. Department of Social Services of City of New York, 436 U.S. 658, 98 S. Ct. 2018, 56 L. Ed. 2d 611 (1978)); Heflin v. Stewart County, Tenn., 958 F.2d 709, 34 Fed. R. Evid. Serv. 1446 (6th Cir. 1992), on reconsideration, 968 F.2d 1 (6th Cir. 1992) (upholding jury verdict where by policy failed to cut down arguably alive victim for 20 minutes or more and no resuscitation efforts); Marshall v. Borough of Ambridge, 798 F. Supp. 1187, 1197 (W.D. Pa. 1992) (failure to train stated cause of action).

[10]Rich v. City of Mayfield Heights, 955 F.2d 1092 (6th Cir. 1992) (no particularized right to be cut down before taking one minute to

that it had been clearly established for six years that "police officers could not be deliberately indifferent to a detainee . . . who is a substantial suicide risk."[11] The latter opinion is more in keeping with the Supreme Court's recent decision in *Hope v. Pelzer*,[12] which overturned an overly narrow definition of the constitutional right at stake in a qualified immunity case.

In *Rellergert v Cape Girardeau County*,[13] the court accurately described the jail suicide cases as falling into two general categories: where "jailers failed to discover the decedent's suicidal tendencies" or where "jailers have discovered the tendencies and have not taken preventive measures."

Where jail officials do not have reason to suspect that an inmate is suicidal, the question is whether the officials have any duty to attempt to distinguish those inmates who are suicidal from those that are not. As noted, many of the class action cases have held that mental health screening is an essential part of any system of mental health care and an essential part of any initial screening, in part to determine suicide impulses. Despite those holdings, in jail suicide cases courts frequently and erroneously hold that there is no right to such screening.[14] Where there is no evidence that an inmate is suicidal, virtually any efforts-and

---

summon help; therefore, there was qualified immunity and, since help was summoned, there was no liability). But see Heflin v. Stewart County, Tenn., 958 F.2d 709, 34 Fed. R. Evid. Serv. 1446 (6th Cir. 1992), on reconsideration, 968 F.2d 1 (6th Cir. 1992) (upholding jury verdict whereby policy failed to cut down an arguably alive victim for 20 minutes or more and there were no resuscitation efforts).

[11]Hall v. Ryan, 957 F.2d 402, 405 (7th Cir. 1992).

[12]Hope v. Pelzer, 122 S. Ct. 2508, 153 L. Ed. 2d 666 (U.S. 2002).

[13]Rellergert by Rellergert v. Cape Girardeau County, Mo., 924 F.2d 794, 796 (8th Cir. 1991).

[14]Often this position is justified by citing the Supreme Court's decision in Helling v. McKinney, 509 U.S. 25, 113 S. Ct. 2475, 125 L. Ed. 2d 22 (1993). See also Estate of Cole by Pardue v. Fromm, 94 F.3d 254 (7th Cir. 1996) (prison medical officials were granted

§ 3:16   Rights of Prisoners, Third Edition

summary judgment where plaintiffs failed to satisfy the subjective component of *Farmer*); Hare v. City of Corinth, Miss., 949 F. Supp. 456 (N.D. Miss. 1996), rev'd on other grounds, 135 F.3d 320 (5th Cir. 1998) (plaintiff must demonstrate that prison officials had "actual" knowledge of a substantial risk of harm and disregarded that risk); Gagne v. City of Galveston, 805 F.2d 558, 559 (5th Cir. 1986) (officer "not under a clearly established constitutional duty to discover the prisoner's suicidal tendencies"); Danese v. Asman, 875 F.2d 1239, 1244 (6th Cir. 1989) (no clearly established right that "police officers must detect suicidal prisoners"); Belcher v. Oliver, 898 F.2d 32, 34-35 (4th Cir. 1990) ("the officer's failure to afford Belcher medical screening . . . did not violate constitutional standards. The general right [to medical care] . . . does not place upon jail officials the responsibility to screen every detainee for suicidal tendencies").

Burns v. City of Galveston, Tex., 905 F.2d 100, 104 (5th Cir. 1990) is an example of a case that not only ignores the general law requiring screening but also, in order to rule against the inmate, sets up a classic straw man, ignoring the real issue. The court says that the: "failure to train police officers in screening procedures geared toward detection of detainees with suicidal tendencies may rise to the level of a constitutional deprivation only if the right of detainees to adequate medical care includes an absolute right to psychological screening. We perceive no such right . . . .It is one thing to require a municipality to train its police officers to recognize and not ignore obvious medical needs of detainees with known, demonstrable, and serious mental disorders. It is quite another to require as a constitutional minimum that a municipality train its officers to to medically screen each pretrial detainee so that the officers will unerringly detect suicidal tendencies. The latter requires the skills of an experienced medical professional with psychiatric training, an ability beyond that required of the average police officer by the due process clause."

There is no evidence that medical personnel could unerringly distinguish suicidal people, and the lack of perfection on the part of jail officials hardly justifies them in making no attempts. See also Roberts v. City of Troy, 773 F.2d 720 (6th Cir. 1985) (upholding jury verdict denying liability for failure to screen). In *Roberts,* the circuit went so far as to say in dicta that, absent intent to punish, the police chief's failure to provide better suicide prevention training and to learn about and implement a new regulation and the City of Troy's failure to employ better trained jailers did not amount to constitutional violations because the failures arose from

§ 3:16

often no efforts[15] -at screening inmates, training jail officials to recognize those who are suicidal, or elementary suicide precautions will be found sufficient.[16] In addi-

---

the allocation of resources-time, personnel, and money-which constitutes a legitimate governmental purpose.

[15]Estate of Cartwright v. City of Concord, Cal., 856 F.2d 1437 (9th Cir. 1988) (upholding verdict that rejects liability in claims of preventing suicide since no reason to believe suicidal); Danese v. Asman, 875 F.2d 1239, 1244 (6th Cir. 1989) (no clearly established right that "police officers must detect suicidal prisoners and put them in suicide-proof facilities" and no right to training for that purpose); Bell v. Stigers, 937 F.2d 1340 (8th Cir. 1991) (where no real evidence of suicidal threat, and because no duty to be familiar with a prisoner suicide profile, no liability).

Edwards v Gilbert, 867 F2d 1271, 1275 (11th Cir 1989) is an example of the confused thinking that permeates this area. The court granted summary judgment to the defendants, though they had violated state law by placing a juvenile in an adult jail, because "[i]n the absence of a previous threat of or an earlier attempt at suicide, we know of no federal court in the nation or any other court within this circuit that has concluded that official conduct in failing to prevent a suicide constitutes deliberate indifference." Of course, no one suggests that the jail must "prevent a suicide." That does not mean, however, that steps should not be taken to minimize the risk of suicide. On the other hand, see Marshall v. Borough of Ambridge, 798 F. Supp. 1187, 1197 (W.D. Pa. 1992) (possible liability for failure to train and inadequate policies).

[16]State Bank of St. Charles v. Camic, 712 F.2d 1140 (7th Cir. 1983) (where lack actual knowledge of suicidal intent, and take some reasonable precautions, failure to follow own established procedures does not result in liability); Dobson v. Magnusson, 923 F.2d 229 (1st Cir. 1991) (where no evidence of suicidal nature, failure to observe precautionary 15-minute checks not enough to justify liability); Wayland v. City of Springdale, Ark., 933 F.2d 668 (8th Cir. 1991) (no liability where no evidence of suicidal tendency even though city negligently did not fix vent from which another detainee had killed self); Barber v. City of Salem, Ohio, 953 F.2d 232 (6th Cir. 1992) (no suicide training, no overnight observation, no screening as required by state law, and horizontal bars, combined with jail's own report noting risks of insufficient observation and horizontal bars; detainee not cut down for 45 minutes; detainee lost because in 1982 no clearly established right to these suicide prevention measures and not liable for failure to follow policy where no evidence of suicidal intent); Tittle v. Jefferson

§ 3:16   Rights of Prisoners, Third Edition

tion, the failure to utilize any of those steps, even if required by law, will ordinarily be found negligent but not evidencing deliberate indifference to a serious medical need.[17] These cases are troubling. The duty exists to

---

County Com'n, 10 F.3d 1535 (11th Cir. 1994) (county did not act with deliberate indifference to prisoners' suicide risk, as required to establish violation of Eighth or Fourteenth Amendment in prisoners' suicide, where prisoners were screened by jail medical personnel and neither exhibited suicidal tendencies; alleged weaknesses in screening of inmates for suicidal tendencies, without more, did not amount to showing of deliberate indifference toward prisoners' rights); Hardin v. Hayes, 957 F.2d 845 (11th Cir. 1992).

[17]Gagne v. City of Galveston, 805 F.2d 558, 559 (5th Cir. 1986) (officer "not under a clearly established constitutional duty to . . . deprive him [the inmate] of the means of killing himself" and, thus, no liability for failure to remove belt or screen for suicidal tendency in violation of jail rules); Molton v. City of Cleveland, 839 F.2d 240, 247 (6th Cir. 1988) (jailers failed to respond to shouts from other inmates that detainee trying to kill himself, but court found that the city's inadequate training to detect suicide was "negligence"); Beddingfield v. City of Pulaski, Tenn., 861 F.2d 968 (6th Cir. 1988) (even if training was negligent in not recommending removal of shoelaces and belt, not sufficient for liability); Belcher v. Oliver, 898 F.2d 32 (4th Cir. 1990) (qualified immunity precluded liability, where failure to remove belt pursuant to policy caused suicide, because no evidence that inmate was suicidal); Popham v. City of Talladega, 908 F.2d 1561, 1565 (11th Cir. 1990) (where no evidence of suicidal tendencies, failure to have staff on duty all night and failure of surveillance camera to be able to see whole cell not deliberate indifference because there are no cases holding that "deliberate indifference is demonstrated if prisoners are not seen by jailers at all times"); Rellergert by Rellergert v. Cape Girardeau County, Mo., 924 F.2d 794 (8th Cir. 1991) (failure to take measures may be "so inadequate as to be deliberately indifferent to the risk"; jury verdict overturned where jail had policy of constant observation, but guard who conducted the observation had other duties that precluded him from maintaining constant observation); Colburn v. Upper Darby Tp., 946 F.2d 1017 (3d Cir. 1991) (no evidence of suicidal tendencies except intoxication, which is not enough, and no evidence of training that would have identified prisoner as suicide risk, so allegation of failure to train insufficient); Schmelz v. Monroe County, 954 F.2d 1540 (11th Cir. 1992) (in action against sheriff by guardian of arrestee who was rendered incompetent by suicide attempt in county jail, guardian failed to

MEDICAL CARE § 3:16

screen new inmates for possible suicidal tendencies and there is knowledge to be applied in distinguishing possibly suicidal inmates. Thus, failure to take simple measures would seem to justify a finding that the institution was deliberately indifferent to the inmate's serious medical needs. Equally troubling are cases that fail to recognize that the failure to train prison personnel to identify and respond to suicide risks can be actionable.[18] Some cases have held that liability can be

---

show that sheriff's unwritten policy for dealing with suicidal inmates was unconstitutional; policy made effort to identify and protect potentially suicidal inmates from self-harm, and guardian did not show that sheriff's department employees' failure to do more resulted from inadequate training amounting to deliberate indifference to needs of jail's inmates); Bowen v. City of Manchester, 966 F.2d 13 (1st Cir. 1992) (where no evidence of suicidal intent, failure to screen and leaving the jail unobserved, though perhaps negligent and a "gross deficiency," was not sufficient to establish liability; training would not have permitted officer to identify plaintiff as suicidal and the existence of anti-suicide policies, though inadequate, showed the jailers were not deliberately indifferent); Manarite By and Through Manarite v. City of Springfield, 957 F.2d 953, 957 (1st Cir. 1992) (no liability "where police departments have promulgated commonplace suicide-prevention policies . . . even if the officers did not always follow the department's policy and even if other, better policies might have diminished suicide risks," and thus failure to remove shoelaces as required by policy and jail's failure to recognize past pattern of shoelace suicides in the face of noncompliance with policy insufficient to establish liability). But see Brewer v. Perrin, 132 Mich. App. 520, 349 N.W.2d 198 (1984) (failure to follow monitoring and segregation procedures sufficient to state cause of action though apparently no evidence of suicidal nature).

[18]See, e.g., Daniels v. Glase, 198 F.3d 257 (10th Cir. 1999) (holding that a claim of failure to properly train and supervise jail employees was not proven); Criswell v. Wayne County, Kentucky, 165 F.3d 26 (6th Cir. 1998) (holding that there was a failure to prove that any training inadequacy "was closely related to" or "actually caused" the inmate's suicide); Vallejo by Morales v. Rahway Police Dept., 292 N.J. Super. 333, 678 A.2d 1135 (App. Div. 1996) (affirming lower court's dismissal of plaintiff's Eighth Amendment claim against the department for failing to adequately train personnel); Pyka v. Village of Orland Park, 906 F. Supp. 1196 (N.D. Ill. 1995)

§ 3:16

based on a failure to take the most simple preventative measures, including training.[19] These cases suggest that as more and more is known about measures that can be used to minimize the risk of suicide in jails, jailers will be increasingly held accountable for failing to take at least the simplest and most widely accepted of those measures. The words of a judge concurring in one jail suicide case[20] may yet prove true: "Jailers beware!" Failure to screen inmates, failure to observe inmates, and a failure to provide 24-hour access to needed psychiatric care create a risk of suicide. Thus, in the future, they may form the basis for liability because "[s]howing concern for those in custody by taking limited steps will not pass muster unless the strides taken to deal with the risk are calculated to work."[21]

The second category of cases is those in which there

(holding that failure to train officers to recognize suicidal inmates does not violate Eighth Amendment when there had been few inmate suicide attempts at the jail and that there were no statutes that required municipality to educate officers in suicide prevention).

[19]Simmons v. City of Philadelphia, 947 F.2d 1042, 21 Fed. R. Serv. 3d 966 (3d Cir. 1991) (upholding jury verdict for failure to take simple preventive measures and failure to train). See also Marshall v. Borough of Ambridge, 798 F. Supp. 1187, 1197 (W.D. Pa. 1992) (lack of training due to lack of funds not a valid defense and summary judgment denied).

[20]Rhyne v. Henderson County, 973 F.2d 386, 396 (5th Cir. 1992) (Goldberg, J., concurring) (inmate losts because policies not deliberately indifferent, insufficient evidence on training, observation every 10 minutes rather than continuous, and inability to obtain commitment to hospital on weekends may have been negligent, but insufficient due to lack of history that policy was inadequate).

[21]Rhyne v. Henderson County, 973 F.2d 386, 396 (5th Cir. 1992) (Goldberg, J., concurring). Although *Rhyne* concerned the second category of jail suicide cases, where there was evidence that the inmate was suicidal, the same principles will apply to this category; where a detainee is interviewed during incarceration and no suicidal tendencies are discovered, there is no constitutional violation when the detainee commits suicide. Herman v. Clearfield County, Pa., 836 F. Supp. 1178 (W.D. Pa. 1993), judgment aff'd, 30 F.3d 1486 (3d Cir. 1994).

MEDICAL CARE § 3:16

is evidence that an inmate is suicidal.[22] This evidence must show a strong likelihood, not a "mere possibility" that the inmate is suicidal.[23] When that evidence exists, failure to take basic steps to prevent suicide, including

---

[22]Rhyne v. Henderson County, 973 F.2d 386, 391 (5th Cir. 1992) ("failure to provide pre-trial detainees with adequate protection from their known suicidal impulses is actionable under § 1983 as a violation of the detainee's constitutional rights").

[23]State Bank of St. Charles v. Camic, 712 F.2d 1140, 1146 (7th Cir. 1983) (strong likelihood, not mere possibility); Popham v. City of Talladega, 908 F.2d 1561, 1563 (11th Cir. 1990) ("deliberate indifference . . . is a difficult burden for a plaintiff to meet" and requires "strong likelihood" not "mere possibility"); Torraco v. Maloney, 923 F.2d 231 (1st Cir. 1991) (upholding summary judgment for defendants where treated by psychologist rather than psychiatrist and where not placed in suicide cell because mixed facts presented case of mere possibility, not strong likelihood); Elliott v. Cheshire County, N.H., 940 F.2d 7, 10-11 (1st Cir. 1991) (must be "strong likelihood"; key is "whether the defendants knew, or reasonably should have known, of the detainee's suicidal tendencies"; allowing case to go to trial where other detainees said they told jail personnel of detainee's threats); Colburn v. Upper Darby Tp., 946 F.2d 1017, 1023-25 (3d Cir. 1991) (must show inmate had a "particular vulnerability to suicide," and that jail personnel knew or should have known of that vulnerability and acted with reckless indifference to it; must show strong likelihood of suicide; "'should have known' . . . is a phrase of art . . . the 'strong likelihood' of suicide must be 'so obvious that a lay person would easily recognize the necessity for' preventative action . . . ; the risk of self-inflicted injury must be not only great, but also sufficiently apparent that a lay custodian's failure to appreciate it evidences an absence of any concern for the welfare of his or her charges"); Barber v. City of Salem, Ohio, 953 F.2d 232, 239 (6th Cir. 1992) (as to city that is not entitled to qualified immunity, "the proper inquiry . . . is: whether the decedent showed a strong likelihood that he would attempt to take his own life in such a manner that failure to take adequate precautions amounted to deliberate indifference to the decedent's serious medical needs"; here, not liable for failure to follow policy where no evidence of suicidal intent); Tittle v. Jefferson County Com'n, 966 F.2d 606 (11th Cir. 1992), reh'g granted and opinion vacated on other grounds, 986 F.2d 1384 (11th Cir. 1993) and on reh'g, 10 F.3d 1535 (11th Cir. 1994); Marshall v. Borough of Ambridge, 798 F. Supp. 1187, 1193-95 (W.D. Pa. 1992); Guglielmoni v. Alexander, 583 F. Supp.

monitoring of the inmate and training of officers involved, will ordinarily constitute a violation.[24] If the

---

821, 827 (D. Conn. 1984) (two previous suicide attempts that doctor wrote off as not serious sufficient to deny motion to dismiss).

In Manarite By and Through Manarite v. City of Springfield, 957 F.2d 953, 956 (1st Cir. 1992), the First Circuit held that "a plaintiff may establish deliberate indifference in a prison suicide case by showing: (1) an unusually serious risk of harm (self-inflicted harm, in a suicide case); (2) defendant's actual knowledge of (or, at least, willful blindness to) that elevated risk; and (3) defendant's failure to take obvious steps to address that known, serious risk. The risk, the knowledge, and the failure to do the obvious, taken together, must show that the defendant is "deliberately indifferent" to the harm that follows.

But see Kanayurak v. North Slope Borough, 677 P.2d 893 (Alaska 1984) (issue under state negligence law is foreseeability).

[24]See, e.g., Townsend v. City of Morehead Kentucky, 208 F.3d 215 (6th Cir. 2000) (holding that there would be liability where prison authorities were present when inmate attempted suicide on a prior occasion, authorities had access to a psychological report identifying inmate as suicidal, the inmate directly informed the jailer of his intent to kill himself, and the jailer did not inform prison authorities of his need for help); Sanders v. Howze, 177 F.3d 1245 (11th Cir. 1999) (after three unsuccessful suicide attempts, inmate was placed in an isolation cell near the jailer's office to keep him away from exposure to razor blades pens, pencils, and other objects available to the general population, and was issued only socks, jogging pants, a shirt, and a bed sheet; inmate hung himself from the cell light fixture with the bed sheet and jailers did not detect inmate's death for four to six hours after it occurred, despite the policy that all inmates in isolation must be visually monitored every 30 minutes.); Rodgers v. Chapleau, 238 F.3d 423 (6th Cir. 2000) (holding that where the inmate told a guard of his intentions just before the suicide attempt, and the guard consciously disregarded the risk, there was liability); Jacobs v. West Feliciana Sheriff's Dept., 228 F.3d 388 (5th Cir. 2000) (inmate was put in a detoxification cell in which a suicide had occurred in the past; cell had blind spots and ties that could be used to commit suicide; sheriff and one deputy had knowledge that the pretrial detainee was a suicide risk);McDuffie v. Hopper, 982 F. Supp. 817 (M.D. Ala. 1997); Robey v. Chester County, 946 F. Supp. 333 (E.D. Pa. 1996) (denying summary judgment when there was credible evidence that the prison psychologist knew of decedent's previous suicide attempt, yet discontinued a prison suicide watch);

MEDICAL CARE § 3:16

evidence does not demonstrate that the deceased presented a known risk of suicide, there is normally no liability even under current case law.[25]

Jackson v. City of Detroit, 449 Mich. 420, 537 N.W.2d 151 (1995) (denying summary judgment where there was evidence that city knew that overhead bars in cells were a significant risk where inmates were suicidal and that there had been 128 attempted suicides over the previous five years); Viero v. Bufano, 901 F. Supp. 1387 (N.D. Ill. 1995) (estate of deceased inmate stated a claim where they alleged that department of corrections and probation officer were deliberately indifferent to the threat of inmate suicide where officials incarcerated fourteen year old who had a history of mental disorders, took Ritalin, and had made suicidal threats); Russell v. Knox County, 826 F. Supp. 20 (D. Me. 1993) (giving inmate back his shoe laces when a known suicide risk existed could support finding of deliberate indifference). See also Partridge v. Two Unknown Police Officers of City of Houston, Tex., 791 F.2d 1182 (5th Cir. 1986); Greason v. Kemp, 891 F.2d 829, 835 (11th Cir. 1990) (qualified immunity inapplicable where doctor "provided [grossly incompetent] care and, moreover, . . . realized that he was doing so at the time" in ignoring clear threat of suicide, and where supervisor ignored repeated information that staff and facilities were inadequate and incompetent); Lewis v. Parish of Terrebonne, 894 F.2d 142 (5th Cir. 1990); Buffington v. Baltimore County, Md., 913 F.2d 113, 17 Fed. R. Serv. 3d 577 (4th Cir. 1990) (in part upholding verdict against defendants where they knew inmate was suicidal and, in violation of policy, did not keep him under observation, but since no evidence that failure to train officers in suicide prevention actually and proximately caused jail suicide in question, no municipal liability); Hall v. Ryan, 957 F.2d 402, 405 (7th Cir. 1992) (since jail officials knew of risk, case must go to trial); Manarite By and Through Manarite v. City of Springfield, 957 F.2d 953, 1992 WL 40039 (1st Cir. 1992) (liability "where the municipality did not provide any suicide-prevention training to police officers, and also failed to adopt known, inexpensive suicide-prevention measures (such as directives to keep intoxicated detainees under restraint or observation, or not to house them alone in an empty cellblock)" applicable to a detainee who had demonstrated suicide-risk symptoms). See also National Commn on Correctional Health Care, Standards for Health Services in Jails J-51 (May 1999).

[25]See, e.g., Barrie v. Grand County, Utah, 119 F.3d 862 (10th Cir. 1997) (holding that the defendants did not act with deliberate indifference because they did not know that the inmate was intent

§ 3:16

In general, to prevail in a case challenging inadequate medical care in a jail or prison, an inmate must

---

on killing himself); Williams v. Mehra, 186 F.3d 685, 1999 FED App. 286P (6th Cir. 1999) (holding that there was no liability where there was no evidence that doctors knew there was a danger that pills that deceased was taking could be used to commit suicide); Bowens v. City of Atmore, 171 F. Supp. 2d 1244 (S.D. Ala. 2001), aff'd, 275 F.3d 57 (11th Cir. 2001) (where pretrial detainee had a history of suicide attempts, but displayed no suicidal tendencies while being held in the defendant jail, court held there was no deliberate indifference); Estate of Cills v. Kaftan, 105 F. Supp. 2d 391 (D.N.J. 2000) (holding there was no liability for prison officials taking an inmate off suicide watch when the officials did not believe that the inmate posed a suicide risk; however, there could be liability on the part of the county for a policy that did not require consultation with a psychiatric professional prior to removing inmates from suicide watch); McCollum v. Pontotoc County, MS, 2000 WL 1146706 (N.D. Miss. 2000) (holding that there was no liability if defendants were not aware of the deceased's suicidal tendencies); Norton v. County of Le Sueur, 565 N.W.2d 447 (Minn. Ct. App. 1997) (upon arrest decedent was examined by a mental health worker; during this interview he claimed that he had no intention of committing suicide, that he had many reasons to live; he was then placed in general population and left unattended for almost two hours, during which time he hung himself; court held that defendants were not deliberately indifferent); Perkowski v. City of Detroit, 794 F. Supp. 223 (E.D. Mich. 1992) (no violation where no precautions taken for inmate who exhibited no suicidal tendencies); Estate of Frank v. City of Beaver Dam, 921 F. Supp. 590 (E.D. Wis. 1996) (no liability for suicide despite inmate warning to prison officials that he had mood swings where inmate did nothing specific that would cause the guards to suspect that he was suicidal); Litz v. City of Allentown, 896 F. Supp. 1401 (E.D. Pa. 1995) (city did not violate Eighth Amendment regarding failure to prevent inmate suicide where estate of deceased inmate alleged only that he was intoxicated and asked why he could not go home, and later committed suicide; court noted that insufficient evidence was presented to establish that there was a strong likelihood that inmate would commit suicide.); Burke v. Warren County Sheriff's Dept., 890 F. Supp. 133 (N.D. N.Y. 1995) (no indication that inmate was suicidal); Medina v. State, 1993 OK 121, 871 P.2d 1379 (Okla. 1993); Gordon v. Kidd, 971 F.2d 1087, 1095 (4th Cir. 1992), as amended, (July 7, 1992) (failure to take action in the face of credible information indicating a risk of suicide is sufficient to permit case to go to trial).

show deliberate indifference to a serious medical need. Cases involving jail suicide vividly illustrate that courts apply this standard in a manner that focuses almost exclusively on facts known to the prison or jail officials at the time of the alleged violation. Thus, plaintiffs in jail suicide cases will win if there was a "strong likelihood," given the facts at the time, that suicide would occur. On the other hand, plaintiffs will lose if the risk of suicide was small or if the measures not taken probably would not have minimized the likelihood of suicide anyway. In addition, families of inmates are also beginning to win, as they should, in cases where prison officials failed to engage in simple measures that would have easily minimized the likelihood of suicide. On the flip side, however, plaintiffs often will lose if the prison officials did take some action to prevent suicides even if it was unsuccessful and more could have been done.[26] What has been discussed, of course, are the constitutional obligations of defendants; even if there is no liability under those rather stringent criteria, there may

---

There are even a ill-considered cases that hold that knowledge of suicidal tendencies and failure to act is not enough to establish liability. See, e.g., Freedman v. City of Allentown, Pa., 853 F.2d 1111, 1116 (3d Cir. 1988) (even if officials should have known that scars were from prior suicide attempts, failure to act on that was mere negligence).

[26]See, e.g., Estate of Novack ex rel. Turbin v. County of Wood, 226 F.3d 525 (7th Cir. 2000) (holding that there was no liability where defendants were told that the decedent was a suicide risk and after placing him in an observation cell for a couple of days, defendants placed him in the general prison population; though other prisoners told officials that the decedent was displaying odd behavior, officials never witnessed the decedent acting strangely; thus, because defendants took some action, even though it was not successful they were not liable); Yellow Horse v. Pennington County, 225 F.3d 923 (8th Cir. 2000) (inmate was placed on suicide watch, then was removed from suicide watch, and hanged himself; the county had a policy with specific requirements for putting inmates on suicide watch and for taking them off suicide watch; court held the policy was reasonable, so the county could not be held liable for the inmate's suicide); Butler v. City of Terrell, 1999 WL 62387 (Tex. App. Dallas 1999).

§ 3:16   Rights of Prisoners, Third Edition

still be liability under state law.[27]

§ 3:17   Drug and Alcohol Treatment and Treatment for Tobacco Addiction

Given the high percentage of people with drug or alcohol abuse problems who are incarcerated, drug and alcohol treatment programs would seem to be an essential part of any medical care system. The most common cases are those challenging an institution's policy of requiring inmates who are addicted to go "cold turkey" and, without any assistance, immediately stop all use of alcohol or drugs. Such policies have been universally condemned.[1] Most courts have also held

---

[27]See, e.g., Edwards v. Okaloosa County, 5 F.3d 1431 (11th Cir. 1993) (holding that even where no constitutional violation occurs, a suicide case may be brought under state wrongful death law and district courts have pendent jurisdiction to review those claims).

[Section 3:17]

[1]Lancaster v. Monroe County, Ala., 116 F.3d 1419 (11th Cir. 1997) (alcohol withdrawal is a "serious medical need" which requires attention); Alberti v. Sheriff of Harris County, Texas, 406 F. Supp. 649, 677, (S.D. Tex. 1975) (must have treatment for drug and alcohol withdrawal); O'Bryan v. Saginaw County, Mich., 437 F. Supp. 582, 598 (E.D. Mich. 1977), judgment entered, 446 F. Supp. 436 (E.D. Mich. 1978) (must screen out those in withdrawal and "house them in a separate environment designed to treat withdrawal problems"); Miller v. Carson, 401 F. Supp. 835, 879 (M.D. Fla. 1975), aff'd in part, modified in part on other grounds and remanded, 563 F.2d 741 (5th Cir. 1977) (addicts must not be forced to go "cold turkey"); Inmates of Allegheny County Jail v. Peirce, 487 F. Supp. 638 (W.D. Pa. 1980) (must transfer those in withdrawal); Palmigiano v. Garrahy, 443 F. Supp. 956, 971-73, (D.R.I. 1977) (must set up drug treatment program other than "cold turkey"); Pedraza v. Meyer, 919 F.2d 317 (5th Cir. 1990) (delay of several days in treatment for withdrawal stated cause of action). See also U.S. Dept of Justice, Federal Standards for Prisons and Jails § 5.33 (1980); American Correctional Assn, Standards for Adult Correctional Institutions, Standard 3-4370 (1990); National Commn on Correctional Health Care, Standards for Health Services in Jails J-52 (May 1999); Commission on Accreditation for Corrections, Certification Standards for Health Care Programs HC-075 (1989).

MEDICAL CARE § 3:17

that there must be some treatment program for those addicted to drugs or alcohol but have generally deferred to prison authorities concerning the nature of the treatment to be provided.[2]

There is a movement to ban smoking in all public places, including prisons. These bans have been challenged unsuccessfully. Courts have held that there is no constitutional right to smoke in prison.[3] If bans on smoking are to be imposed, the question arises whether inmates have a right to treatment overcoming their craving for cigarettes. In one case upholding such a ban, the court noted that prison authorities imple-

---

[2]Hamilton v. Landrieu, 351 F. Supp. 549, 550 (E.D. La. 1972) (must have drug abuse program); Barnes v. Government of Virgin Islands, 415 F. Supp. 1218, 1235 (D.V.I. 1976) (must be an "alcohol and drug rehabilitation program"); Inmates of Allegheny County Jail v. Pierce, 612 F.2d 754, 760-61 (3d Cir. 1979) (defer to jail doctors on form of methadone treatment); U.S. ex rel. Walker v. Fayette County, Pa., 599 F.2d 573 (3d Cir. 1979) (no right to methadone, but right to some treatment). But see Jinks v. McCauley, 163 F.3d 598 (4th Cir. 1998) (holding that there is no liability for failure to immediately administer Librium prescribed by prison physician for alcohol withdrawal). See also Laaman v. Helgemoe, 437 F. Supp. 269, 314 (D.N.H. 1977) (noting that there must be some proof that a cure or generally accepted mode of treatment for the condition, in fact, exists; as with any condition, prison officials have a duty to diagnose and treat serious medical needs, and the treatments must be provided so long as they are based on medical necessity); Dawson v. Kendrick, 527 F. Supp. 1252, 1272-73, (S.D. W. Va. 1981) (court found lack of drug and alcohol treatment but not clear if this is a violation); American Correctional Assn, Standards for Adult Correctional Institutions, Standard 3-4371 (1990); National Commn on Correctional Health Care, Standards for Health Services in Jails J-52 (May 1999); Commission on Accreditation for Corrections, Certification Standards for Health Care Programs HC-076 (1989). But see Pace v. Fauver, 479 F. Supp. 456 (D.N.J. 1979), aff'd, 649 F.2d 860 (3d Cir. 1981) (alcoholism not serious in case in which inmates sought to run alcohol program).

[3]See, e.g., Reynolds v. Bucks, 833 F. Supp. 518 (E.D. Pa. 1993); House of Corrections Block Representatives Comm. v. Creamer, 1998 WL 242663 (E.D. Pa. 1998); Alley v. State, 1997 WL 695590 (D. Kan. 1997).

mented a policy offering inmates the opportunity to take classes on how to overcome the craving to smoke.[4] In another case, a tobacco-free policy at a New Hampshire state prison was upheld where the warden provided support to the inmates during the implementation of the policy by distributing information about the policy in advance of its implementation and by providing literature, videos and counseling on overcoming tobacco addiction.[5] However, another court held that the institution of a no-smoking policy did not constitute additional punishment, an ex post facto law, a prohibited bill of attainder, cruel and unusual punishment, or any other constitutional violation, even though there was no indication that the prison provided inmates with addiction treatment after the ban.[6]

§ 3:18 Disabled Prisoners

Research References

West's Key Number Digest, Civil Rights ⚖135

Inmates have a right to whatever care is necessary to treat serious disabilities.[1] A few cases have alleged that there is a duty to provide prosthetic devices, with mixed

---

[4]Reynolds v. Bucks, 833 F. Supp. 518, 520 (E.D. Pa. 1993).

[5]Nowaczyk v. Shaheen, 2001 DNH 52, 2001 WL 276960 (D. N.H. 2001).

[6]Alley v. State, 1997 WL 695590 (D. Kan. 1997).

[Section 3:18]

[1]See, e.g., Frost v. Agnos, 152 F.3d 1124, 41 Fed. R. Serv. 3d 538 (9th Cir. 1998) (holding that a pre-trail detainee who wore a leg brace and relied on crutches was entitled to accessible shower facilities); Davis v. Hall, 992 F.2d 151 (8th Cir. 1993) (inmate sent to facility not equipped to accommodate disability); Hicks v. Frey, 992 F.2d 1450 (6th Cir. 1993) (paraplegic kept in room, denying mobility and without proper facilities); Maclin v. Freake, 650 F.2d 885 (7th Cir. 1981) (paraplegic given no physical therapy); Hallett v. New York State Dept. of Correctional Services, 109 F. Supp. 2d 190 (S.D. N.Y. 2000) (denying summary judgment to defendants in case claiming that denial of admission to the state prison's shock incarceration program because he was confined to a wheelchair violated ADA and Eighth Amendment); Clarkson v. Coughlin, 898

results.[2] Failure to provide a needed wheelchair and

F. Supp. 1019, 10 A.D.D. 642 (S.D. N.Y. 1995) (holding that the failure to provide interpreters or assistive devices for deaf and hearing-impaired inmates violated the Eighth Amendment); Leach v. Shelby County Sheriff, 891 F.2d 1241 (6th Cir. 1989) (paraplegic inmate given inadequate mattress and no assistance in cleaning himself); Warren v. State of Mo., 754 F. Supp. 150, 153 (W.D. Mo. 1990), judgment aff'd, 995 F.2d 130 (8th Cir. 1993) (failure to provide physical therapy stated cause of action); Yarbaugh v. Roach, 736 F. Supp. 318 (D.D.C. 1990); Noland v. Wheatley, 835 F. Supp. 476, 3 A.D.D. 27 (N.D. Ind. 1993) (semi-quadriplegic kept in padded room with no bed or sink, only a drain in the floor); Casey v Lewis 834 F Supp 1569 (D Ariz 1993) (disabled inmates must be provided with facilities that fully accommodate their needs; lack of funding for such facilities is not a defense to a constitutional violation); Candelaria v. Coughlin, 787 F. Supp. 368, 378 (S.D. N.Y. 1992), aff'd, 979 F.2d 845 (2d Cir. 1992) (paraplegic had need for " adequate wheelchair and for orthopedic treatment [and] . . . liquid dietary supplement"); Harris v. O'Grady, 803 F. Supp. 1361, 1366 (N.D. Ill. 1992) (blind inmate); Clarkson v. Coughlin, 145 F.R.D. 339, 348, 2 A.D.D. 639 (S.D. N.Y. 1993) (hearing-impaired inmates); State v. Johnson, 108 Md. App. 54, 670 A.2d 1012 (1996) (state department of corrections and prison officials had no duty to create a personal care and treatment plan for paraplegic inmate where the state had contracted with private health care provider to maintain health care services). See also U.S. Dept of Justice, Federal Standards for Prisons and Jails § 5.30 (1980); National Commn on Correctional Health Care, Standards for Health Services in Jails J-49 (May 1999). But see Crowder v. True, 74 F.3d 812 (7th Cir. 1996) (holding that paraplegic inmate denied use of a wheelchair was not entitled to have a wheelchair in his cell since the wheelchair did not fit through the cell door); Coppage v. Mann, 906 F. Supp. 1025 (E.D. Va. 1995) (holding that superintendent of prison was not deliberately indifferent to inmate's medical condition where prison officials failed to provide inmate with a wheelchair for one month when his spinal cancer prevented him from walking.).

[2]Henderson v. Secretary of Corrections, 518 F.2d 694 (10th Cir. 1975) (inmate not entitled to prescription shoes); Nicholson v. Choctaw County, Ala., 498 F. Supp. 295, 308 (S.D. Ala. 1980) (pretrial detainees not entitled to prosthetic devices since services not provided to non-inmates and detainees were in jail so short a time); Newman v. State of Ala., 349 F. Supp. 278, 287 (M.D. Ala. 1972), aff'd in part, 503 F.2d 1320 (5th Cir. 1974) and judgment vacated

§ 3:18   Rights of Prisoners, Third Edition

failure to provide handicapped-accessible facilities will result in liability.³ Again, the critical factor would seem

---

in part on other grounds, 522 F.2d 71 (5th Cir. 1975) (delay of a year for "prosthetic devices" must be cured and inmates must receive them within "reasonable time"); Kopec v. Coughlin, 767 F. Supp. 463 (S.D. N.Y. 1990), judgment vacated on other grounds, 922 F.2d 152, 18 Fed. R. Serv. 3d 707 (2d Cir. 1991) (failure to provide adequate prosthesis merely negligent; Court of Appeals held that district court erred in converting defendant's motion to dismiss into one for summary judgment without giving prisoner notice and opportunity to offer evidence to controvert that submitted by defendant); Young v. Harris, 509 F. Supp. 1111 (S.D. N.Y. 1981) (allegation of failure to provide leg brace stated cause of action). See also U.S. Dept of Justice, Federal Standards for Prisons and Jails § 5.27 (1980); ABA Standards for Criminal Justice § 23.5-1 (commentary) (1986); American Correctional Assn, Standards for Adult Correctional Institutions, Standard 3-4358 (1990); National Commn on Correctional Health Care, Standards for Health Services in Jails J-57 (May 1999); Commission on Accreditation for Corrections, Certification Standards for Health Care Programs HC-077 (1989).

³LaFaut v. Smith, 834 F.2d 389 (4th Cir. 1987) (Justice Powell); Weeks v. Chaboudy, 984 F.2d 185, 187 (6th Cir. 1993); Hicks v. Frey, 992 F.2d 1450 (6th Cir. 1993) (paraplegic kept in room, denying mobility and without adequate facilities; officer in charge of jail liable because he received daily reports of conditions). Parkinson v. Columbia County Dist. Attorney, 178 Misc. 2d 52, 679 N.Y.S.2d 505 (Sup 1998) (inmate brought an action alleging that his constitutional rights were violated after his artificial leg was confiscated at the time of his arrest for shooting at state police, and not returned after his conviction on the grounds that it might constitute evidence upon an appeal and to prevent inmate from tampering with the evidence; without the prosthetic leg the inmate could not make use of his crutches and was therefore confined to his cell; court found that the confiscation of the prosthetic leg was a deprivation of property without due process in violation of the Fourteenth Amendment, and retention of the leg constituted cruel and unusual punishment as defined by the Eighth Amendment; court ordered the county to return the prosthetic leg and ruled that each party could photograph the leg for purposes of any appeal). See also More v. Farrier, 984 F.2d 269 (8th Cir. 1993) (prison need not provide wheelchair-bound inmates same cable TV as provided to other inmates); Clarkson v. Coughlin, 145 F.R.D. 339, 348, 2 A.D.D. 639 (S.D. N.Y. 1993) (alleging lack of facilities

§ 3:18

to be the seriousness of the inmate's need for the treat-

---

and lack of equal facilities for hearing-impaired inmates); Yarbaugh v. Roach, 736 F. Supp. 318 (D.D.C. 1990) (multiple sclerosis). But see Shakka v. Smith, 71 F.3d 162 (4th Cir. 1995) (prison officials did not violate Eighth Amendment where officials took away inmate's wheelchair after he broke his sink, toilet, and window with a metal pipe; court noted that prison officials took the wheelchair after prison psychiatrist determined that the wheelchair was a risk to inmate because inmate could disassemble the chair and cause more damage; officials returned the chair the next day after the inmate calmed down); Hallett v. New York State Dept. of Correctional Services, 109 F. Supp. 2d 190 (S.D. N.Y. 2000) (HIV-positive amputee prisoner brought an action under the ADA and Rehabilitation Act and a § 1983 action for failure to provide an adequate wheelchair; court held that Title II of the ADA and Title 504 of the Rehabilitation Act applies to inmates in state prisons, and further found that the temporary nature of the four-month deprivation of another wheelchair and the alleged back pain arising out of the deprivation called into doubt the plaintiff's ability to prove that the denial was "sufficiently serious" in objective terms; nonetheless, the court held that at this early juncture the plaintiff's allegations of serious injury from the inappropriate wheelchair and the claim that the defendants acted with a culpable state of mind in depriving him of a customized wheelchair was sufficient to withstand a motion to dismiss); Candelaria v. Cunningham, 2000 WL 280052 (S.D. N.Y. 2000) (paraplegic prisoner, confined to a wheelchair, brought an action under ADA and Rehabilitation Act alleging that defendants denied him access to special programs and a § 1983 action for deliberate indifference to medical needs for failure to provide dialysis treatment, alleging that he had been excluded from programs and activities and services such as the law library because he was confined to a wheelchair and the prison was not wheelchair accessible; defendants' argument that the "plaintiff has not been excluded from the benefit of dialysis treatment" and that "the ADA does not create any right for an inmate to be housed at a specific prison" was rejected; court found the plaintiff's claim sufficient to deny the defendants' motion for summary judgment); Rainey v. County of Delaware, 18 Nat'l Disability Law Rep. ¶ 208, 2000 WL 1056456 (E.D. Pa. 2000) (incomplete paraplegic, able to walk slowly only with the aid of leg braces, alleged he was denied food on 15 occasions and medical treatment on several occasions because the prison official defendants allowed him too little time to travel to the dining room and the dispensary; court dismissed the individually-named defendants because there was no indication

§ 3:18

ment or device.

A few inmates have challenged discrimination against them on the basis of their disabilities.[4] It is clear that, in an appropriate case, discrimination against disabled inmates could violate the Equal Protection Clause of the Fourteenth Amendment.

Two federal statutes provide rights to inmates who are disabled beyond those provided under the Eighth Amendment. The Americans With Disabilities Act

---

that any of them were personally involved; however, the county and the corporate owner of the prison could not assert an Eleventh Amendment or qualified immunity defense because it is well-settled that a paraplegic confined to a wheelchair has a serious medical condition that warrants recognition under the Eighth Amendment). But see Stanley v. Litscher, 213 F.3d 340 (7th Cir. 2000) (inmate brought a suit alleging that the denial of his application to participate in a sex offender program violated the Americans with Disabilities Act ("ADA"); psychologist's report stated that the plaintiff was a psychopath and was not appropriate for the programs; court held that, assuming that psychopathy was a disability, the prison's denial of the inmate's application to participate in the sex offender's program did not violate his right to equal protection; state could rationally conclude that psychopaths did not benefit from intra-prison programs and that they spoiled the programs for less aggressive inmates, or both; court also held that the ADA claim could not be litigated in a federal court because the ADA rests on the Commerce Clause rather than the Enforcement Clause of the Fourteenth Amendment and the Eleventh Amendment precludes private litigation against the state in a federal court; finally, the denial of the application did not violate the Rehabilitation Act); See also Commission on Accreditation for Corrections, Certification Standards for Health Care Programs HC-018 (1989).

[4]Joihner v. McEvers, 898 F.2d 569 (7th Cir. 1990) (unsuccessful procedural due process challenge by epileptic inmate denied work assignment); Madewell v. Roberts, 909 F.2d 1203, 1207 (8th Cir. 1990). See also Raines v. State of Fla., 987 F. Supp. 1416 (N.D. Fla. 1997) (approving class action settlement which provided retroactive good time for inmates who werephysically and mentally handicapped and were not provided with a job or education). See, generally, Note, Bonner v. Lewis: Testing Society's Commitment to Aid Individuals With Handicaps, 1989 BYU L Rev 943.

MEDICAL CARE § 3:19

(ADA)[5] prohibits discrimination against disabled people and does apply, in appropriate cases, to inmates.[6] The Rehabilitation Act also prohibits discrimination against disabled people in a federally funded "program or activity."[7] The Rehabilitation Act has been held to apply to prisons[8] and, as discussed in the section that follows, in 1998 the Supreme Court held that the ADA also applies to state prisons.[9]

§ 3:19 Prisoners and the Americans With Disabilities Act

Research References

West's Key Number Digest, Civil Rights ⚞135
Actions Brought Under Americans with Disabilities Act, 42 U.S.C.A. §§ 12101 et seq.—Supreme Court Cases, 173 A.L.R. Fed. 639

---

[5]42 U.S.C.A. § 12101 et seq. For a full discussion of the ADA and prisoners see § 3:19.

[6]The Act provides that "[s]ubject to the provisions of this subchapter, no qualified individual with a disability shall, by reason of such disability, be excluded from participation in or be denied the benefits of the services, programs, or activities of a public entity, or be subjected to discrimination by any such agency." 42 U.S.C. § 12101. The Act applies to prisons. Pennsylvania Dept. of Corrections v. Yeskey, 524 U.S. 206, 118 S. Ct. 1952, 141 L. Ed. 2d 215, 163 A.L.R. Fed. 671 (1998).

[7]29 U.S.C. § 794 (1986). Department of Justice regulations implementing this statute are found at 28 CFR §§ 42.501 et seq.

[8]Harris v. Thigpen, 941 F.2d 1495, 1522 n41 (11th Cir. 1991); Bonner v. Lewis, 857 F.2d 559, 562 (9th Cir. 1988); Casey v. Lewis, 773 F. Supp. 1365 (D. Ariz. 1991), rev'd in part, vacated in part on other grounds, 4 F.3d 1516, 2 A.D.D. 908 (9th Cir. 1993); Duffy v. Riveland, 98 F.3d 447, 17 A.D.D. 1006 (9th Cir. 1996) (deaf inmate who challenged denial of interpreter at prison disciplinary proceeding under the Rehabilitation Act had implied right of action against prison and prison officials; Act required appointment of qualified interpreter if hearing impaired inmate was party or witness at judicial or quasi judicial proceeding). See also Noland v. Wheatley, 835 F. Supp. 476, 3 A.D.D. 27 (N.D. Ind. 1993) (quadriplegic ADA claim).

[9]Pennsylvania Dept. of Corrections v. Yeskey, 524 U.S. 206, 118 S. Ct. 1952, 141 L. Ed. 2d 215, 163 A.L.R. Fed. 671 (1998).

§ 3:19   Rights of Prisoners, Third Edition

In 1998, the Supreme Court decided *Pennsylvania Department of Correction v Yeskey*,[1] a highly significant case wherein the Court unanimously held that the Americans With Disabilities Act applies to prisoners. The plaintiff in *Yeskey* was sentenced to serve 18 to 36 months in a Pennsylvania correctional facility. He was recommended, however, for placement in a motivational boot camp for first offenders, after which he would be paroled in six months. The case arose when the plaintiff was denied admission to the boot camp because of his medical history of hypertension. He brought suit against the Pennsylvania Department of Corrections and several department officials, claiming his exclusion violated Title II of the ADA. Title II prohibits a "public entity" from discriminating against a "qualified individual with a disability" on account of that disability[2]. The district court dismissed for failure to state a claim, holding that the ADA was inapplicable to inmates in state prisons. Following reversal by the Third Circuit Court of Appeals, the Supreme Court granted certiorari and unanimously affirmed.

The majority opinion, written by Justice Scalia, held that the ADA covers inmates in state prisons. The court distinguished *Pennsylvania* from *Gregory v Ashcroft*,[3] which held that the Age Discrimination in Employment Act (ADEA) did not cover state judges. Here, unlike *Gregory*, the court stated, the "ADA plainly covers state institutions without any exception that could cast the

---

[Section 3:19]

[1]Pennsylvania Dept. of Corrections v. Yeskey, 524 U.S. 206, 118 S. Ct. 1952, 141 L. Ed. 2d 215, 163 A.L.R. Fed. 671 (1998). For discussions of the ADA and prisons, see Tim Kollas, Note: Federal Power, States' Rights, Individual Rights: Mentally Disabled Prisoners and the Supreme Court's New Activism, 10 Wm. & Mary Bill of Rts. J. 861 (2002); Sandra J. Carnahan, Article: The Americans With Disabilities Act In State Correctional Institutions, 27 Cap. U.L. Rev. 291 (1999).

[2]U.S.C. § 12132 (1998).

[3]Gregory v. Ashcroft, 501 U.S. 452, 111 S. Ct. 2395, 115 L. Ed. 2d 410 (1991).

MEDICAL CARE § 3:19

coverage of prisons into doubt."[4]

The Court noted that state prisons fall within the statutory definition of "public entity," and that the term "qualified individual with a disability" includes state prisoners so long as they qualify as disabled under the same definition applicable to free-world individuals.

Furthermore, the Court rejected the defendants' contention that the absence of prisons and prisoners in the ADA's statement of findings and purpose renders the statute ambiguous. According to the court, the "fact that a statute can be applied in situations not expressly anticipated by Congress is not ambiguity. It demonstrates breadth."[5]

Since 1998, courts have consistently extended the protection of Title II of the ADA to disabled prisoners, including those with AIDS or HIV.[6] In doing so, the courts have explained that prisoners "have the same

---

[4] Pennsylvania Dept. of Corrections v. Yeskey, 524 U.S. 206, 118 S. Ct. 1952, 1953, 141 L. Ed. 2d 215, 163 A.L.R. Fed. 671 (1998).

[5] *Id.* at 1956.

[6] Hallett v. New York State Dept. of Correctional Services, 109 F. Supp. 2d 190 (S.D. N.Y. 2000) (holding that no HIV discrimination allowed). See also Crawford v. Indiana Dept. of Corrections, 115 F.3d 481, 22 A.D.D. 22 (7th Cir. 1997) (inmate has the "same interest in access to the programs, services, and activities available to the other inmates of his prison as disabled people on the outside have to the counterpart programs, services, and activities available to free people"); Clarkson v. Coughlin, 898 F. Supp. 1019, 10 A.D.D. 642 (S.D. N.Y. 1995) (holding that the failure to provide interpreters or assistive devices for deaf and hearing-impaired inmates was discriminatory); Noland v. Wheatley, 835 F. Supp. 476, 3 A.D.D. 27 (N.D. Ind. 1993) (holding that a claim may lie under the ADA when a semi-quadriplegic is subjected to unhygienic conditions and denied access to prison programs).

For cases denying relief see Aswegan v. Bruhl, 113 F.3d 109 (8th Cir. 1997) (ADA did not apply to cable television access because cable TV "is not a public service, program, or activity within the contemplation of the ADA"); Oyague v. State, 2000 WL 1231406 (S.D. N.Y. 2000), aff'd, 13 Fed. Appx. 16 (2d Cir. 2001), cert. denied, 122 S. Ct. 484, 151 L. Ed. 2d 397 (U.S. 2001) (difficulty in urinating did not qualify as a disability under the ADA;

§ 3:19   Rights of Prisoners, Third Edition

interest in access to the programs, services, and activities available to the other inmates of their prison as disabled people on the outside have to the counterpart programs, services, and activities available to free

---

therefore requiring urine samples was not a violation on the part of prison officials); Clark v. Woods, 20 Nat'l Disability Law Rep. ¶ 106, 2001 WL 123668 (N.D. Tex. 2001), aff'd, 275 F.3d 1079 (5th Cir. 2001), cert. denied, 122 S. Ct. 1968, 152 L. Ed. 2d 1027 (U.S. 2002) (denying claim of inmate that denial of contact visits was discriminatory because of his vision and hearing problems on the ground that the evidence established that the denial was related to valid security concerns about inmate's relationship with the KKK).

    There is a rich literature about this subject. See, generally, Ira P. Robbins, George Bush's America Meets Dante's Inferno: The Americans With Disabilities Act In Prison, 15 Yale L & Pol'y Rev 49 (1996). For an argument that when a prison regulation infringes upon an inmate's statutory rights under the ADA, courts should not use the deferential *Turner* standard of review, but instead should incorporate the claims of the inmates and the prison administration into their "reasonable modification" determinations under Title II of the ADA, see Christopher J. Burke, Winning the Battle, Losing the War?: Judicial Scrutiny of Prisoners' Statutory Claims Under the Americans With Disabilities Act, 98 Mich L Rev 482 (November, 1999). For a discussion of mandatory HIV Testing, segregation of HIV-positive inmates and the Americans with Disability Act, see Susan Jacobs, AIDS in Correctional Facilities: Current Status of Legal Issues Critical to Policy Development, 23 J Crim Justice 209 (1995). For a discussion of potential issues regarding HIV-linked conditions of release and denial of release, see Deborah Dalrymple-Blackburn, AIDS, Prisoners, and the Americans with Disabilities Act, 25 Utah L Rev 839 (1995). See also Connie M. Mayer, Unique Mental Health Needs of HIV-Infected Women Inmates: What Services are Required Under the Constitution and the Americans with Disabilities Act 6 Wm & Mary J Women & L 215 (Fall 1999) (outlining the unique health needs of HIV-infected female inmates and how prisons will likely have to respond to be in compliance with the requirements of both the ADA and the Eighth Amendment). See also James C. Harrington, The ADA and Section 1983: Walking Hand-In-Hand, 19 Rev Litig 435 (Summer 2000) (demonstrating how the ADA fills a void left by decisional law under the Eighth and Fourteenth Amendments).

MEDICAL CARE § 3:20

people".[7]

§ 3:20 AIDS

Research References

Federal constitutional and statutory claims by HIV-positive inmates as to medical treatment or conditions of confinement, 162 A.L.R. Fed. 181

Acquired Immunodeficiency Syndrome (AIDS)[1] is a disease in which the body's immune system fails.[2] The viral agent associated with AIDS is called the human immunodeficiency virus (HIV). If the virus is found in a person's blood, the person is said to be HIV positive. Full-blown AIDS is a serious life-threatening disease. "The rate of confirmed AIDS in the U.S. prison population is particularly high-more than five times the rate of the general population."[3] The extraordinary nature of

---

[7]Candelaria v. Greifinger, 1998 WL 312375 (N.D. N.Y. 1998). See also Crawford v. Indiana Dept. of Corrections, 115 F.3d 481, 484, 22 A.D.D. 22 (7th Cir. 1997); Hanson v. Sangamon County Sheriff's Dept., 991 F. Supp. 1059, 1062 (C.D. Ill. 1998); Roop v. Squadrito, 70 F. Supp. 2d 868, 877 (N.D. Ind. 1999).

[Section 3:20]

[1]Many of the issues in this section also arise in the case of contagious diseases other than AIDS. The most common and most serious at this point is tuberculosis (TB). See also Nicholson v. Choctaw County, Ala., 498 F. Supp. 295, 309 (S.D. Ala. 1980) (must exclude those with contagious diseases including TB). Some of the issues may be resolved in different ways in the case of other diseases, due to different methods of transmission.

[2]See, generally, Harris v. Thigpen, 941 F.2d 1495, 1502-04 (11th Cir. 1991); Nolley v. County of Erie, 776 F. Supp. 715, 718-20 (W.D. N.Y. 1991). For later opinions in *Nolley*, see Nolley v. County of Erie, 802 F. Supp. 898 (W.D. N.Y. 1992) (awarding damages) and Nolley v. County of Erie, 798 F. Supp. 123, 124 (W.D. N.Y. 1992) (after "second thoughts," withdrawal of order of punitive damages).

[3]Columbia Human Rights Law Review, A Jailhouse Lawyer's Manual, 558 (5th ed. 2000) (citing Laura M. Maruschak, U.S. Dep't of Justice, HIV in Prisons 1997, Bureau of Justice Statistics Bulletin 4 (1999)).

the AIDS epidemic[4] has resulted in extensive literature on AIDS and numerous article about AIDS in prisons.[5] There has also been a significant amount of litigation. The case law concentrates on five recurrent issues.

Testing and Screening

Tests for HIV became available in 1985. However, the tests are not completely reliable. For example, there is a delay, sometimes significant, between the time a person is infected and the time when testing will identify the HIV virus. Thus, a negative result does not necessarily mean the person is free of infection. However, a positive test can lead to treatment, which,

---

[4]As of 1997, at least 385,000 people in the United States have died as result of contracting this disease. Columbia Human Rights Law Review, A Jailhouse Lawyer's Manual, 558 (5th ed. 2000) (citing Centers for Disease Control and Prevention, U.S. Dep't of Health and Human Services, Trends in the HIV and AIDS Epidemic 2 (1998)).

[5]See, e.g., Connie M. Mayer, Unique Mental Health Needs of HIV-Infected Women Inmates: What Services are Required Under the Constitution And the Americans with Disabilities Act, 6 Wm & Mary J Women & L 215 (Fall 1999) (outlining the unique health needs of HIV-infected female inmates and how prisons will likely have to respond to be in compliance with the requirements of both the ADA and the Eighth Amendment); Sarah E Frink, Note, Aids Behind Bars: Judicial Barriers Prisoners' Constitutional Claims, 45 Drake L Rev 165 (1997); Eileen Kelly, Expanding Prisoners' Access to AIDS-Related Clinical Trials: An Ethical and Clinical Imperative, 75 Prison J 48 (1995); Susan Jacobs, AIDS in Correctional Facilities: Current Status of Legal Issues Critical to Policy Development, 23 J Crim Justice 209 (1995); Deborah Dalrymple-Blackburn, AIDS, Prisoners, and the Americans with Disabilities Act, 25 Utah L Rev 839 (1995). Mark Parts, The Eighth Amendment and the Requirement of Active Measures to Prevent the Spread of AIDS in Prison, 22 Colum Hum Rts L Rev 217 (1991). A number of courts have relied heavily on the National Institute of Justice publication, AIDS in Correctional Facilities: Issues and Options, which is supplemented each year. See, e.g., Harris v. Thigpen, 941 F.2d 1495, 1499 n.3 (11th Cir. 1991). Alexa Freeman, National Lawyer's Guild AIDS Network, AIDS and Prisons, in AIDS Practice Manual: A Legal and Educational Guide (Paul Alpert et al ed., 3d ed. 1991).

while not yet able to cure the disease, may substantially prolong the life of the person involved.[6]

Involuntary Testing

As indicated in an earlier section,[7] a number of courts have held that, when an inmate arrives at the institution, he or she must be screened by appropriate medical authorities to determine any existing medical problems, including the presence of any communicable disease. Particularly in the early years of knowledge of AIDS, the most common litigation was brought on behalf of prisoners who did not have AIDS and sought to use this principle, and the general duty to protect inmates, to force testing of all inmates. In that way, the uninfected inmates hoped they would be able to ensure that they would not be exposed to the virus. Those cases have been unsuccessful.[8] The courts have generally deferred to the judgments of prison medical authorities that such testing is not necessary and can create a false

---

[6]Alexa Freeman, National Lawyer's Guild AIDS Network, AIDS and Prisons, in AIDS Practice Manual: A Legal and Educational Guide § 14.2 (Paul Alpert et al ed., 3d ed. 1991). See also Eileen Kelly, Expanding Prisoners' Access to AIDS-related Clinical Trials: An Ethical and Clinical Imperative 75 Prison J 48 (1995) (calling for prisoner participation in clinical trials of AIDS research; author points to the direct correlation between IV drug users and ethnic minorities; the overrepresentation of these groups in the nation's prisons is the main reason to allow such research to be conducted). For a survey of the various prison policies and procedures utilized to contend with AIDS in prison see Sarah E Frink, Note, Aids Behind Bars: Judicial Barriers Prisoners' Constitutional Claims, 45 Drake L Rev 165 (1997).

[7]§ 3:5.

[8]Jarrett v. Faulkner, 662 F. Supp. 928 (S.D. Ind. 1987); Glick v. Henderson, 855 F.2d 536 (8th Cir. 1988); Feigley v. Fulcomer, 720 F. Supp. 475 (M.D. Pa. 1989); Davis v. Stanley, 740 F. Supp. 815 (N.D. Ala. 1987); Portee v. Tollison, 753 F. Supp. 184 (D.S.C. 1990), judgment aff'd, 929 F.2d 694 (4th Cir. 1991).

sense of security.[9] Some states, relying on this position, have chosen to test all inmates, while others have not. In New York, for example, inmates generally cannot be tested for AIDS without their consent.[10] However, some states have made the opposite choice and have decided to test all entering inmates.[11] Here, as well, courts have given prisons systems that choose to test the entire prison population the discretion to do so if they wish.[12]

Another approach used by some prison systems is not to test all inmates but to test in specified situations; for example, testing to provide information for ongoing criminal investigations or testing sex offenders.[13] Efforts by inmates to challenge these tests on a variety of grounds, including the Fourth, Eighth, and Fourteenth Amendments, and the right of privacy, for the most part have been unsuccessful.[14] The courts have held that there is a reasonable basis for prison authorities to

---

[9]Feigley v. Fulcomer, 720 F. Supp. 475 (M.D. Pa. 1989). The Federal Bureau of Prisons does not automatically test each inmate for the presence of AIDS. 28 CFR §§ 549.10 to 549.20. Testing is done "as clinically indicated." The Bureau does test prior to an inmate's release, tests random samples of inmates, and tests certain groups, such as pregnant women. 28 CFR §§ 549.10 to 549.20. See also American Correctional Assn, Standards for Adult Correctional Institutions, Standard 3-4366 (1990).

[10]N.Y. Pub. Health Law § 2781.1.

[11]As of 2000, eighteen states test all inmates when they enter the prison system. Columbia Human Rights Law Review, A Jailhouse Lawyer's Manual, 570 n.94 (5th ed. 2000) (following states test: Alabama, Arkansas, Colorado, Georgia, Idaho, Iowa, Michigan, Mississippi, Missouri, Nebraska, New Hampshire, Nevada, North Dakota, Oklahoma, Rhode Island, South Dakota, Utah and Virginia).

[12]Dunn v. White, 880 F.2d 1188 (10th Cir. 1989).

[13]See, e.g., NY Crim. Proc. Law § 390.15.1 (a).

[14]Dunn v. White, 880 F.2d 1188 (10th Cir. 1989) (religious objections to testing rejected); Walker v. Sumner, 917 F.2d 382 (9th Cir. 1990); Barlow v. Ground, 943 F.2d 1132 (9th Cir. 1991); Harris v. Thigpen, 941 F.2d 1495 (11th Cir. 1991) (upholding state law requiring testing of all inmates); Connor v. Foster, 833 F. Supp. 727 (N.D. Ill. 1993) (holding that inmate could be tested when his hypodermic needle pricked the finger of a corrections officer during

MEDICAL CARE § 3:20

test. However, in one case, an inmate alleged that blood testing was being done for purposes unrelated to treatment or investigation, and the court held that a forced blood test could be improper when prison officials "offered no evidence that the AIDS test, if such was the purpose of the blood sample, was 'reasonably related to legitimate penological interests.'"[15]

Right to Have a Test Upon Request

Most states allow an inmate to request an HIV test.[16] If the request is denied, inmates can challenge the denial of a right to be tested. But the challenge is unlikely to be successful unless it can be shown that there is no valid reason for the refusal to test. If prison officials give a rationale for refusing to test, such as that the inmate is not in a high-risk group, courts have refused to intervene.[17]

---

a frisk); Johnson v. U.S., 816 F. Supp. 1519 (N.D. Ala. 1993) (detainee may be forced to submit to HIV test when arresting officer was pricked by drug needle). See also Matter of Michael WW, 203 A.D.2d 763, 611 N.Y.S.2d 47 (3d Dep't 1994); Matter of Juveniles A, B, C, D, E, 121 Wash. 2d 80, 847 P.2d 455 (1993) (upholding AIDS testing of juveniles who committed sex offenses); Columbia Human Rights Law Review, A Jailhouse Lawyer's Manual, 569-70 (5th ed. 2000) (collecting cases).

[15]Walker v. Sumner, 917 F.2d 382 (9th Cir. 1990) (quoting Turner v. Safley, 482 U.S. 78, 107 S. Ct. 2254, 96 L. Ed. 2d 64 (1987)). For a discussion of mandatory HIV Testing, segregation of HIV-positive inmates, and the Americans with Disability Act, see Susan Jacobs, AIDS in Correctional Facilities: Current Status of Legal Issues Critical to Policy Development, 23 J Crim Justice 209 (1995).

[16]Columbia Human Rights Law Review, A Jailhouse Lawyer's Manual, 570 (5th ed. 2000) (collecting cases) (only eight states do not have a policy on voluntary testing: Alabama, Delaware, Iowa, Mississippi, Nebraska, New Hampshire, North Dakota, and South Dakota).

[17]See, e.g., St. Hilaire v. Lewis, 26 F.3d 132 (9th Cir. 1994) (holding that there is no constitutional violation for refusal to test inmate where state offered a rationale reason for the denial).

§ 3:20   Rights of Prisoners, Third Edition

Segregation

There are two issues that arise with segregation. The first and most frequently litigated issue is whether or not inmates can be forced into segregated housing because they test positive on HIV or AIDS tests. The second is whether or not inmates who are not HIV-positive have the right to be segregated from known HIV-positive inmates.

Inmates uninfected with the AIDS virus have also sought to require that all inmates who are HIV-positive be segregated from the general population so that there would be no risk of infection. Those lawsuits, like the cases seeking mandatory testing, have generally been unsuccessful.[18] Similarly, most of the cases in which inmates objected to being segregated after HIV-positive finding have also deferred to prison authorities and permitted segregation.[19] Those courts have justified segregation on the basis of protecting inmates from

---

[18]Camarillo v. McCarthy, 998 F.2d 638 (9th Cir. 1993) (holding that segregation of AIDS inmates was not unconstitutional); Muhammad v. Carlson, 845 F.2d 175 (8th Cir. 1988) (same); Jarrett v. Faulkner, 662 F. Supp. 928 (S.D. Ind. 1987); Feigley v. Fulcomer, 720 F. Supp. 475 (M.D. Pa. 1989); Welch v. Sheriff, Lubbock County, Tex., 734 F. Supp. 765 (N.D. Tex. 1990); Deutsch v. Federal Bureau of Prisons, 737 F. Supp. 261 (S.D. N.Y. 1990), aff'd, 930 F.2d 909 (2d Cir. 1991) (required to share cell with HIV-positive inmate); Portee v. Tollison, 753 F. Supp. 184 (D.S.C. 1990), judgment aff'd, 929 F.2d 694 (4th Cir. 1991); Myers v. Maryland Div. of Correction, 782 F. Supp. 1095 (D. Md. 1992); Robbins v. Clarke, 946 F.2d 1331 (8th Cir. 1991); Oladipupo v. Austin, 104 F. Supp. 2d 626 (W.D. La. 2000) (holding that prisons are under no affirmative duty under the Constitution to segregate those detainees with HIV from non-infected detainees); Goss v. Sullivan, 839 F. Supp. 1532 (D. Wyo. 1993) (plaintiff's unsubstantiated fear that an HIV-positive inmate was aggressively attempting to infect others was not sufficient to support a claim for segregation); LaRocca v. Dalsheim, 120 Misc. 2d 697, 467 N.Y.S.2d 302 (Sup 1983).

[19]Cordero v. Coughlin, 607 F. Supp. 9 (S.D. N.Y. 1984); Powell v. Department of Corrections, State of Okl., 647 F. Supp. 968 (N.D. Okla. 1986); McDuffie v. Rikers Island Medical Dept., 668 F. Supp. 328 (S.D. N.Y. 1987); Judd v. Packard, 669 F. Supp. 741 (D. Md. 1987); Muhammad v. Carlson, 845 F.2d 175 (8th Cir. 1988); Baez

hostile, uninfected inmates, preventing the spread of AIDS, and diagnostic ease.[20]

There may have been some justification for segregation in the early years when testing for AIDS was much less reliable and the methods by which the disease is transmitted were not known. However, more recently the vast majority of prison systems have rejected segregation in favor of either mainstreaming HIV-positive inmates or making individual determinations.[21] The Federal Bureau of Prisons has adopted this approach.[22] There are a number of advantages to reject-

---

v. Rapping, 680 F. Supp. 112 (S.D. N.Y. 1988); Harris v. Thigpen, 941 F.2d 1495 (11th Cir. 1991); Moore v. Mabus, 976 F.2d 268 (5th Cir. 1992). See also American Correctional Assn, Standards for Adult Correctional Institutions, Standard 3-4366 (1990).

[20]Cordero v. Coughlin, 607 F. Supp. 9 (S.D. N.Y. 1984); Powell v. Department of Corrections, State of Okl., 647 F. Supp. 968 (N.D. Okla. 1986); Judd v. Packard, 669 F. Supp. 741 (D. Md. 1987). The desire to segregate prisoners in order to prevent spread of the disease is usually justified on the basis of the increased incidence of homosexual activity, both forced and consensual, in prison and the increased rate of violence and needle sharing, either through the use of illegal drugs or tattooing. In every instance, these activities are known to exist in prisons despite their prohibition and are known as the most common methods by which the disease is transmitted. Interestingly, recent studies show that "rates of HIV transmission in prison are lower than those outside of prison." Alexa Freeman, National Lawyer's Guild AIDS Network, AIDS in Prison, in AIDS Practice Manual: A Legal and Educational Guide § 14.1, at 14-2 (Paul Alpert et al ed., 3d ed. 1991).

[21]Alexa Freeman, National Lawyer's Guild AIDS Network, AIDS in Prison, in AIDS Practice Manual: A Legal and Educational Guide § 14.3(1) (Paul Alpert et al ed., 3d ed. 1991); Harris v Thigpen, 941 F2d 1495, 1516 (11th Cir 1991); Marcussen v. Brandstat, 836 F. Supp. 624 (N.D. Iowa 1993) (double celling with an HIV-positive inmate was not a constitutional violation).

[22]28 CFR §§ 549.10 to 549.20. See also 28 CFR §§ 541.60 to 541.68 (segregation permitted where there is "reliable evidence" that the inmate "engages in conduct posing a health risk to others").

§ 3:20   RIGHTS OF PRISONERS, THIRD EDITION

ing segregation.[23] Segregation automatically identifies those inmates with HIV, violating their interest in keeping medical details about themselves confidential and subjecting them to possible harm. There are management problems in ensuring the segregated inmates have equal access to appropriate programs.[24] Given the shortcomings of testing, segregation can lead to a false sense of security for those inmates who are not segregated and thereby increase the risk of transmission.

Two cases, relying on this authority and reasoning, have found segregation unconstitutional in certain circumstances. In *Doe v. Coughlin*,[25] the court found that segregation furthered "legitimate interests" but in a "constitutionally impermissible manner." The court prohibited involuntary transfers to segregated units for the purpose of HIV testing. Another district court in New York reconciled two contradictory policies adopted by the local jail by finding the reasons for segregation unpersuasive and blanket segregation impermissible.[26] Thus, despite the deference paid to prison officials, it can no longer be said that challenges to segregation of AIDS inmates will invariably lose.[27] By parity of reasoning, courts have generally rejected claims by non-

---

[23]See, generally, Alexa Freeman, National Lawyer's Guild AIDS Network, AIDS in Prison, in AIDS Practice Manual: A Legal and Educational Guide § 14.1, at 14-2 (Paul Alpert et al ed., 3d ed. 1991).

[24]Harris v. Thigpen, 941 F.2d 1495 (11th Cir. 1991). The issue of access to programs is discussed in greater detail later in this section.

[25]Doe v. Coughlin, 697 F. Supp. 1234 (N.D. N.Y. 1988).

[26]Nolley v. County of Erie, 776 F. Supp. 715 (W.D. N.Y. 1991).

[27]But see Onishea v. Hopper, 171 F.3d 1289, 162 A.L.R. Fed. 651 (11th Cir. 1999), cert. denied, 528 U.S. 1114, 120 S. Ct. 931, 145 L. Ed. 2d 811 (2000) (upholding involuntary segregation of HIV-positive inmates on the ground that a significant risk of HIV transmission existed for any prison program in which HIV-positive inmates participated; integrated programs might risk violence; segregation of HIV-positive inmates was not an exaggerated response; cost was a proper consideration in determination of

infected inmates complaining about being housed with HIV positive inmates.[28]

Access to Programs and Services

Segregation of inmates with AIDS may lead to their being deprived of access to programs and services offered to inmates in the general population. In addition, even when not segregated, HIV-positive inmates are sometimes excluded from certain programs or services as a result of their status. Most commonly, they are refused employment in prison food or health services.

In the earliest cases involving denial of access to programs, the courts found no violation, reasoning that segregation was justified and inevitably meant differential access to programs[29] or that, because inmates had no interest in a particular program, they could be excluded from that program because of their HIV status.[30] Similarly, constitutional challenges to the exclusion of HIV inmates from prison food or health services were unsuccessful because courts found the fears of other inmates to be a rational basis for such

---

whether hiring of additional guards to deter high-risk behavior was a reasonable accommodation to allowing integrated programs, and the hiring of additional guards imposed an undue burden on the prison system).

[28]See, e.g., Zaczek v. Murray, 983 F.2d 1059 (4th Cir. 1992); Deutsch v. Federal Bureau of Prisons, 737 F. Supp. 261 (S.D. N.Y. 1990), aff'd, 930 F.2d 909 (2d Cir. 1991). However, if the HIV-positive inmate is a sexual predator there can be liability for housing him with another inmate if a rape occurs and prison officials do nothing to stop it. Billman v. Indiana Dept. of Corrections, 56 F.3d 785 (7th Cir. 1995).

[29]Cordero v. Coughlin, 607 F. Supp. 9, 11 (S.D. N.Y. 1984) ("Obviously, in a case such as this, defendants cannot be compelled to provide plaintiffs with the identical privileges available to the other inmates.").

[30]Williams v. Sumner, 648 F. Supp. 510 (D. Nev. 1986).

§ 3:20

exclusion.[31]

More recently, inmates challenging exclusions have had more success. In one case, the court held that excluding an inmate from a temporary release program was impermissible when there was no medical reason for the exclusion.[32] In other cases, courts have found violations where inmates were denied equal access to the courts, to religious services, or to other programs as a result of their AIDS status.[33]

Other inmates have achieved success by focusing, not on constitutional rights, but on rights created by the prohibition against discrimination against handicapped persons contained in the federal Rehabilitation Act. Noting that the Act was passed to prevent federally funded programs from yielding to stereotypes or irrational fears about handicapped people, and the extremely low risk of transmission of AIDS, courts have found that the Act prohibits some discrimination against inmates as a result of their HIV status.[34]

---

[31]Farmer v. Moritsugu, 742 F. Supp. 525 (W.D. Wis. 1990). But see Austin v. Pennsylvania Dept. of Corrections, 876 F. Supp. 1437, 10 A.D.D. 1042 (E.D. Pa. 1995) (consent agreement provided that HIV-infected inmates could not be denied work detail in food service and personal service and that notification to general population of HIV-inmates was violative of confidentiality).

[32]Lopez v. Coughlin, 139 Misc. 2d 851, 529 N.Y.S.2d 247 (Sup 1988). Interestingly, the court made this decision even in the face of conclusory affidavits from prison officials opposing the release on health grounds.

[33]Nolley v. County of Erie, 776 F. Supp. 715 (W.D. N.Y. 1991); Harris v. Thigpen, 941 F.2d 1495 (11th Cir. 1991). See also Anderson v. Romero, 72 F.3d 518 (7th Cir. 1995) (holding that denial of same access to the yard and to haircut as other prisoners could be an Eighth Amendment violation).

[34]Casey v. Lewis, 773 F. Supp. 1365 (D. Ariz. 1991), rev'd in part, vacated in part on other grounds, 4 F.3d 1516, 2 A.D.D. 908 (9th Cir. 1993); Harris v. Thigpen, 941 F.2d 1495 (11th Cir. 1991) (concerning access to programs, the court found that individual decision-making had to take place for each program and its ability to reasonably accommodate HIV-positive inmates). See also Hallett v. New York State Dept. of Correctional Services, 109 F. Supp.

MEDICAL CARE § 3:20

Finally, seriously ill inmates should be aware that it may be possible for them to seek early release from prison through parole, medical furlough, clemency, or reduction of their sentence.[35]

Confidentiality

In a number of cases, inmates have argued that they have a protected interest in keeping confidential information about themselves, including their HIV-positive status.[36] The problem arises when those who know about the HIV status simply tell others who have no real need to know, as in *Doe v. Borough of Barrington*,[37] where the police apparently told the neighbor of an inmate taken into custody, or *Lipinski v Skinner*,[38] where the authorities apparently told the press. In

---

2d 190 (S.D. N.Y. 2000) (denying motion to dismiss complaint of HIV-positive amputee prisoner under the ADA and § 504 of the Rehabilitation Act contending that he was denied access to the shock incarceration program and the work release program because of his disabilities).

[35]Alexa Freeman, National Lawyer's Guild AIDS Network, AIDS and Prisons, in AIDS Practice Manual: A Legal and Educational Guide § 14.6 (Paul Alpert et al ed., 3d ed. 1991); Margorie R. Russell, Too Little, Too Late, Too Slow: Compassionate Release of Terminally Ill Prisoners: Is the Cure Worse than the Disease? 3 Widener J Pub L 799 (1994) (discussing the inadequate administrative methods for release of terminally ill prisoners). See also N.Y. Exec. Law § 259-r (medical parole provisions for terminally ill inmates); Columbia Human Rights Law Review, A Jailhouse Lawyer's Manual, 585-587 (5th ed. 2000).

[36]Moenius v. Stevens, 688 F. Supp. 1054 (D. Md. 1988) (sign over cell door that prisoner had AIDS); Woods v. White, 689 F. Supp. 874 (W.D. Wis. 1988), aff'd, 899 F.2d 17 (7th Cir. 1990); Doe v. Coughlin, 697 F. Supp. 1234 (N.D. N.Y. 1988); Doe v. Borough of Barrington, 729 F. Supp. 376 (D.N.J. 1990); Lipinski v. Skinner, 781 F. Supp. 131 (N.D. N.Y. 1991); Moore v. Mabus, 976 F.2d 268 (5th Cir. 1992); Nolley v. County of Erie, 776 F. Supp. 715 (W.D. N.Y. 1991); Harris v. Thigpen, 941 F.2d 1495 (11th Cir. 1991). See also Doe v. American Red Cross Blood Services, S.C. Region, 125 F.R.D. 646, 15 Fed. R. Serv. 3d 70 (D.S.C. 1989).

[37]Doe v. Borough of Barrington, 729 F. Supp. 376 (D.N.J. 1990).

[38]Lipinski v. Skinner, 781 F. Supp. 131 (N.D. N.Y. 1991).

§ 3:20   Rights of Prisoners, Third Edition

those cases, the courts found violations of the rights of the inmates.

The problem also arises when prisoners are segregated on the basis of HIV status, because such segregation, by definition, identifies those who are HIV-positive. In those cases, courts have been less sympathetic and, if finding the segregation permissible, have found that the consequent labeling is also permissible.[39] However, several courts have found that an allegation of unnecessary disclosure of a person's HIV status does state a violation of the right to privacy, which, though limited in prison, still exists.[40] The crucial factor is whether disclosure is necessary. Obviously, disclosure to the treating physician will always

---

[39]Tokar v. Armontrout, 97 F.3d 1078 (8th Cir. 1996) (HIV-positive inmate claimed segregation in HIV-only unit violated his right to privacy by disclosing his medical condition to prison officials and other inmates; court held that the plaintiff's privacy interest had to yield to the interest of the prison in preventing the risk of HIV infection); Moenius v. Stevens, 688 F. Supp. 1054 (D. Md. 1988); Moore v. Mabus, 976 F.2d 268 (5th Cir. 1992); Harris v. Thigpen, 941 F.2d 1495 (11th Cir. 1991). See also Davis v. District of Columbia, 158 F.3d 1342 (D.C. Cir. 1998) (holding that there was no violation in disclosing medical records because no physical injury was caused by the disclosure); Baez v. Rapping, 680 F. Supp. 112 (S.D. N.Y. 1988) (holding that warning prison guards to avoid contact with body fluids of an HIV-positive inmate was not a violation of the inmate's privacy rights).

[40]Woods v. White, 689 F. Supp. 874 (W.D. Wis. 1988), aff'd, 899 F.2d 17 (7th Cir. 1990) (unnecessary, disclosure to other inmates and staff could violate right to privacy); Doe v. Coughlin, 697 F. Supp. 1234 (N.D. N.Y. 1988) (segregated dorm impermissible in part due to violation of privacy interest); Nolley v. County of Erie, 776 F. Supp. 715 (W.D. N.Y. 1991) (red sticker placed on inmate's possessions to indicate her HIV status was violation of right to privacy and due process); but see Gill v. DeFrank, 2000 WL 897152 (S.D. N.Y. 2000), judgment aff'd, 8 Fed. Appx. 35 (2d Cir. 2001) (where an inmate's right to privacy regarding his HIV status was not clearly established law in 1997, the defendants were entitled to qualified immunity on § 1983 claim for disclosure).

be necessary.[41] Disclosure to other inmates will rarely be necessary. Thus, for this and other reasons, it was held that it is unconstitutional to force an HIV infected inmate to wear a mask.[42] In other cases, individual decisions will have to be made, recognizing the deference paid to the decisions of prison officials.[43]

A number of systems notify parole officials of an inmate's HIV status, and there is some evidence that the result of the notification is that HIV-positive inmates find it more difficult to obtain parole.[44] There seems little justification for a blanket policy of notifying parole officials in all cases.

Treatment

There is no dispute that AIDS-positive inmates are entitled to treatment for the disease, just as any inmate

---

[41]See, e.g., 28 CFR § 549.18 (authorizing disclosure to medical personnel).

[42]Perkins v. Kansas Dept. of Corrections, 165 F.3d 803 (10th Cir. 1999) (cannot make AIDS-positive person wear a mask).

[43]Powell v. Schriver, 175 F.3d 107 (2d Cir. 1999) (disclosure just to gossip is not proper); Anderson v. Romero, 72 F.3d 518 (7th Cir. 1995) (holding that disclosure of HIV status to individuals at risk of infection are acceptable so long as they are not punitive in nature, that disclosure to inmate's cellmate was acceptable because of the risk of homosexual activity between inmates, and that disclosure to the barber was also acceptable given the possibility of transmission if barber were to cut inmate during a shave or haircut); Harris v. Thigpen, 941 F.2d 1495 (11th Cir. 1991). The Federal Bureau of Prisons has adopted rules to protect the confidentiality of HIV status. 28 CFR §§ 549.10 to 5.20. See also American Correctional Assn, Standards for Adult Correctional Institutions, Standard 3-4366 (1990); Austin v. Pennsylvania Dept. of Corrections, 876 F. Supp. 1437, 10 A.D.D. 1042 (E.D. Pa. 1995) (consent agreement provided that notification to general population of HIV-inmates was violative of confidentiality); Doe v. Meachum, 126 F.R.D. 452 (D. Conn. 1989) (allowing HIV-positive inmates to sue department of corrections under fictitious names in order to protect their identity).

[44]Alexa Freeman, National Lawyer's Guild AIDS Network, AIDS and Prisons, in AIDS Practice Manual: A Legal and Educational Guide § 14.4(1), at 14-28 (Paul Alpert et al ed., 3d ed. 1991).

§ 3:20

is entitled to treatment for any other disease.[45] Failure to treat an AIDS-positive inmate is a violation of the Eighth Amendment.[46] This includes the psychiatric counseling that is often essential for persons with AIDS, as well as physical care.[47]

However, consistent with the general rule that medical care need not be ideal but need be only minimally adequate, an inmate receiving some treatment will ordinarily not be able to seek alternative treatments even if the inmate is prepared to pay for those treatments.[48] In addition, delay in receiving AIDS treatment, like other delays, may be seen as harmless and thus not a violation.[49] Finally, the failure to treat, like

---

[45]Gomez v. U.S., 899 F.2d 1124 (11th Cir. 1990) (inmate sought release when prison officials admitted there was no place in the prison system that could adequately treat him; release denied, because the remedy was treatment); Alexa Freeman, National Lawyer's Guild AIDS Network, AIDS and Prisons, in AIDS Practice Manual: A Legal and Educational Guide § 14.5 (Paul Alpert et al ed., 3d ed. 1991).

[46]Maynard v. New Jersey, 719 F. Supp. 292 (D.N.J. 1989); Nolley v. County of Erie, 776 F. Supp. 715 (W.D. N.Y. 1991).

[47]Alexa Freeman, National Lawyer's Guild AIDS Network, AIDS and Prisons, in AIDS Practice Manual: A Legal and Educational Guide § 14.5(2) (Paul Alpert et al ed., 3d ed. 1991); Franklin v. District of Columbia, 960 F. Supp. 394 (D.D.C. 1997), supplemented, 1997 WL 403418 (D.D.C. 1997), vacated in part on other grounds, 163 F.3d 625, 42 Fed. R. Serv. 3d 1013 (D.C. Cir. 1998), reh'g and reh'g en banc denied, 168 F.3d 1360 (D.C. Cir. 1999) supra (holding prison medical system was deliberately indifferent to the health needs of a class of Hispanic inmates when they failed to offer proper AIDS treatment, prevention, and counseling; court ordered the defendants to submit a memorandum detailing a plan to redress the constitutional violation).

[48]Hawley v. Evans, 716 F. Supp. 601 (N.D. Ga. 1989) (inmate could not get AZT, outside doctor, or experimental treatments because he was receiving some treatment, there was a dispute in the medical community about treatments, and legitimate penological concerns justified prohibition of outside drugs).

[49]Walker v. Peters, 989 F. Supp. 971 (N.D. Ill. 1997) (holding that failure to treat for suspected HIV before a diagnosis was not deliberate indifference, nor was failure to administer an HIV test

MEDICAL CARE § 3:20

other failures to treat, must evidence "deliberate indifference" and not merely malpractice or negligence.[50] Deliberate indifference has been found where defendants deny treatment for the condition;[51] where they discontinue an inmate's prescribed medication,[52] and where they fail to follow the federal guidelines for HIV care.[53]

AIDS education is also an essential component of any program that seeks to prevent the spread of and provide

---

against plaintiff's will, and also holding that disagreement with treatment alone is not a constitutional question); Wilson v Franceschi, 730 F Supp 420 (MD Fla 1990). See also Harris v. Thigpen, 941 F.2d 1495, 1508, (11th Cir. 1991) (the Court of Appeals found that the knowledge of prison medical officials "relating to some seemingly basic terminology about HIV is disturbing," that the institution was "not ideally staffed" for treatment of AIDS, and even that "the quality of its mental health care perhaps is substandard," but nevertheless found that prison officials were not deliberately indifferent to the medical needs of inmates with AIDS).

[50]Harris v. Thigpen, 941 F.2d 1495, 1508, (11th Cir. 1991); Hetzel v. Swartz, 31 F. Supp. 2d 444 (M.D. Pa. 1998) (finding no deliberate indifference for failure to grant dying AIDS patient psychological counseling to cope with AIDS where prison counselor had over 100 patients and was unable to help everyone); Polanco v. Dworzack, 25 F. Supp. 2d 148 (W.D. N.Y. 1998) (finding no deliberate indifference).

[51]Rivera v. Sheahan, 1998 WL 531875 (N.D. Ill. 1998) (allegation that defendants paid no attention to inmate's notification of her AIDS condition and her continuous requests for daily medication until she was comatose in her cell).

[52]McNally v. Prison Health Services, 52 F. Supp. 2d 147 (D. Me. 1999) (holding that there was sufficient evidence for a jury to find that prison officials refused to administer his HIV medication, thus exhibiting deliberate indifference to plaintiff's serious medical needs).

[53]Gates v. Fordice, 1999 WL 33537206 (N.D. Miss. 1999) (granting preliminary injunction ordering that the NIH Guidelines be followed unless there was good reason in an individual case not to do so). But see Perkins v. Kansas Dept. of Corrections, 165 F.3d 803 (10th Cir. 1999) (holding that there was no right to protease inhibitors if there was a disagreement over the course of treatment).

for the treatment of AIDS.[54] Some unreported cases have suggested that an education program is a required part of a prison health system.[55]

§ 3:21 Transsexuals

Research References

West's Key Number Digest, Civil Rights ⚖105(2)

Transsexuals are people who have a long-standing desire to change their sex.[1] Many transsexuals seek surgery that will change their sex. There are a number of steps that an individual must take before most medical authorities will approve them for surgery. First, the person must live for a period of a year or more in the new sex. The person will then be administered hormones of the new sex. For example, male to female transsexuals will be administered female hormones that will cause them to grow breasts, inhibit male hair growth, and cause a redistribution of body fat. Often,

---

[54]Alexa Freeman, National Lawyer's Guild AIDS Network, AIDS and Prisons, in AIDS Practice Manual: A Legal and Educational Guide § 14.5(3) (Paul Alpert et al ed., 3d ed. 1991).

[55]Doe v. Meachum, No H88-562 (PCD) (JGM) (Conn May 16, 1989) (consent decree); Telepo v Fauver, No 85-1742 (NJ Feb 8, 1988). See also DeGidio v. Pung, 704 F. Supp. 922, 942 (D. Minn. 1989), judgment aff'd, 920 F.2d 525 (8th Cir. 1990) ("lack of an aggressive education campaign in light of inmates' concerns [about an outbreak of tuberculosis] constitute neglect of their basic health needs"). These cases are discussed in Alexa Freeman, National Lawyer's Guild AIDS Network, AIDS and Prisons, in AIDS Practice Manual: A Legal and Educational Guide § 14.5(3) (Paul Alpert et al ed., 3d ed. 1991).

[Section 3:21]

[1]For an excellent discussion of transsexuality, see Phillips v. Michigan Dept. of Corrections, 731 F. Supp. 792 (W.D. Mich. 1990), decision aff'd, 932 F.2d 969 (6th Cir. 1991). See also Gender Dysphoria (Betty Steiner ed. 1985); For a comprehensive discussion on the transgendered identity, legal issues facing transgendered prisoners, and the placement and treatment issues of transgendered prisoners, see Darren Rosenblum, "Trapped" in Sing Sing: Transgendered Prisoners Caught in the Gender Binarism, 6 Mich J Gender & L 499 (2000).

other steps must be taken. Male to female transsexuals will ordinarily require electrolysis to remove facial hair. Female to male transsexuals will require mastectomy. Only after these steps have been taken will reputable authorities approve someone for gender reassignment surgery.[2]

If a person has gone through the entire reassignment process, that person should be treated as a member of the assigned sex. Thus, after surgery, a male to female transsexual should be confined in a women's prison and provided the hormones that continue to be necessary for good health. That is the policy of the Federal Bureau of Prisons.[3] There may also be cases in which someone who has not yet completed all surgery should be placed in a prison with other people of their assigned sex. For example, in *Crosby v Reynolds*,[4] a doctor insisted that a male to female transsexual who had not yet had final surgery but who had been living as a woman for some years, whose body had taken on female characteristics, and who, with long hormone administration, had become impotent, be placed in a female prison. The doctor reasoned that the inmate's needs to live as a woman would be better met in the female prison, that management problems would be infinitely less than those that would occur by placing the totally feminine inmate in a male prison, and that no danger would occur to other women inmates. The doctor was correct in concluding that individual decisions should be made concerning assignment, based on these factors.[5]

However, problems arise if the transsexual is incarcerated after beginning the process of reassignment but

---

[2]Gender Dysphoria (Betty Steiner ed. 1985).

[3]Farmer v. Haas, 990 F.2d 319 (7th Cir. 1993).

[4]Crosby v. Reynolds, 763 F. Supp. 666 (D. Me. 1991) (the inmate's cellmate sued, objecting to having been housed with a man, but the court found that the doctor's decision was reasonable).

[5]All of the litigation in this area has concerned male to female transsexuals. As many as one-half of all persons seeking gender reassignment are female to male. Gender Dysphoria (Betty Steiner ed. 1985). In those cases, some of the considerations may be

before it has been completed. In two reported cases, male to female transsexuals in their mid-30s who had not yet had surgery were incarcerated in male prisons after living as women for approximately half of their lives.[6] As the doctor in *Crosby* noted, placing a totally feminine person in a male prison presents obvious and serious problems of protecting that person from unwanted attention.

There is no question that a genuine[7] transsexual has a "serious medical condition" that requires some treatment.[8] The failure to provide transsexuals with needed medical treatment caused at least two inmates to attempt self-castration.[9] There can also be no serious dispute that many prison officials, including doctors, are ignorant about transsexuality and are often cruel to transsexual inmates.[10] In one recent case, for example, prison officials revealed, in the presence of other staff

---

different. For example, a female to male transsexual who has not completed reassignment could be still raped.

[6] Phillips v. Michigan Dept. of Corrections, 731 F. Supp. 792 (W.D. Mich. 1990), decision aff'd, 932 F.2d 969 (6th Cir. 1991); Meriwether v. Faulkner, 821 F.2d 408 (7th Cir. 1987).

[7] Is it not always easy to determine if a person is genuinely a transsexual or if their desire for sexual reassignment is due to other gender dysphorias such as transvestism or is due to other emotional problems. Lamb v. Maschner, 633 F. Supp. 351 (D. Kan. 1986). The matter is complicated by more recent evidence indicating that people can become transsexuals in middle age. Gender Dysphoria (Betty Steiner ed. 1985).

[8] Wolfe v. Horn, 130 F. Supp. 2d 648 (E.D. Pa. 2001) (holding that transsexualism is a serious medical need); Phillips v. Michigan Dept. of Corrections, 731 F. Supp. 792 (W.D. Mich. 1990), decision aff'd, 932 F.2d 969 (6th Cir. 1991); White v. Farrier, 849 F.2d 322 (8th Cir. 1988); Meriwether v. Faulkner, 821 F.2d 408 (7th Cir. 1987).

[9] Supre v. Ricketts, 792 F.2d 958 (10th Cir. 1986); White v. Farrier, 849 F.2d 322 (8th Cir. 1988); Farmer v. Carlson, 685 F. Supp. 1335 (M.D. Pa. 1988).

[10] Phillips v. Michigan Dept. of Corrections, 731 F. Supp. 792, 800 (W.D. Mich. 1990), decision aff'd, 932 F.2d 969 (6th Cir. 1991) (doctor subjected transsexual to "ridicule and offensive remarks"); Meriwether v. Faulkner, 821 F.2d 408 (7th Cir. 1987). Prison doc-

and inmates, that inmate had had a sex change operation and that she was HIV-positive. Thereafter, the inmate became the target of harassment by guards and prisoners. The inmate sued the guard and supervisor, alleging that her privacy and Eighth Amendment rights were violated by the disclosure that she was a transsexual. The Court of Appeals reversed the dismissal of the claim, holding the actions of the defendants, if true, compromised the inmate's safety and had no valid purpose.[11] Similarly, courts have held that transsexual inmates are protected against sexual harassment by prison staff.[12]

Pre-operative transsexual inmates have sought a variety of treatments, including female clothing, cosmetics, electrolysis, hormone therapy, transfer to a female prison, and surgery.[13] If the inmate is placed in a male prison, the courts have uniformly found that prison management concerns against having inmates appear feminine outweigh any medical need for female clothing or cosmetics.[14] The principal emphasis has been on continuation of hormone therapy begun prior to

---

tors are not the only ones with prejudices when it comes to treatment of conditions involving sex. The Americans with Disabilities Act specifically exempts transsexuals, and other similar sexual conditions, from its protections. 42 U.S.C. § 12211.

[11]Powell v. Schriver, 175 F.3d 107 (2d Cir. 1999).

[12]Schwenk v. Hartford, 204 F.3d 1187 (9th Cir. 2000) (holding that preoperative male-to-female transsexual had a valid claim against a state prison guard and other prison authorities for an alleged attempted rape by the guard; court held that the Eighth Amendment right of prisoners to be free from sexual abuse was well-established at the time of the assault and that same-sex harassment of prisoners was unconstitutional).

[13]Lamb v. Maschner, 633 F. Supp. 351 (D. Kan. 1986); White v. Farrier, 849 F.2d 322 (8th Cir. 1988).

[14]Jones v. Warden of Stateville Correctional Center, 918 F. Supp. 1142 (N.D. Ill. 1995); Star v. Gramley, 815 F. Supp. 276 (C.D. Ill. 1993).

§ 3:21

incarceration.[15] Every court has held that genuine transsexuals are entitled to some treatment for their condition, but the courts have been divided on their entitlement to hormone therapy.[16]

Those courts denying hormone therapy have relied on the general rule that the courts will not second guess medical decisions of prison doctors and that, if there is a disagreement among the medical experts, the court will defer to the prison doctor's opinion. The courts need to be sensitive to the fact that many people, including many doctors, are unable to unemotionally diagnosis problems relating to sex and erroneously still see this condition as a sign of serious psychiatric illness or as a desire for simple cosmetic changes. Expert opinion is unanimous concerning the essential nature of treatment for transsexuals. The better approach is to treat transsexuality like any other medical problem and to ensure that appropriate treatment, such as hormones, is provided.[17] Recently, courts have been sensitive to this need, at least in cases where hormonal treatment

---

[15]Phillips v. Michigan Dept. of Corrections, 731 F. Supp. 792 (W.D. Mich. 1990), decision aff'd, 932 F.2d 969 (6th Cir. 1991); Lamb v. Maschner, 633 F. Supp. 351 (D. Kan. 1986).

[16]Compare Phillips v. Michigan Dept. of Corrections, 731 F. Supp. 792 (W.D. Mich. 1990), decision aff'd, 932 F.2d 969 (6th Cir. 1991) (hormones ordered) with White v. Farrier, 849 F.2d 322 (8th Cir. 1988) (not ordered); Supre v. Ricketts, 792 F.2d 958 (10th Cir. 1986) ("We are unable to conclude that federal law requires prison officials to administer female hormones to a transsexual inmate.") and Meriwether v. Faulkner, 821 F.2d 408 (7th Cir. 1987) (not necessarily entitled to hormones); Farmer v. Carlson, 685 F. Supp. 1335 (M.D. Pa. 1988).

[17]Phillips v. Michigan Dept. of Corrections, 731 F. Supp. 792 (W.D. Mich. 1990), decision aff'd, 932 F.2d 969 (6th Cir. 1991). The Federal Bureau of Prisons policy is to maintain an inmate at the stage of transition they are at when they arrive at the institution. Farmer v. Haas, 990 F.2d 319 (7th Cir. 1993). This presumably includes the administration of hormones to those people who had been receiving them outside the institution. For a discussion on the constitutionality of present procedures regarding transsexual prisoners and a proposal for a model policy for treatment of trans-

was begun and then abruptly discontinued.[18] As with other medical care cases, if the facts of the case do not disclose deliberate indifference, there is no constitutional violation.[19]

§ 3:22 Experimentation and Research

There is a long history of using inmates for purposes of medical research, and much of that history reveals serious abuses.[1] There are advantages and disadvantages to allowing medical research on inmates, both for the inmates themselves and for society.[2] Prisoners may seek to enroll in experiments to obtain better pay for work or better and safer living conditions, as an alternative to boredom, or to seek future favor in, for example,

---

sexuals, see Anita C. Barnes, The Sexual Continuum: Transsexual Prisoners, 24 N Eng J of Crim & Civ Confinement 599 (1998).

[18]See, e.g., South v. Gomez, 211 F.3d 1275 (9th Cir. 2000) (holding that when prison authorities abruptly and peremptorily terminated plaintiff inmate's cycle of female hormone therapy, they acted with deliberate indifference to inmate's serious medical needs); Wolfe v. Horn, 130 F. Supp. 2d 648 (E.D. Pa. 2001) (holding that transsexualism is a serious medical need and that an abrupt termination of hormone therapy without an understanding of the condition, or treatment for withdrawal and after-effects, could constitute deliberate indifference).

[19]See, e.g., Farmer v. Moritsugu, 163 F.3d 610, 333 (D.C. Cir. 1998) (holding that prison officials were not deliberately indifferent to transsexual inmate's medical needs); Long v. Nix, 86 F.3d 761 (8th Cir. 1996) (holding that prison officials were not deliberately indifferent to inmate suffering for 20 years from dysphoria, a gender identity disorder, because the evidence showed that on numerous occasions the prison medical staff attempted to evaluate the inmate's psychological problems and the inmate refused to cooperate).

[Section 3:22]
[1]Colleen M. McCarthy, Note, Experimentation On Prisoners: The Inadequacy of Voluntary Consent, 15 New Eng J on Crim & Civ Confinement 55, 56-60 (1989).

[2]James Overholser, Ethical Issues in Prison Research: A Risk/ Benefit Analysis, 5 Behav Sci & the Law 187 (1987).

§ 3:22   Rights of Prisoners, Third Edition

parole decisions.[3] That there is a risk may be a positive, not a negative, feature for inmates.[4] Many of these motives, and many of the characteristics of the prison environment, raise serious questions about the inmate's ability to give truly voluntary consent to experimentation.[5] Inmates are also motivated by altruism, just as are non-inmates who volunteer for experiments.[6] Risks and benefits to inmates may depend on the nature of the experiment and whether it is designed to find out information that would benefit inmates generally or inmates with particular characteristics.[7]

Experimenters may seek access to prisoners because the cost is minimal, because the control of the environment permits more accurate measurement of the results of the experiment,[8] or because the prison population presents the characteristics necessary to the experiment.

Traditionally, the key question in human experimentation is whether the subject was informed and volun-

---

[3]Bailey v. Lally, 481 F. Supp. 203 (D. Md. 1979); Colleen M. McCarthy, Note, Experimentation On Prisoners: The Inadequacy of Voluntary Consent, 15 New Eng J on Crim & Civ Confinement 55, 61 (1989); James Overholser, Ethical Issues in Prison Research: A Risk/Benefit Analysis, 5 Behav Sci & the Law 187, 191, 193 (1987).

[4]Colleen M. McCarthy, Note, Experimentation On Prisoners: The Inadequacy of Voluntary Consent, 15 New Eng J on Crim & Civ Confinement 55, 64-65 (1989).

[5]*Id.*; James Overholser, Ethical Issues in Prison Research: A Risk/Benefit Analysis, 5 Behav Sci & the Law 187, 191, 196 (1987).

[6]Colleen M. McCarthy, Note, Experimentation On Prisoners: The Inadequacy of Voluntary Consent, 15 New Eng J on Crim & Civ Confinement 55, 58, 61 (1989); James Overholser, Ethical Issues in Prison Research: A Risk/Benefit Analysis, 5 Behav Sci & the Law 187, 192-93 (1987).

[7]James Overholser, Ethical Issues in Prison Research: A Risk/Benefit Analysis, 5 Behav Sci & the Law 187, 188-89 (1987).

[8]Colleen M. McCarthy, Note, Experimentation On Prisoners: The Inadequacy of Voluntary Consent, 15 New Eng J on Crim & Civ Confinement 55, 58 (1989).

§ 3:22

tary consented to the experiment.[9] Without such consent, experimentation is problematical at best. In the institutional context, there are also serious problems of maintaining confidentiality, especially if the research is designed to elicit evidence of criminality or other confidential information.[10]

Until quite recently, human experimentation on prisoners presented potentially serious problems. For example, in 1969, it was estimated that 85 per cent of all new drugs were tested first in prisons and that at least 42 prisons allowed medical research on prisoners.[11] However, by 1979, one survey showed only three prisons still allowing such research.[12]

This decline can largely be traced to the extensive standards[13] and regulations[14] that have been developed in the last 35 years governing human experimentation

---

[9]These issues are extensively discussed in Bailey v. Lally, 481 F. Supp. 203 (D. Md. 1979) (voluntariness). See also Clay v. Martin, 509 F.2d 109 (2d Cir. 1975) (alleging lack of informed consent); Scott v. Casey, 562 F. Supp. 475 (N.D. Ga. 1983) (LSD experiments); Valenti v. Prudden, 58 A.D.2d 956, 397 N.Y.S.2d 181 (3d Dep't 1977) (informed consent); James Overholser, Ethical Issues in Prison Research: A Risk/Benefit Analysis, 5 Behav Sci & the Law 187, 195-96 (1987); Johnson v. Meltzer, 134 F.3d 1393 (9th Cir. 1998) (holding that summary judgment was improper in a case in which inmate injured in accident while trying to evade arrest suffered brain injuries and was given an experimental drug allegedly without his consent).

[10]James Overholser, Ethical Issues in Prison Research: A Risk/Benefit Analysis, 5 Behav Sci & the Law 187, 195 (1987).

[11]Gettinger & Krajick, The Demise of Prison Medical Research, Corrections Mag 5, 6 (Dec 1979); Bailey v. Lally, 481 F. Supp. 203, 212 n16 (D. Md. 1979) (in 1975, research conducted in nine states).

[12]Gettinger & Krajick, The Demise of Prison Medical Research, Corrections Mag 5, 6 (1979).

[13]See American Psychological Assn, Ethical Principles in the Conduct of Research with Human Participants (1982); American Assn of Correctional Psychologists, Standards for Psychology Services in Adult Jails and Prisons, in Criminal Justice and Behavior, 7, 81-127, both cited in Overholser, Ethical Issues in Prison Research: A Risk /Benefit Analysis, 5 Behav Sci & the Law 187 (1987).

§ 3:22 RIGHTS OF PRISONERS, THIRD EDITION

in general and prison experimentation in particular. Because of the extensive consultation that preceded adoption of the regulations, the overwhelming role played by federal funding of medical research, and federal funding of prisons and jails, the federal regulations play a very large role in determining the law in this area.[15]

Before research involving human subjects is permitted under the federal regulations, it must be reviewed by an institutional review board (IRB) consisting of at least five people of "varying backgrounds.[16] With prison research, one of the five members of the IRB must be "a prisoner, or a prisoner representative with appropriate background and experience" and a majority of the IRB "shall have no association with the prison(s)."[17] The IRB must assure itself that there is nothing about the research that will increase the risk of improper factors that would influence inmate participation. Thus, the

---

[14]Federal regulations have been issued by the Department of Health and Human Services (45 CFR pt 46, with prison research at subpart C) and the Food & Drug Administration (21 CFR pt 50, with prison research at subpart C). See Bailey v. Lally, 481 F. Supp. 203, 214-17 (D. Md. 1979). Some states also have regulations, some of which are discussed in Colleen M. McCarthy, Note, Experimentation On Prisoners: The Inadequacy of Voluntary Consent, 15 New Eng J on Crim & Civ Confinement 55 (1989).

[15]There are also some state regulations and statutes. See, e.g., Or Rev Stat § 421.085(b)(2), cited in Colleen M. McCarthy, Note, Experimentation On Prisoners: The Inadequacy of Voluntary Consent, 15 New Eng J on Crim & Civ Confinement 55, at 59 nn. 28, 29 (1989). The same article contains a fairly extensive discussion of state regulations in the area of prison experimentation, emphasizing Oregon, Iowa, California, and Michigan. Colleen M. McCarthy, Note, Experimentation On Prisoners: The Inadequacy of Voluntary Consent, 15 New Eng J on Crim & Civ Confinement 55, 70-74 (1989).

[16]45 CFR § 46.107(a).

[17]45 CFR § 46.304.

MEDICAL CARE § 3:22

IRB must assure itself that:[18]

(1) the advantages to the inmate "when compared to the general living conditions . . . are not of such a magnitude that his or her ability to weigh the risks of the research against the value of such advantages in the limited choice environment of the prison is impaired";
(2) risks "are commensurate with risks that would be accepted by non-prisoner volunteers";
(3) selection procedures are fair;
(4) information about the research is adequately conveyed;
(5) inmates know that parole boards will not consider an inmate's participation; and
(6) adequate provision is made for needed follow-up.

Even with these IRB procedures, the regulations prohibit all "biomedical or behavioral research" involving inmates, with four exceptions:[19]

(1) the possible causes, effects, and processes of incarceration and of criminal behavior;
(2) study of prisons as institutional structures or prisoners as incarcerated persons;

In both of these cases it must be found that "the study presents no more than inconvenience to the subjects." In addition, research is permissible:

(3) on conditions particularly affecting prisoners as a class; and
(4) on practices which have the intent and reasonable probability of improving the health or well-being of the subject.

---

[18]45 CFR § 46.305. This is in addition to the other review required by IRBs for all research, including the requirement that there be informed consent. 45 CFR §§ 46.109, 46.111, 46.116.
[19]45 CFR § 46.306.

§ 3:22

These regulations are very strict, and the net effect has largely been to bar experimentation in prisons.[20]

§ 3:23 Right to Refuse Treatment

Outside the prison environment, there has been extensive litigation concerning the concept of informed consent. It has long been a fundamental rule that no person may be given medical treatment without their informed and voluntary consent.[1]

---

[20]Colleen M. McCarthy, Note, Experimentation On Prisoners: The Inadequacy of Voluntary Consent, 15 New Eng J on Crim & Civ Confinement 55, 68 (1989). See also U.S. Dept of Justice, Federal Standards for Prisons and Jails § 5.50 (1980) ABA Standards for Criminal Justice § 23.5-.8 (1986); American Correctional Assn, Standards for Adult Correctional Institutions, Standard 3-4373 (1990); National Commn on Correctional Health Care, Standards for Health Services in Jails J-69 (May 1999); Commission on Accreditation for Corrections, Certification Standards for Health Care Programs HC-083 (1989).

[Section 3:23]

[1]Holley v. Deal, 948 F. Supp. 711 (M.D. Tenn. 1996) (where appointed guardian of "incompetent" inmate consented to prison administration of medication, inmate failed to state a due process claim; court held state law empowered a legal guardian to consent to or refuse medical treatment for an incompetent person; thus, the court granted the defendant's motion for summary judgment).

See also Reynolds v. Goord, 103 F. Supp. 2d 316 (S.D. N.Y. 2000), where a Rastafarian inmate asserted a challenge to the defendants' tuberculosis health policy, N.Y. Department of Correctional Serv. Health Serv. Policy 1.18, under which the inmate's refusal to submit to a purified protein derivative (PPD) test resulted in the placement of the inmate in tuberculin hold restrictive confinement (TB Hold) for one year, unless he consented to treatment with isoniazid (INH). The inmate asserted the sanctions against him violated his First Amendment right to the free exercise of his religion. The court granted the plaintiff's motion for a preliminary injunction barring his placement in the TB Hold pending a trial, holding that under the *Turner* standard, he had shown a likelihood of success on the merits on the issue of a lack of a valid and rational connection between the challenged regulation and the defendants' legitimate and neutral objectives. Turner v. Safley, 482 U.S. 78, 107 S. Ct. 2254, 96 L. Ed. 2d 64 (1987). Placement in

For a long time, this principle was not applied to people with mental heath problems and, in particular, was seldom honored in mental hospitals. Beginning in the 1970s, people confined in mental hospitals began to challenge that practice, arguing that when civil commitment was not the equivalent of a finding of incompetence, they ought not to be involuntarily treated.[2] This movement was propelled, in part, by the growing use of psychiatric drugs, many of which were used indiscriminately or for purposes other than treatment,[3] and by other abuses of "treatment" in the institutional setting.[4]

---

the TB Hold for the exercise of his religious beliefs was a substantial burden on the inmate's constitutional rights that could not be adequately compensated monetarily.

For a discussion on ethical implications of a person's right to refuse treatment, see Frederick R. Parker, Jr., and Charles J. Paine, The Informed Consent and the Refusal of Medical Treatment in the Correctional Setting, 27 J L Med & Ethics 240 (Fall 1999).

[2]Mills v. Rogers, 457 U.S. 291, 102 S. Ct. 2442, 73 L. Ed. 2d 16 (1982); Winters v. Miller, 446 F.2d 65 (2d Cir. 1971); Scott v. Plante, 532 F.2d 939 (3d Cir. 1976); Souder v. McGuire, 423 F. Supp. 830 (M.D. Pa. 1976); Rennie v. Klein, 653 F.2d 836 (3d Cir. 1981), cert. granted, judgment vacated, 458 U.S. 1119, 102 S. Ct. 3506, 73 L. Ed. 2d 1381 (1982); Anderson v. Nosser, 438 F.2d 183 (5th Cir. 1971), decision modified on denial of reargument, 456 F.2d 835 (5th Cir. 1972); Wyatt v. Stickney, 344 F. Supp. 387 (M.D. Ala. 1972), aff'd in part, rev'd in part and remanded, 503 F.2d 1305 (5th Cir. 1974); U.S. v. Charters, 863 F.2d 302 (4th Cir. 1988) (person confined as incompetent to stand trial); Robert Plotkin, Limiting the Therapeutic Orgy: Mental Patients' Right to Refuse Treatment, 72 NW U L Rev 461 (1977).

[3]Nelson v. Heyne, 355 F. Supp. 451 (N.D. Ind. 1972), judgment aff'd, 491 F.2d 352 (7th Cir. 1974); Pena v. New York State Division for Youth, 419 F. Supp. 203 (S.D. N.Y. 1976); Welsch v. Likins, 373 F. Supp. 487 (D. Minn. 1974), opinion supplemented, 68 F.R.D. 589 (D. Minn. 1975), judgment aff'd, 525 F.2d 987 (8th Cir. 1975); Brian M. Schwartz, In the Name of Treatment: Autonomy, Civil Commitment, and the Right to Refuse Treatment, 50 Notre Dame Law 808 (1975).

[4]Knecht v. Gillman, 488 F.2d 1136, 71 Ohio Op. 2d 101 (8th Cir. 1973) (apomorphine, which induces vomiting, as a behavior

§ 3:23   RIGHTS OF PRISONERS, THIRD EDITION

The common psychiatric drugs have proven benefits, but they also can have serious side effects.[5]

Because prison incarceration does not result in a finding of incompetence, the principle of informed consent was long thought to apply as much in the prison context as outside. However, prison psychiatrists began to involuntarily medicate inmates with psychiatric problems just as they had done in mental hospitals.[6] This has become even more of a potential problem as more people admitted to prison suffer from mental illness.

In 1990, the Supreme Court addressed the issue of involuntary treatment of inmates in the jail or prison context in *Washington v Harper*.[7] The Court first found that inmates had a state-created liberty interest and a "significant liberty interest in avoiding the unwanted

---

modification technique); Mackey v. Procunier, 477 F.2d 877 (9th Cir. 1973); Clonce v. Richardson, 379 F. Supp. 338 (W.D. Mo. 1974) (behavior modification).

[5]Washington v. Harper, 494 U.S. 210, 110 S. Ct. 1028, 108 L. Ed. 2d 178 (1990); Eugene Z. DuBose Jr., Of the Parens Patriae Commitment Power and Drug Treatment of Schizophrenia: Do the Benefits to the Patient Justify Involuntary Treatment, 60 Minn L Rev 1149 (1976).

[6]Williams v. Anderson, 959 F.2d 1411 (7th Cir. 1992); Bee v. Greaves, 744 F.2d 1387 (10th Cir. 1984) (later opinion upholding jury verdict against doctor for involuntarily medicating pretrial detainee); U.S. v. Watson, 893 F.2d 970, 976-82 (8th Cir. 1990), opinion vacated in part on reh'g, 900 F.2d 1322 (8th Cir. 1990); Gilliam v. Martin, 589 F. Supp. 680 (W.D. Okla. 1984) (permitting forced medication); Breads v. Moehrle, 781 F. Supp. 953 (W.D. N.Y. 1991); Sconiers v. Jarvis, 458 F. Supp. 37 (D. Kan. 1978). A discussion on the scope of the civilly committed prisoner's right to refuse medication under the substantive component of the Due Process Clause of the Fourteenth Amendment may be found in William M. Brooks, Reevaluating Substantive Due Process as a Source of Protection for Psychiatric Patients to Refuse Drugs, 31 Ind L Rev 937 (1998).

[7]Washington v. Harper, 494 U.S. 210, 110 S. Ct. 1028, 108 L. Ed. 2d 178 (1990). See also Riggins v. Nevada, 504 U.S. 127, 112 S. Ct. 1810, 118 L. Ed. 2d 479 (1992) (without *Washington* findings or evidence needed to adjudicate guilt, may not forcibly medicate pretrial detainee).

administration of antipsychotic drugs under the Due Process Clause of the Fourteenth Amendment."[8] However, the Court found that incarceration often resulted in deprivation of fundamental liberties. The proper analysis concerning the permissible deprivations was that of *Turner v Safley*,[9] and therefore, "given the requirements of the prison environment, the Due Process Clause permits the State to treat a prison inmate who has a serious mental illness with antipsychotic drugs against his will, if the inmate is dangerous to himself or others and the treatment is in the inmate's medical interest.[10] Key to this conclusion is the standard that must be met[11] —the equivalent of a civil commitment standard[12] —and the requirement that the treatment be for medical reasons and not for penological reasons, such as control.[13] If these requirements are met, the inmate is still entitled to procedural protections surrounding the decision to involuntarily medicate him or her. The Court found that a full judicial hearing was not required and that the procedures utilized by the state of Washington in that case were constitutionally sufficient. Those procedures required that the decision first be made by a psychiatrist and then reviewed, on request, by a hearing committee consisting of a psychiatrist, a psychologist, and the assistant superintendent, at a proceeding which the inmate could attend

---

[8]Washington v. Harper, 494 U.S. 210, 110 S. Ct. 1028, 1036, 108 L. Ed. 2d 178 (1990).

[9]Turner v. Safley, 482 U.S. 78, 107 S. Ct. 2254, 96 L. Ed. 2d 64 (1987).

[10]Washington v. Harper, 494 U.S. 210, 110 S. Ct. 1028, 1039-40, 108 L. Ed. 2d 178 (1990).

[11]Under *Harper*, forcing antipsychotic drugs on a convicted prisoner is impermissible absent a finding of overriding justification and a determination of medical appropriateness. Riggins v. Nevada, 504 U.S. 127, 112 S. Ct. 1810, 1815, 118 L. Ed. 2d 479 (1992); Breads v. Moehrle, 781 F. Supp. 953, 957 (W.D. N.Y. 1991).

[12]Washington v. Harper, 494 U.S. 210, 110 S. Ct. 1028, 1033 n3, 108 L. Ed. 2d 178 (1990).

[13]*Id.* at 1037 n.8.

§ 3:23　　　　　　Rights of Prisoners, Third Edition

and at which he could present evidence, cross-examine witnesses, and have the assistance of a lay advisor, and that that the inmate be able to appeal the decision to the state court system.[14]

Harper establishes that inmates in appropriate cases can be forced to take antipsychotic drugs.[15] Lower courts since that time have required due process protections in all cases except emergencies where the drug must be administered by a professional immediately.[16] Although the Court's opinion is strictly limited to the administra-

---

[14]*Id.* at 1033, 1040-44.

[15]See, e.g., U.S. v. Weston, 134 F. Supp. 2d 115 (D.D.C. 2001), order aff'd, 255 F.3d 873 (D.C. Cir. 2001), cert. denied, 122 S. Ct. 670, 151 L. Ed. 2d 583 (U.S. 2001) (pretrial detainee was deemed incompetent to stand trial for the murder of federal law enforcement officers; Bureau of Prisons attempted to treat the defendant with anti-psychotic drugs; court held the BOP could involuntarily treat the defendant with the drugs, as it was the only effective treatment available, in that the BOP had legitimate interests in rendering the defendant less dangerous, and competent to stand trial); Walton v. Norris, 59 F.3d 67 (8th Cir. 1995) (sufficient evidence existed to order inmate to be medicated with psychotropic drugs where prison psychiatrist explained that each time inmate's medication was stopped he became psychotic and delusional, and where inmate received due process though a hearing before the mental health review committee); Steinkruger v. Miller, 2000 SD 83, 612 N.W.2d 591 (S.D. 2000) (state's statute on forced medication met all due process requirements).

There are special considerations when the forced medication of pre-trail detainee is contemplated. See, e.g., U.S. v. Brandon, 158 F.3d 947, 1998 FED App. 319P (6th Cir. 1998) (holding that forced medication implicated detainee's First Amendment and liberty interests because it might produce severe and irreversible side effects and might affect his right to a fair trial, since it could produce a prejudicial negative demeanor by interfering with his ability to communicate); Joanne R. Propst, Restoring Competency: Does the State Have the Right to Force Anti-Psychotic Medications on the Mentally Ill Pretrial-Detainee?, 49 Drake L. Rev. 147 (2000).

[16]Hogan v. Carter, 85 F.3d 1113 (4th Cir. 1996) (prison physicians may administer a sedative to a mentally ill inmate in an emergency situation; such an involuntary administration of anti-psychotic drugs does not violate due process); Wilson v. Chang, 955 F. Supp. 18 (D.R.I. 1997) (prison physician who administered

MEDICAL CARE § 3:23

tion of antipsychotic drugs,[17] the same principles have applied to other forms of mental health treatments.[18] If the institution establishes that the *Harper* standards are met, involuntary mental health treatment will be permitted if accompanied by appropriate procedural protections. However, it would be unlikely, and erroneous, if the *Harper* principle were applied to inmates who do not have serious mental health problems that prevent them from making informed consent decisions. For non-mentally ill inmates, the general rules prohibiting treatment in the absence of informed consent still apply.[19]

In addition to mental health treatment courts have

---

a sedative to a violent inmate without a prior hearing or inmate's consent did not violate the inmate's rights of due process; court held that when a prison physician "has reasonable grounds to believe that an inmate is a danger to himself or others, utilizing his medical judgment in a medically appropriate manner, he may inject the inmate with a sedative to deal with an emergency situation").

[17]*Id.* at 1032 n.1. See also National Commn on Correctional Health Care, Standards for Health Services in Jails J-65 (May 1999).

[18]See Vitek v. Jones, 445 U.S. 480, 494, 100 S. Ct. 1254, 63 L. Ed. 2d 552 (1980) (behavior modification program at mental hospital one of the critical factors in requiring procedural due process protections prior to transfer from prison to mental hospital). This may also apply to inmates on parole. Felce v. Fiedler, 974 F.2d 1484, 1495-96 (7th Cir. 1992).

[19]White v. Napoleon, 897 F.2d 103, 111-115 (3d Cir. 1990). See also U.S. Dept of Justice, Federal Standards for Prisons and Jails §§ 5.44, 5.51 (1980); ABA Standards for Criminal Justice § 23.5-5 (1986); American Correctional Assn, Standards for Adult Correctional Institutions, Standard 3-4372 (1990); National Commn on Correctional Health Care, Standards for Health Services in Jails J-68, J-69 (1987); Commission on Accreditation for Corrections, Certification Standards for Health Care Programs HC-082 (1989). But see Givens v. Jones, 900 F.2d 1229 (8th Cir. 1990).

Depending on the circumstances, forced invasion of the body by a physician can implicate other constitutional rights. Winston v. Lee, 470 U.S. 753, 105 S. Ct. 1611, 84 L. Ed. 2d 662 (1985) (surgical operation to remove bullet violated Fourth Amendment).

§ 3:23

grappled with several other forced treatment issues, including such diverse issues as whether inmates can be force fed if they are in danger of dying while on a hunger strike[20] and whether inmates can be forced to undergo tuberculosis testing.[21] The weight of authority is that inmates can be compelled in both circumstances so long as under the *Turner v. Safley* analysis there is sufficient reason offered for the intrusion and so long as

---

[20]See, e.g., Grand Jury Subpoena John Doe v. U.S., 150 F.3d 170 (2d Cir. 1998) (holding that a civil contemnor could be force-fed when his life would otherwise be in danger; Court of Appeals held that the prison was responsible for the plaintiff's care while incarcerated and other compelling governmental interests such as preservation of life, prevention of suicide, and enforcement of prison security, order and discipline outweighed the constitutional rights asserted by the plaintiff); In re Soliman, 134 F. Supp. 2d 1238 (N.D. Ala. 2001) (holding that Immigration and Naturalization Service could force feed a detainee who was not terminally ill; court held that force-feeding otherwise healthy prisoners who are starving themselves furthers valid penological interests, as long as safe intravenous type procedures are used); Laurie v. Senecal, 666 A.2d 806 (R.I. 1995) (court issued prison officials a preliminary injunction allowing officials to force-feed inmate under direction of prison physician, finding that inmate who did not have terminal illness did not have the right to end his life by starvation).

[21]McCormick v. Stalder, 105 F.3d 1059 (5th Cir. 1997) (holding that inmate who was forced to undergo prophylactic treatment because of a previous positive tuberculosis test failed to state substantive and procedural due process violations; court held that the prison's course of treatment was rationally related to fulfilling the prison's objective of preventing the spread of tuberculosis); Hasenmeier-McCarthy v. Rose, 986 F. Supp. 464 (S.D. Ohio 1998) (holding that the test was for the protection of the plaintiff's and other inmates' health). But see Jolly v Coughlin, 1995 WL 495799 (S.D.N.Y. 1995) (granting preliminary injunction against continued keeplock status of an inmate for refusal to take a tuberculosis test; court found that the plaintiff was in danger of substantial harm due to physical ailments acquired as a result of the keeplock, and the order was therefore excessive). Cf. State ex rel. Schuetzle v. Vogel, 537 N.W.2d 358, 66 A.L.R.5th 707 (N.D. 1995) (holding that prison officials could require that diabetic inmate submit to testing for blood sugar and administer food, insulin and other medication under direction of prison doctor if inmate's health was in danger).

MEDICAL CARE § 3:24

the inmate's health is not jeopardized by the procedure.

§ 3:24 Prison Co-Payment Plans For Medical Care

In recent years some states have imposed new rules that require prisoners in certain situations to pay for the costs of their medical care. These so-called "inmate co-payment" systems have now been implemented through legislation or administrative directive in at least 25 states.[1] The typical program automatically deducts from an inmate trust account a "nominal" fee for each medical visit, service, or cost of a prescribed drug or medicine. The fee is usually a charge of from one to five dollars. While the charge might seem small, in the prison world, where pay for inmate work is typically a fraction of the minimum wage, these charges in reality are substantial.[2] At inmate wages, a fee of two dollars might take the better part of a day or more to

---

[Section 3:24]

[1]See, e.g., Ariz Rev Stat Ann 31-161; Alaska Stat 33.30.028; Cal Penal Code 5007.5; Fla Stat Ann 945.6037; Ga Code Ann 42-5-51; Ill Ann Stat ch 125 para. 20; Ky Rev Stat Ann 24A.191; La Rev Stat Ann 705; Md Ann Code, Corr. Services § 5-405; Mich Comp Laws Ann 801.310; Minn Stat Ann 645.15; Miss Code Ann 47-5-179; Nev Rev Stat 211.2415; NH Stat Ann 622:31; NJ Stat Ann 30:7E-1-6; Ohio Rev Code Ann 341.06; Okla Stat Ann tit 531; Pa Cons Stat Ann 1013; SC Code Ann 24-13-80; Tenn Code Ann 41-4-115; Tex Code Crim Proc Ann art. 104.002; Utah Code Ann 64-13-30; Wash Rev Code Ann 70.48.130; W Va Code 7-8-2; Wis Stat Ann 302.38. For a discussion of Georgia's prisoner medical co-payment statute see Allison Chance Gabrielsen, Jails: Provide for Recoupment of Money From Inmates for Medical Services Provided to Inmates Not Eligible for Health Benefits, 13 Ga St U L Rev 273 (1996).

[2]See, e.g., Blaise v. McKinney, 187 F.3d 640 (8th Cir. 1999) (dismissing inmate's § 1983 challenge to the state's "pay for stay" incarceration fee and the medical co-payment fee, the court noted that the Eighth Amendment's prohibition against cruel and unusual punishment requires prisons to provide basic medical care to inmates, but does not require medical care to be provided at no cost); McLeod v. Henderson, 729 So. 2d 393 (Fla. 1999) (upholding Florida statute requiring payment of fee for medical services). For

§ 3:24   Rights of Prisoners, Third Edition

earn.

The purpose of these policies is not necessarily to transfer the full burden of health care costs to an inmate. Rather, the stated goal is to contain health care costs by imposing upon inmates a financial disincentive to use medical care. For instance, the purpose of a New Jersey prison inmate co-payment statute[3] was described as working to "partially defray the cost of inmates' health care and to reduce the incidence of overutilization."[4]

Under some, but not all, of these plans, inmates are not charged for certain services, such as emergency care or physician-ordered follow-up visits, nor are they charged for services offered to the entire prison population, such as entering physical examinations or regular inoculations. Further, some plan limitations are placed upon the amount of money that can be deducted from an inmate's account to pay for medical services.[5]

This ensures that the inmate is left with some funds to purchase necessities from the prison commissary. In each plan, moreover, provision is made for medical care without payment for inmates who are unable at the time to tender the co-payment.

Not surprisingly these co-payment plans have been challenged on a variety of constitutional grounds. So

---

a discussion of whether prison officials may charge inmates for health care, see Wesley P. Shields, Prison Health Care: Is It Proper to Charge Inmates For Health Services?, 32 Houston L Rev 271 (1995).

[3]NJSA § 30:7E-1-6.

[4]Mourning v. Correctional Medical Services, (CMS) of St. Louis, Mo., 300 N.J. Super. 213, 692 A.2d 529, 530 (App. Div. 1997). See also Reynolds v. Wagner, 936 F. Supp. 1216, 1219 (E.D. Pa. 1996), aff'd, 128 F.3d 166 (3d Cir. 1997) (at the Berks County Prison in Pennsylvania, the primary purpose of prison fee system was "to instill inmate responsibility and discourage abuse of sick call. . .not to generate revenue").

[5]Breakiron v. Neal, 166 F. Supp. 2d 1110 (N.D. Tex. 2001) (deducting from prisoner account for medical services does not violate due process property rights).

far, the challenges have not been successful. A copayment plan must comport with the Supreme Court's holding in *Estelle v Gamble*[6] that states are constitutionally obligated to provide health care for prisoners. Prison officials claim that co-payment schemes do not contradict this principle. To support the validity of these plans, they rely upon *City of Revere v. Massachusetts General Hospital.*[7]

In *City of Revere,* the Massachusetts General Hospital sought to recover from the City of Revere costs of medical care provided to an arrestee who was wounded by the city police during the course of an arrest. The Court held that the City of Revere was not required to reimburse the hospital for these costs. The city had discharged its constitutional duty to provide health care when the arrestee was taken to a hospital and treated for his injuries. According to the Court, "as long as the governmental entity ensures that the medical care needed is in fact provided, the Constitution does not dictate how the cost of that care should be allocated as between the entity and the provider of the care. That is a matter of state law."[8]

Courts have relied upon this precedent in upholding co-payment plans from Eighth Amendment attack. As one court stated, *City of Revere* stands for the proposition that "[a]lthough the government must provide medical care, the Supreme Court has never held the government must pay for it." Building on this notion, courts have held that if an inmate has funds to pay for a portion of his or her medical care, the state may seek

---

[6]Estelle v. Gamble, 429 U.S. 97, 97 S. Ct. 285, 50 L. Ed. 2d 251 (1976).

[7]City of Revere v. Massachusetts General Hosp., 463 U.S. 239, 103 S. Ct. 2979, 77 L. Ed. 2d 605 (1983).

[8]City of Revere v. Massachusetts General Hosp., 463 U.S. 239, 245, 103 S. Ct. 2979, 77 L. Ed. 2d 605 (1983).

§ 3:24   Rights of Prisoners, Third Edition

reimbursement.[9]

In each of the cases cited in the previous note, the courts noted that insolvent inmates were not denied access to health care because of an inability to pay, nor in any of the cases did the prisoner claim that he was denied or delayed access to health care. If, however, a "co-payment" system were to be implemented in a way that deprived an inmate of "meaningful access to health care" by discouraging inmates from seeking necessary care, a different case would be presented and the plan might very well run afoul of the Eighth Amendment.[10]

Challenges to co-payment systems have also been mounted on due process and equal protection grounds. For example, in *Reynolds v Wagner*,[11] the court rejected the plaintiffs' due process claim and held that the pro-

---

[9] See, e.g., Gardner v. Wilson, 959 F. Supp. 1224 (C.D. Cal. 1997); Mourning v. Correctional Medical Services, (CMS) of St. Louis, Mo., 300 N.J. Super. 213, 692 A.2d 529 (App. Div. 1997) (holding that statute mandating inmate co-payment of medical expenses did not raise Eighth Amendment or due process violations and finding that the statute furthered an important state objective of containing health care costs); Reynolds v. Wagner, 936 F. Supp. 1216 (E.D. Pa. 1996), aff'd, 128 F.3d 166 (3d Cir. 1997); Bihms v. Klevenhagen, 928 F. Supp. 717 (S.D. Tex. 1996); Turcios v. Dep't of Corrections, 1996 WL 193849 (N.D. Cal. 1996) (medical co-payment system did not violate the Eighth Amendment).

[10] Collins v. Romer, 962 F.2d 1508, 1513 (10th Cir. 1992) (a Colorado statute that, before it was amended, provided no exceptions for chronically ill inmates and inmates who constantly needed a physician's medical care might violate the Eighth Amendment because in operation it would have essentially denied indigent inmates medical care); Johnson v. Department of Public Safety and Correctional Services, 885 F. Supp. 817 (D. Md. 1995) (prison policy of co-payment requiring prisoners to contribute to the cost of their treatment was not an Eighth Amendment violation, where no prisoner who faced a substantial risk of danger was denied access to medical care because he could not pay).

[11] Reynolds v. Wagner, 936 F. Supp. 1216 (E.D. Pa. 1996), aff'd, 128 F.3d 166 (3d Cir. 1997).

cess due in a co-payment scheme was "minimal."[12] The court noted that the "taking of property is not involved in the normal sense of word. Inmate accounts are debited because inmates are purchasing something medical care on their own volition." The court distinguished this situation from the situation where an inmate's account may be involuntarily debited even though nothing had been purchased.

A final constitutional theory used to challenge medical co-payment policies is the Equal Protection Clause. Courts have rejected these claims, finding that since no suspect class or fundamental right is involved, the plans do not violate equal protection if they are supported by a rational basis, and the plans are grounded in the rational interest of the state in containing health care costs.[13]

In *Wagner,* inmates at Berks County Prison brought a class action where they challenged the policy, which charged them a fee for health care. They claimed that charging the fee constituted deliberate indifference to their medical needs. The policy instituted a three-dollar charge for a medical evaluation by a nurse. If the inmate was referred to a doctor there was no charge. If the inmate chose to see a doctor without a referral, there was a five-dollar fee. The five-dollar fee was waived if the doctor decided that the inmate should have been referred. There was no charge for follow-up visits, prescription medicine or, if deemed necessary, over-the-counter medicine. Prescreening psychiatric

---

[12]Reynolds v. Wagner, 936 F. Supp. 1216, 1228 (E.D. Pa. 1996), aff'd, 128 F.3d 166 (3d Cir. 1997).

[13]See, e.g., Hutchinson v. Belt, 957 F. Supp. 97 (W.D. La. 1996) (holding that the co-payment policy was rationally related to a legitimate governmental issue since it applied "negative reinforcement to the human tendency to overuse health care services by a third party"); Robinson v. Fauver, 932 F. Supp. 639 (D.N.J. 1996) (requiring inmates who received money from outside sources to pay for medical care did not violate the Equal Protection Clause; state furthered legitimate governmental interest in "defraying the burgeoning cost of inmate medical care").

§ 3:24   Rights of Prisoners, Third Edition

evaluation and emergency services were also free. When a medical service was provided, the inmate was required to sign a "medical service fee form." If the inmate did not have money in his account, treatment was still provided and the fee was deducted, leaving a negative balance. Fifty percent of the inmate's incoming funds were then used to satisfy the debt. The District Court held that there is no constitutional right to free health care. The Court of Appeals affirmed the judgment for the defendants.[14]

These co-payment systems are generally set up by state statute and although the statutes have come under attack for being either facially unconstitutional or unconstitutional as applied,[15] the courts have apparently upheld the validity of the systems so long as they do not deprive indigent prisoners of necessary care.[16] Legal scholars, however, have questioned the stance of the courts on this issue and have argued that both co-payment systems and managed health care in prison can effectively impose cruel and unusual punishment.[17]

---

[14]Reynolds v. Wagner, 128 F.3d 166 (3d Cir. 1997) (court also held that an absence of a Spanish-language handbook did not create a notice problem and was not unconstitutional where Spanish-speaking staff were available).

[15]*Id.* at 171, (3d Cir. 1997); Reynolds v. Wagner, 936 F. Supp. 1216, 1228 (E.D. Pa. 1996), aff'd, 128 F.3d 166 (3d Cir. 1997).

[16]Canell v. Multnomah County, 141 F. Supp. 2d 1046 (D. Or. 2001) (charging for care is not unconstitutional where indigents are treated regardless of ability to pay).

[17]Ira P. Robbins, Criminal Law: Managed Health Care In Prisons As Cruel And Unusual Punishment, 90 J. Crim. L. & Criminology 195 (1999); James McNally, Note: Inmate Payment of Health Care-Divisiveness in the Federal Courts in the Application of the Estelle Standard and City of Revere v. Massachusetts General Hospital, 24 N.E. J. on Crim. & Civ. Con. 687 (1998).

Chapter 4

Equal Protection Clause-Discrimination Issues

Research References

Nahmod, Civil Rights and Civil Liberties Litigation: The Law of Section 1983 §§ 4:36, 4:37, 4:60, 4:61

Cook, Constitutional Rights of the Accused (3d ed.) §§ 1:13 to 1:16

Prisoners and the Law, Ch 1B, 5, 14

Am. Jur. 2d, Penal and Correctional Institutions §§ 26 to 33

Civil Rights ⚖104, 135; Constitutional Law ⚖82(13), 209, 223, 224; Federal Courts ⚖181

A.L.R. Index: Equal Protection of the Law; Prisons and Prisoners

Equal Protection and Due Process Clause Challenges Based on Racial Discrimination--Supreme Court Cases, 172 A.L.R. Fed. 1

What constitutes reverse or majority race or national origin discrimination violative of Federal Constitution or statutes--nonemployment cases, 152 A.L.R. Fed. 1

> **KeyCite®:** Cases and other legal materials listed in KeyCite Scope can be researched through West Group's KeyCite service on Westlaw®. Use KeyCite to check citations for form, parallel references, prior and later history, and comprehensive citator information, including citations to other decisions and secondary materials.

§ 4:1 Introduction
§ 4:2 The Theory of Equal Protection and Equal Protection standards
§ 4:3 Equal Protection Applied
§ 4:4 —Racial Discrimination
§ 4:5 —Sexual Discrimination

§ 4:1 Introduction

This chapter will examine the applicability of the

Equal Protection Clause of the Fourteenth Amendment to prisons. The Fourteenth Amendment prohibits the government from denying "any person within [its] jurisdiction the equal protection of the laws."[1] The purpose of the Equal Protection Clause is to guarantee "that similar individuals will be dealt with in a similar manner by the government."[2] Equal protection claims arise when, without adequate justification, similarly situated persons are treated differently by a state or government entity, or when dissimilarly situated persons are treated alike.

"Prisoners do not surrender their rights to equal protection at the prison gate."[3] In the prison context, equal protection arguments are advanced when certain prisoners claim that they are being treated unfairly as compared to other similarly situated inmates.[4] For example, an equal protection question might arise if

---

[Section 4:1]

[1] U.S. Const. Amend. XIV.

[2] John E. Nowak & Ronald D. Rotunda, Constitutional Law § 14.2, at 634 (6th ed. 2000).

[3] Williams v. Lane, 851 F.2d 867, 881, 11 Fed. R. Serv. 3d 753 (7th Cir. 1988); see also Hosna v. Groose, 80 F.3d 298, 303 (8th Cir. 1996) ("The inmates bringing this action have a right to equal protection.").

[4] The Equal Protection Clause only applies if the groups who are being compared are similarly situated. See, e.g., Hansen v. Rimel, 104 F.3d 189 (8th Cir. 1997) (hearing impaired inmate claimed prison officials violated the Equal Protection Clause by failing to provide a special telephone adapted for his disability; court held that for purposes of accessing a telephone, the plaintiff was not similarly situated to inmates who did not have hearing impairments; since he was not similarly situated there could be no equal protection violation); Anderson v. Vasquez, 827 F. Supp. 617 (N.D. Cal. 1992), aff'd in part, rev'd in part on other grounds, 28 F.3d 104 (9th Cir. 1994) (no equal protection violation where death row inmates were not allowed conjugal visits, but "lifers" were, because there was no showing that lifers were similarly situated to death row inmates); Matter of Galvez, 79 Wash. App. 655, 904 P.2d 790 (Div. 3 1995) (prison officials did not violate the Equal Protection Clause where inmates in administrative segregation for disciplinary reasons were denied good time credit, but inmates in

EQUAL PROTECTION § 4:1

one religious group in a prison is denied access to the prison chapel, but other more favored groups are given entry. Less frequently, inmates maintain that they are being discriminated against vis-à-vis non-prisoners.

An equal protection argument may be combined with a charge that the inmates in question are being denied substantive constitutional rights. Thus, a religious sect that is not permitted to hold services similar to those allowed more conventional religious groups may claim a violation not only of its Fourteenth Amendment right to equal protection, but also of its First Amendment right of religious freedom.[5] The substantive constitutional dimensions of such claims will be examined in other chapters.[6] This chapter will examine what additional support, if any, the equal protection claim adds to the case.

The Equal Protection Clause has the most relevance in prison cases involving race or sex discrimination. Issues of race and gender discrimination loom large in prisons. Indeed, for many years, prisons were racially segregated, and today virtually all prisons remain sexually segregated. Following a brief, but seminal, 1968 Supreme Court decision,[7] the door was open for lower courts to critically examine racially discriminatory rules

---

administrative segregation for their own protection were given good time credit; court found that the two groups were not similarly situated); but see Merritt v. Hawk, 153 F. Supp. 2d 1216, 1225 (D. Colo. 2001) (plaintiff's allegations of racial and anti-semitic epithets were sufficient to suggest he was treated differently than similarly situated inmates; thus, the court denied defendants' motion for summary judgment on plaintiff's equal protection claim).

[5]This was the claim in the landmark opinion of Cruz v. Beto, 405 U.S. 319, 92 S. Ct. 1079, 31 L. Ed. 2d 263 (1972) discussed in Ch 6.

[6]In regard to the cited example, see Ch 6.

[7]Lee v. Washington, 390 U.S. 333, 88 S. Ct. 994, 19 L. Ed. 2d 1212 (1968).

and practices in penal institutions.[8] Although lagging somewhat behind in its initial development, and although major questions remain unanswered, there is a body of law examining claims of sex discrimination in prison.[9] These areas remain ripe for continuing litigation. Before the specific instances of discrimination are tackled, a brief review of equal protection theory and standards is in order.

§ 4:2 The Theory of Equal Protection and Equal Protection standards

Research References

West's Key Number Digest, Constitutional Law ⚬―209

The Equal Protection Clause prohibits the government from unfairly discriminating between equivalent groups. It does not prevent the government from drawing lines nor does it invariably guarantee precise equality in treatment between groups.[1] The government may make distinctions if it has sufficient reasons for doing so and if it is not acting in an invidious or arbitrary manner. The key to determining whether the government, in treating one group differently from another, has stepped over the line is to ascertain the level of justification that the government will be required to provide to explain its actions.

No single standard defines the level of justification that is required. Instead, the Supreme Court has articulated three distinct standards. The first, and most lenient standard from the standpoint of prison administrators, is the rational basis standard. It requires only that the classification be drawn for the purpose of serving a legitimate governmental interest and that the

---

[8]See § 4:4.

[9]See § 4:5.

[Section 4:2]

[1]Laurence H. Tribe, American Constitutional Law 1437 (2d ed 1988) ("any universal demand for sameness would prevent government from discriminating in the public interest").

§ 4:2

means chosen actually serve that interest.[2] In marked contrast, the second standard, the strict scrutiny standard, commands a close connection between the legislation or practice under examination and a compelling state interest.[3] In addition, the regulation in question generally must be narrowly drawn to encompass only the recognized state interests.[4] In between these two positions lies the third standard, the intermediate standard of review; under it, there must be a substantial relationship to an important (although not compelling) state interest.[5]

The standard that applies in a non-prison setting

---

[2]See, e.g., San Antonio Independent School Dist. v. Rodriguez, 411 U.S. 1, 93 S. Ct. 1278, 36 L. Ed. 2d 16 (1973); Rinaldi v. Yeager, 384 U.S. 305, 86 S. Ct. 1497, 16 L. Ed. 2d 577 (1966); Lindsley v. Natural Carbonic Gas Co., 220 U.S. 61, 31 S. Ct. 337, 55 L. Ed. 369 (1911); Metropolitan Life Ins. Co. v. Ward, 470 U.S. 869, 105 S. Ct. 1676, 84 L. Ed. 2d 751 (1985); Gregory v. Ashcroft, 501 U.S. 452, 111 S. Ct. 2395, 115 L. Ed. 2d 410 (1991); Nordlinger v. Hahn, 505 U.S. 1, 112 S. Ct. 2326, 120 L. Ed. 2d 1 (1992); F.C.C. v. Beach Communications, Inc., 508 U.S. 307, 113 S. Ct. 2096, 124 L. Ed. 2d 211 (1993).

[3]See, e.g., Graham v. Richardson, 403 U.S. 365, 91 S. Ct. 1848, 29 L. Ed. 2d 534 (1971); Kramer v. Union Free School Dist. No. 15, 395 U.S. 621, 89 S. Ct. 1886, 23 L. Ed. 2d 583 (1969); Loving v. Virginia, 388 U.S. 1, 87 S. Ct. 1817, 18 L. Ed. 2d 1010 (1967); Shapiro v. Thompson, 394 U.S. 618, 89 S. Ct. 1322, 22 L. Ed. 2d 600 (1969) (overruled in part on other grounds by, Edelman v. Jordan, 415 U.S. 651, 94 S. Ct. 1347, 39 L. Ed. 2d 662 (1974); Adarand Constructors, Inc. v. Pena, 515 U.S. 200, 115 S. Ct. 2097, 132 L. Ed. 2d 158 (1995); Miller v. Johnson, 515 U.S. 900, 115 S. Ct. 2475, 132 L. Ed. 2d 762 (1995).

[4]See, e.g., Roe v. Wade, 410 U.S. 113, 93 S. Ct. 705, 35 L. Ed. 2d 147 (1973); Griswold v. Connecticut, 381 U.S. 479, 85 S. Ct. 1678, 14 L. Ed. 2d 510 (1965); Aptheker v. Secretary of State, 378 U.S. 500, 84 S. Ct. 1659, 12 L. Ed. 2d 992 (1964); Bush v. Vera, 517 U.S. 952, 116 S. Ct. 1941, 135 L. Ed. 2d 248 (1996).

[5]See, e.g., Califano v. Goldfarb, 430 U.S. 199, 97 S. Ct. 1021, 51 L. Ed. 2d 270 (1977); Craig v. Boren, 429 U.S. 190, 97 S. Ct. 451, 50 L. Ed. 2d 397 (1976); Plyler v. Doe, 457 U.S. 202, 102 S. Ct. 2382, 72 L. Ed. 2d 786, 4 Ed. Law Rep. 953 (1982); Mississippi University for Women v. Hogan, 458 U.S. 718, 102 S. Ct. 3331, 73 L. Ed. 2d 1090, 5 Ed. Law Rep. 103 (1982); U.S. v. Virginia, 518

§ 4:2

depends on the nature of the class involved or the interest affected. Under traditional equal protection theory, the rational basis test is most commonly applied to regulations in the social and economic field when nonfundamental rights are at issue, and when the regulations do not exclude "suspect groups" such as racial or religious minorities.[6] Strict scrutiny will be the appropriate test when fundamental rights are at stake or a suspect classification is involved.[7] Finally, under current law, the intermediate standard applies to gender-based classifications.[8] Commentators have suggested that the intermediate standard may also apply in cases involving important, but not fundamental, rights.[9] Whether to raise an equal protection claim-rather than one focusing solely on violation of a substantive right-depends in part, therefore, on an assessment of the standard of review used to resolve the equal protection claim. The reason is that the likelihood of a prisoner's suit resulting in relief on an equal

---

U.S. 515, 116 S. Ct. 2264, 135 L. Ed. 2d 735 (1996); I.N.S. v. Nam Nguyen, 533 U.S. 944, 121 S. Ct. 2582, 150 L. Ed. 2d 743 (2001).

[6]See, e.g., Dandridge v. Williams, 397 U.S. 471, 90 S. Ct. 1153, 25 L. Ed. 2d 491 (1970); San Antonio Independent School Dist. v. Rodriguez, 411 U.S. 1, 93 S. Ct. 1278, 36 L. Ed. 2d 16 (1973); Lindsley v. Natural Carbonic Gas Co., 220 U.S. 61, 31 S. Ct. 337, 55 L. Ed. 369 (1911); U.S. R.R. Retirement Bd. v. Fritz, 449 U.S. 166, 101 S. Ct. 453, 66 L. Ed. 2d 368 (1980); Romer v. Evans, 517 U.S. 620, 116 S. Ct. 1620, 134 L. Ed. 2d 855, 109 Ed. Law Rep. 539 (1996).

[7]See, e.g., Police Dept. of City of Chicago v. Mosley, 408 U.S. 92, 92 S. Ct. 2286, 33 L. Ed. 2d 212 (1972) (free speech); Shapiro v. Thompson, 394 U.S. 618, 89 S. Ct. 1322, 22 L. Ed. 2d 600 (1969) (overruled in part on other grounds by, Edelman v. Jordan, 415 U.S. 651, 94 S. Ct. 1347, 39 L. Ed. 2d 662 (1974) (right to travel); Loving v. Virginia, 388 U.S. 1, 87 S. Ct. 1817, 18 L. Ed. 2d 1010 (1967) (right to marry).

[8]See, e.g., Califano v. Goldfarb, 430 U.S. 199, 97 S. Ct. 1021, 51 L. Ed. 2d 270 (1977); Craig v. Boren, 429 U.S. 190, 97 S. Ct. 451, 50 L. Ed. 2d 397 (1976).

[9]See, e.g., L. Tribe, American Constitutional Law 1591-92 (2d ed 1988) (contending that the intermediate standard should apply to cases involving children or "childhood").

EQUAL PROTECTION § 4:3

protection claim can very well turn on the stringency of the equal protection standard applied by the court. However, if the *Turner v. Safley*[10] standard is applied to even equal protection claims, then the nature of the interest that an inmate claims does not matter. That issue is discussed below.[11]

§ 4:3 Equal Protection Applied

Of course, to invoke the protections of the Equal Protection Clause the plaintiff must present proof that the action complained of is one that discriminates against a definable group of inmates. Where there is no credible support for such a claim, there is no valid equal protection claim to even consider.[1] When a nonfundamental right is involved and when the classifica-

---

[10]Turner v. Safley, 482 U.S. 78, 107 S. Ct. 2254, 96 L. Ed. 2d 64 (1987). See Ch 5.

[11]See § 4:3.

[Section 4:3]

[1]See, e.g., Hansard v. Barrett, 980 F.2d 1059 (6th Cir. 1992) (equal protection claim rejected where there was no evidence of prison policy against employing homosexual inmates, but where one homosexual inmate was denied employment for valid disciplinary reasons); Lewis v. Cook County Dept. of Corrections, 28 F. Supp. 2d 1073 (N.D. Ill. 1998) (county inmate alleging discrimination on account of inmate's homosexuality, brought § 1983 action against correctional officers after they terminated him from his position as law library cleaner due to a "hickey"' on his neck; the court held that the corrections officers' conduct did not violate the inmate's equal protection rights since the motivation for that treatment was not inmate's alleged homosexuality, rather it was the mark on his neck); Malsh v. Austin, 901 F. Supp. 757 (S.D. N.Y. 1995) (holding that inmate failed to allege that prison officials conspired against him based upon his class); Mathis v. Sauser, 942 P.2d 1117 (Alaska 1997) (no proof that policy which prevents inmate from possessing computer printers in their cells is discriminatory); Hester v. McBride, 966 F. Supp. 765 (N.D. Ind. 1997) (inmate failed to show that he was singled out for harsher punishment than other inmates); Alameen v. Coughlin, 892 F. Supp. 440 (E.D. N.Y. 1995) (Muslim inmates failed to state a cause of action under the Equal Protection Clause where they alleged that prison regulation denied them the right to possess black dhikr

§ 4:3   Rights of Prisoners, Third Edition

tion does not single out a "suspect group," the rational basis standard will be applied.[2] Prisoners have not been considered by the courts to be a suspect class.[3] Therefore, when a prison regulation does not implicate fundamental constitutional rights and does not adversely impact on racial minorities or women, there is no doubt that courts will apply the rational basis test.

---

beads; court noted that the prison regulation prohibited all religious beads, including rosary beads). See also Lee v. Akture, 827 F. Supp. 556 (E.D. Wis. 1993) (refusing to rule on whether equal protection would be violated by providing better medical care to medically insured inmates than to inmates without medical insurance when there was no credible evidence in the record that the presence or absence of insurance controlled receipt of needed medical care in the prison).

[2]See, e.g., San Antonio Independent School Dist. v. Rodriguez, 411 U.S. 1, 93 S. Ct. 1278, 36 L. Ed. 2d 16 (1973).

[3]See, e.g., Pierce v. King, 918 F. Supp. 932, 15 A.D.D. 246 (E.D. N.C. 1996), aff'd, 131 F.3d 136 (4th Cir. 1997), cert. granted, judgment vacated, 525 U.S. 802, 119 S. Ct. 33, 142 L. Ed. 2d 25 (1998) (disabled inmate failed to state a claim under Equal Protection Clause where he alleged that prison officials failed to provide disabled inmate with an opportunity to participate in specific work release program where inmates maintain the garden at the Governor's Mansion; court found that disabled inmate was not a member of a suspect class and stated that prison officials had a rational basis for denying this employment); Seltzer-Bey v. Delo, 66 F.3d 961 (8th Cir. 1995); Pryor v. Brennan, 914 F.2d 921, 923 (7th Cir. 1990); Beck v. Symington, 972 F. Supp. 532 (D. Ariz. 1997) (Prisoners and indigents are not a suspect class); Thomas v. Brown, 824 F. Supp. 160 (N.D. Ind. 1993); Harrison v. Bent County Correctional Facility, 24 Fed. Appx. 965 (10th Cir. 2001) (neither prisoners nor indigents constituted a suspect class so as to warrant strict scrutiny review of equal protection claim challenging prison policy limiting advances for postage and copying costs to prisoners whose prison accounts were more than $300 in arrears); Brown v. Wisconsin Dept. of Corrections, 26 Fed. Appx. 548 (7th Cir. 2001) (Court found that prisoner was not part of a suspect class and, thus, applied the rational basis test); Manning v. Bolden, 25 Fed. Appx. 269 (6th Cir. 2001) (inmate put in administrative segregation did not state a valid equal protection claim by stating that he was being treated differently from other inmates; inmate had to show that the segregation was due to his membership of a suspect class).

§ 4:3

Under this test, courts will uphold the regulation unless the distinction that the prison policy makes is either irrational or arbitrary.[4] Put another way, an equal protection violation will not be made out when nonfundamental rights are infringed by government classifications if the government has "articulated a legitimate governmental purpose" for the classification and the classification bears a "rational relation" to that purpose.[5] The purpose of this test is not to test the wisdom of the choices made by government. As long as there is some rationality in the classification, it will be upheld even if it is "seemingly unwise."[6]

Two types of claims are common here. One raises the issue of whether differences in treatment between groups of prisoners are justified; the other involves distinctions between prisoners and nonprisoners. Regarding the former, under this lax test, most official actions are sustained.[7] For example, denial of access to temporary release programs or early release on parole,

---

[4]See, e.g., McGinnis v. Royster, 410 U.S. 263, 93 S. Ct. 1055, 35 L. Ed. 2d 282 (1973); Sellers v. Ciccone, 530 F.2d 199 (8th Cir. 1976); Chapman v. Plageman, 417 F. Supp. 906 (W.D. Va. 1976); Beatham v. Manson, 369 F. Supp. 783 (D. Conn. 1973).

[5]See, e.g., Shapiro v. Thompson, 394 U.S. 618, 89 S. Ct. 1322, 22 L. Ed. 2d 600 (1969) (overruled in part on other grounds by, Edelman v. Jordan, 415 U.S. 651, 94 S. Ct. 1347, 39 L. Ed. 2d 662 (1974); Loving v. Virginia, 388 U.S. 1, 87 S. Ct. 1817, 18 L. Ed. 2d 1010 (1967).

[6]Klinger v. Nebraska Dept. of Correctional Services, 824 F. Supp. 1374 (D. Neb. 1993), order rev'd on other grounds, 31 F.3d 727 (8th Cir. 1994). See also Parham v. Hughes, 441 U.S. 347, 351, 99 S. Ct. 1742, 60 L. Ed. 2d 269 (1979) ("The Constitution presumes that, absent some reason to infer antipathy, even improvident decisions will eventually be rectified by the democratic process and judicial intervention is generally unwarranted, no matter how unwisely we may think a political branch has acted.").

[7]See, e.g., Keeton v. State of Okl., 32 F.3d 451 (10th Cir. 1994) (holding that there was no violation of equal protection to exempt from prison release provisions, under Oklahoma Prison Overcrowding Emergency Powers Act, inmates who have been convicted of crimes for which maximum security treatment is appropriate); Farmer v. Hawk-Sawyer, 69 F. Supp. 2d 120 (D.D.C. 1999) (uphold-

§ 4:3

when inmates with similar records are given these

ing from an equal protection challenge a policy that required preincarceration hormone therapy before it would be continued in prison; the distinction between prisoners who had had this therapy prior to prison and those who had not was reasonable); Daniel v. Rolfs, 29 F. Supp. 2d 1184 (E.D. Wash. 1998) (distinction in eligibility for participation in Extended Family Visitation (EFV) program between inmates who were legally married to offenders prior to incarceration for the current convictions, and those who were not, was rational); Marshall v. Reno, 915 F. Supp. 426 (D.D.C. 1996) (Federal Bureau of Prisons policy which denies access to community and minimum security facilities to aliens who have not been domiciled in the United States for five years or have history of stable employment does not violate equal protection); Coleman v. McGinnis, 843 F. Supp. 320 (E.D. Mich. 1994) (holding that inmates failed to establish an equal protection violation where prisoners from two particular cellblocks and inmates in administrative segregation were not allowed to participate on a prisoners benefit fund board; court found that the prison had a legitimate interest in organizing the board without unnecessary disruption that would be caused by the inclusion of the inmates in the segregated groups); Johnson v. Texas Dept. of Criminal Justice, 910 F. Supp. 1208 (W.D. Tex. 1995), judgment rev'd in part, vacated in part on other grounds, 110 F.3d 299 (5th Cir. 1997) (parole board did not violate equal protection where they considered completion of furlough as a positive factor in parole decisions; out-of-state inmates alleged that this was unconstitutional because they were ineligible for furlough because they had no family in the area); Petition of Fogle, 128 Wash. 2d 56, 904 P.2d 722 (1995) (county jail officials acted within their statutory discretion and did not violate equal protection where they granted pre-trial detainees fewer early release credits; court noted that the jail officials explained that the policy was rationally related to maintaining inmate discipline); Vargas v. Pataki, 899 F. Supp. 96 (N.D. N.Y. 1995) (prison regulation which prohibited inmates convicted of homicide from participating in work release did not violate the Equal Protection Clause; ourt found that policy was rationally related to public safety); Riddle v. Mondragon, 83 F.3d 1197 (10th Cir. 1996) (classification of sex offenders as violent offenders without regard to the specific offense, application of longer sentences for sex offenders than other violent offenders, and restriction on pre-sentencing and post-sentencing programs available to inmates were all acceptable and did not violate Equal Protection Clause, since they were reasonably related to legitimate public safety and security interests); Knox v. Lanham, 895 F. Supp. 750 (D. Md. 1995), aff'd, 76 F.3d

§ 4:3

benefits, have been held not to violate equal protection.[8] In addition, courts have refused to upset pay dif-

---

377 (4th Cir. 1996) (court upheld Division of Corrections directive which prohibited inmates sentenced to life from participating in family leave and work release programs; court found that the policy did not violate equal protection since inmates sentenced to life constituted a greater security and escape risk than inmates sentenced under lesser charges); Pryor-El v. Kelly, 892 F. Supp. 261 (D.D.C. 1995) (inmate failed to state a claim where he alleged that prison officials violated equal protection by restricting the quantity of property inmate could possess in his cell; court noted that prison officials implemented the action because they believed that inmate was stealing from prison supply truck and then reselling goods to other inmates); More v. Farrier, 984 F.2d 269 (8th Cir. 1993) (holding that it is not a violation of equal protection for disabled inmates to be denied in-cell cable TV while nondisabled inmates are given that privilege). See also Mahoney v. Carter, 938 S.W.2d 575 (Ky. 1997) (veto of inmate's reclassification from a medium to minimum security facility did not violate the Equal Protection Clause of the Fourteenth Amendment; plaintiff alleged that this veto subjected him to a different standard than other similarly situated prisoners and that no rational basis for such treatment existed; in rejecting the inmate's claim, the court held that the prison's duty in protecting the safety and security of the facility was sufficient justification to satisfy rational basis review); Brooks v. State of Okl., 862 F. Supp. 342 (W.D. Okla. 1994), aff'd, 92 F.3d 1196 (10th Cir. 1996) (holding that the Oklahoma Prison Overcrowding Emergency Powers Act, Okla. Stat. Ann. Tit. 57, § 570 (West 1994), which granted emergency time credits to accelerate releases, did not violate the Equal Protection Clause when violent offenders were denied the time credits; court found that there was a legitimate penological interest in distinguishing between violent and non-violent offenders); But see Page v. Wylie, 3 Fed. Appx. 638 (9th Cir. 2001) (plaintiff was civilly confined after serving a criminal sentence; he claimed his equal protection rights were violated because upon his release from civil confinement, he was not provided funds similar to those provided to paroled inmates; because the plaintiff claimed he was similarly situated to the paroled inmates, the court held a valid equal rights claim was stated, and it reversed the trial court's dismissal of the equal rights claim).

[8]See, e.g., Martino v. Gard, 526 F. Supp. 958 (E.D. N.Y. 1981) (work release); Rowe v. Cuyler, 534 F. Supp. 297 (E.D. Pa. 1982), aff'd, 696 F.2d 985 (3d Cir. 1982) (early parole).

§ 4:3   Rights of Prisoners, Third Edition

ferentials between two prisons or to hold that the rehabilitative programs held in one prison must be duplicated in another.[9] Even challenges to gross discrepancies of treatment which can often occur between treatment of persons in the general population and those in protective custody units or on death rows, with some notable exceptions,[10] by and large have been unsuccessful on equal protection grounds.[11] For this

---

[9]See, e.g., Hrbek v. Farrier, 787 F.2d 414 (8th Cir. 1986) (differential treatment of wages of prisoners and nonprisoners did not violate equal protection); Williams v. Manson, 499 F. Supp. 773 (D. Conn. 1980) (pay differentials); McLamore v. State, 257 S.C. 413, 186 S.E.2d 250 (1972) (rehabilitation programs).

[10]Faver v. Bayh, 689 N.E.2d 727 (Ind. Ct. App. 1997) (inmates in general population received state pay of $0.65 per day for participation in educational or vocational programs; inmates involuntarily placed in protective custody also received state pay while those placed there voluntarily did not; all prisoners in protective custody were also not allowed to participate in education programs; court held that the state's refusal to pay inmates voluntarily placed in protective custody was unlawful, and further held that the plaintiffs were entitled to the state pay; it was also determined that some form of education program should be available to the plaintiffs); but see Cohn v. Strawhorn, 721 N.E.2d 342 (Ind. Ct. App. 1999) (plaintiffs, prisoners in department of correction's county jails, instituted a suit alleging entitlement to certain educational and substance abuse treatment programs and a violation of their constitutional rights by the denial of these programs; plaintiffs asserted that inmates of DOC prisons had the ability to access educational and substance abuse programs in order to obtain reductions in their sentences while, at the same time, many DOC jail prisoners did not have access to educational and/or substance abuse treatment programming and could not take advantage of these sentence reduction statutes; court held that "Faver, which compared the disparate treatment of prisoners confined in different parts of the same institution, constitutes little, if any, precedental authority for the present comparison of prisoners confined to DOC institutions and the DOC Jail Prisoners"; court applied a rational basis standard and held that the plaintiffs' constitutional rights had not been violated).

[11]See, e.g., Hosna v. Groose, 80 F.3d 298 (8th Cir. 1996) (upholding a host of restrictions on inmates in disciplinary and administrative segregation, including property restrictions and prohibitions

reason, commentators have stated that prisoners "cannot expect to gain much help" from the Equal Protection Clause.[12]

However, there have been some exceptions. One court, for example, found a state policy of providing free transportation to state, but not to federal, court proceedings irrational.[13] Another court found that the state was arbitrary in its treatment of state prisoners who were held more than 90 days in local jails vis-à-vis similarly situated inmates who were held in state facilities.[14] Another court held that the disparate treatment of protective custody inmates could not be justified by the "reflexive, rote assertions that existing condi-

---

on access to prison school, religious services, law library, and telephone use and restriction of inmates' access to the canteen, visitation, and outdoor exercise; restrictions were all rationally related to prison security); Robinson v. Illinois State Correctional Center (Stateville) Warden, 890 F. Supp. 715 (N.D. Ill. 1995) (restrictions on the type of commissary items which inmates in segregation may purchase do not violate Equal Protection Clause; court noted that inmates in general population and segregation are not similarly situated); Williams v. Manson, 499 F. Supp. 773 (D. Conn. 1980) (pay differentials); Bullock v. Horn, 720 A.2d 1079 (Pa. Commw. Ct. 1998) (discriminatory exercise policy and practice that denied inmate petitioner access to basketballs, handballs and weights while allowing other restricted housing unit prisoners access did not violate Equal Protection Clause); Tilley v. State, 912 P.2d 1140 (Wyo. 1996) (prison officials did not violate the Equal Protection Clause where inmate was sentenced to seven consecutive one-year sentences rather than one seven-year sentence, which caused him to be placed in county jail rather than state prison, where inmates were provided with many rehabilitative programs; court found that inmate was sentenced in accordance with statute); McLamore v. State, 257 S.C. 413, 186 S.E.2d 250 (1972) (rehabilitation programs).

[12]Barbara B. Knight & Stephen T. Early, Jr., Prisoners' Rights in America 58 (1986). See also Daniel E. Manville, Prisoners' Self-Help Litigation Manual (1983) ("As a practical matter, it is very hard to win an equal protection claim in a prison case ").

[13]Matter of Warden of Wisconsin State Prison, 541 F.2d 177, 181-82 (7th Cir. 1976).

[14]Hill v. Hutto, 537 F. Supp. 1185 (E.D. Va. 1982).

tions are dictated by security concerns and that the cost of change is prohibitive.[15]

One explanation for the apparent inconsistency in these cases is that, in dealing with equal protection claims alleging discrimination between prisoners, courts sometimes fall into the trap of reasoning that if a state is not under a constitutional or statutory obligation to provide a particular service or privilege, it does not violate equal protection by providing it to some but not others. This was the rationale used by the court, referred to above, that held that a state program that provided rehabilitative programs at some, but not all, prisons did not violate equal protection.[16] Likewise, a federal district court reasoned that since pay for convict labor was a privilege, granting it to some while withholding it from others did not deny equal treatment.[17] Other recent cases continue with this trend.[18]

These decisions appear misguided, both from a

---

[15]Williams v. Lane, 851 F.2d 867, 886, 11 Fed. R. Serv. 3d 753 (7th Cir. 1988) (Flaum, J, concurring). See also Page v. Wylie, 3 Fed. Appx. 638 (9th Cir. 2001) (plaintiff was civilly confined after serving a criminal sentence; he claims his equal protection rights were violated because, upon his release from civil confinement, he was not provided funds similar to those provided to paroled inmates; because the plaintiff claimed he was similarly situated to the paroled inmates, the court held a valid equal rights claim was stated and reversed the trial court's dismissal of the equal rights claim); Quartararo v. Catterson, 917 F. Supp. 919 (E.D. N.Y. 1996) (court held that inmate stated an equal protection claim where he alleged that prison officials treated him differently from other high security inmates when they removed him from his work release job and allegedly leaked his participation in work release to the press).

[16]McLamore v. State, 257 S.C. 413, 186 S.E.2d 250 (1972).

[17]Ramsey v. Ciccone, 310 F. Supp. 600 (W.D. Mo. 1970).

[18]See, e.g., Franklin v. District of Columbia, 960 F. Supp. 394 (D.D.C. 1997), vacated in part on other grounds, 163 F.3d 625 (D.C. Cir. 1998), reh'g and reh'g en banc denied, 168 F.3d 1360 (D.C. Cir. 1999) supra (no right to rehabilitation programs). Robinson v. Illinois State Correctional Center (Stateville) Warden, 890 F. Supp. 715 (N.D. Ill. 1995) (holding that restrictions on the type of commissary items which inmates in segregation may purchase

constitutional and from a policy perspective. Constitutionally, the mere fact that a government is under no obligation to provide a benefit does not excuse its invidious discrimination among potential recipients after the decision has been reached to establish the benefit.[19] To paraphrase a leading constitutional scholar, tolerance for discretion in the granting of benefits does not imply tolerance for capricious distribution of these benefits.[20]

From a policy perspective, discriminatory irrationality in the distribution of prison privileges will surely prove counter-rehabilitative, because it will fuel inmate-administration animosity and generate jealousy among inmates. Of course, to the extent that a decision by prison administrators to provide differential treatment between groups of inmates is motivated by rational justifications, such as using the dispensation of prison privileges as an incentive to inmates, it does not carry these dangers and need not be disturbed, since it lies within the sound discretion of administrative officials, unless shown to be arbitrarily or capriciously applied. In addition, if a distinction can be justified by the sheer cost and security headaches of equalizing treatment between inmates who have vastly different security needs, it has a rational basis and will survive an equal protection challenge.[21] However, not all of these cases can be explained on that rationale.

---

does not violate due process; court noted that inmates have no protected rights to commissary privileges).

[19]See, e.g., Pitts v. Thornburgh, 866 F.2d 1450 (D.C. Cir. 1989); Brown v. State, 117 Ariz. 476, 573 P.2d 876 (1978). See also Arnett v. Kennedy, 416 U.S. 134, 94 S. Ct. 1633, 40 L. Ed. 2d 15 (1974). See, generally, Van Alstyne, The Demise of the Right-Privilege Distinction in Constitutional Law, 81 Harv. L. Rev. 1439 (1968).

[20]L. Tribe, American Constitutional Law 969-70 n27 (3rd ed. 2000).

[21]Compare, e.g., French v. Owens, 777 F.2d 1250 (7th Cir. 1985) (upholding unequal treatment of protective custody inmates when rationally justified by security needs) with Williams v. Lane, 851 F.2d 867, 876, 11 Fed. R. Serv. 3d 753 (7th Cir. 1988) (refusing to uphold unequal treatment when the evidence showed that it

Sometimes prisoners mount a different type of claim, arguing that they are discriminated against when compared to nonprisoners. Such a claim is even more difficult to sustain than when the distinction is between groups of prisoners. The need to maintain internal order, discipline, and security differentiates prisons from outside society.[22] Moreover, prisoners are distinguishable from nonprisoners in that they are serving time for having committed a crime. Their violence and dangerousness may be presumptively greater than that of their civilian counterparts, and the state has legitimate interests in the enforcement of penal sanctions to impose treatment that, almost by definition, differs from the treatment owed people who have not run afoul of the criminal law.

Consequently, it is relatively simple for a court to conclude that prisoners and nonprisoners are not similarly situated and that differences in treatment are justified. Thus, in *Glouser v Parratt*[23] for example, the Eighth Circuit found no equal protection violation where a prisoner received a more severe punishment for possession of marijuana than would have been imposed on a nonprisoner convicted of a similar offense.[24] Courts have also found no equal protection violation in laws that authorize the taking of compul-

---

stemmed from a "lack of desire to make improvements" when there were rational opportunities for improvement).

[22]See Bell v. Wolfish, 441 U.S. 520, 545-46, 99 S. Ct. 1861, 60 L. Ed. 2d 447 (1979); Jones v. North Carolina Prisoners' Labor Union, Inc., 433 U.S. 119, 125, 97 S. Ct. 2532, 53 L. Ed. 2d 629 (1977); Price v. Johnston, 334 U.S. 266, 285, 68 S. Ct. 1049, 92 L. Ed. 1356 (1948).

[23]Glouser v Parratt, 605 F.2d 419 (8th Cir. 1979).

[24]See also Chem v. Horn, 725 A.2d 226 (Pa. Commw. Ct. 1999) (inmate who was transferred to a restricted housing unit after drug test revealed presence of marijuana sought a declaratory judgment invalidating Department of Corrections (DOC) drug testing policy; inmate did not allege that he was receiving different treatment from that received by other inmates but compared his treatment to that received by DOC employees, who could request an independent drug test at their own expense to resolve an evi-

§ 4:3

sory DNA samples from prisoners but not civilians.[25] Likewise even though there is no security justification for the disparate treatment, the decision by Congress to eliminate Pell grants for higher education for prisoners but not for civilian has been upheld.[26] Similarly, courts have sustained prison no-smoking rules which applied to prisoners but which were not imposed on staff, including guards.[27]

In a few instances, judges have been persuaded that prisoners and civilians are sufficiently alike to warrant similar treatment.[28] One conspicuous area in which this

---

dentiary dispute; however, prisoner's due process rights were not violated because the interests of law-abiding citizens in continued employment are not comparable to the interests of a convict in prison, where more intrusion into private interests is required).

[25]See Vanderlinden v. State of Kan., 874 F. Supp. 1210 (D. Kan. 1995), judgment aff'd, 103 F.3d 940 (10th Cir. 1996); Roe v. Marcotte, 193 F.3d 72 (2d Cir. 1999); Gaines v. State, 116 Nev. 359, 998 P.2d 166 (2000), cert. denied, 531 U.S. 856, 121 S. Ct. 138, 148 L. Ed. 2d 90 (2000).

[26]Nicholas v. Riley, 874 F. Supp. 10 (D.D.C. 1995), aff'd, 1995 WL 686227 (D.C. Cir. 1995), reh'g and suggestion for reh'g in banc denied, (Dec. 7, 1995) (holding that prisoners did not have an equal protection claim where they were denied Pell grants to receive post-secondary education; plaintiff had been enrolled and attending college-level courses and was a recipient of Pell grants as provided by the Higher Education Act of 1965, § 401(b)(8), 20 U.S.C. § 1070a(b); however, the Violent Crime Control and Law Enforcement Act of 1994 prohibited any prisoner from any longer receiving financial aid for educational advancement; court found that since a prisoner has no fundamental interest in education, substantive due process rights were not violated).

[27]Reynolds v. Bucks, 833 F. Supp. 518 (E.D. Pa. 1993); Shockey v. Winfield, 97 Ohio App. 3d 409, 646 N.E.2d 911 (4th Dist. Ross County 1994) (prison smoking policy allowing prison guards to smoke in housing areas, but denying the same privilege to inmates, withstood an equal protection challenge; because guards had unrestricted movement throughout the facility and prisoners were confined in close spaces, the court found that the two groups were differently situated; in addition, the court held that smoking is not a fundamental right).

[28]See, e.g., Mabra v. Schmidt, 356 F. Supp. 620 (W.D. Wis. 1973).

§ 4:3

has occurred is where mentally ill prisoners have been transferred to mental hospitals.[29] Courts have concluded that such inmates are entitled to the same procedural protections afforded nonprisoners facing civil commitment.[30] Another situation where prisoners may be able to assert that they are being treated discriminatorily in comparison to nonprisoners involves worker's compensation. The argument can be made that prisoners receiving work-related injuries should be treated the same as nonprisoners who incur similar injuries.[31] They endure the same pain and suffering and may well be as permanently disadvantaged by the injury when they are released and must compete in the job market. While there are bases for differentiating prisoners and nonprisoners in certain aspects of the administration of this benefit (for example, in regard to the timing of payments), the equal protection arguments appear formidable.

Donald C. v. Illinois State Board of Education[32] provides an interesting example of analysis of an equal protection claim of this type. In that case, the plaintiffs, who were school age children who were detainees held in the Cook County Jail, argued that the failure to provide them with an education equal to children in the civilian world violated the Equal Protection Clause. The court accepted the notion that education was not a fundamental right and that security concerns are a legitimate state interest. The court, therefore, applied the rational relationship test. However, it insisted that

---

[29] See, e.g., Matthews v. Hardy, 420 F.2d 607 (D.C. Cir. 1969); U.S. ex rel. Schuster v. Herold, 410 F.2d 1071 (2d Cir. 1969); Sites v. McKenzie, 423 F. Supp. 1190 (N.D. W. Va. 1976); Matter of Knapp, 102 Wash. 2d 466, 687 P.2d 1145 (1984); State v. Waldon, 287 N.W.2d 628 (Minn. 1979) (inmates transferred to mental institution are entitled to the same rights as similarly situated prisoners in the state's prison). See Ch 10.

[30] See Ch 10.

[31] See Ch 7.

[32] Donnell C. v. Illinois State Bd. of Educ., 829 F. Supp. 1016, 2 A.D.D. 1305 (N.D. Ill. 1993).

§ 4:3

there be a true rational relationship between the restriction and the security needs of the institution. The defendants argued that that chaos would result if inmates were allowed to bring equal protection suits for this claim. The court held that this rationale had nothing to do with security and that "[a]pocyphal claims of burdensome litigation do not justify disparate treatment under the Equal Protection Clause."[33]

So far this discussion has focused on distinctions in the granting of nonfundmanental rights or benefits. As a general matter, when the government classifies persons in a way that deprives one group of fundamental rights, such as First Amendment rights to freedom of speech or free exercise of religion, courts have required a much higher level of justification than the rational basis test. The compelling state interest test has been invoked in its stead. Under the compelling state interest test, a state must not only demonstrate a compelling interest but also show a close connection between means and end. Thus, if a fundamental right is at stake in a nonprison setting, judicial scrutiny will be close and searching.

While the compelling state interest test is the test to apply in a nonprison setting when fundamental constitutional rights are at stake, this does not mean that it will be invoked in prison cases. There are two competing theories. One holds that courts should use the rational basis test even when fundamental rights are at stake. Support for this theory is found in two United States Supreme Court cases. The first is *Jones v North Carolina Prisoners' Labor Union, Inc.*[34] In *Jones,* the plaintiffs argued that they were not given the same First Amendment rights to gather together as was provided other groups. The Supreme Court, in an opinion by then-Justice Rehnquist, held that, even

---

[33]*Id.* at 1018.

[34]Jones v. North Carolina Prisoners' Labor Union, Inc., 433 U.S. 119, 97 S. Ct. 2532, 53 L. Ed. 2d 629 (1977). *Jones* is discussed at length in Ch 5.

§ 4:3   RIGHTS OF PRISONERS, THIRD EDITION

though the prison gave different speech and assembly rights to one group of inmates as opposed to another, the distinction would be sustained if there were "a rational basis for [the] distinction between organizational groups.[35] The Court continued:

> It is precisely in matters such as this, the decision as to which of many groups should be allowed to operate within the prison walls, where confronted with claims based on the Equal Protection Clause, the court should allow prison administrators the full latitude of discretion, unless it can be firmly stated that the two groups are so similar that the discretion has been abused.[36]

Subsequently, in *Turner v Safley*[37] and *O'Lone v Estate of Shabazz*,[38] the Supreme Court made clear that, even when fundamental First Amendment constitutional rights are at stake, the compelling state interest standard is not applicable, at least with regard to regulations that "govern the day-to-day operation of prisons and that restrict the exercise of prisoner's individual rights within prisons.[39] Instead, the Court has opted for a four-part reasonable relationship test discussed elsewhere in this book.[40] The test was designed to accommodate the security and administrative difficulties of managing penal institutions on the one hand, and the constitutional rights of inmates on the other hand.[41]

This tension is involved in equal protection cases when prison officials decide to impose policies that restrict the rights of certain groups on security grounds.

---

[35] 433 U.S. at 134.

[36] *Id.* at 136.

[37] Turner v. Safley, 482 U.S. 78, 107 S. Ct. 2254, 96 L. Ed. 2d 64 (1987). See Ch 5.

[38] O'Lone v. Estate of Shabazz, 482 U.S. 342, 107 S. Ct. 2400, 96 L. Ed. 2d 282 (1987).

[39] Pitts v. Thornburgh, 866 F.2d 1450, 1453 (D.C. Cir. 1989).

[40] The *Turner* and *Shabazz* standards are discussed in Chs 5, 6; see also §§ 1:09 to 1:14.

[41] See Ch 5.

§ 4:3

For this reason, a number of lower courts have held that a reasonable relationship test is to be applied in prisoner equal protection cases, even when the claims implicate fundamental constitutional rights.[42] Thus, in prison cases dealing with fundamental rights many courts say that "[t]he appropriate analysis for an equal protection claim is whether the unequal treatment bears a reasonable relationship to legitimate penalogical interests.[43]

Not all courts agree, at least when the claim relates to gender discrimination and also when the claim does not involve policies based on security rationales.[44] Some courts recognize the issue but have not yet decided it.[45] Some commentators have urged that *Turner* ought not be automatically applied to every prison equal protec-

---

[42]See, e.g., DeHart v. Horn, 227 F.3d 47 (3d Cir. 2000) (holding that *Turner* applies to a claim of religious discrimination); May v. Sheahan, 226 F.3d 876, 882 (7th Cir. 2000) ("In the prison context, the Equal Protection Clause of the Fourteenth Amendment requires inmates to be treated equally, unless unequal treatment bears a rational relation to a legitimate penal interest"); Benjamin v. Coughlin, 905 F.2d 571, 574 (2d Cir. 1990) (disapproved of by, Frazier v. Dubois, 922 F.2d 560 (10th Cir. 1990)) ("While the *Turner/Shabazz* standard was established in the context of first amendment issues, it is also relevant to the assessment of equal protection claims in the prison setting. As to such claims, the reasonableness of the prison rules and policies must be examined to determine whether distinctions made between religious groups in prison are reasonably related to legitimate penological interests."); Williams v. Lane, 851 F.2d 867, 877, 11 Fed. R. Serv. 3d 753 (7th Cir. 1988); Langone v. Coughlin, 712 F. Supp. 1061, 1066 (N.D. N.Y. 1989). See also Quinn v. Nix, 983 F.2d 115 (8th Cir. 1993) (applying *Turner* analysis to equal protection claim dealing with hair length regulation First Amendment case).

[43]Griffin v. Coughlin, 743 F. Supp. 1006, 1010 (N.D. N.Y. 1990).

[44]See Pitts v. Thornburgh, 866 F.2d 1450, 1459 (D.C. Cir. 1989); and discussion in § 4:4.

[45]See, e.g., Glover v. Johnson, 198 F.3d 557, 559, 1999 FED App. 415P (6th Cir. 1999) ("This case does not require us to decide whether the *Turner* reasonable relationship standard applies to equal protection claims in the prison setting.").

tion claim.[46] One noted that if *Turner* were applied to all prison equal protection claims even when security is not an issue and when a suspect classification is involved, this "would nullify the scrutiny standards carefully developed by the Supreme Court."[47] In a recent decision district court Judge James C. Turk, holding that the rational basis test should not apply to an equal protection claim based on gender discrimination, stated that "[a]pplying the rational basis test to all inmates' equal protection claims would allow the state to house inmates of one gender (or race or national origin) separately, treating them more harshly or denying them a multitude of beneficial programs and policies all on the basis on nothing more than economic efficiency."[48]

The Supreme Court has not definitively held which test will govern equal protection challenges dealing with fundamental rights. Even if the rational basis test does apply, this does not mean that an equal protection claim adds nothing to the resolution of a case dealing with individual constitutional rights of inmates. To the contrary, it provides another way for the court to view the impact of a restrictive prison regulation and may contribute to the outcome of the case. To illustrate, if prison authorities decide, for security reasons, to prohibit mass gatherings and, accordingly, ban all religious meetings, affected prisoners may raise a viable claim that they are being denied their First Amendment right

---

[46]See, e.g., Jennifer Arnett Lee, Women Prisoners, Penological Interests, and Gender Stereotyping: An Application of Equal Protection Norms to Female Prisoners, 32 Colum. Human Rights L. Rev. 251 (2000); Angie Baker, Leapfrogging over Equal Protection Analysis: The Eighth Circuit Sanctions Separate and Unequal Prison Facilities for Males and Females in Kilinger v. Department of Corrections, 31 F3d 727 (8th Cir. 1994), 76 Neb. L. Rev. 371, 383 (1997).

[47]Angie Baker, Leapfrogging over Equal Protection Analysis: The Eighth Circuit Sanctions Separate and Unequal Prison Facilities for Males and Females in Kilinger v. Department of Corrections, 31 F3d 727 (8th Cir. 1994), 76 Neb. L. Rev. 371, 383 (1997).

[48]Ashann-Ra v. Com. of Va., 112 F. Supp. 2d 559, 570 (W.D. Va. 2000).

§ 4:3

to free exercise of religion.[49] An equal protection claim, however, would not lie, since all religious sects are being treated alike.[50] Although the argument could be made that religious prisoners are being invidiously discriminated against compared to other inmates who are allowed to gather for nonreligious activities, the response might be that there is no equal protection violation in this differentiation, because the permitted activities do not involve "an organized, functioning alternative authority structure among inmates,"[51] as is the danger with group prayer meetings.

On the other hand, where prison authorities allow some, but not all, sects to hold religious services, the affected groups can argue that they are being discriminated against in the exercise of their constitutional right of free exercise of religion, in violation of equal protection.[52] This claim potentially adds weight to the argument that prison officials have acted unreasonably and therefore have violated the constitutional rights of the plaintiffs. The diligent advocate would doubtless assert both claims. This point is well illustrated by *Freeman v. Arpaio*.[53] In that case, the plaintiff, who was a practicing Muslim, alleged that prison officials prevented Muslim inmates from attending religious services and shackled the Muslim inmates when the officials did allow them to go to services. The court held that these restrictions did not violate free exercise if they were imposed on all religious groups but that they would violate equal protection if they were only imposed

---

[49]See Ch 6.

[50]See, e.g., Knuckles v. Prasse, 302 F. Supp. 1036 (E.D. Pa. 1969), judgment aff'd, 435 F.2d 1255 (3d Cir. 1970).

[51]Cooper v. Tard, 855 F.2d 125, 130 (3d Cir. 1988).

[52]See Cruz v. Beto, 405 U.S. 319, 92 S. Ct. 1079, 31 L. Ed. 2d 263 (1972).

[53]Freeman v. Arpaio, 125 F.3d 732 (9th Cir. 1997).

§ 4:3

on inmates of the Muslim faith.[54]

Another reason to mount an equal protection challenge is that it may be preferable to a procedural due process case when both are possible. When due process is involved, a prisoner must first establish that a liberty or property interest has been infringed before a court will examine the constitutionality of the procedures followed.[55] For example, the Supreme Court has held that to remain in the prison to which one is initially assigned is not such an interest.[56] Likewise, the loss of "mere privileges" may not give rise to due process protections.[57] On the other hand, as discussed earlier in this section, where equal protection claims are advanced, this right-privilege distinction ought to be of far less importance, if not irrelevant.[58] Thus, if a transferred prisoner could prove that the transfer was arbitrary or capricious or based on an improper standard, such as race, the transfer would be held to violate equal protection, although not due process. Similarly, the irrational distribution of privileges among the prison population may infringe on equal protection but not on due process.[59]

---

[54]*Id.* See also Lucero v. Hensley, 920 F. Supp. 1067 (C.D. Cal. 1996) (allegation that prison officials failed to provide Native American inmates with a chaplain when prison officials provided a similar number of Jewish inmates a full time rabbi).

[55]See, e.g., Sandin v. Conner, 515 U.S. 472, 115 S. Ct. 2293, 132 L. Ed. 2d 418 (1995); Meachum v. Fano, 427 U.S. 215, 96 S. Ct. 2532, 49 L. Ed. 2d 451 (1976). See Ch 9.

[56]Olim v. Wakinekona, 461 U.S. 238, 103 S. Ct. 1741, 75 L. Ed. 2d 813 (1983); Meachum v. Fano, 427 U.S. 215, 96 S. Ct. 2532, 49 L. Ed. 2d 451 (1976).

[57]Wolff v. McDonnell, 418 U.S. 539, 571 n 19, 94 S. Ct. 2963, 41 L. Ed. 2d 935 (1974).

[58]See, generally, Van Alstyne, The Demise of the Right-Privilege Distinction in Constitutional Law, 81 Harv. L. Rev. 1439 (1968).

[59]See, e.g., Brown v. State, 117 Ariz. 476, 573 P.2d 876 (1978). See Ch 9.

§ 4:4 —Racial Discrimination

Research References
West's Key Number Digest, Civil Rights ⚖︎104.2

Race relations in American prisons have been a topic that has engendered little sustained study and remarkably little litigation, given its importance. One leading scholar remarked that race is "the most important factor in the prison subculture determining more than anything else how one 'did time' in most of the nation's major prisons.[1] However, the same author described as "shocking" the "indifference" to the topic by legal scholars and courts.[2] What is known about the topic is not pleasant. For one thing, minorities are vastly overrepresented in American prisons. One study, for example, calculated that in 2001 one out of every seven African-American men in the 25-29 age group and one out of every twenty-four Hispanic males in the same age group are in prison or jail, as compared to one out of every fifty-five white males.[3] Equally relevant, in 1999, over 60 percent of the nation's prisoners were African-American or Hispanic.[4] In some states the numbers are dramatically higher. In New York, for example, 82 percent of the inmates are African-American or Hispanic, even though collectively they account for no more than 22 percent of the population.[5]

What little we know about treatment of minorities is similarly disturbing. Discrimination in housing, job as-

---

[Section 4:4]

[1] James B. Jacobs, The Limits of Racial Integration in Prison, 18 Crim. Law Bull. 117, 119 (1982) (citing authorities).

[2] *Id.* at 118.

[3] See The Sentencing Project, Facts About Prisons and Prisoners, at www.sentencingproject.org/brief/pub1035.pdf.

[4] *Id.*

[5] Correctional Assn of NY, Prisoner Profile (Feb 1993). See also Jacobs, supra note 61, at 120 (reporting that in some large states 80 to 90% of the inmates are black).

§ 4:4 Rights of Prisoners, Third Edition

signments, and discipline has been reported.[6] One of the causes of the tragic prison disturbance at Attica was racial discrimination.[7] Moreover, many prisons are situated in rural areas of states that draw guards from the surrounding areas. The guards tend to be white persons from cultures far removed from the predominantly minority urban inmates.[8] As a result of these and other factors, in many prisons there is "deep-seated animosity between prisoners of different races[9] that contribute to making "[r]acial conflict, including extreme violence and riots . . . a reality of institutional life in prisons around the county.[10]

Not all instances of discrimination involve African-American inmates.[11] While most racial discrimination cases have involved African-Americans, in some areas of the country, particularly the southwest, and states with large urban populations, the affected minority may

---

[6] Disparities in sentencing have been reported as well. See, e.g., Sheri L. Johnson, Unconscious Racism and the Criminal Law, 73 Cornell L. Rev. 1016 (1988); Sheri L. Johnson, Black Innocence and the White Jury, 83 Mich. L. Rev. 1611 (1985), but that topic is beyond the scope of this work.

[7] Report on Attica 39-40 (1972). For more information on racial discrimination in prisons, see National Advisory Commission on Criminal Justice Standards and Goals Corrections 41 (1973).

[8] Report on Attica 80 (1972).

[9] Sheldon Krantz & Lynn S. Branham, The Law of Sentencing, Corrections, and Prisoners' Rights 405 (4th ed 1991).

[10] James B. Jacobs, The Limits of Racial Integration in Prison, 18 Crim Law Bull. 117, 120.

[11] Some unusual cases have involved discrimination against white inmates. See, e.g., Antonelli v. Sheahan, 81 F.3d 1422 (7th Cir. 1996) (white inmate's claim that he was denied right to move outside the cellblock by black corrections officers); Grabowski v. Jackson County Public Defenders Office, 47 F.3d 1386 (5th Cir. 1995), reh'g en banc granted, (Mar. 14, 1995) and on reh'g en banc, 79 F.3d 478 (5th Cir. 1996) (white inmate's claim that he was deliberately placed in a position of danger because of his race); Bentley v. Beck, 625 F.2d 70 (5th Cir. 1980) (white inmate's claim that he was denied a job in the institution's kitchen because these jobs were reserved for blacks stated a claim under the Equal Protection Clause).

consist of Spanish-speaking inmates.[12] The Equal Protection Clause forbids discrimination against them as as it does against any insular minority. Indeed, given the inability of many Hispanic inmates to speak English and the fact that many prisons do not provide sufficient numbers of bilingual staff,[13] these inmates have special problems that courts should, but have not yet, sufficiently addressed. This, of course, is not an issue that is limited to Hispanic inmates; it affects inmates of other groups for whom English is not the first language.

In one interesting case involving the rights of non-English speaking inmates, a Laotian inmate in an Iowa prison challenged a rule requiring that all his correspondence, both incoming and outgoing, be in English, except for communications with his parents and grandparents.[14] The court held that while the purpose of the rule was to promote security by insuring that prison officials could actually read mail to monitor it for escape plans or other unlawful activities, the rule was invalid. This was so because the record demonstrated that that there was a readily available means of translating the letters and the failure to do so violated the plaintiff's constitutional rights.[15] This decision, however, must be contrasted with *Franklin v. District*

---

[12]See generally Haft, Spanish Speaking Prisoners, in Hermann & Haft, Prisoner Rights Sourcebook, Ch. 18 (1973).

[13]Correctional Assn. of NY, Not Simply a Matter of Words: Academic & Vocational Programs for Latino Inmates in New York State Prisons 26 (1992).

[14]Thongvanh v. Thalacker, 17 F.3d 256 (8th Cir. 1994).

[15]*Id.* See also U.S. ex rel. Gabor v. Myers, 237 F. Supp. 852 (E.D. Pa. 1965) (Hungarian refugee alleged that letters written by his sister in their native language were not being delivered to him by prison officials; court found this practice unconstitutional and ordered the use of a Hungarian social worker as a translator). There are no comparable cases for Hispanic inmates. Indeed, what little case law there is points in the opposite direction. See, e.g., Pabon v. McIntosh, 546 F. Supp. 1328 (E.D. Pa. 1982) (non-availability of classes taught in Spanish for Spanish-speaking inmates who did not speak English does not violate equal protection); Rodriguez v. Blaedow, 497 F. Supp. 558 (E.D. Wis. 1980) (no

of Columbia,[16] a recent decision by the Court of Appeals for the D. C. Circuit that dealt with the right of Hispanic inmates to interpreters and, unlike the Eighth Circuit case invoking the Laotian inmate, held that there was no entitlement to this service.

In *Franklin,* the district court held that Hispanic inmates who were not proficient in English were entitled to interpreters at least to the extent needed to communicate with medical staff and to participate in parole hearings at which they sought release from custody and at disciplinary hearings in which they were charged with institutional offenses. The Court of Appeals reversed. The court acknowledged that inmates have a "right to an understanding of the proceedings,"[17] in which there is a liberty interest at stake, but held that the plaintiffs had not proven that they were deprived of interpreters at any proceeding in which they were subjected to a loss of a liberty interest protected by the due process clause.[18] Moreover, the court held that the failure to provide interpreters did not violate the inmates' right to medical care, since the

---

violation of equal protection where Hispanic brother and sister were required to converse in English rather than Spanish). These cases, however, are of dubious validity in light of the better reasoned cases cited above.

[16]Franklin v. District of Columbia, 163 F.3d 625 (D.C. Cir. 1998), reh'g and reh'g en banc denied, 168 F.3d 1360 (D.C. Cir. 1999).

[17]Franklin v. District of Columbia, 163 F.3d 625, 633 (D.C. Cir. 1998), reh'g and reh'g en banc denied, 168 F.3d 1360 (D.C. Cir. 1999).

[18]*Id.* at 634-635. The court based this part of its decision on the Supreme Court's decision in Sandin v. Conner, 515 U.S. 472, 115 S. Ct. 2293, 132 L. Ed. 2d 418 (1995). For a discussion of this decision, see Ch 9. While there may be a liberty interest in parole decisions, that branch of the district court's decision was moot because a law passed during the pendency of the appeal transferred responsibility for parole decisions from the department of correction. Franklin v. District of Columbia, 163 F.3d 625, 631-32 (D.C. Cir. 1998), reh'g and reh'g en banc denied, 168 F.3d 1360 (D.C. Cir. 1999).

defendants had a policy of providing assistance at medical consultations. Even if that policy was imperfectly enforced, there was no constitutional violation so long as the defendants did not intentionally deprive inmates of access to medical care.[19]

As these cases show, there are serious equal protection issues that arise in the context of racial discrimination in prison. The Supreme Court has made clear that discrimination based on race is condemned, absent a compelling state interest.[20] The Court also has held that the Equal Protection Clause applies to prisons, albeit not with quite the same force as it applies in other public institutions.[21] However, aside from a brief opinion almost 35 years ago on the subject of segregated prisons, the Court has not addressed this pressing topic.[22] In the relatively few cases that have been decided-given the overriding importance of this topic-lower courts have addressed three topics that directly involve racial issues: (1) racial segregation in housing assignments; (2) discrimination in the provision of services and sanctions; and (3) racial harassment of inmates. Each of these topics will be discussed in turn.

Segregation

In the 1968 case of *Lee v Washington*,[23] the Supreme Court dealt with whether it was constitutional for a

---

[19]*Id.* at 635-636.

[20]See, e.g., Loving v. Virginia, 388 U.S. 1, 87 S. Ct. 1817, 18 L. Ed. 2d 1010 (1967); Anderson v. Martin, 375 U.S. 399, 84 S. Ct. 454, 11 L. Ed. 2d 430 (1964); Brown v. Board of Ed. of Topeka, Shawnee County, Kan., 347 U.S. 483, 74 S. Ct. 686, 98 L. Ed. 873, 38 A.L.R.2d 1180 (1954).

[21]Lee v. Washington, 390 U.S. 333, 88 S. Ct. 994, 19 L. Ed. 2d 1212 (1968).

[22]What cases exist are almost entirely devoted to racial discrimination in men's prisons. For an exploration of racial problems among female prisoners, see Candace Kruttschnitt, Race Relations and the Female Inmate, 29 Crim & Delinq 577 (1983).

[23]Lee v. Washington, 390 U.S. 333, 88 S. Ct. 994, 19 L. Ed. 2d 1212 (1968).

state to maintain an explicit policy of racially segregating its prisons. In that case, the state of Alabama argued that the Court's condemnation of segregation in public schools did not extend to prisons. The state maintained that segregation was needed to prevent racial violence from flaring up in its prisons. The Court's opinion in the case consisted of a short, three-sentence paragraph summarily affirming the district court's order that de jure prison segregation was unconstitutional. Responding to the state's concern, Justices Black, Harlan, and Stewart wrote a concurring opinion to emphasize that prison authorities retained "the right, acting in good faith and in particularized circumstances, to take into account racial tensions in maintaining security, discipline, and good order. . . .."[24] This view was subsequently approved by a majority of the Supreme Court in dictum in *Cruz v Beto,* where the Court noted that ". . . racial segregation, which is unconstitutional outside prisons, is unconstitutional within prisons, save for 'the necessities of prison security and discipline.'"[25]

Lower courts implementing this mandate have struck down segregation that did not result from a firm policy of separating inmates but instead came about because prison officials permitted inmates free choice as to where they would be housed. In *Jones v Diamond,*[26] a jail permitted inmates to choose which of the two "bullpens" they would be placed in. When the cells became racially segregated, the defendants claimed that this was only the result of the "free choices" of the inmates. The Fifth Circuit thought otherwise and held

---

[24]*Id.* at 334 (Black, Harlan, and Stewart, JJ, concurring).

[25]Cruz v. Beto, 405 U.S. 319, 321, 92 S. Ct. 1079, 31 L. Ed. 2d 263 (1972) (quoting Lee v. Washington, 390 U.S. 333, 334, 88 S. Ct. 994, 19 L. Ed. 2d 1212 (1968)).

[26]Jones v Diamond, 636 F.2d 1364 (5th Cir. 1981).

EQUAL PROTECTION § 4:4

that the policy was "but a gauze for discrimination."[27] Similarly, in *Simpson v. Horn*[28] the district court refused to credit a written policy that declared that inmates would only be segregated where there was a specific declaration that segregation was necessary for prison security, when the evidence established that in practice prison officials were not following the policy and instead were allowing segregated cell assignments to be made.[29] And in *Johnson v. State of California*[30] the Ninth Circuit made clear that a policy of racial discrimination of housing assignments, if proven, would not be tolerated.[31] Thus, prisons are under a mandate to create the "maximum feasible integration" within prison walls.[32]

The dictum in the concurring opinion in *Lee* and the majority opinion in *Cruz,* to the effect that racial ten-

---

[27]*Id.* at 1373. See also Stewart v. Rhodes, 473 F. Supp. 1185, 1188 (S.D. Ohio 1979), judgment aff'd, 785 F.2d 310 (6th Cir. 1986) (striking a limited policy of double celling inmates by race during the initial classification process). But see Jacobs v. Lockhart, 9 F.3d 36, 37 (8th Cir. 1993) (holding that plaintiff had not made out a prima facia case of discrimination; the dissent pointed out that inmates by "saying the right thing" (on an inmate form) could avoid having a person of a different race in the cell with him; thus the dissent argued that segregation resulted more from a prisoner's personal preference than from valid security concerns).

[28]Simpson v. Horn, 25 F. Supp. 2d 563 (E.D. Pa. 1998).

[29]However, the court indicated that there was no constitutional violation unless there was evidence that the defendant actually intended by this policy to cause segregation by race. *Id.* at 572.

[30]Johnson v. State of Cal., 207 F.3d 650 (9th Cir. 2000).

[31]According to the allegation of the complaint, the racial segregation was done to foment not to end racial tensions. *Id.* at 654.

[32]Jacobs, supra note 10, at 130. There is virtual unanimity on this subject among the lower courts; there are only two published opinions sanctioning segregation of the prison to alleviate prison violence. White v. Morris, 832 F. Supp. 1129 (S.D. Ohio 1993); Stroman v. Griffin, 331 F. Supp. 226 (S.D. Ga. 1971). Where there is no credible allegation of discrimination, however, there is no claim. See, e.g., Arney v. Thornburgh, 817 F. Supp. 83 (D. Kan. 1993) (allegations of racial discrimination in housing assignments dismissed based on unrefuted showing that racial composition in

§ 4:4

sions can be taken into account in maintaining security, discipline, and order open the possibility that segregation in prison might sometimes be permissible where implemented to serve the state's compelling interest in curtailing prison violence. Consistent with the Supreme Court's pronouncements, lower courts have held that to invoke this exception prison officials must point to "particularized circumstances" which justify making housing assignments on a racial basis.[33]

In *Sockwell v. Phelps*[34] the Fifth Circuit attempted to define when "particularized circumstances" justify taking race into account in housing assignments. In that case the district court found that the Louisiana State Penitentiary (Angola) remained segregated despite a court order desegregating it. Even with the court order, prison officials were convinced that segregated housing assignments were necessary for security reasons. The deputy warden testified that the prison administration was motivated by past incidents of violence between black and white inmates. The defendants offered five reasons why they had not integrated the two-man cells: (1) prison guards were unable to visually monitor the cells at all hours; (2) inmates in Angola were the "worst of the worst"; (3) in two instances where white and black inmates were housed together there had been violence; (4) there were racial supremacy groups in the prison; and (5) interracial conflicts could trigger more generalized racial violence and with the segregated policy there was a low number of two-man cell

---

area in question was consistent with the racial composition of the state prison population in general).

[33]See, e.g., Sockwell v. Phelps, 20 F.3d 187, 190 (5th Cir. 1994) (quoting Lee v. Washington, 390 U.S. at 334, ". . . prison authorities have the right, acting in good faith and in *particularized circumstances* to take into account racial tensions in maintaining security, discipline and good order in prisons and jails") (Emphasis supplied).

[34]Sockwell v. Phelps, 20 F.3d 187 (5th Cir. 1994).

EQUAL PROTECTION § 4:4

assaults.[35]

The Fifth Circuit held that these arguments did not justify across-the-board racial segregation of the two-man cells. The court held that the "particularized circumstances" exception cannot be met by such "a generalized or vague fear of racial violence. . . ."[36] None of the factors demonstrated an "unusual situation in which security and discipline would have demanded segregation."[37] The court acknowledged that the defendants were correct that violence might erupt between white and black cellmates. If this did happen the court said that it would expect prison officials to take action. In any event, in such a case racial segregation should be limited to the "offending individual prisoners."[38]

Thus, "[e]ven when there is a specific basis for racial conflict, segregation is impermissible if there are other means of maintaining institutional security."[39] This means that prison officials must search for other alternatives to control violence before they will be permitted to impose across-the-board segregation. The most common alternative that courts have endorsed is for prison officials to determine on an individual basis which prisoners are likely to cause violence. Only those

---

[35]*Id.* at 191.

[36]*Id.*

[37]*Id.*

[38]*Id.* While the court found that the constitutional rights of the plaintiffs were violated, it did not greatly value the right in monetary terms. The court affirmed a jury award of only $1 in compensatory damages and a punitive damages award of $4,000 for violating a clearly established right. Nominal damages were upheld because the plaintiffs failed to show that they had sustained any harm from the segregated double-celling. *Id.* at 192-93.

[39]Sheldon Krantz & Lynn S. Branham, The Law of Sentencing, Corrections and Prisoners' Rights 406 (4th ed 1991). See also Blevins v. Brew, 593 F. Supp. 245, 248 (W.D. Wis. 1984).

§ 4:4 RIGHTS OF PRISONERS, THIRD EDITION

prisoners should be segregated.[40] Moreover, as demonstrated in the *Sockwell* decision, past violence is generally not viewed as a valid justification for failure to integrate cells.[41] Nor is an official's vague fear that desegregation will lead to violence sufficient to prevent integration.[42] Instead, prison officials must first seek alternatives to segregation to stem prison violence, including close supervision of all inmates and firm disciplinary measures against troublemakers.[43]

In a provocative article, Professor James B. Jacobs, a leading scholar and a keen student of prison life, has challenged the opposition of the federal courts to voluntary self-segregation of prison inmates.[44] Professor Jacobs contends that the analogy between prisons and schools on which the case law is based is flawed. Segregation in school assignments can impose a badge of inferiority on minority children; this is not necessarily the case in a prison, Professor Jacobs argues, because in the closed world of prisons, where often white inmates are a distinct minority, inmates will not

---

[40]See, e.g., Sockwell v. Phelps, 20 F.3d 187 (5th Cir. 1994); Holt v. Hutto, 363 F. Supp. 194 (E.D. Ark. 1973), judgment rev'd on other grounds, 505 F.2d 194 (8th Cir. 1974).

[41]See Battle v. Anderson, 376 F. Supp. 402 (E.D. Okla. 1974), judgment aff'd in part, rev'd in part on other grounds, 993 F.2d 1551 (10th Cir. 1993).

[42]See U.S. v. Wyandotte County, Kan., 480 F.2d 969 (10th Cir. 1973); Stewart v. Rhodes, 473 F. Supp. 1185, 1189 (S.D. Ohio 1979), judgment aff'd, 785 F.2d 310 (6th Cir. 1986); Mickens v. Winston, 462 F. Supp. 910 (E.D. Va. 1978), aff'd, 609 F.2d 508 (4th Cir. 1979).

[43]Blevins v. Brew, 593 F. Supp. 245, 248 (W.D. Wis. 1984). See also McClelland v. Sigler, 456 F.2d 1266, 1267 (8th Cir. 1972) ("We think it is incumbent upon the officials in charge to make other provisions for housing those who would commit assaults or aggravations on other inmates, white or black, and thus only penalize those guilty of offending the personal and constitutional rights of the others").

[44]Jacobs, supra note 10, at 117-53.

§ 4:4

perceive it that way.[45] In addition, Jacobs argues that an inmate's social preference should be given more weight than a student's because school attendance is "nowhere near as total and pervasive an experience as prison."[46] "There is no private refuge for prisoners," Professor Jacobs asserts.[47]

Most important to Professor Jacobs is the fact that interracial violence is a reality of prison life in America.[48] With forced integration, inmates are compelled to live in potentially more dangerous situations than would be the case if they were permitted to make their own choices. This, Jacobs contends, may well violate their constitutional right to be protected from harm.[49] While courts may wish to repress this unpleasant subject, Professor Jacobs concludes that lower courts would better serve society by taking more seriously the Supreme Court's recognition that, when essential for prison safety, prison officials may allow inmates to voluntarily choose where they will be housed, even if these preferences are based on race.[50]

Sadly, Professor Jacobs's observations about the potential danger of involuntary prison integration were borne out in one case.[51] In that case[52] the plaintiff sued to end segregation in cell assignments at an Ohio state

---

[45]*Id.* at 137.

[46]*Id.* at 139.

[47]*Id.*

[48]For a discussion of inmate-on-inmate violence in prison, see Ch 2. See also Joanne Mariner, Human Rights Watch, No Escape: Male Rape in U.S. Prisons (Human Rights Watch 2001).

[49]Jacobs, supra note 10, at 141-43.

[50]*Id.* at 143. An indication that courts may be making gestures in the direction that Professor Jacobs indicates is found in the district court's opinion in Knop v. Johnson, 667 F. Supp. 467, 507-09 (W.D. Mich. 1987). In that case, the court refused to order an end to segregation in the prison dining room when the evidence established that the segregation was truly voluntary.

[51]For another case in which it was alleged that prison officials took advantage of racial tensions by deliberately housing a white inmate with racist attitudes in a cell area with black inmates with

prison. Subsequently, the district court approved a consent decree prohibiting cell assignments based on race unless prison officials specifically found that segregation of an inmate was necessary for security reasons. A short time later the worst riot in the history of Ohio's prisons and one of the worst riots in American history erupted at the facility. Nine inmates and one guard were killed and scores of others injured. Records were destroyed. During the uprising, inmates "repeatedly cited integrated celling as a factor contributing to the tense atmosphere at the prison."[53] One of the demands made by prisoners during negotiations leading to the restoration of control by prison officials was that the consent decree be reviewed. In the anxious period after control was restored, the court granted the defendants' motion to modify the decree. The court held that without the inmates' security records it would be impossible to make the security judgments required by the decree.

No doubt the court's opinion was influenced by the racial tension at the facility in the aftermath of the riot. In that climate and for those reasons, the court held that the request was not a "routine and automatic" assertion of a security rationale, but rather was the product of a real need to maintain order in the facility.[54] Thus, the court with "great difficulty and reluctance" allowed racial assignments to cells to be made for a period of six months until the defendants could recreate

---

knowledge that he would be assaulted, see Grabowski v. Jackson County Public Defenders Office, 47 F.3d 1386 (5th Cir. 1995), reh'g en banc granted, (Mar. 14, 1995) and on reh'g en banc, 79 F.3d 478 (5th Cir. 1996) (where white prisoner was placed with black inmates who had previously overheard plaintiff call a paralegal a "nigger" and was then severely beaten, prison officials did not put the plaintiff in danger in violation of equal protection; on rehearing, court held en banc that there was no evidence of a "policy" of deliberate indifference to plaintiff's rights).

[52]White v. Morris, 832 F. Supp. 1129 (S.D. Ohio 1993).

[53]Id. at 1130.

[54]Id. at 1136.

EQUAL PROTECTION § 4:4

security records of the inmates. However, it underlined that the measure was only temporary for the current emergency. Thereafter, the court decreed that it "fully intends to see the complete implementation of the terms of the consent decree on schedule."[55]

While Professor Jacobs calls for more flexibility on this subject, he does not, of course, support racial favoritism in prison housing assignments. Unfortunately, however, there are cases in which such favoritism has been documented. One case involved a prison facility that was integrated with the exception of the most comfortable cell block, which contained 50 whites who objected to living with blacks.[56] The court refused to tolerate this situation, reasoning correctly that those who resisted segregation should not be rewarded.[57] In a similar vein, a New York federal district court decision found that at a New York state prison, housing assignments were routinely made by placing the white inmates, disproportionately, in so called "honor housing blocks" while consigning black inmates to regular housing blocks, labeled "slums" by the inmates sent there. The court enjoined the practice.[58]

Discrimination in Provision of Services and Sanctions

Lee involved racial segregation of facilities. However, its principle that the Equal Protection Clause restricts racial discrimination extends to every other area of

[55]*Id.* at 1137.

[56]McClelland v. Sigler, 456 F.2d 1266 (8th Cir. 1972).

[57]*Id.* See also U.S. v. Wyandotte County, Kan., 480 F.2d 969 (10th Cir. 1973).

[58]Santiago v. Miles, 774 F. Supp. 775 (W.D. N.Y. 1991). See also Sockwell v. Phelps, 20 F.3d 187 (5th Cir. 1994) (allegation that housing assignments were made so that housing areas holding white inmates were called first for desired events, including showers, and were housed so that they had a better view of television sets).

§ 4:4

prison life as well.[59] It has been held, for example, that job assignments cannot be made on a racially discriminatory basis.[60] Similarly, visiting privileges cannot be denied because of race.[61] Nor can a prisoner's correspondence rights be withdrawn simply because the correspondent is of another race.[62] Protection against racial discrimination is equally available to white inmates as to blacks or other racial minorities. Thus, an allegation by a white inmate that "he is seldom allowed movement during a lockdown situation because he is white and most of the staff is black and because it is the custom and practice in the jail to discriminate against whites" was held by the Seventh Circuit to state a valid claim under the Equal Protection Clause.[63]

Discrimination can occur in failing to provide services, but it also can occur when sanctions are meted out in a racially unbalanced way. In one case, an

---

[59]See, e.g., Powells v. Minnehaha County Sheriff Dept., 198 F.3d 711 (8th Cir. 1999) (allegation that officer gave white inmate an extra mattress and blanket but did not give a black inmate these materials stated a claim of racial discrimination).

[60]See, e.g., Smith v. Ottinger, 230 F.3d 1360 (6th Cir. 2000) (prison inmate brought a claim alleging the disciplinary board denied him a job as an inmate advisor saying he was unqualified, then gave the job to a white prisoner; court held this stated a valid claim alleging violation of his equal protection rights and reversed the trial court's dismissal of the claim); Taylor v. Perini, 413 F. Supp. 189 (N.D. Ohio 1976); Battle v. Anderson, 376 F. Supp. 402 (E.D. Okla. 1974), judgment aff'd in part, rev'd in part on other grounds, 993 F.2d 1551 (10th Cir. 1993); U.S. ex rel. Motley v. Rundle, 340 F. Supp. 807 (E.D. Pa. 1972).

[61]See, e.g., Thomas v. Brierley, 481 F.2d 660 (3d Cir. 1973); Henry v. Van Cleve, 469 F.2d 687 (5th Cir. 1972). See also Martin v. Wainwright, 525 F.2d 983 (5th Cir. 1976). (visitation privileges may not be withheld because visitor is of another race).

[62]Worley v. Bounds, 355 F. Supp. 115 (W.D. N.C. 1973).

[63]Antonelli v. Sheahan, 81 F.3d 1422, 1433 (7th Cir. 1996). See also Mitchell v. Angelone, 82 F. Supp. 2d 485 (E.D. Va. 1999) (refusal to allow non-Native American to participate in Native American religious practices is race-based discrimination).

extensive record was made of this phenomenon.[64] In that case, the plaintiff proved through statistical and anecdotal evidence that "blacks tended to be disciplined more frequently than white inmates," even for the same offense.[65]

One issue that has arisen in this regard concerns neutral policies which African-American inmates claim impact more heavily on them than white inmates. Generally speaking, these claims have not been successful. Thus, grooming regulations which allegedly discriminated against black inmates were upheld when shown to be applicable to all prisoners.[66] One should be cautious, however, in applying this kind of reasoning across the board. It led to a fallacious result, for example, when another court denied African-American inmates the right to routine sickle cell anemia examinations. The court inferred that to hold otherwise would require giving blacks a more comprehensive physical than that provided the general prison population.[67] This rationale is suspicious, since a sickle cell examination is as important for giving a black prisoner a clean bill of health as it is unimportant for a white prisoner. For

---

[64]Santiago v. Miles, 774 F. Supp. 775 (W.D. N.Y. 1991).

[65]*Id.* at 786-87 (noting evidence that showed that black inmates received 4.87 misbehavior reports per inmate while white inmates received only 2.99 per inmate).

[66]Brooks v. Wainwright, 428 F.2d 652 (5th Cir. 1970). See also Betts v. McCaughtry, 827 F. Supp. 1400 (W.D. Wis. 1993), judgment aff'd, 19 F.3d 21 (7th Cir. 1994) (regulations regarding length of fingernails, length of hair, and curling irons did not constitute equal protection violations where plaintiffs failed to show that African-American inmates were the only ones affected and the prison had valid security reasons for the limitation); May v. Baldwin, 895 F. Supp. 1398, 1410 (D. Or. 1995), judgment aff'd, 109 F.3d 557 (9th Cir. 1997) (prison officials did not violate equal protection where inmate alleged that he was denied body lotion for his dry skin because he was black, where white inmates were given Vaseline for chapped lips; court noted that plaintiff's medical condition was not sufficiently serious and that he had canteen privileges to purchase such products).

[67]Ross v. Bounds, 373 F. Supp. 450 (E.D. N.C. 1974).

each, the goal is the same: providing a comprehensive physical examination. Therefore, the failure to give the exam to black inmates was a form of discrimination that ought to have been held to be a violation of the Equal Protection Clause.

Thus, it is one thing to say that racial discrimination is generally impermissible in a penal setting; it is quite another to prevail on a claim of racial discrimination.[68] These cases are difficult to prove.[69] In the absence of supporting factual evidence, courts will not inquire into

---

[68]For an indication of the barriers that some courts erect, see, e.g., Jackson v. Hogan, 388 Mass. 376, 446 N.E.2d 692 (1983) ("bare fact, if it were one, that all inmates in cadre unit were white would not be enough to support a claim that [plaintiff's] requests to transfer to that unit were denied because of his race").

[69]See, e.g., Foster v. Delo, 130 F.3d 307 (8th Cir. 1997) (African-American inmate claimed that prison superintendent refused to allow him to purchase a television and stereo in retaliation for filing lawsuits. Plaintiff claimed that white inmates are allowed to purchase such equipment. The court held that plaintiff failed to produce any evidence that defendant was enforcing the policy as retaliation or that it was done selectively); See also, Brown v. Byrd, 2000 WL 1780234 (E.D. Pa. 2000), aff'd, 276 F.3d 576 (3d Cir. 2001) (Inmate who was not housed in the cell he requested claims it was because of his race. The court held the inmate did not allege any facts that suggested prison officials based the cell assignment decision on race, and not based on the list of factors identified by the department of corrections in determining compatibility of inmates); Tooley v. Boyd, 936 F. Supp. 685 (E.D. Mo. 1996) (white inmate suffered no equal protection violation based upon denial of kitchen work assignment. Plaintiff failed to present evidence to demonstrate his race had anything to do with denial); Lacy v. Berge, 921 F. Supp. 600 (E.D. Wis. 1996), decision aff'd, 132 F.3d 36 (7th Cir. 1997) (prison officials did not violate equal protection where inmate alleged that prison officials failed break up fight between plaintiff and another inmate because plaintiff was black and the attacking inmate was white; court noted that inmate presented no evidence other than conclusory allegations); Hunt v. Budd, 895 F. Supp. 35 (N.D. N.Y. 1995) (inmate failed to state a claim where he alleged violation of equal protection regarding body cavity search; court found that inmate alleged no facts or evidence in furtherance of his claim that prison officials conducted body cavity searches in a manner that was racially motivated).

whether decisions of prison officials are racially motivated.[70] The initial burden of establishing facts to support the charge of racial discrimination, therefore, rests with the plaintiff.[71]

This burden is anything but easy to carry. The Supreme Court has held that the Fourteenth Amendment is not violated by unintentional conduct that has a disparate impact on minorities.[72] Rather, what is required is proof of an intent to discriminate.[73] In other words, "[i]n order to establish an [equal protection]

---

[70]Harris v. Ostrout, 65 F.3d 912 (11th Cir. 1995) (prison officials did not violate Equal Protection Clause where inmate alleged that he was incarcerated in an insect-infested cell and denied vegetarian diet because he was black; court found that inmate presented no evidence of racial bias other than conclusory allegations); Gibson v. McEvers, 631 F.2d 95 (7th Cir. 1980); Jackson v. Hogan, 388 Mass. 376, 446 N.E.2d 692 (1983) (conclusory allegations of racism without support are not actionable); Chapman v. Reynolds, 378 F. Supp. 1137 (W.D. Va. 1974).

[71]See, e.g., Harris v. Ostrout, 65 F.3d 912 (11th Cir. 1995) (prison officials did not violate Equal Protection Clause where inmate alleged that he was subject to strip searches because he was black; court found that inmate was searched in accordance with prison regulations).

[72]Washington v. Davis, 426 U.S. 229, 96 S. Ct. 2040, 48 L. Ed. 2d 597 (1976); Hernandez v. New York, 500 U.S. 352, 111 S. Ct. 1859, 114 L. Ed. 2d 395 (1991).

[73]Washington v. Davis, 426 U.S. 229, 96 S. Ct. 2040, 48 L. Ed. 2d 597 (1976). This is not true if the case is brought under Title VII of the Civil Rights Act of 1964. That provision, which protects against racial and religious discrimination in employment relations, does not require proof of intent. Guardians Ass'n v. Civil Service Com'n of City of New York, 463 U.S. 582, 103 S. Ct. 3221, 77 L. Ed. 2d 866 (1983). See also Villanueva v. Carere, 85 F.3d 481, 110 Ed. Law Rep. 38 (10th Cir. 1996) (citing *Guardians,* "Although Title VI itself proscribes only intentional discrimination, certain regulations promulgated pursuant to Title VI prohibit actions that have a disparate impact on groups protected by the act, even in the absence of discriminatory intent"). While there is no definitive authority on the subject, the Ninth Circuit indicated that Title VII might apply to at least some forms of prisoner employment discrimination. Baker v. McNeil Island Corrections Center, 859 F.2d 124 (9th Cir. 1988).

§ 4:4   Rights of Prisoners, Third Edition

violation, plaintiffs must prove not only discriminatory effect, but also that racial motive was responsible for that effect."[74]

In this day and age, direct proof of discriminatory intent is not always easy to find. Often discrimination takes place behind closed doors, or is the product of unconscious bias. Therefore, plaintiffs must use circumstantial evidence from which intent can be inferred. Statistical evidence plays a major, but not necessarily a determinative, role here. Through statistical evidence, plaintiffs can show where, for example, a majority of the desirable jobs and living quarters go.[75] Important as statistical evidence is, it is difficult to obtain. To gather statistical proof, as a practical matter, requires the diligence and resources of plaintiffs' counsel to obtain the raw data and to have an expert in statistics analyze and present the testimony.[76] This can be quite an expensive undertaking.

If the statistical showing is gross enough, it may be sufficient to shift the burden to the defendant to offer some convincing nondiscriminatory reason for the disparate impact.[77] The Supreme Court supported this approach when it held that: [if] a disparity is sufficiently large, then it is unlikely that it is due solely to chance or accident, and, in the absence of evidence to the contrary, one must conclude that racial or other class-

---

[74]Santiago v. Miles, 774 F. Supp. 775, 797 (W.D. N.Y. 1991); Gant ex rel. Gant v. Wallingford Bd. of Educ., 195 F.3d 134, 139 Ed. Law Rep. 160 (2d Cir. 1999).

[75]Santiago v. Miles, 774 F. Supp. 775, 778 (W.D. N.Y. 1991); see also Taylor v. Perini, 413 F. Supp. 189 (N.D. Ohio 1976); Battle v. Anderson, 457 F. Supp. 719 (E.D. Okla. 1978) (rebuttable presumption of discrimination where number of mixed cells is more than four standard deviations from the expected).

[76]See, e.g., Santiago v. Miles, 774 F. Supp. 775 (W.D. N.Y. 1991) (expert in statistics testified to gross statistical disparities).

[77]See, e.g., Hudson v. International Business Machines Corp., 620 F.2d 351, 355 (2d Cir. 1980); Santiago v. Miles, 774 F. Supp. 775, 797 (W.D. N.Y. 1991).

§ 4:4

related factors entered into the selection process.[78]

Thus, if plaintiffs can show gross statistical disparities on the order of two or three standard deviations,[79] courts may infer that the plaintiffs have made a prima facie showing of an equal protection violation.[80] At that point, the burden shifts to the state.[81]

This should be especially true in a prison context because, as one court observed, the greater control prison authorities have over prisoners' lives increases the likelihood that a statistical difference in treatment is the result of prison policies.[82] This is different from other situations where equal protection claims are made, such as in school desegregation suits. In prison, every aspect of an inmate's life is state controlled, while separation of the races in a school system can exist as a result of an individual's free choice of where to live. The absolute control a prison has over its inmates, therefore, renders it extremely unlikely that racial disparities are due to anything other than state action.[83] However, not every court sees it this way. In *Knop v Johnson*,[84] for example, the district court refused to make a finding of racial discrimination even though it found the statisti-

---

[78]Castaneda v. Partida, 430 U.S. 482, 494 n13, 97 S. Ct. 1272, 51 L. Ed. 2d 498 (1977).

[79]Standard deviation is a unit of measurement used to define the margin of error for any given conclusion, e.g., a probability of 50% with a standard deviation of 5% means that the actual probability is between 45% and 55%. See, generally, Michael O. Finkelstein & Bruce Levin, Statistics for Lawyers (1990).

[80]Santiago v. Miles, 774 F. Supp. 775, 799 (W.D. N.Y. 1991).

[81]Thomas v. Pate, 493 F.2d 151 (7th Cir. 1974), judgment vacated on other grounds, 419 U.S. 813, 95 S. Ct. 288, 42 L. Ed. 2d 39 (1974). See also National Advisory Commission on Criminal Just Standards and Goals, Corrections, at 41, Commentary to Standard 2.8 (1973).

[82]See Thomas v. Pate, 493 F.2d 151 (7th Cir. 1974), judgment vacated on other grounds, 419 U.S. 813, 95 S. Ct. 288, 42 L. Ed. 2d 39 (1974).

[83]*Id.* at 155.

[84]Knop v. Johnson, 667 F. Supp. 467 (W.D. Mich. 1987).

cal evidence "deeply disturbing.[85] The court reasoned that the evidence did not show that racial animus was the motivating factor for the disparate treatment.

Similarly in *Franklin v. District of Columbia*[86] a claim of disparity between programs for English speaking inmates and those for Hispanic inmates with limited language ability (the inmates were called Low English Proficiency or LEP inmates) was rejected even thought the programs available to the latter inmates were less valuable than the programs given to English speaking inmates. To further support their claim, the plaintiffs introduced evidence showing that Spanish-language programs suffered disproportionate cuts in the past. However, the court held that there was no intentional discrimination against these inmates. Racial motives were not responsible for any limitations in the programming, and there was no showing that the limitations were as a result of the defendant's conscious attempt to discriminate. Indeed, all programs were open to all inmates without regard to race or color or national origin. To the extent that inmates were unable to participate, the court held, it was not because of race or ethnicity but only because of their limited English language skills.[87]

Even when inmates make a powerful statistical showing, it may not be enough to prove a claim of unlawful racial discrimination. The Supreme Court has held that statistics alone are not necessarily enough to carry the day for the plaintiffs.[88] Aside from statistical proof, discrimination can be proved in other ways. Also rele-

---

[85]*Id.* at 505.

[86]Franklin v. District of Columbia, 960 F. Supp. 394 (D.D.C. 1997), vacated in part on other grounds, 163 F.3d 625 (D.C. Cir. 1998), reh'g and reh'g en banc denied, 168 F.3d 1360 (D.C. Cir. 1999).

[87]*Id.* at 431.

[88]Washington v. Davis, 426 U.S. 229, 96 S. Ct. 2040, 48 L. Ed. 2d 597 (1976). But see Castaneda v. Partida, 430 U.S. 482, 97 S. Ct. 1272, 51 L. Ed. 2d 498 (1977) (statistical evidence was sufficient to create a presumption of discrimination).

vant is the "historical background or context that existed at the time that the challenged actions were made.[89] Often this type of proof is combined with statistical proof.[90] In *Santiago v Miles*,[91] for example, the plaintiffs offered a statistical expert who demonstrated that the better housing and employment assignments at the Elmira Correctional Facility went disproportionately to white inmates. This evidence was combined with testimony from more than 20 witnesses, including inmates and staff, who testified to "scores of incidents from which a clear pattern of racial animus" emerged.[92] From this overwhelming presentation, the court had little difficulty concluding that "an entrenched attitude of discrimination and racism exists at Elmira."[93]

As in society at large, the question of the appropriate remedy to be applied after impermissible racial discrimination has been found is often a matter of controversy. Courts that have found racial discrimination have imposed a variety of remedies. One solution has been to order the defendants to submit a plan to root out the discrimination.[94] Another remedy employed is an affirmative action program to rectify past injustices. One court, for example, ordered an affirmative action program to integrate a prison's corrections staff.[95] Another required an affirmative action program

---

[89]*Id.* at 797 (citing McCleskey v. Kemp, 481 U.S. 279, 298 n20, 107 S. Ct. 1756, 95 L. Ed. 2d 262 (1987)); Hunter v. Underwood, 471 U.S. 222, 225, 105 S. Ct. 1916, 85 L. Ed. 2d 222 (1985).

[90]See, e.g., Payne v. Travenol Laboratories, Inc., 673 F.2d 798, 33 Fed. R. Serv. 2d 1582 (5th Cir. 1982) (if the statistical disparity is insufficient alone to establish a prima facie case, the plaintiff may get over his or her initial hurdle by combining statistics with historical, individual, or circumstantial evidence).

[91]Santiago v. Miles, 774 F. Supp. 775 (W.D. N.Y. 1991).

[92]*Id.* at 800.

[93]*Id.*

[94]Santiago v. Miles, 774 F. Supp. 775, 801 (W.D. N.Y. 1991).

[95]Holt v. Hutto, 363 F. Supp. 194 (E.D. Ark. 1973), judgment rev'd on other grounds, 505 F.2d 194 (8th Cir. 1974). In *Finney*,

§ 4:4 RIGHTS OF PRISONERS, THIRD EDITION

to ensure that cell blocks were racially mixed.[96] In a similar effort to avoid the effects of past discrimination, the court in *Battle v Anderson*[97] held that in order to ensure future nondiscriminatory job assignments, no preference could be given on the basis of an inmate's previous work experience at the penitentiary if such preference would have a racially discriminatory impact.[98] That court also ordered the formulation and implementation of affirmative action plans to overcome the effects of past discrimination in the operation of housing, dining, recreation facilities, and the disciplinary system.[99] Regardless of the remedy that is chosen, it is clear that the court "has substantial discretion to take whatever action is necessary to correct constitutional violations."[100]

The Equal Protection Clause's guarantee of equal treatment and protection from racially based treatment is subject to a significant caveat when applied to prisons. As suggested in the *Lee* concurring opinion, security justifications can be lawfully used to justify racial distinctions that would be otherwise unconstitutional. To trigger these encroachments on equal protection rights, prison officials must provide legitimate and particularized reasons for making racial distinctions. There are several cases in which this has occurred. As mentioned above, a district court in Ohio sanctioned racial separation of prisoners for a six month period in the aftermath of a prison riot that had racial

---

the appellate court also expressed concern over the nonintegration of the prison's disciplinary court. *Id.* at 209-10.

[96]Thomas v. Pate, 493 F.2d 151 (7th Cir. 1974), judgment vacated on other grounds, 419 U.S. 813, 95 S. Ct. 288, 42 L. Ed. 2d 39 (1974).

[97]Battle v. Anderson, 457 F. Supp. 719 (E.D. Okla. 1978).

[98]*Id.*

[99]*Id.*

[100]Santiago v. Miles, 774 F. Supp. 775, 801 (W.D. N.Y. 1991).

§ 4:4

overtones.[101] The Ninth Circuit, in an unpublished opinion, held that it was permissible for prison officials at the Pelican Bay prison in California to target Hispanic inmates for tighter security controls.[102] This overtly racial classification was justified, the Ninth Circuit said, by the safety needs of the facility. There had been serious racial disturbances at the prison. In what the court called the "dire circumstances" reigning at the prison, the evidence showed that "Hispanics, as a group, were more likely to be violent than other groups and thus more worthy of closer scrutiny."[103] Seven of nine states of emergency that were called at the prison were as a result of violence involving Hispanic inmates. In a three month period a study commissioned by prison officials found that 52 of the 58 inmates involved in violence were Hispanic. Applying the *Turner* standards, the court held that singling out Hispanic inmates for special treatment was rationally related to a legitimate governmental interest.[104] The approach taken in this case is questionable in that it sanctions in a prison environment a form of "racial profiling" which has drawn serious criticism when used in civilian society.[105] One judge speaking in a case that involved a different issue pointed out the dangers of treating all members of a group in a particular way because of characteristics that many group members

---

[101]White v. Morris, 832 F. Supp. 1129 (S.D. Ohio 1993).

[102]Ramirez v. Reagan, 82 F.3d 423 (9th Cir. 1996) (Table) (unpublished opinion).

[103]*Id.* The court noted that seven out of the nine states of emergency called at the prison over a recent period of time involved Hispanic inmates and 52 out of the 58 inmates involved in violence during a three month period were Hispanic.

[104]*Id.* citing Turner v. Safley, 482 U.S. 78, 107 S. Ct. 2254, 96 L. Ed. 2d 64 (1987). *Turner* is discussed in depth in Ch 5.

[105]See Kathryn Russell, "Driving While Black": Corollary Phenomena and Collateral Consequences, 40 B.C. L. Rev. 717 (May 1999); Brandon Garrett, Remedying Racial Profiling, 33 Colum. Human Rights L. Rev. 41 (Fall 2001); Gregory M. Lipper, Recent Development: Racial Profiling, 38 Harv. J. on Legis. 551 (Summer 2001).

share:

> An individual, even a prisoner, may not be denied equal treatment afforded to those sharing his relevant characteristics, simply because statistics show that that he belongs to a group that typically does not bear those relevant characteristics. Such a justification would be similar to justifying the denial of library privileges to a woman on the basis of statistics that show that more men have high school diplomas than women, or the denial of voting rights to an Asian-American on the basis of a statistic that shows that more European-Americans exercise the right to vote.[106]

Harassment

Unfortunately, racial harassment of inmates by guards occurs.[107] However, by and large, courts have failed to effectively address the problem. Some courts have taken the position that the use of rough language in prison, even if it offends the sensibilities of some inmates, does not violate the Constitution.[108] Therefore, they have been willing to tolerate "an occasional racial slur."[109] Some courts have gone beyond even that and have indicated that while they could require a state to

---

[106] Bills v. Dahm, 32 F.3d 333 (8th Cir. 1994) (Morris Shepard Arnold, J.).

[107] Without casting aspersions on all prison guards it is a fact that some prison guards have been known to be members of racist organizations such as the Klu Klux Klan. See Weicherding v. Riegel, 160 F.3d 1139 (7th Cir. 1998) (firing a prison sergeant because he promoted a Klu Klux Klan rally on television did not violate his First Amendment rights); Hernandez v. Estelle, 788 F.2d 1154 (5th Cir. 1986) (an article in Torch-La Antorcha, a bilingual publication of the Revolutionary Socialist League of New York, alleged that prison guards encouraged inmates to organize a Klu Klux Klan chapter). For a case in which a prison guard refused to condone racist conduct see Moyo v. Gomez, 40 F.3d 982 (9th Cir. 1994) (prison guard was dismissed because he refused to participate in unlawful racially motivated discrimination against black inmates which included allowing shower privileges to white inmates after work detail but not to black inmates),

[108] See, e.g., Burton v. Livingston, 791 F.2d 97, 100 (8th Cir. 1986).

[109] Knop v. Johnson, 667 F. Supp. 467 (W.D. Mich. 1987).

§ 4:4

eliminate other discriminatory practices, they could not order guards to refrain from having racist attitudes.[110] As the Seventh Circuit recently said "[t]he use of racially derogatory language, while unprofessional and deplorable, does not violate the Constitution. . . Standing alone, simple verbal harassment does not constitute cruel and unusual punishment, deprive a prisoner of protected liberty interest, or deny a prisoner equal protection of the laws."[111]

These opinions fail to come to grips with the damage that is inflicted on inmates who are subjected to racial verbal attacks from the very people who are entrusted with enormous power by the state over almost every aspect of their lives. In other contexts, courts have recognized the harm that is done by employers who racially harass their employees and have acted firmly to prohibit it.[112] The case for constitutional protection against this kind of indefensible practice, if anything, is even stronger when it occurs in a prison than when it occurs in the workplace.

Knop v Johnson[113] gives an indication of the difficulty that plaintiffs have in this area. There, the district court found that there was so much racial harassment of inmates that "an atmosphere of racial tension and hostility existed."[114] The court further found that the racial slurs were made "for the sole purpose of antago-

---

[110]Hoptowit v. Ray, 682 F.2d 1237, 1252, 9 Fed. R. Evid. Serv. 1511 (9th Cir. 1982). See also Morgan v. Ward, 699 F. Supp. 1025 (N.D. N.Y. 1988) (racial insults do not violate the Eighth Amendment because they do not deprive inmates of the basic necessities of life). But see Finney v. Mabry, 534 F. Supp. 1026 (E.D. Ark. 1982) (prohibiting racial slurs by guards).

[111]DeWalt v. Carter, 224 F.3d 607, 612 (7th Cir. 2000).

[112]See, e.g., Poe v. Haydon, 853 F.2d 418, 429 (6th Cir. 1988) (racial harassment of government employee violates equal protection). See also Patterson v. McLean Credit Union, 491 U.S. 164, 180, 109 S. Ct. 2363, 105 L. Ed. 2d 132 (1989); Sharp v. City of Houston, 960 F. Supp. 1164 (S.D. Tex. 1997).

[113]Knop v Johnson, 667 F. Supp. 467 (W.D. Mich. 1987).

[114]*Id.* at 506.

nizing black inmates and inflict[ing] emotional and psychological pain on the inmates."[115] Finally, the court found that prison officials were aware of the problem but failed to take steps to control it. Despite these factual findings, the Sixth Circuit Court of Appeals reversed the district court and held that the evidence was insufficient to show that the harassment was officially condoned.[116] In another case, there was evidence that Hispanic inmates had been called derogatory names by other inmates and by certain corrections officials. However, the court held that the class action fell short because the plaintiffs failed to prove that the racial attacks were officially condoned or that the incidents involving guards were systemic. While the department's record was not "enviable," it did not violate the Hispanic inmates' constitutional rights.[117] One can hope that, in the future, courts will show greater sensitivity to this important question. After all, as one court warned, "[r]acism is never justified; it is no less inexcusable and indefensible merely because it occurs inside the prison gates."[118]

---

[115]*Id.*

[116]Knop v. Johnson, 977 F.2d 996 (6th Cir. 1992).

[117]Franklin v. District of Columbia, 960 F. Supp. 394, 434 (D. D.C. 1997), vacated in part on other grounds, 163 F.3d 625 (D.C. Cir. 1998), reh'g and reh'g en banc denied, 168 F.3d 1360 (D.C. Cir. 1999) supra. See also Lacy v. Berge, 921 F. Supp. 600 (E.D. Wis. 1996), decision aff'd, 132 F.3d 36 (7th Cir. 1997) (prison officials did not violate due process where inmate alleged that officials failed to investigate and prosecute white inmate who attacked plaintiff, a black inmate; court noted that plaintiff had no liberty interest in having another inmate prosecuted, district attorney investigated the incident and choose not to prosecute, and correctional officials charged neither inmate with violation of a prison regulation).

[118]Santiago v. Miles, 774 F. Supp. 775, 777 (W.D. N.Y. 1991). For a recent case indicating that racist language is not to be condoned see Harris v. Ostrout, 65 F.3d 912 (11th Cir. 1995) (holding that the use of racist language to a prisoner supports an allegation of retaliation).

§ 4:5 —Sexual Discrimination

Research References

West's Key Number Digest, Civil Rights ⚷105

Ask the proverbial person on the street to visualize a prisoner and chances are he or she will conjure up a description of a male. Men, it is true, continue to constitute the majority of prisoners, but the number of women in prison is not insignificant and is growing. It has been reported that females account for approximately 5.4 percent of the total prison population as compared to about 2 percent in 1970.[1] Over the last twenty years, the female prison population has grown by almost 700 percent.[2] As of January 1, 2002, an estimated 1,040,000 women were in prison, jail, or on parole or probation in the United States.[3] In general, the prison population has been growing dramatically in recent years,[4] but the expansion in the female prison population leads the way. Since 1980, the number of women entering prisons in the United States had risen almost 400 percent, double the rate of men.[5] In New York, as of January 1, 2002, 3,133 women were incarcerated which is 4.6 percent of New York's total prison population.[6].

However, even with the rising numbers, women

[Section 4:5]

[1]Bureau of the Census, US Dept of Commerce, Statistical Abstract of the United States: 1992, at 198 (112th ed. 1992).

[2]US Dept of Justice, Sourcebook of Criminal Justice Statistics 636 (1991).

[3]Correctional Assn of NY, Women in Prison Fact Sheet 1 (March 2002).

[4]See Ch 2.

[5]Correctional Assn of NY, Women in Prison Fact Sheet 1 (March 2000).

[6]*Id.* No one knows for certain what accounts for this dramatic increase, but, of the several theories that have been offered, the most persuasive is the increased numbers of women who are sentenced to prison for drug offenses. The New York data portrays this trend. Of the 3,133 women in New York State prisons, 45% were incarcerated for drug offenses. *Id.* In fact, New York has the

§ 4:5

continue to be a minority of the prisoners in this country. As such, they have special problems.[7] These are caused by two factors. One, they are a minority of every state's prison population; two, the discrimination that women have experienced in society generally has, in many instances, been carried over to prison society. Prisons in the United States were sexually integrated until 1873, when Indiana opened the first women's prison.[8] Other states followed suit, with the result that today most prison systems are sexually segregated. This prohibition against sexual integration is now often required by statute.[9]

Because there are significantly fewer female prisoners than male, there are correspondingly fewer female prisons. In many states there is only one prison for females.[10] This has serious repercussions for women. Male prisoners often may be assigned to maximum, medium, or minimum security units. However, in states

---

fourth largest female prison population in the nation, exceeded only by Texas, California and Florida

[7]The special health needs of women are discussed in Ch 3. For a discussion of discrimination problems for female prisoners, see Jennifer Arnett Lee, Women Prisoners, Penological Interests, and Gender Stereotyping: An Application of Equal Protection Norms to Female Prisoners, 32 Colum. Human Rights L. Rev. 251 (2000); See also Iman R. Soliman, Male Officers in Women's Prisons: The Need for Segregation of Officers in Certain Positions, 10 Tex. J. Women & L. 45 (2000).

[8]Barry Ruback, The Sexually Integrated Prison: A Legal and Policy Evaluation, 3 Am. J. Crim. L. 301 (1975). See, generally, Walter C. Reckless & A. Kay, The Female Offender (1967) (consultants' report to the President's Commission on Law Enforcement and the Administration of Justice); Rose Giallombardo, Society of Women: A Study of a Women's Prison (1966); Otto Pollack, The Criminality of Women (1980).

[9]See, e.g., Mass. Gen. Laws Ann. ch. 127, § 22 (West 1991); Minn. Stat. Ann. § 243.90 (West 1992).

[10]In the 1970s one source reported that no state operates more than one women's prison. Ralph R. Arditi et al, Note, The Sexual Segregation of the American Prison, 82 Yale L.J. 1229, 1233 (1973). With the explosion in prison populations, that has since changed in the larger states. New York, e.g., which had only one women's

that have only one women's prison, all women sentenced for crimes, whether major or minor, will be sent to the same institution. Even in states that have more than one women's prison, the chances are that the greater number of men's prisons will offer a wider variety of programs and greater sophistication in classification. Partly as a consequence of this fact, differences in treatment between women and men's institutions are common.

The smaller number of women's prisons makes it more difficult to provide treatment and rehabilitative programs, since there may be a wide diversity of needs. Also, because there is less ability to classify female prisoners than male prisoners, females entering prison for the first time may be exposed to hardened criminals. Another impact of sexual segregation in prisons is that women sometimes find themselves in institutions farther from their homes, families, friends, and attorneys than do men.[11] With fewer prisons from which to choose, corrections officials obviously lack flexibility in assigning women to penitentiaries near their homes. This, in turn, can cause a disadvantage to female inmates in both visitation and personal consultations with lawyers. Work furlough programs in the few communities having women's prisons may also be less attractive to qualified inmates who do not plan to remain in that community after release.

Because of the smaller number of women in each facility, institutional services in women's prisons tend to be reduced. Prisons for males, for example, are more likely to have full-time medical staff and to offer a wider

---

prison in 1970, now has 10. However, many states still operate only one women's facility.

[11]Ralph R. Arditi et al, Note, The Sexual Segregation of the American Prison, 82 Yale L.J. 1229, 1232 (1973). Lawrence Bershad, Discriminatory Treatment of the Female Offender in the Criminal Justice System, 26 B.C. L. Rev. 389, 402, 406 (1985).

§ 4:5

range of medical services.[12] The same is true for full-time chaplains.[13] Female offenders often are afforded more limited recreational opportunities, perhaps because of the stereotype of female fragility.[14] Often the vocational and educational programs that are available to women reflect stereotypical notions about what is proper "women's work."[15]

However, not all of the differences between prisons for men and women are disadvantageous to women. Security at women's prisons tends to be more relaxed, as women are perceived to be less dangerous than men.[16] Also, greater privacy usually is afforded women inmates, reflected in the greater prevalence of private rooms as opposed to the barracks living arrangements or multi-tiered cell-blocks that typify male

---

[12]Ralph R. Arditi et al, Note 206, The Sexual Segregation of the American Prison, 82 Yale L.J. 1229, 1236 (1973). Disparities in medical treatment for women are discussed in Ch 3.

[13]Ralph R. Arditi et al, Note 206, The Sexual Segregation of the American Prison, 82 Yale L.J. 1229, 1236 (1973)

[14]Ralph R. Arditi et al, Note, The Sexual Segregation of the American Prison, 82 Yale L.J. 1229, 1239 (1973); Klinger v. Nebraska Dept. of Correctional Services, 824 F. Supp. 1374, 1427 (D. Neb. 1993), order rev'd, 31 F.3d 727 (8th Cir. 1994)(Court of Appeals found no equal protection violation).

[15]See, e.g., Jennifer Arnett Lee, Women Prisoners, Penological Interests, and Gender Stereotyping: An Application of Equal Protection Norms to Female Prisoners, 32 Colum. Human Rights L. Rev. 251, 253 (2000) (noting that with respect to vocational training programs female inmates do not have access to the same quality of programming as men and "those [programs] that do exist tend to limit participation to traditional female roles, such as cosmetology or secretary programs, excusing them from more career-oriented training.") citing William Collins and Andrew Collins, National Institute of Corrections, Women in Jail: Legal Issues 4 (1996); Rosemary M. Kennedy, The Treatment of Women Prisoners after the VMI Decision: Application of a New "Heightened Scrutiny", 6 Am. U. J. Gender & Law 65 (Fall 1997).

[16]Ralph R. Arditi et al, Note, The Sexual Segregation of the American Prison, 82 Yale L.J. 1229, 1237 (1973).

penitentiaries.[17] Another difference relates to staff. There are usually more staff members, particularly treatment personnel, per inmate at women's institutions.[18] The staff in women's prisons are also more likely to be sexually integrated and to view their role in parental, rather than custodial, terms.[19] A sexually integrated staff may have a greater humanizing effect than an all-male or all-female staff.[20] Despite these limited benefits, it is clear that disparate treatment of women prisoners results in many women inmates having fewer opportunities for programs that men, even though several national groups have condemned this.[21]

Standard of Review

What role, if any, does the Equal Protection Clause play in confronting these problems?[22] To answer this question, the standard that is applicable when dealing with questions of sexual discrimination must be determined. It also is important to know whether male and female prisoners are similarly situated for purposes of the Equal Protection Clause.

---

[17]*Id.* at 1238.

[18]*Id.* at 1240.

[19]Ralph R. Arditi et al, Note, The Sexual Segregation of the American Prison, 82 Yale L.J. 1229, 1240-41 (1973).

[20]But see Iman R. Soliman, Male Officers in Women's Prisons: The Need for Segregation of Officers in Certain Positions, 10 Tex. J. Women & L. 45 (2000) (arguing that it is dangerous for women inmates to place male officers in direct contact with prisoners).

[21]E.g., ABA, Standards for Criminal Justice Standard 23-6.14 (1986) ("Prisoners should not be subjected to discriminatory treatment based solely on . . . sex . . ."; Model Sentencing and Corrections Act § 4-111(a) (July 2001) ("A confined person has a protected interest in freedom from discrimination on the basis of sex"); American Correctional Assn, Standards for Adult Correctional Institutions Standards 3-4265(1995), 3-4266 (1990) (all decisions are made without regard to inmate's sex; all inmates should have equal opportunity to participate in institution's programs).

[22]For a discussion of this topic, see Sex Discrimination in Treatment of Jail or Prison Inmates, 12 A.L.R. 4th 1219 § 3.

§ 4:5

Until the 1970s, the Supreme Court did not treat claims of gender discrimination seriously. The rational relationship test was used, and the "Court almost always upheld gender discriminatory statutes."[23] With the growth of the women's movement, the Court became more sensitive to the problems of gender discrimination and, in the process, began to change the law concerning the level of scrutiny for cases involving sex discrimination.[24] The standard the Court approved in place of the rational relationship test subjects gender-based regulations to heightened scrutiny under what has been called an intermediate standard of review.[25] The intermediate standard of review falls between the rational basis test and the compelling state interest test.[26] Under this level of review, a state policy that distinguishes between men and women will not be upheld unless it can be shown that the distinction is drawn in the service of "important government objectives" and that the means chosen are " substantially related to the achievement of those objectives."[27] Applying this standard, the Supreme Court has stressed that when a classification is based on gender alone, there must be "an exceedingly persuasive justification . . . to sustain the

---

[23]Lawrence Bershad, Discriminatory Treatment of the Female Offender in the Criminal Justice System, 26 B.C. L. Rev. 389, 392 (1985) (citing cases).

[24]See, e.g., Reed v. Reed, 404 U.S. 71, 92 S. Ct. 251, 30 L. Ed. 2d 225 (1971); Frontiero v. Richardson, 411 U.S. 677, 93 S. Ct. 1764, 36 L. Ed. 2d 583 (1973); Craig v. Boren, 429 U.S. 190, 97 S. Ct. 451, 50 L. Ed. 2d 397 (1976).

[25]Laurence H. Tribe, American Constitutional Law §§ 16-33 (2d ed 1988).

[26]Under a state constitution, a court may still deem gender to be a "suspect" classification like race and require a showing of a compelling state interest. See, e.g., Inmates of Sybil Brand Institute for Women v. County of Los Angeles, 130 Cal. App. 3d 89, 181 Cal. Rptr. 599 (2d Dist. 1982).

[27]Craig v. Boren, 429 U.S. 190, 197, 97 S. Ct. 451, 50 L. Ed. 2d 397 (1976).

EQUAL PROTECTION § 4:5

gender based classification."[28]

One motive for this heightened scrutiny is to guard against stereotypical thinking with "fixed notions concerning the roles and abilities of males and females."[29] The Court, speaking through Justice Ginsburg, made this point when it stressed that "overbroad generalizations" about the differences between men and women are not sufficient to provide the justification need to uphold gender based distinctions.[30] The standard is designed to prevent the government from acting as though "women were second-class citizens or unworthy of the consideration provided" to men.[31] With the heightened scrutiny test, actions that might appear rational will not be sustained unless the government can go further and show, in addition, that the distinction based on sex is designed to advance an important state interest, and that the means chosen to advance the state interest are related to that interest.

While the intermediate standard of review is clearly applicable to sex discrimination cases outside of prison, is it the test to be applied in a prison sex discrimination case? There is an argument that it should not be the test for prison cases. As will be seen in later chapters, the Supreme Court in *Turner v Safley*[32] and

---

[28]Mississippi University for Women v. Hogan, 458 U.S. 718, 731, 102 S. Ct. 3331, 73 L. Ed. 2d 1090, 5 Ed. Law Rep. 103 (1982). See also U.S. v. Virginia, 518 U.S. 515, 526, 116 S. Ct. 2264, 135 L. Ed. 2d 735 (1996) (holding that distinctions based on gender cannot stand unless the differentiation is justified by an "exceedingly persuasive justification").

[29]Mississippi University for Women v. Hogan, 458 U.S. 718, 725, 102 S. Ct. 3331, 73 L. Ed. 2d 1090, 5 Ed. Law Rep. 103 (1982).

[30]U.S. v. Virginia, 518 U.S. 515, 533, 116 S. Ct. 2264, 135 L. Ed. 2d 735 (1996)

[31]Pitts v. Thornburgh, 866 F.2d 1450, 1459 (D.C. Cir. 1989).

[32]Turner v. Safley, 482 U.S. 78, 107 S. Ct. 2254, 96 L. Ed. 2d 64 (1987).

O'Lone v Estate of Shabazz[33] approved the looser rational basis test for adjudicating claims involving fundamental rights of inmates to free speech and the free exercise of religion.[34] The weight of authority is that these are the governing tests for prison equal protection claims involving fundamental rights.[35] Thus, for many equal protection prison claims, courts will apply the slack rational basis test even though, had the same issue arisen in civilian society, the compelling state interest test would be applied. Why should not the same be true for gender-based prison claims?

In a reflective opinion for the District of Columbia Circuit Court of Appeals, Judge Kenneth Starr held that, even in a prison setting, the heightened scrutiny test ought to apply to sex-based prison discrimination cases.[36] Judge Starr sought to distinguish between cases involving individual rights under the Bill of Rights, to which the *Turner* rational basis test would apply, and cases raising equal protection sex discrimination claims. The personal rights governed by the *Turner* test involve a court determination about a rule designed to control day-to-day life in prison.[37] Thus, judicial deference is needed to enable prison administrators the leeway they need to run a safe and secure facility. By contrast, a gendered-based equal protection claim is a claim that "charges invidiousness, rather than an unwarranted interference with constitutionally secured liberties."[38]

Because it is not as direct an affront to the ability of prison officials to make on-the-spot judgments but, rather, goes to the overarching policies of a system, there is not the same reason for deference with equal protection claims. Therefore, the intermediate standard

---

[33]O'Lone v. Estate of Shabazz, 482 U.S. 342, 107 S. Ct. 2400, 96 L. Ed. 2d 282 (1987).

[34]*Turner* is discussed in Ch 5 and *Shabazz* in Ch 6.

[35]See § 4:2.

[36]Pitts v. Thornburgh, 866 F.2d 1450 (D.C. Cir. 1989).

[37]For a discussion of the *Turner* test, see Ch 5.

[38]Pitts v. Thornburgh, 866 F.2d 1450, 1455 (D.C. Cir. 1989).

of review test can be applied. Several commentators agree with the position taken by Judge Starr. They make a strong argument that it would be "misguided" to apply *Turner* at least when there are not serious security issues involved.[39] In the words of one author, the *Turner* test "is not the appropriate standard for an equal protection challenge claiming gender discrimination. By using rational basis review courts lower the constitutional minimum requirement for gender discrimination."[40]

Nevertheless, this argument is not entirely persuasive. Many gender-based distinctions in a prison setting are made because prison administrators feel-often for misguided reasons-that they are necessary to operate their institutions. If courts are required to give less protection to inmates' rights when First Amendment rights are at stake in prison than they would if those rights were infringed by government officials operating in the free world, why should not the same be true for gender-based distinctions? To be sure, judicial protection against sex discrimination is crucial to our constitutional democracy, but is not the same true of judicial protection of cherished First Amendment protections as well? This observation may simply reveal the intellectual weakness of the *Turner* test, not of Judge Starr's ultimate position that the intermediate

---

[39]Jennifer Arnett Lee, Women Prisoners, Penological Interests, and Gender Stereotyping: An Application of Equal Protection Norms to Female Prisoners, 32 Colum. Human Rights L. Rev. 251, 266 (2000); Donna L. Laddy, Can Women Prisoners Be Carpenters? A Proposed Analysis For Equal Protection Claims Of Gender Discrimination In Educational And Vocational Programming At Women's Prisons, 5 Temple Pol. & Civ. Rts. L. R. 1 (Fall 1995).

[40]Marya P. McDonald, A Multidimensional Look At The Gender Crisis In The Correctional System, 15 Law & Ineq. 505, 531 (1997). See also Donna L. Laddy, Can Women Prisoners be Carpenters? A Proposed Analysis for Equal Protection Claims of Gender Discrimination in Educational and Vocational Programming at Women's Prisons, 5 Temp. Pol. & Civ. Rts. L. Rev. 1, 17 (1995) (pointing out that decisions about prison programs do not implicate security issues that necessitate use of the *Turner* standard).

§ 4:5   Rights of Prisoners, Third Edition

standard of review should be applied in prison sex discrimination cases.[41] For these and other reasons there are decisions contrary to that of Judge Starr.[42] Thus, this critical issue remains unresolved in the absence of a definitive opinion by the United States Supreme Court.

This is not the only area in which there is uncertainty. In addition to the present doubt about the proper standard for equal protection analysis of gender based claims, as we shall see below there is also indecision about whether male and female prisoners are "similarly situated." Since the Equal Protection Clause only protects against discrimination between similarly situated groups, there is no violation of the Constitution if there is disparate treatment of two groups that are not similarly situated.[43] These two issues and the uncertainty about there proper resolution cloud the case law on this topic. The later topic is explored below.

---

[41]See also Ashann-Ra v. Com. of Va., 112 F. Supp. 2d 559, 570-71 (W.D. Va. 2000) (applying intermediate review to a gender claim and rejecting *Turner*); West v. Virginia Dept. of Corrections, 847 F. Supp. 402 (W.D. Va. 1994) (same).

[42]See, e.g., Yates v. Stalder, 217 F.3d 332 (5th Cir. 2000) (holding that the *Turner* test applies in equal protection cases); Pearce v. Sapp, 182 F.3d 918 (6th Cir. 1999) (holding that groups may be treated differently if there is a rational relationship shown). C.f., Women Prisoners of District of Columbia Dept. of Corrections v. District of Columbia, 93 F.3d 910, 926, 113 Ed. Law Rep. 30 (D.C. Cir. 1996) (holding that *Turner's* deferential approach is appropriate in a equal protection case in order to avoid micromanaging prison facilities). Other circuits have noted the issue but have not ruled on it. Glover v. Johnson, 198 F.3d 557, 559, 1999 FED App. 415P (6th Cir. 1999).

[43]See Marsh v. Newton, 134 F.3d 383 (10th Cir. 1998) (plaintiff, a female inmate, claimed that there was a disparity of treatment between females in private correction facilities and males in state run facilities in New Mexico; 10th Circuit affirmed the lower court's holding that the male and female inmates were not similarly situated and that an equal protection claim must therefore fail).

Comparing Discrete Prison Conditions

As just noted, differences in conditions, rules, and treatment between prisons for males and females has proved to be fertile ground for equal protection challenges. In regard to one prison system, for example, a judge indicated that a practice that only allowed men to apply for work furlough was constitutionally offensive.[44] The practice of charging male, but not female, prisoners for their stay in mental hospitals also has been invalidated[45] as has the failure to provided special facilities for male deaf inmates but not female deaf inmates.[46]

On the other hand, there is case law sustaining some distinct policies that rely on sexual classifications. Differences in the application of grooming regulations for male and female prisoners, for example, have been upheld.[47] It has also been held that allowing female, but not male, inmates to decorate their cells and to call

---

[44]Dawson v Carberry, No C-71-1916 (ND Cal filed Sept 1971), reported in 14 Am. Crim. L Rev. 563 (1977). See also Cooper v. Morin, 91 Misc. 2d 302, 398 N.Y.S.2d 36 (Sup 1977), judgment aff'd and modified, 64 A.D.2d 130, 409 N.Y.S.2d 30 (4th Dep't 1978).

[45]McAuliffe v. Carlson, 377 F. Supp. 896 (D. Conn. 1974), order rev'd on other grounds, 520 F.2d 1305 (2d Cir. 1975).

[46]Clarkson v. Coughlin, 898 F. Supp. 1019, 10 A.D.D. 642 (S.D. N.Y. 1995).

[47]Hill v. Estelle, 537 F.2d 214 (5th Cir. 1976); Ashann-Ra v. Com. of Va., 112 F. Supp. 2d 559 (W.D. Va. 2000) (upholding regulation allowing women to have longer hair than male inmates and to have braids, plaits or pony tails); Davie v. Wingard, 958 F. Supp. 1244, 166 A.L.R. Fed. 709 (S.D. Ohio 1997) (court held prison regulation restricting the hair length of men, but not women did not violate the Equal Protection Clause). Poe v. Werner, 386 F. Supp. 1014 (M.D. Pa. 1974). Wise v. Com., Dept. of Corrections, 690 A.2d 846 (Pa. Commw. Ct. 1997) (prison policy, which restricted the hair length of men but not women did not violate the Equal Protection Clause of the Fourteenth Amendment; court held such different treatment was reasonably related to the legitimate penological interests of prison safety and security).

§ 4:5   Rights of Prisoners, Third Edition

home periodically is not unconstitutional.[48] Another court rejected an equal protection challenge based on differential sentences for male and female escapees.[49] And another court held that a policy that allowed overnight visitation by infant children with female inmates but not with male inmates did not violate equal protection.[50]

A particularly egregious example of lack of parity is the not uncommon practice of transferring women prisoners out of state because of the lack of in-state facilities in which to place them. This was the normal practice in North Dakota and is authorized by legislation in several other states.[51] A controversy about the custom arose in North Dakota when one judge specified in a criminal sentence that the female defendant be required to serve her sentence in the state. The state's attorney general brought an action to set aside this limitation on the sentence. The North Dakota Supreme Court, finding the system to be an unconstitutional discrimination against women, placed sharp limits on the practice. In its opinion, the court took note of the hardships caused to female prisoners who were required to spend their time in prison far from their families, without the same opportunities to appear in person before the parole board or to confer with counsel.[52] The court concluded that the state was required to make maximum efforts to create facilities in order to avoid

---

[48]Hill v. Estelle, 537 F.2d 214 (5th Cir. 1976).

[49]Wark v. Robbins, 458 F.2d 1295 (1st Cir. 1972).

[50]Bills v. Dahm, 32 F.3d 333 (8th Cir. 1994).

[51]According to one report, at least six states have statutes authorizing transfer of women to out-of-state prisons to serve their sentences. Lawrence Bershad, Discriminatory Treatment of the Female Offender in the Criminal Justice System, 26 B.C. L. Rev. 389, 403 (1985) (Georgia, Hawaii, Maine, Montana, Nevada, and Wyoming).

[52]State ex rel. Olson v. Maxwell, 259 N.W.2d 621, 624 (N.D. 1977).

sending women out of state.[53] A similar result was reached in an earlier case from Hawaii.[54]

However, an opinion from the District of Columbia Circuit upholds the practice of transferring women, but not men, out of the District to serve their sentences.[55] The court acknowledged that the practice placed an unfair burden on women but held it was not unconstitutional because it was related to the important government interest of reducing prison overcrowding and was not the product of "bias, indifference, or outdated stereotypes of women."[56] Critical to the court's determination was evidence that demonstrated that public officials had made diligent, yet unsuccessful, efforts to construct a women's prison close to the District of Columbia.[57] In that sense, the opinion is distinguishable from the North Dakota and Hawaii cases where there was no evidence that prison officials had made good-faith efforts to stem the out-of-state transfers.[58]

There is one type of case that distinguishes between the rights available to women that are not available to men in a way that makes a great deal of sense. These are cases that raise privacy issues that arise when male guards conduct body searches of women inmates. While cross-gender searches of male inmates may be permissible, there are special difficulties posed by cross gender body searches of women inmates. The leading case in-

---

[53]*Id.* at 632-33.

[54]See, e.g., Park v. Thompson, 356 F. Supp. 783 (D. Haw. 1973).

[55]Pitts v. Thornburgh, 866 F.2d 1450 (D.C. Cir. 1989).

[56]*Id.* at 1461.

[57]*Id.*

[58]See, e.g., State ex rel. Olson v. Maxwell, 259 N.W.2d 621 (N.D. 1977); Park v. Thompson, 356 F. Supp. 783 (D. Haw. 1973). Cf DeVault v. Nicholson, 170 W. Va. 719, 296 S.E.2d 682 (1982) (absent legislative act, state may not close its only women's prison because of budgetary considerations). But see Jackson v. Thornburgh, 907 F.2d 194 (D.C. Cir. 1990) (holding constitutional having female offenders in facilities that make them ineligible for early release based on good-time credits while men were housed in facilities that made them eligible).

§ 4:5

validated the practice on the grounds that the searches were highly traumatic to women, 85 per cent of whom had a prior history of physical and sexual abuse by men.[59] The court held that the searches were unconstitutional even though the same searches of male inmates by female guards would not be. The court reasoned that "women experience unwanted intimate touching by men differently from men subject to comparable touching by women."[60] Other courts have added that correctional employees may be assigned according to sex in order to protect inmates' privacy.[61] And to ensure that women inmates are not sexually abused, courts have held that prison officials have a special responsibility to police and control inappropriate conduct by male prison

---

[59] Jordan v. Gardner, 986 F.2d 1521, 1525 (9th Cir. 1993) (en banc) ("Eighty-five percent of the inmates report a history of serious abuse . . . including rapes, molestations, beatings and slavery.").

[60] Id. at 1526. See also Smith v. Fairman, 678 F.2d 52 (7th Cir. 1982) (not unconstitutional to allow female guards to frisk male prisoners where frisks did not extend to genital area); Madyun v. Franzen, 704 F.2d 954 (7th Cir. 1983); Grummett v. Rushen, 779 F.2d 491 (9th Cir. 1985) (routine pat-down searches, which included groin area of male prisoners by female guards did not violate inmate's right of privacy); Ashann-Ra v. Com. of Va., 112 F. Supp. 2d 559, 570 (W.D. Va. 2000) (women have greater rights not to be observed by members of the opposite sex while showering, but a regular practice of that occurring for male prisoners would be unconstitutional).

[61] See, e.g., Forts v. Ward, 434 F. Supp. 946 (S.D. N.Y. 1977), judgment rev'd on other grounds, 566 F.2d 849 (2d Cir. 1977); Reynolds v. Wise, 375 F. Supp. 145 (N.D. Tex. 1973). See United Nations, Standard Minimum Rules for Treatment of Prisoners Rule 53 (1955) (women prisoners generally supervised by women officers, with few exceptions). For a discussion of the problem of sexual harassment of women in prison, see Laurie A. Hanson, Comment, Women Prisoner's Freedom from Sexual Harassment-A Constitutional Analysis, 13 Golden Gate U. L. Rev. 667 (1983). See also Sims v. Montgomery County Com'n, 766 F. Supp. 1052 (M.D. Ala. 1990) (finding that sexual harassment at a county jail was unlawful).

EQUAL PROTECTION § 4:5

guards.[62]

The "Parity" Cases

The most important cases, however, have been those that deal with systemic challenges with regard to programs available to women. There have been a series of district court opinions in major class action challenges to disparities in programs in Kentucky,[63] Michi-

---

[62]See, e.g.,Women Prisoners of District of Columbia Dept. of Corrections v. District of Columbia, 877 F. Supp. 634, 98 Ed. Law Rep. 681 (D.D.C. 1994), vacated in part on other grounds, modified in part on other grounds, 899 F. Supp. 659, 104 Ed. Law Rep. 213 (D.D.C. 1995) (holding that pervasive sexual harassment existed and ordering injunctive relief, where guards forced sexual activity on female inmates, partook in unsolicited sexual contact in the form of touching and exposure of genitals, and made sexual comments and prison officials did not commit a substantial effort to remedy the problem). But see Johnston v. Ohio Dept. of Rehab. & Corr., 66 Ohio Misc. 2d 101, 643 N.E.2d 595 (Ct. Cl. 1993) (holding that since prison officials acted to halt inappropriate activity immediately, female inmate did not prove that prison officials acted with deliberate indifference when a custodian acting outside the scope of his employment touched the inmate on her buttocks); Thompson v. Wyandotte County Detention, 869 F. Supp. 893 (D. Kan. 1994) (female prisoner was denied equal protection claim where she was viewed by male prison guards while she was nude in the shower because she was not treated differently from male inmates who were viewed by female guards). See also Iman R. Soliman, Male Officers in Women's Prisons: The Need for Segregation of Officers in Certain Positions, 10 Tex. J. Women & L. 45 (2000); Rebecca Jurado, The Essence of Her Womanhood: Defining the Privacy Rights of Women Prisoners and The Employment Opportunities of Women Guards, 7 Am. U. J. Gender Soc. Policy & Law 1 (1999). For a fuller discussion of sexual harassment claims by prisoners, see § 2.06

[63]Canterino v. Wilson, 546 F. Supp. 174 (W.D. Ky. 1982), judgment aff'd, 875 F.2d 862 (6th Cir. 1989) (dealing with disparities in vocational programs); Canterino v. Wilson, 644 F. Supp. 738 (W.D. Ky. 1986),judgment aff'd, 875 F.2d 862 (6th Cir. 1989) (dealing with disparities in law library access).

§ 4:5   Rights of Prisoners, Third Edition

gan,[64] Nebraska,[65] and the District of Columbia.[66] In these cases, which arose in the 1970's and 1980's, district courts fleshed out in some detail what those courts felt was required to meet the demands of the Equal Protection Clause. These cases established the principle that there must be "parity" between programs available in male and female prisons. As is discussed later in this section several of these decisions have been reversed and the underpinnings of the remaining cases are now to say the least a bit insecure.[67] While this body of case law is no longer clearly established, to understand the present state of the law on parity claims as it has evolved it is important to first describe that case law as it developed in the district courts.

These district court cases espouse the position that women have the constitutional right to "parity of treat-

---

[64]Glover v. Johnson, 478 F. Supp. 1075 (E.D. Mich. 1979) (prison officials moved to terminate district court's continuing twenty-year jurisdiction over the plan to remedy equal protection violations in prison education; Court of Appeals granted defendants' motion for discontinuance of the jurisdiction over the remedial plan after, on remand, the district court held that prison post-secondary and college educational opportunities between female and male inmates were sufficiently comparable, vocational opportunities were sufficiently comparable, and apprenticeship opportunities were sufficiently comparable).

[65]Klinger v. Nebraska Dept. of Correctional Services, 824 F. Supp. 1374 (D. Neb. 1993), order rev'd, 31 F.3d 727 (8th Cir. 1994). Other courts have addressed these issues as well. See, e.g., Fiandaca v. Cunningham, 827 F.2d 825, 8 Fed. R. Serv. 3d 858 (1st Cir. 1987) (New Hampshire violated female prisoners' right to equal protection because of lack of comparable facilities for women).

[66]Women Prisoners of District of Columbia Dept. of Corrections v. District of Columbia, 877 F. Supp. 634, 98 Ed. Law Rep. 681 (D. D.C. 1994), vacated in part, modified in part, 899 F. Supp. 659, 104 Ed. Law Rep. 213 (D.D.C. 1995).

[67]See Klinger v. Nebraska Dept. of Correctional Services, 824 F. Supp. 1374 (D. Neb. 1993), order rev'd, 31 F.3d 727 (8th Cir. 1994); Women Prisoners of District of Columbia Dept. of Corrections v. District of Columbia, 877 F. Supp. 634, 98 Ed. Law Rep. 681 (D. D.C. 1994), vacated in part, modified in part, 899 F. Supp. 659, 104 Ed. Law Rep. 213 (D.D.C. 1995).

ment" with men in the programs that are made available to them.[68] However, this does not mean that prison officials are obligated to duplicate each program for women that it provides for men. The Equal Protection Clause is not violated if the programs are "equivalent in substance if not in form."[69]

The question, according to these district court opinions, then becomes: what are programs that are equivalent in substance? From those cases, several concepts emerge that bear directly on this question. One is that prison officials cannot rely on the comparatively small numbers of women to justify diminished program opportunities. If they were permitted to do this, they could point to the fact that smaller numbers of women make it more expensive to operate the same kind of programs that are available to men. As one district court said, "the argument that women's prisons are small and therefore expensive to operate, 'is frankly not a justification, but an excuse' that will not be countenanced."[70] A second point, which follows from the first, is that defendants will not be able to defeat an equal protection challenge by merely demonstrating that they spend more money per female inmate than they do per male inmate. This fact only demonstrates

---

[68]See, e.g., Klinger v. Nebraska Dept. of Correctional Services, 824 F. Supp. 1374 (D. Neb. 1993), order rev'd, 31 F.3d 727 (8th Cir. 1994); Canterino v. Wilson, 546 F. Supp. 174, 210 (W.D. Ky. 1982), judgment aff'd, 875 F.2d 862 (6th Cir. 1989); Glover v. Johnson, 478 F. Supp. 1075, 1079 (E.D. Mich. 1979). See also Bukhari v. Hutto, 487 F. Supp. 1162 (E.D. Va. 1980) (quoting unreported decision in Barefield v. Leach, No 10282 (D.N.M. 1974)("[w]hat the Equal Protection Clause requires in a prison setting is parity of treatment, as contrasted with identity of treatment, between male and female inmates . . .").

[69]Glover v. Johnson, 478 F. Supp. 1075, 1079 (E.D. Mich. 1979).

[70]Klinger v. Nebraska Dept. of Correctional Services, 824 F. Supp. 1374 (D. Neb. 1993), order rev'd, 31 F.3d 727 (8th Cir. 1994) (quoting Glover v. Johnson, 478 F. Supp. 1075, 1078 (E.D. Mich. 1979)); ABA, Standards for Criminal Justice Standard 23.614 (1986) ("Prisoners should not be subjected to discriminatory treatment based solely on . . . sex . . .").

that there are more "economies of scale" in operating large male institutions than is the case for small women's prisons.[71] It follows from this that "spending is not a very good measure of equivalency."[72]

A third proposition is that differences between men and women can be a relevant consideration for prison administrators making an equivalency determination, if it is not based on outmoded stereotypical sentiments about the roles of women in society. There is no place in law for exercises in "romantic paternalism" that discriminate against women."[73] An example of impermissible thinking is found in one case where prison administrators sought to excuse the failure to provide prison programs on the ground that women were less responsive to them. The defendants asserted that female prisoners, as a group, tend to be less aggressive, not as well-trained, and less educated than their male counterparts. Furthermore, they are more likely to have child care responsibility then men.[74] For these reasons, women are less likely to be employable than men. Based on these facts, the defendants argued that there was no need to provide the same level of vocational and training programs for women prisoners as for men.

The court declined to credit this argument. The court noted that the differences the defendants pointed to might be real, but did not conclude that this meant that vocational and educational programs would be wasted on women offenders. To the contrary, the court held, if anything, these differences establish that the state could constitutionally provide remedial programs

---

[71]Klinger v. Nebraska Dept of Correctional Servs, 824 F. Supp. 1392-93 (D. Neb. 1993), rev'd by, 31 F.3d 727 (8th Cir. 1994), motion denied by, on remand at, 887 F. Supp.1281 (D. Neb. 1995), aff'd in part, rev'd in part by, vacated by in part, 107 F.3d 609 (8th Cir. 1997).

[72]*Id.*

[73]Dothard v. Rawlinson, 433 U.S. 321, 335, 97 S. Ct. 2720, 53 L. Ed. 2d 786 (1977).

[74]For a discussion of the problems that incarceration causes to women who have small children, see Ch 15.

designed especially to help women overcome these barriers; they could not excuse the state's providing a lesser quality and quantity of programs for women.[75] Thus, the state could justify "differential treatment of females . . . if the means chosen are directly and substantially related to the objective of providing women with remedial assistance. . . ."[76] Another example of an argument that is the product of "archaic notions of appropriate gender roles" is where prison officials argued that child rearing classes for women should be considered a valid substitute for vocational training.[77] The court held that while these classes were undeniably important, they did not supplant the need for job training programs.[78]

The principle that emerges from this line of cases is the notion that it is permissible to craft programs that take into account the needs of women. In fact, courts have pointed with favor to surveys that some prisons have undertaken of the needs and desires of women for the types of programs. Based on these surveys, in one case women stated a preference for "secretarial technology" and "clerical arts" vocational training, over other offerings, such as truck driving. The court held that it was constitutional to honor these preferences, even though it meant that the programs offered at the women's prison would differ from those at the men's prison.[79]

Utilizing these "parity of treatment" principles, district courts have ordered extensive improvements in

---

[75]Klinger v. Nebraska Dept. of Correctional Services, 824 F. Supp. 1374, 1394 (D. Neb. 1993), order rev'd, 31 F.3d 727 (8th Cir. 1994).

[76]Id. at 1396.

[77]Id. at 1398.

[78]Id at 1405-06.

[79]Id. at 1404. See also Glover v. Johnson, 478 F. Supp. 1075, 1086, (E.D. Mich. 1979) (a similar survey was done, but the court doubted its accuracy and ordered a second, more comprehensive survey). But see Rosemary Herbert, Comment, Women's Prisons: An Equal Protection Evaluation, 94 Yale L.J. 1182, 1197 n77 (1985) (arguing that it is improper to consider preferences of

vocational, recreational, educational, and work release programs and in classification systems.[80] They have additionally ordered markedly inferior conditions corrected in women's prisons that occurred when female, but not male, inmates were denied contact visitation, regular outdoor exercise, and subscriptions to newspapers, television privileges, and educational opportunities.[81] Also found to be an equal protection violation was a prison system in which men, but not women, were allowed to be trustees.[82] Adding to the list of discrepancies struck down have been schemes that provide unequal pay to women. An illustration is the Nebraska prison system, which had a system that paid women by the hour but paid men by the day-even if they worked less than a full day.[83] In other instances, in order to achieve parity, courts have ordered remedial programs training female inmates in legal research

---

women because it can be used as a justification for the continuation of unconstitutional conditions).

[80]See, e.g., Klinger v. Nebraska Dept. of Correctional Services, 824 F. Supp. 1374 (D. Neb. 1993), order rev'd, 31 F.3d 727 (8th Cir. 1994); Canterino v. Wilson, 546 F. Supp. 174, 210 (W.D. Ky. 1982), judgment aff'd, 875 F.2d 862 (6th Cir. 1989); Glover v. Johnson, 478 F. Supp. 1075, 1079 (E.D. Mich. 1979); Mitchell v. Untreiner, 421 F. Supp. 886 (N.D. Fla. 1976). See, generally, Lawrence Bershad, Discriminatory Treatment of the Female Offender in the Criminal Justice System, 26 B.C. L. Rev. 389, 401-18 (1985) (collecting cases). It is worth noting that male prisoners have a more difficult time establishing a claim to sex discrimination than do women. See, e.g., Smith v. Bingham, 914 F.2d 740 (5th Cir. 1990) (holding that there was no equal protection violation when a male inmate was denied permission on security grounds to enroll in a vocational training program at a women's prison).

[81]Mitchell v Untreiner, 421 F. Supp. 886 (N.D. Fla. 1976).

[82]*Id.* at 895. See also Cooper v. Morin, 91 Misc. 2d 302, 398 N.Y. S.2d 36 (Sup 1977), judgment aff'd and modified, 64 A.D.2d 130, 409 N.Y.S.2d 30 (4th Dep't 1978), judgment modified, 49 N.Y.2d 69, 424 N.Y.S.2d 168, 399 N.E.2d 1188 (1979).

[83]Klinger v. Nebraska Dept. of Correctional Services, 824 F. Supp. 1374, 1397 (D. Neb. 1993), order rev'd, 31 F.3d 727 (8th Cir. 1994).

EQUAL PROTECTION § 4:5

skills to assist inmates using the law library.[84]

This line of cases has been thrown into serious question by a series of Court of Appeal decisions that seem to weaken the force of the Equal Protection Clause in assessing discrepancies between programs in male and female prisons. The leading case is the Eighth Circuit's decision in *Klinger v. Department of Corrections*.[85] The lawsuit involved a challenge to limitations in programs available to women inmates at the Nebraska Center for Women (NCW). The plaintiffs claimed that the programs at the women's prison were inferior to programs at the Nebraska State Penitentiary (NSP), the major state prison for men.[86] After a four week trial the district court found equal protection violations in over a dozen different ways relating to the programs. The lower court found that the men and women inmates in Nebraska were similarly situated and that since this was a gender discrimination case "heightened scrutiny" was required.[87]

The Eighth Circuit, by a 2-1 vote, found that the district court erred in finding that men and women prisoners were similarly situated. The district court had found that the two groups were similar since they

---

[84]Glover v. Johnson, 478 F. Supp. 1075, 1095 (E.D. Mich. 1979); Canterino v. Wilson, 546 F. Supp. 174, 203 (W.D. Ky. 1982), judgment aff'd, 875 F.2d 862 (6th Cir. 1989); Klinger v. Nebraska Dept. of Correctional Services, 824 F. Supp. 1374, 1436 (D. Neb. 1993), order rev'd, 31 F.3d 727 (8th Cir. 1994). See also Casey v. Lewis, 834 F. Supp. 1477 (D. Ariz. 1993) (court found substantial disparity rising to the level of constitutional violation where services offered to men encompassed occupational therapy, computer training, and stress management, and women only received aerobics, board games, and self-help programs such as "Women Who Love Too Much").

[85]Klinger v. Department of Corrections, 31 F.3d 727 (8th Cir. 1994).

[86]Prior to trial plaintiffs had sought to broaden the inquiry to include all state prisons in which men were held but the lower court held that the request was not made in a timely matter. *Id.* at 729.

[87]*Id.* at 730.

§ 4:5

were both groups of prisoners of roughly similar security levels, the purposes of their confinement were the same and, to the extent that there were other differences, they were better dealt with at the heightened scrutiny stage where a balancing could take place than at the district court stage where a finding that the two groups were not similarly situated would end the case.[88]

Judge Magill, speaking for the majority, began the court's analysis by stating that "[d]issimilar treatment of dissimilarly situated persons does not violate equal protection."[89] To determine whether men and women inmates were similarly situated, the court focused on what it perceived to be the nature of the plaintiffs' claim. The court noted that the plaintiffs did not challenge the level of funding available for programs at women's prisons.[90] Without a claim of discriminatory funding, the court felt that the plaintiffs' claim amounted to an argument that they were entitled to the same programs that men receive. The court found that men and women inmates were not similarly situated so as to make that claim. The court noted first that there were fewer women inmates in NCW than male inmates in NSP. Second, men stayed two to three times longer in NSP than women did at NCW. Third, women inmates are more likely to be victims of abuse, while male inmates were "more likely to be violent and predatory than female inmates."[91]

Thus, since the institutions were "different institutions with different inmates each operating with limited

---

[88]*Id.* at 730 (describing the holding of the district court).

[89]*Id.* at 731.

[90]*Id.*

[91]*Id.* at 732. The Eighth Circuit in a later case added additional factors to the list so that there are five factors now that should be considered in determining whether men and women inmates are similarly situated in a prison system. These factors include (1) population size of the prison; (2) security level; (3) types of crimes for which inmates are committed to prison; (4) length of sentence; and (5) special characteristics. Pargo v. Elliott, 894 F. Supp. 1243 (S.D. Iowa 1995), judgment aff'd, 69 F.3d 280 (8th Cir. 1995).

resources to fulfill different specific needs . . . whether NCW lacks one program that NSP has proves almost nothing."[92] Indeed, the court observed "female inmates can always point out certain ways in which male prisons are 'better' than theirs, just as male inmates can always point out *other* ways in which female prisons are 'better' than theirs."[93] The court therefore concluded that "comparing programs at NSP to those at NCW is like the proverbial comparison of apples to oranges."[94] For these reasons the court held that, with one limited exception,[95] men and women inmates, although both were in the same prison system, were not similarly situated for purposes of invoking the Equal Protection Clause.

The court went on to explain why it thought that its opinion was also good policy. Since the Equal Protection Clause did not require "parity" in programming between female and male inmates, prison officials would be able "to experiment and innovate with programs at an individual institution" without fear that a federal court would second guess their choices to provide some programs at one facility and other programs at another facility.[96]

The majority's decision provoked a strong dissent. In the dissenting judge's view, male and female inmates were similarly situated, since both groups were confined for commission of a crime and for both groups the state

---

[92]*Id.* at 732.

[93]*Id.* at 732.

[94]*Id.* at 733. The court also held that even if the Equal Protection Clause applied the claim would fail, since there was no evidence of intentional discrimination against the plaintiffs.

[95]The court in dicta stated that had the plaintiffs alleged that the process by which programming decisions was made differed from men to women's prisons than there could be a valid claim. This is so because men and women are "similarly situated at the beginning of the decision making process where infinite intervening variable have not yet excessively tainted the comparison . . .[between men and women]"). *Id.* at 733, n.4.

[96]*Id.*

§ 4:5   Rights of Prisoners, Third Edition

had an interest in rehabilitation.[97] The dissent noted while the male and female prisoners did not have identical needs and interests, this did not mean that the groups were not similarly situated for equal protection purposes. As long as the two groups shared "commonalities," they were similarly situated.[98] If this was the case, then they ought to receive similar treatment unless there were special reasons for a disparity in treatment based on legitimate and important governmental interests. These differences could and should be explored when applying the gender specific standard for determining whether in fact there is an equal protection violation on these facts.[99] The majority's opinion refusing to invoke the Equal Protection Clause meant that the conditions would not even be subjected to that scrutiny and that the court was sanctioning "unequal treatment of female inmates . . ."[100]

In *Women Prisoners of the District of Columbia Department of Corrections v. District of Columbia*,[101] the D.C. Circuit Court of Appeals reached a similar result, reversing a district court judgment that on equal protection grounds ordered improvements in programming at a women's prison. The Court of Appeals relied heavily on the reasoning in *Klinger*.[102] Again, there was a forceful dissent. The dissenter took the majority to task for not even requiring the government to justify disparate treatment of women inmates, noting that

[u]nder the court's rationale it would almost seem that the District could send men to a country club and women to

---

[97]*Id.* at 735 (dissenting opinion).

[98]*Id.* at 736 (dissenting opinion).

[99]*Id.* at 737 (dissenting opinion).

[100]*Id.* at 736 (dissenting opinion).

[101]Women Prisoners of District of Columbia Dept. of Corrections v. District of Columbia, 93 F.3d 910, 113 Ed. Law Rep. 30 (D.C. Cir. 1996).

[102]For example, the court noted that "It is hardly surprising let alone evidence of discrimination that the smaller correctional facility offered fewer programs than the larger one." *Id.* at 925.

the Black Hole of Calcutta; a difference in treatment the women received there would be ascribed to their dissimilar situation and would require no further justification.[103]

The holdings in *Klinger* and *Women Prisoners* that men and women inmates are not similarly situated was followed by another decision in the Eighth Circuit Court of Appeals.[104] Thus, the state of the law is that there are a number of district court opinions standing for the proposition that women and men are entitled to parity in prison programs and several Courts of Appeals decisions from two circuits finding no right to parity because men and women prisoners in those systems are not similarly situated. While there is as yet no split in the federal Courts of Appeals on this subject, there is a substantial body of scholarly commentary on these decisions and it is almost uniformly critical of those cases that say that men and women inmates are not similarly situated.[105]

---

[103]*Id.* at 951 (dissenting opinion)

[104]See, e.g., Keevan v. Smith, 100 F.3d 644 (8th Cir. 1996) (holding that men and women inmates in Missouri were not similarly situated and that even if they were there was no purposeful discrimination). The Sixth Circuit considered the issue but held that it was not necessary for decision in the case before it. Glover v. Johnson, 138 F.3d 229, 253, 1998 FED App. 72P (6th Cir. 1998) (not ruling explicitly on this issue but noting that "not a single appellate court in the nation has ever held that a lack of parity with respect to educational or vocational opportunities between male and female inmates is a violation of the Equal Protection Clause of the Fourteenth Amendment . . .").

[105]See, e.g., Jennifer Arnett Lee, Women Prisoners, Penological Interests, and Gender Stereotyping: An Application of Equal Protection Norms to Female Prisoners, 32 Colum. Human Rights L. Rev. 251, 266 (2000); Julie Kocaba, The Proper Standard Of Review: Does Title Ix Require "Equality" Or "Parity" Of Treatment When Resolving Gender-Based Discrimination In Prison Institutions?, 25 New Eng. J. on Crim. & Civ. Confinement 607, 643 (1999) (criticizing courts for failing to notice that "they are reinforcing gender classifications and traditional stereotypes through the effect of their decision(s)"); Marya P. McDonald, A Multidimensional Look At The Gender Crisis In The Correctional System, 15

§ 4:5

At least one Court of Appeals, however, has indicated that a finding that men and women are not similarly situated cannot be assumed without a careful record of the actual conditions and circumstances in men and women's prisons.[106] In that case, male inmates claimed that their equal protection rights were violated by harsher conditions in Louisiana's male prisons than in the state's female prisons. The plaintiffs alleged that female inmates did not have to labor in agricultural fields, that they were confined in private or semi-private air conditioned rooms, and they were provided with a standard of living above the state poverty level while men were not. The defendants cited *Klinger* for the proposition that men and women prisoners were not similarly situated. The court held that such a finding could not be made without a developed factual record, noting that "speculations concerning possible disparities among male and female populations cannot be substituted for adequate evidence and findings of fact in the district court."[107]

Until there is further litigation and perhaps a decision by the Supreme Court, this area of the law remains muddled. While the decisions discussed above rely primarily on the Equal Protection Clause, courts have begun, to a more limited extent, to make use of Civil Rights statutes to prevent discrimination against women as well as to support the courts' holdings.[108] Under Title IX of the Educational Amendments of 1972

Law & Ineq. 505 (1997); Donna L. Laddy, Can Women Prisoners be Carpenters? A Proposed Analysis for Equal Protection Claims of Gender Discrimination in Educational and Vocational Programming at Women's Prisons, 5 Temp. Pol. & Civ Rights. L. Rev. 1, 22 (1995) (arguing that the *Klinger* court's analysis of the similarly situated point is "based on outdated views of women and impermissible generalizations").

[106] Yates v. Stalder, 217 F.3d 332 (5th Cir. 2000).

[107] *Id.* at 335.

[108] Klinger v. Nebraska Dept. of Correctional Services, 824 F. Supp. 1374 (D. Neb. 1993), order rev'd, 31 F.3d 727 (8th Cir. 1994) (using 42 U.S.C. § 2000d-7).

§ 4:5

("Title IX") recipients of federal aid must provide men and women with equal access to educational programs and activities.[109] Utilizing this Act, women inmates have brought suits seeking to rectify deficiencies in programming at women's prisons. While the act is not comprehensive enough to cover all prison programs, it does cover education programs.[110] Courts have held that the Act applies to prisons,[111] but they are divided on the appropriate standard for determining whether the statute has been violated. The Ninth Circuit held that the Act requires not mere parity in prison programs, but equality.[112] The Eighth Circuit agreed, and also held that women need not be similarly situated to male inmates to invoke the protection of the Act.[113] Thus, in those jurisdictions the Act provides broader protections

---

[109]20 U.S.C. §§ 1681 et seq., The Act in relevant part provides that "[no] person in the United States shall, on the basis of sex, be excluded from participation in, be denied the benefits of, or be subjected to discrimination under any educational program or activity receiving federal financial assistance." 20 U.S.C. § 1681 (a). There is persuasive evidence that Congress did not intend to exempt prisoners from the protections of the Act. Jeldness v. Pearce, 30 F.3d 1220, 1222, 93 Ed. Law Rep. 146 (9th Cir. 1994); Canterino v. Wilson, 546 F. Supp. 174, 210 (W.D. Ky. 1982), judgment aff'd, 875 F.2d 862 (6th Cir. 1989) (courts "cannot judicially impose a special exception" for prisons).

[110]See Jeldness v. Pearce, 30 F.3d 1220, 93 Ed. Law Rep. 146 (9th Cir. 1994).

[111]See, e.g., Jeldness v. Pearce, 30 F.3d 1220, 1225, 93 Ed. Law Rep. 146 (9th Cir. 1994) ("The statute, the case law, and the legislative history all suggest that Title IX should apply to prisons; there is no contrary authority."). Accord Klinger v. Department of Corrections, 107 F.3d 609 (8th Cir. 1997); Women Prisoners of District of Columbia Dept. of Corrections v. District of Columbia, 93 F.3d 910, 113 Ed. Law Rep. 30 (D.C. Cir. 1996).

[112]Jeldness v. Pearce, 30 F.3d 1220, 93 Ed. Law Rep. 146 (9th Cir. 1994).

[113]Klinger v Department of Corrections, 107 F.3d 609 (8th Cir. 1997) (although the court stated that the female plaintiffs were unable to demonstrate that they were "similarly situated" to male inmates, this failure did not preclude a claim under Title IX; the court held that the "similarly situated" standard is not applicable

than the Equal Protection Clause. However, the D. C. Circuit disagreed, holding that the Act is co-extensive in its protections to the Equal Protection Clause.[114] Under that theory, the Act adds little, if anything, to the constitutional analysis. Commentators have advocated using Title IX as an alternative theory for equalizing educational and vocational programs in men and women's prisons.[115]

Segregation

A fact of imprisonment that has been little litigated is the sexual segregation of American prisons.[116] . There is some case law that holds that sexual segregation

---

to a Title IX analysis; rather, the plaintiffs could prevail if they could show that a systemic discrimination exists; however, since the plaintiffs failed to engage in this analysis, the court affirmed the lower court's grant of summary judgment for the defendants).

[114]Women Prisoners of District of Columbia Dept. of Corrections v. District of Columbia, 93 F.3d 910, 113 Ed. Law Rep. 30 (D.C. Cir. 1996).

[115]See e.g., Julie Kocaba, The Proper Standard Of Review: Does Title Ix Require "Equality" Or "Parity" Of Treatment When Resolving Gender-Based Discrimination In Prison Institutions?, 25 New Eng. J. on Crim. & Civ. Confinement 607 (1999); Christine M. Safarik, Separate But Equal: Jeldness v Pearce: An Analysis of Title IX within the Confines of Correctional Facilities, 18 W. New Eng. L. Rev. 337 (1996); Donna L. Laddy, Can Women Prisoners be Carpenters? A Proposed Analysis for Equal Protection Claims of Gender Discrimination in Educational and Vocational Programming at Women's Prisons, 5 Temp. Pol. & Civ. Rts. L. Rev. 1, 22 (1995) ("Title IX offers prisoners more protection than the Equal Protection Clause and thus is an attractive alternative . . . to an equal protection claim.").

[116]As of 1997, 92 of 108 state prisons holding women were women only. Only 16 state prisons in the United States house both males and females. Morris L. Thigpen and Susan M. Hunter, Dep't of Justice, Current Issues in the Operation of Women's Prisons 1 (1998)

does not amount to a constitutional violation.[117] But most of the major prison sex discrimination cases do not raise the issue.[118] Although most courts dismiss such claims without examining the purposes behind sexual segregation,[119] there have been questions raised in the legal literature about the wisdom of this widely accepted practice,[120] and several national correctional organizations have called for the development of more co-correctional institutions where men and women are integrated at least for the purposes of prison programs.[121] According to the critics of segregated prisons, a dual prison system based on sex carries with it many of the same burdens well-established for a dual system based on race. Segregation by sex, it is claimed, stigmatizes women by separating them "on the basis of their supposed moral weakness. . .."[122] Like the old "separate, but equal" shibboleth for schools, with segregation of prisons women are consigned to facilities that will inevitably have inferior programs, facilities,

---

[117]Stuart v. Heard, 359 F. Supp. 921 (S.D. Tex. 1973); Dodson v. State, 268 Ind. 667, 377 N.E.2d 1365 (1978). See also Tarlton v. Clark, 441 F.2d 384 (5th Cir. 1971).

[118]Pitts v. Thornburgh, 866 F.2d 1450, 1458 (D.C. Cir. 1989) (noting that prisoners do not attack segregated facilities based on gender); Klinger v. Nebraska Dept. of Correctional Services, 824 F. Supp. 1374, 1385 (D. Neb. 1993), order rev'd, 31 F.3d 727 (8th Cir. 1994) (plaintiffs do not claim segregation because of gender is violative of the Equal Protection Clause).

[119]See, e.g., Stuart v. Heard, 359 F. Supp. 921 (S.D. Tex. 1973).

[120]Rosemary Herbert, Comment, Women's Prisons: An Equal Protection Evaluations, 94 Yale L.J. 1182 (1985).

[121]National Advisory Commission on Criminal Justice Standards and Goals, Corrections 378-79, Standard 11.6(7) and Commentary (1973) ("The Correctional system should abandon the current system of separate institutions based on sex and develop a fully integrated system based on all offenders' needs."); American Correctional Assn, Standards for Adult Correctional Institutions Standard 3-4266 (1990) (male and female inmates housed in the same institution should have equal access to all programs).

[122]Herbert, supra note 119, at 1193.

§ 4:5   Rights of Prisoners, Third Edition

and services.[123] Finally, critics maintain that even the "parity of treatment" doctrine[124] used by the some courts in an attempt to equalize treatment of women is a vague concept that "is ill suited to the issues that arise in prison sex discrimination cases."[125] In particular, the parity doctrine "refuse[s] to recognize harms resulting from the process of segregation itself, it does not even demand that separate prison facilities be equal."[126]

On the other side of this question, defenders of sexually segregated prisons argue that sound penological rationales can be identified for the practice. They maintain that male competition for the attention of the limited number of female prisoners in an integrated environment might lead to violence. There is arguably an increased risk of sexual attacks. Moreover, the few women in a predominantly male facility might find their unique rehabilitative needs overlooked, as specialized treatment programs for them might become prohibitively expensive. Defenders of segregation argue that either the state's interest in preventing violence or its interest in rehabilitating female offenders amply justify the maintenance of separate facilities. Thus, they argue, sexual segregation is not unconstitutional per se.[127]

Although sexually integrated prisons may not be constitutionally required, they may be desirable as a matter of policy.[128] Several states now have such prisons, and the evidence that is available suggests

---

[123]*Id.*

[124]As discussed above even this limited doctrine is not in current favor with the courts that lately have tended to dismiss even claims based upon parity on the ground that men and women inmates are not similarly situated.

[125]*Id.* at 1196.

[126]*Id.* at 1197.

[127]See, e.g., Barbara B. Knight & Stephen T. Early, Jr., Prisoners' Rights in America 257 (1986) (citing James J. Gobert & Neil P. Cohen, Rights of Prisoners 302 (Shepard's/McGraw-Hill 1981)). See also Dodson v. State, 268 Ind. 667, 377 N.E.2d 1365 (1978).

[128]National Advisory Commission on Criminal Justice Standards and Goals, Corrections Standard 11.6 (1973). See also ABA, Stan-

that they have been successful.[129] One reported experimental program involving a sexually integrated prison population of minimum security inmates resulted in reduced forced homosexuality, violence, and tension, and a very low recidivism rate following release.[130] The reduced recidivism may be attributable to the fact that, because the sexually mixed milieu more closely approximates civilian society, released prisoners may have less difficulty readjusting to a sexually integrated society than their counterparts who have served time in a sexually segregated environment. While there is an obvious risk of increased heterosexual activity, the benefits of an integrated prison, including reduced forced homosexuality, may outweigh the liabilities.

---

dards for Criminal Justice Standard 23-6.14 (1986) (male and female inmates should have the same living conditions). But see United Nations, Standard Minimum Rules for the Treatment of Prisoners Rule 8 (1955) ("Men and women shall so far as possible be detained in separate institutions . . .").

[129]Rosemary Herbert, Comment, Women's Prisons: An Equal Protection Evaluation, 94 Yale L.J. 1182, 1184 (1985) (reporting that the federal government, Massachusetts, Kansas, Alaska, and New York have established co-correctional prisons). See also Vernon B. Fox, Correctional Institutions 218 (1983).

[130]Barry Ruback, The Sexually Integrated Prison: A Legal and Policy Evaluation, 3 Am. J. Crim. L. 301, 314-16 (1975).

Chapter 5

Communication and Expression: Speech in Prison

Research References
Federal Courts ⚖181; Prisons ⚖4, 17.5; Sentencing and Punishment ⚖1543, 1544
A.L.R. Index: Prisons and Prisoners

> **KeyCite®:** Cases and other legal materials listed in KeyCite Scope can be researched through West Group's KeyCite service on Westlaw®. Use KeyCite to check citations for form, parallel references, prior and later history, and comprehensive citator information, including citations to other decisions and secondary materials.

§ 5:1   Introduction
§ 5:2   The Supreme Court's Approach to Speech in Prison
§ 5:3   Censorship and Limitations on Receipt of Publications
§ 5:4   Publisher-Only Rules
§ 5:5   Access to Literature in Punitive Segregation
§ 5:6   Prisoner Writings
§ 5:7   The Right to Political Activity: The Right to Associate, to Communicate, and to Present Grievances in Prison

§ 5:1 Introduction

The "Constitution's most majestic guarantee"[1] is the Free Speech Clause of the First Amendment. Because it is so "central to the workings of a tolerably responsive

---

[Section 5:1]
[1]Lawrence H. Tribe, American Constitutional Law § 12-1, at 785 (2d ed 1988).

§ 5:1

and responsible democracy,"[2] free speech, which includes the rights of speech, press, assembly, petition, and association,[3] occupies a preferred place[4] in the constellation of American constitutional protections and is enshrined in the First Amendment to the Constitution.

Free speech is valued by our society for many reasons. Long ago John Milton observed that it helps in "preventing human error through ignorance."[5] More recently, Oliver Wendell Holmes eloquently constructed a "marketplace of ideas" theory built on the premise that free speech encourages a healthy competition between ideas, which is conducive to the discovery of truth.[6] Another important benefit of free speech is that it acts as a check on "the abuse of power by public officials."[7] By allowing for the release of pent-up emotions of the citizenry, free speech also provides a "safety valve for society."[8]

Indeed, freedom of speech serves so many important

---

[2]*Id.* at 788.

[3]US Const amend I: "Congress shall make no law . . . abridging the freedom of speech, or the right of the press; or the right of the people peaceably to assemble; and to petition the Government for a redress of grievances."

[4]Dennis v. United States, 341 U.S. 494, 581, 71 S. Ct. 857, 95 L. Ed. 1137 (1951); Thomas v. Collins, 323 U.S. 516, 529-30, 65 S. Ct. 315, 89 L. Ed. 430 (1945); Murdock v. Com. of Pennsylvania, 319 U.S. 105, 115, 63 S. Ct. 870, 87 L. Ed. 1292, 146 A.L.R. 81 (1943); John E. Nowak & Roland D. Rotunda, Constitutional Law § 16.7, at 941 (4th ed 1991); Robert B. McKay, The Preference for Freedom, 34 NYU L Rev 1182 (1959).

[5]John E. Nowak & Roland D. Rotunda, Constitutional Law § 16.6, at 1060 (6th ed. 2000).

[6]Abrams v. U.S., 250 U.S. 616, 630, 40 S. Ct. 17, 63 L. Ed. 1173 (1919) (Holmes, J, dissenting).

[7]*Id.* at 941.

[8]*Id.* Professor Tribe identified an additional, and more transcendental, value of free speech when he wrote that apart from its instrumental value to democracy, free speech is important "because it enhances personal growth and self-realization." Lawrence H. Tribe, American Constitutional Law § 12-1, at 787 (2d ed 1988).

societal values that Justice Cardoza aptly summarized it as "the matrix, the indispensable condition of nearly every other form of freedom."[9] Free speech is such a highly valued right that government interference with speech normally is subjected to exacting scrutiny by the courts.[10] Indeed, it is well established that to abridge First Amendment freedoms of people in the free world, the government must have a "compelling interest."[11]

As we will see, however, these high standards are not applied in prison free speech cases. The reason for this is not that the benefits associated with freedom of speech are inapplicable to the prison environment. To the contrary, speech by prisoners aids the public in understanding how this important government operation is run. Similarly, ideas expressed by persons in prison contribute-sometimes in unique ways-to the "marketplace of ideas."[12] Speech in prison also aids in checking abuses of government power by prison officials who, by definition, have almost complete control over their charges. Additionally, free speech allows prisoners to vent their grievances in public thereby serving as an important safety valve. Finally, when permitted, free speech contributes to prisoners' self-growth, and gives inmates a sense of individual dignity that they

---

[9]Palko v. State of Connecticut, 302 U.S. 319, 327, 58 S. Ct. 149, 82 L. Ed. 288 (1937) (overruled on other grounds by, Benton v. Maryland, 395 U.S. 784, 89 S. Ct. 2056, 23 L. Ed. 2d 707 (1969)).

[10]Boos v. Barry, 485 U.S. 312, 324, 108 S. Ct. 1157, 99 L. Ed. 2d 333 (1988); National Ass'n for Advancement of Colored People v. State of Ala. ex rel. Patterson, 357 U.S. 449, 78 S. Ct. 1163, 2 L. Ed. 2d 1488 (1958); Buckley v. Valeo, 424 U.S. 1, 64-5, 96 S. Ct. 612, 46 L. Ed. 2d 659 (1976).

[11]Perry Educ. Ass'n v. Perry Local Educators' Ass'n, 460 U.S. 37, 45, 103 S. Ct. 948, 74 L. Ed. 2d 794, 9 Ed. Law Rep. 23 (1983); Carey v. Brown, 447 U.S. 455, 461-62, 100 S. Ct. 2286, 65 L. Ed. 2d 263 (1980); U.S. v. O'Brien, 391 U.S. 367, 376-77, 88 S. Ct. 1673, 20 L. Ed. 2d 672 (1968).

[12]For examples of prisoners' works, see Daniel Berrigan, Prison Poems (1973); Pete Earley, The Hot House: Life Inside Leavenworth Prison (1992); Jean Harris, Marking Time-Letters from Jean Harris to Shana Alexander (1991).

would not otherwise have.

Moreover, freedom of speech, as a practical matter, has a heightened significance for prisoners. For a prisoner, cut off from others by conviction and imprisonment, free speech rights can be a lifeline to the world. Without them, an inmate could be denied benefits others normally take for granted. John Stuart Mill made a similar point when he asserted that free speech leads to public enlightenment.[13] Without the protection of free speech, an inmate would have no right to do such accepted things as receive uncensored publications and books or write, either for other inmates, through prison newspapers or pamphlets, or for the wider world, through books and articles. Free speech rights also come into play when prisoners seek to come together for the purposes of forming organizations within the prison. An additional important freedom of speech interest arises when inmates seek to maintain contact with their family and friends on the outside through mail or by visits to the prison.

As important as freedom of speech is for prisoners, and for the public at large, there are reasons why some prison officials have sought to limit a prisoner's ability to communicate. Prison administrators have argued that unfettered free speech is incompatible with their task of providing security within the sometimes volatile prison environment. They have argued that opportunities for communication give inmates the chance to hatch escape plans or plots for raising havoc in the institution. Prison officials also have asserted that speech and association interferes with rehabilitation by introducing ideas to inmates that the prison officials would prefer they not receive. Finally, prison officials have pointed to administrative problems that make it infeasible to provide opportunities for free speech.

This chapter will treat the issue of freedom of speech in prison. The chapter will begin with a discussion of the Supreme Court's general approach to speech in

---

[13]John Stuart Mill, On Liberty

SPEECH IN PRISON § 5:2

prison, and will then address the issues presented by prison censorship policies, restrictions of the rights of inmates to publish their writings, and restraints placed on the right of inmates to associate for political purposes with one another while imprisoned. While freedom of speech also has implications for prison mail and visiting policies, those subjects will be discussed in subsequent chapters.[14]

§ 5:2 The Supreme Court's Approach to Speech in Prison

Research References

West's Key Number Digest, Federal Courts ⚖181

The Supreme Court has grappled over the years for a consistent approach to the adjudication of prison First Amendment free speech claims. Although the Court has decided a number of prison cases that raise First Amendment issues, three cases best mark the path that the Court has followed and best describe the test that now governs: *Procunier v Martinez*,[1] *Turner v Safley*,[2] and *Thornburgh v Abbot*.[3]

Procunier v Martinez

The first occasion that the Court had to consider the question of free speech within prison was *Procunier v Martinez*.[4] *Martinez* involved a challenge to mail censorship rules in California state prisons. The rules permitted the opening and reading of all incoming and outgoing mail between prisoners and their families and friends. Under the rules, prison officials were authorized to censor any mail considered to "unduly com-

---

[14]See Chs 12, 13.

[Section 5:2]

[1]416 U.S. 396 (1974).

[2]482 U.S. 78 (1987).

[3]490 U.S. 401 (1989).

[4]Procunier v. Martinez, 416 U.S. 396, 94 S. Ct. 1800, 40 L. Ed. 2d 224 (1974).

§ 5:2   Rights of Prisoners, Third Edition

plain" or "magnify grievances."⁵ In addition, mail that expressed "inflammatory political, racial, [or] religious" views and mail that was "lewd, obscene or defamatory" could be withheld.⁶

Although the Court noted that the case raised an issue of the First Amendment rights of prisoners, it refused to rule explicitly on the question because it found that there was a narrower ground for decision, that is, the fact that the censorship regulation affected not only prisoners, but also free-world persons to whom the letters were addressed and who were seeking to send letters to inmates. Therefore, the Court said, "[w]hatever the status of a prisoner's claim to uncensored correspondence with an outsider, it is plain that the latter's interest is grounded in the First Amendment's guarantee of freedom of speech."⁷

Having sidestepped the question of the prisoners' free speech rights, the Court turned to the question of the First Amendment rights of outsiders who seek to maintain contact with inmates. To determine that issue, the court held that the mail regulations at issue in the case should be judged by a standard that took into account the outsider's interest in communication with the prisoner and balanced it against the "legitimate and substantial" state interests in the operation of the prisons. The Court held those interests to include "preservation of internal order and discipline, the maintenance of institutional security against escape or unauthorized entry and the rehabilitation of the prisoners."⁸ To accomplish this balance in a way that accommodated the interests of both parties, the Court chose a middle-level standard of review. The standard had two parts:

First, the regulation or practice in question must further an important or substantial governmental interest unrelated to the suppression of expression . . . . Second, the

⁵*Id.* at 399.
⁶*Id.* at 399-400.
⁷*Id.* at 408.
⁸*Id.* at 412.

limitation of First Amendment freedoms must be no greater than is necessary or essential to the protection of the particular governmental interest involved.[9]

Applying this two-part standard to the censorship regulations at issue, the Court held that the rules were unconstitutional. The state failed to show that the regulations were necessary to preserve order in the facility or to rehabilitate the inmates. In fact, the "extraordinary latitude" given to prison officials under the regulations had been used simply to "suppress unwelcome criticism" from inmates, not to protect the legitimate security interests of the state.[10] Although the state argued that statements in letters that "unduly complain" or "magnify grievances" might lead to "flash riots" and detract from rehabilitation efforts, the Court found that the state had not shown how such letters "could possibly lead to flash riots, nor do they specify what contribution the suppression of complaints makes to the rehabilitation of criminals."[11] Furthermore, applying the second branch of the test, the Court found that the regulations were not "narrowly drawn to reach only material" that posed a legitimate threat to institutional interests.[12]

The *Martinez* decision held for the first time that the First Amendment can limit the scope of prison rules affecting speech, at least to the extent that these rules have an impact on outsiders. Equally important, *Martinez* held that the "complex and intractable" problems of running prisons require a lower standard of review than the "compelling interest" and "least drastic alternative" tests which usually apply in free speech cases.[13] While the middle-level standard of review applied by the Court this standard certainly gives prison

---

[9]*Id.* at 413.
[10]*Id.* at 415.
[11]*Id.* at 416.
[12]*Id.*
[13]*Id.* at 405.

officials "some latitude"[14] to anticipate problems that may arise if free speech is granted in the prison, it is a fairly rigorous standard. Under this standard, the burden is placed on prison administrators to establish that a rule affecting the free speech rights of outsiders advances a substantial interest of the prison and that the rule is narrowly fashioned so as not to intrude on First Amendment rights more than is necessary to achieve that objective.

Martinez was an important step forward in the advancement of free speech interests within the prison environment. However, some labeled the decision "disappointing,"[15] and others characterized it as a "pyrrhic victory" for prisoners' rights.[16] The reason is that the Court missed an important opportunity to delineate what the First Amendment rights of inmates themselves were. Just how significant this missed opportunity was can be seen from an examination of the next major prison free speech case decided by the Court, *Turner v Safley*.[17]

---

[14]*Id.* at 414 (prison officials are permitted "some latitude" to anticipate possible consequences of allowing speech in prison).

[15]James J. Gobert & Neil P. Cohen, Rights of Prisoners 104 (Shepard's/McGraw-Hill 1st ed 1981).

[16]Ira P. Robbins, The Cry of Wolfish in the Federal Courts: the Future of Federal Judicial Intervention in Prison Administration, 71 J Crim L & Criminology 211, 214 (1980).

[17]Turner v. Safley, 482 U.S. 78, 107 S. Ct. 2254, 96 L. Ed. 2d 64 (1987). Prior to *Turner* the Court decided four other cases that touched on aspects of the First Amendment rights of inmates, but in none of them did the Court use the occasion to set forth with any specificity what the free speech rights of inmates were. See, e.g., Pell v. Procunier, 417 U.S. 817, 94 S. Ct. 2827, 41 L. Ed. 2d 495 (1974) (ban on face-to-face interviews by the media with specific inmates); Jones v. North Carolina Prisoners' Labor Union, Inc., 433 U.S. 119, 97 S. Ct. 2532, 53 L. Ed. 2d 629 (1977) (involving prison regulations designed to discourage the creation of a prisoners' labor union); Bell v. Wolfish, 441 U.S. 520, 99 S. Ct. 1861, 60 L. Ed. 2d 447 (1979) (pre-trial detainee "publishers only" rule); Block v. Rutherford, 468 U.S. 576, 104 S. Ct. 3227, 82 L. Ed.

Turner v Safley

Turner dealt with two rules of a Missouri state prison. One placed a ban on correspondence between inmates in the prison system;[18] the second, in practice, prohibited inmates from marrying while they were imprisoned. The lower courts struck down both rules, but the Supreme Court in a 5-4 decision reversed. The mail rule raised only the rights of prisoners. Thus, the *Turner* Court had to determine whether the *Martinez* test applied to cases in which only the rights of prisoners were involved.

The Court held that the *Martinez* test did not apply to these cases. Although the Court recognized that "prison walls do not form a barrier separating inmates from the protections of the Constitution,"[19] it had serious reservations about an overly aggressive role for the federal courts in prison cases. Prisons, the Court said, are difficult to operate, and courts lack the "expertise, planning and the commitment of resources" that the legislative and executive branches of government have to run them.[20] Moreover, prison administration is a function that has been committed to the legislatures and the executive. Therefore, "separation of powers concerns counsel a policy of judicial restraint."[21] The Court further noted that federalism problems are raised when federal courts are involved in determining the

---

2d 438 (1984) (non-contact visiting rule). *Pell* is discussed in Ch 14; *Jones* is discussed in § 5:7; *Bell* is discussed in § 5:4; *Block* is discussed in Ch 12.

[18]Turner v. Safley, 482 U.S. 78, 81, 107 S. Ct. 2254, 96 L. Ed. 2d 64 (1987). The only exceptions to this ban were legal correspondence between inmates and other correspondence with the permission of prison staff. However, as a practical matter these exceptions were rarely invoked, and the rule functioned as a virtual absolute ban on correspondence. *Id.* at 81-82.

[19]*Id.* at 84.
[20]*Id.* at 85.
[21]*Id.*

rights of inmates in state prison systems.[22]

The Court held that the *Martinez* test was not an appropriate way of addressing these concerns. In the Court's view, *Martinez's* "inflexible strict scrutiny analysis," when used in cases that deal with prisoners' rights only, "would seriously hamper [prison officials'] ability to anticipate security problems and to adopt innovative solutions to the intractable problems of prison administration."[23] If this were the case, the Court opined, "[c]ourts inevitably would become the primary arbiters of what constitutes the best solution to every administrative problem" in the prisons.[24] Instead of the *Martinez* test, the Court chose a "reasonable relationship" test. Under that standard, a prison rule that restricts First Amendment rights "is valid if it is reasonably related to legitimate penological interests."[25]

The Court set forth four factors for a court to consider in determining whether a reasonable relationship was present. "First, there must be a 'valid rational connection' between the prison regulation and the legitimate governmental interest put forward to justify it."[26] Second, there must be "alternative means" of exercising the right that the prisoner claims is infringed.[27] Third, the court must consider "the impact accommodation of the asserted constitutional right will have on guards and other inmates and on the allocation of prison resources generally."[28] Finally, the court must consider whether there are readily available alternatives that at de minimis cost could meet the prison's interests without sacrificing the plaintiffs' free speech rights.[29]

The Court held that the prison mail rule was consti-

---

[22]*Id.*

[23]*Id.*

[24]*Id.*

[25]*Id.* at 89.

[26]*Id.*

[27]*Id.* at 90.

[28]*Id.*

[29]*Id.* at 90-91.

tutional under these tests. First, as it was designed to control the communication of escape, assault, and violence plans, it was logically connected to valid security concerns of the prison. Second, the regulation did not deprive prisoners of all means of written expression; it only barred communication among inmates; therefore, there were alternative means of exercising the restricted right to communicate. Third, the cost of accommodating the right would be "significantly less liberty and safety for everyone else, guards and other prisoners alike," since to allow correspondence between inmates would, in the judgment of prison administrators, jeopardize their ability to maintain security in the institution. Thus, the impact of accommodation was too high. Finally, there were "no obvious, easy alternatives" to the prohibition. The alternative suggested by the plaintiffs, monitoring all inmate mail, would require prison officials to read every piece of mail. The risk of missing dangerous communications, combined with the "sheer burden on staff resources" required for this undertaking, led the Court to conclude that the alternative "would impose more than a de minimis cost on the pursuit of legitimate inmate corrections goals."[30]

Turner resolved the issue left open in *Martinez*

---

[30]*Id.* at 91-93. The marriage rule, however, did not satisfy the four *Turner* factors. The Court recognized that the marriage rule, to the extent that it forbade the marriage between an inmate and a civilian, affected the rights of outsiders as well as inmates. Thus, it might be subject to the *Martinez* test rather than the *Turner* test. The Court concluded, however, that it need not consider whether *Martinez* applied because the rule failed to meet the less demanding four *Turner* factors. *Id.* at 96-97.

The marriage rule was not "reasonably related" to security and rehabilitation goals because it "sweeps much more broadly" than necessary to protect these interests. *Id.* at 98. The defendants had argued that the rule prohibiting marriages was necessary to guard against the security threat to the institution posed by "love triangles" that might develop with prisoners who married someone while maintaining a relationship with someone else. The defendants also justified the rule on rehabilitation grounds as a way of preventing women from developing excessive dependence on men.

concerning the constitutional standard for determining the free speech rights of prisoners. At least when the case did not also involve a free speech claim of outsiders, the Court opted for a "reasonable relationship" test, arguably the lowest level of scrutiny possible for free speech issues and one that is more deferential to prison administrators than the test announced in *Martinez*.

The *Turner* case has significance beyond the free speech issues discussed in this chapter. Indeed, *Turner* itself applied the reasonable relationship test to adjudicate the marriage claim, which was not a free speech issue per se. In addition, *Turner* has rapidly come to be understood as the key case for determining the constitutional rights of prisoners to practice religion.[31]

It is important to note several key ways in which the holding in *Turner* contrasts with *Martinez*. *Martinez* subjects prison rules to a middle level of scrutiny in which the burden is placed on prison officials to show that the rule advances a substantial governmental interest and that the restriction is tailored so that it is no broader than necessary to serve that interest. *Turner* selects a more deferential level of review. In the pro-

---

Neither ground rationally supported the prohibition. Love triangles could exist whether inmates were married or not. As for the prevention of dependence in women inmates, the Court held that this belief reflected an "excessive paternalism" of the Missouri prison system that treated women differently than men without substantial justification. *Id.* at 99. The Court also reasoned that there were obvious alternatives to the marriage rule that would accommodate at de minimis cost the right to marry without an undue "ripple effect" on other prisoners. The alternative was found in the Federal Bureau of Prisons regulation that permitted inmates to marry unless the warden specifically determined that the marriage would be a threat to security *Id.* at 98. For a discussion of the right to marry while incarcerated, see Ch 15.

[31]See O'Lone v. Estate of Shabazz, 482 U.S. 342, 107 S. Ct. 2400, 96 L. Ed. 2d 282 (1987) decided several weeks after *Turner*. *Shabazz* is discussed in detail in Ch 6. The four-factor analysis set out in *Turner* is discussed in detail there.

cess, it alters the *Martinez* burden in some ways and reverses it in others. It alters the burden in that, under *Turner,* prison officials need not show that the restriction is necessary to serve a substantial governmental interest. As long as they show a reasonable relationship between a valid governmental purpose and the rule, they have met their burden. Moreover, in making the reasonableness judgment, the four-factor *Turner* test does not impose on defendants the obligation to justify their failure to adopt less drastic alternatives as is the case with *Martinez.* The only exception is when there is an alternative that is so obvious that it is readily available and can be implemented at little or no cost.

Thus, after *Turner* and *Martinez,* it appeared that the Supreme Court had bifurcated prison free speech cases into those that involved the claims of prisoners and outsiders to communicate with one another, for which the heightened scrutiny of *Martinez* applied, and those that involved only the claims of prisoners, for which the "reasonableness" standard of *Turner* applied. That distinction, however, was challenged, and dispelled, in the last of the three Supreme Court free speech cases, *Thornburgh v Abbott.*[32]

Thornburgh v Abbott

In *Thornburgh,* the plaintiffs filed a class action challenging, on First Amendment grounds, incoming publication censorship rules of the Federal Bureau of Prisons. The rules permitted the warden to reject any publications sent to an inmate that the warden deemed "detrimental to the security, good order, or discipline of the institution, or . . . [that] might facilitate criminal activity."[33] In the event that the warden determined that the publications should not be admitted, the rules contained procedural safeguards the inmate could use

---

[32]Thornburgh v. Abbott, 490 U.S. 401, 109 S. Ct. 1874, 104 L. Ed. 2d 459 (1989).

[33]Thornburgh v Abbott, 490 US 401, 109 S Ct 1874, 1877 (1989) (citing 28 CFR § 540.71(b)).

to challenge the decision.[34]

The rules provided that in making the decision whether to allow the publication, the warden could not reject a publication solely because its content was "religious, philosophical, political, social or sexual, or because its content [was] unpopular or repugnant."[35] The regulations went on to provide a nonexhaustive list of criteria that a warden could rely on to reject a publication.[36] The Bureau supplemented these rules with an all-or-nothing practice that kept the inmate from receiving acceptable portions of a publication if any part of the publication was found to be objectionable.

The Court of Appeals for the District of Columbia Circuit subjected the regulation to review under the *Martinez* standard and struck it down. The court reasoned that *Martinez,* rather than *Turner,* should apply, because the regulation restricted the First Amendment rights of publishers and authors of publications, who were not inmates.[37] Therefore, the defendants were required to show that the rule served an important governmental interest and that it was narrowly tailored to serve that purpose. The Court of Appeals held that

---

[34]*Id.* at 1877-78. These safeguards included the right to notice of a rejected publication and of the name of the articles or materials in the publication that were considered objectionable. An inmate could also appeal the denial to the Regional Director of the Federal Bureau of Prisons, and was entitled to review the publication to aid in preparing his or her appeal, unless the warden deemed review of the publication by the inmate detrimental to security. *Id.* at 1878 (citing 28 CFR § 540.71(d)).

[35]*Id.*

[36]These included publications that described how to produce weapons and bombs, that would aid in escape, that described how to manufacture alcoholic beverages and drugs, that were written in code, that encouraged violence or group disruption, that instructed how to commit crimes, or that were so sexually explicit as to pose a threat to the facility. *Id.*

[37]Abbott v. Meese, 824 F.2d 1166, 1170-71 (D.C. Cir. 1987) judgment vacated, 490 U.S. 401, 109 S. Ct. 1874, 104 L. Ed. 2d 459 (1989).

defendants had not met that burden and that the regulations were unconstitutional on their face.

By a 6-3 decision, the Supreme Court reversed. Writing for the Court, Justice Blackmun noted that "[t]here is little doubt that the kind of censorship just described would raise grave First Amendment concerns outside the prison context."[38] Despite these concerns, and even though the case admittedly dealt with the rights of outsiders to communicate with inmates, Justice Blackmun held that the District of Columbia Circuit had incorrectly chosen the *Martinez* standard to apply to this case. Instead, Justice Blackmun decreed that the reasonable relationship test of *Turner* should apply. Under that standard, the regulation, on its face, was constitutional.[39]

Justice Blackmun gave two reasons for refusing to apply the *Martinez* standard. First, *Martinez* had been incorrectly interpreted by the lower courts as requiring the strict scrutiny and least drastic alternative analysis that is more properly reserved for First Amendment cases in the free world.[40] Justice Blackmun noted that strict scrutiny is inappropriate in a prison context because it fails to accord "sufficient sensitivity to the need for discretion in meeting legitimate prison needs."[41]

Second, *Martinez* was inapplicable because it dealt with outgoing correspondence, whereas *Thornburgh* dealt with incoming publications. To Justice Blackmun, there was a critical difference between the two. Although both outgoing and incoming communications raise issues of an outsider's ability to engage in speech, Justice Blackmun declared that incoming communications present a greater danger to prison security than do outgoing communications. The reason is that "[o]nce

---

[38] 109 S. Ct. at 1878.

[39] *Id.* at 1882-85. The Court remanded for a determination whether the rule had been constitutionally applied. *Id.* at 1885.

[40] *Id.* at 1879-80.

[41] *Id.* at 1880 (quoting Turner v. Safley, 482 U.S. 78, 89-90, 107 S. Ct. 2254, 96 L. Ed. 2d 64 (1987)).

§ 5:2 RIGHTS OF PRISONERS, THIRD EDITION

in the prison, material of this kind reasonably may be expected to circulate among prisoners, with the concomitant potential for coordinated disruptive conduct."[42] By contrast, outgoing material is far less likely to "present a danger to the community *inside* the prison" since it is not intended for an inmate audience and since dangerous outgoing communication is more likely to be easily identifiable.[43]

For these reasons, the *Thornburgh* Court declined to accept the distinction suggested by *Turner* between free speech cases involving outsiders' claims to communicate with prisoners and free speech cases raising only the rights of prisoners. To drive the point home, the Court explicitly overruled *Martinez* to the extent that it suggested this distinction and limited that case only to situations involving outgoing communications between inmates and civilians.[44] Justice Blackmun, however, made clear his confidence that the *Turner* standard was "not toothless" and could adequately protect the rights of inmates and those who wished to communicate with them.[45]

Applying the reasonable relationship *Turner* test to the issues in *Thornburgh*, Justice Blackmun had little difficulty in upholding the censorship regulation in practice. The Court found that the regulation was a legitimate and neutral effort to maintain prison security. Although censorship, by definition, involves some judgments about content, the regulation was content neutral since it was not aimed at the suppression of any particular doctrine, but rendered judgments "solely on the basis of their potential implications for prison security."[46] Moreover, the discretion delegated to prison wardens to censor publications was rationally linked to the need to control the volatile prison environment. The

---

[42]*Id.* at 1881.

[43]*Id.* at 1880 (emphasis in original).

[44]*Id.* at 1881.

[45]*Id.* at 1882.

[46]*Id.* at 1882-83.

discretion was also controlled by the requirement of the regulations that called for individualized judgments in each case, which expressly prohibited categorical judgments.[47]

Continuing with the *Turner* test, the Court found that, as the regulations "permit a broad range of publications to be sent, received, and read," the prisoners had alternative means of communicating.[48] The Court also found that the cost of accommodating the plaintiffs' desires to receive publications that the warden might deem a threat would endanger the "liberty and safety of everyone else, guards, and other prisoners alike."[49] In addition, as there were no obvious alternatives to the censorship rules that could guard against this danger, the challenged rule was not an "exaggerated response."[50]

The Court also upheld the all-or-nothing rule as reasonable. The plaintiffs argued that this rule was not rational because the defendants could just as easily serve their purposes by simply ripping out the offending pages and delivering the remainder of the publication to the inmate. The Court disagreed. Justice Blackmun credited the defendants' fear as reasonable that delivering a mutilated publication to an inmate would create "more discontent" than would banning the entire publication.[51] Since the defendants did not have to prove that the all-or-nothing rule was necessary, this reasonable fear-even if unsupported-was sufficient to forge a rational link between the rule and the defendants' interest in security. A further reason for upholding the all-or-nothing rule was that it was administratively more convenient than the alternative of ripping

---

[47]*Id.* at 1883.

[48]*Id.* at 1883-84.

[49]*Id.* at 1884 (quoting Turner v. Safley, 482 U.S. 78, 92, 107 S. Ct. 2254, 96 L. Ed. 2d 64 (1987)).

[50]*Id.*

[51]*Id.* at 1884.

out the offending pages.[52]

For these reasons, the majority held that the censorship regulations were facially valid. The majority, however, remanded the case to the lower courts for a determination of the validity of the regulations as applied to 46 publications that were excluded under them.[53]

Justice Stevens dissented. He was particularly troubled by the majority's rejection of the *Martinez* standard. *Martinez,* he argued, relied on the distinction between the rights of inmates and outsiders, "not between nonprisoners who are senders and those who are receivers."[54] Justice Stevens criticized the majority for "[t]he casual discarding" of such an important precedent.[55] In addition, Justice Stevens took the majority to task for approving, as reasonable, a set of rules that "too easily may be interpreted to authorize arbitrary rejections of literature addressed to inmates."[56] In sum, he characterized the Court as engaging in "a headlong rush to strip inmates of all but a vestige of free communication with the world beyond the prison gate."[57]

Finally, Justice Stevens rejected the majority's acceptance of the all-or-nothing rule. In his opinion, there was no security justification for failure to deliver to the inmate portions of a publication that, by definition, posed no security threat to the institution.[58] Justice Stevens found it "difficult to even imagine" the administrative convenience argument since prison officials had to read the offending article before rejecting it. The "incremental burden associated with clipping out the offending matter could not be of constitutional

---

[52]*Id.*
[53]*Id.* at 1885.
[54]*Id.* at 1887.
[55]*Id.* at 1889.
[56]*Id.*
[57]*Id.* at 1886.
[58]*Id.* at 1891.

significance."⁵⁹

Legal scholars have criticized *Thornburgh,* particularly its rejection of the middle-level scrutiny of *Martinez* for the lowest-level reasonableness test of *Turner* to adjudicate a case that involves the First Amendment claims of outsiders to communicate with inmates. The majority in *Thornburgh* relied for this determination on lower court opinions that had interpreted *Martinez* to require the use of a strict scrutiny and least drastic alternative analysis. The Court held that this level of review was inappropriate in a prison context. However, one commentator has pointed out that, rather than rejecting *Martinez* entirely, "the Court could have remedied any lower court misinterpretation by simply restating with more precision its holding in *Martinez.*"[60] Moreover, the Court's equation of the security risks in *Turner* and *Thornburgh* has been criticized as not persuasive. *Turner* dealt with the risks of permitting inmates to correspond with one another. The danger is that these communications might be the vehicle for the transmission of escape plans and criminal plots. By contrast, *Thornburgh* dealt with only the receipt of outside publications, so the threat to security is not nearly as great.[61] This is because even a publication that generally exhorts criminal conduct would be easily identifiable, as opposed to individual communications that may be phrased obliquely or even in code.

Another criticism of *Thornburgh* is that it does not sufficiently protect the rights of the authors and publishers to gather and disseminate information. Expression by these parties "not only enhances individual self-expression but also protects the fundamental values underlying the First Amendment-preservation of the 'market place of ideas' and promotion of 'intelligent

---

[59]*Id.* at 1892.

[60]Note, The Supreme Court-Leading Cases, 105 Harv L Rev 177, 245 (1989).

[61]*Id.* at 245.

§ 5:2 RIGHTS OF PRISONERS, THIRD EDITION

self-government.'"[62] *Thornburgh* threatens these values because it gives prison officials "broad authority to limit publishers' access to inmates."[63] Finally, *Thornburgh* has been criticized as interfering unnecessarily with the right of inmates "to receive information and ideas."[64] Nevertheless, in *Shaw v. Murphy*,[65] the latest Supreme Court opinion on this topic, the court indicated that it continues to adhere to this approach.[66]

---

[62] *Id.* at 247.

[63] *Id.* In the non-prison context, the Supreme Court has intimated that there is a First Amendment right to receive information and ideas. See, e.g., First Nat. Bank of Boston v. Bellotti, 435 U.S. 765, 781, 98 S. Ct. 1407, 55 L. Ed. 2d 707 (1978) (indicating that the Court views with suspicion limitations on the ability of publishers to inform and educate the public and to provide a forum for ideas).

[64] *Id.* at 248. See also Alphonse A. Gerhardstein, False Teeth? Thornburgh's Claim that Turner's Standard for Determining A Prisoner's First Amendment Rights is Not "Toothless," 17 N Ky L Rev 527 (1990); Megan M. McDonald, Note, Thornburgh v Abbott: Slamming the Prison Gates on Constitutional Rights, 17 Pepp L Rev 1011 (1990).

[65] Shaw v. Murphy, 532 U.S. 223, 121 S. Ct. 1475, 149 L. Ed. 2d 420 (2001).

[66] In *Shaw*, an inmate law clerk was punished for sending a letter containing legal advice to a maximum security prisoner. The court refused to allow an exception to the test prescribed in *Turner* for communications between prisoners related to legal assistance provided by inmates. The Court held that to allow exceptions for certain types of speech based on the content of that speech would entangle federal courts in the administrative affairs of prison officials. The Court held that prison officials should have broad discretion in deciding what regulations to employ to address legitimate penological objectives. It held that there is no First Amendment right for prisoners to provide legal advice to other inmates. It noted that there is a penological objective to be served by disallowing certain communications between inmates, as communications disguised as legal advice could contain the type of inappropriate comments prison officials seek to avoid. The case was remanded, with the caveat that the plaintiff could only prevail by showing that the regulation was not related to legitimate penological interests, and he would have to "overcome the presumption that prison officials acted within their broad discretion." *Id.* at 1476.

Summary

With the trilogy of *Martinez, Turner,* and *Thornburgh,* the Supreme Court established several important principles that govern the free speech rights of prisoners. First, inmates have First Amendment rights that survive incarceration. Second, these free speech interests often implicate not only the right of inmates to communicate, but also the rights of persons who are not incarcerated or convicted of any crimes. Third, the free speech rights of inmates are governed by the reasonable relationship test annunciated in *Turner.* Fourth, free speech rights of outsiders are also governed by the *Turner* rule when those rights involve the right to send communications into the prison. Fifth, the heightened scrutiny of the *Martinez* case will be applied only, if at all, in situations in which inmates seek the right to correspond or communicate with the outside world. We turn now to cases applying these principles.

§ 5:3 Censorship and Limitations on Receipt of Publications

Research References

West's Key Number Digest, Prisons ⊕=4(8)

It is an axiomatic principle of American constitutional law that only in the most grievous of circumstances can the government impose a "prior restraint" on speech to intercept the communications of publishers and authors prior to their receipt by their intended audiences.[1] However, as we have seen, censorship rules that operate in this fashion, and that would present "grave First Amendment concerns outside the prison context," have

---

[Section 5:3]

[1]Laurence H. Tribe, American Constitutional Law § 12-11, at 859, § 12-34, at 1039-43 (2d ed 1988); John E. Nowak & Roland D. Rotunda, Constitutional Law § 16.16 at 1094, § 16.17, at 1095 (6th ed. 2000); Jerome A. Barron & C. Thomas Dienes, Constitutional Law in a Nutshell 346-51 (4th ed. 1999).

§ 5:3

been approved by the Supreme Court for prisons.² In *Thornburgh v Abbott,* the Supreme Court upheld just such a prior restraint rule.³

Yet the Court made clear that prison censorship rules are not invariably constitutional. In *Thornburgh,* the Federal Bureau of Prisons' censorship policy was held constitutional on its face because it contained clear standards designed to ensure that the rights of inmates and outsiders to free speech were not capriciously denied. The censorship rule found constitutional in *Thornburgh* has several important safeguards that the Court relied on in upholding it. The Court found that the censorship policy was not content-based,[4] that it required an individualized determination by the warden that a particular publication posed "an intolerable risk of disorder under the conditions of a particular prison at a particular time,"[5] that it did not sweep within its scope a broad array of predetermined unacceptable publications,[6] that it contemplated that inmates would have access to "a broad range of publications,"[7] and that it provided "procedural safeguards for both the recipient and the sender" to review the initial censorship decision."[8] Even with these safeguards, the Court left open the possibility that constitutional violations might occur in the manner in which the regulations were applied to particular publications.[9]

Thus, after *Thornburgh,* prison censorship rules that

---

[2]Thornburgh v. Abbott, 490 U.S. 401, 109 S. Ct. 1874, 1878, 104 L. Ed. 2d 459 (1989).

[3]*Id.*

[4]*Id.* at 1882-83.

[5]*Id.* at 1883.

[6]*Id.*

[7]*Id.* at 1884. See, generally, Aiello v. Kingston, 947 F.2d 834, 836, 21 Fed. R. Serv. 3d 259 (7th Cir. 1991) (lottery tickets are commerce, not included as a protected publication).

[8]Thornburgh v. Abbott, 490 U.S. 401, 109 S. Ct. 1874, 1877, 104 L. Ed. 2d 459 (1989).

[9]*Id.* at 1884-85.

§ 5:3

do not have sufficient safeguards to adequately preserve the free speech rights of inmates or outsiders cannot pass constitutional muster. There are at least three categories of censorship rules that, even after *Thornburgh,* remain facially unconstitutional for failure to meet the standards set in that case.

First are those censorship rules that prohibit inmates categorically from receiving certain publications. A prison censorship rule that prohibits the receipt of daily newspapers or that specifies that certain magazines can never be received is one example of this kind of rule. Courts have properly struck down such rules despite the arguments of prison administrators that the rules are necessary to prevent clogging of toilets[10] or that they are fire or health hazards.[11] The argument that newspapers are not necessary because inmates can

---

[10]Mann v. Smith, 796 F.2d 79, 81 (5th Cir. 1986); Kincaid v. Rusk, 670 F.2d 737, 743 (7th Cir. 1982); Parnell v. Waldrep, 511 F. Supp. 764, 769 (W.D. N.C. 1981).

[11]In Thomas v. Leslie, 176 F.3d 489 (10th Cir. 1999) (table) the Tenth Circuit held that an absolute ban on newspapers violated First Amendment rights, and rejecting argument that that the ban on newspapers was rationally related to concerns that they could be used as weapons or to start fires. The court determined that since the inmates were permitted to have soft-back Bibles, paperbacks, and puzzle books presenting the same security and safety risks; the newspaper ban was not rationally related to the defendant sheriff's stated objective. The defendants further asserted that access to television constituted an alternative means of exercising the right to remain informed about community and national news. This assertion was refuted because a majority vote of the inmates governed what programs were in fact watched. If the defendants' alternative means test was allowed, the defendants could prohibit all reading material under the theory that television provided an adequate substitute for all written communication. Finally, the court determined that an obvious and easy alternative existed to the defendants' underlying concern about the amount of combustible materials in the jail. A policy approved by another county jail that required inmates to turn in one publication before receiving another reduced the amount of combustible materials at hand. Therefore, the ban was not reasonable but rather an "exaggerated response to prison concerns."

§ 5:3

watch television has been consistently rejected.[12] As one court put it, "[t]elevison cannot supply the depth and diversity of coverage that newspapers can provide."[13]

Another example of a categorical rule of exclusion would be one that prohibits inmates from receiving publications in a foreign language. In one such case the Seventh Circuit found that a prison policy which flatly refused to consider receipt of publications not in the English language "without even looking to see how the [First Amendment] rights [of a Japanese speaking inmate] might be accommodated" was unconstitutional.[14] The court held that prison officials must make an effort to translate these works or find someone who could. The opinion suggests, but does not squarely hold,[15] that unless translation services pose an excessive financial burden on the facility, there is an obligation to provide them unless the inmate is literate in other languages and could obtain similar material in English.

A final example of a categorical rule of exclusion would be a blanket prohibition of nude photographs no matter what the source or the context.[16]

On occasion a rule that does not purport to be a categorical censorship rule as a practical matter is one.

---

[12]Mann v. Smith, 796 F.2d 79, 83 (5th Cir. 1986).

[13]Thomas v. Leslie, 176 F.3d 489 (10th Cir. 1999) (table). But see Hause v. Vaught, 993 F.2d 1079 (4th Cir. 1993) (upholding a complete ban on the receipt of any outside publications in a short-term detention facility on the grounds that such material presented a fire hazard and could be a conduit for smuggling and that the restrictions were imposed on a short-term detainee).

[14]Kikumura v. Turner, 28 F.3d 592, 598-599 (7th Cir. 1994) (court found that such a policy ran afoul of the Thornburgh factors, which require particularized" findings that the prohibited publication violates security).

[15]Since the rule being reviewed did not require that an attempt at accommodation be made, there was no need to consider what the result would be were the results of such an attempt known.

[16]Owen v. Wille, 117 F.3d 1235 (11th Cir. 1997)

This was the case in *Allen v. Coughlin*,[17] a Second Circuit case in which the plaintiff claimed that a policy at Green Haven Prison that unconditionally excluded press clippings from newspapers and from magazines from being sent to the facility was unconstitutional.[18] The inmate, a New York State prison inmate, was from Camden, South Carolina. He brought suit because prison officials removed from his incoming mail press clippings from his hometown newspaper. The defendants maintained that since the plaintiff could receive newspapers from the publisher, the rule was not a categorical restriction on writings in newspapers. The defendants also argued that the logistical problems associated with inspecting and reading the newspaper press clippings justified the policy. They also relied upon a New York state court opinion that upheld the rule.[19] Based upon these arguments, the district court granted summary judgment for the defendants.

The Second Circuit reversed. The court cut through the defendants' contentions that this rule was not an absolute censorship rule, holding that in practice the rule was "tantamount to a complete prohibition" against the receipt of press clippings, since the inmate could not as a practical matter obtain the press clippings in any way other than through his personal mail.[20] The court also was unimpressed with the claim that the rule was necessary to prevent dissemination of dangerous material. Press clippings could be easily examined for content.[21] Moreover, this defense lacked seriousness in light of the fact that the record established that gen-

---

[17]Allen v. Coughlin, 64 F.3d 77 (2d Cir. 1995).

[18]*Id.*

[19]Montgomery v. Coughlin, 194 A.D.2d 264, 605 N.Y.S.2d 569 (3d Dep't 1993).

[20]Allen v. Coughlin, 64 F.3d 77, 79 (2d Cir. 1995).

[21]*Id.* The court held that damages could not be recovered because the existence of the New York state court opinion on which the defendants relied meant that the rule not a violation of clearly established constitutional law. However, the claim for injunctive and declaratory relief remained open.

§ 5:3

eral correspondence from the outside was seldom read by prison officials.

A second category of rules that are facially unconstitutional in light of *Thornburgh* are those that are so vague that they fail to provide any guidance to decisionmakers about how they ought to be applied,[22] as well as those that permit the banning of publications merely because the ideas are unpopular or repugnant.[23] An example of the latter is found in *McCabe v Arave*.[24] In that case, the court dealt with a censorship rule that permitted the banning of publications that espoused views of racial superiority. Without a showing that the publication posed some realistic threat of causing violence in the facility, censorship of it could not stand.

A final category of prison rules that remain unconstitutional on their face after *Thornburgh* are those that fail to provide some mechanism for affected parties to review the initial decision to exclude the publication.[25]

Even where a prison censorship rule is constitutional under the *Thornburgh* standards, the inquiry is not complete. As mentioned earlier, *Thornburgh* left the door open to a determination that a censorship rule that is constitutional on its face may be unconstitutional as applied.[26] A difficult question that arises after *Thornburgh* is how can it be determined whether a

---

[22]Procunier v. Martinez, 416 U.S. 396, 405, 94 S. Ct. 1800, 40 L. Ed. 2d 224 (1974) (overruled by, Thornburgh v. Abbott, 490 U.S. 401, 109 S. Ct. 1874, 104 L. Ed. 2d 459 (1989)); Ustrak v. Fairman, 781 F.2d 573, 580 (7th Cir. 1986).

[23]Thornburgh v. Abbott, 490 U.S. 401, 109 S. Ct. 1874, 104 L. Ed. 2d 459 (1989); Abbott v. Meese, 824 F.2d 1166, 1176 (D.C. Cir. 1987), judgment vacated on other grounds, 490 U.S. 401, 109 S. Ct. 1874, 104 L. Ed. 2d 459 (1989).

[24]McCabe v. Arave, 827 F.2d 634 (9th Cir. 1987) (there is no reasonable relationship between goals of prison security and rehabilitation and the banning of materials that advocate racial purity but do not encourage violence or illegal activity).

[25]See, e.g., Hunter v. Koehler, 618 F. Supp. 13 (W.D. Mich. 1984).

[26]If a law is found to be facially unconstitutional because it is vague or overbroad, the law is invalidated. Under the as-applied

censorship rule that is constitutional on its face is being applied in a constitutional manner?

While the *Thornburgh* Court did not rule on this question, it did throw some light on the issue when it suggested that a constitutional violation could result from variations in enforcement of censorship regulations that stem from the "censors' subjective views."[27] In other words, if a regulation is implemented in such a way that prison censors apply "their own personal prejudices and opinions," it is suspect.[28]

Another way of assessing whether a censorship rule is being applied constitutionally is to apply the familiar four *Turner* factors.[29] The most relevant and important of these factors in the censorship area is the first factor. This test, it will be recalled, looks to the presence or absence of a rational link between the legitimate interests of the facility and the censorship of a particular piece of literature.[30] In determining whether the rational link is present, the real question in such a case is whether the court should accept the warden's judgment that the receipt of the publication at issue would pose a threat to that legitimate interest or whether, instead, the court should make an independent assessment of that question. If the court decides, how should it make that judgment?

One prison censorship case that arose after *Thornburgh* helps answer these questions. *Eckford-El v Toombs*[31] dealt with the refusal to deliver a brochure to an inmate from a correspondence school. The material

---

analysis, a judicial determination of unconstitutionality does not invalidate the law but only renders that particular application void. Jerome A. Barron & C. Thomas Dienes, Constitutional Law in a Nutshell 343 (4th ed 1999).

[27]Thornburgh v Abbott, 490 US 401, 109 S Ct 1874, 1883 n15 (1989).

[28]*Id.* n14.

[29]These factors are described in detail at § 1:9 to 1:14.

[30]For a discussion of the *Turner v Safley* test, see § 5:2.

[31]Eckford-El v. Toombs, 760 F. Supp. 1267 (W.D. Mich. 1991).

was entitled "How To Prepare For Your Paralegal Career."[32] It described the benefits of a paralegal education at the school. Although the brochure did not contain an application form or any other form of contract, the material was not delivered to the inmate because of a censorship rule that forbade inmates from receiving material that might entice the inmate to enter into contractual agreements.[33]

The court held that the regulation, which was aimed at preventing inmates from making contractual purchases by mail for such things as book-of-the-month clubs or record clubs, was justifiable on its face as a "safeguard against inmate abuse of credit."[34] However, as applied to this particular publication, the censorship was not constitutional. The court refused to take the defendant's word for it on the question of whether the receipt of the publication was reasonably related to that legitimate goal. After the court made its own independent assessment of the challenged publication, it held that the rejection was not rationally linked to the state's claimed interests. The reason for this determination was that the excluded brochure was not in any sense "contractual." For this reason, "[i]t is impossible for the court to discern how receipt of a school brochure could in any way violate the prohibition against inmates entering into certain contracts."[35] Since the exclusion of the brochure was "a mistaken application" of the censorship rule, the court held that the document should be given to the plaintiff.[36] The *Toombs* opinion indicates that, in an as-applied censorship case, courts must assess for themselves whether the defendants

---

[32]*Id.* at 1269.
[33]*Id.*
[34]*Id.* at 1271.
[35]*Id.*
[36]*Id.* at 1272.

§ 5:3

have rationally excluded the publication at issue.[37]

In *Toombs* the material was excluded to further the prison's interest in the prevention of fraud. In a more typical case, publications are excluded on security grounds. In those cases, the most common censored publications are those that contain information that can be used in criminal activities, those that contain political messages, and those that are sexual in nature.

Criminal Writings

Criminal material is the easiest to deal with. If the material contains information about how to make a bomb or how to fashion other weapons, there are easily understandable reasons why prison officials might rationally conclude that it ought not be introduced into the prison.[38] However, here, as well as with other categories, courts should not accept unexamined presumptive judgments of prison officials that a publication violates the censorship guidelines without a showing that the official involved actually examined the particular publication at issue to determine that it contained prohibited information.

Political Material

Political material is not as simple. Some material may be permitted, while other material may be excluded. For example, a publication that contains unpopular or even repugnant political views, even those of a racial nature, should not be excluded on that ground alone.[39] However, when the publication urges its readers to engage in disruptive activities such as

---

[37]See also Pepperling v. Crist, 678 F.2d 787, 791 (9th Cir. 1982) (district court could not, "without close examination of the magazine, determine whether the prohibition" was proper).

[38]Allen v. Higgins, 902 F.2d 682 (8th Cir. 1990) (improper to exclude a military surplus catalogue that the superintendent had not even examined himself).

[39]McCabe v. Arave, 827 F.2d 634 (9th Cir. 1987) (there is no reasonable relationship between goals of prison security and reha-

§ 5:3 RIGHTS OF PRISONERS, THIRD EDITION

"strikes, riots, [and] fights," it may be banned.[40] An example of a case that a court believed crossed the line between mere advocacy of beliefs on the one hand and the encouragement of unlawful activities on the other is *Malik v Coughlin*.[41] *Malik* dealt with an issue of *Freedom Press* that contained an article entitled "Experimentation, Genocide and the Death of Kuwasi Balagoon." The article accused prison officials of conspiring to commit "mass genocide" on black and Hispanic prisoners by medical experimentation practices and through other practices that were calculated to give inmates acquired immune deficiency syndrome (AIDS) and tuberculosis. The court characterized the article as "clearly intended to incite disobedience to

---

bilitation and the banning of materials that advocate racial purity but do not encourage violence or illegal activity); Murphy v. Missouri Dept. of Corrections, 814 F.2d 1252 (8th Cir. 1987) (same); Schwartz v. Jones, 2001 WL 118600 (E.D. La. 2001) (denial of access to a right wing magazine, The Free American, where there was no evidence of the advocation of violence or racism, did not serve any penological interest, and the inmate was awarded nominal damages); Nichols v. Nix, 810 F. Supp. 1448 (S.D. Iowa 1993), aff'd, 16 F.3d 1228 (8th Cir. 1994) (ban on publications from white supremacist church was invalid because there was no real threat to security); Lyon v. Grossheim, 803 F. Supp. 1538 (S.D. Iowa 1992) (denial of religious comic books was not related to legitimate security concern); Fallon v. Lockhart, 919 F.2d 1304 (8th Cir. 1990) (publications from white supremacist church could be banned when it preached its doctrine and degraded other religions). Cf .Weir v. Nix, 890 F. Supp. 769, 776 (S.D. Iowa 1995), judgment aff'd, appeal dismissed in part, 114 F.3d 817 (8th Cir. 1997) (banning of religious comic book overturned because the book did not espouse violence).

[40]Thomas v. U.S. Secretary of Defense, 730 F. Supp. 362, 363 (D. Kan. 1990); see also Al-Ra'id v. Ingle, 69 F.3d 28, 33 Fed. R. Serv. 3d 133 (5th Cir. 1995) (holding that it was constitutional to confiscate religious material that denounced Christianity as Satanism and that promoted violence); Grooms v. Caldwell, 806 F. Supp. 807, 811 (N.D. Ind. 1991) (possession of photographs relating to the Ku Klux Klan could be prohibited based on their potential to incite a riot).

[41]Malik v. Coughlin, 154 A.D.2d 135, 137, 552 N.Y.S.2d 182, 184 (3d Dep't 1990).

SPEECH IN PRISON § 5:3

prison personnel and possibly hysteria and violence."[42] The court failed to explain, however, in what way this article, which was undoubtedly critical of prison practices, incited unlawful disobedience to prison authority.[43]

Another example of a publication that crossed the line from racist advocacy to incitement to violence is found in *Stefano v. McFadden*.[44] In that case a white inmate protested the confiscation of *Christianities* (sic) *Ancient Enemy*, a book sent to him by its author, the plaintiff's pastor. The anti-Semitic book argued that Jews control the United States government and that this group is oppressing Christian white citizens, including white people in prison. The author asserted that the only proper way to resist Jewish domination is to form an "unorganized militia" to fight a "war for survival."[45] The plaintiff, a high-risk inmate who had committed numerous security violations by threatening staff and inmates with weapons, including homemade knives and shanks, also possessed narcotics in prison and was being held in a high security unit.[46] The warden testified that he was not permitted to have the book because it might incite violent prisoners, such as the plaintiff, to assault other prisoners and prison staff.

The court held that while the book could not be banned in the free world, it was proper to impose a

---

[42]*Id.* at 184. Another debatable decision is Travis v. Norris, 805 F.2d 806 (8th Cir. 1986) (book entitled *Gorilla Law* properly excluded when the "tone [of the book] is relentlessly hostile to prison officials and to authority in general" and "promotes the notion that prisoners are hapless victims of society and speaks of their 'motivation of burning revenge'").

[43]In fact, the article only advocated that inmates refuse to accept medical care, which, in most cases, is legal for them to do. See Ch 3.

[44]Stefanow v. McFadden, 103 F.3d 1466 (9th Cir. 1996).
[45]*Id.* at 1470, 1472.
[46]*Id.* at 1466.

§ 5:3 RIGHTS OF PRISONERS, THIRD EDITION

"content regulation" and ban it from this prisoner.[47] The book, the court noted, went beyond racism by advocating a "war for survival" against the government. Even though the book apparently did not contain a specific and detailed call to arms, the court noted that the plaintiff was not entitled to the same constitutional free speech protections that he would enjoy were he not in prison. The court recognized that even hate is entitled to protection in the "free marketplace of ideas" but the plaintiff, through his violent acts and his imprisonment, "has for the time being encumbered his right [to engage in free speech] . . .."[48] The court's opinion, which raises the specter of past instances of violence against Jews,[49] is infused with trepidation about the possible negative impacts of uncontrolled speech.[50]

In dealing with the reasonableness of censorship of political publications, *Thornburgh* teaches that it is proper for the reviewing court to consider the "conditions of a particular prison at a particular time."[51] Thus, a publication acceptable in a prison that is calm might be unacceptable in another prison that is experiencing "turmoil."[52] As we have seen, it is also proper to pay attention to the inmate who is seeking access to the information.[53] In any event, while certain political pieces can be barred under the *Thornburgh* guidelines, it bears

---

[47]*Id.* at 1471.

[48]*Id.* at 1472.

[49]The court cites the Crusades and the Holocaust. *Id.* at 1466.

[50]*Id.* ("One cannot underestimate the power of ideas to incite . . .").

[51]Thornburgh v. Abbott, 490 U.S. 401, 109 S. Ct. 1874, 1883, 104 L. Ed. 2d 459 (1989). See also Stefanow v. McFadden, 103 F.3d 1466 (9th Cir. 1996).

[52]Hernandez v. Estelle, 788 F.2d 1154, 1156 (5th Cir. 1986) (because of "serious unrest at the [prison]" prior to the censorship decision, articles from the Revolutionary Socialist League of New York were a "potential spark which could ignite a 'powder keg situation'").

[53]See, e.g., Stefanow v. McFadden, 103 F.3d 1466 (9th Cir. 1996).

SPEECH IN PRISON § 5:3

repeating that the judgment must not be a "wholesale" one that keeps out a publication permanently because of one issue. To be constitutional, the decision to bar a publication must be based on a "conscientious review" of the challenged material.[54]

Sexual Materials

The final category of commonly excluded literature is material that is sexual in nature. Actual obscene literature can be censored, of course, since it is outside the protection of the First Amendment.[55] The more difficult issue concerns material that is not obscene, but

---

[54]See, e.g., Thomas v. U.S. Secretary of Defense, 730 F. Supp. 362 (D. Kan. 1990) (wholesale rejections of publications are forbidden; individual judgments based on conscientious review are required before a political publication may be withheld). For additional cases requiring such a review, see, e.g., Yoder v. Oestreich, 820 F. Supp. 405 (W.D. Wis. 1993) (removal from a newspaper of an article advocating violence against a prison guard does not violate the Constitution because it is rationally related to security interests); Winburn v. Bologna, 979 F. Supp. 531 (W.D. Mich. 1997). Olson v. Loy, 951 F. Supp. 225 (S.D. Ga. 1996) (refusal of prison authorities to deliver an issue of Prison Life Magazine to an inmate did not violate the First Amendment; magazine contained inflammatory information about illegal aliens and guards at the prison; court held the defendants' actions were reasonable given the potential disorder and violence that such an article could cause; thus, the defendants' motion for summary judgment was granted); Knecht v. Collins, 903 F. Supp. 1193 (S.D. Ohio 1995), aff'd in part, vacated in part, rev'd in part on other grounds, 187 F.3d 636 (6th Cir. 1999) (prison officials did not violate First Amendment where officials banned a publication which promoted hostile takeovers of prison, and advocated dissension among inmates; court rejected inmate's argument that the publication was appropriate because the publication contained articles that concerned legitimate inmate issues as well).

[55]Jenkins v. Georgia, 418 U.S. 153, 94 S. Ct. 2750, 41 L. Ed. 2d 642 (1974); Miller v. California, 413 U.S. 15, 93 S. Ct. 2607, 37 L. Ed. 2d 419 (1973); Roth v. U.S., 354 U.S. 476, 77 S. Ct. 1304, 1 L. Ed. 2d 1498 (1957). For prison cases ruling that particular publications sought by inmates were obscene, see, e.g., Montana v. Patterson, 894 S.W.2d 812 (Tex. App. Tyler 1994) (holding that prisoner's First Amendment rights were not violated when prison

§ 5:3

rather is sexually explicit. This type of material is available in the general population. However, can it be banned in prison?[56]

One court was confronted with this question when the prison permitted inmates to receive *Playboy* magazine, but prohibited the more "explicit" *Hustler* magazine. The court stated that "prison officials have no legitimate governmental interest in imposing their own standards of sexual morality on the inmates."[57] Only if the prison officials can point to some other rational reason why sexually explicit material might jeopardize some legitimate interest can they constitutionally keep this material out.

In two recent cases prison officials have taken this challenge and have made attempts to ban sexually explicit material that is not obscene, while in a third case the court dealt with an Act of Congress that bars this

---

mail office refused to deliver obscene material in the form of a pornographic periodical); Harrison v. Calderon, 2000 WL 74017 (N.D. Cal. 2000), aff'd, 32 Fed. Appx. 346 (9th Cir. 2002) (plaintiff inmate brought an action alleging that defendant prison warden wrongfully applied a state statute that prohibited inmates from receiving specifically defined obscene materials, by confiscating only materials depicting black women, and that the material confiscated did not meet the definition of prohibited material; court held that although the specific pages of publication "Black Tail" submitted by the plaintiff were not prohibited material, the plaintiff failed to show the remaining content of that issue, and defendant's evidence clearly demonstrated that the publication met the definition of prohibited material; plaintiff failed to produce evidence that other prisoners obtained prohibited materials depicting only white women, or that defendants confiscated materials depicting women of color which were not prohibited; accordingly, summary judgment for defendant was granted because the material in question clearly met the regulatory definition of prohibited obscene material).

[56]For a discussion on inmates' rights to sexually explicit materials, see, Stacey A. Miness, Pornography Behind Bars, 85 Cornell L. Rev. 1702 (2000) (advocating a intermediate scrutiny approach to evaluating regulations regarding pornography in prisons, as opposed to the more restrictive reasonableness standard).

[57]Pepperling v. Crist, 678 F.2d 787, 790 (9th Cir. 1982).

kind of material in federal prisons.[58] Each of these efforts was successful. These cases represent a significant weakening of First Amendment protections for inmates, at least in cases dealing with access to sexual material that is not deemed obscene.

The first of these cases, *Amatel v. Reno,* concerned the so-called "Ensign Amendment."[59] That provision barred the use of federal funds to pay for the distribution of commercial material that was "sexually explicit" or "features nudity."[60] While the Act was only directed to spending federal funds, in practice the effect of the Act was to prohibit access to this material.[61] In regulations construing and enforcing the act the Federal Bureau of Prisons defined the terms "sexually explicit" and "nudity" narrowly and in addition excepted from the operation of the prohibition material that was illustrative for "medical, educational or anthropological content."[62]

As limited by these regulations, the District of Columbia Circuit in a 2-1 opinion held that the Act was constitutional under *Thornburgh*. While the Act was "content based" and while it prohibited receipt of material that clearly would be available to people in the free world, the court held that it was constitutional because it was rationally connected to the government's interest in rehabilitation. The court cited studies that made a connection between male violence and sexually explicit materials. That there are studies that find to the con-

---

[58]Amatel v. Reno, 156 F.3d 192 (D.C. Cir. 1998); Mauro v. Arpaio, 188 F.3d 1054 (9th Cir. 1999), cert. denied, 529 U.S. 1018, 120 S. Ct. 1419, 146 L. Ed. 2d 311 (2000) (en banc); Waterman v. Farmer, 183 F.3d 208 (3d Cir. 1999).

[59]See Omnibus Consolidated Appropriations Act of 1997, Pub. L. No. 104-208 § 614.

[60]*Id.*

[61]Amatel v. Reno, 156 F.3d 192, 194 n.1 (D.C. Cir. 1998).

[62]The Bureau defined nudity to mean "a pictorial depiction where genitalia or female breasts are exposed." Features were defined to mean depictions of nudity on a "routine or regular" basis. *Id.* at 192-93.

trary does not matter since the government does not have to be "right" when it bans sexually explicit material, it only has to act "reasonably."[63] The court also held that there was no requirement that the government engage in a "case by case" review of every publication to determine whether it interfered with the rehabilitation of a specific prisoner. The court noted that the Act's impact was lessened by the Bureau's interpretation of it, which would allow the receipt of a number of publications including *National Geographic, Our Bodies, Our Selves, Sports Illustrated* (Swimsuit Edition) and Victoria's Secret catalogues.[64] In addition, the ban did not prevent the receipt of sexually explicit reading material, only sexually explicit pictures.[65]

The second case, *Waterman v. Farmer,* dealt with a law passed by the New Jersey legislature that also severely restricted access to sexual material by inmates who were housed in a prison for sex offenders, 70% of whom were pedophiles.[66] The act prohibited "sexually oriented and obscene materials." This act, which applied to words as well as pictures, was upheld on similar grounds to the statute in the earlier case. The Third Circuit held that the act was justified by the state's "legitimate penological interest in rehabilitating its most dangerous and compulsive sex offenders."[67]

The third and most recent case, *Mauro v. Arpaio,* was

---

[63]*Id.* at 198.

[64]*Id.* at 202.

[65]*Id.* Although the court held that the Act was reasonable, it remanded for a hearing on whether the Act was unconstitutionally vague.

[66]Waterman v. Farmer, 183 F.3d 208 (3d Cir. 1999).

[67]*Id.* at 213. The court also held that the statute was not broad enough to prohibit receipt of important material that has sexual references such as the Bible, since under the statute a publication was only considered "predominantly oriented to the depiction or description of sexual activity or associated anatomical area" if it "features or contains such descriptions or displays on a routine or regular basis or promotes itself based upon such depictions in the case of individual one-time issues." *Id.* at 218-19.

SPEECH IN PRISON § 5:3

the most far-reaching. It concerned a jail regulation that prohibited inmates and pretrial detainees from possessing "sexually explicit material."[68] Unlike the two previous cases in which the terms "nudity" and "sexually explicit" were given more narrow definitions by prison officials, here the terms were broadly defined to include any pictorial materials that featured "frontal nudity." Thus, the policy, unlike the policy in the other cases, included within its ambit a prohibition on the receipt of artistic and scientific material.[69] Also, unlike the other two cases, which dealt with convicted prisoners, in this case the policy was imposed on pre-trial detainees who had not been convicted of a crime and whom the state had no right to compel to participate in rehabilitation programs. Despite these significant differences, the policy was upheld. The en banc court held that the policy was a rational measure designed to reduce sexual harassment of female detention officers.[70]

These three cases along with others,[71] taken together, stand for the proposition that "prisoners' access to sexually explicit material may be restricted without violating the First Amendment [if] . . . such restrictions are rationally related to legitimate penological interests of

---

[68]Mauro v. Arpaio, 188 F.3d 1054 (9th Cir. 1999), cert. denied, 529 U.S. 1018, 120 S. Ct. 1419, 146 L. Ed. 2d 311 (2000) (en banc)

[69]*Id.* at 1060.

[70]Prison officials claimed that some inmates when they viewed sexually explicit material harassed female guards by, among other things, masturbating in front of them. *Id.* at 1054. The court held that inmates had alternative means to receive sexual explicit communications, including letters, articles, and photographs of clothed females. It would be too burdensome, the court held, to require the defendants to implement alternatives such as a reading room for inmates to view this material or psychological screening to determine which inmates could use this material without engaging in sexual harassment of prison guards. *Id.* at 1061-62. Four judges dissented from this ruling.

[71]See e.g., Frost v. Symington, 197 F.3d 348 (9th Cir. 1999) (dealing with a ban on sexually explicit sexual material "showing penetration"); Owen v. Wille, 117 F.3d 1235 (11th Cir. 1997) (individualized ban on material).

security, rehabilitation, and the prevention of harassment of female guards."[72] This does not mean that anything goes. There must, these cases emphasize, be a rational connection between the challenged policy and legitimate state interests. While prison officials have great leeway, they may not be so overly broad in their determination to cleanse prisons of "smut" that they sweep out material that inmates ought to be allowed to possess. For this reason the court in one recent case refused to grant summary judgment to defendants who had promulgated an all-encompassing regulation that banned any correspondence dealing with any depictions of "human sexual behavior," or "nudity which appeals to the prurient interest in sex."[73] This regulation was so broad that it led to the rejection of artistic materials, letters with vague references to sex, and private diary entries. Among the items banned under the rule was a picture of Michelangelo's Sistine Chapel, artwork by Herrera, the *Sports Illustrated* swimsuit issue and issues of *Vanity Fair, Rolling Stone,* and *Maxim*.[74] The court observed that:

> . . .as defendants apparently interpret their regulation, much of the great works of western art and literature must be kept from prisoners, allegedly to promote rehabilitation, increase security and protect female officers. Defendants have suggested no rational connection between so broad a ban and neither defendants' stated goals nor common sense suggests any (in fact, in the case of works such as the Bible, common sense suggests the opposite).[75]

---

[72]Aiello v. Litscher, 104 F. Supp. 2d 1068, 1075 (W.D. Wis. 2000).
[73]*Id.*
[74]*Id.*

[75]*Id.* at 1080. The court went on to say that "neither scientific nor expert testimony nor common sense provides a basis for the conclusion that a ban on such materials as important works of art and literature, sexually intimate love letters between spouses and private diary entries jeopardizes security, hampers the rehabilitation of most prisoners or increases harassment of female guards." *Id.* at 1082. See also Broulette v. Starns, 161 F. Supp. 2d 1021 (D. Ariz. 2001), where the court held that the defendants violated a

Speech In Prison § 5:3

Another issue regarding sexually explicit material that has engendered litigation, with conflicting results, is whether inmates can be prohibited from receiving nude photographs of their spouses or partners. Some prisons have permitted inmates to have commercially distributed nude photographs but have not allowed other nude photos. These photos have been prohibited on the ground that their possession might lead to violent confrontations between inmates.

Courts have split on whether inmates have a constitutional right to receive these photographs. The Ninth Circuit held that they did. The court acknowledged that photographs of wives and girlfriends could become "highly emotionally charged" and might lead to "violent altercations among prisoners."[76] However, the court held that the danger was only present if the photographs were displayed. "[I]t is not the mere receipt of such photographs by a particular prisoner which provokes violence but rather the interest aroused in other inmates by the photographs."[77] Therefore, the court held that inmates could be prohibited from displaying these photographs, but not from possessing them. By contrast, the Seventh Circuit reached a contrary result. It held that absolute prohibition of the photographs is "a narrowly drawn and carefully limited response to a valid

---

consent decree allowing inmates to obtain non-obscene material when plaintiff was denied ten issues of Hustler magazine because it depicted particular sexual activities. The court held the magazines had to be "taken as a whole" and as such contained serious literary, political, or artistic value. The defendants violated the plaintiff's First Amendment rights and were not entitled to qualified immunity. Even though the obscenity test might not apply as a matter of constitutional law, it did apply here because of the provisions of the consent decree. The plaintiff was entitled to $65.00 in compensatory damages representing the replacement cost of the magazines.

[76]Pepperling v. Crist, 678 F.2d 787, 790 (9th Cir. 1982).
[77]Id.

§ 5:3   RIGHTS OF PRISONERS, THIRD EDITION

security problem."[78]

Both cases were decided prior to *Thornburgh*. *Thornburgh* does not require that a warden determine that a given communication would be "likely" to lead to violence; however, it does require that a rational judgment be made that the publication would "create an intolerable risk of disorder."[79] Moreover, *Thornburgh* requires a prison to implement easily available alternatives to censorship. It is difficult to understand how an intolerable risk of disorder is posed when there exists the easily available alternative of prohibiting the display of the photograph suggested by the Ninth Circuit. Nevertheless, the Second Circuit, in a case decided after *Thornburgh,* disagreed with the Ninth Circuit and held without so much as requiring a trial that the prohibition on the receipt of nude photos from a wife or girlfriend was a reasonable security measure designed to reduce friction among inmates.[80]

Different questions have arisen when courts have considered homosexual material. Prison officials have argued that this material presents greater danger to security and to the rehabilitation of inmates than does heterosexual material. Homosexual material, it has been argued, might encourage inmates to engage in homosexual acts that pose the risk of assaults and violence in the prisons.

Although homosexuality among consenting adults has been considered more acceptable in recent years, there is still case law on the books from past decades in

---

[78]Trapnell v. Riggsby, 622 F.2d 290 (7th Cir. 1980). Accord, Hunter v. Koehler, 618 F. Supp. 13 (W.D. Mich. 1984).

[79]Thornburgh v. Abbott, 490 U.S. 401, 109 S. Ct. 1874, 1883, 104 L. Ed. 2d 459 (1989).

[80]Giano v. Senkowski, 54 F.3d 1050 (2d Cir. 1995). The decision prompted a sharp dissent from Judge Calabresi, who protested the court's willingness to uphold the restriction on free speech without requiring a trial to determine whether, in fact, the defendants had offered valid security justifications for the rule. *Id.* at 1057-62. Another post-*Thornburgh* decision upholding such a rule is LeVier v. Nelson, 21 Kan. App. 2d 172, 897 P.2d 188 (1995).

§ 5:3

which courts have been less inclined to admit homosexual literature than heterosexual literature. As one court in a case 15 years ago put it:

> We think it clear that a legitimate rehabilitative interest of prison authorities is involved in the prevention of homosexual acts. We are not willing to condone the introduction of material into the prison that would exacerbate the situation.[81]

The decision stands on shaky ground in light of the changing mores regarding homosexuality since it was decided. Today, courts should no longer be willing to tolerate the discrimination against homosexual inmates that this decision represents.

An indication that modern courts have modified their position on this subject is *Espinoza v Wilson*.[82] There, the Sixth Circuit suggested that not all literature that "advocate[d] homosexuality" could be excluded.[83] Literature "of a religious or educational nature, and those containing supportive materials or medical information" could be received.[82] To exclude that material would not be reasonably related to security interests of the prison.[84] Therefore, "[m]erely advocating homo-

---

[81]Guajardo v. Estelle, 580 F.2d 748, 762 (5th Cir. 1978). Accord, Hunter v. Koehler, 618 F. Supp. 13 (W.D. Mich. 1984).

[82]Espinoza v. Wilson, 814 F.2d 1093 (6th Cir. 1987).

[83]*Id.* at 1099.

[82]*Id.* at 1095.

[84]*Id.* at 1099. See also Thompson v. Patteson, 985 F.2d 202 (5th Cir. 1993) (withholding sexually explicit material is constitutional when based on interference with rehabilitation); Dawson v. Scurr, 986 F.2d 257 (8th Cir. 1993) (regulating sexually explicit material is valid when done for rehabilitative or security reasons; prisoners were allowed sexually explicit material, that would normally be prohibited, in a reading room); Harper v. Wallingford, 877 F.2d 728 (9th Cir. 1989) (literature from North American Man/Boy Love Association could be banned on security and rehabilitation grounds, since it would increase the likelihood of antisocial behavior and violence).

sexual activity is not a sufficient basis for a ban."[85] Prison officials must be persuaded that the material poses an actual threat of "potential danger to . . . security" or rehabilitation for the ban to be lawful.[86]

Due Process

Regardless of the reason for exclusion, *Thornburgh* dictates that it is not proper unless there are adequate due process safeguards under which prison officials review each publication and decide whether or not to exclude it.[87] An interesting question that has arisen in light of this requirement is whether or not the proce-

---

[85]Harper v. Wallingford, 877 F.2d 728, 733 (9th Cir. 1989).

[86]*Id.*

[87]Thornburgh v. Abbott, 490 U.S. 401, 109 S. Ct. 1874, 1878, 104 L. Ed. 2d 459 (1989); see, e.g., Owen v. Wille, 117 F.3d 1235 (11th Cir. 1997) (inmate claimed that he was unconstitutionally denied access to publication containing nude photographs; a reviewer checked all incoming mail and if it contained prohibited material it was sent to a supervisor; if the supervisor agreed to prohibit the material it was next sent to a senior supervisor; if it was found to be prohibited for a third time the prisoner was sent a notice and the publication was stored with his belongings until his release; inmates could use the grievance procedure if they disagreed with the findings; the court affirmed summary judgment in favor of defendants; the court held that because the item was reviewed three times before rejection there was no question of fact for the jury); Snelling v. Riveland, 983 F. Supp. 930 (E.D. Wash. 1997), judgment aff'd, 165 F.3d 917 (9th Cir. 1998) (inmate sued prison officials for allegedly violating First Amendment by rejecting letters and magazines that contained sexually explicit material; court granted defendants' motion for summary judgment, since each issue was reviewed separately); Lawson v. Dugger, 844 F. Supp. 1538 (S.D. Fla. 1994), rev'd, 85 F.3d 502 (11th Cir. 1996) (where prisoner was denied publication from incoming mail, procedural due process requirements were met because prisoner received written notice and prisoner as well as publisher could submit written comments to office of secretary and publisher or sender could appeal to independent review by library services administrator); Allen v. Wood, 970 F. Supp. 824 (E.D. Wash. 1997) (inmate claimed, inter alia, that First Amendment right to free speech was violated by defendants' rejection of his mail; prison policy that required that every catalogue sent to inmates be

dure must give notice and an opportunity to be heard by the non-inmate sender of the publication.

In *Montcalm Publishing Corp. v. Hodges*,[88] the Fourth Circuit considered this question and held that notice and an opportunity to be heard must be accorded to senders as well as the intended receivers of the targeted publication. In *Montcalm,* two inmates who had subscribed to *Gallery* magazine filed suit when two issues were held by the prison publication review committee to be obscene. The publisher of the magazine, Montcalm, sought to intervene when the inmates who wrote to them seeking a refund of the subscription fee notified the publisher of this decision. The district court held that the publisher had no due process right to be heard by prison officials. The Fourth Circuit reversed. It held that the publisher had an independent First Amendment right to have inmates receive its publications.

While the Supreme Court has held that there is no First Amendment right for prisoners to receive "bulk mail,"[89] this was a case where the publisher had a pre-existing relationship with its subscriber.[90] Thus, the publisher had a First Amendment interest in communicating and was entitled to be heard by prison officials before the issue of its magazine could be barred. The plaintiff inmates could not protect that interest since "[a]n inmate who cannot even see the publication can hardly mount an effective challenge to the decision to withhold that publication."[91]

---

reviewed on an issue-by-issue basis and rejected if it contained sexually explicit material; policy was enacted to reduce the risk of sodomy and sexual assault; court held that the First Amendment was not violated by prison policy.).

[88]Montcalm Pub. Corp. v. Beck, 80 F.3d 105 (4th Cir. 1996).

[89]See Jones v. North Carolina Prisoners' Labor Union, Inc., 433 U.S. 119, 97 S. Ct. 2532, 53 L. Ed. 2d 629 (1977) discussed at § 5:7.

[90]Montcalm Pub. Corp. v. Beck, 80 F.3d 105, 109 (4th Cir. 1996).

[91]*Id.* at 109.

§ 5:4 Publisher-Only Rules

Considerable litigation has focused on commonly found prison rules that limit inmates to obtaining books, periodicals, and newspapers only from the publisher or other approved sellers. These rules vary considerably in what kinds of materials, and what sources, are appropriate. Although there is considerable variation, the single, perhaps imprecise term *publisher-only rule* has been coined to describe any rule that limits receipt of some type of literature to a specified source.

The common purpose of publisher-only rules, however formulated, is to reduce the possibility of smuggling contraband into the facility. Proponents of the rules argue that there is a much diminished risk of this danger if the inmate obtains literature from reputable publishers or booksellers than if he or she is free to get them from family members or friends. Proponents also make a secondary argument that the rule limits clutter in the prison and thus contributes to fire safety.

In *Bell v Wolfish*,[1] the Supreme Court upheld one such rule. The rule was in effect for pretrial detainees at a federal detention center. The rule, as written when the case came before the Court,[2] prevented inmates from receiving hard-cover books unless mailed directly from publishers, book clubs, or bookstores.[3] Paperback books, magazines, and other soft-cover materials could be received from any source.

[Section 5:4]

[1] Bell v. Wolfish, 441 U.S. 520, 99 S. Ct. 1861, 60 L. Ed. 2d 447 (1979).

[2] The rule was changed during the pendency of the litigation. At the time of the lower court's decision, the rule permitted inmates to receive books and magazines from outside the institution only if it was mailed directly from a publisher or book club. *Id.* at 548-49. The amended rule permitted receipt of books and magazines from bookstores as well. The Bureau of Prisons proposed to further amend the rule to allow receipt of soft-cover material from any source. *Id.* at 549.

[3] *Id.* at 549-50.

SPEECH IN PRISON § 5:4

The Court upheld the rule as a reasonable time, place, and manner restriction on the exercise of First Amendment rights. The Court relied on the "considered judgment" of prison officials that there were security and administrative difficulties involved in allowing inmates to receive hard-cover books from any source.[4] In addition, the Court was "influenced" by three other factors. First, the rule was not a content-based restriction on speech. Second, there were readily available alternatives to receiving hard-cover books, including the right to receive soft-cover materials from family and friends, and a "relatively large" jail library. Finally, the Court noted that the jail served mostly short-term detainees whose average length of stay was only 60 days.[5]

Lower courts have been presented with the issue of whether the *Bell* decision applies across the board to all publisher-only rules, or whether it should be more limited. A divided three-judge federal district court in North Carolina, over a strong dissent, took the view that *Bell* validated a publisher-only rule that applied in a long-term state prison to hard-cover as well as soft-cover books.[6] The dissenting judge chided his colleagues on the panel for failing to recognize that the distinctions in the way publisher-only rules operate could control the decision of the constitutionality of such rules. Since the case dealt with soft-cover as well as hard-cover books, since the rule was applied to a long-

---

[4]*Id.* at 551.

[5]*Id.* at 551-552. The Court pointed out that the jail's general library consisted of more than 3,000 hardback books, which included general reference texts and fiction and nonfiction works and more than 5,000 assorted paperbacks, including fiction and nonfiction. Furthermore, detainees could purchase four daily newspapers and an unspecified number of magazines. *Id.* at 552 n. 33.

[6]Rich v. Luther, 514 F. Supp. 481 (W.D. N.C. 1981). *Rich* was heard by a three-judge court because, at the time, federal law required challenges to the constitutionality of state laws to be considered by three judges. Former 28 U.S.C.A. § 2284.

term facility and the prison library was a meager alternative source of literature, the dissenting judge was unwilling to interpret *Bell* as upholding the rule.[7]

The majority of courts that have considered this question have proceeded more carefully. These courts have been sensitive to the First Amendment implications of a publisher-only rule that, in operation, can prevent an inmate who lacks funds from receiving otherwise unobjectionable literature. The seriousness of the deprivation wrought by publisher-only rules was recognized by the Third Circuit when it observed that, "to rephrase a French saying: a day without reading is like a week without sunshine."[8] Thus, before making a judgment on a publisher-only rule's constitutionality, most courts have examined closely such factors as the type of rule at issue, the security rationale offered for it, the type of institution in which the rule is applied, and the alternative means of obtaining literature available to the inmates.[9]

One question that has arisen after *Bell* is whether soft-cover books and magazines can be included within a publisher-only rule.[10] Extending the publisher-only rule to soft-cover books "clearly restricts the flow of in-

---

[7]Rich v. Luther, 514 F. Supp. 481, 486 (W.D. N.C. 1981). The dissent was influenced by the fact that the "publisher-only" rule "runs totally counter" to the goal of rehabilitation. "Books," the dissent argued, "are the windows through which the soul looks out. . . .. Rehabilitation, or correction, or retribution, may require imprisonment of the body; but is it also necessary, without demonstrated reason, to black out the windows of the soul?" *Id.* (emphasis in original).

[8]Hurd v. Williams, 755 F.2d 306 (3d Cir. 1985). For these reasons many prison systems forgo these restrictions on inmate access to literature, and operate without a publisher-only rule. See, e.g., Spruytte v. Walters, 753 F.2d 498 (6th Cir. 1985) (Michigan prison regulations did not contain a publisher-only rule).

[9]Alternatives include libraries and soft-cover materials from family and friends. Bell v. Wolfish, 441 U.S. 520, 552, 99 S. Ct. 1861, 60 L. Ed. 2d 447 (1979).

[10]It is now fairly clearly established that the *Bell* Court's analysis is applicable to prisons as well as jails. See, e.g., Johnson v.

Speech In Prison § 5:4

formation to the prisoner" in a much more serious manner than is the case if the rule is limited to hard-cover books.[11] Moreover, the security need for the rule is not as great with soft-cover materials, since it is more difficult to secrete weapons or drugs in them than in hard-cover books. For these reasons, "[t]he particular security problem presented by the bindings of hard-bound volumes appears to be inapplicable to newspapers and possibly also to paperbound books."[12]

Courts have been reluctant to sanction a soft-cover publisher-only rule for these reasons. One court that granted summary judgment for the defendants in a case that challenged a soft-cover publisher-only rule, for example, indicated its "concern about what may be the prison's overreaction to its undeniably real security problem" and stated that it would reconsider its decision if a more compelling record was made in the future.[13] The court specifically left the way open for such a case to be filed.[14]

Therefore, courts have been unwilling to permanently uphold the ban on soft-cover books without something more than "assertions in argument that security

---

Moore, 948 F.2d 517 (9th Cir. 1991); Hurd v. Williams, 755 F.2d 306 (3d Cir. 1985).

[11]Johnson v. Moore, 948 F.2d 517 (9th Cir. 1991).

[12]Hurd v. Williams, 755 F.2d 306, 308 (3d Cir. 1985). See also Skelton v. Pri-Cor, Inc., 963 F.2d 100, 102-3 (6th Cir. 1991) (forbidding inmate from having a hardbound Bible because he could have a soft-cover Bible).

[13]Hurd v. Williams, 755 F.2d 306, 309 (3d Cir. 1985).

[14]*Id.* ("[w]e leave open the possibility that the record in another case may raise sufficient question that the security risk in such materials has been exaggerated as to require a plenary trial on the issue"). In applying *Bell* to a soft-cover book rule in a long-term prison setting, another court stated that the availability or lack of availability of alternative sources of the information is a more important consideration than is the length of stay in the facility. Kines v. Day, 754 F.2d 28, 30 (1st Cir. 1985).

considerations necessitated the rule."[15] Courts that have upheld the extension of *Bell* to soft-cover materials have done so only when the rule is applied to a short-term jail facility[16] or, in the case of a prison, when the record establishes that inmates have ample alternative practicable means of obtaining the material desired through other means.[17]

Another example of a case in which the courts have carefully examined the rationale for a publisher-only rule is a recent Ninth Circuit decision dealing with a variation of a publisher-only rule that limited inmates to only those books that they could buy themselves out of their own prison accounts.[18] The rule was defended by prison officials on the grounds that (1) it was a fire safety measure, (2) it limited the amount of contraband coming into the facility, and (3) it was needed to prevent some inmates from "strong arming" other inmates and forcing them to ask their friends and family to send books to other inmates as "gifts."[19]

The Ninth Circuit found that there was no evidence to support any of these arguments. Fire safety could be promoted without this rule simply by limiting the amount of books that inmates could possess at any given time. Moreover, the rule was not needed to restrict the flow of contraband, since inmates could only purchase material from a publisher. Thus, no matter who paid for the book, the prison would know the source of the publication; this knowledge prevented the

---

[15]*Id.* See also Pratt v. Sumner, 807 F.2d 817 (9th Cir. 1987) (challenge to soft-cover publisher-only rule is not frivolous; case reversed for examination of rationale for the rule).

[16]Ward v. Washtenaw County Sheriff's Dept., 881 F.2d 325 (6th Cir. 1989) (soft-cover publisher-only rule constitutional in jail); Wagner v. Thomas, 608 F. Supp. 1095 (N.D. Tex. 1985) (same).

[17]Kines v. Day, 754 F.2d 28 (1st Cir. 1985) ("no showing that the listed books [that inmate desired] were unavailable from the outside libraries").

[18]Crofton v. Roe, 170 F.3d 957 (9th Cir. 1999), as amended, (May 5, 1999).

[19]*Id.* at 959.

introduction of contraband. Prison officials also offered no evidence in support of their argument that inmates might strong-arm weaker inmates into buying books for them. Indeed, the argument was weakened by another prison rule that allowed family and friends of inmates to send funds, a practice that also raised the same strong-arming issue. Accordingly, the court held that the rule was a violation of the First Amendment rights of the plaintiff.[20]

The strongest justification for a publisher-only rule arises when the inmate is being held in a short-term facility such as a pretrial detention center. In these cases the deprivation will not be long standing. In such situations, because the stays are so short, there is some case law support for the idea that jail officials can go beyond enforcement of publisher-only rules and actually prevent the introduction of any books and periodicals into the institution, regardless of whether they come from a publisher or not.[21] While the rationale for a publisher-only rule is most compelling when the rule is imposed in short-term detention facilities, similar kinds of rules have also been upheld in long-term prison settings.[22] In one such case a long-term penitentiary's publisher-only rule for cassette tapes was held to be a

---

[20]*Id.* at 960. See also Allen v. Coughlin, 64 F.3d 77 (2d Cir. 1995) (holding that a publisher-only rule that prohibited an inmate from receiving press clippings could be unconstitutional).

[21]Hause v. Vaught, 993 F.2d 1079 (4th Cir. 1993). The court relied on the fact that the stays were short. Books ordered from the publisher would most likely arrive after the inmate was released. Moreover, there were alternative source of information, including a prison library, daily newspapers, and cable television.

[22]See e.g., Allen v. Wood, 970 F. Supp. 824 (E.D. Wash. 1997) (the rejection of oversized greeting cards was not a violation; oversized cards rejected because they might contain contraband; summary judgment in favor of defendants granted): Salahuddin v. Kuhlmann, 216 A.D.2d 649, 628 N.Y.S.2d 412 (3d Dep't 1995) (where prison officials prohibited inmate from receiving a tape machine from a Islamic vendor, rather than vendors approved to send products to inmates, officials were not acting in a discriminatory manner in violation of inmate's First Amendment rights).

§ 5:4   Rights of Prisoners, Third Edition

valid security measure designed to limit contraband.[23]

The best way to summarize the cases dealing with the publisher-only rule decided after *Bell* is to note that they do not automatically validate a publisher-only rule without regard to its content or to the circumstances in which it applies. To the contrary, this body of case law reveals that courts confronting a challenge to a publisher-only rule engage in a fact-specific analysis to determine whether the factors that "influenced" the *Bell* Court to uphold the rule are present or absent in the case before it.[24]

An important issue that has not arisen in any of the cases is the effect of a publisher-only rule that, in practice, prevents prisoners from obtaining a particular item or type of literature; e.g., an approved vendor rule which limits prisoners to books from mainstream publishers who do not carry the literature that the inmate wants, such as peripheral political literature or obscure poetry. In such a case, it is unlikely that an inmate would have any alternative source for the

---

[23]Ennis v. Berg, 509 N.W.2d 33 (N.D. 1993) (holding that an exception for religious tapes was valid because it served the interest of allowing the greatest freedom in the practice of religion).

[24]Other factors to be considered include the identity of the person who seeks to deliver the books to the inmate. Pratt v. Sumner, 807 F.2d 817 (9th Cir. 1987) (whether publisher-only rule can be applied to prevent law professor who authored treatise from sending it directly to the inmate was not specifically answered by Bell). The fact-specific analysis called for in the text may reveal that what is called a publisher-only rule is not such a rule at all. In Jackson v. Elrod, 881 F.2d 441 (7th Cir. 1989), a detainee at the Cook County Jail was denied the right to receive hard-cover books discussing the treatment of alcoholism. The denial was justified on the ground that hard covered books presented an intolerable security problem. However, the Seventh Circuit, speaking through Judge Manion, rejected the argument. The court held that the "restrictions applied to Jackson go well beyond those permitted in Wolfish." *Id.* at 445. The court held that this practice violated clearly established First Amendment rights of pretrial detainees. While courts must "heed . . . valid security and disciplinary needs of penal authorities . . . they do not justify deleting the constitutional rights of pretrial detainees." *Id.* at 446.

material. If such a hypothetical case were to arise, nothing in *Bell* would prevent a court from ruling in favor of the prisoner.

§ 5:5 Access to Literature in Punitive Segregation

Research References

West's Key Number Digest, Prisons ⟐4(4)

A related problem to censorship of literature for the general population is prison censorship policies for prisoners who are placed in punitive segregation. Some prisons have promulgated policies that limit severely the amount of reading material that an inmate may possess while in this status. Although many prison systems allow prisoners in solitary confinement to receive publications,[1] and standards exist for prisons to allow this material,[2] a number of systems restrict or prohibit access during punitive confinement.[3] Those prison systems that impose restrictions on reading material justify the prohibition on the grounds that punitive segregation is a temporary status that is designed to be unpleasant and that limiting the amount of reading material aids in the deterrent effect of punitive

---

[Section 5:5]

[1]Ohio allows inmates in solitary confinement to have at least one book, and textbooks if they are enrolled in educational classes. Taylor v. Perini, 413 F. Supp. 189, 196 (N.D. Ohio 1976). New York also allows receipt of literature while in solitary confinement. Royal v. Clark, 447 F.2d 501 (5th Cir. 1971). In Texas, an inmate sentenced to segregation has access to legal books and one religious book. Guajardo v. Estelle, 568 F. Supp. 1354, 1366 (S.D. Tex. 1983).

[2]Ohio's regulations on receipt of literature while in segregation are the same as the general rules governing reading material. Taylor v. Perini, 413 F. Supp. 189, 196 (N.D. Ohio 1976). See also National Sheriffs' Assn, Standards for Inmates' Legal Rights, Right 12 (1987) (inmates in segregation have same rights to reading material as others).

[3]See also Guajardo v. Estelle, 568 F. Supp. 1354, 1367 n2 (S.D. Tex. 1983) (listing 18 states that permit inmates in solitary to receive reading materials).

§ 5:5   Rights of Prisoners, Third Edition

segregation.

Courts have not been willing to disturb this judgment.[4] As one court that upheld the practice explained:

> [T]here can be no doubt . . . that solitary confinement is a disciplinary measure whose very essence is the deprivation of interests the First Amendment protects: association with the general prison population and communication with outsiders. To promote the important government interest in maintaining discipline, officials must have available sanctions that impose incremental disadvantages on those already imprisoned. Left alone to write, to . . . receive literature of any kind, a prisoner might find punitive isolation desirable, offering solitude and leisure as an alternative to the ordinary conditions of prison work and life.[5]

Most of the cases that sustain the denial of reading material have relied on the limited duration of confinement in solitary confinement.[6] Because the detention is short, courts have been able to say that the policy is "not directed at what an inmate could receive, but when he could receive it.["7] However, in one questionable case, the sanction was upheld even though the plaintiff was

---

[4]This is not true for administrative segregation. Inmates are not in that restrictive environment for punishment; therefore, restrictions on receipt of literature are much more carefully scrutinized. See, e.g, Spellman v. Hopper, 142 F. Supp. 2d 1323 (M.D. Ala. 2000) (holding that inmates in administrative segregration are entitled to subcribe at least four publications).

[5]Daigre v. Maggio, 719 F.2d 1310, 1313 (5th Cir. 1983). See also Gregory v. Auger, 768 F.2d 287 (8th Cir. 1985); Little v. Norris, 787 F.2d 1241 (8th Cir. 1986).

[6]See, e.g., Little v. Norris, 787 F.2d 1241, 1243 (8th Cir. 1986) ("because the disciplinary detention serves a valid purpose, and because thirty days is not an excessive length of time," the sanction was constitutional); Gregory v. Auger, 768 F.2d 287 (8th Cir. 1985) (maximum duration of solitary was sixty days; prohibition upheld because it was "temporary"); Guajardo v. Estelle, 568 F. Supp. 1354, 1367 (S.D. Tex. 1983) (maximum period of solitary confinement was fifteen days; intervals of at least three days were required between successive terms).

[7]Gregory v. Auger, 768 F.2d 287, 290 (8th Cir. 1985).

to undergo a protracted confinement in punitive segregation.

In *Jackson v Brookhart*,[8] the plaintiff was sentenced to 286 days in punitive segregation. The prison limited her to only reading materials that were religious, legal, or educational and to a newspaper for one hour per day. The court upheld the restriction even though it was protracted because the court was concerned that, if the court were to permit reading material after 60 days, "an inmate might find prolonged disciplinary detention status desirable and actively seek it.[9] The assumption that this case relied on for its conclusion-that, with reading material, prolonged confinement in punitive segregation might be a pleasurable experience-is unconvincing in light of the severe deprivations that can constitutionally be visited on inmates who are confined in punitive segregation.[10]

§ 5:6 Prisoner Writings

A quintessential expression of speech is one's own writings. It is well known that the isolation and frequent solitude of a prison setting has been fertile soil for inmates to write and compose music and art, and prisoners often have interesting and vital tales to tell, music to write, and art to compose. To take one example from the music world, many blues and country music songs evolved from songs first sung by prisoners.[1] Moreover, the fruit of some prisoner literary efforts have become justly famous examples of world-renowned literature.[2] These works not only add to the culture, but also have immediate benefits to prisoners as a means of

---

[8]Jackson v. Brookhart, 640 F. Supp. 241 (S.D. Iowa 1986).

[9]*Id.* at 243.

[10]For a discussion of these conditions, see Ch 2.

[Section 5:6]

[1]See, generally, Wake Up Dead Man: Afro-American Work Songs from Texas Prisons (Bruce Jackson ed 1972).

[2]See, e.g., John Bunyan, Pilgrim's Progress (1684); Henri Charriére, Papillon (1970); O. Henry, The Ransom of Red Chief in

rehabilitation and as a "nonviolent means to defuse tensions within a prison."³

The legal problems that an inmate's original expression engenders depend on whether the inmate is writing primarily for a prison audience or whether, instead, the author seeks a wider audience for the work. This section will consider these questions separately and also will briefly consider whether inmates may be punished for their writings.

Writings Primarily for a Civilian Audience

When inmates write for an outside audience, they are composing, in the parlance of *Martinez*[4] and *Thornburgh*,[5] an essentially outgoing communication. It will be recalled that while most restrictions on inmate speech are subject to a reasonable relationship test, the Supreme Court has reserved a more stringent test for regulating communications intended solely for the outside world.[6]

Prisoners, therefore, have a First Amendment right to compose books and other writings intended for an outside audience as long as restrictions on the right are not necessitated by some important governmental interest that cannot reasonably be served in some other way.[7]

Whirligigs (1910); Martin Luther King, Letter from Birmingham Jail (1963); Oscar Wilde, Ballad of Reading Gaol (1898).

[3]Martin v. Rison, 741 F. Supp. 1406, 1411 (N.D. Cal. 1990), opinion vacated on other grounds, 962 F.2d 959 (9th Cir. 1992).

[4]Procunier v. Martinez, 416 U.S. 396, 94 S. Ct. 1800, 40 L. Ed. 2d 224 (1974). This case is discussed in depth in § 5:2.

[5]Thornburgh v. Abbott, 490 U.S. 401, 109 S. Ct. 1874, 104 L. Ed. 2d 459 (1989). This case is discussed in depth in § 5:2.

[6]*Id.*

[7]Procunier v. Martinez, 416 U.S. 396, 94 S. Ct. 1800, 40 L. Ed. 2d 224 (1974)(overruled on other grounds by, Thornburgh v. Abbott, 490 U.S. 401, 109 S. Ct. 1874, 104 L. Ed. 2d 459 (1989)).

§ 5:6

As a practical matter, prisoners, with rare exceptions,[8] have not been prevented from working on books, manuscripts, music, or art while imprisoned.

One of those rare exceptions is *Frink v. Arnold*.[9] In that case an inmate who was a sex offender enrolled in a voluntary treatment program for sexual deviancy was prevented from retaining over 1,600 pages of manuscripts that he had written and on which he was continuing to work. The manuscripts contained short stories, plays and character outlines. The work was reviewed by treatment staff, who found that about half of it contained graphic sexual material. The treatment staff considered this material to be inappropriate for the plaintiff's treatment. If he wished to remain in the program the plaintiff was given the choice of either having the material destroyed or sent outside the prison.

The court, relying on *Thornburgh* and *Turner*,[10] held that the prison officials acted properly. The restriction on the plaintiff's ability to write was held to be reasonably related to the goal of rehabilitating the plaintiff.[11] It was not clear from the record whether prison officials objected only to particular segments of the plaintiff's writings or to the entire project. Nevertheless, the court held that the restriction was proper even if it had the effect of completely preventing the plaintiff from doing any writing on these projects.[12] The holding in this unusual case may be explained by the fact that the plaintiff was a pedophile and that the treatment staff

---

[8]In one early case, prison officials sought to prevent an inmate from writing a book on the ground that the writing was an anti-rehabilitative attempt to justify or glorify his crime. Theriault v. Carlson, 339 F. Supp. 375 (N.D. Ga. 1972), vacated and remanded, 495 F.2d 390 (5th Cir. 1974).

[9]Frink v. Arnold, 842 F. Supp. 1184 (S.D. Iowa 1994), aff'd, 43 F.3d 673 (8th Cir. 1994).

[10]The court proceeded as though the only test that could be applied in these circumstances was the *Thornburgh* test rather than the *Martinez* test. Id. at 1187-88.

[11]Id. at 1191-92.

[12]Id. at 1192.

were insistent that he could not receive treatment if he continued to write on the subjects in question. Moreover, the prison did not absolutely prohibit the plaintiff from writing. He could, had he chosen, have continued to write. Thus, the only issue presented to the court was whether he could continue to write about sexual graphic scenes of abuse as he chose while still continuing to participate in the treatment program.

Even though the *Frink* court ruled that the plaintiff could be compelled to stop writing, it remains true that in the overwhelming number of situations, absent such forceful circumstances, prison officials will not be able to forbid inmates from writing. But while prison officials cannot in the normal case prohibit inmates from working on their expressive projects, they can impose reasonable time and place rules.[13] For example, prison administrators have been allowed to prohibit inmates from engaging in these activities when doing so would interfere with the normal prison routine, such as prison work details.[14] In addition, one court in a questionable decision upheld a rule that required an inmate who was preparing a sermon for an outside audience to submit an advance outline of the manuscript.[15]

Writings for Civilian Outlets, Including Newspapers, Periodicals and Electronic Media

When inmates write or broadcast for civilian media, special problems are posed. These outlets communicate on a regular basis to persons in the outside world;[16] however, the may also be available to inmates. There-

---

[13] See, e.g., Thompson v. Clarke, 848 F. Supp. 1452 (D. Neb. 1994) (prisoners were not entitled to use of prison facilities to tape religious segments for public access television).

[14] Inmates in the federal system may use only nonwork time to prepare a manuscript. 28 CFR § 551.81.

[15] Berrigan v. Norton, 322 F. Supp. 46 (D. Conn. 1971), judgment aff'd, 451 F.2d 790 (2d Cir. 1971).

[16] These articles can provide a real benefit to public understanding. As one court noted "[t]he public appears to be

fore, should the *Martinez* test, reserved for outside communications, apply or should the less rigorous *Thornburgh* test, for intraprison communications, apply? In *Martin v Rison*,[17] this issue was presented when the court was faced with deciding whether the Federal Bureau of Prisons constitutionally could enforce a rule which prevented an inmate from serving as a paid correspondent for a local newspaper.

The inmate had written 18 articles about prison life for the *San Francisco Chronicle* over a two-year period. "Some of the articles were critical of prison authorities and some were not."[18] After one particularly harsh article entitled "The Gulag Mentality," which discussed "murders, assaults, and possible violence or rioting,"[19] appeared in the newspaper, prison officials decided to enforce a Federal Bureau of Prisons rule which prevented inmates from serving as a reporter for the news media.[20]

The court noted that newspapers were read by inmates as well as an outside audience, and therefore could not be characterized as purely outgoing communications. The court held that the standard to

---

interested in the subject of life in prison; and light and air, literally or figuratively, are generally healthy to any institution." Martin v. Rison, 741 F. Supp. 1406, 1411 (N.D. Cal. 1990), opinion vacated on other grounds, 962 F.2d 959 (9th Cir. 1992). See also Simmat v. Manson, 554 F. Supp. 1363, 1374 n11 (D. Conn. 1983) ("However provocative Simmat's columns may be in the prison environment they are in most instances an attempt to bring to the public's attention matters of serious concern to the society at large and thus are clearly entitled to First Amendment protection.").

[17]Martin v. Rison, 741 F. Supp. 1406 (N.D. Cal. 1990),opinion vacated on other grounds, 962 F.2d 959 (9th Cir. 1992).

[18]*Id.* at 1409.

[19]*Id.* at 1415.

[20]*Id.* at 1410. (citing 28 CFR § 540.20(b)) ("The inmate may not receive compensation or anything of value for correspondence with the news media. The inmate may not act as a reporter or publish under a byline.").

use in determining this case was the *Turner*[21] and *Thornburgh* reasonableness standard. Under that standard, the rule was valid. The court held that the rule was not a "knee-jerk" reaction to the security dangers posed by inmates serving as correspondents for local newspapers and writing about prison life.

The rule was rational, the court stated, because "[a]rticles about matters within a prison can create a danger of violence, or at least threats of violence."[22] This can occur when the articles focus on individual prisoners or when the article causes prison staff to "fear that everything they say will be reported by prisoner-reporters in the public media."[23] Moreover, the court held that the regulation advanced a legitimate interest by ensuring that a prisoner-correspondent was not given "undue prominence" within the prison population.[24]

The court also found that, as applied to the plaintiff, the regulation was reasonable. The "Gulag" article the plaintiff wrote recirculated into the prison and created "genuine concern about security within the prison," including a heightened danger of a prison disturbance.[25] Because this showing was made, the court sustained

---

[21]Turner v. Safley, 482 U.S. 78, 107 S. Ct. 2254, 96 L. Ed. 2d 64 (1987). This case is discussed in depth in § 5:2. See also Lomax v. Fiedler, 204 Wis. 2d 196, 554 N.W.2d 841 (Ct. App. 1996) (when the court is faced with a "dual audience" question, the proper standard of review is based on a *Turner/Thornburgh* analysis; in the instant case, an inmate who was disciplined for writing critical articles about prison officials claimed such action violated the First Amendment; inmates as well as a non-prison audience read the articles; the court held that such articles could undermine prison discipline and order; this, in the court's mind, justified the disciplinary action; accordingly, the court affirmed the lower court's grant of summary judgment).

[22]Martin v. Rison, 741 F. Supp. 1406, 1414 (N.D. Cal. 1990), opinion vacated on other grounds, 962 F.2d 959 (9th Cir. 1992).

[23]*Id.* at 1415.

[24]*Id.* at 1415.

[25]*Id.* at 1421.

the firing of the inmate.[26] The court, however, cautioned that its holding should not be misinterpreted to provide carte blanche to the prison to suppress dissent. Under the ruling, inmates remain free to correspond with the press. As the judge wrote: "in a civilized society governed by the rule of law, voices of dissent cannot and should not be suppressed. History has been punctuated by writers who have emerged from prison cells to become spokesmen for humanity."[27]

In another instructive case, Mumia Abu-Jamal, an inmate who was a journalist sentenced to death for the murder of a police officer, was approached by National Public Radio to broadcast his commentaries to a national radio audience.[28] When police organizations protested these contacts, prison officials began to inspect all of his mail, including his legal mail, and thereafter invoked a prison rule that prevented all inmates from engaging in "business" while incarcerated. In fact, this rule had previously not been enforced against another inmate who had written a novel while in prison. Mr. Abu-Jamal sued, claiming that the rule as enforced against him violated his First Amendment right to speak and to write.

The Third Circuit agreed. It found that the rule was imposed on the plaintiff "in retaliation against the content of his writing."[29] Unlike the *Rison* case, the court noted that here there was no evidence that the plaintiff's writings and broadcasts "had strained prison resources, contributed to unrest among the inmate population or enhanced Jamal's status as a prisoner,

---

[26]*Id.* at 1425. See also Simmat v. Manson, 554 F. Supp. 1363 (D. Conn. 1983) (inmate could be transferred after his articles in civilian press caused unrest in the prison and threats to his safety).

[27]Martin v. Rison, 741 F. Supp. 1406, 1425 (N.D. Cal. 1990), opinion vacated on other grounds, 962 F.2d 959 (9th Cir. 1992).

[28]Abu-Jamal v. Price, 154 F.3d 128 (3d Cir. 1998).

[29]*Id.* at 134.

resulting in danger to himself or others."[30] The court concluded that while prison officials could validly prohibit a business operation that placed a substantial burden on prison staff, it could not prohibit a First Amendment activity that did not threaten corrections officers or incite the inmate population.[31]

Writings Primarily for a Prisoner Audience

On occasion, prisons have established inmate newspapers staffed by inmates and intended, by and large, to be read by the prison population. These publications have been funded by the state for a variety of reasons. Prisons see these publications as a means of informing the prison population of events within the prison, as a healthy outlet for the release of tensions, as a vehicle for the expression of the creative talents of the inmates, or as a means of gaining recognition for the rehabilitative program of the prison administrators.[32] Regardless of the reason for establishing such a newspaper, having established an organ of the press, what power does the institution retain to regulate it?

This question arose first in *Luparar v Stoneman*.[33] In *Luparar,* the state of Vermont sought to ban an issue of a prison newspaper established by the state because it found the content of the articles objectionable. The articles in question had been critical of the administration and had focused on the personalities of prison staff rather than on issues, as the prison guidelines required. The defendants argued that, since they funded the paper, they had the unrestrained right to full control over it.

The district court disagreed. Drawing analogies from

---

[30]*Id.* at 134.

[31]*Id.* at 134-35.

[32]See, e.g., Pittman v. Hutto, 594 F.2d 407 (4th Cir. 1979) (prison newspapers won national awards in American Penal Press contest sponsored by Southern Illinois University).

[33]The Luparar v. Stoneman, 382 F. Supp. 495 (D. Vt. 1974).

school and college newspaper cases,[34] the court held that, "once the state has sanctioned publication of the newspaper, it cannot terminate publication even when financially supported by the state . . . in a manner inconsistent with the freedom of expression guaranteed by the First Amendment.[35]

Having decided that the First Amendment imposed limitations on the ability of the state to censor the prison newspaper, the court turned to the question of the standard to use in determining whether the state had exceeded its authority. The *Luparar* decision held that the *Martinez*[36] standard applied. Under that standard, "[t]he fact that the article is critical, attacks personalities, or is defamatory is not sufficient reason, standing alone, to suppress the publication in which it appears.[37] Only articles that threaten security, order, or rehabilitation interests of the institution could be censored legitimately.

In addition, prior to imposing censorship on the prisoner newspaper, the court required that a mechanism be established to ensure that due process protections were provided. The procedure must provide for an "expeditious review" of the content of the newspaper by prison officials. The burden of demonstrating that there were sufficient grounds to bar the publication rested on the prison officials. Before a censorship decision could be made, the prisoner editorial staff of the paper was entitled to be notified of any rejection of any article or issue and the reason for the rejection.[38] In addition, prisoners were entitled to a review of any censorship

---

[34]See, e.g., Joyner v. Whiting, 477 F.2d 456 (4th Cir. 1973); Antonelli v. Hammond, 308 F. Supp. 1329 (D. Mass. 1970).

[35]The Luparar v. Stoneman, 382 F. Supp. 495, 500 (D. Vt. 1974).

[36]Procunier v. Martinez, 416 U.S. 396, 94 S. Ct. 1800, 40 L. Ed. 2d 224 (1974)(overruled on other grounds by, Thornburgh v. Abbott, 490 U.S. 401, 109 S. Ct. 1874, 104 L. Ed. 2d 459 (1989)). This case is discussed in depth in § 5:2.

[37]The Luparar v. Stoneman, 382 F. Supp. 495, 500 (D. Vt. 1974).
[38]*Id.*

§ 5:6   Rights of Prisoners, Third Edition

decision by a prison official who was not involved in the original decision.[39]

Luparar was decided before the Supreme Court's decision in *Thornburgh v Abbott*.[40] The question arises, therefore, whether it is still good law. The answer to that question is that some of it is, and some of it is not. The central holding that the First Amendment protects prison newspapers that contain the writings of inmates from unreasonable censorship seems an accurate statement of current law. In *Thornburgh,* the Supreme Court unanimously held that prisoners enjoy the protections of the First Amendment from arbitrary censorship decisions by prison administrators.[41] However, *Luparar's* holding that the *Martinez* standard applies to censorship of prison newspapers can no longer be considered an accurate statement of the law.[42] Since prison newspapers are primarily intended for inmate audiences, they are intraprison communications to other prisoners that, under *Thornburgh,* are subject to the reasonableness standard first enunciated in *Turner v Safley* and not the more rigorous standard of *Martinez.*[43] While censorship standards for prison newspapers utilized by *Luparar* are no longer good law, *Luparar's* procedural safeguards against arbitrary censorship remain valid. Their content is very similar to the safeguards that the Supreme Court relied on in upholding the publication rules of the Federal Bureau of

---

[39]*Id.* at 501-2.

[40]Thornburgh v. Abbott, 490 U.S. 401, 109 S. Ct. 1874, 104 L. Ed. 2d 459 (1989).

[41]*Id.*

[42]This is true even though it is undoubtedly true that persons outside of the prison also read prison newspapers. Thornburgh stressed the importance of providing prison administrators leeway when dealing with the potentially volatile nature of communications going directly to other inmates. See § 5:2. Those dangers are present with a prison newspaper read by inmates even if some copies find their way to others who are not imprisoned.

[43]See § 5:2 for a discussion of the *Turner* standard.

Prisons in *Thornburgh*.[44]

Thus, although there are no cases that directly discuss this issue, under current law, prison officials can probably censor an article whenever the censorship decision could pass muster under the four-part reasonable relationship test utilized in *Thornburgh*.[45] Under that test, rules that prohibit inflammatory comments or comments that attack prison officials[46] would probably be upheld as long as the prison administrators make an individualized, nonarbitrary determination that a particular article posed a threat to prison security and as long as there was a reasonable connection between the actual article and the threat to institutional goals.[47]

Furthermore, since the institutional interests in a state-sponsored, inmate-run newspaper are often rehabilitative, censorship decisions to further that goal can be reasonable. An interesting California state case, dealing with censorship rules for the *San Quentin News*, illustrates what might be permissible censorship rules designed to further that interest. That court upheld rules that provided for articles that were written "in accordance with the highest journalistic standards" as well as those that prohibited articles that were "inflammatory" or "offensive to any race, gender, nationality, religious faith or similar group" or that were "sexually

---

[44]See § 5:2.

[45]For a discussion of that test, see § 5:2.

[46]See Epps v. Smith, 112 Misc. 2d 724, 728, 447 N.Y.S.2d 577, 580 (Sup 1981) (in allowing inmate newspapers, "authorities may take steps to prevent the participants from using the paper as a platform for ridiculing the administration or as a vehicle for organizing dissident inmates").

[47]See, e.g., In re Williams, 159 Cal. App. 3d 600, 609, 205 Cal. Rptr. 903 (1st Dist. 1984) ("restricting material, whether 'inflammatory' or not, which might threaten institutional safety is permissible") (emphasis in original). See also Bailey v. Loggins, 32 Cal. 3d 907, 187 Cal. Rptr. 575, 654 P.2d 758 (1982).

suggestive.[48] These rules arguably went further than necessary to rationally promote prison security, but they were justified on grounds other than security. The court accepted the notion that the state had a valid interest in using the paper as a teaching tool to train inmates in good journalism practices and that they also had a valid interest in having "a prison newspaper of which it [the institution] can be proud."[49]

Punishment for Improper Writings

One way for prison officials to regulate writings by prisoners, either for the outside or for other inmates, is, as already discussed, to establish censorship rules. Another way that officials might attempt to regulate writing is to punish inmates whose writings are considered improper.

However, courts have held that it is inconsistent with the First Amendment to retaliate against inmates for their writings. In *Simmat v Manson*,[50] for example, the plaintiff claimed that he was being transferred from one prison to another in retaliation for a series of articles that he had authored for a local newspaper about his life in prison. The articles had, on occasion, criticized both inmates and prison officials who were operating the facility. The court, ordering a hearing on the reasons for the transfer, held that "the plaintiff's First Amendment right to freedom of expression encompasses the right to express himself without punitive

---

[48]In re Williams, 159 Cal. App. 3d 600, 609, 205 Cal. Rptr. 903 (1st Dist. 1984).

[49]*Id.* at 609. For a discussion of the California prison newspaper censorship cases, and an argument that there is a state law rationale for more lenient censorship rules, see Christine D. Truter, Note, First Amendment Rights of Prisoners: Freedom of the Prison Press, 18 USF L Rev 599 (1984).

[50]Simmat v. Manson, 535 F. Supp. 1115 (D. Conn. 1982).

retaliation."[51]

While inmates cannot be punished solely for expressing themselves, prison officials are not prohibited from taking action based on legitimate security concerns that arise from prisoner expression. Thus, if an inmate's writings cause dangers to the inmate or to others in the facility, the prison has been held to be entitled to take measures, including transferring the inmate if necessary, to preserve institutional security. The *Simmat* case explains this concept.

In *Simmat,* the court, following a hearing on the reasons for the plaintiff's transfer, determined that plaintiff's newspaper articles-particularly articles that accused other inmates, on racial grounds, of improper performance and that published information that a fellow inmate had assumed would be kept confidential- "engendered hostility among the inmate population" and posed a serious risk of physical danger to the plaintiff.[52] This danger was so serious that it justified the decision to transfer plaintiff "to protect his personal safety.[53]

As discussed earlier, the Third Circuit in *Abu-Jamal*

---

[51]*Id.* at 117-18. See also Gray v. Creamer, 465 F.2d 179 (3d Cir. 1972); Martin v. Rison, 741 F. Supp. 1406 (N.D. Cal. 1990), opinion vacated on other grounds, 962 F.2d 959 (9th Cir. 1992) (inmate cannot be transferred as "a pretext or for purposes of retaliation").

[52]Simmat v. Manson, 554 F. Supp. 1363, 1372 (D. Conn. 1983).

[53]*Id.* See also Gomes v. Fair, 738 F.2d 517 (1st Cir. 1984) (disciplinary action against an inmate who passed a sexually explicit poem to a female prison counselor upheld when the evidence established that the action was not taken to retaliate against an inmate for his writing, but rather was taken to punish the inmate for an improper sexual advance to the employee foreshadowed by plaintiff's earlier conduct); Martin v. Rison, 741 F. Supp. 1406, 1423 (N.D. Cal. 1990), opinion vacated on other grounds, 962 F.2d 959 (9th Cir. 1992) (evidence established that transfer of inmate who wrote newspaper column was not retaliatory but rather to protect the inmate and to lessen tensions at the facility that resulted from the publications of the plaintiff's articles).

v. Price[54] held that it was improper to punish a prison journalist for providing his commentaries to a national radio audience. The court found that where there was no evidence that the plaintiff's writings and broadcasts "had strained prison resources, contributed to unrest among the inmate population or enhanced Jamal's status as a prisoner, resulting in danger to himself or others,"[55] it was improper to enforce a rule which prohibited inmates from conducting a "business" while in prison.

Son-of-Sam Laws

An interesting, and contentious, problem raised by prisoner-authored books is whether the state can regulate contracts for works authored by convicted criminals. Many states have laws that attempt to do just that.

In 1977, New York State was in the throes of a one-man crime wave caused by a serial killer who labeled himself the "Son of Sam." His crimes created a media sensation in the state.[56] While he was still at large, and following a public outcry over news reports that the killer was negotiating with publishers to sell the story of his crimes for significant profits, the New York State Legislature passed a "Son-of-Sam Law" aimed at seizing the profits that a criminal might gain from books or movies that depict his or her crimes. The law required that any payments made "to a criminal pursuant to a contract for the re-enactment of his or her crimes through a movie, book, magazine article, tape recording, phonograph record, radio and television production, or from the expression of an accused or convicted person's thoughts, feelings, opinions or emotions regarding such crime" must be paid into an escrow account, maintained by the New York State Crime Victims

---

[54]Abu-Jamal v. Price, 154 F.3d 128 (3d Cir. 1998).

[55]*Id.* at 134.

[56]The killer, David R. Berkowitz, was later captured and sentenced to a life term in prison.

§ 5:6

Board, from which victims, among others, who obtain money judgments against the defendant would be reimbursed.[57]

The law required that any payments to criminal-authors be deposited in escrow for five years and used, among other things,[58] to satisfy any judgments against the author obtained by his or her crime victims. The law applied not only to inmates who had been convicted of a crime, but also to persons who had been accused of criminal acts and even to persons who had never been accused but "admitted" a crime in their books.[59] Under the law, the publisher of the work was obligated to make the payment into the fund if the author did not.[60]

Inspired by the New York example, Congress and 43 states enacted Son-of-Sam laws in one form or another.[61] Although they all have a similar purpose of compensat-

---

[57]NY Exec Law § 632-a (McKinney 1982 & Supp 1990), amended by NY Exec Law § 632-a (Supp 1993).

[58]The law provided that the funds in the escrow account were to be used for payment of other expenses, such as the defendant's attorney's fees. See NY Exec Law § 632-a(8), amended by NY Exec Law § 632-a.

[59]NY Exec Law § 632-a(1), amended by NY Exec Law § 632-a.

[60]*Id.*

[61]18 USC § 3681; Ala. Code §§ 41-9-80 to- 84; Alaska Stat. § 12.61.020; Ariz. Rev. Stat. Ann. § 13.4202; Ark. Code Ann. § 16.90-308; Cal. Civ Code § 2225; Colo. Rev. Stat. Ann. § 24-4.201; Ariz. Rev. Stat. Ann. § 13.4202; Del. Code Ann. tit. 11, § 9103; Fla. Stat. Ann. § 54-218; Ga. Code Ann. §§ 17-14-30 to -32; Haw. Rev. Stat. §§ 351-81 to -88; Idaho Code § 19-5301; 725 Ill. Comp. Stat. 145/1-2.3; Ind. Code Ann. §§ 5-2-6.3-1 to 5-2-6.3-7; Iowa Code Ann. § 910.15; Kan. Stat. Ann. § 74-7319 to -7321; Ky. Rev. Stat. Ann. § 346.165; La. Rev. Stat. Ann. §§ 46:1831 to :1838 (repealed 1997); Md. Code Ann. §§ 11-621 to -633; Mass. Gen. Laws. Ann. ch. 258A, §§ 1, 8; Mich. Comp. Laws Ann. § 780.768; Minn. Stat. Ann. § 611A.68; Miss. Code Ann. §§ 99-38 to -11; Mo. Ann. Stat. § 595.045(14); Mont. Code Ann. §§ 53-9-103, -104(1)(b); Neb. Rev. Stat. §§ 81-1836 to -1840; Nev. Rev. Stat. § 217.007; N.J. Stat. Ann. §§ 52:4B-27 to -33; N.M. Stat. Ann. §§ 31-22-22 to -23; N.Y. Exec. Law § 632-a; Ohio Rev. Code Ann. §§ 2969.01 to .05; Okla. Stat. Ann. tit. 22, § 17; Or. Rev. Stat. §§ 147.005, .275; Pa. Cons. Stat. Ann. tit. 71, § 180-7.18 (repealed 1995); R.I. Gen. Laws §§ 12-

§ 5:6   Rights of Prisoners, Third Edition

ing crime victims by making available to them the literary profits a criminal might obtain from his or her crime, they vary in the means they choose to achieve this objective. Some cover convicted criminals only; others, like the New York provision, also apply to pretrial detainees.[62] The New York statute provided for release of the monies if the accused was acquitted or if there was an excess in the fund following release of payments to the victims;[63] however, other statutes provide for forfeiture of the assets in the fund even if the accused is acquitted and even if the assets exceed what is necessary to compensate the victim.[64]

The First Amendment implications of these laws sparked litigation that resulted in a 1991 Supreme

---

25.1-1 to -12; S.C. Code Ann. § 15-59-40 (repealed 2000); S.D. Codified Laws Ann. §§ 23A-28A-1 to -14; Tenn. Code Ann. §§ 29-13-201 to -208 (repealed 2000); Tex. Rev. Civ. Stat. Ann. art. 8309-1, -3, -16 to -18; Utah Code Ann. § 78-11-12.5 (repealed 1996); Wash. Rev. Code Ann. §§ 7.68.200-280; Wis. Stat. Ann. § 949.165; Wyo. Stat. Ann. § 1-40-112(d)(repealed 1997).

There has been very little litigation under any of the Son-of-Sam laws except for the New York statute. See Fasching v. Kallinger, 227 N.J. Super. 270, 546 A.2d 1094 (App. Div. 1988) (New Jersey statute did not reach assignment of contract rights to defendant's attorney); Fasching v. Kallinger, 211 N.J. Super. 26, 510 A.2d 694, 60 A.L.R.4th 1189 (App. Div. 1986) (statute did not reach proceeds payable to agent and publisher). Perhaps the reason for this is that very few criminals are able to obtain profitable contracts for publicizing their crimes.

[62]Alaska Stat. § 12.61.020; N.M. Stat. Ann. §§ 31-22-22 to -23; Okla. Stat. Ann. tit. 22, § 17.

[63]NY Exec Law § 632-a (McKinney 1982 & Supp 1990), amended by NY Exec Law § 632-a (Supp 1993). New York's statute has been interpreted to exclude one type of convicted person: a person who is convicted of a "victimless" crime. Children of Bedford, Inc. v. Petromelis, 77 N.Y.2d 713, 570 N.Y.S.2d 453, 573 N.E.2d 541 (1991), judgment vacated on other grounds, 502 U.S. 1025, 112 S. Ct. 859, 116 L. Ed. 2d 767 (1992).

[64]Ala. Code §§ 41-9-80 to- 84; Ariz. Rev. Stat. Ann. § 13.4202; Minn. Stat. Ann. § 611A.68. For a useful summary of the nation's Son-of-Sam laws, see Garrett Epps, Wising Up: "Son of Sam" Laws and the Speech and Press Clauses, 70 NC L Rev 493, 500-05 (1992).

Court opinion which determined the constitutionality of New York's Son-of-Sam law. In that case, *Simon & Schuster, Inc v New York Crime Victims Board*,[65] the Court unanimously struck down the New York statute.[66] The case involved a challenge to the statute by the publisher of "Wiseguy," a book written about Henry Hill, an organized crime foot soldier. The book recounts his life of crime and "depicts, in colorful detail, the day-to-day existence of organized crime."[67]

Justice O'Connor, writing for the majority, began the analysis by recognizing that New York's Son-of-Sam law is a content-based restriction on speech.[68] "The Son of Sam law," she wrote, "establishes a financial disincentive to create or publish works with a particular

---

[65] Simon & Schuster, Inc. v. Members of New York State Crime Victims Bd., 502 U.S. 105, 112 S. Ct. 501, 116 L. Ed. 2d 476 (1991).

[66] For a scholarly evaluation of this decision, see, e.g., William E. Lawrence, Constitutional Law - Freedom of Speech-Crime May Pay: New York's Son of Sam Law Found Unconstitutional, 14 U Ark Little Rock LJ 673 (1992); Lisa A. Owens, Freedom of Speech; New York's Son of Sam Statute Fails to Withstand a First Amendment Challenge, 28 Gonz L Rev 171 (1992); Elizabeth P. Peterson, The Supreme Court Stands by the First Amendment, 12 Bridgeport L Rev 1057 (1992); Kevin S. Reed, Criminal anti-profit statutes and the First Amendment, 15 Harv JL & Pub Poly 1060 (1992); Adam Robert Teehorn, Beyond Son of Sam: A Constitutionally Valid Alternative to New York Executive Law Section 632-a, 17 Vt L Rev 321 (1992).

[67] Simon & Schuster, Inc. v. Members of New York State Crime Victims Bd., 502 U.S. 105, 112 S. Ct. 501, 506, 116 L. Ed. 2d 476 (1991).

[68] The district court had held that the statute was not aimed at speech, but was limited to nonexpressive aspects of the publishing process related to making a profit. Simon & Schuster, Inc. v. Members of New York State Crime Victims Bd., 724 F. Supp. 170, 177 (S.D. N.Y. 1989), judgment aff'd, 916 F.2d 777 (2d Cir. 1990), judgment rev'd, 502 U.S. 105, 112 S. Ct. 501, 116 L. Ed. 2d 476 (1991). However, this line of reasoning was rejected by both the Second Circuit and the Supreme Court

content."⁶⁹ Because "[i]t singles out income derived from expressive activity for a burden the state places on no other income and it is directed only at works with a specified content,"⁷⁰ Justice O'Connor held that the exacting compelling state interest standard must be applied to determine its constitutionality.

The Court found that New York had a compelling state interest "in depriving criminals of the profits of their crimes and in using these funds to compensate victims."⁷¹ Nevertheless, the Court determined that the statute was not narrowly drawn to achieve the state's compelling interest because it was overinclusive. The Court gave two reasons for its conclusion that the statute was overinclusive. First, the statute reached works by accused persons who had not been convicted of a crime. Second, it reached works that only contained brief or passing references to a crime. The Court gave the following illustration of the breath of the statute:

> Should a prominent figure write his autobiography at the end of his career, and include in an early chapter a brief recollection of having stolen (in New York) a nearly worthless item as a youthful prank, the Board would control his entire income from the book for five years and would make that income available to all of the author's creditors, despite the fact that the statute of limitations for this minor incident had long since run.⁷²

The Court found the statute so overinclusive that it would have inhibited, publication of "a sobering bibliography. . . [of] hundreds of works by American

---

⁶⁹Simon & Schuster, Inc. v. Members of New York State Crime Victims Bd., 502 U.S. 105, 112 S. Ct. 501, 509, 116 L. Ed. 2d 476 (1991).

⁷⁰*Id.* at 508.

⁷¹*Id.* at 510. The Court rejected the idea that the state had a more narrow compelling interest in compensating victims from the proceeds of criminals' "storytelling." The reason was that the state had offered no justification for treating assets generated by expressive activity differently than assets a criminal obtained in another manner. *Id.*

⁷²*Id.* at 512.

prisoners and ex-prisoners, many of which contain descriptions of the crime for which the authors were incarcerated, including works by such authors as Emma Goldman and Martin Luther King, Jr."[73] Because the open-ended statute covered a "wide range of literature that does not enable a criminal to profit from his crime while a victim remains uncompensated," the Court found that it was unconstitutional.[74]

Having found the statute overbroad, the Court refused, as Justice Blackmun urged in his concurrence,[75] to rule on the plaintiff's contention that the law was also underinclusive, because the majority thought that such a determination was unnecessary to decide the case.[76] This refusal is significant because, as the Court recognized, "[t]he federal government and many of the states have enacted statutes designed to serve purposes similar to that served by the Son of Sam law."[77] Some of these laws are not as broadly written as was the New York law.[78] For example, not all of the Son-of-Sam laws cover persons who have not been convicted of crimes

---

[73]*Id.* at 511. The Court also pointed out that had the statute been in effect works by Malcolm X, Sir Walter Raleigh, Jessie Jackson, and Bertrand Russell might never have been published. *Id.* at 510-11.

[74]*Id.* at 511.

[75]*Id.* at 512. (Blackmun, J, concurring).

[76]*Id.* at 511-12. The majority also failed to engage in an exchange with Justice Kennedy, who wrote a separate concurrence urging that the Court reject a compelling state interest analysis of any law that it found imposed a content-based burden on speech. *Id.* at 512-13. Justice Kennedy argued that this finding alone was sufficient to support a finding of unconstitutionality of the statute. With this finding, he wrote, "it is both unnecessary and incorrect to ask whether the State can show" a compelling state interest in the restriction. *Id.* at 512 (Kennedy, J, concurring).

[77]*Id.* at 512.

[78]Since the Supreme Court's ruling, New York has enacted a new Son-of-Sam law. NY Exec Law § 632-a. The current statute affects "profits from the crime," including any income generated as a result of the commission of a crime, rather than only moneys earned on contracts that provide for a reenactment of the crime

and not all sweep within their ambit works that are only tangentially related to the crime. These statutes might be constitutionally infirm on the second ground argued by the plaintiffs in *Simon & Schuster* for declaring the New York statute unconstitutional-that the law is underinclusive-but the Court's refusal to address the issue leaves the status of these states' Son-of-Sam laws uncertain.

The argument on underinclusiveness of the Son-of-Sam laws is relatively easy to state. If, as the Supreme Court found, the state's interest in these laws is ensuring that funds are available to reimburse victims from the proceeds of a criminal's profits, then the law only partially accomplishes this purpose by singling out for seizure only those proceeds which are obtained from publicizing the crime. It does nothing to reach other proceeds of a crime that a criminal might have available for seizure. As Judge Newman stated in dissent when the *Simon & Schuster* case was before the Second Circuit, "many poor criminals whose crimes involve the taking of property have at least some of that property available for restitution when they are arrested. Thus, I think it unlikely that the opportunity to write about their crimes is the sole or even principal asset of most criminals."[79]

Under this rationale, Son-of-Sam laws are infirm where the legislatures have chosen to provide a remedy only for speech-generated assets while ignoring other equally available assets. The defect could be cured by the simple expedient of amending the laws so that all of the assets of a criminal defendant were made available for recovery. Such a law would be a content-neutral way of dealing with the problem without clashing with the First Amendment. Whether courts will embrace

---

through various methods of publication. In addition, the new law itself does not authorize attachment.

[79]Simon & Schuster, Inc. v. Fischetti, 916 F.2d 777, 785 (2d Cir. 1990), judgment rev'd, 502 U.S. 105, 112 S. Ct. 501, 116 L. Ed. 2d 476 (1991) (Newman, J, dissenting).

this argument, or will instead subscribe to the contrary position that the law is not underinclusive because "as a practical matter, the sole asset of most criminals is the right to tell the story of their crimes,[80] will be seen as future litigation on the question of the constitutionality of other states' Son-of-Sam laws, which was left open by the Supreme Court, unfolds.[81]

In its initial response to *Simon & Schuster, Inc.*, the New York State legislature amended the Son-of Sam law to provide that victims could recover from any funds that constituted "profits of the crime," whether or not the profits were generated by First Amendment activities.[82] This provision was held not to be broad enough to reach the funds that a criminal obtained from a civil damages award for injuries inflicted upon him by police officers during his arrest for the crime.[83]

In June 2001 New York's Son-of-Sam law was substantially revised and expanded again to reach funds that could not be reached under the initial amendment to the law.[84] The new law gave victims far greater rights to proceed against newly obtained funds of inmates

---

[80]*Id.* at 783.

[81]For a discussion of the constitutional arguments in favor of and opposed to Son-of-Sam laws, see, e.g., Garrett Epps, Wising Up: "Son of Sam" Laws and the Speech and Press Clauses, 70 NC L Rev 493 (1992); Karen M. Ecker & Margot J. O'Brien, Note, Simon & Schuster, Inc. v. Fischetti: Can New York's Son of Sam Law Survive First Amendment Challenge?, 66 Notre Dame L Rev 1075 (1991); John Timothy Loss, Note, Criminals Selling Their Stories: The First Amendment Requires Legislative Reexamination, 72 Cornell L Rev 1331 (1987); Patricia Nicole Gillard, Comment, The Expansion of Victim Compensation Programs: Today's "Son of Sam" Legislation and its Susceptibility to Constitutional Challenge, 18 U Tol L Rev 155 (1986); Joel Rothman, Note, In Cold Type: Statutory Approaches to the Problem of the Offender as Author, 71 J Crim L & Criminology 255 (1980).

[82]NY Exec Law § 632-a (L.1991, Ch 379).

[83]Sandusky v. McCummings, 164 Misc. 2d 700, 625 N.Y.S.2d 457 (Sup 1995).

[84]N.Y. Exec. Law § 632-a. This law was passed to rectify what the legislature considered to be "limitations that restrict sharply

regardless of the source of the funds. Under the new law any funds that a criminal obtained, even if they were not profits from the crime that the inmate committed, was eligible for attachment. Under the law, any time a convicted criminal received any funds in excess of $10,000, whether from an inheritance, civil judgment, or even lottery winnings, the payer must notify the New York State Crime Victims Board of the payment and the Board then notified all know crime victims of the payment. The Board had the right to freeze the funds pending the commencement of a lawsuit by the victim against the criminal. The statute also tolled all applicable statutes of limitation until the Board notified the victims of the payment.[85]

§ 5:7 The Right to Political Activity: The Right to Associate, to Communicate, and to Present Grievances in Prison

The First Amendment encompasses the political right to communicate, associate, and present grievances to the government.[1] These rights go to the very heart of a political system that values the participation of its citizens. Prisoners are, by their very confinement, restricted in their ability to engage in these activities. But prisoners do not lose all First Amendment protec-

---

the ability of crime victims to obtain full and just compensation for their injuries and other expenses." Memorandum in Support of S5110A, McKinney's 2001 Section Law, 1305 (2002)

[85]There may very well be litigation on the constitutionality of this new Act, but no cases have been reported at the time of the writing of this edition of the book.

[Section 5:7]
[1]US Const amend I; Dawson v. Delaware, 503 U.S. 159, 112 S. Ct. 1093, 1096, 117 L. Ed. 2d 309 (1992); National Ass'n for Advancement of Colored People v. State of Ala. ex rel. Patterson, 357 U.S. 449, 460-61, 78 S. Ct. 1163, 2 L. Ed. 2d 1488 (1958); John E. Nowak & Roland D. Rotunda, Constitutional Law § 16.41, at 1199-1200 (6th ed. 2000).

§ 5:7 SPEECH IN PRISON

tion on conviction.[2] The extent to which prisoners retain the right to engage in concerted political activity in prison through communication, association, and the presentation of grievances is the subject of this section.

Jones v North Carolina Prisoners' Union[3] is the most important case on this subject. In *Jones,* the plaintiffs sought to establish a prisoner labor union in the North Carolina prison system. At first, the prison authorities tolerated their efforts. But when they had attracted 2,000 members, the administration became concerned. In response to the growing success of the union, the state imposed severe restrictions on the prisoner-organizers of the union. These restrictions included a prohibition on inmate solicitation of membership, either through individual meetings or through bulk mailings, and a ban on any meetings of the union.[4] The lower court struck down these restrictions on the grounds that they were unnecessary infringements on the inmates' First Amendment rights and violated the Equal Protection Clause, because other prison organizations, including the Jaycees and Alcoholics Anonymous, were allowed to engage in these activities.[5]

However, the Supreme Court, in an opinion written by then-Justice Rehnquist, reversed and upheld all of these restrictions. Justice Rehnquist took a very limited view of the rights of inmates to engage in concerted political activity. In the first place, the Court noted, prisons "are populated, involuntarily, by people who have been found to have violated one or more of the criminal laws established by society for its orderly

---

[2]Pell v. Procunier, 417 U.S. 817, 94 S. Ct. 2827, 41 L. Ed. 2d 495 (1974); Wolff v. McDonnell, 418 U.S. 539, 555, 94 S. Ct. 2963, 41 L. Ed. 2d 935 (1974) (prisoners are not stripped of all constitutional rights).

[3]Jones v. North Carolina Prisoners' Labor Union, Inc., 433 U.S. 119, 97 S. Ct. 2532, 53 L. Ed. 2d 629 (1977).

[4]*Id.*

[5]North Carolina Prisoners' Labor Union, Inc. v. Jones, 409 F. Supp. 937 (E.D. N.C. 1976), judgment rev'd, 433 U.S. 119, 97 S. Ct. 2532, 53 L. Ed. 2d 629 (1977).

governance."[6] With such a population, political activity is fraught with danger, since in prison there is "the ever-present potential for violent confrontation and conflagration.[7] This peril, Justice Rehnquist noted, is pronounced in the case of prison unions that seek to "collectively engage in a legitimately prohibited activity.[8] Indeed, a prisoners' union that focused on the presentation of grievances in an adversarial manner "surely would rank high on anyone's list of potential trouble spots."[9] For these reasons, the Court held that prison officials were entitled to " wide-ranging" deference by the courts in their judgments about what kind of group activities to permit within the prison.[10]

With this background, the Court easily disposed of the plaintiffs' claims that the restrictions imposed on them interfered with their rights to associate, to communicate, and to present grievances. The Court began by noting that "the most obvious of the First Amendment rights that are necessarily curtailed by confinement are those associational rights that the First Amendment protects outside of prison walls.[11] Whatever associational rights remain after imprisonment are subject to restriction whenever prison officials reasonably believe that they pose undue risks to the

---

[6]Jones v. North Carolina Prisoners' Labor Union, Inc., 433 U.S. 119, 129, 97 S. Ct. 2532, 53 L. Ed. 2d 629 (1977).

[7]*Id.* at 132.

[8]*Id.* While the union had renounced any intention of engaging in collective bargaining, a practice that the district court had held improper and which North Carolina law specifically prohibited, its charter set forth this as one of its purposes. The Court held that the fact that the union, in its charter, sought the right to engage in what was illegal activity was a factor "which prison officials may legitimately consider in determining whether the Union is likely to be a disruptive influence." *Id.* at 126 n4.

[9]*Id.* at 133.

[10]*Id.* at 126.

[11]*Id.* at 125-26.

§ 5:7

facility.[12] The Court also held that the defendants' restrictions on the formation of a union did not hamper the plaintiffs' ability to present grievances to correctional officials, because they were free to use the established inmate grievance system. Justice Rehnquist wrote, "[i]n banning Union solicitation or organization, appellants have merely affected one of several ways in which inmates may voice their complaints to, and seek relief from prison officials."[13]

The Court quickly disposed of the inmates' claim that the ban on bulk mail privileges interfered with their right to communicate. To that claim, the Court replied briskly, "First Amendment speech rights are barely implicated."[14] This was so, the Court held, because only *bulk* mailings, not individual mailings, were prohibited.[15] Justice Rehnquist acknowledged that there were cost savings involved in bulk mailings, but he held these savings were not of constitutional significance.[16] Therefore, because prison officials reasonably believed that the formation of the union "posed the likelihood of disruption to prison order or stability," the Court held that whatever First Amendment rights the plaintiffs might have to engage in organizational activities leading to the formation of a prison labor union were "properly curtailed."[17]

Finally, the Court rejected the notion that the restrictions violated the equal protection rights of the plaintiffs. Since prisons are not "public forums," the Court held that it was permissible for prison officials to draw distinctions among organizations as long as they were reasonable.[18] The Court found that the defendants had a rational basis for distinguishing between a

---

[12]*Id.* at 132.
[13]*Id.* at 130 n6.
[14]*Id.* at 130.
[15]*Id.* at 130 (emphasis in original).
[16]*Id.* at 131.
[17]*Id.*
[18]*Id.* at 136.

prisoner union, on the one hand, and service or treatment groups, such as the Jaycees and Alcoholics Anonymous, on the other. The later groups, unlike the union, had a recognized history of providing services to prisoners, and did not have as their goals "the avowed intent to pursue an adversary relationship with the prison officials."[19] The Court drew from this distinction the principle that "[t]here is nothing in the Constitution which requires prison officials to treat all inmate groups alike where differentiation is necessary to avoid an imminent threat of institutional disruption or violence."[20]

Jones determined that the First Amendment rights of inmates to engage in concerted political activity are limited. If prison officials have a sincere belief that group activities of inmates present a risk to any of their legitimate interests, then, under *Jones,* they may prohibit the activity without violating inmates' constitutional rights. The *Jones* Court was not troubled that there was no evidence in the record establishing that a strike or work stoppage, or any disruption of the facility, for that matter, was imminent. It was enough for the Court that the defendants were not being "irrational" in their concerns about the potential threat posed by an established union.[21] When prison officials are faced with the possibility of organized prison opposition to their policies, the Court held, they must be given sufficient leeway to "be permitted to act before the time when they can compile a dossier on the eve of a riot."[22] *Jones,* therefore, is a potentially extremely broad holding that provides prison administrators with wide authority to decide for themselves when organizational activities of inmates are intolerable.

In dissent, Justice Marshall complained that the Court was engaging in "wholesale abandonment of

---

[19]*Id.* at 135.
[20]*Id.* at 136.
[21]*Id.* at 129.
[22]*Id.* at 132-33.

traditional principles of First Amendment analysis."[23] He criticized the majority's almost total reliance on the subjective reasonableness of prison officials' fears to justify depriving inmates of what would otherwise be clear constitutional entitlements to organize themselves. Without an "independent judgment" by the courts concerning the necessity of restricting rights, Justice Marshall feared that "prison officials [would] err on the side of too little freedom.[24] The reason for this is the pressure that prison administrators feel to maintain order in a facility at all costs. There is little pressure, however, to avoid "needlessly repressed free speech."[25] Thus, Justice Marshall warned that the Court's excessive reliance on the viewpoint of prison wardens would inevitably lead to less speech in prison than the Constitution ought to permit. Group Activity

It is possible to interpret the broad holding of the majority's opinion as a reflex reaction to the unique problems caused by a prisoner union. These organizations, if allowed to exist, might, in the judgment of prison officials, pose grave threats to the stability of a penal institution beyond what would be the case with other organizations of inmates. Indeed Justice Marshall characterized the opinion as "an aberration, a manifestation of the extent to which the very phrase 'prisoner union' is threatening to those holding traditional conceptions of the nature of penal institutions.[26]

However, courts have not shown any willingness to treat the opinion in such a limited manner, at least when the issue presented is the right of inmates to form organizations of their own choosing. After *Jones,* lower courts have allowed prison officials to disband prisoner organizations whenever they have "a sincere belief that the course [the organization has] undertaken threat-

---

[23]*Id.* at 141 (Marshall, J, dissenting).
[24]*Id.* at 142-43 (Marshall, J, dissenting).
[25]*Id.* at 142 (Marshall, J, dissenting).
[26]*Id.* at 147 (Marshall, J, dissenting).

ened the security of the institution.[27] By the same token, courts have ruled that organized protest activities of inmates can be prohibited on security grounds.[28]

While the state has been given almost unfettered discretion under *Jones* to ban prison organizations and concerted group political activity, some courts have been less willing to grant carte blanche when inmates claim other associational rights, such as the right to communicate with one another or to present grievances. These courts have struck down unreasonable attempts to prevent inmates from expressing their viewpoints. The reason for more scrutiny of these situations may be that they do not present as immediate a threat to prison security as an established inmate organization.

The clearest examples of this judicial activity are found in cases dealing with simple discussions by inmates of political issues among themselves, activity that is at the opposite end of the spectrum from the

---

[27]Hudson v. Thornburgh, 770 F. Supp. 1030, 1036 (W.D. Pa. 1991), judgment aff'd, 980 F.2d 723 (3d Cir. 1992) (prison officials permitted to disband prison "lifers" association made up of inmates who were sentenced to life sentences). See also Nicholas v. Miller, 109 F. Supp. 2d 152 (S.D. N.Y. 2000) (holding that prison officials had the right to prohibit plaintiff from establishing a "prisoners' advocacy center"); Thomas v. U.S. Secretary of Defense, 730 F. Supp. 362 (D. Kan. 1990) (no constitutional violation involved in refusing to permit the formation of a "European Heritage club" in a prison even though prison permitted clubs of other ethnic groups including an Afro-American Cultural Organization and a Latin Studies Group).

However, prison officials may not punish an inmate for his membership in an organization without any justification. Frazier v. Dubois, 922 F.2d 560 (10th Cir. 1990) (allegation that inmate was transferred for his activities as chairman of the "Afrikaans Cultural Society" stated a claim that inmate's First Amendment rights were violated).

[28]See, e.g., Figueroa v. Kapelman, 526 F. Supp. 681 (S.D. N.Y. 1981) (no right for pretrial detainees to participate in organized boycott of court appearances by criminal defendants).

formation of groups. In *Diamond v Thompson*,[29] Judge Frank Johnson held that it was unconstitutional to prevent inmates in administrative segregation from engaging in political conversations among themselves. While the prison had the right to regulate the time, place, and manner of the conversations, it was impermissible to ban outright any discussion of political issues by inmates.[30] Since it is difficult to believe that prison officials could have a rational belief that all political conversations present a realistic threat to prison security, the result in *Diamond* seems correct even under the loose strictures of judicial review approved in *Jones*.[31]

Individual Activity

Individual expressions of protest or criticisms also

---

[29]Diamond v. Thompson, 364 F. Supp. 659 (M.D. Ala. 1973), judgment aff'd, 523 F.2d 1201 (5th Cir. 1975).

[30]See also Rudolph v. Locke, 594 F.2d 1076 (5th Cir. 1979) (unconstitutional to prohibit inmates in segregation units from exchanging literature on politics and religion among themselves).

[31]The right to engage in political discussions with inmates who are confined in the same area must be distinguished from the right to be confined with a particular person in order to have communication with him or her. Both claims involve the right of association and communication. However, courts have not been willing to entertain claims of any right to associate or communicate with a particular inmate. See, e.g., Jeffries v. Reed, 631 F. Supp. 1212 (E.D. Wash. 1986) (inmates on death row have no right to associate with inmates in the general population); Cordero v. Coughlin, 607 F. Supp. 9 (S.D. N.Y. 1984) (inmates with acquired immune deficiency syndrome (AIDS) have no First Amendment right of association to be confined with the general population of prisoners); Dooley v. Quick, 598 F. Supp. 607 (D.R.I. 1984), aff'd, 787 F.2d 579 (1st Cir. 1986) (no right of two homosexual inmates confined in different areas of the same prison to communicate with one another). See also Jackson v. Meachum, 699 F.2d 578 (1st Cir. 1983) (inmates confined in punitive segregation have no free association right to human contact with other inmates in punitive segregation). For a discussion of whether inmates in punitive segregation have an Eighth Amendment right to associate with each other, see Ch 12.

§ 5:7   Rights of Prisoners, Third Edition

pose less of a generic threat to prison security than does organized group activity. Thus, unless individual complaints pose a realistic danger to security, they ought to be permitted under *Jones*.[32] There is a body of case law that has grown up on this subject.[33] The vast weight of authority stands for the proposition that it is unconstitutional to punish an inmate who exercises his First Amendment right to express a complaint. Some courts have indicated that, to establish such a claim, an inmate must establish three propositions: first, that the inmate has engaged in protected activity;[34] second, that prison officials have taken adverse action against the

---

[32]See, e.g., Meriwether v. Coughlin, 879 F.2d 1037, 1046, 14 Fed. R. Serv. 3d 1251 (2d Cir. 1989) (damage award upheld when jury found that inmate was transferred for exercising his First Amendment right to meet with prison superintendent to complain about prison conditions); Collins v. Schoonfield, 344 F. Supp. 257 (D. Md. 1972), opinion supplemented, 363 F. Supp. 1152 (D. Md. 1973). However, if the statements are inflammatory in nature or are made in a context that poses risks to security, courts have prohibited them. See, e.g., Riggs v. Miller, 480 F. Supp. 799 (E.D. Va. 1979) ("bickering argumentative" complaint is not protected); Durkin v. Taylor, 444 F. Supp. 879 (E.D. Va. 1977) (complaint that "I am tired of chickenshit rules" not protected). See also Daniel E. Manville & John Boston, Prisoners' Self-Help Litigation Manual 96-97 (2d ed 1983) (a complaint about stolen property by a guard might be protected if made privately to the warden, but not protected if made "in front of twenty or thirty other prisoners").

[33]For an extensive review of that case law see Thaddeus-X v. Blatter, 175 F.3d 378, 1999 FED App: 88P (6th Cir. 1999).

[34]Compare Zimmerman v. Tribble, 226 F.3d 568 (7th Cir. 2000) (allegation that inmate's library access was denied in retaliation for the inmate filing a grievance against the librarian stated a valid claim, leading the court to reverse and remand that portion of the claim); Brown v. Crowley, 229 F.3d 1150 (6th Cir. 2000) (inmate stated a valid claim in alleging officials retaliated against him for filing a grievance); Wells v. Wade, 2000 WL 1239085 (S.D. N.Y. 2000) (allegations that officials filed a false misbehavior report in retaliation for filing a grievance stated a valid claim), with Chambers v. Adams, 230 F.3d 1357 (6th Cir. 2000), cert. denied, 532 U.S. 1012, 121 S. Ct. 1745, 149 L. Ed. 2d 668 (2001) (inmate did not state a claim where he claimed he lost his job as a legal clerk after he suggested another inmate be hired for the same job;

§ 5:7

inmate that would deter a person of ordinary firmness from continuing to engage in the conduct;[35] and third,

---

court held that the inmate's speech did not express opinion on a matter of political, social, or public concern).

[35]Compare Allah v. Seiverling, 229 F.3d 220 (3d Cir. 2000) (district court's dismissal of inmate's claim of retaliation for filing lawsuits against prison officials vacated; allegations that officials put inmate in segregation in retaliation for the suits could lead a reasonable finder of fact to find that the conduct could deter a reasonable person from exercising constitutional rights); Spruytte v. Hoffner, 181 F. Supp. 2d 736 (W.D. Mich. 2001) (where evidence showed inmates were transferred after one of them sent a critical letter to the editor of a local newspaper disclosing that they had information regarding possible inappropriate behavior of prison officials and intended to send it to the newspaper, court held this was an adverse action that would curtail the protected First Amendment rights of a person with ordinary mental firmness); Hancock v. Thalacker, 933 F. Supp. 1449 (N.D. Iowa 1996) (inmate claimed the imposition of disciplinary sanctions for "false statements" made in grievances to prison authorities unconstitutionally "chilled" his First Amendment right of petition; court concluded he stated a viable First Amendment claim; holding that in order to avoid a chill on the First Amendment rights of prisoners, disciplinary sanctions could not be imposed on an inmate for false or defamatory statement unless the statements were knowingly false or defamatory); Griffin v. Thomas, 122 N.M. 826, 1997 -NMCA- 009, 932 P.2d 516 (Ct. App. 1997) (lower court improperly dismissed inmate's First Amendment claim where prison officials imposed disciplinary segregation in retaliation for his filing grievances; thus, the judgment was reversed and remanded for further proceedings), with Friedmann v. Corrections Corp. of America, 11 Fed. Appx. 467 (6th Cir. 2001) (inmate was interviewed by a nationally published magazine regarding his views on the privatization of prisons; he also gathered other articles on the topic and compiled a publication to send to legislators; the warden reviewed the publication, and ordered a reclassification hearing, which led to the inmate's transfer to another facility; the inmate claimed the transfer violated his constitutional rights, as it came in retaliation for his criticism of privately run prisons; court held the transfer would not prevent a person of ordinary mental firmness from discontinuing his First Amendment speech, therefore the inmate's First Amendment rights were not violated); Root v. Towers, 2000 WL 424193 (E.D. Mich. 2000), judgment aff'd, 238 F.3d 423 (6th Cir. 2000) (plaintiff inmate filed a grievance against

§ 5:7

that there exists a causal connection between the action taken against the inmate and the protected activity.[36] Some courts, however, do not require the second showing holding that the constitution is violated for punishing an inmate for filing a grievance even if the "adverse action" would not itself violate the constitution.[37]

Petitions

Submission of petitions to prison authorities is an-

---

prison officials based on their alleged misconduct in the storage of his personal property; the "adverse conduct" alleged was that a defendant "threatened, harassed, and/or intimidated" the plaintiff by telling him "never to put his name on a grievance, that the defendant would deny all allegations claiming no knowledge or involvement in damage, loss or destruction to [plaintiffs'] personal or legal property, and that [plaintiff was on his "shit-list"; court held that, assuming the defendant did make the statements, they did not rise to the level of a constitutional action; rough words are common in prisons, and such language does not deter "ordinary prisoners" from filing actions and did not deter the plaintiff from pursuing the lawsuit or even from pursuing his grievances).

[36]Hazen v. Reagen, 16 F.3d 921 (8th Cir. 1994) (affirming district court decision holding no First Amendment violation where prisoner was transferred, not to foil his nomination to a prisoner advisory board, but for prison officials' "reasonable belief" that he was manipulative and caused problems); Cook v. Lehman, 863 F. Supp. 207 (E.D. Pa. 1994) (granting summary judgment to prison officials where prisoner did not prove that segregated confinement was imposed as a retaliatory measure after prisoner had lead a peaceful protest intended to compel prison authorities to provide medical care to two fellow inmates); Geder v. Godinez, 875 F. Supp. 1334 (N.D. Ill. 1995) (granting summary judgment for prison officials where prisoner did not establish that false disciplinary charge was issued against him in retaliation for written or oral complaints he submitted concerning prison living conditions). Retaliatory actions against inmates who assert their First Amendment rights may also violate state law. See, e.g., Gaston v. Coughlin, 81 F. Supp. 2d 381 (N.D. N.Y. 1999) (firing an inmate from his job in the prison kitchen because he complained that work conditions in the prison violated state law was unlawful retailiation under state law).

[37]DeWalt v. Carter, 224 F.3d 607 (7th Cir. 2000).

other example of political activity that some courts have permitted after *Jones*. In *Wolfel v Bates*,[38] the plaintiff was charged with violating prison rules by circulating a petition signed by 17 inmates that was sent to the prison superintendent complaining about the prison's shower policy. Absent any evidence that the statements in the petition were false or malicious, the court held that punishing the plaintiff for circulating the petition violated his right to petition for the redress of grievances.[39] The court held that, "[n]owhere do we find authority for the proposition that prison administrators have an overriding interest in the *indiscriminate* suppression of peacefully communicated inmate complaints.[40] However, there is contrary authority on this point. The Eighth Circuit has held that if prison officials provide alternative means of communicating grievances, they may constitutionally prohibit inmates from circulating "mass protest" petitions.[41] The Second Circuit has gone both ways with one case finding a right

---

[38]Wolfel v. Bates, 707 F.2d 932 (6th Cir. 1983).

[39]*Id.* at 934. The court indicated that the result might very well have been different had it been proved that plaintiff was guilty of malicious dissemination of false or defamatory information. *Id.* at 234 n1. See also Ross v. Reed, 719 F.2d 689, 695 (4th Cir. 1983) (no right to send complaining letter to prison officials when the letter is not a legitimate attempt to petition but rather "an arguably illegal effort to coerce official action by making allegations known to be false or unsupportable").

[40]*Id.* at 934 (emphasis in original). See also Haymes v. Montanye, 547 F.2d 188, 191 (2d Cir. 1976); Stovall v. Bennett, 471 F. Supp. 1286 (M.D. Ala. 1979). Cf Richardson v. Coughlin, 763 F. Supp. 1228, 1235 (S.D. N.Y. 1991) (violation of due process to punish an inmate for circulating a petition when there was no prison rule which prohibited such activity).

[41]Nickens v. White, 622 F.2d 967 (8th Cir. 1980). See also Richardson v. Coughlin, 763 F. Supp. 1228, 1237 (S.D. N.Y. 1991) (as of 1987, the right of prisoners to circulate petitions complaining harshly of prison conditions was not clearly established); Edwards v. White, 501 F. Supp. 8 (M.D. Pa. 1979), aff'd, 633 F.2d 209 (3d Cir. 1980) and aff'd, 633 F.2d 212 (3d Cir. 1980) (ban on petitions justified by the fact that violence may erupt when signatures are gathered).

to circulate a petition as long as it is not part of a plan to ferment a prison work stoppage[42], while another case holds that there is no right to circulate petitions if there is an inmate grievance procedure that allows inmates to communicate their complaints.[43]

The tone of the petition is one factor that might justify banning petitions under *Jones* in some cases while permitting them in others. If the petition is hostile and threatening or false and misleading, there is obviously more reason to prohibit it than would be the case if the authors of the petition assume a more respectful posture.[44] Whether the prison provides alternative channels for inmates to express their complaints is another relevant factor in deciding whether the ban on petitions is constitutional.[45]

---

[42]Graham v. Henderson, 89 F.3d 75, 80 n. 1 (2d Cir. 1996) ("Graham does have a constitutional right to circulate a petition").

[43]Duamutef v. O'Keefe, 98 F.3d 22, 23 (2d Cir. 1996) ("So long as that avenue of communication [grievance procedure] is open we believe it is permissible for prison officials to bar the circulation of petitions."). See also Bowman v. City of Middletown, 91 F. Supp. 2d 644 (S.D. N.Y. 2000) (noting that it is not clear whether inmates have a right to petition prison officials).

[44]For an example of a hostile petition, see, e.g., Williams v. Stacy, 468 F. Supp. 1206 (E.D. Va. 1979) (guards described as "Nazis" and "maniacs"). See also Jones v. Nelson, 861 F. Supp. 983 (D. Kan. 1994) (inmate's First Amendment rights were not violated when he received a written disciplinary report after calling a female prison officer a "bitch.").

[45]See, e.g., Nickens v. White, 622 F.2d 967 (8th Cir. 1980). See also Duamutef v. O'Keefe, 98 F.3d 22 (2d Cir. 1996).

Chapter 6

First Amendment Rights: Religion

Research References

Prisoners and the Law, Ch 3
Steinglass, Section 1983 Litigation in State Courts § 4:22
Am. Jur. 2d, Constitutional Law §§ 443
Am. Jur. 2d, Penal and Correctional Institutions §§ 32, 33, 36 to 44
Civil Rights ⚖104.3; Constitutional Law ⚖84.5(14); Prisons ⚖4(14); Sentencing and Punishment ⚖1551
A.L.R. Index: Prisons and Prisoners; Religion and Religious Societies

> **KeyCite®:** Cases and other legal materials listed in KeyCite Scope can be researched through West Group's KeyCite service on Westlaw®. Use KeyCite to check citations for form, parallel references, prior and later history, and comprehensive citator information, including citations to other decisions and secondary materials.

§ 6:1 Introduction
§ 6:2 The Search for a Governing Standard
§ 6:3 *O'Lone v Estate of Shabazz*
§ 6:4 Congress and the Supreme Court Battle Over a Governing Standard
§ 6:5 Equal Protection
§ 6:6 Establishment of Religion
§ 6:7 Defining Religion
§ 6:8 Religious Practices
§ 6:9 —Personal Appearance and Clothing
§ 6:10 —Meals
§ 6:11 —Religious Services
§ 6:12 —Name Changes
§ 6:13 —Access to Clergy
§ 6:14 —Access to Religious Mail and Publications
§ 6:15 —Access to Religious Accouterments

§ 6:16 —Work-Religion Conflicts
§ 6:17 —Medical Treatment-Religion Conflicts

§ 6:1 Introduction

The First Amendment to the United States Constitution guarantees the right to freely practice religion.[1] To what extent do prisoners enjoy this right?

In the early days, the question itself might have seemed surprising. The Philadelphia reformers who developed the first American penitentiaries saw them as religious places in which prisoners would be required to engage in prayerful reflection about their crimes, penitence most literally.[2]

But in the Philadelphia style penitentiaries of the eighteenth and nineteenth centuries, the religion that was obligatory was the Protestant faith.[3] There was little tolerance granted to prisoners practicing religions

---

[Section 6:1]

[1] US Const amend I: "Congress shall make no law respecting an establishment of religion or prohibiting the free exercise thereof." The First Amendment was made applicable to the states in 1867. See Murdock v. Com. of Pennsylvania, 319 U.S. 105, 108, 63 S. Ct. 870, 87 L. Ed. 1292, 146 A.L.R. 81 (1943).

[2] Prisoners were encouraged to "reflect upon their sins and repent." John Martin, Break Down the Walls: American Prisons: Present, Past, and Future 111 (1954). See also David J. Rothman, The Discovery of the Asylum: Social Order and Disorder in the New Republic 85 (1971) (through isolation in prison, "the grandiose goals of peace, right, and Christianity would be furthered").

[3] To be sure, the penitentiary model was not used everywhere. In New York, the Auburn system, the major alternative to the Philadelphia system, relied more on a requirement that prisoners work together in complete silence than it did on religion. The Auburn system, however, did have a role for religion, using silence and nightly isolation to "spark redemption." David J. Rothman, Conscience and Convenience; The Asylum and Its Alternatives in Progressive American 119 (1st ed 1980). Thus, religion was an essential element in at least some of the first American prisons.

FIRST AMENDMENT: RELIGION § 6:1

that did not fit the mold.[4]

Although modern penology no longer subscribes to the notion that prisons are primarily places for religious reflection and meditation, certain religious activities are still voluntarily encouraged, primarily because they are viewed as having a rehabilitative effect on the inmates and because regular religious services and counseling assist in maintaining security in the institution.[5]

The notion of religious exercise as a prisoner's right rather than an administrator's prerogative first surfaced as a legal issue over a century ago. In *Ho Ah Kow v Nunan*,[6] a Chinese citizen incarcerated in a San Francisco jail challenged his jailors' actions in cutting off his *queue,* a long braid of hair. Ho Ah Kow claimed that the queue symbolized his religious beliefs and that its absence was a mark of disgrace in his religion.[7] The prison officials justified cutting his hair as necessary for security, identification, and hygiene.[8]

Justice Stephen J. Field, a Supreme Court Justice who was sitting as a Circuit Justice at the time, heard the case. Justice Field held for the plaintiff in what is probably the first court decision dealing with the religious rights of prisoners. Although the decision was based on equal protection grounds, Justice Field recognized that the hairstyle regulation might offend the free exercise rights of the plaintiff. He wrote that this regulation, like a regulation that forced Orthodox

---

[4]The Pennsylvania system was very strict and inflexible. Rules provided that prisoners must speak only with selected visitors, and read only "morally uplifting literature" (the Christian Bible). David J. Rothman, The Discovery of the Asylum: Social Order and Disorder in the New Republic 85 (1971).

[5]National Advisory Commission on Crim. Just. Standards & Goals Corrections 64 (1973).

[6]Ho Ah Kow v. Nunan, 12 F. Cas. 252, No. 6546 (C.C.D. Cal. 1879). This case is discussed in Comment, The Religious Rights of the Incarcerated, 125 U Pa L Rev 812, 813 (1977).

[7]Ho Ah Kow, 12 F. Cas. at 253.

[8]*Id.*

Jewish prisoners to eat pork, would be an "offense against . . . religion."[9]

Over 120 years after *Ho Ah Kow,* prisoners continue to raise similar and, in some cases, identical issues.[10] Does free exercise require that prison officials accommodate sincerely held religious practices? Does equal protection prohibit granting protection to the practice of some religions and not others? Is there an obligation to supply the materials and assistance needed by inmates to practice their religion, or does the affirmative provision of these services by the government run afoul of the Establishment Clause of the Constitution? For the purposes of deciding whether the religious rights of a prisoner have been violated, how does a court determine whether the prisoner's practice or belief constitutes a religion?

That courts are regularly called on to make these judgments comes as no surprise. After all, a prisoner is cut off from the outside world and the opportunities it offers for largely uninhibited religious expression. A free-world person hardly has to ask permission to wear a religious medal or grow long hair as an expression of his or her faith. Nor is a civilian prevented by the state from attending religious services or meeting privately with a religious advisor. However, in a penal environment, none of these practices can be taken for granted; they all depend on the acquiescence of the persons who are in charge of the prison. Moreover, prison officials who are charged with responsibility for maintaining order and safety in the prison, and have to do so with limited budgets, often express concern that granting these dispensations in the controlled atmosphere of a prison will severely compromise these paramount concerns.

Since the days of *Ho Ah Kow,* the manner in which the courts should resolve these inevitable tensions has remained a matter of some uncertainty. Until the late

---

[9] *Id.* at 255.
[10] See § 6:7.

1980's, that uncertainty was compounded by the absence of a Supreme Court determination of the standards to be used in adjudicating a prisoner's religious claim case under the First Amendment. The Court seemingly settled the issue in its 1987 opinion in *O'Lone v Estate of Shabazz*.[11] However, *Shabazz* and a non-prison opinion, *Employment Division v. Smith*,[12] have simply shifted the debate from disagreement among the courts of appeals, to discord between the Supreme Court and Congress. As this is written, that debate continues, as will be discussed in this chapter.

This chapter will examine the road the courts took to *Shabazz*, and will then discuss the *Shabazz* case itself. It will also discuss Congress's attempts to give greater protection to the religious practices of inmates. The chapter will then consider the equal protection, free exercise, and establishment issues that are raised when challenges are made to policies affecting religious practices in prison.

§ 6:2 The Search for a Governing Standard

Research References

West's Key Number Digest, Constitutional Law ⚖84.5(14)

Justice Field decided the *Ho Ah Kow* case in 1879. It was not until the 1960s, however, that courts were regularly called on to address prisoners' religious claims. At that time, the issue of religious freedom in prison took on a new importance when courts began to give credence to complaints that prison officials were refusing to allow adherents of the Black Muslim faith to practice their religion. Prior to that time, with the lone exception of *Ho Ah Kow*, courts refused to adjudicate claims of prisoners for religious freedom because of

---

[11]O'Lone v. Estate of Shabazz, 482 U.S. 342, 107 S. Ct. 2400, 96 L. Ed. 2d 282 (1987).

[12]Employment Div., Dept. of Human Resources of Oregon v. Smith, 494 U.S. 872, 110 S. Ct. 1595, 108 L. Ed. 2d 876 (1990).

the rigid hold of the hands-off doctrine.[1] In 1964, the Supreme Court addressed the issue for the first time in *Cooper v Pate*.[2] The Court held, in a brief opinion, that such claims by Black Muslims stated a viable claim for judicial review.

In *Cruz v Beto*,[3] decided eight years after *Cooper*, the Court was presented with a similar claim by a Buddhist prisoner in a Texas prison. The Court used the occasion to add substance to its earlier holding in *Cooper*. In *Cruz*, the plaintiff alleged that he was denied use of the prison chapel, prevented from corresponding with religious advisors, and not allowed to share religious materials with other inmates. The Court held that if the plaintiff's allegations were proven to be true, "there was palpable discrimination by the state against the Buddhist religion . . . . The First Amendment, applicable to the States by reason of the Fourteenth Amendment, . . . prohibits government from making a law 'prohibiting the free exercise of religion.'"[4]

Cruz "clearly establishes that the free exercise of religion is among those rights retained by the incarcerated."[5] However, *Cruz* did not determine the scope of this right and the standard that courts should use to determine whether the right to practice religion was abridged. The decision rested as much on the equal protection claim of *Cruz* that Buddhists were not given rights granted to other religious groups as it did on the claim that the prison officials had violated independent

---

[Section 6:2]

[1] See Ch 1.

[2] Cooper v. Pate, 378 U.S. 546, 84 S. Ct. 1733, 12 L. Ed. 2d 1030 (1964) (per curiam).

[3] Cruz v. Beto, 405 U.S. 319, 92 S. Ct. 1079, 31 L. Ed. 2d 263 (1972) (per curiam).

[4] *Id.* at 322.

[5] Comment, The Religious Rights of the Incarcerated, 125 U Pa L Rev 812, 822 (1977).

free exercise rights.[6]

Without a clear uniform standard to determine whether free exercise rights of inmates have been violated, it is difficult to know when a constitutional deprivation has occurred.[7]

Nevertheless, the Supreme Court did not address this issue or discuss freedom of religion in prison again until 1987, some 15 years after the *Cruz* decision. Left without the assistance of a definitive Supreme Court decision during those years, lower courts developed a number of contradictory tests to resolve these cases.[8] Some courts applied the exacting "compelling state interest standard" used by courts in adjudicating free exercise claims of free-world persons.[9] Under this test, restrictions on religious practices were subjected to meticulous scrutiny by the courts to determine whether there were sufficiently powerful governmental interests that necessitated the restriction. In a similar vein, some courts held that restrictions on religious practices were not legitimate unless they were the least restrictive

---

[6]See, e.g., Comment, Backwash Benefits for Second Class Citizens: Prisoners' First Amendment and Procedural Due Process Rights, 46 U Colo L Rev 377, 382 (1975) ("Under *Cruz v. Beto* freedom of religion extends only so far as the umbrella of equal protection can shelter it").

[7]O'Lone v. Estate of Shabazz, 482 U.S. 342, 357, 107 S. Ct. 2400, 96 L. Ed. 2d 282 (1987) (Brennan, J, dissenting).

[8]One commentator pointed to seven distinct tests that courts had used in prison free exercise cases. Comment, The Religious Rights of the Incarcerated, 125 U Pa L Rev 812, 837-856(1977). For an interesting discussion of the variety of approaches used by the courts to adjudicate prison free exercise cases in the years prior to *Shabazz,* see Note, O'Lone v Estate of Shabazz: The State of Prisoners' Religious Free Exercise Rights, 37 Am UL Rev 453, 467-71 (1988).

[9]See, e.g., Kennedy v. Meacham, 540 F.2d 1057 (10th Cir. 1976); Weaver v. Jago, 675 F.2d 116 (6th Cir. 1982).

§ 6:2   Rights of Prisoners, Third Edition

means available to achieve valid correctional goals.[10]

Other courts, however, rejected the compelling interest standard and ruled that a less exacting standard of review applied in the prison context.[11] The Seventh Circuit, for example, held that limitations on the practice of religion were constitutional if supported by an important governmental objective and if reasonably adapted to the achievement of that objective.[12] Other courts were even less demanding and were willing to uphold any curtailment of religion in prison as long as the prison officials' actions were reasonable.[13]

With such a wide variety and conflicting array of standards used by the lower courts, the law in this area prior to 1987 was, at best, unsettled. On the eve of the Supreme Court's decision in *O'Lone v Estate of Shabazz*, the Fifth Circuit noted the "intercircuit conflict on the appropriate standard for free exercise claims" and of-

---

[10]See, e.g., Shabazz v. Barnauskas, 790 F.2d 1536 (11th Cir. 1986); Native American Council of Tribes v. Solem, 691 F.2d 382 (8th Cir. 1982).

[11]Perhaps the most sophisticated of the many tests proposed was developed by Judge Kaufman of the Second Circuit in Abdul Wali v. Coughlin, 754 F.2d 1015 (2d Cir. 1985). Under that test, the degree of scrutiny would depend on "the nature of the right being asserted by prisoners, the type of activity in which they seek to engage and whether the challenged restriction works a total deprivation (as opposed to a mere limitation) on the exercise of that right." *Id.* at 1033. If the activity that was prohibited was dangerous, or if the regulation did not work a total deprivation of the right but merely regulated the time, place, or manner of its expression, then all that was required to validate the practice was a finding that the prison officials had a reasonable justification for the restriction. However, if the practice was not dangerous, or if the deprivation of the religious practice was complete, a higher level of scrutiny was mandatory. In those cases, the prison officials needed to demonstrate that the restriction was "necessary to further an important governmental interest, and that the limitations on freedoms occasioned by the restrictions are no greater than necessary to effectuate the governmental objective involved." *Id.*

[12]Madyun v. Franzen, 704 F.2d 954 (7th Cir. 1983).

[13]See, e.g., Little v. Norris, 787 F.2d 1241 (8th Cir. 1986); Walker v. Mintzes, 771 F.2d 920 (6th Cir. 1985).

fered a prayer that the Supreme Court "will bring order to this unholy mess."[14] As if in answer to the Fifth Circuit's supplication, the Supreme Court decided the major opinion in this area, *O'Lone v Shabazz*.[15]

§ 6:3 O'Lone v Estate of Shabazz

The *Shabazz* case arose when Muslim inmates at a New Jersey prison who were assigned to a minimum-security work detail outside the prison walls requested permission to attend Islamic Jumu'ah services that were held each Friday in the prison.[1] After the request was denied, the inmates brought suit in federal court. The plaintiffs argued that the Jumu'ah service was an essential rite of their religion, and one in which all Muslims were required to participate.[2]

The defendants did not challenge the sincerity of the prisoners' beliefs or the importance to Muslims of regular attendance at the Friday services.[3] They argued, instead, that they lacked sufficient staff to escort the prisoners to the services and at the same time continue the normal prison schedule. Moreover, attendance at the services, the defendants claimed, would disrupt the rehabilitative program of the inmates and might create problems by fostering the development of a cohesive group that could challenge prison authority. The defendants argued further that to permit the plaintiffs to attend services might engender a perception among other inmates that Muslims were being offered favored status.[4] Finally, the defendants pointed to other ways in which devout Muslims could practice their faith at

---

[14]Udey v. Kastner, 805 F.2d 1218, 1219 n1 (5th Cir. 1986).

[15]O'Lone v. Estate of Shabazz, 482 U.S. 342, 107 S. Ct. 2400, 96 L. Ed. 2d 282 (1987).

[Section 6:3]

[1]O'Lone v. Estate of Shabazz, 482 U.S. 342, 343, 107 S. Ct. 2400, 96 L. Ed. 2d 282 (1987).

[2]*Id.*

[3]*Id.* at 345.

[4]*Id.* at 343.

the prison, including special diets, other religious services, and the presence at the facility of a Muslim religious leader.[5]

By a five to four vote, the Supreme Court ruled for the defendants. Of the competing tests for determining free exercise claims, the Court chose the rational relationship test, the one that most favored prison administrators. Quoting from *Turner v Safley*,[6] decided the same term, Chief Justice Rehnquist (writing for the Court) held that "when a prison regulation impinges on inmates' constitutional rights, the regulation is valid if it is reasonably related to legitimate penological interests."[7] To determine whether such a rational relationship is present, the Court adopted the four-factor analysis set forth in *Turner v Safely*.[8]

The *Turner* analysis considers the following factors:

(1) whether there is a logical connection between the restriction and the governmental interests invoked to justify it;
(2) the availability of alternative means to exercise the restricted right;
(3) the impact that accommodation of the right might have on other inmates, on prison personnel, and on allocation of prison resources generally; and
(4) whether there are "obvious, easy alternatives" to the policy that could be adopted at de minimis cost.[9]

The Court found that the restriction on Friday ser-

---

[5]*Id.*

[6]Turner v. Safley, 482 U.S. 78, 107 S. Ct. 2254, 96 L. Ed. 2d 64 (1987). *Turner* is discussed in detail in Ch 5.

[7]O'Lone v. Estate of Shabazz, 482 U.S. 342, 349, 107 S. Ct. 2400, 96 L. Ed. 2d 282 (1987) (quoting Turner v. Safley, 482 U.S. 78, 89, 107 S. Ct. 2254, 96 L. Ed. 2d 64 (1987)).

[8]Turner v. Safley, 482 U.S. 78, 89, 107 S. Ct. 2254, 96 L. Ed. 2d 64 (1987).

[9]*Id.* at 89-91.

vices satisfied all four of the *Turner* factors. First, there was a logical connection between the restriction and the state's interests in order and security. The Court credited the testimony of prison officials that the restriction on returning to the prison during the day eased overcrowding at the prison, prevented congestion and delays at the main gate, and aided rehabilitation by requiring the inmates to maintain regular working hours during the workweek.[10] Second, while there were no alternative means of attending Jumu'ah, the Court observed that the plaintiffs were not "deprived of all forms of religious exercise."[11] They could attend other services-although not ones with the same importance-and could meet with the state provided Imam, the Muslim religious leader. Moreover, they were given a pork-free diet, and special arrangements were made for Muslims to observe the month-long holiday of Ramadan.

Turning to the third factor, the Court considered the impact that accommodation of the plaintiff's wishes would have on the facility and accepted the defendants' arguments that alternative arrangements to permit the plaintiffs to attend services would be untenable.[12] The reasons given by the defendants for this conclusion were that the extra security required would be a drain on scant prison resources. Moreover, accommodation would threaten prison security by allowing "affinity groups" in the prison to flourish. Furthermore, to accommodate the plaintiffs' request might open prison officials to the criticism that they were "playing favorites."[13] Finally, the Court determined, without further discussion, that there were no de minimis alternatives to the policy forbidding attendance at the Friday services.[14]

The dissenting opinion, written by Justice Brennan

---

[10]O'Lone v. Estate of Shabazz, 482 U.S. 342, 350-51, 107 S. Ct. 2400, 96 L. Ed. 2d 282 (1987).

[11]*Id.* at 351-52.

[12]*Id.* at 350.

[13]*Id.* at 352-53.

[14]*Id.* at 353.

for himself and three other members of the court, took the majority to task for choosing the reasonableness standard, which is characterized as "categorically deferential.[15] With the majority's high level of deference to the decisions of prison officials, Justice Brennan wrote, prisoners will not receive the protections of the Constitution because:

> [t]he Constitution was not adopted as a means of enhancing the efficiency with which government officials conduct their affairs, or as a blueprint for ensuring sufficient reliance on administrative expertise. Rather it was meant to provide a bulwark against infringements that might otherwise be justified as necessary expedients of governing.[16]

The Significance of *Shabazz*

In *Shabazz,* the Supreme Court seemingly settled the controversy in the lower courts over the governing rule for prison free exercise cases. The Court chose the lowest standard of review of the available options. Restrictions on religious expressions of prisoners are constitutional, under this standard, as long as they are reasonable.[17] Strict scrutiny of the claim, which would otherwise be required if the case arose in another setting, is not the goal of the *Shabazz* standard.[18] As the Court acknowledged, the *Shabazz* standard is not the same that is "ordinarily applied to alleged infringements of fundamental constitutional rights."[19]

The Court's "reasonableness" standard makes no use

---

[15]*Id.* at 356 (Brennan, J, dissenting).

[16]*Id.* at 356 (Brennan, J, dissenting). Justice Brennan also took issue with the majority's application of its own standard. Since the record contained little justification for the deprivation, even under the court's standard, Brennan argued that the Court was in error in not remanding the case to the district court for further consideration of the case. *Id.* at 359-68.

[17]*Id.* at 349.

[18]*Id.* at 349 n. 2.

[19]*Id.* at 349.

of the least restrictive alternative test. The presence of an alternative that could serve the prison's interest without violating the prisoners' rights, therefore, is not dispositive.[20] While alternatives are relevant, under *Shabazz* prison officials need not resort to them if they require the prison to expend considerable resources or exert a major effort to implement; only easily available alternatives to the practice that can be implemented with de minimis effort will be required.[21] Moreover, the burden of proving the existence of these easily available alternatives falls squarely on the shoulders of the complaining prisoners.[22]

Commentators criticized the *Shabazz* Court's choice of standard. In the words of one commentator, *Shabazz* "places prisoners' constitutional rights in a very precarious situation . . . [and] provides [prison] officials with great discretion to curtail and abolish many basic religious rights of the incarcerated.[23] "[W]ith only minimal justification" prison officials can extinguish these rights.[24]

As the discussion that follows points out, commentators were not alone in showing their displeasure with the test put forth in *Shabazz*. Congress took note of that decision, and the decision in *Employment Division v. Smith*, and soon the issue of the religious protections afforded to prisoners was swept up in a power struggle between the Supreme Court and lawmakers.

---

[20]*Id.* at 350.

[21]*Id.* at 352.

[22]*Id.* at 350 ("We have rejected the notion that prison officials . . . have to set up and then shoot down every conceivable alternative method of accommodating the claimants constitutional complaint") (quoting Turner v. Safley, 482 U.S. 78, 90-91, 107 S. Ct. 2254, 96 L. Ed. 2d 64 (1987)).

[23]Note, O'Lone v Shabazz: The State of Prisoners' Religious Free Exercise Rights, 37 Am U L Rev 453, 483 (1988).

[24]*Id.* at 478.

§ 6:4 Congress and the Supreme Court Battle Over a Governing Standard

Three years after *Shabazz,* the Supreme Court dealt another blow to the compelling interest standard as it applies to violations of free exercise rights with its decision in *Employment Division v. Smith.*[1] In *Smith,* the Court held that where religious exercise is burdened by the affect of a neutral, generally applicable law or regulation, the Free Exercise Clause does not require the law to be analyzed under a compelling interest standard.[2] Though adding nothing new in the context of the rights of prisoners after *Shabazz,* it was *Smith* that aroused Congress's attention and led to the first of two attempts to re-impose the compelling interest standard in all instances where free exercise rights of prisoners are implicated.[3]

Religious Freedom Restoration Act (RFRA)

In 1993, Congress passed, and the President signed, the Religious Freedom Restoration Act. The Act provided as follows:

FREE EXERCISE OF RELIGION PROTECTED

(a) IN GENERAL.-Government shall not substantially burden a person's exercise of religion even if the burden results from a rule of general applicability, except as provided in subsection (b).

(b) EXCEPTION.-Government may substantially burden a person's exercise of religion only if it determines that the application of the burden to the person-

(1) is in furtherance of a compelling governmental interest; and

---

[Section 6:4]

[1]Employment Div., Dept. of Human Resources of Oregon v. Smith, 494 U.S. 872, 110 S. Ct. 1595, 108 L. Ed. 2d 876 (1990).

[2]*Id.* at 885.

[3]See S. Rep. No. 103-111, pt. V(b) (1993).

(2) is the least restrictive means of furthering that compelling interest.[4]

The legislative history of the Act makes it clear that it applied to prisoners.[5] The Act also expressly overruled *O'Lone v. Estate of Shabazz*.[6] Congress found that a state or governmental entity "must do more than simply offer conclusory statements that a limitation on religious freedom is required for security, health or safety in order to establish that its interest are of the 'highest order.'"[7] But Congress also recognized the special circumstances facing prisons, and pointed out that if the government could show that a regulation was a legitimate means of maintaining security, health, or safety, then it had met its burden of proving a compelling interest[8]

So the first major difference between the standard imposed by the RFRA and the rational basis test of *Shabazz* was the higher initial hurdle prison and government officials must meet in order for the challenged law or regulation to be upheld. The second major difference between the two standards was the role that available alternatives to the challenged policy played in the analysis. In *Shabazz,* the Supreme Court held that as long as there was some other way for the prisoner to practice his or her religion despite the challenged policy, whether or not that involved the same practice, the policy would be upheld.[9] Under the RFRA, the policy, even if it serves a compelling interest, still must be the least restrictive means of furthering that interest.[10] The Act also shifted the burden of proving this portion of the test to the government officials, as

---

[4]42 U.S.C. § 2000bb-1 (1993).

[5]See S. Rep. No. 103-111, pt. V(d) (1993).

[6]*Id.*

[7]*Id.* quoting, Weaver v. Jago, 675 F.2d 116, 119 (6th Cir. 1982).

[8]*Id.*

[9]See O'Lone v. Estate of Shabazz, 482 U.S. 342, 351-62, 107 S. Ct. 2400, 96 L. Ed. 2d 282 (1987).

[10]42 U.S.C. § 2000bb-1(b)(2) (1993).

they were in the best position to determine whether this particular policy was the least restrictive means of achieving the policy's purpose.

If the Court were to have decided *Shabazz* under RFRA, it is unclear if it would have come to a different result. The Court would first have had to look at whether the freedom to exercise one's religion had been substantially burdened, something the courts had struggled with in the past.[11] The key to the analysis would be whether the government had provided enough evidence that the policy furthered a compelling government interest, and whether there was enough evidence that the policy represented the least restrictive means available of furthering that goal. Whether *Shabazz* would have come out the same or not, its clear that the test adopted by the Court, and that adopted by Congress were polar opposites, and would, at least in some cases, lead to differing results.

Congress enacted the RFRA using it powers under Section 5 of the Fourteenth Amendment to the Constitution. That section gives Congress the power to remedy current, and prevent possible future, violations of the Fourteenth Amendment. Congress saw the Supreme Court's decisions in *Smith* and *Shabazz* as leaving the door open for such an exercise of legislative power, and it felt that the enactment of the RFRA was well within their authority. The Supreme Court disagreed.

City of Boerne v Flores

In 1997, The Supreme Court decided a case concerning a land use law in the city of Boerne, Texas. *City of Boerne v. Flores* was a claim brought by the Archbishop of San Antonio alleging that a city ordinance violated the RFRA.[12] The Archbishop had approved the renova-

---

[11]See § 6:6.

[12]City of Boerne v. Flores, 521 U.S. 507, 534, 117 S. Ct. 2157, 138 L. Ed. 2d 624 (1997).

tion of a church to accommodate an influx of new parishioners, but the Historic Landmarks Commission set up by the challenged ordinance denied the expansion.[13] In a six to three decision, the Supreme Court found that Congress had exceeded its authority in passing RFRA.[14]

First of all, the Court found that the RFRA was "so out of proportion to a supposed remedial or preventive object, that it cannot be understood as responsive to, or designed to prevent, unconstitutional behavior."[15] The Court found that the law did not only apply to what Congress saw as constitutional violations, but to every imaginable governmental action.[16] Furthermore, the Court held that the RFRA did not protect and enforce existing constitutional rights, but instead attempted to create new rights, something Congress has no power to do without amending the Constitution.[17]

The Supreme Court admonished Congress for attempting to specifically overrule one of its decisions. It is the Court's responsibility to interpret the Constitution. It had done so in *Smith,* holding that government was not required to meet a compelling interest standard in order for a neutral, generally applicable policy to survive an attack based on free exercise. The Court held in *Boerne* that any attempt to impose a standard directly contrary to *Smith* was to impermissibly make a substantive change to the Constitution, and relieve the judiciary of its appointed role.[18]

The effect the RFRA would have on the states also played a major role in the outcome of *Boerne.* The Court found that states would be heavily burdened if they had to come up with a compelling interest for a policy and show that it was the least restrictive means every

---

[13]*Id.* at 512.
[14]*Id.* at 536.
[15]*Id.* at 530.
[16]*Id.* at 532.
[17]*Id.* at 532.
[18]*Id.* at 534.

time someone showed that the practice of their religion had been substantially burdened. Holding that RFRA violated separation of powers and federalism doctrines, the Court invalidated it, at least as it applied to state governments. Once again, it seemed, prisoners' freedom of exercise claims were to be analyzed under the *Shabazz* rational relationship test.

The Religious Land Use and Institutionalized Persons Act (RLUIPA)

Congress did not mourn the loss of the RFRA for long. After failing to pass another comprehensive law that would have re-installed the compelling interest standard for all laws that burden the free practice of religion, Congress paired down the legislation so that it dealt only with land use laws and the regulations imposed on institutionalized persons.[19] The resulting legislation is known as the Religious Land Use and Institutionalized Persons Act (RLUIPA), and it was passed by Congress and signed into law by the President in September 2000.[20] The Act reads as follows:

Protection of religious exercise of institutionalized persons

(a) General rule. No government shall impose a substantial burden on the religious exercise of a person residing in or confined to an institution, as defined in section 2 of the Civil Rights of Institutionalized Persons Act (42 U.S.C.A. § 1997), even if the burden results from a rule of general applicability, unless the government demonstrates that imposition of the burden on that person-

(1) is in furtherance of a compelling governmental interest; and

(2) is the least restrictive means of furthering that compelling governmental interest.

(b) Scope of application. This section applies in any case in which—

(1) the substantial burden is imposed in a program or activity that receives Federal financial assistance; or

---

[19] 146 Cong. Rec. S 7774 (statement of Senator Hatch).
[20] See 42 U.S.C. § 2000cc-1 (2002).

§ 6:4 FIRST AMENDMENT: RELIGION

(2) the substantial burden affects, or removal of that substantial burden would affect, commerce with foreign nations, among the several States, or with Indian tribes.[21]

RLUIPA differs from the RFRA in several important respects. First, instead of basing the statute on § 5 of the Fourteenth Amendment, Congress based the new Act on its powers under the Spending and Commerce Clauses of the Constitution. Theoretically, this avoids the problem Congress faced with regard to the RFRA, as Congress's Spending and Commerce Clause powers are not remedial, but are plenary. This means that as long as the regulation being analyzed is part of a program that receives federal assistance, or has some affect on interstate commerce, it is within Congress's power to impose the compelling interest/least restrictive means standard.

The only court, so far, to consider the validity of RLUIPA has deemed it constitutional.[22] In *Mayweathers v. Terhune,* prison officials sought dismissal of a lawsuit brought by a group of Muslim inmates seeking an injunction for alleged violations of the inmates' free exercise rights.[23] Prison officials claimed the statute exceeded Congress' Spending and Commerce Clause authority, violated principles of separation of powers and federalism, and violated the Establishment Clause.[24] The district court denied the motion to dismiss, holding that the Act met all the requirements for Congress to act under the Spending Clause, as it was for the general welfare of the public, related to the federal spending at issue, sufficiently clear as to its application, and it was not coercive.[25] The prison officials' separation of powers claim stated that the statute impermissibly sought to overturn the Supreme Court's holdings in *Employment Division v. Smith,* and *Turner*

---

[21]42 U.S.C. § 2000cc-1 (2002).

[22]Mayweathers v. Terhune, 2001 WL 804140 (E.D. Cal. 2001).

[23]*Id.* at 2.

[24]*Id.* at 4.

[25]*Id.* at 4-15.

§ 6:4 Rights of Prisoners, Third Edition

v. Safley.²⁶ The district court held that as long as Congress originally had the power to enact the legislation, the fact that it employs a standard different from that set forth by the Supreme Court does not impair that power.²⁷ The Act was proper under Congress's Commerce Clause powers because its applicability is limited to only those situations in which interstate commerce was affected, according to the court.²⁸ Finally, an attack based on federalism grounds fails because, according to the district court, where Congress has the power to act under the Constitution, there is no state power to legislate in that area.²⁹ *Mayweather* is the first of what is sure to be a number of judicial rulings on this subject, which must eventually be resolved by the federal Courts of Appeal or quite possibly another decision by the United States Supreme Court. Awaiting those decisions, many commentators have predicted the doom of RLUIPA.³⁰ Other commentators, however, assert that the Act at least has a chance of surviving Supreme Court review.³¹ Until this issue is finally resolved the correct standard to use in evaluating prison religion

---

²⁶*Id.* at 22-23.

²⁷Mayweathers v. Terhune, 2001 WL 804140 (E.D. Cal. 2001).

²⁸*Id.* at 22.

²⁹*Id.* at 20-21.

³⁰See Walston, Federalism and Federal Spending: Why the Religious Land Use and Institutionalized Persons Act of 2000 is Unconstitutional, 23 Hawaii L. Rev. 479 (2001) (RLUIPA is unconstitutional on federalism grounds; prison regulations have historically been left to state penal authorities, and a compelling interest standard burdens that local police power). See also, Ada-Marie Walsh, Note: Religious Land Use and Institutionalized Persons Act of 2000: Unconstitutional and Unnecessary, 10 Wm. & Mary Bill of Rts. J. 189 (2001); Evan M. Shapiro, Notes & Comments: The Religious Land Use and Institutionalized Persons Act: An Analysis Under the Commerce Clause, 76 Wash. L. Rev. 1255 (2001) (Congress exceeded its Commerce Clause power in enacting RLUIPA).

³¹See Shawn Jensvold, The Religious Land Use and Institutionalized Persons Act of 2000 (RLUIPA): A Valid Exercise of Congressional Power?, 16 BYU J. Pub. L. 1 (2001) (land use portion of the

cases will not be known.

RLUIPA Applied

Unless the RLUIPA is declared unconstitutional it provides the applicable standard for determining a prison religion case. Therefore, it is important to know what the standard set out in the Act provides.

The first requirement under the statute is that an inmate's religious exercise must be substantially burdened.[32] How to determine whether an act is religious in nature is discussed in more detail later in this chapter.[33] Assuming that the burdened practiced is religious in nature, how is a court to determine whether that practice has been substantially burdened? Congress expressly reserved that question for court determination.[34] The problem with this is that there is disagreement among the courts over what constitutes a substantial burden.[35]

For example, the United States Court of Appeals for the Ninth Circuit has held that for a substantial burden to be shown, a plaintiff must prove that the burdened practice is one mandated by the plaintiff's faith, that it is a central tenet of that faith, and that the burden is

---

Act is constitutional); Heather Guidry, If at First You Don't Succeed. . . Can the Commerce and Spending Clauses Support Congress's Latest Attempt at Religious Freedom Legislation?, 32 Cumb. L. Rev. 419 (2001) (RLUIPA has a chance of surviving Supreme Court review); Roman P. Storzer and Anthony R. Picarello, Jr., The Religious Land Use and Institutionalized Persons Act of 2000: A Constitutional Response to Unconstitutional Zoning Practices, 9 Geo. Mason L. Rev. 929 (2001).

[32]See note 75 and accompanying text.

[33]See § 6:6.

[34]See 146 Cong Rec S 7774, S 7776 (statement of Senator Hatch) (term "substantial burden" is to be given no broader interpretation than that given by the Supreme Court).

[35]See Ingalls v. Florio, 968 F. Supp. 193, 204 (D.N.J. 1997) ("Courts that have considered the question have come to differing conclusions about the exact definition of a 'substantial burden.'").

§ 6:4

substantial.[36] The Tenth Circuit has come to a similar conclusion.[37] Two district courts, however, have held that a court need not inquire into whether a religious practice is central to or mandated by a particular faith when deciding if the practice is substantially burdened, holding that the court need only show that the practice "is motivated by a sincerely held religious belief, and. . .governmental conduct has substantially burdened his ability to engage in that practice."[38]

Though it is silent on the actual meaning of the phrase "substantial burden," Congress seems to endorse this latter reading of the test. Congress defines the phrase "exercise of religion" in RLUIPA as "any exercise of religion, whether or not compelled by, or central to, a system of religious belief."[39] This reading also seems to be the one favored by the Supreme Court. In *City of Boerne v. Flores,* the Court noted "The distinction between questions of centrality and questions of sincerity and burden is admittedly fine."[40] In *Smith,* one thing all of the Justices agreed upon was that, "'[i]t is not within the judicial ken to question the centrality of particular beliefs or practices to a faith, or the validity of particular litigants' interpretations of those creeds.'"[41]

---

[36]See, Bryant v. Gomez, 46 F.3d 948, 949 (9th Cir. 1995). See also, Weir v. Nix, 890 F. Supp. 769, 783 (S.D. Iowa 1995), judgment aff'd, appeal dismissed in part, 114 F.3d 817 (8th Cir. 1997).

[37]Werner v. McCotter, 49 F.3d 1476, 1480 (10th Cir. 1995).

[38]Muslim v. Frame, 897 F. Supp. 215, 218 (E.D. Pa. 1995); see also, Sasnett v. Sullivan, 908 F. Supp. 1429 (W.D. Wis. 1995), aff'd, 91 F.3d 1018 (7th Cir. 1996), cert. granted, judgment vacated on other grounds, 521 U.S. 1114, 117 S. Ct. 2502, 138 L. Ed. 2d 1007 (1997).

[39]42 U.S.C. § 2000cc-5(7)(A) (2002).

[40]City of Boerne v. Flores, 521 U.S. 507, 534, 117 S. Ct. 2157, 138 L. Ed. 2d 624 (1997), quoting, Employment Div., Dept. of Human Resources of Oregon v. Smith, 494 U.S. 872, 907, 110 S. Ct. 1595, 108 L. Ed. 2d 876 (1990) (O'Connor, J., concurring in the judgment).

[41]Employment Div., Dept. of Human Resources of Oregon v. Smith, 494 U.S. 872, 887, 110 S. Ct. 1595, 108 L. Ed. 2d 876 (1990),

Once an inmate has shown that a prison policy has substantially burdened a religious practice, the burden shifts to prison officials to prove that there is a compelling interest behind the legislation.[42] Though this is a tougher standard to meet than the *Shabazz* rational relationship standard, it may not be as difficult to meet as prison officials might think. First, Congress has stated that the new standard should not change the current practice of giving great deference to the decisions of prison officials, especially in the areas of maintaining security and discipline.[43] The legislative history of the Act explains that it targets policies enacted based on "mere speculation, exaggerated fears, or post-hoc rationalizations."[44] Second, most courts have found that there is always a compelling interest present where prison officials cite and prove legitimate security concerns as the basis for a challenged policy.[45]

Where prison officials will have a more difficult task in fending off a religious based challenge to a policy is where the court applies the least restrictive means portion of the test. Where courts have upheld inmate challenges to prison policies under RFRA, they have done so mostly because those policies were not the least restrictive means of furthering the prison's compelling governmental interest.[46] For example, in *Weir v. Nix*,[47] a federal district court upheld an inmate's claim under

---

quoting, Hernandez v. C.I.R., 490 U.S. 680, 699, 109 S. Ct. 2136, 104 L. Ed. 2d 766 (1989).

[42]42 U.S.C.A. § 2000cc-2(c) (2002).

[43]146 Cong. Rec. S. 7774, S 7775 (Statement of Senator Hatch).

[44]*Id.*

[45]See Fawaad v. Jones, 81 F.3d 1084 (11th Cir. 1996); Arguello v. Duckworth, 106 F.3d 403 (7th Cir. 1997); Lawson v. Singletary, 85 F.3d 502 (11th Cir. 1996); Hundson v. Action Bldg. Systems, 78 F.3d 593 (9th Cir. 1996).

[46]See Sasnett v. Sullivan, 908 F. Supp. 1429 (W.D. Wis. 1995), aff'd, 91 F.3d 1018 (7th Cir. 1996), judgment vacated, 521 U.S. 1114, 117 S. Ct. 2502, 138 L. Ed. 2d 1007 (1997) (prohibiting the wearing of crucifixes and other religious items not the least restrictive means of preventing inmates from wearing gang identify-

§ 6:4　　　　　　　　　Rights of Prisoners, Third Edition

the RFRA, in part because the prison's practice could not have been the least restrictive means of furthering security interests.[48] In *Weir,* inmates were prevented from witnessing baptisms, as the baptisms were held in the prison infirmary. The court held that even if there were valid security concerns behind the restriction, it was not the least restrictive means of furthering that goal. The court found that the prison had had an immersion pool for baptisms in the chapel in the past, and it was proven such a pool could be installed again at relatively low cost.[49]

This is not to say, however, that prison officials have always had trouble proving their methods were the least restrictive means necessary to further a compelling interest. In fact, in the majority of cases, courts have given deference to prison officials, either by finding no substantial burden on the inmate's religious practice, or by accepting prison officials' evidence of a compelling interest and least restrictive means.[50] The majority's fears in *City of Boerne v. Flores* that state of-

---

ing markers); Campbell-El v. District of Columbia, 874 F. Supp. 403 (D.D.C. 1994) (summary judgment for prison officials denied where officials failed to show that limiting inmates to a gathering of 10 to 12 inmates every other week was the least restrictive means of preserving order); Weir v. Nix, 890 F. Supp. 769, 783 (S.D. Iowa 1995), judgment aff'd, appeal dismissed in part, 114 F.3d 817 (8th Cir. 1997) (excluding other inmates from a baptism because it was held in the infirmary could not be the least restrictive means of maintaining security where it was proven the prison had used an immersion tank for baptisms in the chapel, and could do so again at minimal costs).

[47]Weir v. Nix, 890 F. Supp. 769 (S.D. Iowa 1995), judgment aff'd, appeal dismissed in part, 114 F.3d 817 (8th Cir. 1997).

[48]Weir v. Nix, 890 F. Supp. 769, 783 (S.D. Iowa 1995), judgment aff'd, appeal dismissed in part, 114 F.3d 817 (8th Cir. 1997).

[49]*Id.*

[50]See, e.g., Ochs v. Thalacker, 90 F.3d 293 (8th Cir. 1996) (denying inmate request to be housed in a racially segregated manner served a compelling security concern and was the least restrictive means of doing so); Abdur-Rahman v. Michigan Dept. of Corrections, 65 F.3d 489 (6th Cir. 1995) (no violation where inmate

ficials would rarely be able to meet the compelling interest/least restrictive means standard appear to be unfounded, at least as applied in the prison environment.

§ 6:5 Equal Protection

When a prisoner claims that his or her religion has been singled out for unfair treatment as compared to other religions in the prison, a potential equal protection violation is raised.[1] One of the first prison religion cases, *Cruz v Beto*,[2] involved such a claim. In *Cruz,* the plaintiff alleged that Buddhist inmates in the Texas penal system were not granted the same rights to practice as Christian prisoners. The Supreme Court held that every prisoner is entitled to "a reasonable opportunity of pursuing his faith comparable to the opportunity afforded fellow prisoners who adhere to

---

claimed he was not released from work to attend services, where there were two services per week and a teacher of the Islamic faith testified that work was a valid excuse for missing services); Muhammad v. City of New York Dept. of Corrections, 904 F. Supp. 161 (S.D. N.Y. 1995) (failure to provide inmate with religious services tailored to his specific Islamic beliefs served a compelling interest and was the least restrictive means as accommodating all inmates in a setting of constant flux would be too difficult under the circumstances); Woods v. Evatt, 876 F. Supp. 756 (D.S.C. 1995), aff'd, 68 F.3d 463 (4th Cir. 1995) (requiring Muslims to use all purpose room for services, prohibiting general inmate population from attending the services, not allowing inmates time off from their jobs to attend services and not providing Muslims with a chaplain all served a compelling interest due to time and administrative constraints and security concerns, and were the least restrictive means available).

[Section 6:5]
[1]The Equal Protection Clause is discussed at greater length in Ch 4.
[2]Cruz v. Beto, 405 U.S. 319, 92 S. Ct. 1079, 31 L. Ed. 2d 263 (1972).

conventional religious precepts. . ..."[3] Thus, courts have held that Muslim inmates who alleged that they were not permitted to receive a religious diet, while Jewish inmates were, stated a claim under the Equal Protection Clause.[4] Similarly, a claim of inequality in the way a prison handled the religious needs of Native Americans as opposed to other religions was actionable as potentially violative of the Fourteenth Amendment.[5] In a Seventh Circuit Case discussed elsewhere in this chapter,[6] irrational distinctions between Catholics and Protestants were found to violate equal protection.[7]

Although prisoners are entitled to equal protection, it does not follow that a prison must duplicate every religious benefit it provides so that all religions are treated exactly the same. There may very well be valid reasons for the distinction between faiths. As the Supreme Court observed in *Cruz,* "A special chapel or place of worship need not be provided for every faith regardless of size; nor must a chaplain, priest or minister be provided without regard to the extent of the demand."[8]

---

[3]Cruz v. Beto, 405 U.S. 319, 322, 92 S. Ct. 1079, 31 L. Ed. 2d 263 (1972).

[4]Moorish Science Temple of America, Inc. v. Smith, 693 F.2d 987 (2d Cir. 1982).

[5]Native American Council of Tribes v. Solem, 691 F.2d 382 (8th Cir. 1982). But see, Thomas v. Gunter, 103 F.3d 700 (8th Cir. 1997) (denial of daily access for a Native American prisoner to pray in a sweat lodge not violative of equal protection where facts showed he was provided more time to pray than any other religious group).

[6]See § 6:9..

[7]Sasnett v. Litscher, 197 F.3d 290, 293 (7th Cir. 1999) (policy of Wisconsin that forbade inmates from wearing crosses but permitted rosary beads that could have crosses on them found by court to favor Catholics over Protestants, since rosaries were just as much a security concern as any other cross).

[8]Cruz v. Beto, 405 U.S. 319, 322, 92 S. Ct. 1079, 31 L. Ed. 2d 263 (1972). See also Allen v. Toombs, 827 F.2d 563, 568 (9th Cir. 1987) (no requirement that a full-time chaplain be hired for Native

§ 6:6 Establishment of Religion

So far this discussion has centered on the First Amendment right of free exercise of religion, and the Fourteenth Amendment right of equal protection, but the First Amendment also contains the "separate and distinct"[1] Establishment Clause.[2] The intent of the Establishment Clause is to prevent the government from excessive involvement in religious affairs in order to maintain a separation between government and religion.[3] To comply with the Establishment Clause, the government normally must be neutral in religious matters and cannot prefer one religion over another, or religion over nonreligion.[4] The tension between the Free Exercise Clause and the Establishment Clause, which has long been noted,[5] is dramatically revealed in a prison setting. In order for inmates to practice their

---

Americans even though one was hired for Catholics and Protestants); Campbell-El v. District of Columbia, 874 F. Supp. 403 (D. D.C. 1994) (restriction of prisoners religious gathering to 10 to 12 people did not violate equal protection where there was no proof that other groups were not subject to the restriction); Woods v. Evatt, 876 F. Supp. 756 (D.S.C. 1995), aff'd, 68 F.3d 463 (4th Cir. 1995) (no equal protection violation in preventing Muslim inmates from using visitation area for services while Christians were allowed to, as allowing such services would prevent 90 percent of the prison population from having visiting hours); Blagman v. White, 112 F. Supp. 2d 534 (E.D. Va. 2000), aff'd, 3 Fed. Appx. 23 (4th Cir. 2001) (Christian participants in boot camp prison program given Thanksgiving and Christmas off to worship while Islamic inmates were not allowed time off to observe Ramadan; court held this was not an equal protection violation as allowing Muslims to observe Ramadan would totally disrupt the program, while the smaller Christian celebrations would not).

[Section 6:6]

[1]Gittlemacker v. Prasse, 428 F.2d 1, 5 (3d Cir. 1970).

[2]US Const amend I: "Congress shall make no law respecting an establishment of religion. . .."

[3]Tribe, American Constitutional Law (2d ed.) p 1157.

[4]See, generally, J. Nowak & R. Rotunda, Constitutional Law § 17.2 (4th ed 1991).

[5]*Id.*

religion, they necessarily have to rely, to a significant extent, on government help. After all, prisoners who have been deprived of their liberty and free movement cannot, without government aid, attend religious services, receive visits from clergy, or adhere to religious diets, to mention just a few examples. When the state, at taxpayer expense, facilitates the practice of religion in prison, has it transgressed the strictures of the Establishment Clause?

This issue is seen perhaps most starkly when the prison hires, or is asked to hire, chaplains. The issue posed is whether the employment of clergy is state activity that promotes and finances religion, in violation of the Establishment Clause. Although there are no cases definitively answering this question, there are powerful arguments, drawn from cases in analogous areas, for suggesting that there is no Establishment Clause violation in this practice. For example, the Second Circuit rejected an Establishment Clause challenge to the hiring of clergy to serve as chaplains in the military.[6] In another case, the Eighth Circuit rebuffed a claim that a public hospital could not hire a chaplain.[7] A major rationale for both rulings is the inability of soldiers or patients to practice their religion unless they are provided assistance from the state.[8] That rationale applies with equal, if not greater, force in prison. As Judge Posner recognized:

> Patients in public hospitals, members of the armed forces in some circumstances (e.g., the crew of a ballistic missile submarine on duty)-and prisoners-have restricted or even no access to religious services unless government takes an

---

[6]Katcoff v. Marsh, 755 F.2d 223 (2d Cir. 1985).

[7]Carter v. Broadlawns Medical Center, 857 F.2d 448 (8th Cir. 1988).

[8]Katcoff v. Marsh, 755 F.2d 223, 234 (2d Cir. 1985) (the Army, having moved soldiers to areas of the world where religion of their own denomination is not present, has a constitutional duty to "make religion available"); Carter v. Broadlawns Medical Center, 857 F.2d 448, 457 (8th Cir. 1988) (state must compensate for "state-imposed burden on patients' religious practices").

§ 6:6

active role in supplying these services. That role is not an interference with, but a precondition of, the free (or relatively free) exercise of religion by members of these groups.[9]

Although the state may constitutionally hire prison chaplains, it does not follow that a prisoner can force an institution to hire clergy of each faith. In one case, a court held that the state was not required to hire a Jewish chaplain for a prison that had only two or three Jewish inmates.[10] However, a federal court in another case held that the state must hire and pay for the services of a Muslim Imam.[11] These two decisions are not as inconsistent as they might at first seem. In the first case, there were only two or three Jewish inmates in the prison,[12] while in the second case there were a far greater number of Muslim prisoners in the system and the state had hired chaplains for Christian inmates.[13]

Thus, when the state undertakes to hire chaplains

---

[9]Johnson-Bey v. Lane, 863 F.2d 1308, 1312 (7th Cir. 1988).

[10]Gittlemacker v. Prasse, 428 F.2d 1 (3d Cir. 1970). The court held that in the absence of an intent to discriminate against Jewish inmates, for a court to require a rabbi to be hired by the state would be to embrace a "concept that dangerously approaches the jealously guarded frontiers of the Establishment Clause." Gittlemacker v. Prasse, 428 F.2d 1, 4 (3d Cir. 1970). The basis of this statement is unclear. Perhaps what the court meant by it was that in the absence of a clear need for a chaplain of a particular faith, the hiring of that chaplain would constitute an unconstitutional preference of that religion over others. See also Reimers v. State of Or., 863 F.2d 630 (9th Cir. 1988) (Pentecostal inmates did not have a right to Pentecostal minister in prison); Allen v. Toombs, 827 F.2d 563 (9th Cir. 1987) (no affirmative duty to provide Native American inmate with a spiritual counselor of his choice).

[11]Northern v. Nelson, 315 F. Supp. 687 (N.D. Cal. 1970), order aff'd, 448 F.2d 1266 (9th Cir. 1971). Cf. Rasul v. District of Columbia, 680 F. Supp. 436 (D.D.C. 1988) (violation of Title VII of the Civil Rights Act to reject a Muslim Imam for a chaplain's vacancy because he was not Protestant).

[12]Gittlemacker v. Prasse, 428 F.2d 1 (3d Cir. 1970).

[13]Northern v. Nelson, 315 F. Supp. 687 (N.D. Cal. 1970), order aff'd, 448 F.2d 1266 (9th Cir. 1971).

§ 6:6   RIGHTS OF PRISONERS, THIRD EDITION

for one faith but not for another faith that has as many adherents, it runs the danger of violating the Establishment Clause prohibition against the state favoring one religion over another.[14] If this is the case, the state may be compelled by the Establishment Clause (and the Equal Protection Clause) to hire prison chaplains.[15] However, the state is under no constitutional obligation to hire chaplains of a faith that has few adherents in the prison.[16]

There are other ways in which prison practices may conflict with the Establishment Clause. Encouraging or condoning religious proselytizing by prison officialdom is one illustration of a practice that certainly violates the Establishment Clause; such conduct sponsors religion and, in addition, favors one religion over others.[17] The Establishment Clause is designed to

---

[14]It is a violation of the Establishment Clause to prefer one religion over another. US Const amend I; see also Larson v. Valente, 456 U.S. 228, 229, 102 S. Ct. 1673, 72 L. Ed. 2d 33 (1982). In addition, the favoring of one religion over another runs counter to equal protection guarantees of the Fourteenth Amendment. See Cruz v. Beto, 405 U.S. 319, 92 S. Ct. 1079, 31 L. Ed. 2d 263 (1972).

[15]See, e.g., Johnson-Bey v. Lane, 863 F.2d 1308, 1312 (7th Cir. 1988); Card v. Dugger, 709 F. Supp. 1098, 1100 (M.D. Fla. 1988), judgment aff'd, 871 F.2d 1023 (11th Cir. 1989).

[16]Card v. Dugger, 709 F. Supp. 1098 (M.D. Fla. 1988), judgment aff'd, 871 F.2d 1023 (11th Cir. 1989) (no Establishment Clause violation even though all the prison chaplains were Southern Baptists, when the majority of the prison population was Protestant, the chaplains were instructed to attempt to meet the needs of all inmates or secure the services of volunteer clergy, and the position of chaplain was open to any clergy who was qualified without regard to religious denomination).

[17]Campbell v. Cauthron, 623 F.2d 503, 509 (8th Cir. 1980). See also Campbell v. Thornton, 644 F. Supp. 103 (W.D. Mo. 1986) (unconstitutional for proprietors of "halfway house" to force their religion on inmates housed there). The Establishment Clause is implicated for similar reasons when the prison only permits Bibles and "little Christian tracts" to come into the prison. Parnell v. Waldrep, 511 F. Supp. 764 (W.D. N.C. 1981). A state statute that requires the hiring of a Catholic chaplain, but not a chaplain of

prevent both outcomes.[18] The Establishment Clause also forbids the state from affirmatively promoting religion in ways not necessary to satisfy the free exercise needs of inmates.[19] An example of a successful effort by prison officials to avoid this difficulty is a case in which the prison discharged a counselor who, against orders, used "religious counseling techniques" with inmates who were sent to him for treatment.[20]

One area that has engendered a great deal of litigation is prison regulations requiring participation in rehabilitation programs that have religious connotations. Courts have declared forced participation in these religiously based treatment programs unconstitutional as violating the Establishment Clause. The United States Court of Appeals for the Seventh Circuit, for instance, found that a Wisconsin prison violated the Establishment Clause by impermissibly coercing an inmate to participate in Narcotics Anonymous (NA).[21] The program's treatment centers on a twelve-step approach that requires the participant to admit that only

---

other faiths, also might violate the Establishment Clause, Reimers v. State of Or., 863 F.2d 630 (9th Cir. 1988). However, a case that questioned, on Establishment Clause grounds, a claim by a Jewish inmate that he be permitted to procure, at state expense, Jewish religious books for the prison library, McElyea v. Babbitt, 833 F.2d 196, 199 (9th Cir. 1987), seems wrong, since these books might be necessary for the inmate to practice his faith.

[18]Young v. Lane, 1989 WL 197412 (N.D. Ill. 1989).

[19]See, e.g., Theriault v. A Religious Office in the Structure of the Government Requiring a Religious Test as a Qualification, 895 F.2d 104 (2d Cir. 1990) (allegation that prison delegated nonreligious authority to prison chaplains raises a significant Establishment Clause issue).

[20]Spratt v. Kent County, 621 F. Supp. 594, 600 (W.D. Mich. 1985), judgment aff'd, 810 F.2d 203 (6th Cir. 1986) ("Sheriff Heffron chose to walk the narrow line between the free exercise and Establishment Clauses by forbidding county paid social workers from using religious counseling techniques while, at the same time, allowing inmates access to voluntary chaplains of all faiths who serviced the jail.").

[21]See Kerr v. Farrey, 95 F.3d 472 (7th Cir. 1996).

§ 6:6

God can lead them to recovery.[22] Failure to attend the NA meetings led to a higher security classification and was considered in parole determinations.[23] The court was only concerned with whether the state action amounted to coercion, and if it did whether the object of the coercion was religious or secular.[24] The court easily found that there was coercion and also found unavailing any argument that the object of the coercion was secular.[25] The court found that "[a] straightforward reading of the 12 steps shows clearly that the steps are based on the monotheistic idea of a single God or Supreme Being."[26] Since NA was the only treatment program available, and since refusal to participate carried serious penalties, the court found the prison had impermissibly coerced the inmate into participating, in violation of the Establishment Clause.[27]

The free exercise, equal protection, and establish-

---

[22]*Id.* at 474.

[23]*Id.*

[24]*Id.* at 479.

[25]*Id.* at 480.

[26]*Id.* at 472.

[27]*Id.* See also Griffin v. Coughlin, 88 N.Y.2d 674, 649 N.Y.S.2d 903, 673 N.E.2d 98 (1996) (prison officials cannot deprive an inmate of visitation rights for refusal to participate in a religious-based treatment program); Ross v. Keelings, 2 F. Supp. 2d 810 (E.D. Va. 1998). See also Rachel F. Calabro, Comment: Correction Through Coercion: Do State Mandated Alcohol and Drug Treatment Programs in Prisons Violate the Establishment Clause?, 47 DePaul L. Rev. 565 (1998) (mandating participation in such programs is impermissible under the Establishment Clause); in accord, Derek P. Apanovitch, Note: Religion and Rehabilitation: The Requisition of God by the State, 47 Duke L.J. 785 (1998). But see, Stafford v Harrison, 766 F Supp 1014 (D Kan 1991) (defendants were not guilty of an Establishment Clause violation when they required an inmate to complete a treatment program modeled on Alcoholics Anonymous, because Alcoholics Anonymous is not a religion).

While forced participation in a religiously based treatment program is impermissible the United States Supreme Court has ruled that it is not improper in a secular treatment program to require an inmate to disclose past criminal behavior. This compul-

ment provisions of the Constitution only come into play when the state interacts with religion in some way. Before going further, therefore, it is important to discuss the legal standards for defining a religion.

§ 6:7 Defining Religion

As we have seen, there is a constitutional right to practice religion in prison. No matter what standard is used to analyze a claim that this right has been violated, the first prerequisite for the exercise of the right is, of course, that the prisoner be a sincere adherent of a religious persuasion. Therefore, it has become necessary for the courts to assess whether a prisoner claiming the right to practice his religion in prison is sincere, and whether the beliefs that prisoner adheres to constitute a religion.[1]

Although these questions are essential, they are not ones that courts embrace eagerly. Judge Adams, writing for the Third Circuit in one of the prison cases that raised this issue, aptly explained the awkwardness with which courts approach the issue of determining what is a religion:

Few tasks that confront a court require more circumspec-

---

sion does not violate the Fifth Amendment. McKune v. Lile, 122 S. Ct. 2017, 153 L. Ed. 2d 47 (U.S. 2002).

[Section 6:7]
   [1]This question has arisen since the early days of prison litigation. In fact, some of the most heavily contested and best known of the first prisoners' rights cases dealt with the question of whether the Black Muslim faith was a religion. Some courts initially held-perhaps motivated by the sect's racial theories-that the Black Muslims were not a legitimate religion. See, e.g., Pierce v. LaVallee, 212 F. Supp. 865 (N.D. N.Y. 1962), judgment aff'd, 319 F.2d 844 (2d Cir. 1963); In re Ferguson, 55 Cal. 2d 663, 12 Cal. Rptr. 753, 361 P.2d 417 (1961).

   However, the courts eventually came to recognize that the Black Muslim faith is, for its adherents, as much a religion as Catholicism is for Catholics and, therefore, is entitled to be treated as a religion. See, e.g., Holt v. Hutto, 363 F. Supp. 194 (E.D. Ark. 1973), judgment rev'd on other grounds, 505 F.2d 194 (8th Cir. 1974).

tion than that of determining whether a particular set of ideas constitute a religion within the meaning of the First Amendment. Judges are ill equipped to examine the breadth and content of an avowed religion; we must avoid any predisposition toward conventional religions so that unfamiliar faiths are not branded mere secular beliefs.[2]

Judge Adams' hesitancy is understandable; this country is based on "our society's abiding acceptance and tolerance of the unorthodox belief.[3] Courts, therefore, are properly fearful that they might inadvertently brand as secular beliefs that are unconventional or exotic and thereby improperly exclude them from the protections of the Free Exercise Clause of the First Amendment.

One way to handle the problem would be to go to the extreme of allowing anyone, on their own declaration, to proclaim his or her own religion. But to do this, one court has correctly said, would allow a person complete discretion to "shield himself or herself from otherwise legitimate state regulation.[4] Thus, courts, by necessity, are called on to make "uneasy differentiations" between the religious on the one hand and the secular on the other.[5]

In the prison setting, courts have faced a bewildering number of claims that a particular set of beliefs constitutes a religion. The cases have involved the courts in deciding whether such unique and controversial groups

---

[2] Africa v. Com. of Pa., 662 F.2d 1025, 1031 (3d Cir. 1981).

[3] Patrick v. LeFevre, 745 F.2d 153, 157, 40 Fed. R. Serv. 2d 39 (2d Cir. 1984).

[4] Africa v. Com. of Pa., 662 F.2d 1025, 1031 (3d Cir. 1981). But see, Developments in the Law, The Law Of Prisons: IV. In the Belly of the Whale: Religious Practice in Prison, 115 Harv. L. Rev. 1891 (2002) (author argues that many problems could be avoided if prisons identified acceptable practices and items and made them available to all inmates without regard to religion, regulating them based on feasibility).

[5] *Id.* at 1031.

§ 6:7

as Black Muslims,[6] Rastafarians,[7] Five Percenters,[8] the Ayran Brotherhood,[9] and MOVE[10] are legitimate religions.[11]

It is hardly surprising that courts would face such a wide variety of claims for religious protection by groups within the prisons. This is, after all, a pluralistic society with literally hundreds of groups in the culture that call themselves religions. That many of these groups would sign up members from within the prisons, or that prisoners themselves would start their own groups,[12] is entirely predictable.

Once it is recognized that courts will have to "ponder

---

[6]Holt v. Hutto, 363 F. Supp. 194 (E.D. Ark. 1973), judgment rev'd on other grounds, 505 F.2d 194 (8th Cir. 1974).

[7]Reed v. Faulkner, 653 F. Supp. 965 (N.D. Ind. 1987).

[8]Patrick v. LeFevre, 745 F.2d 153, 40 Fed. R. Serv. 2d 39 (2d Cir. 1984).

[9]Murphy v. Missouri Dept. of Corrections, 814 F.2d 1252 (8th Cir. 1987).

[10]Africa v. Com. of Pa., 662 F.2d 1025 (3d Cir. 1981).

[11]See also Johnson-Bey v. Lane, 863 F.2d 1308 (7th Cir. 1988) (discussing the Moorish Science Temple of America, a black Islamic sect which had its own version of the Koran and a list of prophets, including Buddha and Confucius; this sect was considered a "bona fide" religion by the court even though three-fourths of its congregations were inside prisons). For examples of other faiths seeking recognition, see, e.g., Dettmer v. Landon, 799 F.2d 929 (4th Cir. 1986) (Church of Wicca, based upon witchcraft is a religion); Carpenter v. Wilkinson, 946 F. Supp. 522 (N.D. Ohio 1996) (Satanism is a religion).

[12]In one series of cases, courts in two circuits were even asked to decide whether the Eclatarian faith, a creed that was conceived by an inmate in prison, was a religion. The replies of the courts were, unfortunately, inconsistent. Compare Theriault v. Carlson, 495 F.2d 390 (5th Cir. 1974) (not a religion) with Remmers v. Brewer, 529 F.2d 656 (8th Cir. 1976) (district court properly found that evidence was insufficient to justify reopening issue of whether Church of New Song was religion, within ambit of First Amendment).

the imponderable and define the undefinable"[13] to decide whether a prisoner professes a "religion" within the meaning of the First Amendment, the question arises how courts should make this difficult judgment. As stated at the beginning, two requirements emerge from the cases. They are: (1) that the beliefs be sincerely held, and (2) that they be religious in nature.[14] The following pages examine each of these standards in turn.

Sincerity of Beliefs

Religious sincerity is the most difficult of all forms of credibility for a trial court to determine.[15] Yet, no matter if the claim is analyzed under a statute or the Supreme Court's interpretation of the Constitution, it is a job that courts must perform. Without a requirement of a showing of sincerity, the First Amendment would become, in the words of Professor Tribe, "a limitless excuse for avoiding all unwanted legal obligations."[16] While the task of determining sincerity is "exceedingly amorphous,"[17] there are several important guidelines that a court can use to aid in the effort.

First, this is a question that can rarely be determined on a summary judgment motion. Where such subjective issues regarding a person's state of mind and conscience

---

[13]Jacques v. Hilton, 569 F. Supp. 730, 731 (D.N.J. 1983), judgment aff'd, 738 F.2d 422 (3d Cir. 1984).

[14]Africa v. Com. of Pa., 662 F.2d 1025, 1030 (3d Cir. 1981) (quoting U.S. v. Seeger, 380 U.S. 163, 185, 85 S. Ct. 850, 13 L. Ed. 2d 733 (1965)).

[15]Reed v. Faulkner, 653 F. Supp. 965, 971 (N.D. Ind. 1987).

[16]Tribe, American Constitutional Law (2d ed.) p 1244. See also Patrick v Le Fevre, 745 F2d 153, 157 (2d Cir 1984) (requirement of sincerity is to prevent the First Amendment from becoming a "talisman for self-indulgence or material gain."); Reed v. Faulkner, 842 F.2d 960, 963 (7th Cir. 1988) ("in the prison setting . . . an inmate may adopt a religion merely to harass the prison staff with demands to accommodate his new faith").

[17]Patrick v. LeFevre, 745 F.2d 153, 157, 40 Fed. R. Serv. 2d 39 (2d Cir. 1984).

First Amendment: Religion § 6:7

are involved, a hearing is almost invariably required.[18] The purpose of this hearing is for the court to hear the witnesses, including most importantly, the plaintiff to evaluate for itself the sincerity of his or her beliefs. Therefore, simplistic objective tests of sincerity, such as a requirement that plaintiff submit references of sincerity from "a reputable nonfamily member who was not incarcerated," cannot substitute for the inherently subjective evaluation called for by the holding of a trial and the calling of witnesses.[19]

Second, the issue of sincerity must not be confused with the question of the truth or falsity of the plaintiff's religious beliefs. The latter question is not for the courts to decide.[20] As the Tenth Circuit observed, "courts carefully avoid inquiring into the merits of particular religious beliefs in an effort to gauge sincerity."[21] The court's inquiry, rather, is limited to whether, regardless of the truth of the beliefs, the plaintiff sincerely adheres to them.[22]

Third, a plaintiff need not be a member of an orga-

---

[18]Patrick v. LeFevre, 745 F.2d 153, 159, 40 Fed. R. Serv. 2d 39 (2d Cir. 1984); Mosier v. Maynard, 937 F.2d 1521, 1527 (10th Cir. 1991) (whether religious beliefs are sincere is a question of fact); Reed v. Faulkner, 653 F. Supp. 965, 971 (N.D. Ind. 1987) ("Determining religious sincerity certainly involves an opportunity to see and hear the plaintiff witness testify, to be examined and cross examined."); Sinnett v. Simmons, 45 F. Supp. 2d 1210 (D. Kan. 1999) (though the court granted summary judgment to defendants, it refused to do so on sincerity grounds, as the inmate's mere assertion that his fasting was based on religious beliefs created a material issue of fact).

[19]Mosier v. Maynard, 937 F.2d 1521, 1527 (10th Cir. 1991). But see Abdool-Rashaad v. Seiter, 690 F. Supp. 598, 602 (S.D. Ohio 1987) (holding incorrectly that the plaintiff was not sincere in his adherence to "Universalism" dogma because "plaintiff's desire for exemption is not shared by an organized group").

[20]Thomas v. Review Bd. of Indiana Employment Sec. Division, 450 U.S. 707, 715, 101 S. Ct. 1425, 67 L. Ed. 2d 624 (1981).

[21]Mosier v. Maynard, 937 F.2d 1521, 1526 (10th Cir. 1991).

[22]Thomas v. Review Bd. of Indiana Employment Sec. Division, 450 U.S. 707, 715, 101 S. Ct. 1425, 67 L. Ed. 2d 624 (1981); LaFe-

nized church to be a sincere religious believer. In *Mosier v Maynard*,[23] the plaintiff claimed that he was a sincere believer of a Native American religion even though he did not belong to the Native American worship group in the prison. The court held that "membership in a religious organization is [not] a prerequisite for religious convictions to be judged sincere.[24] Furthermore, religious rights are based on the inmate's sincere beliefs, not on descent. In *Morrison v. Garraghty*,[25] prison officials denied an inmate's request for Native American religious items pending proof the inmate was of Native American descent. The district court enjoined the prison officials from refusing to consider the inmate's request, and the Fourth Circuit affirmed, holding, "we cannot endorse the proposition that an inmate's sincerity of religious beliefs in Native American spirituality can be defined solely by his race or heritage."[26]

Fourth, in a similar fashion, sincerity does not require that plaintiff reach perfection in his or her practice of the religious canons. "[N]o court can realistically expect perfect moral purity of any adherent to any religion.[27] Evidence of nonobservance is, of course, relevant to the question of sincerity. However, it is not

---

vers v. Saffle, 936 F.2d 1117, 1119 (10th Cir. 1991); Martinelli v. Dugger, 817 F.2d 1499, 1504 (11th Cir. 1987).

[23]Mosier v. Maynard, 937 F.2d 1521 (10th Cir. 1991).

[24]*Id.* (citing Frazee v. Illinois Dept. of Employment Sec., 489 U.S. 829, 834, 109 S. Ct. 1514, 103 L. Ed. 2d 914 (1989)). Accord, Thomas v. Lord, NY Law Journal, July 12, 1997, at 32 (Sup. Ct. 1997) (the fact that an inmate is not a Jew is not a valid reason for denying the inmate access to Jewish services).

[25]Morrison v. Garraghty, 239 F.3d 648 (4th Cir. 2001).

[26]*Id.* at 658.

[27]Reed v. Faulkner, 653 F. Supp. 965, 971 (N.D. Ind. 1987) ("Human history and indeed, the teaching of major religions of the world in and of themselves tell us that most mortals are fallible and do not always live up to the highest moral ideals of their religious faith.").

conclusive. In *Reed v Faulkner*,[28] for example, the district court held that the plaintiff was insincere in his claim to be a Rastafarian because the evidence at trial showed that, in the past, he had not been unfaltering in the practice of his faith. Contrary to the demands of Rastafarianism, he had eaten meat and shaved his beard.

The Seventh Circuit reversed, holding that "the fact that a person does not adhere steadfastly to every tenet of his faith does not mark him as insincere."[29] The court observed that "it would be bizarre for prisons to undertake, in effect, to promote strict orthodoxy, by forfeiting the religious rights of any inmate observed backsliding, thus placing guards and fellow inmates in the role of religious police."[30] A further reason for not requiring staunch observation of a faith is that (at least with faiths that are not hierarchical) such a requirement places the court in the awkward position of deciding the "precise point orthodoxy becomes apostasy."[31]

Fifth, prisoners are not required to demonstrate that a particular practice is absolutely required by their religion for them to be sincere in their religious desire to participate in the practice. It is enough that the practice has roots in the religious beliefs of the faith. *Thomas v Review Board*,[32] an unemployment insurance case, is relevant here. In *Thomas,* the Supreme Court dealt with the claim of a Jehovah's Witness that he could not, consistent with his beliefs, continue to work in a plant that was making war machinery. Although other members of his faith did work in the plant and did not think that this employment was barred by their religion, Chief Justice Burger held for the court that this was not dispositive. He wrote, "The guarantee of

---
[28]Reed v. Faulkner, 653 F. Supp. 965, 971 (N.D. Ind. 1987).
[29]*Id.* at 963.
[30]*Id.*
[31]*Id.*
[32]Thomas v. Review Bd. of Indiana Employment Sec. Division, 450 U.S. 707, 101 S. Ct. 1425, 67 L. Ed. 2d 624 (1981).

§ 6:7　　　　　　Rights of Prisoners, Third Edition

free exercise is not limited to beliefs shared by all members of a sect."[33] This viewpoint has been properly held to apply in prison religious sincerity cases.[34] Thus, it is not conclusive that other members of the faith in the prison are not as rigorous in their practices as is plaintiff. The reason for this is that "[i]nterfaith differences are common and cannot be resolved by courts."[35]

Though the Third Circuit recently affirmed this principle in *Dehart v. Horn*,[36] it did so in a way that did not favor the inmate. *Dehart* overruled *Johnson v. Horn*, decided only two years earlier, which held that where a religious practice is mandated or central to an inmate's faith, an inquiry into alternative means for the inmate to practice his faith, the second *Shabazz* factor, was irrelevant.[37] The court, this time sitting en banc, held that there is no distinction between mandated religious beliefs and beliefs that are merely grounded in a religious faith.[38] The court held that a distinction between mandated beliefs and non-mandated practices is inconsistent with Supreme Court precedent.[39] Therefore, even where a religious practice was commanded by a religious faith, the court must analyze whether there are alternative means for the inmate to practice his religion. The Third Circuit also held that it was "unacceptable" to "discount . . .[a] sincerely held belief

---

[33]*Id.* at 715-16.

[34]See, e.g., Thomas v. Review Bd. of Indiana Employment Sec. Division, 450 U.S. 707, 714, 101 S. Ct. 1425, 67 L. Ed. 2d 624 (1981); Mosier v. Maynard, 937 F.2d 1521 (10th Cir. 1991); Moskowitz v. Wilkinson, 432 F. Supp. 947 (D. Conn. 1977).

[35]Mosier v. Maynard, 937 F.2d 1521, 1523 (10th Cir. 1991).

[36]DeHart v. Horn, 227 F.3d 47 (3d Cir. 2000) (en banc).

[37]150 F.3d 276, 282 (3d Cir. 1998).

[38]See DeHart v. Horn, 227 F.3d 47, 54-55 (3d Cir. 2000).

[39]See DeHart v. Horn, 227 F.3d 47, 54-55 (3d Cir. 2000), citing O'Lone v. Estate of Shabazz, 482 U.S. 342, 107 S. Ct. 2400, 96 L. Ed. 2d 282 (1987) (though religious practice was compelled by the inmate's faith, the Court held second factor was satisfied as there were alternative means for the inmate to practice his religion).

because it was not in the mainstream."⁴⁰ This would contrary to Supreme Court jurisprudence, according to the Third Circuit.⁴¹

Finally, an inmate should have some acquaintance with the religious tenets of the faith to which the plaintiff professes to sincerely belong. This enables the court to examine critically the inmate's sincerity. The claim that he or she is a sincere adherent of the faith is weakened if the inmate does not have a reasonable basis for his or her beliefs. If an inmate's testimony reveals that he or she lacks knowledge of the most fundamental tenets of the faith, this is relevant, although not necessarily dispositive, proof of his or her insincerity. Thus, in one case in which an inmate claimed to be a sincere member of the Rastafarian faith, a court properly took into account that the plaintiff lacked basic information about the history and practices of the faith.⁴² This does not mean, however, that the inmate must be a master of the theology of his or her faith. Were that the test of sincerity, only the most educated practitioners of a religion would pass the sincerity test.⁴³

Nature of the Beliefs

Sincerity is only one part of the puzzle. The other, equally important part requires a determination of whether the plaintiff's beliefs constitute a religion. It is clear that not every set of beliefs, no matter how worthy

---

⁴⁰See DeHart v. Horn, 227 F.3d 47, 55 (3d Cir. 2000).

⁴¹See DeHart v. Horn, 227 F.3d 47, 56 (3d Cir. 2000). Citing Hernandez v. C.I.R., 490 U.S. 680, 699, 109 S. Ct. 2136, 104 L. Ed. 2d 766 (1989) ("It is not within the judicial ken to question the centrality of the particular beliefs or practices to a faith, or the validity of particular litigants' interpretation of those creeds.")

⁴²Robinson v. Foti, 527 F. Supp. 1111 (E.D. La. 1981).

⁴³One commentator argues that courts should defer to religious leaders in determining whether an inmate genuinely belongs to a religion. Heather Davis, Comment: Inmates' Religious Rights: Deference to Religious Leaders and Accommodation of Individualized Religious Beliefs, 64 Alb. L. Rev. 773 (2000).

§ 6:7

or sincerely held, form a religion. Pure moral, secular, or political beliefs are not a religion.[44] In addition, sham doctrines and creeds that are manufactured purely for the purpose of obtaining permission for exclusion from what would otherwise be valid governmental regulation of conduct are not religions.[45] The trick is to differentiate those beliefs that are secular or sham from those which are genuinely religious.

As with the sincerity issue, there are no easy answers to this perplexing question. Belief in a Supreme Being "controlling the destiny of man[46] is one obvious signpost, but this is not required for a set of beliefs to constitute a religion. In *United States v Seeger,*[47] a case involving a conscientious objector to the military draft, the Supreme Court held that a belief that occupies "a place in the life of its possessor parallel to that filled by the orthodox belief in God" is a religious belief.[48] With *Seeger*

---

[44]Africa v. Com. of Pa., 662 F.2d 1025, 1036 (3d Cir. 1981). See also, Tinsley v. Pittari, 952 F. Supp. 384 (N.D. Tex. 1996) (defendants were entitled to summary judgment where they denied inmate's request for time off from work where the inmate failed to establish the "good faith nature of her beliefs"); Winters v. State, 549 N.W.2d 819 (Iowa 1996) (inmate's request for racially-segregated cell denied where the description of his beliefs were "lacking sufficient detail to illuminate what the tenets of the religion in fact were.").

[45]Theriault v. Carlson, 495 F.2d 390, 395 (5th Cir. 1974) (First Amendment does not extend to "so-called religions which tend to mock established institutions and are obviously shams and absurdities"); see also Faheem-El v. Lane, 657 F. Supp. 638 (C.D. Ill. 1986) (gatherings of street gangs are not religious).

[46]Fulwood v. Clemmer, 206 F. Supp. 370 (D. D.C. 1962).

[47]U.S. v. Seeger, 380 U.S. 163, 85 S. Ct. 850, 13 L. Ed. 2d 733 (1965).

[48]U.S. v. Seeger, 380 U.S. 163, 166, 85 S. Ct. 850, 13 L. Ed. 2d 733 (1965). *Seeger* is a movement away from 19th Century Supreme Court decisions which relied on a belief in a deity. Davis v. Beason, 133 U.S. 333, 342, 10 S. Ct. 299, 33 L. Ed. 637 (1890) ("religion has reference to one's views of his relations to his Creator").

§ 6:7

and its progeny,[49] the Court has "moved considerably beyond the wholly theistic interpretation" of what is a religion within the meaning of the First Amendment.[50] Thus, the definition of religion is not tied to theistic doctrine. It is equally certain that discrimination against unfamiliar or unconventional faiths is forbidden.[51] To hold otherwise would defeat the promise of the First Amendment "to allow our citizenry to explore diverse religious beliefs in accordance with the dictates of their conscience.[52] It is common ground that "[r]eligions now accepted were persecuted, unpopular and condemned at their inception."[53] For these reasons, exclusion of First Amendment protection for new, or even frightening, faiths is wholly inconsistent with the history of this country. Similarly off base is an examination of the truth or falsity of the beliefs. Almost 50 years ago, the Supreme Court held that "men may believe what they cannot prove."[54]

Another important point to bear in mind is that courts have recognized that religious faiths may have beliefs that relate to secular concerns. As one court put it, "a belief can be both secular and religious. The categories are not mutually exclusive."[55] For example, one court held correctly that the Aryan Nations Church of Jesus Christ Christian could qualify for protection as a

---

[49]See, e.g., Welsh v. U.S., 398 U.S. 333, 90 S. Ct. 1792, 26 L. Ed. 2d 308 (1970) (conscientious objector status extended to a person who declined to profess a belief in a supreme being). See also Torcaso v. Watkins, 367 U.S. 488, 495, 81 S. Ct. 1680, 6 L. Ed. 2d 982 (1961) (a state may not favor "those religions based on a belief in the existence of God as against those religions founded on different beliefs").

[50]Africa v. Com. of Pa., 662 F.2d 1025, 1031 (3d Cir. 1981).

[51]*Id.* at 1031.

[52]Patrick v. LeFevre, 745 F.2d 153, 40 Fed. R. Serv. 2d 39 (2d Cir. 1984).

[53]U.S. v. Kuch, 288 F. Supp. 439, 35 A.L.R.3d 922 (D. D.C. 1968).

[54]U.S. v. Ballard, 322 U.S. 78, 86, 64 S. Ct. 882, 88 L. Ed. 1148 (1944).

[55]Wiggins v. Sargent, 753 F.2d 663, 666 (8th Cir. 1985).

§ 6:7

religion notwithstanding the fact that its belief in racial superiority of the white race had clear secular implications.[56] Other courts have ruled in a similar fashion concerning the Black Muslim faith, despite its belief in the superiority of the black race.[57]

A belief can qualify as a religion even if it does not require adherence to a Supreme Being, even if it is not conventional or correct, and even if it seems "bizarre"[58] to the mind of mainstream Americans. It is easier, however, to say what a court may not rely on in making the difficult judgment of whether a particular set of beliefs is a religion than it is to describe what it may use to make the ruling.[59] Two circuit courts dealing with this question in the prison context provide helpful, but in some ways contradictory, guidance on that point.

The first, *Africa v Pennsylvania*,[60] dealt with the claim by a member of the MOVE creed at the Holmesburgh Prison in Pennsylvania to declare that MOVE was a religion. MOVE was founded by John Africa. It is a group without a governing body or official hierarchy. Everyone in the group is considered equal. There are no official written guidelines setting forth the group's beliefs. There are no official codes of religious worship or church services. In addition, the group observes no holidays. Nevertheless, there appears to be general

---

[56]Murphy v. Missouri Dept. of Corrections, 814 F.2d 1252, 1255 (8th Cir. 1987) ("We have recognized that a belief with political or secular aspects may be religious in nature.").

[57]See, e.g., Otey v. Best, 680 F.2d 1231, 1233-34 n3 (8th Cir. 1982); Long v. Parker, 390 F.2d 816, 822 (3d Cir. 1968).

[58]Reed v. Faulkner, 842 F.2d 960, 962 (7th Cir. 1988) ("This assemblage of beliefs will strike most Americans as bizarre, but then most Americans are not Rastafarians, and religious beliefs often strike the nonbeliever as bizarre.").

[59]One clear principle is that a prison may condition recognition of a group as a bone fide faith by a rule which requires that the group make a formal request to prison officialdom for recognition. Murphy v. Missouri Dept. of Corrections, 814 F.2d 1252, 1255 (8th Cir. 1987).

[60]Africa v. Com. of Pa., 662 F.2d 1025 (3d Cir. 1981).

First Amendment: Religion § 6:7

agreement among the members as to the organization's credo. Adherents of MOVE "are committed to a 'natural,' 'moving,' 'active,' and 'generating' way of life."[61] Toward that end, they abhor civilization or anything that they believe is "artificial."[62] Accordingly, a central tenet of the creed is that members consume a "diet composed largely of raw vegetables and fruits."[63]

The Third Circuit set out a three-part test to use in determining whether MOVE was a religion. To be a religion, the *Africa* court held that a set of beliefs must: (1) "address fundamental and ultimate questions having to do with deep and imponderable matters"; (2) be "comprehensive in nature"; and (3) have "certain formal and external signs."[64]

This test draws heavily on the *Seeger* dictum that a set of beliefs "parallel" in the minds of its believers to that of an orthodox religion for its adherents is a religion. Put another way, the *Africa* test advances a definition-by-analogy approach under which the basic attributes of traditional faiths are described and then applied to the belief structure of the contested group. If the belief structure at issue in the case has similar generic attributes to those found in traditional religions, then it is deemed a religion within the meaning of the First Amendment; if it does not have similar attributes, then it does not qualify as a religion.

Applying the test to MOVE, the court decided that it was not a religion. Because the group had no functional equivalent of the Ten Commandments, the New Testament Gospels or the Muslim Koran, the court held that "MOVE does not . . . take a position with respect to matters of personal morality, human morality or the

---

[61]*Id.* at 1026.
[62]*Id.*
[63]*Id.*
[64]*Id.* at 1032.

meaning and purposes of life.[65] The group, therefore, did not have a theology that addressed fundamental and ultimate questions and, therefore, did not satisfy the first branch of the test. The group also failed the second prong of the test because it appeared to consist of only one idea rather a comprehensive belief system. The court held that it was a "single-faceted" ideology similar in that way to secular nonreligious beliefs such as "economic determinism, Social Darwinism, or even vegetarianism.[66]

Finally, the court held that MOVE failed to satisfy the third test because it "lacks almost all of the formal identifying characteristics common to most recognized religions.[67] In support of this conclusion, the court relied on the facts that the organization lacked an organizational structure, had no ministers or clergy, celebrated no holidays, had no special services or official customs, and had no documents which "might pass for . . .[a] scripture book or catechism."[68]

In *Patrick v Le Fevre*,[69] the Second Circuit characterized the *Africa* test as "narrow,"[70] and propounded a different test. *Patrick* dealt with a claim that the "Five Percenters" practiced a valid religion. The Five Percent Nation of Islam was founded by Clarence 13X in the early 1960s. The creed "conceive[s] of its ideals by reference to the realm of mathematics.[71] According to the group, its adherents are among the five percent of the people of the world who can bring "knowledge and spiritual guidance to the eighty-five percent of the popula-

---

[65]*Id.* at 1033. The court rejected the idea that the MOVE belief structure was a pantheistic devotion to nature, but held rather that it was the "mindset" of a "secular philosophy." *Id.*

[66]*Id.* at 1035.

[67]*Id.* at 1036.

[68]*Id.*

[69]Patrick v. LeFevre, 745 F.2d 153, 40 Fed. R. Serv. 2d 39 (2d Cir. 1984).

[70]*Id.* at 156 n. 4.

[71]*Id.* at 155.

First Amendment: Religion § 6:7

tion who are oppressed by the remaining ten percent."[72]

Although the Five Percent faith draws on a mixture of traditional and obscure religious texts (including the Bible, Elijah Mohammed's Body of Lessons, and the Egyptian Book of the Dead), and the faith recognizes the existence of a Superior Being, the trappings of the faith are informal. Rather, according to the teachings of the Five Percent creed, "the seeds of spiritual communication are nurtured from within."[73] Therefore, the Five Percenters have "no need for a fixed place of worship where adherents could congregate regularly to exchange their ideas."[74] Moreover, Five Percenters think of their beliefs as a "way of life."[75]

On these facts, the Second Circuit reversed the district court's grant of a motion for summary judgment against the Five Percenters. The court found that the district court had erred by adhering to the objective three-part *Africa* test. Writing for the court, Judge Kaufman held that "a more subjective definition of religion, which examines an individual's inward attitudes towards a particular belief system," was required.[76] Under this test, the court concentrates on the individual's state of mind to determine whether he or she "conceives of the beliefs as religious in nature."[77]

The court acknowledged that this determination would require the factfinder to delve into the internal operations of the claimant's mind to determine the place

---

[72]*Id.*

[73]*Id.*

[74]*Id.*

[75]*Id.* at 159.

[76]*Id.* at 157.

[77]*Id.* at 158. The court quoted with approval the American philosopher William James' definition of religion: "The feelings, act, and experiences of individual men in their solitude, so far as they apprehend themselves to stand in relation to whatever they may consider the divine." W. James, The Varieties of Religious Experience 31 (1910).

occupied by such beliefs in the claimant's life.[78] The court observed that this "expansive conception of religious belief" was necessary if the First Amendment is to function as "a vehicle promoting the inviolability of individual conscience."[79]

Courts and litigants, therefore, have two competing tests from which to choose. Both have in common the recognition that nontraditional and nontheistic faiths can qualify for protection under the First Amendment. Thus, both are broadly consistent with governing Supreme Court precedent.[80] The difference between the tests is between their respective emphasis on either the objective or the subjective components of the inquiry. The *Africa* test is focused more on the externalities of the questioned religion. These can be measured without regard to the subjective intentions of the plaintiff. The *Patrick* test, by contrast, is concerned almost entirely with the subjective state of the plaintiff's mind and pays less regard to external evidence.

It is important to recognize that, under either test, it is entirely possible that a court will reach the same result about a particular persuasion. For example, under the *Africa* test, it is by no means certain that the Five Percenters would not be considered a religion. The Five Percenters, after all, in contrast to the MOVE creed, did have religious texts to draw on for their beliefs that addressed fundamental questions of human existence; additionally, they did have a comprehensive "way of life" that appeared to govern, as is the case with most traditional religions, many aspects of everyday life. Thus, they appeared to satisfy the first two of the three *Africa* tests. However, the informality of the organization of the group is not similar to the more

---

[78]*Id.* at 159.

[79]*Id.* at 158 (citing Tribe, American Constitutional Law p 818 § 14-3). See also, Allah v. Menei, 844 F. Supp. 1056 (E.D. Pa. 1994) (summary judgment precluded where prisoners provided evidence that Temple of Islam was a bona fide religion).

[80]See discussion at § 6:3.

organized structure of traditional faiths, and therefore probably would not satisfy the third part of the *Africa* test. Accordingly, two of the three *Africa* criteria are probably met by the Five Percent belief system. Since in the *Africa* case itself all three criteria were not met, it is possible that by applying the *Africa* test to the *Patrick* facts, a court might find that Five Percenters' teachings are sufficiently, although not completely, analogous to traditional religion to be considered a religion for the purposes of the First Amendment.

Nevertheless, the two tests differ in the focus of the analysis and might easily lead to differing results in a particular case depending on which standard a court chooses. One way to approach this problem would be to subject the facts of a case that raise this issue to both analyses. If the facts meet, or fail to meet, both the *Africa* and the *Patrick* standards, then the issue is resolved. Only if the facts pass one test and fail the other must a court choose between them.

In making the choice between these standards, the *Patrick* test has much to recommend itself. Unlike the *Africa* test, which concentrates so heavily on external factors, the *Patrick* test allows a court to focus on the pivotal fact involved in these cases: the place in the mind of the believer of the ideas claimed to constitute a religion. This central fact, which is not explicitly acknowledged by the *Africa* test, is the most important to bear in mind if the teachings of the Supreme Court are to be observed. Those teachings require that ideas which occupy a place in the mind of the believer similar to that held by persons who adhere to traditional religions are as worthy of constitutional protection as those of more easily recognizable religions.[81]

Since the *Patrick* test forces a court to confront that issue directly and the *Africa* test does not, the *Patrick* test, although it is more difficult to apply, seems the more appropriate of the two.

In any event, until the Supreme Court resolves this

---

[81]See discussion at § 6:3.

issue and chooses between the two tests or harmonizes them, it is vital for litigators and courts to be aware of the choice of standards currently available for resolving this important question and how they might differ in result.

§ 6:8 Religious Practices

Research References

West's Key Number Digest, Prisons ☞4(14)

The applicable constitutional provisions implicated by prisoner free exercise claims, the general standards that govern these disputes, as well as the standards for defining religion have been analyzed now. What remains for discussion are the application of the standards to specific religious practices that prisoners commonly desire to follow while confined. The remaining sections of this chapter discuss these practices.[1]

§ 6:9 —Personal Appearance and Clothing

Challenges to prison rules that regulate physical appearance have been a frequent source of litigation by inmates claiming restrictions on their free exercise rights. The challenges have occurred because some religions impose dress and personal appearance codes on their members that prison rules often do not honor. For example, male Orthodox Jews are required to wear beards, and Rastafarians and members of some Native American faiths are obligated to wear their hair long. When these religious codes clash with prison rules that proscribe long hair or beards, litigation often results.

[Section 6:8]

[1]One commentator argues that security interests do not need to be in tension with the religious practices of inmates. He argues that providing neutral accommodations would actually bring more prisoners in line with the security structure of the prison. See, Developments in the Law, The Law Of Prisons: IV. In the Belly of the Whale: Religious Practice in Prison, 115 Harv. L. Rev. 1891 (2002).

FIRST AMENDMENT: RELIGION § 6:9

In the years prior to *Shabazz*,¹ cases involving inmates' personal appearance and clothing produced varied results. Some courts upheld the restrictions;² others did not.³ Prison rules that regulated the personal appearance of prisoners were generally upheld following *Shabazz*. One would think prison officials would have had a much harder time defending such regulations under the compelling interest/least restrictive means standard of the RFRA or RLUIPA. In some cases this has been true, but for the most part, prison officials have been highly successful under both standards in defending policies regulating the personal appearance of inmates against attacks based on religious exercise.⁴

[Section 6:9]
¹O'Lone v. Estate of Shabazz, 482 U.S. 342, 107 S. Ct. 2400, 96 L. Ed. 2d 282 (1987). This case is discussed in detail in § 6:3. For a discussion of the difference between the *Shabazz* standard and the compelling interest standard as it applies to grooming policies in prison, see Eric J. Zogry, Comment: Orthodox Jewish Prisoners and the Turner Effect, 56 La. L. Rev. 905 (1996) (claiming that the *Shabazz* factors make it too difficult for an inmate to win a legitimate claim); Note: Will Jewish Prisoners be Boerne Again? Legislative Responses to City of Boerne v. Flores, 66 Fordham L. Rev. 2333 (1998) (the death of the RFRA legitimizes the limiting of prisoners' religious practices, which will especially affect Jewish prisoners).

²Shabazz v Barnauskas, 790 F2d 1536 (11th Cir 1986); Hill v Blackwell, 774 F2d 338 (8th Cir 1985); Wilson v Schilliager, 761 F2d 921 (3d Cir 1985).

³Chapman v. Pickett, 801 F.2d 912 (7th Cir. 1986), judgment vacated on other grounds, 484 U.S. 807, 108 S. Ct. 54, 98 L. Ed. 2d 19 (1987); Safley v. Turner, 777 F.2d 1307 (8th Cir. 1985), judgment aff'd in part, rev'd in part on other grounds, 482 U.S. 78, 107 S. Ct. 2254, 96 L. Ed. 2d 64 (1987); Prushinowski v. Hambrick, 570 F. Supp. 863 (E.D. N.C. 1983).

⁴Compare Phipps v. Parker, 879 F. Supp. 734 (W.D. Ky. 1995) (RFRA not violated where cutting of Hasidic Jewish inmate's hair served security concerns; court held the cutting of inmate's hair was the only means of furthering the concerns); May v. Baldwin, 109 F.3d 557 (9th Cir. 1997) (RFRA not violated as policy requiring an inmate to unbraid his hair so officials could check for contraband was the least restrictive means of serving a compelling

§ 6:9   Rights of Prisoners, Third Edition

One recent case, however, shows that this deference to prison officials when the words "security interests" are uttered may not be as much a sure thing as it once was, even under the *Shabazz* factors.

Sasnett v. Litchser[5] began as a claim by several Wisconsin inmates under the RFRA.[6] The inmates claimed that a prison regulation prohibiting them from wearing crosses violated their free exercise rights and violated the RFRA. Prison officials initially claimed that the regulation did not violate the free exercise rights of the inmates, as the wearing of crosses was not mandated by their respective religions. They also argued that even if the inmates' religious practice was substan-

---

state interest); Harris v. Chapman, 97 F.3d 499, 45 Fed. R. Evid. Serv. 1063 (11th Cir. 1996) (policy requiring Rastafarian inmate to cut his hair served valid security concerns and therefore did not violate RFRA), with Green v. Polunsky, 229 F.3d 486 (5th Cir. 2000); Wellmaker v. Dahill, 836 F. Supp. 1375 (N.D. Ohio 1993) (inmate's claim that hair length regulation violated the First Amendment was dismissed under *Shabazz,* as it was reasonably related to valid penological concern); Dillon v. Russell, 85 Ohio App. 3d 781, 621 N.E.2d 491 (3d Dist. Allen County 1993) (hair length restriction reasonably related to valid penological concerns; defendants' motion for summary judgment granted); Dunavant v. Moore, 907 F.2d 77 (8th Cir. 1990) (rule limiting beards to two inches in length did not violate the First Amendment because a long beard could make identification more difficult); Friedman v. State of Ariz., 912 F.2d 328 (9th Cir. 1990) (a complete ban on all beards, except where medically necessary, was not unconstitutional since it aided in "rapid and accurate identification" in day-to-day activities, in cases of prison disturbances, and in cases of escape from custody); Iron Eyes v. Henry, 907 F.2d 810 (8th Cir. 1990) (restriction on hair length below the collar prevented an inmate from quickly altering his appearance); Pollock v. Marshall, 845 F.2d 656 (6th Cir. 1988) (same); Brightly v. Wainwright, 814 F.2d 612 (11th Cir. 1987) (same); Perry v. Davies, 757 F. Supp. 1223, 1224 (D. Kan. 1991) (a requirement that inmates be clean shaven at admission serves "a legitimate security interest" in identification).

[5]Sasnett v. Litscher, 197 F.3d 290 (7th Cir. 1999).

[6]Sasnett v. Sullivan, 908 F. Supp. 1429 (W.D. Wis. 1995), aff'd, 91 F.3d 1018 (7th Cir. 1996), judgment vacated, 521 U.S. 1114, 117 S. Ct. 2502, 138 L. Ed. 2d 1007 (1997).

FIRST AMENDMENT: RELIGION § 6:9

tially burdened, the policy served the compelling state interest of maintaining order and security by preventing inmates from signifying gang membership by wearing jewelry. The defendants further argued that the policy was the least restrictive means of serving that compelling interest, as they had deliberated over the policy for an extended period of time.

The district court first addressed the substantial burden question. The court spent considerable time deciding whether a religious practice must have been central to or mandated by the plaintiffs' religion for it to have been substantially burdened.[7] The court recognize that not requiring that a religious practice be mandated by the inmate's faith could increase litigation; however it held that the Supreme Court and Congress made it clear that courts were not to become "embroiled in questions of theology."[8] The court therefore adopted a test that required only that the religious practice be "1) motivated by a sincerely held religious belief and 2) significantly or meaningfully curtailed."[9] The court held that the plaintiff's religious practice of wearing crosses was a sincerely held religious belief that had been significantly curtailed, and therefore that their religious practice had been substantially burdened.[10]

The district court then applied the RFRA's compelling interest/least restrictive means test to the inmates' claims. It found that the defendants' interest in maintaining security and order in the prison was compelling.[11] But the court refused to accept the prison officials' explanation that the policy had been put in place only after extensive deliberation as satisfying the

---

[7]Sasnett v. Sullivan, 908 F. Supp. at 1440-47.

[8]*Id.* at 1444 (citing Thomas v. Review Bd. of Indiana Employment Sec. Division, 450 U.S. 707, 101 S. Ct. 1425, 67 L. Ed. 2d 624 (1981))

[9]*Id.*

[10]*Id.* at 1444-46.

[11]*Id.* at 1449.

least restrictive means test.[12] The court found that the defendants failed to show that the least restrictive means was employed to further their legitimate security concerns, as they could have prevented theft of the jewelry by limiting the value of jewelry allowed in the prison, and they could have prevented gang affiliation by requiring the jewelry be worn under the inmate's clothes.[13] The district court, therefore, granted summary judgment for the plaintiffs, and enjoined the defendants from preventing the inmates from wearing religious jewelry.[14]

The defendant prison officials appealed to the Seventh Circuit.[15] After finding that the RFRA was constitutional, Judge Posner agreed with the finding of the district court that the policy was not the least restrictive means of furthering the compelling interest:

> The regulation to which the defendants refuse to make an exception forbids the wearing of a crucifix even if it is too small or light to be a weapon . . . too inexpensive to barter for a weapon, invisible because worn under clothing, and not a gang symbol or easily confused with one. The state allows prisoners to have rosaries, which could be used to strangle a fellow prisoner or a guard, and bans crucifixes even in correctional facilities wholly occupied by white-collar prisoners who do not belong to gangs or get into fights with each other or the guards. These features of the state's practice blast the case for regarding a ban on crucifixes and other religious jewelry as a serious and measured response to a concern with violence or a concern with gangs, legitimate and important as these concerns are.[16]

The court affirmed the district court's ruling.[17]

Nearly a year after Judge Posner held that the RFRA

---

[12]*Id.* at 1449.

[13]*Id.* at 1449-50.

[14]*Id.* at 1451.

[15]Sasnett v. Sullivan, 91 F.3d 1018 (7th Cir. 1996), judgment vacated, 521 U.S. 1114, 117 S. Ct. 2502, 138 L. Ed. 2d 1007 (1997).

[16]*Id.* at 1022.

[17]*Id.*

First Amendment: Religion § 6:9

was constitutional in *Sasnett,* the Supreme Court struck it down in *City of Boerne v. Flores*.[18] Two days after the decision in *Flores,* the Court vacated the Seventh Circuit's decision in *Sasnett* and remanded the case for a determination on First Amendment grounds in light of the demise of the RFRA.[19] This time the district court granted summary judgment for the defendants, finding that under pre-RFRA analysis, the policy did not interfere with the inmates' religious exercise.[20]

The plaintiffs appealed the decision, and the case was squarely back in the lap of Judge Posner.[21] Judge Posner discussed whether the case should be analyzed under *Employment Division v. Smith,* or *O'Lone v. Estate of Shabazz*.[22] In what can only be called dicta, Posner stated that if Wisconsin prison officials forbade the wearing of any jewelry, the outcome would change depending on whether it was *Smith* or *Shabazz* that governed the case.[23] If *Smith* governed, Posner posited, the burden on plaintiffs' religious exercise would be the result of a neutral law of general applicability, and the policy would be upheld.[24] Posner pointed to his previous decision in the case to show that prison officials' security concerns were not seriously implicated by the allowance of the wearing of crosses, and therefore if the case were to be analyzed under *Shabazz* rational relationship test, the plaintiffs would prevail.[25] Judge Posner never made a decision on which standard *would* govern. Instead, he pointed out that Wisconsin's policy allowed prisoners to wear crosses if they were attached

---

[18]City of Boerne v. Flores, 521 U.S. 507, 117 S. Ct. 2157, 138 L. Ed. 2d 624 (1997).

[19]*Id.*

[20]See Sasnett v. Litscher, 197 F.3d 290, 291 (7th Cir. 1999).

[21]*Id.*

[22]*Id.* at 292-93.

[23]*Id.*

[24]*Id.*

[25]*Id.*

to a rosary.[26] He decided that this favored Catholics over Protestants, and found that rosaries were just as much a security concern as any other cross on a chain or rope.[27] The district court's grant of summary judgment was reversed, and the Seventh Circuit ordered the prison officials be enjoined from enforcing the regulation.[28]

Though Judge Posner did not actually decide *Sasnett* on an explicit finding that the Wisconsin prison policy was not reasonably related to a legitimate government concern, as prescribed by *Shabazz,* it is clear that that was the approach he favored. Posner intimated that *Shabazz* and not *Smith* should govern prison claims because, "*Smith* . . . was not a prison case and it did not purport to overrule or limit *Turner* and *O'Lone* [*v. Estate of Shabazz*]; and the Supreme Court has instructed us to leave the overruling of its decisions to it."[29] It is clear from his language that Posner thought little of the security arguments advanced by the prison officials, and that if he had his way, prison policies regulating the personal appearance of prisoners, and thus burdening their religious practices, would not pass Constitutional muster on the mere mention of a security interest.

Sasnett suggests the deference accorded prison officials does not mean abdication. It also shows that the result might be the same in many of these case regardless of whether the governing standard is *Shabazz* or RLUIPA.

However, case law shows that the differing standards can make a difference in how claims against prison grooming policies have been adjudicated. The point is highlighted by two cases involving similar claims decided by the Fifth Circuit. In 1995, the court heard

---

[26]Sasnett v. Litscher, 197 F.3d 290, 293 (7th Cir. 1999).
[27]*Id.*
[28]*Id.*
[29]*Id.* at 292.

§ 6:9 FIRST AMENDMENT: RELIGION

Hicks v. Garner.[30] In *Garner,* an inmate claimed a prison regulation violated the Free Exercise Clause by forcing him to cut his hair. Hicks, a Rastafarian, claimed his religion mandated he not cut his hair. He brought claims under the First Amendment to the Constitution that required analysis under the *Shabazz* factors, and he also claimed the regulation violated his rights under the RFRA. The court made quick work of the First Amendment claim, holding that "prison grooming regulations, including specifically the requirement that a prisoner cut his hair and beard, are rationally related to the achievement of valid penological goals, such as security and inmate identification."[31] It further held that Hicks failed to distinguish his case from the many cases upholding such regulations under the rational relationship test.[32]

The court came to a different conclusion when it analyzed Hicks' RFRA claim. It held that "the district court abused its discretion when it summarily dismissed Hicks' RFRA claim as frivolous."[33] It concluded that Hicks had a "fighting" chance of prevailing on the claim under the new compelling interest/least restrictive means standard.[34] The court also focused on the substantial burden requirement of the RFRA, noting that it was a break from the *Shabazz* standard, and that it could make a difference in the disposition of the case.[35]

Five years after the *Hicks* ruling, the Fifth Circuit once again faced a claim that prison regulations of personal appearance impermissibly burdened an inmate's free exercise of his religion. In *Green v. Polun-*

---

[30]Hicks v. Garner, 69 F.3d 22 (5th Cir. 1995).

[31]*Id.* at 25.

[32]*Id.*

[33]*Id.* at 26.

[34]*Id.*

[35]*Id.* at 26 n 22 (5th Cir. 1995) (surveying the different tests adopted by various courts in determining whether a plaintiff's practice of religion has been substantially burdened).

§ 6:9 RIGHTS OF PRISONERS, THIRD EDITION

sky,[36] an inmate claimed that a prison policy preventing him from keeping a short beard violated his constitutional right to exercise his Islamic faith. Predictably, prison officials contended that the underlying goal of the policy was to aid in identification of the prisoner should he escape. The claim was brought after the Supreme Court had found RFRA unconstitutional. The Fifth Circuit, therefore, applied the *Shabazz* factors in its analysis, and upheld the district court's dismissal of the claim.[37] The court held that the policy was reasonably related to the legitimate interest in maintaining security in the prison.[38]

Case law reflects the pattern of the Fifth Circuit cases decided under the two standards. Claims brought under the RFRA were more likely to survive motions to dismiss or for summary judgment than claims brought under *Shabazz*.[39] Prison officials almost always claim that the personal appearance regulations are in place

---

[36]Green v. Polunsky, 229 F.3d 486 (5th Cir. 2000).

[37]*Id.* at 491.

[38]*Id.* at 490.

[39]Compare Hicks v. Garner, 69 F.3d 22 (5th Cir. 1995); Abordo v. State of Hawai'i, 902 F. Supp. 1220 (D. Haw. 1995) (inmate's RFRA claim that grooming regulation violated RFRA survived summary judgment); Estep v. Dent, 914 F. Supp. 1462 (W.D. Ky. 1996) (preliminary injunction granted for plaintiff where Orthodox Hasidic Jew claimed the forcible cutting of his earlocks violated RFRA; court determined that the inmate's claim had a strong likelihood of succeeding); Hall v. Griego, 896 F. Supp. 1043 (D. Colo. 1995) (Muslim inmate stated a claim under RFRA where he alleged that prison officials prohibited him from wearing religious headgear); Muslim v. Frame, 891 F. Supp. 226 (E.D. Pa. 1995) (summary judgment precluded where a pre-trial detainee alleged prohibition of religious headgear violated RFRA); Sasnett v. Sullivan, 908 F. Supp. 1429 (W.D. Wis. 1995), aff'd, 91 F.3d 1018 (7th Cir. 1996), judgment vacated, 521 U.S. 1114, 117 S. Ct. 2502, 138 L. Ed. 2d 1007 (1997) (policy prohibiting inmate from wearing a cross violated the RFRA as it was not the least restrictive means to target gang identification); with Green v. Polunsky, 229 F.3d 486 (5th Cir. 2000); Wellmaker v. Dahill, 836 F. Supp. 1375 (N.D. Ohio 1993) (inmate's claim that hair length regulation violated the First Amendment was dismissed under *Shabazz*, as regulation

to further security interests, which, as noted earlier, is almost always deemed a compelling interest by the courts.[40] However, if RFRA or RLUIPA is the governing standard, prison officials also have the burden of showing that the regulations are the least restrictive means of furthering that compelling interest. This can be difficult for prison officials in the case of a regulation of personal appearance. In the case of regulations regarding the length of a prisoner's beard or hair, the argument is that the prison could always periodically photograph the prisoner with short hair, or without a beard, thus allowing prison officials to identify prisoners should they escape and alter their appearance. With advancements in modern technology, computer generated photos of how inmates look with shorter hair and without beards are a reliable way of identifying inmates who have escaped, and are a less restrictive means of achieving identification than an across the board groom-

---

was reasonably related to valid penological concern); Dillon v. Russell, 85 Ohio App. 3d 781, 621 N.E.2d 491 (3d Dist. Allen County 1993) (hair length restriction reasonably related to valid penological concern; defendants' motion for summary judgment granted); Dunavant v. Moore, 907 F.2d 77 (8th Cir. 1990) (rule limiting beards to two inches in length did not violate the First Amendment because a long beard can make identification more difficult); Friedman v. State of Ariz., 912 F.2d 328 (9th Cir. 1990) (a complete ban on all beards, except where medically necessary, was not unconstitutional, since it aided in "rapid and accurate identification" in day-to-day activities, in cases of prison disturbances and escape from custody); Iron Eyes v. Henry, 907 F.2d 810 (8th Cir. 1990) (restriction on hair length below the collar prevented an inmate from quickly altering his appearance); Pollock v. Marshall, 845 F.2d 656 (6th Cir. 1988) (same); Brightly v. Wainwright, 814 F.2d 612 (11th Cir. 1987) (same); Perry v. Davies, 757 F. Supp. 1223, 1224 (D. Kan. 1991) (a requirement that inmates be clean shaven at admission serves "a legitimate security interest" in identification). See, e.g., Dunavant v. Moore, 907 F.2d 77, 79 (8th Cir. 1990) ("A long beard, like long hair, could . . . help prisoners hide contraband."); Pollock v. Marshall, 845 F.2d 656, 659 (6th Cir. 1988) (hair regulations removed a "place to hide small contraband").

[40]See notes 98-100 and accompanying text.

ing policy. These considerations, if they do not lead to eventual success in a prisoner's religious exercise claim, should at least preclude dismissal and summary judgment in many cases.

An analogous personal appearance issue concerns religious head coverings. Muslim, Jewish, Rastafarian, and certain Native American faiths are examples of religions that require that their members cover their heads with a pre- scribed cap or hat. Regulations banning the use of these head coverings have been challenged as interfering with legitimate religious practices. However, as is the case with beard- and hair-length rules, prison administrators have justified head-covering rules on security and sanitation grounds.

In *Young v Lane*,[41] Jewish inmates in the Illinois prison system disputed a rule that prohibited them from wearing yarmulkes, the Jewish head covering. The defendants, however, allowed inmates to wear baseball caps at all times. The plaintiffs argued that this defeated any claim that head coverings could be prohibited, but the court disagreed. The court noted that the rule was designed to eliminate the effectiveness of gangs "by restricting the variety of available headgear."[42] Because of the "strong interest in uniform dress regulations," the Seventh Circuit upheld the restriction.[43] Even though the court upheld the rule on these grounds, it is not clear why allowing sincerely religious Jewish inmates to wear yarmulkes would encourage the development of illegal gang activity at the prison. The decision in *Young,* however, is in accord with that of other reported decisions on this topic following *Shabazz.*[44]

A final personal appearance rule found in the cases

---

[41]Young v. Lane, 922 F.2d 370 (7th Cir. 1991).

[42]*Id.* at 376.

[43]*Id.* at 375.

[44]See, e.g., Benjamin v. Coughlin, 905 F.2d 571, 578-79 (2d Cir. 1990) (unreasonable). 1990) (Rastafarians could be prevented from wearing loose fitting crowns because of the "ease with which

§ 6:9

regulates the wearing of religious medallions. Many prison systems permit the wearing of this type of jewelry.[45] Nevertheless, courts have upheld prohibitions on the use of medallions by inmates in cases where it was shown that the medal could be used as a weapon.[46]

As in the case of grooming regulations, claims against prison regulations prohibiting the wearing of religious headgear or medallions, analyzed under the compelling interest/least restrictive means standard, have a better chance of success. As *Sasnett* points out, prison officials almost always could impose less restrictive means than a total ban. As Wisconsin officials could have limited inmates to wearing cheaper, plastic crosses under their clothes, instead of banning them altogether, prison officials could require that inmates' medallions be made of plastic or require that prisoners only wear certain

---

contraband can be secreted" in them); Standing Deer v. Carlson, 831 F.2d 1525 (9th Cir. 1987) (Native Americans prohibited from wearing headbands because dirty headgear caused sanitation problem); Butler-Bey v. Frey, 811 F.2d 449 (8th Cir. 1987) (wearing of fez banned because of fears that they might be used to smuggle contraband). But see Abbott v. Smaller, 1990 WL 131359 (E.D. Pa. 1990) (awarding damages to a Muslim inmate after defendant refused to allow him to eat dinner when he would not remove his kufi, a Muslim religious headdress).

These cases cast serious doubt on earlier pre-*Shabazz* decisions that were more exacting in their analysis of rules restricting the wearing of head coverings in prison. See, e.g., Burgin v. Henderson, 536 F.2d 501 (2d Cir. 1976); Reinert v. Haas, 585 F. Supp. 477 (S.D. Iowa 1984) (permitting adherents of Native American religion to wear headbands where restriction was not shown to be a realistic threat to prison security).

[45]Lawson v. Dugger, 840 F.2d 781, 784 (11th Cir. 1987), judgment vacated on other grounds, 490 U.S. 1078, 109 S. Ct. 2096, 104 L. Ed. 2d 658 (1989); Martin v. Lane, 1992 WL 14111 (N.D. Ill. 1992); Sample v. Borg, 675 F. Supp. 574, 581 (E.D. Cal. 1987), judgment vacated on other grounds, 870 F.2d 563 (9th Cir. 1989).

[46]See, e.g., Hall v. Bellmon, 935 F.2d 1106, 19 Fed. R. Serv. 3d 1217 (10th Cir. 1991) (regulation banning the possession of a religious sharp bear tooth necklace upheld on the ground that it could be used as a weapon); Rowland v. Jones, 452 F.2d 1005 (8th Cir. 1971).

§ 6:9   Rights of Prisoners, Third Edition

types of headgear that could not conceal contraband or be identified with gangs.

§ 6:10 —Meals

The right to a religious diet has been the source of much litigation over the years. The reason for this is that a number of religions require their members to follow a rigid dietary code, which prisons often do not honor.[1] Perhaps the most familiar dietary requirements, and the ones most frequently litigated, involve the Jewish and Muslim faiths. A kosher[2] diet is a firm mandate of Orthodox Judaism; Muslims also must follow religious food practices and are prohibited from eating pork. Other lesser known religions also have dietary laws that inmates are not able to follow if they are limited to standard prison fare.[3] Although a number of prison systems voluntarily provide these diets to prisoners, many have refused to do so.

The question of whether prisons are constitutionally required to honor requests for special religious diets has always been a controversial one. On the one hand, these diets are a matter of central importance to sin-

---

[Section 6:10]

[1] However, some states, such as New York, have codified rules that mandate that prisoners be provided with a diet which satisfies their religious requirements. NY Comp Codes Rules & Reg tit 9f, § 7024.6.

[2] A restriction on a Jewish adherent's diet that not only limits what one can eat, but also regulates the manner in which food is prepared; e.g., animals must be slaughtered in conformity with Jewish rituals; meat and dairy products may not be prepared or eaten together; there must be separate dishes for meat and dairy foods, etc.

[3] See Benjamin v. Coughlin, 708 F. Supp. 570, 571 (S.D. N.Y. 1989), aff'd, 905 F.2d 571 (2d Cir. 1990) (disapproved of by, Frazier v. Dubois, 922 F.2d 560 (10th Cir. 1990)) (court held that defendants were not required to provide an "Ital" diet for Rastafarians; Ital diet involves abstaining from meat, liquor, and caffeine and eating only natural foods); but see LaFevers v. Saffle, 936 F.2d 1117 (10th Cir. 1991) (Seventh Day Adventists allowed a vegetarian diet even though religion does not mandate such a diet).

cere adherents of religions that require them. Thus, the claim for a religious diet invokes an understandable empathy from the courts. Without these diets, an inmate's ability to practice his or her religion in prison is severely compromised. On the other hand, meeting the demand can impose administrative and budgetary headaches on prison officials that can exceed those involved in meeting other religious needs of inmates.[4]

Initially, the courts were not notably receptive to these claims. Before the mid-1970s, there were a series of opinions that denied the right of Muslim and Jewish prisoners to a religious diet. These opinions stressed the costs involved, the security risks posed by individual treatment of food that could lead to smuggling, and the danger of provoking claims of favoritism if some inmates were granted such a significant privilege.[5]

However, the trend was reversed in 1975 by the Second Circuit's influential ruling in *Kahane v Carlson*.[6] In *Kahane,* the court ruled that plaintiff, an Orthodox Jewish rabbi, was entitled to a kosher diet while confined. The court observed that the Jewish dietary laws "are an important, integral part of the covenant between the Jewish people and the God of Israel.[7] For this reason, the prison was required not to "unnecessarily prevent Kahane's observation of his dietary obligations.[8] Since there were only a dozen or so Orthodox Jews in the prison and since other prisons in the area were able to accommodate kosher diets, the

---

[4]For a discussion on the benefits of offering Kosher meals to Jewish inmates see, Jamie Aron Forman, Note: Jewish Prisoners and Their First Amendment Right to a Kosher Meal: An Examination of the Relationship Between Prison Dietary Policy and Correctional Goals, 65 Brooklyn L. Rev. 477 (1999).

[5]See, e.g., Walker v. Blackwell, 411 F.2d 23 (5th Cir. 1969); U.S. v. Huss, 394 F. Supp. 752 (S.D. N.Y. 1975), order vacated on other grounds, 520 F.2d 598 (2d Cir. 1975); Cochran v. Sielaff, 405 F. Supp. 1126 (S.D. Ill. 1976).

[6]Kahane v. Carlson, 527 F.2d 492 (2d Cir. 1975).

[7]*Id.* at 495.

[8]*Id.*

§ 6:10   Rights of Prisoners, Third Edition

court ruled that the administrative problems associated with providing Kahane with a kosher diet were "surmountable.[9] The prison, however, was left to decide for itself how to provide the required food, as long as it gave "a diet sufficient to sustain the prisoner in good health without violating the Jewish dietary laws. "[10]

Kahane gives inmates a right to a religious diet unless the cost is "prohibitive" or "administratively unfeasible.[11] It does not seem to matter whether claims of denial of a religious diet are analyzed under *Shabazz* or under the compelling interest/least restrictive means standard. If a religious diet is not extravagant to provide and if the request can be handled without significant administrative difficulty, then under either *Shabazz* or RLUIPA, it ought to be provided. By parity of reasoning, if the costs associated with the diet are exorbitant or the administrative barriers formidable, the diet may be denied.

A good example of this is the Ninth Circuit's decision in *Ashelman v. Warzaszek*.[12] Ashelman, an Orthodox Jew, requested a kosher diet. Prison officials provided one kosher meal per day but the other two meals were non-kosher. The trial court found that it would be unfeasible to provide two additional frozen kosher meals for Orthodox Jewish prisoners per day, as it would require either the construction of a separate kosher kitchen, or the purchase of expensive frozen, kosher meals.[13] On appeal, Ashelman argued that the RFRA should govern. The Ninth Circuit found it unnecessary to apply the RFRA, as it found that the prison's actions where not even constitutional under the less

---

[9]*Id.*

[10]The court refused to order that frozen dinners be supplied to Kahane. *Id.* at 496.

[11]Benjamin v. Coughlin, 905 F.2d 571, 579 (2d Cir. 1990).

[12]Ashelman v. Wawrzaszek, 111 F.3d 674 (9th Cir. 1997), as amended, (Apr. 25, 1997).

[13]*Id.* at 676.

§ 6:10

stringent *Shabazz* factors.[14] The Ninth Circuit held that the plaintiff provided adequate evidence that a kosher diet could be provided by supplementing fresh fruits and vegetables and other low-cost kosher products for the regular meals.[15] The court found that the denial of such a diet did not serve the prison's legitimate interests in providing a "simplified food service."[16]

Accordingly, courts have been willing to order the provision of a religious diet to inmates when the costs associated with it are not overwhelming[17] and where prison officials could offer no rational purpose for denying it.[18] Where the showing cannot be made, however,

---

[14]*Id.* at 677.

[15]*Id.*

[16]*Id.* at 677-78. See also, Ward v. Hatcher, 172 F.3d 61 (9th Cir. 1999); Washington v. Garcia, 977 F. Supp. 1067 (S.D. Cal. 1997) (plaintiff sued prison officials who refused to give the plaintiff a special diet for Ramadan while he was confined in administrative segregation; court denied defendants' motion for summary judgment in analyzing the claim under RFRA; defendants moved for reconsideration in light of the Supreme Court's decision in Boerne, but the court denied the motion, holding that there was no rational relationship between the denial and furthering legitimate penological goals); Jenkins v. Angelone, 948 F. Supp. 543 (E.D. Va. 1996) (exorbitant cost and health concerns in the prison setting are compelling interests for denying a vegan diet under RFRA).

[17]Benjamin v. Coughlin, 905 F.2d 571, 579 (2d Cir. 1990) (disapproved of by, Frazier v. Dubois, 922 F.2d 560 (10th Cir. 1990)); McElyea v. Babbitt, 833 F.2d 196, 198 (9th Cir. 1987) ("Inmates . . . have the right to be provided food sufficient to sustain them in good health that satisfies the dietary laws of their religion. . ."); Ross v. Coughlin, 669 F. Supp. 1235, 1243 (S.D. N.Y. 1987) ("the state's obligation to provide an adequate kosher diet is a clearly established constitutional right"); Young v. Lane, 733 F. Supp. 1205 (N.D. Ill. 1990), rev'd on other grounds, 922 F.2d 370 (7th Cir. 1991) (kosher meals required for Jewish inmates).

[18]An example of an irrational denial is found in the case of LaFevers v. Saffle, 936 F.2d 1117 (10th Cir. 1991). In that case a Seventh Day Adventist was denied a vegetarian diet he claimed was a necessity of his faith because prison officials asserted that the diet was nutritionally inadequate. In response, the inmate

§ 6:10

courts have denied requests for religious diets. Thus, in *Kahey v Jones*,[19] the court rejected a prisoner's demand that she be provided a religious diet of "regular meals consisting of eggs, fruit and vegetables served with shells or peels, on paper plates.[20] The prisoner, who was a Muslim, had already been given a pork-free diet by the prison, but she claimed that this was inadequate because her religion forbade not only eating pork, but also consuming food that was cooked with utensils that had come into contact with pork. The diet she requested was designed to ensure that all the food she received was not contaminated. The court held that the administrative costs associated with complying with this demand were prohibitive, and would, if ordered, convert the prison's food service system into a "full scale restaurant."[21]

In making the judgment that *Kahane* requires of whether to grant or deny a request for a religious diet, a court must carefully scrutinize the reasons defendants offer for refusing to supply it. If the rationale does not stand up to careful inquiry, the court will reject it. *Hanafa v Murphy*[22] is a good example of this analysis. In *Hanafa*, a Muslim inmate in punitive segregation complained that he had been given food contaminated with pork. Although the food that was sent to him from

---

submitted evidence that the American Dietetic Association considered a vegetarian diet healthful. With this showing, the court held that a factfinder could conclude that the restriction was illogical. LaFevers v. Saffle, 936 F.2d 1117, 1119-20 (10th Cir. 1991).

[19]Kahey v. Jones, 836 F.2d 948 (5th Cir. 1988).

[20]*Id.* at 949.

[21]*Id.* at 950. See also Martinelli v. Dugger, 817 F.2d 1499, 1507 (11th Cir. 1987) (failure to provide full kosher diet was rationally related to "goal of avoiding excessive administrative expenses"); Udey v. Kastner, 805 F.2d 1218 (5th Cir. 1986) (special diets of organically grown produce washed in distilled water was not required where costs of providing it were over $15,000 per year and where granting the request would give rise to many fraudulent or exaggerated claims for similar treatment).

[22]Hunafa v. Murphy, 907 F.2d 46 (7th Cir. 1990).

§ 6:10 FIRST AMENDMENT: RELIGION

the prison kitchen contained a pork substitute, the pork was not physically removed from the tray. The defendants conceded that this practice made it likely that the pork-free portion of the meal would be infected with the pork portion but argued that it was administratively infeasible to alter the practice.

Judge Posner, writing for the Seventh Circuit, reversed the grant of summary judgment in favor of the defendants. Since "a prisoner is entitled to practice his religion insofar as doing so does not unduly burden the administration of the prison,"[23] Judge Posner refused to accept the defendants' arguments glibly and, instead, closely examined each.

On examination, none of the defendants' rationales for denying the plaintiff the diet his religion required was sufficiently apparent to warrant summary judgment. The defendants' assertion that it was inconvenient to make up trays with no pork on them was dismissed by the court as "trivial," since there were no more than eleven inmates who wished to have a pork-free meal.[24] The court also ruled that the validity of the defendants' argument that meeting the plaintiff's needs would cause hostility toward Muslims was not readily apparent, since what the plaintiff was requesting was not a major concession. Finally, the evidence submitted by the defendants did not factually support the danger of smuggling.[25] Without "a far more taxing" demand on the defendants' resources and "without detailed objections based on cost and feasibility," the court ruled that summary judgment was improper.[26]

To prevail on a claim for a religious diet, therefore, it is necessary for an inmate to show that his or her desire

---

[23]*Id.* at 47.

[24]*Id.*

[25]*Id.*

[26]*Id.* at 47-48. Judge Posner thus distinguished the record in *Hanafa* from that in Kahey v. Jones, 836 F.2d 948 (5th Cir. 1988).

§ 6:10   Rights of Prisoners, Third Edition

is sincere,[27] that there is no reasonable alternative to the requested diet,[28] that the cost involved and the administrative and security burdens imposed by granting the request are not excessive, and that without the diet he or she cannot obtain proper nourishment and still comply with the mandates of his or her religion.

One proposal made for dealing with the problem of offering religious diets to inmates is to offer the choice of up to three diets to all inmates regardless of religion.[29] The benefit to this approach is that it would prevent officials from having to decide the sincerity of an inmate's religious beliefs and would prevent the feeling that some inmates were being favored over others.[30] The author of this proposal points out that some states follow this policy without extravagant costs by offering a vegetarian, no pork, and regular food line.[31]

Several additional, and subsidiary, points are worth mentioning here. One is that unequal treatment in the provision of special diets is prohibited by equal protection considerations. If, for example, kosher food is made available to Jewish inmates in a prison, the prison may not arbitrarily fail to satisfy the needs of Muslim inmates by refusing to provide them with a protein

---

[27]Johnson v. Moore, 948 F.2d 517 (9th Cir. 1991) (claim for religious diet properly dismissed where plaintiff did not present proof that his vegetarianism was "rooted in his religious beliefs").

[28]Spies v. Voinovich, 173 F.3d 398, 1999 FED App. 137P (6th Cir. 1999) (Zen Buddhist prisoner was not entitled to a Vegan diet where the religion only required a vegetarian diet and such diet was offered by the prison; court made it clear that it was making its decision based on the reasonable alternative test of Turner and not the fact that the Vegan diet was not a central tenet of the inmate's religion).

[29]See Developments in the Law, The Law of Prisons: IV. In the Belly of the Whale: Religious Practice in Prison, 115 Harv. L. Rev. 1891, 1906-09 (2002).

[30]Id. at 1906-09.

[31]Id.

substitute for pork.[32] Another point is that prison officials who undertake to provide a religious diet to inmates will not be liable for a single instance of denial of these meals.[33] Additionally, prison officials, in cases of special holidays where religious meals are consumed, may meet their constitutional obligation to accommodate prisoners' needs by permitting inmates to purchase the provisions at their own expense.[34] Finally, inmates may not be punished for refusing to work with food that they are forbidden by their religion to handle.[35]

§ 6:11 —Religious Services

Congregate services are the hallmark of most religions.[1] Group religious rites are an opportunity for like-minded adherents of a faith to come together on a regular basis and, with clergy present and officiating, express their commitment to the tenets of their faith.[2] In the prison context, religious services, at least for conventional religions and for prisoners in the general

---

[32]U.S. ex rel. Wolfish v. Levi, 439 F. Supp. 114 (S.D. N.Y. 1977), order aff'd, 573 F.2d 118 (2d Cir. 1978) and judgment rev'd on other grounds, 441 U.S. 520, 99 S. Ct. 1861, 60 L. Ed. 2d 447 (1979).

[33]Muhammad v. McMickens, 708 F. Supp. 607 (S.D. N.Y. 1989).

[34]Al-Alamin v. Gramley, 926 F.2d 680 (7th Cir. 1991) (permitting Muslims the right to purchase, at their own expense, commercially prepared and packaged food for Ramadan and the feast of Eid-Ul-Fitr satisfied the Constitution).

[35]Chapman v. Pickett, 586 F.2d 22 (7th Cir. 1978) (violation of the First and Eighth Amendments to require Muslim to handle pork); Franklin v. Lockhart, 890 F.2d 96 (8th Cir. 1989) (allegation that plaintiff was required to handle manure and dead animals in his work assignment, contrary to Muslim beliefs, stated a constitutional claim); Hayes v. Long, 72 F.3d 70 (8th Cir. 1995) (reversing summary judgment for prison officials where a Muslim inmate was forced to handle pork as part of his kitchen duties).

[Section 6:11]

[1]Wilson v. Beame, 380 F. Supp. 1232, 1239 (E.D. N.Y. 1974).

[2]Id. See also Termunde v. Cook, 684 F. Supp. 255, 261 (D. Utah 1988) ("group religious experience is basic to an inmate's First Amendment Rights").

§ 6:11

population, have long been encouraged, in part in recognition of the value of religion in rehabilitating prisoners, in part in keeping with the historic religious roots of American prisons, and in part because officials have long acknowledged that regular religious services can actually enhance the security of an institution.[3]

However, religious services have posed real, and imagined, problems for prison administrators. In a prison setting, group activity of inmates can present risks of "altercations, illegal transactions and even rioting." Officials also may believe that it is possible that inmates will use religious services as a pretext for planning escapes or other prohibited activities. Officials may be concerned, as well, that the content of the services of some religions, in and of themselves, will constitute a threat to prison security, either because of the ideas expressed at the services or because the services are officiated by inmates serving as clergy. Moreover, there may be logistical problems in getting inmates together for worship if the number of inmates who profess a particular faith is small or spread throughout a facility. This, after all, was the reason why the Supreme Court in *Shabazz* held that Muslim inmates who worked outside of the prison could be prohibited from returning to the prison for Friday Jumu'ah services.[4] Finally, prison officials may attempt to prohibit services for inmates who are confined in special segregation units.

Because of these conflicting interests, courts have been asked to resolve a number of questions that concern religious services. Among the first prisoner rights cases were those that dealt with whether nonconventional religions, such as the Black Muslim faith,

---

[3]National Advisory Commn on Criminal Justice Standards & Goals Corrections 64 (1973).

[4]O'Lone v. Estate of Shabazz, 482 U.S. 342, 107 S. Ct. 2400, 96 L. Ed. 2d 282 (1987). The issue of when, if at all, work conflicts can be justified as reasons to exclude inmates from religious services is discussed in § 6:16.

First Amendment: Religion § 6:11

could have the same opportunity for holding congregate services as recognized faiths. The courts ruled that, consistent with the First Amendment or the Equal Protection Clause, these services could not be prohibited.[5] Although the courts ruled that Black Muslim services must be permitted, they set out two conditions for holding the services. First, prison authorities could monitor the services. Second, they could be canceled if the authority of the institution was defied at the service.[6]

The early prison cases clearly established a broad[7] right of prisoners in the general prison population to attend group religious services.[8] These cases, however,

---

[5]See, e.g., Knuckles v. Prasse, 302 F. Supp. 1036 (E.D. Pa. 1969), judgment aff'd, 435 F.2d 1255 (3d Cir. 1970); Cooper v. Pate, 382 F.2d 518 (7th Cir. 1967).

[6]Knuckles, 302 F Supp at 1058. While services may be monitored by prison guards for unlawful activity, one court has held that records of attendance may not be kept. Theriault v. Carlson, 339 F. Supp. 375 (N.D. Ga. 1972), vacated on other grounds and remanded, 495 F.2d 390 (5th Cir. 1974). But see, Freeman v. Arpaio, 125 F.3d 732 (9th Cir. 1997) (summary judgment for defendants reversed where defendants claimed services without the presence of an Imam would be cancelled, but other services where the Imam was present were also cancelled).

[7]Occasional or isolated failures to hold services are not actionable if, for example, they are the "result of the prison's attempt to accommodate the religious, social and recreational needs of the approximately 2,000 prisoners . . . within the resources available in a penal facility." Hadi v. Horn, 830 F.2d 779, 787-88 (7th Cir. 1987).

[8]Lawson v. Dugger, 840 F.2d 781, 786 (11th Cir. 1987), judgment vacated on other grounds, 490 U.S. 1078, 109 S. Ct. 2096, 104 L. Ed. 2d 658 (1989) (members of the Hebrew Israelite sect had a fundamental constitutional right to attend worship services which could not be denied by "bare" assertions that the prohibition was necessary to prevent potential violence.); Salahuddin v. Cuomo, 861 F.2d 40, 12 Fed. R. Serv. 3d 915 (2d Cir. 1988) (complaint of denial of right to attend religious services stated a claim for relief). See also, Developments in the Law, The Law of Prisons: IV. In the Belly of the Whale: Religious Practice in Prison, 115 Harv. L. Rev. 1891 (2002) (majority of prisons now allow inmates

§ 6:11   Rights of Prisoners, Third Edition

did not answer all the questions that are raised by recognition of this right. Recent cases have grappled with important questions about the nature of the right.

One such question is whether inmates themselves have the right to officiate at congregate services. Courts that have considered the question of inmate-led services have ruled that when outside clergy are available to conduct services, inmates have no right to officiate.[9] The reason is that granting prisoners positions of authority over other inmates can create significant security problems. "[C]onflicts might arise because inmates lacked the requisite religious expertise to resolve issues that arose during the religious meeting."[10] In addition, prisoner-led services could be used for gang meetings or for "dissemination of views interfering with order in the prison."[11]

Even if the prison permits some denominations to

---

to attend religious services regardless of their professed religion, and each recognized religion is given equal worship time; this approach keeps officials out of the business of deciding whose religious beliefs are sincere, and cuts down on litigation).

[9]Hadi v. Horn, 830 F.2d 779, 787-88 (7th Cir. 1987); Hobbs v. Pennell, 754 F. Supp. 1040, 1042 (D. Del. 1991) ("[W]here an inmate is permitted to act as Imam, this organizational structure results in a pyramid of power that has the inmate Imam at its apex."); Tisdale v. Dobbs, 807 F.2d 734 (8th Cir. 1986) ("outside sponsor" for Muslim services upheld where inmate led services in the past had become a "forum for advocating institutional mutiny" and where officials had made efforts to obtain a sponsor); Childs v. Duckworth, 705 F.2d 915 (7th Cir. 1983) (denial of Satanic services upheld where no outside sponsorship was proposed and no information was provided about what would take place at the services). Cf Johnson-Bey v. Lane, 863 F.2d 1308 (7th Cir. 1988); Anderson v. Angelone, 123 F.3d 1197 (9th Cir.1997) (concerns over the influence an inmate-minister might exert and the possibility that inmate-led services could mask gang activity were enough for prison-wide rule prohibiting inmate ministers).

[10]Hadi v. Horn, 830 F.2d 779, 787-88 (7th Cir. 1987).

[11]*Id.* Other security problems with inmate-led services credited by courts include the arguments that an inmate minister might have an incentive to be radical to attract membership, and that having an outside minister might aid in rehabilitation efforts.

First Amendment: Religion § 6:11

conduct services with inmate clergy, it may, if the belief structure of a particular religion is potentially threatening, prohibit inmate leadership of these services without running afoul of the Equal Protection Clause.[12] However, the distinction must be rational, and the ban on inmate-conducted services may not be enforced in an arbitrary or discriminatory manner.[13] If a prison chooses to forbid inmate-led services, it must make reasonable efforts to arrange for outside clergy to lead the services.[14]

An analogous question that has been litigated concerns the right of inmates to informally gather for religious prayers in the prison yard. That right has also been denied for reasons that are akin to those given for refusing to permit inmate-led formal services. The Third Circuit held that unsupervised informal group prayer, like formal group services, can give rise to "a leadership structure within the prison alternative to that provided by the lawful authorities."[15] Group prayer

---

Hobbs v. Pennell, 754 F. Supp. 1040, 1044 (D. Del. 1991). In addition, courts have accepted the idea that, without outside leadership, congregate meetings might be used for extortion or for the conduct of kangaroo courts. Benjamin v. Coughlin, 708 F. Supp. 570 (S.D. N.Y. 1989), aff'd, 905 F.2d 571 (2d Cir. 1990) (disapproved of by, Frazier v. Dubois, 922 F.2d 560 (10th Cir. 1990)).

[12]Hobbs v. Pennell, 754 F. Supp. 1040, 1045 (D. Del. 1991) (evidence presented that inmate-led services by members of the Nation of Islam were particularly disruptive and had in the past led to confrontations with prison personnel).

[13]Johnson-Bey v. Lane, 863 F.2d 1308, 1312 (7th Cir. 1988).

[14]Johnson-Bey v. Lane, 863 F.2d 1308, 1312 (7th Cir. 1988) (inmates may not be given the "run-around" and prison officials may not delay or refuse to arrange for outsider to conduct services); Lane v. Griffin, 834 F.2d 403, 24 Fed. R. Evid. Serv. 46 (4th Cir. 1987) (Powell, J) (eight-month delay in arranging for a Muslim chaplain to conduct services may be actionable in damages if delay is not "reasonably related" to valid governmental interests). Whether the government must pay for these clergy is considered in § 6:12.

[15]Cooper v. Tard, 855 F.2d 125, 129 (3d Cir. 1988). See also Shabazz v. Coughlin, 852 F.2d 697, 701 (2d Cir. 1988) ("No deci-

can be forbidden even though other group activities like boxing, basketball, and discussion are permitted. There is no equal protection violation in this differentiation, because the permitted activities do not, as is the danger with group prayer meetings, involve "an organized, functioning alternative authority structure among inmates."[16]

Another interesting question is how discriminating prison officials need to be in defining the religion whose services are being offered. In other words, is it sufficient to hold "Christian" services, or must services for each Christian sect be arranged? Courts have tended to allow a broadly defined service to be sufficient, as long as there is a reasonable relationship between the service and the tenets of the subsidiary sect.[17] The rationale for this is that "the large number of religious groups represented in the prison population and such factors as security, staffing, and space" can make separate services for all groups logistically infeasible.[18]

Can prison administrators be required to allow inmates from far-flung corners of the institution to

---

sions in this circuit clearly foreshadow [the right to pray in the prison yard]. Nor are there cases in other circuits condemning or condoning such practices"). But see, Chatin v. Coombe, 186 F.3d 82 (2d Cir. 1999) (inmate was disciplined for praying in prison yard; court held the inmate's action could not be considered a religious service or religious speech as prohibited by a prison rule, therefore the rule was vague, and unconstitutional as applied).

[16]Cooper v. Tard, 855 F.2d 125, 130 (3d Cir. 1988).

[17]Clifton v. Craig, 924 F.2d 182 (10th Cir. 1991) (no requirement that Church of Christ services be held separately when there are services for Christians); Matiyn v. Commissioner Dept. of Corrections, 726 F. Supp. 42 (W.D. N.Y. 1989) (no denial of free exercise rights of Sunni Muslim when he is was to attend Muslim services with Shia Muslims); Weir v. Nix, 114 F.3d 817 (8th Cir. 1997) (fact that protestant minister conducted inclusive Protestant services, which were against inmate's exclusive beliefs, was not enough for the inmate to get a separate service, where the minister's beliefs mirrored the inmate's beliefs in all other respects).

[18]Clifton v. Craig, 924 F.2d 182, 185 (10th Cir. 1991).

gather together for services? In a well-reasoned opinion, the Sixth Circuit found that importance of the right to congregate religious services meant that administrators can be required to make this effort.[19] The court found that the security concerns regarding the movement of the inmates were manageable, and therefore that the prohibition on services was an exaggerated response by prison officials that could not stand.[20]

The discussion thus far has dealt with the right of inmates in the general prison population to have group religious services. A highly controversial question that arises frequently concerns another group of inmates: those who are held in segregation units either for their own protection or for disciplinary reasons. Can they be permitted to attend religious services?

Problems arise with segregated inmates that do not occur with inmates in the normal prison population. The difficulty is caused by the fact that the central purpose of punitive and protective segregation units is to isolate inmates from the rest of the prison population. That goal is compromised when segregated prisoners are permitted to attend normal group religious services. However, inmates in segregated units, no less than their compatriots in the general population, have a constitutional right to practice their religion while

---

[19]Whitney v. Brown, 882 F.2d 1068 (6th Cir. 1989).

[20]*Id.* at 1078. Whitney dealt with a request by Jewish inmates that they be allowed to gather together for Passover services once each year and weekly for Sabbath services. The inmates had differing security classifications and, for that reason, were not normally allowed to mingle with one another. However, for 45 years before the recently imposed security classifications had been implemented, the prison had allowed the few Jewish inmates to come together for Sabbath services. The court closely examined the security justifications put forward by the defendants and found that none of them justified the denial of the plaintiffs' rights to attend services. The court pointed out that the defendants' arguments amounted to a claim that "any time the normal routine of an institution is altered the good order and security of that facility are potentially compromised. . . .. The fact remains that prison officials do not set constitutional standards by fiat." *Id.* at 1074.

incarcerated. It would be obviously impermissible for prison officials to deliberately punish segregated inmates by depriving them of the right to attend religious services.[21] But a different question is raised when security justifications are cited instead as the reason for this denial.

In cases dealing with access to religious services for inmates who have been placed in disciplinary segregation as punishment for having committed prison offenses, courts have reached mixed conclusions. Some courts have upheld a blanket refusal to permit any inmates held in these units to attend services.[22] These cases have tended to rely on the fact that prison officials have made optional methods of practicing religion available to inmates in segregation.[23] However, the better reasoned decisions hold that a universal denial of attendance at religious services to all inmates in punitive segregation, without any individual consideration of the security dangers of each inmate, is unconstitutional.[24] These cases require an individual "determination as to the necessity of [an inmate's]

---

[21]Beck v. Lynaugh, 842 F.2d 759, 761 (5th Cir. 1988); Mawhinney v. Henderson, 542 F.2d 1, 3 (2d Cir. 1976).

[22]See, e.g., Matiyn v. Henderson, 841 F.2d 31, 37 (2d Cir. 1988) (exclusion of inmate in punitive segregation from congregate religious services was reasonably related to valid penological goals); Aliym v. Miles, 679 F. Supp. 1 (W.D. N.Y. 1988) (denial of congregate religious services to prisoner who was sentenced to one year in disciplinary segregation was reasonable).

[23]McDonald v. Hall, 579 F.2d 120 (1st Cir. 1978); Sharp v. Sigler, 408 F.2d 966 (8th Cir. 1969). This trend, however, is by no means universal. In both Matiyn v. Henderson, 841 F.2d 31 (2d Cir. 1988) and Aliym v. Miles, 679 F. Supp. 1 (W.D. N.Y. 1988) the courts denied attendance at services without any discussion of alternative means for the inmate to meet his religious needs.

[24]LaReau v. MacDougall, 473 F.2d 974, 979 (2d Cir. 1972); Mawhinney, 542 F2d at 3 ("not every prisoner in segregation can be excluded from chapel services; because not all segregated prisoners are potential troublemakers, the prison authorities must make some discrimination among them"); Beck v Lynaugh, 842 F2d 759 (5th Cir 1988).

exclusion" from the services.[25]

Prisoners in protective custody present a similar, although somewhat different, situation from inmates in punitive segregation. Like inmates in punitive segregation, they have been separated from the normal prison population. Unlike inmates in punitive segregation, however, they are usually placed in segregation through no fault of their own but because they cannot be protected if they are confined with the normal prison population. Moreover, unlike the normal situation for inmates in punitive segregation, who are sent to segregation for a defined term, inmates remain in protective custody indefinitely, as long as there is danger to them in the general population.

For these reasons, courts have tended to closely examine the reasons given for the denial of religious services to inmates in protective custody and have pressed prison officials to develop measures that permit these inmates, whenever possible, to attend services,[26] and have required that meaningful alternatives to services be offered in cases where inmates cannot attend services.[27] Only if the record indicates that a presence at religious services of an inmate in protective custody

---

[25]Mawhinney v. Henderson, 542 F.2d 1, 3 (2d Cir. 1976). See also, Alston v. DeBruyn, 13 F.3d 1036 (7th Cir. 1994) (district court abused its discretion in dismissing inmate's claim of denial of the opportunity to attend religious services based only on the fact that he was held in administrative segregation).

[26]Young v. Coughlin, 866 F.2d 567, 570 (2d Cir. 1989) ("we have long held that prisoners should be afforded every reasonable opportunity to attend religious services, whenever possible"). But see, Salahuddin v. Jones, 992 F.2d 447, 25 Fed. R. Serv. 3d 898 (2d Cir. 1993) (prohibiting inmate in punitive segregation from attending congregate services not contrary to *Young* where the inmate presented a security risk and he was allowed the solitary practice of his religion).

[27]Thus, in Williams v. Lane, 851 F.2d 867, 877-78, 11 Fed. R. Serv. 3d 753 (7th Cir. 1988) the Seventh Circuit held that the holding of a single "non-denominational service" in the protective custody unit was an "inadequate and needlessly inferior alternative" for meeting the inmates' free exercise rights. See also Young

§ 6:11   Rights of Prisoners, Third Edition

would present serious security problems have courts upheld the restriction.[28] In addition, the restriction can remain in place only as long as security interests legitimately require it.[29] In cases where the restriction is upheld, courts have stressed the need for providing inmates with an alternative means of meeting the need for religious services.[30] An equivalent analysis should be applied when the denial of access to religious ser-

---

v. Coughlin, 866 F.2d 567 (2d Cir. 1989) (denial of religious services for inmate in "limited privilege program" could not be upheld unless the defendants justified reason for the exclusion).

[28]Stroud v. Roth, 741 F. Supp. 559 (E.D. Pa. 1990) (upholding denial of access to religious services for protective custody inmate who was placed in segregation for protection after he had attacked the inmate Imam and after he received threats from other inmates); Bellamy v. McMickens, 692 F. Supp. 205 (S.D. N.Y. 1988) (denial of access to services to inmate who was in protection because he was informer in organized crime case upheld); Termunde v. Cook, 684 F. Supp. 255, 259, 262 (D. Utah 1988) (temporary denial of religious services for all inmates in protective custody unit upheld when evidence showed serious security problems in the unit, including "[f]ires and throwing of debris at officers"); Tyler v. Rapone, 603 F. Supp. 268 (E.D. Pa. 1985); Jones v. Stine, 843 F. Supp. 1186 (W.D. Mich. 1994) (inmate in protective custody voluntarily; court held no First Amendment violation in prohibiting attendance at a religious service where there were legitimate security concerns).

[29]Termunde v. Cook, 684 F. Supp. 255, 263 (D. Utah 1988) (if security reasons no longer justify restriction, it will be struck down because "fossilized policy cannot be a rationale for contemporary restriction").

[30]Griffin v. Coughlin, 743 F. Supp. 1006 (N.D. N.Y. 1990) (holding that inmates were entitled to private meaningful religious meetings with religious advisors in a private meeting room); Stroud v. Roth, 741 F. Supp. 559, 562 (E.D. Pa. 1990) (inmate permitted to watch closed circuit television or videotapes of the prison service); Bellamy v. McMickens, 692 F. Supp. 205, 215 (S.D. N.Y. 1988) (alternative means included visits by ministers and bible study classes); McCabe v. Arave, 626 F. Supp. 1199 (D. Idaho 1986), judgment aff'd in part, vacated in part on other grounds, 827 F.2d 634 (9th Cir. 1987) (protective custody inmate could be denied permission to attend service of a particular denomination if he was permitted to attend interdenominational service).

vices is brought about because of a prison wide lockdown, during which inmate activity is suspended throughout the facility.[31]

§ 6:12 —Name Changes

Converts to a new religion often signal their conversion by changing their names. In the Muslim faith particularly, while not essential, a name change is encouraged and frequently made. Muslim converts who change their names do so because they "find their previous names religiously offensive . . . [as] a sign or mark of a spiritually unenlightened state which they have transcended."[1] This viewpoint is hardly unique to the Muslim faith. There is a nearly universal understanding of the significance of name changes. As Judge Heaney of the Eighth Circuit explained:

A personal name is special. It may honor the memory of a

---

[31]Divers v. Department of Corrections, 921 F.2d 191 (8th Cir. 1990) (allegation of denial of all religious services to inmates in "lockdown" status stated a constitutional claim; defendants were required to show a justifiable rationale for the restriction); Martin v. Lane, 766 F. Supp. 641 (N.D. Ill. 1991) (denial of summary judgment where defendants presented no evidence justifying denial of services during lockdown). See also Bruscino v. Carlson, 854 F.2d 162, 166 (7th Cir. 1988) (denial of religious services to inmates in highest security institution in federal prison system justified by the "extraordinary security problems at the prison"); Ra Chaka v. Franzen, 727 F. Supp. 454 (N.D. Ill. 1989) (reclassification of facility following lockdown into three separate security units justified suspension of normal Muslim religious services where each individual unit was permitted to have its own Muslim services). Cf. Pedraza v. Meyer, 919 F.2d 317 (5th Cir. 1990) (convicted prisoners awaiting transfer to state prison were considered "high escape risks" and are properly excluded from congregate services for the general population, when they were offered services in the "security vestibule" of their cell block).

[Section 6:12]

[1]Salaam v. Lockhart, 856 F.2d 1120, 1121 (8th Cir. 1988). See also Azeez v. Fairman, 604 F. Supp. 357, 362 (C.D. Ill. 1985), judgment rev'd on other grounds, 795 F.2d 1296 (7th Cir. 1986) (new names "reflect [inmate's] new spiritual identities and the type of lives they hope to lead").

loved one, reflect a deep personal commitment, show respect or admiration for someone famous or worthy or as in this case reflect a reverence for God and God's teachings. Like a baptism, bar mitzvah, or confirmation, the adoption of a new name may signify a conversion and the acceptance of responsibilities of membership in a community.[2]

Sometimes, however, prison officials have refused to honor a prisoner's name change, adhering instead to a "committed name" policy. Under that policy, the only name that the prison recognizes is the one the inmate had when he or she was committed to the institution. Given the almost total control exerted over prisoners, the refusal to acknowledge a prisoner's name change can have serious repercussions, ranging from the failure to use the new name when the inmate is addressed by prison guards to the more serious denial of important services such as mail delivery, access to the law library, or sick call. Indeed, in some cases, inmates have been subjected to stern punishment for insisting on using their new names.

When prison officials decline to recognize an inmate's new name, courts have been confronted with the need to determine the extent to which a prisoner's religiously motivated change of name is entitled to constitutional protection. While the litigation that has arisen on this subject has not answered all of the questions, some principles are now well-established. One is that an inmate's adoption of a new name for religious purposes "is part of the practice of their religious faith."[3] However, this is only the first step in the analysis, since,

---

[2]Salaam v. Lockhart, 905 F.2d 1168, 1170 (8th Cir. 1990).

[3]Masjid Muhammad-D. C. C. v. Keve, 479 F. Supp. 1311, 1323 (D. Del. 1979). See also Salaam v. Lockhart, 905 F.2d 1168 (8th Cir. 1990); Ali v. Dixon, 912 F.2d 86, 90 (4th Cir. 1990) (First Amendment protects an inmate's right to legal recognition of an adopted religious name"); Felix v. Rolan, 833 F.2d 517, 518 (5th Cir. 1987) ("The adoption of Muslim names by inmates practicing that religion is generally recognized to be an exercise of both First Amendment speech and religious freedom"); Barrett v. Com. of Va., 689 F.2d 498 (4th Cir. 1982) ("Virginia does not dispute that a

§ 6:12

as we have seen,[4] a finding that First Amendment interests of prisoners are implicated does not necessarily mean restrictions on those interests are unconstitutional. To determine the extent to which religious freedom is protected in a prison environment, one also must use the *Shabazz* test to balance the right to practice religion against the governmental interests that are claimed to justify restrictions on the right.

Various state interests have been raised to explain prisons' committed name policies. Prison administrators have argued that such policies are administratively convenient, prevent misidentification of inmates, combat fraud, and avoid confrontations between inmates and staff. Courts, however, have uniformly rejected these arguments as too broadly sweeping when used to justify a stance that gives absolutely no recog-

---

change of name may be a religious exercise protected by the First Amendment.").

It should be noted that the First Amendment is involved even if the inmate's religion does not make this an essential practice. Masjid Muhammad-D. C. C. v. Keve, 479 F. Supp. 1311, 1323 (D. Del. 1979). See also § 6:6.

Whether an inmate needs to have a judicially approved change of name to trigger the protections of the First Amendment is not entirely clear, and depends to some extent on the law of each state. Some states recognize a common law right to change one's name without a court order. When that is the case, one court held that the First Amendment right to use the new name applies even if the inmate has not obtained judicial approval for the name change. Masjid Muhammad-D. C. C. v. Keve, 479 F. Supp. 1311, 1322 n13 (D. Del. 1979). However, other courts disagree. Azeez v. Fairman, 795 F.2d 1296, 1299 (7th Cir. 1986) (upholding refusal to honor name changes that were not judicially approved; judicial approval is necessary to protect prison officials from "capricious, incessant, casual, and sudden on the spot name changes"). See also Salahuddin v. Coughlin, 591 F. Supp. 353 (S.D. N.Y. 1984) (requiring a court ordered name change when the evidence established that plaintiff did not use his Muslim name consistently and had used several different Muslim names at his whim).

[4]See § 6:3.

§ 6:12   RIGHTS OF PRISONERS, THIRD EDITION

nition to an inmate's new name.[5]

"It does not follow, however, that plaintiffs are entitled to have the institution and its staff utilize their Muslim names for all purposes."[6] A blanket committed name policy sweeps too broadly. Yet it remains possible that there are particular applications of the committed name policy that are legitimate reasonable responses to prison needs. Thus, courts must examine each individual application of a committed name policy to determine whether that application is justifiable. This analysis as to what interests officials may cite for not recognizing a name change seems to apply where the compelling interest/least restrictive means standard governs.[7]

Utilizing this approach, courts have consistently held that there is no valid governmental purpose served by withholding benefits that would otherwise be available to an inmate merely because he or she refuses to use his or her old name. Thus, a prison may not refuse to deliver mail to an inmate because it is addressed with the prisoner's new name or deny an inmate a visitor

---

[5]Barrett v. Com. of Va., 689 F.2d 498 (4th Cir. 1982) (state law which prohibited inmates from obtaining court-ordered name change was unconstitutionally overbroad); Azeez v. Fairman, 604 F. Supp. 357, 362 (C.D. Ill. 1985), judgment rev'd on other grounds, 795 F.2d 1296 (7th Cir. 1986); Masjid Muhammad-D. C. C. v. Keve, 479 F. Supp. 1311 (D. Del. 1979) (blanket prison "committed name" policy was unconstitutional); Matthews v. Morales, 23 F.3d 118 (5th Cir. 1994) (court upheld state's blanket prohibition on prisoner name changes as furthering a valid security interest).

[6]Masjid Muhammad-D. C. C. v. Keve, 479 F. Supp. 1311, 1323-24 (D. Del. 1979).

[7]Compare Fawaad v. Jones, 81 F.3d 1084 (11th Cir. 1996) (RFRA not violated where prison officials cited identification concerns in refusing to recognize an inmate's name change), with Malik v. Brown, 65 F.3d 148 (9th Cir. 1995) (officials violated RFRA where they refused to process inmate's mail under his changed name).

because the visitor uses the new name.[8] Moreover, an inmate cannot be denied access to other important services, such as "commissary, the law library, 'sick call,' the clothing room, religious activities and notary services" merely because he or she requests access to these services by using the new name.[9]

For similar reasons, some courts have gone further and held that "the state may not punish an inmate for failing to acknowledge a particular name or for failing to perform a task where to do so would involve the acknowledgment of a religiously offensive name."[10] Courts that have taken this step have made clear that this does not mean that an inmate cannot be punished for disregarding orders of prison staff or for acting disrespectfully toward prison staff.[11] However, it does mean that "an inmate may not be disciplined for his

---

[8]See, e.g., Salaam v. Lockhart, 905 F.2d 1168, 1170 (8th Cir. 1990) (mail must be delivered if addressed to inmate with his new name); Masjid Muhammad-D. C. C. v. Keve, 479 F. Supp. 1311 (D. Del. 1979).

[9]Azeez v. Fairman, 604 F. Supp. 357, 362 (C.D. Ill. 1985), judgment rev'd on other grounds, 795 F.2d 1296 (7th Cir. 1986). See also Ali v. Dixon, 912 F.2d 86 (4th Cir. 1990) (Muslim prisoner with new name could not be required to use his old name to withdraw money from his prison account); Moorish Science Temple of America, Inc. v. Benson, 86 F.3d 1159 (8th Cir. 1996) (officials could not forbid prisoners from adding a religiously motivated suffix to their name when signing for materials in conjunction with their prison numbers, as it would not be administratively unfeasible, nor would it implicate security concerns). But see Felix v. Rolan, 833 F.2d 517 (5th Cir. 1987) (prison records must contain the new name; however, prison officials could continue to require that inmate use his committed name as a method of identification when he seeks to use the law library).

[10]Azeez v. Fairman, 604 F. Supp. 357, 362 (C.D. Ill. 1985), judgment rev'd on other grounds, 795 F.2d 1296 (7th Cir. 1986).

[11]Masjid Muhammad-D. C. C. v. Keve, 479 F. Supp. 1311, 1325 (D. Del. 1979) ("Muslim inmates are [not] free to disregard orders whenever a member of the staff fails to address them by their Muslim names"); Salaam v. Lockhart, 905 F.2d 1168, 1170 (8th Cir. 1990) (existing policies give guards the right to discipline any inmate who did not follow orders).

§ 6:12   Rights of Prisoners, Third Edition

failure to *acknowledge* his non-Muslim name."[12]

The specific applications of the committed name policy that have caused the most difficulty for courts have involved prison records and prisoner name tags. The refusal to change prison records to reflect the inmate's new name has been defended on the grounds that it is administratively difficult, that it will lead to a flood of paperwork as more and more inmates change their names, and that it will cause confused records that will not be of assistance to other law enforcement agencies in the event that they have a need for an inmate's record; for example, in escape cases.[13]

In response to these concerns, courts have held that prison officials cannot be compelled to reorganize their files every time a prisoner changes his name. As the Fourth Circuit put it: "[h]ow prison officials choose to organize their records is a quintessential administrative matter in which the courts should not intervene."[14] A middle ground, however, between totally reorganizing prison files on the one hand, and ignoring a prisoner's new name on the other, has been found. This compromise proposal would:

> alter [the] "committed name" policy by an "also known as (a/k/a)" designation to the records of each inmate who changed his name for religious reasons during incarceration. Thus, instead of deleting the committed names from the records and uniforms and replacing them

---

[12]Azeez v. Fairman, 604 F. Supp. 357, 364 (C.D. Ill. 1985), judgment rev'd on other grounds, 795 F.2d 1296 (7th Cir. 1986). Accord, Masjid Muhammad-D. C. C. v. Keve, 479 F. Supp. 1311, 1324 (D. Del. 1979).

[13]See, e.g., Salaam v. Lockhart, 905 F.2d 1168, 1172-73 (8th Cir. 1990).

[14]Barrett v. Com. of Va., 689 F.2d 498, 503 (4th Cir. 1982). See also Ali v. Dixon, 912 F.2d 86, 89-90 (4th Cir. 1990); Imam Ali Abdullah Akbar v. Canney, 634 F.2d 339, 340 (6th Cir. 1980) ("We do not believe that any inmate has a constitutional right to dictate how prison officials keep their prison records."); Mujihadeen v. Compton, 627 F. Supp. 356 (W.D. Tenn. 1985) (no right to identification card that had only the new name on it); Spies v. Voinovich, 173 F.3d 398, 1999 FED App. 137P (6th Cir. 1999).

FIRST AMENDMENT: RELIGION § 6:12

with new names. . . the prison instead would add the new names as a/k/a's to the current files and name tags.[15]

This compromise does not force prison officials to either reorganize their files or add the inmate's new name whenever it is found in the file; rather, it simply requires the prison to supplement the files and name tags by adding the new name to them. The purpose of this policy is to ensure that the records make clear to anyone who uses them that the inmate has taken a new name. The administrative burden of implementing the a/k/a approach "while not imaginary, is nevertheless not onerous.[16] The feasibility of this approach is evidenced by the common practice of most prisons to record regularly all the aliases of an inmate.[17] Perhaps most important, the a/k/a compromise does not make the records difficult to find or to use in the event that they are needed by law enforcement agencies.[18] For these reasons, courts have ordered that the a/k/a approach be implemented.[19] Courts have recently held that where a dual name approach is used, the changed name should apply to all services and purposes within

---

[15]Salaam v. Lockhart, 856 F.2d 1120, 1122 (8th Cir. 1988) ("Salaam I"). See also, Fawaad v. Herring, 874 F. Supp. 350 (N.D. Ala. 1995), judgment aff'd, 81 F.3d 1084 (11th Cir. 1996).

[16]Salaam v. Lockhart, 905 F.2d 1168, 1173 (8th Cir. 1990) ("Salaam II") (less than one hour per inmate of prison clerical personnel time was required to make the changes necessary to implement this policy).

[17]Salaam v. Lockhart, 905 F.2d 1168, 1174 (8th Cir. 1990).

[18]*Id.* at 1173. ("Lockhart's claim that the prison would be unable to assist law enforcement agencies during escapes under the a/k/a alternative presumes either the elimination of the committed name or the forced reorganization of the prison's internal records under Salaam's new name. Neither is requested.").

[19]Salaam v. Lockhart, 905 F.2d 1168 (8th Cir. 1990); Azeez v. Fairman, 604 F. Supp. 357 (C.D. Ill. 1985), judgment rev'd on other grounds, 795 F.2d 1296 (7th Cir. 1986); Malik v. Brown, 65 F.3d 148 (9th Cir. 1995) (collecting cases).

§ 6:12 RIGHTS OF PRISONERS, THIRD EDITION

the prison.[20]

A similar a/k/a approach has been ordered for name tags. In a carefully reasoned decision, the Eighth Circuit held that fears of confrontation and misidentification did not justify a refusal to alter name tags. Since the a/k/a alternative helped guards identify and use the name that the inmate preferred, the a/k/a approach actually could help avoid misidentification, leading to a reduction in the number of confrontations between guards and staff[21] Although the court required the prison to add the new name to the prisoner's name tag, it held that it was not ordering the guards to address an inmate by his or her new name.[22] The court also held that guards remained free, in their discretion, to

---

[20]Hakim v. Hicks, 223 F.3d 1244 (11th Cir. 2000), cert. denied, 532 U.S. 932, 121 S. Ct. 1382, 149 L. Ed. 2d 307 (2001) (court found that prison officials failed to comply with a dual name policy, where the prisoner's name tag stated that the inmate's changed name applied only for notary purposes, and not to all services within the prison).

[21]Salaam v. Lockhart, 905 F.2d 1168, 1175-76 (8th Cir. 1990). Even if adding the new name to name tags did cause some confrontations, the court stated that it would still be unconstitutional not to make this change because "if the rights of those who would cooperate [by answering to their committed name] could be sacrificed in fear of those who would cause trouble under any regime, officials could ignore any individual right. Inmates do not abandon their rights to individualized judgments about their behavior." Salaam v. Lockhart, 905 F.2d 1168, 1175 (8th Cir. 1990). See also, Hakim v. Hicks, 223 F.3d 1244 (11th Cir. 2000), cert. denied, 532 U.S. 932, 121 S. Ct. 1382, 149 L. Ed. 2d 307 (2001).

[22]Salaam v. Lockhart, 905 F.2d 1168, 1175 (8th Cir. 1990). See also Ali v. Dixon, 912 F.2d 86, 90-91 (4th Cir. 1990) (citing "obvious difficulties present if prison staff must memorize a second name after having made the effort to learn the first"). Whether prison officials can be required to correspond with inmates using their new names remains an open question. Ali v. Dixon, 912 F.2d 86, 91 (4th Cir. 1990) (remanding to the district court for findings on this issue).

FIRST AMENDMENT: RELIGION § 6:13

continue to use an inmate's committed name.[23]

§ 6:13 —Access to Clergy

A prison may not be required to hire clergy of a particular faith.[1] Nevertheless, inmates of that faith will usually need the assistance of clergy to practice their religion in prison. If the prison does not have a chaplain on its staff who can service the population, the preferable way to meet this need is for outside clergy of that faith to enter the prison.[2] Volunteer clergy for this purpose are constitutionally entitled to visit inmates and to conduct services, unless it can be demonstrated that their presence poses a clear and present danger to security.[3] To make this determination, prison officials may require a visiting cleric to file a program state-

---

[23]Salaam v. Lockhart, 905 F.2d 1168, 1175 (8th Cir. 1990). In a cryptic aside, however, the *Salaam* court stated that it might have the power to order prison guards to address an inmate by his new religious name. The reason for this, the court stated, was that "[g]uards should not deliberately 'bait' inmates, and we cannot justify the prison policies on any such propensity. The imposition on the prison state would be clearly de minimis." Salaam v. Lockhart, 905 F.2d 1168, 1175 (8th Cir. 1990). The *Salaam* Court's ambiguity on this point surfaced in Bilal v. Davis, 918 F.2d 723 (8th Cir. 1990). In that case, an inmate was expelled from a disciplinary proceeding for refusing to respond to his committed name. The district court dismissed the complaint, but the Eighth Circuit, on the strength of *Salaam,* reversed and remanded for reconsideration. One judge concurred. He explained that he had some unease with [*Salaam*], and that he might be persuaded to ask the full Eighth Circuit to reconsider the validity of *Salaam* en banc. *Id.* at (Gibson, J, specially concurring).

[Section 6:13]

[1]See § 6:5.

[2]"No one thinks that a prison is required to excuse inmates to attend religious services outside the prison." Johnson-Bey v. Lane, 863 F.2d 1308, 1310 (7th Cir. 1988).

[3]Cooper v. Pate, 382 F.2d 518 (7th Cir. 1967); Saleem v. Evans, 866 F.2d 1313 (11th Cir. 1989) (allegation that prison refused to allow entry of Muslim Imam of Nation of Islam and only allowed Imam from American Muslim Mission stated a claim). One court has held that a cleric who was a convicted felon could be barred on

§ 6:13

ment that describes "the time, place and nature of the services to be conducted and identifying the clergy who will conduct them.[4] Moreover, visiting clergy are subject, as are all visitors, to searches for weapons or contraband, but courts have made clear that they cannot be harassed to discourage them from visiting.[5]

A more difficult question is whether prisoners can affirmatively compel the institution to provide the services of visiting clergy. The answer depends on whether the inmates themselves are permitted to conduct religious services, a topic considered earlier.[6] If they are not, then "the reasonableness of the ban on inmates conducting their own religious services is related to the availability of substitutes, whether chaplains employed by the prison or ministers invited on a visiting basis.[7]

In the absence of a paid prison chaplain to conduct services, the better reasoned approach is to hold that the prison is obligated to arrange for visiting clergy to

---

the ground that his presence in the facility constitutes a security threat. Johnson-Bey v. Lane, 863 F.2d 1308, 1311 (7th Cir. 1988) ("It [the prison] need not yield to their [the inmates'] desire to invite convicted felons, frocked or unfrocked, to conduct religious services in the prison.").

[4]Johnson-Bey v. Lane, 863 F.2d 1308, 1309 (7th Cir. 1988). See also Childs v. Duckworth, 705 F.2d 915, 921 (7th Cir. 1983). A prison could turn over the screening process to a "chaplaincy counsel" made up of representatives of religious organizations that provided clergy to the prison. Siddiqi v. Leak, 880 F.2d 904, 14 Fed. R. Serv. 3d 1059 (7th Cir. 1989).

[5]See, e.g., Finney v. Hutto, 410 F. Supp. 251 (E.D. Ark. 1976), judgment aff'd, 548 F.2d 740 (8th Cir. 1977), and judgment aff'd, 437 U.S. 678, 98 S. Ct. 2565, 57 L. Ed. 2d 522 (1978).

[6]See § 6:11.

[7]Johnson-Bey v. Lane, 863 F.2d 1308, 1311 (7th Cir. 1988). See also, Muhammad v. City of New York Dept. of Corrections, 126 F.3d 119 (2d Cir. 1997) (Nation of Islam ministers were hired by the department of corrections after the World Community of Islam approved them; where no ministers had been approved, court held there was no constitutional violation where inmates were permitted unlimited visits with individual spiritual advisors).

§ 6:13

officiate.[8] Whether the prison, in addition, must pay for the assistance of these clergy is an unresolved issue.[9] The absence of financial inducements, at least to the extent of providing reimbursement for travel expenses, has been termed "troubling" by one panel of the Seventh Circuit.[10] Another panel of the same court, however, expressed serious reservations about whether there should be such an entitlement.[11] Since this problem is likely to arise only with small minority sects, at least minimal reimbursement ought to be required if that is the only practical way that outside clergy can be induced to meet the religious needs of inmates who depend on them. Otherwise the prison would be guilty of "discrimination against minority sects,"[12] a result

---

[8]Johnson-Bey v. Lane, 863 F.2d 1308 (7th Cir. 1988); SapaNajin v. Gunter, 857 F.2d 463 (8th Cir. 1988) (rotation of different medicine men provided by the state was a constitutional way to meet the needs of a maximum number of Native American inmates). But see Young v. Lane, 922 F.2d 370, 377-78 (7th Cir. 1991); Reimers v. State of Or., 846 F.2d 561, 562 (9th Cir. 1988), opinion superseded, 863 F.2d 630 (9th Cir. 1988) ("a prisoner is not entitled to have the clergyman of his choice provided for him in the prison"); Thompson v. Com. of Ky., 712 F.2d 1078 (6th Cir. 1983) (failure to provide Muslim leader at state expense was not actionable); Blair-Bey v. Nix, 963 F.2d 162 (8th Cir. 1992) (denial of minister of particular sect not unconstitutional).

The statement that an inmate is not entitled to have a cleric of his choice, while no doubt true, sweeps too far if it is used, as it has been in some cases cited above, to suggest that the state is under no obligation to provide clergy at all.

[9]But see Johnson v. Moore, 948 F.2d 517 (9th Cir. 1991) (court held that the absence of a paid chaplain was not violative of plaintiff's right to "reasonable opportunity" to practice religion). If the prison has no obligation to provide a paid chaplain and if there is no affirmative duty to pay for a visiting chaplain, how can a court conclude that inmates have a "reasonable opportunity" to practice religion? This point is especially strong in situations where inmates are not allowed to conduct their own services.

[10]Johnson-Bey v. Lane, 863 F.2d 1308, 1312 (7th Cir. 1988).

[11]Young v. Lane, 922 F.2d 370, 377-78 (7th Cir. 1991).

[12]Johnson-Bey v. Lane, 863 F.2d 1308, 1312 (7th Cir. 1988).

§ 6:13   Rights of Prisoners, Third Edition

forbidden by the Equal Protection Clause.[13]

Access to clergy is especially important for inmates held in punitive or protective segregation. They often are not permitted to attend congregate services.[14] Therefore, for these persons clergy is essential if they are to have any exposure to a person trained in ministering to adherents of the faith.[15] The total deprivation of the assistance of clergy while in segregation would raise serious free exercise questions.[16] Furthermore, to ensure that meaningful spiritual counseling can take place, the right of access to clergy for segregated inmates includes the right to "truly private meetings."[17]

However, due to the need for increased security in

---

[13]Cruz v. Beto, 405 U.S. 319, 322, 92 S. Ct. 1079, 31 L. Ed. 2d 263 (1972) ("reasonable opportunities must be afforded to all prisoners to exercise the freedom guaranteed by the First and Fourteenth Amendments").

[14]See § 6:8. Sweet v. South Carolina Dept. of Corrections, 529 F.2d 854, 863 (4th Cir. 1975).

[15]See, e.g., Peterkin v. Jeffes, 661 F. Supp. 895 (E.D. Pa. 1987), decision aff'd in part and vacated in part on other grounds, 855 F.2d 1021 (3d Cir. 1988) (restriction on congregate services for inmates on death row was constitutional in part because inmates were permitted to receive visits from outside clergy).

[16]Apparently, prison officials recognize this entitlement, since there are no reported decisions in which a prison has urged that it would be constitutionally permissible to deny permanent access to clergy to segregated inmates. However, in cases of genuine emergencies, courts have upheld suspension of this right. Rogers v. Scurr, 676 F.2d 1211 (8th Cir. 1982).

[17]Griffin v. Coughlin, 743 F. Supp. 1006 (N.D. N.Y. 1990). In *Griffin*, the court held that since inmates in protective custody could not attend congregate services, they were entitled to have private unmonitored meetings with clergy and religious advisors in a private room available in the unit. The court held that there was no valid security rationale for depriving inmates of the "need for privacy in confidential communications between inmate and spiritual advisor." *Id.* at 1028. See also Card v. Dugger, 709 F. Supp. 1098 (M.D. Fla. 1988), judgment aff'd, 871 F.2d 1023 (11th Cir. 1989) (death watch inmates were permitted to have private, although noncontact, visits with clergy).

FIRST AMENDMENT: RELIGION § 6:14

segregation units, courts have allowed prisons to impose restrictions on access to clergy that are greater than those imposed on inmates in the general population, as long as access is permitted in a significant and essential way. Thus, a delay in providing access to a Catholic priest was upheld when the delay was brought about by a policy change that limited meetings between segregated inmates and clergy to those clergy who were on the prison staff even though general population inmates could visit with outside clergy.[18]

§ 6:14 —Access to Religious Mail and Publications

A corollary to the right of physical access to clergy is the right to correspond with outside clergy.[1] Although it might be argued that religious mail should be given greater protection than ordinary mail, as is the case with mail to the courts and attorneys,[2] courts have not so held. Religious mail, instead, is treated under the same constitutional standards that govern the receipt of all other non-confidential mail.[3] In other words, incoming and outgoing religious mail can be opened

---

[18]McClaflin v. Pearce, 743 F. Supp. 1381, 1385 (D. Or. 1990) ("Non-essential elements of a religion may be withheld from inmates in a disciplinary segregation unit, even though they are provided in the general population."); Allen v. Toombs, 827 F.2d 563 (9th Cir. 1987) (access for Native American in segregation was properly limited to a civilian religious assistant rather than an inmate assistant).

[Section 6:14]

[1]See, e.g., Murphy v. Missouri Dept. of Corrections, 814 F.2d 1252 (8th Cir. 1987); Cooper v. Pate, 382 F.2d 518 (7th Cir. 1967).

[2]For a discussion of the constitutional standards governing the censorship of prison mail, see Ch 13.

[3]Woods v. O'Leary, 890 F.2d 883, 885 (7th Cir. 1989) ("The mere fact that the [plaintiff's religion] may be a religion does not remove any venture [plaintiff] wishes to engage in from the prison officials' scrutiny"; therefore, rules governing bulk mailings applied to religious organizations); Valiant-Bey v. Morris, 829 F.2d 1441, 1443 (8th Cir. 1987); Murphy v. Missouri Dept. of Corrections, 814 F.2d 1252, 1256 (8th Cir. 1987).

§ 6:14

and read to determine whether a particular piece of mail poses a legitimate threat to institutional security.[4] If the incoming mail does not pose a threat to security, it must be delivered to the inmate. Even though religious mail is subject to inspection, it is not permissible to treat it in a more suspicious or restrictive manner than ordinary mail.[5]

The receipt of religious literature and publications from the outside is another means of practicing religion in prison. Attempts to censor this material have arisen most frequently with religions that make racial appeals. For instance, literature of the Black Muslim faith and of the Aryan Nations Church, which contain appeals directed exclusively to black and white inmates respectively, have been totally banned from prisons. The explanations offered for this exclusion is that these publications either appeal to racial hostility or make claims of racial superiority. Prison officials, therefore, argue that these materials are inherently threatening to the security of the prison.

Courts that have considered this question have uniformly refused to uphold bans of religious publications that sweep so broadly.[6] Because of the First Amendment right to believe whatever one wishes, "pris-

---

[4]Murphy v. Missouri Dept. of Corrections, 814 F.2d 1252, 1256 (8th Cir. 1987). See also George v. Sullivan, 896 F. Supp. 895 (W.D. Wis. 1995) (RFRA not violated where officials denied a white supremacist mail from the Church of Jesus Christ Christian, as the denial furthered a legitimate security interest). For a discussion of mail censorship practices, see Ch 13.

[5]Valiant-Bey v. Morris, 829 F.2d 1441, 1444 (8th Cir. 1987) (allegation that prison officials singled out and delayed delivery of mail sent by the Moorish Science Temple stated a claim of religious discrimination); McCabe v. Arave, 827 F.2d 634 (9th Cir. 1987) (prison could not artificially limit the number of religious publications inmates could receive).

[6]See, e.g., Lawson v. Dugger, 840 F.2d 781 (11th Cir. 1987), judgment vacated on other grounds, 490 U.S. 1078, 109 S. Ct. 2096, 104 L. Ed. 2d 658 (1989) (publications of Hebrew Israelite religion); Murphy v. Missouri Dept. of Corrections, 814 F.2d 1252, 1256 (8th Cir. 1987) (publications of the Aryan Nations Church of

FIRST AMENDMENT: RELIGION § 6:14

on authorities have no legitimate penological interest in excluding religious books . . . merely because they contain racist views.[7] For similar reasons, religious publications may not be banished merely because prison personnel find the ideas in them distasteful.[8] Instead, courts have ruled that restrictions on publications "must be limited to those materials that advocate violence or that are so racially inflammatory as to be reasonably likely to cause violence at the prison.[9] Some courts have banned all publications of the Muslim group the Five Percenters, as the group's insignia itself has been identified with gang activity.[10]

Jesus Christ Christian); McCabe v. Arave, 827 F.2d 634 (9th Cir. 1987) (publications of Church Jesus Christ Christian); Walker v. Blackwell, 411 F.2d 23 (5th Cir. 1969) (publications of Black Muslim faith).

[7]McCabe v. Arave, 827 F.2d 634, 638 (9th Cir. 1987).

[8]Lawson v. Dugger, 840 F.2d 781, 784 n1 (11th Cir. 1987), judgment vacated on other grounds, 490 U.S. 1078, 109 S. Ct. 2096, 104 L. Ed. 2d 658 (1989) ("It is not, however, the role of the court to evaluate these items by their effect upon the sensibilities of some persons.").

[9]Murphy v. Missouri Dept. of Corrections, 814 F.2d 1252, 1257 (8th Cir. 1987). See also McCabe v. Arave, 827 F.2d 634 (9th Cir. 1987) ("literature advocating racial purity, but not advocating violence or illegal activity as a means of achieving this goal, and not so racially inflammatory as to be reasonably likely to cause violence at the prison, cannot be constitutionally banned as rationally related to rehabilitation"). While material that does not fit this description may be provided, short delays in obtaining religious publications are not actionable. Quam v. Minnehaha County Jail, 821 F.2d 522 (8th Cir. 1987) (two-day delay in providing Bible did not violate the Constitution).

[10]See, e.g., Self-Allah v. Annucci, 1999 WL 299310 (W.D. N.Y. 1999) (the mere presence of the Five Percenter material implicated security concerns). But see, Graham v. Cochran, 96 Civ. 6166 2000 U.S. Dist. LEXIS 1477 (S.D.N.Y. February 14, 2000) (summary judgment for defendants denied where court found a total ban on Five Percenter material did reasonably relate to security concerns).

§ 6:14

Utilizing this standard,[11] courts have ruled that prison authorities cannot automatically exclude publications of the Hebrew Israelite religion, even though a "repeated message of these materials is that white society has continually mistreated black Americans since their arrival as slaves.[12] Nor, courts have held, can a blanket ban of publications of the Aryan Nations be justified even though it is an organization with the "religious belief that the white race is the chosen people of God and that racial integration is wrong or sinful.[13] However, one court concluded that *The Satanic Bible* could properly be excluded, since an independent review of the book by the district court established that "persons following its teachings would murder, rape or rob at will without regard for moral or legal consequences.[14] Thus, unless the prison can establish that a particular religious publication poses a serious threat to the institution, it is improper to confiscate the publication or to punish the inmate for possessing it.[15]

---

[11]The cases dealing with this issue discussed above were decided prior to the Supreme Court's decision dealing generally with censorship in prison. Thornburgh v. Abbott, 490 U.S. 401, 109 S. Ct. 1874, 104 L. Ed. 2d 459 (1989). It is not entirely clear whether Thornburgh will compel a different result if the issue arises again. For a discussion of *Thornburgh,* see Ch 5.

[12]Lawson v. Dugger, 840 F.2d 781, 783 (11th Cir. 1987), judgment vacated on other grounds, 490 U.S. 1078, 109 S. Ct. 2096, 104 L. Ed. 2d 658 (1989).

[13]Murphy v. Missouri Dept. of Corrections, 814 F.2d 1252, 1254 n2 (8th Cir. 1987).

[14]McCorkle v. Johnson, 881 F.2d 993, 995 (11th Cir. 1989). In addition, the inmate involved in the case had, in the past, asked other inmates for their blood, causing a certain amount of irritability in the prison population. *Id.* at 995.

[15]See, e.g., Valiant-Bey v. Morris, 829 F.2d 1441, 1444 (8th Cir. 1987) (confiscation of religious material that is not inflammatory is unconstitutional); Mukmuk v. Commissioner of Dept. of Correctional Services, 529 F.2d 272 (2d Cir. 1976); Burns v. Swenson, 288 F. Supp. 4 (W.D. Mo. 1968), opinion modified, 300 F. Supp. 759 (W.D. Mo. 1969), aff'd in part as modified, rev'd in part on other grounds, 430 F.2d 771 (8th Cir. 1970).

In the event that the prison decides to exclude religious publications, an inmate has the right to be notified in writing when materials are withheld.[16] In addition, the inmate affected is entitled to be given a statement of reasons for the decision to exclude the publication and the right to file an administrative appeal of the decision. Finally, prison officials who were not involved in the original decision to bar the publication should decide the appeal.[17]

§ 6:15 —Access to Religious Accouterments

Religious jewelry and accessories are frequently used in the practice of religion. They either symbolize a person's belief in a particular faith[1] or are used by the practitioner of a faith to carry out the rituals of that religion.[2] Observant prisoners, therefore, normally seek to continue using these items during imprisonment. They are often permitted to possess religious materials, no doubt because these items are seen as innocuous and because they might help in rehabilitation.[3] Occasionally, however, prisons deny these articles to prisoners because of fear that the items might endanger prison security.

A primary consideration for the courts to take into account under both the *Shabazz* test and the compelling interest/least restrictive means standard is the physical characteristics of the accessory itself. If its physical properties render it inherently threatening to

---

[16]Murphy v. Missouri Dept. of Corrections, 814 F.2d 1252, 1258 (8th Cir. 1987).

[17]*Id.*

[Section 6:15]

[1]For example, a cross for a Christian or a Star of David for a Jew.

[2]Catholics, for example, might use rosary beads in prayer, while Jews might use a tallith and teffilian for morning prayers.

[3]See, e.g., Ross v. Coughlin, 669 F. Supp. 1235 (S.D. N.Y. 1987) (discussing New York prison policy which, as applied to Jewish inmates, granted right to possess a wide variety of religious items).

security, it can be banned. Thus, cases have held that inmates may be deprived of the use of marijuana for religious ceremonies.[4] Prisoners also may be prevented from possessing articles that could readily be used as weapons, such as sharp bear tooth necklaces.[5] Candles, too, have been barred because they can be used to start fires.[6]

The real question is whether religious materials that are not as obviously threatening as drugs, sharp objects, or flammable material can be barred from a prison environment. In a questionable decision, *Friend v Kolodzieczak*,[7] the Ninth Circuit held that such materials could be kept out. The case involved a jail that blocked Catholic detainees from possessing rosary beads or scapulars in their cells. The jail operated with a rigid rule that prevented detainees from having any property which was not supplied to them by the facility. Applying the rule to the religious items at issue in the case, the jail allowed detainees to have rosary beads and scapulars during religious services and meetings with religious visitors but barred them at all other times. Although there was no evidence that the religious items were inherently dangerous, the court held that they

---

[4]L'Aquarius v. Maynard, 1981 OK 115, 634 P.2d 1310 (Okla. 1981). See also, Brock v. Carroll, 107 F.3d 241 (4th Cir. 1997) (confiscation of inmate's prayer pipe constitutional pursuant to a general ban on contraband).

[5]Hall v. Bellmon, 935 F.2d 1106, 1113, 19 Fed. R. Serv. 3d 1217 (10th Cir. 1991).

[6]Childs v. Duckworth, 509 F. Supp. 1254 (N.D. Ind. 1981), judgment aff'd, 705 F.2d 915 (7th Cir. 1983). In *Childs,* the court further noted that candles could be used as key molds to fashion unlawful keys. *Id.* at 1263. The court also banned the use of incense because it could be used as an intoxicant and to mask the odor of illegal drugs and alcohol. *Id.* See also, Ward v. Walsh, 1 F.3d 873 (9th Cir. 1993); Dettmer v. Landon, 799 F.2d 929 (4th Cir. 1986) (no right to unsupervised use of candles, salt, and incense for witchcraft religious ceremony).

[7]Friend v. Kolodzieczak, 923 F.2d 126 (9th Cir. 1991).

could be properly excluded from the jail.[8]

The court gave three reasons for upholding the restriction. First, it relied on the general policy of the facility that kept all property out of the hands of inmates. The court held that this policy was designed to prevent the possession of drugs and weapons in the jail, which is a valid penal objective.[9] Second, the court held that to give Catholics the right to have their religious materials would create "an impression of favoritism toward Roman Catholic prisoners, thereby generating resentment, envy and intimidation."[10] Third, the court stated that Catholic inmates could practice their faith in other ways within the prison.[11]

The *Friend* ruling is problematic, because it is not based on a close examination of the relationship between the property rule as applied to religious items only and the security of the institution. As a general matter, the prohibition against property might be a valid way of keeping drugs and weapons out of the jail, but when the prohibition is applied to such clearly religious items as rosary beads, can the same be said with as much conviction? Why must rosary beads be excluded to keep the institution free of drugs and weapons? This is the real question posed, and never really answered, by the Ninth Circuit in *Friend*. The reasonable relationship test of *Shabazz,* and Congress's compelling interest/least restrictive means standard, are better served by looking at the policy as it is applied in the case before the court rather than looking at the question abstractly, as the court did.

Another problem with the *Friend* ruling is that it accepts without any factual support or analysis the defendants' argument that to grant the plaintiffs' request would cause other inmates to feel resentment toward Catholic detainees. As we have seen earlier,

---

[8]*Id.* at 128.
[9]*Id.*
[10]*Id.*
[11]*Id.*

§ 6:15   Rights of Prisoners, Third Edition

this is a flawed line of thinking that is not consistent with either the *Shabazz* rule or the compelling interest standard.[12] Other courts have taken a more careful view of the right of inmates to possess religious objects.[13]

Thus, in order for an inmate to prevail on a claim of entitlement to possess a religious article, the better reasoned approach requires a showing that the item is one genuinely needed for the practice of religion,[14] that the religious article does not have physical properties that are inherently threatening to prison security, and

---

[12]See § 6:3.

[13]See, e.g., Higgins v. Burroughs, 816 F.2d 119 (3d Cir. 1987), judgment vacated, 484 U.S. 807, 108 S. Ct. 54, 98 L. Ed. 2d 18 (1987). In Higgins the Third Circuit carefully examined the security rationale for preventing inmates from carrying rosary beads with them into the visiting room. The court held, contrary to the defendants' assertions, that "the risk of using hand-carried rosary beads either as a weapon or for purposes of concealing contraband has not been established." *Id.* at 123. *Higgins* was decided prior to *Shabazz*. The case was remanded to the Third Circuit following the *Shabazz* decision for reconsideration, Burroughs v. Higgins, 484 U.S. 807, 108 S. Ct. 54, 98 L. Ed. 2d 18 (1987). On remand, the Third Circuit observed in dicta that the same result should occur under the *Shabazz* standard. Higgins v. Burroughs, 834 F.2d 76, 77 (3d Cir. 1987). Although the district court ultimately reached a different result, it did so following a detailed review of the reasons for the restriction in the specific context of the situation in which it was applied. Higgins v. Burroughs, 1988 WL 33884 (E.D. Pa. 1988), judgment aff'd, 862 F.2d 308 (3d Cir. 1988). See also Street v. Maloney, 923 F.2d 841 (1st Cir. 1990) (claim that Hari Krishna inmate was not permitted to possess Hindu prayer beads and Hindu religious necklace stated a claim that could not be dismissed); Craddick v. Duckworth, 113 F.3d 83 (7th Cir. 1997) (summary judgment for defendant reversed, where officials prevented inmate from wearing a medicine bag and made no showing that the medicine bags threatened security).

[14]See, e.g., Holloway v. Pigman, 884 F.2d 365 (8th Cir. 1989) (no particularized showing by inmate that sweet grass and sage was necessary for the practice of religion); McClaflin v. Pearce, 739 F. Supp. 537 (D. Or. 1990) (in a segregation unit, a rosary is a "nonessential element" of religion that may be barred); Jackson v. Lewis, 163 F.3d 606 (9th Cir. 1998) (practitioner of Wicca did not show that use of tarot cards was necessary to practice his religion.

FIRST AMENDMENT: RELIGION § 6:16

that, using the *Shabazz* factors, there is no reasonable relationship between the ban on the religious item and the prison's security needs. This analysis would work just as well under the RLUIPA standard, as security concerns have been deemed a compelling interest.[15] If a showing is made that the item is necessary for religious purposes, and that there is no rational connection between its restriction and valid security concerns, the inmate should be permitted to retain the item during his or her imprisonment. The fact that an inmate can possess a religious item, however, does not mean that the prison has an affirmative obligation to supply it to the inmate, only that the inmate is permitted to purchase it.[16] One proposal would be to allow inmates to petition for possession of an item and, if the inmate's request is approved, to add the item is to a list of approved items that all inmates may then possess.[17] This system is used in the state of Oregon.[18]

§ 6:16 —Work-Religion Conflicts

In *O'Lone v Estate of Shabazz*,[1] the Supreme Court held that Muslim inmates in a New Jersey prison could be constitutionally prevented from attending Friday religious services within the institution when their work required that they remain outside the prison gates. The holding in *Shabazz* suggests that prisoners are not likely to be victorious with claims that they are

---

[15]See § 6:3.

[16]Frank v. Terrell, 858 F.2d 1090 (5th Cir. 1988) (Jewish inmate can purchase Jewish religious items, but prison need not supply them to him).

[17]See, Developments in the Law, The Law of Prisons: IV. In the Belly of the Whale: Religious Practice in Prison, 115 Harv. L. Rev. 1891, 1911-14 (2002).

[18]*Id.*

[Section 6:16]

[1]O'Lone v. Estate of Shabazz, 482 U.S. 342, 107 S. Ct. 2400, 96 L. Ed. 2d 282 (1987). See § 6:3 for an extensive discussion of this case.

§ 6:16

entitled to changes to their work schedules in order to accommodate religious observations.[2]

However, this does not mean that there is no possibility for a prisoner to be successful with such a case. In the first place, *Shabazz* teaches that each case must be analyzed on its own facts. On the facts in *Shabazz*, there was a reasonable relationship between the restriction on attendance at the religious service and the governmental interests in security and administrative convenience.[3] To grant the plaintiffs' request in that case would have imposed a drain on the physical resources of the facility by creating a logistics problem of moving inmates who had already been processed out of the facility in the middle of a work day.[4]

It is possible that a record could be developed in another case that would demonstrate that the failure to accommodate prisoners' religious needs is not as rational as was the case in *Shabazz*.[5] If such a showing is made, then the refusal to oblige the plaintiffs' request would be unconstitutional. In fact, when courts after *Shabazz* have been presented with such claims, they have not merely rubber-stamped the defendants' decisions, but instead have carefully searched the record to

---

[2] Claims under RFRA, though under a tougher standard, have also shown the difficulty a prisoner faces in challenging the denial of release from work duties to attend services. See, e.g., Abdur-Rahman v. Michigan Dept. of Corrections, 65 F.3d 489 (6th Cir. 1995) (court found attending Friday services was not a central tenet of the inmate's religion; therefore the inmate's First Amendment rights were not violated when he was not released from work detail to attend). See also, Beierle v. Zavares, 215 F.3d 1336 (10th Cir. 2000).

[3] See § 6:3.

[4] O'Lone v. Estate of Shabazz, 482 U.S. 342, 107 S. Ct. 2400, 96 L. Ed. 2d 282 (1987).

[5] An example of such a case is Chapman v. Pickett, 801 F.2d 912 (7th Cir. 1986), judgment vacated on other grounds, 484 U.S. 807, 108 S. Ct. 54, 98 L. Ed. 2d 19 (1987). In that case, the Seventh Circuit upheld a judgment that determined that it was unconstitutional to punish a devout black Muslim for refusing to handle pork.

§ 6:16

determine whether the denial of religious expression was rational.[6] Indeed, in a recent case decided by the Ninth Circuit, just such a showing was made.[7]

In that case Muslim inmates who had jobs in the prison were marked as having an unauthorized absence from their work if they attended Friday services. An authorized absence from work had serious repercussions for inmates; it could be grounds for adverse action, including disciplinary action. The Ninth Circuit held that charging unauthorized absences to inmates who went to services to practice their religion was an unconstitutional interference with religion, and distinguished *Shabazz*. *Shabazz,* the court held, dealt with a rule that was necessary to avoid serious security problems and was also needed to preserve the work incentive program of the prison. By contrast, in the case before it, ruling for the inmates did not "require that Muslims receive preferential work assignments . . . and will not disrupt the work incentive program."[8] Thus, the court ruled that prison officials could not take disciplinary action against inmates who attended the Friday services.

A second reason for pausing to carefully consider these claims is that they might raise equal protection questions. If, for example, a prison accommodates some religions by permitting its members to be excused from work to attend services but does not offer a similar

---

[6]Mumin v. Phelps, 857 F.2d 1055 (5th Cir. 1988) (refusal to transport Muslim inmates to the main prison for services upheld after review of the record); Johnson v. Bruce, 771 F. Supp. 327 (D. Kan. 1991), aff'd, 961 F.2d 220 (10th Cir. 1992) (conducting Muslim Friday afternoon services in the evening after completion of work day was reasonable given the facts of the case). Moreover, when the policy is constitutional, it is proper to discipline an inmate for refusing to obey it. Boyd v. Coughlin, 83 A.D.2d 977, 442 N.Y.S.2d 824 (3d Dep't 1981) (refusal to obey an order to work on Sunday justified punishment of inmate).

[7]Mayweathers v. Newland, 258 F.3d 930, 51 Fed. R. Serv. 3d 230 (9th Cir. 2001).

[8]*Id.* at at 938.

dispensation for members of other faiths who have like conflicts, then an equal protection violation is made out unless the record shows a valid purpose for distinguishing between the groups. Similarly, although there are no cases that raise and answer this question, if a state by law specifically sets aside Sundays as a day on which inmates shall not be required to work,[9] there might very well be a denial of equal protection if inmates whose Sabbath does not fall on Sunday are not given time off on their holidays.[10]

§ 6:17 —Medical Treatment-Religion Conflicts

On occasion, prisoners have objected on religious grounds to medical or psychological testing and treatment. The issues raised by these objections are by no means unique to a prison setting. It is well known that some religions, the Jehovah's Witnesses for example, will not accept blood transfusions even when necessary to preserve their lives. When this refusal has occurred in the civilian world, it has often led to litigation concerning the right of the individual to refuse state-offered treatment.[1]

Recent litigation on this topic has centered on two issues: (1) whether for purposes of treatment an inmate can be forced to participate in rehabilitation programs that have religious connotations; and (2) whether inmates can be forced to undergo medical treatments that violate their religious practices?

---

[9]See, e.g., Ala Code § 14-3-48.

[10]If a prisoner is given time off to observe religious holy days, compensatory labor can, of course, be required to ensure that the prisoner is not given a lighter workload than his fellow inmates. Laaman v. Hancock, 351 F. Supp. 1265, 1270 (D.N.H. 1972).

[Section 6:17]

[1]See, Niebla, By and Through Niebla v. County of San Diego, 967 F.2d 589 (9th Cir. 1992); Graham v. Deukmejian, 713 F.2d 518 (9th Cir. 1983); McKenzie v. Doctors' Hosp. of Hollywood, Inc., 765 F. Supp. 1504 (S.D. Fla. 1991), aff'd, 974 F.2d 1347 (11th Cir. 1992).

FIRST AMENDMENT: RELIGION § 6:17

The answer to the first question seems to be that inmates may not be forced to participate in religiously based treatment programs and cannot be punished for refusing to do so. As discussed earlier,[2] there are several recent federal Court of Appeals holdings that have declared forced participation in so called "twelve-step" programs unconstitutional.[3]

Regarding the second issue, a number of courts have held that when a prisoner makes a religious objection to a medical test necessary to determine whether he or she is carrying an infectious disease, prison officials can compel compliance so long as the procedure is reasonable and is not overly intrusive or dangerous. If this showing is made, the prison's interest "in ensuring that prisoners are not admitted to the prison general population if they are carrying a contagious disease" outweighs the prisoner's sincere medical objection to the

---

[2]See § 6:6 for a discussion of this case law from an Establishment Clause perspective.

[3]See, e.g., Kerr v. Farrey, 95 F.3d 472 (7th Cir. 1996); Griffin v. Coughlin, 88 N.Y.2d 674, 649 N.Y.S.2d 903, 673 N.E.2d 98 (1996) (prison officials cannot deprive an inmate of visitation rights for refusal to participate in a religious-based treatment program); Ross v. Keelings, 2 F. Supp. 2d 810 (E.D. Va. 1998). See also, Rachel F. Calabro, Comment: Correction Through Coercion: Do State Mandated Alcohol and Drug Treatment Programs in Prisons Violate the Establishment Clause?, 47 DePaul L. Rev. 565 (1998) (mandating participation in such programs is impermissible under the Establishment Clause). Accord, Derek P. Apanovitch, Note: Religion and Rehabilitation: The Requisition of God by the State, 47 Duke L.J. 785 (1998). But see, Stafford v. Harrison, 766 F. Supp. 1014 (D. Kan. 1991) (defendants were not guilty of an Establishment Clause violation when they required an inmate to complete a treatment program modeled on Alcoholics Anonymous, because Alcoholics Anonymous is not a religion); see also Cokley v. Hayden, 731 F. Supp. 1013 (D. Kan. 1990) (objection to participation in "religiously oriented" substance abuse program dismissed because the prisoner was no longer incarcerated at the prison in question).

§ 6:17

procedure.[4] However, the showing must be made. In the case of tuberculosis tests there is a conflict in the courts about when this showing is made. The issue arises when an inmate is segregated for failure to take a screening test.[5] One court upheld the practice.[6] Another, in a carefully reasoned decision, did not.[7] In the latter case the district court closely examined the rationale for a policy that segregated for one year any inmate who refused a tuberculosis test. The inmate, who was a Rastafarian, had a sincere religious objection to the test which involved injecting a foreign element into his body. Subjecting the regulation to careful scrutiny the court held that it was not rationally related to protecting the health of inmates or staff. The court found that a number of people with latent TB were already in the general population and that prisoners who posed an even greater risk of contagion were also in the population. Moreover, the plaintiff was willing to submit to chest X-rays and other procedures should he exhibit active symptoms of the disease. Thus, subjecting the plaintiff to a keeplock for refusing testing did not materially advance the stated objective of the prison officials in controlling the amount of TB in the prison.

---

[4]Smallwood-El v. Coughlin, 589 F. Supp. 692, 699 (S.D. N.Y. 1984). See also Dunn v. White, 880 F.2d 1188 (10th Cir. 1989) (plaintiff's religious objection to compulsory HIV testing dismissed because it was not sufficiently specific to even invoke First Amendment protection); Karolis v. New Jersey Dept. of Corrections, 935 F. Supp. 523 (D.N.J. 1996) (officials had a compelling interest in testing a Christian Scientist inmate for tuberculosis); Jones-Bey v. Wright, 944 F. Supp. 723 (N.D. Ind. 1996); Hasenmeier-McCarthy v. Rose, 986 F. Supp. 464 (S.D. Ohio 1998).

[5]Contrast Smallwood-EL, 589 F Supp at 692 with Reynolds v. Goord, 103 F. Supp. 2d 316 (S.D. N.Y. 2000).

[6]Smallwood-El v. Coughlin, 589 F. Supp. 692, 699 (S.D. N.Y. 1984) (inmate refused to submit to a tuberculosis test because the test involved the use of a pork derivative; the court issued a preliminary injunction preventing officials from segregating the inmate pending trial, finding that the segregation was a substantial burden on the inmate's constitutional rights).

[7]Reynolds v. Goord, 103 F. Supp. 2d 316 (S.D. N.Y. 2000).

The court held that the regulation placed an unconstitutional burden on the plaintiff's practice of his religion.

Chapter 7

Prison Labor

Research References

Prisoners and the Law, Ch 21

Am. Jur. 2d, Penal and Correctional Institutions §§ 159, 160, 162 to 173

Convicts ⊶7 to 13; Prisons ⊶4(5); Sentencing and Punishment ⊶1535

A.L.R. Index: Prisons and Prisoners; Work Release Programs

Coverage, under Fair Labor Standards Act (FLSA) (29 U.S.C.A. secs. 201 et seq.), of prisoners working for private individuals or entities other than prisons, 110 A.L.R. Fed. 839

Grant or denial of furlough or work release to federal prisoner under 18 U.S.C.A. sec. 4082(c), 64 A.L.R. Fed. 807

Denial of state prisoner's application for, or revocation of, participation in work or study release program or furlough program as actionable under Civil Rights Act of 1871 (42 U.S.C.A. sec. 1983), 55 A.L.R. Fed. 208

> **KeyCite®:** Cases and other legal materials listed in KeyCite Scope can be researched through West Group's KeyCite service on Westlaw®. Use KeyCite to check citations for form, parallel references, prior and later history, and comprehensive citator information, including citations to other decisions and secondary materials.

§ 7:1   Introduction
§ 7:2   Historical Background
§ 7:3   Prison-Made Goods
§ 7:4   Thirteenth Amendment—Involuntary Servitude Exception: Can Inmates Be Forced to Work?
§ 7:5   The Right to Work or Be Employed
§ 7:6   Job Seniority and Security; The Right to a Particular Job
§ 7:7   The Right to a Particular Job as Affected by Civil Rights Laws

§ 7:8   The Right to a Particular Job as Affected by AIDS and Other Conditions
§ 7:9   Wages—The Right to Be Paid in General
§ 7:10   —The Right to Be Paid Minimum Wages
§ 7:11   Withholding Wages and Payment of Interest on Inmate Accounts
§ 7:12   The Right to Be Compensated for Work-Related Injuries
§ 7:13   The Right to Unemployment Compensation
§ 7:14   The Right to Form Prisoners' Unions
§ 7:15   The Right to Engage in Work Stoppages and Strikes
§ 7:16   The Right to Participate in Work Release Programs Generally
§ 7:17   Work Release Participation and Due Process Requirement
§ 7:18   Conclusion—The Legislative Challenge

§ 7:1 Introduction

This chapter addresses the basic rights of prisoners to prison work, prison workers, and associated questions, such as whether prison workers have the right to be paid, the right to job security, and the right to form unions.

The value of productive prison work and its relationship to rehabilitation are widely accepted.[1] Work combats boredom and idleness, reduces institutional tensions, and teaches and reinforces skills, attitudes, and habits that can be used constructively after release. As one commentator recently put it "[s]teady labor and self-support have . . .been described as bases of indi-

---

[Section 7:1]

[1]See, generally, Stephen P. Garvey, Freeing Prisoners' Labor, 50 Stan. L. Rev. 339 (1998) (citing authorities); Stephanie Evans, Making More Effective Use of Our Prisons Through Regimented Labor, 27 Pepp. L. Rev. 521 (2000).

vidual self respect."[2] Tocqueville, who toured American prisons in the early 19th Century, recognized the value of work when he observed that "labor gives to the disciplinary cell an interest; it fatigues the body and relieves the soul."[3] Products of prison labor, moreover, help offset the costs of housing, feeding, and maintaining prisoners and running a prison system. Thus, prison labor, in theory, benefits both prisoners and the state.

The normal incentives to work, however, are not present in the same way in the modern prison milieu. For one thing there is little productive work in prison. One recent article reported that most of the nation's prisoners are idle. According to that report, while 90% of the prison population worked in 1890 by 1997, only 6.2% were gainfully employed.[4] Compensation for an inmate's labor is usually de minimis, frequently falling below one dollar per day.[5] The possibilities for advancement are rare. Intellectually challenging positions are few, and many prisoners do not find their abilities tapped by

---

[2] Stephen P. Garvey, Freeing Prisoners' Labor, 50 Stan. L. Rev. 339, 381 (1998).

[3] Gustative deBeaumont & Alexis de Tocqueville, On The Penitentiary System In The United States And Its Application In France 57 (Herman R. Lantz ed. & Francis Lieber tras., S. Ill Univ. Pres 1964).

[4] Stephen P. Garvey, Freeing Prisoners' Labor, 50 Stan. L. Rev. 339, 370 (1998) (citing Greg Weese, Prison Industries 1997, Corrections Compendium, June 1997).

[5] Most federal inmates are assigned to institution jobs such as food service worker, painter, groundskeeper or plumber. These jobs typically pay twelve to forty cents an hour. About 25% of federal inmates work in Federal Prison Industries (FPI) and are assigned to job involving metals, furniture, textiles, or graphic arts. These FPI jobs typically pay twenty-three cents to a dollar fifty an hour. See, U.S. Department of Justice Federal Bureau of Prisons, www.bop.gov/ipapg/ipaover.html#work (accessed on June 30, 2002); see also Lenihan, The Financial Condition of Released Prisoners, 21 Crime & Delinq 266, 272-73 (1975).

§ 7:1

the menial jobs available.[6] Moreover, any interest in self-improvement is often extinguished by prison industries that use outmoded equipment and teach skills not needed in the free world. Another distinction between civilian and convict labor is the compulsory characteristics of the latter-prisoners are assigned jobs that they must perform.[7] Failure to work may be punished and may result in a bad record for parole board review.

Several potential constitutional issues arise in regard to prison labor. The Thirteenth Amendment prohibits involuntary servitude, but a specific exception exists for those duly convicted of crimes.[8] Nonetheless, questions regarding the reach of that exception remain. In addition, the disparity in treatment between prisoners and other workers may have equal protection implications. Discrimination in the assignment of prison jobs may also violate equal protection.

Statutory interpretation questions relating to prison employment also arise. Laws governing such matters as minimum wages, workers' compensation, and unemployment insurance often do not indicate whether prisoners are included. Whether they are covered must

---

[6]See, generally, Stephen P. Garvey, Freeing Prisoners' Labor, 50 Stan. L. Rev. 339 (1998); National Inst of Law Enforcement & Crim Just, Study of the Economic and Rehabilitative Aspects of Prison Industry: Analysis of Prison Industries and Recommendations for Change (1978); National Inst of Law Enforcement & Crim Just, Study of the Economic and Rehabilitative Aspects of Prison Industry: Technical Tasks and Results (1978).

[7]See American Correctional Assn, Standards for Adult Correctional Institutions, Standard 3-4395 (1990) (inmates can refuse to participate in institutional programs except work assignments). However, unsentenced detainees in jail are sometimes not required to do jobs other than keeping their cell areas clean. Commission on Accreditation for Corrections, Manual of Standards for Adult Local Detention Facilities Standards 5262, 5344 (1977).

[8]US Const amend XIII, § 1: "Neither slavery nor involuntary servitude, except as a punishment for crime whereof the party shall have been duly convicted, shall exist within the United States, or any place subject to their jurisdiction." (emphasis added.)

be determined by the courts. In addition, a number of underlying policy issues must be addressed by legislatures. Should prisoners injured while performing administratively assigned jobs, for example, be entitled to workers' compensation benefits?

Another labor-related issue concerns unionism. During the early 1970s, inmates at several penal institutions attempted to organize. Their purpose was not simply to raise labor issues but, more generally, to serve as a vehicle through which to communicate with prison officials. The latter, not surprisingly, reacted negatively. They viewed the prisoners' efforts as an attempt to undermine their traditional authority and envisioned unrest. Administrative policies aimed at frustrating the spread and effectiveness of prison unions spawned litigation that ultimately reached the Supreme Court.[9] This chapter traces that now largely resolved controversy. This chapter also discusses other issues including restrictions on the sale of prison made goods, the right to work, the employment rights and benefits of prison work for those inmates who have it, and the development and law surrounding work release programs.

§ 7:2 Historical Background

Originally, the idea of having prisoners work was considered a reform, a constructive alternative to the harsh punishments of the 17th century.[1] Work, along with prayer, was perceived as the means through which

---

[9]Jones v. North Carolina Prisoners' Labor Union, Inc., 433 U.S. 119, 97 S. Ct. 2532, 53 L. Ed. 2d 629 (1977), discussed in § 7:14.

[Section 7:2]

[1]For a history of the checkered past regarding prison work programs and their growth and decline see, generally, Stephen P. Garvey, Freeing Prisoners' Labor, 50 Stan. L. Rev. 339, (1998); See also Clark & Parker, The Labor Law Problems of the Prisoner, 28 Rutgers L Rev 840 (1975).

§ 7:2   Rights of Prisoners, Third Edition

prisoners atoned for their crimes.[2] The profits from prison labor, however, generally went to the private employers who leased or contracted with the state for the use of inmate workers.

This exploitation of prison labor for private profit had its share of critics. Social reformers decried the inhumane and degrading conditions under which convicts often had to work. Competitors were upset by the economic advantage which accrued to the employers of the relatively inexpensive inmate labor force. Finally, the use of convict labor resulted in lost employment opportunities for many law-abiding civilians, who were understandably angered by the competition for scarce jobs.

In part because of free-market pressures, prison labor in the early 20th century was redirected from use by private employers to use by the state in public works projects. This metamorphosis was aided by federal legislation. One statute, for example, enabled states to ban the importation of goods made by prisoners in a sister state.[3] Another called for special labeling of goods made by prisoners so that the public could know the source of the items.[4] Many states, following the lead of Congress, limited the sale of prisoner-made goods to

---

[2]Today, prison labor is more often justified on the basis of four goals: it is justified for the purpose of punishment; it is a means to reinforce prison discipline; it is necessary, to preserve the health of prison inmates; and it teaches inmates a useful trade. J. Spitzer, Penal and Correctional Institutions, 60 Am Jur 2d § 165 (1987). For a discussion of labor both as a punitive and rehabilitative tool, see, Stephanie Evans, Making More Effective Use of Our Prisons Through Regimented Labor, 27 Pepp. L. Rev. 521 (2000) (advocating a "ladder" approach where inmates would begin with hard labor, and work their way up to jobs that would train them in skills they could use once released).

[3]49 U.S.C. § 11507.

[4]49 Stat 494 (1935), as amended 18 U.S.C. § 1762. Some states have enacted similar statutes. See, e.g., Pa Stat Ann tit 61, § 251 (convict-made goods to be branded).

state agencies.[5] The final blow, however, may have come when Congress banned outright the interstate shipment of many goods manufactured by prisoners.[6] These statutes dealing with the transportation and labeling of goods made in prison by prisoners are criminal statutes and do not give rise to any private right of action on the part of prison inmates against prison officials.[7]

With the exodus of private employers from the prison labor market came a predictable decline in the number of inmates actually working. The percentage of prisoners productively employed dropped steadily from 1900 to 1970.[8] Work release programs may now be changing this trend,[9] but relatively few inmates are engaged in these programs.[10] By 1997 less than 10% of all inmates

---

[5]See, e.g., Cal Penal Code § 2873 repealed by Stats 1982, C 1549, at 6044, § 29; Fla Stat § 946.21; Ga Code Ann § 42-5-60(b); Mo Ann Stat § 216.505 repealed by L 1982, HB No 1196, § A (1983). See also 18 U.S.C. § 4122 (similar restriction for federal prison industries).

[6]49 Stat 494 (1935), as amended 18 U.S.C. § 1761. Exceptions were made for agricultural items, goods to be used by a government, and items made by probationers, parolees, and participants in certain programs. Repeal of this section has been urged. Uniform Law Commrs' Model Sentencing and Corrections Act § 4-816 (July 2001) (reprinted in Appendix B).

[7]Wentworth v. Solem, 548 F.2d 773 (8th Cir. 1977) (interpreting '18 U.S.C. §§ 1761, 1762); Arney v. Davies, 759 F. Supp. 763 (D. Kan. 1991).

[8]See Clark & Parker, The Labor Law Problems of the Prisoner, 28 Rutgers L Rev 840, 844 (1975).

[9]For a discussion of the historical development of modern prison industries, see J.J. Mirashi, Factories With Fences: An Analysis of the Prison Industry Enhancement Certification Program in Historical Perspective, 33 Am Crim L Rev 1183 (1996). See also §§ 7:16, 7:17.

[10]For a proposal to alleviate idleness and lack of work opportunities by the creation of prisoner-run industries, see Note, Prisoners as Entrepreneurs: Developing A Model for Prisoner-Run Industry, 62 BU L Rev 1163 (1982). See also Burger, The High Cost of Prison Tuition, 40 U Miami L Rev 903 (1986).

were gainfully employed.¹¹ Even the objective of avoiding competition with private businesses has not been fully realized, for sales of prison-made items to the state deprive private employers of access to a significant market. This system has been criticized and some well reasoned commentaries have called for opening the market again to prison made goods.¹² Realistically, for these changes to occur would require legislation ending the restrictions on prison labor discussed above.

§ 7:3 Prison-Made Goods

Research References

West's Key Number Digest, Convicts ⌾13

An Act of Congress¹ made some changes in 1990 to the federal laws governing prison-made goods. These provisions may be found at 18 U.S.C. §§ 1761, 1762.

Subsections (a) and (b) remained unchanged. Subsection (a) of § 1761 continues to provide that anyone who knowingly transports in interstate commerce or from any foreign country,² any goods made wholly or in part by convicts, except convicts or prisoners on parole, supervised release, or probation, shall be fined not more than $1,000 or imprisoned not more than one year, or both.³ Subsection (b) exempts agricultural commodities or parts for the repair of farm machinery, as well as

---

[11]Stephen P. Garvey, Freeing Prisoners' Labor, 50 Stan. L. Rev. 339 (1998).

[12]*Id.*

[Section 7:3]

[1]Act of Nov 29, 1990, Pub L No 101-647, tit XXIX, § 2906, 104 Stat 4915.

[2]The statute did not create any right on the part of the longshoremen's union to challenge a decision of the US Customs Service to permit the importation of goods produced in the Soviet Union wholly or in part by forced labor. McKinney v. U.S. Dept. of Treasury, 9 Ct. Int'l Trade 315, 614 F. Supp. 1226 (1985), decision aff'd, 4 Fed. Cir. (T) 103, 799 F.2d 1544 (1986).

[3]The purpose of the statute was to embody the congressional interest in free labor and to protect private businesses from having

goods made for the use of state and federal governments and their subdivisions.[4]

Subsection (c) of § 1761 now provides that this section will not apply to goods made by convicts or prisoners who: (1) are participating in one of not more than 50 nonfederal prison work pilot projects designated by the Director of the Bureau of Justice Assistance; (2) have received wages at a rate not less than that paid for work of a similar nature in the locality in which the work was performed, and which wages are subject to the payment of taxes, reasonable charges for room and board, child and family support, and restitution to the victims of the crime for which the inmate has been imprisoned; (3) have not, solely by their status as offenders, been deprived of the right to participate in benefits made available by federal or state governments to other individuals on the basis of their employment, such as workers' compensation [however, the statute does specifically provide that convicts are not qualified to receive any unemployment compensation benefits while incarcerated]; and (4) have participated in such employment voluntarily, agreed in advance to the specific deductions made from gross wages, and also agreed to all other financial arrangements as a result of such participation.

Section 1762 requires that all packages containing any prison-made goods must be plainly and clearly so marked and provides for penalties for violating this statute. These two statutes represent a policy decision by Congress not to foster competition between private employers and prison-made, inexpensively produced goods, but the effect also is to limit the number of meaningful jobs which prison inmates can fill and to limit the opportunities for rehabilitation of prisoners.

---

to compete with goods produced with inexpensive convict labor. Wentworth v. Solem, 548 F.2d 773 (8th Cir. 1977).

[4]As to the sale and labeling of inmate-made goods, see, generally, J. Spitzer, Penal and Correctional Institutions, 60 Am Jur 2d §§ 171, 172 (1987).

In a more enlightened approach to prison-made goods, the American Bar Association has recommended that most of these restrictions on prison-made goods be repealed. In its Standards for Criminal Justice, Standard 23-4.4(a), adopted in 1985, it recommended as follows:

(a) To increase opportunities for meaningful prisoner employment, legal provisions restricting goods or services that may be produced or delivered by prisoners, restricting types of employment available to prisoners or restricting the interstate or intrastate marketing, sale or transportation of goods produced in correctional institutions should be repealed. Correctional authorities should be empowered to contract with private enterprises for the establishment and operation of industrial and service facilities.

§ 7:4 Thirteenth Amendment—Involuntary Servitude Exception: Can Inmates Be Forced to Work?

Prisoners lack a constitutional right to choose whether to work.[1] The Thirteenth Amendment in relevant part provides:

Neither slavery nor involuntary servitude, except as a punishment for crime whereof the party shall have been duly convicted, shall exist within the United States, or any place subject to their jurisdiction.[2]

The term "crime" in the Amendment has been read broadly to include both felonies and misdemeanors, and all other offenses in violation of the penal law.[3] The exception does not apply, however, to persons detained

---

[Section 7:4]

[1] See, generally, Penal and Correctional Institutions, 60 Am Jur 2d §§ 159, 160, 162-73, for an overview of the law relating to prison labor and work release programs.

[2] US Const amend XIII, § 1.

[3] City of Fort Lauderdale v. King, 222 So. 2d 6 (Fla. 1969); Stone v. City of Paducah, 120 Ky. 322, 27 Ky. L. Rptr. 717, 86 S.W. 531 (1905).

in prison who have not been convicted of a crime.[4] Moreover, for the exception to apply, the prisoner must have been "duly convicted." Thus, it has been held that imprisonment of a defendant who has been denied the right of assistance of counsel violates the Thirteenth Amendment.[5] Similarly unconstitutional is the jailing of a person convicted without evidence.[6]

Once individuals have been duly tried, convicted, sentenced, and imprisoned, courts will not find Thirteenth Amendment violations where prison rules require inmates to work.[7] An inmate is "duly convicted"

---

[4]See. e.g., Johnston v. Ciccone, 260 F. Supp. 553 (W.D. Mo. 1966); State ex rel. Hobbs v. Murrell, 170 Tenn. 152, 93 S.W.2d 628 (1936). Nevertheless, even pretrial detainees cannot sue for violation of the 13th Amendment if they voluntarily choose to work while confined, even if the choice that they make as to whether or not to work is a "painful" one. Brooks v. George County, Miss., 84 F.3d 157 (5th Cir. 1996). See also Watson v. Graves, 909 F.2d 1549, 110 A.L.R. Fed. 823 (5th Cir. 1990).

[5]United States v. Morgan, 222 F.2d 673 (2d Cir. 1955).

[6]U.S. ex rel. Caminito v. Murphy, 222 F.2d 698 (2d Cir. 1955).

[7]See, e.g. Tourscher v. McCullough, 184 F.3d 236 (3d Cir. 1999) (duly convicted prisoner continued in that status for the purposes of the Thirteenth Amendment prohibition against involuntary servitude until the appeal became final, and could be required to perform general housekeeping without violating the Thirteenth Amendment or the minimum wage requirements of the Fair Labor Standards Act of 1938); Brooks v. George County, Miss., 84 F.3d 157 (5th Cir. 1996) (inmate was not subject to involuntary servitude when he was mistakenly held for eight months after his case was dismissed and during that time the inmate worked for prison industries and other charitable organizations on a volunteer basis); Mikeska v. Collins, 928 F.2d 126 (5th Cir. 1991) (forcing inmates to work without pay does not violate the Thirteenth Amendment); Ruark v. Solano, 928 F.2d 947 (10th Cir. 1991) (Thirteenth Amendment's restriction on involuntary servitude does not apply to prisoners); Draper v. Rhay, 315 F.2d 193 (9th Cir. 1963) (holding that there is no federally protected right of a state prisoner not to work while imprisoned after conviction, even though his conviction is being appealed); Lindsey v. Leavy, 149 F.2d 899 (C.C.A. 9th Cir. 1945); see also Plaisance v. Phelps, 845 F.2d 107, 11 Fed. R. Serv. 3d 101 (5th Cir. 1988) (fact that an ap-

§ 7:4   RIGHTS OF PRISONERS, THIRD EDITION

even if his case is on appeal.[8] Prisoners not only have no right to refuse to work,[9] but also have no right to a particular job assignment.[10]

Since prisoners have no constitutional right not to work, courts have upheld the placing of them in disciplinary confinement for refusing to work in the prison industry or elsewhere.[11] In most of these cases, the refusal to work stemmed from dissatisfaction with the task assigned or the belief that prisoners had a

---

peal of prisoner's conviction is pending does not bar prison officials from requiring him or her to work); Omasta v. Wainwright, 696 F.2d 1304 (11th Cir. 1983) (no violation of Thirteenth Amendment in requiring prisoner to work even though prisoner's conviction was subsequently reversed).

A United Nations publication provides that "[a]ll prisoners under sentence shall be required to work," subject to their physical and mental fitness. United Nations, Standard Minimum Rules for the Treatment of Prisoners, Rule 71(2) (1955). The Anti-Peonage Act, passed by Congress in 1867 and codified at 42 U.S.C. § 1994, reinforces the provisions of the Thirteenth Amendment. The applicability of this provision to a prisoner's labor was rejected in Craine v. Alexander, 756 F.2d 1070 (5th Cir. 1985).

[8]Tourscher v. McCullough, 184 F.3d 236 (3d Cir. 1999).

[9]Convicted prisoners have no right to refuse to work. Cooper v. Morin, 91 Misc. 2d 302, 398 N.Y.S.2d 36 (Sup 1977), judgment aff'd and modified on other grounds, 64 A.D.2d 130, 409 N.Y.S.2d 30 (4th Dep't 1978), judgment modified on other grounds, 49 N.Y.2d 69, 424 N.Y.S.2d 168, 399 N.E.2d 1188 (1979).

[10]Banks v. Norton, 346 F. Supp. 917 (D. Conn. 1972). See § 7:8.

[11]See, e.g., Granville v. Hunt, 411 F.2d 9 (5th Cir. 1969); Claybrone v. Long, 371 F. Supp. 1320 (M.D. Ala. 1974); Laaman v. Hancock, 351 F. Supp. 1265 (D.N.H. 1972); Fallis v. U.S., 263 F. Supp. 780 (M.D. Pa. 1967). One court expanded on the rationale for punishing inmates who refuse to work in the following way: "The refusal to work, by a group or even a single inmate, presents a serious threat to the orderly functioning of a prison. Any unjustified refusal to follow the established work regime is an invitation to sanctions." Mikeska v. Collins, 900 F.2d 833, 837 (5th Cir. 1990), opinion withdrawn on other grounds and superseded on reh'g on other grounds, 928 F.2d 126 (5th Cir. 1991).

right to select their jobs.[12] However there would be a different case if an inmate's refusal instead were based on the claimed exercise of an independent constitutional right, such as could occur if a prisoner refused on sincere religious grounds to work on a religious holy day.[13] Likewise, work assignments that amount to cruel and unusual punishment are forbidden,[14] as are assignments to jobs on a discriminatory,[15] arbitrary, or capricious basis.[16]

---

[12]See, e.g., Claybrone v. Long, 371 F. Supp. 1320 (M.D. Ala. 1974); Fallis v. U.S., 263 F. Supp. 780 (M.D. Pa. 1967). But see United Nations, Standard Minimum Rules for the Treatment of Prisoners, Rule 71 (6) (1955) (subject to various administrative limitations, prisoners should be able to choose the type of work they perform).

[13]See, e.g., Sherbert v. Verner, 374 U.S. 398, 83 S. Ct. 1790, 10 L. Ed. 2d 965 (1963); Laaman v. Hancock, 351 F. Supp. 1265, 1270 (D.N.H. 1972). See also 28 CFR § 548.13(b) (allowing relief from a work assignment where there is a religious conflict); Smith v. Rowe, 761 F.2d 360, 2 Fed. R. Serv. 3d 31 (7th Cir. 1985) (upholding jury verdict in favor of prisoner who refused to accept a job assignment on the grounds that her former position as assistant prison librarian was wrongfully terminated because of exercise of her constitutional rights; failure to take the proffered job was held not to be an unreasonable failure to mitigate damages; prison officials were ordered to return inmate to former position).

[14]See Ray v. Mabry, 556 F.2d 881 (8th Cir. 1977); Talley v. Stephens, 247 F. Supp. 683 (E.D. Ark. 1965); Fidtler v. Rundle, 316 F. Supp. 535 (E.D. Pa. 1970); McLaughlin v. Royster, 346 F. Supp. 297, 311 (E.D. Va. 1972).

In a factually interesting case, Glick v. Lockhart, 759 F.2d 675 (8th Cir. 1985), a prisoner refused to work outside the prison. He contended that his history of escapes and assaults on other prisoners, along with his treatment with "psychotrophy" drugs, rendered him a menace to other persons. The court rejected his argument and upheld his placement in the maximum security unit for his refusal to work. The court declined to create an exception from the general rule that compelling inmates to work was not unconstitutional.

[15]See § 7:7.

[16]See Battle v. Anderson, 376 F. Supp. 402 (E.D. Okla. 1974), judgment aff'd in part, rev'd in part on other grounds, 993 F.2d

§ 7:5 The Right to Work or Be Employed

Research References

West's Key Number Digest, Sentencing and Punishment ⚖︎1535

If inmates generally have no right either to refuse to work or to choose their jobs, do they have a right to work rather than to remain idle? The Thirteenth Amendment obviously does not establish such a right. A few courts, usually on the basis of statutory construction, have held that work opportunities must be provided to avoid the stultifying idleness that might otherwise prevail.[1] However, the large majority of courts generally have concluded that there is no constitutional

---

1551 (10th Cir. 1993). See also Finney v. Arkansas Bd. of Correction, 505 F.2d 194 (8th Cir. 1974); Cleveland v. State, 260 Ga. 770, 399 S.E.2d 472 (1991) (upholding criminal conviction of a warden who forced inmates to walk his dog, wash his dishes, and care for his children); National Advisory Commn on Criminal Justice Standards & Goals, Corrections, Standard 2.8 (1973).

[Section 7:5]

[1]See, e.g., Pugh v. Locke, 406 F. Supp. 318 (M.D. Ala. 1976), judgment aff'd and remanded, 559 F.2d 283 (5th Cir. 1977), cert. granted in part, judgment rev'd in part, 438 U.S. 781, 98 S. Ct. 3057, 57 L. Ed. 2d 1114 (1978); Laaman v. Helgemoe, 437 F. Supp. 269, 318 (D.N.H. 1977); Barnes v. Government of Virgin Islands, 415 F. Supp. 1218 (D.V.I. 1976). See also US Dept of Justice, Federal Standards for Prisons and Jails 14.01 (1980) (reprinted in Appendix D); French v. Owens, 538 F. Supp. 910 (S.D. Ind. 1982), aff'd in part, vacated in part on other grounds, 777 F.2d 1250 (7th Cir. 1985). But in Hoptowit v. Ray, 682 F.2d 1237, 1254, 9 Fed. R. Evid. Serv. 1511 (9th Cir. 1982), the court stated that idleness and lack of programs were not Eighth Amendment violations. See also Robbins v. South, 595 F. Supp. 785 (D. Mont. 1984).

In Garza v. Miller, 688 F.2d 480 (7th Cir. 1982), a federal prisoner advanced both a statutory and a constitutional claim for a job. The statutory argument was predicated on 18 U.S.C. § 4122(b)(1), which states:

§ 4122. Administration of Federal Prison Industries * * *

(b) (l) [The Federal Prison Industries] board of directors shall provide employment for the greatest number of those inmates in the United States penal and correctional institutions who are eligible to work as is reasonably possible, diversify, so far as practicable, prison industrial

§ 7:5 PRISON LABOR

right to work[2] or to vocational training for inmates.[3] Since there is no right to work or not to work it essentially follows that prisoners have no due process right to furlough or vacation from work.[4] A statute may, of course, create such a right.[5] Thus, we have the curious and somewhat anomalous result that inmates neither have a right to work or a right not to work. Whether or not they will work and if so how and where and for how long is a matter the law entrusts to the

operations and so operate the prison shops that no single private industry shall be forced to bear an undue burden of competition from the products of the prison workshops, and to reduce to a minimum competition with private industry or free labor.

The Court of Appeals for the Seventh Circuit held that the provision should be construed in light of its legislative history and 18 U.S.C. § 4122(a), which vests discretion in the Federal Prison Industries Board to determine the manner and extent to which industrial operations should be carried out in federal prisons. It concluded that 18 U.S.C. § 4122(b)(1) did not guarantee a job for every physically fit federal prisoner. The court also rejected the inmate's claim of a property or liberty interest in prison employment. But see Smith v. Owens, 135 Pa. Commw. 631, 582 A.2d 85 (1990) (holding that state law requires all inmates not in restrictive housing to be employed).

[2]Fuller v. Lane, 686 F. Supp. 686 (C.D. Ill. 1988); Jackson v. O'Leary, 689 F. Supp. 846 (N.D. Ill. 1988); Williams v. Sumner, 648 F. Supp. 510 (D. Nev. 1986); Semkus v. Coughlin, 139 A.D.2d 868, 527 N.Y.S.2d 596 (3d Dep't 1988).

[3]See, e.g., Russell v. Oliver, 392 F. Supp. 470 (W.D. Va. 1975), aff'd in part, vacated in part on other grounds, 552 F.2d 115 (4th Cir. 1977); Turner v. Maschner, 11 Kan. App. 2d 134, 715 P.2d 425 (1986). See also Preston v. Ford, 378 F. Supp. 729 (E.D. Ky. 1974) (no constitutional requirement that a state establish a work release program); Jackson v. Hogan, 388 Mass. 376, 446 N.E.2d 692 (1983); Johnson v. Galli, 596 F. Supp. 135 (D. Nev. 1984); Kennibrew v. Russell, 578 F. Supp. 164 (E.D. Tenn. 1983).

[4]Gilliam v. Quinlan, 608 F. Supp. 823 (S.D. N.Y. 1985). In *Gilliam,* the court found that the statute in question had not created a right to furlough or vacation because the prison officials were accorded considerable discretion in awarding these leaves.

[5]State regulations may place limitations on the sanctions which may be imposed on a prisoner who refuses a work assignment See, e.g., Jones v. Jones, 127 Misc. 2d 541, 486 N.Y.S.2d 674 (Sup 1985).

keepers.

Nonetheless, the ABA's Standards for Criminal Justice, Legal Status of Prisoners Standard 23-4.2 suggests:

> Subject to standard 23-1.1, prisoners generally should work under the same conditions that prevail in similar types of employment in free society. Prisoners should not be excluded from otherwise applicable legislation concerning their employment. These standards are not intended to extend to prisoners the right to strike or take other concerted action to affect the wages, hours, benefits, terms, or other conditions of their employment within correctional institutions.

§ 7:6 Job Seniority and Security; The Right to a Particular Job

As demonstrated above, the general rule is that a prisoner has no right to be assigned to work at,[1] or to continue working at,[2] a particular job, although there is

---

[Section 7:6]

[1]DeWalt v. Carter, 224 F.3d 607 (7th Cir. 2000); Jamal v. Cuomo, 234 F.3d 1273 (7th Cir. 2000), cert. denied, 532 U.S. 963, 121 S. Ct. 1498, 149 L. Ed. 2d 383 (2001); James v. Quinlan, 866 F.2d 627 (3d Cir. 1989) (inmates have no property interest in their federal prison industries job assignments); Flittie v. Solem, 827 F.2d 276 (8th Cir. 1987); Ingram v. Papalia, 804 F.2d 595 (10th Cir. 1986); Williams v. Meese, 926 F.2d 994 (10th Cir. 1991); Gardner v. Johnson, 429 F. Supp. 432 (E.D. Mich. 1977); McKinnon v. Patterson, 425 F. Supp. 383 (S.D. N.Y. 1976), judgment modified on other grounds, 568 F.2d 930 (2d Cir. 1977); Coyle v. Hughs, 436 F. Supp. 591 (W.D. Okla. 1977); Chapman v. Plageman, 417 F. Supp. 906 (W.D. Va. 1976); Sowell v. Israel, 500 F. Supp. 209 (E.D. Wis. 1980); Cooper v. Morin, 91 Misc. 2d 302, 398 N.Y.S.2d 36 (Sup 1977), judgment aff'd and modified on other grounds, 64 A.D.2d 130, 409 N.Y.S.2d 30 (4th Dep't 1978), judgment modified, 49 N.Y.2d 69, 424 N.Y.S.2d 168, 399 N.E.2d 1188 (1979).

[2]See, e.g., Wallace v. Robinson, 940 F.2d 243 (7th Cir. 1991) (state has not assured its inmates any job, much less the job which the inmate prefers, and prison regulations do not create a liberty or property interest in a particular job placement); Flittie v. Solem, 827 F.2d 276 (8th Cir. 1987) (inmate had no substantive right to

PRISON LABOR § 7:6

some slight movement in the opposite direction.[3] A state, in its constitution or by statute or administrative

---

retain his job as an inmate law clerk, and his due process rights were not violated when he was dismissed); Ingram v. Papalia, 804 F.2d 595 (10th Cir. 1986); Banks v. Norton, 346 F. Supp. 917 (D. Conn. 1972); Manley v. Bronson, 657 F. Supp. 832 (D. Conn. 1987) (prisoner had no property or liberty interest in his employment as an institutional barber); Nicolaison v. Erickson, 425 N.W.2d 597 (Minn. Ct. App. 1988); Terrell v. State, 573 So. 2d 732 (Miss. 1990); Moore v. Grammer, 232 Neb. 795, 442 N.W.2d 861 (1989); Semkus v. Coughlin, 139 A.D.2d 868, 527 N.Y.S.2d 596 (3d Dep't 1988); Esparza v. Diaz, 802 S.W.2d 772 (Tex. App. Houston 14th Dist. 1990). See also Dupont v. Saunders, 800 F.2d 8 (1st Cir. 1986) (no vested property or liberty interest in job in prison library); Gibson v. McEvers, 631 F.2d 95 (7th Cir. 1980) (inmate's expectation of keeping a certain job does not amount to a property or liberty interest entitled to due process protection); Anderson v. Hascall, 763 F.2d 325 (8th Cir. 1985) (upholding administrative transfer of prisoner from prison industries job); Adams v. James, 784 F.2d 1077 (11th Cir. 1986) (reassignment of prisoner law clerk did not implicate property interest); Watts v. Morgan, 572 F. Supp. 1385 (N.D. Ill. 1983) (a prison inmate is not entitled to procedural protections relative to his temporary or permanent removal from one job assignment to another); Lane v. Reid, 575 F. Supp. 37 (S.D. N.Y. 1983) (no statutory right to, and consequently no liberty interest in, full-time job); Coyle v. Hughs, 436 F. Supp. 591 (W.D. Okla. 1977) (prisoner had no constitutional right to a job in the prison laundry; job assignments within a prison are matters peculiarly within the discretion of prison officials); Inmates, Washington County Jail v. England, 516 F. Supp. 132 (E.D. Tenn. 1980), aff'd, 659 F.2d 1081 (6th Cir. 1981) (no right to hold position of trustee); Cooper v. Smith, 99 A.D.2d 644, 471 N.Y.S.2d 932 (4th Dep't 1984), order aff'd, 63 N.Y.2d 615, 479 N.Y.S.2d 519, 468 N.E.2d 701 (1984) (loss of kitchen job could be ordered without a hearing); Johnson v. Smith, 112 A.D.2d 50, 490 N.Y.S.2d 414 (4th Dep't 1985), order aff'd, 66 N.Y.2d 697, 496 N.Y.S.2d 425, 487 N.E.2d 282 (1985) (inmate had no statutory guarantee or right to keep job in mess hall).

[3]For example, a prisoner was held to have a "protected interest" in a prison industries program at a meatpacking plant. Ferguson v. State, Dept. of Corrections, 816 P.2d 134 (Alaska 1991). See § 7:17, where other courts, in the context of work release programs, have found protectible interests to reside in particular prisoners and their job assignments.

§ 7:6   Rights of Prisoners, Third Edition

regulation, may, of course, grant prisoners the right to work while in prison[4] and may administratively establish an internal seniority system. If it does so, it may not discriminate among inmates on the basis of age, race, or handicap without equal protection consequences.[5] In addition, prison officials may not retaliate against an inmate who is seeking to exercise his constitutional rights by terminating him from a prison job.[6] With these caveats, the general rule followed by a

---

[4]While the Constitution may not specifically require that all prisoners be provided jobs, a Colorado statute does so provide. Ramos v. Lamm, 485 F. Supp. 122 (D. Colo. 1979), judgment aff'd in part, set aside in part on other grounds, 639 F.2d 559 (10th Cir. 1980). See also, to similar effect Laaman v. Helgemoe, 437 F. Supp. 269 (D.N.H. 1977) (recognizing that under a New Hampshire law, prisoners have a statutory right to work, the court saying that this right does not extend to a right to have a meaningful job, but noting that it does at least provide prisoners with the right to avoid stultifying idleness). But even where a statute requires a prison industries board to "provide employment for all physically fit inmates," such a requirement has been interpreted as not providing any statutory right to an inmate to be so employed. Garza v. Miller, 688 F.2d 480 (7th Cir. 1982). A New Jersey statute stating that "inmates of all correctional . . . institutions . . . shall be employed . . ." was interpreted as not investing in prison inmates any state-created "liberty" interest to actually be employed. Rowe v. Fauver, 533 F. Supp. 1239 (D.N.J. 1982). It was held that South Dakota statutes did not create any legal entitlement or right of a prisoner to either trustee status or to be employed in the prison industry's shops. Peck v. Hoff, 660 F.2d 371 (8th Cir. 1981).

[5]Williams v. Meese, 926 F.2d 994 (10th Cir. 1991) (prison inmate has no right to a job in the prison or to any job assignment in particular, but prison officials cannot discriminate against an inmate on the basis of age, race, or handicap, in choosing whether to assign him a job or choosing what job to assign him). See also Jackson v. Hogan, 388 Mass. 376, 446 N.E.2d 692 (1983), and § 7:9.

[6]Vignolo v. Miller, 120 F.3d 1075 (9th Cir. 1997) (firing an inmate from a job in the law library in retaliation for his exercise of his First Amendment rights would be unconstitutional if the claim was proved); Smith v. Rowe, 761 F.2d 360, 2 Fed. R. Serv. 3d 31 (7th Cir. 1985) (upholding jury verdict in favor of prisoner who

§ 7:6

large majority of the courts which have considered the issue still appears to be that prison inmates do not have any unqualified right to work in a particular job, that they have no seniority rights or job security, that they have no right to receive any attendant benefits from working, and that any such rights as may exist can be restricted by rules stemming from valid penological concerns such as security and order.[7]

For this reason, the courts generally view as administrative decisions selection of job assignments and removal of prisoners from particular job assignments, and fact-finding hearings are not usually required.[8] The general rule continues to be that removal from a job assignment is deemed to be an administrative matter with which courts are loath to interfere,[9] except where complete arbitrariness appears to exist. And, where appropriate authority exists by statute, government authorities may enter into contracts with respect to

---

refused to accept a job assignment on the grounds that her former position as assistant prison librarian was wrongfully terminated because of exercise of her constitutional rights; failure to take the proffered job was held not to be an unreasonable failure to mitigate damages; and prison officials were ordered to return inmate to former position); Hunter v. Heath, 95 F. Supp. 2d 1140 (D. Or. 2000), rev'd on other grounds, 26 Fed. Appx. 754 (9th Cir. 2002).

[7]Jackson v. Hogan, 388 Mass. 376, 446 N.E.2d 692 (1983).

[8]See Altizer v. Paderick, 569 F.2d 812 (4th Cir. 1978).

[9]See, e.g., Gardner v. Johnson, 429 F. Supp. 432 (E.D. Mich. 1977). However, working conditions can be so harsh in some instances as to constitute cruel and unusual punishment. See Howard v. King, 707 F.2d 215 (5th Cir. 1983); Fruit v. Norris, 905 F.2d 1147, 17 Fed. R. Serv. 3d 300 (8th Cir. 1990) (holding that forcing inmates to clear out a wet-well containing the prison's raw sewage without protective clothing and equipment could constitute an Eighth Amendment violation). Likewise, requiring an inmate to perform tasks beyond his or her physical capabilities may constitute an Eighth Amendment violation. See Martin v. Sargent, 780 F.2d 1334 (8th Cir. 1985). Compare Sampson v. King, 693 F.2d 566 (5th Cir. 1982) (exposure to pesticides as part of working conditions was not cruel and unusual punishment). See also Jackson v. Cain, 864 F.2d 1235 (5th Cir. 1989).

§ 7:6   Rights of Prisoners, Third Edition

providing the labor services of prisoners.[10]

Job seniority questions may arise when a prisoner is transferred to a different institution. Illustrative is *Beatham v Manson*.[11] Beatham argued that he should be assigned a job at his new prison commensurate with the seniority he had accrued at his former prison. The court rejected the claim, reasoning that the transfer to a more desirable minimum security institution offset any loss of pay or seniority.[12] Moreover, the court felt that granting the requested seniority would be unfair to inmates of the second institution.[13] No showing had been made that Beatham had been treated arbitrarily or capriciously and, in the absence of such proof, the court found the prison's policy to be rational. The court gratuitously observed that, in its opinion, such treatment of transferees would pass muster under the National Labor Relations Act.[14] Most courts have simply held that a prisoner who is assigned to a particular job or to a particular grade or pay level at one institution has no right to be assigned to the same type of job, or to retain a particular grade or pay level,[15] if he is transferred to another penal institution.[16]

---

[10]State of Ariz., By and Through Arizona Dept. of Transp. v. U.S., 216 Ct. Cl. 221, 575 F.2d 855 (1978).

[11]Beatham v. Manson, 369 F. Supp. 783 (D. Conn. 1973).

[12]*Id.* at 789. See also Kibbe v. Scully, 97 A.D.2d 795, 468 N.Y. S.2d 538 (2d Dep't 1983) (prisoner not entitled to pretransfer rate of pay following transfer to new facility).

[13]*Id.*

[14]*Id.* 29 U.S.C.A. § 151 et seq.

[15]Burkins v. Scully, 108 A.D.2d 743, 485 N.Y.S.2d 89 (2d Dep't 1985) (reduction in prisoner's pay rate from $1.25 per day to $0.45 per day was permissible when he was transferred to another correctional facility); Kibbe v. Scully, 97 A.D.2d 795, 468 N.Y.S.2d 538 (2d Dep't 1983).

[16]Gladson v. Henman, 814 F. Supp. 46 (D. Kan. 1993), order aff'd, 13 F.3d 405 (10th Cir. 1993) (no right to the same job after release from disciplinary segregation). A prisoner had no property or liberty interest in his employment as an institutional barber, which he lost as a result of his transfer to administrative

While it may not be legally required, a case can be made from a policy perspective for establishing a system of job security in prisons. Unjustified dismissals from attractive work assignments may undercut progress toward rehabilitation and may generate animosity toward prison officials. This, in turn, could lead to increased internal tensions and disruptions. In contrast, job security may result in sharpened work skills, since inmates would have the opportunity to master their craft. Finally, job security may increase productivity, as prisoners could concentrate on their work without having to worry about being fired. On the other hand, job security could lessen motivation to excel and might also preclude newer inmates from obtaining desirable jobs.

§ 7:7 The Right to a Particular Job as Affected by Civil Rights Laws

While the overwhelming majority of courts support the view that a prison inmate has no right to be assigned to, or to retain, a particular job, they nonetheless clearly support the view that decisions relating to job assignments or retention cannot be based on unlawful criteria, such as race, religion, and age.[1] For example, in a reverse discrimination case,[2] a prisoner who repeatedly asked to be assigned to work as an orderly in the jail kitchen was told that he would be appointed as soon as there was an opening for a "white boy," but it was also alleged that the deputy had said that he would permit only blacks to work in the kitchen.

---

segregation. Manley v. Bronson, 657 F. Supp. 832 (D. Conn. 1987). When transferred to another prison, an inmate had no due process right to either notice or hearing before his wage grade level was reduced following the transfer. Salahuddin v. Coughlin, 674 F. Supp. 1048 (S.D. N.Y. 1987).

[Section 7:7]

[1]See Note, The Need for a Different Standard and Analysis in Equal Employment Opportunity Cases Arising in the Prison Setting, 45 Ohio St LJ 737 (1984).

[2]Bentley v. Beck, 625 F.2d 70 (5th Cir. 1980).

On these facts, the court found that the inmate's right to be free from racial discrimination had been violated.

The courts are divided about whether Title VII of the Civil Rights Act of 1964 dealing with employment discrimination, applies to prisoners. The key issue is whether a prisoner is an "employee" within the meaning of the Act. In *Baker v McNeil Island Corrections Centey,*[3] the Ninth Circuit held that Title VII covered a prisoner. In that case, an inmate in a minimum security prison in Washington State applied for a job as a library aide in the corrections center annex library to assist the librarian and receive training and $30 per month. He did not get the job, even though he alleged that a prison employee said he was "next in line" for the job. The inmate, who was black, claimed that he had been a victim of racial discrimination. The district court dismissed the complaint for failure to state a claim, holding that Title VII (under which the inmate had sued) did not apply to prisoners. The Ninth Circuit remanded for reconsideration, noting that the Equal Employment Opportunity Commission had published a policy statement that prisoners eligible for work release did fall under Title VII.

The Tenth Circuit in *Williams v. Meese*[4] took a contrary position, holding that Title VII did not apply in prison. However, in that case, the court held that, while a prison inmate has no right to a job in the prison or to any job assignment in particular, where jobs are available, as a matter of constitutional law prison officials cannot discriminate against an inmate on the basis of age, race, or handicap in choosing whether to assign him a job or choosing what job to assign him. Following this rule, another court held that a black inmate who was denied his former higher paying position on his return from a temporary transfer to another jail successfully raised an equal protection claim by showing

---

[3]Baker v. McNeil Island Corrections Center, 859 F.2d 124 (9th Cir. 1988).

[4]Williams v. Meese, 926 F.2d 994 (10th Cir. 1991).

PRISON LABOR § 7:8

that white prisoners similarly transferred had been allowed to resume their former jobs.[5] Another black inmate was held to have stated an actionable equal protection claim in connection with an alleged racially discriminatory treatment of his request for work assignment as an electrician, where he was able to show that similarly situated white inmates, unlike himself, were given work assignments without having to complete a training program and that no blacks had been assigned as institution electricians for ten years.[6]

§ 7:8 The Right to a Particular Job as Affected by AIDS and Other Conditions

In the past two decades, much attention has been focused on acquired immune deficiency syndrome (AIDS) and those prisoners within the prison population who are human immunodeficiency virus (HIV) pos-

---

[5]U.S. ex rel. Motley v. Rundle, 340 F. Supp. 807 (E.D. Pa. 1972). See also Terrell v. State, 573 So. 2d 732 (Miss. 1990) (allegation that inmate was deprived of a job assignment because of his race states a constitutional claim).

An allegation against Illinois prison officials charging race discrimination in the assignment of jobs was found to be factually baseless, particularly in view of the fact that two of the three members of the board who were responsible for making such assignments were black. Gibson v. McEvers, 631 F.2d 95 (7th Cir. 1980).

While there is no right to a particular job and inmates may be transferred from job to job at the discretion of prison officials, inmates are protected against transfers in retaliation for exercise of their constitutional rights. Huffman v. Davis, 571 So. 2d 1371 (Fla. Dist. Ct. App. 1st Dist. 1990). Moreover, a loss of a job as punishment for a violation of prison rules conceivably could trigger protected liberty interests. See, e.g., Wallace v. Robinson, 914 F.2d 869 (7th Cir. 1990), reh'g granted and opinion vacated, 922 F.2d 409 (7th Cir. 1991) and on reh'g en banc, 940 F.2d 243 (7th Cir. 1991) (court held en banc that rule giving prison officials discretion to act for any reason, but placing restraints on their options if their motive is disciplinary, creates neither a liberty nor a property interest); Baptist v. O'Leary, 742 F. Supp. 975 (N.D. Ill. 1990).

[6]LaBounty v. Adler, 933 F.2d 121, 19 Fed. R. Serv. 3d 933 (2d Cir. 1991).

itive, as well as on those prisoners who have other mental and physical handicaps. The subject of prisoners with AIDS is generally reviewed in Chapter 3.[1] However, as the subject relates to prison labor, it has been held that prisoners who are HIV positive are handicapped within the meaning of federal law protecting the handicapped.[2] Therefore, prison officials must make an individual determination, with regard to each such

---

[Section 7:8]

[1]See also generally Note, AIDS in Correctional Institutions: The Legal Aspects, 23 Crim L Bull 533 (Nov/Dec 1987); Note, AIDS in Prisons: Are We Doing the Right Thing?, 13 New Eng J on Crim & Civ Confinement 269 (Summer 1987); Rowe, Death Row: AIDS is Turning a Prison Term into a Potential Death Sentence; 7 Cal Law 49 (Summer 1987); Raburn, Prisoners with AIDS: The Use of Electronic Processing, 24 Crim L Bull 213 (May/Jun 1988); Note, AIDS Behind Bars: Prison Responses and Judicial Deference, 62 Temple L Rev 327 (Spring 1989); Note, The AIDS Crisis in Prison: A Need for Change, 6 J Contemp Health L & Poly 221 (Spring 1990); Note, AIDS in Correctional Facilities: A New Form of the Death Penalty?, 36 Wash U J Urb & Contemp L 167 (Fall 1989); Note, The Legal Aspects of AIDS in the Correctional Setting, 14 L & Psych 185 (Spring 1990); Khan, The Application of Section 504 of the Rehabilitation Act to the Segregation of HlV-Positive Inmates, 65 Wash L Rev 839 (Oct 1990); Note, Women in Prison with AIDS: An Assault on the Constitution?, 64 S Cal L Rev 741 (Mar 1991).

[2]See, e.g., Rehabilitation Act of 1973, 29 U.S.C. § 794; Americans with Disabilities Act, 42 U.S.C. §§ 12101 et seq. The American with Disabilities Act applies to prisoners. Pennsylvania Dept. of Corrections v. Yeskey, 524 U.S. 206, 118 S. Ct. 1952, 141 L. Ed. 2d 215, 163 A.L.R. Fed. 671 (1998). However, The ADA has been attacked on Eleventh Amendment grounds. Board of Trustees of University of Alabama v. Garrett, 531 U.S. 356, 121 S. Ct. 955, 148 L. Ed. 2d 866, 151 Ed. Law Rep. 35 (2001) (Supreme Court holding, inter alia, that legislative record of the ADA failed to show that Congress identified a pattern of irrational state discrimination in employment against the disabled, and thus did not support abrogation of the states' Eleventh Amendment immunity from suits for money damages under Title I of the ADA). In addition the 10th Circuit held that the disability statutes do not apply to prison employment. White v. State of Colo., 82 F.3d 364, 366, 15 A.D.D. 18 (10th Cir. 1996). One district court held that this decision was overruled by *Yeskey*.

PRISON LABOR § 7:8

prisoner, that he or she presents a significant danger to other prisoners in the performance of certain jobs.[3] For example, if the prisoner works in food services, a determination must be made that a significant risk exists of transmitting the virus to others before the prisoner can be removed from that particular job. A blanket prohibition against assigning prisoners with AIDS to food service jobs could not be tolerated, where the rule was not based on significant scientific evidence but on "unfounded fears and mythologies" of other prisoners that they might contract AIDS and on the alleged dangers of possible rioting.[4] With regard to prisoners with mental or physical handicaps, it has been held that the exclusion of mentally ill prisoners from participating in a vocational rehabilitation program operated by the West Virginia Department of Corrections constituted dis-

---

[3]Farmer v. Moritsugu, 742 F. Supp. 525 (W.D. Wis. 1990) (prisoner's claim that his equal protections rights were violated must fail since the institution had a rational basis for excluding this prisoner from working in the food service).

[4]See, generally, Casey v. Lewis, 773 F. Supp. 1365 (D. Ariz. 1991), rev'd in part on other grounds, vacated in part on other grounds, 4 F.3d 1516, 2 A.D.D. 908 (9th Cir. 1993) (reversed on standing grounds). But see Gates v. Rowland, 39 F.3d 1439, 7 A.D.D. 1 (9th Cir. 1994) (court reversed the judgment that enjoined defendants from prohibiting plaintiff HIV-positive inmates from working in the cafeteria; while a person infected with HIV was an individual with a disability within the meaning of § 706(8)(B) of the Rehabilitation Act of 1973 (Act), 29 U.S.C. § 706(8)(B), abridgment of the rights granted by the Act was permissible if it was reasonably related to legitimate penological interests; given the phobias and irrationality prevalent in the prison population, the restriction was permissible); Casey v. Lewis, 4 F.3d 1516, 2 A.D.D. 908 (9th Cir. 1993) (inmates lacked standing to challenge prohibition against food service employment by inmates testing positive for human immunodeficiency virus (HIV); even if named inmate in class had been identified HIV-positive as early as pleading stage, no named inmate ever stated that he or she was interested in food service job, and no named inmate applied for one).

crimination for purposes of 29 U.S.C. § 794.[5]

§ 7:9 Wages—The Right to Be Paid in General

On its face, the Thirteenth Amendment does not address the question of wages for convict labor. Courts have held that prisoners have no independent constitutional right to be paid wages for their services,[1] but a jurisdiction may create a statutory right of compensation.[2] Thus, although the Thirteenth Amendment may not require payment of wages for prison

---

[5]Sites v. McKenzie, 423 F. Supp. 1190 (N.D. W. Va. 1976). See also Laurence L. Motiuk & Frank J. Porporino, The Prison Careers of Mentally Disordered Offenders, 18 Intl. J. L. & Psychiatry 29 (1995) (discussing the unique work problems mentally disordered prisoners have when prison officials are ill equipped to deal with their special needs).

[Section 7:9]

[1]See, e.g., Murray v. Mississippi Dept. of Corrections, 911 F.2d 1167 (5th Cir. 1990); Wendt v. Lynaugh, 841 F.2d 619 (5th Cir. 1988); Rochon v. Louisiana State Penitentiary Inmate Account, 880 F.2d 845 (5th Cir. 1989) (prisoners have no constitutional right to be paid for work performed in prison); Hrbek v. Farrier, 787 F.2d 414 (8th Cir. 1986) (there is no constitutional right to prison wages and any such compensation is by the grace of the state); Sigler v. Lowrie, 404 F.2d 659 (8th Cir. 1968); Woodall v. Partilla, 581 F. Supp. 1066 (N.D. Ill. 1984) (since no pay at all is required, low pay violates no constitutional right); X v. Brierley, 457 F. Supp. 350 (E.D. Pa. 1978); Bryant v. Miller, 637 F. Supp. 226 (M.D. Pa. 1984); Kennibrew v. Russell, 578 F. Supp. 164 (E.D. Tenn. 1983) (county workhouse inmate has no constitutional right to be paid either for work time or for idle time); Borror v. White, 377 F. Supp. 181 (W.D. Va. 1974).

[2]See Sprouse v. Federal Prison Industries, Inc., 480 F.2d 1 (5th Cir. 1973); Sigler v. Lowrie, 404 F.2d 659 (8th Cir. 1968); Borror v. White, 377 F. Supp. 181 (W.D. Va. 1974); Ingenito v. Department of Corrections, State of N.J., 568 F. Supp. 946 (D.N.J. 1983); Piatt v. MacDougall, 773 F.2d 1032 (9th Cir. 1985) (Arizona statute created right to inmate compensation in an amount equal to at least the current prevailing minimum wage for work performed for private parties, and state could not deprive inmate of wages without affording inmate due process). The rate of inmate compensation may legitimately vary from institution to institution. See Burkins v. Scully, 108 A.D.2d 743, 485 N.Y.S.2d 89 (2d Dep't

§ 7:9

labor, it does not preclude a state from choosing to do so. Most states currently provide only de minimis wages.[3] Moreover, the failure to pay promised wages may only constitute a breach of contract and, thus, not be actionable under 42 U.S.C. § 1983.[4]

In rare cases, it is possible to invoke other constitutional provisions for an increase in prison wages. For example, in *Glover v Johnson*,[5] women prisoners argued that the Equal Protection Clause was violated by a wage scheme in which female prisoners were paid less than male prisoners for the same work. In response, the district court required the prison authorities to review the wage structure so that female inmates were paid fairly.[6]

Thus, the general rule is that absent a particular statute which provides a right to a specific wage prison-

---

1985). See also American Correctional Assn, Standards for Adult Correctional Institutions Standard 3-4407 (1990). Special rules may require a minimum wage or wages prevailing in the trade if inmates are employed by public or private organizations. American Correctional Assn, Standards for Adult Correctional Institutions Standard 3-4408 (1990). A United Nations document recommends a system of "equitable remuneration" for prisoners' work. For nongovernmental work, the full normal wages should be paid to the prison administration for distribution, at least in part, to the prisoners, who can in turn choose to send support to their families. Part of the earnings are saved and given to the offender on release. United Nations, Standard Minimum Rules for the Treatment of Prisoners Rules 73, 75, 76 (1955). See, generally, J. Spitzer, Penal and Correctional Institution, 60 Am Jur 2d Penal Inst §§ 168-169 (1987), as to the right of inmates to be compensated for their labor.

[3]See, generally, Lenihan, The Financial Condition of Released Inmates, 21 Crime & Delinq 266 (1975). In lieu of significant wages, however, some prisoners can earn a statutory reduction in sentence for prison work performed. See, e.g., Conn Gen Stat § 18-98a.

[4]Holton v. Fields, 638 F. Supp. 1319 (S.D. W. Va. 1986).

[5]Glover v. Johnson, 478 F. Supp. 1075, 1093 (E.D. Mich. 1979).

[6]Glover v. Johnson, 510 F. Supp. 1019, 1022-23 (E.D. Mich. 1981), judgment aff'd, 774 F.2d 1161 (6th Cir. 1985). The subsequent history of this case is found in § 4:5.

ers have no constitutional right to be paid for their labor, any claim to relief must be based on federal or state statutes or regulations. To that subject we now turn.

§ 7:10 —The Right to Be Paid Minimum Wages

The Fair Labor Standards Act of 1983 (FLSA),[1] which regulates the wages and hours of many workers, is the most important statute on this subject. The FLSA, "enacted in 1938, requires employers throughout the country to pay their employees the minimum hourly wage as established by Congress."[2] Like most of its state counterparts, it is silent as to whether prison labor is covered. There is no specific evidence in the legislative history of the FLSA that Congress intended to exclude prison laborers from the protections of the Act.[3] Thus, the question becomes whether or not a working inmate is an "employee" within the meeting of the Act.

To make this determination, most courts that have examined the question have employed an "economic

---

[Section 7:10]

[1] 29 U.S.C.A. § 201 et seq. One federal statute authorizes federal prisoners in a few programs to receive not less than the prevailing wages in the area. 18 U.S.C. § 1761(c).

[2] Alexander B. Wellen, Prisoners and the FLSA: Can the American Taxpayer Afford Extending Prison Inmates the Federal Minimum Wage, 67 Temp. L. Rev. 295 (1994). The Act was intended "to eliminate substandard labor conditions throughout the nation and to prevent unfair competition in commerce from the use of underpaid labor." Id.

[3] Hale v. State of Ariz., 993 F.2d 1387 (9th Cir. 1993) (pointing out that inmates are not on the list of excluded employees). See also Carter v. Dutchess Community College, 735 F.2d 8, 13, 17 Ed. Law Rep. 1031 (2d Cir. 1984) ("It would be an encroachment upon the legislative prerogative for a court to hold that a class of unlisted workers is excluded from the Act."). The "economic reality test" was first set forth by the Supreme Court in a non-prison case. Goldberg v. Whitaker House Co-op., Inc., 366 U.S. 28, 33, 81 S. Ct. 933, 6 L. Ed. 2d 100 (1961).

§ 7:10

reality" test.[4] This test looks at the totality of the circumstances to determine whether in fact there is an "employer-employee" relationship established between the plaintiff and the defendant. Among the factors that are considered to make this determination are: (1) whether the location where the labor is provided is inside or outside of the prison; (2) whether the labor is voluntary or involuntary; and (3) whether the employer is a private or public body.

Utilizing the "economic reality" test, courts have "consistently rejected the notion that all prisoners are categorically excluded from the covered under the FLSA."[5] Thus, it is improper to say that an inmate is not entitled to receive the minimum wage merely because he or she is an inmate; a more particularized examination of the work relationship is required. However, upon undertaking this examination, most courts have held that inmates who work in prison settings for prison authorities are not "employees" within the meaning of the FLSA.[6] The reason that the Seventh Circuit gave this reason for the conclusion that inmates

---

[4]See N.L.R.B. v. Hearst Publications, 322 U.S. 111, 64 S. Ct. 851, 88 L. Ed. 1170 (1944)(overruled in part on other grounds by, Nationwide Mut. Ins. Co. v. Darden, 503 U.S. 318, 112 S. Ct. 1344, 117 L. Ed. 2d 581 (1992)).

[5]Barnett v. Young Men's Christian Ass'n, Inc., 175 F.3d 1023 (8th Cir. 1999).

[6]See, e.g. Villarreal v. Woodham, 113 F.3d 202 (11th Cir. 1997) (holding that a pretrial detainee is not an employee); Vanskike v. Peters, 974 F.2d 806, 810 (7th Cir. 1992); Zawitz v. Ohio Dept. of Rehab. & Corr., 61 Ohio Misc. 2d 798, 585 N.E.2d 573 (Ct. Cl. 1990) (inmates working in a prison setting are not "employees" subject to statutory protections under statutory provisions relating exclusively to employers); Franks v. Oklahoma State Industries, 7 F.3d 971 (10th Cir. 1993) (FLSA definition of employee does not extend to inmates working in prison); Washington v. Cornell Corrections, Inc., 2001 OK CIV APP 102, 30 P.3d 1162 (Okla. Civ. App. Div. 1 2001), cert. denied, (July 3, 2001) (inmate's confinement at a privately owned correctional facility did not alter his status as a prisoner and, thus, did not make him an employee under the FLSA). See also Kip Davis, Recent Development: Fair Labor Standards Act, 27 Stetson L. Rev. 1156 (Winter 1998) ("the

§ 7:10   Rights of Prisoners, Third Edition

are not "employees" is representative:

> Prisoners are essentially taken out of the national economy upon incarceration. When they are assigned work *within the prison* for purposes of training and rehabilitation, they have not contracted with the government to become its employees. Rather, they are working as part of their sentences of incarceration.[7]

While so far the courts have been unwilling to hold that inmates who work inside prison walls for prison employers-or even outside where their work benefits and contributes to the operation of the prison-are entitled to a minimum wage as a matter of federal law, the situation changes where inmates work outside of the prison for private employers who are engaged in private commerce. This kind of arrangement is increasing in recent years.[8] In one such case an inmate worked at a YMCA. He worked forty hours a week as a maintenance worker. The YMCA had the power to hire and fire him and to control his schedule and conditions of employment. The inmate sued, claiming that the $1.00 per hour that he was earning violated the FLSA. The Eighth Circuit held that because the work was for a private employer, because it was not work that was designed to keep the prison running, and because the employer had the power to hire and fire, the FLSA applied.[9] The fact that YMCA was a not for profit institution did not change this result.[10] The Second[11]

---

majority of the courts have held that prisoners should not be considered employees under the FLSA").

[7]Vanskike v. Peters, 974 F.2d 806, 810 (7th Cir. 1992) (emphasis supplied).

[8]Annotation: Coverage, under Fair Labor Standards Act (FLSA) (29 U.S.C.A. §§ 201 et seq.), of prisoners working for private individuals or entities other than prisons, 110 A.L.R. Fed. 839.

[9]Barnett v. Young Men's Christian Ass'n, Inc., 175 F.3d 1023 (8th Cir. 1999).

[10]*Id.*

[11]Carter v. Dutchess Community College, 735 F.2d 8, 17 Ed. Law Rep. 1031 (2d Cir. 1984). But cf. Danneskjold v. Hausrath, 82

and the Fifth Circuits[12] also have held that that when the prisoner voluntarily works outside the prison for a private company that supervises and pays him for private work, the FLSA can apply.[13] However, other circuits, most notably the Ninth, take a contrary view and hold that an inmate can never be protected by the FLSA, even if he or she works for a private entity and works outside the prison.[14]

Federal prisoners, even those working for a private employer, face an added barrier to obtaining a minimum wage. Even if the general language in the FLSA might otherwise be construed as covering federal prisoners, the more specific language on the employment of federal prisoners found in 18 U.S.C. § 4126 precludes application of the FLSA to prison workers.[15] In one case, for instance, the court, in finding that inmates assigned to work in a pharmaceutical company were not employees, noted that the company could nei-

---

F.3d 37, 108 Ed. Law Rep. 1105 (2d Cir. 1996) (holding that the FLSA does not apply to an inmate who works within the prison for a private company).

[12]Watson v. Graves, 909 F.2d 1549, 110 A.L.R. Fed. 823 (5th Cir. 1990) (inmates employed by private construction company outside of prison walls were covered by FLSA) . See also Reimonenq v. Foti, 72 F.3d 472 (5th Cir. 1996).

[13]Whether sovereign immunity bars such claims is an open question. The Supreme Court in Alden v. Maine, 527 U.S. 706, 119 S. Ct. 2240, 144 L. Ed. 2d 636 (1999) held that suit directly against a state under the FLSA is barred by the Eleventh Amendment. The Eleventh Amendment only bars suit against a state entity; thus, a suit against a private employer would not be barred under the Amendment. However, under current Eleventh Amendment doctrines, an FLSA suit against a state by a prisoner could not proceed.

[14]See, e.g. Hale v. State of Ariz., 993 F.2d 1387 (9th Cir. 1993) (en banc); Gilbreath v. Cutter Biological, Inc., 931 F.2d 1320 (9th Cir. 1991) (inmates in the Arizona Prison System who worked for a privately operated plasma center on the prison grounds were not covered employees under the Fair Labor Standards Act);

[15]Emory v. U.S., 2 Cl. Ct. 579 (1983), judgment aff'd, 727 F.2d 1119 (Fed. Cir. 1983).

§ 7:10

ther hire nor fire the prisoners and lacked ultimate control over them.[16] The court also cited the absence of a formal contractual relationship between the inmates and the company.[17]

Prisoners seeking minimum wages under state laws generally have a tough row to hoe. State labor legislation often defines employers and employees in terms comparable to the Fair Labor Standards Act.[18] It is not surprising, therefore, to find courts interpreting those terms to exclude prisoners, at least when they work for the prison within prison walls from coverage under the state statute.[19] In states where legislation has been enacted specifically addressing prisoners and minimum wage, courts have applied those statutes in a very limited way.[20] In some of these states, whether or not a prisoner is qualified to receive minimum wage usually depends on the category of work he is involved in. Typi-

---

[16]Sims v. Parke Davis & Co., 334 F. Supp. 774, 15 Fed. R. Serv. 2d 709 (E.D. Mich. 1971), judgment aff'd, 453 F.2d 1259 (6th Cir. 1971). But compare Carter v. Dutchess Community College, 735 F.2d 8, 17 Ed. Law Rep. 1031 (2d Cir. 1984) (rejecting the ultimate control test); see also Danneskjold v. Hausrath, 82 F.3d 37, 108 Ed. Law Rep. 1105 (2d Cir. 1996) (the court, modifying the test established in *Carter,* held that the "FLSA doesn't apply to inmates in circumstances in which labor provides services to the prison, whether or not the work is voluntary, whether it is performed inside or outside the prison and whether or not a private contractor is involved").

[17]Sims v. Parke Davis & Co., 334 F. Supp. 774, 786, 15 Fed. R. Serv. 2d 709 (E.D. Mich. 1971), judgment aff'd, 453 F.2d 1259 (6th Cir. 1971).

[18]See, e.g., Ill Ann Stat ch 48, §§ 1001-1015; NY Lab Law §§ 650-665; Or Rev Stat §§ 653.010-.070.

[19]See, e.g., Sims v. Parke Davis & Co., 334 F. Supp. 774, 15 Fed. R. Serv. 2d 709 (E.D. Mich. 1971), judgment aff'd, 453 F.2d 1259 (6th Cir. 1971).

[20]Bilke v. State, 189 Ariz. 133, 938 P.2d 1134 (Ct. App. Div. 1 1997) (inmate who worked for Department of Corrections, and second inmate who worked for a fellow inmate, did not work under contract between Director of Department of Corrections and private person or entity, and thus were not entitled to minimum wage under statute providing for payment of minimum wage pur-

PRISON LABOR § 7:10

cally, as is the case with the FLSA case law, a distinction is made between prisoners who work for the prisons and prisoners who work in private sector industries.[21] In some situations, state courts have had to decide whether a general state law requiring minimum wages to be paid for certain kinds of labor applied to prison labor. At times the task was complicated by the existence of another statute specifically dealing with prison laborers' wages. Generally, courts have held, in such situations, that the specific statute applied, not the general statute.[22]

Eschewing statutory or constitutional arguments, some prisoners have based wage demands on a quantum meruit theory, demanding payment for the reasonable value of their services.[23] This ingenious argument has been rejected on the rationale that, because the inmate's labor belongs to the state, prisoners have not been deprived of any labor that belonged to them.[24]

In sum, demands by prisoners for minimum wages for work done in prison are unlikely to be achieved through litigation in the absence of a statute specifically including prisoners within its coverage. Work for outside groups, however, can possibly be covered under the FSLA. The case law on that question is divided,

---

suant to such contract, notwithstanding fact that entities they worked for had contracts with private parties).

[21]See, e.g., Ar. St. § 12-30-502; Az.St. § 31-254; In. St. § 11-10-7-3; La. R.S. § 15:873.

[22]See, e.g., Manville v. Board of Governors of Wayne State University, 85 Mich. App. 628, 272 N.W.2d 162 (1978), which held that a later-enacted specific wage law known as the Correctional Industries Act applied to determine the pay of prison laborers rather than the state's more general minimum wage law applicable to a whole, more general range of employment situations.

[23]See, e.g., Sims v. Parke Davis & Co., 334 F. Supp. 774, 15 Fed. R. Serv. 2d 709 (E.D. Mich. 1971), judgment aff'd, 453 F.2d 1259 (6th Cir. 1971); Huntley v. Gunn Furniture Co., 79 F. Supp. 110 (W.D. Mich. 1948).

[24]Sims v. Parke Davis & Co., 334 F. Supp. 774, 791, 15 Fed. R. Serv. 2d 709 (E.D. Mich. 1971), judgment aff'd, 453 F.2d 1259 (6th Cir. 1971).

§ 7:10 RIGHTS OF PRISONERS, THIRD EDITION

and is quite case-specific. As one court put it "the more indicia of traditional free-market employment the relationship between the prisoner and his putative 'employer' bears, the more likely it is that the FLSA will govern the employment relationship."[25]

On a policy level, commentators and policy makers have taken various views on this question. Some commentators have written that legislation ought to be passed exempting inmates, regardless of where they work, from minimum wage protections.[26] The American Bar Association has taken a contrary position. In its Standards for Criminal Justice, Legal Status of Prisoners Standard 23-4.5 (adopted in 1985), the American Bar Association (ABA) recommends that prisoners employed by private employers be paid at least minimum wages. The ABA also recommends that prisoners, if paid the minimum or higher wages, should be required to pay applicable taxes and contribute some of their net income from such employment toward their own maintenance, family support obligations, and victim restitution. The ABA recommends increasing the pay, over a period of time, of prisoners who are privately employed to comparable rates in private industry. Other policy-setting groups, including unions, have taken a similar position.[27] Minimum wages would provide an incentive for quality job performance and a

---

[25]Villarreal v. Woodham, 113 F.3d 202, 206-07 (11th Cir. 1997).

[26]James K. Kaslam, Comment, Prison Labor under State Direction: Do Inmates have the Right to FLSA Coverage and Minimum Wage?, 1994 BYU L. Rev. 369 (arguing that it would undermine public policy to allow coverage): Alexander B. Wellen, Prisoners and the FLSA: Can the American Taxpayer Afford Extending Prison Inmates the Federal Minimum Wage, 67 Temp. L. Rev. 295 (1994).

[27]See, e.g., Stephen P. Garvey, Freeing Prisoners' Labor, 50 Stan. L. Rev. 339, n.265 (1998) (describing the AFL-CIO support for minimum wages for prison labor under the FSLA); National Advisory Commission on Criminal Justice Standards and Goals, Corrections, Standard 11.10(5) (1973); Uniform Law Commrs' Model Sentencing and Corrections Act §§ 4-801(2), 4-811(d) (July 2001) (reprinted in Appendix B); Note, Minimum Wages for Prison-

work atmosphere more like that to which the offender will return on release from prison.

Moreover, if prisoners earned regular salaries, they would pay taxes and social security and could be charged for their room and board, plus the costs associated with their employment, thereby helping to defray institutional expenses.[28] Since opportunities to spend wages are limited by both prison rules and the lack of access to stores, inmates would be likely to save money, with the result that they might amass a sufficient financial cushion to provide for themselves after release until they are able to secure employment. Alternatively, some inmates might choose to use their earnings to support their families,[29] thereby helping to preserve family ties and lessening the likelihood that their families will have to go on welfare. Finally, providing minimum wages may inculcate in the inmate a sense of financial responsibility, foster greater self-respect, and alleviate feelings of being exploited by the prison system.[30]

In the absence of being able to pay minimum wages,

---

ers: Legal Obstacles and Suggested Reforms, 7 U Mich JL Ref 193 (1973). For a description of a prison work program wherein inmates received payments approximating the federal minimum wage, see Mastrian v. Schoen, 725 F.2d 1164 (8th Cir. 1984).

[28]See ABA, Standards for Criminal Justice Standard 23-4.5(a) (1985); Uniform Law Commrs' Model Sentencing and Corrections Act § 4-812(a)(2) (July 2001). Some states already require prisoners to reimburse the state for costs of incarceration if they are financially able to do so. See, e.g., Mich Comp Laws Ann § 800.401 et seq.

[29]ABA, Standards for Criminal Justice Standard 23-4.5 (1985). See also Smith v. State, Dept. of Revenue, Child Support Enforcement Div., 790 P.2d 1352 (Alaska 1990) (state may attach prisoner earnings to satisfy child support orders).

[30]These arguments were raised and rejected as part of an Eighth Amendment claim in X v. Brierley, 457 F. Supp. 350 (E.D. Pa. 1978). For a vivid description of inmates' hostile attitudes toward their prison jobs, see J. Mitford, Kind and Usual Punishment 207-35 (1973). See also Dorman v. Thornburgh, 955 F.2d 57 (D.C. Cir. 1992) (regulation requiring working inmates to commit a per-

§ 7:10

the ABA Standards for Criminal Justice, Legal Status of Prisoners, Standard 23-4.1 (b) suggests that compensation should be provided "for well-performed work at least sufficient to enable the prisoner to make commissary purchases and to accumulate some funds for release."

On the other hand, requiring prisons to pay minimum wages might prove counter-productive if corrections officials decided it was economically sounder to employ better- trained nonprisoners for comparable salaries. If the economic incentive to utilize inmates were diminished, fewer inmates might have jobs. While a legislature could mandate jobs for prisoners, pressures from unions and unemployed nonconvicts would constitute formidable opposition. Also, if too many costs were assessed against inmate salaries, such as would occur if they were required to support all the expenses of running the corrections and criminal justice systems, inmates would be left with nothing to show for their efforts, which might be even more frustrating to them than the status quo.

§ 7:11 Withholding Wages and Payment of Interest on Inmate Accounts

When prisoners do get paid for their work, new questions arises that have recently come to the fore. Can prison wages be withheld from the inmate? Since inmates are almost always prevented from carrying cash in prison, can they earn interest on their wages and other funds when they are deposited in an inmate account?

Regarding the first question, in many states and also

---

centage of their earnings to pay court-ordered obligations did not create a liberty interest requiring application of due process); Smith v. State, Dept. of Revenue, Child Support Enforcement Div., 790 P.2d 1352, 1354 (Alaska 1990) ("the rehabilitative benefits associated with taking some responsibility for the support of [a prisoner's] children justifies imposition of child support obligations").

on the federal level, legislation has been passed that allows for inmate wages to be withheld for various programs and services. Such programs and services include withholding wages for court fees, costs of incarceration, medical care, and victim restitution.

On the federal level, a program called the Inmate Financial Responsibility Program requires inmates to commit a percentage of their prison employment earnings to the payment of court-ordered compensation to the inmates' victims.[1] Many states have also enacted similar legislation requiring a certain percentage of earned wages to be allotted to victims and their families.[2] Similar state legislation also gives correctional institutions the power to deduct general prison

---

[Section 7:11]

[1]28 C.F.R. § 545 (2002). See Hyde v. Hawk, 201 F.3d 448 (10th Cir. 1999); Montano-Figueroa v. Crabtree, 162 F.3d 548 (9th Cir. 1998).

[2]See Cal. Pen. Code § 2085.5 (deduction from prisoners' wages for payment of restitution fines); Ariz. Rev. Stat. Ann. § 31-254(D)(2) (30% of prisoner's compensation to be expended for court-ordered restitution); 11 Del. C. § 6534 (a portion of an inmate's wages from employment under the private sector may be applied to the Victim Compensation Fund); Fla. Stat. § 946.002 (monetary payments made directly to the prisoner go in part or whole to satisfy restitution ordered by the court); Miss. Code Ann. § 47-5-1251(1)(d) (deduction of prisoner's wages to pay no less than 5% and no more than 20% into the Crime Victims' Compensation Fund); N.M. Stat. Ann. § 33-8-8 (no more than 50% and no less than 15% can be deducted from an inmate's wages to pay victim restitution); Utah Code Ann. § 63-63a-4 (a percentage of income from inmates working in a federally certified private sector program will be deposited into the victim reparation fund); Ala. Code § 15-18-180 (can establish a victim restitution fund from inmates' wages); Minn. Stat § 243.23 (inmate's earnings can go toward court-ordered restitution); Mont. Code Ann. § 53-1-107 (if inmate's account exceeds two hundred dollars, the excess can be forfeited to pay victim restitution); Nev. Rev. Stat. Ann. § 209.463 (if inmate is paid minimum wage or higher, a portion is deducted for a victim compensation fund); N.J. Stat. § 30:8-42 (the county governing body is authorized to make deductions, not exceeding one-third of the inmate's total income, for victim restitution); N.D. Cent. Code § 12-44.1-12.1 (correctional facility administrator may

§ 7:11　　　　　　　Rights of Prisoners, Third Edition

costs and medical care from an inmate's income.[3] A typical statute is Iowa's, which requires convicted criminal defendants to pay restitution to victims and reimbursement to the state for attorney's fees of court-appointed public defenders.[4] The court sets the amount due at sentencing and the Department of Correction is then empowered to present a restitution plan to the court for its approval. The inmate is entitled to be heard before the plan is ordered by the court. Once approved, to collect the money due under the plan the Department sets aside 20% of all funds coming to the inmate, including prison wages.

Not surprisingly, the validity of these statutes has been challenged as violative of the Fifth and Fourteenth

---

withdraw an inmate's funds to pay restitution); 57 Okl. St. § 549 (up to 80% of an inmate's wages can be deducted to pay victim restitution); S.D. Codified Laws § 23A-28B-40 (deductions from an inmate's income will be placed in the Crime Victims' Compensation Fund); Rev. Code Wash. § 72.09.110 (a portion of an inmate's income may be deposited in a victim restitution account); Rev. Code Wash. § 72.09.111 (inmates earning at least minimum wage may have 5% deducted for victim compensation); Wyo. Stat § 25-13-107 (if an inmate is paying child support only 5% of his or her wages may be deducted to pay victim compensation, but if the inmate is not paying child support 20% will be deducted).

[3]See Fla. Stat. § 946.002 (inmates receiving compensation are required to reimburse the state for lodging, food, transportation and other expenses); Miss. Code Ann. § 47-5-1251 (deductions may be made in order to pay for reasonable room and board); N.M. Stat. Ann. § 33-8-8 (the department may deduct from inmate compensation for reasonable costs incident to confinement); Ala. Code § 14-8-6 (can withhold portion of wages to pay for costs of confinement); Minn. Stat § 241.26 (correctional institution may withhold a portion of wages to go towards transportation and other incidental expenses of the inmate); Minn. Stat § 243.23 (compensation paid to inmates may go toward room and board and medical expenses); N.D. Cent. Code § 12-44.1-12.1 (withholding funds for health care costs). See also Reimonenq v. Foti, 72 F.3d 472 (5th Cir. 1996) (holding that Louisiana could require a work release prison to contribute 10% of his wages to Sheriff's Victim Compensation Fund).

[4]Iowa Code §§ 910.2; 904.72.

PRISON LABOR § 7:11

Amendments.[5] In these cases, plaintiffs have argued that these types of statutes amount to a deprivation of a constitutionally protected property right without due process of law.[6] The challenges, by and large, have not been successful.[7] For example, in *Mahers v. Halford*,[8] the United States Court of Appeals for the Eighth Circuit held that the Iowa plan mentioned above, which deducted 20% of a prisoner's money to pay court-ordered restitution, did not violate due process.[9] As mentioned, the statute called for the sentencing court to review the payment plan and approve or modify it. At that determination, the prisoner had the right to be heard. However, after the plan was approved the deduction was automatic, with no further right to a hearing. This is the provision that the inmate challenged. The court held that this scheme passed constitutional muster. The court relied on *Mathews v. Eldridge*,[10] in which the Supreme Court announced a three-part balancing test to determine exactly "what process is due" under the Fifth and Fourteenth Amendments.[11] The Eighth Circuit found that a balancing of the *Mathews* factors compelled it to hold that the deductions from the prisoners' funds did not violate due process. The court concluded that, because of the

---

[5]The Fifth and Fourteenth Amendments guarantee that a person will not be deprived of "life, liberty, or property without due process of law." U.S. Const. amend V; U.S. Const. amend. XIV.

[6]See Ervin v. Blackwell, 733 F.2d 1282 (8th Cir. 1984); Cumbey v. State, 1985 OK 36, 699 P.2d 1094 (Okla. 1985) (plaintiff prisoners attacked the constitutionality of various sections of the state correctional code, including the prison reimbursement section, on the grounds that, inter alia, the statute violated their right to due process).

[7]See, e.g., Reynolds v. Wagner, 128 F.3d 166 (3d Cir. 1997); Jennings v. Lombardi, 70 F.3d 994 (8th Cir. 1995).

[8]Mahers v. Halford, 76 F.3d 951 (8th Cir. 1996).

[9]*Id.*

[10]Mathews v. Eldridge, 424 U.S. 319, 96 S. Ct. 893, 47 L. Ed. 2d 18 (1976).

[11]*Id.* at 335.

§ 7:11

limited nature of the deprivation and the more limited due process protections applicable to the inmates, the notice and hearing proceedings satisfied due process.[12]

An additional question is whether the failure to pay interest on prisoner financial accounts is a "taking" of property forbidden by the Fifth Amendment. These accounts are typical in most prisons. Inmates draw on the accounts to make individual commissary purchases and to send money to family. Inmates may not use other accounts to pay for personal items from the prison commissary. In many cases, the accounts are non interest-bearing. Is the failure of the government to pay interest on these accounts a constitutional taking of an inmate's property?

In the litigation raising this issue, inmate advocates cite an opinion from the Supreme Court dealing with an analogous situation of lawyer escrow accounts. Funds that lawyers hold for clients are often put in these accounts. Often the interest is devoted to some purpose involving the administration of justice, such as funding pro bono activities, and is not given to the client. The Supreme Court held in one such case that a valid takings issue was presented.[13] Is the same true for prison accounts?

The Ninth Circuit answered this question in the affirmative and held that inmates do have a "property" interest in such accounts.[14] However, on remand summary judgment was granted because the district court found that in practice the cost of administering the accounts exceeded the interest that would have been

---

[12]Mahers v. Halford, 76 F.3d 951, 955 (8th Cir. 1996). See also Amy McCool, Casenote: Prisoners' Rights: An Unbalanced Approach to Prisoners' Procedural Due Process Rights: Misapplying the Balancing Test in Mahers v. Halford, 30 Creighton L. Rev. 949 (May 1997).

[13]Phillips v. Washington Legal Foundation, 524 U.S. 156, 118 S. Ct. 1925, 141 L. Ed. 2d 174 (1998).

[14]Schneider v. California Dept. of Corrections, 151 F.3d 1194 (9th Cir. 1998).

earned.[15] The district court also rejected the plaintiffs' claim that their equal protection rights had been violated.[16] The plaintiffs alleged that state parolees were offered inmate trust accounts, which earned interest, while inmates were denied interest payments,[17] and argued that this difference in treatment between inmates and parolees constitutes an equal protection violation. The court pointed out that in order "to establish an equal protection violation, plaintiffs must show that the alleged actions taken by the state (1) had a disparate impact on a suspect class and (2) [were] motivated by discriminatory intent."[18] The court found that the plaintiffs showed no evidence establishing a difference in treatment between them and the parolees.[19] As discussed in Chapter 4, equal protection claims are usually unsuccessful for prisoners because of the difficulty in proving a suspect classification and showing discriminatory intent by the correctional facility or other governmental actor.[20]

This holding leaves open the possibility that inmates can recover interest on their accounts if they make a showing that the expenses of administration do not exceed a reasonable amount of interest. However, no other circuit has made a similar holding, and the Fourth Circuit in a recent opinion rejected the reasoning of the Ninth Circuit and found that there was no "taking" involved in operating these accounts without paying interest.[21]

---

[15]Schneider v. California Dept. of Corrections, 91 F. Supp. 2d 1316 (N.D. Cal. 2000).

[16]*Id.*

[17]*Id.* at 1330.

[18]*Id.*

[19]*Id.* at 1331.

[20]See Ch 4.

[21]Washlefske v. Winston, 234 F.3d 179 (4th Cir. 2000), cert. denied, 532 U.S. 983, 121 S. Ct. 1627, 149 L. Ed. 2d 488 (2001) (holding that there is no taking if the interest in the inmate ac-

§ 7:12 The Right to Be Compensated for Work-Related Injuries

Ordinarily, prison inmates who are injured or disabled while working have three avenues of redress: they may sue in tort where that is permitted; they may seek recovery under a state workers' compensation statute if they are state prisoners; or they may file a claim under 18 U.S.C. § 4126 if they are federal prisoners.

Tort Suits

Tort suits are difficult, although not always impossible, to maintain. For one thing, it is not easy to make out a constitutional claim for work-related injuries that will provide access to the federal courts. It has been held that unsafe working conditions (in the cases cited below, a slippery floor) did not constitute the "unnecessary and wanton infliction of pain" necessary to establish an Eighth Amendment violation and allow a prisoner to bring a § 1983 suit.[1] Thus, to make out a viable Eighth Amendment Claim, an inmate would have to show that the violation by defendants exceeded, the absence of ordinary care and rose to the level of "delib-

---

count is used for general benefit of inmates; the court also held that under state law the plaintiff had no common law private property interest in wages earned for work in prison, but only an interest created by the statute that gave him a limited right to those funds; thus, he could not claim that a property interest was taken from him based on traditional principles.).

[Section 7:12]

[1]Bagola v. Kindt, 131 F.3d 632 (7th Cir. 1997) (holding that there is Eighth Amendment violation when an inmate loses his hand as a result of defective textile machine in a prison shop); Robinson v. Cuyler, 511 F. Supp. 161 (E.D. Pa. 1981); Snyder v. Blankenship, 473 F. Supp. 1208 (W.D. Va. 1979), aff'd, 618 F.2d 104 (4th Cir. 1980). See also Thaxton v. Rose, 563 F. Supp. 1361 (M.D. Tenn. 1983) (allegation that defective laundry room press machine closed on prisoner's hand did not state Eighth Amendment claim).

erate indifference" to his or her needs.[2]

If the injury is caused by simple negligence, an inmate may attempt to sue in tort in state court. The law varies from jurisdiction to jurisdiction but there are cases holding that prison officials are under a common law tort duty to protect inmates against unreasonable risks of physical harm with regard to their performance of work duties[3] To prevail on such a claim, an injured inmate suing in tort, like any tort plaintiff, must prove a breach of an owed duty, negligence, and proximate cause, and may have to avoid any applicable defenses such as contributory negligence, assumption of risk,

---

[2]For a discussion of the Eighth Amendment standards, see Ch 2.

[3]See, e.g., Becnel v. Charlet, 569 So. 2d 9 (La. Ct. App. 4th Cir. 1990), writ denied, 572 So. 2d 65 (La. 1991) (holding the state liable for the negligent injury of an inmate caused by a state employee's improper handling of a chisel). Despite thus holding, an Ohio court went on to hold, with regard to a prisoner's injuries suffered as a result of performing his duties as an assistant in the electrical shop, that prison officials were not negligent in failing to instruct the inmate on the proper assembly and use of a scaffold, even though the inmate had never before worked on a scaffold, as the assembly and use of the scaffold did not require technical skills, the risk associated with assembling and using it was not unreasonable, and the inmate was working with another inmate who was experienced in the use of scaffolds. Porter v. Ohio Dept. of Rehab. & Corr., 62 Ohio Misc. 2d 296, 598 N.E.2d 241 (Ct. Cl. 1991). Another Ohio court held that the Department of Rehabilitation and Correction was under a duty of reasonable care to protect a prison inmate against unreasonable risks of physical harm in connection with the performance of his duties at a prison sign shop. Boyle v. Ohio Dept. of Rehab. & Corr., 70 Ohio App. 3d 590, 591 N.E.2d 832 (10th Dist. Franklin County 1990). See also Reed v. State Dept. of Corrections, 351 So. 2d 788 (La. Ct. App. 1st Cir. 1977); United Nations Standard Minimum Rules for the Treatment of Prisoners, Rule 74(1) (1955) (precautions taken to protect safety and health of free workmen shall be equally observed in institutions); US Department of Justice, Federal Standards for Prisons and Jails 14.09 (1980) (reprinted in Appendix D) (working conditions for inmates should comply with all applicable federal, state, and local work safety laws);.

and the fellow servant rule.[4] The applicability of some common law defenses, however, is questionable in the context of prisons. Since prisoners are not free to choose whether to work, nor are they able to bargain over conditions of employment, it makes little sense to apply to them traditional assumption-of-risk doctrines. In a well-reasoned decision, the Hawaii Supreme Court agreed.[5] This is not relevant in several states, however, since they block such suits altogether on sovereign immunity grounds, based on the state's position as the inmate's employer.[6]

State Workers' Compensation Laws

For some state prisoners who are not able to sue in tort or in constitutional tort actions to recovery for their work-related injuries, there is one other possibility, that of recovering under state statutory workers'

---

[4]See, e.g., Adair v. Ohio Dept. of Rehab. & Corr., 96 Ohio Misc. 2d 8, 708 N.E.2d 302 (Ct. Cl. 1998) (court held that defendant did not have notice that soap press machine presented an unreasonable risk of harm to plaintiff, and was therefore not liable for plaintiff's injuries); Fondern v. Dept. of Rehabilitation and Correction, 51 Ohio App. 2d 180, 5 Ohio Op. 3d 325, 367 N.E.2d 901 (10th Dist. Franklin County 1977); Reed v. State Dept. of Corrections, 351 So. 2d 788 (La. Ct. App. 1st Cir. 1977).

[5]Haworth v. State, 60 Haw. 557, 592 P.2d 820 (1979).

[6]See, e.g., Warren v. Town of Booneville, 151 Miss. 457, 118 So. 290 (1928). But see Hillman v. City of Anniston, 214 Ala. 522, 108 So. 539, 46 A.L.R. 89 (1926). There are recent cases indicating that courts do not look favorably upon such a defense. See, e.g., Warren v. State, 939 S.W.2d 950 (Mo. Ct. App. W.D. 1997) (inmate sued the state in tort for injuries received while working with a table saw in a prison factory, alleging that the saw was in a dangerous condition because it lacked a safety guard; court found that plaintiff met the threshold requirements to state a claim against the defendants under the dangerous condition exception to the sovereign immunity doctrine); Williams v. Department of Corrections, 224 Ga. App. 571, 481 S.E.2d 272 (1997) (holding that a suit might go forward despite the sovereign immunity doctrine if it could be shown that the county was serving as an agent for the department of corrections).

compensation laws.[7] Of course, workers' compensation recovery differs in significant ways from tort recovery. For one thing, fault is not required; for another the amounts that can be recovered are smaller and specified by statute.[8] Policymakers have urged states to permit such recovery[9] Whether or not such recovery is permitted, however, is a matter that is determined by each state.

The states fall into three distinct groups. First, there is a group of states where statutes specifically exclude prisoners from the workers' compensation system.[10] Second, there are those states where the question is apparently left open. In these, judges usually,[11] though

---

[7]See, generally, Note, The Prisoners' Paradox: Forced Labor and Uncompensated Injuries, 10 New Eng J Crim & Civ Confinement 123 (1984); Note, A Time for Recognition: Extending Workmen's Compensation Coverage to Inmates, 61 ND L Rev 403 (1985).

[8]Larson's Workers' Compensation Law (2000).

[9]Support for permitting recovery under such provisions, for example, is provided by a United Nations rule regarding the treatment of prisoners: "Provision shall be made to indemnify prisoners against industrial injury, including occupational disease, on terms not less favorable than those extended by law to free workmen." United Nations Standard Minimum Rules for the Treatment of Prisoners, Rule 74(2) (1955). Accord, Uniform Law Commrs' Model Sentencing and Corrections Act § 4-901 (1985). Funding could result from acquisition of insurance. Uniform Law Commrs' Model Sentencing and Corrections Act § 4-902 (1985) (reprinted in Appendix B).

[10]See, e.g., Fla Stat Ann § 946.002(5); Kofoed v. Industrial Commn, 872 P2d 484 (Utah Ct. App. 1994) (noting that prisoners cannot recover under Utah workmen's compensation law).

[11]See, e.g., Watson v. Industrial Commission, 100 Ariz. 327, 414 P.2d 144 (1966); Tackett v. Lagrange Penitentiary, 524 S.W.2d 468 (Ky. 1975); Abrams v. Madison County Highway Dept., 495 S.W.2d 539 (Tenn. 1973). See also Becnel v. Charlet, 446 So. 2d 466 (La. Ct. App. 4th Cir. 1984) (place of injury does not affect inmate's eligibility for workers compensation); Orr v. Industrial Com'n, 691 P.2d 1145 (Colo. Ct. App. 1984), judgment aff'd, 716 P.2d 1106 (Colo. 1986).

not always,[12] deny recovery to injured inmates. For various reasons, courts generally conclude that prisoners are not employees within the meaning of the applicable statutes. Some courts find that a voluntary employment relationship is contemplated by the appropriate statute and that the prisoner's labor, being involuntary, does not qualify.[13] Others seem to proceed from the fact that prisoners do not receive significant compensation for their work and conclude that the legislature, therefore, could not have intended to consider them as employees.[14] Another rationale is that a prisoner's labor is not employment but is rehabilitation.[15] However, with the growth of contracting prisoners out to private industries, some courts have taken the approach that the prisoners are entitled to workers' compensation just like any other employee of private industry.[16] Finally, some courts within this second group see a contract for

---

[12]Johnson v. Industrial Commission, 88 Ariz. 354, 356 P.2d 1021 (1960); State Compensation Ins. Fund v. Workmen's Comp. App. Bd., 8 Cal. App. 3d 978, 87 Cal. Rptr. 770 (2d Dist. 1970); Town of Germantown v. Industrial Commission, 178 Wis. 642, 190 N.W. 448, 31 A.L.R. 1284 (1922).

[13]See, e.g., Watson v. Industrial Commission, 100 Ariz. 327, 414 P.2d 144 (1966); Frederick v. Men's Reformatory, 203 N.W.2d 797 (Iowa 1973); Greene's Case, 280 Mass. 506, 182 N.E. 857 (1932); Drake v. Essex County, 192 N.J. Super. 177, 469 A.2d 512 (App. Div. 1983); Spikes v. State, 458 A.2d 672 (R.I. 1983).

[14]See, e.g., Keeney v. Industrial Commission, 24 Ariz. App. 3, 535 P.2d 31 (Div. 1 1975); Jones v. Houston Fire & Cas. Ins. Co., 134 So. 2d 377 (La. Ct. App. 3d Cir. 1961); Goff v. Union County, 26 N.J. Misc. 135, 57 A.2d 480 (Dept. of Labor 1948); but see Scroggins v. Twin City Fire Ins. Co., 656 S.W.2d 213 (Tex. App. El Paso 1983) (whether prisoner is "employee" for purposes of worker's compensation is a question of fact).

[15]See, e.g., Frederick v. Men's Reformatory, 203 N.W.2d 797 (Iowa 1973); Jones v. Houston Fire & Cas. Ins. Co., 134 So. 2d 377 (La. Ct. App. 3d Cir. 1961).

[16]See Benavidez v. Sierra Blanca Motors, 1996 -NMSC- 045, 122 N.M. 209, 922 P.2d 1205 (1996). See also Blackmon v. North Carolina Dept. of Correction, 343 N.C. 259, 470 S.E.2d 8 (1996) (family of inmate killed while employed in a work release program could recover workmen's compensation).

hire as essential to an employment relationship and find this missing in the case of prison labor.[17]

A third group of states has followed Congress's example and enacted statutes allowing prisoners to be compensated for work-related injuries under the state's workers' compensation laws.[18] In at least one of these states, at a county's option compensation may be limited to inmates of county jails.[19] In others, the statutory benefits are restricted to prisoners working for the county government.[20] In most, claims are not adjudicated nor benefits paid until after completion of the prisoner's sentence;[21] the apparent rationale is that jealousies and animosity among inmates would increase if some had more pocket money than others. Another explanation is that prisoners do not need workers' compensation benefits, since their expenses are already being met by state funds. For perhaps the same reasons, benefits usually are terminated if the prisoner

---

[17]See, e.g., Orr v. Industrial Com'n, 691 P.2d 1145 (Colo. Ct. App. 1984), judgment aff'd, 716 P.2d 1106 (Colo. 1986); Tackett v. Lagrange Penitentiary, 524 S.W.2d 468 (Ky. 1975); Drake v. Essex County, 192 N.J. Super. 177, 469 A.2d 512 (App. Div. 1983); Abrams v. Madison County Highway Dept., 495 S.W.2d 539 (Tenn. 1973).

[18]As of November 2000, twelve states had some kind of legislation providing some coverage for prisoners. Larson's Workers' Compensation Law § 64.03 [6], (citing the laws of California, Iowa, North Carolina, South Carolina, Oregon, Washington, Nebraska, Maine, Maryland, Utah, Rhode Island and Wisconsin). See also Tinsley, States Workers' Compensation Legislation Enacted in 1990, 114 Monthly Labor Rev 57 (Jan 1991).

[19]Iowa Code Ann § 85.62.

[20]E.g., Md Code Ann § 9-221. One set of prison accreditation standards provided that prisoners working for public or private organizations should be paid at the prevailing rate and should receive "all fringe benefits." Commission on Accreditation for Corrections, Manual of Standards for Adult Correctional Institutions, Standard 4392 (1977).

[21]See, e.g., Md Code Ann § 9-735(c)(2); Or Rev Stat § 655.515(1); NC Gen Stat § 97-13(c); Wis Stat Ann § 303.21.

is subsequently reincarcerated.[22] The rate of compensation authorized by these statutes is generally lower than that paid to comparably injured nonprisoners.[23] For obvious reasons, this practice raises serious equal protection questions.

To summarize this area, despite some positive movement it is still fair to say that most inmates are excluded from the benefits of workmen's compensation. As one leading treatise describes the state of the law in this area:

> Convicts and prisoners by judicial decision by statute or sometimes by both have usually been denied compensation for injuries sustained in connection with work done within the prison even when some kind of reward attended their exertions.[24]

Recovery under 18 U.S.C. § 4126

A specific federal statute authorizes payment of benefits to federal inmates or their dependents for work-related injuries[25] incurred by federal prisoners "in connection with the maintenance or operation of the institution where confined."[26] The Supreme Court and other federal courts have held that this section is in the

---

[22]See, e.g., NC Gen Stat § 97-13(c); Or Rev Stat § 655.515(2).

[23]Compare, e.g., Wis Stat Ann § 303.21 (maximum of $10,000 in benefits for injured prisoners), with Wis Stat Ann § 102.43(1) (indefinite payment for length of disability) and Wis Stat Ann § 102.44(2) (permanent disability payments as long as disabled person lived). See also NC Gen Stat § 97-13(c) (maximum of $30/week benefits for prisoner).

[24]Larson's Workers's Compensation Law, § 64.03 (2000).

[25]It is important to emphasize that recovery is not allowed under 18 U.S.C. § 4126 for non-work-related injuries. For example, recovery was denied under this statute for failure to give adequate medical care, Wooten v. U.S., 825 F.2d 1039 (6th Cir. 1987); for failure to diagnose and treat a benign brain tumor, U.S. v. Muniz, 374 U.S. 150, 83 S. Ct. 1850, 10 L. Ed. 2d 805 (1963); and for failure to protect a prisoner from assaults (*Muniz*). These types of claims are normally the subject of Federal Tort Claims Act suits.

[26]18 U.S.C. § 4126, which states in pertinent part:

nature of a workers' compensation statute, and that it is sufficiently comprehensive to constitute an exclusive remedy.[27] Accordingly, federal prisoners may not recover from the government under the Federal Tort Claims Act for ordinary work-related injuries,[28] but tort actions against the individual actually causing the

---

§ 4126. Prison Industries Fund; use and settlement of accounts

(a) All moneys under the control of Federal Prison Industries, or received from the sale of the products or by-products of such Industries, or for the services of federal prisoners, shall be deposited or covered into the Treasury of the United States to the credit of the Prison Industries Fund and withdrawn there from only pursuant to accountable warrants or certificates of settlement issued by the General Accounting Office.

(b) All valid claims and obligations payable out of said fund shall be assumed by the corporation.

(c) The corporation,. . ., is authorized to employ the fund, and any earnings that may accrue to the corporation-

* * *

(d) in the vocational training of inmates without regard to their industrial or other assignments;

(e) in paying,. . ., compensation to inmates employed in any industry, or performing outstanding services in institutional operations, and compensation to inmates or their dependents for injuries suffered in any industry or in any work activity in connection with the maintenance or operation of the institution in which the inmates are confined.

[emphasis added.]

See also 28 CFR §§ 301.1-301.26 (1979); and Tate v Blackwell, 475 F2d 193 (5th Cir), cert denied 412 US 922 (1983).

[27]U.S. v. Demko, 385 U.S. 149, 87 S. Ct. 382, 17 L. Ed. 2d 258 (1966). Accord, Aston v. U.S., 625 F.2d 1210 (5th Cir. 1980); Sturgeon v. Federal Prison Industries, 608 F.2d 1153 (8th Cir. 1979); Granade v. U.S., 356 F.2d 837 (2d Cir. 1966); U.S. v. Gomez, 378 F.2d 938 (10th Cir. 1967); Shepard v. Stidham, 502 F. Supp. 1275 (M.D. Ala. 1980); Nobles v. Federal Prison Industries, Inc., 213 F. Supp. 731 (N.D. Ga. 1963); Scott v. Reno, 902 F. Supp. 1190 (C.D. Cal. 1995); see also 28 CFR pt 551.

[28]U.S. v. Demko, 385 U.S. 149, 87 S. Ct. 382, 17 L. Ed. 2d 258 (1966); Vander v. U.S. Dept. of Justice, 268 F.3d 661 (9th Cir. 2001) (holding that Prison Industries Fund provided exclusive remedy for inmate who was injured while working in prison, and therefore barring an action under the Federal Tort Claims Act); Scott v. Reno, 902 F. Supp. 1190 (C.D. Cal. 1995) (recovery from PIF is exclusive remedy). See also Thompson v. U.S., 495 F.2d 192

§ 7:12

injury may still be possible.[29] The terminology of § 4126 makes it clear that compensation for a work-related injury is both claimable and collectible while the injured prisoner is still in federal custody.[30] It has been held that a federal prisoner who is injured on his way to lunch may recover under § 4126, since his journey to and from meals is considered to be in the course of his employment.[31]

It has also been held that a federal prisoner who files a claim for work-related injuries is entitled to a hearing to determine the validity of the claims, and that due process requires that the claimant have written notice of the hearing, an opportunity to present evidence and

---

(5th Cir. 1974) (18 U.S.C. § 4126 is the exclusive remedy for a prison-employee's work-related injury); Aston v. U.S., 625 F.2d 1210 (5th Cir. 1980) (same); Wooten v. U.S., 825 F.2d 1039 (6th Cir. 1987) (§ 4126 is the exclusive remedy for negligent job assignments); Owens v. Department of Justice, U. S. A., 527 F. Supp. 373 (N.D. Ind. 1981), aff'd, 673 F.2d 1334 (7th Cir. 1981). The relevant portions of the Federal Tort Claims Act are found in , 2671 et seq.'28 U.S.C. §§ 1346(b), 2671 et seq. See also Richardson v. North Carolina Dept. of Correction, 345 N.C. 128, 478 S.E.2d 501 (1996) (state prisoner could not sue under North Carolina's Torts Claim Act because workman compensation was his only remedy); but see Wooten v. U.S., 825 F.2d 1039 (6th Cir. 1987), in which it was held that, while a prisoner's exclusive remedy for job-related injuries lay in § 4126, injuries which he sustained when prison authorities allegedly denied him adequate medical care were compensable in an action against the United States under the Federal Tort Claims Act. For other information on this subject, see Annotation, United States' Liability, Under Federal Tort Claims Act, for Death or Injury of Federal Prisoner, 10 L Ed 2d 13611964); Annotation, Federal Compensation Acts as Affecting Recovery Under Federal Tort Claims Act, 17 L Ed 2d 929, § 6 (1967); Annotation, Remedy Under Other Federal Statute as Affecting Relief Under Federal Tort Claims Act, 84 A.L.R. 2d 1059 § 9.

[29]Tindall v. Moore, 417 F. Supp. 548 (N.D. Ga. 1976); Byrd v. Warden, Federal Detention Headquarters, New York, New York, 376 F. Supp. 37 (S.D. N.Y. 1974).

[30]Thompson v. U.S. Federal Prison Industries, 492 F.2d 1082 (5th Cir. 1974).

[31]Wooten v. U.S., 437 F.2d 79 (5th Cir. 1971).

cross-examine adverse witnesses, the right to hire counsel and the privilege to obtain independent medical examinations by physicians of the prisoner's own choosing if his or her personal finances permit, and the right to have a written statement of the reasons for denial of the claim if that is the result of the hearing officer's decision.[32] It has been held appropriate for federal courts to review the decision of the hearing officers under the Administrative Procedure Act (5 U.S.C. §§ 701 et seq.), but the courts have held that the hearing officer's decision should be affirmed in the absence of a showing that the officer acted arbitrarily or capriciously.[33]

To take advantage of this federal compensation law, a federal prison inmate who is injured in the performance of assigned duties must report the injury to the inmate's superior and obtain necessary medical treatment.[34] A record of the injury is then made.[35] A formal claim for compensation, however, may not be filed until 45 days prior to the injured inmate's release date.[36]

A claims examiner, appointed by the Commissioner of the Federal Prison Industries (FPI), initially decides the claim for compensation.[37] Appeal of this decision may be made to an Inmate Accident Compensation

---

[32]Saladino v. Federal Prison Industries, 404 F. Supp. 1054 (D. Conn. 1975); Davis v. U.S., 415 F. Supp. 1086 (D. Kan. 1976).

[33]Thompson v. U.S. Federal Prison Industries, 492 F.2d 1082 (5th Cir. 1974); Berry v. Federal Prison Industries, Inc., 440 F. Supp. 1147 (N.D. Cal. 1977); McCoy v. Cardamone, 646 F. Supp. 1143 (D.D.C. 1986); Owens v. Department of Justice, U. S. A., 527 F. Supp. 373 (N.D. Ind. 1981), aff'd, 673 F.2d 1334 (7th Cir. 1981); Davis v. U.S., 415 F. Supp. 1086 (D. Kan. 1976).

[34]28 CFR § 301.104. Failure may result in forfeiture of an accident claim.

[35]28 CFR § 301.105. (provision calls for a report and an investigation as to the cause of the injury).

[36]28 CFR § 301.303 (claim must be filed no more than 45 days prior to release but no less than 15 days prior to release).

[37]28 CFR § 301.305.

Committee, also appointed by the Commissioner of the FPI.[38] A formal hearing will then be convened. The claimant may call witnesses[39] and present documentary evidence.[40] It has been held that the opportunity to challenge a prison physician's conclusions and diagnosis is constitutionally required.[41] An appeal from this hearing may be taken to the Chief Operating Officer of Federal Prison Industries, Inc.[42] Finally, judicial review is available, although administrative determinations, as noted previously, will probably be overturned only if found to be arbitrary or capricious.[43]

Policy Considerations

From a policy perspective, workers' compensation laws arguably should cover prisoners.[44] Injured inmates and their families experience the same pain and suffering as their civilian counterparts. The absence of benefits may engender extreme hostility. Moreover, disabled inmates will re-enter society with their earning potential limited not only by the stigma of a criminal record, but also by their disability. This inability to work, coupled with probable indigency resulting from token wages for their prison labor,[45] makes it highly predictable that many disabled former prisoners and their families will become public charges. Finally, it

---

[38]28 CFR § 301.310 (10 days notice is required and the committee in its discretion may limit the number of witnesses).

[39]28 CFR § 301.309.

[40]28 CFR § 301.308.

[41]Davis v. U.S., 415 F. Supp. 1086 (D. Kan. 1976). See also Saladino v. Federal Prison Industries, 404 F. Supp. 1054 (D. Conn. 1975).

[42]28 CFR § 301.313.

[43]See, e.g., Thompson v. U.S. Federal Prison Industries, 492 F.2d 1082 (5th Cir. 1974). See also Saladino v. Federal Prison Industries, 404 F. Supp. 1054 (D. Conn. 1975); Davis v. U.S., 415 F. Supp. 1086 (D. Kan. 1976).

[44]See Workmen's Compensation & Rehabilitation Law, revised reprint from Council of State Governments § 8, at 8 (1974).

[45]See § 7:10.

seems only fair that when states benefit from convict labor, they should compensate prisoners injured as a result of that labor. Indeed, it is possible to argue, although there appear to be no cases on point, that, because ex-prisoners injured at prison work are in substantially the same position as non-prisoners similarly injured, the failure of a workers' compensation statute to provide benefits to both constitutes discriminatory treatment which violates the Equal Protection Clause.[46]

Providing workers' compensation benefits to prisoners would not be as expensive as providing prisoners with minimum wages, because the number of injured inmates is relatively small. Furthermore, once it is recognized that released disabled prisoners are likely to become public charges in any event, there is little savings to be gained by denying them workers' compensation. Extending workers' compensation benefits to prisoners might also achieve the incidental benefit of creating an incentive for states to examine and improve job safety in prison work programs.

§ 7:13 The Right to Unemployment Compensation

Nonprisoners who are discharged from their employment are often eligible to receive unemployment compensation for a temporary transition period until they can find other suitable work. A federal enabling

---

[46]See Note, Granting Workmen's Compensation Benefits to Prison Inmates, 46 S Cal L Rev 1223, 1249-61 (1973). Cf., Weber v. Aetna Cas. & Sur. Co., 406 U.S. 164, 92 S. Ct. 1400, 31 L. Ed. 2d 768 (1972) (unconstitutional distinction in worker's compensation statute between legitimate and illegitimate children). In an interesting twist on this theme, the court, in Orr v. Industrial Com'n, 691 P.2d 1145 (Colo. Ct. App. 1984), judgment aff'd, 716 P.2d 1106 (Colo. 1986), denied compensation to a prisoner engaged in unskilled tasks. Under the terms of the relevant statute, compensation for injuries was available to persons participating in training programs or programs designed to teach a trade or occupation.

act encourages states to establish unemployment compensation programs,[1] and all states have accepted the challenge. Rarely, however, does a statute speak to whether prison inmates are covered under its program.

While the rehabilitative value of prison work is generally conceded, it is common to find significant numbers of prisoners unemployed.[2] Nonworking inmates are generally deemed ineligible for unemployment compensation. Under federal statutory definitions, prisoners may be excepted from benefits.[3] On the state level, too, prisoners have been denied unemployment compensation.[4] In one instance this result was rationalized on the basis of a statutory requirement that recipients must be available to accept other work without undue restrictions-a condition prisoners are unable to meet.[5]

From a policy perspective, the unwillingness of states to provide unemployment compensation for convicts is understandable. A job lost as a result of the prisoner's incarceration can be viewed as the result of the individual's conscious choice to engage in criminal activity, certainly not the type of employment separation which justifies state financial relief. Moreover, unemployment compensation is generally reserved for individuals who

---

[Section 7:13]

[1] 42 U.S.C. §§ 501-504. See also 26 U.S.C. §§ 3301-3311.

[2] Stephen P. Garvey, Freeing Prisoners' Labor, 50 Stan. L. Rev. 339, 370 (1998) (reporting an unemployment rate in U.S. prisons of over 90%). See, generally, Clark & Parker, The Labor Law Problems of the Prisoner, 28 Rutgers L Rev 840, 844-45 (1975).

[3] See 5 U.S.C. § 8501(1)(F), (G). See also 18 U.S.C. § 1761(c)(3) (prisoners in certain work programs involving prison-made goods are specifically barred from receiving unemployment compensation benefits). For the text of this statute, and a discussion of prison-made goods, see § 7:2.

[4] Kroh v. Unemployment Compensation Bd. of Review, 711 A.2d 1093 (Pa. Commw. Ct. 1998) (denial of unemployment compensation did not violate the inmate's equal protection rights because the institution had a rational basis for denying the benefits).

[5] The case is reported in Clark & Parker, The Labor Law Problems of the Prisoner, 28 Rutgers L Rev 840, 857 n.93 (1975).

have a continuing attachment to the labor force but who are temporarily out of work. A prisoner's prospects for gainful employment during imprisonment are bleak, and generally beyond the control of the inmate, who is unable to accept private employment. Finally, compensation is designed in large part to alleviate the adverse economic consequences of being unemployed-an out-of-work laborer may experience difficulty paying for food and shelter without state assistance. Prisoners, on the other hand, already have these living expenses provided for them by the state.

§ 7:14 The Right to Form Prisoners' Unions

In the free world, of course, unionization of workers in permitted if not encouraged. The situation, not unexpectedly, is dramatically different in prisons. In that environment the concept has been rejected, at least for now, but not without a struggle. This section describes that struggle.

The threshold question that was raised by advocates who wished to establish the right of prisoners to unionize is whether prisoners have a constitutional right to form a union. There is no doubt that a state or federal statute or administrative rule or prison regulation may give inmates that right; but, in the absence of such, is there a fundamental right, based on the right of free association or some other constitutional right, to form prisoners' unions? Most courts have said there is no such right.[1]

The idea of unions among inmates was first has been credited to inmates at California's Soledad Prison.[2] In November 1970, 2,000 Folsom Prison inmates staged a

---

[Section 7:14]

[1]See, e.g., Brooks v. Wainwright, 439 F. Supp. 1335 (M.D. Fla. 1977).

[2]Zonn, Inmate Unions: An Appraisal of Prisoner Rights and Labor Implications, 32 U Miami L Rev 613, 621 (1978).

17-day strike.[3] Initially, unions consisted of local organizations at individual institutions; however, the National Prisoners' Reform Association has called for a nationwide coalition of all prisoners' unions.[4]

Prisoners' organizations were designed to be more than simply labor unions. Like labor unions, they often sought higher wages, improved working conditions, and recognition as a collective bargaining agent. But they were also intended to serve as a medium for the expression of inmate grievances about prisons and the political system. In short, prisoners, through unionization, sought a participatory role in the operation of the institution and greater control over the decisions that affected their lives.

Policy Considerations

There are policy arguments both for and against prison unions. In their favor, unions provide a mechanism for the transmission of rectifiable grievances of which an administration may be unaware. They also may be able to bargain successfully on such matters as wages, working conditions, and disability benefits. As a result, expensive and time-consuming litigation may be avoided. On a psychological level, prison unions may help preserve prisoners' self-respect, both individually and collectively. This, in turn, may further the rehabilitative process. Promoting self-determination may help develop a sense of responsibility. From an institutional perspective, prisoners' unions may lessen internal tensions and personal frustrations. The likelihood of riots and other serious disturbances may be correspondingly

---

[3]*Id.*

[4]See Clark & Parker, The Labor Law Problems of the Prisoner, 28 Rutgers L Rev 840, 857 n.94 (1975). The issue of prisoners' unions must be kept separate from the question of whether prisoners on work release may join the union of the company for which they work. In regard to the latter issue, see Rosslyn Concrete Const. Co. v. N.L.R.B., 713 F.2d 61 (4th Cir. 1983) (NLRB properly included work release inmates within bargaining unit).

reduced.

The American Bar Association's Standards for Criminal Justice, Standard 23-6.6 stops short of advocating that prisoners be allowed to join unions. It does provide that prisoners should be permitted to form, join, or belong to organizations, the purposes of which are lawful (subject to the restrictions of Standard 1.1); however, Standards 6.6(c) and 4.5 both state that the standards are not intended to extend to prisoners the right to strike or take other concerted action to affect institutional conditions, programs, or policies.

On the other hand, prison administrators strongly and uniformly resisted the formation of prisoners' unions.[5] Rather than viewing unions as a stabilizing influence to curb potential disruptions, many officials saw union meetings as a potential vehicle for fomenting disorder and for organizing riots, not to mention for the planning of escapes. They feared the autonomy of a union would erode the necessary respect for prison authorities that they believed to be indispensable to maintaining institutional order. Moreover, unionization could foster an adversarial relationship between the administration and the inmates that could be detrimental for both sides. Prison officials also worried that certain inmates would misuse the unions to achieve personal power, and they foresaw the possibility of friction between union and nonunion members. The intensified problems of security and control during union meetings were another concern. Finally, they doubted that a bargaining model which might operate smoothly in civilian society, where negotiations take place between highly skilled and trained professionals, was transferable to the prison setting, where bargaining could be delegated to uneducated, unskilled prisoners.

---

[5]See the survey contained in Comment, Labor Unions for Prison Inmates: An Analysis of a Recent Proposal for the Organization of Inmate Labor, 21 Buffalo L Rev 963, 966 n13 (1972).

In *Jones v North Carolina Prisoners' Labor Union*,[6] the Supreme Court addressed some of the issues raised by prisoners' unions. The plaintiff union was an incorporated organization with the goal of forming a prisoners' labor union at every prison and jail in North Carolina. Through collective bargaining, the union hoped to improve prison working conditions and to eliminate objectionable practices. State regulations prohibited inmates from soliciting fellow prisoners to join the union, barred union meetings, and precluded the delivery of union publications mailed in bulk to selected inmates for distribution to other prisoners. The union argued that these restrictions violated their First Amendment and equal protection rights. The Supreme Court disagreed, reasoning that First Amendment associational rights are necessarily curtailed by the fact of confinement and the needs of the penal institution.[7] Consequently, organizational privileges exist only if they are not inconsistent with the inmate's incarceration. Addressing the question of the negative impact of prison unions and mirroring the view generally held by prison administrators, the Supreme Court noted that prison officials had testified that the labor union was fraught with the potential dangers described above.[8] Absent an affirmative showing that these beliefs were unreasonable, the *Jones* majority held that the restrictions on unions were proper.[9] Significantly, the Court accorded great deference to the judgment of prison officials. The burden lay not on them to demonstrate that the union would be detrimental to proper penological objectives or security and order, but rather rested on the union to prove with "substantial evidence"

---

[6] Jones v. North Carolina Prisoners' Labor Union, Inc., 433 U.S. 119, 97 S. Ct. 2532, 53 L. Ed. 2d 629 (1977). This case is also discussed in Ch 5.

[7] *Id.* at 125-26, 129-30.

[8] *Id.* at 126.

[9] *Id.* at 130.

PRISON LABOR § 7:14

that the officials' concerns were exaggerated.[10] (Needless to say, it would be extremely difficult for prisoners to satisfy this burden.)

Proceeding from this deference to administrative expertise, the Supreme Court in *Jones* found that the bans on inmate solicitation and group meetings were rationally related to prison administration.[11] Any restriction of First Amendment rights was held to be reasonable under the circumstances. The Court held that the prohibitions were reasonable, since those they were addressed to group meetings and group organizational activities, and since they neither precluded membership in the union nor banned its formation.[12] The decision may have, as a practical matter, sounded the death knell for prison unions, because it is obviously difficult if not impossible to create a viable group organization without soliciting members or holding periodic meetings.

The union's equal protection argument in *Jones* was premised on the fact that privileges denied the union had been accorded other groups, such as the Jaycees, Alcoholics Anonymous, and the Boy Scouts.[13] The Court rejected the argument. It reasoned that the prison was not a "public forum" entitling all organizations to equal treatment, and that the other groups, unlike the union, fulfilled a rehabilitative function and did not pose a threat to the security and order of the institution.[14] Once again according prison officials great discretion, the Court upheld the administrator's decision as "not unreasonable" and entitled to respect, absent a showing of

---

[10]*Id.* at 128.

[11]*Id.* at 130. The same result was reached in a case where prisoners alleged a state statutory right to hold union meetings. In re Price, 25 Cal. 3d 448, 158 Cal. Rptr. 873, 600 P.2d 1330 (1979).

[12]*Id.* at 128-29.

[13]*Id.* at 122-23.

[14]*Id.* at 134-6.

§ 7:14　　　　　Rights of Prisoners, Third Edition

abuse of discretion.[15]

While union organizing is not permitted through group meetings there are several opinions that do provide some limited protections. For example, the Second Circuit Court of Appeals ordered a warden to deliver to union members legal correspondence pertaining to union matters.[16] Also, the California Supreme Court has upheld on state statutory grounds an inmate's right to wear a prisoner's union lapel button.[17]

Grievance Mechanisms

An increasingly explored alternative to a prisoners' union is an internal institutional grievance procedure.[18] Such a mechanism, like a union, may serve to open

---

[15]*Id.* at 135-36.

[16]Goodwin v. Oswald, 462 F.2d 1237 (2d Cir. 1972). See also National Prisoners Reform Ass'n v. Sharkey, 347 F. Supp. 1234 (D. R.I. 1972); In re Brandt, 25 Cal. 3d 136, 157 Cal. Rptr. 894, 599 P.2d 89 (1979).

[17]In re Reynolds, 25 Cal. 3d 131, 157 Cal. Rptr. 892, 599 P.2d 86 (1979).

[18]See, e.g., NY Correct Law § 139 (construed in Johnson v. Ward, 64 A.D.2d 186, 409 N.Y.S.2d 670 (3d Dep't 1978)); Ind Code Ann § 11-11-1-2; Vt Stat Ann tit 28, § 854. See also Laaman v. Helgemoe, 437 F. Supp. 269, 320 (D.N.H. 1977); O'Bryan v. Saginaw County, Mich., 437 F. Supp. 582, 601 (E.D. Mich. 1977), judgment entered, 446 F. Supp. 436 (E.D. Mich. 1978); ABA Standards for Criminal Justice, Standard 23-7.1; National Advisory Commn on Criminal Justice Standards & Goals, Corrections Standard 2.14 (1973); US Department of Justice, Federal Standards for Prisons and Jails 1.11 (1980); Uniform Law Commrs' Model Sentencing and Corrections Act §§ 4-301 to 4-307 (1985).

One scholar in 1980 observed that grievance mechanisms are so widespread that they "characterize most state prisons today." Singer, Prisoners ' Rights Litigation: A Look at the Past Decade, and a Look at the Coming Decade, 44 Fed Probation 3, 4 (Dec 1980). And see, generally, J. Keating, V. McArthur, M. Lewis, M. Sebelius, & L. Singer, Grievance Mechanisms in Correctional Institutions (1975); Hepburn & Lane, Prisoner Redress: Analysis of an Intimate Grievance Procedure, 26 Crim & Delinq 162 (1980); Brakel, Administrative Justice in the Penitentiary: A Report on Inmate Grievance Procedures, 1982 ABA Res J 111. Mediation

PRISON LABOR § 7:14

formal channels of communication between inmates and prison officials while avoiding the potentially disruptive influence of a union and the aggregation of power in those inmates who become union officers.

Although grievance procedures may be desirable, they are not constitutionally required,[19] and it has been held

may be another alternative. See Cole, Hanson, & Silbert, Mediation: Is It an Effective, Alternative to Adjudication in Resolving Prisoner Complaints?, 65 Judicature 481 (1982); Reynolds & Tonry, Professional Mediation Services for Prisoners' Complaints, 67 ABAJ 294 (1981); Brakel, Ruling on Prisoners' Grievances, 1983 Am Bar Found Resources J 393; Note, Dispute Resolution in Prisons: An Overview and Assessment, 36 Rutgers L Rev 145 (1983).

[19]See O'Bryan v. Saginaw County, Mich., 437 F. Supp. 582, 601 (E.D. Mich. 1977), judgment entered, 446 F. Supp. 436 (E.D. Mich. 1978); Williams v. Meese, 926 F.2d 994 (10th Cir. 1991) (claim that grievance procedure was inadequate dismissed as conclusory). But see Stovall v. Bennett, 471 F. Supp. 1286, 1290 (M.D. Ala. 1979) (prisoners have right to file complaints with prison officials).

Where a grievance procedure is established, state courts may require that it be exhausted prior to bringing suit. See Roberts v. Coughlin, 165 A.D.2d 964, 561 N.Y.S.2d 852 (3d Dep't 1990). See also Spencer v. Moore, 638 F. Supp. 315 (E.D. Mo. 1986) (as grievance procedure is not constitutionally required, violations of voluntarily established procedures do not deprive inmates of federal constitutional rights).

Until passage of the Prison Litigation Reform Act, there was federal statutory authority supporting establishment of a formal grievance mechanism in all prisons and jails. See former 42 U.S.C. § 1997c. Such grievance mechanisms were to provide for an advisory role for employees and inmates of any jail, prison, or other correctional institution (at the most decentralized level as is reasonably possible), in the formulation, implementation, and operation of the system; for specific maximum time limits for written replies to grievances with reasons thereto at each decision level within the system; for priority processing of grievances which are of an emergency nature, including matters in which delay would subject the grievant to substantial risk of personal injury or other damages; for safeguards to avoid reprisals against any grievant or participant in the resolution of a grievance; and for independent review of disposition of grievances. The Prison Litigation Reform Act did away with these provisions and simply required exhaus-

that a prohibition against circulating protest petitions among prisoners may be warranted by legitimate prison security concerns, particularly if there are alternative means of communicating the grievances.[20] If a grievance committee is established, however, the nonemergency transfer of an inmate member of the grievance resolution committee may be improper without a due process hearing.[21] Where a grievance procedure is established, under the Prison Litigation Reform Act resort to it is now required before seeking judicial relief.[22] Complaints made to a grievance committee have been held to be privileged and immune from use as a basis for a disciplinary report for lying.[23] The reasoning is that otherwise the possible disciplinary action could have a chilling effect on the First Amendment right to file a grievance.

§ 7:15 The Right to Engage in Work Stoppages and Strikes

Research References
West's Key Number Digest, Sentencing and Punishment ⚷1535

Even supporters of prison unionization are wary of advocating a right of prisoners to strike or engage in

---

tion of any grievance mechanism that a prison system chose to establish.

[20]Nickens v. White, 622 F.2d 967 (8th Cir. 1980).

[21]Johnson v. Ward, 64 A.D.2d 186, 409 N.Y.S.2d 670 (3d Dep't 1978). See Ch 9. A prisoner would, of course, have to establish factually that this was the basis of the transfer, which may prove difficult. See Sebastiano v. Harris, 76 A.D.2d 1004, 429 N.Y.S.2d 288 (3d Dep't 1980), order aff'd, 54 N.Y.2d 1014, 446 N.Y.S.2d 261, 430 N.E.2d 1314 (1981).

[22]42 U.S.C. § 1997e(a). For a discussion of this Provision see Ch. 16.

[23]Hunyadi v. Smith, 112 Misc. 2d 484, 447 N.Y.S.2d 226 (Sup 1982).

PRISON LABOR § 7:15

work stoppages.¹ These activities in the closed, already tense environment of the prison carry grave potential for violence and rioting. There is little doubt that the Supreme Court, which has never had occasion to specifically address the question directly, would support prison rules forbidding prisoner strikes or other concerted group protest actions. The Court's approval in *Jones v North Carolina Prisoners' Labor Union*² of prison rules restricting group activities that threatened institutional order and security, would surely be extended to uphold rules banning work stoppages and strikes. Clearly these acts present far greater potential for disruption than the solicitation or meetings involved in *Jones*. Moreover, in refusing to strike down prison rules restricting prisoner access to news media in *Pell v Procunier*,³ the Court emphasized the existence of alternative methods of communicating grievances.⁴ Comparable alternatives to strikes no doubt also could be shown.

Lower courts have sustained correction officials' decisions to punish inmates who either individually or collectively engages in work stoppages.⁵ Convicts placed in disciplinary confinement for their refusal to work have

[Section 7:15]
¹See. e.g., ABA Standards for Criminal Justice, Standards 6.6(c) and 4.2 (1986) expressly state that those standards are not intended to extend to prisoners the right to strike or to take other concerted action to affect institutional conditions, programs, or policies.
²Jones v. North Carolina Prisoners' Labor Union, Inc., 433 U.S. 119, 97 S. Ct. 2532, 53 L. Ed. 2d 629 (1977), discussed in § 7:14.
³Pell v. Procunier, 417 U.S. 817, 94 S. Ct. 2827, 41 L. Ed. 2d 495 (1974).
⁴*Id.* at 824.
⁵See, e.g., Gray v. Levine, 455 F. Supp. 267 (D. Md. 1978), aff'd, 605 F.2d 1202 (4th Cir. 1979) and aff'd, 605 F.2d 1201 (4th Cir. 1979); Banks v. Norton, 346 F. Supp. 917 (D. Conn. 1972); Harrington v. Oregon State Penitentiary, Corrections Division, 41 Or. App. 349, 597 P.2d 1252 (1979).

§ 7:15   Rights of Prisoners, Third Edition

found no relief in the courts,[6] unless the conditions of disciplinary confinement or the disciplinary procedures[7] are suspect. Lower court judges also have rejected the argument for a constitutionally protected right to protest prison regulations by a work stoppage,[8] and have upheld the imposition of a general lockup in the face of such a stoppage.[9] Punishment has been sustained for inmates who either solicited support for, or attempted to incite, a work stoppage.[10]

§ 7:16 The Right to Participate in Work Release Programs Generally

Research References

West's Key Number Digest, Convicts ⇐7(2)

Many states and the federal government have established work release programs for prisoners,[1] sometimes

---

[6]See, e.g., Granville v. Hunt, 411 F.2d 9 (5th Cir. 1969); Laaman v. Hancock, 351 F. Supp. 1265 (D.N.H. 1972); Fallis v. U.S., 263 F. Supp. 780 (M.D. Pa. 1967).

[7]See Ch 9.

[8]See, e.g., McKinnon v. Patterson, 425 F. Supp. 383, 389 (S.D. N.Y. 1976), judgment modified on other grounds, 568 F.2d 930 (2d Cir. 1977).

[9]See, e.g., Gray v. Levine, 455 F. Supp. 267 (D. Md. 1978), aff'd, 605 F.2d 1202 (4th Cir. 1979) and aff'd, 605 F.2d 1201 (4th Cir. 1979).

[10]See, e.g., Meyers v. Alldredge, 348 F. Supp. 807 (M.D. Pa. 1972), judgment rev'd on other grounds, 492 F.2d 296 (3d Cir. 1974). See also Vodicka v. Phelps, 624 F.2d 569 (5th Cir. 1980) (upholding restriction on distribution of a newsletter approving of a prior prisoner work stoppage and advocating a prisoner union).

[Section 7:16]

[1]See, e.g., 18 U.S.C. § 3622(c) (formerly 18 U.S.C. § 4082(c)); Conn Gen Stat Ann § 18-100; Del Code Ann tit 11, § 6533; Mass Gen Laws Ann Chap 127, § 49; Va Code § 53.1-60. See, generally, as to the federal program, Annotation, Grant or Denial of Furlough or Work Release to Federal Prisoner under 18 U.S.C.A. § 4082(c), 64 A.L.R. Fed. 807 [editor's note: § 4082(c) is now § 3622(c)].

The federal law provides as follows:

by court order.[2] A work release program,[3] sometimes known as a work furlough program, is remedial in nature, not penal, since it ameliorates the harshness of a jail or imprisonment term, minimizes the stigma of complete imprisonment, and aims at rehabilitation of prisoners, rather than having punishment as its primary purpose.[4] Its primary purpose is to maintain a prisoner's morale, self-respect, dignity, and rehabilitation.[5]

The ABA Standards for Criminal Justice, Legal Status of Prisoners, Standard 23-4.3, states:

Correctional authorities, after consultation with the prisoners and consideration of their records, should determine the types of rehabilitation programs, including self-improvement and educational programs, that will be beneficial to them, and should thereafter seek to provide

---

[18 U.S.C.] § 3622. Temporary release of a prisoner. The Bureau of Prisons may release a prisoner from the place of his imprisonment for a limited period if such release appears to be consistent with the purpose for which the sentence was imposed and any pertinent policy statement issued by the Sentencing Commission pursuant to 28 U.S.C. § 994(a)(2), if such release otherwise appears to be consistent with the public interest and if there is reasonable cause to believe that a prisoner will honor the trust to be imposed in him, by authorizing him, under prescribed conditions, to-

(c) work at paid employment in the community, while continuing in official detention at the penal or correctional facility if-

(1) the rates of pay and other conditions of employment will not be less than those paid or provided for work of a similar nature in the community; and

(2) the prisoner agrees to pay to the Bureau such costs incident to official detention as the Bureau finds appropriate and reasonable under all the circumstances, such costs to be collected by the Bureau and deposited in the Treasury to the credit of the appropriation available for such costs at the time such collections are made.

See also Note, Washington's Discretionary Immunity Doctrine and Negligent Early Release Decisions: Parole and Work Release, 65 Wash L Rev 619 (July 1990).

[2]Cooper v. Gwinn, 171 W. Va. 245, 298 S.E.2d 781 (1981).

[3]See, generally, J. Spitzer, Penal and Correctional Institutions 60 Am Jur 2d §§ 159, 160 (1987), for an overview of the law relating to work release programs.

[4]Davidson v. U.S., 467 A.2d 1282 (D.C. 1983).

[5]*Id.*

access to as many such programs as feasible, either by establishing such programs or by contracting with outside agencies or individuals for such services.

After debating the issue for a long time, the ABA adopted a new Standard 23-4.4(b) in 1985, which provides: "To promote relevant occupational training for prisoners, the establishment of work release programs, including community correctional center programs, should be encouraged."

In some states, despite the absence of an enabling statute, the authority to establish work release programs has been inferred under other statutes authorizing the director of state prisons to make rules and regulations for the government and management of penal institutions under the director's jurisdiction.[6] These work release programs allow for expanded job opportunities for inmates and a wider range of types of employment. In addition, they help to ease the prisoner's transition to civilian life.[7] As a result, these programs have been hailed as a progressive and rehabilitative advancement in penology. Work release granted to an inmate is often conditioned on the inmate's agreeing to certain conditions, such as the repayment by the inmate from his wages of certain

---

[6]See, e.g., Ervin v. Blackwell, 733 F.2d 1282 (8th Cir. 1984).

[7]Another federal statute provides, at 18 U.S.C. § 3624(c), for pre-release custody:

§ 3624. Release of a prisoner

(c) Pre-release custody.— The Bureau of Prisons shall, to the extent practicable, assure that a prisoner serving a term of imprisonment spends a reasonable part, not to exceed six months, of the last 10 per centum of the term to be served under conditions that will afford the prisoner a reasonable opportunity to adjust to and prepare for his re-entry into the community. The United States Probation System shall, to the extent practicable, offer assistance to a prisoner during such pre-release custody. [Emphasis added].

§ 7:16

court expenses incurred during his trial,[8] payment of restitution to the victims,[9] or payment of the prisoner's lawful debts.[10]

There is no constitutional requirement that a state establish a work release program.[11] Even if such a program is established, moreover, an individual prisoner generally has no constitutional right to participate in it.[12]

Since prison officials have discretion to choose among

---

[8]Alexander v. Johnson, 742 F.2d 117 (4th Cir. 1984) (inmate had to agree to repay court expenses incurred in providing her with court-appointed counsel at her trial).

[9]Reimonenq v. Foti, 72 F.3d 472 (5th Cir. 1996) (payment required of 10% of wages to Sheriff's Victim Compensation Fund); Brewer v. State, 274 Ark. 38, 621 S.W.2d 698 (1981); Davidson v. U.S., 467 A.2d 1282 (D.C. 1983) (restitution does not undermine the purpose of work release statutes); State v. Arnette, 67 N.C. App. 194, 312 S.E.2d 547 (1984).

[10]Davidson v. U.S., 467 A.2d 1282 (D.C. 1983).

[11]See, e.g., Preston v. Ford, 378 F. Supp. 729 (E.D. Ky. 1974). See also Ruiz v. Estelle, 650 F.2d 555 (5th Cir. 1981) (staying a district court order that a specified number of inmates be placed on work furlough by certain deadlines); Ervin v. Blackwell, 585 F. Supp. 680 (W.D. Mo. 1983), judgment aff'd, 733 F.2d 1282 (8th Cir. 1984) (no right to participate in work release program and, therefore, requirement that prisoner contribute to maintenance as a condition of work release not unconstitutional); Rowe v. Cuyler, 534 F. Supp. 297 (E.D. Pa. 1982), aff'd, 696 F.2d 985 (3d Cir. 1982).

[12]Green v. U.S., 481 F.2d 1140 (D.C. Cir. 1973); Romer v. Morgenthau, 119 F. Supp. 2d 346 (S.D. N.Y. 2000) (no liberty interest in being approved for work release program); Logan v. Horn, 692 A.2d 1157 (Pa. Commw. Ct. 1997); Mercer v. U.S. Medical Center for Federal Prisoners, 312 F. Supp. 1077 (W.D. Mo. 1970); Ervin v. Blackwell, 585 F. Supp. 680 (W.D. Mo. 1983), judgment aff'd, 733 F.2d 1282 (8th Cir. 1984); Austin v. Armstrong, 473 F. Supp. 1114 (D. Nev. 1979). See also Matz v. Kelsch, 638 F.2d 48 (8th Cir. 1981); Johnson v. Stark, 717 F.2d 1550 (8th Cir. 1983) (work release statute creates no constitutionally protected liberty interest where there are no substantive restrictions placed on corrections officials in choosing prisoners for work release); Baumann v. Arizona Dept. of Corrections, 754 F.2d 841 (9th Cir. 1985) (no liberty interest in release on work or home furlough); Gorman v. Moody, 710 F. Supp. 1256 (N.D. Ind. 1989); Spencer v. Snell, 626

§ 7:16   RIGHTS OF PRISONERS, THIRD EDITION

eligible inmates, regulations setting out eligibility requirements for an inmate to participate in a work

F. Supp. 1096 (E.D. Mo. 1986), judgment aff'd, 786 F.2d 1171 (8th Cir. 1986); Dugar v. Coughlin, 613 F. Supp. 849 (S.D. N.Y. 1985) (no liberty interest in temporary release program); Rucker v. Meachum, 513 F. Supp. 32 (W.D. Okla. 1980) (no constitutionally protected liberty interest in assignment to community treatment program); Carter v. Carlson, 545 F. Supp. 1120 (S.D. W. Va. 1982); Berry v. State, Dept. of Corrections, 145 Ariz. 12, 699 P.2d 387 (Ct. App. Div. 1 1985) (work furlough statutes created no constitutionally protected liberty for prisoners): People ex rel. Burbank v. Irving, 108 Ill. App. 3d 697, 64 Ill. Dec. 303, 439 N.E.2d 554 (3d Dist. 1982) (refusal to place prisoner in work release program does not entitle prisoner to habeas corpus discharge); Avery v. Webb, 480 N.E.2d 281 (Ind. Ct. App. 3d Dist. 1985); Medley v. Hirsch, 88 A.D.2d 1099, 453 N.Y.S.2d 59 (3d Dep't 1982); People ex rel. Feliciano v. Waters, 99 A.D.2d 850, 472 N.Y.S.2d 455 (2d Dep't 1984); Gonzalez v. Wilson, 106 A.D.2d 386, 482 N.Y.S.2d 302 (2d Dep't 1984) (judicial review of denial of opportunity to participate in work release program is limited to a determination of whether there has been a violation of a positive statutory requirement or constitutional right and whether the determination was affected by "irrationality bordering on impropriety"); Reider v. Com., Bureau of Correction, 93 Pa. Commw. 326, 502 A.2d 272 (1985) (no liberty interest in pre-release status). If jurisdiction for administration of a work release program lies in the Department of Corrections, however, a trial court at the time of sentencing may not preclude a prisoner's participation in such program. See Davis v. State, 274 S.C. 549, 265 S.E.2d 679 (1980); Romer v. Morgenthau, 119 F. Supp. 2d 346 (S.D. N.Y. 2000). In Smith v. Stoner, 594 F. Supp. 1091 (N.D. Ind. 1984), the court found a liberty interest to participate in a work release program created by the terms of the inmate's sentence. See, generally, Annotation, Grant or Denial of Furlough or Work Release to Federal Prisoner under 18 U.S.C.A. § 4082(c), 64 A.L.R. Fed. 807.

In Winsett v. McGinnes, 617 F.2d 996 (3d Cir. 1980), the court held that, in light of Delaware's specific criteria for work release which, if met, give rise to liberty interest in work release, a Delaware prisoner had protectible due process liberty interest in work release where he met all eligibility criteria under the Delaware regulations and where the considerations influencing prison officials' discretionary denial of work release, namely concern for public reaction and fear of legislative reprisals, were outside the legitimate bounds of their discretionary power.

release program do not create a liberty or property interest in the work release program for every inmate who arguably meets those requirements.[13] Even if state officials act arbitrarily in allowing prisoners with records worse than that of a particular inmate to participate in such a program while denying it to the inmate, this does not violate the inmate's equal protection rights, since he has no liberty or property interest in work release, and since the state is cautious in awarding work release status because there are few available positions and the potential risks are high.[14]

Statutes barring certain classes of offenders from work release programs have withstood equal protection attacks.[15] The courts reason that work release is a priv-

---

[13]DeTomaso v. McGinnis, 970 F.2d 211 (7th Cir. 1992).

[14]See, e.g., Quartararo v. New York State Dept. of Correctional Services, 222 A.D.2d 758, 634 N.Y.S.2d 824 (3d Dep't 1995) (holding that New York could constitutionally exclude inmates who have been convicted of murder or of a sexual offense from work release).

[15]See, e.g., Fuller v. Lane, 686 F. Supp. 686 (C.D. Ill. 1988); Wagner v. Holmes, 361 F. Supp. 895 (E.D. Ky. 1973); Sanno v. Preiser, 397 F. Supp. 560 (S.D. N.Y. 1975); Paulino v. Connery, 766 F. Supp. 209 (S.D. N.Y. 1991). See also Hale v. Davis, 387 F. Supp. 408 (W.D. Va. 1974). The groups most likely to be excluded are violent prisoners and sex offenders. See, e.g., Quartararo v. New York State Dept. of Correctional Services, 222 A.D.2d 758, 634 N.Y.S.2d 824 (3d Dep't 1995) (holding that New York could constitutionally exclude inmates who have been convicted of murder or of a sexual offense from work release). For a sex offender exclusion case, see Mahfouz v. Lockhart, 826 F.2d 791 (8th Cir. 1987). In Tennessee, prisoners who have been convicted of driving while under the influence of an intoxicant are ineligible for a work release permit until they have completed at least the minimum sentence provided by law for such conviction. State v. Lowe, 661 S.W.2d 701 (Tenn. Crim. App. 1983). See also, e.g., Tenn Code Ann § 55-10-403(b). See, generally, Root, State Work Release Programs: An Analysis of Operational Policies, 37 Fed Probation 52 (Dec 1973). The court in Jamieson v. Robinson, 641 F.2d 138 (3d Cir. 1981) held that no equal protection violation occurred where work release opportunities were available to prisoners at some, but not all, state prison facilities. See also Luttrell v. Department of

§ 7:16　　　　　　　　　Rights of Prisoners, Third Edition

Corrections, 421 Mich. 93, 365 N.W.2d 74 (1984) (rule excluding prisoners in class of "drug traffickers" from eligibility for community placement was within legislative intent underlying statute authorizing community placement of prisoners). But compare Winsett v. McGinnes, 617 F.2d 996 (3d Cir. 1980) (while there is no inherent liberty interest creating right to enter work release program, in light of Delaware's specific criteria for work release which, if met, give rise to liberty interest in work release, Delaware prisoner had protectible due process liberty interest in work release where he met all eligibility criteria under Delaware regulations and where considerations influencing prison officials' discretionary denial of work release, namely concern for public reaction and fear of legislative reprisals, were outside legitimate bounds of their discretionary power).

Some courts have held that an inmate has no due process liberty or property interest limiting his or her transfer from a work release program back to penitentiary confinement. Since an inmate has no constitutional right to rehabilitation, he can have no constitutional right to due process when he is deprived of the right to participate in a work release program. Coakley v. Murphy, 884 F.2d 1218 (9th Cir. 1989). To similar effect, see People ex rel. Feliciano v. Waters, 99 A.D.2d 850, 472 N.Y.S.2d 455 (2d Dep't 1984); Medley v. Hirsch, 88 A.D.2d 1099, 453 N.Y.S.2d 59 (3d Dep't 1982). But other courts disagree for example, a decision of the Court of Appeals for the Eighth Circuit held that a prisoner who was participating in a work release program and who was living outside of prison did possess a liberty interest sufficient to require due process protection before she could be removed from the program. Edwards v. Lockhart, 908 F.2d 299 (8th Cir. 1990). See also Friedl v. City of New York, 210 F.3d 79, 46 Fed. R. Serv. 3d 146 (2d Cir. 2000). See also § 7:17.

DeTomaso v. McGinnis, 970 F.2d 211 (7th Cir. 1992). But see Edwards v. Lockhart, 908 F.2d 299 (8th Cir. 1990), holding that a prisoner's participation in a work release program does create the need for due process protection before he or she can be removed from the program. *Id.* See, e.g., Fuller v. Lane, 686 F. Supp. 686 (C.D. Ill. 1988); Wagner v. Holmes, 361 F. Supp. 895 (E.D. Ky. 1973); Sanno v. Preiser, 397 F. Supp. 560 (S.D. N.Y. 1975); Paulino v. Connery, 766 F. Supp. 209 (S.D. N.Y. 1991). See also Hale v. Davis, 387 F. Supp. 408 (W.D. Va. 1974). The groups most likely to be excluded are violent prisoners and sex offenders. For a sex offender exclusion case, see Mahfouz v. Lockhart, 826 F.2d 791 (8th Cir. 1987). In Tennessee, prisoners who have been convicted of driving while under the influence of an intoxicant are ineligible for

PRISON LABOR § 7:16

ilege rather than a right and that, in any event, it is not irrational to restrict eligibility to prisoners who are most likely to benefit from the opportunity and least likely to abuse it.[16] However, at least one court, in a minority view, has held that under state law a prisoner whose application for work release has been denied is entitled to know the reasons for the denial.[17] One Cali-

---

a work release permit until they have completed at least the minimum sentence provided by law for such conviction. State v. Lowe, 661 S.W.2d 701 (Tenn. Crim. App. 1983). See also, e.g., Tenn Code Ann § 55-10-403(b). See, generally, Root, State Work Release Programs: An Analysis of Operational Policies, 37 Fed Probation 52 (Dec 1973). The court in Jamieson v Robinson 641 F2d 138 (3d Cir 1981), held that no equal protection violation occurred where work release opportunities were available to prisoners at some but not all state prison facilities. See also Edmond v. Department of Corrections, 116 Mich. App. 1, 321 N.W.2d 817 (1982), decision rev'd on other grounds, 421 Mich. 93, 365 N.W.2d 74 (1984) (work release programs must be exercised consistent with the underlying purposes of the work release program; state Supreme Court held that rule excluding prisoners in class of "drug traffickers" from eligibility for community placement was within legislative intent underlying statute authorizing community placement of prisoners); Baumann v. Arizona Dept. of Corrections, 754 F.2d 841, 846 (9th Cir. 1985) (discriminatory furlough policy against "notorious white collar criminals" would violate equal protection only if it lacked "a rational relationship to a legitimate state interest").

[16]See Wagner v. Holmes, 361 F. Supp. 895 (E.D. Ky. 1973). See also Sellers v. Ciccone, 530 F.2d 199 (8th Cir. 1976); Martino v. Gard, 526 F. Supp. 958 (E.D. N.Y. 1981). Cf. also Luttrell v. Department of Corrections, 421 Mich. 93, 365 N.W.2d 74 (1984) (upholding rule interpreted so as to exclude drug trafficker from eligibility for community placement); Jansson v. Department of Corrections, 147 Mich. App. 774, 383 N.W.2d 152 (1985) (same re exclusion for sex offenders). A rule denying a prisoner eligibility for work release solely on the basis that he had been imprisoned for violating the conditions of his parole did not deny him equal protection. Graham v. Broglin, 922 F.2d 379 (7th Cir. 1991).

[17]White v. Vincent, 88 Misc. 2d 914, 390 N.Y.S.2d 499 (Sup 1975). See also Horton v. Hongisto, 70 A.D.2d 1040, 417 N.Y.S.2d 565 (4th Dep't 1979), appeal granted, 48 N.Y.2d 603, 421 N.Y.S.2d 1027, 396 N.E.2d 206 (1979); In re Thomas, 161 Cal. App. 3d 721, 206 Cal. Rptr. 719 (2d Dist. 1984) (under state constitution, unsuc-

§ 7:16

fornia court suggested that prison authorities should be required, in work furlough denials, to give the prisoner whose application was denied a written statement of the grounds for his exclusion from the program.[18] On the other hand, it has been held that actions taken by corrections officials in carrying out work release programs are exempt from the requirements of a state's Administrative Procedure Act.[19] Limiting participation

---

cessful inmate applicant for work furlough program entitled to procedural due process protection, including advance notice of proposed rejection, reasons for the rejection, specific concerns underlying the rationale for the rejection, and an opportunity to refute the reasons for the rejection).

[18]In In re Head, 147 Cal. App. 3d 1125, 1129-30, 195 Cal. Rptr. 593, 595 (1st Dist. 1983), the court found a state-created liberty interest in a work furlough program, and struck down blanket exclusion of certain classes of prisoners from participation. The court required individual consideration of prisoner applications for work furlough. More specifically, the court held that due process required the following procedural safeguards: (a) prisoners must be given a written statement of the grounds for their exclusion from the work furlough program; (b) prisoners must have access to the information used by the director in making his decision; (c) prisoners must be given notice of their right to respond to the decision; (d) prisoners must have the opportunity to make an oral response before a responsible official if the prisoner desires to do so; and (e) prisoners must be given a written statement of the final decision and the reasons therefor.

But see In re Thomas, 161 Cal. App. 3d 721, 206 Cal. Rptr. 719 (2d Dist. 1984), where a different California Court of Appeals said that a prisoner has no right or entitlement to acceptance in a work furlough program, since the determination of fitness and acceptance under such a program is left to the sole discretion of the work furlough administrator; therefore, a prisoner's interest in acceptance into such a program does not fall within the scope of due process liberty warranting some degree of protection under the federal due process clause.

[19]Paola v. Cupp, 11 Or. App. 43, 500 P.2d 739 (1972) (overruled by, Rutherford v. Oregon State Penitentiary, Corrections Division, Field Services, 39 Or. App. 431, 592 P.2d 1028 (1979)). Contra, Dougherty v. State, 323 N.W.2d 249 (Iowa 1982) (Iowa Administrative Procedure Act does apply to work release revocations and is the exclusive means for challenging a work release revocation).

§ 7:16

in work release programs to inmates who are within nine months of their minimum parole eligibility dates has been held valid, since work release is contemplated as a last step before parole and is intended to prepare inmates for productive lives beyond prison.[20]

Once prison administrators have decided that a particular inmate cannot participate in work release, courts are reluctant to question the wisdom of, or the factual basis for, the decision.[21] But discriminatory selection of participants in work release based on race,

---

See also State Division of Human Rights on Complaint of Wilson v. Monroe County, 49 N.Y.2d 937, 428 N.Y.S.2d 622, 406 N.E.2d 439 (1980) (state Division of Human Rights does not have jurisdiction over prisoner's complaint of discriminatory exclusion from work release program).

An ingenious argument was raised by the petitioner in Baumann v. Arizona Dept. of Corrections, 754 F.2d 841 (9th Cir. 1985). He maintained that the denial of an anticipated work release caused such emotional trauma and financial injury as to constitute torture forbidden by the Eighth Amendment's proscription against cruel and unusual punishment. The court was not persuaded that the prisoner's disappointment in not receiving work release rose to the level required for an Eighth Amendment violation.

[20]Rich v. Powell, 130 N.H. 455, 544 A.2d 29 (1988).

[21]See, e.g., Gahagan v. Pennsylvania Bd. of Probation and Parole, 444 F. Supp. 1326 (E.D. Pa. 1978); Young v. Hunt, 507 F. Supp. 785 (N.D. Ind. 1981) (upholding decisions to deny work release to some prisoners, while granting it to others); Rowe v. Cuyler, 534 F. Supp. 297 (E.D. Pa. 1982), aff'd, 696 F.2d 985 (3d Cir. 1982). See, generally, Annotation, Denial of State Prisoner's Application for, or Revocation of, Participation in Work or Study Release Program or Furlough Program as Actionable under Civil Rights Act of 1871 (42 U.S.C.A. § 1983), 55 A.L.R. Fed. 208.

Pursuant to a statute which authorized a prison warden to recall a prisoner at any time from a work release program if he believed that the peace, safety, welfare, or security of the community might be endangered by leaving the prisoner in work release status, the warden could monitor the prisoner's behavior and had wide discretion to revoke a work release permit. Brennan v. Cunningham, 126 N.H. 600, 493 A.2d 1213 (1985).

§ 7:16　　　　　　　Rights of Prisoners, Third Edition

religion, sex, or even mental impairment is improper.[22]

Courts have uniformly held that a prisoner may lawfully be denied admission to a work release program if his assignment would constitute a threat to the safety of the community.[23]

Inmates on work release are generally paid the prevailing wage for the job performed.[24] Often they are

---

[22]See, e.g., DeTomaso v. McGinnis, 970 F.2d 211 (7th Cir. 1992) (by implication); Battle v. Anderson, 376 F. Supp. 402 (E.D. Okla. 1974), judgment aff'd in part, rev'd in part on other grounds, 993 F.2d 1551 (10th Cir. 1993) (race); Sites v. McKenzie, 423 F. Supp. 1190 (N.D. W. Va. 1976) (mental impairment); Canterino v. Wilson, 869 F.2d 948 (6th Cir. 1989) (recognizing rule that denial of work release to female prisoners would be improper, but finding that no discrimination existed); Cooper v. Morin, 91 Misc. 2d 302, 398 N.Y.S.2d 36 (Sup 1977), judgment aff'd and modified on other grounds, 64 A.D.2d 130, 409 N.Y.S.2d 30 (4th Dep't 1978), judgment modified, 49 N.Y.2d 69, 424 N.Y.S.2d 168, 399 N.E.2d 1188 (1979) (sex). See also National Advisory Commn on Criminal Justice Standards & Goals, Corrections Standard 2.8 (1973).

In Martino v. Gard, 526 F. Supp. 958, 960-61 (E.D. N.Y. 1981), a prisoner claimed an equal protection violation when he was denied admission to a work release program. His brother, who had committed the same offense and had received the same sentence, had been admitted to the program. The court said that such choices fell within the discretion of the selection committee and that, absent an allegation of "consistent or patterned discrimination," there was no constitutional violation.

[23]Marciano v. Coughlin, 510 F. Supp. 1034 (E.D. N.Y. 1981) (inmate had committed a serious felony and had a history of previous parole violation); U.S. v. Michienzi, 508 F. Supp. 161 (N.D. Ohio 1981) (inmate convicted of aiding and abetting mail fraud was not entitled to work release); Bowman v. Wilson, 514 F. Supp. 403 (E.D. Pa. 1981), rev'd in part, vacated in part on other grounds, 672 F.2d 1145 (3d Cir. 1982); Gahagan v. Pennsylvania Bd. of Probation and Parole, 444 F. Supp. 1326 (E.D. Pa. 1978).

[24]See, e.g., 18 U.S.C. § 3622 (c)(1) ("rates of pay and other conditions of employment will not be less than those paid or provided for work of a similar nature in the community"); Cal Penal Code § 1208(c); Mass Gen Laws ch 127, § 49; NY Corrections Law § 153. See, generally, Lenihan, The Financial Condition of Released Prisoners, 21 Crime & Delinq 266, 276 (1975). Inmates on work release have also been held to be properly included within a

required to pay for room and board and, in some instances, to compensate the local welfare department if it is paying public assistance to the inmate's family.[25] Compensating the offender's victim may also be required.[26] Thus, work release programs combine rehabilitative training with institutional cost reduction.[27]

Where the terms of a statute creating a work release program are subsequently changed, no ex post facto problem arises if the changes are procedural in nature

---

bargaining unit for NLRB purposes. Rosslyn Concrete Const. Co. v. N.L.R.B., 713 F.2d 61 (4th Cir. 1983); Watson v. Graves, 909 F.2d 1549, 110 A.L.R. Fed. 823 (5th Cir. 1990) (holding that inmates who participated in a work release program were entitled to the minimum wage under the federal Fair Labor Standards Act).

[25]See, e.g., 18 U.S.C. § 3622(c)(2) (prison must pay costs "incident" to work release); Ark Stat Ann § 12-30-486; Cal Penal Code § 1208(e); Minn Stat Ann § 241.26, subd 5. See also State v. Killian, 37 N.C. App. 234, 245 S.E.2d 812 (1978) (department of corrections could deduct from earnings of inmate on work release money to reimburse state for attorney fees).. Requirements of this nature have been upheld by the courts. See, e.g. Mastrian v. Schoen, 725 F.2d 1164 (8th Cir. 1984) ("chargeback" program, whereby inmates enrolled in wage-paying prison work program were required to contribute to cost of room and board, was not unconstitutional); Ervin v. Blackwell, 585 F. Supp. 680 (W.D. Mo. 1983), judgment aff'd, 733 F.2d 1282 (8th Cir. 1984) (no right to participate in work release program and, therefore, requirement that prisoner contribute to maintenance as a condition of work release not unconstitutional); Cumbey v. State, 1985 OK 36, 699 P.2d 1094 (Okla. 1985) (upholding requirement that inmates contribute to costs of incarceration from income derived from employment other than in prison industries).

[26]Reimonenq v. Foti, 72 F.3d 472 (5th Cir. 1996).

[27]In one typical case, an inmate on work release earned $177 each pay period. From this he paid $17 in state and federal taxes, $9 in social security, $25 for room and board, $100 for family support (enabling his family to go off welfare), and $12 for spending money. The remainder was deposited in a savings account. B. Bagdikian & L. Dash, The Shame of the Prisons 186-88 (1972). See also Ervin v. Blackwell, 733 F.2d 1282 (8th Cir. 1984) (state may withhold maintenance costs from salary of work release prisoner).

§ 7:16   Rights of Prisoners, Third Edition

only,[28] but the result may be different where substantive changes are made in the statute and an attempt is made to apply those changes retrospectively. The Court of Appeals for the Eleventh Circuit held that work release guidelines were simply not laws within the meaning of the ex post facto clause.[29]

§ 7:17 Work Release Participation and Due Process Requirement

Work release status may be revoked for good cause, including erroneous assignments to work release. Examples of good cause include situations in which the inmate was placed on work release on the basis of incomplete information,[1] was mistakenly placed in a work release program for which he was categorically ineligible;[2] repeatedly escaped from official custody for prolonged periods of time;[3] or violated rules relating to work release or breached work release conditions.[4]

The courts remain divided as to whether a prisoner

---

[28]Alston v. Robinson, 791 F. Supp. 569 (D. Md. 1992), aff'd, 19 F.3d 10 (4th Cir. 1994) (statutory change requiring that a larger percentage of members of the board of review approve work releases was a procedural change and its retrospective application did not violate the ex post facto clause).

[29]Francis v. Fox, 838 F.2d 1147 (11th Cir. 1988). See also Jandelli v. Coughlin, 217 A.D.2d 733, 629 N.Y.S.2d 303 (3d Dep't 1995) (amendment to corrections law that prohibited inmates convicted of murder from participating in work release did not violate Ex Post Facto Clause); Knox v. Lanham, 895 F. Supp. 750 (D. Md. 1995), aff'd, 76 F.3d 377 (4th Cir. 1996).

[Section 7:17]

[1]O'Bar v. Pinion, 953 F.2d 74 (4th Cir. 1991).

[2]Codd v. Brown, 949 F.2d 879 (6th Cir. 1991) (inmate was ineligible because serving a life sentence for second degree murder).

[3]Beckett v. Cuyler, 523 F. Supp. 104 (E.D. Pa. 1981).

[4]See, e.g., State ex rel. Kaus v. McManus, 306 Minn. 487, 238 N.W.2d 597 (1976); Liston v. Oregon Corrections Division, Field Services, 26 Or. App. 83, 552 P.2d 275 (1976) (overruled by, Rutherford v. Oregon State Penitentiary, Corrections Division, Field Services, 39 Or. App. 431, 592 P.2d 1028 (1979)). Commonly, a work release prisoner is forbidden to visit or telephone friends

PRISON LABOR § 7:17

has to be provided due process protections before termination from a work release program. In the period prior to the *Sandin v. Conner*[5] some federal courts held that prisoners have no federal constitutional or statutory right to a work release status and, therefore, have no right to any hearing prior to the revocation of such status by prison officials.[6] But other courts disagreed.[7]

---

and family, indulge in intoxicants or drugs, or delay in traveling to and from work. See, generally, Case, Doing Time in the Community, 31 Fed Probation 9 (1967). See also O'Bar v. Pinion, 953 F.2d 74 (4th Cir. 1991) (the work release status of plaintiff who had been convicted of attempted murder was revoked when further investigation, prompted by letter from the mother of the plaintiff's victim, revealed that the plaintiff might be a threat to the victim if he remained on work release status); State v. Patrick, 381 So. 2d 501 (La. 1980); Young v. Temporary Release Committee of Albion Correctional Facility, 122 A.D.2d 606, 505 N.Y.S.2d 279 (4th Dep't 1986).

A prison inmate's participation in a work release program was conditional upon his complying with disciplinary rules. Where an inmate disobeyed a direct order, in violation of a rule of the work release center, termination of his participation in the program was warranted. McCall-Bey v. Franzen, 777 F.2d 1178, 3 Fed. R. Serv. 3d 1206 (7th Cir. 1985).

[5]Sandin v. Conner, 515 U.S. 472, 115 S. Ct. 2293, 132 L. Ed. 2d 418 (1995). *Sandin* is discussed in § 9:3. For a discussion of the pre-*Sandin* caselaw see Herman, The New Liberty: The Procedural Due Process Rights of Prisoners and Others Under the Burger Court, 59 NYU L Rev 482 (June 1984).

[6]See, e.g., Vinson v. Barkley, 646 F. Supp. 39 (W.D. N.Y. 1986). A federal district court, interpreting West Virginia law, held that no liberty right to work release existed under state law, and therefore inmates were not denied due process when they were administratively transferred from a work release center to a more restrictive correctional environment without an administrative hearing or determination, Beasley v. Duncil, 792 F. Supp. 485 (S.D. W. Va. 1992), aff'd, 9 F.3d 1106 (4th Cir. 1993). The Court of Appeals for the Fourth Circuit has held that removing an inmate from a work release program did not deprive him of any state constitutional right to the "fruits of his labor," nor did it implicate any federal constitutional due process liberty interest, since his removal from the work release program, his transfer, and his subsequent reclassification were discretionary administrative acts,

§ 7:17 RIGHTS OF PRISONERS, THIRD EDITION

Since *Sandin,* the courts remain divided. The Second Circuit, for example, has clearly held that the revocation of work release status is an "atypical and signifi-

---

O'Bar v. Pinion, 953 F.2d 74 (4th Cir. 1991). Citing Kentucky statutes, the Sixth Circuit held that prisoners had no liberty interest in work release programs, Canterino v. Wilson, 869 F.2d 948 (6th Cir. 1989).

In Dukes v. State, 576 So. 2d 683 (Ala. Crim. App. 1991), an Alabama court held that the Fourteenth Amendment did not require a due process hearing prior to the revocation of an inmate's work release status. In People v. Malmquist, 155 Mich. App. 521, 400 N.W.2d 317 (1986), a Michigan court held that a prisoner's work release privileges could be withdrawn without a notice or a hearing. But see Perrote v. Percy, 465 F. Supp. 112 (W.D. Wis. 1979), holding that a due process hearing had to be held either before, or within 14 days after, a revocation of a work release occurred, since the inmate could not be deprived of his or her liberty interest in the continuation of a work/study release status in the absence of a disciplinary due process hearing.

[7]In 1987, the Court of Appeals for the First Circuit, relying on the Fourteenth Amendment, held that a prisoner who was participating in a halfway house work release program did have a liberty interest in remaining in the program and was entitled to receive written notice in advance of any disciplinary charges against him, an opportunity consistent with institutional safety to call witnesses and present evidence at a hearing on such charges, and a written statement by the warden of the evidence relied on and the reasons for the disciplinary action. Brennan v. Cunningham, 813 F.2d 1 (1st Cir. 1987). In another case, Edwards v. Lockhart, 908 F.2d 299 (8th Cir. 1990), the Court of Appeals for the Eighth Circuit held that a prisoner did have a sufficient liberty interest in being continued in a work release program that would require due process protection before she could be removed from it. See also Durso v. Rowe, 579 F.2d 1365 (7th Cir. 1978); Application of Grosh, 415 N.W.2d 824 (S.D. 1987); Horton v. Hongisto, 70 A.D.2d 1040, 417 N.Y.S.2d 565 (4th Dep't 1979), appeal granted, 48 N.Y.2d 603, 421 N.Y.S.2d 1027, 396 N.E.2d 206 (1979); Tompkins v. Oregon Corrections Division, Field Services, 43 Or. App. 135, 602 P.2d 334 (1979); Perrote v. Percy, 444 F. Supp. 1288 (E.D. Wis. 1978). See also Dougherty v. State, 323 N.W.2d 249 (Iowa 1982) (state administrative procedure act provided means for challenging work release revocation).

PRISON LABOR § 7:17

cant hardship" triggering due process protections.[8] Other courts have taken the opposite tack, holding that revocation of work release does not implicate a liberty interest, since the inmate remains a prisoner regardless of whether or not he is on work release.[9] The Second Circuit held that there was a liberty interest in a case in which prison officials revoked an inmate's work release status following his application for food stamps and Medicaid even though the inmate alleged that there was no rule against him doing so. The court indicated that due process in this context requires at least the following elements:

(1) written notice of the reasons why removal is being considered;
(2) a report or summary of evidence against the inmate;
(3) advance notice of the committee hearing;
(4) the right to confront and cross-examine witnesses;
(5) neutral decisionmakers; and
(6) a post-hearing written account of the actual reason for removal and a summary of the evidence supporting that determination.[10]

Support for this position is found in the United States Supreme Court's decision in *Harper v. Young*[11] holding that inmates who are placed in "pre-parole" status

---

[8]Friedl v. City of New York, 210 F.3d 79, 46 Fed. R. Serv. 3d 146 (2d Cir. 2000). See also Kim v. Hurston, 182 F.3d 112 (2d Cir. 1999); Quartararo v. Hoy, 113 F. Supp. 2d 405 (E.D. N.Y. 2000).

[9]See e.g., Dominique v. Weld, 73 F.3d 1156 (1st Cir. 1996); Callender v. Sioux City Residential Treatment Facility, 88 F.3d 666 (8th Cir. 1996) and Bulger v. U.S. Bureau of Prisons, 65 F.3d 48 (5th Cir. 1995); Weller v. Grant County Sheriff, 75 F. Supp. 2d 927 (N.D. Ind. 1999); Boglin v. Weaver, 2001 WL 228172 (S.D. Ala. 2001) (no due process violation for the loss of the inmates "free world" job for violating prison rules).

[10]*Id.*

[11]Young v. Harper, 520 U.S. 143, 117 S. Ct. 1148, 137 L. Ed. 2d 270 (1997).

outside of prison walls have a due process right to a hearing prior to the termination of that status and their return to the prison. Work release resembles pre-parole in some ways in that the inmate is released from the prison walls to participate in the program. However, the grant of work release, unlike the grant of pre-parole, does not provide a guarantee of a release date.[12] Thus, the *Harper* holding provides support for both points of view on this question.

§ 7:18 Conclusion—The Legislative Challenge

Prison administrators and legislators seem to take a schizophrenic approach to inmates' labor. On the one hand, they piously extol its rehabilitative value. On the other hand, laws and policies currently in force limit the prisoner's job opportunities and combine to make prison work less than a meaningful experience.

Unlike in other areas, it is unrealistic to expect dramatic change through judicial action. The Thirteenth Amendment specifically excepts prison labor from its proscription against involuntary servitude. Other constitutional guarantees have rarely been applied. Absent any violation of constitutional rights, courts are appropriately reluctant to interfere with prison labor policies that they see as falling within the legislative and executive spheres.

A legislative blueprint for change would have many dimensions. The first step would be to normalize the prisoner's work environment so that it resembles that of the free world work force. This would require several changes in existing laws. First would be the repeal of those statutes which restrict the sale of prisoner-produced goods, a move which has been endorsed by

---

[12]One court opined that these are important distinctions and indicated that the closer that the actual terms of work release are to pre-parole, the more likely that a liberty interest exists. Weller v. Grant County Sheriff, 75 F. Supp. 2d 927 (N.D. Ind. 1999) (holding that if the work release facility is outside of prison walls, there is a liberty interest in remaining in that status).

the American Bar Association.[1] Second would be the promulgation of laws which create work incentives for prisoners, including the establishment of a minimum wage structure. Third would be the extension of traditional labor protection legislation, such as workers' compensation, to prisoners.

With the creation of a more normal work environment would come concomitant responsibilities. Prisoners would be charged for their room and board and other services, they would be required to contribute to the support of their families, and they would be required to make restitution to their victims. They would also have to pay taxes and contribute to social security.

While these proposals may appear radical, one must remember that society currently suffers a major economic loss from the failure to use the prison labor market efficaciously. The diminished effectiveness of the present prison labor system as a rehabilitative tool and the increased chance of recidivism caused by releasing from prison impecunious unskilled convicts also support the case for radical alternatives to the status quo. The public's attitudes toward prisoners and their general welfare change slowly, but nevertheless do change, and any programs that make it more likely that prisoners will be returned to civilian life better equipped to cope with the problems and opportunities that arise in today's society, and better able to support themselves and their families, should be welcomed by the public.

[Section 7:18]

[1] See ABA Standards for Criminal Justice, Standard 23-4.4(a); Uniform Law Commrs' Model Sentencing and Corrections Act § 4-816 (1985) (reprinted in Appendix B).

RIGHTS OF PRISONERS

Third Edition

2005 Supplement
Issued in December 2004

Volume 1
Chapters 1-7

Michael B. Mushlin
Professor of Law
Pace University School of Law

THOMSON
™
WEST

For Customer Assistance Call 1-800-328-4880

Mat #40207461

© 2004 West, a Thomson business

West, a Thomson business, has created this publication to provide you with accurate and authoritative information concerning the subject matter covered. However, this publication was not necessarily prepared by persons licensed to practice law in a particular jurisdiction. West is not engaged in rendering legal or other professional advice, and this publication is not a substitute for the advice of an attorney. If you require legal or other expert advice, you should seek the services of a competent attorney or other professional.

Preface to the 2005 Supplement To Rights of Prisoners (3d Ed)

I am grateful to David S. Cohen, Class of 2004 and to Siobhan Molt, Class of 2005 of Pace University School of Law, for their superb legal research and writing of the new material for the 2003 Supplement to this book.

I am grateful to Nicholle Crisalli, Class of 2006 of Pace University School of Law, for her superb legal research and writing of the new material for the 2004 Supplement to this book.

Chapter 1
Prisoners' Rights-Historical Background and General Overview

> **KeyCite®:** Cases and other legal materials listed in KeyCite Scope can be researched through West's KeyCite service on Westlaw®. Use KeyCite to check citations for form, parallel references, prior and later history, and comprehensive citator information, including citations to other decisions and secondary materials.

§ 1:1 Introduction
n. 1.
   Page 2, note 1, add:
The United States prison population grew more than twice as fast in 2002 as in 2001, bringing the total number of people behind bars in the United States to a record high. As of December 31, 2002, 2,033,331 prisoners were held in Federal or State prisons or in local jails. This total increased 3.7% from year end 2001. Based on these figures, there were an estimated 476 prison inmates per 100,000 U.S. residents in 2002. The number of women held behind bars in state or federal prison increased 4.9% from December 31, 2001, to December 31, 2002, reaching a high of 97,491 female inmates. The number of men imprisoned also rose, increasing 2.4%. United States Department of Justice, Office of Justice Programs, Bureau of Justice Statistics Bulletin, Prisoners in 2002 (July 2003).
   section 1:1, note 1, add:
The United States prison population continued to expand in the last year. It grew 2.9 percent from June 2002 to June 2003, the largest increase in four years. As of June 30, 2003, America's prisons and jails were home to 2,078,570 men and women. Based on these figures, there were an estimated 715 prison and jail inmates per 100,000 U.S. residents at midyear 2003. The number of women held behind bars in State or Federal prison increased 5%, at a rate almost twice the rate of increase as the rate of increase of male prisoners. On June 30, 2003 there were 100,102 female inmates. During the same time period, the number of men imprisoned increased 2.7%. As of June 30, 2003, privately owned prisons housed 94,316 inmates, an increase of 1.3% from yearend 2002. United States Department of Justice, Office of Justice Programs, Bureau of Justice Statistics Bulletin, Prison and Jail Inmates at Midyear 2003, http://www.opj.usdoj/bjs/pub/pdf/pjim03.pdf (last visited 7/28/04). Vincent Schiraldi, Digging Out: As US States Begin to Reduce Prison Use, Can America Turn the Corner on its Imprisonment Binge?, 24 Pace L. Rev._____ (forthcoming 2004) (discussing prison reform and prison population reduction measures in several states, including Michigan,

Washington, California, Arizona, Texas, Ohio, Kentucky, and Alabama, and encouraging those involved in prison reform to consider the examples set by these states for reducing the reliance on imprisonment).

§ 1:4 The Demise of the Hands-Off Doctrine and the Beginning of Prisoners' Rights Law

n. 7.

section 1:4, note 7, add:
Alphonse A. Gehardstein, A Practitioner's Guide to Successful Jury Trials on Behalf of Prisoner Plaintiffs, 24 Pace L. Rev. _____ (forthcoming 2004) (this article provides a practical guide to aid those who represent prisoner plaintiffs. Specifically, the article discusses case selection, discovery, jury instructions, trial presentation, damages, and attorney's fees).

n. 13.

section 1:4, note 13, add:
In October of 2003 a symposium on prison reform was held at Pace Law School in White Plains, New York. The papers presented at the symposium will be published in an issue of the Pace Law Review. See Symposium, Prison Reform: The Unfinished Agenda, 24 Pace L. Rev. _____(forthcoming 2004); see e.g. William Dean, Untitled, 24 Pace L. Rev. _____ (forthcoming 2004) (discussing three examples of the private bar's involvement in prisoner litigation); Michele Deitch, Thinking Outside the Cell: Prison Reform Litigation and the Vision of Prison Reform, 24 Pace L. Rev. _____(forthcoming 2004) (discussing the need to define a broad strategy to achieve long term prison reform); Hon. Morris E. Lasker, Untitled, 24 Pace L. Rev. _____(forthcoming 2004) (discussing the role of prison reform through litigation over the past several decades); Alvin J. Bronstein, Prison Reform Revisited: The Unfinished Agenda, 24 Pace L. Rev. _____(forthcoming 2004) (keynote speech); Vincent M. Nathan, Have the Courts Made a Difference in the Quality of Conditions? What Have We Accomplished to Date?, 24 Pace L. Rev. _____(forthcoming 2004) (discussing the overall improvements to prison conditions achieved through prisoner litigation); Malcolm M. Feeley & Van Swearingen, The Prison Conditions Cases and the Bureaucratization of American Corrections: Influences, Impacts, and Implications, 24 Pace L. Rev. _____(forthcoming 2004) (This article identifies the role of prisoner litigation in, "1) strengthening the process of professionalization within corrections; (2) embracing and fostering national standards for corrections; (3) expanding national governmental interests in and oversight of state and local institutions; and 4) represented the last step in constitutionalizing the criminal process." The authors also discuss the bureaucratization of prisons through which prison were transformed into organizations with clear organizational structures, written rules and procedures, highly trained staff, and systems of inmate classification. Lastly, the article describes the "double-edged" nature of bureaucracies which in the case of prisoners' rights both strengthen prisoners' rights and strengthen the authority of prison administrators); Alvin J. Bronstein & Jennie Gainsborough, Using International Human Rights Laws and Standards for U.S. Prison Reform, 24 Pace L. Rev._____ (forthcoming 2004) (discussing the increased willingness of courts in the United States to

consider international law, and the use of international law as a tool in prison litigation and reform); Reginald A. Wilkinson et al., Prison Reform Through Offender Reentry: A Partnership Between Courts and Corrections, 24 Pace L. Rev. _____ (forthcoming 2004) (discussing a collaboration between the department of correction and the courts to create a comprehensive rehabilitation plan for inmates through the use of reentry courts which provide judicial oversight for rehabilitation from entry into prison to reentry into society); James B. Jacobs & Elana Olitsky, Leadership and Correctional Reform, 24 Pace L. Rev. _____(forthcoming 2004) (discussing the importance of strong leadership in our nation's prisons. Specifically, the article discussed the experience and knowledge base that prison leaders should possess including, but not limited to, knowledge of law, corrections, interpersonal management, human resources management, accounting, public relations, and physical plant management; techniques for recruiting and retaining prison leaders, and discussing the role of training to develop the prison leaders of the future; the article concludes with a recommendation for a national commitment to finding and training that leadership); Andrew Coyle, Prison Reform Around the World: The Role of the Prison Administrator, 24 Pace L. Rev. (forthcoming 2004).

Chapter 2

The Eighth Amendment—Solitary Confinement, Prevention of Violence, Protection Against Overcrowding, and Provision of the Necessities of Life

> **KeyCite®:** Cases and other legal materials listed in KeyCite Scope can be researched through West's KeyCite service on Westlaw®. Use KeyCite to check citations for form, parallel references, prior and later history, and comprehensive citator information, including citations to other decisions and secondary materials.

§ 2:1 Introduction
n. 2.
   section 2:1 note 2, add:
Austin v. Johnson, 328 F.3d 204 (5th Cir. 2003) (granting qualified immunity on plaintiff's Eighth Amendment claim and holding that one day of attendance at a boot camp of plaintiff's choice was punishment thereby implicating the Eighth Amendment. However, one day at the camp is not disproportionate to the crime of stealing a candy bar, and running with a weight sack cannot be deemed cruel and unusual).

§ 2:2 The Supreme Court's Definition of Cruel and Unusual Punishment
n. 81.
   section 2:2 note 81, add:
Nelson v. Campbell, 124 S. Ct. 2117, 158 L. Ed. 2d 924 (U.S. 2004) (holding that § 1983 is an appropriate vehicle for the petitioner's Eighth Amendment claim seeking a temporary stay and permanent injunctive relief to prevent the State of Alabama from using the "cut-down" procedure to gain access to the inmate's veins in order to carry out the punishment of death by lethal injection. Under Alabama's "cut-down" procedure, prison officials, but not necessarily a doctor, would cut a two-inch incision in the inmate's arm while he was under local anesthesia in order to gain access to his veins so that he can be given a lethal injection.

In this case, the Court rejected the prison officials' argument that this claim should be brought as a habeas corpus petition as opposed to ?1983 claim and held that a ?1983 claim was proper because the inmate was not

§ 2:2 RIGHTS OF PRISONERS

challenging his sentence or the method of execution as cruel and unusual, rather his only challenge was to the method of gaining venous access. The court reasoned that if the prison officials sought to gain access to an inmate's veins for reasons other than for lethal injection this method of access could be challenged under ?1983 and there is no reason to treat this claim differently because it involves lethal injection.); Cooper v. Rimmer, 358 F.3d 655 (9th Cir. 2004), opinion amended and superseded, 379 F.3d 1029 (9th Cir. 2004) (holding that California's method of lethal injection which includes pancuronium bromide is not unconstitutional under the Eighth Amendment's cruel and unusual punishment clause because plaintiff's evidence of unnecessary pain and suffering was purely speculative); Robinson v. Crosby, 358 F.3d 1281 (11th Cir. 2004), cert. denied before judgment, 124 S. Ct. 1532, 158 L. Ed. 2d 173 (U.S. 2004) (holding that "[a] ?1983 claim seeking relief- including a TRO preliminary injunction or stay of execution from a sentence of death as cruel and unusual punishment is the 'functional equivalent' of a successful habeas corpus petition."); see also In re Williams, 359 F.3d 811, 2004 FED App. 0058P (6th Cir. 2004).

§ 2:3 Restrictive Confinement: Punitive Segregation, Solitary Confinement and "Supermax" Units

n. 3.

Page 85, note 3, add:
Alexander v. Gilmore, 202 F. Supp. 2d 478 (E.D. Va. 2002) (state prisoner's placement in segregated housing, following institutional conviction for being under influence of drugs, was not sufficiently severe sanction to support claim that his Eighth Amendment rights were violated).

n. 6.

section 2:3 note 6, add:
Jennifer R. Wynn & Alisa Szatrowski, Hidden Prisons: 23-Hour Lockdown Units In New York State Correctional Facilities, 24 Pace L. Rev. _____ (forthcoming 2004) (this article describes the use of "supermax security" prisons in New York State. The author argues that too many mentally ill inmates are held in supermax confinement and urges reform of the disciplinary confinement process).

n. 7.

Page 86, note 7, add:
; Holly Boyer, Comment, Home Sweet Hell: An Analysis of the Eighth Amendment's "Cruel and Unusual Punishment" Clause As Applied to Supermax Prisons, 32 SW. U. L. Rev. 317 (2003) (article addresses the questionable implementation of solitary confinement at supermax facilities and analyzes whether conditions inherent in the supermax design violate the Eighth Amendment's protection against "cruel and unusual punishment"); Daniel Brook, A History of Hard Time: Solitary Confinement, Then and Now, 2003-FEB Legal Aff. 39 (2003) (short article on the history of prisons culminating in the supermax prison and the potentially damaging effect such confinement has on the human psyche); Charles A. Pettigrew, Comment, Technology and the Eighth Amendment: The Problem of Supermax Prisons, 4 N.C. J. L. & Tech. 191 (2002) (author

§ 2:3

argues that supermax prisons, designed and constructed with the noble goals of protecting staff and inmates, instead result in a level of isolation for inmates that may be a violation of the Eighth Amendment); Leena Kurki & Norval Morris, The Purposes, Practices, and Problems of Supermax Prisons, 28 Crime & Just. 385 (2001) (authors argue, among other things, that although supermax prisons do hold some very dangerous prisoners, they also hold many others who merely have been identified by the prison authorities as threatening, disruptive, or persistent nuisances, and that prison safety and security do not require such harsh and separate conditions for these prisoners).

Page 87, last word in first full paragraph after the word "activities," add new footnote 9.1.

[9.1]Phillips v. Norris, 320 F.3d 844 (8th Cir. 2003) (denial to state prison inmate of contact visitation, exercise privileges, and religious services for 37 days while he was in segregation did not constitute cruel and unusual punishment, regardless of whether segregation was ordered without hearing); Gill v. Hoadley, 261 F. Supp. 2d 113 (N.D. N.Y. 2003) (allegations of unconstitutional confinement conditions consisting of the denial of one noon meal, denial of exercise while on keeplock confinement, and being confined to his cell for periods of four, 21, and 21 days, were insufficient, without more, to establish a claim of cruel and unusual punishment); Dixon v. Goord, 224 F. Supp. 2d 739 (S.D. N.Y. 2002) (disciplined prisoner's claims of having been cut off from prison population, computer program, religious services, legal research, medical showers and personal property, as well as limits on food access, and other normal incidents of special housing unit (sHU) confinement, did not allege violations of Eighth Amendment).

n. 10.

section 2:3 note 10, add:
But see David C. Fathi, The Common Law of Supermax Litigation, 24 Pace L. Rev. _____ (forthcoming 2004) (this article describes the terms of settlement of three supermax cases. The author describes the settlement agreements which address the exclusion of mentally ill prisoners from supermax confinement, out of cell time for inmates housed in supermax units, visitation rights of prisoners housed in supermax units, and various other issues. The author concludes by stating that although the use of supermax prisons seems to be declining, prison systems which continue to use this form of punishment should use the above mentioned cases as a guide when forming their policies).

n. 12.

Page 88, note 12 add:
See also Gertrude Strassburger, Judicial Inaction and Cruel and Unusual Punishment: Are Super-Maximum Walls Too High for the Eighth Amendment?, 11 Temp. Pol. & Civ. Rts. L. Rev. 199 (2001) (author argues that the placement of inmates in complete solitary confinement in supermax prisons for years on end is causing severe injury to prisoners and concludes that courts must balance the security needs of the prisons with the psychological needs of the inmates to ensure that the Constitution is not violated).

Page 88, sixth sentence of the first full paragraph, after the word "attractive," add new footnote 12.1.

§ 2:3

[12.1]But see Edward L. Rubin, The Inevitability of Rehabilitation, 19 Law & Ineq. 343 (2001) (author argues that the only rationale for the design of prison programs that is possible and acceptable in this society is rehabilitation).

n. 31.

Page 93, note 31, add:
; Hernandez v. Hanks, 65 Fed. Appx. 72 (7th Cir. 2003) (state prison officials did not subject inmate to cruel and unusual punishment by keeping him in disciplinary segregation after completion of his originally imposed sanctions, absent allegation that inmate was being deprived of anything beyond privilege of being in general prison population); Khalild v. Reda, 2003 WL 42145 (S.D. N.Y. 2003) (corrections official's alleged forgery of request for extension of time for inmate's disciplinary hearing resulting in inmate's continued confinement in special housing unit (sHU), stated no Eighth Amendment violation, as deprivation of being housed in SHU was not so serious as to constitute cruel and unusual punishment).

n. 42.

Page 95, note 42, add:
See Beckford v. Portuondo, 151 F. Supp. 2d 204 (N.D. N.Y. 2001) (fact issues existed as to whether officials violated Eighth Amendment by denying wheelchair-bound inmate shower benefits for one week, requiring him to sleep on steel floor for one night, reducing him to one meal per day, spraying him with fire extinguisher, and taking no action when he was exposed to bleach by fellow inmate).

n. 46.

section 2:3 note 46, add:
Trammell v. Keane, 338 F.3d 155 (2d Cir. 2003) (holding that prison officials were not deliberately indifferent to the inmate's health or safety when the inmate was deprived of "all state and personal property in [his] cell except one pair of shorts, No recreation, No shower, No hot water, [and] No cell bucket . . ." because plaintiff was uncontrollable and would "throw . . . drinks, soup, spit, urine, and feces - at corrections officers or others near his cell." The inmate was subject to this treatment in various degrees from December 16, 1994 through January 13, 1995. On December 16 all of the inmate's possessions were confiscated. The inmate was able to regain privileges with good behavior but would lose privileges with bad behavior. All of the inmate's property was returned on January 13. In addition, the inmate was given only nutriloaf, "a bread-like food containing carrots and potatoes," and raw cabbage for 95 days. The court held that this punishment was reasonably calculated to correct the plaintiff's behavior because plaintiff could regain his privileges if he would conform to prison regulations, and since plaintiff had access to a nurse his health was not in danger).

n. 50.

Page 101, note 50, add:
But see Green v. Nadeau, 70 P.3d 574 (Colo. Ct. App. 2003), cert. denied, 2003 WL 21142504 (Colo. 2003) (denying inmate in administrative segregation for misconduct outdoor exercise did not constitute cruel and unusual punishment).

CRUEL & UNUSUAL PUNISHMENT § 2:3

n. 59.

Page 105, note 59, add:
; Liles v. Camden County Dept. of Corrections, 225 F. Supp. 2d 450 (D.N.J. 2002) (county prison lock-down of 22 days that caused inmates inconvenience and discomfort did not support inmates' Eighth Amendment claims against prison officials, although inmates were allowed only 20 minutes daily outside of cells to shower, use bathroom, exercise, and make phone calls); Oliver v. Powell, 250 F. Supp. 2d 593 (E.D. Va. 2002) (allegations that prison guards deprived prisoner of sleep by keeping him up with their singing, talking, and other noise, and that prisoner's segregation cell had roaches, leaky toilet, peeling paint, and writing on wall, did not rise to level of Eighth Amendment claim, since claims did not lie outside scope of ordinary discomfort accompanying prison life); Beckford v. Portuondo, 152 F.Supp.2d 204 (N.D.N.Y. 2001) (officials did not violate Eighth Amendment by denying inmate shower privileges for one day, limiting his in-cell water privileges for six days, or limiting his exercise opportunities).

section 2:3 note 59, add:
Trammell v. Keane, 338 F.3d 155 (2d Cir. 2003) (holding that prison officials were not deliberately indifferent to the inmate's health or safety when the inmate was deprived of "all state and personal property in [his] cell except one pair of shorts, No recreation, No shower, No hot water, [and] No cell bucket . . ." because plaintiff was uncontrollable and would "throw . . . drinks, soup, spit, urine, and feces - at corrections officers or others near his cell." The inmate was subject to this treatment in various degrees from December 16, 1994 through January 13, 1995. On December 16 all of the inmate's possessions were confiscated. The inmate was able to regain privileges with good behavior but would lose privileges with bad behavior. All of the inmate's property was returned on January 13. In addition, the inmate was given only nutriloaf, "a bread-like food containing carrots and potatoes," and raw cabbage for 95 days. The court held that this punishment was reasonably calculated to correct the plaintiff's behavior because plaintiff could regain his privileges if he would conform to prison regulations, and since plaintiff had access to a nurse his health was not in danger); Rivera v. Pa. Dep't of Corr., 2003 PA Super 447 (Pa. Super. Ct. 2003) (denying the inmates' petition for a writ of habeas corpus when they alleged that the conditions in the Long Term Segregation Unit (LTSU) violated their Eighth Amendment rights. The plaintiffs' claim stated that the LTSU is the most restrictive class in the Pennsylvania prison system. While prisoners are in the LTSU they are not allowed access to personal property, education or religious programs, they are confined to their cells for 23 hours per day, they are only allowed three showers per week, the sentence in the LTSU is indefinite, the lights are on for 24 hours per day, there is constant noise, the heating system does not function properly, and inmates often throw feces which does not get cleaned up for some time. Despite these facts, the court held that the conditions in the LTSU did not rise to the level of an Eighth Amendment violation because the inmates were provided with the necessities of life, the inmates had to ability to change many of the conditions (i.e. constant noise, feces throwing), and the prison officials took reasonable steps to manage the conditions (i.e. providing extra blankets on cold nights, bringing in cleaning crews)).

n. 60.

Page 105, note 60, add:

§ 2:3 RIGHTS OF PRISONERS

; Ashley v. Seamon, 32 Fed. Appx. 747 (7th Cir. 2002) (deprivations of inmate who was placed in segregation were not sufficiently serious to rise to the level of an Eighth Amendment violation, although inmate was not allowed to smoke cigarettes, watch television, listen to the radio, make telephone calls, or have reading material).

n. 73.

Page 107, note 73, add:
; Rahman X v. Morgan, 300 F.3d 970 (8th Cir. 2002) (deprivations experienced by prisoner when housed in segregation cell for 26 months after being sentenced to death for killing prison guard were not sufficiently serious to violate Eighth Amendment, where prisoner complained of lack of access to television, being prohibited from possessing ballpoint pens and batteries, and being deprived of outdoor yard privileges for several months).

n. 75.

section 2:3 note 75, add:
Trammell v. Keane, 338 F.3d 155 (2d Cir. 2003) (holding that prison officials were not deliberately indifferent to the inmate's health or safety when the inmate was deprived of "all state and personal property in [his] cell except one pair of shorts, No recreation, No shower, No hot water, [and] No cell bucket . . ." because plaintiff was uncontrollable and would "throw . . . drinks, soup, spit, urine, and feces - at corrections officers or others near his cell." The inmate was subject to this treatment in various degrees from December 16, 1994 through January 13, 1995. On December 16 all of the inmate's possessions were confiscated. The inmate was able to regain privileges with good behavior but would lose privileges with bad behavior. All of the inmate's property was returned on January 13. In addition, the inmate was given only nutriloaf, "a bread-like food containing carrots and potatoes," and raw cabbage for 95 days. The court held that this punishment was reasonably calculated to correct the plaintiff's behavior because plaintiff could regain his privileges if he would conform to prison regulations, and since plaintiff had access to a nurse his health was not in danger); Rivera v. Pa. Dep't of Corr., 2003 PA Super 447 (Pa. Super. Ct. 2003) (denying the inmates' petition for a writ of habeas corpus when they alleged that the conditions in the Long Term Segregation Unit (LTSU) violated their Eighth Amendment rights. The plaintiffs' claim stated that the LTSU is the most restrictive class in the Pennsylvania prison system. While prisoners are in the LTSU they are not allowed access to personal property, education or religious programs, they are confined to their cells for 23 hours per day, they are only allowed three showers per week, the sentence in the LTSU is indefinite, the lights are on for 24 hours per day, there is constant noise, the heating system does not function properly, and inmates often throw feces which does not get cleaned up for some time. Despite these facts, the court held that the conditions in the LTSU did not rise to the level of an Eighth Amendment violation because the inmates were provided with the necessities of life, the inmates had to ability to change many of the conditions (i.e. constant noise, feces throwing), and the prison officials took reasonable steps to manage the conditions (i.e. providing extra blankets on cold nights, bringing in cleaning crews)).

n. 81.

section 2:3 note 81, add:

CRUEL & UNUSUAL PUNISHMENT § 2:4

Gates v. Cook, 376 F.3d 323 (5th Cir. 2004) (affirming in part and vacating in part the district court's injunctions regarding the prison conditions on death row. The court affirmed the district court's injunctions requiring prison officials to: discontinue the practice of moving inmates to a new cell and requiring them to clean up after the former occupant; provide inmates with adequate cleaning supplies to clean their cells; provide proper ventilation, and access to fans, ice water and showers during days when the temperature exceeds 90 degrees; repair and/or provide screens to control mosquitoes entry into cells; correct the "ping-pong" toilet whereby human waste flushed in one toilet would appear in another; improve lighting; and improve medical care. The court vacated the district court's injunctions requiring the prison to provide a written maintenance schedule and to provide inmates with sneakers in stead of "flip-flops" during exercise times.).

n. 95.

Page 114, note 95, before "See Black v. Brown," add:
; Dixon v. Goord, 224 F. Supp. 2d 739 (S.D. N.Y. 2002) (state prisoner's punishment of ten months in special housing unit upon being found guilty in a disciplinary hearing of assaulting prison officer was not cruel or unusual punishment, as discipline was not grossly disproportionate to seriousness of offense).

n. 112.

Page 119, note 112, add:
; Knight v. Keane, 247 F. Supp. 2d 379 (S.D. N.Y. 2002) (prisoner failed to state cruel and unusual punishment claim against prison officials arising from alleged confinement for 365 days in "keeplock," absent specific allegations of serious deprivation rather than general allegations of "emotional and psychological trauma").

§ 2:4 Corporal Punishment and Physical and Mechanical Restraints

n. 14.

Page 123, note 14, add:
Jackson v. Morgan, 19 Fed. Appx. 97 (4th Cir. 2001), cert. denied, 535 U.S. 970, 122 S. Ct. 1437, 152 L. Ed. 2d 381 (2002) (court of appeals found that inmate suffered only de minimus injury as a result of his placement into an isolation cell for two days and in three-point mechanical restraints after having been sprayed with pepper spray, and that no reasonable jury could find that excessive force was used; court noted that restraints did not entirely restrict prisoner's movements and that meals were offered during period of confinement); Laws v. Cleaver, 140 F. Supp. 2d 145, 56 Fed. R. Evid. Serv. 941 (D. Conn. 2001) (four-hour immobilization in "four-point" restraints following an altercation did not by itself constitute atypical and significant hardship).

n. 15.

section 2:4 note 15, add:
Alison Chin, Supreme Court Review: Hope v. Pelzer: Increasing the Accountability of State Actors in Prison Systems- A Necessary Enterprise in Guaranteeing the Eighth Amendment Rights of Prison Inmates, 93 Crim. L. & Criminology 913 (2002) ("argu[ing] that Hope encourages judicial

§ 2:4   Rights of Prisoners

intervention through its monitoring of state prison management, which may, in some cases, be necessary to protect inmates rights").

n. 19.

Page 124, note 19, add:
; Camp v. Brennan, 54 Fed. Appx. 78 (3d Cir. 2002) (prison officials did not violate inmate's Eighth Amendment rights by restraining him on table for approximately two days while naked, where inmate provoked violent disturbance, was stripped to be certain he did not possess weapon or other contraband, was shackled to ensure his safety, and had himself removed blanket that prison officials had used to cover him); Dye v. Lomen, 40 Fed. Appx. 993 (7th Cir. 2002) (in affirming the district court's grant of summary judgment to correctional officials, court of appeals found that officials did not use excessive force in violation of prisoner's Eighth Amendment rights when they physically and mechanically restrained prisoner and used a stun gun against him during the two cell entries, where evidence showed that officials used force only because prisoner was struggling with them and they needed to restrain him so that he would not injure them or himself); Cunningham v. Eyman, 17 Fed. Appx. 449 (7th Cir. 2001) (due to prisoner's behavior on the prior day, yelling and kicking a partition, prisoner spent 16 hours in shackles and four to five hours in soiled clothing, since he was denied a request to use the bathroom; court found that though certainly unpleasant, these hardships were temporary and not of sufficient severity to implicate Eighth Amendment); Barker v. Fugazzi, 18 Fed. Appx. 663 (9th Cir. 2001), cert. denied, 534 U.S. 1140, 122 S. Ct. 1092, 151 L. Ed. 2d 990 (2002) (affirming grant of defendant's motion for summary judgment, court held that alleged injuries sustained by inmate from being shackled during bus trip were not serious enough either to satisfy objective component of the test for Eighth Amendment violation or to give rise to inference that officials on bus knew about and disregarded an excessive risk to his health and safety); Ruffin v. Taylor, 166 F. Supp. 2d 999 (D. Del. 2001) (allegations by inmate that he was forcibly handcuffed and leg-shackled after trying to prevent correctional officers from placing a chain and padlock on his cell door did not support Eighth Amendment excessive force claim; inmate's injuries were relatively minimal and inmate admitted that he had resisted officer's attempts to remove him from his cell).

section 2:4 note 19, add:
Myers v. Milbert, 281 F. Supp. 2d 859 (N.D. W. Va. 2003) (holding that prison officials did not violate the inmate's Eighth Amendment rights when they placed the inmate in a "stokes basket," a metal stretcher, for approximately one day in response to plaintiff throwing food, yelling, and kicking his cell door until the jail alarm sounded).

n. 20.

Page 124, note 20, add:
And see Benjamin v. Fraser, 2002 WL 31845111 (S.D. N.Y. 2002) (in order to avoid violation of Eighth Amendment, corrections department would be required to free inmates of enhanced restraints once every two hours for not less than ten minutes, that defendants must honor more frequent requests, within reason, to use the facilities or to drink water, and could not handcuff inmate's arms behind back during court appearances, as there was less of a need for heightened security in the court room).

§ 2:5 Use of Force by Guards

n. 4.

Page 126, note 4, add:

See McCoy v. Goord, 255 F. Supp. 2d 233 (S.D. N.Y. 2003) (allegations that corrections officers caused second-degree burns to inmate's arm stated Eighth Amendment claim for use of excessive force; it was alleged that the officers did not apply force to "maintain or restore discipline," but to retaliate against inmate for comments made to one of the officers; allegations that, in a separate incident, corrections officers forced inmate to the ground, handcuffed him, cleared the area of witnesses, and beat him until he "looked like the elephant man" supported Eighth Amendment claim for excessive force); Evicci v. Baker, 190 F. Supp. 2d 233 (D. Mass. 2002) (court denied motion for summary judgment on inmate's Eighth Amendment claim regarding an alleged beating by several correction officers because his assertions and a medical report supported a finding that he was beaten, not merely subdued; inmate also alleged that defendants conspired to assault him and then cover up the beating; defendants on their part submitted numerous exhibits and affidavits to demonstrated that inmate assaulted the corrections officers, but court noted that weight to be given these documents was for trier of fact to decide); Davis v. Agosto, 2002 WL 1880761 (W.D. Ky. 2002) (inmate failed to establish that defendants violated his Eighth Amendment right when force was applied in order to free prison officer from inmate's grasp and was ceased as soon as this was accomplished; it was clear that the motivation behind the force was to maintain or restore discipline rather than merely to cause plaintiff harm and the minor extent of inmate's injuries also indicated that the force was not sadistically applied).

section 2:5 note 4, add:

Fillmore v. Page, 358 F.3d 496 (7th Cir. 2004) (reversing the district court's grant of summary judgment for defendants on plaintiff's excessive force claim when plaintiff claimed that members of the "Orange Crush," a special security team, pushed his face against a metal cage, pushed him into his cell, and then punched and kicked him even though plaintiff could not identify the officers. The court held that a further inquiry was required to identify which officers used excessive force before granting summary judgment); Jarno v. Lewis, 256 F. Supp. 2d 499 (E.D. Va. 2003) (holding that the actions of officers at a local jail that contracted with the federal government to hold INS detainees constituted state, not federal, action making the officers amenable to plaintiff's suit under § 1983. Here, the inmate alleged that jail officers physically abused him on two occasions).

n. 6.

section 2:5 note 6, add:

Scott v. Coughlin, 344 F.3d 282 (2d Cir. 2003) (reversing the district court's grant of summary judgment in favor of the defendant and holding that the inmate's allegations of excessive force were supported by his affidavit in which he stated that he was beaten by a prison guard for filing a grievance against the prison guard. The court ruled that the district court erred when it only considered the severity of plaintiff's injury and not the remaining *Hudson v. McMillian* factors when deciding to grant summary judgment).

n. 7.

Page 127, note 7, add:

§ 2:5 RIGHTS OF PRISONERS

; Outlaw v. Newkirk, 259 F.3d 833 (7th Cir. 2001) (summary judgment was properly granted on inmate's claim that prison guard slammed his hand in a cuff-port hatch, a small hatch within the cell door, as the evidence did not suggest that prisoner's injury was more than minor and a jury could only find that either incident was accident or that guard used minor amount of force to achieve legitimate security objective); Beckwith v. Hart, 263 F. Supp. 2d 1018 (D. Md. 2003) (inmate failed to establish that he was subject to excessive force in violation of his Eighth Amendment rights by actions of prison employee, who closed door to conference room on inmate's foot after he had interrupted meeting among prison personnel).

section 2:5 note 7, add:
Fillmore v. Page, 358 F.3d 496 (7th Cir. 2004) (holding that officers who transported the inmate from his cell to the prison segregation unit did not violate plaintiff's rights under the Eighth Amendment when the video of the transfer reveals "incidental bumping." The prison officers' behavior did not rise to the level of excessive force. Since this behavior did not rise to the level of excessive force, the observing officers who did not have physical contact with the inmate cannot be held liable for failure to protect the inmate); Perkins v. Brown, 285 F. Supp. 2d 279 (E.D. N.Y. 2003) (holding that prison officials acted objectively reasonable under the *Hudson* test and therefore did not violate the inmate's Eighth Amendment rights when the officers asked the inmate to submit to a strip search according to policy several times without cooperation from the inmate before they forcibly striped him. The inmate also claimed that the officers used excessive force against him in violation of this Eighth Amendment rights when they were escorting him from one cell to another. During the transfer, the inmate and the guards began to argue. As a result of the argument, one of the officers began to punch the inmate. The court rejected the inmate's claim that the officer's conduct violated his Eighth Amendment rights because the inmate's medical records and statements indicated that the force was *de minimis)*; Burks v. Nassau County Sheriff's Dept., 288 F. Supp. 2d 298 (E.D. N.Y. 2003) (granting jail officials' motion to dismiss plaintiff's claim that the officials violated his Eighth Amendment rights because failure to warn plaintiff about the possibility that the cell doors could malfunction at most states a claim for negligence which does not constitute an Eighth Amendment violation).

n. 15.

Page 129, note 15, add:
; Irene M. Baker, Comment, *Wilson v. Spain: Will Pretrial Detainees Escape the Constitutional "Twilight Zone,"* 75 St. John's L. Rev. 449, 465-481 (2001) (author argues that there can be no logical distinction between arrestees and pretrial detainees and asserts that a single constitutional standard applies to claims of excessive force).

n. 20.

section 2:5 note 20, add:
Fillmore v. Page, 358 F.3d 496 (7th Cir. 2004) (holding that officers who transported the inmate from his cell to the prison segregation unit did not violate plaintiff's rights under the Eighth Amendment when the video of the transfer reveals "incidental bumping." The prison officers' behavior did not rise to the level of excessive force. Since this behavior did not rise to the level of excessive force, the observing officers who did not have

Cruel & Unusual Punishment § 2:5

physical contact with the inmate cannot be held liable for failure to protect the inmate); Minifield v. Butikofer, 298 F. Supp. 2d 900 (N.D. Cal. 2004) (holding that the inmate's Eighth Amendment claim based on sexual harassment by officers does not state a valid claim. Plaintiff alleged that the officer "unzipped his clothing and told Plaintiff to grab his penis," and "[held] a candy bar towards his [the officer's] genital area . . . [and] [w]hen plaintiff asked if this action was directed at him, [the officer responded] 'I don't kiss and tell." The court denied relief because the plaintiff did not allege that the officer "exposed his genitals or touched plaintiff in a sexual manner." The court held that words alone have not been held to violate the Eighth Amendment); Johnson v. Unknown Dellatifa, 357 F.3d 539, 57 Fed. R. Serv. 3d 1108, 2004 FED App. 0036P (6th Cir. 2004), cert. denied, 125 S. Ct. 157 (U.S. 2004) (affirming the district court's dismissal of the inmate's Eighth Amendment claim against a prison official and holding that the prison official's behavior, which the inmate claimed included kicking the inmate's cell door, making aggravating remarks to the inmate, making insulting remarks about the inmate's hair, growling and snarling at the inmate through his cell window, smearing the inmate's cell door window so that the inmate could not see through it, and behaving in a racially prejudicial manner toward the inmate, while "shameful and utterly unprofessional," does not rise to the level of an Eighth Amendment violation).

n. 28.

Page 132, note 28, add:
But see Piedra v. True, 169 F. Supp. 2d 1239 (D. Kan. 2001), aff'd, 52 Fed. Appx. 439 (10th Cir. 2002) (granting officers' motion for summary judgment, court found that inmate's claim that officers beat and kicked him while he was handcuffed was too general for a constitutional violation and was not supported by medical records; court said that reasonable officer could have believed that inmate threatened his or others' safety, since inmate, even though handcuffed, was combative as officers were escorting him).

n. 30.

Page 133, note 30, add the following before "But see":
; Reyes v. Chinnici, 54 Fed. Appx. 44 (3d Cir. 2002) (officer's single punch to shoulder was de minimis use of physical force, and was not the sort of action that was repugnant to the conscience of mankind, and thus did not violate prisoner's Eighth Amendment rights); Jackson v. Morgan, 19 Fed. Appx. 97 (4th Cir. 2001), cert. denied, 535 U.S. 970, 122 S. Ct. 1437, 152 L. Ed. 2d 381 (2002) (inmate suffered only de minumus injury as result of his placement in isolation cell for two days and in three-point mechanical restraints after having been sprayed with pepper spray, and thus could not state Eighth Amendment excessive force claim against prison officials); White v. Matti, 58 Fed. Appx. 636 (7th Cir. 2002) (in order to be sustained, an Eighth Amendment claim of excessive force must involve force that is more than de minimis or force that is repugnant to the conscience of mankind); Outlaw v. Newkirk, 259 F.3d 833 (7th Cir. 2001) (while prisoner need not demonstrate significant injury to state claim for excessive force under Eighth Amendment, claim ordinarily cannot be predicated on de minimis use of physical force); West v. Fuchs, 38 Fed. Appx. 323 (7th Cir. 2002) (prisoner failed to establish that prison guards used excessive force against him when he was transported from one prison to another prison,

§ 2:5   RIGHTS OF PRISONERS

since prisoner offered no evidence that force used by guards was excessive or that he suffered anything more than de minimis injury); Amaker v. Coombe, 2003 WL 21222534 (S.D. N.Y. 2003) (de minimis use of force will rarely suffice to state a constitutional claim); Crayton v. Terhune, 24 Nat'l Disability Law Rep. ¶ 235, 2002 WL 31093590 (N.D. Cal. 2002) (Eighth Amendment's prohibition of cruel and unusual punishment necessarily excludes from constitutional recognition de minimis uses of physical force, provided that the use of force is not a sort "repugnant to the conscience of mankind"); Floyd v. Nelson, 2002 WL 1483896 (N.D. Ill. 2002) (county deputies did not use excessive force against pre-trial detainee by pushing him, since the push constituted a de minimis use of force); Oliver v. Powell, 250 F. Supp. 2d 593 (E.D. Va. 2002) (allegation that prison guards assaulted prisoner by "poking" him in the back when he did not hear them did not state claim of excessive force, as it did not involve more than de minimus injury); Marshall v. Odom, 156 F. Supp. 2d 525 (D. Md. 2001) (inmate who, while being transported, tripped and fell into a correctional officer who then struck him, suffered injuries that were de minimis and did not rise to an Eighth Amendment violation; court in granting officers' motion for summary judgment said that inmate failed to show that correctional officers acted to deprive him of his constitutional rights); Ostrander v. Horn, 145 F. Supp. 2d 614 (M.D. Pa. 2001), aff'd, 49 Fed. Appx. 391 (3d Cir. 2002) (inmate's claim that during an emergency preparedness and fire evacuation drill, he was removed from his cell, handcuffed, and strip searched did not rise to the level of an Eighth Amendment violation because inmate had shown only a de minimum use of force and there was no indication that he had suffered any actual injuries); Davis v. Lester, 156 F. Supp. 2d 588 (W.D. Va. 2001) (de minimis injury can be conclusive evidence that force used was also de minimis and therefore did not violate Eighth Amendment protections).

  section 2:5 note 30, add:
Perkins v. Brown, 285 F. Supp. 2d 279 (E.D. N.Y. 2003) (holding that prison officials acted objectively reasonable under the *Hudson* test and therefore did not violate the inmate's Eighth Amendment rights when the officers asked the inmate to submit to a strip search according to policy several times without cooperation from the inmate before they forcibly striped him. The inmate also claimed that the officers used excessive force against him in violation of this Eighth Amendment rights when they were escorting him from one cell to another. During the transfer, the inmate and the guards began to argue. As a result of the argument, one of the officers began to punch the inmate. The court rejected the inmate's claim that the officer's conduct violated his Eighth Amendment rights because the inmate's medical records and statements indicated that the force was *de minimis*).

Page 133, the 3rd sentence after the word "injury," add new footnote 30.1:

[30.1]Foulk v. Charrier, 262 F.3d 687, 57 Fed. R. Evid. Serv. 1080 (8th Cir. 2001) (claim of excessive force in which corrections officer sprayed pepper spray directly into prisoner's face through a screened window, while prisoner was in a locked room and being compliant, was supported by the evidence; award of nominal damages of $1 was permissible and did not necessarily mean that the use of force was de minimis or that inmate's Eighth Amendment rights had not been violated).

§ 2:5

n. 32.

Page 134, note 32, add following the Watford *citation:*
See also Smith v. Mensinger, 293 F.3d 641 (3d Cir. 2002) (inmate alleged that he was the victim of an unprovoked and unjustified beating; district court granted prison officials' motion for summary judgment; in reversing, the court of appeals stated that district court erred in its analysis of prisoner's excessive force claim by focusing almost exclusively on the lack of a serious physical injury; inmate's allegation that while he was handcuffed the prison guards punched and kicked him and rammed his head into a wall created an issue of fact as the extent of the injuries to be resolved by the fact finder and not the court; further, a supervisor who was present but failed to intervene in the beating could be held liable under the Eighth Amendment); Shelton v. Angelone, 183 F. Supp. 2d 830 (W.D. Va. 2002)(allegations that prisoner was repeatedly shocked with a stun gun without justification while restrained in leg irons and handcuffs was conduct that, if it occurred, would be "repugnant to the conscience of mankind," and therefore sufficient to defeat the defendants' motion for summary judgment, despite the claim that absence of any serious long term physical effect established a de minimis injury inflicted by the device).

n. 36.

section 2:5 note 36, add:
Johnson v. Unknown Dellatifa, 357 F.3d 539, 57 Fed. R. Serv. 3d 1108, 2004 FED App. 0036P (6th Cir. 2004), cert. denied, 125 S. Ct. 157 (U.S. 2004) (affirming the district court's dismissal of the inmate's Eighth Amendment claim against a prison official and holding that the prison official's behavior, which the inmate claimed included kicking the inmate's cell door, making aggravating remarks to the inmate, making insulting remarks about the inmate's hair, growling and snarling at the inmate through his cell window, smearing the inmate's cell door window so that the inmate could not see through it, and behaving in a racially prejudicial manner toward the inmate, while "shameful and utterly unprofessional," does not rise to the level of an Eighth Amendment violation).

n. 37.

Page 135, note 37, add following the Davis *citation:*
Walton v. Terry, 38 Fed. Appx. 363 (9th Cir. 2002) (prison officials' verbal threats towards inmate did not constitute cruel and unusual punishment under Eighth Amendment); Wright v. O'Hara, 2002 WL 1870479 (E.D. Pa. 2002) (prisoner claims that prison guards harassed him by being verbally abusive and threatening to charge him with misconduct did not state an Eighth Amendment violation as it is well-established that verbal abuse or threats alone do not state a constitutional claim); Williams v. Newell, 2002 WL 1559762 (E.D. Mich. 2002) (verbal threats by prison officials do not implicate the Eighth Amendment);

section 2:5 note 37, add:
Minifield v. Butikofer, 298 F. Supp. 2d 900 (N.D. Cal. 2004) (holding that the inmate's Eighth Amendment claim based on sexual harassment by officers does not state a valid claim. Plaintiff alleged that the officer "unzipped his clothing and told Plaintiff to grab his penis," and "[held] a candy bar towards his [the officer's] genital area . . . [and] [w]hen plaintiff asked if this action was directed at him, [the officer responded] 'I don't kiss and tell." The court denied relief because the plaintiff did not allege that the officer "exposed his genitals or touched plaintiff in a sexual

§ 2:5 RIGHTS OF PRISONERS

manner." The court held that words alone have not been held to violate the Eighth Amendment).

n. 43.

Page 137, note 43, add at end of note:
; Clement v. Gomez, 298 F.3d 898 (9th Cir. 2002) (court of appeals held that correctional officer's use of two bursts of pepper spray to quell violent fighting in a cell between two inmates did not state a claim for excessive use of force violative of the Eighth Amendment; inmates alleged that second spray was administered after sounds of coughing and gagging were heard from the cell; court reasoned that, even if true, this allegation alone would not lead to inference that official used the pepper spray maliciously and sadistically for the very purpose of causing harm); Gailor v. Armstrong, 187 F. Supp. 2d 729 (W.D. Ky. 2001) (allegations that described a scene in which an inmate was shackled and then beaten to death stated Eighth Amendment claim for use of excessive force against prison guards and supervisor, who observed much of the incident but failed to intervene; court concluded that, taking the evidence in the light most favorable to the plaintiff, the officers acted maliciously and sadistically for the very purpose of causing harm); Ducally v. Rhode Island Dept. of Corrections, 160 F. Supp. 2d 220 (D.R.I. 2001) (inmate who alleged that corrections officer slammed the cell door on his hand stated a cause of action under the Eighth Amendment, since if done intentionally, the act could rise to the level of wanton infliction of pain that was used maliciously).

n. 52.

Page 140, note 52, add at end of sentence before "But see":
; Camp v. Brennan, 54 Fed. Appx. 78 (3d Cir. 2002) (use of stun gun against inmate by corrections officials during cell extraction was not so excessive as to present cognizable Eighth Amendment claim, where inmate's refusal to walk through doorway created confrontation, force was applied for approximately twenty seconds, and use of stun gun was reasonably necessary to regain control of inmate); Keller v. Trefz, 66 Fed. Appx. 44 (7th Cir. 2003) (inmate failed to establish claim that prison officers used excessive force on him in violation of his Eighth Amendment rights where he did not dispute that he failed to comply with lawful orders and resisted officers, and submitted no evidence to suggest that the amount of force used by officers was other than a good faith effort to restore discipline); Skrtich v. Thornton, 280 F.3d 1295 (11th Cir. 2002) (allegations that corrections officers in extracting prisoner from cell, when he refused to voluntarily leave to permit a search to be conducted, used electronic shield to shock and incapacitate inmate, punched, kicked and beaten him to extent that he had to be airlifted from prison to hospital, were sufficient to make out a claim for violation of his Eighth Amendment rights); Cox v. Malone, 199 F. Supp. 2d 135 (S.D. N.Y. 2002), aff'd, 56 Fed. Appx. 43 (2d Cir. 2003) (use of force by prison officials on an inmate during a pat down frisk was not excessive, where inmate was not cooperating and made threatening statements; force used was no more than necessary to make the inmate comply with the search, and injuries sustained by inmate, a scratched hand and psychological trauma, were not sufficiency serious to warrant Eighth Amendment protection and to preclude granting prison officials' motion for summary judgment); Washington v. Barry, 2002 OK 45, 55 P.3d 1036 (Okla. 2002) (prisoner did not show wantonness in the infliction of pain, and thus failed to state cause of action for use of

excessive force by correctional officers in removing prisoner's restraints, where prisoner had refused to allow the restraints to be removed peaceably; injuries the prisoner suffered, the court found, arose because of his refusal to comply with prison discipline).

n. 54.

Page 141, note 54, add:
; Treats v. Morgan, 308 F.3d 868 (8th Cir. 2002) (court denied motion for summary judgment against prisoner in case where correctional officer used pepper spray without warning on inmate who failed to fully comply with an order but whose actions "did not rise to the level of recalcitrance" and who otherwise posed no threat to any person's safety or prison security).

n. 57.

Page 141, note 57, add:
; Lawrence v. Bowersox, 297 F.3d 727, 53 Fed. R. Serv. 3d 186 (8th Cir. 2002) (evidence was sufficient for reasonable jury to conclude that prison guards violated inmates' Eighth Amendment rights, where inmates confined to their cell had their faces, bodies, and their entire cell doused with pepper spray, and one inmate experienced spotting on his lower body for almost two years following incident, and the other inmate suffered problems with his skin and eyes).

n. 59.

Page 142, note 59, add:
; Dellis v. Corrections Corp. of America, 257 F.3d 508, 2001 FED App. 0228P (6th Cir. 2001) (inmate who alleged that prison guards ordered him to kneel on his bunk with his hands behind his back, and beat him even though he complied, stated a viable Eighth Amendment claim); Proctor v. Harmon, 257 F.3d 867 (8th Cir. 2001) (reversing dismissal of inmate's excessive force claim, court of appeals found that inmate's testimony stating that correctional officers bodyslammed him, stomped on his head and back, and beat him with a flashlight and their fists, while he was handcuffed, was sufficient to preclude dismissal of Eighth Amendment claim).

n. 66.

Page 143, note 66, add:
Milo Miller, Electrified Prison Fencing: A Lethal Blow to the Eighth Amendment, 38 Cal. W. L. Rev. 63 (2001) (author argues that use of high voltage electric fencing systems, which are increasingly being installed around the perimeters of correctional institutions, constitutes cruel and unusual punishment under the Eighth Amendment, as they are inconsistent with the evolving standards of decency in a maturing society and reflect deliberate indifference to the health and safety of inmates; article also provides useful summary of cases dealing with "use of force," "conditions of confinement," and "use of deadly force").

n. 80.

Page 146, note 80, add:
; Santiago v. Fields, 170 F. Supp. 2d 453 (D. Del. 2001) (handcuffed inmate alleged that during transfer to disciplinary unit, he was struck in the face and back and had a stun gun used on him; defendant prison officers admitted that force was used but only after inmate became "unruly and vio-

lent"; court found that there existed a genuine issue of material fact as to whether defendants used excessive force against prisoner, precluding a grant of summary judgment).

n. 81.

Page 146, note 81, add:
; Bafford v. Nelson, 241 F. Supp. 2d 1192 (D. Kan. 2002) (correctional officer did not use excessive force in restraining inmate by punching inmate in the nose and pulling his nostrils, where inmate had threatened to throw official over ledge and made aggressive move toward him; however, motion for summary judgment was denied on the issue of whether correctional officer beat inmate by allegedly punching him several times in the back of the head after inmate was restrained and posed no apparent disciplinary threat).

n. 82.

Page 147, note 82, add:
; Amaro v. Taylor, 170 F. Supp. 2d 460 (D. Del. 2001) (inmate who missed an order to lock in because he was in the shower and who was subsequently shackled, hands and feet, and repeatedly punched and kicked by prison guards as well as struck in the face with a shield and baton, alleged facts sufficient to state a claim for an Eighth Amendment violation).

n. 84.

Page 148, note 84, add:
; Jackson v. Austin, 241 F. Supp. 2d 1313 (D. Kan. 2003) (corrections officers used excessive force by grabbing prisoner, forcing him to the floor and handcuffing him, causing severe shoulder and knee injuries, after prisoner attempted to show them a medical excuse to explain his noncompliance with officer's order to stand in line while waiting at a medical clinic, when restraint was not necessary to maintain discipline in prison, prisoner was sixty years old, and officials were aware that the prisoner had a bad knee that prevented him from standing for long periods of time).

n. 85.

Page 148, note 85, add:
; Marquez v. Gutierrez, 322 F.3d 689 (9th Cir. 2003) (corrections officer was entitled to qualified immunity in inmate's action for alleged use of excessive force, in connection with officer's shooting of inmate in the leg during assault on another inmate, since reasonable officer could have believed that shooting one inmate to stop an assault was a good faith effort to restore order).

n. 89.

Page 150, note 89, add:
; Townsend v. Moya, 291 F.3d 859 (5th Cir. 2002) (court of appeals in a 2-1 decision affirmed summary judgment in favor of prison guard, finding that guard who stabbed inmate in the back while the two were engaged in "horseplay" was not acting under color of law, as it involved a "purely private aim and no misuse of state authority" so as to subject the warden and prison director to suit; dissent argued that guard, who had a reputation for playing with knives and pulling them on inmates, abused his power in the prison by possessing a knife, verbally abusing inmate in question by calling him "bitch" and "whore," stabbing him, and attempting to conceal his conduct by ordering the inmate to lie about his injury).

section 2:5 note 89, add:

n. 90.

Page 150, note 90, add:
; Gallardo v. DiCarlo, 203 F. Supp. 2d 1160 (C.D. Cal. 2002) (prisoner who sustained physical injuries from alleged unprovoked beating from correctional officers, requiring a 31-day hospital stay and resulting in permanent physical injuries, stated an Eighth Amendment excessive force claim against warden who allegedly did not discipline guards for using force or investigate complaints of excessive use of force by guards against inmates).

n. 96.

Page 153, note 96, add:
; Pizzuto v. County of Nassau, 239 F. Supp. 2d 301 (E.D. N.Y. 2003) (corrections officer who admitted that he knew in advance that two other officers planned to use excessive force against inmate, accompanied other officers to inmate's cell, watched them viciously beat inmate for approximately one minute, without interceding, and admitted that his presence was intended both to ensure that the prisoner did not fight back and to keep other inmates from interfering was liable as a matter of law for deliberate indifference to a substantial risk of serious harm to the prisoner in violation of his Eighth Amendment rights).

n. 100.

Page 154, note 100, add:
; Stewart v. Stewart, 60 Fed. Appx. 20 (9th Cir. 2003) (prison administrators' alleged policy of spraying prisoners with pepper spray for refusing to follow directions fell within the wide-ranging zone of deference accorded to prison officials in shaping preventive measures intended to reduce incidence of breaches of prison discipline, and did not amount to use of excessive force in violation of inmate's Eighth Amendment rights).

n. 101.

Page 155, note 101, add following the Peterson v. Davis citation:
Combs v. Wilkinson, 315 F.3d 548, 59 Fed. R. Evid. Serv. 1208, 2002 FED App. 0408P (6th Cir. 2002) (corrections officer's use of mace against death row inmate to quell disturbance was not excessive, as officer was entitled to substantial deference as to his decision to use mace, considering that his decision was made in haste and under significant pressure; however, genuine issue of material fact existed as to whether commander of the unit assigned to quell the disturbance failed to control the extraction of inmates and the use of chemical agents by members of the unit, precluding summary judgment on the alleged use of excessive force); Hallett v. Morgan, 296 F.3d 732 (9th Cir. 2002) (prison staff's use of pepper spray very sparingly and with authorization, for managing the behavior of mentally ill inmates, was not an Eighth Amendment violation for excessive use of force).

section 2:5 note 101, add:
Martinez v. Stanford, 323 F.3d 1178, 55 Fed. R. Serv. 3d 160 (9th Cir. 2003) (holding that the inmates stated a valid claim when they alleged that that prison officials used excessive force in violation of the Eighth Amendment against them because the district court failed to view the evidence in a light most favorable to the inmates, rather it resolved material disputes in favor of the prison officials based on their declarations. In this

case, a fight broke out in the cell adjacent to the plaintiff/inmates' cell. Prison officials used pepper spray to gain control of the situation. Next, according to the prison officials, the inmate used a mattress to barricade their cell, they brandished homemade weapons, and threw human waste at the prison officials. The prison officials content that they had to use plastic bullets and tasers to gain control of the situation, which caused minor injury to the inmates. In contrast, the inmates contend that they did not barricade their cell with a mattress; rather they put up a sheet to prevent the pepper spray from entering their cell. The inmates further claim that they did throw human waste at the officers, they were not brandishing homemade weapons even though they had such weapons in their cell, and they did not resist the officers making the use of plastic bullets and tasers unnecessary. The discrepancy between the parties' versions of the incident is sufficient to create a genuine issue of material fact making summary judgment inappropriate).

n. 102.

Page 155, note 102, add:
; Torres-Viera v. Laboy-Alvarado, 311 F.3d 105 (1st Cir. 2002) (prisoner who sustained injury when struck in head by tear gas canister fired by prison official during disturbance did not state claim for Eighth Amendment violation, as nothing in complaint permitted inference that tear gas canister was fired for very purpose of causing harm); DeSpain v. Uphoff, 264 F.3d 965 (10th Cir. 2001) (prison inmate's allegation that prison guard indiscriminately discharged pepper spray, burning inmate's eyes and causing lung congestion, was sufficient to state a claim of excessive force, as guard's indiscriminate spraying of prison tier with pepper spray was not a good faith effort to maintain or restore order).

section 2:5 note 102, add:
Martinez v. Stanford, 323 F.3d 1178, 55 Fed. R. Serv. 3d 160 (9th Cir. 2003) (holding that the inmates stated a valid claim when they alleged that that prison officials used excessive force in violation of the Eighth Amendment against them because the district court failed to view the evidence in a light most favorable to the inmates, rather it resolved material disputes in favor of the prison officials based on their declarations. In this case, a fight broke out in the cell adjacent to the plaintiff/inmates' cell. Prison officials used pepper spray to gain control of the situation. Next, according to the prison officials, the inmate used a mattress to barricade their cell, they brandished homemade weapons, and threw human waste at the prison officials. The prison officials content that they had to use plastic bullets and tasers to gain control of the situation, which caused minor injury to the inmates. In contrast, the inmates contend that they did not barricade their cell with a mattress; rather they put up a sheet to prevent the pepper spray from entering their cell. The inmates further claim that they did throw human waste at the officers, they were not brandishing homemade weapons even though they had such weapons in their cell, and they did not resist the officers making the use of plastic bullets and tasers unnecessary. The discrepancy between the parties' versions of the incident is sufficient to create a genuine issue of material fact making summary judgment inappropriate).

n. 103.

Page 156, note 103, add:
; Wright v. Snyder, 2002 WL 1821583 (D. Del. 2002) (inmate failed to

CRUEL & UNUSUAL PUNISHMENT § 2:5

demonstrate that genuine issue of material fact existed as to whether correctional officers used unnecessary, excessive force in response to plaintiff's conduct; inmate refused to obey defendants' order to allow them to search his body cavity for contraband, use of pepper spray was reasonable, since both officers believed that the prisoner was lunging towards them in a threatening manner, and correctional officers took prisoner to see a nurse after he was sprayed to relieve his burning sensations).

n. 110.

section 2:5 note 110, add:
Smith v. Cochran, 339 F.3d 1205 (10th Cir. 2003) (denying a state license examiner a grant of qualified immunity to a female prisoner's claim that the state license examiner raped her while she was under his supervision in a work release program. The court held that the prisoner was able to show that the state license examiner violated her clearly established Eighth Amendment right to be free from excessive force. The fact that the defendant was not a prison guard did not make the Eighth Amendment inapplicable in this case because the DOC delegated their penological responsibilities to the defendant while the prisoners were working at the Department of Public Services site); Craft v. Mann, 265 F. Supp. 2d 970 (N.D. Ind. 2003) (granting the plaintiff time to amend his complaint alleging that prison guards forcibly raped or molested him and subjected him to racial discrimination in violation of the Eighth Amendment because plaintiff did not plead sufficient facts to sustain this claim. In the amended complaint, the court instructed the inmate to write a short and plain statement of facts describing each incident of rape or molestation including where the incident took place, when the incident took place, and which officers were involved in the incident).

n. 113.

Page 159, note 113, add:
; Beers-Capitol v. Whetzel, 256 F.3d 120 (3d Cir. 2001) (female former resident of state juvenile detention facility who was sexually assaulted failed to state facts sufficient to oppose a motion for summary judgment against supervisors, because two allegations of sexual misconduct were insufficient to show that the supervisors failed to adequately respond to a pattern of past occurrences of injuries, and although the facility did not implement a number of policies that were standard in the juvenile detention field, this alone was insufficient to show that the risk of an sexual assault was great or obvious); Riley v. Olk-Long, 282 F.3d 592 (8th Cir. 2002) (affirming the district court's judgment not to set aside jury award of $25,000 in punitive damages, court of appeals determined that jury had sufficient evidence to find that defendants, prisoner security director and warden, were deliberately indifferent to risk that a male officer, who had had complaints filed against him for sexual misconduct and whom the supervisors saw as a "problem employee," would sexually assault female inmate); Wright v. O'Hara, 2002 WL 1870479 (E.D. Pa. 2002) (allegations that state prison guard sexually assaulted prisoner stated Eighth Amendment violation, precluding a motion to dismiss). For cases in which assaulted inmates sued supervisors, claiming that they failed to protect them from the risk of sexual assault, see Ortiz v. Voinovich, 211 F. Supp. 2d 917 (S.D. Ohio 2002) (female inmate was sexually assaulted by prison officer; after the first attack, prison officer threatened to "get her" the next day; inmate reported the attack and threat to prison supervisor, but was

§ 2:5   RIGHTS OF PRISONERS

sexually assaulted the following day; court held that a genuine issue of material fact existed as to whether supervisor failed to take reasonable measures to protect inmate from second sexual assault); Morris v. Eversley, 205 F. Supp. 2d 234 (S.D. N.Y. 2002) (female inmate stated facts sufficient to oppose motion for summary judgment on Eighth Amendment claim against supervisors for sexual assault by correctional officer, as defendants knew corrections officers at prison were engaging in sexual contact with female prisoners, evidenced by complaints and incidence of pregnancies among inmates, but failed to act).

n. 114.

Page 160, note 114, add:
; Goode v. Correctional Medical Services, 168 F. Supp. 2d 289 (D. Del. 2001) (pregnant inmate who alleged that at a medical exam nurses sexually assaulted her by conducting an internal exam without gloves, asking if she was HIV-positive, giving her hugs and kisses, and providing one of their home phone numbers, stated an Eighth Amendment claim, precluding a motion to dismiss); Katherine C. Parker, Comment, Female Inmates Living in Fear: Sexual Abuse by Correctional Officers in the District of Columbia, 10 Am. U. J. Gender Soc. Pol'y & L. 443 (2002) (article explores crisis within District of Columbia Department of Corrections and judicial system that allows guards to sexually harass and abuse female inmates in correctional facilities seemingly without punishment); Anthea Dinos, Note, Custodial Sexual Abuse: Enforcing Long-Awaited Policies Designed to Protect Female Prisoners, 45 N.Y.L. Sch. L. Rev. 281 (2001) (author addresses prevalence of sexual abuse in women's prisons and inadequate remedies that are available to prisoners).

n. 116.

section 2:5 note 116, add:
Faas v. Washington County, 260 F. Supp. 2d 198 (D. Me. 2003) (granting in part and denying in part the defendants' motion to dismiss plaintiff's claim that defendants, Washington County, Maine, and the Sheriff of Washington County, violated her rights under, *inter alia*, the Eighth Amendment because sexual conduct between prison guards and prisoners, even if it was consensual, may have contributed to the environment in which plaintiff was sexually assaulted by prison guards. The court granted the defendants' motion to dismiss based on the fact that no policy adopted by Washington County caused this harm to plaintiff. However, the court denied the defendants' motion based on custom and practice in the municipality because there was a question of fact as to whether "the practice of sexual misconduct with inmates was so 'widespread that policy making officials of the municipality- [had] constructive knowledge of it but did nothing to end the practice'").

n. 122.

section 2:5 note 122, add:
Minifield v. Butikofer, 298 F. Supp. 2d 900 (N.D. Cal. 2004) (holding that the inmate's Eighth Amendment claim based on sexual harassment by officers does not state a valid claim. Plaintiff alleged that the officer "unzipped his clothing and told Plaintiff to grab his penis," and "[held] a candy bar towards his [the officer's] genital area . . . [and] [w]hen plaintiff asked if this action was directed at him, [the officer responded] 'I don't kiss and tell." The court denied relief because the plaintiff did not allege

CRUEL & UNUSUAL PUNISHMENT   § 2:7

that the officer "exposed his genitals or touched plaintiff in a sexual manner." The court held that words alone have not been held to violate the Eighth Amendment).

§ 2:7 Assaults by Other Inmates

n. 8.

page 170 note 8, add:
PRISON RAPE ELIMINATION ACT OF 2003, S. 1435, 108th CONG. (2003) (The purposes of the Act are primarily to establish a zero-tolerance standard for the incidence of prison rape in prisons in the United States by developing and implementing national standards for the detection, prevention, reduction, and punishment of prison rape; to increase the accountability of prison officials who fail to detect, prevent, reduce, and punish prison rape; and to increase the efficiency and effectiveness of state and local officials in investigating and prosecuting prison rape. The Act proposes to create national standards by identifying common characteristics of the victims and perpetrators of rape and prison systems with a high incidence of prison rape through annual statistical gathering and analysis, surveys, review panels, and public hearings. To assist in prison rape prevention and prosecution, the Act provides for periodic training and education programs for federal, state, and local authorities responsible for the prevention, investigation, and punishment of instances of prison rape).

section 2:7 note 8, add:
James E. Robertson, Compassionate Conservatism and Prison Rape: The Prison Rape Elimination Act, 30 N.E.J. on Crim. & Civ. Con. 1 (2004) (discussing the events and findings that lead to the Prison Rape Elimination Act becoming law); James E. Robertson, A Punk's Song About Prison Reform, 24 Pace L. Rev. _____ (forthcoming 2004) (discussing gender roles adopted by male inmates in prison, particularly the role of the punk, a heterosexual man who takes on the role of a "girl" in prison society. This article further discusses the jurisprudence of prison reform from the fall of the hands off doctrine to the present as experience through the eyes of a punk).

n. 12.

Page 171, note 12, add:
; Christopher D. Man & John P. Cronan, Forecasting Sexual Abuse in Prison: The Prison Subculture of Masculinity As a Backdrop for "Deliberate Indifference," 92 J. Crim. L. & Criminology 127 (2002) (article discusses *Farmer* standard of "deliberate indifference," psychological dynamics of prisoner rape, and characteristics that can be used to predict sexual roles inmate is likely to assume or be forced to assume); Shara Abraham, 2001 Male Rape in U.S. Prisons: Cruel and Unusual Punishment, 9 NO. 1 Hum. Rts. Brief 5 (2001).

n. 38.

Page 179, note 38, add:
; Taylor v. Little, 58 Fed. Appx. 66 (6th Cir. 2003) (county officials were not deliberately indifferent to danger posed to detainee by fellow inmate, even though fellow inmate had threatened detainee on day before attack, where officials were not aware of threat); Webster v. Crowley, 62 Fed.

§ 2:7   Rights of Prisoners

Appx. 598 (6th Cir. 2003) (prison inspector was not deliberately indifferent to alleged threat of assaults against inmate, where inspector had no prior knowledge that inmate needed protection from specific inmates); Dunkle v. Endel, 60 Fed. Appx. 166 (9th Cir. 2003) (state prisoner failed to state a deliberate indifference claim based on officer's failure to intervene to protect prisoner because prisoner did not allege that officer was aware beforehand that other inmates would throw rocks at prisoner); Butera v. Cottey, 285 F.3d 601 (7th Cir. 2002) (pretrial detainee's statements to county jail correctional officers that he was having "problems in the block" and needed to be moved, and detainee's mother's telephone call to unknown jail employee stating that her son had been threatened with sexual assault, were insufficient to give county sheriff actual notice of specific risk of serious harm so as to find the sheriff deliberately indifferent); Segovia v. County of Los Angeles, 41 Fed. Appx. 126 (9th Cir. 2002) (prison officials were not deliberately indifferent to safety of inmate who was attacked by other prisoners and seriously injured, where inmate did not allege that officials were aware he was in danger or that he warned them prior to incident).

section 2:7 note 38, add:
Verdecia v. Adams, 327 F.3d 1171 (10th Cir. 2003) (holding that prison officials are entitled to qualified immunity from plaintiff's claim that they violated his Eighth Amendment rights by placing plaintiff, a Cuban inmate, in a cell with two members of the Latin Kings because plaintiff could not show that the prison officials were aware of the fact that plaintiff was in danger); Pagels v. Morrison, 335 F.3d 736 (8th Cir. 2003) (granting qualified immunity to a prison official from an inmate's claim that the official violated his Eighth Amendment rights by failing to protect him from an assault by other inmates because plaintiff could not show that the official knew about the serious risk of harm even though the inmate submitted a letter regarding contraband possession by his assailants. The letter did not indicate that plaintiff feared for his own safety); Riccardo v. Rausch, 359 F.3d 510 (7th Cir. 2004) (holding that the prison official did not act with deliberate indifference to a substantial risk of serious harm to plaintiff when he placed plaintiff in a cell with another inmate and three days later the cellmate raped him because defendant, who did not usually make cell assignments, could have thought that the assignment was only for one night, and even though plaintiff notified defendant that he feared for his safety in the cell with the new cellmate, the plaintiff's fear was that he was going to be beaten and not raped by the his cellmate); Adames v. Perez, 331 F.3d 508 (5th Cir. 2003) (vacating and remanding the trial court's judgment that prison officials' were liable for failure to protect the inmate from violence because the evidence offered at trial did not show that the prison officials' were subjectively aware of the danger to the inmate. In this case, the plaintiff/inmate was a member of a prison gang but decided to leave the gang and prepare for release from prison. In order to increase his chance for parole, the plaintiff informed prison officials about the illegal activities of his former gang. On the day the plaintiff was attacked by another inmate, officers had the inmate handcuffed and were escorting him from the shower back to his cell. Unbeknownst to the officers, another inmate had escaped from his cell and attacked the plaintiff with a shank, stabbing him 13 times before he listened to the prison officials' orders to stop. The plaintiff believed that the attack was in response to the information he provided the prison officials on the activities of his former gang. At trial the inmate tried to establish that inmates

CRUEL & UNUSUAL PUNISHMENT § 2:7

escaping from their cells and harming other inmates was such a pervasive problem that the officials should have know that the inmate was in danger. To establish this pattern the plaintiff introduced two other inmates to testify regarding this problem, however, the court held that this testimony was insufficient to establish a widespread problem. The plaintiff also attempted to show that the officers should have been aware of the risk that he would be harmed by another inmate because the officer's failed to follow the prison safety procedure by checking each cell door every half hour, and because prison officials knew that he was classified as a "potential victim." The court held that these arguments failed to show that the prison officials had actual knowledge of the risk of harm to the inmate); Mooring v. San Francisco Sheriff's Dept., 289 F. Supp. 2d 1110 (N.D. Cal. 2003) (holding that a prison official was not deliberately indifferent to a pretrial detainee's safety when he put the pretrial detainee in a cell with rival gang members because the pretrial detainee did not raise a triable issue of fact that the prison official knew that he was in a rival gang).

Page 179, the fifth sentence of the second full paragraph after the words "unresponsive to it," add new footnote 40.1:

[40.1]Flint ex rel. Flint v. Kentucky Dept. of Corrections, 270 F.3d 340, 2001 FED App. 0381P (6th Cir. 2001) (defendants could be held liable for subjecting deceased inmate to cruel and unusual punishment, because defendants were aware of threat to inmate's life but did not nothing to protect him).

section 2:7 note 40.1, add:
Verdecia v. Adams, 327 F.3d 1171 (10th Cir. 2003) (holding that prison officials are entitled to qualified immunity from plaintiff's claim that they violated his Eighth Amendment rights by placing plaintiff, a Cuban inmate, in a cell with two members of the Latin Kings because plaintiff could not show that the prison officials were aware of the fact that plaintiff was in danger); Adames v. Perez, 331 F.3d 508 (5th Cir. 2003) (vacating and remanding the trial court's judgment that prison officials' were liable for failure to protect the inmate from violence because the evidence offered at trial did not show that the prison officials' were subjectively aware of the danger to the inmate. In this case, the plaintiff/inmate was a member of a prison gang but decided to leave the gang. In order to increase his chance for parole, the plaintiff informed prison officials about the illegal activities of his former gang. On the day the plaintiff was attacked by another inmate, officers had the inmate handcuffed and were escorting him from the shower back to his cell. Unbeknownst to the officers, another inmate had escaped from his cell and attacked the plaintiff with a shank, stabbing him 13 times before he listened to the prison officials' orders to stop. The plaintiff believed that the attack was in response to the information he provided the prison officials on the activities of

§ 2:7 RIGHTS OF PRISONERS

his former gang. At trial the inmate tried to establish that inmates escaping from their cells and harming other inmates was such a pervasive problem that the officials should have know that the inmate was in danger. To establish this pattern the plaintiff introduced two other inmates to testify regarding this problem, however, the court held that this testimony was insufficient to establish a widespread problem. The plaintiff also attempted to show that the officers should have been aware of the risk that he would be harmed by another inmate because the officer's failed to follow the prison safety procedure by checking each cell door every half hour, and because prison officials knew that he was classified as a "potential victim." The court held that these arguments failed to show that the prison officials had actual knowledge of the risk of harm to the inmate); Mooring v. San Francisco Sheriff's Dept., 289 F. Supp. 2d 1110 (N.D. Cal. 2003) (holding that a prison official was not deliberately indifferent to a pretrial detainee's safety when he put the pretrial detainee in a cell with rival gang members because the pretrial detainee did not raise a triable issue of fact that the prison official knew that he was in a rival gang).

n. 43.

Page 180, note 43, add:
Liles v. Camden County Dept. of Corrections, 225 F. Supp. 2d 450 (D.N.J. 2002) (if Eighth Amendment plaintiff presents evidence showing that substantial risk of inmate attacks was longstanding, pervasive, well-documented, or expressly noted by prison officials in the past, then such evidence could be sufficient to permit trier of fact to find that official had actual knowledge of risk).

section 2:7 note 43, add:
Carter v. Galloway, 352 F.3d 1346 (11th Cir. 2003) (holding that prison officials did not violate plaintiff's Eighth Amendment rights when they placed him in an administrative segregation cell with a "problematic inmate" and that inmate stabbed plaintiff in the stomach with a shank because plaintiff's general complaints about the behavior of his cellmate and the cellmates classification as problematic did not establish that defendant had a "substantial awareness of a substantial risk of serious physical threat").

n. 52.

Page 182, note 52, add:
; Tucker v. Evans, 276 F.3d 999 (8th Cir. 2002) (administrators of decedent inmate's estate filed suit against defendants alleging that they failed to protect the inmate from a fatal attack by other inmates who severely beat deceased with a broken bed frame; district court denied defendants' motion for summary judgment but court of appeals reversed, stating that even though corrections officer failed to properly perform his inspection duties, misinterpreted an argument between the two inmates, failed to properly supervise the barracks, and failed to assist the inmate during the attack, this conduct, although pointing to negligence or gross negligence,

CRUEL & UNUSUAL PUNISHMENT § 2:7

did not demonstrate deliberate indifference).

section 2:7 note 52, add:
Glenn v. Berndt, 289 F. Supp. 2d 1120 (N.D. Cal. 2003) (holding that a prison official's negligence or gross negligence in accidentally opening a white inmates cell door during and white/black war which lead to a fight between white and black inmates did not rise to the level of an Eighth Amendment violation); Montez ex rel. Estate of Hearlson v. U.S., 359 F.3d 392, 2004 FED App. 0061P (6th Cir. 2004) (affirming the district court's decision that the United States is protected by the discretionary function exception to the Federal Torts Claim Act. Plaintiff, the mother of an inmate murdered in prison, failed to show that a statute or regulation provided a mandatory course of conduct for prison officials, and did not plead sufficient facts to rebut the presumption that the prison officials' decisions regarding the care of her son was contrary to BOP policy when she alleged that the prison officials were negligent because they knew or should have know that her son was in protective lock-up and at risk of imminent danger but transferred him to a facility where he was inadequately protected).

n. 54.

Page 183, note 54, add:
; Blades v. Schuetzle, 302 F.3d 801 (8th Cir. 2002) (officials' decision to release inmate, who was known to be dangerous, into general population did not rise to the level of deliberate indifference, since even if prison officials had been aware of a threat, inmate's statements that assailant posed no risk of harm to him barred his claim); Nichols v. Maryland Correctional Institution—Jessup, 186 F. Supp. 2d 575 (D. Md. 2002) (inmate who asserted that defendant violated his rights by failing to protect him from a violent, threatening cellmate who later assaulted him failed to overcome a motion for summary judgment; corrections officer did not show deliberate indifference by failing to see that there was an imminent threat to plaintiff such that his refusal to take immediate action was inappropriate, where officer stated that he was unaware of any threats and that he was only aware that one of the inmates wanted to move)

section 2:7 note 54, add:
Riccardo v. Rausch, 359 F.3d 510 (7th Cir. 2004) (holding that the prison official did not act with deliberate indifference to a substantial risk of serious harm to plaintiff when he placed plaintiff in a cell with another inmate and three days later the cellmate raped him because defendant, who did not usually make cell assignments, could have thought that the assignment was only for one night, and even though plaintiff notified defendant that he feared for his safety in the cell with the new cellmate, the plaintiff's fear was that he was going to be beaten and not raped by the his cellmate); Pagels v. Morrison, 335 F.3d 736 (8th Cir. 2003) (granting qualified immunity to a prison official from an inmate's claim that the official violated his Eighth Amendment rights by failing to protect him from an assault by other inmates because plaintiff could not show that the official knew about the serious risk of harm even though the inmate submitted a letter regarding contraband possession by his assailants. The letter did not indicate that plaintiff feared for his own safety).

n. 55.

Page 184, note 55, add:
; Adames v. Perez, 331 F.3d 508 (5th Cir. 2003) (vacating a jury verdict

§ 2:7 RIGHTS OF PRISONERS

for inmate against three prison officials for failing to protect him from an attack by a fellow inmate who escaped his cell, court of appeals held that evidence that a few inmates had escaped their cells and attacked other inmates on previous occasions was insufficient to establish deliberate indifference on the part of prison officials, since those incidents were isolated and fell short of a pervasive problem); Smith v. Gray, Rucker & Harkins., 259 F.3d 933 (8th Cir. 2001) (affirming grant of summary judgment to defendants, court held that plaintiff, who was ordered out of his cell to mop up a flood created by other inmates as protest, failed to present evidence to show that officers knew that allowing another inmate out of his cell, who attacked plaintiff with a sharp instrument, would present a significant risk to plaintiff)

n. 57.
Page 185, note 57, add:
; Boyce v. Moore, 314 F.3d 884 (7th Cir. 2002) (prison official's decision to transfer prisoner, after prisoner was attacked by unidentified inmates, to different tier of prison instead of to protective custody, believing that the different tier would be more secure, did not evidence deliberate indifference to risk of harm to prisoner who, after the transfer, was the victim of a second attack); Fisher v. Stewart, 37 Fed. Appx. 947 (9th Cir. 2002), cert. denied, 123 S. Ct. 1570, 155 L. Ed. 2d 311 (U.S. 2003) (prison official was not deliberately indifferent to inmate's safety where, after official learned of a substantial risk of harm to the inmate from violence at the hands of other prisoners, he took reasonable steps to abate any known risk); Doe v. Bowles, 254 F.3d 617, 2001 FED App. 0199P (6th Cir. 2001) (defendant corrections officer was not deliberately indifferent to the threat of an inmate assault, when officer segregated the two inmates through cell isolation, even though this approach ultimately was not sufficient to protect the plaintiff, who later was the victim of an assault); Tobias v. Campbell, 202 F. Supp. 2d 934 (E.D. Mo. 2001) (county correctional officers were not deliberately indifferent to risk that inmate was in danger of assault by fellow prisoners, and thus were not liable under § 1983 for injuries sustained by inmate during assault, even though inmate had informed officers that his cellmate was in danger, where inmate did not tell officers that he was also in danger).

n. 58.
Page 185, note 58, add:
; Cantu v. Jones, 293 F.3d 839 (5th Cir. 2002) (affirming jury verdict in favor of inmate who was slashed with a razor by another prisoner, court of appeals held that whether prison officials, allegedly in response to inmate's complaints about guards at the prison, helped to orchestrate the attack by leaving prisoner's cell door open, allowing him to escape to assault the plaintiff inmate, was a question for the jury, precluding entry of judgment as a matter of law for defendants); Peate v. McCann, 294 F.3d 879 (7th Cir. 2002) (reversing grant of summary judgment in favor of corrections officer, court of appeals held that issue of fact existed as to whether official acted deliberately indifferently to safety and health of an inmate, when official gave attacking prisoner back his weapon, and then stood by while prisoner attacked inmate for a second time, minutes after the officer broke up the first attack; first fight gave corrections officer knowledge that there was a substantial risk that prisoner would use the weapon to injure the plaintiff inmate)

CRUEL & UNUSUAL PUNISHMENT § 2:7

n. 63.

Page 188, note 63, add:
; Mackey v. Lyons, 52 Fed. Appx. 468 (10th Cir. 2002) (prison officials' alleged statement to prisoners that inmate was a "snitch" demonstrated deliberate indifference to substantial risk of serious harm to inmate sufficient to state claim for violation of inmate's Eighth Amendment rights).

section 2:7 note 63, add:
Hopkins v. Warden, NH State Prison, 2004 DNH 88, 2004 WL 1125241 (D.N.H. 2004) (holding that the inmate stated a valid Eighth Amendment claim when he alleged that prison officials ignored the risk of staff retaliation against him when he participated in an investigation which lead to the discharge of three prison employees for embezzling money from inmate accounts. The inmate's participation in this investigation resulted in his transfer to a dangerous unit where he was severely beaten by other inmates).

n. 64.

Page 188, note 64, add:
See also Johnson-Bey v. Ray, 38 Fed. Appx. 507 (10th Cir. 2002) (prisoner stated claim that official violated his Eighth Amendment rights by deliberately exposing him to risk of harm at hands of other inmates, when official allegedly informed another prisoner that plaintiff attempted to "set him up" for disciplinary charge by placing a knife in his cell).

n. 65.

section 2:7 note 65, add:
Odom v. South Carolina Department of Corrections, 349 F.3d 7656 (4th Cir. 2003) (denying prison officials a grant of qualified immunity from the inmate's claim that officials violated his rights under the Eighth Amendment. In this case, prison officials locked plaintiff in an outdoor cage during a fire. The inmate begged prison officials not to place him near a certain group of inmates because those inmates were threatening his life. Nevertheless, the prison officials place the threatening group of inmates in the cage adjacent to the plaintiff's cage. The group of inmates continued to threaten the plaintiff, encouraged prisoners in the plaintiff's cage to assault him, and ripped down the cage and beat plaintiff before the officers intervened even thought the officers were aware of the possibility of harm to the plaintiff).

n. 70.

Page 190, note 70, add:
; Case v. Ahitow, 301 F.3d 605 (7th Cir. 2002) (plaintiff who was assaulted by another inmate stated Eighth Amendment claim for deliberate indifference against corrections personnel, where plaintiff had written to prison staff informing them that assailant, who had a record of violent behavior, had threatened to beat and rape him and the danger could have been easily averted).

n. 72.

section 2:7, note 72, add:
Scicluna v. Wells, 345 F.3d 441, 2003 FED App. 0350P (6th Cir. 2003) (denying qualified immunity to a prison official on the plaintiff's claim that the prison official was deliberately indifferent to his risk of serious harm at the hands of another inmate when the other inmate, the plaintiff/

31

§ 2:7   Rights of Prisoners

inmate's co-defendant at trial, fractured the plaintiff's scull because the plaintiff showed that both he and his sister informed the prison official of the risk of harm and the prison issued a warning to officials stating that they should segregate former co-defendants).

n. 74.

Page 191, note 74, add:
; Lawrence v. Norris, 307 F.3d 745 (8th Cir. 2002) (court held that inmate, who was attacked by another inmate allegedly because there was only one guard on duty but in a different area of the prison, properly alleged that the defendant failed to provide adequate security in violation of the Eighth Amendment).

section 2:7, note 74, add:
Cottone v. Jenne, 326 F.3d 1352 (11th Cir. 2003) (denying the prison officials' motion to dismiss plaintiff's Fourteenth Amendment complaint that the officials acted objectively and subjectively unreasonably to the risk of inmate on inmate violence which resulted in an inmate's death at the hands of another inmate when the prison officials knew that they were guarding an inmate who had been classified as having a history of violent outbursts and mental instability at a detention center which housed mentally ill inmates, and they knew that the inmate was experiencing a schizophrenic outburst prior to the murder but nevertheless took consecutive breaks and had a computer game on at the time of the murder indicating a lack of supervision of the inmates); Adames v. Perez, 331 F.3d 508 (5th Cir. 2003) (vacating and remanding the trial court's judgment that prison officials' were liable for failure to protect the inmate from violence because the evidence offered at trial did not show that the prison officials' were subjectively aware of the danger to the inmate. In this case, the plaintiff/inmate was a member of a prison gang but decided to leave the gang and prepare for release from prison. In order to increase his chance for parole, the plaintiff informed prison officials about the illegal activities of his former gang. On the day the plaintiff was attacked by another inmate, officers had the inmate handcuffed and were escorting him from the shower back to his cell. Unbeknownst to the officers, another inmate had escaped from his cell and attacked the plaintiff with a shank, stabbing him 13 times before he listened to the prison officials' orders to stop. The plaintiff believed that the attack was in response to the information he provided the prison officials on the activities of his former gang. At trial the inmate tried to establish that inmates escaping from their cells and harming other inmates was such a pervasive problem that the officials should have know that the inmate was in danger. To establish this pattern the plaintiff introduced two other inmates to testify regarding this problem, however, the court held that this testimony was insufficient to establish a widespread problem. The plaintiff also attempted to show that the officers should have been aware of the risk that he would be harmed by another inmate because the officer's failed to follow the prison safety procedure by checking each cell door every half hour, and because prison officials knew that he was classified as a "potential victim." The court held that these arguments failed to show that the prison officials had actual knowledge of the risk of harm to the inmate.).

n. 76.

Page 192, note 76, add:
; Flanders v. Maricopa County, 203 Ariz. 368, 54 P.3d 837 (Ct. App. Div. 1

2002) (to show deliberate indifference, inmate need not prove that official acted or failed to act believing that harm actually would befall an inmate; it is enough that official was aware of a substantial risk of serious harm).

n. 81.

Page 193, note 81, add:
; Skinner v. Uphoff, 234 F. Supp. 2d 1208 (D. Wyo. 2002) (holding that policies, practices, and customs of prison officials—failing to adequately supervise and train employees in how to investigate and abate dangerous conditions, failing to develop and follow effective internal review process for reporting policy violations, and failing to discipline employees whose behavior violated constitutional rights—placed inmates at the risk of assault, injury, or death at the hands of other inmates).

n. 84.

section 2:7 note 84, add:
Miller v. Blanchard, 2004 WL 1354368 (W. D. Wis. 2004) (denying the inmate's request to proceed in forma pauperis on this Eighth Amendment claim against prosecutors and investigators for failure to protect the inmate from harm. In this case the defendant's agreed to help the plaintiff obtain a shortened sentence and a transfer to a facility where he would be safe from gang members in return for information about a murder that happened in the prison. However, the defendants did not enter a request and subsequently gang members attempted to kill the plaintiff by cutting his face and throat. The court denied the inmate's request because investigators and prosecutors are not responsible for an inmate's safety while in prison).

n. 88.

Page 195, note 88, add:
; Verdecia v. Adams, 327 F.3d 1171 (10th Cir. 2003) (inmate was placed in cell with gang members who assaulted him because of his Cuban nationality; district court denied prison agents' motion for summary judgment and court of appeals reversed, holding that, despite two recent incidents of violence between Cuban inmates and members of the gang, inmate failed to establish that prison agents were subjectively aware of alleged risk to him so as to state an Eighth Amendment violation, absent any evidence that one of the agents knew the inmate was Cuban or that he was housed with members of the gang); see also Thompson v. Eason, 258 F. Supp. 2d 508 (N.D. Tex. 2003).

n. 89.

section 2:7 note 89, add:
Carl Reynolds, Effective Self-Monitoring of Correctional Conditions, 24 Pace L. Rev. _____(forthcoming 2004) (discussing the post-Ruiz v. Johnson changes in the Texas Department of Criminal Justice (TDCJ) (formerly the Texas Department of Corrections) including a detailed discussion of the TDCJ's self-monitoring policies, a discussion of the TDCJ's partnership with the National Institute of Corrections to evaluate administrative segregation and use of force issues within the TDCJ, and a detailed discussion of future improvements within the TDCJ to improve conditions within Texas prisons); but see Palmer v. Marion County, 327 F.3d 588 (7th Cir. 2003) (holding that the pretrial detainee could not show that the county, city and county sheriff allowed a widespread practice of

§ 2:7   RIGHTS OF PRISONERS

racial segregation and then failed to respond to problems in the cell containing black inmates because plaintiff only cited two incidents of misconduct by guards in one year).

n. 92.

Page 197, note 92, add:
; Calderon-Ortiz v. Laboy-Alvarado, 300 F.3d 60, 53 Fed. R. Serv. 3d 432 (1st Cir. 2002) (plaintiff, former pre-trial detainee who was sodomized, stated a claim of deliberate indifference to his safety in violation of the Eighth Amendment; plaintiff claimed injury occurred because institution failed to classify inmates, separate them according to their safety needs, and supervise them; if proved these were facts from which deliberate indifference could be inferred)

n. 93.

Page 197, note 93, add:
; Miller v. McBride, 64 Fed. Appx. 558 (7th Cir. 2003) (inmate who was injured in fight failed to show that prison officials were deliberately indifferent to his safety with regard to his various placements in prison housing or transfer of alleged gang member into same unit as inmate); Cardenas v. Lewis, 66 Fed. Appx. 86 (9th Cir. 2003) (officers who placed pretrial detainee in holding tank with an inmate from whom detainee was supposed to be kept separated were not acting with deliberate indifference to detainee's safety); Fuller v. Commissioner of Correction, 75 Conn. App. 133, 815 A.2d 208 (2003) (record was insufficient to support inmate's claim that a housing classification system separating violent from nonviolent offenders would have eliminated the risk of assault by cellmate).

n. 95.

Page 198, note 95, add:
But see Estate of Ford v. Ramirez-Palmer, 301 F.3d 1043 (9th Cir. 2002) (family of estate of inmate who was killed by his cellmate brought Eighth Amendment action against corrections officers and warden; court held that defendants did not violate plaintiff's Eighth Amendment rights by celling him with inmate who had a "extraordinary history of violence," because the two inmates were previously housed together without incident and the cellmate had not recently acted aggressively toward others).

Page 198, the fourth sentence after the word "assault," add new footnote

---

[95.1]Marsh v. Butler County, Ala., 268 F.3d 1014 (11th Cir. 2001) (plaintiffs, an inmate and a detainee, were severely beaten by armed inmates while in jail; district court dismissed their claims of deliberate indifference on the part of the sheriff; court of appeals reversed, finding that there was substantial evidence that the sheriff knew that the conditions of the jail, which were overcrowded and unsupervised, were deficient).

n. 97.

Page 198, note 97, add:
; Swan v. U.S., 159 F. Supp. 2d 1174 (N.D. Cal. 2001), aff'd, 32 Fed. Appx. 315 (9th Cir. 2002), cert. denied, 537 U.S. 821, 123 S. Ct. 99, 154 L. Ed. 2d 29 (2002) (prisoner sued defendants, prison psychologists and United States, for Eighth Amendment violation in failing to prevent assault upon

him by another inmate which caused the loss of his eye; court held that defendant psychologist could have reasonably believed that no excessive risk to plaintiff's health or safety existed, where plaintiff only told psychologist that he felt afraid from a confrontation with a group of inmates but did not request any kind of protection from them).

§ 2:9 Conditions of Confinement-Basic Human Needs and the Prisoner's Physical Well-Being

n. 3.

Page 213, note 3, following the Jordan v. Gardner citation and parenthetical, add:
; Russell v. Johnson, 2003 WL 22208029 (N.D. Miss. 2003) (death row prisoners filed suit against Mississippi State Penitentiary alleging, in violation of the Eighth Amendment, that prison officials subjected them to profound isolation, lack of exercise, intolerable stench and filth, malfunctioning plumbing, constant exposure to human excrement, dangerously high temperatures and humidity, uncontrolled mosquitoes and insect infestations, and deprivation of basic mental health care; court found that prison officials violated prisoners' Eighth Amendment rights and ordered as remedial action that prison officials in moving inmates from cell to cell insure that the cell to which an inmate was moved was clean prior to the move, provide inmates with adequate cleaning supplies, insure that each cell was equipped with a fan, that ice water was available to each inmate, and that each inmate was permitted to take one shower during each day when the heat index was 90 degrees or above, equip all windows with screens to control mosquito and other insect infestation, repair plumbing so that fecal matter from one toilet would not bubble up in adjoining cell, upgrade lighting conditions, insure that proper chemical agents were used at laundry so that laundry was returned without foul smell, give each inmate a comprehensive mental health examination on a yearly basis, allow inmates to wear sneakers rather than flip-flops when exercising, and provide a shaded area for exercise and access to water).

section 2:9 note 3, add:
Gates v. Cook, 376 F.3d 323 (5th Cir. 2004) (affirming in part and vacating in part the district court's injunctions regarding the prison conditions on death row. The court affirmed the district court's injunctions requiring prison officials to: discontinue the practice of moving inmates to a new cell and requiring them to clean up after the former occupant; provide inmates with adequate cleaning supplies to clean their cells; provide proper ventilation, and access to fans, ice water and showers during days when the temperature exceeds 90 degrees; and repair and/or provide screens to control mosquitoes entry into cells; correct the "ping-pong" toilet whereby human waste flushed in one toilet would appear in another; improve lighting; and improve medical care. The court vacated the district court's injunctions requiring the prison to provide a written maintenance schedule and to provide inmates with sneakers in stead of "flip-flops" during exercise times).

§ 2:10 Conditions of Confinement-Basic Human Needs and the Prisoner's Physical Well-Being—Diet

n. 2.

Page 214, note 2, add:
; Drake v. Velasco, 207 F. Supp. 2d 809 (N.D. Ill. 2002) (prisoner who claimed that food was routinely served on trays containing spoiled food from previous meals stated constitutional claim).

n. 3.

section 2:10, note 3, add:
Craft v. Mann, 265 F. Supp. 2d 970 (N.D. Ind. 2003) (holding that "[d]enial of full nutritious meals for two days is insufficient to violate the *Eighth Amendment's* prohibition against cruel and unusual punishment").

n. 6.

Page 215, note 6, add:
; Phelps v. Kapnolas, 308 F.3d 180 (2d Cir. 2002) (complaint alleging that prison officials deprived inmate of a nutritionally adequate diet for 14 straight days and knew that inmate's diet was inadequate and likely to inflict pain and suffering asserted Eighth Amendment claim). Craft v. Mann, 265 F. Supp. 2d 970 (N.D. Ind. 2003) (holding that "[d]enial of full nutritious meals for two days is insufficient to violate the *Eighth Amendment's* prohibition against cruel and unusual punishment").

n. 8.

Page 216, note 8, add:
; Lee v. Mackay, 29 Fed. Appx. 679 (2d Cir. 2002) (inmate who claimed that he received his food one hour late on three occasions alleged no more than de minimis injury, such that dismissal of his Eighth Amendment claim was warranted).

n. 9.

Page 216, note 9, add:
; Rogers v. Holt, 49 Fed. Appx. 231 (10th Cir. 2002) (prison staff's denial of recreation and substitution of sack lunches for five days did not rise to severity required to support claim for cruel and unusual punishment).

n. 11.

Page 216, note 11, add:
; McCoy v. Goord, 255 F. Supp. 2d 233 (S.D. N.Y. 2003) (denial of warm food is not, by itself, a deprivation of the minimal civilized measure of nutrition, so as to support prisoner's Eighth Amendment claim challenging conditions of confinement); Waring v. Meacham (D.Conn. 2001) (complaint alleging that prisoner did not receive hot food during lockdown did not raise Eighth Amendment violation).

n. 28.

Page 221, note 28, add:
; Stanley v. Page, 44 Fed. Appx. 13 (7th Cir. 2002) (state prisoner's claims that prison menu during month-long lockdown became repetitious, portion sizes were decreased, inmates were denied utensils at breakfast, scrambled eggs had greenish tint, and he found roaches in his ice cubes

CRUEL & UNUSUAL PUNISHMENT   § 2:10

were temporary inconveniences that did not constitute such extreme deprivations as to constitute an Eighth Amendment violation).

n. 33.

Page 222, note 33, add:
; Drake v. Velasco, 207 F. Supp. 2d 809 (N.D. Ill. 2002) (food that occasionally contains foreign objects or sometimes is served cold, while unpleasant, does not amount to a constitutional deprivation).

n. 34.

Page 222, note 34, add:
; Liles v. Camden County Dept. of Corrections, 225 F. Supp. 2d 450 (D.N.J. 2002) (allegations that prison inmates received spoiled food on one occasion and were served food on trays that smelled did not rise to level required to support inmates' inadequate prison conditions claim against prison officials, when inmates provided no evidence that the food caused any physical illness).

n. 38.

Page 224, note 38, following the Ayers v. Uphoff citation and parenthetical, add:
; Thompson v. Gibson, 289 F.3d 1218 (10th Cir. 2002), cert. denied, 537 U.S. 978, 123 S. Ct. 440, 154 L. Ed. 2d 337 (2002) (state inmate's claim that prison officials were deliberately indifferent to his serious medical need for adequate portions of food was not actionable under Eighth Amendment when the record established that prison facility was providing inmate with nutritionally adequate diet and doctors had medical difference of opinion as to whether inmate should receive double food portions); Paige v. Hudson, 234 F. Supp. 2d 893 (N.D. Ind. 2002), aff'd, 2003 WL 22019824 (7th Cir. 2003) (inmate's claim that he was not provided his special diet did not allege deprivation of the basic necessities of life to the degree that a jury could find an Eighth Amendment violation).

section 2:10, note 38, add:
Woulard v. Food Service, 294 F. Supp. 2d 596 (D. Del. 2003) (denying prison official's motion to dismiss plaintiff's claim of deliberate indifference when plaintiff's allegations state that defendant responded to plaintiff's special diet for Diabetes and Crones Disease by saying that he did not care if plaintiff lived or died, and that the prison official refused to carry out the doctors prescribed diet. The court also denied the food service company's motion to dismiss because plaintiff's complaint showed that no action was taken to provide the inmate with his prescribed diet and the inadequate procedure of the food service company could rise to a constitutional violation. Finally, the court granted the prison supervisor's motion to dismiss plaintiff's claim because supervisors cannot be liable under ?1983 without actual knowledge and the plaintiff did not claim that the supervisor had actual knowledge of the constitutional violations); Gerber v. Sweeney, 292 F.Supp.2d 700 (E. D. Pa. 2003) (holding that prison officials did not deny the inmate an adequate diet when they substituted fruit and cheese for juice and milk with the advice of a dietitian to combat the inmates hypertension when plaintiff was in the segregation unit even though the inmate's total caloric intake was reduced because the inmate could not show that the reduction in calories resulted in a serious deprivation. The inmate's diet had to be changed when he was moved to the segregation unit because prison regulations prohibit

§ 2:10

inmates in the segregation unit from having access to any container that can hold liquid since inmates have used such containers to hurl urine and feces); Pladsen v. Warden, 2003 WL 21716430 (Conn. Super. Ct. 2003) (holding that plaintiff could not prove deliberate indifference on the part of prison officials for not providing a special diet to accommodate his allergies to fish, milk, and cheese because plaintiff failed to provide objective medical evidence that he actually suffered from the food allergies, or that his health was suffering from eating the diet he selected without milk, fish and cheese).

n. 39.

Page 224, note 39, add:
Kind v. Frank, 329 F.3d 979 (8th Cir. 2003) (prison officials held an objectively reasonable belief that they were not violating Muslim inmate's constitutional rights by offering him a pork-free, instead of a vegetarian, diet out of respect for his religious beliefs, because it was not clearly established that Muslims must be offered a meat-free diet).

section 2:10, note 39, add:
Williams v. Morton, 343 F.3d 212 (3d Cir. 2003) (affirming the district courts grant of summary judgment for the prison officials on the inmate's free exercise claim that the prison officials' refusal to provide halal meat to Muslim inmates unconstitutionally burdens the inmate's right to free exercise because there are "alternative avenues through which [Muslim inmates] can express their religious beliefs" without having access to halal meats including, *inter alia*, access to a pork-free, vegetarian diet on a regular basis and halal meats on certain religious holidays); Rashad v. Maloney, 16 Mass. L. Rep. 162 (Mass. Super. Ct. 2003) (dismissing the claim of Muslim inmates that they were not given halaal [sic] but that Jewish inmates were given kosher food. The claim was denied because the plaintiffs did not provide any evidence that the prison could obtain an adequate supply of the halaal meat from a reliable vendor at a reasonable cost)

n. 43.

Page 225, note 43, add following the Von Holden v. Chapman citation:
; Walker v. Horn, 286 F.3d 705 (3d Cir. 2002) (prisoner who claimed he fasted for religious reasons was force fed by prison officials who believed he was on a hunger strike and feared for his health; district court found that a genuine issue of material fact existed as to whether prison officials force fed prisoner through a feeding tube even after he allegedly agreed to end his fast; appeal was interlocutory and court of appeals dismissed the case for lack of jurisdiction); People ex rel. Illinois Dept. of Corrections v. Millard, 335 Ill. App. 3d 1066, 270 Ill. Dec. 407, 782 N.E.2d 966 (4th Dist. 2003), appeal denied, 204 Ill. 2d 682, 275 Ill. Dec. 82, 792 N.E.2d 313 (2003) (Department of Corrections' interests in preserving life, preventing suicide, and maintaining orderly and disciplined institution outweighed hunger-striking inmate's constitutional right to privacy and thus Department could force-feed inmate).

§ 2:11 Conditions of Confinement-Basic Human Needs and the Prisoner's Physical Well-Being—Exercise and Outside Recreation

n. 12.

section 2:11, note 12, add:

Cruel & Unusual Punishment § 2:11

Knight v. Castellaw, 99 Fed. Appx. 790 (9th Cir. 2004) (holding that prison officials did not violate the inmate's constitutional right of access to the court or his Eighth Amendment right to outdoor exercise when they required him to choose between the two during a modified lockdown because during that time, the inmate filed two complaints in two different district courts and had six hours of outdoor exercise each week).

n. 19.

Page 230, note 19, add:
; Rogers v. Holt, 49 Fed. Appx. 231 (10th Cir. 2002) (prison staff's denial of recreation for five days did not rise to severity required to support claim for cruel and unusual punishment); Pearson v. Ramos, 237 F.3d 881 (7th Cir. 2001) (Eighth Amendment not violated when inmate denied access to prison yard for exercise for 360 days when inmate committed 4 separate serious infractions of prison rules, because each disciplinary sanction was 90 days and stacking sanctions did not constitute cruel and unusual punishment); Smith v. Maloney, 55 Mass. App. Ct. 1112, 772 N.E.2d 1098 (2002), review denied, 438 Mass. 1110, 785 N.E.2d 383 (2003) (inmate's alleged deprivation of exercise for six days while confined in health services unit did not amount to denial of minimal civilized measure of life's necessities, and thus did not constitute cruel and unusual punishment in violation of Eighth Amendment).

n. 20.

Page 230, note 20, add:
; Phillips v. Norris, 320 F.3d 844 (8th Cir. 2003) (denial of exercise privileges for 37 days during segregation did not constitute cruel and unusual punishment).

n. 39.

Page 236, note 39, add:
; Green v. Nadeau, 70 P.3d 574 (Colo. Ct. App. 2003), cert. denied, 2003 WL 21142504 (Colo. 2003) (denying inmates outdoor exercise is not a per se Eighth Amendment violation).

n. 42.

Page 237, note 43, add:
; Gill v. Hoadley, 261 F. Supp. 2d 113 (N.D. N.Y. 2003) (denial of exercise while on keeplock confinement was insufficient, without more, to establish a claim of cruel and unusual punishment).

section 2:11 note 42, add:
Gates v. Cook, 376 F.3d 323 (5th Cir. 2004) (vacating the district court's injunctions requiring prison officials to provide inmates with sneakers in stead of "flip-flops" during exercise times).

n. 54.

Page 240, note 54, add:
; Williams v. Goord, 142 F. Supp. 2d 416 (S.D. N.Y. 2001) (genuine issue of material fact existed as to whether plaintiff inmate was denied "meaningful" exercise, where inmate, who was housed in a special housing unit, was entitled to one hour of out-of-cell exercise per day, but while wearing handcuffs and waist restraints; whether defendant could engage in meaningful exercise while in his cell was in dispute).

§ 2:12 Conditions of Confinement-Basic Human Needs and the Prisoner's Physical Well-Being—Shelter, Clothing, Personal Hygiene, Sanitation, Ventilation, Fire Safety, and Hazardous Substances

n. 11.

Page 244, note 11, add following the Inmates of Occoquan v. Barry citation and parenthetical:

; Laube v. Haley, 234 F. Supp. 2d 1227 (M.D. Ala. 2002) (in determining adequacy of ventilation at a prison facility for purposes of an Eighth Amendment claim, court may consider temperature, specifically, the heat inmates must endure and prison defendants' responses to the heat).

n. 12.

section 2:12 note 12, add:

But See Riebsame v. Prince, 267 F.Supp.2d 1225 (M. D. Fla. 2003), aff'd, 91 Fed. Appx. 656 (11th Cir. 2004) (granting defendant qualified immunity to the pretrial detainee's claim that defendant violate his due process rights under the Fourteenth Amendment when the defendant left him in the back of a patrol car with the windows rolled up for 30 to 40 minutes as a result of which plaintiff suffered minor dehydration which was cured by a drink of water at the jail. The court held that plaintiff did not have a clearly established right to have the car windows open).

n. 16.

section 2:12 note 16, add:

Gates v. Cook, 376 F.3d 323 (5th Cir. 2004) (affirming in part and vacating in part the district court's injunctions regarding the prison conditions on death row. The court affirmed the district court's injunctions requiring prison officials to: discontinue the practice of moving inmates to a new cell and requiring them to clean up after the former occupant; provide inmates with adequate cleaning supplies to clean their cells; provide proper ventilation, and access to fans, ice water and showers during days when the temperature exceeds 90 degrees; and repair and/or provide screens to control mosquitoes entry into cells; correct the "ping-pong" toilet whereby human waste flushed in one toilet would appear in another; improve lighting; and improve medical care. The court vacated the district court's injunctions requiring the prison to provide a written maintenance schedule and to provide inmates with sneakers in stead of "flip-flops" during exercise times.).

n. 17.

Page 245, note 17, add:

; Flores v. O'Donnell, 36 Fed. Appx. 204 (7th Cir. 2002) (prisoners have an Eighth Amendment right to adequate shelter, including a right to protection from cold); Davis v. Biller, 41 Fed. Appx. 845 (7th Cir. 2002) (prisoner's allegation that his exposure to extreme cold while in segregation constituted cruel and unusual punishment stated claim upon which relief could be granted); Moore v. Gardner, 199 F. Supp. 2d 17 (W.D. N.Y. 2002) (denying a motion for summary judgment in favor of prison officials, court held that issues of fact existed concerning inmate's claim that for three weeks during the winter he was kept in a cold, drafty cell, without his bed sheets, and with only one blanket).

CRUEL & UNUSUAL PUNISHMENT   § 2:12

n. 19.

Page 245, note 19, add:
But see Clark v. Spey, 2002 WL 31133198 (N.D. Ill. 2002) (prison officials did not subject inmate to cruel and unusual punishment when they allegedly confined him overnight in unlit cold cell, without warm clothing, mattress, sheets and blanket); Scotti v. Russell, 175 F. Supp. 2d 1099 (N.D. Ill. 2001) (temperature during two winters at prison was not sufficiently severe so as to constitute a violation of prisoner's Eighth Amendment rights, where heating system was proven adequate, cell windows were insulated with industrial plastic, and inmates were permitted to have extra blankets); Brown v. McElroy, 160 F. Supp. 2d 699 (S.D. N.Y. 2001) (cold cell was not enough to state a claim of unconstitutional conditions of confinement).

n. 23.

section 2:12 note 23, add:
But See Burleson v. Glass, 268 F. Supp. 2d 699 (W.D. Tex. 2003) (dismissing plaintiff's Eighth Amendment claim that he developed cancer of the lungs and throat because his prison work assignment required that he weld with thoriated tungsten electrodes, which contain a radioactive substance. The court reasoned that based on admissible evidence, a jury could only conclude that plaintiff's cancer was caused by his forty-five years of smoking, not exposure to radioactive particles).

n. 26.

Page 247, note 26, add:
; Flores v. O'Donnell, 36 Fed. Appx. 204 (7th Cir. 2002) (cold need not present an imminent threat to an inmate's health to implicate the Eighth Amendment).

n. 32.

Page 248, note 32, add:
; Sanders v. Kingston, 53 Fed. Appx. 781 (7th Cir. 2002) (prisoner's contention that doubling him in a single cell without giving him a bunk for his mattress violated the Eighth Amendment fell far short of "extreme deprivation"); Paige v. Hudson, 234 F. Supp. 2d 893 (N.D. Ind. 2002), aff'd, 2003 WL 22019824 (7th Cir. 2003) (inmate's claim that because of overcrowding he was required to sleep on a floor mattress rather than a bunk was not sufficiently serious as to allege deprivation of the basic necessities of life to the degree that a jury could find an Eighth Amendment violation); Wells v. Jefferson County Sheriff Dept., 159 F. Supp. 2d 1002 (S.D. Ohio 2001), judgment aff'd, 35 Fed. Appx. 142 (6th Cir. 2002) (having to sleep on a mattress on the floor simply does not rise to the level of a constitutional violation); Carlyle v. Aubrey, 189 F. Supp. 2d 660 (W.D. Ky. 2001) (inmate was not subjected to cruel and unusual punishment when forced to sleep on floor for one night).

n. 33.

Page 248, note 33, add:
; Liles v. Camden County Dept. of Corrections, 225 F. Supp. 2d 450 (D.N.J. 2002) (allegations that prison officials did not provide inmates with adequate amount of bedding materials did not rise to level of sufficiently serious constitutional deprivation, where inmates received two sheets and one blanket, but no pillow).

§ 2:12   RIGHTS OF PRISONERS

n. 34.

section 2:12 note 34, add:
Trammell v. Keane, 338 F.3d 155 (2d Cir. 2003) (holding that prison officials were not deliberately indifferent to the inmate's health or safety when the inmate was deprived of "all state and personal property in [his] cell except one pair of shorts, No recreation, No shower, No hot water, [and] No cell bucket . . ." because plaintiff was uncontrollable and would "throw . . . drinks, soup, spit, urine, and feces - at corrections officers or others near his cell." The inmate was subject to this treatment in various degrees from December 16, 1994 through January 13, 1995. On December 16 all of the inmate's possessions were confiscated. The inmate was able to regain privileges with good behavior but would lose privileges with bad behavior. All of the inmate's property was returned on January 13. In addition, the inmate was given only nutriloaf, "a bread-like food containing carrots and potatoes," and raw cabbage for 95 days. The court held that this punishment was reasonably calculated to correct the plaintiff's behavior because plaintiff could regain his privileges if he would conform to prison regulations, and since plaintiff had access to a nurse his health was not in danger).

n. 35.

Page 249, note 35, add:
; Liles v. Camden County Dept. of Corrections, 225 F. Supp. 2d 450 (D.N.J. 2002) (inmates presented no evidence to support their Eighth Amendment claim of inadequate prison conditions against prison officials that prison mattresses, which were between two and two and one half inches thick, caused their back injuries).

section 2:12 note 35, add:
Davidson v. Conway, 2004 U.S. Dist. 9257 (W.D.N.Y. 2004) (denying the inmate leave to amend a complaint to add a new Eighth Amendment violation claim. Plaintiff seeks to assert that a prison policy that "limits inmates in the general population . . . to one blanket, along with one laundered towel, two laundered sheets, and one laundered pillow case per-week" is a violation of the Eighth Amendment. The court rejected plaintiff's claim because the prison policy is not objectively unreasonable and therefore the proposed amendment to the complaint would be futile).

n. 36.

section 2:12 note 36, add:
Marion County Jail Inmates v. Anderson, 270 F. Supp. 2d 1034 (S.D. Ind. 2003) (holding the county sheriff in contempt of court for failure to comply with a court order mandating that he provide a bed or bunk off the floor for all prisoner and ensure that all prisoners are treated in a safe and humane manner even thought the sheriffs non-compliance was not willful).

n. 37.

Page 250, note 37, add:
; Smith v. Maloney, 55 Mass. App. Ct. 1112, 772 N.E.2d 1098 (2002), review denied, 438 Mass. 1110, 785 N.E.2d 383 (2003) (inmate's alleged deprivation of a table and chair for six days while confined in health services unit did not constitute cruel and unusual punishment in violation of Eighth Amendment).

n. 39.

Page 250, note 39, add:

; Rasheed v. Commissioner of Correction, 55 Mass. App. Ct. 1112, 772 N.E.2d 1098 (2002), review denied, 438 Mass. 1106, 782 N.E.2d 516 (2003) (inmates failed to state an Eighth Amendment violation for failure to provide adequate winter clothing, where inmates were provided with winter coats, knit hats, and footwear, and were not required to exercise outdoors in harsh conditions).

n. 40.

Page 251, note 40, add:
But see Smith v. Board of County Com'rs of County of Lyon, 216 F. Supp. 2d 1209 (D. Kan. 2002) (no Eighth Amendment violation occurred when jail inmate, who was incontinent, failed on some occasions to receive clean clothing from prison guards upon his request).

n. 43.

Page 252, note 43, add:
; Woodruff v. Paulson, 51 Fed. Appx. 822 (10th Cir. 2002) (state prison officers did not subject inmate to cruel and unusual punishment by providing lights in his cell that were too bright).

n. 44.

Page 252, note 44, add:
; Carney v. Craven, 40 Fed. Appx. 48 (6th Cir. 2002) (state prisoner failed to show that prison officials were deliberately indifferent to his request to fix a faulty light which was producing a strobe-like effect and allegedly causing him headaches and eye pain, as required to state an Eighth Amendment violation, as new light bulb was not immediately available, and prisoner was ultimately moved to new cell 11 days after reporting problem).

section 2:12 note 44, add:
Minifield v. Butikofer, 298 F. Supp. 2d 900 (N.D. Cal. 2004) (dismissing plaintiff's claim that a prison officer violated his Eighth Amendment rights by turning off the water and electricity in plaintiff's cell for five hours because plaintiff could not prove that the prison officer was the person responsible for the deprivation and a deprivation of this sort for five hours does not rise to the level of a constitutional violation).

n. 52.

Page 254, note 52, add:
But see Ledbetter v. City of Topeka, Kan., 318 F.3d 1183 (10th Cir. 2003) (allegations that arrestee was falsely imprisoned in "heinous conditions" and placed in his bare feet in a cell without a toilet for five hours did not allege a sufficiently serious deprivation to support a claim for cruel and unusual punishment); Frye v. Pettis County Sheriff Dept., 41 Fed. Appx. 906 (8th Cir. 2002) (pretrial detainee failed to show that jail officials were deliberately indifferent to his health and safety due to fact that toilet in his cell leaked both sewage and water, where there was no showing that the leakage was sufficiently serious that the prisoners had a substantial risk of a fall causing serious harm); Dellis v. Corrections Corp. of America, 257 F.3d 508, 2001 FED App. 0228P (6th Cir. 2001) (prisoner's claim that he was subjected to a flooded cell and was deprived of a working toilet were only temporary inconveniences and did not demonstrate that conditions fell beneath a minimal standard of decency).

section 2:12 note 52, add:

§ 2:12 RIGHTS OF PRISONERS

Gates v. Cook, 376 F.3d 323 (5th Cir. 2004) (affirming in part and vacating in part the district court's injunctions regarding the prison conditions on death row. The court affirmed the district court's injunctions requiring prison officials to: discontinue the practice of moving inmates to a new cell and requiring them to clean up after the former occupant; provide inmates with adequate cleaning supplies to clean their cells; provide proper ventilation, and access to fans, ice water and showers during days when the temperature exceeds 90 degrees; and repair and/or provide screens to control mosquitoes entry into cells; correct the "ping-pong" toilet whereby human waste flushed in one toilet would appear in another; improve lighting; and improve medical care. The court vacated the district court's injunctions requiring the prison to provide a written maintenance schedule and to provide inmates with sneakers in stead of "flip-flops" during exercise times.).

n. 54.

Page 254, note 54, add:
But see Estrada v. Kruse, 38 Fed. Appx. 498 (10th Cir. 2002) (allegations that state inmate was held for four nights and five days in stripped basement cell with no cleaning supplies for cell did not establish violation of Eighth Amendment); Cannon v. Cooper, 2002 WL 1729562 (Tex. App. Texarkana 2002) (dismissal of inmate's Eighth Amendment suit against prison officials was warranted on ground that it was frivolous, where inmate's complaint about failure to provide adequate cleaning supplies was not that defendants failed to supply the items but that prison had not included the types of supplies inmate believed were necessary and appropriate).

n. 55.

Page 255, note 55, add following the Warren v. Stempson citation and parenthetical:
; McCoy v. Goord, 255 F. Supp. 2d 233 (S.D. N.Y. 2003) (mere presence of vermin in prisoner's housing area was not "punishment" under the Eighth Amendment); Stanley v. Page, 44 Fed.Appx. 13 (7th Cir. 2002) (state prisoner claiming emotional distress from seeing mice, roaches and birds in cellhouse did not state Eighth Amendment claim); Oliver v. Powell, 250 F. Supp. 2d 593 (E.D. Va. 2002) (allegations that prisoner's cell had roaches did not rise to level of Eighth Amendment claim, where prisoner neglected to use roach traps).

section 2:12 note 55, add:
Gates v. Cook, 376 F.3d 323 (5th Cir. 2004) (affirming in part and vacating in part the district court's injunctions regarding the prison conditions on death row. The court affirmed the district court's injunctions requiring prison officials to: discontinue the practice of moving inmates to a new cell and requiring them to clean up after the former occupant; provide inmates with adequate cleaning supplies to clean their cells; provide proper ventilation, and access to fans, ice water and showers during days when the temperature exceeds 90 degrees; and repair and/or provide screens to control mosquitoes entry into cells; correct the "ping-pong" toilet whereby human waste flushed in one toilet would appear in another; improve lighting; and improve medical care. The court vacated the district court's injunctions requiring the prison to provide a written maintenance schedule and to provide inmates with sneakers in stead of "flip-flops" during exercise times.).

CRUEL & UNUSUAL PUNISHMENT § 2:12

***n*. 56.**

section 2:12 note 56, add:
Minifield v. Butikofer, 298 F. Supp. 2d 900 (N.D. Cal. 2004) (dismissing plaintiff's claim that a prison officer violated his Eighth Amendment rights by turning off the water and electricity in plaintiff's cell for five hours because plaintiff could not prove that the prison officer was the person responsible for the deprivation and a deprivation of this sort for five hours does not rise to the level of a constitutional violation).

***n*. 57.**

Page 256, note 57, add:
; Mitchell v. Newryder, 245 F. Supp. 2d 200 (D. Me. 2003) (detainee's complaint sufficiently pled Eighth Amendment claim by alleging that detainee was purposefully subjected to dehumanizing conditions when he was denied access to facilities both to go to the restroom and to clean himself up during five-hour period in which he sat in his feces). But see Ledbetter v. City of Topeka, Kan., 318 F.3d 1183 (10th Cir. 2003) (allegations that arrestee was placed in his bare feet in a cell without a toilet for five hours did not allege a sufficiently serious deprivation to support a claim by arrestee for cruel and unusual punishment); Dye v. Lomen, 40 Fed. Appx. 993 (7th Cir. 2002) (prison officials' failure to provide prisoner with toilet paper for several days did not constitute cruel and unusual punishment in violation of prisoner's Eighth Amendment rights).

***n*. 63.**

Page 257, note 63, add following the Carver v. Knox County citation and parenthetical:
; James v. O'Sullivan, 62 Fed. Appx. 636 (7th Cir. 2003) (inmate's allegations about being denied soap, a toothbrush, and toothpaste, if true, could state an Eighth Amendment violation); but see Brown v. Brown, 46 Fed. Appx. 324 (6th Cir. 2002) (any inconvenience prisoner suffered due to his inability to purchase personal hygiene and toiletry items for several months because of unlawful hold on his account did not demonstrate condition of confinement that fell beneath minimal civilized measure of life's necessities, and therefore did not violate Eighth Amendment); Davison v. Stout, 44 Fed. Appx. 404 (10th Cir. 2002) (alleged acts of depriving prisoner of toothpaste, toothbrush, toilet paper, and soap over three-day detention in city jail, if proven, did not constitute cruel and unusual punishment); Stolte v. Cummings, 70 P.3d 695 (Kan. Ct. App. 2003), as corrected, (June 19, 2003) (hygiene products that were not contained in the inmate's monthly indigency package, such as shampoo, deodorant, skin lotion, and nail clippers, were not absolutely necessary for personal hygiene, and thus did not amount to cruel and unusual punishment, where inmate was given two tubes of toothpaste, a plastic toothbrush, a comb, and four bars of soap).

***n*. 65.**

section 2:12 note 65, add:
Gates v. Cook, 376 F.3d 323 (5th Cir. 2004) (affirming in part and vacating in part the district court's injunctions regarding the prison conditions on death row. The court affirmed the district court's injunctions requiring prison officials to: discontinue the practice of moving inmates to a new cell and requiring them to clean up after the former occupant; provide inmates with adequate cleaning supplies to clean their cells; provide proper ventila-

§ 2:12   Rights of Prisoners

tion, and access to fans, ice water and showers during days when the temperature exceeds 90 degrees; and repair and/or provide screens to control mosquitoes entry into cells; correct the "ping-pong" toilet whereby human waste flushed in one toilet would appear in another; improve lighting; and improve medical care. The court vacated the district court's injunctions requiring the prison to provide a written maintenance schedule and to provide inmates with sneakers in stead of "flip-flops" during exercise times.).

n. 66.

   Page 258, note 66, add:

; McCoy v. Goord, 255 F. Supp. 2d 233 (S.D. N.Y. 2003) (two-week suspension of inmate's shower privileges did not suffice as a denial of basic hygienic needs, under Eighth Amendment, nor did failure to provide razors for shaving rise to the level of constitutional concern); see also Beckford v. Portuondo, 152 F.Supp.2d 204 (N.D.N.Y. 2001) (no Eighth Amendment violation for denying shower privileges for one day).

n. 69.

   Page 260, note 69, add:

; Stanley v. Page, 44 Fed. Appx. 13 (7th Cir. 2002) (state prisoner claiming that he suffered severe athlete's foot from standing water in cellhouse shower did not show that he suffered serious harm as required to support Eighth Amendment claim); Flandro v. Salt Lake County Jail, 53 Fed.Appx. 499 (10th Cir. 2002) (soapy shower floor in jail did not present excessive or substantial risk, and thus inmate's slip and fall in shower did not constitute cruel and unusual punishment in violation of Eighth Amendment).

   section 2:12 note 69, add:

Reynolds v. Powell, 370 F.3d 1028 (10th Cir. 2004) (dismissing the inmate's claim in which he alleged that prison officials violated his rights under the Eighth Amendment when they did not correct a problem with the drainage in a prison shower which caused a standing water problem in the shower. As a result of the standing water, the inmate fell sustaining injuries to his head, back, and neck. The court held that the slippery floor cause by the standing water, without more, does not rise to the level of a sufficiently serious condition to warrant constitutional protection); Govan v. Campbell, 289 F. Supp. 2d 289 (N.D. N.Y. 2003) (holding that plaintiff did not assert unconstitutional prison conditions when he alleged that the shower stalls had rust, birds were allowed to fly into the prison through open windows, and the prison had a cockroach problem); Jones v. Nassau County Sheriff Dept., 285 F. Supp. 2d 322 (E.D. N.Y. 2003) (holding that "failure to remedy a wet shower area with rubber mats does not rise to the level of a constitutional deprivation"); Porter v. Selsky, 287 F. Supp. 2d 180 (W.D. N.Y. 2003) (granting the prison officials' motion for summary judgment on plaintiff's claim that they placed him in a cell near a feces throwing inmate and subjected him to unhygienic conditions in violation of his Eighth Amendment right to be free from cruel and unusual punishment. The court held that the defendants were not responsible for plaintiff's cell placement and the prison officials took reasonable steps to correct the unhygienic conditions in the SHU such as "cleaning and disinfecting cells, moving inmates behind plexiglass shields and punishing violators").

n. 70.

   Page 261, note 70, add:

Cruel & Unusual Punishment § 2:12

; Stanley v. Page, 44 Fed. Appx. 13 (7th Cir. 2002) (inmate stated no Eighth Amendment claim where prison officials took steps to correct prison conditions that inmate cited, such as plumbing malfunctions, infestations of mice, roaches, and birds, and peeling walls in cell).

n. 73.

Page 262, note 73, add:
; Linger v. Andrews, 2002-Ohio-4495, 2002 WL 2005702 (Ohio Ct. App. 10th Dist. Franklin County 2002) (smoking is not a basic human need akin to food, water, or the adequate provision of clothing, shelter and medical care, and thus, smoking ban at corrections facility did not violate Eighth Amendment); Brashear v. Simms, 138 F. Supp. 2d 693 (D. Md. 2001) (prisoner who smoked tobacco sought injunctive relief claiming that his rights under the American With Disabilities Act were violated by prison policies prohibiting smoking; court stated that smoking was not a "disability" within the meaning of the ADA, and held that the regulation served a legitimate state interest and dismissed the case as frivolous).

n. 75.

Page 264, note 75, add:
; Reilly v. Grayson, 310 F.3d 519, 2002 FED App. 0397P (6th Cir. 2002) (affirming an award of punitive damages against prison officials, court of appeals held that district court did not err in finding that prisoner suffered from a serious medical condition that was worsened when prisoner exposed to smoke and that prison officials failed to respond to repeated requests by medical personnel to move prisoner to smoke-free environment).

n. 78.

Page 264, note 78, add:
; Atkinson v. Taylor, 316 F.3d 257 (3d Cir. 2003) (prison officials were deliberately indifferent to serious medical needs of prisoner, who suffered severe allergic reactions to smoke, when there was evidence that inmate was housed for over seven months with "constant" smokers, that he suffered numerous symptoms as a result and that, after telling prison officials about his sensitivity to smoke, no change was made to his living arrangements); Jones v. Bayer, 56 Fed. Appx. 408 (9th Cir. 2003) (reversing a grant of summary judgment for prison officials, court of appeals held that a jury could reasonably find that assigning prisoner to a cell with a heavy smoker amounted to cruel and unusual punishment, where medical records showed that prisoner suffered from a chronic throat condition that significantly affected his quality of life and which worsened with exposure to cigarette smoke); Davis v. New York, 316 F.3d 93 (2d Cir. 2002) (genuine issue of material fact as to whether state prisoner was exposed to unreasonable levels of second-hand smoke precluded summary judgment, where prisoner alleged that he had always been housed in areas where the majority of inmates were smokers, including being surrounded by seven inmates who were chain smokers, and that the smoke caused him to suffer dizziness, difficulty breathing, blackouts, and respiratory problems); Sanders v. Kingston, 53 Fed. Appx. 781 (7th Cir. 2002) (prisoner stated claim that his exposure to environmental tobacco smoke in prison constituted an Eighth Amendment violation, where he claimed that he was exposed to ETS for approximately six weeks and that prison officials exhibited deliberate indifference toward the risk that this exposure constituted a threat to his future health).

§ 2:12   Rights of Prisoners

n. 81.

Page 265, note 81, add:
; Wilcox v. Lewis, 47 Fed. Appx. 714 (6th Cir. 2002) (alleged exposure of state prisoner, who was diagnosed with cancer of the rectum and colon, and who underwent surgery, chemotherapy, radiation, and total colectomy, to environmental tobacco smoke (ETS) did not violate his Eighth Amendment rights, where there was no evidence that ETS had anything to do with his serious medical condition).

n. 83.

Page 266, note 83, add:
; Zaire v. Artuz, 2003 WL 230868 (S.D. N.Y. 2003) (prisoner's periodic exposure to environmental tobacco smoke while housed in single-person cells during five-month stay at correctional facility did not pose substantial risk of harm to his health that could support Eighth Amendment claim, particularly where he spent majority of time in cell containing door and window); Holman v. Gillen, 2002 WL 31834875 (N.D.Ill.E.Div. 2002) (state prisoner's exposure to second-hand smoke through his placement with cellmate who smoked did not create substantial risk of serious harm to prisoner); Baker v. Williams, 2002 WL 31015630 (D. Del. 2002) (state could not be held liable for Eighth Amendment violation for exposure of prisoner to environmental tobacco smoke absent showing that level of smoke was so great as to create grave risk of injury); Richardson v. Spurlock, 260 F.3d 495 (5th Cir. 2001) (prisoner's occasional exposure to cigarette smoke during bus rides, which allegedly caused him coughing and nausea, did not reach the level of a constitutional violation).

n. 84.

Page 267, note 84, add:
; Garcia v. Maddock, 64 Fed. Appx. 10 (9th Cir. 2003) (corrections officials were not deliberately indifferent to inmate's exposure to second-hand smoke, and therefore inmate was not subjected to cruel and unusual punishment, where evidence did not establish that defendants had any knowledge of inmate's condition or his exposure to second-hand smoke after he was diagnosed with smoking-related ailments); White v. Caruso, 39 Fed. Appx. 75 (6th Cir. 2002) (allegations by inmate that his exposure to second hand smoke was the result of the prison officials' failure to enforce prison's regulations and policies with regard to smoking, and that because of their failure to enforce these policies, he was suffering various health-related problems, was dismissed for failing to state claim, where it was demonstrated that prison officials enforced no-smoking policy with disciplinary sanctions imposed on prisoners who violated it).

n. 118.

Page 276, note 118, add:
; Turner v. Miller, 301 F.3d 599 (7th Cir. 2002) (prisoner failed to show that prison officials were deliberately indifferent to prisoner's conditions of confinement, for purpose of prisoner's claim under Eighth Amendment to recover for injuries he allegedly sustained when he was shocked by exposed electrical wires in showers at correctional center, where defendants denied that they had ever personally seen any exposed wires in showers or that anyone had ever told them about the wires).

n. 122.

Page 277, note 122, add:

§ 2:13

; Stanley v. Page, 44 Fed. Appx. 13 (7th Cir. 2002) (risk of lead in water in state prison was minimal and could be easily addressed by running tap water for a few minutes in the morning to flush out lead, and thus did not support state prisoner's Eighth Amendment claim).

n. 127.
Page 280, note 127, add:
; Wells v. Jefferson County Sheriff Dept., 35 Fed. Appx. 142 (6th Cir. 2002) (inmate's six-day stay in holding cell that was cold and was regularly sprayed with insecticides and in which inmate slept on mattress on floor did not rise to level of Eighth Amendment violation); Maus v. Murphy, 29 Fed. Appx. 365 (7th Cir. 2002) (although exposing inmates to air pollution may amount to deliberate indifference, failing to provide an environment completely free from pollution or safety hazards is not actionable under the Eighth Amendment); Stanley v. Page, 44 Fed. Appx. 13 (7th Cir. 2002) (state prisoner claiming that he suffered headaches as a result of peeling paint in his cell presented no evidence establishing that peeling paint was actual cause of his headaches, as required to support Eighth Amendment claim); see also Wells v. Jefferson County Sheriff Dept., 159 F. Supp. 2d 1002 (S.D. Ohio 2001), judgment aff'd, 35 Fed. Appx. 142 (6th Cir. 2002) (even if plaintiff was exposed to pesticides, he failed to allege that the levels of pesticides posed an unreasonable risk to his health).

§ 2:13 Conditions of Confinement-Basic Human Needs and the Prisoner's Physical Well-Being—Overcrowding

n. 7.
Page 282, note 7, add:
; William J. Rich, *Prison Conditions and Criminal Sentencing in Kansas: A Public Policy Dialogue*, 11 Kan. J.L. & Pub. Pol'y 693 (2002) (article discusses, among other things, deficient conditions of the Kansas prison system due to overcrowding and its relationship to sentencing policies).

n. 36.
Page 292, note 36, add:
; Foster v. Fulton County, Georgia, 223 F. Supp. 2d 1292 (N.D. Ga. 2002) (overcrowding in jail deprived inmates who had tested positive for HIV of their constitutional right to minimal civilized measure of life's necessities); but see Stewart v. Taft, 235 F. Supp. 2d 763 (N.D. Ohio 2002) (prison inmate failed to show that overcrowding caused him to test positive for tuberculosis, precluding claim that officials showed deliberate indifference to his medical condition).

section 2:13 note 36, add:
Marion County Jail Inmates v. Anderson, 270 F. Supp. 2d 1034 (S.D. Ind. 2003) (holding the county sheriff in contempt of court for failure to comply with a court order mandating that he provide a bed or bunk off the floor for all prisoner and ensure that all prisoners are treated in a safe and humane manner even thought the sheriffs non-compliance was not willful).

Page 292, third line of first full paragraph after the word "uncomfortable," add new footnote.

[37.1] Armstrong v. Metropolitan Government of Nashville and Davidson

§ 2:13   RIGHTS OF PRISONERS

County, 196 F. Supp. 2d 673 (M.D. Tenn. 2002) (overcrowded conditions in jail, even when restrictive and harsh, do not violate Eighth Amendment unless they result in deprivation of minimal civilized necessities of life, such as food and reasonable measures of sanitation and safety).

n. 38.

section 2:13 note 38, add:
Fraternal Order of Police/Dept. of Corrections Labor Committee v. Williams, 263 F. Supp. 2d 45 (D.D.C. 2003) (dismissing the correction officers' union's complaint that understaffing and overcrowding at Washington D.C. prisons violates correction officers' rights under the Due Process Clause of the Fourteenth Amendment by increasing their risk of harm at work because "the Due Process Clause does not guarantee municipal employees a workplace that is free from unreasonable risks of harm").

n. 52.

Page 296, note 52, add:
; Fuller v. Commissioner of Correction, 75 Conn. App. 133, 815 A.2d 208 (2003) (double celling of inmates was not sufficiently serious as to state Eighth Amendment violation, where inmate only alleged that double celling made incarceration uncomfortable, and did not connect it to other conditions affecting an inmate's quality of life).

n. 65.

Page 299, note 65, add following the Carty v. Farrell citation and parenthetical:
; Hoover v. Keating, 59 Fed. Appx. 288 (10th Cir. 2003) (state prison officials' insistence that inmate accept housing assignment did not demonstrate deliberate indifference to inmate's safety, in violation of Eighth Amendment, absent evidence that officials were aware of any risk beyond inmate's broad assertions that "prison riot" could ensue if inmates of different races continued to be celled together).

n. 89.

Page 308, note 89, add:
; Laube v. Haley, 234 F. Supp. 2d 1227 (M.D. Ala. 2002) (granting plaintiffs' motion for preliminary injunctive relief on their claim that they were subjected to serious harm caused by prison's greatly overcrowded and understaffed dorms, court, instead of fashioning relief, ordered defendants to submit a plan to redress the problem).

§ 2:14   Conditions of Confinement-Basic Human Needs and the Prisoner's Physical Well-Being—Idleness, Programs, and Rehabilitation

n. 8.

section 2:14 note 8, add:
Freeman v. Berge, 283 F. Supp. 2d 1009 (W.D. Wis. 2003) (granting prison officials qualified immunity on plaintiff's claim that deprivation of social interaction and sensory stimulation violated his Eighth Amendment right to be free from cruel and unusual punishment because prisoners have no clearly established right to social interaction and sensory stimulation).

n. 24.

Page 318, note 24, add:

CRUEL & UNUSUAL PUNISHMENT § 2:15

; Figueroa v. Dinitto, 52 Fed. Appx. 522 (1st Cir. 2002) (state prison official's alleged acts of confining prisoner to cell for 23-24 hours a day, without opportunity to work or participate in educational, vocational, or rehabilitation programs, if proven, did not constitute "extreme deprivation" that might violate Eighth Amendment's prohibition against cruel and unusual punishment).

n. 51.

Page 325, note 51, add:
See also Eric S. Janus, Minnesota's Sex Offender Commitment Program: Would an Empirically-Based Prevention Policy Be More Effective?, 29 Wm. Mitchell L. Rev. 1083, 1133 (2003).

n. 54.

Page 326, note 54, add:
; Searcy v. Simmons, 299 F.3d 1220 (10th Cir. 2002) (inmate sued secretary of corrections and warden alleging violations of constitutional rights stemming from the department of corrections sexual abuse treatment program that required inmate to sign an admission of responsibility form; inmate, who entered a plea of nolo contendere to charges of sexual exploitation of a child, refused, arguing that although the program was voluntary, failure to participate would result in the withholding of good time credits, and this pressure imposed upon him to provide an admission of responsibility was unconstitutional; court rejected this argument and held that the pressure imposed on the inmate for an admission of guilt did not rise to a level where it was likely to "compel" a person to be a witness against himself).

§ 2:15 Conditions of Confinement-Basic Human Needs and the Prisoner's Physical Well-Being—Large Scale Litigations: Totality of the Conditions, Inadequate Finances, and Remedies

n. 1.

section 2:15 note 1, add:
Gates v. Cook, 376 F.3d 323 (5th Cir. 2004) (affirming in part and vacating in part the district court's injunctions regarding the prison conditions on death row. The court affirmed the district court's injunctions requiring prison officials to: discontinue the practice of moving inmates to a new cell and requiring them to clean up after the former occupant; provide inmates with adequate cleaning supplies to clean their cells; provide proper ventilation, and access to fans, ice water and showers during days when the temperature exceeds 90 degrees; and repair and/or provide screens to control mosquitoes entry into cells; correct the "ping-pong" toilet whereby human waste flushed in one toilet would appear in another; improve lighting; and improve medical care. The court vacated the district court's injunctions requiring the prison to provide a written maintenance schedule and to provide inmates with sneakers in stead of "flip-flops" during exercise times.); but see Webb v. Goord, 340 F.3d 105 (2d Cir. 2003), cert. denied, 124 S. Ct. 1077, 157 L. Ed. 2d 897 (U.S. 2004) (affirming the dismissal of the plaintiffs' Eighth Amendment claim that prison officials in the New York State, Department of Corrections attacked the inmates, failed to

§ 2:15   Rights of Prisoners

protect the inmates from attacks by other inmates, used improper physical punishment on inmates, and denied the inmates medical and dental care. The plaintiffs in this case were former and current (all but one of the plaintiffs have been released from jail) inmates in the New York State Correctional system. The plaintiffs sought compensatory damages in this action for the violation of their civil rights. Their claim was dismissed because the group was not certified as a class and all the plaintiffs' complaints are virtually unrelated to one another).

Chapter 3

The Eighth Amendment: Medical Care

> **KeyCite®:** Cases and other legal materials listed in KeyCite Scope can be researched through West's KeyCite service on Westlaw®. Use KeyCite to check citations for form, parallel references, prior and later history, and comprehensive citator information, including citations to other decisions and secondary materials.

§ 3:1 Introduction

n. 1.

section 3:1 note 1, add:

n. 15.

section 3:1 note 15, add:
Doe v. Gustavus, 294 F. Supp. 2d 1003 (E.D. Wis. 2003) (denying the prison nurses' motion for summary judgment and holding that a jury could find that the prison nurses were deliberately indifferent to the inmate's serious medical need when they refused to provide pain medication, a complete examination, or assistance to a pregnant inmate who was experiencing labor pains because the nurses falsely diagnosed the inmate's symptoms as false labor. As a result of the nurses' conduct, the inmate was forced to deliver her own baby while she was locked in a segregation cell).

n. 26.

Page 362, note 26, add:
; Massey v. U.S., 312 F.3d 272 (7th Cir. 2002) (federal prison inmate brought medical malpractice claim under Federal Tort Claims Act, but summary judgment in favor of defendants was affirmed, because substituting one medication for another following surgery and requiring inmate to walk to meals was not negligent); Berman v. U.S., 205 F. Supp. 2d 362 (M.D. Pa. 2002) (former federal prisoner who filed action pursuant to FTCA recovered $150,000 for medical malpractice); Podlog v. U.S., 205 F. Supp. 2d 346 (M.D. Pa. 2002), judgment aff'd (3d Cir. July 7, 2003); Robinson v. U.S. Bureau of Prisons, 244 F. Supp. 2d 57 (N.D. N.Y. 2003); Marshall v. U.S., 242 F. Supp. 2d 395 (S.D. N.Y. 2003).

§ 3:3 Rights of Pretrial Detainees to Medical Care

n. 4.

Page 373, note 4, add:

§ 3:3   RIGHTS OF PRISONERS

And see Davis v. Hill, 173 F. Supp. 2d 1136 (D. Kan. 2001) (claim by arrestee for inadequate medical care was meritless, because the Eighth Amendment was only applicable to post-conviction incarcerations).

§ 3:4   What is a "Serious Medical Need"?
n. 3.

   Page 374, note 3, after "cases holding that particular conditions did not constitute a serious medical need, see, e.g." add:
; Taylor v. Smolinski, 2003 WL 21383015 (W.D. N.Y. 2003) (inmate's alleged injuries—inadequate post-operative care after knee surgery, prescription of "psychotropic" drugs, shoulder and palm pain, surgery without informed consent and failure to provide physical therapy and outside referrals—were not sufficiently serious to support Eighth Amendment claim for deliberate indifference to serious medical needs); Dye v. Lomen, 40 Fed. Appx. 993 (7th Cir. 2002) (prisoner who alleged that he suffered back pain and a cut on his ankle from actions of prison officials failed to submit any evidence that either of these injuries gave rise to a serious medical need); Martinez v. Hedrick, 36 Fed. Appx. 209 (7th Cir. 2002) (prisoner's lipoma, a tumor made up of fat tissue, was not serious medical need, as required to support claim that doctors and prison staff violated prisoner's Eighth Amendment right against cruel and unusual punishment, where prisoner complained only that lipoma was tender when touched and that he could not sleep on his left side); Lomholt v. Holder, 287 F.3d 683 (8th Cir. 2002) (sore feet which prisoner suffered from going barefoot did not amount to a serious medical need); Rodriguez v. Mercado, 2002 WL 1997885 (S.D. N.Y. 2002) (any injuries jail inmate received when he was allegedly kneed in the back and had his head struck against the wall by corrections officers were not sufficiently serious to support an Eighth Amendment claim of indifference to serious medical needs, where inmate claimed to have sustained only bruises); Victoria W. v. Larpenter, 205 F. Supp. 2d 580 (E.D. La. 2002) (abortion sought due to financial and emotional reasons was not a serious medical need for Eighth Amendment purposes); Davidson v. Scully, 155 F. Supp. 2d 77 (S.D. N.Y. 2001) (tinnitus, a constant ringing in the ear, is not life-threatening or degenerative, and thus is not a serious medical need under the Eighth Amendment); Canell v. Multnomah County, 141 F. Supp. 2d 1046 (D. Or. 2001) (plaintiff allegation that he had headaches because he was forced to read without his reading glasses does not demonstrate a serious medical need).

   Page 374, note 3, after "cases holding conditions to be serious see, e.g." add:
; Brock v. Wright, 315 F.3d 158, 60 Fed. R. Evid. Serv. 279 (2d Cir. 2003) (genuine issue of material fact as to whether prisoner's keloid, an excessive growth of scar tissue on the skin that developed at the site of a knife wound on his cheek, causing prisoner chronic and substantial pain, was a serious medical condition); De'Lonta v. Angelone, 330 F.3d 630 (4th Cir. 2003) (inmate's need for protection against continued self-mutilation was serious medical need to which prison officials could not be deliberately indifferent); Green v. Mazzone, 2002 WL 1636709 (D.N.J. 2002) (severe arthritic condition in prisoner's knees constituted serious medical need for purposes of Eighth Amendment deliberate indifference claim); Darnell v. Simmons, 30 Kan. App. 2d 778, 48 P.3d 1278 (2002) (prisoner's medical complaints regarding lump in his abdomen, stomach pains, and bloody

MEDICAL CARE § 3:5

stool presented serious medical need that would support a claim of deliberate indifference); Gonzalez v. Cecil County, Maryland, 221 F. Supp. 2d 611 (D. Md. 2002) (pretrial detainee's heroin withdrawal presented "serious medical need" sufficient to support claim against county detention center's medical staff); Davidson v. Scully, 155 F. Supp. 2d 77 (S.D. N.Y. 2001) (podiatric condition could constitute a serious medical need); Jones v. Natesha, 151 F. Supp. 2d 938 (N.D. Ill. 2001) (hemorrhoid condition was a serious medical need, where hemorrhoids were serious enough to lead physicians to perform three surgeries within two years); Johnson v. Wright, 234 F. Supp. 2d 352 (S.D. N.Y. 2002) (Hepatitis C qualifies as a serious medical condition for purposes of Eighth Amendment); Christy v. Robinson, 216 F. Supp. 2d 398 (D.N.J. 2002) (same).

section 3:4 note 3, add:
Myers v. Milbert, 281 F. Supp. 2d 859 (N.D. W. Va. 2003) (holding that prison officials did not violate the inmate's right to medical care under the Eighth Amendment when plaintiff complained of wrist injuries from being placed in a "stokes basket," a metal stretcher, and stomach problems from being fed a diet of nutra-loaf because plaintiff could not prove that he was suffering from a serious medical condition).

Smith v. County of Bucks, 28 Nat'l Disability Law Rep. P 55, 2004 WL 868278 (E.D. Pa. 2004) (denying the prison officers' motion to dismiss the claim that they were deliberately indifferent to the plaintiff's son's serious medical need when both the plaintiff and her son informed the officials of the changing conditions of a mole on the inmate's chest and requested a biopsy. Despite the inmate's symptoms, he did not receive a biopsy on the mole for several months. The mole was in fact cancerous and the inmate died of cancer after being released from prison. From the evidence, a jury could find that the prison officials were deliberately indifferent to the inmate's serious medical need because cancer is a serious medical need and both the inmate and the plaintiff told the prison officials about the mole. Furthermore, the court denied the prison officials qualified immunity because any reasonable official would know that the denial of medical care to an inmate with a serious medical need would result in an Eighth Amendment violation).

Mladek v. Day, 320 F. Supp. 2d 1373 (D. Ga., 2004) (dismissing the pretrial detainee's claim that a police officer violated his due process right to medical treatment when the officer failed to call a doctor or provide the inmate with ice to treat swelling and bruising of the inmate's wrist. The court dismissed the detainee's claim because the injury did not rise to the level of a serious medical need); Thomas v. Nassau County Correctional Center, 288 F. Supp. 2d 333 (E.D. N.Y. 2003) (holding that the inmate failed to state a serious medical condition to implicate an Eighth Amendment violation when the claimed that his hand was in pain).

§ 3:5 Initial Screening When Entering Facility
n. 3.
Richardson v. Nassau County, 277 F. Supp. 2d 196 (E.D. N.Y. 2003) (holding that the nurse who performed the pretrial detainee's entrance medical interview was not deliberately indifferent to the pretrial detainee's serious medical need, glaucoma, when she recorded the fact that the pretrial detainee suffered from glaucoma on his medical chart but did not at-

§ 3:5

tempt to provide or obtain any further treatment for the him. The court further held that "[t]he plaintiff has failed to set forth any allegations or evidence establishing that [the sheriff] had any personal involvement in delaying his treatment or that [the sheriff] knew that the pre-trial detainee's treatment was delayed" and therefore granted summary judgment in favor of the sheriff).

n. 5.

Page 380, note 5, add:
; Gibbs v. Grimmette, 254 F.3d 545 (5th Cir. 2001), cert. denied, 534 U.S. 1136, 122 S. Ct. 1083, 151 L. Ed. 2d 983 (2002) (prison officials' refusal to administer tuberculosis test to pretrial detainee upon request did not amount to deliberate indifference, where detainee did not show symptoms of active tuberculosis or come into contact with an infected individual).

§ 3:6 Emergency Care and Sick Call Procedures

n. 2.

Page 383, note 2, add:
; Natale v. Camden County Correctional Facility, 318 F.3d 575, 60 Fed. R. Evid. Serv. 679 (3d Cir. 2003) (fact question existed, precluding summary judgment, as to whether employees of prison health service were deliberately indifferent to serious medical needs of diabetic detainee in failing to administer insulin during first 21 hours of his incarceration, allegedly resulting in stroke); Mabrey v. Farthing, 280 F.3d 400 (4th Cir. 2002) (existence of disputed facts as to whether physicians and nurses who were involved in care of state inmate prior to his death from severe dehydration were entitled to qualified immunity defense, where depositions of some 20 witnesses did not agree on numerous issues, which could lead to conclusion that defendants were deliberately indifferent to prisoner's serious medical needs); El-Uri v. City of Chicago, 186 F. Supp. 2d 844 (N.D. Ill. 2002) (motion for summary judgment for defendant denied on claim of deliberate indifference to serious medical needs, where court found that officer would have to know that someone who was beaten in the head hard enough to knock him to the floor would need medical attention); Bozeman v. Orum, 199 F. Supp. 2d 1216 (M.D. Ala. 2002) (fact issues remained as to whether officers were deliberately indifferent to detainee's serious medical needs, where after beating inmate, they failed to resuscitate him after realizing that he was not breathing).

section 3:6 note 2, add:
Hopkins v. Warden, NH State Prison, 2004 DNH 88, 2004 WL 1125241 (D.N.H. 2004) (holding that the inmate stated a valid Eighth Amendment claim for lack of medical treatment when the inmate notified a prison official that he was experiencing severe abdominal pain but the official refused to call a nurse and watched the inmate "writhing in pain." When the nurse eventually made her rounds she determined that the inmate needed immediate medical care).

n. 3.

section 3:6 note 3, add:
Lolli v. County of Orange, 351 F.3d 410 (9th Cir. 2003) (reversing the district court's grant of summary judgment for prison officials on the detainee's claim that they were deliberately indifferent to his serious medi-

Medical Care § 3:6

cal need, diabetes, when they did not provide the inmate with food or insulin even though the detainee told officials that he was ill and appeared outwardly ill); Austin v. Johnson, 328 F.3d 204 (5th Cir. 2003) (denying a grant of qualified immunity on plaintiff's claim that they were deliberately indifferent to plaintiff's serious medical condition when they waited two hours before calling an ambulance after plaintiff show signs of dehydration such as vomiting and losing consciousness after a "march" at boot camp); Doe v. Gustavus, 294 F. Supp. 2d 1003 (E.D. Wis. 2003) (denying the prison nurses' motion for summary judgment and holding that a jury could find that the prison nurses were deliberately indifferent to the inmate's serious medical need when they refused to provide pain medication, a complete examination, or assistance to a pregnant inmate who was experiencing labor pains because the nurses falsely diagnosed the inmate's symptoms as false labor. As a result of the nurses' conduct, the inmate was forced to deliver her own baby while she was locked in a segregation cell).

Rodriguez v. Ames, 287 F. Supp. 2d 213 (W.D. N.Y. 2003) (holding that the inmate's right to privacy was not violated when the prison doctor discussed the inmate's health concerns with him in his cell and then performed a rectal examination in the inmate's cell with the inmates cellmate and a male nurse present because minor inconveniences and embarrassments are normal in prison in life and this particular medical condition, if disclosed, is not likely to subject the inmate to discrimination or harm).

n. 6.

Page 386, note 6, add:
; Boyd v. Rhode Island Dept. of Corrections, 160 F. Supp. 2d 213 (D.R.I. 2001) (inmate stated claim against physician for cruel and unusual punishment where physician knew of inmate's painful and serious condition and refused to provide proper medical treatment); Johnson v. Wright, 234 F. Supp. 2d 352 (S.D. N.Y. 2002) (prisoner stated claim for Eighth Amendment violation by alleging that he was denied therapy by prison officials for 15 months); Iseley v. Dragovich, 236 F. Supp. 2d 472 (E.D. Pa. 2002) (prison officials did not violate inmate's constitutional rights by refusing to treat his hepatitis C unless he submitted to psychological evaluation as requirement was reasonably related to legitimate penological interest, in light of evidence that treatment for hepatitis C could cause severe psychological side effects that could place inmate or others in danger).

section 3:6 note 6, add:
Brown v. Missouri Dept. of Corrections, 353 F.3d 1038 (8th Cir. 2004) (reversing the district court's dismissal of an inmate's claim of inadequate medical care and deliberate indifference to the inmate's safety when the inmate asked a prison official to put his seatbelt on for him in the prison van but the prison official refused and plaintiff was subsequently injured in a car accident. Plaintiff also alleges that prison officials would not provide him with access to the prison medical staff after the accident when he complained that he was having "severe complication").

n. 7.

Page 387, note 7, add:
; Livingston v. Goord, 225 F. Supp. 2d 321 (W.D. N.Y. 2002) (allegation that prison nurse caused certain treatment recommended by physician to

§ 3:6

be delayed, on the basis that the nurse "would give" prisoner "the run around," was not evidence sufficient to show that she caused any delay in prisoner's treatment or adversely affected his health); Davila v. Master, 2002 WL 1870459 (E.D. Pa. 2002) (prison nurse's failure to take inmate to doctor immediately after altercation with another prisoner did not constitute deliberate indifference to his serious medical needs, where nurse examined inmate and gave him ice for nosebleed, and inmate suffered no adverse consequences from one- or two-day delay in seeing doctor); Evicci v. Baker, 190 F. Supp. 2d 233 (D. Mass. 2002) (prisoner who had 16 sick call examinations over three-month period following alleged assault, at least four of which were with doctors, was not denied access to physician after alleged assault by guards, notwithstanding his allegation that he never received a promised follow-up visit with a doctor a few days after attack).

n. 8.

Page 388, note 8, add:
; Wallin v. Norman, 317 F.3d 558, 55 Fed. R. Serv. 3d 284, 2003 FED App. 0031P (6th Cir. 2003) (former prisoner stated claim of deliberate indifference against prison officials, where he claimed that prison officials delayed his access to medical treatment for a urinary tract infection and leg infection, causing unnecessary pain and resulting in residual injury); Terrance v. Northville Regional Psychiatric Hosp., 286 F.3d 834, 2002 FED App. 0115P (6th Cir. 2002) (genuine issue of material fact existed as to whether physician's conduct of allowing involuntarily committed mental patient to go outside hospital on extremely hot day, despite physician's knowledge of patient's health risks, such as diabetes, obesity, hypertension and increased risk of heat stroke from medication, and delaying treatment for hyperthermia, was grossly inadequate, precluding summary judgment, in action against psychiatrist for deliberate indifference arising from patient's death); Halpin v. Simmons, 33 Fed. Appx. 961 (10th Cir. 2002) (state prisoner alleged deliberate indifference to his medical condition, in violation of Eighth Amendment, through allegations that authorities ignored repeated requests for treatment of severe heart condition and for gastric pain); Bias v. Woods, 2002 WL 1750792 (N.D. Tex. 2002) (prison physician showed deliberate indifference to medical condition of inmate, in violation of inmate's Eighth Amendment rights, when she ordered him transported 150 miles to another facility, in comatose condition following suicide attempt, without attempting any local treatment); Ducally v. Rhode Island Dept. of Corrections, 160 F. Supp. 2d 220 (D.R.I. 2001) (plaintiff stated a claim of deliberate indifference when he alleged that prison officer, after intentionally slamming inmate's fingers in cell door, delayed his medical treatment); Baker v. Blanchette, 186 F. Supp. 2d 100 (D. Conn. 2001) (summary judgment for defendant denied because jury could find that four month delay for colostomy closure was excessive and that it demonstrated deliberate indifference); Scicluna v. Wells, 219 F. Supp. 2d 846 (E.D. Mich. 2002) (material issue of fact existed as to whether prison doctor was deliberately indifferent to inmate's medical needs by failing to evaluate inmate for three weeks after receiving referral for immediate neurological consultation).

section 3:6 note 8, add:
Austin v. Johnson, 328 F.3d 204 (5th Cir. 2003) (denying prison officials a grant of qualified immunity on plaintiff's claim that they were deliberately indifferent to the plaintiff's serious medical condition when they waited

MEDICAL CARE § 3:6

two hours before calling an ambulance after plaintiff show signs of dehydration such as vomiting and losing consciousness after a "march" at boot camp); Scicluna v. Wells, 345 F.3d 441, 2003 FED App. 0350P (6th Cir. 2003) (denying a grant of qualified immunity to a prison doctor on the inmate's Eighth Amendment claim that the doctor was deliberately indifferent to his serious medical need when the doctor waited for three weeks to examine the inmate even though the inmate had an emergency treatment report specifying that he required an immediate neurological consultation. The court held that viewing the evidence in a light most favorable to the inmate, there is a material issue of fact as to whether the three week delay constituted deliberate indifference).

n. 9.

Page 390, note 9, add:
; Shepard v. Sullivan, 65 Fed. Appx. 677 (10th Cir. 2003) (medical staff members were not deliberately indifferent to inmate's serious medical needs, as result of their denial of post-cancer reconstructive surgery, where inmate failed to demonstrate harm of substantial nature resulting from delay); Jurgevich v. McGary, 63 Fed. Appx. 448 (10th Cir. 2003) (state prison officials' delay in permitting surgery to alleviate inmate's heel spurs did not amount to deliberate indifference to inmate's serious medical needs, where request for surgery was ultimately approved after inmate's podiatrist supplied needed documentation); Pabon v. Goord, 2003 WL 1787268 (S.D. N.Y. 2003) (inmate failed to prove that his health care providers were deliberately indifferent to his spinal condition and pain, so as to support an Eighth Amendment claim, despite claim that prisoner endured a nearly three-year wait for surgery); Nelson v. California Dept. of Corrections, 2003 WL 946412 (N.D. Cal. 2003) (inmate failed to show that medical coordinator at prison knew that not expediting a pulmonary function test ordered by a physician would result in a substantial risk of medical harm to the inmate, and thus, could not show that the coordinator was deliberately indifferent to his medical needs); Rossby v. Santa Clara County, 2003 WL 297537 (N.D. Cal. 2003) (delay of three hours in treating inmate's injuries sustained when he fell out of his upper bunk did not rise to the level of deliberate indifference to his medical needs); McCoy v. Goord, 255 F. Supp. 2d 233 (S.D. N.Y. 2003) (at most, allegations that member of state prison's medical staff kept inmate waiting for 25 minutes and then sent him back to his cell without treating his chest pains amounted to claim of negligence, and were insufficient to support Eighth Amendment claim for deliberate indifference). See also Bright v. Martin, 37 Fed. Appx. 136 (6th Cir. 2002), cert. denied, 537 U.S. 956, 123 S. Ct. 427, 154 L. Ed. 2d 306 (2002) (prisoner failed to prove that he suffered detrimental effect from alleged delay in diagnosis of his alleged liver disease, in violation of Eighth Amendment, since prisoner did not place verifying medical evidence into record to establish any detrimental effect resulting from delay in treatment); Love v. Taft, 30 Fed. Appx. 336 (6th Cir. 2002) (Ohio correctional officials and medical personnel were not deliberately indifferent to prisoner's serious medical needs in alleged delay and proper diagnosis and treatment of his hepatitis, where inmate failed to allege any actual detrimental effect resulting from delay in treatment); Zimmerman v. Prison Health Services, Inc., 36 Fed. Appx. 202 (7th Cir. 2002) (corrections official did not act with deliberate indifference to health needs of inmate suffering from hepatitis C, where delay to inoculate resulted from bureaucratic obstacles and possible negligence rather than

§ 3:6

deliberate indifference); Perkins v. Lawson, 312 F.3d 872 (7th Cir. 2002) (prison officials were not deliberately indifferent to serious medical needs of inmate, who was beaten, when nurse sent him to hospital, where twice he was found not to be in serious distress, a finding which seemed to be in error but which jail officials were not deliberately indifferent for relying on); Dixon v. Howe, 44 Fed. Appx. 274 (9th Cir. 2002) (any delay that prisoner experienced before seeing a specialist did not constitute deliberate indifference because prisoner failed to demonstrate that delay caused him any harm); Wallace v. City of Columbus, 2002 WL 31844688 (S.D. Ohio 2002) (delay of hours by county and sheriff in providing detainee with medical treatment after she was sprayed with mace by police officer did not rise to level of a constitutional violation); Smith v. Franklin County, 227 F. Supp. 2d 667 (E.D. Ky. 2002) (complaint failed to state claim for cruel and unusual punishment on basis of deprivation and delay of medical care where alleged deprivation of medication for two and a half days and decision not to take plaintiff to hospital after her seizure did not adversely affect plaintiff); Rodriguez v. Ames, 224 F. Supp. 2d 555 (W.D. N.Y. 2002) (physician's seven-day delay in treating prisoner's bowel disorder did not constitute deliberate indifference to serious medical need under Eighth Amendment, where prisoner admitted that he suffered no pain as a result of his condition); Rodriguez v. Ames, 224 F. Supp. 2d 555 (W.D. N.Y. 2002) (nurse practitioner's alleged delay in treatment of prisoner's hands after an altercation with his cellmate did not constitute deliberate indifference to serious medical need under Eighth Amendment). And see Lindsay v. Dunleavy, 177 F. Supp. 2d 398 (E.D. Pa. 2001) (state prisoner's allegations that physician failed to diagnose his broken jaw and order an X-ray from which he could have diagnosed the fracture did not establish "deliberate indifference" to prisoner's serious medical needs in violation of the Eighth Amendment); Howard v. Calhoun County, 148 F. Supp. 2d 883 (W.D. Mich. 2001) (no showing of deliberate indifference on part of corrections officer who, after seeing inmate collapse in TV room, spent the first 10-15 minutes thereafter preoccupied with clearing the room, instead of directly administering to inmate, who later died of a heart attack, when officer thought that inmate was only suffering from a seizure).

n. 10.

Page 391 note 10, add:
; Sulton v. Wright, 265 F. Supp. 2d 292 (S.D. N.Y. 2003) (prison inmate stated claim of deliberate indifference to torn ligaments in left knee by establishing four-year delay in necessary corrective surgery); Warren v. Shelby County, Tenn., 191 F. Supp. 2d 980 (W.D. Tenn. 2001) (findings of Department of Justice that inmates at jail did not receive medical treatment in a timely fashion and a showing of failure to provide medical care to a single individual over a short period of time were insufficient to demonstrate a custom or policy of inaction on the part of the defendants).

§ 3:7 Periodic Examinations and Necessary Treatment

n. 1.

section 3:7 note 1, add:
Doe v. Gustavus, 294 F. Supp. 2d 1003 (E.D. Wis. 2003) (denying the prison nurses' motion for summary judgment and holding that a jury could

find that the prison nurses were deliberately indifferent to the inmate's serious medical need when they refused to provide pain medication, a complete examination, or assistance to a pregnant inmate who was experiencing labor pains because the nurses falsely diagnosed the inmate's symptoms as false labor. As a result of the nurses' conduct, the inmate was forced to deliver her own baby while she was locked in a segregation cell); Smith v. County of Bucks, 28 Nat'l Disability Law Rep. P 55, 2004 WL 868278 (E.D. Pa. 2004) (denying the prison officers' motion to dismiss the claim that they were deliberately indifferent to the plaintiff's son's serious medical need when both the plaintiff and her son informed the officials of the changing conditions of a mole on the inmate's chest and requested a biopsy. Despite the inmate's symptoms, he did not receive a biopsy on the mole for several months. The mole was in fact cancerous and the inmate died of cancer after being released from prison. From the evidence, a jury could find that the prison officials were deliberately indifferent to the inmate's serious medical need because cancer is a serious medical need and both the inmate and the plaintiff told the prison officials about the mole. Furthermore, the court denied the prison officials qualified immunity because any reasonable official would know that the denial of medical care to an inmate with a serious medical need would result in an Eighth Amendment violation);Scicluna v. Wells, 345 F.3d 441, 2003 FED App. 0350P (6th Cir. 2003) (denying a grant of qualified immunity to a prison doctor on the inmate's Eighth Amendment claim that the doctor was deliberately indifferent to his serious medical need when the doctor waited for three weeks to examine the inmate even though the inmate had an emergency treatment report specifying that he required an immediate neurological consultation. The court held that viewing the evidence in a light most favorable to the inmate, there is a material issue of fact as to whether the three week delay constituted deliberate indifference); Benjamin v. Schwartz, 299 F. Supp. 2d 196 (S.D. N.Y. 2004) (granting in part and denying in part a prison doctor's motion to dismiss an inmate's claim that the doctor was deliberately indifferent to his serious medical need when the doctor prescribed shoulder surgery and then did not complete the surgery for over one year from the diagnosis. Furthermore, when the doctor did complete the surgery he was negligent. The court granted the defendant's motion to dismiss the medical malpractice claim because negligence does not rise to the level of an Eighth Amendment violation, however defendant's motion to dismiss was denied as to the delay in treatment claim because delaying surgery for over a year could constitute deliberate indifference).

n. 4.

Page 394 note 4, add:
; Lawson v. Dallas County, 286 F.3d 257 (5th Cir. 2002) (finding that members of jail's medical staff acted with deliberate indifference to the serious medical needs of paraplegic inmate was supported by evidence that all of the nurses who primarily treated inmate had actual knowledge of the risk posed by the development and worsening of inmate's ulcers and that the nurses responded to it by disobeying doctor's orders); Smith v. Michigan, 256 F. Supp. 2d 704 (E.D. Mich. 2003) (estate of correctional facility inmate alleged sufficiently serious deprivation of medical services, in violation of Eighth Amendment, by alleging that officials ignored inmate's request for follow-up medication and monitoring, after his return from hospital, causing him to develop fatal pneumonia).

§ 3:7　　　　　　　　　　　　　　　　　　　Rights of Prisoners

n. 5.

Page 394, note 5, after the Patrick v. Staples citation and parenthetical, add:
; Newsome v. Peterson, 66 Fed. Appx. 550 (6th Cir. 2003) (state prisoner's allegations that correctional officer deliberately failed to obtain prescribed medication for his migraine, and that he therefore suffered for nine hours from migraine, stated claim of Eighth Amendment violation); Halpin v. Simmons, 33 Fed. Appx. 961 (10th Cir. 2002) (state prisoner alleged deliberate indifference to his medical condition through allegations that authorities refused to provide medications ordered by cardiologist); Walker v. Dallas County Sheriff's Medical Dept., 2002 WL 31553930 (N.D. Tex. 2002) (county inmate's allegations that despite prescription, two jail nurses consistently refused to administer his medication were sufficient to state claim against nurses for denial of medical care in violation of Eighth Amendment); U.S. v. Wallen, 177 F. Supp. 2d 455 (D. Md. 2001) (court ordered that defendant be detained at a different detention facility, since detainee's allegation that he was improperly medicated, necessitating a three-day hospital stay, supported the conclusion that current facility could not provide adequate medical care).

Page 394, note 5, add:
; Parker v. Michigan Dept. of Corrections, 65 Fed. Appx. 922 (6th Cir. 2003) (probation officer did not violate state inmate's Eighth Amendment rights by depriving him of his blood pressure and back pain medication while he was in segregation pending resolution of prison misconduct charge) Robinson v. Hager, 292 F.3d 560, 59 Fed. R. Evid. Serv. 244 (8th Cir. 2002) (reversing denial of judgment as a matter of law for defendants, the court of appeals held that inmate, who suffered stroke after being deprived of medication for a month, could not recover absent expert medical testimony on causation); Livingston v. Goord, 225 F. Supp. 2d 321 (W.D. N.Y. 2002) (alleged deprivation of prisoner's pain medication did not amount to deliberate indifference to serious medical need in violation of Eighth Amendment, as prisoner's pain was not debilitating or intense); Baskerville v. Blot, 224 F. Supp. 2d 723 (S.D. N.Y. 2002) (prison nurse's failure to refill prisoner's blood pressure medication for several days did not show deliberate indifference to prisoner's serious medical needs); Turner v. Kight, 192 F. Supp. 2d 391 (D. Md. 2002), reconsideration granted in part, 217 F. Supp. 2d 680 (D. Md. 2002) (correctional officer was not deliberately indifferent to pretrial detainee's medical needs when he failed to dispense medication, as officers were not permitted to, but did alert detention facility's medical staff).

n. 6.

Page 396, note 6, add following the Inmates of Allegheny County Jail v. Peirce citation and parenthetical:
; Bowers v. Milwaukee County Jail Medical Staff, 52 Fed. Appx. 295 (7th Cir. 2002) (county jail's medical staff subjected inmate to objectively serious risk to his future health sufficient to support his Eighth Amendment claim by erroneously giving him another inmate's prescription drugs); Arce v. Superintendent, 2002 WL 1808234 (S.D. N.Y. 2002) (prison inmate failed to state claim that authorities treated medical condition with deliberate indifference, as required for Eighth Amendment violation, when he alleged that intravenous medication was administered by unauthorized personnel); Evans v. Bonner, 196 F. Supp. 2d 252 (E.D. N.Y. 2002) (county

MEDICAL CARE § 3:7

correctional center nurses' alleged untimely dispensing of inmate's HIV medication did not rise to a sufficiently serious level as to constitute deliberate indifference, even if the aches, pains and joint problems suffered by the inmate were caused by the untimely medication).

n. 7.

Page 396, note 7, add:
; Hogan v. Oklahoma Dept. of Corrections, 65 Fed. Appx. 662 (10th Cir. 2003) (prison officials would not be held liable for allegedly violating prisoner's Eighth Amendment rights by forcing him to engage in work which caused him pain or aggravated a prior medical condition, where his medical restrictions from his prior prison were two to four years old and expired); Pate v. Peel, 256 F. Supp. 2d 1326 (N.D. Fla. 2003) (inmate who was diagnosed as HIV positive and was infected with Hepatitis C failed to show that prison nurse acted with deliberate indifference in clearing inmate for unrestricted duty, where at time of decision, inmate was "healthy-looking" in appearance).

n. 8.

section 3:7 note 8, add:
Richardson v. Goord, 347 F.3d 431 (2d Cir. 2003) (per curiam) (vacating a grant of summary judgment in favor of a prison official on plaintiff's claim that the prison official acted with deliberate indifference by allowing the inmate's prescription to be changed because plaintiff raised a question of fact as to whether the prison official had subjective knowledge of the inmate's condition. Moreover, the inmate could not show that the prison officials knew that he was not receiving his medication on the schedule proscribed by his doctor because of logistical problems with the administration of the medication).

n. 9.

section 3:7 note 9, add:
Lumaj v. Williams, 2004 U.S. Dist 8178 (S.D.N.Y. 2004) (holding that the inmate failed to state an Eighth Amendment claim against the prison doctor because the doctor did not provide on-going treatment for the inmate's injuries. Here, the doctor properly stitched the inmate wounds, which he obtained in a fight with another inmate, and provided antibiotics to prevent infection. After the doctor treated the inmate, the inmate was transfer out of the facility to which the doctor was assigned. Therefore the doctor was no longer required to provide care to the inmate); Hernandez v. Keane, 341 F.3d 137, 62 Fed. R. Evid. Serv. 235 (2d Cir. 2003) (holding that plaintiff produced insufficient evidence to establish that any one of the defendants was deliberately indifferent to plaintiff's serious medical need when plaintiff's hand did not recover from surgery); Alsina Ortiz v. Laboy, 286 F. Supp. 2d 133 (D.P.R. 2003) (holding that prison officials and the prison doctor were not deliberately indifferent to plaintiff's son's serious medical need when plaintiff's son was transferred from prison to a medical center where he received a CT scan a few days after he was hit in the head during a prison riot. Upon realizing that plaintiff's son was completely paralyzed in one side of his body and that he was suffering from Tozoplamosis and AIDS, the defendants provided plaintiff's son with frequent medical exams, proper medication, and a wheelchair. Therefore, the defendants cannot be held deliberately indifferent notwithstanding the fact that the plaintiff's son died while in custody); Ciarpaglini v. Saini,

§ 3:7   Rights of Prisoners

352 F.3d 328 (7th Cir. 2003) (dismissing that inmate's claim that he was denied adequate medical care because the inmate's claim did not state that he was denied medical care, rather it merely stated that he had a disagreement with doctors regarding the termination of the his medication for Attention Deficit Hyperactivity Disorder and Panic Disorder); Kretchmar v. Com., 831 A.2d 793 (Pa. Commw. Ct. 2003), appeal denied, 577 Pa. 728, 847 A.2d 1289 (2004) (holding that prison officials were not deliberately indifferent to plaintiff's allergies when they refused to provide him with Clairtin, but provided him with other medication to treat his allergies because an inmate "may not invoke a deliberate indifference claim to second-guess the adequacy of a course of treatment, which remains a question of sound profession judgment"); Perez v. Hawk, 302 F. Supp. 2d 9 (E.D. N.Y. 2004) (holding that the prison inmate failed to assert an Eighth Amendment claim for inadequate medical care or inadequate prison conditions when plaintiff suffered from a serious rash, swollen tongue, swollen feet which "had swollen to the size of footballs," rapid heartbeat, joint swelling, a "grotesquely swollen" groin area, and blood and mucus in his waste. At this point, the prison officials provided him with anti-histamine treatment but did not explore other courses of treatment when the anti-histamine treatment was not effective. Plaintiff informed the prison officials that he believed that his symptoms were coming from chemicals in the prison water supply; however, the prison officials insisted that the rash was from the plaintiff's soap and did not check the water supply. Furthermore, the prison officials told the inmate that they would deny his transfer to another facility unless he accepted as true that his symptoms were a result of his soap. However, the inmate was transferred to a new facility where his symptoms persisted. The inmate continued to claim that his symptoms were a result of unsafe chemicals in the prison water supply. Prison officials at the new facility did not explore the inmate's claim; however, they did provide the inmate with antihistamines and antibiotics. The inmate met with the prison doctor and told the doctor that he had conclusive evidence that his symptoms were caused by chemicals in the water supply. The doctor dismissed this claim and rather than ordering the inmate to see a dermatologist or an allergist, the doctor ordered the inmate to see the staff psychologist. The court held that the inmate's claim did not meet the deliberate indifference standard because he received frequent medical attention while he was incarcerated. The fact that the medical treatment was ineffective or amounted to negligence on the part of the prison officials is not sufficient to prove an Eighth Amendment violation without a showing that the prison officials possessed a sufficiently culpable state of mind; Byers v. Strachan, 69 Fed. Appx. 274 (6th Cir. 2003) (holding that the inmate's claim that a delay in treatment to a back injury he received during a transfer did not rise to the level of a constitutional violation because the plaintiff could not show that the delay had a detrimental effect on his health); Murtaugh v. State, 268 Wis. 2d 295, 2003 WI App 244, 671 N.W.2d 865 (Ct. App. 2003) (holding that prison officials conduct did not rise to the level of an Eighth Amendment violation because of a delay in treatment when plaintiff fell off the top bunk bed seriously injuring his shoulder and in response prison officials examined plaintiff and provided him with pain medication. After the plaintiff complained that the pain medication was insufficient, he was examined again and surgery was recommended, however, plaintiff was discharged from prison before the surgery was scheduled).

MEDICAL CARE § 3:7

n. 12.

Page 400, note 12, add:
; Shepard v. Sullivan, 65 Fed. Appx. 677 (10th Cir. 2003) (medical staff members were not deliberately indifferent to inmate's serious medical needs, as result of their denial of post-cancer reconstructive surgery, where inmate failed to sign release form necessary to obtain medical records to ascertain need for surgery).

n. 13.

section 3:7 note 13, add:
R.T. v. Gross, 298 F. Supp. 2d 289 (N.D. N.Y. 2003) (holding that the inmate did not assert a serious medical need to meet the first prong of an Eighth Amendment medical care claim when plaintiff was diagnosed with bi-polar disorder which manifested itself as periods of stability and instability because the periods of instability were usually associated with plaintiff's failure to take his medication).

Page 400, the second sentence after the word "unconstitutional," add new footnote.

[13.1]Wright v. Sapp, 59 Fed. Appx. 799 (6th Cir. 2003) (prisoner failed to allege facts that, if proven, would rise to the level of deliberate indifference required to support an Eighth Amendment claim, where prisoner's assertions, at most, alleged negligence and disagreement with the medical treatment that he received during his incarceration); Rossby v. Santa Clara County, 2003 WL 297537 (N.D. Cal. 2003) (inmate claiming that he received inadequate medical care for injuries sustained when he fell out of his upper bunk at most alleged negligence, and thus failed to state a claim under the Eighth Amendment); McCoy v. Goord, 255 F. Supp. 2d 233 (S.D. N.Y. 2003) (at most, allegations that member of state prison's medical staff kept inmate waiting for 25 minutes and then sent him back to his cell without treating his chest pains amounted to claim of negligence, and were insufficient to support Eighth Amendment claim for deliberate indifference to inmate's serious medical needs); Long v. Lafko, 254 F. Supp. 2d 444 (S.D. N.Y. 2003) (prison nurse's conduct of applying wrong eye drops to inmate's eyes, allegedly causing permanent eye injury, did not support an Eighth Amendment violation, as failure to check medication before administering it was merely negligent or unprofessional); Morales v. Mackalm, 278 F.3d 126 (2d Cir. 2002) (physician's alleged conduct of injuring inmate by attempting to insert a feeding tube did not support a claim for medical indifference under the Eighth Amendment as it alleged mere negligence); Parks v. McCoy, 35 Fed. Appx. 239 (7th Cir. 2002) (allegation that prisoner was misdiagnosed as suffering from tuberculosis, and was forced to take medication which made him sick, was insufficient to state Eighth Amendment claim for inadequate medical care; claim was, at most, one for malpractice); Lynch v. Robinson, 2002 WL 1949731 (N.D. Ill. 2002) (giving inmate substitute medication, when inmate's file stated that he was allergic to it, may have been negligence or malpractice, but it did not rise to level of deliberate indifference).

n. 14.

Page page 400, note 14, add following the *Givens v. Jones* citation and parenthetical:
; Hall v. Tyszkiewicz, 28 Fed. Appx. 493 (6th Cir. 2002), cert. denied, 537 U.S. 875, 123 S. Ct. 288, 154 L. Ed. 2d 128 (2002) (prisoner's claim that he

§ 3:7   RIGHTS OF PRISONERS

did not receive adequate treatment for esophageal reflux did not state an Eighth Amendment violation, as prisoner's disagreement with the defendants' medical judgment concerning the proper medication and medical aids for his condition did not evidence deliberate indifference); Stewart v. Taft, 235 F. Supp. 2d 763 (N.D. Ohio 2002) (prison officials did not violate Eighth Amendment right of inmate to receive adequate medical care, when they provided him with six months regimen of tuberculosis drug, when nine month regimen was allegedly superior); Tribe v. Englelsgjerd, 2002 WL 31051984 (E.D. Mich. 2002) (prison physician's alleged refusal to prescribe medication of prisoner's choice for arthritis pain did not violate Eighth Amendment); Joyner v. Greiner, 195 F. Supp. 2d 500 (S.D. N.Y. 2002) (parolee who alleged that he had severe back that was not treated did not state an actionable claim, where he was given medication and therapy and the complaint was merely a disagreement over the kind of treatment he received); Christy v. Robinson, 216 F. Supp. 2d 398 (D.N.J. 2002) (misdiagnosis or preference for a certain type of treatment will not alone rise to the level of deliberate indifference).

section 3:7 note 14, add:

n. 15.

section 3:7 note 15, add:
Ciarpaglini v. Saini, 352 F.3d 328 (7th Cir. 2003); Kretchmar v. Com., 831 A.2d 793 (Pa. Commw. Ct. 2003), appeal denied, 577 Pa. 728, 847 A.2d 1289 (2004); Batchelder v. Arnold, 291 F. Supp. 2d 820 (N.D. Ind. 2003).

n. 16.

section 3:7 note 16, add:
Graham ex rel. Estate of Graham v. County of Washtenaw, 358 F.3d 377, 2004 FED App. 0043P (6th Cir. 2004) (dismissing the inmate's claim that a municipal policy of providing medical care through licensed nurses at the county jail and instructing jail officials to give deference to the nurse's medical decisions is unconstitutional. In this case, the plaintiff claimed that this policy contributed to the death of a detainee at the jail. The decedent was arrested for possession of marijuana. After he was arrested, the decedent swallowed about an ounce of cocaine. When they arrived at the police station the decedent began to exhibit erratic behavior. The jail officials asked the decedent what he had taken. The inmate told the jail officials that he smoked marijuana and drank alcohol. Because the decedent was displaying erratic behavior, the jail official requested that decedent by examined by one of the nurses. The nurse asked the decedent what he took that night and the decedent again answered marijuana and alcohol. He also told the nurse that he suffered from asthma. The nurse gave him albuterol, an asthma medication that increases heart rate, and tested his blood alcohol content (BAC). The BAC test showed that he was not intoxicated the nurse released him for an interview. After the interview the decedent appeared too sick to go through the booking process and the jail officials placed him in the general cell. While in the general cell, the decedent told the other inmates that he ingested the cocaine, but did not tell the nurse or the jail officials. The inmates in the cell called to jail officials because the decedent looked very sick and appeared to be having a seizure. When the nurse arrived she asked him what he had taken that night and he told her he took some pills. The nurse took the decedent's heart rate, which was elevated, but she attributed the increased heart rate to the marijuana. About ten minutes later the inmates called

MEDICAL CARE § 3:9

for the prison officials again because the decedent had fainted. The decedent was taken to the medical room where he had multiple seizures. The jail officials called an ambulance and he was brought to the emergency room where he was pronounced dead).

n. 17.

section 3:7 note 17, add:
Means v. Cullen, 297 F. Supp. 2d 1148 (W.D. Wis. 2003) (holding that the prison psychologist did not violate the inmate's Eighth Amendment right to adequate medical treatment when the doctor allegedly told the inmate that nobody would care if he lived or died because the doctor's comments, while insensitive, do not rise to the level of an Eighth Amendment violation. Furthermore, the court held that the plaintiff's claim that he was denied the medical care he requested must fail because while inmates are entitled to adequate medical treatment, they are not entitled to the medical treatment of their choice).

n. 18.

section 3:7 note 18, add:
Austin v. Johnson, 328 F.3d 204 (5th Cir. 2003) (denying prison officials a grant of qualified immunity on plaintiff's claim that they were deliberately indifferent to plaintiff's serious medical condition when they waited two hours before calling an ambulance after plaintiff show signs of dehydration such as vomiting and losing consciousness after a "march" at boot camp); Scicluna v. Wells, 345 F.3d 441, 2003 FED App. 0350P (6th Cir. 2003) (denying a grant of qualified immunity to a prison doctor on the inmate's Eighth Amendment claim that the doctor was deliberately indifferent to his serious medical need when the doctor waited for three weeks to examine the inmate even though the inmate had an emergency treatment report specifying that he required an immediate neurological consultation. The court held that viewing the evidence in a light most favorable to the inmate, there is a material issue of fact as to whether the three week delay constituted deliberate indifference); Lolli v. County of Orange, 351 F.3d 410 (9th Cir. 2003) (reversing the district court's grant of summary judgment for prison officials on the detainee's claim that they were deliberately indifferent to his serious medical need, diabetes, when they did not provide the inmate with food or insulin even though the detainee told officials that he was ill and he appeared outwardly ill).

§ 3:9 Staff

n. 1.

Page 408, note 1, add following Duran v. Anaya citation and parenthetical:
; Hallett v. Morgan, 296 F.3d 732 (9th Cir. 2002) (low number of mental health staff members at state prison did not violate the Eighth Amendment; outpatient services appeared to meet the needs of the inmates, patient requests for mental health services were reviewed by the next business day and were addressed substantively within four days, and as to inpatient mental health services, group counseling was provided on a weekly basis and prisoners were provided with a treatment plan and their medications were monitored by the prison psychiatrist and other staff members).

n. 8.

section 3:9 note 8, add:

§ 3:9   Rights of Prisoners

Graham ex rel. Estate of Graham v. County of Washtenaw, 358 F.3d 377, 2004 FED App. 0043P (6th Cir. 2004) (dismissing the inmate's claim that a municipal policy of providing medical care through licensed nurses at the county jail and instructing jail officials to give deference to the nurse's medical decisions is constitutional. In this case, the plaintiff claimed that this policy contributed to the death of a detainee at the jail. The decedent was arrested for possession of marijuana. After he was arrested, the decedent swallowed about an ounce of cocaine. When they arrived at the police station the decedent began to exhibit erratic behavior. The jail officials asked the decedent what he had taken. The inmate told the jail officials that he smoked marijuana and drank alcohol. Because the decedent was displaying erratic behavior, the jail official requested that decedent by examined by one of the nurses. The nurse asked the decedent what he took that night and the decedent again answered marijuana and alcohol. He also told the nurse that he suffered from asthma. The nurse gave him albuterol, an asthma medication that increases heart rate, and tested his blood alcohol content (BAC). The BAC test showed that he was not intoxicated the nurse released him for an interview. After the interview the decedent appeared too sick to go through the booking process and the jail officials placed him in the general cell. While in the general cell, the decedent told the other inmates that he ingested the cocaine, but did not tell the nurse or the jail officials. The inmates in the cell called to jail officials because the decedent looked very sick and appeared to be having a seizure. When the nurse arrived she asked him what he had taken that night and he told her he took some pills. The nurse took the decedent's heart rate, which was elevated, but she attributed the increased heart rate to the marijuana. About ten minutes later the inmates called for the prison officials again because the decedent had fainted. The decedent was taken to the medical room where he had multiple seizures. The jail officials called an ambulance and he was brought to the emergency room where he was pronounced dead).

n. 9.
   Page 415, note 9, add:
; Smith v. Board of County Com'rs of County of Lyon, 216 F. Supp. 2d 1209 (D. Kan. 2002) (mere fact that county had chosen to provide medical care by means of referral to medical providers who were not on staff at the jail, but who had not been shown to be either unavailable or incompetent, was insufficient to show failure to train rising to level of deliberate indifference); Smith v. LeJeune, 203 F. Supp. 2d 1260 (D. Wyo. 2002) (wife, following death of husband at county detention facility, did not state a failure-to-train claim against physician, where physician provided nurses with protocol and policies to deal with alcohol withdrawal and conducted monthly meetings, and nurses were licensed).

§ 3:10   Records

n. 1.
   Page 418, note 1, add:
; Montgomery v. Pinchak, 294 F.3d 492 (3d Cir. 2002) (mere loss of inmate's medical records by prison officials, physician, and corporate medical provider did not rise to requisite level of deliberate indifference to demonstrate prima facie case of cruel and unusual punishment based on denial of medical care).

MEDICAL CARE § 3:11

Page 419, fourth sentence after the word "relationship," add new footnote.

[1.1] Gowins v. Greiner, 24 Nat ¶ 1172002 WL 1770772 (S.D. N.Y. 2002) (prison doctor did not violate inmate's due process right to privacy or confidentiality when he submitted portion of inmate's medical record in response to grievance asserting that doctor's treatment of inmate had been inadequate and that he did not want to treat inmate and his injuries, as disclosure made by doctor was reasonably related to legitimate penological interest of adjudicating inmate's grievance and establishing whether care he received was adequate).

§ 3:11 Dental Care

n. 14.

Page 423, note 14, add:
; Williamson v. Brewington-Carr, 173 F. Supp. 2d 235 (D. Del. 2001) (inmate stated claim for Eighth Amendment violation when he alleged that he was denied proper dental treatment for gum infection and loss of teeth and that the health services were aware of his dental problems and the health risks associated with them).

section 3:11 note 14, add:
Wall v. Dion, 257 F. Supp. 2d 316 (D. Me. 2003) (denying defendants' motion to dismiss plaintiff's claim that the defendants were deliberately indifferent to the plaintiff's serious dental needs when he alleged that the dentist refused to treat his infected tooth because the inmate had Hepatitis C and the dentist did not have proper protection. Since the plaintiff's tooth went untreated, it turned to gangrene, which eventually led to a misaligned jaw).

Goodnow v. Palm, 264 F. Supp. 2d 125 (D. Vt. 2003) (holding that the inmate raised a triable issue of fact to overcome defendant's motion for summary judgment when the plaintiff alleged that the defendant was deliberately indifferent to his serious dental needs when plaintiff complained a pain in his tooth and was examined by many members of the dental staff who agreed that he needed treatment but failed to treat him).

n. 15.

Page 423, note 15, add following the Clifton v. Robinson citation and parenthetical:
; Manney v. Monroe, 151 F. Supp. 2d 976 (N.D. Ill. 2001) (issue of material fact existed as to whether treatment of serious dental condition with only Tylenol and Motrin demonstrated deliberate indifference).

Page 423, note 15, add:
; Hallett v. Morgan, 296 F.3d 732 (9th Cir. 2002) (quality of dental care at state prison did not violate the Eighth Amendment, where there was no showing that delays in treatment occurred to patients with problems so severe that delays would cause significant harm); Kajfasz v. Department of Rehabilitation and Correction, 2002-Ohio-4145, 2002 WL 31966950 (Ohio Ct. Cl. 2002), adopted, 2002-Ohio-5115, 2002 WL 31956501 (Ohio Ct. Cl. 2002), judgment aff'd, 2003-Ohio-2580, 2003 WL 21152523 (Ohio Ct. App. 10th Dist. Franklin County 2003) (delay in providing dental treat-

§ 3:11   Rights of Prisoners

ment to prison inmate did not support claim of general negligence against Department of Rehabilitation and Correction, where Department informed inmate that he was on list for treatment for a problem concerning a tooth and informed him what to do if he had immediate problem).

n. 16.

   Page 424, note 16, add after Rial v. McGinness citation and parenthetical:
; Hallett v. Morgan, 296 F.3d 732 (9th Cir. 2002) (lack of routine teeth cleaning did not constitute deliberate indifference to serious medical needs).

n. 17.

   Page 424, note 17, add:
; Farrow v. West, 320 F.3d 1235 (11th Cir. 2003) (absent evidence that nurse herself subjectively was aware of a serious risk of harm to prisoner, prisoner's allegations that nurse displayed deliberate indifference towards his serious medical need, by ordering her staff not to provide dental care to him, failed to state claim for violation of his Eighth Amendment rights); Rivera v. Goord, 253 F. Supp. 2d 735 (S.D. N.Y. 2003) (oral surgeon's conduct of removing tissue from inmate's mouth, instead of extracting wisdom tooth, was medical malpractice, but such conduct did not give rise to claim for deliberate indifference).

n. 18.

   Page 425, note 18, add:
; Wilson v. Wilkinson, 62 Fed. Appx. 590 (6th Cir. 2003) (state prison officials were not deliberately indifferent to inmate's serious medical needs, despite inmate's dissatisfaction with his dental treatment, where dentist expressed his professional opinion that inmate's symptoms were not urgent or life threatening in nature and could be remedied through preventive and corrective treatment); Scott v. Gibson, 37 Fed. Appx. 422 (10th Cir. 2002) (difference of opinion as to the need for medical and dental treatment or adequacy of any treatment did not constitute deliberate indifference to prisoner's serious medical needs for purposes of Eighth Amendment claim); Sirois v. Prison Health Services, 233 F. Supp. 2d 52 (D. Me. 2002) (dental care provided to inmate at state correctional facilities was not so inadequate that it amounted to cruel and unusual punishment, where dentists did not comply with inmate's request that they pull all of his teeth and provide him with dentures because dental staff did not think full dentures were proper course of treatment).

§ 3:12   Eye Care

n. 1.

   Page 426, note 1, add:
; Castillo v. U.S., 44 Fed. Appx. 732 (7th Cir. 2002) (prisoner's contention that director's failure to remove eye harmed him was mere disagreement with director's medical judgment and could not sustain deliberate indifference claim); Jones v. Van Fleit, 49 Fed. Appx. 626 (7th Cir. 2002) (prisoner, who suffered permanently blurred vision in one eye after optometrist did not immediately treat retinal tear following eye injury, failed to prove that optometrist acted with deliberate indifference, where optometrist did not initially observe the retinal tear and mere negligence was not enough

Medical Care   § 3:13

to prove constitutional violation); Long v. Lafko, 254 F. Supp. 2d 444 (S.D. N.Y. 2003) (prison nurse's conduct of applying wrong eye drops to inmate's eyes, allegedly causing permanent eye injury, did not support an Eighth Amendment violation, as failure to check medication before administering it was merely negligent or unprofessional).

section 3:12 note 1, add:
Richardson v. Nassau County, 277 F. Supp. 2d 196 (E.D. N.Y. 2003) (holding that the nurse who performed the pretrial detainee's entrance medical interview was not deliberately indifferent to the pretrial detainee's serious medical need, glaucoma, when she recorded the fact that the pretrial detainee suffered from glaucoma on his medical chart but did not attempt to provide or obtain any further treatment for the him. The court further held that "[t]he plaintiff has failed to set forth any allegations or evidence establishing that [the sheriff] had any personal involvement in delaying his treatment or that [the sheriff] knew that the pre-trial detainee's treatment was delayed" and therefore granted summary judgment in favor of the sheriff).

n. 2.

Page 426, note 2, add:
; Taylor v. Smolinski, 2003 WL 21383015 (W.D. N.Y. 2003) (failure to issue new prescription for eyeglasses was not deliberately indifferent to inmate's serious medical needs, where eye examination resulted in determination that inmate needed cataract surgery, which would result in significant change in his prescription); Satz v. Corrections Corporations of America, Inc., 43 Fed. Appx. 64 (9th Cir. 2002) (evidence that federal prisoner received wrong contact lens prescription was insufficient, without more, to establish claim of deliberate indifference to serious medical needs); Shelton v. Angelone, 183 F. Supp. 2d 830 (W.D. Va. 2002) (state prisoner was not denied adequate medical treatment when he was refused permission to wear desired dark glasses to counteract alleged sensitivity to fluorescent lighting used in cells); Davidson v. Scully, 155 F. Supp. 2d 77 (S.D. N.Y. 2001) (defendants not liable for providing inmate with incorrect eyeglass prescriptions, which caused prisoner headaches and blurry vision, since defendants' incompetence amounted only to medical malpractice); Canell v. Multnomah County, 141 F. Supp. 2d 1046 (D. Or. 2001) (inmate was not "disabled" under ADA as result of slight vision problem, and thus prison officials' failure to provide him with reading glasses did not violate ADA, absent evidence that failure to provide glasses precluded inmate from using prison law library).

§ 3:13 Diet

n. 4.

section 3:13 note 4, add:
Woulard v. Food Service, 294 F. Supp. 2d 596 (D. Del. 2003) (denying prison official's motion to dismiss plaintiff's claim of deliberate indifference when plaintiff's allegations state that defendant responded to plaintiff's special diet for Diabetes and Crones Disease by saying that he did not care if plaintiff lived or died, and that the prison official refused to carry out the doctors prescribed diet. The court also denied the food service company's motion to dismiss because plaintiff's complaint showed that no action was taken to provide the inmate with his prescribed diet and the

§ 3:13

inadequate procedure of the food service company could rise to a constitutional violation. Finally, the court granted the prison supervisor's motion to dismiss plaintiff's claim against the prison supervisor because supervisors cannot be liable under § 1983 without actual knowledge and the plaintiff did not claim that the supervisor had actual knowledge of the constitutional violations).

n. 5.

section 3:13 note 5, add:
Pladsen v. Warden, 2003 WL 21716430 (Conn. Super. Ct. 2003) (holding that plaintiff could not prove deliberate indifference on the part of prison officials for not providing a special diet to accommodate his allergies to fish, milk and cheese because plaintiff failed to provide objective medical evidence proving that he actually suffered from the food allergies. Furthermore, the inmate could not show that his health was suffering from eating the diet he selected without milk, fish and cheese).

n. 6.

Page 428, note 6, add:
; Clement v. California Dept. of Corrections, 220 F. Supp. 2d 1098 (N.D. Cal. 2002) (any delay in providing medically appropriate diet to prisoner after he was diagnosed with colon cancer was not sufficiently harmful to constitute deliberate indifference to his medical needs in violation of Eighth Amendment, where prisoner was given high fiber diet within days of physician's recommendation, although prisoner was not given substitute for meat portion of his meals for three months).

n. 7.

Page 428, note 7, add:
Waring v. Meachum, 175 F. Supp. 2d 230 (D. Conn. 2001) (failure to provide prisoner with special diet during lockdown did not violate Eighth Amendment, as the prisoner failed to show that he harmed).

§ 3:14 Health Needs of Women

n. 1.

section 3:14 note 1, add:
Victoria W. v. Larpenter, 369 F.3d 475 (5th Cir. 2004) (holding that a municipal policy which requires inmates to obtain court a order allowing elective medical procedures, including abortions, is reasonably related to the legitimate government interest of inmate security and avoidance of unnecessary liability. The court further held that "a non-therapeutic abortion [does not] qualify as a "serious medical need" for the purposes of the Eighth Amendment").

Kendra Weatherhead, Cruel but not Unusual Punishment: The Failure to Provide Adequate Medical Treatment to Female Prisoners in the United States, 13 Health Matrix 429 (2003) (discussing "the standard of medical care required by the Eighth Amendment and suggest[ing] ways in which it can be changed to more appropriately protect incarcerated women from abuse and inadequate medical treatment").

Cynthia Chandler, Death and Dying in America: The Prison Industrial Complex's Impact on Women's Health, 18 Berkeley Women's L. J. 40 (2003) (arguing that the trend toward profitability in the "prison industrial

MEDICAL CARE § 3:15

complex" diminishes the level of medical care provided to women prisoners, particularly focusing on women prisoners in the custody of the California Department of Correction. The author proposes an activist response to this problem by joining the community with female prisoners to change prison conditions).

n. 6.

Page 430, note 6, add:
; Jamison v. Nielsen, 32 Fed. Appx. 874 (9th Cir. 2002) (Jail official did not intentionally disregard an excessive risk to pregnant inmate's health when miscarriage was threatened, even though official may have been insensitive or negligent, and even though another course of treatment might have been preferable).

section 3:14 note 6, add:
Doe v. Gustavus, 294 F. Supp. 2d 1003 (E.D. Wis. 2003) (denying the prison nurses' motion for summary judgment and holding that a jury could find that the prison nurses were deliberately indifferent to the inmate's serious medical need when they refused to provide pain medication, a complete examination, or assistance to a pregnant inmate who was experiencing labor pains because the nurses falsely diagnosed the inmates symptom's as false labor. As a result of the nurses' conduct, the inmate was forced to deliver her own baby while she was locked in a segregation cell).

n. 8.

section 3:14 note 8, add:
Victoria W. v. Larpenter, 369 F.3d 475 (5th Cir. 2004) (holding that a municipal policy which requires inmates to obtain court a order allowing elective medical procedures, including abortions, is reasonably related to the legitimate government interest of inmate security and avoidance of unnecessary liability. The court further held that "a non-therapeutic abortion [does not] qualify as a "serious medical need" for the purposes of the Eighth Amendment").

§ 3:15 Mental Health

n. 1.

section 3:15 note 1, add:
In 2004 the Correctional Association of New York released a study on the state of mental health care in New York State prisons. Reflecting the national trend, the report showed an increasing number of inmates with mental illness incarcerated in New York's prison. Specifically, the study reports that 7,500 out of 65,000, or 11 percent, of all inmates in New York State prisons are assigned to the mental health caseload. The study also finds that New York prison system lacks inpatient beds for mentally ill inmates, has insufficient staff to support mentally ill inmates, reports a high rate of victimization endured by mentally ill inmates, lacks adequate treatment for mentally ill inmates in the general population, and reports an overrepresentation of inmates with mental illness in disciplinary lockdown. The study concludes by describing models from other jurisdictions and providing recommendations on how New York State can improves the mental health care in its prisons. The Correctional Association of New York, Mental Health in the House of Corrections: A Study of

§ 3:15   RIGHTS OF PRISONERS

Mental Health Care in New York State Prisons, www.corrassoc.org/PMHP/description.pdf (2004).

n. 3.

Page 434, note 3, add:
Neiberger v. Hawkins, 239 F. Supp. 2d 1140 (D. Colo. 2002) (patients in state mental health facility, pursuant to adjudications of not guilty by reason of insanity, would be owed affirmative duty of care); Merriweather v. Sherwood, 235 F. Supp. 2d 339 (S.D. N.Y. 2002) (prison was not constitutionally required to provide prisoners with best possible mental health care, but merely reasonable mental health care); but see Lewis v. Sullivan, 279 F.3d 526 (7th Cir. 2002) (prisoners "do not have a fundamental constitutional right to psychiatric care at public expense").

n. 4.

Page 434, note 4, add following Arnold on behalf of H.B. v. Lewis citation and parenthetical:
; Terry ex rel. Terry v. Hill, 232 F. Supp. 2d 934 (E.D. Ark. 2002) (state of Arkansas violated due process rights of pretrial detainees, found by courts to be in need of mental health evaluation or treatment prior to adjudication of their fitness to stand trial, by making them wait inordinate time for service).

n. 7.

Page 436, note 7, add:
But see Duvalt v. Sonnen, 137 Idaho 548, 50 P.3d 1043 (Ct. App. 2002) (department of correction and prison staff were not bound by prisoner's plea agreement with state that included term that prisoner was to obtain mental health counseling and medication as recommended by prisoner's psychiatrist, where term of plea agreement was one that prisoner, not state, agreed to comply with).

n. 10.

Page 437, note 10, add:
; McCoy v. Goord, 255 F. Supp. 2d 233 (S.D. N.Y. 2003) (prison employee did not act with deliberate indifference to inmate's serious medical needs, notwithstanding allegations that employee, upon interviewing inmate after he had passed out and complained of amnesia, neglected seriousness of inmate's amnesia and sent him back to his cell, where employee's notes demonstrated that he acted in good faith in evaluating inmate's medical condition); Gibson v. County of Washoe, Nev., 290 F.3d 1175 (9th Cir. 2002), cert. denied, 537 U.S. 1106, 123 S. Ct. 872, 154 L. Ed. 2d 775 (2003) (sheriff's deputies who had contact with manic depressive detainee after he was admitted to jail, and who took part in forcible restraint that preceded his death from heart attack, were not deliberately indifferent to his medical needs so as to violate his due process rights, where deputies knew nothing of detainee's mental condition).

section 3:15 note 10, add:
Simpson v. Penobscot County Sheriff's Dept., 285 F. Supp. 2d 75 (D. Me. 2003) (holding that jail staff members were not deliberately indifferent to plaintiff's newly diagnosed Post Traumatic Stress Disorder, anxiety, panic attacks and depression while plaintiff was at the jail because neither the jail staff nor the plaintiff was aware that plaintiff was suffering from health problems and was in need of treatment); Means v. Cullen, 297 F.

Medical Care § 3:15

Supp. 2d 1148 (W.D. Wis. 2003) (holding that the prison psychologist did not violate the inmate's Eighth Amendment right to adequate medical treatment when the doctor allegedly told the inmate that nobody would care if he lived or died because the doctor's comments, while insensitive, do not rise to the level of an Eighth Amendment violation. Furthermore, the court held that the plaintiff's claim that he was denied the medical care he requested must fail because are not entitled to the medical treatment of their choice); Huss v. Rogerson, 271 F. Supp. 2d 1118 (S.D. Iowa 2003) (holding that prison officials were not deliberately indifferent to plaintiff's serious psychological condition when they held him in safekeeper, which is essentially administrative segregation, rather than in the state psychiatric facility after the plaintiff had been found not guilty by reason of insanity for murdering and mutilating his girlfriend because defendant was a safety risk to women and the psychiatric facility was an unsecured, co-ed facility); R.T. v. Gross, 298 F. Supp. 2d 289 (N.D. N.Y. 2003) (holding that the inmate did not assert a serious medical need to meet the first prong of an Eighth Amendment medical care claim when plaintiff was diagnosed with bi-polar disorder which manifested itself as periods of stability and instability because the periods of instability were usually associated with plaintiff's failure to take his medication).

n. 13.

Page 439, note 13, add following Negron v. Ward citation and parenthetical:

; Walker v. State, 2003 MT 134, 316 Mont. 103, 68 P.3d 872 (2003) (state prison subjected mentally ill inmate to cruel and unusual punishment when, rather than providing treatment to inmate following his disruptive behavior and multiple suicide attempts, prison officials took away his mattress, pillow and all personal items including clothing and forced him to sleep naked on concrete slab in filthy cell, greatly exacerbating inmate's mental illness)..

n. 14.

section 3:15 note 14, add:
See also David C. Fathi, The Common Law of Supermax Litigation, 24 Pace L. Rev. _____ (forthcoming 2004).

n. 15.

Page 439, note 15, add following Sullivan v. Flanagan citation and parenthetical:

; Singleton v. Norris, 319 F.3d 1018 (8th Cir. 2003) (Eighth Amendment is not violated by forcible administration of antipsychotic medication to prisoner, ordered for legitimate reasons of prison security or medical need, even if additional motive or effect of administration of drugs is to render prisoner competent to be executed); Dancy v. Gee, 51 Fed. Appx. 906 (4th Cir. 2002) (state corrections officials' forcible administration of antipsychotic medication without inmate's consent did not violate inmate's due process rights, where inmate had been diagnosed with paranoid schizophrenia, and was forcibly medicated only in emergency situations when he exhibited behavior that was dangerous to himself or others); Aaron M. Nance, Comment, Balking at Buying What the Eighth Circuit Is Selling: United States v. Sell and the Involuntary Medication of Incompetent, Non-Dangerous, Pretrial Detainees Cloaked With the Presumption of Innocence, 71 UMKC L. Rev. 685 (2003) (comment discusses, among other things, that forcibly medicating a death-row inmate for the sole purpose of inducing competency in order to execute him constitutionally is likely an unconstitutional violation of Due Process and the Eighth Amendment prohibition of cruel and unusual punishment);

section 3:15 note 15, add:
Lisa N. Jones, Singleton v. Norris: The Eighth Circuit maneuvered Around the Constitution by Forcibly Medicating Insane Prisoners to Create and Artificial Competence for Purposes of Execution, 37 Creighton L. Rev. 431 (2004) (arguing that courts should not impose forced medication on death row inmates to make the inmate competent for execution because an inmate made competent through forced medication is no more competent than he was prior to the administration of the treatment).

n. 20.

section 3:15 note 20, add:
Brad H. v. City of New York, 8 A.D.3d 142, 779 N.Y.S.2d 28 (App. Div. 1st Dep't 2004) (modifying the stipulation of settlement between the City of New York and a class of mentally ill jail inmates granting the City seven days from the completion of the inmate pre-screening process in which to activate an eligible inmate's Medicaid benefits because the seven day period is required to verify an applicants eligibility in conformance with New York law); Heather Barr, Connecting Litigation to a Grass Roots Movement: Monitoring, Organizing, and Brad H. v. City of NY, 24 Pace L. Rev. _____ (forthcoming 2004) (in this article, the author describes the role of lawyer representing mentally ill inmates by focusing on the *Brad H. v. City of NY* litigation. This case was brought on behalf of 25,000 inmates released from New York City jails without proper discharge planning. As a result of this case, the city and the inmates reached a settlement whereby the city would provide discharge services to mentally ill jail inmates. The author describes her involvement in assembling a grass roots organization to advocate for the rights of mentally ill inmates. The name of the organization is 300,000 Mothers. The name of this organization is derived from the fact that there are 300,000 prisoners with mental illness in the U.S., "all of whom where once someone's child." The organization is comprised of families of prisoners with psychiatric disabilities and ex-prisoners with psychiatric disabilities. The author then describes the role of 300,000 mothers in monitoring the settlement agreement reached between the inmates and the city in *Brad H v. City of NY*, and discusses the benefits of combining litigations and grassroots organizing).

§ 3:16 Suicide

n. 2.

Page 442, note 2, add:
; Christy P. Johnson, Comment, Mental Health Care Policies in Jail Systems: Suicide and the Eighth Amendment, 35 U.C. Davis L. Rev. 1227 (2002) (comment argues that jail policies lacking professional mental health evaluations constitute a violation of inmates' Eighth Amendment rights).

n. 6.

Page 443, note 6, add:

MEDICAL CARE § 3:16

; Estate of Sisk v. Manzanares, 262 F. Supp. 2d 1162 (D. Kan. 2002) (claims arising from a jail suicide are considered and treated as claims based on the failure of jail officials to provide medical care for those in their custody).

n. 7.

Page 443, note 7, add:
; Comstock v. McCrary, 273 F.3d 693, 2001 FED App. 0421P (6th Cir. 2001), cert. denied, 537 U.S. 817, 123 S. Ct. 86, 154 L. Ed. 2d 22 (2002) (prison psychologist displayed deliberate indifference to inmate's mental health, when upon briefly evaluating inmate, psychologist removed inmate from suicide watch and sent him back to his cell, whereupon inmate committed suicide, as psychologist knew that a prisoner might lie about how he was feeling in order to be taken off close observation and thereby gain the opportunity to commit suicide); Boncher ex rel. Boncher v. Brown County, 272 F.3d 484, 58 Fed. R. Evid. Serv. 174 (7th Cir. 2001) (jail officials did not show deliberate indifference to inmate who committed suicide, even though inmate answered "yes" when asked if he had mental or emotional problems and to a follow-up question on whether he had ever attempted suicide); Clara v. City of Chicago, 2002 WL 1553419 (N.D. Ill. 2002) (there was no evidence that police officers or lockup employees should have been aware that detainee presented risk of suicide; at most officers and employees were negligent by failing to check detainee's cell often enough).

n. 9.

Page 444, note 9, add:
; Estate of Sisk v. Manzanares, 262 F. Supp. 2d 1162 (D. Kan. 2002) (in lawsuit alleging that supervisor violated prisoner's Eighth Amendment rights, estate of deceased prisoner failed to show that supervisor was deliberately indifferent to substantial risk that prisoner would attempt to commit suicide, where supervisor was subjectively aware of prisoner's suicidal state but was not aware that corrections officer had ordered prisoner to be placed in hard lockdown cell rather than rubber room and supervisor was not aware that officer was not conducting required periodic checks).

n. 14.

Page 445, note 14, add:
; Wilson v. Genesse County, 2002 WL 745975 (E.D. Mich. 2002), rev'd in part, appeal dismissed in part, 2003 WL 21698899 (6th Cir. 2003) (county jail official was not deliberately indifferent to pre-trial detainee's suicidal tendencies, and thus could not be held liable for violating detainee's Fourteenth Amendment rights, where it was not part of official's duties to screen inmates for suicide risks or inquire of transporting officers as to whether he was suicidal).

n. 15.

section 3:16 note 15, add:
Matos ex rel. Matos v. O'Sullivan, 335 F.3d 553 (7th Cir. 2003) (holding that prison officials did not violate an inmate's rights when the plaintiff could not show that prison officials had actual knowledge that the decedent was a suicide risk).

n. 17.

Page 449, note 17, add:

§ 3:16   RIGHTS OF PRISONERS

; Matos ex rel. Matos v. O'Sullivan, 335 F.3d 553 (7th Cir. 2003) (administrator of estate of prisoner who committed suicide by hanging while incarcerated failed to show that prison officials were deliberately indifferent to prisoner's risk of suicide where officials asserted that they never knew about medical form indicating that prisoner had once attempted suicide and prisoner never told any official that he felt suicidal or depressed); Cagle v. Sutherland, 334 F.3d 980 (11th Cir. 2003) (nighttime jailer was not deliberately indifferent to risk of suicide by pretrial detainee who had expressly threatened suicide if confined in county jail, where jailer was aware that detainee's belt, shoelaces and contents of his pockets had been confiscated and that cell had been stripped of implements that might assist suicide); Hott v. Hennepin County, Minnesota, 260 F.3d 901 (8th Cir. 2001) (prison officials failure to conduct regular checks according to prison policy did not amount to deliberate indifference to needs of inmate who committed suicide in cell, where officer was not aware of risk of suicide to inmate and suicide itself was not a substantial risk to general inmate safety); Hofer v. City of Auburn, Ala., 155 F. Supp. 2d 1308 (M.D. Ala. 2001) (prison officers were not deliberately indifferent to needs of plaintiff detainee whose attempted suicide left him brain damaged, where defendants checked on plaintiff at least once every half hour and removed plaintiff's shoelaces and belt prior to placing him in the cell; failure to remove plaintiff's socks, which he used in an attempt to hang himself, did not, without more, allow a finding of deliberate indifference).

n. 18.

Page 449, note 18, add:
; Bozeman v. Orum, 199 F. Supp. 2d 1216 (M.D. Ala. 2002) (county correctional facility was not required to train its officers in diagnosing or treating mental illness).

n. 23.

Page 451, note 23 add following *Guglielmoni v. Alexander* citation and parenthetical:
; Cavalieri v. Shepard, 321 F.3d 616 (7th Cir. 2003) (strange behavior alone, without indications that that behavior has a substantial likelihood of taking a suicidal turn, was not sufficient to impute subjective knowledge of a high suicide risk to jail personnel).

n. 24.

Page 453, note 24, add following *Manarite By and Through Manarite v. City of Springfield* citation and parenthetical:
; Cavalieri v. Shepard, 321 F.3d 616 (7th Cir. 2003) (genuine issue of material fact existed as to whether officer was aware that detainee was on verge of committing suicide, precluding summary judgment, where officer knew that inmate was arrested for threatening to kill himself and his girlfriend and had mental health problems).

section 3:16 note 24, add:
Coleman v. Parkman, 349 F.3d 534 (8th Cir. 2003) (denying jail officials qualified immunity from plaintiff's claim that the officials were deliberately indifferent to the risk that her son, a pretrial detainee, would commit suicide when the jail officials learned from an interview with the decedent that he was suicidal, but despite the fact that the decedent was on suicide watch, jail officials assigned decedent to a cell with bars and gave him some items, including a bed sheet, with which he hung himself from the

Medical Care § 3:16

cell bars); Olson v. Bloomberg, 339 F.3d 730 (8th Cir. 2003) (denying the prison official a grant of qualified immunity because plaintiff was able to raise a question of fact as to whether the prison official was deliberately indifferent to plaintiff's son's threat of suicide because one inmate heard the prison official say, "you do what you go to do and I'll do what I got to do" in response to the decedent's threat of suicide and other inmates and the official say that he tried to talk the decedent out of killing himself. There was also a question of fact regarding the official's response speed in dealing with the situation); but see Cagle v. Sutherland, 334 F.3d 980 (11th Cir. 2003) (per curiam) (holding that Winston County, the county sheriff, and the county jailor were not deliberately indifferent to a detainee's risk of suicide when they were alerted to the detainee's suicidal tendencies and subsequently placed him in a video-monitored cell, which the night jailor checked every 15 minutes, and confiscated his belt and shoelaces but failed to check his cell every hour or staff a second jailor during the overnight shift when the detainee ultimately hung himself by his underwear elastic); Gray v. Tunica County, Mississippi, 279 F. Supp. 2d 789 (N.D. Miss. 2003), judgment aff'd, 100 Fed. Appx. 281 (5th Cir. 2004) (granting the jailor qualified immunity and holding that the plaintiff could not show objective unreasonableness on the part of the jailor to a pretrial detainee's risk of suicide when the jailor placed the pretrial detainee on suicide watch in the "lunacy cell," an 8 X 8 padded cell with no fixtures, after the pretrial detainee displayed unusual behaviors. When the jailor made his rounds, he noticed the pretrial detainee lying naked in his cell in a "frog-like" position (lying on his knees with his back facing the front of the cell). After taking notice of this awkward position, the jailor called the nurse. Both the jailor and the nurse agreed that the inmate was merely sleeping. When the jailor returned to the pretrial detainee's cell about a half hour later with some food, the pretrial detainee was in the same position and he was not breathing. It appeared that he strangled himself with a piece of his jumpsuit. The jailor did not perform CPR and did not call the prison doctor; rather he covered the pretrial detainee's body with his jumpsuit and waited for the paramedics to arrive. When the paramedics arrived they attempted to resuscitate the pretrial detainee, however, their efforts were not successful and the he was pronounced dead. To support its findings of objective reasonableness on the part of the jailor, the district court cited several cases showing objective unreasonableness to the risk of suicide. In those cases, the detainees were being held for crimes that were more severe than the crime the detainee being held for in this case. Also, in the prior cases each cell had fixtures from which an inmate could hang himself and here the cell had no such fixtures. Finally, in the prior cases each detainee was given something that he could use to hang himself and here the detainee was not given materials which presented a reasonable danger).

n. 26.

Page 455, note 26, add:

; Serafin v. City of Johnstown, 53 Fed. Appx. 211 (3d Cir. 2002) (city's reliance on video equipment, known to be sometimes defective, to monitor pretrial detainees at risk for suicide did not demonstrate deliberate indifference to their safety, and thus failure to timely intervene to stop detainee's suicide attempt did not violate Eighth Amendment, absent evidence that jail officials considered and rejected other more effective measures of suicide prevention, or that there was pattern of past suicide

§ 3:16   RIGHTS OF PRISONERS

attempts); Rapier v. Kankakee County, Ill., 203 F. Supp. 2d 978 (C.D. Ill. 2002) (county's policy of placing potentially suicidal detainees in special needs cell, along with its policy to require checks of these inmates every 15 minutes, was effective way to prevent suicide by detainees, and did not demonstrate such deliberate indifference toward detainee who did commit suicide as to establish violation); Middlebrooks v. Bibb County, 261 Ga. App. 382, 582 S.E.2d 539 (2003) (county did not breach its duty to provide suicidal inmate who ultimately committed suicide while incarcerated with adequate medical care, where department provided adequate procedures for caring for potentially suicidal inmates).

§ 3:17   Drug and Alcohol Treatment and Treatment for Tobacco Addiction

n. 1.

section 3:17 note 1, add:
Rebecca Boucher, The Case for Methadone Maintenance Treatment in Prisons, 27 Vt. L. Rev. 452 (2003) (arguing in favor of methadone treatment in prison, specifically discussing the deficiencies of the opioid-treatment programs provided to prisoners in the Vermont Department of Correction).

n. 2.

Page 457, note 2, add:
See William M. Burdon, Ph.D. et al., 2002 Prison-Based Therapeutic Community Substance Abuse programs—Implementation and Operational Issues, 66-DEC Fed. Probation 3 (2002) (article concludes that although a variety of approaches to treating substance-abusing inmates have been developed, the therapeutic community is the treatment that has received the most attention from researchers and policy makers).

section 3:17 note 2, add:
Rebecca Boucher, The Case for Methadone Maintenance Treatment in Prisons, 27 Vt. L. Rev. 452 (2003) (arguing in favor of methadone treatment in prison, specifically discussing the deficiencies of the opioid-treatment programs provided to prisoners in the Vermont Department of Correction).

§ 3:18   Disabled Prisoners

n. 1.

Page 459, note 1, add following State v. Johnson citation and parenthetical:
; Lawson v. Dallas County, 286 F.3d 257 (5th Cir. 2002) (finding that members of jail's medical staff acted with deliberate indifference to the serious medical needs of paraplegic inmate by placing inmate in a solitary cell, not providing him with adequate mobility equipment, not personally assisting him in turning himself, bathing, or moving, not providing necessary dressing changes, and not seeking alternative placement for inmate); Brian Lester, The Americans With Disabilities Act and the Exclusion of Inmates From Services in Prisoners: A Proposed Analytical Approach Regarding the Appropriate Level of Judicial Scrutiny of a Prisoner's ADA Claim, 79 N.D. L. Rev. 83 (2003) (article argues that in order for courts to

MEDICAL CARE § 3:19

resolve controversies arising under the ADA in actions brought by prisoners with disabilities consistent with Congress's intent, courts must rely on factors that properly consider the services and the needs of individuals seeking inclusion in light of the unique setting of prisons).

n. 3.

   Page 460, note 3, add:
; Lavender v. Lampert, 242 F. Supp. 2d 821 (D. Or. 2002) (to unnecessarily deny the use of a wheelchair to someone who obviously has an injury, and who lacks mobility without it, would constitute deliberate indifference to a serious medical need); Green v. Bressler, 2002 WL 31855308 (N.D. Cal. 2002) (failure of prison medical staff to prescribe use of a wheelchair by inmate suffering from osteoporosis did not amount to deliberate indifference to inmate's medical needs, as would violate Eighth Amendment, where staff concluded that inmate's condition did not mandate use of a wheelchair and that inmate would benefit from daily exercise of walking); Pittman v. Forte, 2002 WL 31309183 (N.D. N.Y. 2002) (state prisoner who alleged that he required assistance through cane, crutches, or wheelchair to walk due to extreme pain in his leg and foot did not show that prison officials withheld walking aid for sole purpose of causing prisoner pain, and thus officials were not deliberately indifferent to serious medical condition within meaning of Eighth Amendment due to any delay in provision of such aid); Beck v. Skon, 253 F.3d 330 (8th Cir. 2001) (prison officials did not demonstrate deliberate indifference to inmate's neurological problems, which were exacerbated by walking and climbing stairs, by failing to transfer him to a cell closer to infirmity and cafeteria, where officials permitted inmate to use wheelchair or to eat his meals in his cell); Navedo v. Maloney, 172 F. Supp. 2d 276 (D. Mass. 2001) (qualified immunity denied to prison official where it was shown that he knew that prisoner needed a wheelchair, that prison facility was not wheelchair accessible, and that official denied a transfer to another facility, notwithstanding the recommendations of the medical staff).

   section 3:18 note 3, add:
But see Williams v. Garcia, 97 Fed. Appx. 173 (9th Cir. 2004), petition for cert. filed (U.S. Aug. 12, 2004) (holding that prison officials were not deliberately indifferent to an inmate's serious medical need when they placed the inmate, who had the lower part of his left leg amputated and ambulates using a prosthetic device, in an upper tier cell during a period of heightened security and temporary lockdown and then were slow to return the inmate to a lower tier cell after the emergency situation was complete because this conduct did not rise to the level of a constitutional violation); Arreola v. Choudry, 2004 WL 868374 (N.D. Ill. 2004) (denying prison officials' motion for summary judgment on an inmate's claim that he suffered continuing ankle injury and mental distress when the inmate injured his ankle playing soccer but the prison doctor refused to treat him because he was Jewish, and then prison officials would not move the inmate to a tier where he could have crutches or a cane).

§ 3:19 Prisoners and the Americans With Disabilities Act

n. 6.

   Page 465, note 6, add to end of first paragraph in footnote:

§ 3:19   RIGHTS OF PRISONERS

; Randolph v. Rodgers, 253 F.3d 342 (8th Cir. 2001) (hearing impaired inmate was not barred by Eleventh Amendment from seeking prospective injunctive relief against prison official in her official capacity for violations of ADA and RA arising from official's refusal to provide him with sign language interpreter during medical visits and prison proceedings); Becker v. Oregon, 170 F. Supp. 2d 1061 (D. Or. 2001) (state defendants were not immune to suits brought under Title II of the ADA and the RA because Congress had abrogated the state's Eleventh Amendment immunity); Mitchell v. Massachusetts Dept. of Correction, 190 F. Supp. 2d 204 (D. Mass. 2002) (Congress validly abrogated state sovereign immunity with respect to claims under Title II of the ADA; prisoner's allegation that he was denied participation in various prison work and educational programs due to his medical condition, a diabetic with a heart condition, was sufficient to state claim under Title II of the ADA); Tim Kollas, Note, Federal Power, States' Rights, Individual Rights: Mentally Disabled Prisoners and the Supreme Court's New Activism, 10 Wm. & Mary Bill Rts. J. 861 (2002) (note examines the situation of mentally disabled prisoners who seek to assert their rights in federal court and argues that states do not have the extensive sovereign immunity that the Supreme Court claims, that Congress should be permitted to influence the level of scrutiny afforded to claims brought by the disabled, and that the predicament of mentally disabled prisoners warrants heightened scrutiny).

    Page 465, note 6, add to end of second paragraph in footnote:
; Reickenbacker v. Foster, 274 F.3d 974 (5th Cir. 2001) (mentally ill state prisoners could not sue department of corrections for allegedly deficient mental health services pursuant to Title II of the ADA, because the department was entitled to sovereign immunity).

    section 3:19 note 6, add:

§ 3:20   AIDS

n. 6.

    section 3:20 note 6, add:
Nei v. Dooley, 372 F.3d 1003 (8th Cir. 2004) (holding that the inmates stated a valid Eighth Amendment claim when they alleged that another inmate was threatening to infect the other inmates on the unit with the AIDS virus and during numerous fights the inmate's blood would come into contact with the other inmates on the unit. Furthermore, the inmates were able to show that the prison officials had subjective knowledge of this behavior through affidavits of inmates on the unit and through an email that one of the prison officials wrote describing the situation).

n. 45.

    Page 480, note 45, add:
; Foster v. Fulton County, Georgia, 223 F. Supp. 2d 1292 (N.D. Ga. 2002) (county's failure to employ sufficient number of trained correctional staff to meet health care needs of inmates at county jail who had tested positive for HIV required that county immediately develop and implement plan to increase staffing at jail to level necessary to provide timely access to medical care for current population of inmates).

n. 49.

    Page 481, note 49, add:

MEDICAL CARE § 3:21

; Clark v. Birk, 55 Mass. App. Ct. 1113, 774 N.E.2d 179 (2002) (HIV-infected inmate's lack of prescription drugs for a 40-day period did not constitute inadequate medical treatment in violation of Eighth Amendment's prohibition against cruel and unusual punishment, where expert testified that lack of drugs would not have caused harm to defendant or exacerbated inmate's HIV infection).

n. 50.

Page 481, note 49, add:
; Clark v. Birk, 55 Mass. App. Ct. 1113, 774 N.E.2d 179 (2002) (HIV-infected inmate's lack of prescription drugs for a 40-day period did not constitute inadequate medical treatment in violation of Eighth Amendment's prohibition against cruel and unusual punishment, where expert testified that lack of drugs would not have caused harm to defendant or exacerbated inmate's HIV infection).

n. 52.

Page 481, note 52, add:
; Smith v. Carpenter, 316 F.3d 178 (2d Cir. 2003) (jury was free to consider absence of concrete medical injury to prisoner as relevant factor in determining whether alleged deprivation of his HIV medication for several days on two occasions was sufficiently serious to satisfy the objective serious medical need standard for a deliberate indifference to serious medical needs claim).

§ 3:21 Transsexuals

n. 1.

Page 482, note 1, add:
; Bradley A. Sultan, Note, Transsexual Prisoners: How Much Treatment Is Enough?, 37 New Eng. L. Rev. 1195 (2003) (note argues that prison officials should be given the same wide latitude in treating transsexuals, who often argue that the refusal of prison officials to treat their condition is an unconstitutional violation of the Eighth Amendment, that they receive in determining the course of ordinary medical treatment for other, non-transsexual inmates; it concludes that while incarcerated transsexuals have rights, these rights must be weighed against the overriding fact that they are in prison and should not be treated with any more concern than any other prisoner); Katrina C. Rose, When Is an Attempted Rape Not an Attempted Rape? When the Victim is a Transsexual, 9 Am. U. J. Gender Soc. Pol'y & L. 505 (2001) (article discusses *Schwenk v. Hartford*, a civil rights action brought by a pre-operative transsexual prisoner who was raped by a corrections officer).

section 3:21 note 1, add:
Bradley A. Sultan, Transsexual Prisoners: How Much Treatment is Enough,? 37 New Eng. L. Rev. 1195 (2003) (this note argues that prison officials should be given the same autonomy to determine the course of treatment for transsexual prisons as they are given to handle the medical treatment of non-transsexual inmates).

n. 8.

Page 484, note 8, add:
; Brooks v. Berg, 2003 WL 21649735 (N.D. N.Y. 2003) (prison officials who

§ 3:21

failed to provide treatment to inmate who claimed to be a transsexual were deliberately indifferent to his serious medical needs, where inmate made numerous requests for treatment and officials' decision did not appear to have been based on sound medical judgment)

section 3:21 note 8, add:
Brooks v. Berg, 289 F. Supp. 2d 286 (N.D. N.Y. 2003) ("vacat[ing] denial of summary judgment to defendants . . . and permitting defendants to file a motion for summary judgment).

n. 9.

section 3:21 note 9, add:
Barrett v. Coplan, 292 F. Supp. 2d 281, 2003 DNH 197 (D.N.H. 2003) (holding that the inmate stated a valid Eighth Amendment claim when he alleged that prison officials were objectively and subjectively aware that the inmate was suffering from Gender Identity Disorder (GID). The objective component of this test is satisfied because GID is a serious medical disorder. The subjective component is allegedly met because the inmate claims to have alerted prison officials to the risk of danger from the disorder by writing letters to the prison officials, attempting suicide, and attempting self-castration. Despite the alleged subjective and objective knowledge of the risk of harm to the inmate, the prison officials continued to refuse medical and psychiatric treatment).

n. 15.

section 3:21 note 15, add:
De'Lonta v. Angelone, 330 F.3d 630 (4th Cir. 2003) (reversing the dismissal of plaintiff's claim and holding that the inmate raised sufficient facts to defeat a motion to dismiss when she claimed that prison officials were deliberately indifferent to her serious medical need for protection against continued self-mutilation when prison officials enacted a policy that terminated medical procedures and hormone therapy to Gender Identity Disorder inmates even though the treatment was replaced by counseling, Prozac and Doxepin because the prison officials did not clearly demonstrate that this course of treatment was reasonable to prevent the inmate from continued self mutilation).

n. 16.

Page 485, note 16, add following the Phillips v. Michigan Dept. of Corrections citation and parenthetical:
Kosilek v. Maloney, 221 F. Supp. 2d 156 (D. Mass. 2002) (treatment plans for inmate diagnosed with gender identity disorder were not adequate to meet inmate's serious medical need, as required by Eighth Amendment, where plans were derived from an administrative decision creating blanket policy prohibiting initiation of hormones for inmates for whom they were not prescribed prior to incarceration, and no clinical assessment of inmate's individual circumstances and medical needs was made).

§ 3:23 Right to Refuse Treatment

n. 15.

Page 496, note 15, add:
Recent case law on the topic includes Sell v. U.S., 123 S. Ct. 2174, 156 L. Ed. 2d 197, 188 A.L.R. Fed. 679 (U.S. 2003). In *Sell*, the Supreme Court

MEDICAL CARE § 3:23

addressed the question whether the government could forcibly administer psychotropic medication for the sole purpose of rendering a detainee competent to stand trial. The Supreme Court held that the Constitution permits the involuntary administration of psychotropic medication for the sole purpose of rendering a defendant competent to stand trial if a court finds that the "treatment is medically appropriate, is substantially unlikely to have side effects that may undermine the fairness of the trial, and, taking account of less intrusive alternatives, is necessary significantly to further important governmental trial-related interests"). See also Singleton v. Norris, 319 F.3d 1018 (8th Cir. 2003) (Eighth Amendment is not violated by forcible administration of antipsychotic medication to prisoner, ordered for legitimate reasons of prison security or medical need, even if additional motive or effect of administration of drugs is to render prisoner competent to be executed); Dancy v. Gee, 51 Fed. Appx. 906 (4th Cir. 2002) (state corrections officials' forcible administration of antipsychotic medication without inmate's consent did not violate inmate's due process rights, where inmate had been diagnosed with paranoid schizophrenia and was forcibly medicated only in emergency situations when he exhibited behavior that was dangerous to himself or others); Benson v. Terhune, 304 F.3d 874 (9th Cir. 2002) (after a second-degree murder conviction, petitioner sought federal habeas corpus relief, arguing that she was involuntarily medicated and thereby denied the opportunity to have a full and fair trial, and district court denied her petition; in affirming, court of appeals held that even if defendant was medicated without her consent, she was not prejudiced as a result nor deprived of a fair trial in violation of due process, since she had at least a minimum rational understanding of the trial proceedings and the ability to rationally participate in them). See also Aaron M. Nance, Comment, Balking at Buying What the Eighth Circuit Is Selling: *United States v. Sell* and the Involuntary Medication of Incompetent, Non-Dangerous, Pretrial Detainees Cloaked With the Presumption of Innocence, 71 UMKC L. Rev. 685 (2003) (comment discusses, among other things, that forcibly medicating a death-row inmate for the sole purpose of inducing competency in order to execute him constitutionally is likely an unconstitutional violation of Due Process and the Eighth Amendment prohibition of cruel and unusual punishment); Kathy Swedlow, 2003 Forced Medication of Legally Incompetent Prisoners: A Primer, 30-SPG Hum. Rts. 3 (2003); David E. Gross, Note, Presumed Dangerous: California's Selective Policy of Forcibly Medicating State Prisoners with Antipsychotic Drugs, 35 U.C. Davis L. Rev. 483 (2002) (author argues that patients must receive a judicial hearing to determine their competency to refuse treatment before the state may forcibly medicate them); Dora W. Klein, Note, Trial Rights and Psychotropic Drugs: The Case Against Administering Involuntary Medications to a Defendant During Trial, 55 Vand. L. Rev. 165 (2002) (note proposes that government interests cannot justify administering involuntary psychotropic drugs to a defendant during trial, because administering involuntary psychotropic drugs infringes not only the interest in refusing medical treatment, but also the right to a fair trial, which cannot be justified by any government interest; David M. Siegel, Albert J. Grudzinskas, Jr. & Debra A. Pinals, M.D., Old Law Meets New Medicine: Revisiting Involuntary Psychotropic Medication of the Criminal Defendant, 2001 Wis. L. Rev. 307 (2001) (article addresses the constitutional questions presented by involuntary medication of the pretrial criminal detainee).

n. 21.
Page 498, note 21, add:

§ 3:23

; Parks v. McCoy, 35 Fed. Appx. 239 (7th Cir. 2002) (allegation that prisoner was misdiagnosed as suffering from tuberculosis, and was forced to take medication which made him sick, was insufficient to state Eighth Amendment claim for inadequate medical care; claim was, at most, one for malpractice).

§ 3:24 Prison Co-Payment Plans For Medical Care

n. 2.
  section 3:24 note 2, add:
Hopkins v. Warden, NH State Prison, 2004 DNH 88, 2004 WL 1125241 (D.N.H. 2004) (holding that the inmate did not state a valid due process claim when he challenged the finding that he had to pay restitution for the medical treatment he received after he was seriously beaten by numerous inmates because an inmate does not have a protected liberty interest in free medical care).

Chapter 4
Equal Protection Clause-Discrimination Issues

> **KeyCite®:** Cases and other legal materials listed in KeyCite Scope can be researched through West's KeyCite service on Westlaw®. Use KeyCite to check citations for form, parallel references, prior and later history, and comprehensive citator information, including citations to other decisions and secondary materials.

§ 4:1 Introduction

n. 4.

Page 506, note 4, add:

; Thompson v. Gibson, 289 F.3d 1218 (10th Cir. 2002), cert. denied, 537 U.S. 978, 123 S. Ct. 440, 154 L. Ed. 2d 337 (2002) (affirming district court finding that inmate failed to state equal protection claim where inmate alleged that that inmates who had money could supplement their diet through canteen purchases while he was disadvantaged by hunger and poverty; inmate's claim was not based on his being part of a suspect class, inmate did not show that different treatment was not reasonably related to some legitimate penological purpose, and inmate had no constitutional right to buy food from canteen); Little v. Terhune, 200 F. Supp. 2d 445 (D.N.J. 2002) (holding that prison officials did not violate inmate's right to equal protection by not providing educational and employment opportunities to inmates housed in administrative segregation at the state's only maximum security prison); *but see* Williams v. Manternach, 192 F. Supp. 2d 980 (N.D. Iowa 2002) (reversing district court decision and finding that inmate sufficiently pleaded facts to support equal protection claim based on disparate treatment of inmates serving life sentences, where inmate alleged that, unlike non- "lifers," "lifers" were subjected to quotas on how many of them could be on any employment site or level).

section 4:1, note 4, add:

Okocci v. Klein, 270 F. Supp. 2d 603 (E.D. Pa. 2003), order aff'd, 100 Fed. Appx. 127 (3d Cir. 2004), petition for cert. filed (U.S. Sept. 11, 2004) (granting summary judgment for prison officials on the plaintiff's claim that he was denied a fingerprint analysis of a shank found in his cell in violation of his right to equal protection. In this case, prison officials found a shank in plaintiff's cell during a fire drill. Plaintiff requested a fingerprint analysis of the shank, however his request was denied and he was convicted of possession of contraband. Plaintiff argues that prisoners who are found in possession of controlled substances and prisoners who are found with contraband are similarly situated because both offenses are Class I offenses in the prison handbook. Plaintiff further argues that because urinalysis is required for controlled substance possession cases, fingerprint analysis should be required for contraband possession cases. The court rejected plaintiff's argument because the nature of controlled substance possession and contraband possession are different, despite the fact that both are designated as Class I offenses in the Prison Handbook. Therefore, inmates in possession of contraband are not similarly situated to inmates in possession of controlled substances even though both offenses are Class I offenses in the prison handbook).

Cole v. Clarke, 2003 WL 21278477 (Neb. Ct. App. 2003), review overruled, (Aug. 27, 2003) (holding that plaintiff did not state a valid equal protection claim because plaintiff did not show that he was denied dental services that the prison provided to similarly situated inmates).

McGuire v. Ameritech Services, Inc., 253 F.Supp. 2d 988 (S. D. Ohio 2003) (dismissing the plaintiffs' class-based equal protection claim that persons who receive calls from inmates are similarly situated to those who receive calls from non-inmates. Since plaintiffs cannot show that they are similarly situated to those who receive calls from non-inmates, their class-based equal protection claim was denied. However, the court refused to dismiss plaintiffs' equal protection claim based on their fundamental rights protected by the First Amendment because accepting plaintiffs, friends, family members, attorneys and bailbondsmen of inmates at state and county correctional institutions in Ohio, claim that they are subject to "exorbitant rates" and "are denied adequate service by the defendants" as true could prove to be an unconstitutional barrier to communication between plaintiffs and inmates; Dennison v. Pennsylvania Dept. of Corrections, 268 F. Supp. 2d 387 (M.D. Pa. 2003) (granting summary judgment in favor of prison officials regarding an ex-prison employee's First Amendment conspiracy claim because the ex-employee failed to allege that the defendants conspired against him on the basis of race or class animus); Gean v. Hattaway, 330 F.3d 758, 177 Ed. Law Rep. 64, 2003 FED App. 0183P (6th Cir. 2003) (holding that plaintiffs, three young men who were formerly state custody as juveniles, did not state a valid equal protection claim when plaintiffs, recipient's of social security benefits, were required to contribute to their care and other juveniles in state custody who did not receive social security benefits were not required to contribute to their care); Gwinn v. Awmiller, 354 F.3d 1211 (10th Cir. 2004), cert. denied, 125 S. Ct. 181 (U.S. 2004) (holding that prison officials did not violate the inmate's right to equal protection when the prison officials required the inmate, but not other inmates convicted of robbery, to participate in a treatment program for sex offenders or lose good time credits because unlike the other inmates the plaintiff inmate committed a sexual assault and could benefit from the program. Because a suspect class was not implicated, the prison officials' differential treatment only must be reasonably related to a legitimate penological purpose).

n. 5.

Page 507, note 5, add:

; Youngbear v. Thalacker, 174 F. Supp. 2d 902 (N.D. Iowa 2001) (finding that Native American inmates' claim that correctional officials year-long delay in constructing a sweat lodge was violative of the their right to equal protection failed, where plaintiff inmates were unable meet burden of showing that officials purposefully discriminated against their religion and where defendant officials claimed that they wished to wait to construct the lodge until a consultant was hired by the Iowa Department of Corrections to advise them).

§ 4:2 The Theory of Equal Protection and Equal Protection standards

n. 1.

section 4:2, note 1, add:
Bruce v. Ylst, 351 F.3d 1283, 63 Fed. R. Evid. Serv. 221 (9th Cir. 2003) (In this case, plaintiff was categorized as a gang member based on evidence that had been insufficient to categorize plaintiff as a gang member on three prior occasions. Plaintiff claims that the defendants categorized him as a gang member in retaliation for a grievance he filed on behalf of himself and others relating to prison conditions while in administrative segregation. Plaintiff argued that he was not afforded the same process as other gang affiliates because of his jailhouse lawyering activity. The Court held that because plaintiff was afforded the process he was due in connection with the prison officials' charge of gang affiliation, any difference in treatment does not rise to the level of an equal protection violation because equal protection does not require absolute equality between similarly situated inmates).

n. 2.

section 4:2, note 2, add:
Jackson v. State Bd. of Pardons and Paroles, 331 F.3d 790 (11th Cir. 2003), cert. denied, 124 S. Ct. 319, 157 L. Ed. 2d 145 (U.S. 2003) (affirming the district court's finding that the provision of the Prison Litigation Reform Act which limits attorneys fees does not violate the inmate's right to equal protection even though it restricts the attorney's fees that can be recovered by prisoners and allows non-prisoner civil rights litigants to fully recover attorney's fees. The court rejected the prisoner's request to review the law under heightened scrutiny because prisoners are not a suspect classification. The court further rejected plaintiff's claim that this provision should have been analyzed under heightened scrutiny because it violated the plaintiff's fundamental right of access to the courts. To prove an access to the courts violation the inmate must show actual injury to a non-frivolous legal claim, however, here, plaintiff fully litigated his claim with the assistance of a lawyer).

n. 7.

section 4:2, note 7, add:
Serrano v. Francis, 345 F.3d 1071 (9th Cir. 2003), cert. denied, 125 S. Ct. 43 (U.S. 2004) (reversing the district court's decision and holding that plaintiff raised sufficient evidence of discriminatory intent to convince a jury that a hearing officer's decision to preclude live witness testimony was racially motivated. The hearing officer's remarks included telling the plaintiff the he "'[didn't] know how black people think' and that he said 'he was treating [Serrano] like all the rest . . . and that [Serrano] was 'not O.J. Simpson or Johnnie Cochran.'").

n. 8.

section 4:2, note 8, add:
Townsend v. Cheshire, 2003 WL 21805578 (Conn. Super. Ct. 2003), judg-

§ 4:2   Rights of Prisoners

ment aff'd, 83 Conn. App. 902, 853 A.2d 650 (2004) (holding that plaintiff's equal protection claim that "women prisoners are provided better legal services and access to legal assistance than male prisoners" is barred by res judicata because plaintiff is a member of a certified class in a class action suit that has raised this question and is pending in federal court).

§ 4:3   Equal Protection Applied
n. 1.
Page 511, note 1, add:
; Wolff v. Hood, 242 F. Supp. 2d 811 (D. Or. 2002)(granting summary judgment in favor of correctional officers who showed legitimate, nondiscrimatory reasons for their actions where inmate alleged that he was being discriminated against as a member of a class of sex offenders).

section 4:3, note 1, add:
Damron v. North Dakota Com'r. of Corrections, 299 F. Supp. 2d 970 (D.N.D. 2004) (granting summary judgment for defendant on inmate's claim that prison officials denied the inmate equal access to educational opportunities through educational computers because the inmate could not show that he was treated differently compared with any other inmate. In this case the inmate was suspended from an education program that he accessed through the computer because of a disciplinary violation. The inmate tried to show that two other inmates who have received disciplinary violations have retained their rights to education programs through the computer however the inmate could not produce evidence to show that he was treated differently from these similarly situated inmates. Similarly, the inmate alleged that prison officials violated his equal protection rights when they confiscated a calculator from the inmate but allowed other similarly situated inmates to have similar calculators. The court granted summary judgment in favor of prison officials because the inmate could not produce sufficient evidence to show that similarly situated inmates were allowed to possess calculators).

Williams v. Morton, 343 F.3d 212 (3d Cir. 2003) (affirming the district court's grant of summary judgment for the prison officials on plaintiff's claim that the prison violated his right to equal protection under the Fourteenth Amendment when Jewish inmates were provided with kosher meat but Muslim inmates were not given halal (sic) meat because plaintiff provided no evidence to show that Jewish inmates were provided with kosher meat); Rashad v. Maloney, 16 Mass. L. Rep. 162 (Mass. Super. Ct. 2003) (dismissing the Muslim inmates claim that they were not given halaal meat but that Jewish inmates were given kosher food because the plaintiffs did not provide any evidence that the prison could obtain an adequate supply of the halaal meat from a reliable vendor at a reasonable cost); Huff v. Hooper, 2003 WL 158689 (Del. Super. Ct. 2003), appeal dismissed, 832 A.2d 1251 (Del. 2003) (granting summary judgment for prison officials on plaintiffs' claim that the prison treats Muslims and Christians differently because there are Christian and not Muslim symbols in the chapel. Muslim inmates contended that the prison provides funding for Christian but not Muslim materials, and the prison uses heightened security for Muslim but not Christian visitors. The court rejected this claim because the inmates could not produce evidence supporting the charges).

§ 4:3

n. 4.

section 4:3, note 4, add:
Joseph v. Henderson, 834 So. 2d 373 (Fla. Dist. Ct. App. 2d Dist. 2003) (holding that a county sheriff's regulation violates the petitioners right to equal protection under the law when the regulation requires an inmate who returns to the county jail from prison on a writ of prosequendum (a writ used to bring a prisoner to trial on a case other than the one for which the prisoner is being confined) to pay a per diem fee but does not require an inmate who returns to the county jail from prison on a writ of testificandum (a writ used to bring an inmate to court to testify in a case) to pay a fee because the distinction was not rationally related to the objectives of the legislature); *but see* State v. Daddario, 2003 WL 22963400, 2003 Ohio 6846 (Ohio Ct. App., 2003) (upheld a state statute that created a graduated system by which an inmate could file a motion for judicial release over plaintiff's equal protection challenge because the legislature's stated purpose of keeping the public safe from serious offenders is a rational basis for creating time restrictions based on the severity of the offense. The statute was not unconstitutional as applied to the plaintiff even though his co-defendant could be released at an earlier date than the plaintiff because the plaintiff and his co-defendant were not convicted of the same crimes or sentenced to the same term. Therefore, the plaintiff and his co-defendant were not similarly situated).

n. 7.

section 4:3, note 7, add:
DiMarco v. Wyoming Dept. of Corrections Div. of Prisons, Wyo. Women's Center, 300 F. Supp. 2d 1183 (D. Wyo. 2004) (denying plaintiff's claim that the defendant violated the inmate's right to equal protection under the Fourteenth Amendment when plaintiff, an individual born with ambiguous gender, was confined to a maximum security wing of a woman's prison even though the inmate was classified as the lowest possible security risk. The decision was made to ensure the safety of plaintiff, the other inmates, and the prison in general because the inmate appeared to be a man in a woman's prison. The court applied the rational basis test because individuals born with ambiguous gender are not a suspect or quasi-suspect class and the decision to house plaintiff in the maximum security wing did not burden any of plaintiff's fundamental right).

n. 8.

Page 515, note 8, add:
; Rem v. U.S. Bureau of Prisons, 320 F.3d 791 (8th Cir. 2003) (holding that statute requiring that law enforcement officials be notified of release from prison of a person convicted of a drug trafficking crime or crime of violence, as applied to prisoner convicted for possession with intent to distribute cocaine, did not violate the Equal Protection Clause).

n. 9.

Page 516, note 9, add:
Little v. Terhune, 200 F. Supp. 2d 445 (D.N.J. 2002) (holding that prison officials did not violate inmate's right to equal protection by not providing educational and employment opportunities to inmates housed in administrative segregation at the state's only maximum security prison, where the prison officials relied on a legitimate penological interest, the prison system's security and budget).

§ 4:3

n. 21.

Page 519, note 21, add:
; Little v. Terhune, 200 F. Supp. 2d 445 (D.N.J. 2002) (holding that prison officials did not violate inmate's right to equal protection by not providing educational and employment opportunities to inmates housed in administrative segregation at the state's only maximum security prison where the prison officials relied on a legitimate penological interest, the prison system's security and budget).

n. 22.

Page 520, note 22, add:
; Gerber v. Hickman, 291 F.3d 617 (9th Cir. 2002), cert. denied, 537 U.S. 1039, 123 S. Ct. 558, 154 L. Ed. 2d 462 (2002) (holding that inmate's right to procreate is fundamentally inconsistent with the nature and goals of incarceration and affirming dismissal of inmate's suit in which he claimed his fundamental right to privacy was violated by not allowing him to provide his wife with a sperm specimen with which she could be artificially inseminated).

n. 52.

Page 520, note 22, add:
; Gerber v. Hickman, 291 F.3d 617 (9th Cir. 2002), cert. denied, 537 U.S. 1039, 123 S. Ct. 558, 154 L. Ed. 2d 462 (2002) (holding that inmate's right to procreate is fundamentally inconsistent with the nature and goals of incarceration and affirming dismissal of inmate's suit in which he claimed his fundamental right to privacy was violated by not allowing him to provide his wife with a sperm specimen with which she could be artificially inseminated).

§ 4:4 Equal Protection Applied—Racial Discrimination

n. 6.

section 4:4, note 6, add:
Miller v. Blanchard, 2004 WL 1354368 (W. D. Wis. 2004) (granting the inmate leave to proceed in forma pauperis on his claim that the defendants violated his rights under the Equal Protection Clause of the Fourteenth Amendment when he alleged that the defendants backed out of an agreement to reduce his sentence in return for information about a murder at the prison because the plaintiff was an African-American prisoner. according to the plaintiff, the prison officials had followed through on 50 similar agreements with Caucasian inmates); Glenn v. Berndt, 289 F. Supp. 2d 1120 (N.D. Cal. 2003) (holding that a prison official's negligence or gross negligence in accidentally opening a white inmate's cell door during which lead to a fight between white and black inmates did not rise to the level of an Eighth Amendment violation).

n. 15.

section 4:4, note 15, add:
Ortiz v. Fort Dodge Correctional Facility, 368 F.3d 1024 (8th Cir. 2004) (holding that a former prison policy that prevented inmates who could speak and write in English from sending or receiving letters in a foreign language was constitutional under the *Turner* standard because it

§ 4:4 EQUAL PROTECTION

advanced the legitimate interest of safety and there were no "ready alternatives," to the policy which could be provided at *de minimis* cost. Furthermore, under this policy, alternative avenues of communication were available to the inmate including telephone calls and visits. In this case, the inmate's native language was Spanish, however he was fluent in English. He requested permission to write letters to his family members in Spanish. Permission was granted with regards to the inmate's sister who lived in Mexico because it was the only way the inmate could communicate with his sister. Permission was denied, however, with regards to the inmates other family members, including his mother, because the remaining members of his family lived in the United States. The prison has changed its policy and currently allows inmates to write letters in their preferred language; however, the inmate brought this action for damages based on prior First Amendment violations stemming from the old policy).

n. 32.

Page 535, note 32, add:
; Johnson v. California, 321 F.3d 791 (9th Cir. 2003) (holding that prison policy of using race as a factor in assigning new inmates their initial cell mate did not violate Equal Protection Clause because the policy was rationally related to legitimate penological interest in protecting safety of inmates and staff, the policy was limited to a 60-day period, and the remainder of the prison was integrated).

section 4:4, note 32, add:
Palmer v. Marion County, 327 F.3d 588 (7th Cir. 2003) (holding that the pretrial detainee could not show that the county, city, and county sheriff allowed a widespread practice racial segregation and then failing to respond to problems in the cell containing black inmates because plaintiff only cited two incidents of misconduct by guards in one year).

On March 1, 2004 The United States Supreme Court granted certiorari in Johnson v. California, 124 S. Ct. 1505, 158 L. Ed. 2d 151 (U.S. 2004), miscellaneous rulings, 125 S. Ct. 27 (U.S. 2004). Oral argument is scheduled in the 2004-2005 term after October 3, 2004. In this case, the Court will decide whether the Turner standard or the strict scrutiny standard should apply when analyzing a state prison system's policy of temporarily segregating inmates by race. The Court will also decide whether the California Prison system practice of temporarily segregating inmates based on race is constitutional under the Equal Protection Clause). Randy James, Johnson, Garrison v. Gomez, James & Rowland, James, http://journalism.medill.northwestern.edu/docket/2004-05termcases.html (last visited July 21, 2004).

For an in-depth discussion of the Ninth Circuit's decision in Johnson v. State of California, 321 F.3d 791 (9th Cir. 2003), cert. granted, 124 S. Ct. 1505, 158 L. Ed. 2d 151 (U.S. 2004), miscellaneous rulings, 125 S. Ct. 27 (U.S. 2004), written before the U.S. Supreme Court granted certiorari see Julie Taylor, Ninth Circuit Review: Racial Segregation in California Prisons, 37 Loy. L.A.L. Rev. 139 (2003); Sloan v. Johnson, 95 Fed. Appx. 52 (5th Cir. 2004) (holding that prison officials did not violate the inmates "constitutional rights by removing his racial classification restrictions, which would allow him to be placed in a cell with a black inmate." The court stated that racial segregation in prison violates the constitution and

§ 4:4   Rights of Prisoners

is only allowed when necessary to ensure prison security and discipline. Here, the inmate was unable to show such necessity); Walker v. Gomez, 370 F.3d 969 (9th Cir. 2004), opinion supplemented, 101 Fed. Appx. 200 (9th Cir. 2004) (holding that the inmate stated a valid claim when he alleged that prison officials violated his rights under the Equal Protection Clause when, on several occasions, they allowed non-African American inmates to leave their cells and return to work at an earlier date than African American inmates following several lockdowns. The prison officials argued that this distinction was necessary in each instance for safety reasons because the lockdowns were caused by attacks on prison guards by members of a predominately African American gang and the prison officials needed time to review each African American inmate's file to check for gang affiliation. The inmate argued that he was not a member of a gang and after the first file inspection prison officials knew that he was not a member of a gang. Furthermore, the inmate argued that the rule was not reasonably related to a legitimate penological interest of safety because African American inmates who had pending court deadlines were allowed to leave their cell and use the prison law library under minimal supervision).

n. 66.

Page 543, note 6, add:

; Taylor v. Johnson, 257 F.3d 470 (5th Cir. 2001) (holding that district court abused its discretion in dismissing inmate's equal protection challenge of prison's grooming policy regarding beards by not allowing inmate opportunity to develop factual basis for his claim, where discriminatory enforcement of facially neutral grooming regulations may violate the Equal Protection Clause); DeBlasio v. Johnson, 128 F. Supp. 2d 315 (E.D. Va. 2000), aff'd, 12 Fed. Appx. 149 (4th Cir. 2001) and aff'd, 13 Fed. Appx. 96 (4th Cir. 2001) and aff'd, 13 Fed. Appx. 158 (4th Cir. 2001) (granting summary judgment to defendants for plaintiffs' failure to state a claim where plaintiff inmates alleged that the new Virginia Department of Corrections inmate grooming regulations violated the Fourteenth Amendment by disparately impacting their faiths and by proscribing different standards for inmates based on gender, but failed to show that any unequal treatment was the result of intentional discrimination, and where defendants asserted legitimate, if not compelling, interests in having such regulations).

n. 70.

Page 545, note 70, add:

; Johnson v. Paparozzi, 219 F. Supp. 2d 635 (D.N.J. 2002) (holding that inmate failed to state a claim based on the Equal Protection Clause where he alleged that he had been denied parole because he was not a white inmate who was a friend or acquaintance of a member of the parole board or other official without setting forth any facts in support of this claim).

n. 74.

Page 546, note 74, add:

; Caldwell v. Caesar, 150 F. Supp. 2d 50 (D.D.C. 2001) (denying defendant's motion for summary judgment where there was a genuine issue of material fact as to whether the prison chaplain treated Caucasian prisoners differently from African-American prisoners by requiring Caucasian inmates to submit requests for renewal of religious diet more frequently and delaying responding to these requests).

section 4:4, note 74, add:
Serrano v. Francis, 345 F.3d 1071 (9th Cir. 2003), cert. denied, 125 S. Ct. 43 (U.S. 2004) (reversing the district court's decision and holding that plaintiff raised sufficient evidence of discriminatory intent to convince a jury by a preponderance of the evidence that a hearing officer's decision to preclude live witness testimony was racially motivated based on the hearing officers remarks during the plaintiff's disciplinary hearing. The hearing officer's remarks included telling the plaintiff that 'he was treating [Serrano] like all the rest . . . and that [Serrano] was 'not O.J. Simpson or Johnnie Cochran' ").

n. 112.

Page 564, note 43, add:
; (granting inmate's motion to amend and denying defendant's motion to dismiss inmate's equal protection claim where inmate alleged that defendant prison officials made references to race and to his previous grievances about previous racial comments when they were taking him to the strip cell and putting him in restraints, and that they left an offensive drawing in the cell, making references to it and implying he would be lynched).

§ 4:5 Equal Protection Applied—Sexual Discrimination

n. 43.

Page 564, note 43, add:
; Oliver v. Scott, 276 F.3d 736 (5th Cir. 2002) (finding that the inmate failed to offer the necessary proof that male and female inmates were similarly situated where inmate alleged that his right to equal protection was violated when he was strip-searched by female guards, who observed him showering and using the bathroom, but that defendants protect female inmates from such cross-sex surveillance; court further held that the Fourteenth Amendment does not include a right to avoid exposure to members of the opposite sex and thus did not support inmate's equal protection claim).

n. 47.

Page 565, note 47, add:
; DeBlasio v. Johnson, 128 F. Supp. 2d 315 (E.D. Va. 2000), aff'd, 12 Fed. Appx. 149 (4th Cir. 2001) and aff'd, 13 Fed. Appx. 96 (4th Cir. 2001) and aff'd, 13 Fed. Appx. 158 (4th Cir. 2001) (granting summary judgment to defendants for plaintiffs' failure to state a claim where plaintiff inmates alleged that the new Virginia Department of Corrections inmate grooming regulations violated the Fourteenth Amendment by disparately impacting their faiths and by proscribing different standards for inmates based on gender but failed to show that any unequal treatment was the result of intentional discrimination, and where defendants asserted legitimate, if not compelling, interests in having such regulations).

Chapter 5

Communication and Expression: Speech in Prison

> **KeyCite®:** Cases and other legal materials listed in KeyCite Scope can be researched through West's KeyCite service on Westlaw®. Use KeyCite to check citations for form, parallel references, prior and later history, and comprehensive citator information, including citations to other decisions and secondary materials.

§ 5:1 Introduction

page 590, following the last sentence of the fifth paragraph in the section, after the word "prison." add new footnote

---

[13.1] An interesting development in prisoner's First Amendment rights is the use of the Internet. See generally Titia A. Holtz, Reaching Out From Behind the Bars: The Constitutionality of Laws Barring Prisoners From the Internet, 67 Brook. L. Rev. 885 (2002) (article confronts the issues associated with prisoners' communication rights with respect to the Internet and predicts that new regulations and laws, both federal and state, to curtail inmate use of the Internet will confront daunting constitutional challenges); see also Karen J. Hartman, Prison Walls and Firewalls: H.B. 2376—Arizona Denies Inmates Access to the Internet, 32 Ariz. St. L.J. 1423 (2000).

page 590, following the last sentence of sixth paragraph in the section, add new footnote

---

[13.2] See Lindy K. Lucero & Jeffery P. Bernhardt, Thirty-First Annual Review of Criminal Procedure: Substantive Rights Retained by Prisoners, 90 Geo. L.J. 2006 (2002) (in footnote 2752, authors list and annotate about a dozen cases addressing the extent to which prison officials may censor and limit a prisoner's First Amendment rights for reasons such as security, rehabilitation, and other penological interests); for another reason for limiting a prisoner's freedom of expression, see Kimberlin v. U.S. Dept. of Justice, 318 F.3d 228 (D.C. Cir. 2003) (inmates argued that regulations prohibiting inmates from possessing electric or electronic musical instruments infringed their First Amendment rights; district court dismissed their challenge; in affirming judgment, court of appeals found that blanket ban on electric and electronic instruments was consistent with rationale that prisons should be places of detention and punishment and that prison "perks" undermined the concept of jails as deterrence).

§ 5:3 Censorship and Limitations on Receipt of Publications

Page 610 add new text and footnote to end of fourth paragraph in section:
A restriction on inmates receiving mail order catalogues has been upheld.[13.1]

   [13.1]See Dixon v. Kirby, 210 F. Supp. 2d 792 (S.D. W. Va. 2002), aff'd, 48 Fed. Appx. 93 (4th Cir. 2002) (prison policy that prohibited inmates from receiving mail order catalogs did not violate inmate's First Amendment rights, as there was a rational connection between prohibition against receipt of catalogs and prison's legitimate administrative interest in not being able to process and monitor large volume of retail catalogues that would be received on an unlimited and unrestricted basis; prohibition against receipt of catalogs was not arbitrary censorship of the mail since inmates were prohibited from receiving all catalogs without regard to content).

section 5:3, note 13.1, add:
Prison Legal News v. Lehman, 272 F. Supp. 2d 1151, 31 Media L. Rep. (BNA) 2313 (W.D. Wash. 2003) (granting summary judgment in favor of plaintiff, Prison Legal News, and enjoining the prison officials from banning the delivery of bulk mail that is sent at a standard rate because an outright ban on this material is not reasonably related to the legitimate penological interest of safety since it is an arbitrary way of controlling the volume of mail coming into the prison and other prison regulations (i.e. regulations on the amount of person property an inmate can have in his cell) provide adequate protection against cumbersome cell searches and fire hazards. However, because the right to receive bulk mail was not clearly established, the court granted the prison official qualified immunity and therefore dismissed the damages claim).

n. 16.
section 5:3, note 16, add:
Wolf v. Ashcroft, 297 F.3d 305 (3d Cir. 2002) (reversing and remanding the district court's ruling that a prison regulation that implements the Zimmer Amendment, which prohibits a state from expending funds to provide access to R, X, or NC-17 movies to inmates, is valid under the Turner analysis because the district court did not articulate the valid penological interest that the regulation served, it did not describe the regulations relationship to a valid penological interest, and it only applied the first *Turner* factor.); see also Colin Miller, Film & TV: A Wolf in Sheep's Clothing: Wolf v. Ashcroft and the Constitutionality of Using MPAA Ratings to Censor Films in Prison, 6 Vand. J. Ent, L. & Prac. 265 (2004).

   Bahrampour v. Lampert, 356 F.3d 969 (9th Cir. 2004) (holding that prison officials did not violate the inmate's First or Fourteenth Amend-

SPEECH IN PRISON § 5:4

ment rights when they rejected magazines containing sexually explicit pictures and role playing games because these types of materials have been shown to increase violent behavior and gambling which compromises institutional safety).

n. 65.

page 622, note 65, add:
But see Cline v. Fox, 266 F. Supp. 2d 489 (N.D. W. Va. 2003) (prison regulation that prohibited certain books containing graphically described sexual escapades, but with no pictures, was upheld as rationally related to legitimate penological and rehabilitative interests).

n. 67.

page 622, note 67, add:
See also Ballance v. Virginia, 130 F. Supp. 2d 754 (W.D. Va. 2000), aff'd, 11 Fed. Appx. 174 (4th Cir. 2001) (prison officials did not violate prisoner's rights by confiscating photographs of nude and partially nude children from his cell; decision to confiscate the pictures was reasonable in light of circumstances—inmate was a convicted sex offender—and furthered prison's penological interests of rehabilitation and security).

n. 87.

section 5:3, note 87, add:
Krug v. Lutz, 329 F.3d 692 (9th Cir. 2003) (affirming the district court's decision that the Arizona Department of Correction's (ADOC) policy, which states that an inmate may appeal the exclusion of a magazine to the officer who made the initial decision to exclude the magazine, violates the inmate's right to due process. The court upheld the district court's injunction, which requires ADOC officials to implement a system under which an inmate can appeal the decision to an officer other than the officer who made the initial determination. However, because the officials could have reasonably believed that their conduct did not violate the plaintiff's rights, the officials are entitled to qualified immunity and therefore dismissed the damages claim); Prison Legal News v. Lehman, 272 F. Supp. 2d 1151, 31 Media L. Rep. (BNA) 2313 (W.D. Wash. 2003) (granting summary judgment in favor of plaintiff, Prison Legal News, and enjoining the prison officials from banning the delivery of bulk mail that is sent at a standard rate because an outright ban on this material is not reasonably related to the legitimate penological interest of safety since it is an arbitrary way of controlling the volume of mail coming into the prison and other prison regulations (i.e. regulations on the amount of person property an inmate can have in his cell) provide adequate protection against cumbersome cell searches and fire hazards. However, because the right to receive bulk mail was not clearly established, the court granted the prison official qualified immunity and therefore dismissed the damages claim).

§ 5:4 Publisher-Only Rules

page 632, sixth paragraph of section, add new footnote 7.1 after the first sentence of the paragraph.

[7.1]See Ashker v. California Dept. of Corrections, 224 F. Supp. 2d 1253 (N.D. Cal. 2002) (court granted inmate's motion for summary judgment on

99

§ 5:4   Rights of Prisoners

his First Amendment book label claim against department of corrections and granted permanent injunction against enforcement of policy; policy's purpose was to ensure that books were shipped to inmates directly from publishers, thus decreasing possibility that contraband would be included in book packages, and to decrease number of packages that required individual inspection by prison mailroom employees; court found that it was not clear that ensuring efficient mailroom operations was legitimate penological objective; further, the fact that policy applied to books but not other items meant that it was not neutral but was weighted against First Amendment activities).

section 5:4, note 7.1, add:
Prison Legal News v. Lehman, 272 F. Supp. 2d 1151, 31 Media L. Rep. (BNA) 2313 (W.D. Wash. 2003) (holding that the prison's publisher only rule, which states that inmates may only receive publications directly from the publisher, does not violate the inmates' or Prison Legal News' First Amendment rights because the rule is rationally related to the legitimate penological of safety since publications sent directly from the publisher are less likely to have been altered from their original form and are less likely to contain contraband. Further, inmates have alternative means of acquiring reading material, such as borrowing books from the library).

n. 9.

section 5:4, note 9, add:
Ashker v. California Dept. of Corrections, 350 F.3d 917 (9th Cir. 2003) (holding that "[t]he district court did not err in concluding that the book label requirement is not rationally related to a legitimate penological objective." In this case, the book label rule required that all prison packages containing books and/or magazines contain a label on a specified location on the package. The court held that this rule was not rationally related to the legitimate interest of preventing contraband in the prison because this goal is already achieved by the prisons publisher-only rule combined with the policy that all incoming packages are searched by prison officials).

n. 20.

page 635, note 20, add:
; Sorrels v. McKee, 290 F.3d 965 (9th Cir. 2002) (court declared unconstitutional a "no gift publication" policy that prohibited receipt by a prisoner of any book, magazine, or other publication unless prisoner ordered publication from publisher and paid for it out of his or her own prison account). But see Zimmerman v. Simmons, 260 F. Supp. 2d 1077 (D. Kan. 2003) (court held that prison regulation and policies barring receipt of free or gift subscriptions were rationally related to legitimate penological interest, and thus did not violate First Amendment or due process).

section 5:4, note 20, add:
Rice v. State, 31 Kan. App. 2d 964, 76 P.3d 1048 (2003), review granted, (Nov. 12, 2003) (holding that a prison regulation that bans all periodicals purchased for inmates from friends and family members rather than from

Speech In Prison § 5:6

the inmate's prison account is overbroad and therefore is not reasonably related to a legitimate penological interest).

§ 5:5 Access to Literature in Punitive Segregation

n. 3.

section 5:5, note 3, add:
Iseley v. Beard, 841 A.2d 168 (Pa. Commw. Ct. 2004) (holding in dicta that a prison regulation, which prohibits inmates in segregation from receiving publications, is reasonably related to the legitimate penological interest of safety and rehabilitation).

n. 4.

section 5:5, note 4, add:
Collins v. Franks, 2004 WL 882155 (W.D. Wis. 2004) (granting the inmate leave to proceed on his claim that denial of an English books from the library while he was in administrative segregation merely because the books was a hard cover book states a valid First Amendment claim).

§ 5:6 Prisoner Writings

n. 7.

section 5:6, note 7, add:
Medina v. City of Philadelphia, 2004 WL 1126007 (E.D. Pa. 2004) (holding that the inmate stated a valid First Amendment claim against prison officials when he alleged that officials confiscated a manuscript that he was writing about the Latin Kings even though the inmate was not a member of the Latin Kings, the material in the books was not gang related, the purpose of the book was not to encourage gangs, and it was unlikely that other inmates would see the manuscript because the inmate did not wish to share its contents until publication. However, the court granted qualified immunity for the prison officials because the inmate's right to have this material in his cell was not clearly established. The court reasoned that the Latin Kings are a widely known gang and therefore the prison officials could have reasonably believed that the manuscript posed a security threat).

n. 51.

page 651, note 51, add:
; Farid v. Goord, 200 F. Supp. 2d 220 (W.D. N.Y. 2002) (inmate claimed that he was punished in retaliation for writing satirical articles on various aspects of prison life; in denying defendant's motion for summary judgment, court found that the articles, one of which contained the words "mass mobilization," could not reasonably be interpreted as calling for any kind of inmate action "which may be detrimental to the order of the facility"); Owens v. Shannon, 808 A.2d 607 (Pa. Commw. Ct. 2002) (prisoner stated claim for violation of free-speech rights by alleging transfer to prison farther from his home in retaliation for writing letters to newspapers critical of prison system); Spruytte v. Hoffner, 181 F. Supp. 2d 736 (W.D. Mich. 2001) (prisoners established that their transfer to other facilities was in retaliation for writing letters to editor of newspaper, where evidence that prisoner's lost their library jobs, were both labeled security threats, and had personal property removed from their footlockers

§ 5:6 RIGHTS OF PRISONERS

strongly suggested that corrections official wanted prisoners gone from the facility to prevent any further publicity on prison matters).

n. 57.

section 5:6, note 57, add:
For a comprehensive discussion of the development of New York State's Son-of Sam Laws see Anthony J. Annucci, New York Expanded Son of Sam Law and Other Fiscal Measures to Deter Prisoner Suits While Satisfying Outstanding Debts, 24 Pace L. Rev. _____ (forthcoming 2004).

n. 84.

section 5:6, note 84, add:
Anthony J. Annucci, New York Expanded Son of Sam Law and Other Fiscal Measures to Deter Prisoner Suits While Satisfying Outstanding Debts, 24 Pace L. Rev._____ (forthcoming 2004) (discussing the evolution of the New York State Son-of-Sam Laws).

Add new note 84.1 after the word "criminal" in the second to last sentence of the last paragraph in section 5:6:
84.1

[84.1]New York State Crime Victims Bd. ex rel. Hernon v. Zaffuto, 196 Misc. 2d 602, 763 N.Y.S.2d 442 (Sup 2003) (granting in part and denying in part the New York State Crime Victims Board's motion for a preliminary injunction to prevent the son and wife of a deceased inmate from collecting money from a settled medical malpractice claim arising out of an incident which occurred while the decedent was in prison. As a result of the malpractice settlement the decedent's son was awarded $57,209.20 and the decedent's wife was awarded $30,000. The petitioner brought this action on behalf of the victim of the crime for which the decedent was imprisoned to enjoin the decedent's family from receiving the money until the victim had a chance file suit and recover damages based on the decedent's crime. The court granted the petitioner motion for a preliminary injunction with respect to the decedent's son's award for damages because the State's interest in compensating crime victims outweighed the decedent's son's claim that he should be compensated for his father's failure to provide financial and other support to his son during his formative years. However, the petition's injunction with respect to the decedent's wife's award of damages was denied. Here, the decedent owed his wife back child support payments and the damages award was allocated to satisfy those payments. The court held that the nature of child support payments outweighs the state's interest in compensating crime victims and therefore denied the petition's motion for an injunction. Furthermore, the decedent's wife was clearly able to established that she was entitled to child support payments while the petitioner did not make any factual showing that he was entitled to damages).

New York State Crime Victims Bd. ex rel. Storey v. Jackson, 4 A.D.3d 710, 772 N.Y.S.2d 419 (App. Div. 3d Dep't 2004) (remanding the case to the trial court to determine whether the petitioner could serve as a representative of a deceased crime victim. In this case the record is inconclusive regarding the relationship that the petitioner had with the crime victim and New York law requires that "[s]ome type of relationship must be demonstrated to establish that a person is entitled to represent a crime victim").

§ 5:7 The Right to Political Activity: The Right to Associate, to Communicate, and to Present Grievances in Prison

n. 4.

page 661, note 4, add:
See also Massachusetts Prisoners Ass'n Political Action Committee v. Acting Governor, 435 Mass. 811, 761 N.E.2d 952 (2002) (prison prohibition against political fundraising and policies restricting inmate organizations, which were adversarial and divisive, were reasonably related to legitimate penological interests and therefore did not violate the First Amendment rights to free speech and freedom of association).

n. 27.

page 666, note 27, add:
See Fraise v. Terhune, 283 F.3d 506 (3d Cir. 2002) (court of appeals, affirming district court's judgment, held that policy allowing prison officials to designate groups as security threat groups and transfer core members of these groups was "unrelated to the suppression of expression" and was based on concern about security).

n. 32.

page 668, note 32, add:
See also In re Parmelee, 115 Wash. App. 273, 63 P.3d 800 (Div. 1 2003) (prison authorities did not unreasonably sanction inmate when he violated facility's insolence rule in his written grievances; inmate wrote the court, was not being punished or sanctioned for using grievance process but for use of scandalous, insolent, and abusive language in his grievances, which he knew was prohibited; further, inmate's language referring to a correctional officer as "piss-ant" and "shithead" who should be fired "before his attitude gets him fucked up" was a true threat that was not protected by the First Amendment). On a related topic, see Kevin Francis O'Neill, Muzzling Death Row Inmates: Applying the First Amendment to Regulations that Restrict a Condemned Prisoner's Last Words, 33 Ariz. St. L.J. 1159 (2001) (author argues that the privilege to deliver a last dying speech, which often contain statements that are political or critical of the government or prison system, is a First Amendment right, and that state laws and prison policies that do not allow a condemned prisoner to utter a last dying speech are unconstitutional).

n. 34.

section 5:7, note 34, add:
Govan v. Campbell, 289 F. Supp. 2d 289 (N.D. N.Y. 2003) (holding that plaintiff was not denied access to the prison grievance system policy when defendants were able to provide fourteen grievances filed by plaintiff in less than one year, most of which went through the entire appellate process). Scott v. Coughlin, 344 F.3d 282 (2d Cir. 2003) (vacating and remanding the district courts grant of summary judgment in favor of the prison official based on plaintiff's allegation that a prison official violated his civil rights by retaliating against him for exercising his First Amendment rights. In this case, the prisoner alleged that when he filed a complaint against a prison officer the officer responded by singling him out for a pat frisk and then the officer beat him. The district court granted summary judgment for the defendant because plaintiff's medical records did

§ 5:7   RIGHTS OF PRISONERS

not show significant injury. However, on appeal the court held that the fact that the plaintiff's claim does not match his medical records do not provide a sound basis for summary judgment because further evidence should be considered regarding the injuries in order to make a final determination).

n. 35.
section 5:7, note 35, add:
Miller v. Blanchard, 2004 WL 1354368 (W. D. Wis. 2004) (holding that the inmate did not have a First Amendment claim for retaliation against the defendants/ investigators and prosecutors when the inmate threatened to sue the defendants for subjecting him to life threatening danger and as a result the defendant's withdrew their support to help plaintiff have his sentence reduced because plaintiff does not have a First Amendment right to threaten litigation); Abreu v. Ramirez, 284 F.Supp.2d 1250 (C. D. Cal. 2003)(dismissing the inmate's claim that prison officials retaliated against him for making use of the grievance process).

n. 36.
page 670, note 36, add:
; Morales v. Mackalm, 278 F.3d 126 (2d Cir. 2002) (prison officials' alleged conduct of transferring inmate to a psychiatric center a short time after inmate filed grievance supported inference that prison officials had retaliatory motive); Davis v. Goord, 320 F.3d 346 (2d Cir. 2003) (inmate failed to establish claim of retaliation because sarcastic comments did not, without more, constitute adverse action); Hargis v. Foster, 312 F.3d 404, 54 Fed. R. Serv. 3d 516 (9th Cir. 2002) (material issues of fact existed as to whether prison officials acted unreasonably in characterizing inmate's statements as an attempt to coerce guard into not enforcing prison shaving rule when inmate indicated that he could not shave with regular razor without cutting himself, due to neurological disorder that caused his head to jerk and twist uncontrollably, and suggested that guard's actions with respect to enforcing shaving rule could be raised in inmate's pending state litigation, and thus whether disciplining inmate for such conduct under regulation barring coercion of guards was rationally related to legitimate security concerns, precluding summary judgment for prison officials on inmate's § 1983 claim that regulation, as applied to his conduct, violated First Amendment); Johnson v. Freeburn, 144 F. Supp. 2d 817 (E.D. Mich. 2001) (court denied motion to dismiss claim that correction officer retaliated against inmate who had filed a grievance against officer, by telling guard tower that inmate refused to return to his cell and instructing the guard to shoot the inmate if he moved); Lindy K. Lucero & Jeffery P. Bernhardt, Thirty-First Annual Review of Criminal Procedure: Substantive Rights Retained by Prisoners, 90 Geo. L.J. 2006 (2002) (in footnote 2753, authors list and annotate cases dealing with prison officials' retaliating against prisoners for exercising their First Amendment rights).

section 5:7, note 36, add:
Segreti v. Gillen, 259 F. Supp. 2d 733 (N.D. Ill. 2003) (denying prison officials' motion to dismiss the plaintiff's retaliatory transfer claim because plaintiff described a sufficient sequence of events to support the claim when plaintiff set forth the following chronology of events in his complaint: plaintiff left the Transition Center to attend his work assignments, upon his return, the defendant "falsely" advised plaintiff that his movement off the Transition Center was not approved and proceeded to become

verbally abusive when plaintiff tried to explain that he had been following the proper procedure, plaintiff prepared a written grievance against an officer describing a confrontation, plaintiff submitted the grievance to his counselor, the officer subsequently filed a disciplinary report against plaintiff alleging that plaintiff gave false information to an employee, insolence and unauthorized movement; in response to the grievance, a hearing was held and the officer was allowed to participate in the hearing and dictate the results, plaintiff was then transferred from the Transition Center to the Joliet Correctional Center. In support of their motion to dismiss, the prison officials' argued that plaintiff did not provide evidence to show that the grievance motivated the hearing officers' decision to transfer plaintiff. However, the court did not accept this defense because plaintiff is not required to show motivation at the pleading stage. Further, defendant is not protected by qualified immunity in this case because it is clearly established that retaliatory transfers based on an inmate's complaint violates the inmate's first amendment rights); Bruce v. Ylst, 351 F.3d 1283, 63 Fed. R. Evid. Serv. 221 (9th Cir. 2003) (reversing the district court's grant of summary judgment in favor of the prison officials and holding that plaintiff raised a material question of fact as to whether his transfer based on the prison officials' identification of plaintiff as a gang member was retaliatory in nature. The inmate was identified as a gang member based on evidence that was insufficient to support the finding that plaintiff was a gang membership on three prior occasions. The fact that the goal of preventing gang activity serves a legitimate penological interest does not make the district court's grant of summary judgment appropriate here because the plaintiff has raised a material issue of fact as to whether the prison official were abusing this legitimate procedure); Bennett v. Goord, 343 F.3d 133 (2d Cir. 2003) (holding that plaintiff raised a material question of fact to overcome the defendant's motion for summary judgment when plaintiff alleged that New York Department of Correction Services (DOCS) retaliated against him for constitutionally protected conduct including filing lawsuits and grievances against DOCS and its officers. The parties stipulated that filing grievances is a constitutionally protected activity. The issue was whether the plaintiff's constitutionally protected activities were the reason for adverse action. When circumstantial evidence is sufficiently compelling direct evidence is not needed to show retaliatory motive. The court held that the plaintiff was able raise circumstantial evidence to support a retaliatory motive including evidence that defendant tried to transfer plaintiff from a medium security facility to a maximum security facility when the settlement of a lawsuit plaintiff filed against the DOCS was finalized. Furthermore, the inmate raised sufficient circumstantial evidence to support his claim when he alleged that disciplinary charges, which were ultimately dismissed for lacking a factual basis, were filed against him days after he filed a complaint against an prison officer alleging that the officer violated his right to confidentiality when the officer entered an examination room when the inmate was in the middle of his HIV counseling session); Johnson v. Kingston, 292 F. Supp. 2d 1146 (W.D. Wis. 2003) (the court granted the prison officials' motion for summary judgment on the plaintiff's claim that his transfer to the Waupun Correctional Institution from the Columbia Correctional Institution was in retaliation for a lawsuit plaintiff filed and won against the prison doctor and for testimony the plaintiff provided for another inmate against corrections officers at Waupun. The court held that plaintiff did not have sufficient evidence to raise a question of fact as to whether the defendants, officers at Columbia, knew about the two suits before they decided to transfer plaintiff); Medina v. City of Philadelphia, 2004 WL 1126007 (E.D. Pa. 2004) (dismissing the inmate's claim that prison officials "retaliated against him for filing this civil action by denying him use of the law library and education facilities, depriving him of employment, and confiscating [a] manuscript" because the inmate could not show that "any of the named Defendants were involved in [the inmate's] employment, law library access, or educational opportunities); Buhrman v. Wilkinson, 257 F. Supp. 2d 1110 (S.D. Ohio 2003), opinion supplemented, 2004 WL 2044055 (S.D. Ohio 2004), report and recommendation adopted, 2004 WL 2044056 (S.D. Ohio 2004) (holding that the inmate did not sustain his allegations that the parole board was retaliating against him for bringing suit in federal court by delaying his hearing because, *inter alia*, continuations of his parole hearing were scheduled at the request of his counsel); Hopkins v. Warden, NH State Prison, 2004 DNH 88, 2004 WL 1125241 (D.N.H. 2004) (holding that the inmate stated a valid retaliation claim when prison officials moved the inmate to a cell where he safety was in jeopardy in response to the inmate's action of telling prison administrators about staff misconduct); Miller v. Loughren, 258 F. Supp. 2d 61 (N.D. N.Y. 2003) (granting the defendant's cross motion for summary judgment on plaintiff's claim that he was transferred from a dormitory to a cell block in retaliation for filing a grievance against a prison officer because the plaintiff acknowledged that his own misconduct was sufficient to justify the transfer)

n. 43.

page 672, note 43, add:
See also Farid v. Goord, 200 F. Supp. 2d 220 (W.D. N.Y. 2002) (inmate's right to prepare and send petition was protected conduct because there was no regulation at prison that forbade petitions).

Chapter 6

First Amendment Rights: Religion

> **KeyCite®:** Cases and other legal materials listed in KeyCite Scope can be researched through West's KeyCite service on Westlaw®. Use KeyCite to check citations for form, parallel references, prior and later history, and comprehensive citator information, including citations to other decisions and secondary materials.

§ 6:4 Congress and the Supreme Court Battle Over a Governing Standard

section 6:4: add new note 18.1 after the word "governments" in the first paragraph following note 18:

[18.1]

[18.1] O'Bryan v. Bureau of Prisons, 349 F.3d 399 (7th Cir. 2003) (reversing the district court's dismissal of the inmate's claim that the Federal Bureau of Prisons violated his rights under the Religious Freedom Restoration Act (RFRA) on the grounds that RFRA has been declared unconstitutional because RFRA has only been declared unconstitutional as applied to the states, not as applied to the internal operations of the federal government).

n. 22.

Page 691, note 22, add:
; Johnson v. Martin, 223 F. Supp. 2d 820 (W.D. Mich. 2002) (state prisoners brought action alleging that state department of corrections' classification of religion and its prisoner members as security threat group violated RLUIPA; on state's motion for summary judgment, District Court held RLUIPA does not violate Establishment Clause, Congress did not exceed its powers under Commerce Clause or Spending Clause, and RLUIPA does not violate Tenth Amendment).

n. 45.

Page 695, note 45, add:
; Fraise v. Terhune, 283 F.3d 506 (3d Cir. 2002) (finding that New Jersey prison policy that allowed correctional officials to designate security threat groups and transfer core members of these groups to special units as applied to "Five Percent Nation" did not violate members' First Amendment right to free exercise of religion).

section 6:4: add new text after the last paragraph in section 6.4:

Currently there is a split in the Circuits regarding the

§ 6:4   RIGHTS OF PRISONERS

constitutionality of RLUIPA. The Fourth, Seventh, and Ninth Circuits have all upheld RLUIPA under several constitutional challenges while the Sixth Circuit has struck down RLUIPA as unconstitutional. Courts agree that RLUIPA is constitutional under the Spending Power[51], the Tenth Amendment[52], and the Eleventh Amendment[53]. The disputed issue is whether RLUIPA violates the Establishment Clause of the First Amendment. The Circuits that have upheld RLUIPA under the Establishment Clause reason that RLUIPA has the secular purpose of lifting the burden on religious exercise imposed by unwarranted and substantial infringement, the primary effect of RLUIPA neither advances nor inhibits religion, rather it simply protects the free exercise of religion which is allowed by the constitution; and finally RLUIPA does not require excessive entanglement between government and religion by requiring the government to excessively monitor or sponsor religious practices, rather RLUIPA simply removes government imposed burdens on the exercise of religion.[54] Conversely, the Sixth Circuit reasoned that RLUIPA violates the Establishment Clause of the First Amendment by impermissibly providing greater protection to religious rights compared with other constitutional rights because it requires prison rules which burden religion to be subject to a strict scrutiny analysis while prison rules which burden other constitutional rights are analyzed under the highly deferential Turner standard without showing that religious rights are at a greater risk of deprivation.[55]

[51]See Mayweathers v. Newland, 314 F.3d 1062 (9th Cir. 2002), cert. denied, 124 S. Ct. 66, 157 L. Ed. 2d 30 (U.S. 2003); Charles v. Verhagen, 348 F.3d 601 (7th Cir. 2003); see also Williams v. Bitner, 285 F. Supp. 2d 593 (M.D. Pa. 2003).

[52]See Mayweathers v. Newland, 314 F.3d 1062 (9th Cir. 2002), cert. denied, 124 S. Ct. 66, 157 L. Ed. 2d 30 (U.S. 2003); Charles v. Verhagen, 348 F.3d 601 (7th Cir. 2003); see also Williams v. Bitner, 285 F. Supp. 2d 593 (M.D. Pa. 2003).

[53]See Mayweathers v. Newland, 314 F.3d 1062 (9th Cir. 2002), cert. denied, 124 S. Ct. 66, 157 L. Ed. 2d 30 (U.S. 2003); see also Williams v. Bitner, 285 F. Supp. 2d 593 (M.D. Pa. 2003).

[54]See Mayweathers v. Newland, 314 F.3d 1062 (9th Cir. 2002), cert. denied, 124 S. Ct. 66, 157 L. Ed. 2d 30 (U.S. 2003); Charles v. Verhagen, 348 F.3d 601 (7th Cir. 2003); Madison v. Riter, 355 F.3d 310 (4th Cir. 2003), petition for cert. filed, 72 U.S.L.W. 3658, 73 U.S.L.W. 3059 (U.S. Apr. 6, 2004); see also Williams v. Bitner, 285 F. Supp. 2d 593 (M.D. Pa. 2003).

[55]Cutter v. Wilkinson, 349 F.3d 257, 2003 FED App. 0397P (6th Cir. 2003), cert. granted, 2004 WL 843727 (U.S. 2004).

§ 6:5 Equal Protection

n. 4.

section 6:5, note 4, add:
But see Rashad v. Maloney, 16 Mass. L. Rep. 162 (Mass. Super. Ct. 2003) (dismissing the Muslim inmates claim that they were not given halaal meat but that Jewish inmates were given kosher food because the plaintiffs did not provide any evidence that the prison could obtain an adequate supply of the halaal meat from a reliable vendor at a reasonable cost).

Page 698, add new text and footnote to sentence ending. . . stated a claim under the Equal Protection Clause."
, and that state prisoners had a justiciable claim for damages, in their § 1983 lawsuit alleging violation of their free exercise rights under the First Amendment, on allegations that they were repeatedly denied access to Nation of Islam texts over a period of several years because prison officials determined that those texts were not religious.[4.5]

[4.5]Sutton v. Rasheed, 323 F.3d 236 (3d Cir. 2003), as amended, (May 29, 2003) (finding that state prison regulation prohibiting books other than legal materials and a personal Bible, Holy Koran or other religious equivalent was invalid as applied to restrictive status prisoners who were precluded from possessing Nation of Islam texts on the grounds that such texts were not religious).

n. 8.

Page 699, note 8, add:
; Pugh v. Goord, 184 F. Supp. 2d 326 (S.D. N.Y. 2002) (denying inmates' motion for preliminary injunction where inmates, who were Shi'ite Muslims claimed that the religious programs provided for Sunni Muslims infringed upon their ability to practice Shi'a faith); Cancel v. Mazzuca, 205 F. Supp. 2d 128 (S.D. N.Y. 2002) (right of Shi'ite prisoners to be given separate religious accommodation not clearly established at time that New York Department of Correctional Services employees allegedly violated inmate's free exercise rights).

section 6:5, note 8, add:
Huff v. Hooper, 2003 WL 158689 (Del. Super. Ct. 2003), appeal dismissed, 832 A.2d 1251 (Del. 2003) (granting summary judgment for prison officials on plaintiffs' claim that the prison treats Muslims and Christians differently because there are Christian but not Muslim symbols in the chapel. Muslim inmates contended that the prison provides funding for Christian but not Muslim materials, and the prison uses heightened security for Muslim but not Christian visitors. The court rejected this claim because the inmates could not produce evidence supporting the charges).
Pugh v. Goord, 345 F.3d 121 (2d Cir. 2003) (vacating and remanding the district court's sua sponte dismissal of the Shi'ite Muslim inmates' claim that the religious programs for Muslim inmates at the prison, which were dominated by Sunni Muslim inmates and a Sunni Imam, infringed upon the plaintiffs' ability to practice their Shi'a faith. The court vacated and remanded this case because "[d]istrict courts have to power to enter

§ 6:5   Rights of Prisoners

summary judgment sua sponte if 'the losing party was on notice that [it] had to come forward with all of [its] evidence.' " But here, however, the plaintiffs were not given adequate notice of the courts intention to dismiss their claim allowing the plaintiffs to come forward with all of their evidence).

§ 6:6   Establishment of Religion
n. 27.

Page 704, note 27, add following the Ross v. Keelings citation and parenthetical:
; Nusbaum v. Terrangi, 210 F. Supp. 2d 784 (E.D. Va. 2002) (conditioning availability of good time credit on attending "Therapeutic Community Program," which emphasized religion, violated the Establishment Clause of the First Amendment);

Page 704, note 10, add at end of footnote:
; Searcy v. Simmons, 299 F.3d 1220 (10th Cir. 2002) (finding that the admission of responsibility requirement for prison's sexual abuse treatment program did not violate inmate's First Amendment right to free exercise on ground that inmate, who claimed he was innocent, sincerely held religious beliefs prohibiting him from lying, where inmate's participation in the program was voluntary and the requirement applied to all participating inmates).

section 6:6, note 27, add:
Lynn S. Branham, "Go and Sin No More": The Constitutionality of Governmentally Funded Faith-Based Prison Units, 37 U. Mich. J. L. Ref. 291 (2004) (discussing the constitutionality of faith-based prison programs, how they are best structured to survive a First Amendment Challenge, and recommending a new spin to the Turner test, "the Turner test with teeth," to analyze these programs. Under the "Turner test with teeth,".

> Governmental funding of religious services and programs for prisoners, whether rendered inside or outside a faith-based unit, is constitutional if three requirements are met: one, the monetary outlays are reasonable related to the furtherance of a legitimate governmental interest; two, a prisoner's receipt of these services or participation in those programs is the result if his or her own voluntary choice; and three, the funding programs, when viewed from the perspective of a reasonable person with an awareness of the overall context in which the funding program has been implemented, manifests neutrality between religion and irreligion and between various religious sects).

Scott Roberts, The Constitutionality of Prison-Sponsored Religious Therapeutic Communities, 15 Regent U.L. Rev. 69 (2002/2003) (reasoning that religious rehabilitation units that serve a legitimate penological purpose do not violate the Establishment Clause of the First Amendment).

§ 6:9   Religious Practices—Personal Appearance and Clothing
n. 40.
Page 731, note 40, add:

First Amendment: Religion § 6:10

See Taylor v. Johnson, 257 F.3d 470 (5th Cir. 2001); Goodman v. Money, 180 F. Supp. 2d 946 (N.D. Ohio 2001).

§ 6:10 Religious Practices—Meals

n. 4.

section 6:10, note 4, add:
Rashad v. Maloney, 16 Mass. L. Rep. 162 (Mass. Super. Ct. 2003) (dismissing the Muslim inmates claim that they were not given halaal meat but that Jewish inmates were given kosher food because the plaintiffs did not provide any evidence that the prison could obtain an adequate supply of the halaal meat from a reliable vendor at a reasonable cost).

n. 17.

Page 737, note 17, add:
Resnick v. Adams, 317 F.3d 1056 (9th Cir. 2003) (finding that requirement that inmate fill out a standard prison form in order to receive kosher food was not an unconstitutional infringement of his right to free exercise of religion where there was a legitimate governmental interest in the orderly administration of a program that allowed federal prisons to accommodate the religious dietary needs of inmates); Beerheide v. Suthers, 286 F.3d 1179 (10th Cir. 2002) (finding that inmate's First Amendment right to free exercise of religion was violated when he was not provided kosher meals while incarcerated in the Colorado prison system); Searles v. Van Bebber, 251 F.3d 869 (10th Cir. 2001), cert. denied, 536 U.S. 904, 122 S. Ct. 2356, 153 L. Ed. 2d 179 (2002) (finding that prison chaplain violated inmate's First Amendment right to free exercise of religion by denying him approval of a kosher diet). But see, Ford v. McGinnis, 230 F. Supp. 2d 338 (S.D. N.Y. 2002) (officials of the New York State Department of Correctional Services did not violate Muslim inmate's First Amendment rights when they refused to provide him with "Eid-ul-Fitr Family Day Event" meal, where Muslim clerics informed the officials that when the meal was moved past the required three-day close of Ramadan, it was no longer of religious significance; to force officials to accommodate the inmate's particularized view of Islam, after having been advised of Islam's actual requirements by religious experts, would have unreasonably burdened government officers in the performance of their duties).

n. 28.

section 6:10, note 28, add:
Williams v. Morton, 343 F.3d 212 (3d Cir. 2003) (affirming the district courts grant of summary judgment for the prison officials on the inmate's free exercise claim that the prison officials' refusal to provide halal meat to Muslim inmates unconstitutionally burdens the inmate's right to free exercise because there are "alternative avenues through which [Muslim inmates] can express their religious beliefs" without having access to halal meats including, *inter alia*, access to a pork-free, vegetarian diet on a regular basis and halal meats on certain religious holidays).

n. 33.

section 6:10, note 33, add:
However, inmates may have a valid claim against prison officials if they are temporarily denied a religious diet as a form of punishment. See

§ 6:10   Rights of Prisoners

McEachin v. McGuinnis, 357 F.3d 197 (2d Cir. 2004) (holding that the district court improperly dismissed plaintiff's free exercise claim because plaintiff raised a question of fact as to whether his free exercise rights were infringed when plaintiff refused to obey a prison guard's order to return his tray and cup when the guard allegedly knew that the plaintiff was praying and, in response to that incident, the prison officials imposed a seven day restrictive diet on plaintiff whereby they refused to provide plaintiff with halal meat during Ramadan).

§ 6:11   Religious Practices—Religious Services

section 6:11: Add new note 3.5 after the word "activities" in the third sentence of the paragraph following note 3:
3.1

[3.1]Larson v. Cooper, 90 P.3d 125 (Alaska 2004) (holding that the Free Exercise Clause of the First Amendment does not require prisons "to allow hand-holding, kissing, and embracing throughout [a] visit." In this case, the inmate alleged that prison officials violated his free exercise rights when officers ordered him to release his wife's hand during a visit. The inmate further alleged that his free exercise rights were violated when his request for a religious contact visit with his wife was denied. In his request for a religious contact visit with his wife, the inmate requested permission to "[read] from the New International Readers Version Bible, [kneel] and pray to [the] Lord and Savior Jesus Christ, [embrace] for long periods of time and when needed, [hold] hands and [kiss]." The court held that the restrictions on contact visits were reasonable related to the legitimate penological interest of safety, specifically the prevention of contraband into the facility. The court also held that the prison regulation prohibiting contact visits did not violate the Free Exercise Clause of the Alaska Constitution because the prison regulations were narrowly tailored to achieve the compelling state interest of keeping the prison free from contraband. The regulation was narrowly tailored to achieve this goal because providing accommodations to meet this request would require a significant prison resources including personnel to perform strip searches, placement of the inmate in a "dry cell" after the visit, and assigning a guard to monitor the visit).

n. 15.

section 6:14, note 15, add:
Neal v. Lewis, 259 F. Supp. 2d 1178 (D. Kan. 2003) (granting the inmate's motion for a preliminary injunction to prevent prison officials from destroying religious texts that the inmate had in his cell in excess of the 15 book limit. The court held that the threat of a constitutional violation causes irreparable injury. Additionally, the harm to plaintiff if the books were destroyed is greater then the harm to prison officials if they are made to hold the books until trial. Finally, protecting the constitutional right of free exercise is in the public interest notwithstanding the fact that plaintiff is a prisoner); but see Sutton v. Rasheed, 323 F.3d 236 (3d Cir. 2003), as amended, (May 29, 2003) (affirming the district court's grant of qualified immunity for the prison officials because access to Nation of Islam texts for inmates housed in a special unit for high-risk inmates was not a well-established right even though a *Turner* analysis of whether the plaintiffs should have had access to the books weighed in favor of plaintiffs).

§ 6:13 Religious Practices—Access to Clergy

n. 8.

Page 761, note 8, add:
; Kikumura v. Hurley, 242 F.3d 950 (10th Cir. 2001) (reversing in part and affirming in part district court's denial of prisoner's request for injunctive relief where prisoner, a registered Buddhist, was denied his requests for pastoral visits from a Methodist minister; court affirmed that prisoner had not demonstrated a substantial likelihood on the merits of his First Amendment claim, in part because of deference given to prison officials in evaluating constitutional claim, but found that prisoner did demonstrate a substantial likelihood on the merits of free-exercise claim under Religious Freedom Restoration Act where prisoner was able to show that denial of the pastoral visits constituted a substantial burden on his ability to practice Christianity).

§ 6:15 Religious Practices—Access to Religious Accouterments

n. 4.

Page 768, note 4, add:
Tart v. Young, 168 F. Supp. 2d 590 (W.D. Va. 2001) (ban on burning herbs did not violate inmate's First Amendment right to free exercise of religion where ban was reasonably related to government interests in preventing inmates from burning herbs to mask smell of marijuana). But see Levitan v. Ashcroft, 281 F.3d 1313 (D.C. Cir. 2002) (reversing district court decision to dismiss prisoners' First Amendment free-exercise of religion claim because prisoners did not show that drinking wine as part of the Catholic sacrament of Communion was a vital part of the religion; on appeal, court held that a religious practice need not be mandatory to warrant First Amendment protection; rather, the district court should have determined whether the inmate's views had any basis in their creed and whether prisoners met their burden under the *Turner/O'Lone* test).

section 6:15: Add new text and note 4.1 after the sentence ending with the word "ceremonies" and footnote 4:
Similarly, prison officials can prohibit prisoners from keeping prayer oils in their cell because they can be used to mask the scent of drugs.[4.1]

[4.1] Hammons v. Saffle, 348 F.3d 1250 (10th Cir. 2003) (holding that a prison policy which states that inmates are prohibited from keeping prayer oils in their cells was rationally related to the legitimate penalolgical interest of prison safety because the inmates could used the oils to mask the scent of drugs or to slip out of hand-cuffs. Therefore, the prison rule does not violate the First Amendment. However, the court remanded the case back to the district court for proceeding on the plaintiff's RLUIPA claim raised on appeal).

n. 6.

Page 768, note 6, add:
Young v. Saunders, 169 F. Supp. 2d 553 (W.D. Va. 2001), aff'd in part,

§ 6:15　　　　　　　　　　　　　　　　　Rights of Prisoners

vacated in part on other grounds, 34 Fed. Appx. 925 (4th Cir. 2002); Charles v. Verhagen, 220 F. Supp. 2d 937 (W.D. Wis. 2002).

§ 6:16　Religious Practices—Work-Religion Conflicts
n. 5.
section 6:16, note 5 add:
Williams v. Bitner, 285 F. Supp. 2d 593 (M.D. Pa. 2003) (denying the prison officials' motion to dismiss on the grounds of qualified immunity because plaintiff's First Amendment right to free exercise was violated when the plaintiff, a Muslim inmate, was fired from his job as a cook because he refused to handle pork on the grounds that handling pork violated his religion, and because ". . . [the] plaintiff's right to refrain from handling pork was clearly established at the time of the alleged violation . . .").

§ 6:17　Religious Practices—Medical Treatment-Religion Conflicts
n. 7.
Page 776, note 70, add:
; Selah v. Goord, 255 F. Supp. 2d 42 (N.D. N.Y. 2003) (granting a preliminary injunction of prison policy of placing inmates who refuse annual, mandatory tuberculosis skin tests on religious grounds into tuberculin hold for one year).

Chapter 7

Prison Labor

> **KeyCite®:** Cases and other legal materials listed in KeyCite Scope can be researched through West's KeyCite service on Westlaw®. Use KeyCite to check citations for form, parallel references, prior and later history, and comprehensive citator information, including citations to other decisions and secondary materials.

§ 7:4 Thirteenth Amendment—Involuntary Servitude Exception: Can Inmates Be Forced to Work?

n. 7.

Page 789, note 7, add:
; Ali v. Johnson, 259 F.3d 317 (5th Cir. 2001) (affirming district court's decision to deny relief to inmate who claimed that because he was sentenced during a hiatus in Texas law that did not specifically require inmates to perform "hard labor" he had a valid Thirteenth Amendment claim; court held that, regardless of the hiatus, forcing inmates to work without pay and compelling them to work on private property without pay do not violate the Thirteenth Amendment).

section 7:4, note 7, add:
Ross v. Dretke, 2004 WL 983123 (N.D. Tex. 2004), report and recommendation adopted, 2004 WL 1175492 (N.D. Tex. 2004) (denying habeas corpus relief to the plaintiff on his claim that forced work violates the Eighth Amendment and instructing the plaintiff that Eighth Amendment claims should be brought under 42 U.S.C. § 1983. The court further dismissed plaintiff's claim that forced prison labor violates the Thirteenth Amendment because prisoners cannot state a viable Thirteenth Amendment claim); see also Griffith v. Dretke, 2004 WL 948047 (N.D. Tex. 2004), report and recommendation adopted, 2004 WL 1243365 (N.D. Tex. 2004); Harper v. Dretke, 2004 WL 983229 (N.D. Tex. 2004), report and recommendation adopted, 2004 WL 1175733 (N.D. Tex. 2004).

n. 14.

Page 791, note 14, add:
; Richardson v. Spurlock, 260 F.3d 495 (5th Cir. 2001) (affirming district court's dismissal of inmate's claim alleging that he was subject to cruel and unusual punishment in violation of his Eighth Amendment rights by being forced to inhale unreasonably high levels of tobacco smoke while being transported to and from his work assignment and being forced to stand while washing plastic tray in violation of his medical status.)

n. 15.

section 7:11, note 15, add:

§ 7:4   RIGHTS OF PRISONERS

In the second appellate review of this case, the Ninth Circuit vacated and remanded the district court's decision in Schneider v. California Dept. of Corrections, 91 F. Supp. 2d 1316 (N.D. Cal. 2000), vacated, 345 F.3d 716 (9th Cir. 2003). In this review, the court stated that the district court erred when it held that "the inmates' takings claims were without merit because of estimates submitted by CDC that the costs of operating the ITAs were [more] than the annual interest earned by inmates." The court reasoned that it is not the total interest earned by inmates compared with the total cost of maintaining the prisoner' personal property fund that should determine whether the CDC violated the Takings Clause. Rather, the correct consideration is whether the interest earned by each individual inmate exceeds the amount-spent per-inmate to manage the prisoners' personal property fund. Since this information was not clear in the record, the court remanded this case for further proceedings. Schneider v. California Dept. of Corrections, 345 F.3d 716 (9th Cir. 2003).

See Vance v. Barrett, 345 F.3d 1083 (9th Cir. 2003) (holding that the state can allow state officials to deduct "applicable charges" from an inmate's account. In this case the court defines applicable charges as "those expenses incurred in creating and maintaining the inmate's accounts." The court reasoned that this type of taking is similar to a user's fee to reimburse the government for the use of its services).

§ 7:9 Wages—The Right to Be Paid in General

n. 1.

Page 804, note 1, add:
; Ali v. Johnson, 259 F.3d 317 (5th Cir. 2001) (affirming district court's decision to deny relief to inmate who claimed that because he was sentenced during a hiatus in Texas law that did not specifically require inmates to perform "hard labor" he had a valid Thirteenth Amendment claim; court held that, regardless of the hiatus, forcing inmates to work without pay and compelling them to work on private property without pay do not violate the Thirteenth Amendment).

§ 7:12 The Right to Be Compensated for Work-Related Injuries

n. 4.

section 7:12, note 4, add:
Powers v. Ohio Dep't of Rehab. & Corr., 2003 WL 22889704, 2003 Ohio 6566 (Ohio Ct. App. 2003) (affirming the lower court's findings that prison officers were not negligent for failure to maintain the cafeteria floor or failure to warn employees that the floor could be slippery when wet. In this case the inmate, a cafeteria employee, could not prove that the officers' had actual or constructive knowledge that the floor was slippery on the day that the inmate fell in the cafeteria. Furthermore, the prison officials' brought forward credible evidence to show that there were slippery when wet signs in the cafeteria).

Ref
KF
9731
.G6
1993

SOUTH UNIVERSITY
709 MALL BLVD.
SAVANNAH, GA 31406